SOFTWARE ENGINEERING

SOFTWARE ENGINEERING

THEORY AND PRACTICE

FOURTH EDITION

Shari Lawrence Pfleeger
RAND Corporation

Joanne M. Atlee
University of Waterloo

PEARSON

Original Edition entitled *software engineering: Theory And Practice, Fourth Edition,* by Pfleeger, Shari Lawrence; Atlee, Joanne M.,published by Pearson Education, Inc, publishing as Prentice Hall, Copyright © 2010

ISBN 978-81-317-6062-8

First Impression,2011
Sixth Impression, 2013
Seventh Impression

Published by Dorling Kindersley (India) Pvt. Ltd., licensees of Pearson Education in South Asia.

Head Office: 7th Floor, knowledge Boulevard, A-8(A) Sector-62, Noida (U.P) 201309, India
Registered Office: 11 Community Centre, Panchsheel Park, New Delhi 110 017, India.

Printed in India by Repro India Ltd.

"From so much loving and journeying, books emerge."
Pablo Neruda

To Florence Rogart for providing the spark; to Norma Mertz for helping to keep the flame burning.

S.L.P.

To John Gannon, posthumously, for his integrity, inspiration, encouragement, friendship, and the legacy he has left to all of us in software engineering.

J.M.A.

Contents

Preface

BRIDGING THE GAP BETWEEN RESEARCH AND PRACTICE

Software engineering has come a long way since 1968, when the term was first used at a NATO conference. And software itself has entered our lives in ways that few had anticipated, even a decade ago. So a firm grounding in software engineering theory and practice is essential for understanding how to build good software and for evaluating the risks and opportunities that software presents in our everyday lives. This text represents the blending of the two current software engineering worlds: that of the practitioner, whose main focus is to build high-quality products that perform useful functions, and that of the researcher, who strives to find ways to improve the quality of products and the productivity of those who build them. Edsgar Dykstra continually reminded us that rigor in research and practice tests our understanding of software engineering and helps us to improve our thinking, our approaches, and ultimately our products.

It is in this spirit that we have enhanced our book, building an underlying framework for this questioning and improvement. In particular, this fourth edition contains extensive material about how to abstract and model a problem, and how to use models, design principles, design patterns, and design strategies to create appropriate solutions. Software engineers are more than programmers following instructions, much as chefs are more than cooks following recipes. There is an art to building good software, and the art is embodied in understanding how to abstract and model the essential elements of a problem and then use those abstractions to design a solution. We often hear good developers talk about "elegant" solutions, meaning that the solution addresses the heart of the problem, such that not only does the software solve the problem in its current form but it can also be modified as the problem evolves over time. In this way, students learn to blend research with practice and art with science, to build solid software.

The science is always grounded in reality. Designed for an undergraduate software engineering curriculum, this book paints a pragmatic picture of software engineering research and practices so that students can apply what they learn directly to the real-world problems they are trying to solve. Examples speak to a student's limited experience but illustrate clearly how large software development projects progress from need to idea to reality. The examples represent the many situations that readers are likely to experience: large projects and small, "agile" methods and highly structured ones, object-oriented and procedural approaches, real-time and transaction processing, development and maintenance situations.

The book is also suitable for a graduate course offering an introduction to software engineering concepts and practices, or for practitioners wishing to expand their knowledge of the subject. In particular, Chapters 12, 13, and 14 present thought-provoking material designed to interest graduate students in current research topics.

KEY FEATURES

This text has many key features that distinguish it from other books.

- Unlike other software engineering books that consider measurement and modeling as separate issues, this book blends measurement and modeling with the more general discussion of software engineering. That is, measurement and modeling are considered as an integral part of software engineering strategies, rather than as separate disciplines. Thus, students learn how to abstract and model, and how to involve quantitative assessment and improvement in their daily activities. They can use their models to understand the important elements of the problems they are solving as well as the solution alternatives; they can use measurement to evaluate their progress on an individual, team, and project basis.
- Similarly, concepts such as reuse, risk management, and quality engineering are embedded in the software engineering activities that are affected by them, instead of being treated as separate issues.
- The current edition addresses the use of agile methods, including extreme programming. It describes the benefits and risks of giving developers more autonomy and contrasts this agility with more traditional approaches to software development.
- Each chapter applies its concepts to two common examples: one that represents a typical information system, and another that represents a real-time system. Both examples are based on actual projects. The information system example describes the software needed to determine the price of advertising time for a large British television company. The real-time system is the control software for the Ariane-5 rocket; we look at the problems reported, and explore how software engineering techniques could have helped to locate and avoid some of them. Students can follow the progress of two typical projects, seeing how the various practices described in the book are merged into the technologies used to build systems.
- At the end of every chapter, the results are expressed in three ways: what the content of the chapter means for development teams, what it means for individual developers, and what it means for researchers. The student can easily review the highlights of each chapter, and can see the chapter's relevance to both research and practice.
- The Companion Web site can be found at int.prenhall.com/pfleeger. It contains current examples from the literature and examples of real artifacts from real projects. It also includes links to Web pages for relevant tool and method vendors. It is here that students can find real requirements documents, designs, code, test plans, and more. Students seeking additional, in-depth information are pointed to reputable, accessible publications and Web sites. The Web pages are updated regularly to keep the material in the textbook current, and include a facility for feedback to the author and the publisher.

- A Student Study Guide is available from your local Pearson Sales Representative.
- PowerPoint slides and a full solutions manual are available on the Instructor Resource Center. Please contact your local Pearson Sales Representative for access information.
- The book is replete with case studies and examples from the literature. Many of the one-page case studies shown as sidebars in the book are expanded on the Web page. The student can see how the book's theoretical concepts are applied to real-life situations.
- Each chapter ends with thought-provoking questions about policy, legal, and ethical issues in software engineering. Students see software engineering in its social and political contexts. As with other sciences, software engineering decisions must be viewed in terms of the people their consequences will affect.
- Every chapter addresses both procedural and object-oriented development. In addition, Chapter 6 on design explains the steps of an object-oriented development process. We discuss several design principles and use object-oriented examples to show how designs can be improved to incorporate these principles.
- The book has an annotated bibliography that points to many of the seminal papers in software engineering. In addition, the Web page points to annotated bibliographies and discussion groups for specialized areas, such as software reliability, fault tolerance, computer security, and more.
- Each chapter includes a description of a term project, involving development of software for a mortgage processing system. The instructor may use this term project, or a variation of it, in class assignments.
- Each chapter ends with a list of key references for the concepts in the chapter, enabling students to find in-depth information about particular tools and methods discussed in the chapter.
- This edition includes examples highlighting computer security. In particular, we emphasize designing security in, instead of adding it during coding or testing.

Pearson offers many different products around the world to facilitate learning. In countries outside the United States, some products and services related to this textbook may not be available due to copyright and/or permissions restrictions. If you have questions, you can contact your local office by visiting www.pearsonhighered.com/international or you can contact your local Pearson representative.

CONTENTS AND ORGANIZATION

This text is organized in three parts. The first part motivates the reader, explaining why knowledge of software engineering is important to practitioners and researchers alike. Part I also discusses the need for understanding process issues, for making decisions about the degree of "agility" developers will have, and for doing careful project planning. Part II walks through the major steps of development and maintenance, regardless of the process model used to build the software: eliciting, modeling, and checking the requirements; designing a solution to the problem; writing and testing the code; and turning it over to the customer. Part III focuses on evaluation and improvement. It looks at how we can assess the quality of our processes and products, and how to take steps to improve them.

Chapter 1: Why Software Engineering?

In this chapter we address our track record, motivating the reader and highlighting where in later chapters certain key issues are examined. In particular, we look at Wasserman's key factors that help define software engineering: abstraction, analysis and design methods and notations, modularity and architecture, software life cycle and process, reuse, measurement, tools and integrated environments, and user interface and prototyping. We discuss the difference between computer science and software engineering, explaining some of the major types of problems that can be encountered, and laying the groundwork for the rest of the book. We also explore the need to take a systems approach to building software, and we introduce the two common examples that will be used in every chapter. It is here that we introduce the context for the term project.

Chapter 2: Modeling the Process and Life Cycle

In this chapter, we present an overview of different types of process and life-cycle models, including the waterfall model, the V-model, the spiral model, and various prototyping models. We address the need for agile methods, where developers are given a great deal of autonomy, and contrast them with more traditional software development processes. We also describe several modeling techniques and tools, including systems dynamics and other commonly-used approaches. Each of the two common examples is modeled in part with some of the techniques introduced here.

Chapter 3: Planning and Managing the Project

Here, we look at project planning and scheduling. We introduce notions such as activities and milestones, work breakdown structure, activity graphs, risk management, and costs and cost estimation. Estimation models are used to estimate the cost and schedule of the two common examples. We focus on actual case studies, including management of software development for the F-16 airplane and for Digital's alpha AXP programs.

Chapter 4: Capturing the Requirements

This chapter emphasizes the critical roles of abstraction and modeling in good software engineering. In particular, we use models to tease out misunderstandings and missing details in provided requirements, as well as to communicate requirements to others. We explore a number of different modeling paradigms, study example notations for each paradigm, discuss when to use each paradigm, and provide advice about how to make particular modeling and abstraction decisions. We discuss different sources and different types of requirements (functional requirements vs. quality requirements vs. design constraints), explain how to write testable requirements, and describe how to resolve conflicts. Other topics discussed include requirements elicitation, requirements documentation, requirements reviews, requirements quality and how to measure it, and an example of how to select a specification method. The chapter ends with application of some of the methods to the two common examples.

Chapter 5: Designing the Architecture

This chapter on software architecture has been completely revised for the fourth edition. It begins by describing the role of architecture in the software design process and in the larger development process. We examine the steps involved in producing the architecture, including modeling, analysis, documentation, and review, resulting in the creation of a Software Architecture Document that can be used by program designers in describing modules and interfaces. We discuss how to decompose a problem into parts, and how to use different views to examine the several aspects of the problem so as to find a suitable solution. Next, we focus on modeling the solution using one or more architectural styles, including pipe-and-filter, peer-to-peer, client–server, publish–subscribe, repositories, and layering. We look at combining styles and using them to achieve quality goals, such as modifiability, performance, security, reliability, robustness, and usability.

Once we have an initial architecture, we evaluate and refine it. In this chapter, we show how to measure design quality and to use evaluation techniques in safety analysis, security analysis, trade-off analysis, and cost–benefit analysis to select the best architecture for the customer's needs. We stress the importance of documenting the design rationale, validating and verifying that the design matches the requirements, and creating an architecture that suits the customer's product needs. Towards the end of the chapter, we examine how to build a product-line architecture that allows a software provider to reuse the design across a family of similar products. The chapter ends with an architectural analysis of our information system and real-time examples.

Chapter 6: Designing the Modules

Chapter 6, substantially revised in this edition, investigates how to move from a description of the system architecture to descriptions of the design's individual modules. We begin with a discussion of the design process and then introduce six key design principles to guide us in fashioning modules from the architecture: modularity, interfaces, information hiding, incremental development, abstraction, and generality. Next, we take an in-depth look at object-oriented design and how it supports our six principles. Using a variety of notations from the Unified Modeling Language, we show how to represent multiple aspects of module functionality and interaction, so that we can build a robust and maintainable design. We also describe a collection of design patterns, each with a particular purpose, and demonstrate how they can be used to reinforce the design principles. Next, we discuss global issues such as data management, exception handling, user interfaces, and frameworks; we see how consistency and clarity of approach can lead to more effective designs.

Taking a careful look at object-oriented measurement, we apply some of the common object-oriented metrics to a service station example. We note how changes in metrics values, due to changes in the design, can help us decide how to allocate resources and search for faults. Finally, we apply object-oriented concepts to our information systems and real-time examples.

Chapter 7: Writing the Programs

In this chapter, we address code-level design decisions and the issues involved in implementing a design to produce high-quality code. We discuss standards and procedures, and suggest some simple programming guidelines. Examples are provided in a variety of languages, including both object-oriented and procedural. We discuss the need for program documentation and an error-handling strategy. The chapter ends by applying some of the concepts to the two common examples.

Chapter 8: Testing the Programs

In this chapter, we explore several aspects of testing programs. We distinguish conventional testing approaches from the cleanroom method, and we look at how to test a variety of systems. We present definitions and categories of software problems, and we discuss how orthogonal defect classification can make data collection and analysis more effective. We then explain the difference between unit testing and integration testing. After introducing several automated test tools and techniques, we explain the need for a testing life cycle and how the tools can be integrated into it. Finally, the chapter applies these concepts to the two common examples.

Chapter 9: Testing the System

We begin with principles of system testing, including reuse of test suites and data, and the need for careful configuration management. Concepts introduced include function testing, performance testing, acceptance testing and installation testing. We look at the special needs of testing object-oriented systems. Several test tools are described, and the roles of test team members are discussed. Next, we introduce the reader to software reliability modeling, and we explore issues of reliability, maintainability, and availability. The reader learns how to use the results of testing to estimate the likely characteristics of the delivered product. The several types of test documentation are introduced, too, and the chapter ends by describing test strategies for the two common examples.

Chapter 10: Delivering the System

This chapter discusses the need for training and documentation, and presents several examples of training and documents that could accompany the information system and real-time examples.

Chapter 11: Maintaining the System

In this chapter, we address the results of system change. We explain how changes can occur during the system's life cycle, and how system design, code, test process, and documentation must accommodate them. Typical maintenance problems are discussed, as well as the need for careful configuration management. There is a thorough discussion of the use of measurement to predict likely changes, and to evaluate the effects of change. We look at reengineering and restructuring in the overall context of rejuvenating legacy systems. Finally, the two common examples are evaluated in terms of the likelihood of change.

Chapter 12: Evaluating Products, Processes, and Resources

Since many software engineering decisions involve the incorporation and integration of existing components, this chapter addresses ways to evaluate processes and products. It discusses the need for empirical evaluation and gives several examples to show how measurement can be used to establish a baseline for quality and productivity. We look at several quality models, how to evaluate systems for reusability, how to perform post-mortems, and how to understand return on investment in information technology. These concepts are applied to the two common examples.

Chapter 13: Improving Predictions, Products, Processes, and Resources

This chapter builds on Chapter 11 by showing how prediction, product, process, and resource improvement can be accomplished. It contains several in-depth case studies to show how prediction models, inspection techniques, and other aspects of software engineering can be understood and improved using a variety of investigative techniques. This chapter ends with a set of guidelines for evaluating current situations and identifying opportunities for improvement.

Chapter 14: The Future of Software Engineering

In this final chapter, we look at several open issues in software engineering. We revisit Wasserman's concepts to see how well we are doing as a discipline. We examine several issues in technology transfer and decision-making, to determine if we do a good job at moving important ideas from research to practice. Finally, we examine controversial issues, such as licensing of software engineers as professional engineers and the trend towards more domain-specific solutions and methods.

ACKNOWLEDGMENTS

Books are written as friends and family provide technical and emotional support. It is impossible to list here all those who helped to sustain us during the writing and revising, and we apologize in advance for any omissions. Many thanks to the readers of earlier editions, whose careful scrutiny of the text generated excellent suggestions for correction and clarification. As far as we know, all such suggestions have been incorporated into this edition. We continue to appreciate feedback from readers, positive or negative.

Carolyn Seaman (University of Maryland–Baltimore Campus) was a terrific reviewer of the first edition, suggesting ways to clarify and simplify, leading to a tighter, more understandable text. She also prepared most of the solutions to the exercises, and helped to set up an early version of the book's Web site. I am grateful for her friendship and assistance. Yiqing Liang and Carla Valle updated the Web site and added substantial new material for the second edition; Patsy Ann Zimmer (University of Waterloo) revised the Web site for the third edition, particularly with respect to modeling notations and agile methods.

We owe a huge thank-you to Forrest Shull (Fraunhofer Center–Maryland) and Roseanne Tesoriero (Washington College), who developed the initial study guide for this book; to Maria Vieira Nelson (Catholic University of Minas Gerais, Brazil), who revised the study guide and the solutions manual for the third edition; and to Eduardo S. Barrenechea (University of Waterloo) for updating the materials for the fourth edition. Thanks, too, to Hossein Saiedian (University of Kansas) for preparing the PowerPoint presentations for the third and fourth editions. We are also particularly indebted to Guilherme Travassos (Federal University of Rio de Janeiro) for the use of material that he developed with Pfleeger at the University of Maryland–College Park, and that he enriched and expanded considerably for use in subsequent classes.

Helpful and thoughtful reviewers for all four editions included Barbara Kitchenham (Keele University, UK), Bernard Woolfolk (Lucent Technologies), Ana Regina Cavalcanti da Rocha (Federal University of Rio de Janeiro), Frances Uku (University of California at Berkeley), Lee Scott Ehrhart (MITRE), Laurie Werth (University of Texas), Vickie Almstrum (University of Texas), Lionel Briand (Simula Research, Norway), Steve Thibaut (University of Florida), Lee Wittenberg (Kean College of New Jersey), Philip Johnson (University of Hawaii), Daniel Berry (University of Waterloo, Canada), Nancy Day (University of Waterloo), Jianwei Niu (University of Waterloo), Chris Gorringe (University of East Anglia, UK), Ivan Aaen (Aalborg University), Damla Turget (University of Central Florida), Laurie Williams (North Carolina State University), Ernest Sibert (Syracuse University), Allen Holliday (California State University, Fullerton) David Rine (George Mason University), Anthony Sullivan (University of Texas, Dallas), David Chesney (University of Michigan, Ann Arbor), Ye Duan (Missouri University), Rammohan K. Ragade (Kentucky University), and several anonymous reviewers provided by Prentice Hall. Discussions with Greg Hislop (Drexel University), John Favaro (Intecs Sistemi, Italy), Filippo Lanubile (Università di Bari, Italy), John d'Ambra (University of New South Wales, Australia), Chuck Howell (MITRE), Tim Vieregge (U.S. Army Computer Emergency Response Team) and James and Suzanne Robertson (Atlantic Systems Guild, UK) led to many improvements and enhancements.

Thanks to Toni Holm and Alan Apt, who made the third edition of the book's production interesting and relatively painless. Thanks, too, to James and Suzanne Robertson for the use of the Piccadilly example, and to Norman Fenton for the use of material from our software metrics book. We are grateful to Tracy Dunkelberger for encouraging us in producing this fourth edition; we appreciate both her patience and her professionalism. Thanks, too, to Jane Bonnell and Pavithra Jayapaul for seamless production.

Many thanks to the publishers of several of the figures and examples for granting permission to reproduce them here. The material from *Complete Systems Analysis* (Robertson and Robertson 1994) and *Mastering the Requirements Process* (Robertson and Robertson 1999) is drawn from and used with permission from Dorset House Publishing, at www.dorsethouse.com; all rights reserved. The article in Exercise 1.1 is reproduced from the *Washington Post* with permission from the Associated Press. Figures 2.15 and 2.16 are reproduced from Barghouti et al. (1995) by permission of John Wiley and Sons Limited. Figures 12.14 and 12.15 are reproduced from Rout (1995) by permission of John Wiley and Sons Limited.

Figures and tables in Chapters 2, 3, 4, 5, 9, 11, 12, and 14 that are noted with an IEEE copyright are reprinted with permission of the Institute of Electrical and Electronics Engineers. Similarly, the three tables in Chapter 14 that are noted with an ACM copyright are reprinted with permission of the Association of Computing Machinery. Table 2.1 and Figure 2.11 from Lai (1991) are reproduced with permission from the Software Productivity Consortium. Figures 8.16 and 8.17 from Graham (1996a) are reprinted with permission from Dorothy R. Graham. Figure 12.11 and Table 12.2 are adapted from Liebman (1994) with permission from the Center for Science in the Public Interest, 1875 Connecticut Avenue NW, Washington DC. Tables 8.2, 8.3, 8.5, and 8.6 are reproduced with permission of The McGraw-Hill Companies. Figures and examples from Shaw and Garlan (1996), Card and Glass (1990), Grady (1997), and Lee and Tepfenhart (1997) are reproduced with permission from Prentice Hall.

Tables 9.3, 9.4, 9.6, 9.7, 13.1, 13.2, 13.3, and 13.4, as well as Figures 1.15, 9.7. 9.8, 9.9, 9.14, 13.1, 13.2, 13.3, 13.4, 13.5, 13.6, and 13.7 are reproduced or adapted from Fenton and Pfleeger (1997) in whole or in part with permission from Norman Fenton. Figures 3.16, 5.19, and 5.20 are reproduced or adapted from Norman Fenton's course notes, with his kind permission.

We especially appreciate our employers, the RAND Corporation and the University of Waterloo, respectively, for their encouragement.[1] And we thank our friends and family, who offered their kindness, support, and patience as the book-writing stole time ordinarily spent with them. In particular, Shari Lawrence Pfleeger is grateful to Manny Lawrence, the manager of the real Royal Service Station, and to his bookkeeper, Bea Lawrence, not only for working with her and her students on the specification of the Royal system, but also for their affection and guidance in their other job: as her parents. Jo Atlee gives special thanks to her parents, Nancy and Gary Atlee, who have supported and encouraged her in everything she has done (and attempted); and to her colleagues and students, who graciously took on more than their share of work during the major writing periods. And, most especially, we thank Charles Pfleeger and Ken Salem, who were constant and much-appreciated sources of support, encouragement, and good humor.

Shari Lawrence Pfleeger
Joanne M. Atlee

[1]Please note that this book is not a product of the RAND Corporation and has not undergone RAND's quality assurance process. The work represents us as authors, not as employees of our respective institutions.

About the Authors

Shari Lawrence Pfleeger (Ph.D., Information Technology and Engineering, George Mason University; M.S., Planning, Pennsylvania State University; M.A., Mathematics, Pennsylvania State University; B.A., Mathematics, Harpur College) is a senior information scientist at the RAND Corporation. Her current research focuses on policy and decision-making issues that help organizations and government agencies understand whether and how information technology supports their missions and goals. Her work at RAND has involved assisting clients in creating software measurement programs, supporting government agencies in defining information assurance policies, and supporting decisions about cyber security and homeland security.

Prior to joining RAND, she was the president of Systems/Software, Inc., a consultancy specializing in software engineering and technology. She has been a visiting professor at City University (London) and the University of Maryland and was the founder and director of Howard University's Center for Research in Evaluating Software Technology. The author of many textbooks on software engineering and computer security, Pfleeger is well known for her work in empirical studies of software engineering and for her multidisciplinary approach to solving information technology problems. She has been associate editor-in-chief of *IEEE Software*, associate editor of *IEEE Transactions on Software Engineering*, associate editor of *IEEE Security and Privacy*, and a member of the IEEE Computer Society Technical Council on Software Engineering. A frequent speaker at conferences and workshops, Pfleeger has been named repeatedly by the *Journal of Systems and Software* as one of the world's top software engineering researchers.

Joanne M. Atlee (Ph.D. and M.S., Computer Science, University of Maryland; B.S., Computer Science and Physics, College of William and Mary; P.Eng.) is an Associate Professor in the School of Computer Science at the University of Waterloo. Her research focuses on software modeling, documentation, and analysis. She is best known for her work on model checking software requirements specifications. Other research interests include model-based software engineering, modular software development, feature interactions, and cost-benefit analysis of formal software development techniques. Atlee serves on the editorial boards for *IEEE Transactions on Software Engineering, Software and Systems Modeling*, and the *Requirements Engineering Journal* and is Vice Chair of the International Federation for Information Processing (IFIP) Working Group 2.9, an international group of researchers working on advances in software requirements engineering. She is Program Co-Chair for the 31st International Conference on Software Engineering (ICSE'09).

Atlee also has strong interests in software engineering education. She was the founding Director of Waterloo's Bachelor's program in Software Engineering. She served as a member of the Steering Committee for the ACM/IEEE-CS Computing Curricula—Software Engineering (CCSE) volume, which provides curricular guidelines for undergraduate programs in software engineering. She also served on a Canadian Engineering Qualifications Board committee whose mandate is to set a software engineering syllabus, to offer guidance to provincial engineering associations on what constitutes acceptable academic qualifications for licensed Professional Engineers who practice software engineering.

SOFTWARE ENGINEERING

1 Why Software Engineering?

In this chapter, we look at
- what we mean by software engineering
- software engineering's track record
- what we mean by good software
- why a systems approach is important
- how software engineering has changed since the 1970s

Software pervades our world, and we sometimes take for granted its role in making our lives more comfortable, efficient, and effective. For example, consider the simple tasks involved in preparing toast for breakfast. The code in the toaster controls how brown the bread will get and when the finished product pops up. Programs control and regulate the delivery of electricity to the house, and software bills us for our energy usage. In fact, we may use automated programs to pay the electricity bill, to order more groceries, and even to buy a new toaster! Today, software is working both explicitly and behind the scenes in virtually all aspects of our lives, including the critical systems that affect our health and well-being. For this reason, software engineering is more important than ever. Good software engineering practices must ensure that software makes a positive contribution to how we lead our lives.

This book highlights the key issues in software engineering, describing what we know about techniques and tools, and how they affect the resulting products we build and use. We will look at both theory and practice: what we know and how it is applied in a typical software development or maintenance project. We will also examine what we do not yet know, but what would be helpful in making our products more reliable, safe, useful, and accessible.

We begin by looking at how we analyze problems and develop solutions. Then we investigate the differences between computer science problems and engineering ones. Our ultimate goal is to produce solutions incorporating high-quality software, and we consider characteristics that contribute to the quality.

We also look at how successful we have been as developers of software systems. By examining several examples of software failure, we see how far we have come and how much farther we must go in mastering the art of quality software development.

Next, we look at the people involved in software development. After describing the roles and responsibilities of customers, users, and developers, we turn to a study of the system itself. We see that a system can be viewed as a group of objects related to a set of activities and enclosed by a boundary. Alternatively, we look at a system with an engineer's eye; a system can be developed much as a house is built. Having defined the steps in building a system, we discuss the roles of the development team at each step.

Finally, we discuss some of the changes that have affected the way we practice software engineering. We present Wasserman's eight ideas to tie together our practices into a coherent whole.

1.1 WHAT IS SOFTWARE ENGINEERING?

As software engineers, we use our knowledge of computers and computing to help solve problems. Often the problem with which we are dealing is related to a computer or an existing computer system, but sometimes the difficulties underlying the problem have nothing to do with computers. Therefore, it is essential that we first understand the nature of the problem. In particular, we must be very careful not to impose computing machinery or techniques on every problem that comes our way. We must solve the problem first. Then, if need be, we can use technology as a tool to implement our solution. For the remainder of this book, we assume that our analysis has shown that some kind of computer system is necessary or desirable to solve a particular problem at hand.

Solving Problems

Most problems are large and sometimes tricky to handle, especially if they represent something new that has never been solved before. So we must begin investigating a problem by **analyzing** it, that is, by breaking it into pieces that we can understand and try to deal with. We can thus describe the larger problem as a collection of small problems and their interrelationships. Figure 1.1 illustrates how analysis works. It is important to remember that the relationships (the arrows in the figure, and the relative positions of the subproblems) are as essential as the subproblems themselves. Sometimes, it is the relationships that hold the clue to how to solve the larger problem, rather than simply the nature of the subproblems.

Once we have analyzed the problem, we must construct our solution from components that address the problem's various aspects. Figure 1.2 illustrates this reverse process: **Synthesis** is the putting together of a large structure from small building blocks. As with analysis, the composition of the individual solutions may be as challenging as the process of finding the solutions. To see why, consider the process of writing a novel. The dictionary contains all the words that you might want to use in your writing. But the most difficult part of writing is deciding how to organize and compose the words into sentences, and likewise the sentences into paragraphs and chapters to form the complete book. Thus, any problem-solving technique must have two parts: analyzing the problem to determine its nature, and then synthesizing a solution based on our analysis.

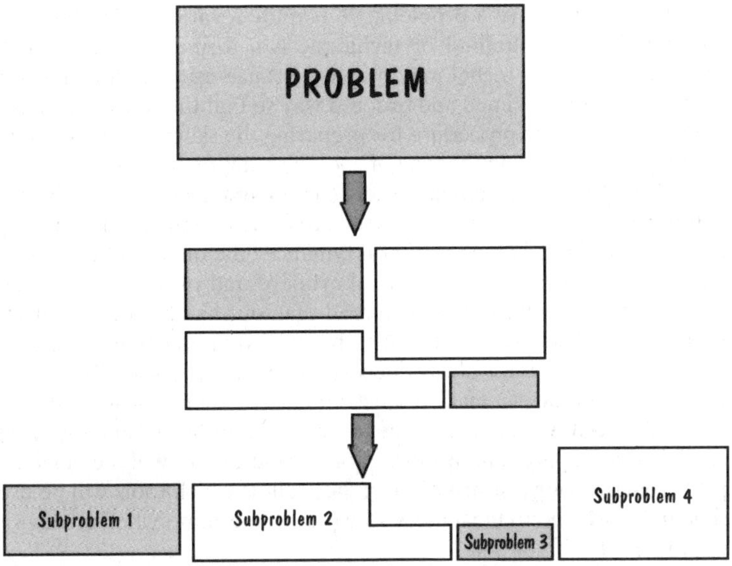

FIGURE 1.1 The process of analysis.

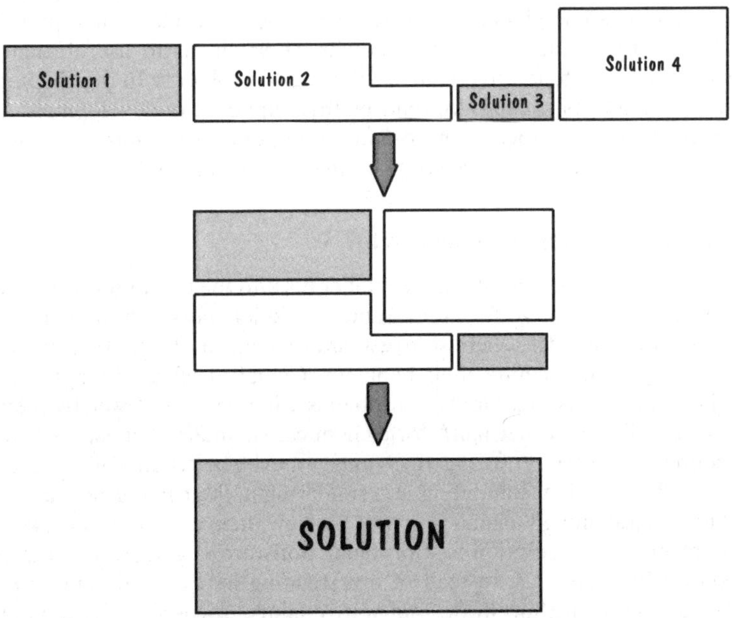

FIGURE 1.2 The process of synthesis.

To help us solve a problem, we employ a variety of methods, tools, procedures, and paradigms. A **method** or **technique** is a formal procedure for producing some result. For example, a chef may prepare a sauce using a sequence of ingredients combined in a carefully timed and ordered way so that the sauce thickens but does not curdle or separate. The procedure for preparing the sauce involves timing and ingredients but may not depend on the type of cooking equipment used.

A **tool** is an instrument or automated system for accomplishing something in a better way. This "better way" can mean that the tool makes us more accurate, more efficient, or more productive or that it enhances the quality of the resulting product. For example, we use a typewriter or a keyboard and printer to write letters because the resulting documents are easier to read than our handwriting. Or we use a pair of scissors as a tool because we can cut faster and straighter than if we were tearing a page. However, a tool is not always necessary for making something well. For example, a cooking technique can make a sauce better, not the pot or spoon used by the chef.

A **procedure** is like a recipe: a combination of tools and techniques that, in concert, produce a particular product. For instance, as we will see in later chapters, our test plans describe our test procedures; they tell us which tools will be used on which data sets under which circumstances so we can determine whether our software meets its requirements.

Finally, a **paradigm** is like a cooking style; it represents a particular approach or philosophy for building software. Just as we can distinguish French cooking from Chinese cooking, so too do we distinguish paradigms like object-oriented development from procedural ones. One is not better than another; each has its advantages and disadvantages, and there may be situations when one is more appropriate than another.

Software engineers use tools, techniques, procedures, and paradigms to enhance the quality of their software products. Their aim is to use efficient and productive approaches to generate effective solutions to problems. In the chapters that follow, we will highlight particular approaches that support the development and maintenance activities we describe. An up-to-date set of pointers to tools and techniques is listed in this book's associated home page on the World Wide Web.

Where Does the Software Engineer Fit In?

To understand how a software engineer fits into the computer science world, let us look to another discipline for an example. Consider the study of chemistry and its use to solve problems. The chemist investigates chemicals: their structure, their interactions, and the theory behind their behavior. Chemical engineers apply the results of the chemist's studies to a variety of problems. Chemistry as viewed by chemists is the object of study. On the other hand, for a chemical engineer, chemistry is a tool to be used to address a general problem (which may not even be "chemical" in nature).

We can view computing in a similar light. We can concentrate on the computers and programming languages, or we can view them as tools to be used in designing and implementing a solution to a problem. Software engineering takes the latter view, as shown in Figure 1.3. Instead of investigating hardware design or proving theorems about how algorithms work, a software engineer focuses on the computer as a problem-solving tool. We will see later in this chapter that a software engineer works with the

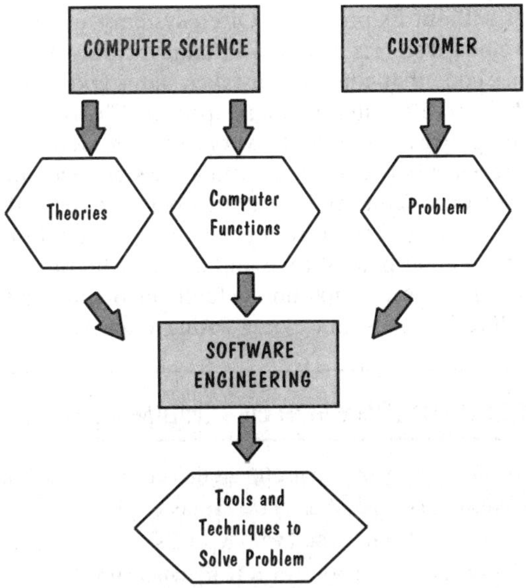

FIGURE 1.3 The relationship between computer science and software engineering.

functions of a computer as part of a general solution, rather than with the structure or theory of the computer itself.

1.2 HOW SUCCESSFUL HAVE WE BEEN?

Writing software is an art as well as a science, and it is important for you as a student of computer science to understand why. Computer scientists and software engineering researchers study computer mechanisms and theorize about how to make them more productive or efficient. However, they also design computer systems and write programs to perform tasks on those systems, a practice that involves a great deal of art, ingenuity, and skill. There may be many ways to perform a particular task on a particular system, but some are better than others. One way may be more efficient, more precise, easier to modify, easier to use, or easier to understand. Any hacker can write code to make something work, but it takes the skill and understanding of a professional software engineer to produce code that is robust, easy to understand and maintain, and does its job in the most efficient and effective way possible. Consequently, software engineering is about designing and developing high-quality software.

Before we examine what is needed to produce quality software systems, let us look back to see how successful we have been. Are users happy with their existing software systems? Yes and no. Software has enabled us to perform tasks more quickly and effectively than ever before. Consider life before word processing, spreadsheets, electronic mail, or sophisticated telephony, for example. And software has supported life-sustaining or life-saving advances in medicine, agriculture, transportation, and most other industries. In addition, software has enabled us to do things that were never imagined in the past: microsurgery, multimedia education, robotics, and more.

However, software is not without its problems. Often systems function, but not exactly as expected. We all have heard stories of systems that just barely work. And we all have written faulty programs: code that contains mistakes, but is good enough for a passing grade or for demonstrating the feasibility of an approach. Clearly, such behavior is not acceptable when developing a system for delivery to a customer.

There is an enormous difference between an error in a class project and one in a large software system. In fact, software faults and the difficulty in producing fault-free software are frequently discussed in the literature and in the hallways. Some faults are merely annoying; others cost a great deal of time and money. Still others are life-threatening. Sidebar 1.1 explains the relationships among faults, errors, and failures. Let us look at a few examples of failures to see what is going wrong and why.

SIDEBAR 1.1 TERMINOLOGY FOR DESCRIBING BUGS

Often, we talk about "bugs" in software, meaning many things that depend on the context. A "bug" can be a mistake in interpreting a requirement, a syntax error in a piece of code, or the (as-yet-unknown) cause of a system crash. The Institute of Electrical and Electronics Engineers (IEEE) has suggested a standard terminology (in IEEE Standard 729) for describing "bugs" in our software products (IEEE 1983).

A **fault** occurs when a human makes a mistake, called an **error**, in performing some software activity. For example, a designer may misunderstand a requirement and create a design that does not match the actual intent of the requirements analyst and the user. This design fault is an encoding of the error, and it can lead to other faults, such as incorrect code and an incorrect description in a user manual. Thus, a single error can generate many faults, and a fault can reside in any development or maintenance product.

A **failure** is a departure from the system's required behavior. It can be discovered before or after system delivery, during testing, or during operation and maintenance. As we will see in Chapter 4, the requirements documents can contain faults. So a failure may indicate that the system is not performing as required, even though it may be performing as specified.

Thus, a fault is an inside view of the system, as seen by the eyes of the developers, whereas a failure is an outside view: a problem that the user sees. Not every fault corresponds to a failure; for example, if faulty code is never executed or a particular state is never entered, then the fault will never cause the code to fail. Figure 1.4 shows the genesis of a failure.

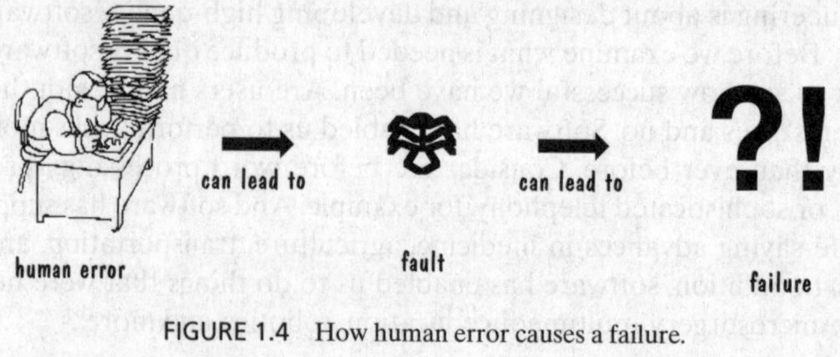

FIGURE 1.4 How human error causes a failure.

In the early 1980s, the United States Internal Revenue Service (IRS) hired Sperry Corporation to build an automated federal income tax form processing system. According to the *Washington Post,* the "system . . . proved inadequate to the workload, cost nearly twice what was expected and must be replaced soon" (Sawyer 1985). In 1985, an extra $90 million was needed to enhance the original $103 million worth of Sperry equipment. In addition, because the problem prevented the IRS from returning refunds to taxpayers by the deadline, the IRS was forced to pay $40.2 million in interest and $22.3 million in overtime wages for its employees who were trying to catch up. In 1996, the situation had not improved. The *Los Angeles Times* reported on March 29 that there was still no master plan for the modernization of IRS computers, only a 6000-page technical document. Congressman Jim Lightfoot called the project "a $4-billion fiasco that is floundering because of inadequate planning" (Vartabedian 1996).

Situations such as these still occur. In the United States, the Federal Bureau of Investigation's (FBI's) Trilogy project attempted to upgrade the FBI's computer systems. The results were devastating: "After more than four years of hard work and half a billion dollars spent, however, Trilogy has had little impact on the FBI's antiquated case-management system, which today remains a morass of mainframe green screens and vast stores of paper records" (Knorr 2005). Similarly, in the United Kingdom, the cost of overhauling the National Health Service's information systems was double the original estimate (Ballard 2006). We will see in Chapter 2 why project planning is essential to the production of quality software.

For many years, the public accepted the infusion of software in their daily lives with little question. But President Reagan's proposed Strategic Defense Initiative (SDI) heightened the public's awareness of the difficulty of producing a fault-free software system. Popular newspaper and magazine reports (such as Jacky 1985; Parnas 1985, Rensburger 1985) expressed skepticism in the computer science community. And now, years later, when the U.S. Congress is asked to allocate funds to build a similar system, many computer scientists and software engineers continue to believe there is no way to write and test the software to guarantee adequate reliability.

For example, many software engineers think that an antiballistic-missile system would require at least 10 million lines of code; some estimates range as high as one hundred million. By comparison, the software supporting the American space shuttle consists of 3 million lines of code, including computers on the ground controlling the launch and the flight; there were 100,000 lines of code in the shuttle itself in 1985 (Rensburger 1985). Thus, an antimissile software system would require the testing of an enormous amount of code. Moreover, the reliability constraints would be impossible to test. To see why, consider the notion of safety-critical software. Typically, we say that something that is **safety-critical** (i.e., something whose failure poses a threat to life or health) should have a reliability of at least 10^{-9}. As we shall see in Chapter 9, this terminology means that the system can fail no more often than once in 10^9 hours of operation. To observe this degree of reliability, we would have to run the system for at least 10^9 hours to verify that it does not fail. But 10^9 hours is over 114,000 years—far too long as a testing interval!

We will also see in Chapter 9 that helpful technology can become deadly when software is improperly designed or programmed. For example, the medical community was aghast when the Therac-25, a radiation therapy and X-ray machine, malfunctioned and killed several patients. The software designers had not anticipated the use of several arrow keys in nonstandard ways; as a consequence, the software retained its high settings and issued a highly concentrated dose of radiation when low levels were intended (Leveson and Turner 1993).

Similar examples of unanticipated use and its dangerous consequences are easy to find. For example, recent efforts to use off-the-shelf components (as a cost savings measure instead of custom-crafting of software) result in designs that use components in ways not intended by the original developers. Many licensing agreements explicitly point to the risks of unanticipated use: "Because each end-user system is customized and differs from utilized testing platforms and because a user or application designer may use the software in combination with other products in a manner not evaluated or contemplated by [the vendor] or its suppliers, the user or application designer is ultimately responsible for verifying and validating the [software]" (*Lookout Direct* n.d.).

Unanticipated use of the system should be considered throughout software design activities. These uses can be handled in at least two ways: by stretching your imagination to think of how the system can be abused (as well as used properly), and by assuming that the system will be abused and designing the software to handle the abuses. We discuss these approaches in Chapter 8.

Although many vendors strive for zero-defect software, in fact most software products are not fault-free. Market forces encourage software developers to deliver products quickly, with little time to test thoroughly. Typically, the test team will be able to test only those functions most likely to be used, or those that are most likely to endanger or irritate users. For this reason, many users are wary of installing the first version of code, knowing that the bugs will not be worked out until the second version. Furthermore, the modifications needed to fix known faults are sometimes so difficult to make that it is easier to rewrite a whole system than to change existing code. We will investigate the issues involved in software maintenance in Chapter 11.

In spite of some spectacular successes and the overall acceptance of software as a fact of life, there is still much room for improvement in the quality of the software we produce. For example, lack of quality can be costly; the longer a fault goes undetected, the more expensive it is to correct. In particular, the cost of correcting an error made during the initial analysis of a project is estimated to be only one-tenth the cost of correcting a similar error after the system has been turned over to the customer. Unfortunately, we do not catch most of the errors early on. Half of the cost of correcting faults found during testing and maintenance comes from errors made much earlier in the life of a system. In Chapters 12 and 13, we will look at ways to evaluate the effectiveness of our development activities and improve the processes to catch mistakes as early as possible.

One of the simple but powerful techniques we will propose is the use of review and inspection. Many students are accustomed to developing and testing software on their own. But their testing may be less effective than they think. For example, Fagan studied the way faults were detected. He discovered that testing a program by running it with test data revealed only about a fifth of the faults located during systems development. However, peer review, the process whereby colleagues examine and comment on each other's designs and code, uncovered the remaining four out of five faults found (Fagan 1986). Thus, the quality of your software can be increased dramatically just by having your colleagues review your work. We will learn more in later chapters about how the review and inspection processes can be used after each major development step to find and fix faults as early as possible. And we will see in Chapter 13 how to improve the inspection process itself.

1.3 WHAT IS GOOD SOFTWARE?

Just as manufacturers look for ways to ensure the quality of the products they produce, so too must software engineers find methods to ensure that their products are of acceptable quality and utility. Thus, good software engineering must always include a strategy for producing quality software. But before we can devise a strategy, we must understand what we mean by quality software. Sidebar 1.2 shows us how perspective influences what we mean by "quality." In this section, we examine what distinguishes good software from bad.

SIDEBAR 1.2 PERSPECTIVES ON QUALITY

Garvin (1984) discusses about how different people perceive quality. He describes quality from five different perspectives:

- the *transcendental view*, where quality is something we can recognize but not define
- the *user view*, where quality is fitness for purpose
- the *manufacturing view*, where quality is conformance to specification
- the *product view*, where quality is tied to inherent product characteristics
- the *value-based view*, where quality depends on the amount the customer is willing to pay for it

The transcendental view is much like Plato's description of the ideal or Aristotle's concept of form. In other words, just as every actual table is an approximation of an ideal table, we can think of software quality as an ideal toward which we strive; however, we may never be able to implement it completely.

The transcendental view is ethereal, in contrast to the more concrete view of the user. We take a user view when we measure product characteristics, such as defect density or reliability, in order to understand the overall product quality.

The manufacturing view looks at quality during production and after delivery. In particular, it examines whether the product was built right the first time, avoiding costly rework to fix delivered faults. Thus, the manufacturing view is a process view, advocating conformance to good process. However, there is little evidence that conformance to process actually results in products with fewer faults and failures; process may indeed lead to high-quality products, but it may possibly institutionalize the production of mediocre products. We examine some of these issues in Chapter 12.

The user and manufacturing views look at the product from the outside, but the product view peers inside and evaluates a product's inherent characteristics. This view is the one often advocated by software metrics experts; they assume that good internal quality indicators will lead to good external ones, such as reliability and maintainability. However, more research is needed to verify these assumptions and to determine which aspects of quality affect the product's actual use. We may have to develop models that link the product view to the user view.

Customers or marketers often take a user view of quality. Researchers sometimes hold a product view, and the development team has a manufacturing view. If the differences in viewpoints are not made explicit, then confusion and misunderstanding can lead to bad decisions and poor products. The value-based view can link these disparate pictures of quality. By equating quality to what the customer is willing to pay, we can look at trade-offs between cost and quality, and we can manage conflicts when they arise. Similarly, purchasers compare product costs with potential benefits, thinking of quality as value for money.

Kitchenham and Pfleeger (1996) investigated the answer to this question in their introduction to a special issue of *IEEE Software* on quality. They note that the context helps to determine the answer. Faults tolerated in word processing software may not be acceptable in safety-critical or mission-critical systems. Thus, we must consider quality in at least three ways: the quality of the product, the quality of the process that results in the product, and the quality of the product in the context of the business environment in which the product will be used.

The Quality of the Product

We can ask people to name the characteristics of software that contribute to its overall quality, but we are likely to get different answers from each person we ask. This difference occurs because the importance of the characteristics depends on who is analyzing the software. Users judge software to be of high quality if it does what they want in a way that is easy to learn and easy to use. However, sometimes quality and functionality are intertwined; if something is hard to learn or use but its functionality is worth the trouble, then it is still considered to have high quality.

We try to measure software quality so that we can compare one product with another. To do so, we identify those aspects of the system that contribute to its overall quality. Thus, when measuring software quality, users assess such external characteristics as the number of failures and type of failures. For example, they may define failures as minor, major, and catastrophic, and hope that any failures that occur are only minor ones.

The software must also be judged by those who are designing and writing the code and by those who must maintain the programs after they are written. These practitioners tend to look at internal characteristics of the products, sometimes even before the product is delivered to the user. In particular, practitioners often look at numbers and types of faults for evidence of a product's quality (or lack of it). For example, developers track the number of faults found in requirements, design, and code inspections and use them as indicators of the likely quality of the final product.

For this reason, we often build models to relate the user's external view to the developer's internal view of the software. Figure 1.5 is an example of an early quality model built by McCall and his colleagues to show how external quality factors (on the left-hand side) relate to product quality criteria (on the right-hand side). McCall associated each right-hand criterion with a measurement to indicate the degree to which an

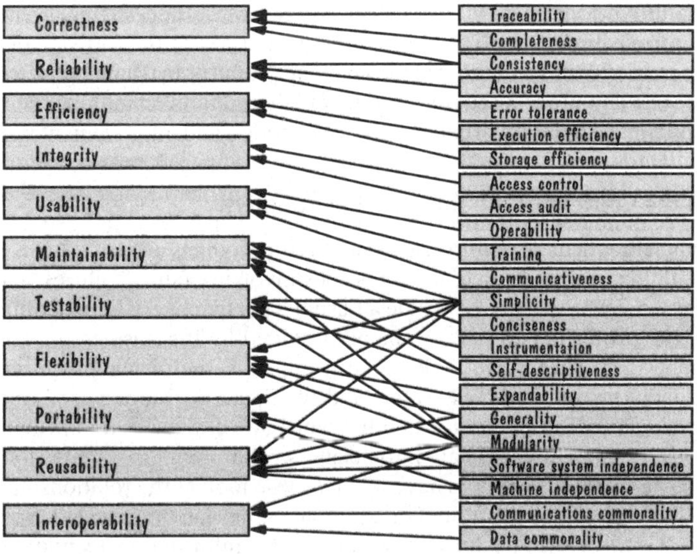

FIGURE 1.5 McCall's quality model.

element of quality was addressed (McCall, Richards, and Walters 1977). We will examine several product quality models in Chapter 12.

The Quality of the Process

There are many activities that affect the ultimate product quality; if any of the activities go awry, the product quality may suffer. For this reason, many software engineers feel that the quality of the development and maintenance process is as important as product quality. One of the advantages of modeling the process is that we can examine it and look for ways to improve it. For example, we can ask questions such as:

- Where and when are we likely to find a particular kind of fault?
- How can we find faults earlier in the development process?
- How can we build in fault tolerance so that we minimize the likelihood that a fault will become a failure?
- How can we design secure, high-quality systems?
- Are there alternative activities that can make our process more effective or efficient at ensuring quality?

These questions can be applied to the whole development process or to a subprocess, such as configuration management, reuse, or testing; we will investigate these processes in later chapters.

In the 1990s, there was a well-publicized focus on process modeling and process improvement in software engineering. Inspired by the work of Deming and Juran, and implemented by companies such as IBM, process guidelines such as the Capability

Maturity Model (CMM), ISO 9000, and Software Process Improvement and Capability dEtermination (SPICE) suggested that by improving the software development process, we can improve the quality of the resulting products. In Chapter 2, we will see how to identify relevant process activities and model their effects on intermediate and final products. Chapters 12 and 13 will examine process models and improvement frameworks in depth.

Quality in the Context of the Business Environment

When the focus of quality assessment is on products and processes, we usually measure quality with mathematical expressions involving faults, failures, and timing. Rarely is the scope broadened to include a business perspective, where quality is viewed in terms of the products and services being provided by the business in which the software is embedded. That is, we look at the technical value of our products, rather than more broadly at their business value, and we make decisions based only on the resulting products' technical quality. In other words, we assume that improving technical quality will automatically translate into business value.

Several researchers have taken a close look at the relationships between business value and technical value. For example, Simmons interviewed many Australian businesses to determine how they make their information technology-related business decisions. She proposes a framework for understanding what companies mean by "business value" (Simmons 1996). In a report by Favaro and Pfleeger (1997), Steve Andriole, chief information officer for Cigna Corporation, a large U.S. insurance company, described how his company distinguishes technical value from business value:

> We measure the quality [of our software] by the obvious metrics: up versus down time, maintenance costs, costs connected with modifications, and the like. In other words, we manage development based on operational performance within cost parameters. HOW the vendor provides cost-effective performance is less of a concern than the results of the effort. . . . The issue of business versus technical value is near and dear to our heart . . . and one [on] which we focus a great deal of attention. I guess I am surprised to learn that companies would contract with companies for their technical value, at the relative expense of business value. If anything, we err on the other side! If there is not clear (expected) business value (expressed quantitatively: number of claims processed, etc.) then we can't launch a systems project. We take very seriously the "purposeful" requirement phase of the project, when we ask: "why do we want this system?" and "why do we care?"

There have been several attempts to relate technical value and business value in a quantitative and meaningful way. For example, Humphrey, Snyder, and Willis (1991) note that by improving its development process according to the CMM "maturity" scale (to be discussed in Chapter 12), Hughes Aircraft improved its productivity by 4 to 1 and saved millions of dollars. Similarly, Dion (1993) reported that Raytheon's twofold increase in productivity was accompanied by a \$7.70 return on every dollar invested in process improvement. And personnel at Tinker Air Force Base in Oklahoma noted a productivity improvement of 6.35 to 1 (Lipke and Butler 1992).

However, Brodman and Johnson (1995) took a closer look at the business value of process improvement. They surveyed 33 companies that performed some kind of process improvement activities, and examined several key issues. Among other things, Brodman and Johnson asked companies how they defined return on investment (ROI), a concept that is clearly defined in the business community. They note that the textbook definition of **return on investment**, derived from the financial community, describes the investment in terms of what is given up for other purposes. That is, the "investment must not only return the original capital but enough more to at least equal what the funds would have earned elsewhere, plus an allowance for risk" (Putnam and Myers 1992). Usually, the business community uses one of three models to assess ROI: a payback model, an accounting rate-of-return model, and a discounted cash flow model.

However, Brodman and Johnson (1995) found that the U.S. government and U.S. industry interpret ROI in very different ways, each different from the other, and both different from the standard business school approaches. The government views ROI in terms of dollars, looking at reducing operating costs, predicting dollar savings, and calculating the cost of employing new technologies. Government investments are also expressed in dollars, such as the cost of introducing new technologies or process improvement initiatives.

On the other hand, industry viewed investment in terms of effort, rather than cost or dollars. That is, companies were interested in saving time or using fewer people, and their definition of return on investment reflected this focus on decreasing effort. Among the companies surveyed, return on investment included such items as

- training
- schedule
- risk
- quality
- productivity
- process
- customer
- costs
- business

The cost issues included in the definition involve meeting cost predictions, improving cost performance, and staying within budget, rather than reducing operating costs or streamlining the project or organization. Figure 1.6 summarizes the frequency with which many organizations included an investment item in their definition of ROI. For example, about 5 percent of those interviewed included a quality group's effort in the ROI effort calculation, and approximately 35 percent included software costs when considering number of dollars invested.

The difference in views is disturbing, because it means that calculations of ROI cannot be compared across organizations. But there are good reasons for these differing views. Dollar savings from reduced schedule, higher quality, and increased productivity are returned to the government rather than the contractor. On the other hand, contractors are usually looking for a competitive edge and increased work capacity as well as greater profit; thus, the contractor's ROI is more effort- than cost-based. In particular, more accurate cost and schedule estimation can mean customer satisfaction and repeat business. And decreased time to market as well as improved product quality are perceived as offering business value, too.

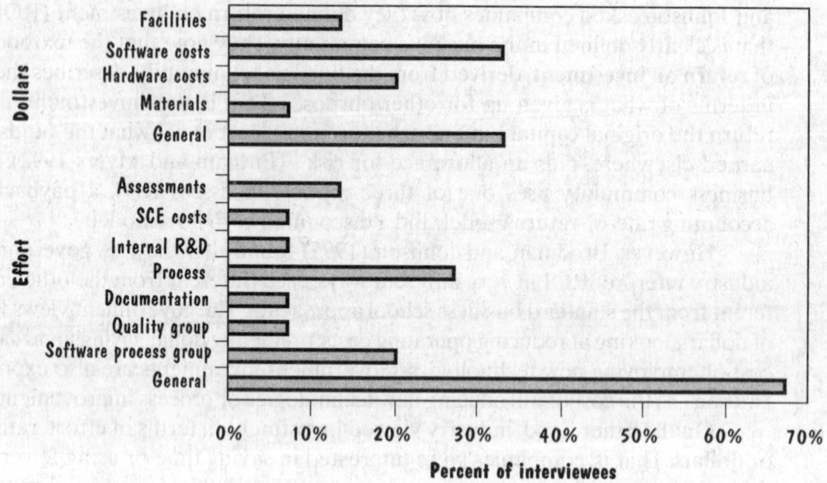

FIGURE 1.6 Terms included in industry definition of return on investment.

Even though the different ROI calculations can be justified for each organization, it is worrying that software technology return on investment is not the same as financial ROI. At some point, program success must be reported to higher levels of management, many of which are related not to software but to the main company business, such as telecommunications or banking. Much confusion will result from the use of the same terminology to mean vastly different things. Thus, our success criteria must make sense not only for software projects and processes, but also for the more general business practices they support. We will examine this issue in more detail in Chapter 12 and look at using several common measures of business value to choose among technology options.

1.4 WHO DOES SOFTWARE ENGINEERING?

A key component of software development is communication between customer and developer; if that fails, so too will the system. We must understand what the customer wants and needs before we can build a system to help solve the customer's problem. To do this, let us turn our attention to the people involved in software development.

The number of people working on software development depends on the project's size and degree of difficulty. However, no matter how many people are involved, the roles played throughout the life of the project can be distinguished. Thus, for a large project, one person or a group may be assigned to each of the roles identified; on a small project, one person or group may take on several roles at once.

Usually, the participants in a project fall into one of three categories: customer, user, or developer. The **customer** is the company, organization, or person who is paying for the software system to be developed. The **developer** is the company, organization, or person who is building the software system for the customer. This category includes any

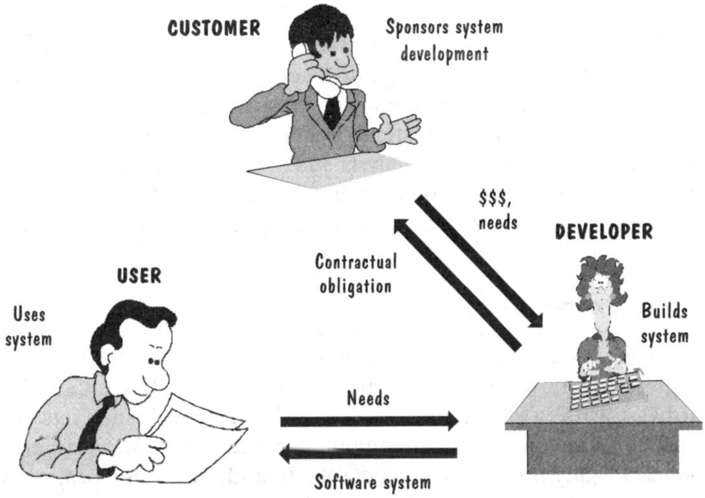

FIGURE 1.7 Participants in software development.

managers needed to coordinate and guide the programmers and testers. The **user** is the person or people who will actually use the system: the ones who sit at the terminal or submit the data or read the output. Although for some projects the customer, user, and developer are the same person or group, often these are different sets of people. Figure 1.7 shows the basic relationships among the three types of participants.

The customer, being in control of the funds, usually negotiates the contract and signs the acceptance papers. However, sometimes the customer is not a user. For example, suppose Wittenberg Water Works signs a contract with Gentle Systems, Inc., to build a computerized accounting system for the company. The president of Wittenberg may describe to the representatives of Gentle Systems exactly what is needed, and she will sign the contract. However, the president will not use the accounting system directly; the users will be the bookkeepers and accounting clerks. Thus, it is important that the developers understand exactly what both the customer and users want and need.

On the other hand, suppose Wittenberg Water Works is so large that it has its own computer systems development division. The division may decide that it needs an automated tool to keep track of its own project costs and schedules. By building the tool itself, the division is at the same time the user, customer, and developer.

In recent years, the simple distinctions among customer, user, and developer have become more complex. Customers and users have been involved in the development process in a variety of ways. The customer may decide to purchase Commercial Off-The-Shelf (**COTS**) software to be incorporated in the final product that the developer will supply and support. When this happens, the customer is involved in system architecture decisions, and there are many more constraints on development. Similarly, the developer may choose to use additional developers, called **subcontractors**, who build a subsystem and deliver it to the developers to be included in the final product. The subcontractors may work side by side with the primary developers, or they may work at a different site, coordinating their work with the primary developers and delivering the subsystem late in the development process. The subsystem may be a **turnkey system**, where the code is incorporated whole (without additional code for integration), or it may require a separate integration process for building the links from the major system to the subsystem(s).

Thus, the notion of "system" is important in software engineering, not only for understanding the problem analysis and solution synthesis, but also for organizing the development process and for assigning appropriate roles to the participants. In the next section, we look at the role of a systems approach in good software engineering practice.

1.5 A SYSTEMS APPROACH

The projects we develop do not exist in a vacuum. Often, the hardware and software we put together must interact with users, with other software tasks, with other pieces of hardware, with existing databases (i.e., with carefully defined sets of data and data relationships), or even with other computer systems. Therefore, it is important to provide a context for any project by knowing the **boundaries** of the project: what is included in the project and what is not. For example, suppose you are asked by your supervisor to write a program to print paychecks for the people in your office. You must know whether your program simply reads hours worked from another system and prints the results or whether you must also calculate the pay information. Similarly, you must know whether the program is to calculate taxes, pensions, and benefits or whether a report of these items is to be provided with each paycheck. What you are really asking is: Where does the project begin and end? The same question applies to any system. A system is a collection of objects and activities, plus a description of the relationships that tie the objects and activities together. Typically, our system definition includes, for each activity, a list of inputs required, actions taken, and outputs produced. Thus, to begin, we must know whether any object or activity is included in the system or not.

The Elements of a System

We describe a system by naming its parts and then identifying how the component parts are related to one another. This identification is the first step in analyzing the problem presented to us.

Activities and Objects. First, we distinguish between activities and objects. An **activity** is something that happens in a system. Usually described as an event initiated by a trigger, the activity transforms one thing to another by changing a characteristic. This transformation can mean that a data element is moved from one location to another, is changed from one value to another, or is combined with other data to supply input for yet another activity. For example, an item of data can be moved from one file to another. In this case, the characteristic changed is the location. Or the value of the data item can be incremented. Finally, the address of the data item can be included in a list of parameters with the addresses of several other data items so that another routine can be called to handle all the data at once.

The elements involved in the activities are called **objects** or **entities**. Usually, these objects are related to each other in some way. For instance, the objects can be arranged in a table or matrix. Often, objects are grouped as records, where each record is arranged in a prescribed format. An employee history record, for example, may contain objects (called fields) for each employee, such as the following:

First name	Postal code
Middle name	Salary per hour
Last name	Benefits per hour
Street address	Vacation hours accrued
City	Sick leave accrued
State	

Not only is each field in the record defined, but the size and relationship of each field to the others are named. Thus, the record description states the data type of each field, the starting location in the record, and the length of the field. In turn, since there is a record for each employee, the records are combined into a file, and file characteristics (such as maximum number of records) may be specified.

Sometimes, the objects are defined slightly differently. Instead of considering each item as a field in a larger record, the object is viewed as being independent. The object description contains a listing of the characteristics of each object, as well as a list of all the actions that can take place using the object or affecting the object. For example, consider the object "polygon." An object description may say that this object has characteristics such as number of sides and length of each side. The actions may include calculation of the area or of the perimeter. There may even be a characteristic called "polygon type," so that each instantiation of "polygon" is identified when it is a "rhombus" or "rectangle," for instance. A type may itself have an object description; "rectangle" may be composed of types "square" and "not square," for example. We will explore these concepts in Chapter 4 when we investigate requirements analysis, and in depth in Chapter 6 when we discuss object-oriented development.

Relationships and the System Boundary. Once entities and activities are defined, we match the entities with their activities. The relationships among entities and activities are clearly and carefully defined. An entity definition includes a description of where the entity originates. Some items reside in files that already exist; others are created during some activity. The entity's destination is important, too. Some items are used by only one activity, but others are destined to be input to other systems. That is, some items from one system are used by activities outside the scope of the system being examined. Thus, we can think of the system at which we are looking as having a border or boundary. Some items cross the boundary to enter our system, and others are products of our system and travel out for another system's use.

Using these concepts, we can define a **system** as a collection of things: a set of entities, a set of activities, a description of the relationships among entities and activities, and a definition of the boundary of the system. This definition of a system applies not only to computer systems but to anything in which objects interact in some way with other objects.

Examples of Systems. To see how system definition works, consider the parts of you that allow you to take in oxygen and excrete carbon dioxide and water: your respiratory system. You can define its boundary easily: If you name a particular organ of

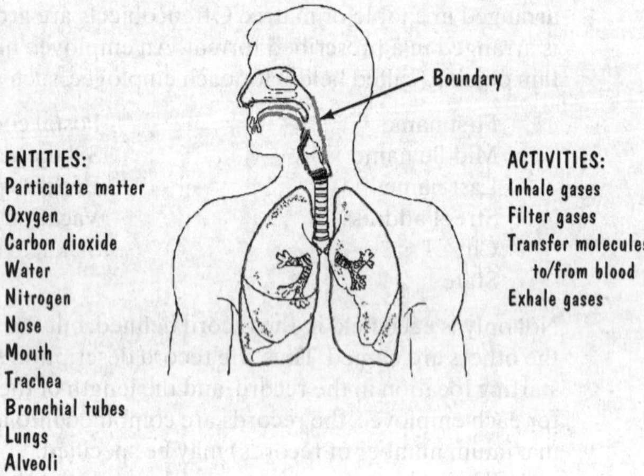

FIGURE 1.8 Respiratory system.

your body, you can say whether or not it is part of your respiratory system. Molecules of oxygen and carbon dioxide are entities or objects moving through the system in ways that are clearly defined. We can also describe the activities in the system in terms of the interactions of the entities. If necessary, we can illustrate the system by showing what enters and leaves it; we can also supply tables to describe all entities and the activities in which they are involved. Figure 1.8 illustrates the respiratory system. Note that each activity involves the entities and can be defined by describing which entities act as input, how they are processed, and what is produced (output).

We must describe our computer systems clearly, too. We work with prospective users to define the boundary of the system: Where does our work start and stop? In addition, we need to know what is on the boundary of the system and thus determine the origins of the input and destinations of the output. For example, in a system that prints paychecks, pay information may come from the company's payroll system. The system output may be a set of paychecks sent to the mail room to be delivered to the appropriate recipients. In the system shown in Figure 1.9, we can see the boundary and can understand the entities, the activities, and their relationships.

Interrelated Systems

The concept of boundary is important, because very few systems are independent of other systems. For example, the respiratory system must interact with the digestive system, the circulatory system, the nervous system, and others. The respiratory system could not function without the nervous system; neither could the circulatory system function without the respiratory system. The interdependencies may be complex. (Indeed, many of our environmental problems arise and are intensified because we do not appreciate the complexity of our ecosystem.) However, once the boundary of a system is described, it is easier for us to see what is within and without and what crosses the boundary.

In turn, it is possible for one system to exist inside another system. When we describe a computer system, we often concentrate on a small piece of what is really a

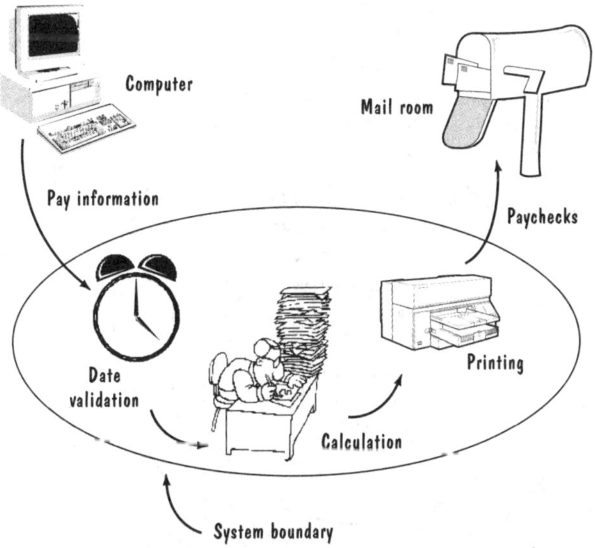

FIGURE 1.9 System definition of paycheck production.

much larger system. Such a focus allows us to define and build a much less complex system than the enveloping one. If we are careful in documenting the interactions among and between systems affecting ours, we lose nothing by concentrating on this smaller piece of a larger system.

Let us look at an example of how this can be done. Suppose we are developing a water-monitoring system where data are gathered at many points throughout a river valley. At the collection sites, several calculations are done, and the results are communicated to a central location for comprehensive reporting. Such a system may be implemented with a computer at the central site communicating with several dozen smaller computers at the remote locations. Many system activities must be considered, including the way the water data are gathered, the calculations performed at the remote locations, the communication of information to the central site, the storage of the communicated data in a database or shared data file, and the creation of reports from the data. We can view this system as a collection of systems, each with a special purpose. In particular, we can consider only the communications aspect of the larger system and develop a communications system to transmit data from a set of remote sites to a central one. If we carefully define the boundary between the communications and the larger system, the design and development of the communications system can be done independently of the larger system.

The complexity of the entire water-monitoring system is much greater than the complexity of the communications system, so our treatment of separate, smaller pieces makes our job much simpler. If the boundary definitions are detailed and correct, building the larger system from the smaller ones is relatively easy. We can describe the building process by considering the larger system in layers, as illustrated in Figure 1.10 for our water-monitoring example. A layer is a system by itself, but each layer and those it contains also form a system. The circles of the figure represent the boundaries of the respective systems, and the entire set of circles incorporates the entire water-monitoring system.

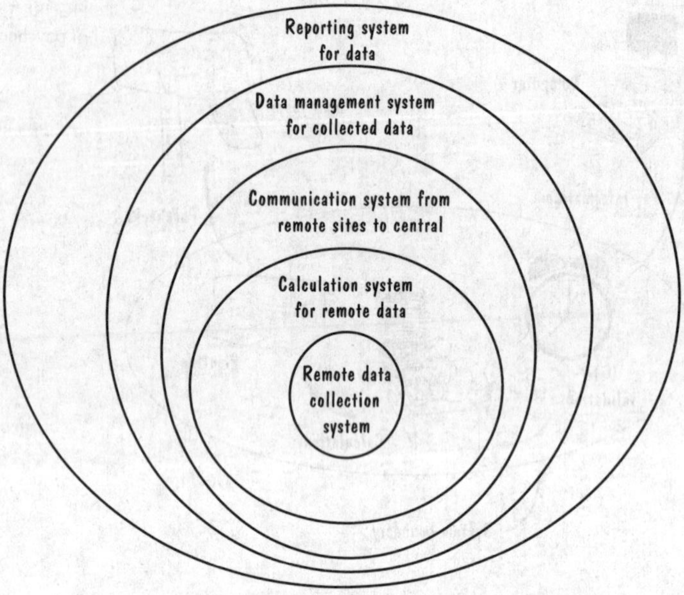

FIGURE 1.10 Layers of a water-monitoring system.

Recognizing that one system contains another is important, because it reflects the fact that an object or activity in one system is part of every system represented by the outer layers. Since more complexity is introduced with each layer, understanding any one object or activity becomes more difficult with each more encompassing system. Thus, we maximize simplicity and our consequent understanding of the system by focusing on the smallest system possible at first.

We use this idea when building a system to replace an older version, either manual or automated. We want to understand as much as possible about how both the old and new systems work. Often, the greater the difference between the two systems, the more difficult the design and development. This difficulty occurs not only because people tend to resist change, but also because the difference makes learning difficult. In building or synthesizing our grand system, it helps dramatically to construct a new system as an incremental series of intermediate systems. Rather than going from system A to system B, we may be able to go from A to A′ to A″ to B. For example, suppose A is a manual system consisting of three major functions, and B is to be an automated version of A. We can define system A′ to be a new system with function 1 automated but functions 2 and 3 still manual. Then A″ has automated functions 1 and 2, but 3 is still manual. Finally, B has all three automated functions. By dividing the "distance" from A to B in thirds, we have a series of small problems that may be easier to handle than the whole.

In our example, the two systems are very similar; the functions are the same, but the style in which they are implemented differs. However, the target system is often vastly different from the existing one. In particular, it is usually desirable that the target be free of constraints imposed by existing hardware or software. An **incremental development** approach may incorporate a series of stages, each of which frees the previous system from another such constraint. For example, stage 1 may add a new piece of hardware, stage 2 may replace the software performing a particular set of functions, and so on. The system is slowly drawn away from old software and hardware until it reflects the new system design.

Thus, system development can first incorporate a set of changes to an actual system and then add a series of changes to generate a complete design scheme, rather than trying to jump from present to future in one move. With such an approach, we must view the system in two different ways simultaneously: statically and dynamically. The static view tells us how the system is working today, whereas the dynamic view shows us how the system is changing into what it will eventually become. One view is not complete without the other.

1.6 AN ENGINEERING APPROACH

Once we understand the system's nature, we are ready to begin its construction. At this point, the "engineering" part of software engineering becomes relevant and complements what we have done so far. Recall that we began this chapter by acknowledging that writing software is an art as well as a science. The art of producing systems involves the craft of software production. As artists, we develop techniques and tools that have proven helpful in producing useful, high-quality products. For instance, we may use an optimizing compiler as a tool to generate programs that run fast on the machines we are using. Or we can include special sort or search routines as techniques for saving time or space in our system. These software-based techniques are used just as techniques and tools are used in crafting a fine piece of furniture or in building a house. Indeed, a popular collection of programming tools is called the Programmer's Workbench, because programmers rely on them as a carpenter relies on a workbench.

Because building a system is similar to building a house, we can look to house building for other examples of why the "artistic" approach to software development is important.

Building a House

Suppose Chuck and Betsy Howell hire someone to build a house for them. Because of its size and complexity, a house usually requires more than one person on the construction team; consequently, the Howells hire McMullen Construction Company. The first event involved in the house building is a conference between the Howells and McMullen so the Howells can explain what they want. This conference explores not only what the Howells want the house to look like, but also what features are to be included. Then McMullen draws up floor plans and an architect's rendering of the house. After the Howells discuss the details with McMullen, changes are made. Once the Howells give their approval to McMullen, construction begins.

During the construction process, the Howells are likely to inspect the construction site, thinking of changes they would like. Several such changes may occur during construction, but eventually the house is completed. During construction and before the Howells move in, several components of the house are tested. For example, electricians test the wiring circuits, plumbers make sure that pipes do not leak, and carpenters adjust for variation in wood so that the floors are smooth and level. Finally, the Howells move in. If there is something that is not constructed properly, McMullen may be called in to fix it, but eventually the Howells become fully responsible for the house.

Let us look more closely at what is involved in this process. First, since many people are working on the house at the same time, documentation is essential. Not only are floor plans and the architect's drawings necessary, but details must be written down so that specialists such as plumbers and electricians can fit their products together as the house becomes a whole.

Second, it is unreasonable to expect the Howells to describe their house at the beginning of the process and walk away until the house is completed. Instead, the Howells may modify the house design several times during construction. These modifications may result from a number of situations:

- Materials that were specified initially are no longer available. For example, certain kinds of roof tiles may no longer be manufactured.
- The Howells may have new ideas as they see the house take shape. For example, the Howells might realize that they can add a skylight to the kitchen for little additional cost.
- Availability or financial constraints may require the Howells to change requirements in order to meet their schedule or budget. For example, the special windows that the Howells wanted to order will not be ready in time to complete the house by winter, so stock windows may be substituted.
- Items or designs initially thought possible might turn out to be infeasible. For example, soil percolation tests may reveal that the land surrounding the house cannot support the number of bathrooms that the Howells had originally requested.

McMullen may also recommend some changes after construction has begun, perhaps because of a better idea or because a key member of the construction crew is unavailable. And both McMullen and the Howells may change their minds about a feature of the house even after the feature is completed.

Third, McMullen must provide blueprints, wiring and plumbing diagrams, instruction manuals for the appliances, and any other documentation that would enable the Howells to make modifications or repairs after they move in.

We can summarize this construction process in the following way:

- determining and analyzing the requirements
- producing and documenting the overall design of the house
- producing detailed specifications of the house
- identifying and designing the components
- building each component of the house
- testing each component of the house
- integrating the components and making final modifications after the residents have moved in
- continuing maintenance by the residents of the house

We have seen how the participants must remain flexible and allow changes in the original specifications at various points during construction.

It is important to remember that the house is built within the context of the social, economic, and governmental structure in which it is to reside. Just as the water-monitoring system in Figure 1.10 depicted the dependencies of subsystems, we must think of the house as a subsystem in a larger scheme. For example, construction of a house is done in the context of the city or county building codes and regulations. The McMullen employees are licensed by the city or county, and they are expected to perform according to building standards. The construction site is visited by building inspectors, who make sure that the standards are being followed. And the building inspectors set standards for quality, with the inspections serving as quality assurance checkpoints for the building project. There may also be social or customary constraints that suggest common or acceptable behavior; for example, it is not customary to have the front door open directly to the kitchen or bedroom.

At the same time, we must recognize that we cannot prescribe the activities of building a house exactly; we must leave room for decisions based on experience, to deal with unexpected or nonstandard situations. For example, many houses are fashioned from pre-existing components; doors are supplied already in the frame, bathrooms use pre-made shower stalls, and so on. But the standard house-building process may have to be altered to accommodate an unusual feature or request. Suppose that the framing is done, the dry-wall is up, the subfloor is laid, and the next step is putting down tile on the bathroom floor. The builders find, much to their dismay, that the walls and floor are not exactly square. This problem may not be the result of a poor process; houses are built from parts that have some natural or manufacturing variation, so problems of inexactitude can occur. The floor tile, being composed of small squares, will highlight the inexactitude if laid the standard way. It is here that art and expertise come to play. The builder is likely to remove the tiles from their backing, and lay them one at a time, making small adjustments with each one so that the overall variation is imperceptible to all but the most discerning eyes.

Thus, house building is a complex task with many opportunities for change in processes, products, or resources along the way, tempered by a healthy dose of art and expertise. The house-building process can be standardized, but there is always need for expert judgment and creativity.

Building a System

Software projects progress in a way similar to the house-building process. The Howells were the customers and users, and McMullen was the developer in our example. Had the Howells asked McMullen to build the house for Mr. Howell's parents to live in, the users, customers, and developer would have been distinct. In the same way, software development involves users, customers, and developers. If we are asked to develop a software system for a customer, the first step is meeting with the customer to determine the requirements. These requirements describe the system, as we saw before. Without knowing the boundary, the entities, and the activities, it is impossible to describe the software and how it will interact with its environment.

Once requirements are defined, we create a system design to meet the specified requirements. As we will see in Chapter 5, the system design shows the customer what the system will look like from the customer's perspective. Thus, just as the Howells looked at floor plans and architect's drawings, we present the customer with pictures of the video display screens that will be used, the reports that will be generated, and any other descriptions that will explain how users will interact with the completed system. If the system has manual backup or override procedures, those are described as well. At first, the Howells were interested only in the appearance and functionality of their house; it was not until later that they had to decide on such items as copper or plastic pipes. Likewise, the system design (also called architectural) phase of a software project describes only appearance and functionality.

The design is then reviewed by the customer. When approved, the overall system design is used to generate the designs of the individual programs involved. Note that it is not until this step that programs are mentioned. Until functionality and appearance are determined, it often makes no sense to consider coding. In our house example, we would now be ready to discuss types of pipe or quality of electrical wiring. We can decide on plastic or copper pipes because now we know where water needs to flow in the structure. Likewise, when the system design is approved by all, we are ready to discuss programs. The basis for our discussion is a well-defined description of the software project as a system; the system design includes a complete description of the functions and interactions involved.

When the programs have been written, they are tested as individual pieces of code before they can be linked together. This first phase of testing is called module or unit testing. Once we are convinced that the pieces work as desired, we put them together and make sure that they work properly when joined with others. This second testing phase is often referred to as integration testing, as we build our system by adding one piece to the next until the entire system is operational. The final testing phase, called system testing, involves a test of the whole system to make sure that the functions and interactions specified initially have been implemented properly. In this phase, the system is compared with the specified requirements; the developer, customer, and users check that the system serves its intended purpose.

At last, the final product is delivered. As it is used, discrepancies and problems are uncovered. If ours is a turnkey system, the customer assumes responsibility for the system after delivery. Many systems are not turnkey systems, though, and the developer or other organization provides maintenance if anything goes wrong or if needs and requirements change.

Thus, development of software includes the following activities:

- requirements analysis and definition
- system design
- program design
- writing the programs (program implementation)
- unit testing
- integration testing
- system testing
- system delivery
- maintenance

In an ideal situation, the activities are performed one at a time; when you reach the end of the list, you have a completed software project. However, in reality, many of the steps are repeated. For example, in reviewing the system design, you and the customer may discover that some requirements have yet to be documented. You may work with the customer to add requirements and possibly redesign the system. Similarly, when writing and testing code, you may find that a device does not function as described by its documentation. You may have to redesign the code, reconsider the system design, or even return to a discussion with the customer about how to meet the requirements. For this reason, we define a **software development process** as any description of software development that contains some of the nine activities listed before, organized so that together they produce tested code. In Chapter 2, we will explore several of the different development processes that are used in building software. Subsequent chapters will examine each of the subprocesses and their activities, from requirements analysis through maintenance. But before we do, let us look at who develops software and how the challenge of software development has changed over the years.

1.7 MEMBERS OF THE DEVELOPMENT TEAM

Earlier in this chapter, we saw that customers, users, and developers play major roles in the definition and creation of the new product. The developers are software engineers, but each engineer may specialize in a particular aspect of development. Let us look in more detail at the role of the members of the development team.

The first step in any development process is finding out what the customer wants and documenting the requirements. As we have seen, analysis is the process of breaking things into their component parts so that we can understand them better. Thus, the development team includes one or more *requirements analysts* to work with the customer, breaking down what the customer wants into discrete requirements.

Once the requirements are known and documented, analysts work with *designers* to generate a system-level description of what the system is to do. In turn, the designers work with programmers to describe the system in such a way that *programmers* can write lines of code that implement what the requirements specify.

After the code is generated, it must be tested. Often, the first testing is done by the programmers themselves; sometimes, additional *testers* are also used to help catch faults that the programmers overlook. When units of code are integrated into functioning groups, a team of testers works with the implementation team to verify that as the system is built up by combining pieces, it works properly and according to specification.

When the development team is comfortable with the functionality and quality of the system, attention turns to the *customer*. The test team and customer work together to verify that the complete system is what the customer wants; they do this by comparing how the system works with the initial set of requirements. Then, *trainers* show users how to use the system.

For many software systems, acceptance by the customer does not mean the end of the developer's job. If faults are discovered after the system has been accepted, a *maintenance team* fixes them. Moreover, the customer's requirements may change as time passes, and corresponding changes to the system must be made. Thus, maintenance can involve analysts who determine what requirements are added or changed, designers to determine where in the system design the change should be made, programmers to implement the changes, testers to make sure that the changed system still runs properly, and trainers to explain to users how the change affects the use of the system. Figure 1.11 illustrates how the roles of the development team correspond to the steps of development.

Students often work by themselves or in small groups as a development team for class projects. The documentation requested by the instructor is minimal; students are usually not required to write a user manual or training documents. Moreover, the assignment is relatively stable; the requirements do not change over the life of the project. Finally, student-built systems are likely to be discarded at the end of the course; their purpose is to demonstrate ability but not necessarily to solve a problem for a real customer. Thus, program size, system complexity, need for documentation, and need for maintainability are relatively small for class projects.

However, for a real customer, the system size and complexity may be large and the need for documentation and maintainability great. For a project involving many thousands of lines of code and much interaction among members of the development team, control of the various aspects of the project may be difficult. To support everyone on the development team, several people may become involved with the system at the beginning of development and remain involved throughout.

Librarians prepare and store documents that are used during the life of the system, including requirements specifications, design descriptions, program documentation, training manuals, test data, schedules, and more. Working with the librarians are

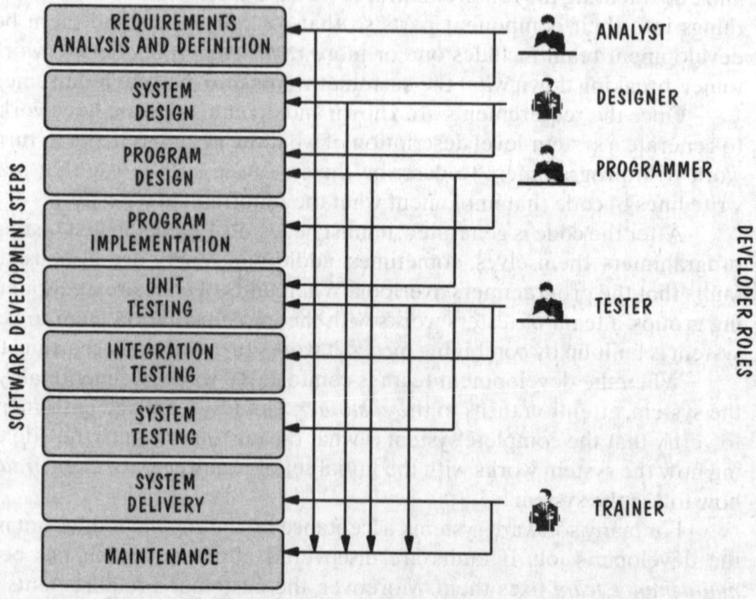

FIGURE 1.11 The roles of the development team.

the members of a *configuration management team*. Configuration management involves maintaining a correspondence among the requirements, the design, the implementation, and the tests. This cross-reference tells developers what program to alter if a change in requirements is needed, or what parts of a program will be affected if an alteration of some kind is proposed. Configuration management staff also coordinate the different versions of a system that may be built and supported. For example, a software system may be hosted on different platforms or may be delivered in a series of releases. Configuration management ensures that the functionality is consistent from one platform to another, and that it doesn't degrade with a new release.

The development roles can be assumed by one person or several. For small projects, two or three people may share all roles. However, for larger projects, the development team is often separated into distinct groups based on their function in development. Sometimes, those who maintain the system are different from those who design or write the system initially. For a very large development project, the customer can even hire one company to do the initial development and another to do the maintenance. As we discuss the development and maintenance activities in later chapters, we will look at what skills are needed by each type of development role.

1.8 HOW HAS SOFTWARE ENGINEERING CHANGED?

We have compared the building of software to the building of a house. Each year, hundreds of houses are built across the country, and satisfied customers move in. Each year, hundreds of software products are built by developers, but customers are too often unhappy with the result. Why is there a difference? If it is so easy to enumerate the steps in the development of a system, why are we as software engineers having such a difficult time producing quality software?

Think back to our house-building example. During the building process, the Howells continually reviewed the plans. They also had many opportunities to change their minds about what they wanted. In the same way, software development allows the customer to review the plans at every step and to make changes in the design. After all, if the developer produces a marvelous product that does not meet the customer's needs, the resultant system will have wasted everyone's time and effort.

For this reason, it is essential that our software engineering tools and techniques be used with an eye toward flexibility. In the past, we as developers assumed that our customers knew from the start what they wanted. That stability is not usually the case. As the various stages of a project unfold, constraints arise that were not anticipated at the beginning. For instance, after having chosen hardware and software to use for a project, we may find that a change in the customer requirements makes it difficult to use a particular database management system to produce menus exactly as promised to the customer. Or we may find that another system with which ours is to interface has changed its procedure or the format of the expected data. We may even find that hardware or software does not work quite as the vendor's documentation had promised. Thus, we must remember that each project is unique and that tools and techniques must be chosen that reflect the constraints placed on the individual project.

We must also acknowledge that most systems do not stand by themselves. They interface with other systems, either to receive or to provide information. Developing such systems is complex simply because they require a great deal of coordination with the systems with which they communicate. This complexity is especially true of systems that are being developed concurrently. In the past, developers had difficulty ensuring the accuracy and completeness of the documentation of interfaces among systems. In subsequent chapters, we will address the issue of controlling the interface problem.

The Nature of the Change

These problems are among many that affect the success of our software development projects. Whatever approach we take, we must look both backward and forward. That is, we must look back at previous development projects to see what we have learned, not only about ensuring software quality, but also about the effectiveness of our techniques and tools. And we must look ahead to the way software development and the use of software products are likely to change our practices in the future. Wasserman (1995) points out that the changes since the 1970s have been dramatic. For example, early applications were intended to run on a single processor, usually a mainframe. The input was linear, usually a deck of cards or an input tape, and the output was alphanumeric. The system was designed in one of two basic ways: as a **transformation**, where input was converted to output, or as a **transaction**, where input determined which function would be performed. Today's software-based systems are far different and more complex. Typically, they run on multiple systems, sometimes configured in a client-server architecture with distributed functionality. Software performs not only the primary functions that the user needs, but also network control, security, user-interface presentation and processing, and data or object management. The traditional "waterfall" approach to development, which assumes a linear progression of development activities, where one begins only when its predecessor is complete (and which we will study in Chapter 2), is no longer flexible or suitable for today's systems.

In his Stevens lecture, Wasserman (1996) summarized these changes by identifying seven key factors that have altered software engineering practice, illustrated in Figure 1.12:

1. criticality of time-to-market for commercial products
2. shifts in the economics of computing: lower hardware costs and greater development and maintenance costs
3. availability of powerful desktop computing
4. extensive local- and wide-area networking
5. availability and adoption of object-oriented technology
6. graphical user interfaces using windows, icons, menus, and pointers
7. unpredictability of the waterfall model of software development

For example, the pressures of the marketplace mean that businesses must ready their new products and services before their competitors do; otherwise, the viability of the business itself may be at stake. So traditional techniques for review and testing cannot be used if they require large investments of time that are not recouped as reduced fault or failure rates. Similarly, time previously spent in optimizing code to improve speed or

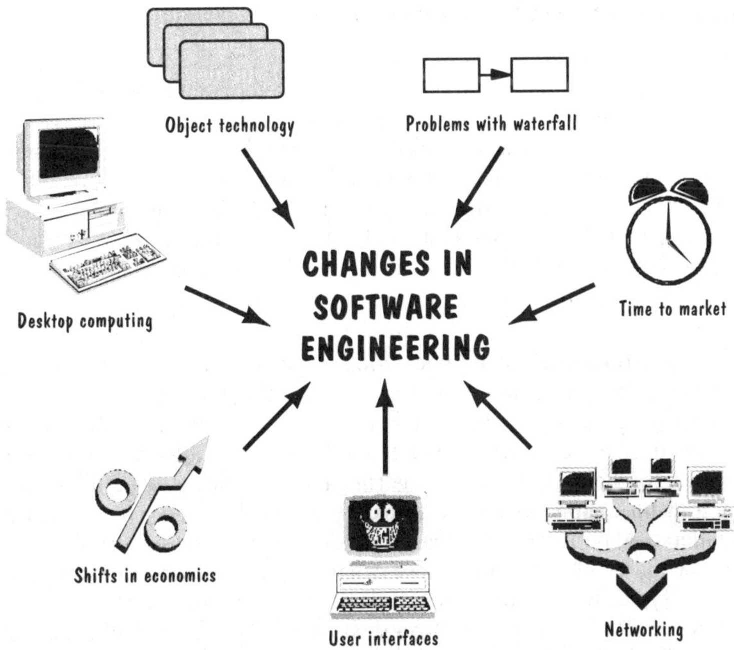

FIGURE 1.12 The key factors that have changed software development.

reduce space may no longer be a wise investment; an additional disk or memory card may be a far cheaper solution to the problem.

Moreover, desktop computing puts development power in the hands of users, who now use their systems to develop spreadsheet and database applications, small programs, and even specialized user interfaces and simulations. This shift of development responsibility means that we, as software engineers, are likely to be building more complex systems than before. Similarly, the vast networking capabilities available to most users and developers make it easier for users to find information without special applications. For instance, searching the World Wide Web is quick, easy, and effective; the user no longer needs to write a database application to find what he or she needs.

Developers now find their jobs enhanced, too. Object-oriented technology, coupled with networks and reuse repositories, makes available to developers a large collection of reusable modules for immediate and speedy inclusion in new applications. And graphical user interfaces, often developed with a specialized tool, help put a friendly face on complicated applications. Because we have become sophisticated in the way we analyze problems, we can now partition a system so we develop its subsystems in parallel, requiring a development process very different from the waterfall model. We will see in Chapter 2 that we have many choices for this process, including some that allow us to build prototypes (to verify with customers and users that the requirements are correct, and to assess the feasibility of designs) and iterate among activities. These steps help us to ensure that our requirements and designs are as fault-free as possible before we instantiate them in code.

Wasserman's Discipline of Software Engineering

Wasserman (1996) points out that any one of the seven technological changes would have a significant effect on the software development process. But taken together, they have transformed the way we work. In his presentations, DeMarco describes this radical shift by saying that we solved the easy problems first—which means that the set of problems left to be solved is much harder now than it was before. Wasserman addresses this challenge by suggesting that there are eight fundamental notions in software engineering that form the basis for an effective discipline of software engineering. We introduce them briefly here, and we return to them in later chapters to see where and how they apply to what we do.

Abstraction. Sometimes, looking at a problem in its "natural state" (i.e., as expressed by the customer or user) is a daunting task. We cannot see an obvious way to tackle the problem in an effective or even feasible way. An **abstraction** is a description of the problem at some level of generalization that allows us to concentrate on the key aspects of the problem without getting mired in the details. This notion is different from a **transformation**, where we translate the problem to another environment that we understand better; transformation is often used to move a problem from the real world to the mathematical world, so we can manipulate numbers to solve the problem.

Typically, abstraction involves identifying classes of objects that allow us to group items together; this way, we can deal with fewer things and concentrate on the commonalities of the items in each class. We can talk of the properties or attributes of the items in a class and examine the relationships among properties and classes. For example, suppose we are asked to build an environmental monitoring system for a large and complex river. The monitoring equipment may involve sensors for air quality, water quality, temperature, speed, and other characteristics of the environment. But, for our purposes, we may choose to define a class called "sensor"; each item in the class has certain properties, regardless of the characteristic it is monitoring: height, weight, electrical requirements, maintenance schedule, and so on. We can deal with the class, rather than its elements, in learning about the problem context, and in devising a solution. In this way, the classes help us to simplify the problem statement and focus on the essential elements or characteristics of the problem.

We can form hierarchies of abstractions, too. For instance, a sensor is a type of electrical device, and we may have two types of sensors: water sensors and air sensors.

Thus, we can form the simple hierarchy illustrated in Figure 1.13. By hiding some of the details, we can concentrate on the essential nature of the objects with which we must deal and derive solutions that are simple and elegant. We will take a closer look at abstraction and information hiding in Chapters 5, 6, and 7.

Analysis and Design Methods and Notations. When you design a program as a class assignment, you usually work on your own. The documentation that you produce is a formal description of your notes to yourself about why you chose a particular approach, what the variable names mean, and which algorithm you implemented. But when you work with a team, you must communicate with many other participants in the development process. Most engineers, no matter what kind of engineering they do,

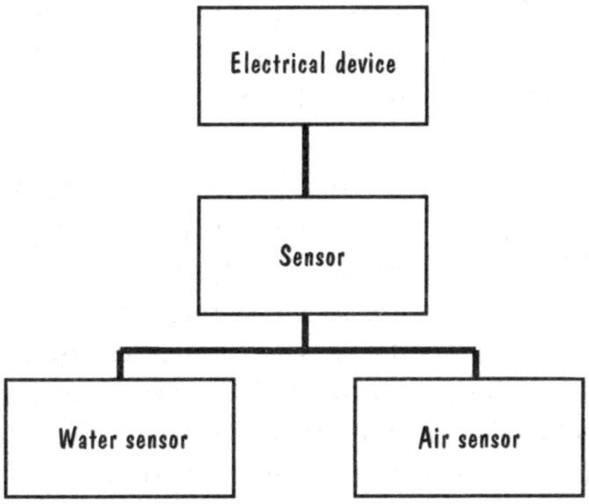

FIGURE 1.13 Simple hierarchy for monitoring equipment.

use a standard notation to help them communicate, and to document decisions. For example, an architect draws a diagram or blueprint that any other architect can understand. More importantly, the common notation allows the building contractor to understand the architect's intent and ideas. As we will see in Chapters 4, 5, 6, and 7, there are few similar standards in software engineering, and the misinterpretation that results is one of the key problems of software engineering today.

Analysis and design methods offer us more than a communication medium. They allow us to build models and check them for completeness and consistency. Moreover, we can more readily reuse requirements and design components from previous projects, increasing our productivity and quality with relative ease.

But there are many open questions to be resolved before we can settle on a common set of methods and tools. As we will see in later chapters, different tools and techniques address different aspects of a problem, and we need to identify the modeling primitives that will allow us to capture all the important aspects of a problem with a single technique. Or we need to develop a representation technique that can be used with all methods, possibly tailored in some way.

User Interface Prototyping. **Prototyping** means building a small version of a system, usually with limited functionality, that can be used to

- help the user or customer identify the key requirements of a system
- demonstrate the feasibility of a design or approach

Often, the prototyping process is iterative: We build a prototype, evaluate it (with user and customer feedback), consider how changes might improve the product or design, and then build another prototype. The iteration ends when we and our customers think we have a satisfactory solution to the problem at hand.

Prototyping is often used to design a good **user interface**: the part of the system with which the user interacts. However, there are other opportunities for using prototypes, even in **embedded systems** (i.e., in systems where the software functions are not explicitly visible to the user). The prototype can show the user what functions will be available, regardless of whether they are implemented in software or hardware. Since the user interface is, in a sense, a bridge between the application domain and the software development team, prototyping can bring to the surface issues and assumptions that may not have been clear using other approaches to requirements analysis. We will consider the role of user interface prototyping in Chapters 4 and 5.

Software Architecture. The overall architecture of a system is important not only to the ease of implementing and testing it, but also to the speed and effectiveness of maintaining and changing it. The quality of the architecture can make or break a system; indeed, Shaw and Garlan (1996) present architecture as a discipline on its own whose effects are felt throughout the entire development process. The architectural structure of a system should reflect the principles of good design that we will study in Chapters 5 and 7.

A system's architecture describes the system in terms of a set of architectural units, and a map of how the units relate to one another. The more independent the units, the more modular the architecture and the more easily we can design and develop the pieces separately. Wasserman (1996) points out that there are at least five ways that we can partition the system into units:

1. modular decomposition: based on assigning functions to modules
2. data-oriented decomposition: based on external data structures
3. event-oriented decomposition: based on events that the system must handle
4. outside-in design: based on user inputs to the system
5. object-oriented design: based on identifying classes of objects and their interrelationships

These approaches are not mutually exclusive. For example, we can design a user interface with event-oriented decomposition, while we design the database using object-oriented or data-oriented design. We will examine these techniques in further detail in later chapters. The importance of these approaches is their capture of our design experience, enabling us to capitalize on our past projects by reusing both what we have done and what we learned by doing it.

Software Process. Since the late 1980s, many software engineers have paid careful attention to the *process* of developing software, as well as to the products that result. The organization and discipline in the activities have been acknowledged to contribute to the quality of the software and to the speed with which it is developed. However, Wasserman notes that

> the great variations among application types and organizational cultures make it impossible to be prescriptive about the process itself. Thus, it appears that the software process is not fundamental to software engineering in the same way as are abstraction and modularization. (Wasserman 1996)

Instead, he suggests that different types of software need different processes. In particular, Wasserman suggests that enterprisewide applications need a great deal of control, whereas individual and departmental applications can take advantage of rapid application development, as we illustrate in Figure 1.14.

By using today's tools, many small and medium-sized systems can be built by one or two developers, each of whom must take on multiple roles. The tools may include a

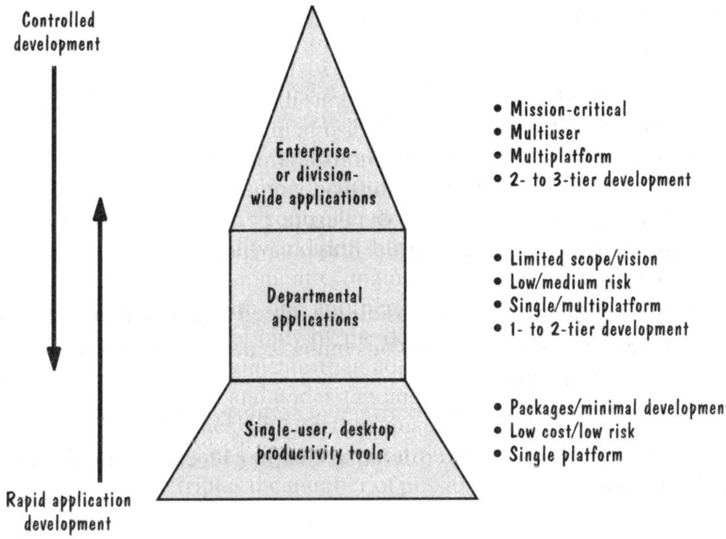

FIGURE 1.14 Differences in development (Wasserman 1996).

text editor, programming environment, testing support, and perhaps a small database to capture key data elements about the products and processes. Because the project's risk is relatively low, little management support or review is needed.

However, large, complex systems need more structure, checks, and balances. These systems often involve many customers and users, and development continues over a long period of time. Moreover, the developers do not always have control over the entire development, as some critical subsystems may be supplied by others or be implemented in hardware. This type of high-risk system requires analysis and design tools, project management, configuration management, more sophisticated testing tools, and a more rigorous system of review and causal analysis. In Chapter 2, we will take a careful look at several process alternatives to see how varying the process addresses different goals. Then, in Chapters 12 and 13, we evaluate the effectiveness of some processes and look at ways to improve them.

Reuse. In software development and maintenance, we often take advantage of the commonalities across applications by reusing items from previous development. For example, we use the same operating system or database management system from one development project to the next, rather than building a new one each time. Similarly, we reuse sets of requirements, parts of designs, and groups of test scripts or data when we build systems that are similar to but not the same as what we have done before. Barnes and Bollinger (1991) point out that reuse is not a new idea, and they provide many interesting examples of how we reuse much more than just code.

Prieto-Díaz (1991) introduced the notion of reusable components as a business asset. Companies and organizations invest in items that are reusable and then gain quantifiable benefit when those items are used again in subsequent projects. However, establishing a long-term, effective reuse program can be difficult, because there are several barriers:

- It is sometimes faster to build a small component than to search for one in a repository of reusable components.
- It may take extra time to make a component general enough to be reusable easily by other developers in the future.
- It is difficult to document the degree of quality assurance and testing that have been done, so that a potential reuser can feel comfortable about the quality of the component.
- It is not clear who is responsible if a reused component fails or needs to be updated.
- It can be costly and time-consuming to understand and reuse a component written by someone else.
- There is often a conflict between generality and specificity.

We will look at reuse in more detail in Chapter 12, examining several examples of successful reuse.

Measurement. Improvement is a driving force in software engineering research: improving our processes, resources, and methods so that we produce and maintain better products. But sometimes we express improvement goals generally, with no quantitative description of where we are and where we would like to go. For this reason, software measurement has become a key aspect of good software engineering practice. By quantifying where we can and what we can, we describe our actions and their outcomes in a common mathematical language that allows us to evaluate our progress. In addition, a quantitative approach permits us to compare progress across disparate projects. For example, when John Young was CEO of Hewlett-Packard, he set goals of "10X," a tenfold improvement in quality and productivity, for every project at Hewlett-Packard, regardless of application type or domain (Grady and Caswell 1987).

At a lower level of abstraction, measurement can help to make specific characteristics of our processes and products more visible. It is often useful to transform our understanding of the real, empirical world to elements and relationships in the formal, mathematical world, where we can manipulate them to gain further understanding. As illustrated in Figure 1.15, we can use mathematics and statistics to solve a problem, look for trends, or characterize a situation (such as with means and standard deviations). This new information can then be mapped back to the real world and applied as part of a solution to the empirical problem we are trying to solve. Throughout this book, we will see examples of how measurement is used to support analysis and decision making.

Tools and Integrated Environments. For many years, vendors touted CASE (Computer-Aided Software Engineering) tools, where standardized, integrated development environments would enhance software development. However, we have seen how different developers use different processes, methods, and resources, so a unifying approach is easier said than done.

On the other hand, researchers have proposed several frameworks that allow us to compare and contrast both existing and proposed environments. These frameworks

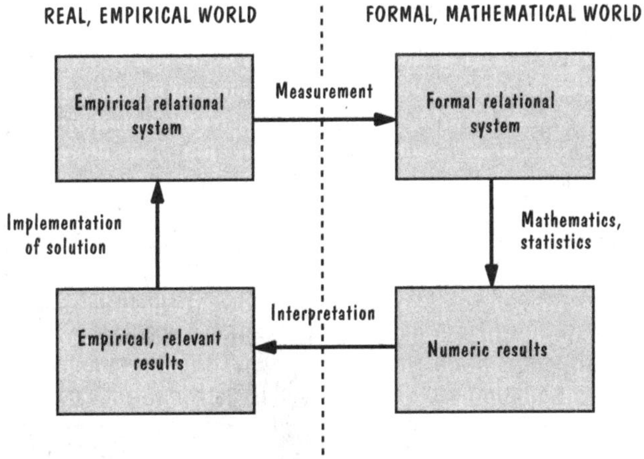

FIGURE 1.15 Using measurement to help find a solution.

permit us to examine the services provided by each software engineering environment and to decide which environment is best for a given problem or application development.

One of the major difficulties in comparing tools is that vendors rarely address the entire development life cycle. Instead, they focus on a small set of activities, such as design or testing, and it is up to the user to integrate the selected tools into a complete development environment. Wasserman (1990) has identified five issues that must be addressed in any tool integration:

1. platform integration: the ability of tools to interoperate on a heterogeneous network
2. presentation integration: commonality of user interface
3. process integration: linkage between the tools and the development process
4. data integration: the way tools share data
5. control integration: the ability for one tool to notify and initiate action in another

In each of the subsequent chapters of this book, we will examine tools that support the activities and concepts we describe in the chapter.

You can think of the eight concepts described here as eight threads woven through the fabric of this book, tying together the disparate activities we call software engineering. As we learn more about software engineering, we will revisit these ideas to see how they unify and elevate software engineering as a scientific discipline.

1.9 INFORMATION SYSTEMS EXAMPLE

Throughout this book, we will end each chapter with two examples, one of an information system and the other of a real-time system. We will apply the concepts described in the chapter to some aspect of each example, so that you can see what the concepts mean in practice, not just in theory.

FIGURE 1.16 Piccadilly Television franchise area.

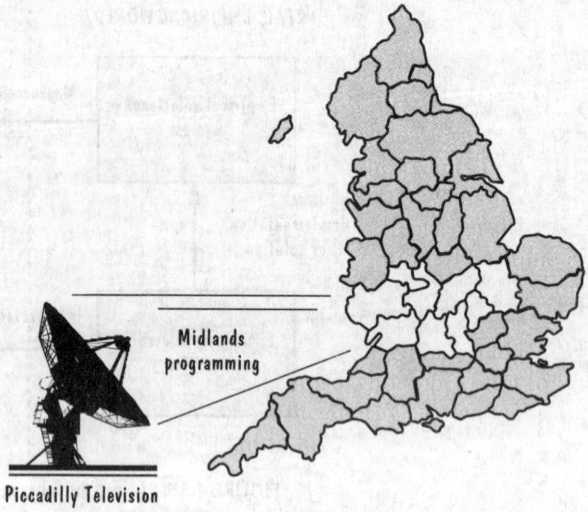

Our information system example is drawn (with permission) from *Complete Systems Analysis: The Workbook, the Textbook, the Answers,* by James and Suzanne Robertson (Robertson and Robertson 1994). It involves the development of a system to sell advertising time for Piccadilly Television, the holder of a regional British television franchise. Figure 1.16 illustrates the Piccadilly Television viewing area. As we shall see, the constraints on the price of television time are many and varied, so the problem is both interesting and difficult. In this book, we highlight aspects of the problem and its solution; the Robertsons' book shows you detailed methods for capturing and analyzing the system requirements.

In Britain, the broadcasting board issues an eight-year franchise to a commercial television company, giving it exclusive rights to broadcast its programs in a carefully defined region of the country. In return, the franchisee must broadcast a prescribed balance of drama, comedy, sports, children's and other programs. Moreover, there are restrictions on which programs can be broadcast at which times, as well as rules about the content of programs and commercial advertising.

A commercial advertiser has several choices to reach the Midlands audience: Piccadilly, the cable channels, and the satellite channels. However, Piccadilly attracts most of the audience. Thus, Piccadilly must set its rates to attract a portion of an advertiser's national budget. One of the ways to attract an advertiser's attention is with audience ratings that reflect the number and type of viewers at different times of the day. The ratings are reported in terms of program type, audience type, time of day, television company, and more. But the advertising rate depends on more than just the ratings. For example, the rate per hour may be cheaper if the advertiser buys a large number of hours. Moreover, there are restrictions on the type of advertising at certain times and for certain programs. For example,

- Advertisements for alcohol may be shown only after 9 P.M.
- If an actor is in a show, then an advertisement with that actor may not be broadcast within 45 minutes of the show.

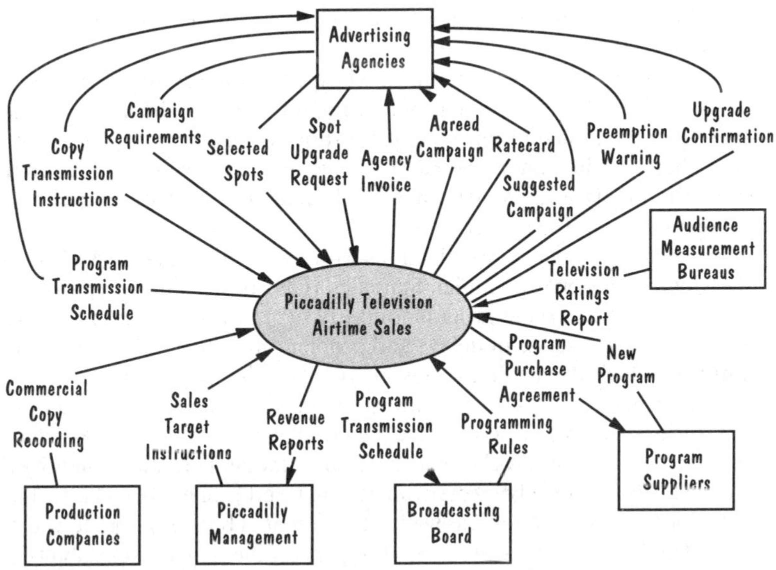

FIGURE 1.17 Piccadilly context diagram showing system boundary (Robertson and Robertson 1994).

- If an advertisement for a class of product (such as an automobile) is scheduled for a particular commercial break, then no other advertisement for something in that class may be shown during that break.

As we explore this example in more detail, we will note the additional rules and regulations about advertising and its cost. The system context diagram in Figure 1.17 shows us the system boundary and how it relates to these rules. The shaded oval is the Piccadilly system that concerns us as our information system example; the system boundary is simply the perimeter of the oval. The arrows and boxes display the items that can affect the working of the Piccadilly system, but we consider them only as a collection of inputs and outputs, with their sources and destinations, respectively.

In later chapters, we will make visible the activities and elements inside the shaded oval (i.e., within the system boundary). We will examine the design and development of this system using the software engineering techniques that are described in each chapter.

1.10 REAL-TIME EXAMPLE

Our real-time example is based on the embedded software in the Ariane-5, a space rocket belonging to the European Space Agency (ESA). On June 4, 1996, on its maiden flight, the Ariane-5 was launched and performed perfectly for approximately 40 seconds. Then, it began to veer off course. At the direction of an Ariane ground controller, the rocket was destroyed by remote control. The destruction of the uninsured rocket was a loss not only of the rocket itself, but also of the four satellites it contained; the total cost of the disaster was $500 million (Lions et al. 1996; Newsbytes home page 1996).

Software is involved in almost all aspects of the system, from the guidance of the rocket to the internal workings of its component parts. The failure of the rocket and its subsequent destruction raise many questions about software quality. As we will see in later chapters, the inquiry board that investigated the cause of the problem focused on software quality and its assurance. In this chapter, we look at quality in terms of the business value of the rocket.

There were many organizations with a stake in the success of Ariane-5: the ESA, the Centre National d'Etudes Spatiales (CNES, the French space agency in overall command of the Ariane program), and 12 other European countries. The rocket's loss was another in a series of delays and problems to affect the Ariane program, including a nitrogen leak during engine testing in 1995 that killed two engineers. However, the June 1996 incident was the first whose cause was directly attributed to software failure.

The business impact of the incident went well beyond the $500 million in equipment. In 1996, the Ariane-4 rocket and previous variants held more than half of the world's launch contracts, ahead of American, Russian, and Chinese launchers. Thus, the credibility of the program was at stake, as well as the potential business from future Ariane rockets.

The future business was based in part on the new rocket's ability to carry heavier payloads into orbit than previous launchers could. Ariane-5 was designed to carry a single satellite up to 6.8 tons or two satellites with a combined weight of 5.9 tons. Further development work hoped to add an extra ton to the launch capacity by 2002. This increased carrying capacity has clear business advantages; often, operators reduce their costs by sharing launches, so Ariane can offer to host several companies' payloads at the same time.

Consider what quality means in the context of this example. The destruction of Ariane-5 turned out to be the result of a requirement that was misspecified by the customer. In this case, the developer might claim that the system is still high quality; it was just built to the wrong specification. Indeed, the inquiry board formed to investigate the cause and cure of the disaster noted that

> The Board's findings are based on thorough and open presentations from the Ariane-5 project teams, and on documentation which has demonstrated the high quality of the Ariane-5 programme as regards engineering work in general and completeness and traceability of documents. (Lions et al. 1996)

But from the user's and customer's point of view, the specification process should have been good enough to identify the specification flaw and force the customer to correct the specification before damage was done. The inquiry board acknowledged that

> The supplier of the SRI [the subsystem in which the cause of the problem was eventually located] was only following the specification given to it, which stipulated that in the event of any detected exception the processor was to be stopped. The exception which occurred was not due to random failure but a design error. The exception was detected, but inappropriately handled because the view had been taken that software should be considered correct until it is shown to be at fault. The Board has reason to believe that this view is also accepted in other areas of Ariane-5 software design. The Board is in favour of the opposite view, that software should be assumed to be faulty until applying the currently accepted best practice methods can demonstrate that it is correct. (Lions et al. 1996)

In later chapters, we will investigate this example in more detail, looking at the design, testing, and maintenance implications of the developers' and customers' decisions. We will see how poor systems engineering at the beginning of development led to a series of poor decisions that led in turn to disaster. On the other hand, the openness of all concerned, including ESA and the inquiry board, coupled with high-quality documentation and an earnest desire to get at the truth quickly, resulted in quick resolution of the immediate problem and an effective plan to prevent such problems in the future.

A systems view allowed the inquiry board, in cooperation with the developers, to view the Ariane-5 as a collection of subsystems. This collection reflects the analysis of the problem, as we described in this chapter, so that different developers can work on separate subsystems with distinctly different functions. For example:

> The attitude of the launcher and its movements in space are measured by an Inertial Reference System (SRI). It has its own internal computer, in which angles and velocities are calculated on the basis of information from a "strap-down" inertial platform, with laser gyros and accelerometers. The data from the SRI are transmitted through the databus to the On-Board Computer (OBC), which executes the flight program and controls the nozzles of the solid boosters and the Vulcain cryogenic engine, via servovalves and hydraulic actuators. (Lions et al. 1996)

But the synthesis of the solution must include an overview of all the component parts, where the parts are viewed together to determine if the "glue" that holds them together is sufficient and appropriate. In the case of Ariane-5, the inquiry board suggested that the customers and developers should have worked together to find the critical software and make sure that it could handle not only anticipated but also unanticipated behavior.

> This means that critical software—in the sense that failure of the software puts the mission at risk—must be identified at a very detailed level, that exceptional behaviour must be confined, and that a reasonable back-up policy must take software failures into account. (Lions et al. 1996)

1.11 WHAT THIS CHAPTER MEANS FOR YOU

This chapter has introduced many concepts that are essential to good software engineering research and practice. You, as an individual software developer, can use these concepts in the following ways:

- When you are given a problem to solve (whether or not the solution involves software), you can analyze the problem by breaking it into its component parts, and the relationships among the parts. Then, you can synthesize a solution by solving the individual subproblems and merging them to form a unified whole.
- You must understand that the requirements may change, even as you are analyzing the problem and building a solution. So your solution should be well-documented and flexible, and you should document your assumptions and the algorithms you use (so that they are easy to change later).
- You must view quality from several different perspectives, understanding that technical quality and business quality may be very different.

- You can use abstraction and measurement to help identify the essential aspects of the problem and solution.
- You can keep the system boundary in mind, so that your solution does not overlap with the related systems that interact with the one you are building.

1.12 WHAT THIS CHAPTER MEANS FOR YOUR DEVELOPMENT TEAM

Much of your work will be done as a member of a larger development team. As we have seen in this chapter, development involves requirements analysis, design, implementation, testing, configuration management, quality assurance, and more. Some of the people on your team may wear multiple hats, as may you, and the success of the project depends in large measure on the communication and coordination among the team members. We have seen in this chapter that you can aid the success of your project by selecting

- a development process that is appropriate to your team size, risk level, and application domain
- tools that are well-integrated and support the type of communication your project demands
- measurements and supporting tools to give you as much visibility and understanding as possible

1.13 WHAT THIS CHAPTER MEANS FOR RESEARCHERS

Many of the issues discussed in this chapter are good subjects for further research. We have noted some of the open issues in software engineering, including the need to find

- the right levels of abstraction to make the problem easy to solve
- the right measurements to make the essential nature of the problem and solution visible and helpful
- an appropriate problem decomposition, where each subproblem is solvable
- a common framework or notation to allow easy and effective tool integration, and to maximize communication among project participants

In later chapters, we will describe many techniques. Some have been used and are well-proven software development practices, whereas others are proposed and have been demonstrated only on small, "toy," or student projects. We hope to show you how to improve what you are doing now and at the same time to inspire you to be creative and thoughtful about trying new techniques and processes in the future.

1.14 TERM PROJECT

It is impossible to learn software engineering without participating in developing a software project with your colleagues. For this reason, each chapter of this book will present information about a term project that you can perform with a team of classmates. The project, based on a real system in a real organization, will allow you to address some of the very real challenges of analysis, design, implementation, testing, and maintenance. In addition, because you will be working with a team, you will deal with issues of team diversity and project management.

The term project involves the kinds of loans you might negotiate with a bank when you want to buy a house. Banks generate income in many ways, often by borrowing money from their depositors at a low interest rate and then lending that same money back at a higher interest rate in the form of bank loans. However, long-term property loans, such as mortgages, typically have terms of up to 15, 25, or even 30 years. That is, you have 15, 25, or 30 years to repay the loan: the principal (the money you originally borrowed) plus interest at the specified rate. Although the income from interest on these loans is lucrative, the loans tie up money for a long time, preventing the banks from using their money for other transactions. Consequently, the banks often sell their loans to consolidating organizations, taking less long-term profit in exchange for freeing the capital for use in other ways.

The application for your term project is called the Loan Arranger. It is fashioned on ways in which a (mythical) Financial Consolidation Organization (FCO) handles the loans it buys from banks. The consolidation organization makes money by purchasing loans from banks and selling them to investors. The bank sells the loan to FCO, getting the principal in return. Then, as we shall see, FCO sells the loan to investors who are willing to wait longer than the bank to get their return.

To see how the transactions work, consider how you get a loan (called a "mortgage") for a house. You may purchase a \$150,000 house by paying \$50,000 as an initial payment (called the "down payment") and taking a loan for the remaining \$100,000. The "terms" of your loan from the First National Bank may be for 30 years at 5% interest. This terminology means that the First National Bank gives you 30 years (the term of the loan) to pay back the amount you borrowed (the "principal") plus interest on whatever you do not pay back right away. For example, you can pay the \$100,000 by making a payment once a month for 30 years (that is, 360 "installments" or "monthly payments"), with interest on the unpaid balance. If the initial balance is \$100,000, the bank calculates your monthly payment using the amount of principal, the interest rate, the amount of time you have to pay off the loan, and the assumption that all monthly payments should be the same amount.

For instance, suppose the bank tells you that your monthly payment is to be \$536.82. The first month's interest is $(1/12) \times (.05) \times (\$100{,}000)$, or \$416.67. The rest of the payment $(\$536.82 - 416.67)$ pays for reducing the principal: \$120.15. For the second month, you now owe \$100,000 minus the \$120.15, so the interest is reduced to $(1/12) \times (.05) \times (\$100{,}000 - 120.15)$, or \$416.17. Thus, during the second month, only \$416.17 of the monthly payment is interest, and the remainder, \$120.65, is applied to the remaining principal. Over time, you pay less interest and more toward reducing the remaining balance of principal, until you have paid off the entire principal and own your property free and clear of any encumbrance by the bank.

First National Bank may sell your loan to FCO some time during the period when you are making payments. First National negotiates a price with FCO. In turn, FCO may sell your loan to ABC Investment Corporation. You still make your mortgage payments each month, but your payment goes to ABC, not First National. Usually, FCO sells its loans in "bundles," not individual loans, so that an investor buys a collection of loans based on risk, principal involved, and expected rate of return. In other words, an investor such as ABC can contact FCO and specify how much money it wishes to invest, for how long, how much risk it is willing to take (based on the history of the people or organizations paying back the loan), and how much profit is expected.

The Loan Arranger is an application that allows an FCO analyst to select a bundle of loans to match an investor's desired investment characteristics. The application accesses information about loans purchased by FCO from a variety of lending institutions. When an investor specifies investment criteria, the system selects the optimal bundle of loans that satisfies the criteria. While the system will allow some advanced optimizations, such as selecting the best bundle of loans from a subset of those available (for instance, from all loans in Massachusetts, rather than from all the loans available), the system will still allow an analyst to manually select loans in a bundle for the client. In addition to bundle selection, the system also automates information management activities, such as updating bank information, updating loan information, and adding new loans when banks provide that information each month.

We can summarize this information by saying that the Loan Arranger system allows a loan analyst to access information about mortgages (home loans, described here simply as "loans") purchased by FCO from multiple lending institutions with the intention of repackaging the loans to sell to other investors. The loans purchased by FCO for investment and resale are collectively known as the loan portfolio. The Loan Arranger system tracks these portfolio loans in its repository of loan information. The loan analyst may add, view, update, or delete loan information about lenders and the set of loans in the portfolio. Additionally, the system allows the loan analyst to create "bundles" of loans for sale to investors. A user of Loan Arranger is a loan analyst who tracks the mortgages purchased by FCO.

In later chapters, we will explore the system's requirements in more depth. For now, if you need to brush up on your understanding of principal and interest, you can review your old math books or look at http://www.interest.com/hugh/calc/formula.html.

1.15 KEY REFERENCES

You can find out about software faults and failures by looking in the Risks Forum, moderated by Peter Neumann. A paper copy of some of the Risks is printed in each issue of *Software Engineering Notes*, published by the Association for Computer Machinery's Special Interest Group on Software Engineering (SIGSOFT). The Risks archives are available on ftp.sri.com, cd risks. The Risks Forum newsgroup is available online at comp.risks, or you can subscribe via the automated list server at risks-request@CSL.sri.com.

You can find out more about the Ariane-5 project from the European Space Agency's Web site: http://www.esrin.esa.it/htdocs/esa/ariane. A copy of the joint ESA/CNES press release describing the mission failure (in English) is at http://www.esrin.esa.it/htdocs/tidc/Press/Press96/press19.html. A French version of the press release is at http://www.cnes.fr/Acces_Espace/Vol_50x.html. An electronic copy of the Ariane-5 Flight 501 Failure Report is at http://www.esrin.esa.it/htdocs/tidc/Press/Press96/ariane5rep.html.

Leveson and Turner (1993) describe the Therac software design and testing problems in careful detail.

The January 1996 issue of *IEEE Software* is devoted to software quality. In particular, the introductory article by Kitchenham and Pfleeger (1996) describes and critiques several quality frameworks, and the article by Dromey (1996) discusses how to define quality in a measurable way.

For more information about the Piccadilly Television example, you may consult (Robertson and Robertson 1994) or explore the Robertsons' approach to requirements at www.systemsguild.com.

1.16 EXERCISES

1. The following article appeared in the *Washington Post* (Associated Press 1996):

PILOT'S COMPUTER ERROR CITED IN PLANE CRASH. AMERICAN AIRLINES SAYS ONE-LETTER CODE WAS REASON JET HIT MOUNTAIN IN COLOMBIA.

Dallas, Aug. 23—The captain of an American Airlines jet that crashed in Colombia last December entered an incorrect one-letter computer command that sent the plane into a mountain, the airline said today.

The crash killed all but four of the 163 people aboard.

American's investigators concluded that the captain of the Boeing 757 apparently thought he had entered the coordinates for the intended destination, Cali.

But on most South American aeronautical charts, the one-letter code for Cali is the same as the one for Bogota, 132 miles in the opposite direction.

The coordinates for Bogota directed the plane toward the mountain, according to a letter by Cecil Ewell, American's chief pilot and vice president for flight. The codes for Bogota and Cali are different in most computer databases, Ewell said.

American spokesman John Hotard confirmed that Ewell's letter, first reported in the *Dallas Morning News*, is being delivered this week to all of the airline's pilots to warn them of the coding problem.

American's discovery also prompted the Federal Aviation Administration to issue a bulletin to all airlines, warning them of inconsistencies between some computer databases and aeronautical charts, the newspaper said.

The computer error is not the final word on what caused the crash. The Colombian government is investigating and is expected to release its findings by October.

Pat Cariseo, spokesman for the National Transportation Safety Board, said Colombian investigators also are examining factors such as flight crew training and air traffic control.

The computer mistake was found by investigators for American when they compared data from the jet's navigation computer with information from the wreckage, Ewell said.

The data showed the mistake went undetected for 66 seconds while the crew scrambled to follow an air traffic controller's orders to take a more direct approach to the Cali airport.

Three minutes later, while the plane still was descending and the crew trying to figure out why the plane had turned, it crashed.

> Ewell said the crash presented two important lessons for pilots.
>
> "First of all, no matter how many times you go to South America or any other place—the Rocky Mountains—you can never, never, never assume anything," he told the newspaper. Second, he said, pilots must understand they can't let automation take over responsibility for flying the airplane.

Is this article evidence that we have a software crisis? How is aviation better off because of software engineering? What issues should be addressed during software development so that problems like this will be prevented in the future?

2. What are the common three categories of software failure? Give two possible examples of each type of failure in word processing software.
3. Why can a count of faults be a misleading measure of product quality?
4. Many developers equate technical quality with overall product quality. Give an example of a product with high technical quality that is not considered high quality by the customer. Are there ethical issues involved in narrowing the view of quality to consider only technical quality? Use the Therac-25 example to illustrate your point.
5. Give an example of problem analysis where the problem components are relatively simple, but the difficulty in solving the problem lies in the interconnections among subproblem components.
6. Using the system approach, describe the elements in a microwave oven and how they interact with each other.
7. When the Ariane-5 rocket was destroyed, the news made headlines in France and elsewhere. *Liberation,* a French newspaper, called it "A 37-billion-franc fireworks display" on the front page. In fact, the explosion was front-page news in almost all European newspapers and headed the main evening news bulletins on most European TV networks. By contrast, the invasion by a hacker of Panix, a New York-based Internet provider, forced the Panix system to close down for several hours. News of this event appeared only on the front page of the business section of the *Washington Post*. What is the responsibility of the press when reporting software-based incidents? How should the potential impact of software failures be assessed and reported?
8. Many organizations buy commercial software, thinking it is cheaper than developing and maintaining software in-house. Describe the pros and cons of using COTS software. For example, what happens if the COTS products are no longer supported by their vendors? What must the customer, user, and developer anticipate when designing a product that uses COTS software in a large system?
9. What are the legal and ethical implications of using COTS software? Of using subcontractors? For example, who is responsible for fixing the problem when the major system fails as a result of a fault in COTS software? Who is liable when such a failure causes harm to the users, directly (as when the automatic brakes fail in a car) or indirectly (as when the wrong information is supplied to another system, as we saw in Exercise 1). What checks and balances are needed to ensure the quality of COTS software before it is integrated into a larger system?

2 Modeling the Process and Life Cycle

In this chapter, we look at
- what we mean by a "process"
- software development products, processes, and resources
- several models of the software development process
- tools and techniques for process modeling

We saw in Chapter 1 that engineering software is both a creative and a step-by-step process, often involving many people producing many different kinds of products. In this chapter, we examine the steps in more detail, looking at ways to organize our activities, so that we can coordinate what we do and when we do it. We begin the chapter by defining what we mean by a process, so that we understand what must be included when we model software development. Next, we examine several types of software process models. Once we know the type of model we wish to use, we take a close look at two types of modeling techniques: static and dynamic. Finally, we apply several of these techniques to our information systems and real-time examples.

2.1 THE MEANING OF PROCESS

When we provide a service or create a product, whether it be developing software, writing a report, or taking a business trip, we always follow a sequence of steps to accomplish a set of tasks. The tasks are usually performed in the same order each time; for example, you do not usually put up the drywall before the wiring for a house is installed or bake a cake before all the ingredients are mixed together. We can think of a set of ordered tasks as a **process**: a series of steps involving activities, constraints, and resources that produce an intended output of some kind.

A process usually involves a set of tools and techniques, as we defined them in Chapter 1. Any process has the following characteristics:

- The process prescribes all of the major process activities.
- The process uses resources, subject to a set of constraints (such as a schedule), and produces intermediate and final products.
- The process may be composed of subprocesses that are linked in some way. The process may be defined as a hierarchy of processes, organized so that each subprocess has its own process model.
- Each process activity has entry and exit criteria, so that we know when the activity begins and ends.
- The activities are organized in a sequence, so that it is clear when one activity is performed relative to the other activities.
- Every process has a set of guiding principles that explain the goals of each activity.
- Constraints or controls may apply to an activity, resource, or product. For example, the budget or schedule may constrain the length of time an activity may take or a tool may limit the way in which a resource may be used.

When the process involves the building of some product, we sometimes refer to the process as a **life cycle**. Thus, the software development process is sometimes called the **software life cycle**, because it describes the life of a software product from its conception to its implementation, delivery, use, and maintenance.

Processes are important because they impose consistency and structure on a set of activities. These characteristics are useful when we know how to do something well and we want to ensure that others do it the same way. For example, if Sam is a good bricklayer, he may write down a description of the bricklaying process he uses so that Sara can learn how to do it as well. He may take into account the differences in the way people prefer to do things; for instance, he may write his instructions so that Sara can lay bricks whether she is right- or left-handed. Similarly, a software development process can be described in flexible ways that allow people to design and build software using preferred techniques and tools; a process model may require design to occur before coding, but may allow many different design techniques to be used. For this reason, the process helps to maintain a level of consistency and quality in products or services that are produced by many different people.

A process is more than a procedure. We saw in Chapter 1 that a procedure is like a recipe: a structured way of combining tools and techniques to produce a product. A process is a collection of procedures, organized so that we build products to satisfy a set of goals or standards. In fact, the process may suggest that we choose from several procedures, as long as the goal we are addressing is met. For instance, the process may require that we check our design components before coding begins. The checking can be done using informal reviews or formal inspections, each an activity with its own procedure, but both addressing the same goal.

The process structure guides our actions by allowing us to examine, understand, control, and improve the activities that comprise the process. To see how, consider the process of making chocolate cake with chocolate icing. The process may contain several procedures, such as buying the ingredients and finding the appropriate cooking utensils.

The recipe describes the procedure for actually mixing and baking the cake. The recipe contains activities (such as "beat the egg before mixing with other ingredients"), constraints (such as the temperature requirement in "heat the chocolate to the melting point before combining with the sugar"), and resources (such as sugar, flour, eggs, and chocolate). Suppose Chuck bakes a chocolate cake according to this recipe. When the cake is done, he tastes a sample and decides that the cake is too sweet. He looks at the recipe to see which ingredient contributes to the sweetness: sugar. Then, he bakes another cake, but this time he reduces the amount of sugar in the new recipe. Again he tastes the cake, but now it does not have enough chocolate flavor. He adds a measure of cocoa powder to his second revision and tries again. After several iterations, each time changing an ingredient or an activity (such as baking the cake longer, or letting the chocolate mixture cool before combining with the egg mixture), Chuck arrives at a cake to his liking. Without the recipe to document this part of the process, Chuck would not have been able to make changes easily and evaluate the results.

Processes are also important for enabling us to capture our experiences and pass them along to others. Just as master chefs pass on their favorite recipes to their colleagues and friends, master craftspeople can pass along documented processes and procedures. Indeed, the notions of apprenticeship and mentoring are based on the idea that we share our experience so we can pass down our skills from senior people to junior ones.

In the same way, we want to learn from our past development projects, document the practices that work best to produce high-quality software, and follow a software development process so we can understand, control, and improve what happens as we build products for our customers. We saw in Chapter 1 that software development usually involves the following stages:

- requirements analysis and definition
- system design
- program design
- writing the programs (program implementation)
- unit testing
- integration testing
- system testing
- system delivery
- maintenance

Each stage is itself a process (or collection of processes) that can be described as a set of activities. And each activity involves constraints, outputs, and resources. For example, the requirements analysis and definitions stage need as initial input a statement of desired functions and features that the user expresses in some way. The final output from this stage is a set of requirements, but there may be intermediate products as the dialog between user and developer results in changes and alternatives. We have constraints, too, such as a budget and schedule for producing the requirements document, and standards about the kinds of requirements to include and perhaps the notation used to express them.

Each of these stages is addressed in this book. For each one, we will take a close look at the processes, resources, activities, and outputs that are involved, and we will learn how they contribute to the quality of the final product: useful software. There are many ways to address each stage of development; each configuration of activities, resources, and outputs constitutes a process, and a collection of processes describes what happens at each stage. For instance, design can involve a prototyping process, where many of the design decisions are explored so that developers can choose an appropriate approach, and a reuse process, where previously generated design components are included in the current design.

Each process can be described in a variety of ways, using text, pictures, or a combination. Software engineering researchers have suggested a variety of formats for such descriptions, usually organized as a model that contains key process features. For the remainder of this chapter, we examine a variety of software development process models, to see how organizing process activities can make development more effective.

2.2 SOFTWARE PROCESS MODELS

Many process models are described in the software engineering literature. Some are *prescriptions* for the way software development should progress, and others are *descriptions* of the way software development is done in actuality. In theory, the two kinds of models should be similar or the same, but in practice, they are not. Building a process model and discussing its subprocesses help the team understand the gap between what should be and what is.

There are several other reasons for modeling a process:

- When a group writes down a description of its development process, it forms a common understanding of the activities, resources, and constraints involved in software development.
- Creating a process model helps the development team find inconsistencies, redundancies, and omissions in the process and in its constituent parts. As these problems are noted and corrected, the process becomes more effective and focused on building the final product.
- The model should reflect the goals of development, such as building high-quality software, finding faults early in development, and meeting required budget and schedule constraints. As the model is built, the development team evaluates candidate activities for their appropriateness in addressing these goals. For example, the team may include requirements reviews, so that problems with the requirements can be found and fixed before design begins.
- Every process should be tailored for the special situation in which it will be used. Building a process model helps the development team understand where that tailoring is to occur.

Every software development process model includes system requirements as input and a delivered product as output. Many such models have been proposed over the years. Let us look at several of the most popular models to understand their commonalities and differences.

Waterfall Model

One of the first models to be proposed is the **waterfall model**, illustrated in Figure 2.1, where the stages are depicted as cascading from one to another (Royce 1970). As the

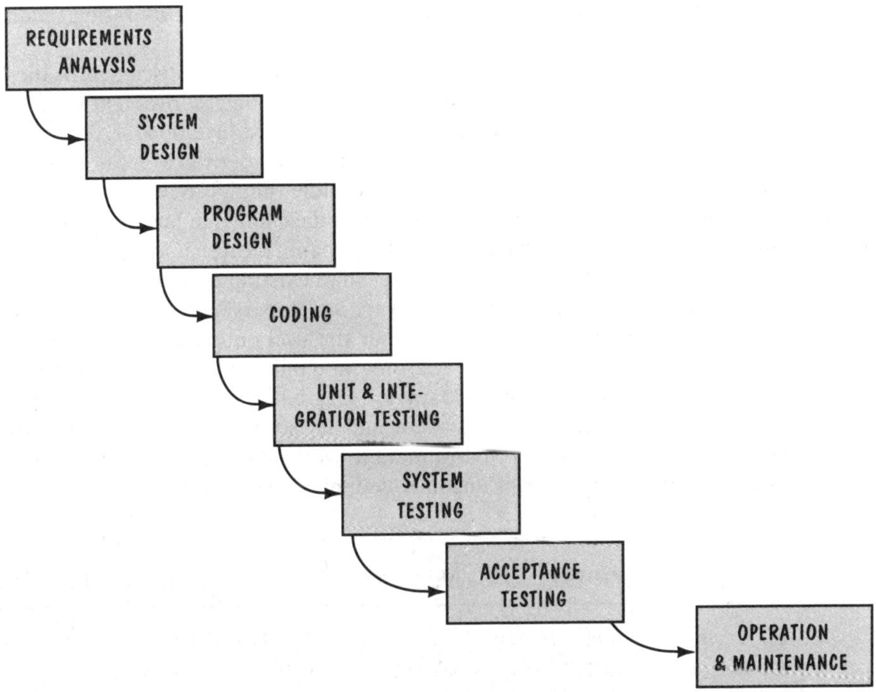

FIGURE 2.1 The waterfall model.

figure implies, one development stage should be completed before the next begins. Thus, when all of the requirements are elicited from the customer, analyzed for completeness and consistency, and documented in a requirements document, then the development team can go on to system design activities. The waterfall model presents a very high-level view of what goes on during development, and it suggests to developers the sequence of events they should expect to encounter.

The waterfall model has been used to prescribe software development activities in a variety of contexts. For example, it was the basis for software development deliverables in U.S. Department of Defense contracts for many years, defined in Department of Defense Standard 2167-A. Associated with each process activity were milestones and deliverables, so that project managers could use the model to gauge how close the project was to completion at a given point in time. For instance, "unit and integration testing" in the waterfall ends with the milestone "code modules written, tested, and integrated"; the intermediate deliverable is a copy of the tested code. Next, the code can be turned over to the system testers so it can be merged with other system components (hardware or software) and tested as a larger whole.

The waterfall model can be very useful in helping developers lay out what they need to do. Its simplicity makes it easy to explain to customers who are not familiar with software development; it makes explicit which intermediate products are necessary in order to begin the next stage of development. Many other, more complex models are really just embellishments of the waterfall, incorporating feedback loops and extra activities.

Many problems with the waterfall model have been discussed in the literature, and two of them are summarized in Sidebar 2.1. The biggest problem with the waterfall model is that it does not reflect the way code is really developed. Except for very well-understood problems, software is usually developed with a great deal of iteration. Often, software is used in a solution to a problem that has never before been solved or whose solution must be upgraded to reflect some change in business climate or operating environment. For example, an airplane manufacturer may require software for a new airframe that will be bigger or faster than existing models, so there are new challenges to address, even though the software developers have a great deal of experience in building aeronautical software. Neither the users nor the developers know all the key factors that affect the desired outcome, and much of the time spent during requirements analysis, as we will see in Chapter 4, may be devoted to understanding the items and processes affected by the system and its software, as well as the relationship between the system and the environment in which it will operate. Thus, the actual software development process, if uncontrolled, may look like Figure 2.2; developers may

SIDEBAR 2.1 DRAWBACKS OF THE WATERFALL MODEL

Ever since the waterfall model was introduced, it has had many critics. For example, McCracken and Jackson (1981) pointed out that the model imposes a project management structure on system development. "To contend that any life cycle scheme, even with variations, can be applied to all system development is either to fly in the face of reality or to assume a life cycle so rudimentary as to be vacuous."

Notice that the waterfall model shows how each major phase of development terminates in the production of some artifact (such as requirements, design, or code). There is no insight into how each activity transforms one artifact to another, such as requirements to design. Thus, the model provides no guidance to managers and developers on how to handle changes to products and activities that are likely to occur during development. For instance, when requirements change during coding activities, the subsequent changes to design and code are not addressed by the waterfall model.

Curtis, Krasner, Shen, and Iscoe (1987) note that the waterfall model's major shortcoming is its failure to treat software as a problem-solving process. The waterfall model was derived from the hardware world, presenting a manufacturing view of software development. But manufacturing produces a particular item and reproduces it many times. Software is not developed like that; rather, it evolves as the problem becomes understood and the alternatives are evaluated. Thus, software is a creation process, not a manufacturing process. The waterfall model tells us nothing about the typical back-and-forth activities that lead to creating a final product. In particular, creation usually involves trying a little of this or that, developing and evaluating prototypes, assessing the feasibility of requirements, contrasting several designs, learning from failure, and eventually settling on a satisfactory solution to the problem at hand.

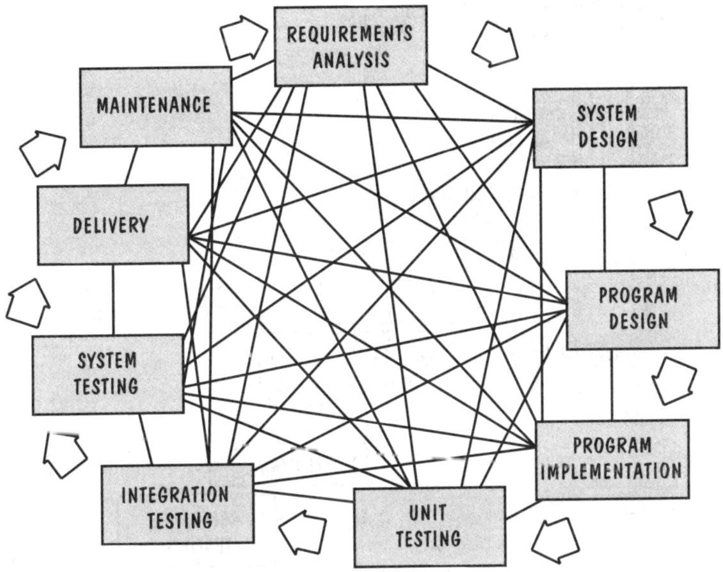

FIGURE 2.2 The software development process in reality.

thrash from one activity to the next and then back again, as they strive to gather knowledge about the problem and how the proposed solution addresses it.

The software development process can help to control the thrashing by including activities and subprocesses that enhance understanding. Prototyping is such a subprocess; a **prototype** is a partially developed product that enables customers and developers to examine some aspect of the proposed system and decide if it is suitable or appropriate for the finished product. For example, developers may build a system to implement a small portion of some key requirements to ensure that the requirements are consistent, feasible, and practical; if not, revisions are made at the requirements stage rather than at the more costly testing stage. Similarly, parts of the design may be prototyped, as shown in Figure 2.3. Design prototyping helps developers assess alternative design strategies and decide which is best for a particular project. As we will see in Chapter 5, the designers may address the requirements with several radically different designs to see which has the best properties. For instance, a network may be built as a ring in one prototype and a star in another, and performance characteristics evaluated to see which structure is better at meeting performance goals or constraints.

Often, the user interface is built and tested as a prototype, so that the users can understand what the new system will be like, and the designers get a better sense of how the users like to interact with the system. Thus, major kinks in the requirements are addressed and fixed well before the requirements are officially validated during system testing; **validation** ensures that the system has implemented all of the requirements, so that each system function can be traced back to a particular requirement in the specification. System testing also verifies the requirements; **verification** ensures that each function works correctly. That is, validation makes sure that the developer is building the

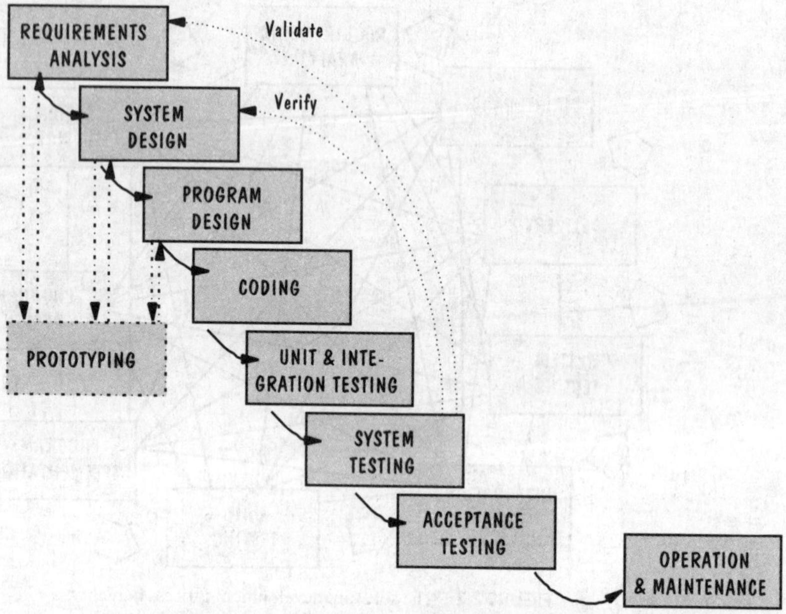

FIGURE 2.3 The waterfall model with prototyping.

right product (according to the specification), and verification checks the quality of the implementation. Prototyping is useful for verification and validation, but these activities can occur during other parts of the development process, as we will see in later chapters.

V Model

The **V model** is a variation of the waterfall model that demonstrates how the testing activities are related to analysis and design (German Ministry of Defense 1992). As shown in Figure 2.4, coding forms the point of the V, with analysis and design on the left, testing and maintenance on the right. Unit and integration testing addresses the correctness of programs, as we shall see in later chapters. The V model suggests that unit and integration testing can also be used to verify the program design. That is, during unit and integration testing, the coders and test team members should ensure that all aspects of the program design have been implemented correctly in the code. Similarly, system testing should verify the system design, making sure that all system design aspects are correctly implemented. Acceptance testing, which is conducted by the customer rather than the developer, validates the requirements by associating a testing step with each element of the specification; this type of testing checks to see that all requirements have been fully implemented before the system is accepted and paid for.

The model's linkage of the left side with the right side of the V implies that if problems are found during verification and validation, then the left side of the V can be reexecuted to fix and improve the requirements, design, and code before the testing steps on the right side are reenacted. In other words, the V model makes more explicit some of the iteration and rework that are hidden in the waterfall depiction. Whereas

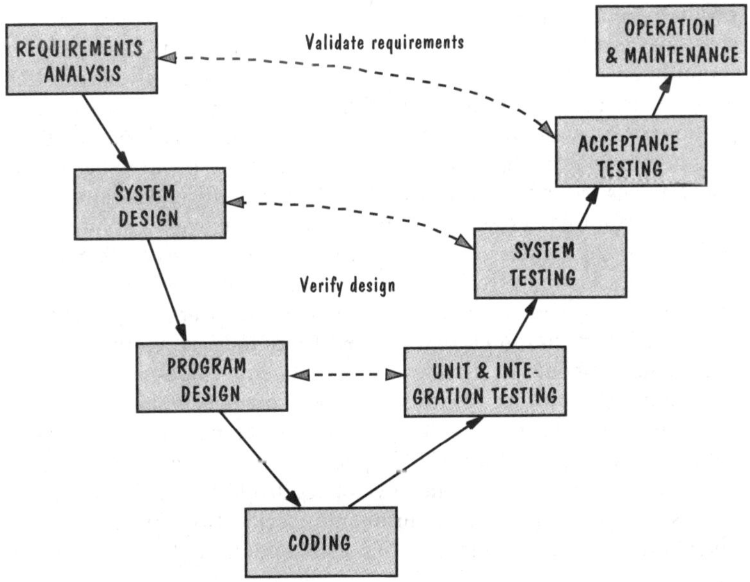

FIGURE 2.4 The V model.

the focus of the waterfall is often documents and artifacts, the focus of the V model is activity and correctness.

Prototyping Model

We have seen how the waterfall model can be amended with prototyping activities to improve understanding. But prototyping need not be solely an adjunct of a waterfall; it can itself be the basis for an effective process model, shown in Figure 2.5. Since the

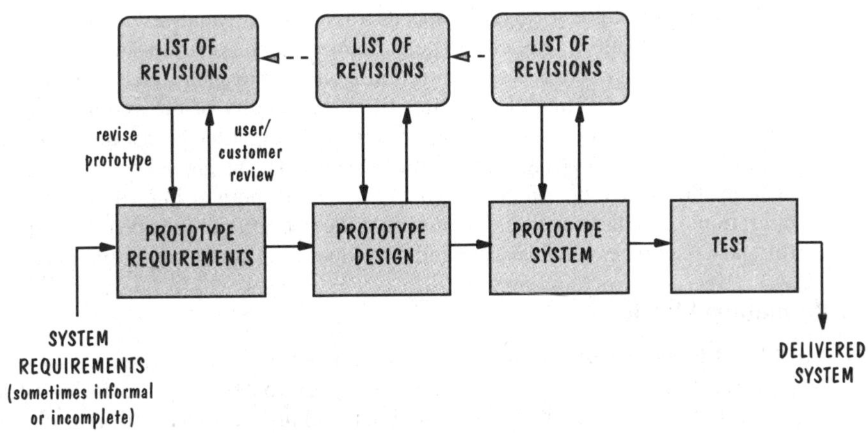

FIGURE 2.5 The prototyping model.

prototyping model allows all or part of a system to be constructed quickly to understand or clarify issues, it has the same objective as an engineering prototype, where requirements or design require repeated investigation to ensure that the developer, user, and customer have a common understanding both of what is needed and what is proposed. One or more of the loops for prototyping requirements, design, or the system may be eliminated, depending on the goals of the prototyping. However, the overall goal remains the same: reducing risk and uncertainty in development.

For example, system development may begin with a nominal set of requirements supplied by the customers and users. Then, alternatives are explored by having interested parties look at possible screens, tables, reports, and other system output that are used directly by the customers and users. As the users and customers decide on what they want, the requirements are revised. Once there is common agreement on what the requirements should be, the developers move on to design. Again, alternative designs are explored, often with consultation with customers and users.

The initial design is revised until the developers, users, and customers are happy with the result. Indeed, considering design alternatives sometimes reveals a problem with the requirements, and the developers drop back to the requirements activities to reconsider and change the requirements specification. Eventually, the system is coded and alternatives are discussed, with possible iteration through requirements and design again.

Operational Specification

For many systems, uncertainty about the requirements leads to changes and problems later in development. Zave (1984) suggests a process model that allows the developers and customers to examine the requirements and their implications early in the development process, where they can discuss and resolve some of the uncertainty. In the **operational specification model**, the system requirements are evaluated or executed in a way that demonstrates the behavior of the system. That is, once the requirements are specified, they can be enacted using a software package, so their implications can be assessed before design begins. For example, if the specification requires the proposed system to handle 24 users, an executable form of the specification can help analysts determine whether that number of users puts too much of a performance burden on the system.

This type of process is very different from traditional models such as the waterfall model. The waterfall model separates the functionality of the system from the design (i.e., what the system is to do is separated from how the system does it), intending to keep the customer needs apart from the implementation. However, an operational specification allows the functionality and the design to be merged. Figure 2.6 illustrates how an operational specification works. Notice that the operational specification is similar to prototyping; the process enables user and developer to examine requirements early on.

Transformational Model

Balzer's **transformational model** tries to reduce the opportunity for error by eliminating several major development steps. Using automated support, the transformational process applies a series of transformations to change a specification into a deliverable system (Balzer 1981a).

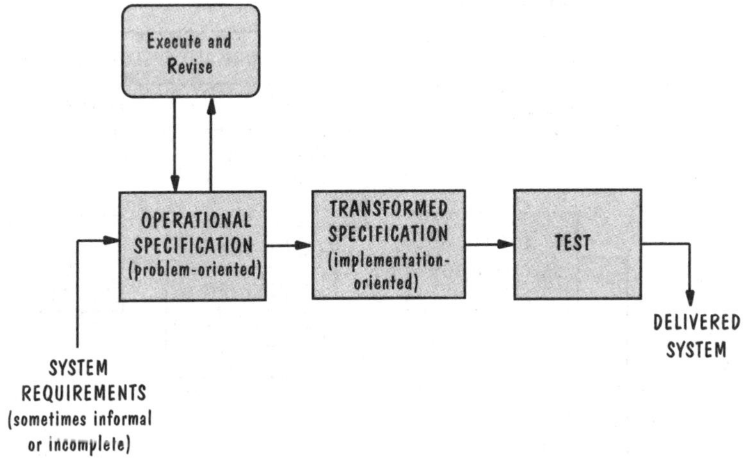

FIGURE 2.6 The operational specification model.

Sample transformations can include

- changing the data representations
- selecting algorithms
- optimizing
- compiling

Because many paths can be taken from the specification to the delivered system, the sequence of transformations and the decisions they reflect are kept as a formal development record.

The transformational approach holds great promise. However, a major impediment to its use is the need for a formal specification expressed precisely so the transformations can operate on it, as shown in Figure 2.7. As formal specification methods become more popular, the transformational model may gain wider acceptance.

Phased Development: Increments and Iterations

In the early years of software development, customers were willing to wait a long time for software systems to be ready. Sometimes years would pass between the time the requirements documents were written and the time the system was delivered, called the **cycle time**. However, today's business environment no longer tolerates long delays. Software helps to distinguish products in the marketplace, and customers are always looking for new quality and functionality. For example, in 1996, 80 percent of Hewlett-Packard's revenues were derived from products introduced in the previous two years. Consequently, new process models were developed to help reduce cycle time.

One way to reduce cycle time is to use phased development, as shown in Figure 2.8. The system is designed so that it can be delivered in pieces, enabling the users to have some functionality while the rest is being developed. Thus, there are usually two systems functioning in parallel: the production system and the development system. The

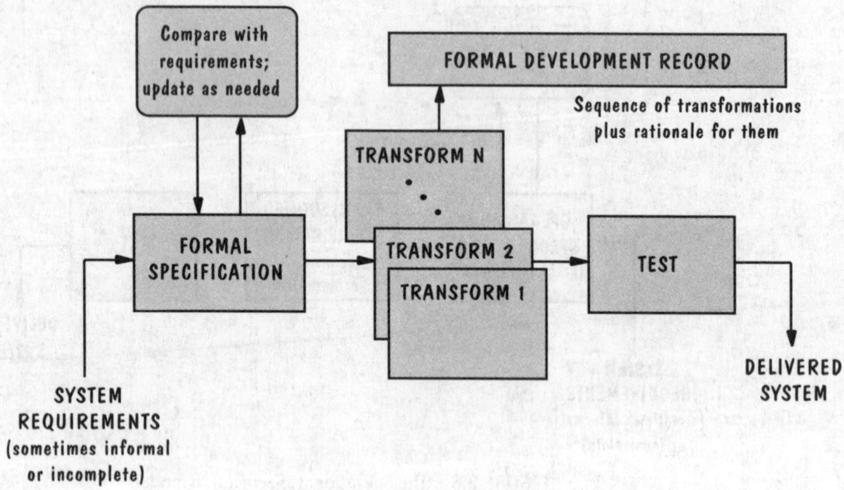

FIGURE 2.7 The transformational model.

operational or **production system** is the one currently being used by the customer and user; the **development system** is the next version that is being prepared to replace the current production system. Often, we refer to the systems in terms of their release numbers: the developers build Release 1, test it, and turn it over to the users as the first operational release. Then, as the users use Release 1, the developers are building Release 2. Thus, the developers are always working on Release $n + 1$ while Release n is operational.

There are many ways for the developers to decide how to organize development into releases. The two most popular approaches are incremental development and iterative development. In **incremental development**, the system as specified in the requirements documents is partitioned into subsystems by functionality. The releases are defined by beginning with one small, functional subsystem and then adding functionality

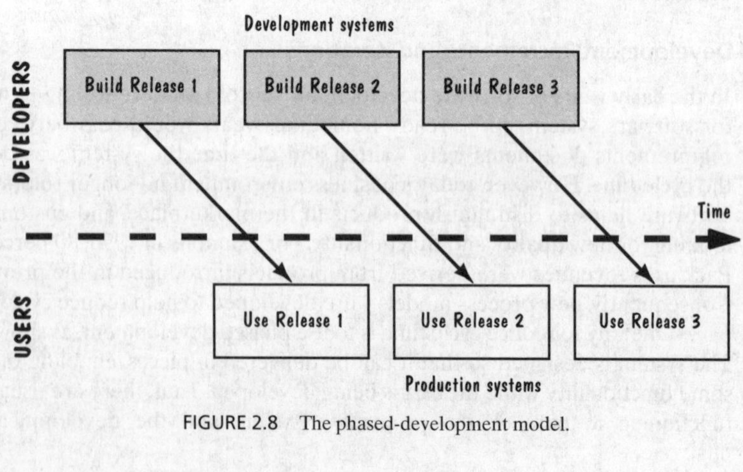

FIGURE 2.8 The phased-development model.

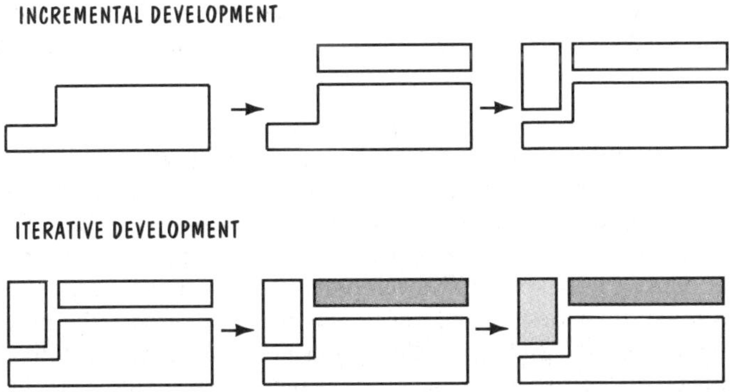

FIGURE 2.9 The incremental and iterative models.

with each new release. The top of Figure 2.9 shows how incremental development slowly builds up to full functionality with each new release.

However, **iterative development** delivers a full system at the very beginning and then changes the functionality of each subsystem with each new release. The bottom of Figure 2.9 illustrates three releases in an iterative development.

To understand the difference between incremental and iterative development, consider a word processing package. Suppose the package is to deliver three types of functionality: creating text, organizing text (i.e., cutting and pasting), and formatting text (such as using different type sizes and styles). To build such a system using incremental development, we might provide only the creation functions in Release 1, then both creation and organization in Release 2, and finally creation, organization, and formatting in Release 3. However, using iterative development, we would provide primitive forms of all three types of functionality in Release 1. For example, we can create text and then cut and paste it, but the cutting and pasting functions might be clumsy or slow. So in the next iteration, Release 2, we have the same functionality, but have enhanced the quality; now cutting and pasting are easy and quick. Each release improves on the previous ones in some way.

In reality, many organizations use a combination of iterative and incremental development. A new release may include new functionality, but existing functionality from the current release may have been enhanced. These forms of phased development are desirable for several reasons:

1. Training can begin on an early release, even if some functions are missing. The training process allows developers to observe how certain functions are executed, suggesting enhancements for later releases. In this way, the developers can be very responsive to the users.
2. Markets can be created early for functionality that has never before been offered.
3. Frequent releases allow developers to fix unanticipated problems globally and quickly, as they are reported from the operational system.
4. The development team can focus on different areas of expertise with different releases. For instance, one release can change the system from a command-driven

one to a point-and-click interface, using the expertise of the user-interface specialists; another release can focus on improving system performance.

Spiral Model

Boehm (1988) viewed the software development process in light of the risks involved, suggesting that a spiral model could combine development activities with risk management to minimize and control risk. The spiral model, shown in Figure 2.10, is in some sense like the iterative development shown in Figure 2.9. Beginning with the requirements and an initial plan for development (including a budget, constraints, and alternatives for staffing, design, and development environment), the process inserts a step to evaluate risks and prototype alternatives before a "concept of operations" document is produced to describe at a high level how the system should work. From that document, a set of requirements is specified and scrutinized to ensure that the requirements are as complete and consistent as possible. Thus, the concept of operations is the product of the first iteration, and the requirements are the principal product of the second. In the third iteration, system development produces the design, and the fourth enables testing.

With each iteration, the risk analysis weighs different alternatives in light of the requirements and constraints, and prototyping verifies feasibility or desirability before a particular alternative is chosen. When risks are identified, the project managers must decide how to eliminate or minimize the risk. For example, designers may not be sure whether users will prefer one type of interface over another. To minimize the risk of choosing an interface that will prevent productive use of the new system, the designers can prototype each interface and run tests to see which is preferred, or even choose to include

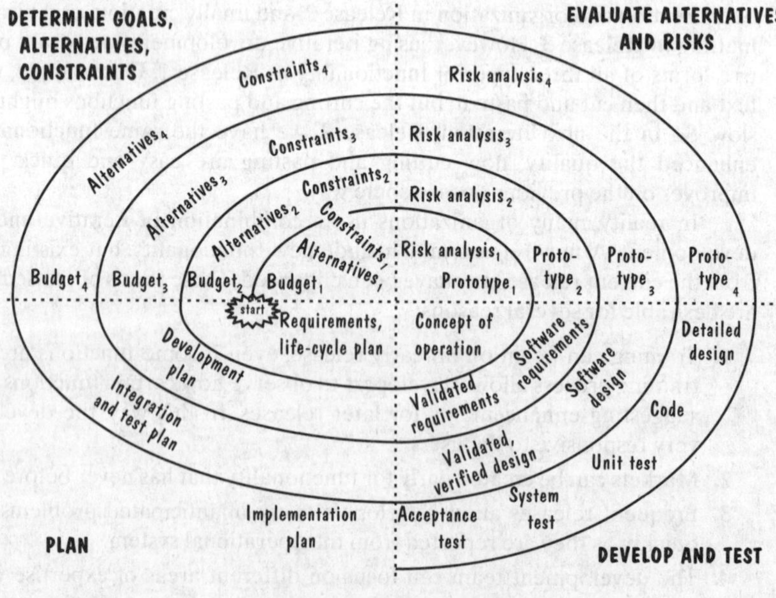

FIGURE 2.10 The spiral model.

two different interfaces in the design, so the users can select an interface when they log on. Constraints such as budget and schedule help to determine which risk-management strategy is chosen. We will discuss risk management in more detail in Chapter 3.

Agile Methods

Many of the software development processes proposed and used from the 1970s through the 1990s tried to impose some form of rigor on the way in which software is conceived, documented, developed, and tested. In the late 1990s, some developers who had resisted this rigor formulated their own principles, trying to highlight the roles that flexibility could play in producing software quickly and capably. They codified their thinking in an "agile manifesto" that focuses on four tenets of an alternative way of thinking about software development (Agile Alliance 2001):

- They value individuals and interactions over processes and tools. This philosophy includes supplying developers with the resources they need and then trusting them to do their jobs well. Teams organize themselves and communicate through face-to-face interaction rather than through documentation.
- They prefer to invest time in producing working software rather than in producing comprehensive documentation. That is, the primary measure of success is the degree to which the software works properly.
- They focus on customer collaboration rather than contract negotiation, thereby involving the customer in key aspects of the development process.
- They concentrate on responding to change rather than on creating a plan and then following it, because they believe that it is impossible to anticipate all requirements at the beginning of development.

The overall goal of agile development is to satisfy the customer by "early and continuous delivery of valuable software" (Agile Alliance 2001). Many customers have business needs that change over time, reflecting not only newly discovered needs but also the need to respond to changes in the marketplace. For example, as software is being designed and constructed, a competitor may release a new product that requires a change in the software's planned functionality. Similarly, a government agency or standards body may impose a regulation or standard that affects the software's design or requirements. It is thought that by building flexibility into the development process, agile methods can enable customers to add or change requirements late in the development cycle.

There are many examples of agile processes in the current literature. Each is based on a set of principles that implement the tenets of the agile manifesto. Examples include the following.

- **Extreme programming (XP),** described in detail below, is a set of techniques for leveraging the creativity of developers and minimizing the amount of administrative overhead.
- **Crystal** is a collection of approaches based on the notion that every project needs a different set of policies, conventions, and methodologies. Cockburn (2002), the creator of Crystal, believes that people have a major influence on software quality, and thus the quality of projects and processes improves as the quality of the

people involved improves. Productivity increases through better communication and frequent delivery, because there is less need for intermediate work products.

- **Scrum** was created at Object Technology in 1994 and was subsequently commercialized by Schwaber and Beedle (2002). It uses iterative development, where each 30-day iteration is called a "sprint," to implement the product's backlog of prioritized requirements. Multiple self-organizing and autonomous teams implement product increments in parallel. Coordination is done at a brief daily status meeting called a "scrum" (as in rugby).
- **Adaptive software development (ASD)** has six basic principles. There is a mission that acts as a guideline, setting out the destination but not prescribing how to get there. Features are viewed as the crux of customer value, so the project is organized around building components to provide the features. Iteration is important, so redoing is as critical is doing; change is embraced, so that a change is viewed not as a correction but as an adjustment to the realities of software development. Fixed delivery times force developers to scope down the requirements essential for each version produced. At the same time, risk is embraced, so that the developers tackle the hardest problems first.

Often, the phrase "extreme programming" is used to describe the more general concept of agile methods. In fact, XP is a particular form of agile process, with guiding principles that reflect the more general tenets of the agile manifesto. Proponents of XP emphasize four characteristics of agility: communication, simplicity, courage, and feedback. *Communication* involves the continual interchange between customers and developers. *Simplicity* encourages developers to select the simplest design or implementation to address the needs of their customers. *Courage* is described by XP creators as commitment to delivering functionality early and often. *Feedback* loops are built into the various activities during the development process. For example, programmers work together to give each other feedback on the best way to implement a design, and customers work with developers to perform planning exercises.

These characteristics are embedded in what are known as the twelve facets of XP.

- *The planning game:* In this aspect of XP, the customer, who is on-site, defines what is meant by "value," so that each requirement can be assessed according to how much value is added by implementing it. The users write stories about how the system should work, and the developers then estimate the resources necessary to realize the stories. The stories describe the actors and actions involved, much like the use cases we define in more detail in Chapters 4 and 6. Each story relates one requirement; two or three sentences are all that is needed to explain the value of the requirement in sufficient detail for the developer to specify test cases and estimate resources for implementing the requirement. Once the stories are written, the prospective users prioritize requirements, splitting and merging them until consensus is reached on what is needed, what is testable, and what can be done with the resources available. The planners then generate a map of each release, documenting what the release includes and when it will be delivered.
- *Small releases:* The system is designed so that functionality can be delivered as soon as possible. Functions are decomposed into small parts, so that some functionality

can be delivered early and then improved or expanded on in later releases. The small releases require a phased-development approach, with incremental or iterative cycles.

- *Metaphor:* The development team agrees on a common vision of how the system will operate. To support its vision, the team chooses common names and agrees on a common way of addressing key issues.
- *Simple design:* Design is kept simple by addressing only current needs. This approach reflects the philosophy that anticipating future needs can lead to unnecessary functionality. If a particular portion of a system is very complex, the team may build a spike—a quick and narrow implementation—to help it decide how to proceed.
- *Writing tests first:* To ensure that the customer's needs are the driving force behind development, test cases are written first, as a way of forcing customers to specify requirements that can be tested and verified once the software is built. Two kinds of tests are used in XP: functional tests that are specified by the customer and executed by both developers and users, and unit tests that are written and run by developers. In XP, functional tests are automated and, ideally, run daily. The functional tests are considered to be part of the system specification. Unit tests are written both before and after coding, to verify that each modular portion of the implementation works as designed. Both functional and unit testing are described in more detail in Chapter 8.
- *Refactoring:* As the system is built, it is likely that requirements will change. Because a major characteristic of XP philosophy is to design only to current requirements, it is often the case that new requirements force the developers to reconsider their existing design. **Refactoring** refers to revisiting the requirements and design, reformulating them to match new and existing needs. Sometimes refactoring addresses ways to restructure design and code without perturbing the system's external behavior. The refactoring is done in small steps, supported by unit tests and pair programming, with simplicity guiding the effort. We will discuss the difficulties of refactoring in Chapter 5.
- *Pair programming:* As noted in Chapter 1, there is a tension between viewing software engineering as an art and as a science. Pair programming attempts to address the artistic side of software development, acknowledging that the apprentice–master metaphor can be useful in teaching novice software developers how to develop the instincts of masters. Using one keyboard, two paired programmers develop a system from the specifications and design. One person has responsibility for finishing the code, but the pairing is flexible: a developer may have more than one partner on a given day. We will see in Chapter 7 how pair programming compares with the more traditional approach of individuals working separately until their modules have been unit-tested.
- *Collective ownership:* In XP, any developer can make a change to any part of the system as it is being developed. In Chapter 11, we will address the difficulties in managing change, including the errors introduced when two people try to change the same module simultaneously.
- *Continuous integration:* Delivering functionality quickly means that working systems can be promised to the customer daily and sometimes even hourly. The

emphasis is on small increments or improvements rather than on grand leaps from one revision to the next.

- *Sustainable pace:* XP's emphasis on people includes acknowledging that fatigue can produce errors. So proponents of XP suggest a goal of 40 hours for each work week; pushing developers to devote heroic amounts of time to meeting deadlines is a signal that the deadlines are unreasonable or that there are insufficient resources for meeting them.
- *On-site customer:* Ideally, a customer should be present on-site, working with the developers to determine requirements and providing feedback about how to test them.
- *Coding standards:* Many observers think of XP and other agile methods as providing an unconstrained environment where anything goes. But in fact XP advocates clear definition of coding standards, to encourage teams to be able to understand and change each other's work. These standards support other practices, such as testing and refactoring. The result should be a body of code that appears to have been written by one person, and is consistent in its approach and expression.

Extreme programming and agile methods are relatively new. The body of evidence for its effectiveness is small but growing. We will revisit many agile methods and concepts, and their empirical evaluation, in later chapters, as we discuss their related activities.

The process models presented in this chapter are only a few of those that are used or discussed. Other process models can be defined and tailored to the needs of the user, customer, and developer. As Sidebar 2.3 notes, we should really capture the development process as a collection of process models, rather than focusing on a single model or view.

SIDEBAR 2.2 WHEN IS EXTREME TOO EXTREME?

As with most software development approaches, agile methods are not without their critics. For example, Stephens and Rosenberg (2003) point out that many of extreme programming's practices are interdependent, a vulnerability if one of them is modified. To see why, suppose some people are uncomfortable with pair programming. More coordination and documentation may be required to address the shared vision that is missing when people work on their own. Similarly, many developers prefer to do some design before they write code. Scrum addresses this preference by organizing around monthly sprints. Elssamadissy and Schalliol (2002) note that, in extreme programming, requirements are expressed as a set of test cases that must be passed by the software. This approach may cause customer representatives to focus on the test cases instead of the requirements. Because the test cases are a detailed expression of the requirements and may be solution oriented, the emphasis on test cases can distract the representatives from the project's underlying goals and can lead to a situation where the system passes all the tests but is not what the customers thought they were paying for. As we will see in Chapter 5, refactoring may be the Achilles heel of agile methods; it is difficult to rework a software system without degrading its architecture.

SIDEBAR 2.3 COLLECTIONS OF PROCESS MODELS

We saw in Sidebar 2.1 that the development process is a problem-solving activity, but few of the popular process models include problem solving. Curtis, Krasner, and Iscoe (1988) performed a field study of 17 large projects, to determine which problem-solving factors should be captured in process models to aid our understanding of software development. In particular, they looked at the behavioral and organizational factors that affect project outcomes. Their results suggest a layered behavioral model of software development, including five key perspectives: the business milieu, the company, the project, the team, and the individual. The individual view provides information about cognition and motivation, and project and team views tell us about group dynamics. The company and business milieu provide information about organizational behavior that can affect both productivity and quality. This model does not replace traditional process models; rather, it is orthogonal, supplementing the traditional models with information on how behavior affects the creation and production activities.

As the developers and customers learn about the problem, they integrate their knowledge of domains, technology, and business to produce an appropriate solution. By viewing development as a collection of coordinating processes, we can see the effects of learning, technical communication, customer interaction, and requirements negotiation. Current models that prescribe a series of development tasks "provide no help in analyzing how much new information must be learned by the project staff, how discrepant requirements should be negotiated, how a design team can resolve architectural conflicts, and how these and similar factors contribute to a project's inherent uncertainty and risk" (Curtis, Krasner, and Iscoe 1988). However, when we include models of cognitive, social, and organizational processes, we begin to see the causes of bottlenecks and inefficiency. It is this insight that enables managers to understand and control the development process. And by aggregating behavior across layers of models, we can see how each model contributes to or compounds the effects of another model's factors.

No matter what process model is used, many activities are common to all. As we investigate software engineering in later chapters, we will examine each development activity to see what it involves and to find out what tools and techniques make us more effective and productive.

2.3 TOOLS AND TECHNIQUES FOR PROCESS MODELING

There are many choices for modeling tools and techniques, once you decide what you want to capture in your process model; we have seen several modeling approaches in our model depictions in the preceding section. The appropriate technique for you depends on your goals and your preferred work style. In particular, your choice for notation depends on what you want to capture in your model. The notations range from textual ones that express processes as functions, to graphical ones that depict processes as hierarchies of boxes and arrows, to combinations of pictures and text that link the graphical depiction to tables and functions elaborating on the high-level illustration. Many of the modeling notations can also be used for representing requirements and designs; we examine some of them in later chapters.

In this chapter, the notation is secondary to the type of model, and we focus on two major categories, static and dynamic. A **static model** depicts the process, showing that the inputs are transformed to outputs. A **dynamic model** enacts the process, so the user can see how intermediate and final products are transformed over time.

Static Modeling: Lai Notation

There are many ways to model a process statically. In the early 1990s, Lai (1991) developed a comprehensive process notation that is intended to enable someone to model any process at any level of detail. It builds on a paradigm where people perform roles while resources perform activities, leading to the production of artifacts. The process model shows the relationships among the roles, activities, and artifacts, and state tables show information about the completeness of each artifact at a given time.

In particular, the elements of a process are viewed in terms of seven types:

1. **Activity:** Something that will happen in a process. This element can be related to what happens before and after, what resources are needed, what triggers the activity's start, what rules govern the activity, how to describe the algorithms and lessons learned, and how to relate the activity to the project team.
2. **Sequence:** The order of activities. The sequence can be described using triggers, programming constructs, transformations, ordering, or satisfaction of conditions.
3. **Process model:** A view of interest about the system. Thus, parts of the process may be represented as a separate model, either to predict process behavior or to examine certain characteristics.
4. **Resource:** A necessary item, tool, or person. Resources can include equipment, time, office space, people, techniques, and so on. The process model identifies how much of each resource is needed for each activity.
5. **Control:** An external influence over process enactment. The controls may be manual or automatic, human or mechanical.
6. **Policy:** A guiding principle. This high-level process constraint influences process enactment. It may include a prescribed development process, a tool that must be used, or a mandatory management style.
7. **Organization:** The hierarchical structure of process agents, with physical grouping corresponding to logical grouping and related roles. The mapping from physical to logical grouping should be flexible enough to reflect changes in physical environment.

The process description itself has several levels of abstraction, including the software development process that directs certain resources to be used in constructing specific modules, as well as generic models that may resemble the spiral or waterfall models. Lai's notation includes several templates, such as an Artifact Definition Template, which records information about particular artifacts.

Lai's approach can be applied to modeling software development processes; later in this chapter, we use it to model the risk involved in development. However, to demonstrate its use and its ability to capture many facets of a complex activity, we apply it to a relatively simple but familiar process, driving an automobile. Table 2.1 contains a description of the key resource in this process, a car.

Other templates define relations, process states, operations, analysis, actions, and roles. Graphical diagrams represent the relationships between elements, capturing the main relationships and secondary ones. For example, Figure 2.11 illustrates the process of starting a car. The "initiate" box represents the entrance conditions, and the "park" box represents an exit condition. The left-hand column of a condition box lists artifacts, and the right-hand column is the artifact state.

TABLE 2.1 Artifact Definition Form for Artifact "CAR" (Lai 1991)

Name	*Car*	
Synopsis	*This is the artifact that represents a class of cars.*	
Complexity type	*Composite*	
Data type	*(car c, user-defined)*	
Artifact-state list		
parked	*((state_of(car.engine) = off)* *(state_of(car.gear) = park)* *(state_of(car.speed) = stand))*	*Car is not moving, and engine is not running.*
initiated	*((state_of(car.engine) = on)* *(state_of(car.key_hole) = has-key)* *(state_of(car-driver(car.)) = in-car)* *state_of(car.gear) = drive)* *(state_of(car.speed) = stand))*	*Car is not moving, but the engine is running.*
moving	*((state_of(car.engine) = on)* *(state_of(car.keyhole) = has-key)* *(state_of(car-driver(car.)) = driving)* *((state_of(car.gear) = drive) or* *(state_of(car.gear) = reverse))* *((state_of(car.speed) = stand) or* *(state_of(car.speed) = slow)* *or (state_of(car.speed) = medium) or* *(state_of(car.speed) = high))*	*Car is moving forward or backward.*
Subartifact list		
	doors	*The four doors of a car*
	engine	*The engine of a car*
	keyhole	*The ignition keyhole of a car*
	gear	*The gear of a car*
	speed	*The speed of a car*
Relations list		
car-key	*This is the relation between a car and a key.*	
car-driver	*This is the relation between a car and a driver.*	

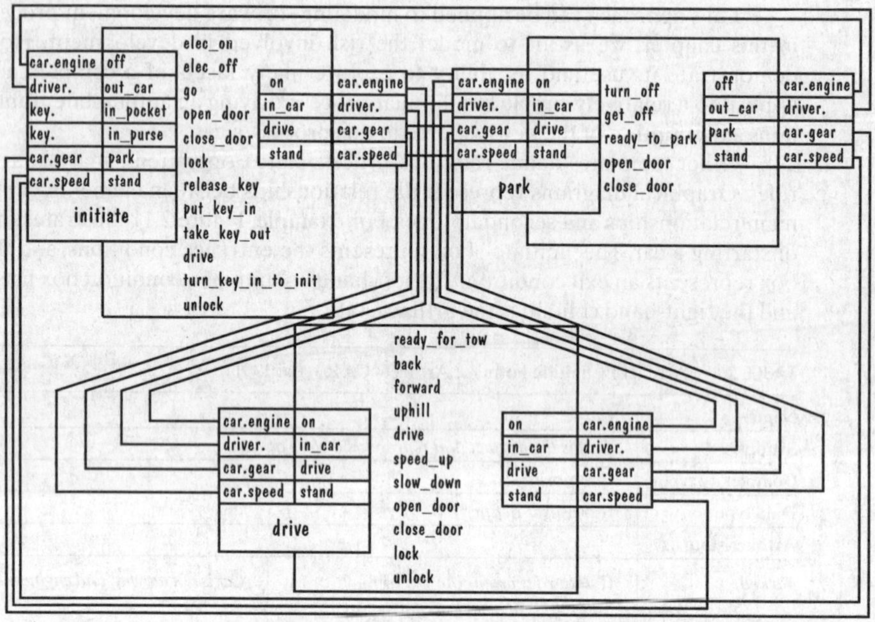

FIGURE 2.11 The process of starting a car (Lai 1991).

Transition diagrams supplement the process model by showing how the states are related to one another. For example, Figure 2.12 illustrates the transitions for a car.

Lai's notation is a good example of how multiple structures and strategies can be used to capture a great deal of information about the software development process. But it is also useful in organizing and depicting process information about user requirements, as the car example demonstrates.

FIGURE 2.12 Transition diagram for a car (Lai 1991).

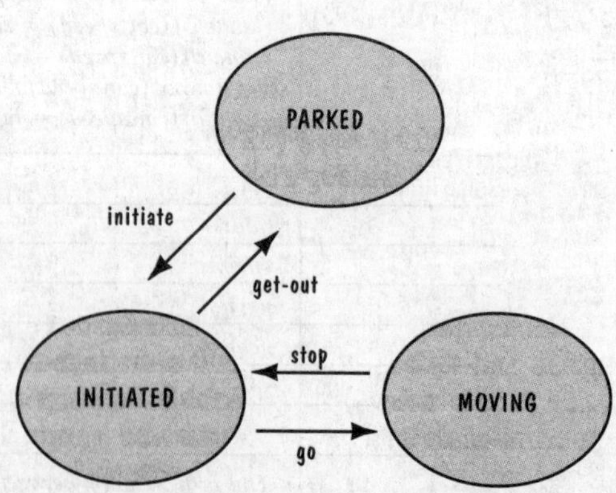

Dynamic Modeling: System Dynamics

A desirable property of a process model is the ability to enact the process, so that we can watch what happens to resources and artifacts as activities occur. In other words, we want to describe a model of the process and then watch as software shows us how resources flow through activities to become outputs. This dynamic process view enables us to simulate the process and make changes before the resources are actually expended. For example, we can use a dynamic process model to help us decide how many testers we need or when we must initiate testing in order to finish on schedule. Similarly, we can include or exclude activities to see their effects on effort and schedule. For instance, we can add a code-review activity, making assumptions about how many faults we will find during the review, and determine whether reviewing shortens test time significantly.

There are several ways to build dynamic process models. The systems dynamics approach, introduced by Forrester in the 1950s, has been useful for simulating diverse processes, including ecological, economic, and political systems (Forrester 1991). Abdel-Hamid and Madnick have applied system dynamics to software development, enabling project managers to "test out" their process choices before imposing them on developers (Abdel-Hamid 1989; Abdel-Hamid and Madnick 1991).

To see how system dynamics works, consider how the software development process affects productivity. We can build a descriptive model of the various activities that involve developers' time and then look at how changes in the model increase or decrease the time it takes to design, write, and test the code. First, we must determine which factors affect overall productivity. Figure 2.13 depicts Abdel Hamid's understanding of these

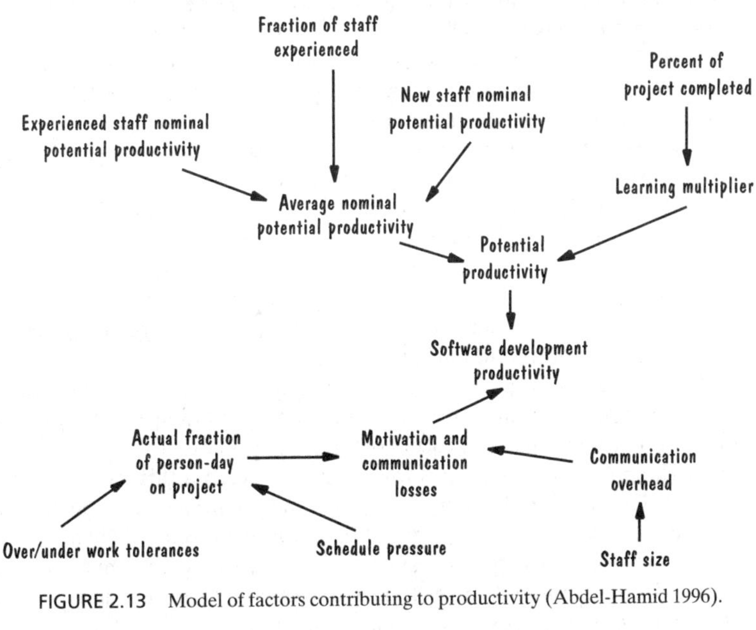

FIGURE 2.13 Model of factors contributing to productivity (Abdel-Hamid 1996).

factors. The arrows indicate how changes in one factor affect changes in another. For example, if the fraction of experienced staff increases from one-quarter to one-half of the people assigned to the project, then we would expect the average potential productivity to increase, too. Similarly, the larger the staff (reflected in staff size), the more time is devoted to communication among project members (communication overhead).

The figure shows us that average nominal potential productivity is affected by three things: the productivity of the experienced staff, the fraction of experienced staff, and the productivity of the new staff. At the same time, new staff must learn about the project; as more of the project is completed, the more the new staff must learn before they can become productive members of the team.

Other issues affect the overall development productivity. First, we must consider the fraction of each day that each developer can devote to the project. Schedule pressures affect this fraction, as do the developers' tolerances for workload. Staff size affects productivity, too, but the more staff, the more likely it is that time will be needed just to communicate information among team members. Communication and motivation, combined with the potential productivity represented in the upper half of Figure 2.13, suggest a general software development productivity relationship.

Thus, the first step in using system dynamics is to identify these relationships, based on a combination of empirical evidence, research reports, and intuition. The next step is to quantify the relationships. The quantification can involve direct relationships, such as that between staff size and communication. We know that if n people are assigned to a project, then there are $n(n - 1)/2$ potential pairs of people who must communicate and coordinate with one another. For some relationships, especially those that involve resources that change over time, we must assign distributions that describe the building up and diminishing of the resource. For example, it is rare for everyone on a project to begin work on the first day. The systems analysts begin, and coders join the project once the significant requirements and design components are documented. Thus, the distribution describes the rise and fall (or even the fluctuation, such as availability around holidays or summer vacations) of the resources.

A system dynamics model can be extensive and complex. For example, Abdel-Hamid's software development model contains more than 100 causal links; Figure 2.14 shows an overview of the relationships he defined. He defined four major areas that affect productivity: software production, human resource management, planning, and control. Production includes issues of quality assurance, learning, and development rate. Human resources address hiring, turnover, and experience. Planning concerns schedules and the pressures they cause, and control addresses progress measurement and the effort required to finish the project.

Because the number of links can be quite large, system dynamics models are supported by software that captures both the links and their quantitative descriptions and then simulates the overall process or some subprocess.

The power of system dynamics is impressive, but this method should be used with caution. The simulated results depend on the quantified relationships, which are often heuristic or vague, not clearly based on empirical research. However, as we will see in later chapters, a historical database of measurement information about the various aspects of development can help us gain confidence in our understanding of relationships, and thus in the results of dynamic models.

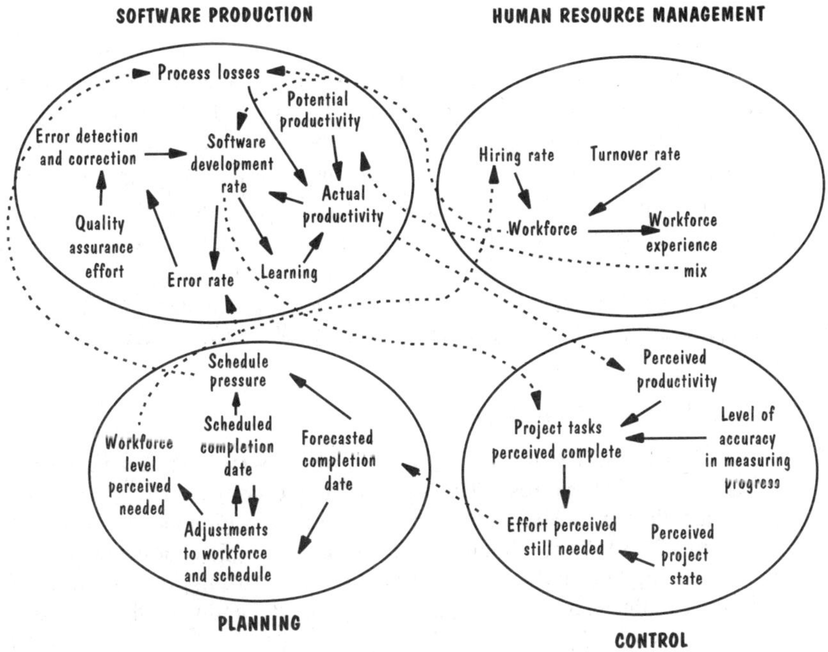

FIGURE 2.14 Structure of software development (Abdel-Hamid 1996)

SIDEBAR 2.4 PROCESS PROGRAMMING

In the mid-1980s, Osterweil (1987) proposed that software engineering processes be specified using algorithmic descriptions. That is, if a process is well-understood, we should be able to write a program to describe the process, and then run the program to enact the process. The goal of process programming is to eliminate uncertainty, both by having enough understanding to write software to capture its essence, and by turning the process into a deterministic solution to the problem.

Were process programming possible, we could have management visibility into all process activities, automate all activities, and coordinate and change all activities with ease. Thus, process programs could form the basis of an automated environment to produce software.

However, Curtis, Krasner, Shen, and Iscoe (1987) point out that Osterweil's analogy to computer programming does not capture the inherent variability of the underlying development process. When a computer program is written, the programmer assumes that the implementation environment works properly; the operating system, database manager, and hardware are reliable and correct, so there is little variability in the computer's response to an instruction. But when a process program issues an instruction to a member of the project team, there is great variability in the way the task is executed and in the results produced. As we will see in Chapter 3, differences in skill, experience, work habits, understanding the customer's needs, and a host of other factors can increase variability dramatically. Curtis and his colleagues suggest that process programming be restricted only to those situations with minimal variability. Moreover, they point out that Osterweil's examples provide information only about the sequencing of tasks; the process program does not help to warn managers of impending problems. "The coordination of a web of creative intellectual tasks does not appear to be improved greatly by current implementations of process programming, because the most important source of coordination is to ensure that all of the interacting agents share the same mental model of how the system should operate" (Curtis et al. 1987).

2.4 PRACTICAL PROCESS MODELING

Process modeling has long been a focus of software engineering research. But how practical is it? Several researchers report that, used properly, process modeling offers great benefits for understanding processes and revealing inconsistencies. For example, Barghouti, Rosenblum, Belanger, and Alliegro (1995) conducted two case studies to determine the feasibility, utility, and limitations of using process models in large organizations. In this section, we examine what they did and what they found.

Marvel Case Studies

In both studies, the researchers used MSL, the Marvel Specification Language, to define the process, and then generated a Marvel process enactment environment for it (Kaiser, Feiler, and Popovich 1988; Barghouti and Kaiser 1991). MSL uses three main constructs—classes, rules, and tool envelopes—to produce a three-part process description:

1. a rule-based specification of process behavior
2. an object-oriented definition of the model's information process
3. a set of envelopes to interface between Marvel and external software tools used to execute the process.

The first case study involved an AT&T call-processing network that carried phone calls, and a separate signaling network responsible for routing the calls and balancing the network's load. Marvel was used to describe the Signaling Fault Resolution process that is responsible for detecting, servicing, and resolving problems with the signaling network. Workcenter 1 monitored the network, detected faults, and referred the fault to one of the two other workcenters. Workcenter 2 handled software or human faults that required detailed analysis, and Workcenter 3 dealt with hardware failures. Figure 2.15 depicts this process. Double dashed lines indicate which activity uses the tool or database represented by an oval. A rectangle is a task or activity, and a diamond is a decision. Arrows indicate the flow of control. As you can see, the figure provides an overview but is not detailed enough to capture essential process elements.

Consequently, each of the entities and workcenters is modeled using MSL. Figure 2.16 illustrates how that is done. The upper half of the figure defines the class

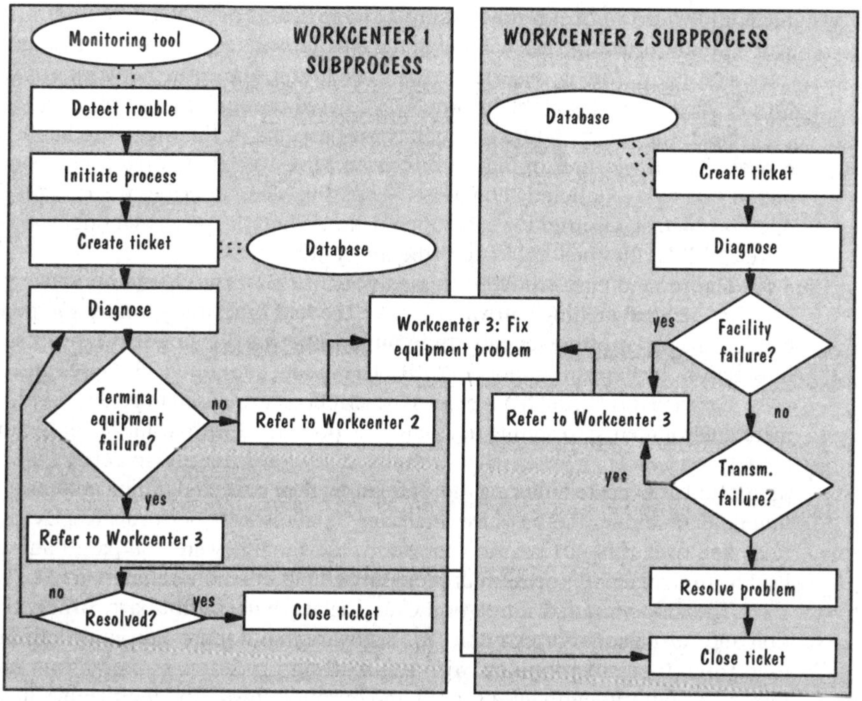

FIGURE 2.15 Signaling Fault Resolution process (Barghouti et al. 1995).

FIGURE 2.16 Examples of Marvel commands (Barghouti et al. 1995).

```
TICKET:: superclass ENTITY
  status: (initial, open, referred_out, referral_done,
                      closed, fixed) = initial;
  diagnostics     : (terminal, non_terminal, none) = none;
  level           : integer;
  description     : text;
  referred_to     : link WORKCENTER;
  referrals       : set_of link TICKET;
  process         : link PROC_INST;
end
```

Class definition for trouble tickets

```
diagnose [?t: TICKET]:
 (exists PROC_INST ?p suchthat (linkto [?t.process ?p]))
 :
 (and (?t.status = open}(?t.diagnostics = none))
 {TICKET_UTIL diagnose ?t.Name}
 (and (?t.diagnostics = terminal)
          (?p.last_task = diagnose)
          (?p.next_task = refer_to_WC3));
 (and (?t.diagnostics = non_terminal)
          (?p.last_task = diagnose)
          (?p.next_task = refer_to_WC2));
```

Rule for diagnosing ticket

TICKET, where a ticket represents the trouble ticket (or problem report) written whenever a failure occurs. As we will see in the chapters on testing, trouble tickets are used to track a problem from its occurrence to its resolution. The entire network was represented with 22 such MSL classes; all information created or required by a process was included.

Next, the model addressed behavioral aspects of the Signaling Fault Resolution process. The lower half of Figure 2.16 is an MSL rule that corresponds loosely to the box of Figure 2.15 labeled "Diagnose." Thus, the MSL describes the rule for diagnosing open problems; it is fired for each open ticket. When the process model was done, there were 21 MSL rules needed to describe the system.

The second case study addressed part of the software maintenance process for AT&T's 5ESS switching software. Unlike the first case study, where the goal was process improvement, the second study aimed only to document the process steps and interactions by capturing them in MSL. The model contained 25 classes and 26 rules.

For each model, the MSL process descriptions were used to generate "process enactment environments," resulting in a database populated with instances of the information model's classes. Then, researchers simulated several scenarios to verify that the models performed as expected. During the simulation, they collected timing and resource utilization data, providing the basis for analyzing likely process performance. By changing the rules and executing a scenario repeatedly, the timings were compared and contrasted, leading to significant process improvement without major investment in resources.

The modeling and simulation exercises were useful for early problem identification and resolution. For example, the software maintenance process definition uncovered three types of problems with the existing process documentation: missing task inputs and outputs, ambiguous input and output criteria, and inefficiency in the process definition. The signaling fault model simulation discovered inefficiencies in the separate descriptions of the workcenters.

Barghouti and his colleagues note the importance of dividing the process modeling problem into two pieces: modeling the information and modeling the behavior. By separating these concerns, the resulting model is clear and concise. They also point out that computer-intensive activities are more easily modeled than human-intensive ones, a lesson noted by Curtis and his colleagues, too.

Desirable Properties of Process Modeling Tools and Techniques

There are many process modeling tools and techniques, and researchers continue to work to determine which ones are most appropriate for a given situation. But there are some characteristics that are helpful, regardless of technique. Curtis, Kellner, and Over (1992) have identified five categories of desirable properties:

1. *Facilitates human understanding and communication.* The technique should be able to represent the process in a form that most customers and developers can understand, encouraging communication about the process and agreement on its form and improvements. The technique should include sufficient information to allow one or more people to actually perform the process. And the model or tool should form a basis for training.
2. *Supports process improvement.* The technique should identify the essential components of a development or maintenance process. It should allow reuse of processes

or subprocesses on subsequent projects, compare alternatives, and estimate the impact of changes before the process is actually put into practice. Similarly, the technique should assist in selecting tools and techniques for the process, in encouraging organizational learning, and in supporting continuing evolution of the process.

3. *Supports process management.* The technique should allow the process to be project-specific. Then, developers and customers should be able to reason about attributes of software creation or evolution. The technique should also support planning and forecasting, monitoring and managing the process, and measuring key process characteristics.
4. *Provides automated guidance in performing the process.* The technique should define all or part of the software development environment, provide guidance and suggestions, and retain reusable process representations for later use.
5. *Supports automated process execution.* The technique should automate all or part of the process, support cooperative work, capture relevant measurement data, and enforce rules to ensure process integrity.

These characteristics can act as useful guidelines for selecting a process modeling technique for your development project. Item 4 is especially important if your organization is attempting to standardize its process; tools can help prompt developers about what to do next and provide gateways and checkpoints to assure that an artifact meets certain standards before the next steps are taken. For example, a tool can check a set of code components, evaluating their size and structure. If size or structure exceeds predefined limits, the developers can be notified before testing begins, and some components may be reviewed and perhaps redesigned.

2.5 INFORMATION SYSTEMS EXAMPLE

Let us consider which development process to use for supporting our information system example, the Piccadilly Television advertising program. Recall that there are many constraints on what kinds of advertising can be sold when, and that the regulations may change with rulings by the Advertising Standards Authority and other regulatory bodies. Thus, we want to build a software system that is easily maintained and changed. There is even a possibility that the constraints may change as we are building the system.

The waterfall model may be too rigid for our system, since it permits little flexibility after the requirements analysis stage is complete. Prototyping may be useful for building the user interface, so we may want to include some kind of prototyping in our model. But most of the uncertainty lies in the advertising regulations and business constraints. We want to use a process model that can be used and reused as the system evolves. A variation of the spiral model may be a good candidate for building the Piccadilly system, because it encourages us to revisit our assumptions, analyze our risks, and prototype various system characteristics. The repeated evaluation of alternatives, shown in the upper-left-hand quadrant of the spiral, helps us build flexibility into our requirements and design.

Boehm's representation of the spiral is high-level, without enough detail to direct the actions of analysts, designers, coders, and testers. However, there are many techniques and tools for representing the process model at finer levels of detail. The choice of technique or tool depends in part on personal preference and experience, and in part on suitability for the type of process being represented. Let us see how Lai's notation might be used to represent part of the Piccadilly system's development process.

Because we want to use the spiral model to help us manage risk, we must include a characterization of "risk" in our process model. That is, risk is an artifact that we must describe, so we can measure and track risk in each iteration of our spiral. Each potential problem has an associated risk, and we can think of the risk in terms of two facets: probability and severity. **Probability** is the likelihood that a particular problem will occur, and **severity** is the impact it will have on the system. For example, suppose we are considering the problem of insufficient training in the development method being used to build the Piccadilly system. We may decide to use an object-oriented approach, but we may find that the developers assigned to the project have little or no experience in object orientation. This problem may have a low probability of occurring, since all new employees are sent to an intensive, four-week course on object-oriented development. On the other hand, should the problem actually occur, it would have a severe impact on the ability of the development team to finish the software within the assigned schedule. Thus, the probability of occurrence is low, but the severity is large.

We can represent these risk situations in a Lai artifact table, shown in Table 2.2. Here, risk is the artifact, with subartifacts probability and severity. For simplicity, we

TABLE 2.2 Artifact Definition Form for Artifact "Risk"

Name	*Risk (ProblemX)*	
Synopsis process	*This is the artifact that represents the risk that problem X will occur and have a negative affect on some aspect of the development process.*	
Complexity type	*Composite*	
Data type	*(risk_s, user_defined)*	
Artifact-state list		
low	$((state\_of(probability.x) = low)$ $(state\_of(severity.x) = small)$	Probability of problem is low, severity problem impact is small.
high-medium	$((state\_of(probability.x) = low)$ $(state\_of(severity.x) = large))$	Probability of problem is low, severity problem impact is large.
low-medium	$((State\_of(probability.x) = high)$ $(state\_of(severity.x) = small))$	Probability of problem is high, severity problem impact is small.
high	$((state\_of(probability.x) = high)$ $(state\_of(severity.x) = large))$	Probability of problem is high, severity problem impact is large.
Subartifact list		
	probability.x	*The probability that problem X will occur.*
	severity.x	*The severity of the impact should problem X occur on the project.*

have chosen only two states for each subartifact: low and high for probability, and small and large for severity. In fact, each of the subartifacts can have a large range of states (such as extremely small, very small, somewhat small, medium, somewhat high, very high, extremely high), leading to many different states for the artifact itself.

In the same way, we can define the other aspects of our development process and use diagrams to illustrate the activities and their interconnections. Modeling the process in this way has many advantages, not the least of which is building a common understanding of what development will entail. If users, customers, and developers participate in defining and depicting Piccadilly's development process, each will have expectations about what activities are involved, what they produce, and when each product can be expected. In particular, the combination of spiral model and risk table can be used to evaluate the risks periodically. With each revolution around the spiral, the probability and severity of each risk can be revisited and restated; when risks are unacceptably high, the process model can be revised to include risk mitigation and reduction techniques, as we will see in Chapter 3.

2.6 REAL-TIME EXAMPLE

The Ariane-5 software involved the reuse of software from Ariane-4. Reuse was intended to reduce risk, increase productivity, and increase quality. Thus, any process model for developing new Ariane software should include reuse activities. In particular, the process model must include activities to check the quality of reusable components, with safeguards to make sure that the reused software works properly within the context of the design of the new system.

Such a process model might look like the simplified model of Figure 2.17. The boxes in the model represent activities. The arrows entering the box from the left are resources, and those leaving on the right are outputs. Those entering from the top are controls or constraints, such as schedules, budgets, or standards. And those entering from below are mechanisms that assist in performing the activity, such as tools, databases, or techniques.

The Ariane-4 reuse process begins with the software's mission, namely, controlling a new rocket, as well as software from previous airframes, unmet needs, and other software components available from other sources (such as purchased software or reuse repositories from other projects). Based on the business strategy of the aerospace builder, the developers can identify reusable subprocesses, describe them (perhaps with annotations related to past experience), and place them in a library for consideration by the requirements analysts. The reusable processes will often involve reusable components (i.e., reusable requirements, design or code components, or even test cases, process descriptions, and other documents and artifacts).

Next, the requirements analysts examine the requirements for the new airframe and the reusable components that are available in the library. They produce a revised set of requirements, consisting of a mix of new and reused requirements. Then, the designers use those requirements to design the software. Once their design is complete, they evaluate all reused design components to certify that they are correct and consistent with the new parts of the design and the overall intention of the system as described in the requirements. Finally, the certified components are used to build or

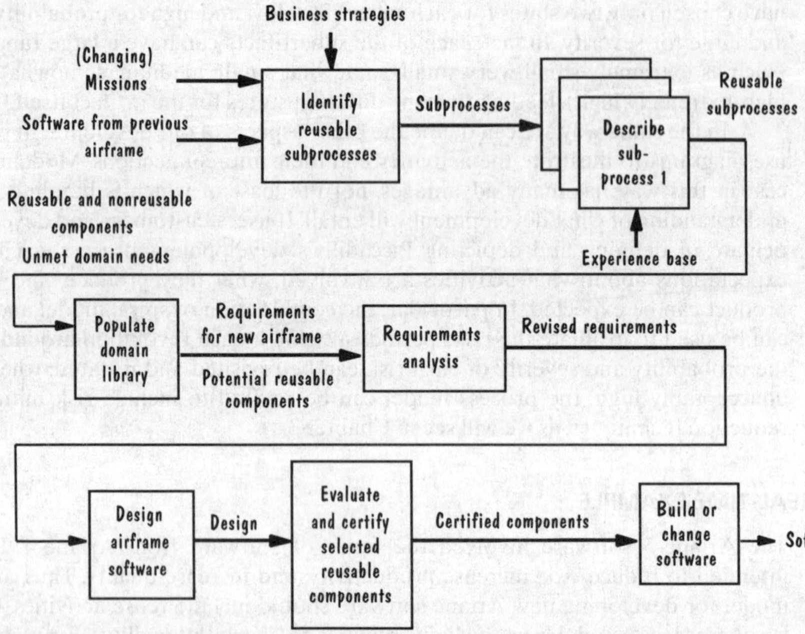

FIGURE 2.17 Reuse process model for new airframe software.

change the software and produce the final system. As we will see in later chapters, such a process might have prevented the destruction of Ariane-5.

2.7 WHAT THIS CHAPTER MEANS FOR YOU

In this chapter, we have seen that the software development process involves activities, resources, and products. A process model is useful for guiding your behavior when you are working with a group. Detailed process models tell you how to coordinate and collaborate with your colleagues as you design and build a system. We have also seen that process models include organizational, functional, behavioral, and other perspectives, so you can focus on particular aspects of the development process to enhance your understanding or guide your actions.

2.8 WHAT THIS CHAPTER MEANS FOR YOUR DEVELOPMENT TEAM

A process model has clear advantages for your development team, too. A good model shows each team member which activities occur when, and by whom, so that the division of duties is clear. In addition, the project manager can use process tools to enact the process, simulating activities and tracking resources to determine the best mix of people and activities in order to meet the project's budget and schedule. This simulation is done before resources are actually committed, so time and money are saved by not having to backtrack or correct mistakes. Indeed, iteration and incremental development can be included in the process model, so the team can learn from prototyping or react to evolving requirements and still meet the appropriate deadlines.

2.9 WHAT THIS CHAPTER MEANS FOR RESEARCHERS

Process modeling is a rich field of research interest in software engineering. Many software developers feel that, by using a good process, the quality of the products of development can be guaranteed. Thus, there are several areas into which researchers are looking:

- *Process notations:* How to write down the process in a way that is understandable to those who must carry it out
- *Process models:* How to depict the process, using an appropriate set of activities, resources, products, and tools
- *Process modeling support tools:* How to enact or simulate a process model, so that resource availability, usage, and performance can be assessed
- *Process measurement and assessment:* How to determine which activities, resources, subprocesses, and model types are best for producing high-quality products in a specified time or environment

Many of these efforts are coordinated with process improvement research, an area we will investigate in Chapter 13.

2.10 TERM PROJECT

It is early in the development process of the Loan Arranger system for FCO. You do not yet have a comprehensive set of requirements for the system. All you have is an overview of system functionality, and a sense of how the system will be used to support FCO's business. Many of the terms used in the overview are unfamiliar to you, so you have asked the customer representatives to prepare a glossary. They give you the description in Table 2.3.

This information clarifies some concepts for you, but you are still far from having a good set of requirements. Nevertheless, you can make some preliminary decisions about how the development should proceed. Review the processes presented in this chapter and determine which ones might be appropriate for developing the Loan Arranger. For each process, make a list of its advantages and disadvantages with respect to the Loan Arranger.

2.11 KEY REFERENCES

As a result of the Fifth International Software Process Workshop, a working group chaired by Kellner formulated a standard problem, to be used to evaluate and compare some of the more popular process modeling techniques. The problem was designed to be complex enough so that it would test a technique's ability to include each of the following:

- multiple levels of abstraction
- control flow, sequencing, and constraints on sequencing

TABLE 2.3 Glossary of Terms for the Loan Arranger

Borrower: A borrower is the recipient of money from a lender. Borrowers may receive loans jointly; that is, each loan may have multiple borrowers. Each borrower has an associated name and a unique borrower identification number.

Borrower's risk: The risk factor associated with any borrower is based on the borrower's payment history. A borrower with no loans outstanding is assigned a nominal borrower's risk factor of 50. The risk factor decreases when the borrower makes payments on time but increases when a borrower makes a payment late or defaults on a loan. The borrower's risk is calculated using the following formula:

$$\begin{aligned} \text{Risk} = 50 &- [10 \times (\text{number of years of loans in good standing})] \\ &+ [20 \times (\text{number of years of loans in late standing})] \\ &+ [30 \times (\text{number of years of loans in default standing})] \end{aligned}$$

For example, a borrower may have three loans. The first loan was taken out two years ago, and all payments have been made on time. That loan is in good standing and has been so for two years. The second and third loans are four and five years old, respectively, and each one was in good standing until recently. Thus, each of the two late-standing loans has been in late standing only for one year. Thus, the risk is

$$50 - [10 \times 2] + [20 \times (1 + 1)] + [30 \times 0] = 70.$$

The maximum risk value is 100, and the minimum risk value is 1.

Bundle: A bundle is a collection of loans that has been associated for sale as a single unit to an investor. Associated with each bundle is the total value of loans in the bundle, the period of time over which the loans in the bundle are active (i.e., for which borrowers are still making payments on the loans), an estimate of the risk involved in purchasing the bundle, and the profit to be made when all loans are paid back by the borrowers.

Bundle risk: The risk of a loan bundle is the weighted average of the risks of the loans in the bundle, with each loan's risk (see *loan risk,* below) weighted according to that loan's value. To calculate the weighted average over n loans, assume that each loan Li has remaining principal Pi and loan risk Ri. The weighted average is then

$$\frac{\sum_{i=1}^{n} PiRi}{\sum_{i=1}^{n} Pi}$$

Discount: The discount is the price at which FCO is willing to sell a loan to an investor. It is calculated according to the formula

$$\text{Discount} = (\text{principal remaining}) \times [(\text{interest rate}) \times (0.2 + (.005 \times (101 - (\text{loan risk}))))]$$

Interest rate type: An interest rate on a loan is either fixed or adjustable. A fixed-rate loan (called an FM) has the same interest rate for the term of the mortgage. An adjustable rate loan (called an ARM) has a rate that changes each year, based on a government index supplied by the U.S. Department of the Treasury.

Investor: An investor is a person or organization that is interested in purchasing a bundle of loans from FCO.

Investment request: An investor makes an investment request, specifying a maximum degree of risk at which the investment will be made, the minimum amount of profit required in a bundle, and the maximum period of time over which the loans in the bundle must be paid.

Lender: A lender is an institution that makes loans to borrowers. A lender can have zero, one, or many loans.

Lender information: Lender information is descriptive data that are imported from outside the application. Lender information cannot be changed or deleted. The following information is associated with each lender: lender name (institution), lender contact (person at that institution), phone number for contact, a unique lender identification number. Once added to the system, a lender entry can be edited but not removed.

(continues)

TABLE 2.3 *(continued)*

Lending institution: A synonym for lender. See *lender*.

Loan: A loan is a set of information that describes a home loan and the borrower-identifying information associated with the loan. The following information is associated with each loan: loan amount, interest rate, interest rate type (adjustable or fixed), settlement date (the date the borrower originally borrowed the money from the lender), term (expressed as number of years), borrower, lender, loan type (jumbo or regular), and property (identified by the address of the property). A loan must have exactly one associated lender and exactly one associated borrower. In addition, each loan is identified with a loan risk and a loan status.

Loan analyst: The loan analyst is a professional employee of FCO who is trained in using the Loan Arranger system to manage and bundle loans. Loan analysts are familiar with the terminology of loans and lending, but they may not have all the relevant information at hand with which to evaluate a single loan or collection of loans.

Loan risk: Each loan is associated with a level of risk, indicated by an integer from 1 to 100. 1 represents the lowest-risk loan; that is, it is unlikely that the borrower will be late or default on this loan. 100 represents the highest risk; that is, it is almost certain that the borrower will default on this loan.

Loan status: A loan can have one of three status designations: good, late, or default. A loan is in good status if the borrower has made all payments up to the current time. A loan is in late status if the borrower's last payment was made but not by the payment due date. A loan is in default status if the borrower's last payment was not received within 10 days of the due date.

Loan type: A loan is either a jumbo mortgage, where the property is valued in excess of $275,000, or a regular mortgage, where the property value is $275,000 or less.

Portfolio: The collection of loans purchased by FCO and available for inclusion in a bundle. The repository maintained by the Loan Arranger contains information about all of the loans in the portfolio.

- decision points
- iteration and feedback to earlier steps
- user creativity
- object and information management, as well as flow through the process
- object structure, attributes, and interrelationships
- organizational responsibility for specific tasks
- physical communication mechanisms for information transfer
- process measurements
- temporal aspects (both absolute and relative)
- tasks executed by humans
- professional judgment or discretion
- connection to narrative explanations
- tasks invoked or executed by a tool
- resource constraints and allocation, schedule determination
- process modification and improvement
- multiple levels of aggregation and parallelism

Eighteen different process modeling techniques were applied to the common problem, and varying degrees of satisfaction were found with each one. The results are reported in Kellner and Rombach (1990).

Curtis, Kellner, and Over (1992) present a comprehensive survey of process modeling techniques and tools. The paper also summarizes basic language types and constructs and gives examples of process modeling approaches that use those language types.

Krasner et al. (1992) describe lessons learned when implementing a software process modeling system in a commercial environment.

Several Web sites contain information about process modeling.

- The U.S. Software Engineering Institute (SEI) continues to investigate process modeling as part of its process improvement efforts. A list of its technical reports and activities can be found at http://www.sei.cmu.edu. The information at http://www.sei.cmu.edu/collaborating/spins/ describes Software Process Improvement Networks, geographically-based groups of people interested in process improvement who often meet to hear speakers or discuss process-related issues.
- The European Community has long sponsored research in process modeling and a process model language. Descriptions of current research projects are available at http://cordis.europa.eu/fp7/projects_en.html.
- The Data and Analysis Centre for Software Engineering maintains a list of resources about software process at https://www.thedacs.com/databases/url/key/39.

More information about Lai notation is available in David Weiss and Robert Lai's book, Software Product Line Engineering: A Family-based Software Development Process (Weiss and Lai 1999).

The University of Southern California's Center for Software Engineering has developed a tool to assist you in selecting a process model suitable for your project's requirements and constraints. It can be ftp-ed from ftp://usc.edu/pub/soft_engineering/demos/pmsa.zip, and more information can be found on the Center's Web site: http://sunset.usc.edu.

Journals such as *Software Process—Improvement and Practice* have articles addressing the role of process modeling in software development and maintenance. They also report the highlights of relevant conferences, such as the International Software Process Workshop and the International Conference on Software Engineering. The July/August 2000 issue of *IEEE Software* focuses on process diversity and has several articles about the success of a process maturity approach to software development.

There are many resources available for learning about agile methods. The Agile Manifesto is posted at http://www.agilealliance.org. Kent Beck's (1999) is the seminal book on extreme programming, and Alistair Cockburn (2002) describes the Crystal family of methodologies. Martin Beck (1999) explains refactoring, which is one of the most difficult steps of XP. Two excellent references on agile methods are Robert C. Martin's (2003) book on agile software development, and Daniel H. Steinberg and Daniel W. Palmer's (2004) book on extreme software engineering. Two Web sites providing additional information about extreme programming are http://www.xprgramming.com and http://www.extremeprogramming.org.

2.12 EXERCISES

1. How does the description of a system relate to the notion of process models? For example, how do you decide what the boundary should be for the system described by a process model?
2. Draw a diagram that describes the process of making a cup of tea.
3. Draw a Lai artifact table to define a module. Make sure that you include artifact states that show the module when it is untested, partially tested, and completely tested.
4. For each of the process models described in this chapter, what are the benefits and drawbacks of using the model?
5. For each of the process models described in this chapter, how does the model handle a significant change in requirements late in development?
6. Examine the characteristics of good process models described in Section 2.4. Which characteristics are essential for processes to be used on projects where the problem and solution are not well understood?
7. You are required to design and build a system that monitors outdoors temperature using a probe connected to a USB port on a PC. The specifications from the client are somewhat unclear. So after careful analysis you decide to build a prototype first, present it to the client, and refine the specifications based on the customer's feedback. Describe some of the functionalities of the final product that you will not implement in the prototype.
8. In this chapter, we suggested that software development is a creation process, not a manufacturing process. Discuss the characteristics of manufacturing that apply to software development and explain which characteristics of software development are more like a creative endeavor.
9. Should a development organization adopt a single process model for all of its software development? Discuss the pros and cons.
10. Consider the processes introduced in this chapter. Which ones give you the most flexibility to change in reaction to changing requirements?
11. Suppose your contract with a customer specifies that you use a particular software development process. How can the work be monitored to enforce the use of this process?
12. Suppose Amalgamated, Inc., requires you to use a given process model when it contracts with you to build a system. You comply, building software using the prescribed activities, resources, and constraints. After the software is delivered and installed, your system experiences a catastrophic failure. When Amalgamated investigates the source of the failure, you are accused of not having done code reviews that would have found the source of the problem before delivery. You respond that code reviews were not in the required process. What are the legal and ethical issues involved in this dispute?

3 Planning and Managing the Project

In this chapter, we look at
- tracking project progress
- project personnel and organization
- effort and schedule estimation
- risk management
- using process modeling with project planning

As we saw in the previous chapters, the software development cycle includes many steps, some of which are repeated until the system is complete and the customers and users are satisfied. However, before committing funds for a software development or maintenance project, a customer usually wants an estimate of how much the project will cost and how long the project will take. This chapter examines the activities necessary to plan and manage a software development project.

3.1 TRACKING PROGRESS

Software is useful only if it performs a desired function or provides a needed service. Thus, a typical project begins when a customer approaches you to discuss a perceived need. For example, a large national bank may ask you for help in building an information system that allows the bank's clients to access their account information, no matter where in the world the clients are. Or you may be contacted by marine biologists who would like a system to connect with their water-monitoring equipment and perform statistical analyses of the data gathered. Usually, customers have several questions to be answered:

- Do you understand my problem and my needs?
- Can you design a system that will solve my problem or satisfy my needs?
- How long will it take you to develop such a system?
- How much will it cost to have you develop such a system?

Answering the last two questions requires a well-thought-out project schedule. A **project schedule** describes the software development cycle for a particular project by enumerating the phases or stages of the project and breaking each into discrete tasks or activities to be done. The schedule also portrays the interactions among these activities and estimates the time that each task or activity will take. Thus, the schedule is a timeline that shows when activities will begin and end, and when the related development products will be ready.

In Chapter 1, we learned that a systems approach involves both analysis and synthesis: breaking the problem into its component parts, devising a solution for each part, and then putting the pieces together to form a coherent whole. We can use this approach to determine the project schedule. We begin by working with customers and potential users to understand what they want and need. At the same time, we make sure that they are comfortable with our knowledge of their needs. We list all project **deliverables**, that is, the items that the customer expects to see during project development. Among the deliverables may be

- documents
- demonstrations of function
- demonstrations of subsystems
- demonstrations of accuracy
- demonstrations of reliability, security, or performance

Next, we determine what activities must take place in order to produce these deliverables. We may use some of the process modeling techniques we learned in Chapter 2, laying out exactly what must happen and which activities depend on other activities, products, or resources. Certain events are designated to be milestones, indicating to us and our customers that a measurable level of progress has been made. For example, when the requirements are documented, inspected for consistency and completeness, and turned over to the design team, the requirements specification may be a project milestone. Similarly, milestones may include the completion of the user's manual, the performance of a given set of calculations, or a demonstration of the system's ability to communicate with another system.

In our analysis of the project, we must distinguish clearly between milestones and activities. An **activity** is a part of the project that takes place over a period of time, whereas a **milestone** is the completion of an activity—a particular point in time. Thus, an activity has a beginning and an end, whereas a milestone is the end of a specially designated activity. For example, the customer may want the system to be accompanied by an online operator tutorial. The development of the tutorial and its associated programs is an activity; it culminates in the demonstration of those functions to the customer: the milestone.

By examining the project carefully in this way, we can separate development into a succession of phases. Each phase is composed of steps, and each step can be subdivided further if necessary, as shown in Figure 3.1.

To see how this analysis works, consider the phases, steps, and activities of Table 3.1, which describes the building of a house. First, we consider two phases: landscaping the lot and building the house itself. Then, we break each phase into smaller steps, such as

FIGURE 3.1 Phases, steps, and activities in a project.

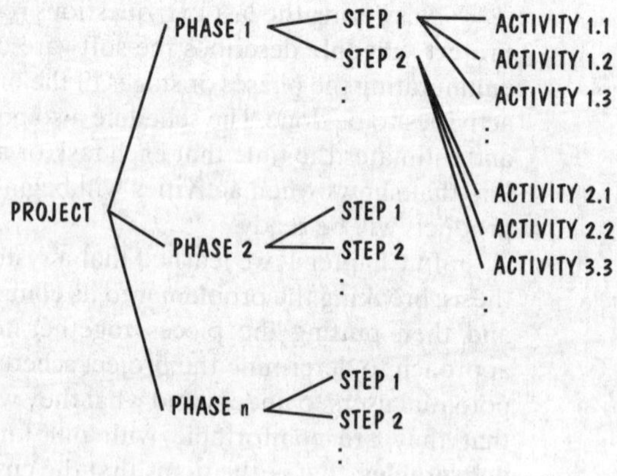

clearing and grubbing, seeding the turf, and planting trees and shrubs. Where necessary, we can divide the steps into activities; for example, finishing the interior involves completing the interior plumbing, interior electrical work, wallboard, interior painting, floor covering, doors, and fixtures. Each activity is a measurable event and we have objective criteria to determine when the activity is complete. Thus, any activity's end can be a milestone, and Table 3.2 lists the milestones for phase 2.

This analytical breakdown gives us and our customers an idea of what is involved in constructing a house. Similarly, analyzing a software development or maintenance project and identifying the phases, steps, and activities, both we and our customers have a better grasp of what is involved in building and maintaining a system. We saw in Chapter 2 that a process model provides a high-level view of the phases and steps, so process modeling is a useful way to begin analyzing the project. In later chapters, we will see that the major phases, such as requirements engineering, implementation, or testing, involve many activities, each of which contributes to product or process quality.

Work Breakdown and Activity Graphs

Analysis of this kind is sometimes described as generating a **work breakdown structure** for a given project, because it depicts the project as a set of discrete pieces of work. Notice that the activities and milestones are items that both customer and developer can use to track development or maintenance. At any point in the process, the customer may want to follow our progress. We developers can point to activities, indicating what work is under way, and to milestones, indicating what work has been completed. However, a project's work breakdown structure gives no indication of the interdependence of the work units or of the parts of the project that can be developed concurrently.

We can describe each activity with four parameters: the precursor, duration, due date, and endpoint. A **precursor** is an event or set of events that must occur before the activity can begin; it describes the set of conditions that allows the activity to begin. The duration is the length of time needed to complete the activity. The **due date** is the date by which the activity must be completed, frequently determined by contractual deadlines. Signifying that the activity has ended, the **endpoint** is usually a milestone or

TABLE 3.1 Phases, Steps, and Activities of Building a House

Phase 1: Landscaping the Lot	Phase 2: Building the House
Step 1.1: Clearing and grubbing	*Step 2.1: Prepare the site*
Activity 1.1.1: Remove trees	Activity 2.1.1: Survey the land
Activity 1.1.2: Remove stumps	Activity 2.1.2: Request permits
Step 1.2: Seeding the turf	Activity 2.1.3: Excavate for the foundation
Activity 1.2.1: Aerate the soil	Activity 2.1.4: Buy materials
Activity 1.2.2: Disperse the seeds	*Step 2.2: Building the exterior*
Activity 1.2.3: Water and weed	Activity 2.2.1: Lay the foundation
Step 1.3: Planting shrubs and trees	Activity 2.2.2: Build the outside walls
Activity 1.3.1: Obtain shrubs and trees	Activity 2.2.3: Install exterior plumbing
Activity 1.3.2: Dig holes	Activity 2.2.4: Exterior electrical work
Activity 1.3.3: Plant shrubs and trees	Activity 2.2.5: Exterior siding
Activity 1.3.4: Anchor the trees and mulch around them	Activity 2.2.6: Paint the exterior
	Activity 2.2.7: Install doors and fixtures
	Activity 2.2.8: Install roof
	Step 2.3: Finishing the interior
	Activity 2.3.1: Install the interior plumbing
	Activity 2.3.2: Install interior electrical work
	Activity 2.3.3: Install wallboard
	Activity 2.3.4: Paint the interior
	Activity 2.3.5: Install floor covering
	Activity 2.3.6: Install doors and fixtures

TABLE 3.2 Milestones in Building a House

1.1.	Survey complete
1.2.	Permits issued
1.3.	Excavation complete
1.4.	Materials on hand
2.1.	Foundation laid
2.2.	Outside walls complete
2.3.	Exterior plumbing complete
2.4.	Exterior electrical work complete
2.5.	Exterior siding complete
2.6.	Exterior painting complete
2.7.	Doors and fixtures mounted
2.8.	Roof complete
3.1.	Interior plumbing complete
3.2.	Interior electrical work complete
3.3.	Wallboard in place
3.4.	Interior painting complete
3.5.	Floor covering laid
3.6.	Doors and fixtures mounted

deliverable. We can illustrate the relationships among activities by using these parameters. In particular, we can draw an **activity graph** to depict the dependencies; the nodes of the graph are the project milestones, and the lines linking the nodes represent the activities involved. Figure 3.2 is an activity graph for the work described in phase 2 of Table 3.1.

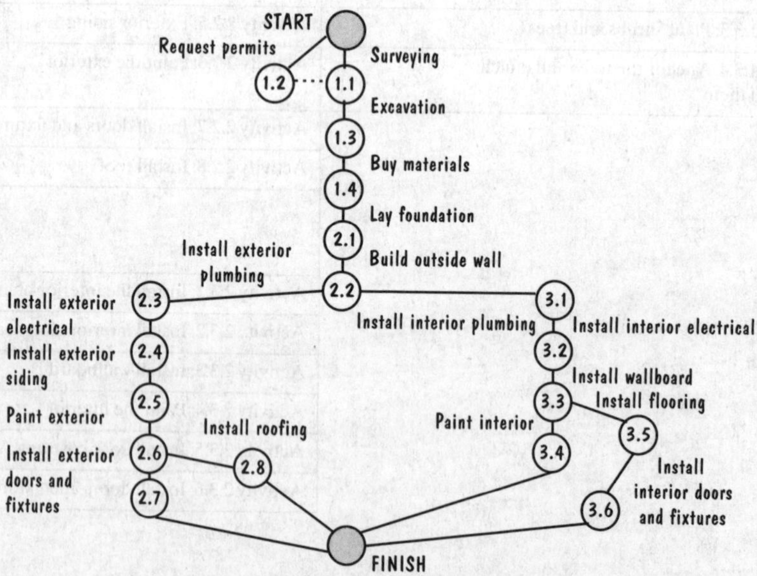

FIGURE 3.2 Activity graph for building a house.

Many important characteristics of the project are made visible by the activity graph. For example, it is clear from Figure 3.2 that neither of the two plumbing activities can start before milestone 2.2 is reached; that is, 2.2 is a precursor to both interior and exterior plumbing. Furthermore, the figure shows us that several things can be done simultaneously. For instance, some of the interior and exterior activities are independent (such as installing wallboard, connecting exterior electrical plumbing, and others leading to milestones 2.6 and 3.3, respectively). The activities on the left-hand path do not depend on those on the right for their initiation, so they can be worked on concurrently. Notice that there is a dashed line from requesting permits (node 1.2) to surveying (node 1.1). This line indicates that these activities must be completed before excavation (the activity leading to milestone 1.3) can begin. However, since there is no real activity that occurs after reaching milestone 1.2 in order to get to milestone 1.1, the dashed line indicates a relationship without an accompanying activity.

It is important to realize that activity graphs depend on an understanding of the parallel nature of tasks. If work cannot be done in parallel, then the (mostly straight) graph is not useful in depicting how tasks will be coordinated. Moreover, the graphs must reflect a realistic depiction of the parallelism. In our house-building example, it is clear that some of the tasks, like plumbing, will be done by different people from those doing other tasks, like electrical work. But on software development projects, where some people have many skills, the theoretical parallelism may not reflect reality. A restricted number of people assigned to the project may result in the same person doing many things in series, even though they could be done in parallel by a larger development team.

Estimating Completion

We can make an activity graph more useful by adding to it information about the estimated time it will take to complete each activity. For a given activity, we label the corresponding edge of the graph with the estimate. For example, for the activities in phase 2 of Table 2.1, we can append to the activity graph of Figure 3.2 estimates of the number of days it will take to complete each activity. Table 3.3 contains the estimates for each activity.

The result is the graph shown in Figure 3.3. Notice that milestones 2.7, 2.8, 3.4, and 3.6 are precursors to the finish. That is, these milestones must all be reached in order to consider the project complete. The zeros on the links from those nodes to the finish show that no additional time is needed. There is also an implicit zero on the link from node 1.2 to 1.1, since no additional time is accrued on the dashed link.

This graphical depiction of the project tells us a lot about the project's schedule. For example, since we estimated that the first activity would take 3 days to complete, we cannot hope to reach milestone 1.1 before the end of day 3. Similarly, we cannot reach milestone 1.2 before the end of day 15. Because the beginning of excavation (activity 1.3) cannot begin until milestones 1.1 and 1.2 are both reached, excavation cannot begin until the beginning of day 16.

Analyzing the paths among the milestones of a project in this way is called the **Critical Path Method (CPM)**. The paths can show us the minimum amount of time it will take to complete the project, given our estimates of each activity's duration. Moreover, CPM reveals those activities that are most critical to completing the project on time.

TABLE 3.3 Activities and Time Estimates

Activity	Time Estimate (in Days)
Step 1: Prepare the site	
Activity 1.1: Survey the land	3
Activity 1.2: Request permits	15
Activity 1.3: Excavate for the foundation	10
Activity 1.4: Buy materials	10
Step 2: Building the exterior	
Activity 2.1: Lay the foundation	15
Activity 2.2: Build the outside walls	20
Activity 2.3: Install exterior plumbing	10
Activity 2.4: Install exterior electrical work	10
Activity 2.5: Install exterior siding	8
Activity 2.6: Paint the exterior	5
Activity 2.7: Install doors and fixtures	6
Activity 2.8: Install roof	9
Step 3: Finishing the interior	
Activity 3.1: Install interior plumbing	12
Activity 3.2: Install interior electrical work	15
Activity 3.3: Install wallboard	9
Activity 3.4: Paint the interior	18
Activity 3.5: Install floor covering	11
Activity 3.6: Install doors and fixtures	7

To see how CPM works, consider again our house-building example. First, we notice that the activities leading to milestones 1.1 (surveying) and 1.2 (requesting permits) can occur concurrently. Since excavation (the activity culminating in milestone 1.3) cannot begin until day 16, surveying has 15 days in which to be completed, even though it is only 3 days in duration. Thus, surveying has 15 days of available time, but requires only 3 days of real time. In the same way, for each activity in our graph, we can compute a pair of times: real time and available time. The **real time** or **actual time** for an activity is the estimated amount of time required for the activity to be completed, and the **available time** is the amount of time available in the schedule for the activity's completion. **Slack time** or **float** for an activity is the difference between the available time and the real time for that activity:

$$\text{Slack time} = \text{available time} - \text{real time}$$

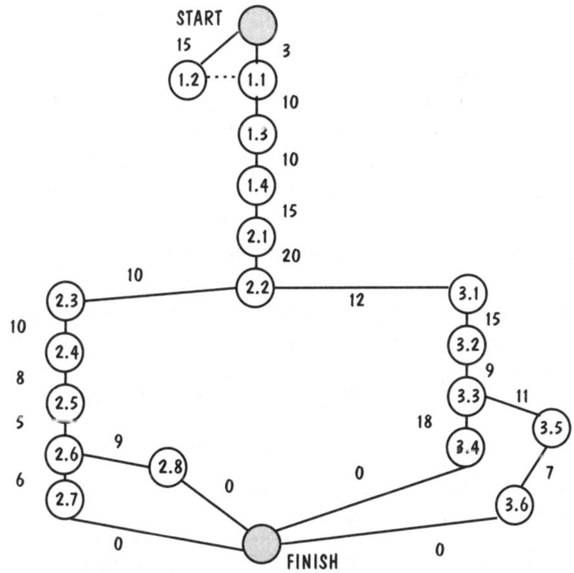

FIGURE 3.3 Activity graph with durations.

Another way of looking at slack time is to compare the earliest time an activity may begin with the latest time the activity may begin without delaying the project. For example, surveying may begin on day 1, so the earliest start time is day 1. However, because it will take 15 days to request and receive permits, surveying can begin as late as day 13 and still not hold up the project schedule. Therefore,

$$\text{Slack time} = \text{latest start time} - \text{earliest start time}$$

Let us compute the slack for our example's activities to see what it tells us about the project schedule. We compute slack by examining all paths from the start to the finish. As we have seen, it must take 15 days to complete milestones 1.1 and 1.2. An additional 55 days are used in completing milestones 1.3, 1.4, 2.1, and 2.2. At this point, there are four possible paths to be taken:

1. Following milestones 2.3 through 2.7 on the graph requires 39 days.
2. Following milestones 2.3 through 2.8 on the graph requires 42 days.
3. Following milestones 3.1 through 3.4 on the graph requires 54 days.
4. Following milestones 3.1 through 3.6 on the graph requires 54 days.

Because milestones 2.7, 2.8, 3.4, and 3.6 must be met before the project is finished, our schedule is constrained by the longest path. As you can see from Figure 3.3 and our preceding calculations, the two paths on the right require 124 days to complete, and the two paths on the left require fewer days. To calculate the slack, we can work backward along the path to see how much slack time there is for each activity leading to a node. First, we note that there is zero slack on the longest path. Then, we examine each of the remaining nodes to calculate the slack for the activities leading to them. For example,

54 days are available to complete the activities leading to milestones 2.3, 2.4, 2.5, 2.6, and 2.8, but only 42 days are needed to complete these. Thus, this portion of the graph has 12 days of slack. Similarly, the portion of the graph for activities 2.3 through 2.7 requires only 39 days, so we have 15 days of slack along this route. By working forward through the graph in this way, we can compute the earliest start time and slack for each of the activities. Then, we compute the latest start time for each activity by moving from the finish back through each node to the start. Table 3.4 shows the results: the slack time for each activity in Figure 3.3. (At milestone 2.6, the path can branch to 2.7 or 2.8. The latest start times in Table 3.4 are calculated by using the route from 2.6 to 2.8, rather than from 2.6 to 2.7.)

The longest path has a slack of zero for each of its nodes, because it is the path that determines whether or not the project is on schedule. For this reason, it is called the critical path. Thus, the **critical path** is the one for which the slack at every node is zero. As you can see from our example, there may be more than one critical path.

TABLE 3.4 Slack Time for Project Activities

Activity	Earliest Start Time	Latest Start Time	Slack
1.1	1	13	12
1.2	1	1	0
1.3	16	16	0
1.4	26	26	0
2.1	36	36	0
2.2	51	51	0
2.3	71	83	12
2.4	81	93	12
2.5	91	103	12
2.6	99	111	12
2.7	104	119	15
2.8	104	116	12
3.1	71	71	0
3.2	83	83	0
3.3	98	98	0
3.4	107	107	0
3.5	107	107	0
3.6	118	118	0
Finish	124	124	0

Since the critical path has no slack, there is no margin for error when performing the activities along its route.

Notice what happens when an activity on the critical path begins late (i.e., later than its earliest start time). The late start pushes all subsequent critical path activities forward, forcing them to be late, too, if there is no slack. And for activities not on the critical path, the subsequent activities may also lose slack time. Thus, the activity graph helps us to understand the impact of any schedule slippage.

Consider what happens if the activity graph has several loops in it. Loops may occur when an activity must be repeated. For instance, in our house-building example, the building inspector may require the plumbing to be redone. In software development, a design inspection may require design or requirements to be respecified. The appearance of these loops may change the critical path as the loop activities are exercised more than once. In this case, the effects on the schedule are far less easy to evaluate.

Figure 3.4 is a bar chart that shows some software development project activities, including information about the early and late start dates; this chart is typical of those produced by automated project management tools. The horizontal bars represent the duration of each activity; those bars composed of asterisks indicate the critical path. Activities depicted by dashes and Fs are not on the critical path, and an F represents float or slack time.

Critical path analysis of a project schedule tells us who must wait for what as the project is being developed. It also tells us which activities must be completed on schedule to avoid delay. This kind of analysis can be enhanced in many ways. For instance, our house-building example supposes that we know exactly how long each activity will take. Often, this is not the case. Instead, we have only an estimated duration for an activity, based on our knowledge of similar projects and events. Thus, to each activity, we can

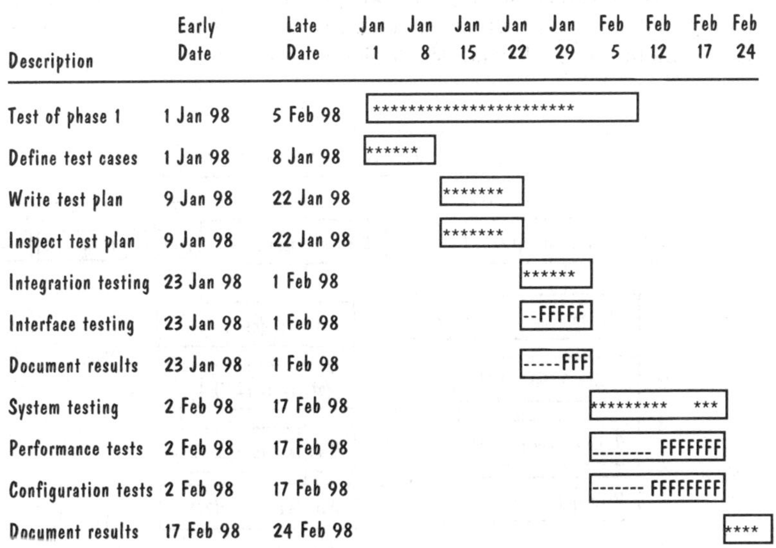

FIGURE 3.4 CPM bar chart.

assign a probable duration according to some probability distribution, so that each activity has associated with it an expected value and a variance. In other words, instead of knowing an exact duration, we estimate a window or interval in which the actual time is likely to fall. The expected value is a point within the interval, and the variance describes the width of the interval. You may be familiar with a standard probability distribution called a normal distribution, whose graph is a bell-shaped curve. The Program Evaluation and Review Technique (PERT) is a popular critical path analysis technique that assumes a normal distribution. (See Hillier and Lieberman [2001] for more information about PERT.) PERT determines the probability that the earliest start time for an activity is close to the scheduled time for that activity. Using information such as probability distribution, latest and earliest start times, and the activity graph, a PERT program can calculate the critical path and identify those activities most likely to be bottlenecks. Many project managers use the CPM or PERT method to examine their projects. However, these methods are valuable only for stable projects in which several activities take place concurrently. If the project's activities are mostly sequential, then almost all activities are on the critical path and are candidates for bottlenecks. Moreover, if the project requires redesign or rework, the activity graph and critical path are likely to change during development.

Tools to Track Progress

There are many tools that can be used to keep track of a project's progress. Some are manual, others are simple spreadsheet applications, and still others are sophisticated tools with complex graphics. To see what kinds of tools may be useful on your projects, consider the work breakdown structure depicted in Figure 3.5. Here, the overall objective is to build a system involving communications software, and the project manager has described the work in terms of five steps: system planning, system design, coding, testing, and delivery. For simplicity, we concentrate on the first two steps. Step 1 is then partitioned into four activities: reviewing the specifications, reviewing the budget, reviewing the schedule, and developing a project plan. Similarly, the system design is

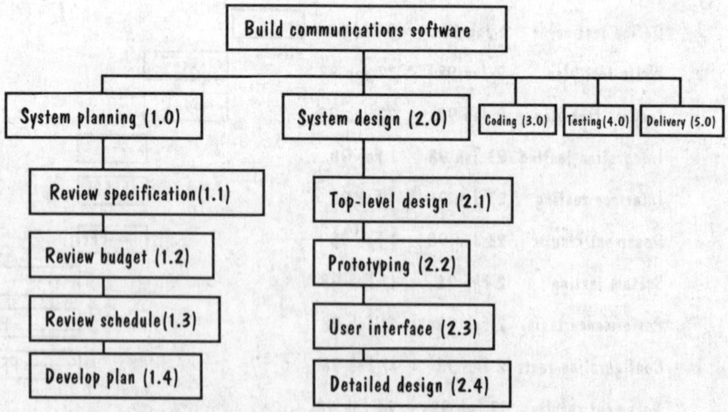

FIGURE 3.5 Example work breakdown structure.

developed by doing a top-level design, prototyping, designing the user interface, and then creating a detailed design.

Many project management software systems draw a work breakdown structure and also assist the project manager in tracking progress by step and activity. For example, a project management package may draw a **Gantt chart**, a depiction of the project where the activities are shown in parallel, with the degree of completion indicated by a color or icon. The chart helps the project manager to understand which activities can be performed concurrently, and also to see which items are on the critical path.

Figure 3.6 is a Gantt chart for the work breakdown structure of Figure 3.5. The project began in January, and the dashed vertical line labeled "today" indicates that the project team is working during the middle of May. A vertical bar shows progress on each activity, and the color of the bar denotes completion, duration, or criticality. A diamond icon shows us where there has been slippage, and the triangles designate an activity's start and finish. The Gantt chart is similar to the CPM chart of Figure 3.4, but it includes more information.

Simple charts and graphs can provide information about resources, too. For example, Figure 3.7 graphs the relationship between the people assigned to the project and those needed at each stage of development; it is typical of graphs produced by project management tools. It is easy to see that during January, February, and March,

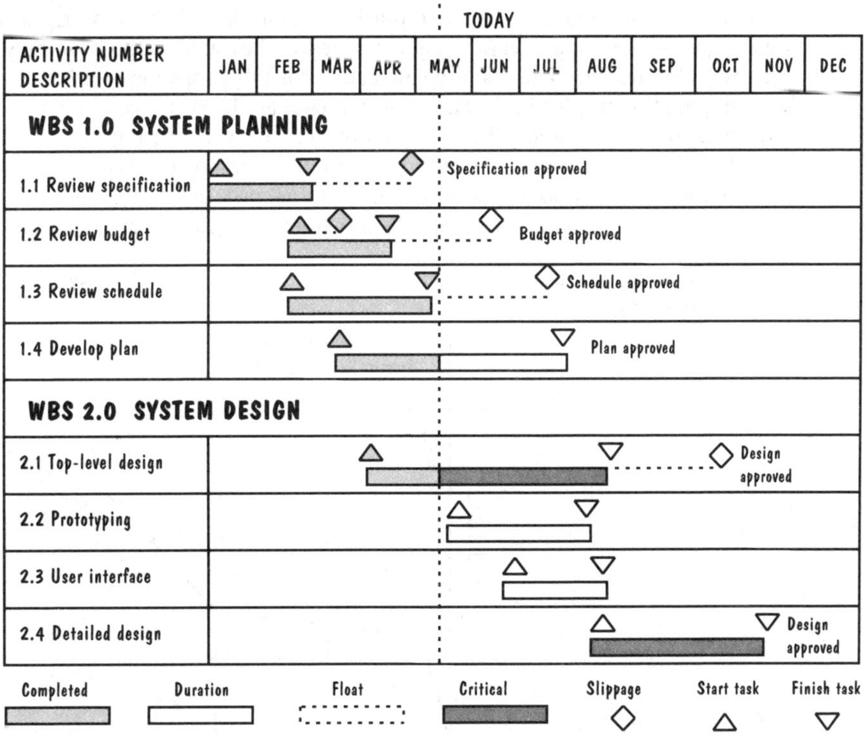

FIGURE 3.6 Gantt chart for example work breakdown structure.

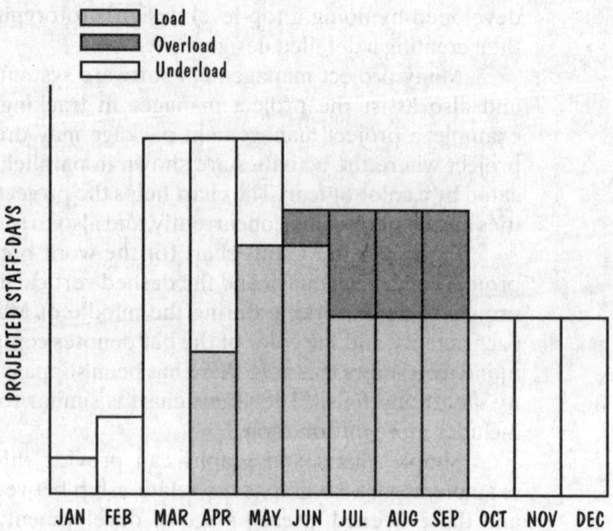

FIGURE 3.7 Resource histogram.

people are needed but no one is assigned. In April and May, some team members are working, but not enough to do the required job. On the other hand, the period during which there are too many team members is clearly shown: from the beginning of June to the end of September. The resource allocation for this project is clearly out of balance. By changing the graph's input data, you can change the resource allocation and try to reduce the overload, finding the best resource load for the schedule you have to meet.

Later in this chapter, we will see how to estimate the costs of development. Project management tools track actual costs against the estimates, so that budget progress can be assessed, too. Figure 3.8 shows an example of how expenditures can be

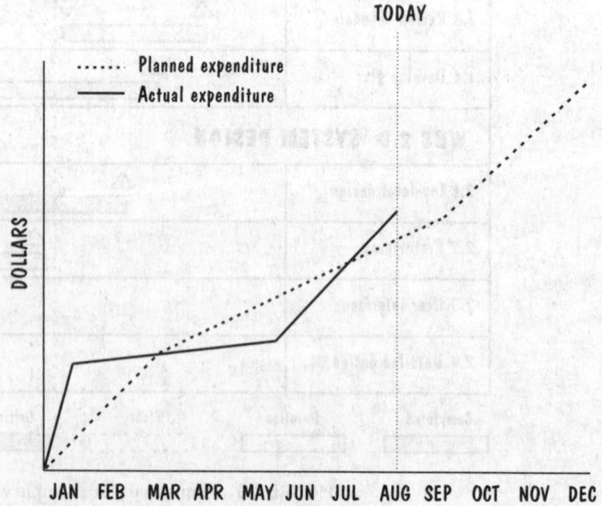

FIGURE 3.8 Tracking planned vs. actual expenditures.

monitored. By combining budget tracking with personnel tracking, you can use project management tools to determine the best resources for your limited budget.

3.2 PROJECT PERSONNEL

To determine the project schedule and estimate the associated effort and costs, we need to know approximately how many people will be working on the project, what tasks they will perform, and what abilities and experience they must have so they can do their jobs effectively. In this section, we look at how to decide who does what and how the staff can be organized.

Staff Roles and Characteristics

In Chapter 2, we examined several software process models, each depicting the way in which the several activities of software development are related. No matter the model, there are certain activities necessary to any software project. For example, every project requires people to interact with the customers to determine what they want and by when they want it. Other project personnel design the system, and still others write or test the programs. Key project activities are likely to include

1. requirements analysis
2. system design
3. program design
4. program implementation
5. testing
6. training
7. maintenance
8. quality assurance

However, not every task is performed by the same person or group; the assignment of staff to tasks depends on project size, staff expertise, and staff experience. There is great advantage in assigning different responsibilities to different sets of people, offering "checks and balances" that can identify faults early in the development process. For example, suppose the test team is separate from those who design and code the system. Testing new or modified software involves a system test, where the developers demonstrate to the customer that the system works as specified. The test team must define and document the way in which this test will be conducted and the criteria for linking the demonstrated functionality and performance characteristics to the requirements specified by the customer. The test team can generate its test plan from the requirements documents without knowing how the internal pieces of the system are put together. Because the test team has no preconceptions about how the hardware and software will work, it can concentrate on system functionality. This approach makes it easier for the test team to catch errors and omissions made by the designers or programmers. It is in part for this reason that the cleanroom method is organized to use an independent test team, as we will see in later chapters (Mills, Dyer, and Linger 1987).

For similar reasons, it is useful for program designers to be different from system designers. Program designers become deeply involved with the details of the code, and they sometimes neglect the larger picture of how the system should work. We will see in later chapters that techniques such as walkthroughs, inspections, and reviews can bring the two types of designers together to double-check the design before it goes on to be coded, as well as to provide continuity in the development process.

We saw in Chapter 1 that there are many other roles for personnel on the development or maintenance team. As we study each of the major tasks of development in subsequent chapters, we will describe the project team members who perform those tasks.

Once we have decided on the roles of project team members, we must decide which kinds of people we need in each role. Project personnel may differ in many ways, and it is not enough to say that a project needs an analyst, two designers, and five programmers, for example. Two people with the same job title may differ in at least one of the following ways:

- ability to perform the work
- interest in the work
- experience with similar applications
- experience with similar tools or languages
- experience with similar techniques
- experience with similar development environment
- training
- ability to communicate with others
- ability to share responsibility with others
- management skills

Each of these characteristics can affect an individual's ability to perform productively. These variations help to explain why one programmer can write a particular routine in a day, whereas another requires a week. The differences can be critical, not only to schedule estimation, but also to the success of the project.

To understand each worker's performance, we must know his or her ability to perform the work at hand. Some are good at viewing "the big picture," but may not enjoy focusing on detail if asked to work on a small part of a large project. Such people may be better suited to system design or testing than to program design or coding. Sometimes, ability is related to comfort. In classes or on projects, you may have worked with people who are more comfortable programming in one language than another. Indeed, some developers feel more confident about their design abilities than their coding prowess. This feeling of comfort is important; people are usually more productive when they have confidence in their ability to perform.

Interest in the work can also determine someone's success on a project. Although very good at doing a particular job, an employee may be more interested in trying something new than in repeating something done many times before. Thus, the novelty of the work is sometimes a factor in generating interest in it. On the other hand, there are always people who prefer doing what they know and do best, rather than venturing into new territory. It is important that whoever is chosen for a task be excited about performing it, no matter what the reason.

Given equal ability and interest, two people may still differ in the amount of experience or training they have had with similar applications, tools, or techniques. The person who has already been successful at using C to write a communications controller is more likely to write another communications controller in C faster (but not necessarily more clearly or efficiently) than someone who has neither experience with C nor knowledge of what a communications controller does. Thus, selection of project personnel involves not only individual ability and skill, but also experience and training.

On every software development or maintenance project, members of the development team communicate with one another, with users, and with the customer. The project's progress is affected not only by the degree of communication, but also by the ability of individuals to communicate their ideas. Software failures can result from a breakdown in communication and understanding, so the number of people who need to communicate with one another can affect the quality of the resulting product. Figure 3.9 shows us how quickly the lines of communication can grow. Increasing a work team from two to three people triples the number of possible lines of communication. In general, if a project has n workers, then there are $n(n - 1)/2$ pairs of people who might need to communicate, and $2^n - 1$ possible teams that can be created to work on smaller pieces of the project. Thus, a project involving only 10 people can use 45 lines of communication, and there are 1023 possible committees or teams that can be formed to handle subsystem development!

Many projects involve several people who must share responsibility for completing one or more activities. Those working on one aspect of project development must trust other team members to do their parts. In classes, you are usually in total control of the projects you do. You begin with the requirements (usually prescribed by your instructor), design a solution to the problem, outline the code, write the actual lines of code, and test the resulting programs. However, when working in a team, either in school or for an employer or customer, you must be able to share the workload. Not only does this require verbal communication of ideas and results, but it also requires written documentation of what you plan to do and what you have done. You must

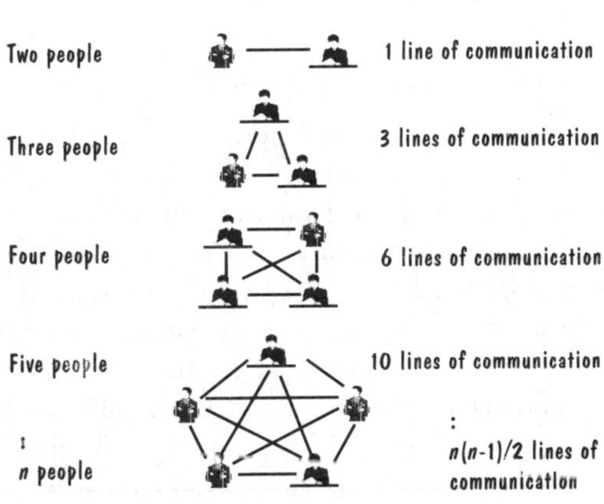

FIGURE 3.9 Communication paths on a project.

accept the results of others without redoing their work. Many people have difficulty in sharing control in this way.

Control is an issue in managing the project, too. Some people are good at directing the work of others. This aspect of personnel interaction is also related to the comfort people feel with the jobs they have. Those who feel uncomfortable with the idea of pushing their colleagues to stay on schedule, to document their code, or to meet with the customer are not good candidates for development jobs involving the management of other workers.

Thus, several aspects of a worker's background can affect the quality of the project team. A project manager should know each person's interests and abilities when choosing who will work together. Sidebar 3.1 explains how meetings and their organization can enhance or impede project progress. As we will see later in this chapter, employee background and communication can also have dramatic effects on the project's cost and schedule.

SIDEBAR 3.1 MAKE MEETINGS ENHANCE PROJECT PROGRESS

Some of the communication on a software project takes place in meetings, either in person or as teleconferences or electronic conversations. However, meetings may take up a great deal of time without accomplishing much. Dressler (1995) tells us that "running bad meetings can be expensive . . . a meeting of eight people who earn $40,000 a year could cost $320 an hour, including salary and benefit costs. That's nearly $6 a minute." Common complaints about meetings include

- The purpose of the meeting is unclear.
- The attendees are unprepared.
- Essential people are absent or late.
- The conversation veers away from its purpose.
- Some meeting participants do not discuss substantive issues. Instead, they argue, dominate the conversation, or do not participate.
- Decisions made at the meeting are never enacted afterward.

Good project management involves planning all software development activities, including meetings. There are several ways to ensure that a meeting is productive. First, the manager should make clear to others on the project team who should be at the meeting, when it will start and end, and what the meeting will accomplish. Second, every meeting should have a written agenda, distributed in advance if possible. Third, someone should take responsibility for keeping discussion on track and for resolving conflicts. Fourth, someone should be responsible for ensuring that each action item decided at the meeting is actually put into practice. Most importantly, minimize the number of meetings, as well as the number of people who must attend them.

Work Styles

Different people have different preferred styles for interacting with others on the job and for understanding problems that arise in the course of their work. For example, you may prefer to do a detailed analysis of all possible information before making a decision, whereas your colleague may rely on "gut feeling" for most of his important decisions. You can think of your preferred work style in terms of two components: the way in which your thoughts are communicated and ideas gathered, and the degree to which your emotions affect decision making. When communicating ideas, some people tell others their thoughts, and some people ask for suggestions from others before forming an opinion. Jung (1959) calls the former **extroverts** and the latter **introverts**. Clearly, your communication style affects the way you interact with others on a project. Similarly, **intuitive** people base their decisions on feelings about and emotional reactions to a problem. Others are **rational**, deciding primarily by examining the facts and carefully considering all options.

We can describe the variety of work styles by considering the graph of Figure 3.10, where communication style forms the horizontal axis and decision style the vertical one. The more extroverted you are, the farther to the right your work style falls on the graph. Similarly, the more emotions play a part in your decisions, the higher up you go. Thus, we can define four basic work styles, corresponding to the four quadrants of the graph. The **rational extroverts** tend to assert their ideas and not let "gut feeling" affect their decision making. They tell their colleagues what they want them to know, but they rarely ask for more information before doing so. When reasoning, they rely on logic, not emotion. The **rational introverts** also avoid emotional decisions, but they are willing to take time to consider all possible courses of action. Rational introverts are information gatherers; they do not feel comfortable making a decision unless they are convinced that all the facts are at hand.

In contrast, **intuitive extroverts** base many decisions on emotional reactions, tending to want to tell others about them rather than ask for input. They use their intuition to be creative, and they often suggest unusual approaches to solving a problem. The **intuitive introvert** is creative, too, but applies creativity only after having gathered

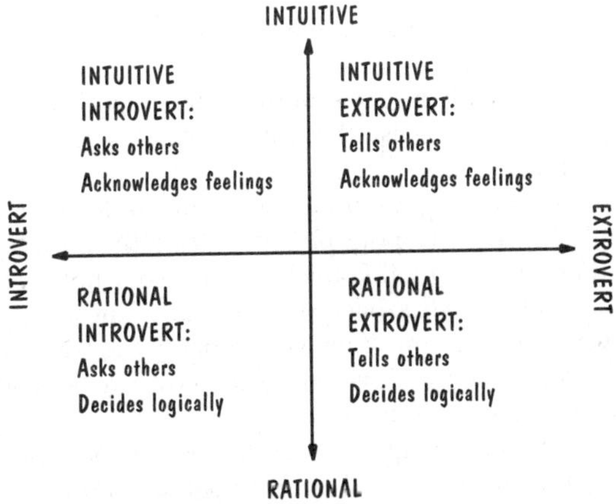

FIGURE 3.10 Work styles.

sufficient information on which to base a decision. Winston Churchill was an intuitive introvert; when he wanted to learn about an issue, he read every bit of material available that addressed it. He often made his decisions based on how he felt about what he had learned (Manchester 1983).

To see how work styles affect interactions on a project, consider several typical staff profiles. Kai, a rational extrovert, judges her colleagues by the results they produce. When making a decision, her top priority is efficiency. Thus, she wants to know only the bottom line. She examines her options and their probable effects, but she does not need to see documents or hear explanations supporting each option. If her time is wasted or her efficiency is hampered in some way, she asserts her authority to regain control of the situation. Thus, Kai is good at making sound decisions quickly.

Marcel, a rational introvert, is very different from his colleague Kai. He judges his peers by how busy they are, and he has little tolerance for those who appear not to be working hard all the time. He is a good worker, admired for the energy he devotes to his work. His reputation as a good worker is very important to him, and he prides himself on being accurate and thorough. He does not like to make decisions without complete information. When asked to make a presentation, Marcel does so only after gathering all relevant information on the subject.

Marcel shares an office with David, an intuitive extrovert. Whereas Marcel will not make a decision without complete knowledge of the situation, David prefers to follow his feelings. Often, he will trust his intuition about a problem, basing his decision on professional judgment rather than a slow, careful analysis of the information at hand. Since he is assertive, David tends to tell the others on his project about his new ideas. He is creative, and he enjoys when others recognize his ideas. David likes to work in an environment where there is a great deal of interaction among the staff members.

Ying, an intuitive introvert, also thrives on her colleagues' attention. She is sensitive and aware of her emotional reactions to people and problems; it is very important that she be liked by her peers. Because she is a good listener, Ying is the project member to whom others turn to express their feelings. Ying takes a lot of time to make a decision, not only because she needs complete information, but also because she wants to make the right decision. She is sensitive to what others think about her ability and ideas. She analyzes situations much as Marcel does, but with a different focus; Marcel looks at all the facts and figures, but Ying examines relational dependencies and emotional involvements, too.

Clearly, not everyone fits neatly into one of the four categories. Different people have different tendencies, and we can use the framework of Figure 3.10 to describe those tendencies and preferences.

Communication is critical to project success, and work style determines communication style. For example, if you are responsible for a part of the project that is behind schedule, Kai and David are likely to tell you when your work must be ready. David may offer several ideas to get the work back on track, and Kai will give you a new schedule to follow. However, Marcel and Ying will probably ask when the results will be ready. Marcel, in analyzing his options, will want to know why it is not ready; Ying will ask if there is anything she can do to help.

Understanding work styles can help you to be flexible in your approach to other project team members and to customers and users. In particular, work styles give you information about the priorities of others. If a colleague's priorities and interests are different from yours, you can present information to her in terms of what she deems important. For example, suppose Claude is your customer and you are preparing a presentation for him on the status of the project. If Claude is an introvert, you know that he prefers gathering information to giving it. Thus, you may organize your presentation so that it tells him a great deal about how the project is structured and how it is progressing. However, if Claude is an extrovert, you can include questions to allow him to tell you what he wants or needs. Similarly, if Claude is intuitive, you can take advantage of his creativity by soliciting new ideas from him; if he is rational, your presentation can include facts or figures rather than judgments or feelings. Thus, work styles affect interactions among customers, developers, and users.

Work styles can also involve choice of worker for a given task. For instance, intuitive employees may prefer design and development (requiring new ideas) to maintenance programming and design (requiring attention to detail and analysis of complex results).

Project Organization

Software development and maintenance project teams do not consist of people working independently or without coordination. Instead, team members are organized in ways that enhance the swift completion of quality products. The choice of an appropriate structure for your project depends on several things:

- the backgrounds and work styles of the team members
- the number of people on the team
- the management styles of the customers and developers

Good project managers are aware of these issues, and they seek team members who are flexible enough to interact with all players, regardless of work style.

One popular organizational structure is the chief programmer team, first used at IBM (Baker 1972). On a **chief programmer team**, one person is totally responsible for a system's design and development. All other team members report to the chief programmer, who has the final say on every decision. The chief programmer supervises all others, designs all programs, and assigns the code development to the other team members. Assisting the chief is an understudy, whose principal job is substituting for the chief programmer when necessary. A librarian assists the team, responsible for maintaining all project documentation. The librarian also compiles and links the code, and performs preliminary testing of all modules submitted to the library. This division of labor allows the programmers to focus on what they do best: programming.

The organization of the chief programmer team is illustrated in Figure 3.11. By placing all responsibility for all decisions with the chief programmer, the team structure minimizes the amount of communication needed during the project. Each team member must communicate often with the chief, but not necessarily with other team members. Thus, if the team consists of $n - 1$ programmers plus the chief, the team can establish only $n - 1$ paths of communication (one path for each team member's interaction with the chief) out of a potential $n(n - 1)/2$ paths. For example, rather than working out a problem themselves, the programmers can simply approach the chief for an answer. Similarly, the chief reviews all design and code, removing the need for peer reviews.

FIGURE 3.11 Chief programmer team organization.

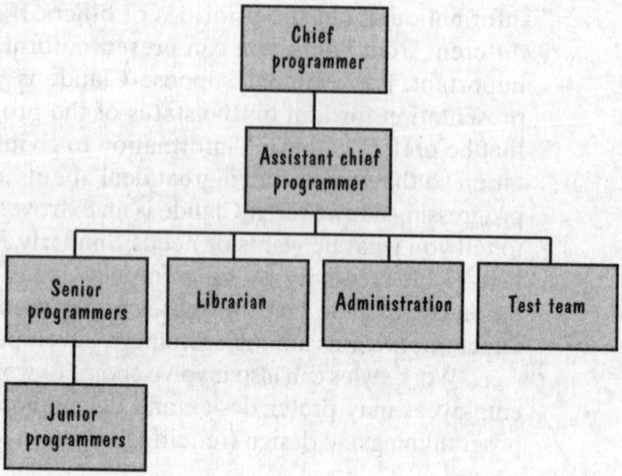

Although a chief programmer team is a hierarchy, groups of workers may be formed to accomplish a specialized task. For instance, one or more team members may form an administrative group to provide a status report on the project's current cost and schedule.

Clearly, the chief programmer must be good at making decisions quickly, so the chief is likely to be an extrovert. However, if most of the team members are introverts, the chief programmer team may not be the best structure for the project. An alternative is based on the idea of "egoless" programming, as described by Weinberg (1971). Instead of a single point of responsibility, an **egoless approach** holds everyone equally responsible. Moreover, the process is separated from the individuals; criticism is made of the product or the result, not the people involved. The egoless team structure is democratic, and all team members vote on a decision, whether it concerns design considerations or testing techniques.

Of course, there are many other ways to organize a development or maintenance project, and the two described above represent extremes. Which structure is preferable? The more people on the project, the more need there is for a formal structure. Certainly, a development team with only three or four members does not always need an elaborate organizational structure. However, a team of several dozen workers must have a well-defined organization. In fact, your company or your customer may impose a structure on the development team, based on past success, on the need to track progress in a certain way, or on the desire to minimize points of contact. For example, your customer may insist that the test team be totally independent of program design and development.

Researchers continue to investigate how project team structure affects the resulting product and how to choose the most appropriate organization in a given situation. A National Science Foundation (1983) investigation found that projects with a high degree of certainty, stability, uniformity, and repetition can be accomplished more effectively by a hierarchical organizational structure such as the chief programmer team. These projects require little communication among project members, so they are well-suited to an organization that stresses rules, specialization, formality, and a clear definition of organizational hierarchy.

TABLE 3.5 Comparison of Organizational Structures

Highly Structured	*Loosely Structured*
High certainty	Uncertainty
Repetition	New techniques or technology
Large projects	Small projects

On the other hand, when there is much uncertainty involved in a project, a more democratic approach may be better. For example, if the requirements may change as development proceeds, the project has a degree of uncertainty. Likewise, suppose your customer is building a new piece of hardware to interface with a system; if the exact specification of the hardware is not yet known, then the level of uncertainty is high. Here, participation in decision making, a loosely defined hierarchy, and the encouragement of open communication can be effective.

Table 3.5 summarizes the characteristics of projects and the suggested organizational structure to address them. A large project with high certainty and repetition probably needs a highly structured organization, whereas a small project with new techniques and a high degree of certainty needs a looser structure. Sidebar 3.2 describes the need to balance structure with creativity.

SIDEBAR 3.2 STRUCTURE VS. CREATIVITY

Kunde (1997) reports the results of experiments by Sally Philipp, a developer of software training materials. When Philipp teaches a management seminar, she divides her class into two groups. Each group is assigned the same task: to build a hotel with construction paper and glue. Some teams are structured, and the team members have clearly defined responsibilities. Others are left alone, given no direction or structure other than to build the hotel. Philipp claims that the results are always the same. "The unstructured teams always do incredibly creative, multistoried Taj Mahals and never complete one on time. The structured teams do a Day's Inn [a bland but functional small hotel], but they're finished and putting chairs around the pool when I call time," she says.

One way she places structure on a team is by encouraging team members to set deadlines. The overall task is broken into small subtasks, and individual team members are responsible for time estimates. The deadlines help to prevent "scope creep," the injection of unnecessary functionality into a product.

The experts in Kunde's article claim that good project management means finding a balance between structure and creativity. Left to their own devices, the software developers will focus only on functionality and creativity, disregarding deadlines and the scope of the specification. Many software project management experts made similar claims. Unfortunately, much of this information is based on anecdote, not on solid empirical investigation.

The two types of organizational structure can be combined, where appropriate. For instance, programmers may be asked to develop a subsystem on their own, using an egoless approach within a hierarchical structure. Or the test team of a loosely structured project may impose a hierarchical structure on itself and designate one person to be responsible for all major testing decisions.

3.3 EFFORT ESTIMATION

One of the crucial aspects of project planning and management is understanding how much the project is likely to cost. Cost overruns can cause customers to cancel projects, and cost underestimates can force a project team to invest much of its time without financial compensation. As described in Sidebar 3.3, there are many reasons for inaccurate estimates. A good cost estimate early in the project's life helps the project manager to know how many developers will be required and to arrange for the appropriate staff to be available when they are needed.

The project budget pays for several types of costs: facilities, staff, methods, and tools. The facilities costs include hardware, space, furniture, telephones, modems, heating and air conditioning, cables, disks, paper, pens, photocopiers, and all other items that provide the physical environment in which the developers will work. For some projects, this environment may already exist, so the costs are well-understood and easy to estimate. But for other projects, the environment may have to be created. For example, a new project may require a security vault, a raised floor, temperature or humidity controls, or special furniture. Here, the costs can be estimated, but they may vary from initial estimates as the environment is built or changed. For instance, installing cabling in a building may seem straightforward until the builders discover that the building is of special historical significance, so that the cables must be routed around the walls instead of through them.

There are sometimes hidden costs that are not apparent to the managers and developers. For example, studies indicate that a programmer needs a minimum amount of space and quiet to be able to work effectively. McCue (1978) reported to his colleagues at IBM that the minimum standard for programmer work space should be 100 square feet of dedicated floor space with 30 square feet of horizontal work surface. The space also needs a floor-to-ceiling enclosure for noise protection. DeMarco and Lister's (1987) work suggests that programmers free from telephone calls and uninvited visitors are more efficient and produce a better product than those who are subject to repeated interruption.

Other project costs involve purchasing software and tools to support development efforts. In addition to tools for designing and coding the system, the project may buy software to capture requirements, organize documentation, test the code, keep track of changes, generate test data, support group meetings, and more. These tools, sometimes called **Computer-Aided Software Engineering** (or **CASE**) **tools**, are sometimes required by the customer or are part of a company's standard software development process.

For most projects, the biggest component of cost is effort. We must determine how many staff-days of effort will be required to complete the project. Effort is certainly

SIDEBAR 3.3 CAUSES OF INACCURATE ESTIMATES

Lederer and Prasad (1992) investigated the cost-estimation practices of 115 different organizations. Thirty-five percent of the managers surveyed on a five-point Likert scale indicated that their current estimates were "moderately unsatisfactory" or "very unsatisfactory." The key causes identified by the respondents included

- frequent requests for changes by users
- overlooked tasks
- users' lack of understanding of their own requirements
- insufficient analysis when developing an estimate
- lack of coordination of systems development, technical services, operations, data administration, and other functions during development
- lack of an adequate method or guidelines for estimating

Several aspects of the project were noted as key influences on the estimate:

- complexity of the proposed application system
- required integration with existing systems
- complexity of the programs in the system
- size of the system expressed as number of functions or programs
- capabilities of the project team members
- project team's experience with the application
- anticipated frequency or extent of potential changes in user requirements
- project team's experience with the programming language
- database management system
- number of project team members
- extent of programming or documentation standards
- availability of tools such as application generators
- team's experience with the hardware

the cost component with the greatest degree of uncertainty. We have seen how work style, project organization, ability, interest, experience, training, and other employee characteristics can affect the time it takes to complete a task. Moreover, when a group of workers must communicate and consult with one another, the effort needed is increased by the time required for meetings, documentation, and training.

Cost, schedule, and effort estimation must be done as early as possible during the project's life cycle, since it affects resource allocation and project feasibility. (If it costs too much, the customer may cancel the project.) But estimation should be done repeatedly throughout the life cycle; as aspects of the project change, the estimate can

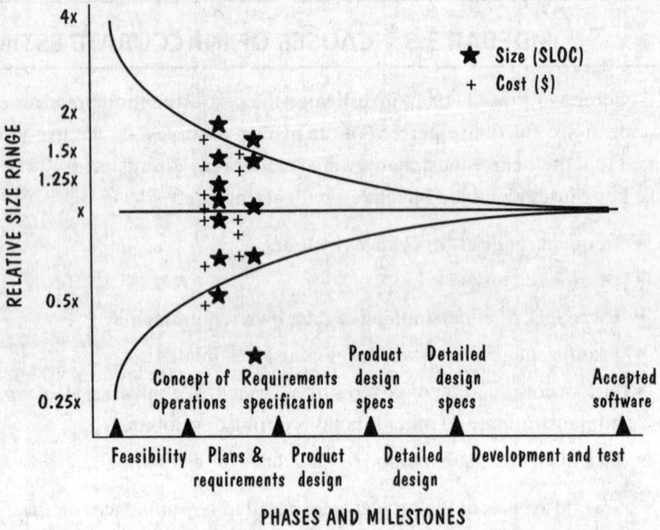

FIGURE 3.12 Changes in estimation accuracy as project progresses (Boehm et al. 1995).

be refined, based on more complete information about the project's characteristics. Figure 3.12 illustrates how uncertainty early in the project can affect the accuracy of cost and size estimates (Boehm et al. 1995).

The stars represent size estimates from actual projects, and the pluses are cost estimates. The funnel-shaped lines narrowing to the right represent Boehm's sense of how our estimates get more accurate as we learn more about a project. Notice that when the specifics of the project are not yet known, the estimate can differ from the eventual actual cost by a factor of 4. As decisions are made about the product and the process, the factor decreases. Many experts aim for estimates that are within 10 percent of the actual value, but Boehm's data indicate that such estimates typically occur only when the project is almost done—too late to be useful for project management.

To address the need for producing accurate estimates, software engineers have developed techniques for capturing the relationships among effort and staff characteristics, project requirements, and other factors that can affect the time, effort, and cost of developing a software system. For the rest of this chapter, we focus on effort-estimation techniques.

Expert Judgment

Many effort-estimation methods rely on expert judgment. Some are informal techniques, based on a manager's experience with similar projects. Thus, the accuracy of the prediction is based on the competence, experience, objectivity, and perception of the estimator. In its simplest form, such an estimate makes an educated guess about the effort needed to build an entire system or its subsystems. The complete estimate can be computed from either a top-down or a bottom-up analysis of what is needed.

Many times analogies are used to estimate effort. If we have already built a system much like the one proposed, then we can use the similarity as the basis for our estimates. For example, if system A is similar to system B, then the cost to produce system A should be very much like the cost to produce B. We can extend the analogy to say that if A is about half the size or complexity of B, then A should cost about half as much as B.

The analogy process can be formalized by asking several experts to make three predictions: a pessimistic one (x), an optimistic one (z), and a most likely guess (y). Then our estimate is the mean of the beta probability distribution determined by these numbers: $(x + 4y + z)/6$. By using this technique, we produce an estimate that "normalizes" the individual estimates.

The Delphi technique makes use of expert judgment in a different way. Experts are asked to make individual predictions secretly, based on their expertise and using whatever process they choose. Then, the average estimate is calculated and presented to the group. Each expert has the opportunity to revise his or her estimate, if desired. The process is repeated until no expert wants to revise. Some users of the Delphi technique discuss the average before new estimates are made; at other times, the users allow no discussion. And in another variation, the justifications of each expert are circulated anonymously among the experts.

Wolverton (1974) built one of the first models of software development effort. His software cost matrix captures his experience with project cost at TRW, a U.S. software development company. As shown in Table 3.6, the row name represents the type of software, and the column designates its difficulty. Difficulty depends on two factors: whether the problem is old (O) or new (N) and whether it is easy (E), moderate (M), or hard (H). The matrix elements are the cost per line of code, as calibrated from historical data at TRW. To use the matrix, you partition the proposed software system into modules. Then, you estimate the size of each module in terms of lines of code. Using the matrix, you calculate the cost per module, and then sum over all the modules. For instance, suppose you have a system with three modules: one input/output module that is old and easy, one algorithm module that is new and hard, and one data management module that is old and moderate. If the modules are likely to have 100, 200, and 100 lines of code, respectively, then the Wolverton model estimates the cost to be $(100 \times 17) + (200 \times 35) + (100 \times 31) = \$11,800$.

TABLE 3.6 Wolverton Model Cost Matrix

	Difficulty					
Type of software	OE	OM	OH	NE	NM	NH
Control	21	27	30	33	40	49
Input/output	17	24	27	28	35	43
Pre/post processor	16	23	26	28	34	42
Algorithm	15	20	22	25	30	35
Data management	24	31	35	37	46	57
Time-critical	75	75	75	75	75	75

Since the model is based on TRW data and uses 1974 dollars, it is not applicable to today's software development projects. But the technique is useful and can be transported easily to your own development or maintenance environment.

In general, experiential models, by relying mostly on expert judgment, are subject to all its inaccuracies. They rely on the expert's ability to determine which projects are similar and in what ways. However, projects that appear to be very similar can in fact be quite different. For example, fast runners today can run a mile in 4 minutes. A marathon race requires a runner to run 26 miles and 365 yards. If we extrapolate the 4-minute time, we might expect a runner to run a marathon in 1 hour and 45 minutes. Yet a marathon has never been run in under 2 hours. Consequently, there must be characteristics of running a marathon that are very different from those of running a mile. Likewise, there are often characteristics of one project that make it very different from another project, but the characteristics are not always apparent.

Even when we know how one project differs from another, we do not always know how the differences affect the cost. A proportional strategy is unreliable, because project costs are not always linear: Two people cannot produce code twice as fast as one. Extra time may be needed for communication and coordination, or to accommodate differences in interest, ability, and experience. Sackman, Erikson, and Grant (1968) found that the productivity ratio between best and worst programmers averaged 10 to 1, with no easily definable relationship between experience and performance. Likewise, a more recent study by Hughes (1996) found great variety in the way software is designed and developed, so a model that may work in one organization may not apply to another. Hughes also noted that past experience and knowledge of available resources are major factors in determining cost.

Expert judgment suffers not only from variability and subjectivity, but also from dependence on current data. The data on which an expert judgment model is based must reflect current practices, so they must be updated often. Moreover, most expert judgment techniques are simplistic, neglecting to incorporate a large number of factors that can affect the effort needed on a project. For this reason, practitioners and researchers have turned to algorithmic methods to estimate effort.

Algorithmic Methods

Researchers have created models that express the relationship between effort and the factors that influence it. The models are usually described using equations, where effort is the dependent variable, and several factors (such as experience, size, and application type) are the independent variables. Most of these models acknowledge that project size is the most influential factor in the equation by expressing effort as

$$E = (a + bS^c)m(\mathbf{X})$$

where S is the estimated size of the system, and a, b, and c are constants. $\mathbf{X}$ is a vector of cost factors, x_1 through x_n, and m is an adjustment multiplier based on these factors. In other words, the effort is determined mostly by the size of the proposed system, adjusted by the effects of several other project, process, product, or resource characteristics.

Walston and Felix (1977) developed one of the first models of this type, finding that IBM data from 60 projects yielded an equation of the form

$$E = 5.25S^{0.91}$$

The projects that supplied data built systems with sizes ranging from 4000 to 467,000 lines of code, written in 28 different high-level languages on 66 computers, and representing from 12 to 11,758 person-months of effort. Size was measured as lines of code, including comments as long as they did not exceed 50 percent of the total lines in the program.

The basic equation was supplemented with a productivity index that reflected 29 factors that can affect productivity, shown in Table 3.7. Notice that the factors are tied to a very specific type of development, including two platforms: an operational computer and a development computer. The model reflects the particular development style of the IBM Federal Systems organizations that provided the data.

TABLE 3.7 Walston and Felix Model Productivity Factors

1. Customer interface complexity	16. Use of design and code inspections
2. User participation in requirements definition	17. Use of top-down development
3. Customer-originated program design changes	18. Use of a chief programmer team
4. Customer experience with the application area	19. Overall complexity of code
5. Overall personnel experience	20. Complexity of application processing
6. Percentage of development programmers who participated in the design of functional specifications	21. Complexity of program flow
7. Previous experience with the operational computer	22. Overall constraints on program's design
8. Previous experience with the programming language	23. Design constraints on the program's main storage
9. Previous experience with applications of similar size and complexity	24. Design constraints on the program's timing
10. Ratio of average staff size to project duration (people per month)	25. Code for real-time or interactive operation or for execution under severe time constraints
11. Hardware under concurrent development	26. Percentage of code for delivery
12. Access to development computer open under special request	27. Code classified as nonmathematical application and input/output formatting programs
13. Access to development computer closed	28. Number of classes of items in the database per 1000 lines of code
14. Classified security environment for computer and at least 25% of programs and data	29. Number of pages of delivered documentation per 1000 lines of code
15. Use of structured programming	

Each of the 29 factors was weighted by 1 if the factor increases productivity, 0 if it has no effect on productivity, and −1 if it decreases productivity. A weighted sum of the 29 factors was then used to generate an effort estimate from the basic equation.

Bailey and Basili (1981) suggested a modeling technique, called a meta-model, for building an estimation equation that reflects your own organization's characteristics. They demonstrated their technique using a database of 18 scientific projects written in Fortran at NASA's Goddard Space Flight Center. First, they minimized the standard error estimate and produced an equation that was very accurate:

$$E = 5.5 + 0.73S^{1.16}$$

Then, they adjusted this initial estimate based on the ratio of errors. If R is the ratio between the actual effort, E, and the predicted effort, E', then the effort adjustment is defined as

$$ER_{adj} = \begin{cases} R - 1 & \text{if } R \geq 1 \\ 1 - 1/R & \text{if } R < 1 \end{cases}$$

They then adjusted the initial effort estimate E_{adj} this way:

$$E_{adj} = \begin{cases} (1 + ER_{adj})E & \text{if } R \geq 1 \\ E/(1 + ER_{adj}) & \text{if } R < 1 \end{cases}$$

Finally, Bailey and Basili (1981) accounted for other factors that affect effort, shown in Table 3.8. For each entry in the table, the project is scored from 0 (not present) to 5 (very important), depending on the judgment of the project manager. Thus, the total

TABLE 3.8 Bailey–Basili Effort Modifiers

Total Methodology (METH)	*Cumulative Complexity* (CPLX)	*Cumulative Experience* (EXP)
Tree charts	Customer interface complexity	Programmer qualifications
Top-down design	Application complexity	Programmer machine experience
Formal documentation	Program flow complexity	Programmer language experience
Chief programmer teams	Internal communication complexity	Programmer application experience
Formal training	Database complexity	Team experience
Formal test plans	External communication complexity	
Design formalisms	Customer-initiated program design changes	
Code reading		
Unit development folders		

score for METH can be as high as 45, for CPLX as high as 35, and for EXP as high as 25. Their model describes a procedure, based on multilinear least-square regression, for using these scores to further modify the effort estimate.

Clearly, one of the problems with models of this type is their dependence on size as a key variable. Estimates are usually required early, well before accurate size information is available, and certainly before the system is expressed as lines of code. So the models simply translate the effort-estimation problem to a size-estimation problem. Boehm's Constructive Cost Model (COCOMO) acknowledges this problem and incorporates three sizing techniques in the latest version, COCOMO II.

Boehm (1981) developed the original COCOMO model in the 1970s, using an extensive database of information from projects at TRW, an American company that built software for many different clients. Considering software development from both an engineering and an economics viewpoint, Boehm used size as the primary determinant of cost and then adjusted the initial estimate using over a dozen cost drivers, including attributes of the staff, the project, the product, and the development environment. In the 1990s, Boehm updated the original COCOMO model, creating COCOMO II to reflect the ways in which software development had matured.

The COCOMO II estimation process reflects three major stages of any development project. Whereas the original COCOMO model used delivered source lines of code as its key input, the new model acknowledges that lines of code are impossible to know early in the development cycle. At stage 1, projects usually build prototypes to resolve high-risk issues involving user interfaces, software and system interaction, performance, or technological maturity. Here, little is known about the likely size of the final product under consideration, so COCOMO II estimates size in what its creators call application points. As we shall see, this technique captures size in terms of high-level effort generators, such as the number of screens and reports, and the number of third-generation language components.

At stage 2, the early design stage, a decision has been made to move forward with development, but the designers must explore alternative architectures and concepts of operation. Again, there is not enough information to support fine-grained effort and duration estimation, but far more is known than at stage 1. For stage 2, COCOMO II employs function points as a size measure. Function points, a technique explored in depth in IFPUG (1994a and b), estimate the functionality captured in the requirements, so they offer a richer system description than application points.

By stage 3, the postarchitecture stage, development has begun, and far more information is known. In this stage, sizing can be done in terms of function points or lines of code, and many cost factors can be estimated with some degree of comfort.

COCOMO II also includes models of reuse, takes into account maintenance and breakage (i.e., the change in requirements over time), and more. As with the original COCOMO, the model includes cost factors to adjust the initial effort estimate. A research group at the University of Southern California is assessing and improving its accuracy.

Let us look at COCOMO II in more detail. The basic model is of the form

$$E = bS^c m(\mathbf{X})$$

where the initial size-based estimate, bS^c, is adjusted by the vector of cost driver information, $m(\mathbf{X})$. Table 3.9 describes the cost drivers at each stage, as well as the use of other models to modify the estimate.

TABLE 3.9 Three Stages of COCOMO II

Model Aspect	Stage 1: Application Composition	Stage 2: Early Design	Stage 3: Postarchitecture
Size	Application points	Function points (FPs) and language	FP and language or source lines of code (SLOC)
Reuse	Implict in model	Equivalent SLOC as function of other variables	Equivalent SLOC as function of other variables
Requirements change	Implicit in model	% change expressed as a cost factor	% change expressed as a cost factor
Maintenance	Application points, annual change traffic (ACT)	Function of ACT, software understanding, unfmiliarity	Function of ACT, software understanding, unfamiliarity
Scale (c) in nominal effort equation	1.0	0.91 to 1.23, depending on precedentedness, conformity, early architecture, risk resolution, team cohesion, and SEI process maturity	0.91 to 1.23, depending on precedentedness, conformity, early architecture, risk resolution, team cohesion, and SEI process maturity
Product cost drivers	None	Complexity, required reusability	Reliability, database size, documentation needs, required reuse, and product complexity
Platform cost drivers	None	Platform difficulty	Execution time constraints, main storage constraints, and virtual machine volatility
Personnel cost drivers	None	Personnel capability and experience	Analyst capability, applications experience, programmer capability, programmer experience, language and tool experience, and personnel continuity
Project cost drivers	None	Required development schedule, development environment	Use of software tools, required development schedule, and multisite development

At stage 1, application points supply the size measure. This size measure is an extension of the object-point approach suggested by Kauffman and Kumar (1993) and productivity data reported by Banker, Kauffman, and Kumar (1992). To compute application points, you first count the number of screens, reports, and third-generation language components that will be involved in the application. It is assumed that these elements are defined in a standard way as part of an integrated computer-aided software engineering environment. Next, you classify each application element as simple, medium, or difficult. Table 3.10 contains guidelines for this classification.

TABLE 3.10 Application Point Complexity Levels

For Screens				For Reports			
	Number and source of data tables				Number and source of data tables		
Number of views contained	Total < 4 (<2 servers, <3 clients)	Total < 8 (2–3 servers, 3–5 clients)	Total 8+ (>3 servers, >5 clients)	*Number of sections contained*	Total <4 (<2 servers, <3 clients)	Total <8 (2–3 servers, 3–5 clients)	Total 8+ (>3 servers, >5 clients)
<3	Simple	Simple	Medium	0 or 1	Simple	Simple	Medium
3–7	Simple	Medium	Difficult	2 or 3	Simple	Medium	Difficult
8+	Medium	Difficult	Difficult	4+	Medium	Difficult	Difficult

The number to be used for simple, medium, or difficult application points is a complexity weight found in Table 3.11. The weights reflect the relative effort required to implement a report or screen of that complexity level.

Then, you sum the weighted reports and screens to obtain a single application-point number. If r percent of the objects will be reused from previous projects, the number of new application points is calculated to be

$$\text{New application points} = (\text{application points}) \times (100 - r)/100$$

To use this number for effort estimation, you use an adjustment factor, called a productivity rate, based on developer experience and capability, coupled with CASE maturity and capability. For example, if the developer experience and capability are rated low, and the CASE maturity and capability are rated low, then Table 3.12 tells us that the productivity factor is 7, so the number of person-months required is the number of new application points divided by 7. When the developers' experience is low but CASE maturity is high, the productivity estimate is the mean of the two values: 16. Likewise, when a team of developers has experience levels that vary, the productivity estimate can use the mean of the experience and capability weights.

At stage 1, the cost drivers are not applied to this effort estimate. However, at stage 2, the effort estimate, based on a function-point calculation, is adjusted for degree of reuse, requirements change, and maintenance. The scale (i.e., the value for c in the effort equation) had been set to 1.0 in stage 1; for stage 2, the scale ranges from 0.91 to

TABLE 3.11 Complexity Weights for Application Points

Element Type	Simple	Medium	Difficult
Screen	1	2	3
Report	2	5	8
3GL component	—	—	10

TABLE 3.12 Productivity Estimate Calculation

Developers' experience and capability	Very low	Low	Nominal	High	Very high
CASE maturity and capability	Very low	Low	Nominal	High	Very high
Productivity factor	4	7	13	25	50

1.23, depending on the degree of novelty of the system, conformity, early architecture and risk resolution, team cohesion, and process maturity.

The cost drivers in stages 2 and 3 are adjustment factors expressed as effort multipliers based on rating your project from "extra low" to "extra high," depending on its characteristics. For example, a development team's experience with an application type is considered to be

- *extra low* if it has fewer than 3 months of experience
- *very low* if it has at least 3 but fewer than 5 months of experience
- *low* if it has at least 5 but fewer than 9 months of experience
- *nominal* if it has at least 9 months but less than one year of experience
- *high* if it has at least 1 year but fewer than 2 years of experience
- *very high* if it has at least 2 years but fewer than 4 years of experience
- *extra high* if it has at least 4 years of experience

Similarly, analyst capability is measured on an ordinal scale based on percentile ranges. For instance, the rating is "very high" if the analyst is in the ninetieth percentile and "nominal" for the fifty-fifth percentile. Correspondingly, COCOMO II assigns an effort multiplier ranging from 1.42 for very low to 0.71 for very high. These multipliers reflect the notion that an analyst with very low capability expends 1.42 times as much effort as a nominal or average analyst, while one with very high capability needs about three-quarters the effort of an average analyst. Similarly, Table 3.13 lists the cost driver categories for tool use, and the multipliers range from 1.17 for very low to 0.78 for very high.

TABLE 3.13 Tool Use Categories

Category	*Meaning*
Very low	Edit, code, debug
Low	Simple front-end, back-end CASE, little integration
Nominal	Basic life-cycle tools, moderately integrated
High	Strong, mature life-cycle tools, moderately integrated
Very high	Strong, mature, proactive life-cycle tools, well-integrated with processes, methods, reuse

Notice that stage 2 of COCOMO II is intended for use during the early stages of design. The set of cost drivers in this stage is smaller than the set used in stage 3, reflecting lesser understanding of the project's parameters at stage 2.

The various components of the COCOMO model are intended to be tailored to fit the characteristics of your own organization. Tools are available that implement COCOMO II and compute the estimates from the project characteristics that you supply. Later in this chapter, we will apply COCOMO to our information system example.

Machine-Learning Methods

In the past, most effort- and cost-modeling techniques have relied on algorithmic methods. That is, researchers have examined data from past projects and generated equations from them that are used to predict effort and cost on future projects. However, some researchers are looking to machine learning for assistance in producing good estimates. For example, neural networks can represent a number of interconnected, interdependent units, so they are a promising tool for representing the various activities involved in producing a software product. In a neural network, each unit (called a neuron and represented by network node) represents an activity; each activity has inputs and outputs. Each unit of the network has associated software that performs an accounting of its inputs, computing a weighted sum; if the sum exceeds a threshold value, the unit produces an output. The output, in turn, becomes input to other related units in the network, until a final output value is produced by the network. The neural network is, in a sense, an extension of the activity graphs we examined earlier in this chapter.

There are many ways for a neural network to produce its outputs. Some techniques involve looking back to what has happened at other nodes; these are called *back-propagation* techniques. They are similar to the method we used with activity graphs to look back and determine the slack on a path. Other techniques look forward, to anticipate what is about to happen.

Neural networks are developed by "training" them with data from past projects. Relevant data are supplied to the network, and the network uses forward and backward algorithms to "learn" by identifying patterns in the data. For example, historical data about past projects might contain information about developer experience; the network may identify relationships between level of experience and the amount of effort required to complete a project.

Figure 3.13 illustrates how Shepperd (1997) used a neural network to produce an effort estimate. There are three layers in the network, and the network has no cycles. The four inputs are factors that can affect effort on a project; the network uses them to produce effort as the single output. To begin, the network is initialized with random weights. Then, new weights, calculated as a "training set" of inputs and outputs based on past history, are fed to the network. The user of the model specifies a training algorithm that explains how the training data are to be used; this algorithm is also based on past history, and it commonly involves back-propagation. Once the network is trained (i.e., once the network values are adjusted to reflect past experience), it can then be used to estimate effort on new projects.

Several researchers have used back-propagation algorithms on similar neural networks to predict development effort, including estimation for projects using

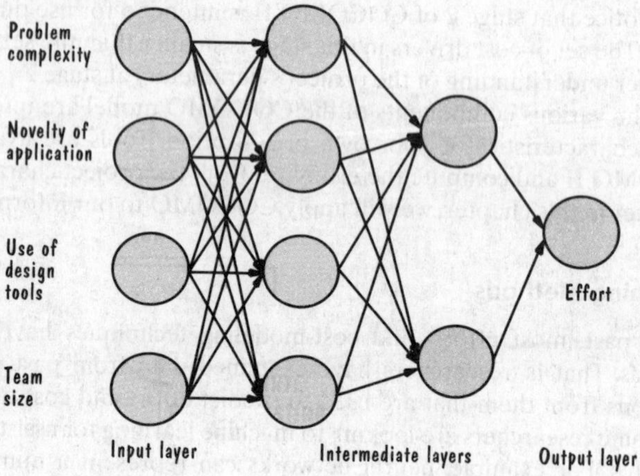

FIGURE 3.13 Shepperd's feed-forward neural network.

fourth-generation languages (Wittig and Finnie 1994; Srinivasan and Fisher 1995; Samson, Ellison, and Dugard 1997). Shepperd (1997) reports that the accuracy of this type of model seems to be sensitive to decisions about the topology of the neural network, the number of learning stages, and the initial random weights of the neurons within the network. The networks also seem to require large training sets in order to give good predictions. In other words, they must be based on a great deal of experience rather than a few representative projects. Data of this type are sometimes difficult to obtain, especially collected consistently and in large quantity, so the paucity of data limits this technique's usefulness. Moreover, users tend to have difficulty understanding neural networks. However, if the technique produces more accurate estimates, organizations may be more willing to collect data for the networks.

In general, this "learning" approach has been tried in different ways by other researchers. Srinivasan and Fisher (1995) used Kemerer's data (Kemerer 1989) with a statistical technique called a regression tree; they produced predictions more accurate than those of the original COCOMO model and SLIM, a proprietary commercial model. However, their results were not as good as those produced by a neural network or a model based on function points. Briand, Basili, and Thomas (1992) obtained better results from using a tree induction technique, using the Kemerer and COCOMO datasets. Porter and Selby (1990) also used a tree-based approach; they constructed a decision tree that identifies which project, process, and product characteristics may be useful in predicting likely effort. They also used the technique to predict which modules are likely to be fault-prone.

A machine-learning technique called *Case-Based Reasoning* (CBR) can be applied to analogy-based estimates. Used by the artificial intelligence community, CBR builds a decision algorithm based on the several combinations of inputs that might be encountered on a project. Like the other techniques described here, CBR requires information about past projects. Shepperd (1997) points out that CBR offers two clear advantages over many of the other techniques. First, CBR deals only with events that actually occur, rather than with the much larger set of all possible occurrences. This same feature also allows CBR to deal with poorly understood domains. Second, it is easier for users to understand particular cases than to depict events as chains of rules or as neural networks.

Estimation using CBR involves four steps:

1. The user identifies a new problem as a case.
2. The system retrieves similar cases from a repository of historical information.
3. The system reuses knowledge from previous cases.
4. The system suggests a solution for the new case.

The solution may be revised, depending on actual events, and the outcome is placed in the repository, building up the collection of completed cases. However, there are two big hurdles in creating a successful CBR system: characterizing cases and determining similarity.

Cases are characterized based on the information that happens to be available. Usually, experts are asked to supply a list of features that are significant in describing cases and, in particular, in determining when two cases are similar. In practice, similarity is usually measured using an n-dimensional vector of n features. Shepperd, Schofield, and Kitchenham (1996) found a CBR approach to be more accurate than traditional regression analysis-based algorithmic methods.

Finding the Model for Your Situation

There are many effort and cost models being used today: commercial tools based on past experience or intricate models of development, and home-grown tools that access databases of historical information about past projects. Validating these models (i.e., making sure the models reflect actual practice) is difficult, because a large amount of data is needed for the validation exercise. Moreover, if a model is to apply to a large and varied set of situations, the supporting database must include measures from a very large and varied set of development environments.

Even when you find models that are designed for your development environment, you must be able to evaluate which are the most accurate on your projects. There are two statistics that are often used to help you in assessing the accuracy, PRED and MMRE. **PRED(x/100)** is the percentage of projects for which the estimate is within x% of the actual value. For most effort, cost, and schedule models, managers evaluate PRED(0.25), that is, those models whose estimates are within 25% of the actual value; a model is considered to function well if PRED(0.25) is greater than 75%. **MMRE** is the mean magnitude of relative error, so we hope that the MMRE for a particular model is very small. Some researchers consider an MMRE of 0.25 to be fairly good, and Boehm (1981) suggests that MMRE should be 0.10 or less. Table 3.14 lists the best values for PRED and MMRE reported in the literature for a variety of models. As you can see, the statistics for most models are disappointing, indicating that no model appears to have captured the essential characteristics and their relationships for all types of development. However, the relationships among cost factors are not simple, and the models must be flexible enough to handle changing use of tools and methods.

TABLE 3.14 Summary of Model Performance

Model	*PRED(0.25)*	*MMRE*
Walston–Felix	0.30	0.48
Basic COCOMO	0.27	0.60
Intermediate COCOMO	0.63	0.22
Intermediate COCOMO (variation)	0.76	0.19
Bailey–Basili	0.78	0.18
Pfleeger	0.50	0.29
SLIM	0.06–0.24	0.78–1.04
Jensen	0.06–0.33	0.70–1.01
COPMO	0.38–0.63	0.23–5.7
General COPMO	0.78	0.25

Moreover, Kitchenham, MacDonell, Pickard, and Shepperd (2000) point out that the MMRE and PRED statistics are not direct measures of estimation accuracy. They suggest that you use the simple ratio of estimate to actual: estimate/actual. This measure has a distribution that directly reflects estimation accuracy. By contrast, MMRE and PRED are measures of the spread (standard deviation) and peakedness (kurtosis) of the ratio, so they tell us only characteristics of the distribution.

Even when estimation models produce reasonably accurate estimates, we must be able to understand which types of effort are needed during development. For example, designers may not be needed until the requirements analysts have finished developing the specification. Some effort and cost models use formulas based on past experience to apportion the effort across the software development life cycle. For instance, the original COCOMO model suggested effort required by development activity, based on percentages allotted to key process activities. But, as Figure 3.14 illustrates, researchers report conflicting values for these percentages (Brooks 1995; Yourdon 1982). Thus, when you are building your own database to support estimation in your organization, it is important to record not only how much effort is expended on a project, but also who is doing it and for what activity.

FIGURE 3.14 Different reports of effort distribution.

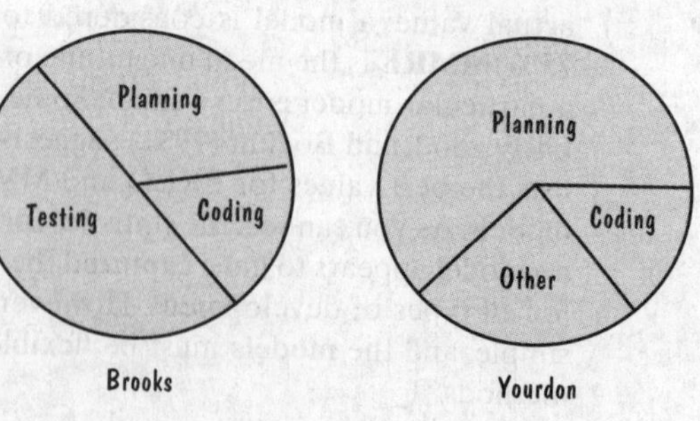

3.4 RISK MANAGEMENT

As we have seen, many software project managers take steps to ensure that their projects are done on time and within effort and cost constraints. However, project management involves far more than tracking effort and schedule. Managers must determine whether any unwelcome events may occur during development or maintenance and make plans to avoid these events or, if they are inevitable, minimize their negative consequences. A **risk** is an unwanted event that has negative consequences. Project managers must engage in **risk management** to understand and control the risks on their projects.

What Is a Risk?

Many events occur during software development; Sidebar 3.4 lists Boehm's view of some of the riskiest ones. We distinguish risks from other project events by looking for three things (Rook 1993):

1. *A loss associated with the event.* The event must create a situation where something negative happens to the project: a loss of time, quality, money, control, understanding, and so on. For example, if requirements change dramatically after

---

SIDEBAR 3.4 BOEHM'S TOP TEN RISK ITEMS

Boehm (1991) identifies 10 risk items and recommends risk management techniques to address them.

1. *Personnel shortfalls.* Staffing with top talent; job matching; team building; morale building; cross-training; prescheduling key people.
2. *Unrealistic schedules and budgets.* Detailed multisource cost and schedule estimation; design to cost; incremental development; software reuse; requirements scrubbing.
3. *Developing the wrong software functions.* Organizational analysis; mission analysis; operational concept formulation; user surveys; prototyping; early user's manuals.
4. *Developing the wrong user interface.* Prototyping; scenarios; task analysis.
5. *Gold plating.* Requirements scrubbing; prototyping; cost-benefit analysis; design to cost.
6. *Continuing stream of requirements changes.* High change threshold; information hiding; incremental development (defer changes to later increments).
7. *Shortfalls in externally performed tasks.* Reference checking; preaward audits; award-fee contracts; competitive design or prototyping; team building.
8. *Shortfalls in externally furnished components.* Benchmarking; inspections; reference checking; compatibility analysis.
9. *Real-time performance shortfalls.* Simulation; benchmarking; modeling; prototyping; instrumentation; tuning.
10. *Straining computer science capabilities.* Technical analysis; cost-benefit analysis; prototyping; reference checking.

---

the design is done, then the project can suffer from loss of control and understanding if the new requirements are for functions or features with which the design team is unfamiliar. And a radical change in requirements is likely to lead to losses of time and money if the design is not flexible enough to be changed quickly and easily. The loss associated with a risk is called the **risk impact**.

2. *The likelihood that the event will occur.* We must have some idea of the probability that the event will occur. For example, suppose a project is being developed on one machine and will be ported to another when the system is fully tested. If the second machine is a new model to be delivered by the vendor, we must estimate the likelihood that it will not be ready on time. The likelihood of the risk, measured from 0 (impossible) to 1 (certainty) is called the **risk probability**. When the risk probability is 1, then the risk is called a **problem**, since it is certain to happen.
3. *The degree to which we can change the outcome.* For each risk, we must determine what we can do to minimize or avoid the impact of the event. **Risk control** involves a set of actions taken to reduce or eliminate a risk. For example, if the requirements may change after design, we can minimize the impact of the change by creating a flexible design. If the second machine is not ready when the software is tested, we may be able to identify other models or brands that have the same functionality and performance and can run our new software until the new model is delivered.

We can quantify the effects of the risks we identify by multiplying the risk impact by the risk probability, to yield the **risk exposure**. For example, if the likelihood that the requirements will change after design is 0.3, and the cost to redesign to new requirements is $50,000, then the risk exposure is $15,000. Clearly, the risk probability can change over time, as can the impact, so part of a project manager's job is to track these values over time and plan for the events accordingly.

There are two major sources of risk: generic risks and project-specific risks. **Generic risks** are those common to all software projects, such as misunderstanding the requirements, losing key personnel, or allowing insufficient time for testing. **Project-specific risks** are threats that result from the particular vulnerabilities of the given project. For example, a vendor may be promising network software by a particular date, but there is some risk that the network software will not be ready on time.

Risk Management Activities

Risk management involves several important steps, each of which is illustrated in Figure 3.15. First, we assess the risks on a project, so that we understand what may occur during the course of development or maintenance. The assessment consists of three activities: identifying the risks, analyzing them, and assigning priorities to each of them. To identify them, we may use many different techniques.

If the system we are building is similar in some way to a system we have built before, we may have a checklist of problems that may occur; we can review the checklist to determine if the new project is likely to be subject to the risks listed. For systems that are new in some way, we may augment the checklist with an analysis of each of the activities in the development cycle; by decomposing the process into small pieces, we may be able to anticipate problems that may arise. For example, we may decide that

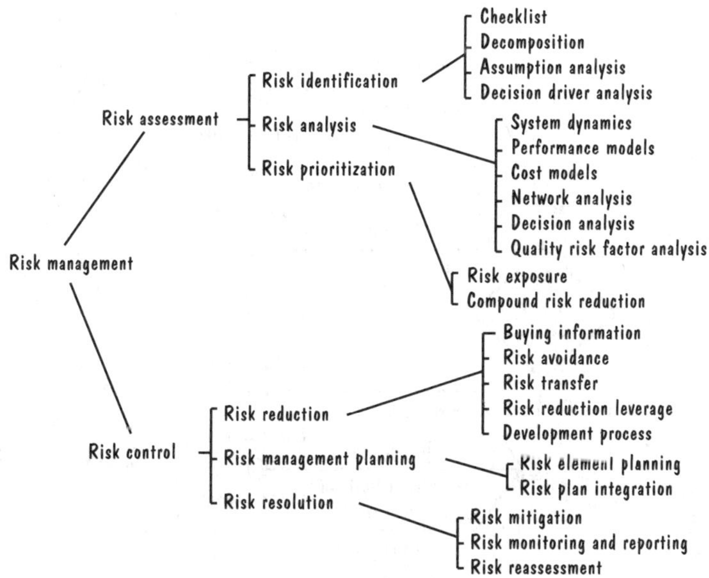

FIGURE 3.15 Steps in risk management (Rook 1993).

there is a risk of the chief designer leaving during the design process. Similarly, we may analyze the assumptions or decisions we make about how the project will be done, who will do it, and with what resources. Then, each assumption is assessed to determine the risks involved.

Finally, we analyze the risks we have identified, so that we can understand as much as possible about when, why, and where they might occur. There are many techniques we can use to enhance our understanding, including system dynamics models, cost models, performance models, network analysis, and more.

Once we have itemized all the risks, we use our understanding to assign priorities them. A priority scheme enables us to devote our limited resources only to the most threatening risks. Usually, priorities are based on the risk exposure, which takes into account not only likely impact, but also the probability of occurrence.

The risk exposure is computed from the risk impact and the risk probability, so we must estimate each of these risk aspects. To see how the quantification is done, consider the analysis depicted in Figure 3.16. Suppose we have analyzed the system development process and we know we are working under tight deadlines for delivery. We have decided to build the system in a series of releases, where each release has more functionality than the one that preceded it. Because the system is designed so that functions are relatively independent, we consider testing only the new functions for a release, and we assume that the existing functions still work as they did before. However, we may worry that there are risks associated with not performing **regression testing**: the assurance that existing functionality still works correctly.

For each possible outcome, we estimate two quantities: the probability of an unwanted outcome, P(UO), and the loss associated with the unwanted outcome,

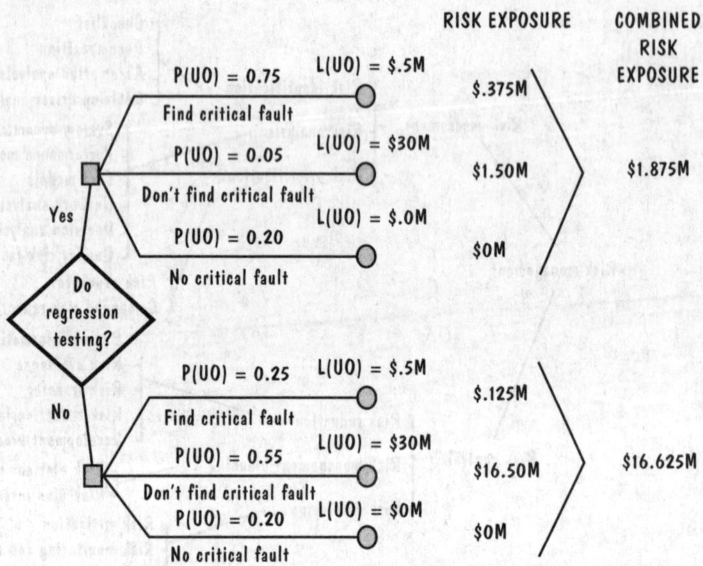

FIGURE 3.16 Example of risk exposure calculation.

L(UO). For instance, there are three possible consequences of performing regression testing: finding a critical fault if one exists, not finding the critical fault (even though it exists), or deciding (correctly) that there is no critical fault. As the figure illustrates, we have estimated the probability of the first case to be 0.75, of the second to be 0.05, and of the third to be 0.20. The loss associated with an unwanted outcome is estimated to be $500,000 if a critical fault is found, so that the risk exposure is $375,000. Similarly, we calculate the risk exposure for the other branches of this decision tree, and we find that our risk exposure if we perform regression testing is almost $2 million. However, the same kind of analysis shows us that the risk exposure if we do not perform regression testing is almost $17 million. Thus, we say (loosely) that more is at risk if we do not perform regression testing.

Risk exposure helps us to list the risks in priority order, with the risks of most concern given the highest priority. Next, we must take steps to control the risks. The notion of control acknowledges that we may not be able to eliminate all risks. Instead, we may be able to minimize the risk or mitigate it by taking action to handle the unwanted outcome in an acceptable way. Therefore, risk control involves risk reduction, risk planning, and risk resolution.

There are three strategies for risk reduction:

- avoiding the risk, by changing requirements for performance or functionality
- transferring the risk, by allocating risks to other systems or by buying insurance to cover any financial loss should the risk become a reality
- assuming the risk, by accepting it and controlling it with the project's resources

To aid decision making about risk reduction, we must take into account the cost of reducing the risk. We call **risk leverage** the difference in risk exposure divided by the cost of reducing the risk. In other words, risk reduction leverage is

$$(\text{Risk exposure before reduction} - \text{risk exposure after reduction}) \\ /(\text{cost of risk reduction})$$

If the leverage value is not high enough to justify the action, then we can look for other less costly or more effective reduction techniques.

In some cases, we can choose a development process to help reduce the risk. For example, we saw in Chapter 2 that prototyping can improve understanding of the requirements and design, so selecting a prototyping process can reduce many project risks.

It is useful to record decisions in a **risk management plan**, so that both customer and development team can review how problems are to be avoided, as well as how they are to be handled should they arise. Then, we should monitor the project as development progresses, periodically reevaluating the risks, their probability, and their likely impact.

3.5 THE PROJECT PLAN

To communicate risk analysis and management, project cost estimates, schedule, and organization to our customers, we usually write a document called a **project plan**. The plan puts in writing the customer's needs, as well as what we hope to do to meet them. The customer can refer to the plan for information about activities in the development process, making it easy to follow the project's progress during development. We can also use the plan to confirm with the customer any assumptions we are making, especially about cost and schedule.

A good project plan includes the following items:

1. project scope
2. project schedule
3. project team organization
4. technical description of the proposed system
5. project standards, procedures, and proposed techniques and tools
6. quality assurance plan
7. configuration management plan
8. documentation plan
9. data management plan
10. resource management plan
11. test plan
12. training plan
13. security plan
14. risk management plan
15. maintenance plan

The scope defines the system boundary, explaining what will be included in the system and what will not be included. It assures the customer that we understand what is wanted. The schedule can be expressed using a work breakdown structure, the deliverables, and a timeline to show what will be happening at each point during the project life cycle. A Gantt chart can be useful in illustrating the parallel nature of some of the development tasks.

The project plan also lists the people on the development team, how they are organized, and what they will be doing. As we have seen, not everyone is needed all the time during the project, so the plan usually contains a resource allocation chart to show staffing levels at different times.

Writing a technical description forces us to answer questions and address issues as we anticipate how development will proceed. This description lists hardware and software, including compilers, interfaces, and special-purpose equipment or software. Any special restrictions on cabling, execution time, response time, security, or other aspects of functionality or performance are documented in the plan. The plan also lists any standards or methods that must be used, such as

- algorithms
- tools
- review or inspection techniques
- design languages or representations
- coding languages
- testing techniques

For large projects, it may be appropriate to include a separate quality assurance plan, to describe how reviews, inspections, testing, and other techniques will help to evaluate quality and ensure that it meets the customer's needs. Similarly, large projects need a configuration management plan, especially when there are to be multiple versions and releases of the system. As we will see in Chapter 10, configuration management helps to control multiple copies of the software. The configuration management plan tells the customer how we will track changes to the requirements, design, code, test plans, and documents.

Many documents are produced during development, especially for large projects where information about the design must be made available to project team members. The project plan lists the documents that will be produced, explains who will write them and when, and, in concert with the configuration management plan, describes how documents will be changed.

Because every software system involves data for input, calculation, and output, the project plan must explain how data will be gathered, stored, manipulated, and archived. The plan should also explain how resources will be used. For example, if the hardware configuration includes removable disks, then the resource management part of the project plan should explain what data are on each disk and how the disk packs or diskettes will be allocated and backed up.

Testing requires a great deal of planning to be effective, and the project plan describes the project's overall approach to testing. In particular, the plan should state how test data will be generated, how each program module will be tested (e.g., by testing all paths or all statements), how program modules will be integrated with each other and tested, how the entire system will be tested, and who will perform each type of testing. Sometimes, systems are produced in stages or phases, and the test plan should explain how each stage will be tested. When new functionality is added to a system in stages, as we saw in Chapter 2, then the test plan must address regression testing, ensuring that the existing functionality still works correctly.

Training classes and documents are usually prepared during development, rather than after the system is complete, so that training can begin as soon as the system is ready (and sometimes before). The project plan explains how training will occur, describing each class, supporting software and documents, and the expertise needed by each student.

When a system has security requirements, a separate security plan is sometimes needed. The security plan addresses the way that the system will protect data, users, and hardware. Since security involves confidentiality, availability, and integrity, the plan must explain how each facet of security affects system development. For example, if access to the system will be limited by using passwords, then the plan must describe who issues and maintains the passwords, who develops the password-handling software, and what the password encryption scheme will be.

Finally, if the project team will maintain the system after it is delivered to the user, the project plan should discuss responsibilities for changing the code, repairing the hardware, and updating supporting documentation and training materials.

3.6 PROCESS MODELS AND PROJECT MANAGEMENT

We have seen how different aspects of a project can affect the effort, cost, and schedule required, as well as the risks involved. Managers most successful at building quality products on time and within budget are those who tailor the project management techniques to the particular characteristics of the resources needed, the chosen process, and the people assigned.

To understand what to do on your next project, it is useful to examine project management techniques used by successful projects from the recent past. In this section, we look at two projects: Digital's Alpha AXP program and the F-16 aircraft software. We also investigate the merging of process and project management.

Enrollment Management

Digital Equipment Corporation spent many years developing its Alpha AXP system, a new system architecture and associated products that formed the largest project in Digital's history. The software portion of the effort involved four operating systems and 22 software engineering groups, whose roles included designing migration tools, network systems, compilers, databases, integration frameworks, and applications. Unlike many other development projects, the major problems with Alpha involved reaching milestones too early! Thus, it is instructive to look at how the project was managed and what effects the management process had on the final product.

During the course of development, the project managers developed a model that incorporated four tenets, called the Enrollment Management model:

1. establishing an appropriately large shared vision
2. delegating completely and eliciting specific commitments from participants
3. inspecting vigorously and providing supportive feedback
4. acknowledging every advance and learning as the program progressed (Conklin 1996)

Figure 3.17 illustrates the model. Vision was used to "enroll" the related programs, so they all shared common goals. Each group or subgroup of the project defined its own objectives in terms of the global ones stated for the project, including the company's business goals. Next, as managers developed plans, they delegated tasks to groups, soliciting comments and commitments about the content of each task and the schedule constraints imposed. Each required result was measurable and identified with a particular owner who was held accountable for delivery. The owner may not have been the person doing the actual work; rather, he or she was the person responsible for getting the work done.

Managers continually inspected the project to make sure that delivery would be on time. Project team members were asked to identify risks, and when a risk threatened to keep the team from meeting its commitments, the project manager declared the project to be a "cusp": a critical event. Such a declaration meant that team members were ready to make substantial changes to help move the project forward. For each project step, the managers acknowledged progress both personally and publicly. They recorded what had been learned and they asked team members how things could be improved the next time.

Coordinating all the hardware and software groups was difficult, and managers realized that they had to oversee both technical and project events. That is, the technical focus involved technical design and strategy, whereas the project focus addressed

FIGURE 3.17 Enrollment Management model (Conklin 1996).

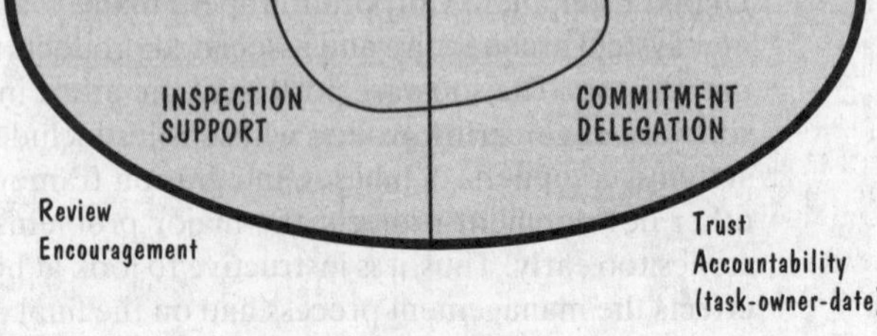

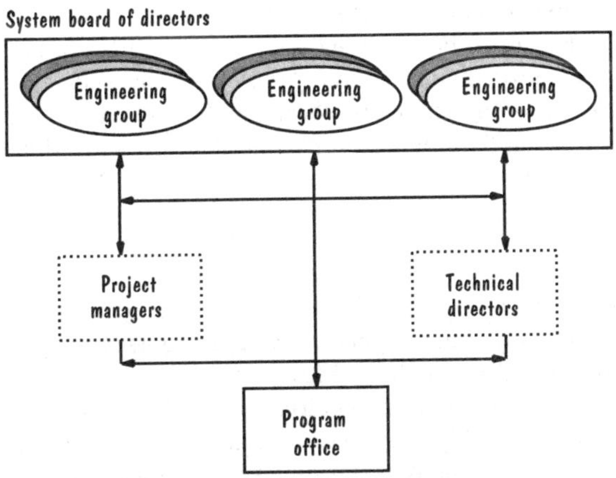

FIGURE 3.18 Alpha project organization (Conklin 1996).

commitments and deliverables. Figure 3.18 illustrates the organization that allowed both foci to contribute to the overall program.

The simplicity of the model and organization does not mean that managing the Alpha program was simple. Several cusps threatened the project and were dealt with in a variety of ways. For example, management was unable to produce an overall plan, and project managers had difficulty coping. At the same time, technical leaders were generating unacceptably large design documents that were difficult to understand. To gain control, the Alpha program managers needed a programwide work plan that illustrated the order in which each contributing task was to be done and how it coordinated with the other tasks. They created a master plan based only on the critical program components—those things that were critical to business success. The plan was restricted to a single page, so that the participants could see the "big picture," without complexity or detail. Similarly, one-page descriptions of designs, schedules, and other key items enabled project participants to have a global picture of what to do, and when and how to do it.

Another cusp occurred when a critical task was announced to be several months behind schedule. The management addressed this problem by instituting regular operational inspections of progress so there would be no more surprises. The inspection involved presentation of a one-page report, itemizing key points about the project:

- schedule
- milestones
- critical path events in the past month
- activities along the critical path in the next month
- issues and dependencies resolved
- issues and dependencies not resolved (with ownership and due dates)

An important aspect of Alpha's success was the managers' realization that engineers are usually motivated more by recognition than by financial gain. Instead of rewarding participants with money, they focused on announcing progress and on making sure that the public knew how much the managers appreciated the engineers' work.

The result of Alpha's flexible and focused management was a program that met its schedule to the month, despite setbacks along the way. Enrollment management enabled small groups to recognize their potential problems early and take steps to handle them while the problems were small and localized. Constancy of purpose was combined with continual learning to produce an exceptional product. Alpha met its performance goals, and its quality was reported to be very high.

Accountability Modeling

The U.S. Air Force and Lockheed Martin formed an Integrated Product Development Team to build a modular software system designed to increase capacity, provide needed functionality, and reduce the cost and schedule of future software changes to the F-16 aircraft. The resulting software included more than four million lines of code, a quarter of which met real-time deadlines in flight. F-16 development also involved building device drivers, real-time extensions to the Ada run-time system, a software engineering workstation network, an Ada compiler for the modular mission computer, software build and configuration management tools, simulation and test software, and interfaces for loading software into the airplane (Parris 1996).

The flight software's capability requirements were well-understood and stable, even though about a million lines of code were expected to be needed from the 250 developers organized as eight product teams, a chief engineer, plus a program manager and staff. However, the familiar capabilities were to be implemented in an unfamiliar way: modular software using Ada and object-oriented design and analysis, plus a transition from mainframes to workstations. Project management constraints included rigid "need dates" and commitment to developing three releases of equal task size, called tapes. The approach was high risk, because the first tape included little time for learning the new methods and tools, including concurrent development (Parris 1996).

Pressure on the project increased because funding levels were cut and schedule deadlines were considered to be extremely unrealistic. In addition, the project was organized in a way unfamiliar to most of the engineers. The participants were used to working in a **matrix organization**, so that each engineer belonged to a functional unit based on a type of skill (such as the design group or the test group) but was assigned to one or more projects as that skill was needed. In other words, an employee could be identified by his or her place in a matrix, with functional skills as one dimension and project names as the other dimension. Decisions were made by the functional unit hierarchy in this traditional organization. However, the contract for the F-16 required the project to be organized as an **integrated product development** team: combining individuals from different functional groups into an interdisciplinary work unit empowered with separate channels of accountability.

To enable the project members to handle the culture change associated with the new organization, the F-16 project used the accountability model shown in Figure 3.19. In the model, a team is any collection of people responsible for producing a given result. A stakeholder is anyone affected by that result or the way in which the result is achieved. The process involves a continuing exchange of accountings (a report of what you have done, are doing, or plan to do) and consequences, with the goal of doing only

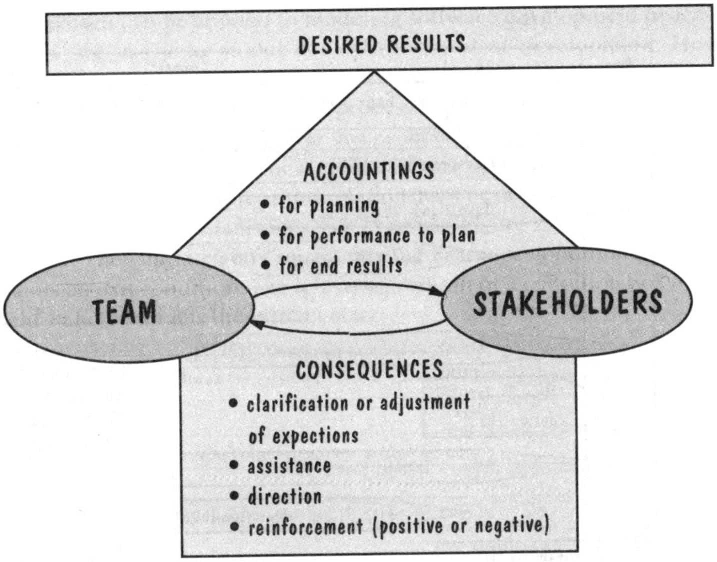

FIGURE 3.19 Accountability model (Parris 1996).

what makes sense for both the team and the stakeholders. The model was applied to the design of management systems and to team operating procedures, replacing independent behaviors with interdependence, emphasizing "being good rather than looking good" (Parris 1996).

As a result, several practices were required, including a weekly, one-hour team status review. To reinforce the notions of responsibility and accountability, each personal action item had explicit closure criteria and was tracked to completion. An action item could be assigned to a team member or a stakeholder, and often involved clarifying issues or requirements, providing missing information or reconciling conflicts.

Because the teams had multiple, overlapping activities, an activity map was used to illustrate progress on each activity in the overall context of the project. Figure 3.20 shows part of an activity map. You can see how each bar represents an activity, and each activity is assigned a method for reporting progress. The point on a bar indicates when detailed planning should be in place to guide activities. The "today" line shows current status, and an activity map was used during the weekly reviews as an overview of the progress to be discussed.

For each activity, progress was tracked using an appropriate evaluation or performance method. Sometimes the method included cost estimation, critical path analysis, or schedule tracking. *Earned value* was used as a common measure for comparing progress on different activities: a scheme for comparing activities determined how much of the project had been completed by each activity. The earned-value calculation included weights to represent what percent of the total process each step constituted, relative to overall effort. Similarly, each component was assigned a size value that

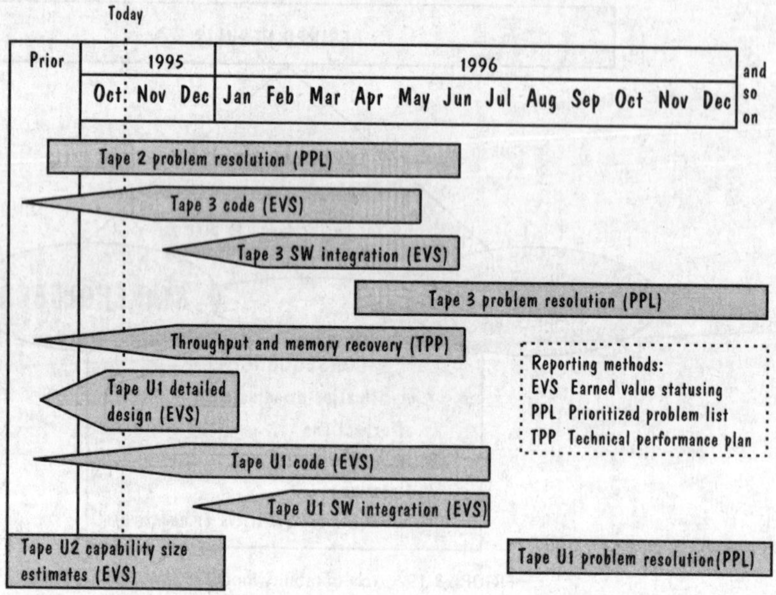

FIGURE 3.20 Sample activity roadmap (adapted from Parris 1996).

represented its proportion of the total product, so that progress relative to the final size could be tracked, too. Then, an earned-value summary chart, similar to Figure 3.21, was presented at each review meeting.

Once part of a product was completed, its progress was no longer tracked. Instead, its performance was tracked, and problems were recorded. Each problem was assigned a priority by the stakeholders, and a snapshot of the top five problems on each product team's list was presented at the weekly review meeting for discussion. The priority lists generated discussion about why the problems occurred, what work-arounds could be put in place, and how similar problems could be prevented in the future.

The project managers found a major problem with the accountability model: it told them nothing about coordination among different teams. As a result, they built software to catalog and track the hand-offs from one team to another, so that every team could understand who was waiting for action or products from them. A model of the hand-offs was used for planning, so that undesirable patterns or scenarios could be eliminated. Thus, an examination of the hand-off model became part of the review process.

It is easy to see how the accountability model, coupled with the hand-off model, addressed several aspects of project management. First, it provided a mechanism for communication and coordination. Second, it encouraged risk management, especially by forcing team members to examine problems in review meetings. And third, it integrated progress reporting with problem solving. Thus, the model actually prescribes a project management process that was followed on the F-16 project.

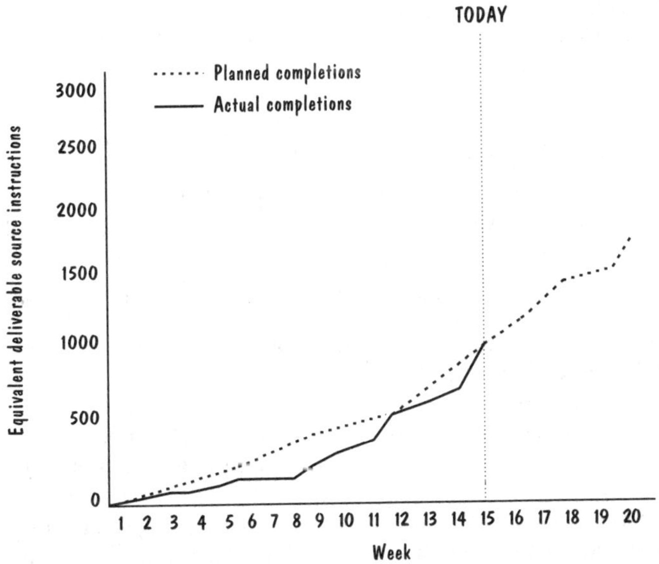

FIGURE 3.21 Example earned-value summary chart (Parris 1996).

Anchoring Milestones

In Chapter 2, we examined many process models that described how the technical activities of software development should progress. Then, in this chapter, we looked at several methods to organize projects to perform those activities. The Alpha AXP and F-16 examples have shown us that project management must be tightly integrated with the development process, not just for tracking progress, but, more importantly, for effective planning and decision making to prevent major problems from derailing the project. Boehm (1996) has identified three milestones common to all software development processes that can serve as a basis for both technical process and project management:

- life-cycle objectives
- life-cycle architecture
- initial operational capability

We can examine each milestone in more detail.

The purpose of the life-cycle objectives milestone is to make sure the stakeholders agree with the system's goals. The key stakeholders act as a team to determine the system boundary, the environment in which the system will operate, and the external systems with which the system must interact. Then, the stakeholders work through scenarios of how the system will be used. The scenarios can be expressed in terms of prototypes, screen layouts, data flows, or other representations, some of which we will learn about in later chapters. If the system is business- or safety-critical, the scenarios should also include instances where the system fails, so that designers can determine how the system is supposed to react to or even avoid a critical failure. Similarly, other essential features of the system are derived and agreed upon. The result is an initial life-cycle plan that lays out (Boehm 1996):

- *Objectives:* Why is the system being developed?
- *Milestones and schedules:* What will be done by when?
- *Responsibilities:* Who is responsible for a function?
- *Approach:* How will the job be done, technically and managerially?
- *Resources:* How much of each resource is needed?
- *Feasibility:* Can this be done, and is there a good business reason for doing it?

The life-cycle architecture is coordinated with the life-cycle objectives. The purpose of the life-cycle architecture milestone is defining both the system and the software architectures, the components of which we will study in Chapters 5, 6, and 7. The architectural choices must address the project risks addressed by the risk management plan, focusing on system evolution in the long term as well as system requirements in the short term.

The key elements of the initial operational capability are the readiness of the software itself, the site at which the system will be used, and the selection and training of the team that will use it. Boehm notes that different processes can be used to implement the initial operational capability, and different estimating techniques can be applied at different stages.

To supplement these milestones, Boehm suggests using the Win–Win spiral model, illustrated in Figure 3.22 and intended to be an extension of the spiral model we examined in Chapter 2. The model encourages participants to converge on a common understanding of the system's next-level objectives, alternatives, and constraints.

Boehm applied Win–Win, called the **Theory W** approach, to the U.S. Department of Defense's STARS program, whose focus was developing a set of prototype software

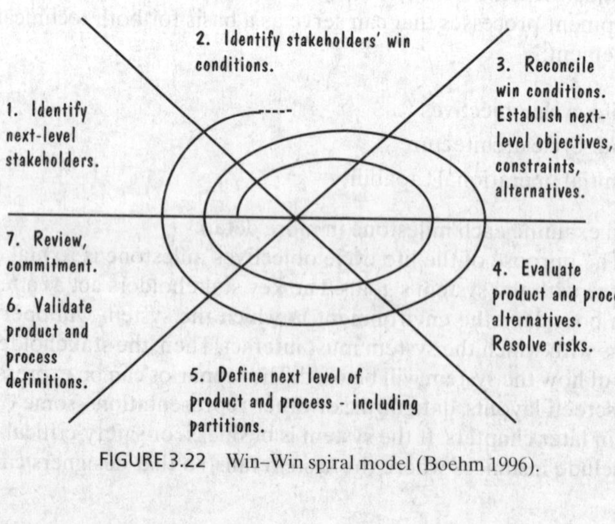

FIGURE 3.22 Win–Win spiral model (Boehm 1996).

engineering environments. The project was a good candidate for Theory W, because there was a great mismatch between what the government was planning to build and what the potential users needed and wanted. The Win–Win model led to several key compromises, including negotiation of a set of common, open interface specifications to enable tool vendors to reach a larger marketplace at reduced cost, and the inclusion of three demonstration projects to reduce risk. Boehm reports that Air Force costs on the project were reduced from $140 to $57 per delivered line of code and that quality improved from 3 to 0.035 faults per thousand delivered lines of code. Several other projects report similar success. TRW developed over half a million lines of code for complex distributed software within budget and schedule using Boehm's milestones with five increments. The first increment included distributed kernel software as part of the life-cycle architecture milestone; the project was required to demonstrate its ability to meet projections that the number of requirements would grow over time (Royce 1990).

3.7 INFORMATION SYSTEMS EXAMPLE

Let us return to the Piccadilly Television airtime sales system to see how we might estimate the amount of effort required to build the software. Because we are in the preliminary stages of understanding just what the software is to do, we can use COCOMO II's initial effort model to suggest the number of person-months needed. A **person-month** is the amount of time one person spends working on a software development project for one month. The COCOMO model assumes that the number of person-months does not include holidays and vacations, nor time off at weekends. The number of person-months is not the same as the time needed to finish building the system. For instance, a system may require 100 person-months, but it can be finished in one month by having ten people work in parallel for one month, or in two months by having five people work in parallel (assuming that the tasks can be accomplished in that manner).

The first COCOMO II model, application composition, is designed to be used in the earliest stages of development. Here, we compute application points to help us determine the likely size of the project. The application point count is determined from three calculations: the number of server data tables used with a screen or report, the number of client data tables used with a screen or report, and the percentage of screens, reports, and modules reused from previous applications. Let us assume that we are not reusing any code in building the Piccadilly system. Then we must begin our estimation process by predicting how many screens and reports we will be using in this application. Suppose our initial estimate is that we need three screens and one report:

- a booking screen to record a new advertising sales booking
- a ratecard screen showing the advertising rates for each day and hour
- an availability screen showing which time slots are available
- a sales report showing total sales for the month and year, and comparing them with previous months and years

For each screen or report, we use the guidance in Table 3.10 and an estimate of the number of data tables needed to produce a description of the screen or report. For example, the booking screen may require the use of three data tables: a table of available

TABLE 3.15 Ratings for Piccadilly Screens and Reports

Name	Screen or Report	Complexity	Weight
Booking	Screen	Simple	1
Ratecard	Screen	Simple	1
Availability	Screen	Medium	2
Sales	Report	Medium	5

time slots, a table of past usage by this customer, and a table of the contact information for this customer (such as name, address, tax number, and sales representative handling the sale). Thus, the number of data tables is fewer than four, so we must decide whether we need more than eight views. Since we are likely to need fewer than eight views, we rate the booking screen as "simple" according to the application point table. Similarly, we may rate the ratecard screen as "simple," the availability screen as "medium," and the sales report as "medium." Next, we use Table 3.11 to assign a complexity rate of 1 to simple screens, 2 to medium screens, and 5 to medium reports; a summary of our ratings is shown in Table 3.15.

We add all the weights in the rightmost column to generate a count of new application points (NOPS): 9. Suppose our developers have low experience and low CASE maturity. Table 3.12 tells us that the productivity rate for this circumstance is 7. Then the COCOMO model tells us that the estimated effort to build the Piccadilly system is NOP divided by the productivity rate, or 1.29 person-months.

As we understand more about the requirements for Piccadilly, we can use the other parts of COCOMO: the early design model and the postarchitecture model, based on nominal effort estimates derived from lines of code or function points. These models use a scale exponent computed from the project's scale factors, listed in Table 3.16.

TABLE 3.16 Scale Factors for COCOMO II Early Design and Postarchitecture Models

Scale Factors	Very Low	Low	Nominal	High	Very High	Extra High
Precedentedness	Thoroughly unprecedented	Largely unprecedented	Somewhat unprecedented	Generally familiar	Largely familiar	Thoroughly familiar
Flexibility	Rigorous	Occasional relaxation	Some relaxation	General conformity	Some conformity	General goals
Significant risks eliminated	Little (20%)	Some (40%)	Often (60%)	Generally (75%)	Mostly (90%)	Full (100%)
Team interaction process	Very difficult interactions	Some difficult interactions	Basically cooperative interactions	Largely cooperative	Highly cooperative	Seamless interactions
Process maturity	Determined by questionnaire	Determined by questionnaire	Determined by questionnaire	Determined by questionnaire	Determined by questionnaire	Determined by questionnaire

"Extra high" is equivalent to a rating of zero, "very high" to 1, "high" to 2, "nominal" to 3, "low" to 4, and "very low" to 5. Each of the scale factors is rated, and the sum of all ratings is used to weight the initial effort estimate. For example, suppose we know that the type of application we are building for Piccadilly is generally familiar to the development team; we can rate the first scale factor as "high." Similarly, we may rate flexibility as "very high," risk resolution as "nominal," team interaction as "high," and the maturity rating may turn out to be "low." We sum the ratings $(2 + 1 + 3 + 2 + 4)$ to get a scale factor of 12. Then, we compute the scale exponent to be

$$1.01 + 0.01(12)$$

or 1.13. This scale exponent tells us that if our initial effort estimate is 100 person-months, then our new estimate, relative to the characteristics reflected in Table 3.16, is $100^{1.13}$, or 182 person-months. In a similar way, the cost drivers adjust this estimate based on characteristics such as tool usage, analyst expertise, and reliability requirements. Once we calculate the adjustment factor, we multiply by our 182 person-months estimate to yield an adjusted effort estimate.

3.8 REAL-TIME EXAMPLE

The board investigating the Ariane-5 failure examined the software, the documentation, and the data captured before and during flight to determine what caused the failure (Lions et al. 1996). Its report notes that the launcher began to disintegrate 39 seconds after takeoff because the angle of attack exceeded 20 degrees, causing the boosters to separate from the main stage of the rocket; this separation triggered the launcher's self-destruction. The angle of attack was determined by software in the on-board computer on the basis of data transmitted by the active inertial reference system, SRI2. As the report notes, SRI2 was supposed to contain valid flight data, but instead it contained a diagnostic bit pattern that was interpreted erroneously as flight data. The erroneous data had been declared a failure, and the SRI2 had been shut off. Normally, the on-board computer would have switched to the other inertial reference system, SRI1, but that, too, had been shut down for the same reason.

The error occurred in a software module that computed meaningful results only before lift-off. As soon as the launcher lifted off, the function performed by this module served no useful purpose, so it was no longer needed by the rest of the system. However, the module continued its computations for approximately 40 seconds of flight based on a requirement for the Ariane-4 that was not needed for Ariane-5.

The internal events that led to the failure were reproduced by simulation calculations supported by memory readouts and examination of the software itself. Thus, the Ariane-5 destruction might have been prevented had the project managers developed a risk management plan, reviewed it, and developed risk avoidance or mitigation plans for each identified risk. To see how, consider again the steps of Figure 3.15. The first stage of risk assessment is risk identification. The possible problem with reuse of the Ariane-4 software might have been identified by a decomposition of the functions; someone might have recognized early on that the requirements for Ariane-5 were different from Ariane-4. Or an assumption analysis might have revealed that the assumptions for the SRI in Ariane-4 were different from those for Ariane-5.

Once the risks were identified, the analysis phase might have included simulations, which probably would have highlighted the problem that eventually caused the rocket's destruction. And prioritization would have identified the risk exposure if the SRI did not work as planned; the high exposure might have prompted the project team to examine the SRI and its workings more carefully before implementation.

Risk control involves risk reduction, management planning, and risk resolution. Even if the risk assessment activities had missed the problems inherent in reusing the SRI from Ariane-4, risk reduction techniques including risk avoidance analysis might have noted that both SRIs could have been shut down for the same underlying cause. Risk avoidance might have involved using SRIs with two different designs, so that the design error would have shut down one but not the other. Or the fact that the SRI calculations were not needed after lift-off might have prompted the designers or implementers to shut down the SRI earlier, before it corrupted the data for the angle calculations. Similarly, risk resolution includes plans for mitigation and continual reassessment of risk. Even if the risk of SRI failure had not been caught earlier, a risk reassessment during design or even during unit testing might have revealed the problem in the middle of development. A redesign or development at that stage would have been costly, but not as costly as the complete loss of Ariane-5 on its maiden voyage.

3.9 WHAT THIS CHAPTER MEANS FOR YOU

This chapter has introduced you to some of the key concepts in project management, including project planning, cost and schedule estimation, risk management, and team organization. You can make use of this information in many ways, even if you are not a manager. Project planning involves input from all team members, including you, and understanding the planning process and estimation techniques gives you a good idea of how your input will be used to make decisions for the whole team. Also, we have seen how the number of possible communication paths grows as the size of the team increases. You can take communication into account when you are planning your work and estimating the time it will take you to complete your next task.

We have also seen how communication styles differ and how they affect the way we interact with each other on the job. By understanding your teammates' styles, you can create reports and presentations for them that match their expectations and needs. You can prepare summary information for people with a bottom-line style and offer complete analytical information to those who are rational.

3.10 WHAT THIS CHAPTER MEANS FOR YOUR DEVELOPMENT TEAM

At the same time, you have learned how to organize a development team so that team interaction helps produce a better product. There are several choices for team structure, from a hierarchical chief programmer team to a loose, egoless approach. Each has its benefits, and each depends to some degree on the uncertainty and size of the project.

We have also seen how the team can work to anticipate and reduce risk from the project's beginning. Redundant functionality, team reviews, and other techniques can help us catch errors early, before they become embedded in the code as faults waiting to cause failures.

Similarly, cost estimation should be done early and often, including input from team members about progress in specifying, designing, coding, and testing the system. Cost estimation and risk management can work hand in hand; as cost estimates raise concerns about finishing on time and within budget, risk management techniques can be used to mitigate or even eliminate risks.

3.11 WHAT THIS CHAPTER MEANS FOR RESEARCHERS

This chapter has described many techniques that still require a great deal of research. Little is known about which team organizations work best in which situations. Likewise, cost- and schedule-estimation models are not as accurate as we would like them to be, and improvements can be made as we learn more about how project, process, product, and resource characteristics affect our efficiency and productivity. Some methods, such as machine learning, look promising but require a great deal of historical data to make them accurate. Researchers can help us to understand how to balance practicality with accuracy when using estimation techniques.

Similarly, a great deal of research is needed in making risk management techniques practical. The calculation of risk exposure is currently more an art than a science, and we need methods to help us make our risk calculations more relevant and our mitigation techniques more effective.

3.12 TERM PROJECT

Often, a company or organization must estimate the effort and time required to complete a project, even before detailed requirements are prepared. Using the approaches described in this chapter, or a tool of your choosing from other sources, estimate the effort required to build the Loan Arranger system. How many people will be required? What kinds of skills should they have? How much experience? What kinds of tools or techniques can you use to shorten the amount of time that development will take?

You may want to use more than one approach to generate your estimates. If you do, then compare and contrast the results. Examine each approach (its models and assumptions) to see what accounts for any substantial differences among estimates.

Once you have your estimates, evaluate them and their underlying assumptions to see how much uncertainty exists in them. Then, perform a risk analysis. Save your results; you can examine them at the end of the project to see which risks turned into real problems, and which ones were mitigated by your chosen risk strategies.

3.13 KEY REFERENCES

A great deal of information about COCOMO is available from the Center for Software Engineering at the University of Southern California. The Web site, http://sunset.usc.

edu/csse/research/COCOMOII/cocomo_main.html, points to current research on COCOMO, including a Java implementation of COCOMO II. It is at this site that you can also find out about COCOMO user-group meetings and obtain a copy of the COCOMO II user's manual. Related information about function points is available from IFPUG, the International Function Point User Group, in Westerville, Ohio.

The Center for Software Engineering also performs research on risk management. You can ftp a copy of its Software Risk Technical Advisor at ftp://usc.edu/pub/soft_engineering/demos/stra.tar.z and read about current research at http://sunset.usc.edu.

PC-based tools to support estimation are described and available from the Web site for Bournemouth University's Empirical Software Engineering Research Group: http://dec.bournemouth.ac.uk/ESERG.

Several companies producing commercial project management and cost-estimation tools have information available on their Web sites. Quantitative Software Management, producers of the SLIM cost-estimation package, is located at http://www.qsm.com. Likewise, Software Productivity Research offers a package called Checkpoint. Information can be found at http://www.spr.com. Computer Associates has developed a large suite of project management tools, including Estimacs for cost estimation and Planmacs for planning. A full description of its products is at http://www.cai.com/products.

The Software Technology Support Center at Hill Air Force Base in Ogden, Utah, produces a newsletter called *CrossTalk* that reports on method and tool evaluation. Its guidelines for successful acquisition and management can be found at http://stsc.hill.af.mil/stscdocs.html. The Center's Web pages also contain pointers to several technology areas, including project management and cost estimation; you can find the listing at http://stsc.hill.af.mil.

Team building and team interaction are essential on good software projects. Weinberg (1993) discusses work styles and their application to team building in the second volume of his series on software quality. Scholtes (1995) includes material on how to handle difficult team members.

Project management for small projects is necessarily different from that for large projects. The October 1999 issue of *IEEE Computer* addresses software engineering in the small, with articles about small projects, Internet time pressures, and extreme programming.

Project management for Web applications is somewhat different from more traditional software engineering. Mendes and Moseley (2006) explore the differences. In particular, they address estimation for Web applications in their book on "Web engineering."

3.14 EXERCISES

1. Figure 3.23 is an activity graph for a software development project. The number corresponding to each edge of the graph indicates the number of days required to complete the activity represented by that branch. For example, it will take four days to complete the activity that ends in milestone E. For each activity, list its precursors and compute the earliest start time, the latest start time, and the slack. Then, identify the critical path.

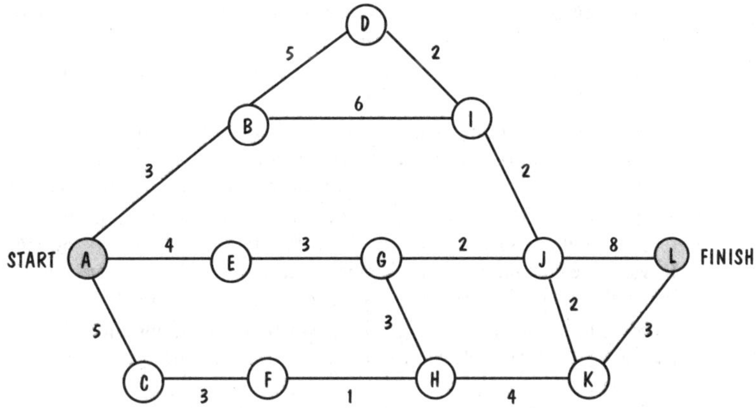

FIGURE 3.23 Activity graph for Exercise 1.

2. Figure 3.24 is an activity graph. Find the critical path.

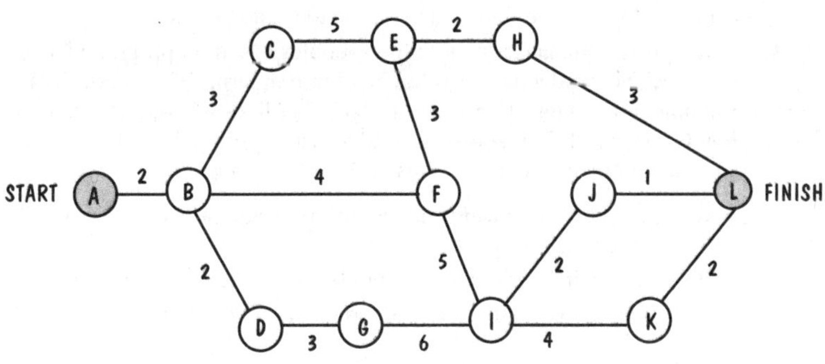

FIGURE 3.24 Activity graph for Exercise 2.

3. You are about to bake a two-layer birthday cake with icing. Describe the cake-baking project as a work breakdown structure. Generate an activity graph from that structure. What is the critical path?
4. Describe how adding personnel to a project that is behind schedule might make the project completion date even later.
5. A large government agency wants to contract with a software development firm for a project involving 20,000 lines of code. The Hardand Software Company uses Walston and Felix's estimating technique for determining the number of people required for the time needed to write that much code. How many person-months does Hardand estimate will be needed? If the government's estimate of size is 10% too low (i.e., 20,000 lines of code represent only 90% of the actual size), how many additional person-months will be

needed? In general, if the government's size estimate is $k\%$ too low, by how much must the person-month estimate change?

6. What are some of the steps of a software project? Why is it important to assign different roles to different team members?
7. Brooks says that adding people to a late project makes it even later (Brooks 1975). Some schedule-estimation techniques seem to indicate that adding people to a project can shorten development time. Is this a contradiction? Why or why not?
8. Many studies indicate that two of the major reasons that a project is late are changing requirements (called requirements volatility or instability) and employee turnover. Review the cost models discussed in this chapter, plus any you may use on your job, and determine which models have cost factors that reflect the effects of these reasons.
9. According to Boehm, what are the risks that can be minimized by using prototyping? Based on your answer, what part of the software life cycle can benefit the most from prototyping?
10. Manny's Manufacturing must decide whether to build or buy a software package to keep track of its inventory. Manny's computer experts estimate that it will cost $325,000 to buy the necessary programs. To build the programs in-house, programmers will cost $5000 each per month. What factors should Manny consider in making his decision? When is it better to build? To buy?
11. Even on your student projects, there are significant risks to your finishing your project on time. Analyze a student software development project and list the risks. What is the risk exposure? What techniques can you use to mitigate each risk?
12. Many project managers plan their schedules based on programmer productivity on past projects. This productivity is often measured in terms of a unit of size per unit of time. For example, an organization may produce 300 lines of code per day or 1200 application points per month. Is it appropriate to measure productivity in this way? Discuss the measurement of productivity in terms of the following issues:
    - Different languages can produce different numbers of lines of code for implementation of the same design.
    - Productivity in lines of code cannot be measured until implementation begins.
    - Programmers may structure code to meet productivity goals.

4 Capturing the Requirements

In this chapter, we look at

- eliciting requirements from our customers
- modeling requirements
- reviewing requirements to ensure their quality
- documenting requirements for use by the design and test teams

In earlier chapters, when looking at various process models, we noted several key steps for successful software development. In particular, each proposed model of the software-development process includes activities aimed at capturing requirements: understanding our customers' fundamental problems and goals. Thus, our understanding of system intent and function starts with an examination of requirements. In this chapter, we look at the various types of requirements and their different sources, and we discuss how to resolve conflicting requirements. We detail a variety of modeling notations and requirements-specification methods, with examples of both automated and manual techniques. These models help us understand the requirements and document the relationships among them. Once the requirements are well understood, we learn how to review them for correctness and completeness. At the end of the chapter, we learn how to choose a requirements-specification method that is appropriate to the project under consideration, based on the project's size, scope, and the criticality of its mission.

Analyzing requirements involves much more than merely writing down what the customer wants. As we shall see, we must find requirements on which both we and the customer can agree and on which we can build our test procedures. First, let us examine exactly what requirements are, why they are so important (see Sidebar 4.1), and how we work with users and customers to define and document them.

SIDEBAR 4.1 WHY ARE REQUIREMENTS IMPORTANT?

The hardest single part of building a software system is deciding precisely what to build. No other part of the conceptual work is as difficult as establishing the detailed technical requirements, including all the interfaces to people, to machines, and to other software systems. No other part of the work so cripples the resulting system if done wrong. No other part is more difficult to rectify later.

(Brooks 1987)

In 1994, the Standish Group surveyed over 350 companies about their over 8000 software projects to find out how well they were faring. The results are sobering. Thirty-one percent of the software projects were canceled before they were completed. Moreover, in large companies, only 9% of the projects were delivered on time and within budget; 16% met those criteria in small companies (Standish 1994). Similar results have been reported since then; the bottom line is that developers have trouble delivering the right system on time and within budget.

To understand why, Standish (1995) asked the survey respondents to explain the causes of the failed projects. The top factors were reported to be

1. Incomplete requirements (13.1%)
2. Lack of user involvement (12.4%)
3. Lack of resources (10.6%)
4. Unrealistic expectations (9.9%)
5. Lack of executive support (9.3%)
6. Changing requirements and specifications (8.7%)
7. Lack of planning (8.1%)
8. System no longer needed (7.5%)

Notice that some part of the requirements elicitation, definition, and management process is involved in almost all of these causes. Lack of care in understanding, documenting, and managing requirements can lead to a myriad of problems: building a system that solves the wrong problem, that doesn't function as expected, or that is difficult for the users to understand and use.

Furthermore, requirements errors can be expensive if they are not detected and fixed early in the development process. Boehm and Papaccio (1988) report that if it costs $1 to find and fix a requirements-based problem during the requirements definition process, it can cost $5 to repair it during design, $10 during coding, $20 during unit testing, and as much as $200 after delivery of the system! So it pays to take time to understand the problem and its context, and to get the requirements right the first time.

4.1 THE REQUIREMENTS PROCESS

A customer who asks us to build a new system has some notion of what the system should do. Often, the customer wants to automate a manual task, such as paying bills electronically rather than with handwritten checks. Sometimes, the customer wants to enhance or extend a current manual or automated system. For example, a telephone billing system that charged customers only for local telephone service and long-distance calls may be updated to bill for call forwarding, call waiting, and other new features. More and more frequently, a customer wants products that do things that have never been done before: tailoring electronic news to a user's interests, changing the shape of an airplane wing in mid-flight, or monitoring a diabetic's blood sugar and automatically controlling insulin dosage. No matter whether its functionality is old or new, a proposed software system has a purpose, usually expressed in terms of goals or desired behavior.

A **requirement** is an expression of desired behavior. A requirement deals with objects or entities, the states they can be in, and the functions that are performed to change states or object characteristics. For example, suppose we are building a system to generate paychecks for our customer's company. One requirement may be that the checks are to be issued every two weeks. Another may be that direct deposit of an employee's check is to be allowed for every employee at a certain salary level or higher. The customer may request access to the paycheck system from several different company locations. All of these requirements are specific descriptions of functions or characteristics that address the general purpose of the system: to generate paychecks. Thus, we look for requirements that identify key entities ("an employee is a person who is paid by the company"), limit entities ("an employee may be paid for no more than 40 hours per week"), or define relationships among entities ("employee X is supervised by employee Y if Y can authorize a change to X's salary").

Note that none of these requirements specify how the system is to be implemented. There is no mention of what database-management system to use, whether a client-server architecture will be employed, how much memory the computer is to have, or what programming language must be used to develop the system. These implementation-specific descriptions are not considered to be requirements (unless they are mandated by the customer). The goal of the requirements phase is to understand the customer's problems and needs. Thus, requirements focus on the customer and the problem, not on the solution or the implementation. We often say that requirements designate *what* behavior the customer wants, without saying *how* that behavior will be realized. Any discussion of a solution is premature until the problem is clearly defined.

It helps to describe requirements as interactions among real-world phenomena, without any reference to system phenomena. For example, billing requirements should refer to customers, services billed, billing periods and amounts—without mentioning system data or procedures. We take this approach partly to get at the heart of the customer's needs, because sometimes the stated needs are not the real needs. Moreover, the customer's problem is usually most easily stated in terms of the customer's business. Another reason we take this approach is to give the designer maximum flexibility in deciding how to carry out the requirements. During the **specification** phase, we will decide which requirements will be fulfilled by our software system (as opposed to requirements that are addressed by special-purpose hardware devices, by other software systems, or by human operators or users); during the **design** phase, we will devise a plan for how the specified behavior will be implemented.

Figure 4.1 illustrates the process of determining the requirements for a proposed software system. The person performing these tasks usually goes by the title of **requirements analyst** or **systems analyst**. As a requirements analyst, we first work with

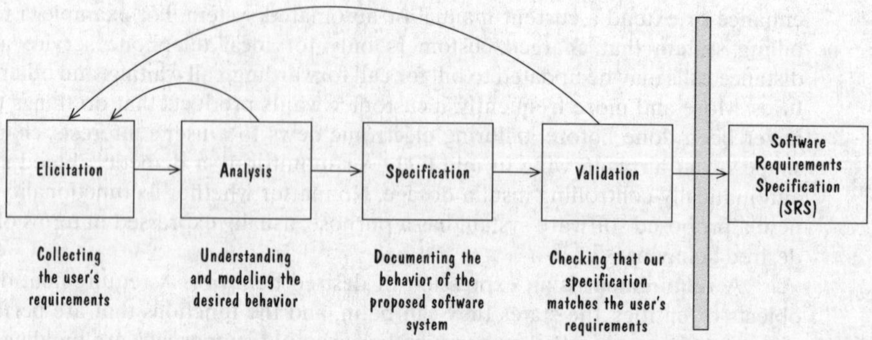

FIGURE 4.1 Process for capturing the requirements.

our customers to elicit the requirements by asking questions, examining current behavior, or demonstrating similar systems. Next, we capture the requirements in a model or a prototype. This exercise helps us to better understand the required behavior, and usually raises additional questions about what the customer wants to happen in certain situations (e.g., what if an employee leaves the company in the middle of a pay period?). Once the requirements are well understood, we progress to the specification phase, in which we decide which parts of the required behavior will be implemented in software. During validation, we check that our specification matches what the customer expects to see in the final product. Analysis and validation activities may expose problems or omissions in our models or specification that cause us to revisit the customer and revise our models and specification. The eventual outcome of the requirements process is a Software Requirements Specification (SRS), which is used to communicate to other software developers (designers, testers, maintainers) how the final product ought to behave. Sidebar 4.2 discusses how the use of agile methods affects the requirements process and the resulting requirements documents. The remainder of this chapter explores the requirements process in more detail.

4.2 REQUIREMENTS ELICITATION

Requirements elicitation is an especially critical part of the process. We must use a variety of techniques to determine what the users and customers really want. Sometimes, we are automating a manual system, so it is easy to examine what the system already does. But often, we must work with users and customers to understand a completely new problem. This task is rarely as simple as asking the right questions to pluck the requirements from the customer's head. At the early stage of a project, requirements are ill-formed and ill-understood by everyone. Customers are not always good at describing exactly what they want or need, and we are not always good at understanding someone else's business concerns. The customers know their business, but they cannot always describe their business problems to outsiders; their descriptions are full of jargon and

SIDEBAR 4.2 AGILE REQUIREMENTS MODELING

As we noted in Chapter 2, requirements analysis plays a large role in deciding whether to use agile methods as the basis for software development. If the requirements are tightly coupled and complex, or if future requirements and enhancements are likely to cause major changes to the system's architecture, then we may be better off with a "heavy" process that emphasizes up-front modeling. In a heavy process, developers put off coding until the requirements have been modeled and analyzed, an architecture is proposed that reflects the requirements, and a detailed design has been chosen. Each of these steps requires a model, and the models are related and coordinated so that the design fully implements the requirements. This approach is most appropriate for large-team development, where the documentation helps the developers to coordinate their work, and for safety-critical systems, where a system's correctness and safety are more important than its release date.

However, for problems where the requirements are uncertain, it can be cumbersome to employ a heavy process and have to update the models with every change to the requirements. As an alternative approach, agile methods gather and implement the requirements in increments. The initial release implements the most essential requirements, as defined by the stakeholders' business goals. As new requirements emerge with use of the system or with better understanding of the problem, they are implemented in subsequent releases of the system. This incremental development allows for "early and continuous delivery of valuable software" (Beck et al. 2004) and accommodates emergent and late-breaking requirements.

Extreme programming (XP) takes agile requirements processes to the extreme, in that the system is built to the requirements that happen to be defined at the time, with no planning or designing for possible future requirements. Moreover, XP forgoes traditional requirements documentation, and instead encodes the requirements as test cases that the eventual implementation must pass. Berry (2002a) points out that the trade-off for agile methods' flexibility is the difficulty of making changes to the system as requirements are added, deleted, or changed. But there can be additional problems: XP uses test cases to specify requirements, so a poorly written test case can lead to the kinds of misunderstandings described in this chapter.

assumptions with which we may not be familiar. Likewise, we as developers know about computer solutions, but not always about how possible solutions will affect our customers' business activities. We, too, have our jargon and assumptions, and sometimes we think everyone is speaking the same language, when in fact people have different meanings for the same words. It is only by discussing the requirements with everyone who has a stake in the system, coalescing these different views into a coherent set of requirements, and reviewing these documents with the stakeholders that we all come to an agreement about what the requirements are. (See Sidebar 4.3 for an alternative viewpoint.) If we cannot agree on what the requirements are, then the project is doomed to fail.

SIDEBAR 4.3 USING VIEWPOINTS TO MANAGE INCONSISTENCY

Although most software engineers strive for consistent requirements, Easterbrook and Nuseibeh (1996) argue that it is often desirable to tolerate and even encourage inconsistency during the requirements process. They claim that because the stakeholders' understanding of the domain and their needs evolve over time, it is pointless to try to resolve inconsistencies early in the requirements process. Early resolutions are expensive and often unnecessary (and can occur naturally as stakeholders revise their views). They can also be counter-productive if the resolution process focuses attention on how to come to agreement rather than on the underlying causes of the inconsistency (e.g., stakeholders' misunderstanding of the domain).

Instead, Easterbrook and Nuseibeh propose that stakeholders' views be documented and maintained as separate Viewpoints (Nuseibeh et al. 1994) throughout the software development process. The requirements analyst defines consistency rules that should apply between Viewpoints (e.g., how objects, states, or transitions in one Viewpoint correspond to similar entities in another Viewpoint; or how one Viewpoint refines another Viewpoint), and the Viewpoints are analyzed (possibly automatically) to see if they conform to the consistency rules. If the rules are violated, the inconsistencies are recorded as part of the Viewpoints, so that other software developers do not mistakenly implement a view that is being contested. The recorded inconsistencies are rechecked whenever an associated Viewpoint is modified, to see if the Viewpoints are still inconsistent; and the consistency rules are checked periodically, to see if any have been broken by evolving Viewpoints.

The outcome of this approach is a requirements document that accommodates all stakeholders' views at all times. Inconsistencies are highlighted but not addressed until there is sufficient information to make an informed decision. This way, we avoid committing ourselves prematurely to requirements or design decisions.

So who are the stakeholders? It turns out that there are many people who have something to contribute to the requirements of a new system:

- *Clients, who are the ones paying for the software to be developed:* By paying for the development, the clients are, in some sense, the ultimate stakeholders, and have the final say about what the product does (Robertson and Robertson 1999).
- *Customers, who buy the software after it is developed:* Sometimes the customer and the user are the same; other times, the customer is a business manager who is interested in improving the productivity of her employees. We have to understand the customers' needs well enough to build a product that they will buy and find useful.
- *Users, who are familiar with the current system and will use the future system:* These are the experts on how the current system works, which features are the most useful, and which aspects of the system need improving. We may want to consult also with special-interest groups of users, such as users with disabilities,

people who are unfamiliar with or uncomfortable using computers, expert users, and so on, to understand their particular needs.

- *Domain experts, who are familiar with the problem that the software must automate:* For example, we would consult a financial expert if we were building a financial package, or a meteorologist if our software were to model the weather. These people can contribute to the requirements, or will know about the kinds of environments to which the product will be exposed.
- *Market researchers, who have conducted surveys to determine future trends and potential customers' needs:* They may assume the role of the customer if our software is being developed for the mass market and no particular customer has been identified yet.
- *Lawyers or auditors, who are familiar with government, safety, or legal requirements:* For example, we might consult a tax expert to ensure that a payroll package adheres to the tax law. We may also consult with experts on standards that are relevant to the product's functions.
- *Software engineers or other technology experts.* These experts ensure that the product is technically and economically feasible. They can educate the customer about innovative hardware and software technologies, and can recommend new functionality that takes advantage of these technologies. They can also estimate the cost and development time of the product.

Each stakeholder has a particular view of the system and how it should work, and often these views conflict. One of the many skills of a requirements analyst is the ability to understand each view and capture the requirements in a way that reflects the concerns of each participant. For example, a customer may specify that a system perform a particular task, but the customer is not necessarily the user of the proposed system. The user may want the task to be performed in three modes: a learning mode, a novice mode, and an expert mode; this separation will allow the user to learn and master the system gradually. Some systems are implemented in this way, so that new users can adapt to the new system gradually. However, conflicts can arise when ease of use suggests a slower system than response-time requirements permit.

Also, different participants may expect differing levels of detail in the requirements documentation, in which case the requirements will need to be packaged in different ways for different people. In addition, users and developers may have preconceptions (right or wrong) about what the other group values and how it acts. Table 4.1 summarizes some of the common stereotypes. This table emphasizes the role that human interaction plays in the development of software systems; good requirements analysis requires excellent interpersonal skills as well as solid technical skills. The book's Web site contains suggestions for addressing each of these differences in perception.

In addition to interviewing stakeholders, other means of eliciting requirements include

- Reviewing available documentation, such as documented procedures of manual tasks, and specifications or user manuals of automated systems
- Observing the current system (if one exists), to gather objective information about how the users perform their tasks, and to better understand the system we are about to automate or to change; often, when a new computer system is developed,

TABLE 4.1 How Users and Developers View Each Other (Scharer 1990)

How Developers See Users	How Users See Developers
Users don't know what they want.	Developers don't understand operational needs.
Users can't articulate what they want.	Developers can't translate clearly stated needs into a successful system.
Users are unable to provide a usable statement of needs.	Developers set unrealistic standards for requirements definition.
Users have too many needs that are politically motivated.	Developers place too much emphasis on technicalities.
Users want everything right now.	Developers are always late.
Users can't remain on schedule.	Developers can't respond quickly to legitimately changing needs.
Users can't prioritize needs.	Developers are always over budget.
Users are unwilling to compromise.	Developers say "no" all the time.
Users refuse to take responsibility for the system.	Developers try to tell us how to do our jobs.
Users are not committed to development projects.	Developers ask users for time and effort, even to the detriment of the users' important primary duties.

the old system continues to be used because it provides some critical function that the designers of the new system overlooked

- Apprenticing with users (Beyer and Holtzblatt 1995), to learn about users' tasks in more detail, as the user performs them
- Interviewing users or stakeholders in groups, so that they will be inspired by one another's ideas
- Using domain-specific strategies, such as Joint Application Design (Wood and Silver 1995) or PIECES (Wetherbe 1984) for information systems, to ensure that stakeholders consider specific types of requirements that are relevant to their particular situations
- Brainstorming with current and potential users about how to improve the proposed product

The Volere requirements process model (Robertson and Robertson 1999), as shown in Figure 4.2, suggests some additional sources for requirements, such as templates and libraries of requirements from related systems that we have developed.

4.3 TYPES OF REQUIREMENTS

When most people think about requirements, they think about required *functionality*: What services should be provided? What operations should be performed? What should be the reaction to certain stimuli? How does required behavior change over time and in response to the history of events? A **functional requirement** describes required behavior in terms of required activities, such as reactions to inputs, and the state of each entity before and after an activity occurs. For instance, for a payroll system, the functional requirements state how often paychecks are issued, what input is necessary for a paycheck to be printed, under what conditions the amount of pay can be changed, and what causes the removal of an employee from the payroll list.

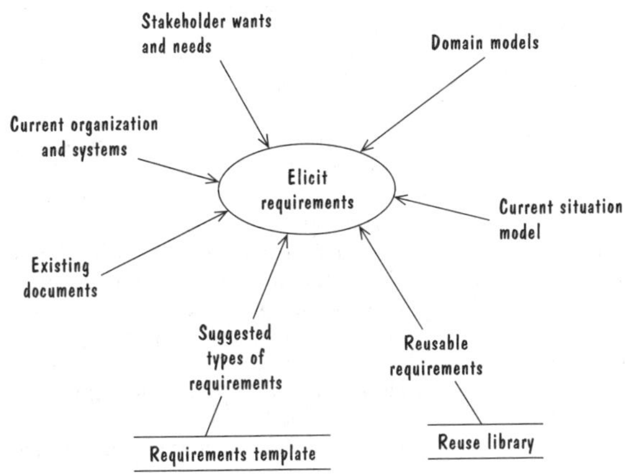

FIGURE 4.2 Sources of possible requirements (Robertson and Robertson 1999).

The functional requirements define the boundaries of the solution space for our problem. The solution space is the set of possible ways that software can be designed to implement the requirements, and initially that set can be very large. However, in practice it is usually not enough for a software product to compute correct outputs; there are other types of requirements that also distinguish between acceptable and unacceptable products. A **quality requirement**, or **nonfunctional requirement**, describes some quality characteristic that the software solution must possess, such as fast response time, ease of use, high reliability, or low maintenance costs. A **design constraint** is a design decision, such as choice of platform or interface components, that has already been made and that restricts the set of solutions to our problem. A **process constraint** is a restriction on the techniques or resources that can be used to build the system. For example, customers may insist that we use agile methods, so that they can use early versions of the system while we continue to add features. Thus, quality requirements, design constraints, and process constraints further restrict our solution space by differentiating acceptable, well-liked solutions from unused products. Table 4.2 gives examples of each kind of requirement.

Quality requirements sometimes sound like "motherhood" characteristics that all products ought to possess. After all, who is going to ask for a slow, unfriendly, unreliable, unmaintainable software system? It is better to think of quality requirements as design criteria that can be optimized and can be used to choose among alternative implementations of functional requirements. Given this approach, the question to be answered by the requirements is: To what extent must a product satisfy these quality requirements to be acceptable? Sidebar 4.4 explains how to express quality requirements such that we can test whether they are met.

Resolving Conflicts

In trying to elicit all types of requirements from all of the relevant stakeholders, we are bound to encounter conflicting ideas of what the requirements ought to be. It usually helps to ask the customer to prioritize requirements. This task forces the customer to

TABLE 4.2 Questions to Tease Out Different Types of Requirements

Functional Requirements

Functionality
- What will the system do?
- When will the system do it?
- Are there several modes of operation?
- What kinds of computations or data transformations must be performed?
- What are the appropriate reactions to possible stimuli?

Data
- For both input and output, what should be the format of the data?
- Must any data be retained for any period of time?

Design Constraints

Physical Environment
- Where is the equipment to be located?
- Is there one location or several?
- Are there any environmental restrictions, such as temperature, humidity, or magnetic interference?
- Are there any constraints on the size of the system?
- Are there any constraints on power, heating, or air conditioning?
- Are there constraints on the programming language because of existing software components?

Interfaces
- Is input coming from one or more other systems?
- Is output going to one or more other systems?
- Is there a prescribed way in which input/output data must be formatted?
- Is there a prescribed medium that the data must use?

Users
- Who will use the system?
- Will there be several types of users?
- What is the skill level of each user?

Process Constraints

Resources
- What materials, personnel, or other resources are needed to build the system?
- What skills must the developers have?

Documentation
- How much documentation is required?
- Should it be online, in book format, or both?
- To what audience should each type of documentation be addressed?

Standards

Quality Requirements

Performance
- Are there constraints on execution speed, response time, or throughput?
- What efficiency measures will apply to resource usage and response time?
- How much data will flow through the system?
- How often will data be received or sent?

Usability and Human Factors
- What kind of training will be required for each type of user?
- How easy should it be for a user to understand and use the system?
- How difficult should it be for a user to misuse the system?

Security
- Must access to the system or information be controlled?
- Should each user's data be isolated from the data of other users?
- Should user programs be isolated from other programs and from the operating system?
- Should precautions be taken against theft or vandalism?

Reliability and Availability
- Must the system detect and isolate faults?
- What is the prescribed mean time between failures?
- Is there a maximum time allowed for restarting the system after a failure?
- How often will the system be backed up?
- Must backup copies be stored at a different location?
- Should precautions be taken against fire or water damage?

Maintainability
- Will maintenance merely correct errors, or will it also include improving the system?
- When and in what ways might the system be changed in the future?
- How easy should it be to add features to the system?
- How easy should it be to port the system from one platform (computer, operating system) to another?

Precision and Accuracy
- How accurate must data calculations be?
- To what degree of precision must calculations be made?

Time to Delivery / Cost
- Is there a prescribed timetable for development?
- Is there a limit on the amount of money to be spent on development or on hardware or software?

SIDEBAR 4.4 MAKING REQUIREMENTS TESTABLE

In writing about good design, Alexander (1979a) encourages us to make our requirements testable. By this, he means that once a requirement is stated, we should be able to determine whether or not a proposed solution meets the requirement. This evaluation must be objective; that is, the conclusion as to whether the requirement is satisfied must not vary according to who is doing the evaluation.

Robertson and Robertson (1999) point out that testability (which they call "measurability") can be addressed when requirements are being elicited. The idea is to quantify the extent to which each requirement must be met. These **fit criteria** form objective standards for judging whether a proposed solution satisfies the requirements. When such criteria cannot be easily expressed, then the requirement is likely to be ambiguous, incomplete, or incorrect. For example, a customer may state a quality requirement this way:

Water quality information must be accessible immediately.

How do you test that your product meets this requirement? The customer probably has a clear idea about what "immediately" means, and that notion must be captured in the requirement. We can restate more precisely what we mean by "immediately":

Water quality records must be retrieved within 5 seconds of a request.

This second formulation of the requirement can be tested objectively: a series of requests is made, and we check that the system supplies the appropriate record within 5 seconds of each request.

It is relatively easy to determine fit criteria for quality requirements that are naturally quantitative (e.g., performance, size, precision, accuracy, time to delivery). What about more subjective quality requirements, like usability or maintainability? In these cases, developers use focus groups or metrics to evaluate fit criteria:

- *75% of users shall judge the new system to be as usable as the existing system.*
- *After training, 90% of users shall be able to process a new account within 5 minutes.*
- *A module will encapsulate the data representation of at most one data type.*
- *Computation errors shall be fixed within 3 weeks of being reported.*

Fit criteria that cannot be evaluated before the final product is delivered are harder to assess:

- *The system shall not be unavailable for more than a total maximum of 3 minutes each year.*
- *The mean-time-between-failures shall be no less than 1 year.*

In these cases, we either estimate a system's quality attributes (e.g., there are techniques for estimating system reliability, and for estimating the number of faults per line of code) or evaluate the delivered system during its operation—and suffer some financial penalty if the system does not live up to its promise.

Interestingly, what gets measured gets done. That is, unless a fit criterion is unrealistic, it will probably be met. The key is to determine, with the customer, just how to demonstrate that a delivered system meets its requirements. The Robertsons suggest three ways to help make requirements testable:

- Specify a quantitative description for each adverb and adjective so that the meaning of qualifiers is clear and unambiguous.
- Replace pronouns with specific names of entities.
- Make sure that every noun is defined in exactly one place in the requirements documents.

An alternative approach, advocated by the Quality Function Deployment (QFD) school (Akao 1990), is to realize quality requirements as special-purpose functional requirements, and to test quality requirements by testing how well their associated functional requirements have been satisfied. This approach works better for some quality requirements than it does for others. For example, real-time requirements can be expressed as additional conditions or constraints on when required functionality occurs. Other quality requirements, such as security, maintainability, and performance, may be satisfied by adopting existing designs and protocols that have been developed specifically to optimize a particular quality requirement.

reflect on which of the requested services and features are most essential. A loose prioritization scheme might separate requirements into three categories:

1. Requirements that absolutely must be met *(Essential)*
2. Requirements that are highly desirable but not necessary *(Desirable)*
3. Requirements that are possible but could be eliminated *(Optional)*

For example, a credit card billing system must be able to list current charges, sum them, and request payment by a certain date; these are *essential* requirements. But the billing system may also separate the charges by purchase type, to assist the purchaser in understanding buying patterns. Such purchase-type analysis is a *desirable* but probably nonessential requirement. Finally, the system may print the credits in black and the debits in red, which would be useful but is *optional*. Prioritizing requirements by category is helpful to all parties in understanding what is really needed. It is also useful when a software-development project is constrained by time or resources; if the system as defined will cost too much or take too long to develop, optional requirements can be dropped, and desirable requirements can be analyzed for elimination or postponement to later versions.

Prioritization can be especially helpful in resolving conflicts among quality requirements; often, two quality attributes will conflict, so that it is impossible to optimize for both. For example, suppose a system is required to be maintainable and deliver responses quickly. A design that emphasizes maintainability through separation of concerns and encapsulation may slow the performance. Likewise, tweaking a system to perform especially well on one platform affects its portability to other platforms, and secure systems necessarily control access and restrict availability to some users. Emphasizing security, reliability, robustness, usability, or performance can all affect maintainability, in that realizing any of these characteristics increases the design's complexity and decreases its coherence. Prioritizing quality requirements forces the customer to choose those software-quality factors about which the customer cares most—which helps us to provide a reasonable, if not optimal, solution to the customer's quality requirements.

We can also avoid trying to optimize multiple conflicting quality requirements by identifying and aiming to achieve *fit criteria*, which establish clear-cut acceptance tests for these requirements (see Sidebar 4.4). But what if we cannot satisfy the fit criteria? Then it may be time to reevaluate the stakeholders' views and to employ negotiation. However, negotiation is not easy; it requires skill, patience, and experience in finding mutually acceptable solutions. Fortunately, stakeholders rarely disagree about the underlying problem that the software system is addressing. More likely, conflicts will pertain to possible approaches to, or design constraints on, solving the problem (e.g., stakeholders may insist on using different database systems, different encryption algorithms, different user interfaces, or different programming languages). More seriously, stakeholders may disagree over priorities of requirements, or about the business policies to be incorporated into the system. For example, a university's colleges or departments may want different policies for evaluating students in their respective programs, whereas university administrators may prefer consolidation and uniformity. Resolution requires determining exactly why each stakeholder is adamant about a particular approach, policy, or priority ranking—for example, they may be concerned about cost, security, speed, or quality and then we need to work toward agreement on fundamental requirements. With effective negotiation, the stakeholders will come to understand and appreciate each other's fundamental needs, and will strive for a resolution that satisfies everyone; such resolutions are usually very different from any of the stakeholders' original views.

Two Kinds of Requirements Documents

In the end, the requirements are used by many different people and for different purposes. Requirements analysts and their clients use requirements to explain their understanding of how the system should behave. Designers treat requirements as constraints on what would be considered an acceptable solution. The test team derives from the requirements a suite of *acceptance tests*, which will be used to demonstrate to the customer that the system being delivered is indeed what was ordered. The maintenance team uses the requirements to help ensure that system enhancements (repairs and new features) do not interfere with the system's original intent. Sometimes a single document can serve all of these needs, leading to a common understanding among customers, requirements analysts, and developers. But often two documents are needed: a *requirements definition* that is aimed at a business audience, such as clients, customers, and users, and a *requirements specification* that is aimed at a technical audience, such as designers, testers, and project managers.

We illustrate the distinction using a small running example from Jackson and Zave (1995). Consider a software-controlled turnstile situated at the entrance to a zoo.

When the turnstile is fed a coin, it unlocks, allowing a visitor to push through the turnstile and enter the zoo. Once an unlocked turnstile has rotated enough to allow one entry, the turnstile locks again, to prevent another person from entering without payment.

A **requirements definition** is a complete listing of everything the customer wants to achieve. The document expresses requirements by describing the entities in the environment in which the proposed system will be installed, and by describing the desired constraints on, monitoring of, or transformations of those entities. The purpose of the proposed system is to realize these requirements (Zave and Jackson 1997). Thus, the requirements are written entirely in terms of the environment, describing how the environment will be affected by the proposed system. Our turnstile example has two requirements: (1) no one should enter the zoo without paying an entrance fee, and (2) for every entrance fee paid, the system should not prevent a corresponding entry.[1] The requirements definition is typically written jointly by the client and the requirements analyst, and it represents a contract describing what functionality the developer promises to deliver to the client.

The **requirements specification** restates the *requirements* as a *specification* of how the proposed system shall behave. The specification also is written entirely in terms of the environment, except that it refers solely to environmental entities that are accessible to the system via its interface. That is, the system boundary makes explicit those environmental entities that can be monitored or controlled by the system. This distinction is depicted in Figure 4.3, with requirements defined anywhere within the environment's domain, including, possibly, the system's interface, and with the specification restricted only to the intersection between the environment and system domains. To see the distinction, consider the requirement that no one should enter the zoo without paying an entrance fee. If the turnstile has a coin slot and is able to detect when a valid coin is inserted, then it can determine when an entrance fee has been paid. In contrast, the concept of an entry event may be outside the scope of the system. Thus, the requirement must be rewritten to realize entry events using only events and states that the turnstile *can* detect and control, such as whether the turnstile is unlocked and whether it detects a visitor pushing the turnstile:

> *When a visitor applies a certain amount of force on an unlocked turnstile, the turnstile will automatically rotate a one-half turn, ending in a locked position.*

In this way, the specification refines the original requirements definition.

The requirements specification is written by the requirements analyst and is used by the other software developers. The analyst must be especially careful that no information is lost or changed when refining the requirements into a specification. There must be a direct correspondence between each requirement in the definition document and those in the specification document.

---

[1] A more intuitive expression of this second requirement, that anyone who pays should be allowed to enter the zoo, is not implementable. There is no way for the system to prevent external factors from keeping the paid visitor from entering the zoo: another visitor may push through the unlocked turnstile before the paid visitor, the zoo may close before the paid visitor enters the turnstile, the paid visitor may decide to leave, and so on (Jackson and Zave 1995).

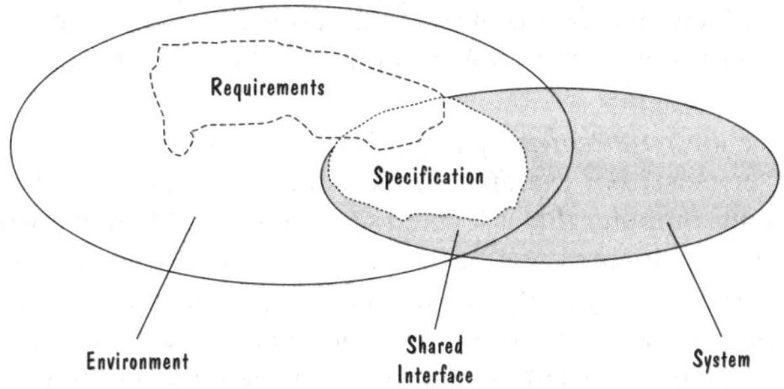

FIGURE 4.3 Requirements vs. Specification.

4.4 CHARACTERISTICS OF REQUIREMENTS

To ensure that the eventual product is successful, it is important that the requirements be of high quality; what is not specified usually is not built. We discuss later in this chapter how to validate and verify requirements. In the meantime, we list below the desirable characteristics for which we should check.

1. *Are the requirements correct?* Both we and the customer should review the documented requirements, to ensure that they conform to our understanding of the requirements.
2. *Are the requirements consistent?* That is, are there any conflicting requirements? For example, if one requirement states that a maximum of 10 users can be using the system at one time, and another requirement says that in a certain situation there may be 20 simultaneous users, the two requirements are said to be inconsistent. In general, two requirements are **inconsistent** if it is impossible to satisfy both simultaneously.
3. *Are the requirements unambiguous?* The requirements are ambiguous if multiple readers of the requirements can walk away with different but valid interpretations. Suppose a customer for a satellite control system requires the accuracy to be sufficient to support mission planning. The requirement does not tell us what mission planning requires for support. The customer and the developers may have very different ideas as to what level of accuracy is needed. Further discussion of the meaning of "mission planning" may result in a more precise requirement: "In identifying the position of the satellite, position error shall be less then 50 feet along orbit, less than 30 feet off orbit." Given this more detailed requirement, we can test for position error and know exactly whether or not we have met the requirement.
4. *Are the requirements complete?* The set of requirements is **complete** if it specifies required behavior and output for all possible inputs in all possible states under all possible constraints. Thus, a payroll system should describe what happens when an employee takes a leave without pay, gets a raise, or needs an advance. We say that the requirements are **externally complete** if all states, state changes, inputs,

products, and constraints are described by some requirement. A requirements description is **internally complete** if there are no undefined terms among the requirements.

5. *Are the requirements feasible?* That is, does a solution to the customer's needs even exist? For example, suppose the customer wants users to be able to access a main computer that is located several thousand miles away and have the response time for remote users be the same as for local users (whose workstations are connected directly to the main computer). Questions of feasibility often arise when the customer requires two or more quality requirements, such as a request for an inexpensive system that analyzes huge amounts of data and outputs the analysis results within seconds.
6. *Is every requirement relevant?* Sometimes a requirement restricts the developers unnecessarily, or includes functions that are not directly related to the customer's needs. For example, a general may decide that a tank's new software system should allow soldiers to send and receive electronic mail, even though the main purpose of the tank is to traverse uneven terrain. We should endeavor to keep this "feature explosion" under control, and to help keep stakeholders focused on their essential and desirable requirements.
7. *Are the requirements testable?* The requirements are **testable** if they suggest acceptance tests that would clearly demonstrate whether the eventual product meets the requirements. Consider how we might test the requirement that a system provide real-time response to queries. We do not know what "real-time response" is. However, if fit criteria were given, saying that the system shall respond to queries in not more than 2 seconds, then we know exactly how to test the system's reaction to queries.
8. *Are the requirements traceable?* Are the requirements organized and uniquely labeled for easy reference? Does every entry in the requirements definition have corresponding entries in the requirements specification, and vice versa?

We can think of these characteristics as the functional and quality requirements for a set of product requirements. These characteristics can help us to decide when we have collected enough information, and when we need to learn more about what a particular requirement means. As such, the degree to which we want to satisfy these characteristics will affect the type of information that we gather during requirements elicitation, and how comprehensive we want to be. It will also affect the specification languages we choose to express the requirements and the validation and verification checks that we eventually perform to assess the requirements.

4.5 MODELING NOTATIONS

One trait of an engineering discipline is that it has repeatable processes, such as the techniques presented in Chapter 2, for developing safe and successful products. A second trait is that there exist standard notations for modeling, documenting, and communicating decisions. Modeling can help us to understand the requirements thoroughly, by teasing out what questions we should be asking. Holes in our models reveal unknown or ambiguous behavior. Multiple, conflicting outputs to the same input reveal inconsistencies in the requirements. As the model develops, it becomes more and more obvious what we don't know and what the customer doesn't know. We cannot complete a model without understanding the subject of the model. Also, by restating the requirements in a completely different form from the customer's original requests, we force the customer to examine our models carefully in order to validate the model's accuracy.

If we look at the literature, we see that there is a seemingly infinite number of specification and design notations and methods, and that new notations are being introduced and marketed all the time. But if we step back and ignore the details, we see that many notations have a similar look and feel. Despite the number of individual notations, there are probably fewer than ten basic paradigms for expressing information about a problem's concepts, behavior, and properties.

This section focuses on seven basic notational paradigms that can be applied in several ways to steps in the development process. We begin our discussion of each by introducing the paradigm and the types of problems and descriptions for which it is particularly apt. Then we describe one or two concrete examples of notations from that paradigm. Once you are familiar with the paradigms, you can easily learn and use a new notation because you will understand how it relates to existing notations.

However, caution is advised. We need to be especially careful about the terminology we use when modeling requirements. Many of the requirements notations are based on successful design methods and notations, which means that most other references for the notations provide examples of designs rather than of requirements, and give advice about how to make design-oriented modeling decisions. Requirements decisions are made for different reasons, so the terminology is interpreted differently. For example, in requirements modeling we discuss *decomposition, abstraction*, and *separation of concerns*, all of which were originally design techniques for creating elegant modular designs. We decompose a requirements specification along separate concerns to simplify the resulting model and make it easier to read and to understand. In contrast, we decompose a design to improve the system's quality attributes (modularity, maintainability, performance, time to delivery, etc.); the requirements name and constrain those attributes, but decomposition plays no role in this aspect of specification. Thus, although we use the terms *decomposition* and *modularity* in both specification and design, the decomposition decisions we make at each stage are different because they have different goals.

Throughout this section, we illustrate notations by using them to model aspects of the turnstile problem introduced earlier (Jackson and Zave 1995) and a library problem. The library needs to track its texts and other materials, its loan records, and information about its patrons. Popular items are placed on *reserve*, meaning that their loan periods are shorter than those of other books and materials, and that the penalty for returning them late is higher than the late penalty for returning unreserved items.

Entity-Relationship Diagrams

Early in the requirements phase, it is convenient to build a conceptual model of the problem that identifies what objects or entities are involved, what they look like (by defining their attributes), and how they relate to one another. Such a model designates names for the basic elements of the problem. These elements are then reused in other descriptions of the requirements (possibly written in other notations) that specify how the objects, their attributes, and their relationships would change in the course of the proposed system's execution. Thus, the conceptual model helps to tie together multiple views and descriptions of the requirements.

The **entity-relationship diagram (ER diagram)** (Chen 1976) is a popular graphical notational paradigm for representing conceptual models. As we will see in Chapter 6, it forms the basis of most object-oriented requirements and design notations, where it is used to model the relationships among objects in a problem description or to model the structure of a software application. This notation paradigm is also popular for describing database schema (i.e., describing the logical structure of data stored in a database).

ER diagrams have three core constructs—entities, attributes, and relations—that are combined to specify a problem's elements and their interrelationships. Figure 4.4 is an ER diagram of the turnstile. An **entity**, depicted as a rectangle, represents a collection (sometimes called a class) of real-world objects that have common properties and behaviors. For example, the world contains many `Coins`, but for the purpose of modeling the turnstile problem, we treat all `Coins` as being equivalent to one another in all aspects (such as size, shape, and weight) except perhaps for their monetary `value`. A **relationship** is depicted as an edge between two entities, with a diamond in the middle of the edge specifying the type of relationship. An **attribute** is an annotation on an entity that describes data or properties associated with the entity. For example, in the turnstile problem, we are most interested in the `Coins` that are inserted into the turnstile's `CoinSlot` (a relationship), and how their monetary `values` compare to the `price of admission` into the zoo (comparison of attribute values). Variant ER notations introduce additional constructs, such as attributes on relationships, one-to-many relationships, many-to-many relationships, special relationships like inheritance, and class-based in addition to individual-entity-based attributes. For example, our turnstile model shows the cardinality (sometimes called the "arity") of the relationships, asserting that the turnstile is to admit multiple `Visitors`. More sophisticated notations have the concept of a **mutable entity**, whose membership or whose relations to members of other entities may change over time. For example, in an ER diagram depicting a family, family members and their interrelations change as they get married, have children, and die. By convention, the entities and relationships are laid out so that relationships are read from left to right, or from top to bottom.

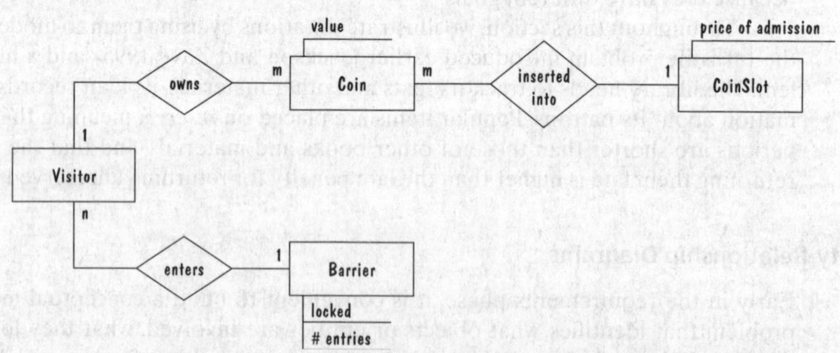

FIGURE 4.4 Entity-relationship diagram of turnstile problem.

ER diagrams are popular because they provide an overview of the problem to be addressed (i.e., they depict all of the parties involved), and because this view is relatively stable when changes are made to the problem's requirements. A change in requirements is more likely to be a change in how one or more entities behave than to be a change in the set of participating entities. For these two reasons, an ER diagram is likely to be used to model a problem early in the requirements process.

The simplicity of ER notations is deceptive; in fact, it is quite difficult to use ER modeling notations well in practice. It is not always obvious at what level of detail to model a particular problem, even though there are only three major language constructs. For example, should the barrier and coin slot be modeled as entities, or should they be represented by a more abstract turnstile entity? Also, it can be difficult to decide what data are entities and what data are attributes. For example, should the lock be an entity? There are arguments for and against each of these choices. The primary criteria for making decisions are whether a choice results in a clearer description, and whether a choice unnecessarily constrains design decisions.

Example: UML Class Diagrams

An ER notation is often used by more complex approaches. For example, the **Unified Modeling Language (UML)** (OMG 2003) is a collection of notations used to document software specifications and designs. We will use UML extensively in Chapter 6 to describe object-oriented specifications and designs. Because UML was originally conceived for object-oriented systems, it represents systems in terms of objects and methods. Objects are akin to entities; they are organized in classes that have an inheritance hierarchy. Each object provides methods that perform actions on the object's variables. As objects execute, they send messages to invoke each other's methods, acknowledge actions, and transmit data.

The flagship model in any UML specification is the **class diagram**, a sophisticated ER diagram relating the classes (entities) in the specification. Although most UML texts treat class diagrams primarily as a design notation, it is possible and convenient to use UML class diagrams as a conceptual modeling notation, in which classes represent real-world entities in the problem to be modeled. It may be that a class in the conceptual model, such as a Customer class, corresponds to a program class in the implementation, such as a CustomerRecord, but this need not always be the case. It is the software designer's task to take a class-diagram specification and construct a suitable design model of the implementation's class structure.

In general, the kinds of real-world entities that we would want to represent in a class diagram include actors (e.g., patrons, operators, personnel); complex data to be stored, analyzed, transformed, or displayed; or records of transient events (e.g., business transactions, phone conversations). The entities in our library problem include people, like the patrons and librarians; the items in the library's inventory, like books and periodicals; and loan transactions.

Figure 4.5 depicts a simple UML class diagram for such a library. Each box is a **class** that represents a collection of similarly typed entities; for example, a single class represents all of the library's books. A class has a **name**; a set of **attributes**, which are simple data variables whose values can vary over time and among different entities of

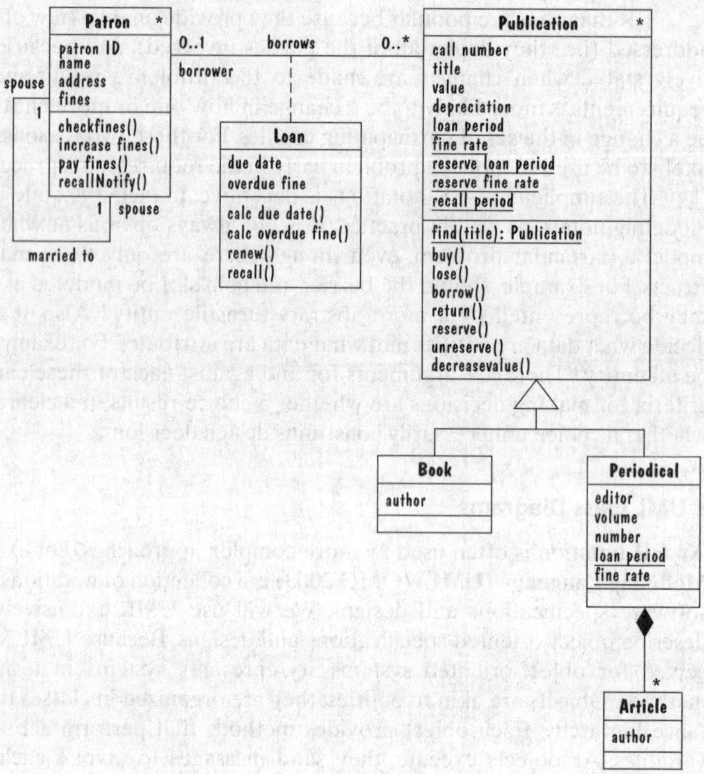

FIGURE 4.5 UML class model of the library problem.

the class; and a set of **operations** on the class's attributes. By "simple data variable," we mean a variable whose values are too simple for the variable to be a class by itself. Thus, we model a `Patron's` address as an attribute, likely as one or more string values, whereas we would model a `Patron`'s credit card information, credit institution, credit card number, expiration date, or billing address as a separate class (not shown). Note that many attributes we might expect in the library class diagram are missing (e.g., records and films) or are imprecisely defined (e.g., periodical, which doesn't distinguish between newspapers and magazines), and operations are omitted (e.g., dealing with book repair or loss). This imprecision is typical in early conceptual diagrams. The idea is to provide enough attributes and operations, and in sufficient detail, that anyone who reads the specification can grasp what the class represents and what its responsibilities are.

UML also allows the specifier to designate attributes and operations as being associated with the class rather than with instances of the class. A **class-scope attribute**, represented as an underlined attribute, is a data value that is shared by all instances of the class. In the library class diagram, the attributes `reserve loan period` and `reserve fine rate` are values that apply to all publications on reserve. Thus in this model, the librarian can set and modify the loan duration for classes of items (e.g., books, periodicals, items on reserve) but not for individual items. Similarly, a **class-scope operation**, written as an underlined operation, is an operation performed by the abstract class, rather than by class instances, on a new instance or on the whole collection of instances; `create()`, `search()`, and `delete()` are common class-scope operations.

A line between two classes, called an **association**, indicates a relationship between the classes' entities. An association may represent interactions or events that involve objects in the associated classes, such as when a `Patron` borrows a `Publication`. Alternatively, an association might relate classes in which one class is a property or element of the other class, such as the relationship between a `Patron` and his `Credit Card`. Sometimes these latter types of associations are **aggregate associations**, or "*has-a*" relationships, as in our example. An aggregate association is drawn as an association with a white diamond on one end, where the class at the diamond end is the aggregate and it includes or owns instances of the class(es) at the other end(s) of the association. **Composition** association is a special type of aggregation, in which instances of the compound class are physically constructed from instances of the component classes (e.g., a bike consists of wheels, gears, pedals, a handlebar); it is represented as an aggregation with a black diamond. In our library model, each `Periodical`, such as a newspaper or magazine, is composed of `Articles`.

An association with a triangle on one end represents a **generalization** association, also called a *sub-type* relation or an "*is-a*" relation, where the class at the triangle end of the association is the parent class of the classes at the other ends of the association, called **subclasses**. A subclass inherits all of the parent class's attributes, operations, and associations. Thus, we do not need to specify explicitly that `Patrons` may borrow `Books`, because this association is inherited from the association between `Patron` and `Publication`. A subclass extends its inherited behavior with additional attributes, operations, and associations. In fact, a good clue as to whether we want to model an entity as a new subclass, as opposed to as an instance of an existing class, is whether we really need new attributes, operations, or associations to model the class variant. In many cases, we can model variants as class instances that have different attribute values. In our library problem, we represent whether an item is on reserve or on loan using `Publication` attributes[2] rather than by creating `Reserved` and `OnLoan` subclasses.

Associations can have labels, usually verbs, that describe the relationship between associated entities. An end of an association can also be labeled, to describe the role that entity plays in the association. Such **role names** are useful for specifying the context of an entity with respect to a particular association. In the library example, we might keep track of which patrons are married, so that we can warn someone whose spouse has overdue books. Association ends can also be annotated with **multiplicities**, which specify constraints on the number of entities and the number of links between associated entities. Multiplicities can be expressed as specific numbers, ranges of numbers, or unlimited numbers (designated "*"). A multiplicity on one end of an association indicates how

---

[2]In later examples, we model an item's loan state and reserve state as states in a state-machine model (Figure 4.9), and this information is included in the library's detailed class model (Figure 4.18).

many instances of that class can be linked to one instance of the associated class. Thus at any point in time, a Patron may borrow zero or more Publications, but an individual Publication can be borrowed by at most one Patron.

The Loan class in the library model is an **association class**, which relates attributes and operations to an association. Association classes are used to collect information that cannot be attributed solely to one class or another. For example, the Loan attributes are not properties of the borrower or of the item borrowed, but rather of the loan transaction or contract. An association class has exactly one instantiation per link in the association, so our modeling Loan as an association class is correct only if we want to model snapshots of the library inventory (i.e., model only current loans). If we wanted instead to maintain a history of all loan transactions, then (because a patron might borrow an item multiple times), we would model Loan as a full-fledged class.

Event Traces

Although ER diagrams are helpful in providing an overall view of the problem being modeled, the view is mostly structural, showing which entities are related; the diagram says nothing about how the entities are to behave. We need other notation paradigms for describing a system's behavioral requirements.

An **event trace** is a graphical description of a sequence of events that are exchanged between real-world entities. Each vertical line represents the timeline for a distinct entity, whose name appears at the top of the line. Each horizontal line represents an event or interaction between the two entities bounding the line, usually conceived as a message passed from one entity to another. Time progresses from the top to the bottom of the trace, so if one event appears above another event, then the upper event occurs before the lower event. Each graph depicts a single **trace**, representing only one of several possible behaviors. Figure 4.6 shows two traces for the turnstile problem: the trace on the left represents typical behavior, whereas the trace on the right shows exceptional behavior of what happens when a Visitor tries to sneak into the zoo by inserting a valueless token (a slug) into the coin slot.

Event traces are popular among both developers and customers because traces have a semantics that is relatively precise, with the exception of timing issues, yet is simple and easy to understand. Much of the simplicity comes from decomposing requirements descriptions into scenarios, and considering (modeling, reading, understanding) each

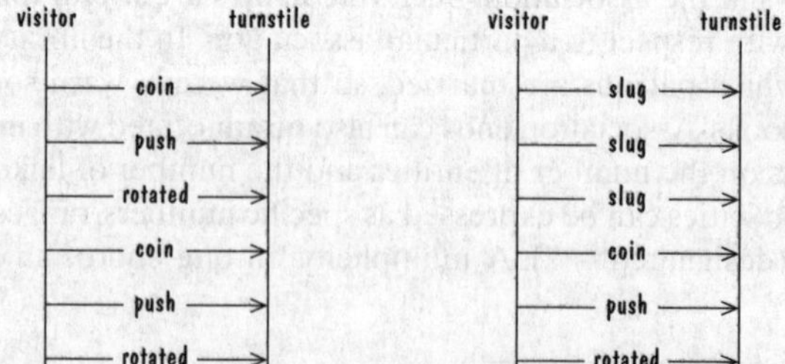

FIGURE 4.6 Event traces in the turnstile problem.

scenario separately as a distinct trace. But these very properties, make event traces inefficient for documenting behavior. We would not want to use traces to provide a complete description of required behavior, because the number of scenarios we would have to draw can quickly become unwieldy. Instead, traces are best used at the start of a project, to come to consensus on key requirements and to help developers identify important entities in the problem being modeled.

Example: Message Sequence Chart

Message Sequence Charts (ITU 1996) are an enhanced event-trace notation, with facilities for creating and destroying entities, specifying actions and timers, and composing traces. Figure 4.7 displays an example Message Sequence Chart (MSC) for a loan transaction in our library problem. Each vertical line represents a participating **entity**, and a **message** is depicted as an arrow from the sending entity to the receiving entity; the arrow's label specifies the message name and data parameters, if any. A message arrow may slope downwards (e.g., message `recall notice`) to reflect the passage of time between when the message is sent and when it is received. Entities may come and go during the course of a trace; a dashed arrow, optionally annotated with data parameters, represents a *create* event that spawns a new entity, and a cross at the bottom of an entity line represents the end of that entity's execution. In contrast, a solid rectangle at the end of the line represents the end of an entity's specification without meaning the end of its execution. **Actions**, such as invoked operations or changes to variable values, are specified as labeled rectangles positioned on an entity's execution line, located at

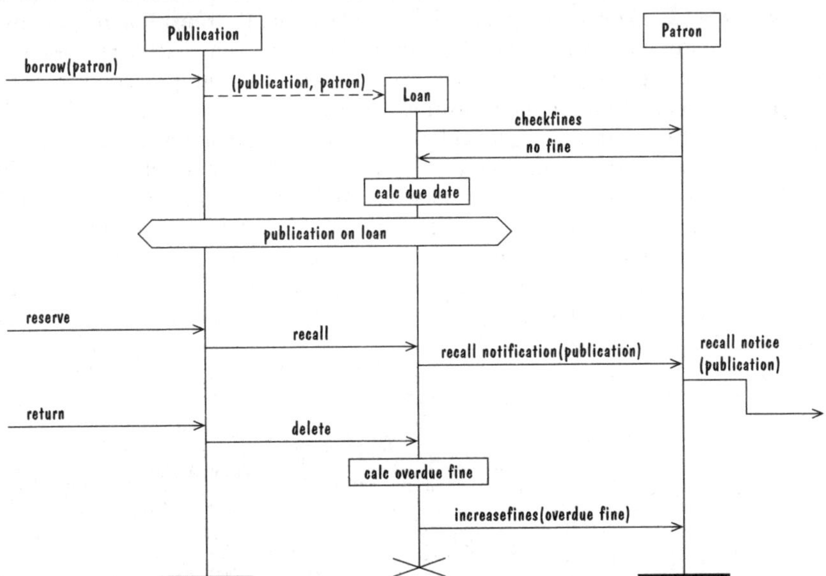

FIGURE 4.7 Message Sequence Chart for library loan transaction.

the point in the trace where the action occurs. Thus, in our MSC model of a library loan, loan requests are sent to the `Publication` to be borrowed, and the `Publication` entity is responsible for creating a `Loan` entity that manages loan-specific data, such as the `due date`. Reserving an item that is out on loan results in a `recall` of that item. Returning the borrowed item terminates the loan, but not before calculating the `overdue fine`, if any, for returning the item after the loan's `due date`.

There are facilities for composing and refining Message Sequence Charts. For example, important states in an entity's evolution can be specified as **conditions**, represented as labeled hexagons. We can then specify a small collection of subtraces between conditions, and derive a variety of traces by composing the charts at points where the entities' states are the same. For example there are multiple scenarios between state `publication on loan` and the end of the loan transition: the patron renews the loan once, the patron renews the loan twice, the patron returns the publication, the patron reports the publication as being lost. Each of these subscenarios could be appended to a prefix trace of a patron successfully borrowing the publication. Such composition and refinement features help to reduce the number of MSCs one would need to write to specify a problem completely. However, these features do not completely address the trace-explosion problem, so Message Sequences Charts are usually used only to describe key scenarios rather than to specify entire problems.

State Machines

State-machine notations are used to represent collections of event traces in a single model. A **state machine** is a graphical description of all dialog between the system and its environment. Each node, called a **state**, represents a stable set of conditions that exists between event occurrences. Each edge, called a **transition**, represents a change in behavior or condition due to the occurrence of an event; each transition is labeled with the triggering event, and possibly with an output event, preceded by the symbol "/", that is generated when the transition occurs.

State machines are useful both for specifying dynamic behavior and for describing how behavior should change in response to the history of events that have already occurred. That is, they are particularly suited for modeling how the system's responses to the same input *change* over the course of the system's execution. For each state, the set of transitions emanating from that state designates both the set of events that can trigger a response and the corresponding responses to those events. Thus, when our turnstile (shown in Figure 4.8) is in the `unlocked` state, its behavior is different from

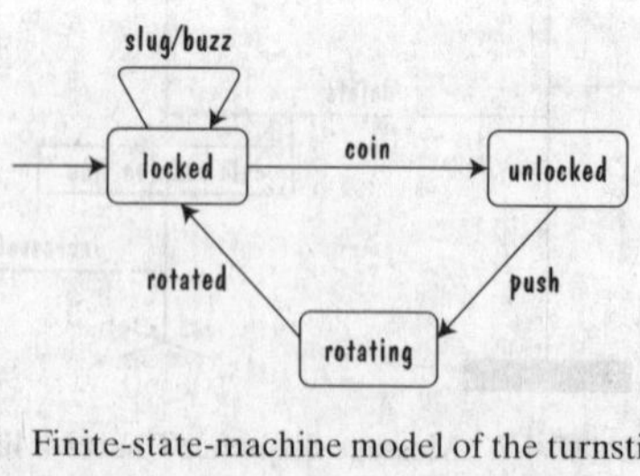

FIGURE 4.8 Finite-state-machine model of the turnstile problem.

when it is in state `locked`; in particular, it responds to different input events. If an unanticipated event occurs (e.g., if the user tries to `push` through the turnstile when the machine is in state `locked`), the event will be ignored and discarded. We could have specified this latter behavior explicitly as a transition from state `locked` to state `locked`, triggered by event `push`; however, the inclusion of such "no-effect" transitions can clutter the model. Thus, it is best to restrict the use of self-looping transitions to those that have an observable effect, such as an output event.

A path through the state machine, starting from the machine's initial state and following transitions from state to state, represents a trace of observable events in the environment. If the state machine is **deterministic**, meaning that for every state and event there is a unique response, then a path through the machine represents *the* event trace that will occur, given the sequence of input events that trigger the path's transitions. Example traces of our turnstile specification include

```
coin, push, rotated, coin, push, rotated,....
slug, slug, slug, coin, push, rotated,...
```

which correspond to the event traces in Figure 4.6.

You may have encountered state machines in some of your other computing courses. In theory-of-computing courses, finite-state machines are used as automata that recognize strings in regular languages. In some sense, state-machine specifications serve a similar purpose; they specify the sequences of input and output events that the proposed system is expected to realize. Thus, we view a state-machine specification as a compact representation of a set of desired, externally observable, event traces, just as a finite state automaton is a compact representation of the set of strings that the automaton recognizes.

Example: UML Statechart Diagrams

A **UML statechart diagram** depicts the dynamic behavior of the objects in a UML class. A UML class diagram gives a static, big-picture view of a problem, in terms of the entities involved and their relationships; it says nothing about how the entities behave, or how their behaviors change in response to input events. A statechart diagram shows how a class's instances should change state and how their attributes should change value as the objects interact with each other. Statechart diagrams are a nice counterpart to Message Sequence Charts (MSC). An MSC shows the events that pass between entities without saying much about each entity's behavior, whereas a statechart diagram shows how a single entity reacts to input events and generates output events.

A UML model is a collection of concurrently executing statecharts—one per instantiated object—that communicate with each other via message passing (OMG 2003). Every class in a UML class diagram has an associated statechart diagram that specifies the dynamic behavior of the objects of that class. Figure 4.9 shows the UML statechart diagram for the `Publication` class from our Library class model.

UML statechart diagrams have a rich syntax, much of it borrowed from Harel's original conception of statecharts (Harel 1987), including state hierarchy, concurrency, and intermachine communication. State hierarchy is used to unclutter diagrams by collecting into **superstates** those states with common transitions. We can think of a superstate

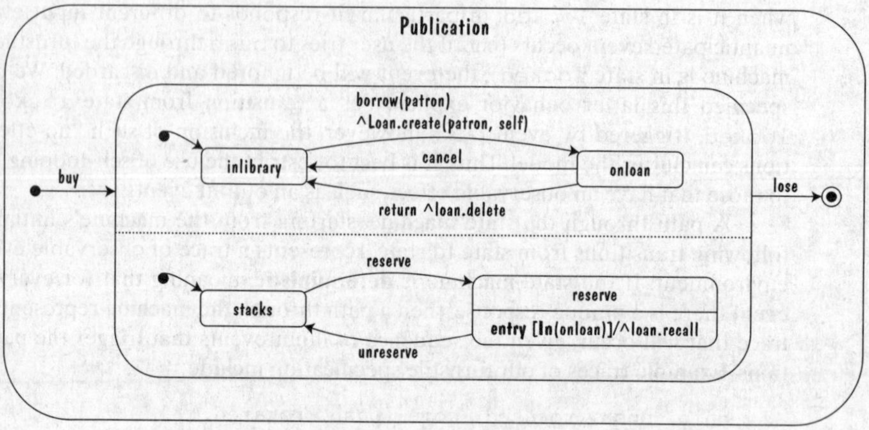

FIGURE 4.9 UML statechart diagram for the `Publication` class.

as a submachine, with its own set of states and transitions. A transition whose destination state is a superstate acts as a transition to the superstate's default initial state, designated by an arrow from the superstate's internal black circle. A transition whose source state is a superstate acts as a set of transitions, one from each of the superstate's internal states. For example, in the `Publication` state diagram, the transition triggered by event `lose` can be enabled from any of the superstate's internal states; this transition ends in a final state and designates the end of the object's life.

A superstate can actually comprise multiple concurrent submachines, separated by dashed lines. The UML statechart for `Publication` includes two submachines: one that indicates whether or not the publication is out on loan, and another that indicates whether or not the publication is on reserve. The submachines are said to operate **concurrently**, in that a `Publication` instance could at any time receive and respond to events of interest to either or both submachines. In general, concurrent submachines are used to model separate, unrelated subbehaviors, making it easier to understand and consider each subbehavior. An equivalent statechart for `Publication` in Figure 4.10 that does not make use of state hierarchy or concurrency is comparatively messy and repetitive. Note that this messy statechart has a state for each combination of states from Figure 4.9 (`stacks = Publication` is in library and not on reserve, `onloan = Publication` is on loan and not on reserve, etc.).[3]

---

[3]The messy statechart also has a `recall` state that covers the case where a publication that is being put on reserve is on loan and needs to be recalled; this behavior cannot be modeled as a transition from `onloan` to `reserveloan`, because state `reserveloan` has a transition `cancel` (used to disallow a loan request if the `Patron` has outstanding fines) that would be inappropriate in this situation. This special case is modeled in Figure 4.9 by testing on **`entry`** (keyword **`entry`** is explained below) to state `reserve` whether the concurrent submachine is **`In`** state `onloan` and issuing a `recall` event if it is.

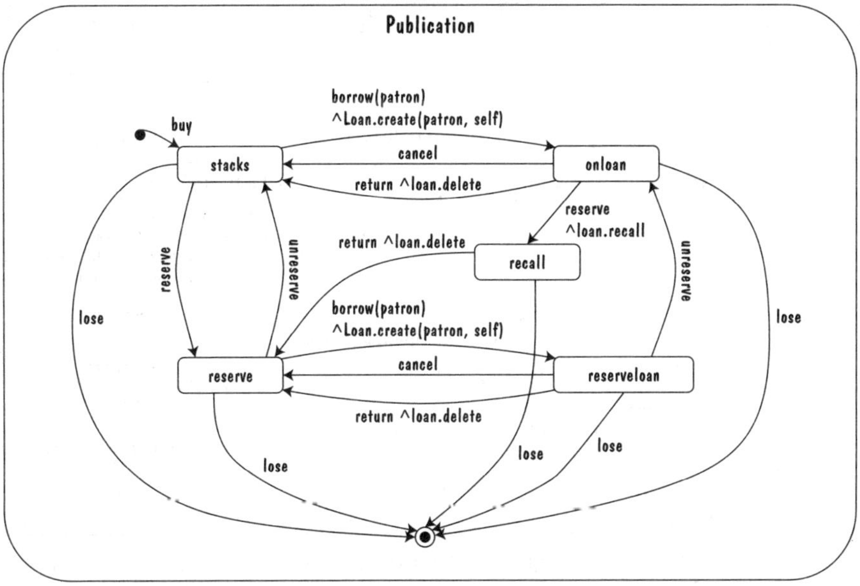

FIGURE 4.10 Messy UML statechart diagram for `Publication` class.

State transitions are labeled with their enabling events and conditions and with their side effects. Transition labels have syntax

event(args) [condition] /action ^Object.event(args)**

where the triggering **event** is a message that may carry parameters. The enabling **condition**, delimited by square brackets, is a predicate on the object's attribute values. If the transition is taken, its **actions**, each prefaced with a slash (/), specify assignments made to the object's attributes; the asterisk "*" indicates that a transition may have arbitrarily many actions. If the transition is taken, it may generate arbitrarily many **output events**, `/^Object.event`, each prefaced with a caret (^); an output event may carry parameters and is either designated for a target `Object` or is broadcast to all objects. For example, in the messy `Publication` statechart (Figure 4.10), the transition to state `recall` is enabled if the publication is in state `onloan` when a request to put the item on `reserve` is received. When the transition is taken, it sends an event to the `Loan` object, which in turn will notify the borrower that the item must be returned to the library sooner than the loan's due date. Each of the transition-label elements is optional. For example, a transition need not be enabled by an input event; it could be enabled only by a condition or by nothing, in which case the transition is always enabled.

The UML statechart diagram for the `Loan` association class in Figure 4.11 illustrates how states can be annotated with local variables (e.g., variable `num renews`), actions, and activities. Variables that are local to a state are declared and initialized in

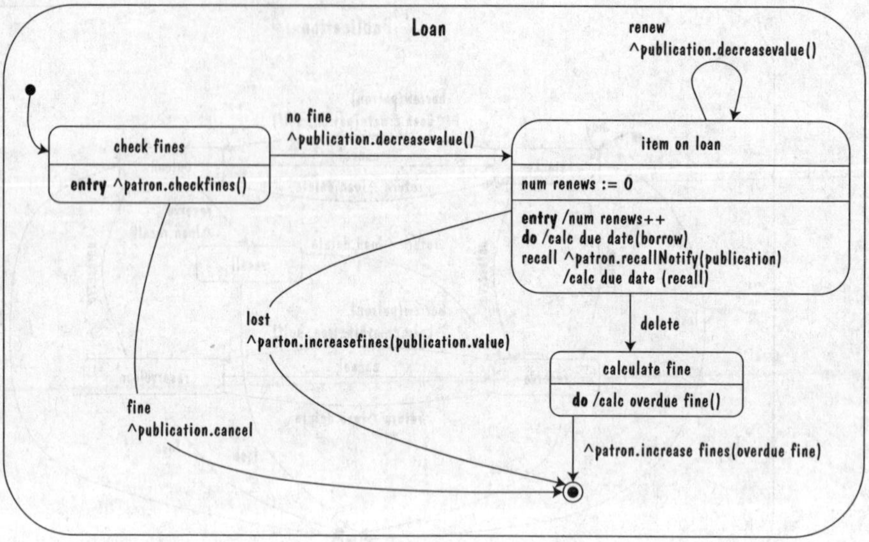

FIGURE 4.11 UML statechart diagram for `Loan` class.

the center section of the state. The state's lower section lists actions and activities on the state's local variables as well as on the object's attributes. The distinction between actions and activities is subtle: an **action** is a computation that takes relatively no time to complete and that is uninterruptible, such as assigning an expression to a variable or sending a message. An action can be triggered by a transition entering or exiting the state, in which case it is designated by keyword *entry* or *exit* followed by arbitrarily many actions and generated events; or it can be triggered by the occurrence of an event, in which case it is designated by the event name followed by arbitrarily many actions and generated events. In our `Loan` statechart, variable `num renews` is incremented every time state `item on loan` is entered, that is, every time the loan is renewed; and a `recallNotify` event is sent to the `Patron` whenever a `recall` event is received in that state. In contrast to actions, an **activity** is a more complex computation that executes over a period of time and that may be interruptible, such as executing an operation. Activities are initiated on entry to the state. When a transition, including a looping transition like the one triggered by `renew`, executes, the order in which actions are applied is as follows: first, the exit actions of the transition's source state are applied, followed by the transition's own actions, followed by the entry actions and activities of the new state.

The semantics of UML diagrams, and how the different diagrams fit together, are intentionally undefined, so that specifiers can ascribe semantics that best fit their problem. However, most practitioners view UML statecharts as communicating finite-state machines with first-in, first-out (FIFO) communication channels. Each object's state machine has an input queue that holds the messages sent to the object from other objects in the model or from the model's environment. Messages are stored in the input queue in the order in which they are received. In each execution step, the state machine reads the message at the head of its input queue, removing the message from the queue. The message either triggers a transition in the statechart or it does not, in which case the message is discarded; the step *runs to completion,* meaning that the machine continues to execute enabled transitions, including transitions that wait for operations to complete, until no more transitions can execute without new input from the input queue. Thus, the machine reacts to only one message at a time.

The hardest part of constructing a state-machine model is deciding how to decompose an object's behavior into states. Some ways of thinking about states include

- Equivalence classes of possible future behavior, as defined by sequences of input events accepted by the machine: for example, every iteration of event sequence `coin,push,rotated` leaves the turnstile in a `locked` position waiting for the next visitor
- Periods of time between consecutive events, such as the time between the start and the end of an operation
- Named control points in an object's evolution, during which the object is performing some computation (e.g., state `calculate fine`) or waiting for some input event (e.g., state `item on loan`)
- Partitions of an object's behavior: for example, a book is out on loan or is in the library stacks; an item is on reserve, meaning that it can be borrowed for only short periods, or it is not on reserve

Some object properties could be modeled either as an attribute (defined in the class diagram) or as a state (defined in the object's statechart diagram), and it is not obvious which representation is best. Certainly, if the set of possible property values is large (e.g., a `Patron's` library fines), then it is best to model the property as an attribute. Alternatively, if the events to which the object is ready to react depend on a property (e.g., whether a book is out on loan), then it is best to model the property as a state. Otherwise, choose the representation that results in the simplest model that is easiest to understand.

Example: Petri Nets

UML statechart diagrams nicely modularize a problem's dynamic behavior into the behaviors of individual class objects, with the effect that it may be easier to consider each class's behavior separately than it is to specify the whole problem in one diagram. This modularization makes it harder, though, to see how objects interact with each other. Looking at an individual statechart diagram, we can see when an object sends a message to another object. However, we have to examine the two objects' diagrams simultaneously to see that a message sent by one object can be received by the other. In fact, to be completely sure, we would have to search the possible executions (event traces) of the two machines, to confirm that whenever one object sends a message to the other, the target object is ready to receive and react to the message.

Petri nets (Peterson 1977) are a form of state-transition notation that is used to model concurrent activities and their interactions. Figure 4.12 shows a basic Petri net specifying the behavior of a book loan. The circles in the net are **places** that represent

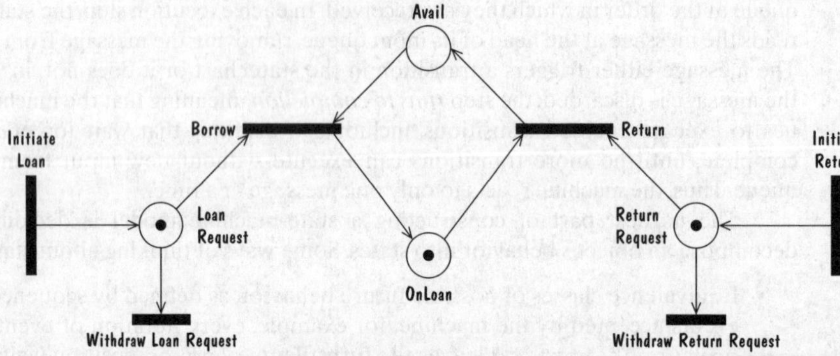

FIGURE 4.12 Petri net of book loan.

activities or conditions, and the bars represent **transitions**. Directed arrows, called **arcs**, connect a transition with its *input places* and its *output places*. The places are populated with **tokens**, which act as enabling conditions for the transitions. When a transition *fires*, it removes tokens from each of its input places and inserts tokens into each of its output places. Each arc can be assigned a **weight** that specifies how many tokens are removed from the arc's input place, or inserted into the arc's output place, when the transition fires. A transition is *enabled* if each of its input places contains enough tokens to contribute its arc's weight's worth of tokens, should the enabled transition actually fire. Thus, in Figure 4.12, transitions `Return`, `Withdraw Return Request`, and `Withdraw Loan Request` are all enabled; firing transition `Return` removes a token from each of the places `ReturnRequest` and `OnLoan`, and inserts a token into `Avail`. The net's **marking**, which is the distribution of tokens among places, changes as transitions fire. In each execution step, the marking determines the set of enabled transitions; one enabled transition is *nondeterministically* selected to fire; the firing of this transition produces a new marking, which may enable a different set of transitions. We can model concurrent behavior by combining into a single net the activities, transitions, and tokens for several executing entities. Concurrent entities are synchronized whenever their activities, or places, act as input places to the same transition. This synchronization ensures that all of the pre-transition activities occur before the transition fires, but does not constrain the order in which these activities occur.

These features of concurrency and synchronization are especially useful for modeling events whose order of occurrence is not important. Consider the emergency room in a hospital. Before a patient can be treated, several events must occur. The triage staff must attempt to find out the name and address of the patient and to determine the patient's blood type. Someone must see if the patient is breathing, and also examine the patient for injuries. The events occur in no particular order, but all must occur before a team of doctors begins a more thorough examination. Once the treatment begins (i.e., once the transition is made from a preliminary examination to a thorough one), the doctors start new activities. The orthopedic doctors check for broken bones, while the hematologist runs blood tests and the surgeon puts stitches in a bleeding wound. The doctors' activities are independent of one another, but none can occur until the transition from the preliminary examination takes place. A state-machine model of the emergency room might specify only a single order of events, thereby excluding several acceptable behaviors, or it might specify all possible sequences of events, resulting in an overly complex model for a relatively simple problem. A Petri net model of the same emergency room nicely avoids both of these problems.

Basic Petri nets are fine for modeling how control flows through events or among concurrent entities. But if we want to model control that depends on the value of data (e.g., borrowing a particular book from a collection of books), then we need to use a high-level Petri net notation. A number of extensions to basic Petri nets have been proposed to improve the notation's expressibility, including inhibitor arcs, which enable a transition only if the input place is empty of tokens; priority among transitions; timing constraints; and structured tokens, which have values.

To model our library problem, which tracks information and events for multiple patrons and publications, we need a Petri net notation that supports structured tokens and transition actions (Ghezzi et al. 1991). A transition action constrains which tokens in the input places can enable the transition and specifies the values of the output tokens. Figure 4.13 is a high-level Petri net specification for the library problem. Each place stores tokens of a different data type. `Avail` stores a token for every library `item` that is not currently out on loan. A token in `Fines` is an n-tuple (i.e., an ordered set of n elements, sometimes called a tuple for short) that maps a `patron` to the value

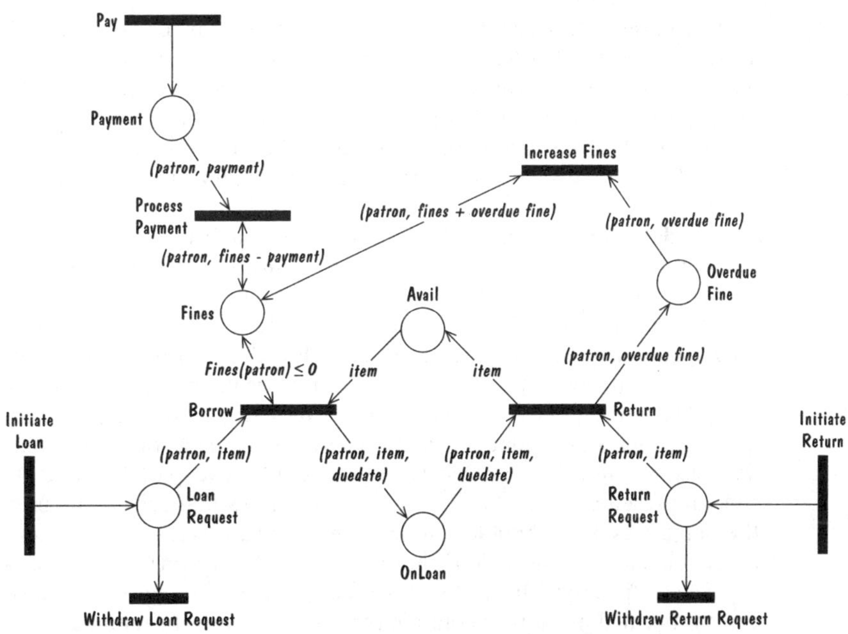

FIGURE 4.13 Petri net of the library problem.

of his or her total outstanding library fines. A token in `OnLoan` is another type of tuple that maps a `patron` and a library `item` to a `due date`. A few of the transition predicates and actions are shown in Figure 4.13, such as the action on `Process Payment`, where the inputs are a `payment` and the patron's current `fines`, and the output is a new `Fines` tuple. The predicates not shown assert that if the token elements in a transition's input or output tokens have the same name, they must have the same value. So in transition `Borrow`, the *`patron`* making the `Loan Request` must match the *`patron`* with no outstanding `Fines` and match the *`patron`* who appears in the generated `OnLoan` tuple; at the same time, the *`item`* being borrowed must match an *`item`* in `Avail`. Otherwise, those tuples do not enable the transition. The net starts with an initial marking of `item` tuples in `Avail` and `(patron, 0)` tuples in `Fines`. As library users trigger input transitions `Pay`, `Initiate Loan`, and `Initiate Return`, new tokens are introduced to the system, which enable the library transitions, which in turn fire and update the `Fines` tokens and the `Avail` and `OnLoan` tokens, and so on.

Data-Flow Diagrams

The notation paradigms discussed so far promote decomposing a problem by entity (ER diagram); by scenario (event trace); and by control state (i.e., equivalence classes of scenarios) (state machines). However, early requirements tend to be expressed as

- Tasks to be completed
- Functions to be computed
- Data to be analyzed, transformed, or recorded

Such requirements, when decomposed by entity, scenario, or state, devolve into collections of lower-level behaviors that are distributed among multiple entities and that must be coordinated. This modular structure makes it harder to see a model's high-level functionality. In our library example, none of the above modeling notations is effective in showing, in a single model, all of the steps, and their variants, that a patron must take to borrow a book. For this reason, notations that promote decomposition by functionality have always been popular.

A **data-flow diagram** (DFD) models functionality and the flow of data from one function to another. A bubble represents a **process**, or function, that transforms data. An arrow represents **data flow**, where an arrow into a bubble represents an input to the bubble's function, and an arrow out of a bubble represents one of the function's outputs. Figure 4.14 shows a high-level data-flow diagram for our library problem. The problem is broken down into steps, with the results of early steps flowing into later steps. Data that persist beyond their use in a single computation (e.g., information about patrons' outstanding fines) can be saved in a **data store**—a formal repository or database of information—that is represented by two parallel bars. Data sources or sinks, represented by rectangles, are **actors**: entities that provide input data or receive the output results. A bubble can be a high-level abstraction of another data-flow diagram that shows in more detail how the abstract function is computed. A lowest-level bubble is a function whose effects, such as pre-conditions, post-conditions, exceptions, can be specified in another notation (e.g., text, mathematical functions, event traces) in a separately linked document.

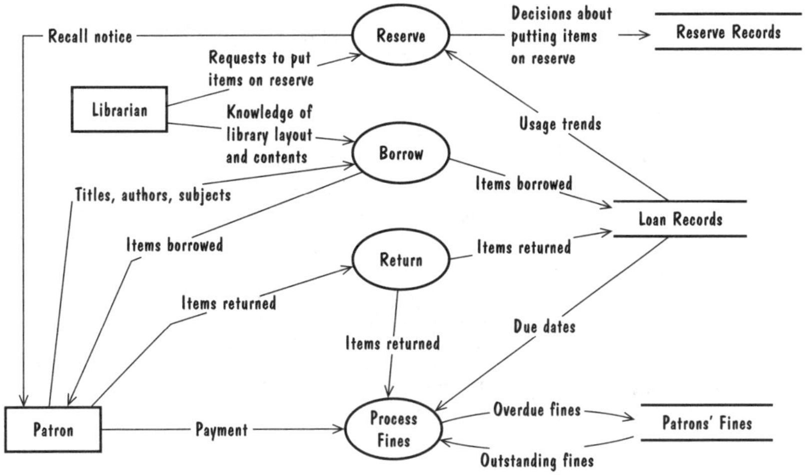

FIGURE 4.14 Data-flow diagram of the library problem.

One of the strengths of data-flow diagrams is that they provide an intuitive model of a proposed system's high-level functionality and of the data dependencies among the various processes. Domain experts find them easy to read and understand. However, a data-flow diagram can be aggravatingly ambiguous to a software developer who is less familiar with the problem being modeled. In particular, there are multiple ways of interpreting a DFD process that has multiple input flows (e.g., process `Borrow`): are all inputs needed to compute the function, is only one of the inputs needed, or is some subset of the inputs needed? Similarly, there are multiple ways of interpreting a DFD process that has multiple output flows: are all outputs generated every time the process executes, is only one of the outputs generated, or is some subset generated? It is also not obvious that two data flows with the same annotation represent the same values: are the `Items Returned` that flow from `Return` to `Loan Records` the same as the `Items Returned` that flow from `Return` to `Process Fines`? For these reasons, DFDs are best used by users who are familiar with the application domain being modeled, and as early models of a problem, when details are less important.

Example: Use Cases

A UML **use-case diagram** (OMG 2003) is similar to a top-level data-flow diagram that depicts observable, user-initiated functionality in terms of interactions between the system and its environment. A large box represents the system boundary. Stick figures outside the box portray actors, both humans and systems, and each oval inside the box is a use case that represents some major required functionality and its variants. A line between an actor and a use case indicates that the actor participates in the use case. Use cases are not meant to model all the tasks that the system should provide. Rather, they are used to specify user views of essential system behavior. As such, they model only

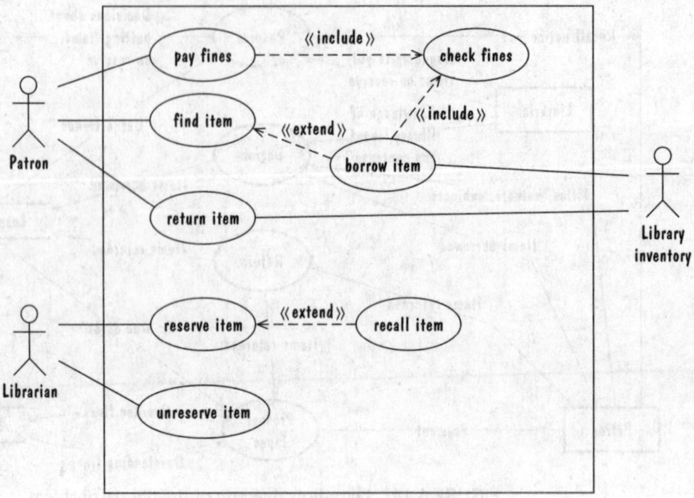

FIGURE 4.15 Library use cases.

system functionality that can be initiated by some actor in the environment. For example, in Figure 4.15, key library uses include borrowing a book, returning a borrowed book, and paying a library fine.

Each use case encompasses several possible scenarios, some successful and some not, but all related to some usage of the system. External to the use-case diagram, the use cases and their variants are detailed as textual event traces. Each use case identifies pre-conditions and alternative behavior if the pre-conditions are not met, such as looking for a lost book; post-conditions, which summarize the effects of the use case; and a normal, error-free scenario comprising a sequence of steps performed by actors or by the system. A completely detailed use case specifies all possible variations of each step in the normal scenario, including both valid behaviors and errors. It also describes the possible scenarios that stem from the valid variations and from recoverable failures. If there is a sequence of steps common to several use cases, the sequence can be extracted out to form a subcase that can be called by a base use case like a procedure call. In the use-case diagram, we draw a dashed arrow from a base case to each of its subcases and annotate these arrows with stereotype «include».[4] A use case can also be appended with an extension subcase that adds functionality to the end of the use case. In the use-case diagram, we draw a dashed arrow from the extension subcase to the base use case and annotate the arrow with stereotype «extend». Examples of stereotypes are included in Figure 4.15.

[4]In UML, a **stereotype** is a meta-language facility for extending a modeling notation, allowing the user to augment one of the notation's constructs with a new «keyword».

Functions and Relations

The notational paradigms discussed so far are representational and relational. They use annotated shapes, lines, and arrows to convey the entities, relationships, and characteristics involved in the problem being modeled. In contrast, the remaining three notational paradigms that we discuss are more strongly grounded in mathematics, and we use them to build mathematical models of the requirements. Mathematically based specification and design techniques, called **formal methods** or **approaches**, are encouraged by many software engineers who build safety-critical systems—that is, systems whose failure can affect the health and safety of people who use them or who are nearby. For example, Defence Standard 00-56, a draft British standard for building safety-critical systems, requires that formal specification and design be used to demonstrate required functionality, reliability, and safety. Advocates argue that mathematical models are more precise and less ambiguous than other models, and that mathematical models lend themselves to more systematic and sophisticated analysis and verification. In fact, many formal specifications can be checked automatically for consistency, completeness, nondeterminism, and reachable states, as well as for type correctness. Mathematical proofs have revealed significant problems in requirements specifications, where they are more easily fixed than if revealed during testing. For example, Pfleeger and Hatton (1997) report on software developers who used formal methods to specify and evaluate the complex communications requirements of an air-traffic-control support system. Early scrutiny of the formal specification revealed major problems that were fixed well before design began, thereby reducing risk as well as saving development time. At the end of this chapter, we see how formal specification might have caught problems with Ariane-5.

Some formal paradigms model requirements or software behavior as a collection of mathematical **functions** or **relations** that, when composed together, map system inputs to system outputs. Some functions specify the state of a system's execution, and other functions specify outputs. A relation is used instead of a function whenever an input value maps to more than one output value. For example, we can represent the turnstile problem using two functions: one function to keep track of the state of the turnstile, mapping from the current state and input event to the next state; and a second function to specify the turnstile's output, based on the current state and input event:

```
                      { unlocked    s=locked AND e=coin
NextState(s,e)   =    { rotating    s=unlocked AND e=push
                      { locked      (s=rotating AND e=rotated)
                                    OR (s = locked AND e=slug)

Output(s,e)   =       { buzz        s=locked AND e=slug
                      { <none>      Otherwise
```

Together, the above functions are semantically equivalent to the graphical state-machine model of the turnstile shown in Figure 4.8.

Because it maps each input to a single output, a function is by definition consistent. If the function specifies an output for *every* distinct input, it is called a total function and is by definition complete. Thus, functional specifications lend themselves to systematic and straightforward tests for consistency and completeness.

(event) borrow	T	T	T	F	F	F	F	F
(event) return	F	F	F	T	T	F	F	F
(event) reserve	F	F	F	F	F	T	T	F
(event) unreserve	F	F	F	F	F	F	F	T
item out on loan	F	T	-	-	-	F	T	F
item on reserve	-	-	-	F	T	-	-	-
patron.fines > \$0.00	F	-	T	-	-	-	-	-
(Re-)Calculate due date	X						X	
Put item in stacks				X				X
Put item on reserve shelf					X	X		
Send recall notice							X	
Reject event		X	X					

FIGURE 4.16 Decision table for library functions.

Example: Decision Tables

A **decision table** (Hurley 1983) is a tabular representation of a functional specification that maps events and conditions to appropriate responses or actions. We say that the specification is *informal* because the inputs (events and conditions) and outputs (actions) may be expressed in natural language, as mathematical expressions, or both.

Figure 4.16 shows a decision table for the library functions `borrow`, `return`, `reserve`, and `unreserve`. All of the possible input events (i.e., function invocations), conditions, and actions are listed along the left side of the table, with the input events and conditions listed above the horizontal line and the actions listed below the line. Each column represents a rule that maps a set of conditions to its corresponding result(s). An entry of "T" in a cell means that the row's input condition is true, "F" means that the input condition is false, and a dash indicates that the value of the condition does not matter. An entry of "X" at the bottom of the table means that the row's action should be performed whenever its corresponding input conditions hold. Thus, column 1 represents the situation where a library patron wants to borrow a book, the book is not already out on loan, and the patron has no outstanding fine; in this situation, the loan is approved and a due date is calculated. Similarly, column 7 illustrates the case where there is a request to put a book on reserve but the book is currently out on loan; in this case, the book is recalled and the due date is recalculated to reflect the recall.

This kind of representation can result in very large tables, because the number of conditions to consider is equal to the number of combinations of input conditions. That is, if there are n input conditions, there are 2^n possible combinations of conditions. Fortunately, many combinations map to the same set of results and can be combined into a single column. Some combinations of conditions may be infeasible (e.g., an item cannot be borrowed and returned at the same time). By examining decision tables in this way, we can reduce their size and make them easier to understand.

What else can we tell about a requirements specification that is expressed as a decision table? We can easily check whether every combination of conditions has been considered, to determine if the specification is complete. We can examine the table for consistency, by identifying multiple instances of the same input conditions and eliminating any conflicting outputs. We can also search the table for patterns to see how strongly individual input conditions correlate to individual actions. Such a search would be arduous on a specification modeled using a traditional textual notation for expressing mathematical functions.

Example: Parnas Tables

Parnas tables (Parnas 1992) are tabular representations of mathematical functions or relations. Like decision tables, Parnas tables use rows and columns to separate a function's definition into its different cases. Each table entry either specifies an input condition that partially identifies some case, or it specifies the output value for some case. Unlike decision tables, the inputs and outputs of a Parnas table are purely mathematical expressions.

To see how Parnas tables work, consider Figure 4.17. The rows and columns define `Calc due date`, an operation in our library example. The information is represented as a Normal Table, which is a type of Parnas table. The column and row headers are predicates used to specify cases, and the internal table entries store the possible function results. Thus, each internal table entry represents a distinct case in the function's definition. For example, if the event is to renew a loan (column header), *and* the publication being borrowed is on reserve (column header), *and* the patron making the request has no outstanding fines (row header), then the due date is calculated to be `publication.reserve loan period` days from `Today`. A table entry of "X" indicates that the operation is invalid under the specified conditions; in other specifications, an entry of "X" could mean that the combination of conditions is infeasible. Notice how the column and row headers are structured to cover all possible combinations of conditions that can affect the calculation of a loaned item's due date. (The symbol ¬ means "not", so `¬publication.InState(reserve)` means that the publication is not on reserve.)

The phrase **Parnas tables** actually refers to a collection of table types and abbreviation strategies for organizing and simplifying functional and relational expressions. Another table type is an Inverted Table, which looks more like a conventional decision table: case conditions are specified as expressions in the row headers and in the table entries, and the function results are listed in the column headers, at the top or the bottom of the table. In general, the specifier's goal is to choose or create a table format that results in a simple and compact representation for the function or relation being specified. The tabular structure of these representations makes it easy for reviewers to check that a specification is complete (i.e., there are no missing cases) and consistent (i.e., there are no duplicate cases). It is easier to review each function's definition case by case, rather than examining and reasoning about the whole specification at once.

A functional specification expressed using Parnas tables is best decomposed into a single function per output variable. For every input event and for every condition on entities or other variables, each function specifies the value of its corresponding output variable. The advantage of this model structure over a state-machine model is that the definition of each output variable is localized in a distinct table, rather than spread throughout the model as actions on state transitions.

	event ∈ {borrow, renew}		event = recall
	publication.In State	publication.In State	
patron.fine = 0	publication.reserve loan period	publication.loan period	Min(due date, publication.recall period)
patron.fine > 0	X	X	X

FIGURE 4.17 (Normal) Parnas table for operation `Calc due date`.

Logic

With the exception of ER diagrams, the notations we have considered so far have been model-based and are said to be operational. An **operational** notation is a notation used to describe a problem or a proposed software solution in terms of situational behavior: how a software system should respond to different input events, how a computation should flow from one step to another, and what a system should output under various conditions. The result is a model of *case-based behavior* that is particularly useful for answering questions about what the desired response should be to a particular situation: for example, what the next state or system output should be, given the current state, input event, process completion, and variable values. Such models also help the reader to visualize global behavior, in the form of paths representing allowable execution traces through the model.

Operational notations are less effective at expressing global properties or constraints. Suppose we were modeling a traffic light, and we wanted to assert that the lights controlling traffic in cross directions are never green at the same time, or that the lights in each direction are periodically green. We could build an operational model that exhibits these behaviors implicitly, in that all paths through the model satisfy these properties. However, unless the model is **closed**—meaning that the model expresses all of the desired behavior, and that any implementation that performs additional functionality is incorrect—it is ambiguous as to whether these properties are requirements to be satisfied or simply are accidental effects of the modeling decisions made.

Instead, global properties and constraints are better expressed using a descriptive notation, such as logic. A **descriptive** notation is a notation that describes a problem or a proposed solution in terms of its properties or its invariant behaviors. For example, ER diagrams are descriptive, in that they express relationship properties among entities. A **logic** consists of a language for expressing properties, plus a set of inference rules for deriving new, consequent properties from the stated properties. In mathematics, a logical expression,[5] called a **formula**, evaluates to either *true* or *false*, depending on the values of the variables that appear in the formula. In contrast, when logic is used to express a property of a software problem or system, the property is an assertion about the problem or system that should be *true*. As such, a property specification represents only those values of the property's variables for which the property's expression evaluates to *true*.

There are multiple variants of logic that differ in how expressive their property notation is, or in what inference rules they provide. The logic commonly used to express properties of software requirements is **first-order logic**, comprising typed variables; constants; functions; predicates, like relational operators $<$ and $>$; equality; logical connectives $\wedge$ (and), $\vee$ (or), $\neg$ (not), $\Rightarrow$ (implies), and $\Leftrightarrow$ (logical equivalence); and quantifiers $\exists$ (there exists) and $\forall$ (for all). Consider the following variables of the turnstile problem, with their initial values:

[5]You can think of a logic as a function that maps expressions to a set of possible values. An n-valued logic maps to a set of n values. Binary logic maps expressions to {true, false}, but n can in general be larger than 2. In this book, we assume that n is 2 unless otherwise stated.

```
num_coins : integer := 0                 /* number of coins inserted         */
num_entries : integer := 0;              /* number of half-rotations of
                                            turnstile                        */
barrier : {locked, unlocked} := locked;  /* whether barrier is locked        */
may_enter : boolean := false;            /* whether anyone may enter         */
insert_coin : boolean := false;          /* event of coin being inserted     */
push : boolean := false;                 /* turnstile is pushed sufficiently
                                            hard to rotate it one-half
                                            rotation                         */
```

The following are examples of turnstile properties over these variables, expressed in first-order logic:

```
num_coins ≥ num_entries
(num_coins > num_entries) ⇔ (barrier = unlocked)
(barrier = locked) ⇔ ¬may_enter
```

Together, these formulae assert that the number of entries through the turnstile's barrier should never exceed the number of coins inserted into the turnstile, and that whenever the number of coins inserted exceeds the number of entries, the barrier is unlocked to allow another person to enter the gated area. Note that these properties say nothing about how variables change value, such as how the number of inserted coins increases. Presumably, another part of the specification describes this. The above properties simply ensure that however the variables' values change, the values always satisfy the formulae's constraints.

Temporal logic introduces additional logical connectives for constraining how variables can change value over time—more precisely, over multiple points in an execution. For example, temporal-logic connectives can express imminent changes, like variable assignments (e.g., an `insert_coin` event results in variable `num_coins` being incremented by 1), or they can express future variable values (e.g., after an `insert_coin` event, variable `may_enter` remains true until a `push` event). We can model this behavior in first-order logic by adding a time parameter to each of the model's variables and asking about the value of a variable at a particular time. However, temporal logic, in allowing variable values to change and in introducing special temporal logic connectives, represents varying behavior more succinctly.

As with logics in general, there are many variants of temporal logic, which differ in the connectives that they introduce. The following (linear-time) connectives constrain future variable values, over a single execution trace:

□f ≡ f is *true* now and throughout the rest of the execution
◇ f ≡ f is *true* now or at some future point in the execution
○ f ≡ f is *true* in the next point of the execution
f W g ≡ f is *true* until a point where g is *true*, but g may never be *true*

In the following, the temporal turnstile properties given above are expressed in temporal logic:

```
□(insert_coin ⇒ ○ (may_enter  W  push))
□(∀n(insert_coin ∧ num_coins=n) ⇒ ○ (num_coins = n+1))
```

Properties are often used to augment a model-based specification, either to impose constraints on the model's allowable behaviors or simply to express redundant but nonobvious global properties of the specification. In the first case, a property specifies behavior not expressed in the model, and the desired behavior is the conjunction of the model and the property. In the second case, the property does not alter the specified behavior but may aid in understanding the model by explicating otherwise implicit behavior. Redundant properties also aid in requirements verification, by providing expected properties of the model for the reviewer to check.

Example: Object Constraint Language (OCL)

The **Object Constraint Language (OCL)** is an attempt to create a constraint language that is both mathematically precise and easy for nonmathematicians, like customers, to read, write, and understand. The language is specially designed for expressing constraints on object models (i.e., ER diagrams), and introduces language constructs for navigating from one object to another via association paths, for dealing with collections of objects, and for expressing queries on object type.

A partial Library class model from Figure 4.5 appears in Figure 4.18, in which three classes have been detailed and annotated with OCL constraints. The leftmost constraint is an invariant on the Patron class, and specifies that no patron's fines may

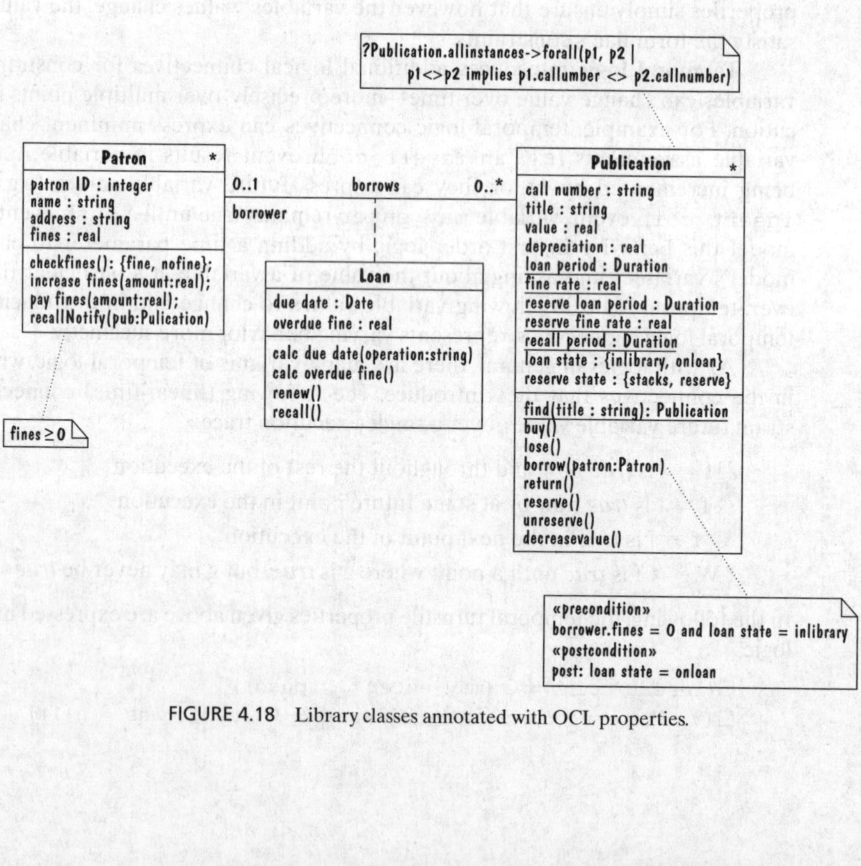

FIGURE 4.18 Library classes annotated with OCL properties.

have a negative value (i.e., the library always makes change if a patron's payment exceeds his or her fines). The topmost constraint is an invariant on the `Publication` class, and specifies that call numbers are unique. This constraint introduces

- Construct *allinstances,* which returns all instances of the `Publication` class
- Symbol $\rightarrow$, which applies the attribute or operation of its right operand to all of the objects in its left operand
- Constructs *forall, and,* and *implies,* which correspond to the first-order connectives described above

Thus, the constraint literally says that for any two publications, `p1` and `p2`, returned by *allinstances,* if `p1` and `p2` are not the same publication, then they have different call numbers. The third constraint, attached to the method `borrow()`, expresses the operation's pre- and post-conditions. One of the pre-conditions concerns an attribute in the `Patron` class, which is accessible via the `borrow` association; the patron object can be referenced either by its role name, `borrower`, or by the class name written in lowercase letters, if the association's far end has no role name. If the association's multiplicity were greater than 0..1, then navigating the association would return a collection of objects, and we would use $\rightarrow$ notation, rather than dot notation, to access the objects' attributes.

Although not originally designed as part of UML, OCL is now tightly coupled with UML and is part of the UML standard. OCL can augment many of UML's models. For example, it can be used to express invariants, preconditions, and post-conditions in class diagrams, or invariants and transition conditions in statechart diagrams. It can also express conditions on events in Message Sequence Charts (Warmer and Kleppe 1999). OCL annotations of UML require a relatively detailed class model, complete with attribute types, operation signatures, role names, multiplicities, and state enumerations of the class's statechart diagram. OCL expressions can appear in UML diagrams as UML notes, or they can be listed in a supporting document.

Example: Z

Z (pronounced "zed") is a formal requirements-specification language that structures set-theoretic definitions of variables into a complete abstract-data-type model of a problem, and uses logic to express the pre- and post-conditions for each operation. Z uses software-engineering abstractions to decompose a specification into manageably sized modules, called **schemas** (Spivey 1992). Separate schemas specify

- The system state in terms of typed variables, and invariants on variables' values
- The system's initial state (i.e., initial variable values)
- Operations

Moreover, Z offers the precision of a mathematical notation and all of its benefits, such as being able to evaluate specifications using proofs or automated checks.

Figure 4.19 shows part of our library example specified in Z. `Patron`, `Item`, `Date`, and `Duration` are all basic types that correspond to their respective real-world designations. (See Sidebar 4.5 for more on designations.) The `Library` schema declares the problem to consist of a `Catalogue` and a set of items `OnReserve`, both

```
[Patron, Item, Date, Duration]
LoanPeriod : Duration;
ReserveLoan : Duration;
DailyFine : ℕ;

┌ Library ──────────────────────
│ Catalogue, OnReserve : ℙ Item
│ Borrower: Item ⇸ Patron
│ DueDate: Item ⇸ Date
│ Fine: Patron ⇸ ℕ
├───────────────────────────────
│ dom Borrower ⊆ Catalogue
│ OnReserve ⊆ Catalogue
│ dom Borrower = dom DueDate
└───────────────────────────────

┌ Buy ──────────────────────────
│ Δ Library
│ i? : Item
├───────────────────────────────
│ i? ∉ Catalogue
│ Catalogue' = Catalogue ∪ {i?}
│ OnReserve' = OnReserve
│ Borrower' = Borrower
│ DueDate' = DueDate
│ Fine' = Fine
└───────────────────────────────

┌ InitLibrary ──────────────────
│ Library
├───────────────────────────────
│ Catalogue = ∅ ∧ OnReserve = ∅
│ dom Borrower = ∅
│ dom DueDate = ∅
│ dom Fine = ∅
└───────────────────────────────

┌ Return ───────────────────────
│ Δ Library
│ i? : Item
│ p? : Patron
│ today? : Date
├───────────────────────────────
│ i? ∈ dom Borrower ∧ p? = Borrower(i?)
│ Borrower' = {i?} ⩤ Borrower
│ DueDate' = {i?} ⩤ DueDate
│ DueDate(i?) - today? < 0 ⇒
│     Fine' = Fine ⊕ {p? ↦ (Fine(p?) + ((DueDate(i?) - today?)*DailyFine)}
│ DueDate(i?) - today? ≥ 0 ⇒
│     Fine' = Fine
│ Catalogue' = Catalogue
│ OnReserve' = OnReserve
└───────────────────────────────

┌ Get Due Date ─────────────────
│ Ξ Library
│ i? : Item
│ due! : Date
├───────────────────────────────
│ i? ∈ dom Borrower
│ due! = DueDate(i?)
└───────────────────────────────
```

FIGURE 4.19 Partial Z specification of the library problem.

SIDEBAR 4.5 GROUND REQUIREMENTS IN THE REAL WORLD

Jackson's advice (Jackson 1995) to ground the requirements in the real world goes beyond the message about expressing the requirements and the specification in terms of the proposed system's environment. Jackson argues that any model of the requirements will include primitive terms that have no formal meaning (e.g., `Patron`, `Publication`, and `Article` in our library example), and that the only way to establish the meaning of a primitive term is to relate it to some phenomenon in the real world. He calls these descriptions **designations**, and he distinguishes *designations* from *definitions* and *assertions*. Definitions are formal meanings of terms based on the meanings of other terms used in the model (e.g., the definition of a *book out on loan*), whereas *assertions* describe constraints on terms (e.g., patrons can borrow only those items not currently out on loan). If a model is to have any meaning with respect to real-world behavior, its primitive terms must be clearly and precisely tied to the real world, and its designations "must be maintained as an essential part of the requirements documentation" (Zave and Jackson 1997).

declared as powersets ($\mathbb{P}$) of `Items`; these declarations mean that the values of `Catalogue` and `OnReserve` can change during execution to be any subset of `Items`. The schema also declares partial mappings ($\rightarrow\!\!\!\!+$) that record the `Borrowers` and `DueDates` for the subset of `Items` that are out on loan, and record `Fines` for the subset of `Patrons` who have outstanding fines. The domain (**dom**) of a partial mapping is the subset of entities currently being mapped; hence, we assert that the subset of items out on loan should be exactly the subset of items that have due dates. The `InitLibrary` scheme initializes all of the variables to be empty sets and functions. All of the remaining schemas correspond to library operations.

The top section of an operation schema indicates whether the operation modifies (Δ) or simply queries (Ξ) the system state, and identifies the inputs (?) and outputs (!) of the operation. The bottom section of an operation schema specifies the operation's pre-conditions and post-conditions. In operations that modify the system state, unprimed variables represent variable values before the operation is performed, and primed variables represent values following the operation. For example, the input to operation `Buy` is a new library `Item`, and the pre-condition specifies that the `Item` not already be in the library `Catalogue`. The post conditions update the `Catalogue` to include the new `Item`, and specify that the other library variables do not change value (e.g., the updated value `Fine'` equals the old value `Fine`). Operation `Return` is more complicated. It takes as input the library `Item` being returned, the `Patron` who borrowed the `Item`, and the `Date` of the return. The post-conditions remove the returned item from variables `Borrowers` and `DueDates`; these updates use Z symbol $\lhd$, "domain subtraction," to return a submapping of their pre-operation values, excluding any element whose domain value is the `Item` being returned. The next two post-conditions are updates to variable `Fines`, conditioned on whether the `Patron` incurs an overdue fine for returning the `Item` later than the loan's due date. These updates use symbol $\mapsto$, which "maps" a domain value "to" a range value, and symbol $\oplus$ which "overrides" a function mapping, usually with a new "maps-to" element. Thus, if `today's` date is later than the returned `Item's DueDate`, then the `Patron's Fine` is overridden with a new value that reflects the old fine value plus the new overdue fine. The last two post-conditions specify that the values of variables `Catalogue` and `OnReserve` do not change.

Algebraic Specifications

With the exception of logic and OCL notations, all of the notation paradigms we have considered so far tend to result in models that suggest particular implementations. For example,

- A UML class model suggests what classes ought to appear in the final (object-oriented) implementation.
- A data-flow specification suggests how an implementation ought to be decomposed into data-transforming modules.
- A state-machine model suggests how a reactive system should be decomposed into cases.
- A Z specification suggests how complex data types can be implemented in terms of sets, sequences, or functions.

Such implementation bias in a requirements specification can lead a software designer to produce a design that adheres to the specification's *model*, subconsciously disregarding possibly better designs that would satisfy the specified *behavior*. For example, as we will see in Chapter 6, the classes in a UML class diagram may be appropriate for expressing a *problem* simply and succinctly, but the same class decomposition in a design may result in an inefficient *solution* to the problem.

A completely different way of viewing a system is in terms of what happens when combinations of operations are performed. This multi-operational view is the main idea behind **algebraic specifications**: to specify the behavior of operations by specifying the interactions between pairs of operations rather than modeling individual operations. An execution trace is the sequence of operations that have been performed since the start of execution. For example, one execution of our turnstile problem, starting with a new turnstile, is the operation sequence

```
new().coin().push().rotated().coin().push().rotated()...
```

or, in mathematical-function notation:

```
...(rotated(push(coin(rotated(push(coin(new()))))))...
```

Specification axioms specify the effects of applying pairs of operations on an arbitrary sequence of operations that have already executed (where `SEQ` is some prefix sequence of operations):

```
num_entries(coin(SEQ))    ≡ num_entries (SEQ)
num_entries(push(SEQ))    ≡ num_entries (SEQ)
num_entries(rotated(SEQ)) ≡ 1 + num_entries (SEQ)
num_entries(new())        ≡ 0
```

The first three axioms specify the behavior of operation `num_entries` when applied to sequences ending with operations `coin`, `push`, and `rotated`, respectively. For example, a `rotated` operation indicates that another visitor has entered the zoo, so `num_entries` applied to `rotated(SEQ)` should be one more than `num_entries` applied to `SEQ`. The fourth axiom specifies the base case of `num_entries` when applied to a `new` turnstile. Together, the four axioms indicate that operation `num_entries` returns, for a given sequence, the number of occurrences of the operation `rotated`—without saying anything about how that information may be stored or computed. Similar axioms would need to be written to specify the behaviors of other pairs of operations.

Algebraic specification notations are not popular among software developers because, for a collection of operations, it can be tricky to construct a concise set of axioms that is complete and consistent—and correct! Despite their complexity, algebraic notations have been added to several formal specification languages, to enable specifiers to define their own abstract data types for their specifications.

Example: SDL Data

SDL data definitions are used to create user-defined data types and parameterized data types in the **Specification and Description Language (SDL)** (ITU 2002). An SDL data type definition introduces the data type being specified, the signatures of all operations

```
NEWTYPE Library
LITERALS New;
OPERATORS
  buy: Library, Item → Library;
  lose: Library, Item → Library;
  borrow: Library, Item → Library;
  return: Library, Item → Library;
  reserve: Library, Item → Library;
  unreserve: Library, Item → Library;
  recall: Library, Item → Library;
  isInCatalogue: Library, Item → boolean;
  isOnLoan: Library, Item → boolean;
  isOnReserve: Library, Item → boolean;

/*generators are New, buy, borrow, reserve */
```

```
AXIOMS
FOR ALL lib in Library (
  FOR ALL i, i2 in Item (
    lose(New, i) ≡ ERROR;
    lose(buy(lib, i), i2) ≡ if i= i2 then lib;
                            else buy(lose(lib, i2), i);
    lose(borrow(lib, i), i2) ≡ if i = i2 then lose(lib, i2)
                               else borrow(lose(lib, i2), i);
    lose(reserve(lib, i), i2) ≡ if i = i2 then lose(lib, i2)
                                else reserve(lose(lib, i2), i);

    return(New, i) ≡ ERROR;
    return(buy(lib, i), i2) ≡ if i = i2 then buy (lib, i);
                              else buy(return(lib, i2), i);
    return(borrow(lib, i), i2) ≡ if i = i2 then lib;
                                 else borrow(return(lib, i2), i);
    return(reserve(lib, i), i2) ≡ reserve(return(lib, i2), i);
    ...
    isInCatalogue(New, i) ≡ false;
    isInCatalogue(buy(lib, i), i2) ≡ if i = i2 then true;
                                     else isInCatalogue(lib, i2);
    isInCatalogue(borrow(lib, i), i2) ≡ isInCatalogue (lib, i2);
    isInCatalogue(reserve(lib, i), i2) ≡ isInCatalogue (lib, i2);
    ...
  }
}
ENDNEWTYPE Library;
```

FIGURE 4.20 Partial SDL data specification for the library problem.

on that data type, and axioms that specify how pairs of operations interact. Figure 4.20 shows a partial SDL data specification for our library problem, where the library itself—the catalogue of publications, and each publication's loan and reserve status—is treated as a complex data type. `NEWTYPE` introduces the `Library` data type. The `LITERALS` section declares any constants of the new data type; in this case, `New` is the value of an empty library. The `OPERATORS` section declares all of the library operations, including each operator's parameter types and return type. The `AXIOMS` section specifies the behaviors of pairs of operations.

As mentioned above, the hardest part of constructing an algebraic specification is defining a set of axioms that is complete and consistent and that reflects the desired behavior. It is especially difficult to ensure that the axioms are consistent because they are so interrelated: each axiom contributes to the specification of two operations, and each operation is specified by a collection of axioms. As such, a change to the specification necessarily implicates multiple axioms. A heuristic that helps to reduce the number of axioms, thereby reducing the risk of inconsistency, is to separate the operations into

- **Generators**, which help to build canonical representations of the defined data type
- **Manipulators**, which return values of the defined data type, but are not generators
- **Queries**, which do not return values of the defined data type

The set of generator operations is a minimal set of operations needed to construct any value of the data type. That is, every sequence of operations can be reduced to some canonical sequence of only generator operations, such that the canonical sequence represents the same data value as the original sequence. In Figure 4.20, we select `New`, `buy`, `borrow`, and `reserve` as our generator operations, because these operations can represent any state of the library, with respect to the contents of the library's catalogue, and the loan and reserve states of its publications. This decision leaves `lose`, `return`, `unreserve`, and `renew` as our manipulator operations, because they are the remaining operations that have return type `Library`, and leaves `isInCatalogue`, `isOnLoan`, and `isOnReserve` as our query operations.

The second part of the heuristic is to provide axioms that specify the effects of applying a nongenerator operation to a canonical sequence of operations. Because canonical sequences consist only of generator operations, this step means that we need to provide axioms only for pairs of operations, where each pair is a nongenerator operation that is applied to an application of a generator operation. Each axiom specifies how to reduce an operation sequence to its canonical form: applying a manipulator operation to a canonical sequence usually results in a smaller canonical sequence, because the manipulator often undoes the effects of an earlier generator operation, such as returning a borrowed book; applying a query operation, like checking whether a book is out on loan, returns some result without modifying the already-canonical system state.

The axioms for each nongenerator operation are recursively defined:

1. There is a base case that specifies the effect of each nongenerator operation on an empty, `New` library. In our library specification (Figure 4.20), losing a book from an empty library is an `ERROR`.
2. There is a recursive case that specifies the effect of two operations on common parameters, such as buying and losing the same book. In general, such operations interact. In this case, the operations cancel each other out, and the result is the state of the library, minus the two operations. Looking at the case of losing a book that has been borrowed, we discard the borrow operation (because there is no need to keep any loan records for a lost book) and we apply the `lose` operation to the rest of the sequence.
3. There is a second recursive case that applies two operations to different parameters, such as buying and losing different books. Such operations do not interact, and the axiom specifies how to combine the effects of the inner operation with the result of recursively applying the outer operation to the rest of the system state. In the case of buying and losing different books, we keep the effect of buying one book, and we recursively apply the lose operation to the rest of the sequence of operations executed so far.

There is no need to specify axioms for pairs of nongenerator operations because we can use the above axioms to reduce to canonical form the application of each nongenerator operation before considering the next nongenerator operation. We could write axioms for pairs of generator operations; for example, we could specify that consecutive loans of the same book are an `ERROR`. However, many combinations of generator operations, such as consecutive loans of different books, will not result in reduced canonical forms. Instead, we write axioms assuming that many of the operations have pre-conditions that constrain when operations can be applied. For example, we assume in our library specification (Figure 4.20) that it is invalid to `borrow` a book that is already out on loan. Given this assumption, the effect of returning a borrowed book

```
return(borrow(SEQ,i),i)
```

is that the two operations cancel each other out and the result is equivalent to SEQ. If we do not make this assumption, then we would write the axioms so that the `return` operation removes *all* corresponding `borrow` operations:

```
return(New,i) ≡ ERROR;
return(buy(lib, i), i2) ≡ if i = i2 then buy(lib, i);
                          else buy(return(lib, i2), i);
return(borrow(lib, i), i2) ≡ if i = i2 then return(lib, i2);
                             else borrow(return(lib, i2), i);
return(reserve(lib, i), i2) ≡ reserve(return(lib, i2), i);
```

Thus, the effect of returning a borrowed book is to discard the `borrow` operation and to reapply the `return` operation to the rest of the sequence, so that it can remove any extraneous matching `borrow` operations; this recursion terminates when the `return` operation is applied to the corresponding `buy` operation, which denotes the beginning of the book's existence, or to an empty library, an `ERROR`. Together, these axioms specify that operation `return` removes from the library state any trace of the item being borrowed, which is the desired behavior. A specification written in this style would nullify consecutive buying, borrowing, or reserving of the same item.

4.6 REQUIREMENTS AND SPECIFICATION LANGUAGES

At this point, you may be wondering how the software-engineering community could have developed so many types of software models with none being the preferred or ideal notation. The situation is not unlike an architect working with a collection of blueprints: each blueprint maps a particular aspect of a building's design (e.g., structural support, heating conduits, electrical circuits, water pipes), and it is the collection of plans that enables the architect to visualize and communicate the building's whole design. Each of the notational paradigms described above models problems from a different perspective: entities and relationships, traces, execution states, functions, properties, data. As such, each is the paradigm of choice for modeling a particular view of a software problem. With practice and experience, you will learn to judge which viewpoints and notations are most appropriate for understanding or communicating a given software problem.

Because each paradigm has its own strengths, a complete specification may consist of several models, each of which illustrates a different aspect of the problem. For this reason, most practical requirements and specification languages are actually combinations of several notational paradigms. By understanding the relationships between specification languages and the notational paradigms they employ, you can start to recognize the similarities among different languages and to appreciate the essential ways in which specification languages differ. At this end of this chapter, we discuss criteria for evaluating and choosing a specification language.

Unified Modeling Language (UML)

The **Unified Modeling Language (UML)** (OMG 2003) is the language best known for combining multiple notation paradigms. Altogether, the UML standard comprises eight graphical modeling notations, plus the OCL constraint language. The UML notations that are used during requirements definition and specification include

- **Use-case diagram (a high-level DFD):** A use-case diagram is used at the start of a new project, to record the essential top-level functions that the to-be-developed product should provide. In the course of detailing the use cases' scenarios, we may identify important entities that play a role in the problem being modeled.
- **Class diagram (an ER diagram):** As mentioned previously, the class diagram is the flagship model of a UML specification, emphasizing the problem's entities and their interrelationships. The remaining UML specification models provide more detail about how the classes' objects behave and how they interact with one another. As we gain a better understanding of the problem being modeled, we detail the class diagram, with additional attributes, attribute classes, operations, and signatures. Ideally, new insight into the problem is more likely to cause changes to these details than to affect the model's entities or relationships.
- **Sequence diagram (an event trace):** Sequence diagrams are early behavioral models that depict traces of messages passed between class instances. They are best used to document important scenarios that involve multiple objects. When creating sequence diagrams, we look for common subsequences that appear in several diagrams; these subsequences may help us to identify states (e.g., the start and end points of the subsequence) in the objects' local behaviors.
- **Collaboration diagram (an event trace):** A collaboration diagram illustrates one or more event traces, overlayed on the class diagram. As such, a collaboration diagram presents the same information as a sequence diagram. The difference is that the sequence diagram emphasizes a scenario's temporal ordering of messages because it organizes messages along a timeline. On the other hand, the collaboration diagram emphasizes the classes' relationships, and treats the messages as elaborations of those relationships in the way that it represents messages as arrows between classes in the class diagram.
- **Statechart diagram (a state-machine model):** A UML statechart diagram specifies how each instance of one class in the specification's class diagram behaves. Before writing a statechart for a class (more specifically, for a representative object of that class), we should identify the states in the object's life cyle, the events that this object sends to and receives from other objects, the order in which these states and events occur, and the operations that the object invokes. Because such information is fairly detailed, a statechart diagram should not be attempted until late in the requirements phase, when the problem's details are better understood.
- **OCL properties (logic):** OCL expressions are properties about a model's elements (e.g., objects, attributes, events, states, messages). OCL properties can be used in any of the above models, to explicate the model's implicit behavior or to impose constraints on the model's specified behavior.

Most of these notations were discussed in the preceding section, as examples of different notation paradigms. In Chapter 6, we will see more details about how UML works, by applying it to a real-world problem for both specification and design.

Specification and Description Language (SDL)

The **Specification and Description Language (SDL)** (ITU 2002) is a language standardized by the International Telecommunications Union for specifying precisely the behavior of real-time, concurrent, distributed processes that communicate with each other via unbounded message queues. SDL comprises three graphical diagrams, plus algebraic specifications for defining complex data types:

- **SDL system diagram (a DFD):** An SDL system diagram, shown in Figure 4.21(a), depicts the top-level blocks of the specification and the communication channels that connect the blocks. The channels are directional and are labeled with the types of signals that can flow in each direction. Message passing via **channels** is *asynchronous*, meaning that we cannot make any assumptions about when sent messages will be received; of course, messages sent along the *same* channel will be received in the order in which they were sent.
- **SDL block diagram (a DFD):** Each SDL block may model a lower-level collection of blocks and the message-delaying channels that interconnect them. Alternatively, it can model a collection of lowest-level processes that communicate via signal routes, shown in Figure 4.21(b). **Signal routes** pass messages *synchronously*, so messages sent between processes in the same block are received instantaneously. In fact, this difference in communication mechanisms is a factor when deciding how to decompose behavior: processes that need to synchronize with one another and that are highly coupled should reside in the same block.

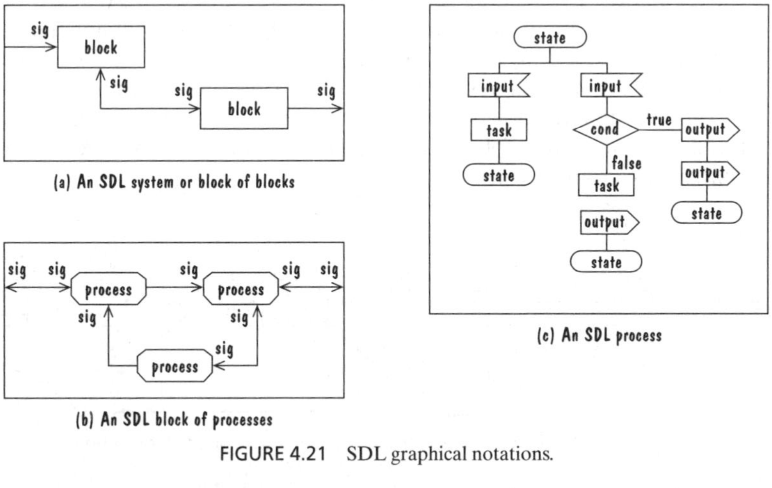

FIGURE 4.21 SDL graphical notations.

- **SDL process diagram (a state-machine model):** An SDL process, shown in Figure 4.21(c), is a state machine, whose transitions are sequences of language constructs (input, decisions, tasks, outputs) that start and end at state constructs. In each execution step, the process removes a signal from the head of its input queue and compares the signal to the input constructs that follow the process's current state. If the signal matches one of the state's inputs, the process executes all of the constructs that follow the matching input, until the execution reaches the next state construct.
- **SDL data type (algebraic specification):** An SDL process may declare local variables, and SDL data type definitions are used to declare complex, user-defined variable types.

In addition, an SDL specification is often accompanied by a set of Message Sequence Charts (MSC) (ITU 1996), each of which illustrates a single execution of the specification in terms of the messages passed between the specification's processes.

Software Cost Reduction (SCR)

Software Cost Reduction (SCR) (Heitmeyer 2002) is a collection of techniques that were designed to encourage software developers to employ good software-engineering design principles. An SCR specification models software requirements as a mathematical function, REQ, that maps **monitored variables**, which are environmental variables that are *sensed* by the system, to **controlled variables**, which are environmental variables that are *set* by the system. The function REQ is decomposed into a collection of tabular functions, similar to Parnas tables. Each of these functions is responsible for setting the value of one controlled variable or the value of a **term**, which is a macro-like variable that is referred to in other functions' definitions.

REQ is the result of composing these tabular functions into a network (a DFD, as shown in Figure 4.22), whose edges reflect the data dependencies among the functions. Every execution step starts with a change in the value of one monitored variable. This change is then propagated through the network, in a single, synchronized step. The specification's functions are applied in a topological sort that adheres to the functions' data dependencies: any function that refers to updated values of variables must execute *after* the functions that update those values. Thus, an execution step resembles a wave of variable updates flowing through the network, starting with newly sensed monitored-variable values, followed by updates to term variables, followed by updates to controlled-variable values.

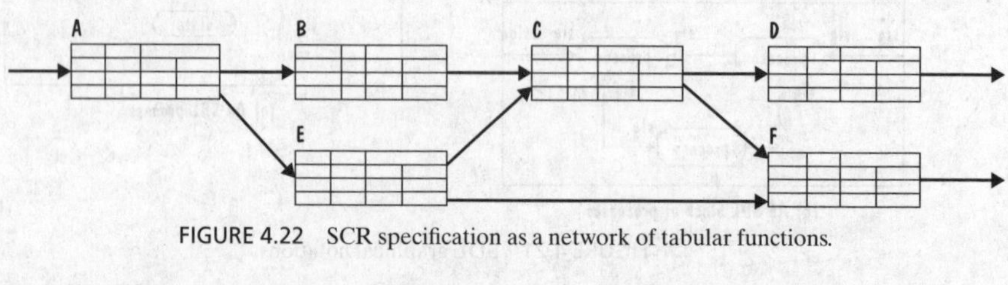

FIGURE 4.22 SCR specification as a network of tabular functions.

Other Features of Requirements Notations

There are many other requirements-modeling techniques. Some techniques include facilities for associating the degree of uncertainty or risk with each requirement. Other techniques have facilities for tracing requirements to other system documents, such as design or code, or to other systems, such as when requirements are reused. Most specification techniques have been automated to some degree, making it easy to draw diagrams, collect terms and designations into a data dictionary, and check for obvious inconsistencies. As tools continue to be developed to aid software engineering activities, documenting and tracking requirements will be made easier. However, the most difficult part of requirements analysis—understanding our customers' needs—is still a human endeavor.

4.7 PROTOTYPING REQUIREMENTS

When trying to determine requirements, we may find that our customers are uncertain of exactly what they want or need. Elicitation may yield only a "wish list" of what the customers would like to see, with few details or without being clear as to whether the list is complete. Beware! These same customers, who are indecisive in their requirements, have no trouble distinguishing between a delivered system that meets their needs and one that does not—known also as "I'll know it when I see it" customers (Boehm 2000). In fact, most people find it easier to critique, in detail, an existing product than to imagine, in detail, a new product. As such, one way that we can elicit details is to build a prototype of the proposed system and to solicit feedback from potential users about what aspects they would like to see improved, which features are not so useful, or what functionality is missing. Building a prototype can also help us determine whether the customer's problem has a feasible solution, or assist us in exploring options for optimizing quality requirements.

To see how prototyping works, suppose we are building a tool to track how much a user exercises each day. Our customers are exercise physiologists and trainers, and their clients will be the users. The tool will help the physiologists and trainers to work with their clients and to track their clients' training progress. The tool's user interface is important, because the users may not be familiar with computers. For example, in entering information about their exercise routines, the users will need to enter the date for each routine. The trainers are not sure what this interface should look like, so we build a quick prototype to demonstrate the possibilities. Figure 4.23 shows a first prototype, in which the user must type the day, month, and year. A more interesting and sophisticated interface involves a calendar (see Figure 4.24), where the user uses a mouse to select the month and year, the system displays the chart for that month, and the user selects the appropriate day in the chart. A third alternative is depicted in Figure 4.25, in which, instead of a calendar, the user is presented with three slider bars. As the user then uses the mouse to slide each bar left or right, the box at the bottom of the screen changes to show the selected day, month, and year. This third interface may provide the fastest selection, even though it may be very different from what the users are accustomed to seeing. In this example, prototyping helps us to select the right "look

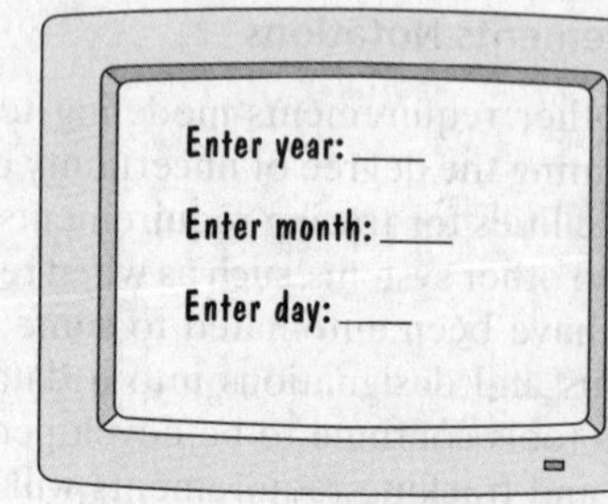

FIGURE 4.23 Keyboard-entry prototype.

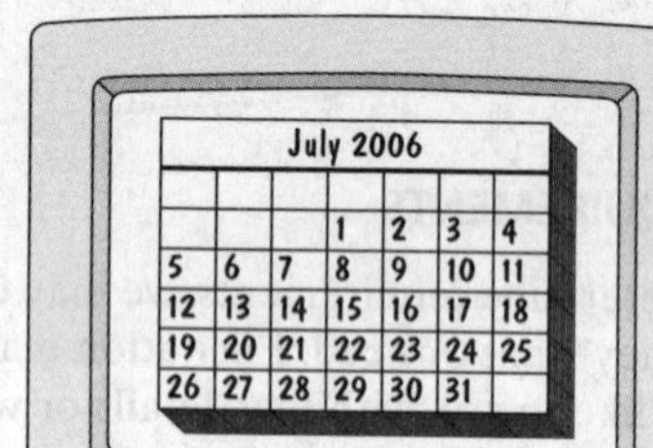

FIGURE 4.24 Calendar-based prototype.

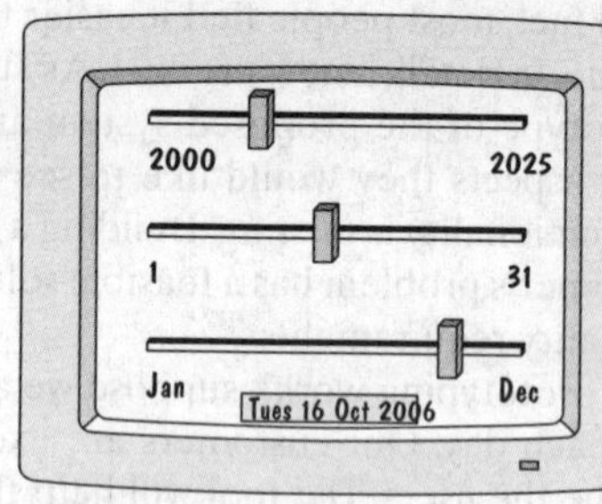

FIGURE 4.25 Slide-bar-based prototype.

and feel" for the user's interaction with the proposed system. The prototype interfaces would be difficult to describe in words or symbols, and they demonstrate how some types of requirements are better represented as pictures or prototypes.

There are two approaches to prototyping: throwaway and evolutionary. A **throwaway prototype** is software that is developed to learn more about a problem or about a proposed solution, and that is never intended to be part of the delivered software. This approach allows us to write "quick-and-dirty" software that is poorly structured, inefficient, with no error checking—that, in fact, may be a facade that does not implement any of the desired functionality—but that gets quickly to the heart of questions we have about the problem or about a proposed solution. Once our questions are answered, we throw away the prototype software and start engineering the software that will be delivered. In contrast, an **evolutionary prototype** is software that is developed not only to help us answer questions but also to be incorporated into the final product. As such, we have to be much more careful in its development, because this software has to eventually exhibit the quality requirements (e.g., response rate, modularity) of the final product, and these qualities cannot be retrofitted.

Both techniques are sometimes called **rapid prototyping**, because they involve building software in order to answer questions about the *requirements*. The term "rapid" distinguishes software prototyping from that in other engineering disciplines, in which a prototype is typically a complete solution, like a prototype car or plane that is built manually according to an already approved design. The purpose of such a prototype is to test the design and product before automating or optimizing the manufacturing step for mass production. In contrast, a rapid prototype is a partial solution that is built to help us understand the requirements or to evaluate design alternatives.

Questions about the requirements can be explored via either modeling or prototyping. Whether one approach is better than the other depends on what our questions are, how well they can be expressed in models or in software, and how quickly the models or prototype software can be built. As we saw above, questions about user interfaces may be easier to answer using prototypes. A prototype that implements a number of proposed features would more effectively help users to prioritize these features, and possibly to identify some features that are unnecessary. On the other hand, questions about constraints on the order in which events should occur, or about the synchronization of activities, can be answered more quickly using models. In the end, we need to produce final requirements documentation for the testing and maintenance teams, and possibly for regulatory bodies, as well as final software to be delivered. So, whether it is better to model or to prototype depends on whether it is faster and easier to model, and to develop the software from the refined models, or faster and easier to prototype, and to develop documentation from the refined prototype.

4.8 REQUIREMENTS DOCUMENTATION

No matter what method we choose for defining requirements, we must keep a set of documents recording the result. We and our customers will refer to these documents throughout development and maintenance. Therefore, the requirements must be documented so that they are useful not only to the customers but also to the technical staff on our development team. For example, the requirements must be organized in such a way that they can be tracked throughout the system's development. Clear and precise illustrations and diagrams accompanying the documentation should be consistent with the text. Also, the level at which the requirements are written is important, as explained in Sidebar 4.6.

Requirements Definition

The requirements definition is a record of the requirements expressed in the customer's terms. Working with the customer, we document what the customer can expect of the delivered system:

1. First, we outline the general purpose and scope of the system, including relevant benefits, objectives, and goals. References to other related systems are included, and we list any terms, designations, and abbreviations that may be useful.

SIDEBAR 4.6 LEVEL OF SPECIFICATION

In 1995, the Australian Defence and Technology Organisation reported the results of a survey of problems with requirements specifications for Navy software (Gabb and Henderson 1995). One of the problems it highlighted was the uneven level of specifications. That is, some requirements had been specified at too high a level and others were too detailed. The unevenness was compounded by several situations:

- Requirements analysts used different writing styles, particularly in documenting different system areas.
- The difference in experience among analysts led to different levels of detail in the requirements.
- In attempting to reuse requirements from previous systems, analysts used different formats and writing styles.
- Requirements were often overspecified in that analysts identified particular types of computers and programming languages, assumed a particular solution, or mandated inappropriate processes and protocols. Analysts sometimes mixed requirements with partial solutions, leading to "serious problems in designing a cost-effective solution."
- Requirements were sometimes underspecified, especially when describing the operating environment, maintenance, simulation for training, administrative computing, and fault tolerance.

Most of those surveyed agreed that there is no universally correct level of specification. Customers with extensive experience prefer high-level specifications, and those with less experience like more detail. The survey respondents made several recommendations, including:

- Write each clause so that it contains only one requirement.
- Avoid having one requirement refer to another requirement.
- Collect similar requirements together.

2. Next, we describe the background and the rationale behind the proposal for a new system. For example, if the system is to replace an existing approach, we explain why the existing approach is unsatisfactory. Current methods and procedures are outlined in enough detail so that we can separate those elements with which the customer is happy from those that are disappointing.
3. Once we record this overview of the problem, we describe the essential characteristics of an acceptable solution. This record includes brief descriptions of the product's core functionality, at the level of use cases. It also includes quality requirements, such as timing, accuracy, and responses to failures. Ideally, we would prioritize these requirements and identify those that can be put off to later versions of the system.

4. As part of the problem's context, we describe the environment in which the system will operate. We list any known hardware and software components with which the proposed system will have to interact. To help ensure that the user interface is appropriate, we sketch the general backgrounds and capabilities of the intended users, such as their educational background, experience, and technical expertise. For example, we would devise different user interfaces for knowledgeable users than we would for first-time users. In addition, we list any known constraints on the requirements or the design, such as applicable laws, hardware limitations, audit checks, regulatory policies, and so on.
5. If the customer has a proposal for solving the problem, we outline a description of the proposal. Remember, though, that the purpose of the requirements documents is to discuss the problem, not the solution. We need to evaluate the proposed solution carefully, to determine if it is a design constraint to be satisfied or if it is an overspecification that could exclude better solutions. In the end, if the customer places any constraints on the development or if there are any special assumptions to be made, they should be incorporated into the requirements definition.
6. Finally, we list any assumptions we make about how the environment behaves. In particular, we describe any environmental conditions that would cause the proposed system to fail, and any changes to the environment that would cause us to change our requirements. Sidebar 4.7 explains in more detail why it is important to document assumptions. The assumptions should be documented separately from the requirements, so that developers know which behaviors they are responsible for implementing.

Requirements Specification

The requirements specification covers exactly the same ground as the requirements definition, but from the perspective of the developers. Where the requirements definition is written in terms of the customer's vocabulary, referring to objects, states, events, and activities in the customer's world, the requirements specification is written in terms of the system's interface. We accomplish this by rewriting the requirements so that they refer only to those real-world objects (states, events, actions) that are sensed or actuated by the proposed system:

1. In documenting the system's interface, we describe all inputs and outputs in detail, including the sources of inputs, the destinations of outputs, the value ranges and data formats of input and output data, protocols governing the order in which certain inputs and outputs must be exchanged, window formats and organization, and any timing constraints. Note that the user interface is rarely the only system interface; the system may interact with other software components (e.g., a database), special-purpose hardware, the Internet, and so on.
2. Next, we restate the required functionality in terms of the interfaces' inputs and outputs. We may use a functional notation or data-flow diagrams to map inputs to outputs, or use logic to document functions' pre-conditions and post-conditions. We may use state machines or event traces to illustrate exact sequences of operations

SIDEBAR 4.7 HIDDEN ASSUMPTIONS

Zave and Jackson (1997) have looked carefully at problems in software requirements and specification, including undocumented assumptions about how the real world behaves.

There are actually two types of environmental behavior of interest: desired behavior to be realized by the proposed system (i.e., the requirements) and existing behavior that is unchanged by the proposed system. The latter type of behavior is often called **assumptions** or **domain knowledge**. Most requirements writers consider assumptions to be simply the conditions under which the system is guaranteed to operate correctly. While necessary, these conditions are not the only assumptions. We also make assumptions about how the environment will behave in response to the system's outputs.

Consider a railroad-crossing gate at the intersection of a road and a set of railroad tracks. Our requirement is that trains and cars do not collide in the intersection. However, the trains and cars are outside the control of our system; all our system can do is lower the crossing gate upon the arrival of a train and lift the gate after the train passes. The only way our crossing gate will prevent collisions is if trains and cars follow certain rules. For one thing, we have to assume that the trains travel at some maximum speed, so that we know how early to lower the crossing gate to ensure that the gate is down well before a sensed train reaches the intersection. But we also have to make assumptions about how car drivers will react to the crossing gate being lowered: we have to assume that cars will not stay in or enter the intersection when the gate is down.

or exact orderings of inputs and outputs. We may use an entity-relationship diagram to collect related activities and operations into classes. In the end, the specification should be complete, meaning that it should specify an output for any feasible sequence of inputs. Thus, we include validity checks on inputs and system responses to exceptional situations, such as violated pre-conditions.

3. Finally, we devise fit criteria for each of the customer's quality requirements, so that we can conclusively demonstrate whether our system meets these quality requirements.

The result is a description of what the developers are supposed to produce, written in sufficient detail to distinguish between acceptable and unacceptable solutions, but without saying how the proposed system should be designed or implemented.

Several organizations, such as the Institute of Electrical and Electronic Engineers and the U.S. Department of Defense, have standards for the content and format of the requirements documents. For example, Figure 4.26 shows a template based on IEEE's recommendations for organizing a software requirements specification by classes or objects. The IEEE standard provides similar templates for organizing the requirements specification by mode of operation, function, feature, category of user, and so on. You may want to consult these standards in preparing documents for your own projects.

1. Introduction to the Document
    1.1 Purpose of the Product
    1.2 Scope of the Product
    1.3 Acronyms, Abbreviations, Definitions
    1.4 References
    1.5 Outline of the rest of the SRS
2. General Description of Product
    2.1 Context of Product
    2.2 Product Functions
    2.3 User Characteristics
    2.4 Constraints
    2.5 Assumptions and Dependencies
3. Specific Requirements
    3.1 External Interface Requirements
        3.1.1 User Interfaces
        3.1.2 Hardware Interfaces
        3.1.3 Software Interfaces
        3.1.4 Communications Interfaces
    3.2 Functional Requirements
        3.2.1 Class 1
        3.2.2 Class 2
        ...
    3.3 Performance Requirements
    3.4 Design Constraints
    3.5 Quality Requirements
    3.6 Other Requirements
4. Appendices

FIGURE 4.26 IEEE standard for Software Requirements Specification organized by object (IEEE 1998).

Process Management and Requirements Traceability

There must be a direct correspondence between the requirements in the definition document and those in the specification document. It is here that the process management methods used throughout the life cycle begin. **Process management** is a set of procedures that track

- The requirements that define what the system should do
- The design modules that are generated from the requirements
- The program code that implements the design
- The tests that verify the functionality of the system
- The documents that describe the system

In a sense, process management provides the threads that tie the system parts together, integrating documents and artifacts that have been developed separately. These threads allow us to coordinate the development activities, as shown by the horizontal "threads" among entities in Figure 4.27. In particular, during requirements activities, we are concerned about establishing a correspondence between elements of the requirements definition and those of the requirements specification, so that the customer's view is tied to the developer's view in an organized, traceable way. If we do not define these links, we have no way of designing test cases to determine whether the code meets the requirements. In later chapters, we will see how process management

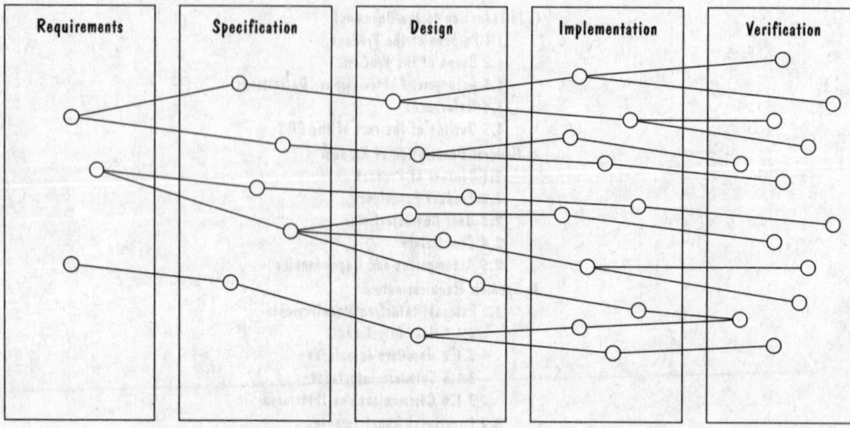

FIGURE 4.27 Links between software-development entities.

also allows us to determine the impact of changes, as well as to control the effects of parallel development.

To facilitate this correspondence, we establish a numbering scheme or data file for convenient tracking of requirements from one document to another. Often, the process management team sets up or extends this numbering scheme to tie requirements to other components and artifacts of the system. Numbering the requirements allows us to cross-reference them with the data dictionary and other supporting documents. If any changes are made to the requirements during the remaining phases of development, the changes can be tracked from the requirements document through the design process and all the way to the test procedures. Ideally, then, it should be possible to trace any feature or function of the system to its causal requirement, and vice versa.

4.9 VALIDATION AND VERIFICATION

Remember that the requirements documents serve both as a contract between us and the customer, detailing what we are to deliver, and as guidelines for the designers, detailing what they are to build. Thus, before the requirements can be turned over to the designers, we and our customers must be absolutely sure that each knows the other's intent, and that our intents are captured in the requirements documents. To establish this certainty, we *validate* the requirements and *verify* the specification.

We have been using the terms "verify" and "validate" throughout this chapter without formally defining them. In **requirements validation**, we check that our requirements definition accurately reflects the customer's—actually, all of the stakeholders'—needs. Validation is tricky because there are only a few documents that we can use as the basis for arguing that the requirements definitions are correct. In **verification**, we check that one document or artifact conforms to another. Thus, we verify that our code conforms to our design, and that our design conforms to our requirements specification; at the requirements level, we verify that our requirements specification conforms to the requirements definition. To summarize, verification ensures that we *build the system right*, whereas validation ensures that we *build the right system!*

Requirements Validation

Our criteria for validating the requirements are the characteristics that we listed in Section 4.4:

- Correct
- Consistent
- Unambiguous
- Complete
- Relevant
- Testable
- Traceable

Depending on the definition techniques that we use, some of the above checks (e.g., that the requirements are consistent or are traceable) may be automated. Also, common errors can be recorded in a **checklist**, which reviewers can use to guide their search for errors. Lutz (1993a) reports on the success of using checklists in validating requirements at NASA's Jet Propulsion Laboratory. However, most validation checks (e.g., that a requirement is correct, relevant, or unambiguous; or that the requirements are complete) are subjective exercises in that they involve comparing the requirements definition against the stakeholders' mental model of what they expect the system to do. For these validation checks, our only recourse is to rely on the stakeholders' assessment of our documents.

Table 4.3 lists some of the techniques that can be used to validate the requirements. Validation can be as simple as reading the document and reporting errors. We

TABLE 4.3 Validation and Verification Techniques

Validation	Walkthroughs
	Reading
	Interviews
	Reviews
	Checklists
	Models to check functions and relationships
	Scenarios
	Prototypes
	Simulation
	Formal inspections
Verification	Cross-referencing
	Simulation
	Consistency checks
	Completeness checks
	Checks for unreachable states or transitions
Checking	Model checking
	Mathematical proofs

can ask the validation team to sign off on the document, thereby declaring that they have reviewed the document and that they approve it. By signing off, the stakeholders accept partial responsibility for errors that are subsequently found in the document. Alternatively, we can hold a **walkthrough**, in which one of the document's authors presents the requirements to the rest of the stakeholders, and asks for feedback. Walkthroughs work best when there are a large number of varied stakeholders, and it is unrealistic to ask them all to examine the document in detail. At the other extreme, validation can be as structured as a **formal inspection**, in which reviewers take on specific roles (e.g., presenter, moderator) and follow prescribed rules (e.g., rules on how to examine the requirements, when to meet, when to take breaks, whether to schedule a follow-up inspection).

More often, the requirements are validated in a requirements **review**. In a review, representatives from our staff and the customer's staff examine the requirements document individually and then meet to discuss identified problems. The customer's representatives include those who will be operating the system, those who will prepare the system's inputs, and those who will use the system's outputs; managers of these employees may also attend. We provide members of the design team, the test team, and the process team. By meeting as a group, we can do more than check that the requirements definition satisfies the validation criteria:

1. We review the stated goals and objectives of the system.
2. We compare the requirements with the goals and objectives, to make certain that all requirements are necessary.
3. We review the environment in which the system is to operate, examining the interfaces between our proposed system and all other systems and checking that their descriptions are complete and correct.
4. The customer's representatives review the information flow and the proposed functions, to confirm that they accurately reflect the customer's needs and intentions. Our representatives review the proposed functions and constraints, to confirm that they are realistic and within our development abilities. All requirements are checked again for omissions, incompleteness, and inconsistency.
5. If any risk is involved in the development or in the actual functioning of the system, we can assess and document this risk, discuss and compare alternatives, and come to some agreement on the approaches to be used.
6. We can talk about testing the system: how the requirements will be revalidated as the requirements grow and change; who will provide test data to the test team; which requirements will be tested in which phases, if the system is to be developed in phases.

Whenever a problem is identified, the problem is documented, its cause is determined, and the requirements analysts are charged with the task of fixing the problem. For example, validation may reveal that there is a great misunderstanding about the way in which a certain function will produce results. The customers may require data to be reported in miles, whereas the users want the data in kilometers. The customers may set a reliability or availability goal that developers deem impossible to meet. These conflicts need to be resolved before design can begin. To resolve a conflict, the developers may need to construct simulations or prototypes to explore feasibility constraints and then work with the customer to agree on an acceptable requirement. Sidebar 4.8 discusses the nature and number of requirements-related problems you are likely to find.

Our choice of validation technique depends on the experience and preferences of the stakeholders and on the technique's appropriateness for the notations used in the requirements definition. Some notations have tool support for checking consistency and completeness. There are also tools that can help with the review process and with tracking problems and their resolutions. For example, some tools work with you and the customer to reduce the amount of uncertainty in the requirements. This book's Web page points to requirements-related tools.

SIDEBAR 4.8 NUMBER OF REQUIREMENTS FAULTS

How many development problems are created during the process of capturing requirements? There are varying claims. Boehm and Papaccio (1988), in a paper analyzing software at IBM and TRW, found that most errors are made during design, and there are usually three design faults for every two coding faults. They point out that the high number of faults attributed to the design stage could derive from requirements errors. In his book on software engineering economics, Boehm (1981) cites studies by Jones and Thayer and others that attribute

- 35% of the faults to design activities for projects of 30,000–35,000 delivered source instructions
- 10% of the faults to requirements activities and 55% of the faults to design activities for projects of 40,000–80,000 delivered source instructions
- 8% to 10% of the faults to requirements activities and 40% to 55% of the faults to design activities for projects of 65,000–85,000 delivered source instructions

Basili and Perricone (1984), in an empirical investigation of software errors, report that 48% of the faults observed in a medium-scale software project were "attributed to incorrect or misinterpreted functional specifications or requirements."

Beizer (1990) attributes 8.12% of the faults in his samples to problems in functional requirements. He includes in his count such problems as incorrect requirements; illogical or unreasonable requirements; ambiguous, incomplete, or overspecified requirements; unverifiable or untestable requirements; poorly presented requirements; and changed requirements. However, Beizer's taxonomy includes no design activities. He says, "Requirements, especially expressed in a specification (or often, as not expressed because there is no specification) are a major source of expensive bugs. The range is from a few percent to more than 50%, depending on application and environment. What hurts most about these bugs is that they're the earliest to invade the system and the last to leave. It's not unusual for a faulty requirement to get through all development testing, beta testing, and initial field use, only to be caught after hundreds of sites have been installed."

Other summary statistics abound. For example, Perry and Stieg (1993) conclude that 79.6% of interface faults and 20.4% of the implementation faults are due to incomplete or omitted requirements. Similarly, *Computer Weekly Report* (1994) discussed a study showing that 44.1% of all system faults occurred in the specification stage. Lutz (1993b) analyzed safety-related errors in two NASA spacecraft software systems, and found that "the primary cause of safety-related interface faults is misunderstood hardware interface specifications" (48% to 67% of such faults), and the "primary cause of safety-related functional faults is errors in recognizing (understanding) the requirements" (62% to 79% of such faults). What is the right number for your development environment? Only careful record keeping will tell you. These records can be used as a basis for measuring improvement as you institute new practices and use new tools.

Verification

In verification, we want to check that our requirements-specification document corresponds to our requirements-definition document. This verification makes sure that if we implement a system that meets the specification, then that system will satisfy the customer's requirements. Most often, this is simply a check of traceability, where we ensure that each requirement in the definition document is traceable to the specification.

However, for critical systems, we may want to do more, and actually demonstrate that the specification fulfills the requirements. This is a more substantial effort, in which we prove that the specification realizes every function, event, activity, and constraint in the requirements. The specification by itself is rarely enough to make this kind of argument, because the specification is written in terms of actions performed at the system's interface, such as force applied to an unlocked turnstile, and we may want to prove something about the environment away from the interface, such as about the number of entries into the zoo. To bridge this gap, we need to make use of our assumptions about how the environment behaves—assumptions about what inputs the system will receive, or about how the environment will react to outputs (e.g., that if an unlocked turnstile is pushed with sufficient force, it will rotate a half-turn, nudging the pusher into the zoo). Mathematically, the specification (S) plus our environmental assumptions (A) must be sufficient to prove that the requirements (R) hold:

$$S, A \vdash R$$

For example, to show that a thermostat and furnace will control air temperature, we have to assume that air temperature changes continuously rather than abruptly, although the sensors may detect discrete value changes, and that an operating furnace will raise the air temperature. These assumptions may seem obvious, but if a building is sufficiently porous and the outside temperature is sufficiently cold, then our second assumption will not hold. In such a case, it would be prudent to set some boundaries on the requirement: as long as the outside temperature is above −100ºC, the thermostat and furnace will control the air temperature.

This use of environmental assumptions gets at the heart of why the documentation is so important: we rely on the environment to help us satisfy the customer's requirements, and if our assumptions about how the environment behaves are wrong, then our system may not work as the customer expects. If we cannot prove that our specification and our assumptions fulfill the customer's requirements, then we need either to change our specification, strengthen our assumptions about the environment, or weaken the requirements we are trying to achieve. Sidebar 4.9 discusses some techniques for automating these proofs.

SIDEBAR 4.9 COMPUTER-AIDED VERIFICATION

Model checking is an exhaustive search of a specification's execution space, to determine whether some temporal-logic property holds of the executions. The model checker computes and searches the specification's execution space, sometimes computing the execution space symbolically and sometimes computing it on-the-fly during the search. Thus, the verification, while completely automated, consumes significant computing resources. Sreemani and Atlee (1996) used the SMV model checker to verify five properties of an SCR specification of the A-7 naval aircraft. Their SMV model consisted of 1251 lines, most of them translated automatically from the SCR specification, and theoretically had an execution space of $1\,3 \times 10^{22}$ states. In their model checking, the researchers found that one of the properties that was thought not to hold did indeed hold: it turned out that the conditions under which it would not hold were unreachable. They also discovered that a safety property did not hold: according to the specification, it was possible for the weapon delivery system to use stale data in tracking a target's location when the navigation sensors were deemed to be reporting unreasonable values.

A **theorem prover** uses a collection of built-in theories, inference rules, and decision procedures for determining whether a set of asserted facts logically entails some unasserted fact; most sophisticated theorem provers require human assistance in sketching out the proof strategy. Dutertre and Stavridou (1997) used the theorem prover PVS to verify some of the functional and safety requirements of an avionics system. For example, the assumption that relates the wing sweep angle WSPOS at time *t + eps* and the wing sweep command CMD at time *t*, in the case where none of the interlocks is active, is expressed in PVS as:

```
cmd_wings : AXIOM
   constant_in_interval (CMD, t, t + eps)
and
   not wings_locked_in_interval (t, t + eps)
implies
   CMD (t) = WSPOS (t + eps)
or
   CMD (t) < WSPOS (t + eps) and
   WSPOS (t + eps) <= WPOS (t) - eps * ws_min_rate
or
   CMD (t) > WSPOS (t + eps) and
   WSPOS (t + eps) >= WPOS (t) 2 eps * ws_min_rate
```

The entire PVS model, including specification and assumptions, consisted of about 4500 lines of PVS, including comments and blank lines. The verification of requirements involved two steps. Some theorems were proved to check that the PVS model was internally consistent and complete, and others were used directly to prove three main safety properties. The proof of safety was quite complex. In total, 385 proofs were performed, of which about 100 were discharged automatically by the theorem prover, and the rest required human guidance. It took approximately 6 person-months to write the PVS model and support libraries, and another 12 person-months to formalize the assumptions and carry out the verification; the verification of the three main safety properties took 9 of the 12 person-months.

When requirements validation and verification are complete, we and our customers should feel comfortable about the requirement specification. Understanding what the customer wants, we can proceed with the system design. Meanwhile, the customer has in hand a document describing exactly what the delivered system should do.

4.10 MEASURING REQUIREMENTS

There are many ways to measure characteristics of requirements such that the information collected tells us a lot about the requirements process and about the quality of the requirements themselves. Measurements usually focus on three areas: product, process, and resources (Fenton and Pfleeger 1997). The number of requirements in the requirements definition and specification can give us a sense of how large the developed system is likely to be. We saw in Chapter 3 that effort-estimation models require an estimate of product size, and requirements size can be used as input to such models. Moreover, requirements size and effort estimation can be tracked throughout development. As design and development lead to a deeper understanding of both problem and solution, new requirements may arise that were not apparent during the initial requirements-capture process.

Similarly, we can measure the number of changes to requirements. A large number of changes indicates some instability or uncertainty in our understanding of what the system should do or how it should behave, and suggests that we should take actions to try to lower the rate of changes. The tracking of changes also can continue throughout development; as the system requirements change, the impact of the changes can be assessed.

Where possible, requirements-size and change measurements should be recorded by requirements type. Such category-based metrics tell us whether change or uncertainty in requirements is product wide, or rests solely with certain kinds of requirements, such as user-interface or database requirements. This information helps us to determine if we need to focus our attention on particular types of requirements.

Because the requirements are used by the designers and testers, we may want to devise measures that reflect their assessment of the requirements. For example, we can ask the designers to rate each requirement on a scale from 1 to 5:

1. You (the designer) understand this requirement completely, you have designed from similar requirements in the past, and you should have no trouble developing a design from this requirement.
2. There are elements of this requirement that are new to you, but they are not radically different from requirements you have successfully designed from in the past.
3. There are elements of this requirement that are very different from requirements you have designed from in the past, but you understand the requirement and think you can develop a good design from it.
4. There are parts of this requirement that you do not understand, and you are not sure that you can develop a good design.
5. You do not understand this requirement at all, and you cannot develop a design for it.

We can create a similar rating scheme that asks testers how well they understand each requirement and how confident they are about being able to devise a suitable test suite for each requirement. In both cases, the profiles of rankings can serve as a coarse indicator of whether the requirements are written at the appropriate level of detail. If the designers and testers yield profiles with mostly 1s and 2s, as shown in Figure 4.28(a), then the requirements are in good shape and can be passed on to the design team. However, if there are many 4s and 5s, as shown in Figure 4.28(b), then the requirements should be revised, and the revisions reassessed to have better profiles, before we proceed to design. Although the assessment is subjective, the general trends should be clear, and the scores can provide useful feedback to both us and our customers.

We can also take note, for each requirement, of when it is reviewed, implemented as design, implemented as code, and tested. These measures tell us the progress we are making toward completion. Testers can also measure the thoroughness of their test cases with respect to the requirements, as we will see in Chapters 8 and 9. We can measure the number of requirements covered by each test case, and the number of requirements that have been tested (Wilson 1995).

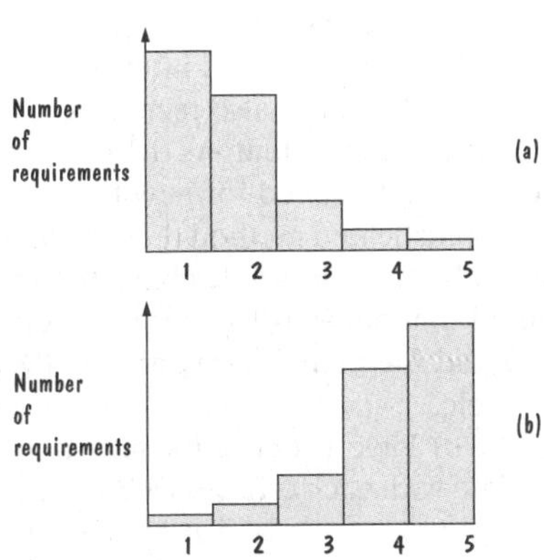

FIGURE 4.28 Measuring requirements readiness.

4.11 CHOOSING A SPECIFICATION TECHNIQUE

This chapter has presented examples of several requirements-specification techniques, and many more are available for use on your projects. Each one has useful characteristics, but some are more appropriate for a given project than others. That is, no technique is best for all projects. Thus, it is important to have a set of criteria for deciding, for each project, which technique is most suitable.

Let us consider some of the issues that should be included in such a set of criteria. Suppose we are to build a computerized system for avoiding collisions among aircraft. Participating aircraft are to be fitted with radar sensors. A subsystem on each aircraft is to monitor other aircraft in its vicinity, detect when an aircraft is flying dangerously close, establish communications with that aircraft, negotiate evasive maneuvers to avoid a collision (after all, we wouldn't want both planes to independently choose maneuvers that would put them or keep them on a collision course!), and instruct its navigation system to execute the negotiated maneuvers. Each aircraft's subsystem performs its own data analysis and decision-making procedures on onboard computers, although it shares flight plans with other aircraft and transmits all data and final maneuvers to a central site for further analysis. One of the key characteristics of this collision-avoidance system is that it is a distributed, reactive system. That is, it is a **reactive system** in that each aircraft's subsystem is continuously monitoring and reacting to the positions of other aircraft. It is a **distributed system** in that the system's functions are distributed over several aircraft. The complexity of this system makes it essential that the requirements be specified exactly and completely. Interfaces must be well-defined, and communications must be coordinated, so that each aircraft's subsystem can make decisions in a timely manner. Some specification techniques may be more appropriate than others for this problem. For example, testing this system will be difficult because, for safety reasons, most testing cannot take place in the real environment. Moreover, it will be hard to detect and replicate transient errors. Thus, we might prefer a technique that offers simulation, or that facilitates exhaustive or automated verification of the specification. In particular, techniques that automatically check the specification or system for consistency and completeness may catch errors that are not easy to spot otherwise.

More generally, if a system has real-time requirements, we need a specification technique that supports the notion of time. Any need for phased development means that we will be tracking requirements through several intermediate systems, which not only complicates the requirements tracking, but also increases the likelihood that the requirements will change over the life of the system. As the users work with intermediate versions of the system, they may see the need for new features, or want to change existing features. Thus, we need a sophisticated method that can handle change easily. If we want our requirements to have all of the desirable characteristics listed early in the chapter, then we look for a method that helps us to revise the requirements, track the changes, cross-reference the data and functional items, and analyze the requirements for as many characteristics as possible.

Ardis and his colleagues (1996) have proposed a set of criteria for evaluating specification methods. They associate with each criterion a list of questions to help us to determine how well a particular method satisfies that criterion. These criteria were intended for evaluating techniques for specifying reactive systems, but as you will see, most of the criteria are quite general:

- **Applicability:** Can the technique describe real-world problems and solutions in a natural and realistic way? If the technique makes assumptions about the environment, are the assumptions reasonable? Is the technique compatible with the other techniques that will be used on the project?
- **Implementability:** Can the specification be refined or translated easily into an implementation? How difficult is the translation? Is it automated? If so, is the generated code efficient? Is the generated code in the same language as is used in the manually produced parts of the implementation? Is there a clean, well-defined interface between the code that is machine-generated and the code that is not?
- **Testability/simulation:** Can the specification be used to test the implementation? Is every statement in the specification testable by the implementation? Is it possible to execute the specification?
- **Checkability:** Are the specifications readable by nondevelopers, such as the customer? Can domain experts (i.e., experts on the problem being specified) check the specification for accuracy? Are there automated specification checkers?
- **Maintainability:** Will the specification be useful in making changes to the system? Is it easy to change the specification as the system evolves?
- **Modularity:** Does the method allow a large specification to be decomposed into smaller parts that are easier to write and to understand? Can changes be made to the smaller parts without rewriting the entire specification?
- **Level of abstraction/expressibility:** How closely and expressively do objects, states, and events in the language correspond to the actual objects, actions, and conditions in the problem domain? How concise and elegant is the resulting specification?
- **Soundness:** Does the language or do the tools facilitate checking for inconsistencies or ambiguities in the specification? Are the semantics of the specification language defined precisely?
- **Verifiability:** Can we demonstrate formally that the specification satisfies the requirements? Can the verification process be automated, and, if so, is the automation easy?
- **Runtime safety:** If code can be generated automatically from the specification, does the code degrade gracefully under unexpected runtime conditions, such as overflow?
- **Tools maturity:** If the specification technique has tool support, are the tools of high quality? Is there training available for learning how to use them? How large is the user base for the tools?
- **Looseness:** Can the specification be incomplete or admit nondeterminism?
- **Learning curve:** Can a new user learn quickly the technique's concepts, syntax, semantics, and heuristics?

- **Technique maturity:** Has the technique been certified or standardized? Is there a user group or large user base?
- **Data modeling:** Does the technique include data representation, relationships, or abstractions? Are the data-modeling facilities an integrated part of the technique?
- **Discipline:** Does the technique force its users to write well-structured, understandable, and well-behaved specifications?

The first step in choosing a specification technique is to determine for our particular problem which of the above criteria are especially important. Different problems place different priorities on the criteria. Ardis and his colleagues were interested in developing telephone switching systems, so they judged whether each of the criteria is helpful in developing reactive systems. They considered not only the criteria's effects on requirements activities, but their effects on other life-cycle activities as well. Table 4.4 shows the results of their evaluation. The second step in choosing a specification technique is to evaluate each of the candidate techniques with respect to the criteria. For example, Ardis and colleagues rated Z as strong in modularity, abstraction, verifiability, looseness, technique maturity, and data modeling; adequate in applicability, checkability, maintainability, soundness, tools maturity, learning curve, and discipline; and weak in implementability and testability/simulation. Some of their assessments of that Z, such as Z inherently supports modularity, hold for all problem types, whereas other assessments, such as applicability, are specific to the problem type. In the end, we choose a specification technique that best supports the criteria that are most important to our particular problem.

Since no one approach is universally applicable to all systems, it may be necessary to combine several approaches to define the requirements completely. Some methods are better at capturing control flow and synchronization, whereas other methods are

TABLE 4.4 Importance of Specification Criteria During Reactive-System Life Cycle (Ardis et al. 1996) (R = Requirements, D = Design, I = Implementation, T = Testing, M = Maintenance, O = Other) © 1996 IEEE

R	D	I	T	M	O	Criteria
+		+				Applicability
		+		+		Implementability
+	+		+			Testability/simulation
+			+	+		Checkability
				+		Maintainability
	+		+			Modularity
+	+					Level of abstraction/expressability
+			+			Soundness
+	+	+	+	+		Verifiability
		+		+		Runtime safety
		+	+	+		Tools maturity
+						Looseness
					+	Learning curve
					+	Technique maturity
	+					Data modeling
+	+	+		+		Discipline

better at capturing data transformations. Some problems are more easily described in terms of events and actions, whereas other problems are better described in terms of control states that reflect stages of behavior. Thus, it may be useful to use one method for data requirements and another to describe processes or time-related activities. We may need to express changes in behavior as well as global invariants. Models that are adequate for designers may be difficult for the test team to use. Thus, the choice of a specification technique(s) is bound up in the characteristics of the individual project and the preferences of developers and customers.

4.12 INFORMATION SYSTEMS EXAMPLE

Recall that our Piccadilly example involves selling advertising time for the Piccadilly Television franchise area. We can use several specification notations to model the requirements related to buying and selling advertising time. Because this problem is an information system, we will use only notations that are data-oriented.

First, we can draw a use-case diagram to represent the key uses of the system, showing the expected users and the major functions that each user might initiate. A partial diagram might look like Figure 4.29. Notice that this high-level diagram captures the essential functionality of the system, but it shows nothing about the ways in which each of these use cases might succeed or fail; for example, a campaign request

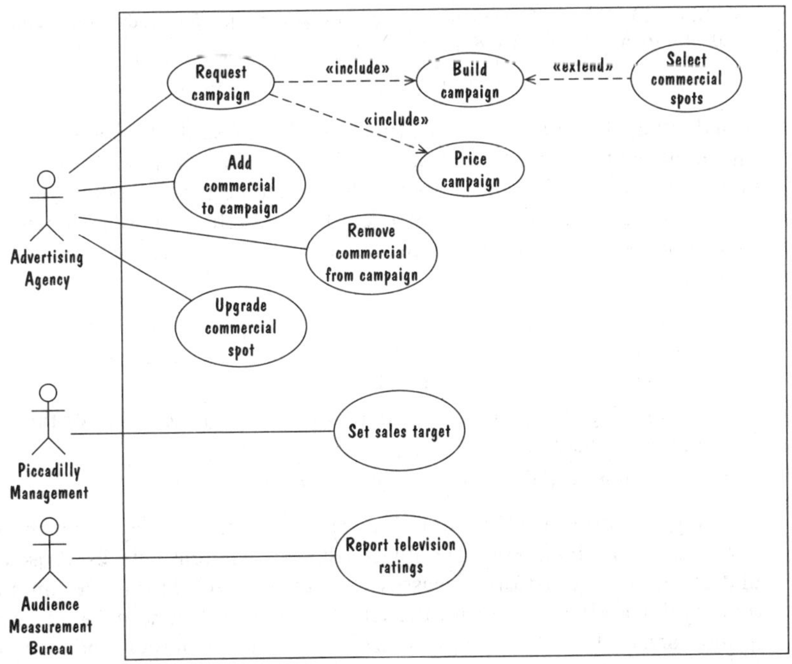

FIGURE 4.29 Use case for the Piccadilly Television advertising system (adapted from Robertson and Robertson 1994).

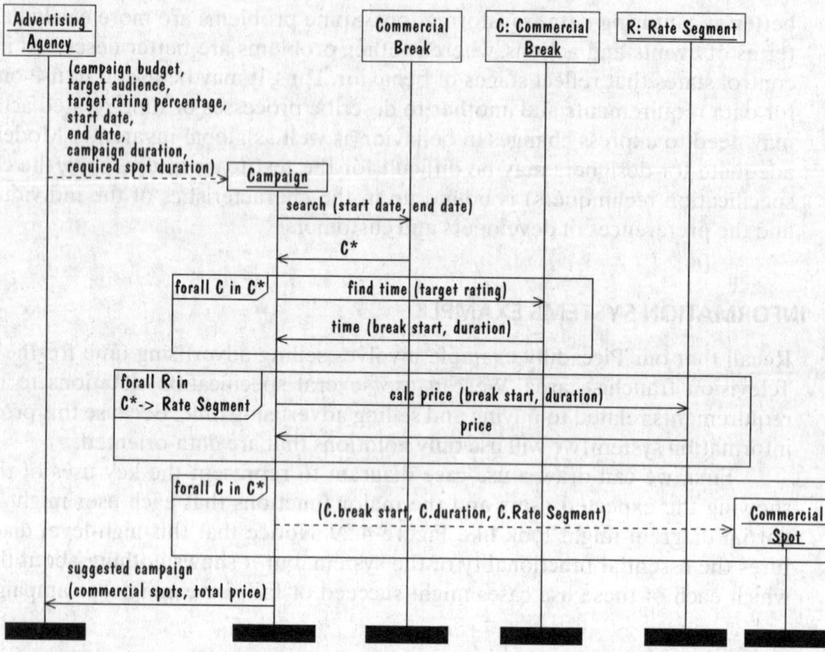

FIGURE 4.30 Message Sequence Chart for a successful request for an advertising campaign (adapted from Robertson and Robertson 1994).

would fail if all of the commercial time was already sold. The diagram also shows nothing about the type of information that the system might input, process, or output. We need more information about each of the uses, to better understand the problem.

As a next step, we can draw event traces, such as the one shown in Figure 4.30, that depict typical scenarios within a use case. For example, the request for a campaign involves

- Searching each relevant commercial break to see whether there is any unsold time and whether commercials during that break are likely to be seen by the campaign's intended target audience
- Computing the price of the campaign, based on the prices of the available commercial spots found
- Reserving available commercial spots for the campaign

Figure 4.30 uses UML-style Message Sequence Charts, in which entities whose names are underlined represent object instances, whereas entities whose names are not underlined represent abstract classes. Thus, the search for available commercial spots is done by first asking the class for the set C* of relevant `Commercial Breaks`, and then asking each of these `Commercial Break` instances whether it has available time that is suitable for the campaign. Boxes surround sequences of messages that are repeated for multiple instances: for example, reserving time in multiple `Commercial Break`

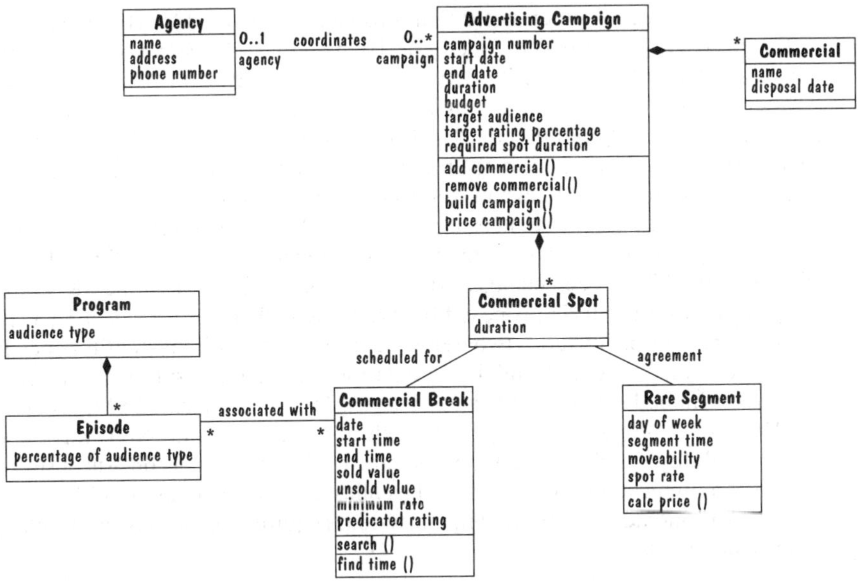

FIGURE 4.31 Partial UML class diagram of Piccadilly Television advertising system (adapted from Robertson and Robertson 1994).

instances, or creating multiple `Commercial Spots`. The resulting campaign of commercial spots and the campaign's price are returned to the requesting `Advertising Agency`. Similar traces can be drawn for other possible responses to a campaign request and for other use cases. In drawing these traces, we start to identify key entities and relationships, which we can record in a UML class diagram, as in Figure 4.31.

The complete specification for Piccadilly is quite long and involved, and the Robertsons' book provides many of the details. However, the examples here make it clear that different notations are suitable for representing different aspects of a problem's requirements; it is important to choose a combination of techniques that paints a complete picture of the problem, to be used in designing, implementing, and testing the system.

4.13 REAL-TIME EXAMPLE

Recall that the Ariane-5 explosion was caused by the reuse of a section of code from Ariane-4. Nuseibeh (1997) analyzes the problem from the point of view of requirements reuse. That is, many software engineers feel that great benefits can be had from reusing requirements specifications (and their related design, code, and test cases) from previously developed systems. Candidate specifications are identified by looking for functionality or behavioral requirements that are the same or similar, and then making modifications where necessary. In the case of Ariane-4, the inertial reference system (SRI) performed many of the functions needed by Ariane-5.

However, Nuseibeh notes that although the needed functionality was similar to that in Ariane-4, there were aspects of Ariane-5 that were significantly different. In particular, the SRI functionality that continued after liftoff in Ariane-4 was not needed after liftoff in Ariane-5. Had requirements validation been done properly, the analysts would have discovered that the functions active after liftoff could not be traced back to any Ariane-5 requirement in the requirements definition or specification. Thus, requirements validation could have played a crucial role in preventing the rocket's explosion.

Another preventive measure might have been to simulate the requirements. Simulation would have shown that the SRI continued to function after liftoff; then, Ariane-5's design could have been changed to reuse a modified version of the SRI code. Consider again the list of criteria proposed by Ardis and colleagues for selecting a specification language. This list includes two items that are especially important for specifying a system such as Ariane-5: testability/simulation and runtime safety. In Ardis's study, the team examined seven specification languages—Modechart, VFSM, Esterel, Lotos, Z, SDL, and C—for suitability against each of the criteria; only SDL was rated "strong" for testability/simulation and runtime safety. An SDL model consists of several concurrent communicating processes like the coin slot process in Figure 4.32.

To validate an SDL model, the system requirements can be written as temporal-logic invariants:

```
CLAIM;
   Barrier = locked
   IMPLIES (Barrier = locked)
      UNLESS (sum >= entryfee);
ENDCLAIM;
```

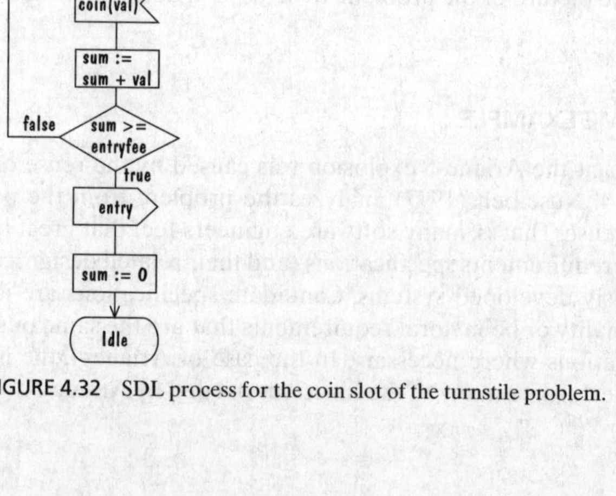

FIGURE 4.32 SDL process for the coin slot of the turnstile problem.

SDL is a mature formal method that includes object-oriented concepts and powerful modeling features: for example, processes can be spawned dynamically, can be assigned identifiers, and can store persistent data; events can carry data parameters and can be directed to specific processes by referring to process identifiers; and timers can model real-time delays and deadlines. Commercial tools are available to support design, debugging, and maintenance of SDL specifications. Thus, one possible prevention technique might have been the use of a specification method like SDL, with accompanying tool support.

We will see in later chapters that preventive steps could also have been taken during design, implementation, or testing; however, measures taken during requirements analysis would have led to a greater understanding of the differences between Ariane-4 and Ariane-5, and to detecting the root cause of the error.

4.14 WHAT THIS CHAPTER MEANS FOR YOU

In this chapter, we have shown the best practices for developing quality software requirements. We have seen that requirements activities should not be performed by the software developer in isolation: definition and specification efforts require working closely with users, customers, testers, designers, and other team members. Still, there are several skills that are important for you to master on your own:

- It is essential that the requirements definition and specification documents describe the problem, leaving solution selection to the designers. The best way of ensuring that you do not stray into the solution space is to describe requirements and specifications in terms of environmental phenomena.
- There are a variety of sources and means for eliciting requirements. There are both functional and quality requirements to keep in mind. The functional requirements explain what the system will do, and the quality requirements constrain solutions in terms of safety, reliability, budget, schedule, and so on.
- There are many different types of definition and specification techniques. Some are descriptive, such as entity-relationship diagrams and logic, while others are behavioral, such as event traces, data-flow diagrams, and functions. Some have graphical notations, and some are based on mathematics. Each emphasizes a different view of the problem, and suggests different criteria for decomposing a problem into subproblems. It is often desirable to use a combination of techniques to specify the different aspects of a system.
- The specification techniques also differ in terms of their tool support, maturity, understandability, ease of use, and mathematical formality. Each one should be judged for the project at hand, as there is no best universal technique.
- Requirements questions can be answered using models or prototypes. In either case, the goal is to focus on the subproblem that is at the heart of the question, rather than necessarily modeling or prototyping the entire problem. If prototyping, you need to decide ahead of time whether the resulting software will be kept or thrown away.
- Requirements must be validated to ensure that they accurately reflect the customer's expectations. The requirements should also be checked for completeness,

correctness, consistency, feasibility, and more, sometimes using techniques or tools that are associated with the specification methods you have chosen. Finally, you should verify that the specification fulfills the requirements.

4.15 WHAT THIS CHAPTER MEANS FOR YOUR DEVELOPMENT TEAM

Your development team must work together to elicit, understand, and document requirements. Often, different team members concentrate on separate aspects of the requirements: the networking expert may work on network requirements, the user-interface expert on screens and reports, the database expert on data capture and storage, and so on. Because the disparate requirements will be integrated into a comprehensive whole, requirements must be written in a way that allows them to be linked and controlled. For example, a change to one requirement may affect other, related requirements, and the methods and tools must support the changes to ensure that errors are caught early and quickly.

At the same time, the requirements part of your team must work closely with

- Customers and users, so that your team builds a product that serves their needs
- Designers, so that they construct a design that fulfills the requirements specification
- Testers, so that their test scripts adequately evaluate whether the implementation meets the requirements
- Documentation writers, so that they can write user manuals from the specifications

Your team must also pay attention to measurements that reflect requirements quality. The measures can suggest team activities, such as prototyping some requirements when indicators show that the requirements are not well-understood.

Finally, you must work as a team to review the requirements definition and specification documents, and to update those documents as the requirements change and grow during the development and maintenance processes.

4.16 WHAT THIS CHAPTER MEANS FOR RESEARCHERS

There are many research areas associated with requirements activities. Researchers can

- Investigate ways to reduce the amount of uncertainty and risk in requirements
- Develop specification techniques and tools that permit easier ways to prove assumptions and assertions, and to demonstrate consistency, completeness, and determinism
- Develop tools to allow traceability across the various intermediate and final products of software development. In particular, the tools can assess the impact of a proposed change on products, processes, and resources.
- Evaluate the many different ways to review requirements: tools, checklists, inspections, walkthroughs, and more. It is important to know which techniques are best for what situations.
- Create new techniques for simulating requirements behavior.
- Help us to understand what types of requirements are best for reuse in subsequent projects, and how to write requirements in a way that enhances their later reuse.

4.17 TERM PROJECT

Your clients at FCO have prepared the following set of English-language requirements for the Loan Arranger system. Like most sets of requirements, this set must be scrutinized in several ways to determine if it is correct, complete, and consistent. Using the requirements here and in supplementary material about the Loan Arranger in earlier chapters, evaluate and improve this set of requirements. Use many of the techniques presented in this chapter, including requirements measurement and Ardis's list. If necessary, express the requirements in a requirements language or modeling technique, to make sure that the static and dynamic properties of the system are expressed well.

Preconditions and Assumptions

- The Loan Arranger system assumes that there already exist lenders, borrowers, and loans from which to choose, and that investors exist who are interested in buying bundles of loans.
- The Loan Arranger system contains a repository of information about loans from a variety of lenders. This repository may be empty.
- At regular intervals, each lender provides reports listing the loans that it has made. Loans that have already been purchased by FCO will be indicated on these reports.
- Each loan in the Loan Arranger repository represents an investment to then be bundled and sold with other loans.
- The Loan Arranger system may be used by up to four loan analysts simultaneously.

High-Level Description of Functionality

1. The Loan Arranger system will receive monthly reports from each lender of new loans issued by that lender. The loans in the report recently purchased by FCO for its investment portfolio will be marked in the report. The Loan Arranger system will use the report information to update its repository of available loans.
2. The Loan Arranger system will receive monthly reports from each lender providing updates about the status of loans issued by that lender. The updated information will include: the current interest rate for an adjustable rate mortgage, and the status of the borrower with respect to the loan (good, late, or default). For loans in the FCO portfolio, the Loan Arranger will update the data in the repository. Loans not in the FCO portfolio will also be examined in order to determine if a borrower's standing should be updated. FCO will provide each lender with the format for the reports, so that all reports will share a common format.
3. The loan analyst can change individual data records as described in Data Operations.
4. All new data must be validated before they are added to the repository (according to the rules described in Data Constraints).
5. The loan analyst can use the Loan Arranger to identify bundles of loans to sell to particular investors.

Functional Requirements

1. The loan analyst should be able to review all of the information in the repository for a particular lending institution, a particular loan, or a particular borrower.
2. The loan analyst can create, view, edit, or delete a loan from a portfolio or bundle.
3. A loan is added to the portfolio automatically, when the Loan Arranger reads the reports provided by the lenders. A report can be read by the Loan Arranger only after the associated lender has been specified.
4. The loan analyst can create a new lender.
5. The loan analyst can delete a lender only if there are no loans in the portfolio associated with this lender.
6. The loan analyst can change lender contact and phone number but not lender name and identification number.
7. The loan analyst cannot change borrower information.
8. The loan analyst can ask the system to sort, search, or organize loan information by certain criteria: amount, interest rate, settlement date, borrower, lender, type of loan, or whether it has been marked for inclusion in a certain bundle. The organizational criteria should include ranges, so that information will be included only if it is within two specified bounds (such as between January 1, 2005 and January 1, 2008). The organizational criteria can also be based on exclusion such as all loans not marked, or all loans not between January 1, 2005 and January 1, 2008.
9. The loan analyst should be able to request reports in each of three formats: in a file, on the screen, and as a printed report.
10. The loan analyst should be able to request the following information in a report: any attribute of loan, lender, or borrower, and summary statistics of the attributes (mean, standard deviation, scatter diagram, and histogram). The information in a report can be restricted to a subset of the total information, as described by the loan analyst's organizing criteria.
11. The loan analyst must be able to use the Loan Arranger to create bundles that meet the prescribed characteristics of an investment request. The loan analyst can identify these bundles in several ways:
    - By manually identifying a subset of loans that must be included in the bundle, either by naming particular loans or by describing them using attributes or ranges
    - By providing the Loan Arranger with the investment criteria, and allowing the Loan Arranger to run a loan bundle optimization request to select the best set of loans to meet those criteria
    - By using a combination of the above, where a subset of loans is first chosen (manually or automatically), and then optimizing the chosen subset according to the investment criteria
12. Creating a bundle consists of two steps. First, the loan analyst works with the Loan Arranger to create a bundle according to the criteria as described above. Then the candidate bundle can be accepted, rejected, or modified. Modifying a

bundle means that the analyst may accept some but not all of the loans suggested by the Loan Arranger for a bundle, and can add specific loans to the bundle before accepting it.

13. The loan analyst must be able to mark loans for possible inclusion in a loan bundle. Once a loan is so marked, it is not available for inclusion in any other bundle. If the loan analyst marks a loan and decides not to include it in the bundle, the marking must be removed and the loan made available for other bundling decisions.
14. When a candidate bundle is accepted, its loans are removed from consideration for use in other bundles.
15. All current transactions must be resolved before a loan analyst can exit the Loan Arranger system.
16. A loan analyst can access a repository of investment requests. This repository may be empty. For each investment request, the analyst uses the request constraints (on risk, profit, and term) to define the parameters of a bundle. Then, the Loan Arranger system identifies loans to be bundled to meet the request constraints.

Data Constraints

1. A single borrower may have more than one loan.
2. Every lender must have a unique identifier.
3. Every borrower must have a unique identifier.
4. Each loan must have at least one borrower.
5. Each loan must have a loan amount of at least $1000 but not more than $500,000.
6. There are two types of loans based on the amount of the loan: regular and jumbo. A regular loan is for any amount less than or equal to $275,000. A jumbo loan is for any amount over $275,000.
7. A borrower is considered to be in good standing if all loans to that borrower are in good standing. A borrower is considered to be in default standing if any of the loans to that borrower have default standing. A borrower is said to be in late standing if any of the loans to that borrower have late standing.
8. A loan or borrower can change from good to late, from good to default, from late to good, or from late to default. Once a loan or borrower is in default standing, it cannot be changed to another standing.
9. A loan can change from ARM to FM, and from FM to ARM.
10. The profit requested by an investor is a number from 0 to 500. 0 represents no profit on a bundle. A nonzero profit represents the rate of return on the bundle; if the profit is x, then the investor expects to receive the original investment plus x percent of the original investment when the loans are paid off. Thus, if a bundle costs $1000, and the investor expects a rate of return of 40, then the investor hopes to have $1400 when all the loans in the bundle are paid off.
11. No loan can appear in more than one bundle.

Design and Interface Constraints

1. The Loan Arranger system should work on a Unix system.
2. The loan analyst should be able to look at information about more than one loan, lending institution, or borrower at a time.
3. The loan analyst must be able to move forward and backwards through the information presented on a screen. When the information is too voluminous to fit on a single screen, the user must be informed that more information can be viewed.
4. When the system displays the results of a search, the current organizing criteria must always be displayed along with the information.
5. A single record or line of output must never be broken in the middle of a field.
6. The user must be advised when a search request is inappropriate or illegal.
7. When an error is encountered, the system should return the user to the previous screen.

Quality Requirements

1. Up to four loan analysts can use the system at a given time.
2. If updates are made to any displayed information, the information is refreshed within five seconds of adding, updating, or deleting information.
3. The system must respond to a loan analyst's request for information in less than five seconds from submission of the request.
4. The system must be available for use by a loan analyst during 97% of the business day.

4.18 KEY REFERENCES

Michael Jackson's book *Software Requirements and Specifications* (1995) provides general advice on how to overcome common problems in understanding and formulating requirements. His ideas can be applied to any requirements technique. Donald Gause and Gerald Weinberg's book *Exploring Requirements* (1989) focuses on the human side of the requirements process: problems and techniques for working with customers and users and for devising new products.

A comprehensive requirements-definition template developed by James and Suzanne Robertson can be found at the Web site of the Atlantic Systems Guild: http://www.systemsguild.com. This template is accompanied by a description of the Volere process model, which is a complete process for eliciting and checking a set of requirements. Use of the template is described in their book *Mastering the Requirements Process* (1999).

Peter Coad and Edward Yourdon's book *Object-Oriented Analysis* (1991) is a classic text on object-oriented requirements analysis. The most thorough references on the Unified Modeling Language (UML) are the books by James Rumbaugh, Ivan Jacobson, and Grady Booch, especially the *Unified Modeling Language Reference Manual*, and the documents released by the Object Management Group; the latter can be downloaded from the organization's Web site: http://www.omg.org. Martin Fowler's book *Analysis Patterns* (1996) provides guidance on how to use UML to model common business problems.

Beginning in 1993, the IEEE Computer Society has started to sponsor two conferences that were directly related to requirements and were held in alternate years: the International Conference on Requirements Engineering and the International Symposium on Requirements Engineering. These conferences merged in 2002 to form the International Requirements Engineering Conference, which is held every year. Information about upcoming conferences and about proceedings from past conferences can be found at the Computer Society's Web page: http://www.computer.org.

The *Requirements Engineering Journal* focuses exclusively on new results in eliciting, representing, and validating requirements, mostly with respect to software systems. *IEEE Software* had special issues on requirements engineering in March 1994, March 1996, March/April 1998, May/June 2000, January/February 2003, and March/April 2004. Other IEEE publications often have special issues on particular types of requirements analysis and specification methods. For example, the September 1990 issues of *IEEE Computer, IEEE Software*, and *IEEE Transactions on Software Engineering* focused on formal methods, as did the May 1997 and January 1998 issues of *IEEE Transactions on Software Engineering* and the April 1996 issue of *IEEE Computer.*

There are several standards related to software requirements. The U.S. Department of Defense has produced MilStd-498, Data Item Description for Software Requirements Specifications (SRS). The IEEE has produced IEEE Std 830-1998, which is a set of recommended practices and standards for formulating and structuring requirements specifications.

There are several tools that support requirements capture and traceability. DOORS/ERS (Telelogic), Analyst Pro (Goda Software), and RequisitePro (IBM Rational) are popular tools for managing requirements, tracing requirements in downstream artifacts, tracking changes, and assessing the impact of changes. Most modeling notations have tool support that at the least supports the creation and editing of models, usually supports some form of well-formedness checking and report generation, and at the best offers automated validation and verification. An independent survey of requirements tools is located at www.systemsguild.com.

There is an IFIP Working Group 2.9 on Software Requirements Engineering. Some of the presentations from their annual meetings are available from their Web site: http://www.cis.gsu.edu/~wrobinso/ifip2_9

4.19 EXERCISES

1. In an early meeting with your customer, the customer lists the following "requirements" for a system he wants you to build:

   (a) The client daemon must be invisible to the user
   (b) The system should provide automatic verification of corrupted links or outdated data
   (c) An internal naming convention should ensure that records are unique
   (d) Communication between the database and servers should be encrypted
   (e) Relationships may exist between title groups [a type of record in the database]
   (f) Files should be organizable into groups of file dependencies

(g) The system must interface with an Oracle database
(h) The system must handle 50,000 users concurrently

Classify each of the above as a functional requirement, a quality requirement, a design constraint, or a process constraint. Which of the above might be premature design decisions? Re-express each of these decisions as a requirement that the design decision was meant to achieve.

2. Among the many nonfunctional requirements that can be included in a specification are those related to safety and reliability. How can we ensure that these requirements are testable, in the sense defined by the Robertsons? In particular, how can we demonstrate the reliability of a system that is required never to fail?

3. Developers work together with customers and users to define requirements and specify what the proposed system will do. If, once it is built, the system works according to specification but harms someone physically or financially, who is responsible?

4. The following statements appear in a requirement document:

(a) Upon completion, the system will send an e-mail.
(b) The user will enter the details.
(c) The software will be reusable in other projects.
(d) The human interface will be user friendly.
(e) The software will run under multiple operating systems.
(f) When a system failure occurs, the front panel red light will turn on.
(g) The MP3 player will support Flash memory.
(h) The data files will be smaller than 20KBytes.

Are these statements correct for a requirement document? If not, explain why and suggest a better statement.

5. Sometimes a customer requests a requirement that you know is impossible to implement. Should you agree to put the requirement in the definition and specification documents anyway, thinking that you might come up with a novel way of meeting it, or thinking that you will ask that the requirement be dropped later? Discuss the ethical implications of promising what you know you cannot deliver.

6. Is it ever possible to have the requirements definition document be the same as the requirements specification? What are the pros and cons of having two documents?

7. Contrast the benefits of an object-oriented requirements specification with those of a functional decomposition.

8. Sometimes part of a system may be built quickly to demonstrate feasibility or functionality to a customer. This prototype system is usually incomplete; the real system is constructed after the customer and developer evaluate the prototype. Should the system requirements document be written before or after a prototype is developed? Why?

9. What are the benefits of separating functional flow from data flow?

10. A simple microwave oven has the following components:

– A keypad with 12 keys: 0–9, Start and Timer. Through the keypad the user enters time and the desired function (timer or microwave).
– A Door Closed switch. This switch indicates that the door of the microwave oven is closed.
– A Magnetron Tube. This device emits the waves required for cooking into the cooking chamber.
– A buzzer. The buzzer notifies the user when the desired operation is done.

To operate the microwave oven, the user enters the desired time, chooses between regular microwave operation (Start key) and timer operation (Timer key), and makes sure the door is closed.

Write a state-machine specification for the microwave oven.

11. Write a state-machine specification to illustrate the requirements of an automatic banking machine (ABM).

12. A state-machine specification is **complete** if and only if there is a transition specified for every possible combination of state and input symbol. We can change an incomplete specification to a complete one by adding an extra state, called a trap state. Once a transition is made to the trap state, the system remains in the trap state, no matter the input. For example, if 0, 1, and 2 are the only possible inputs, the system depicted by Figure 4.33 can be completed by adding a trap state as shown in Figure 4.34. In same manner, complete your state-machine specification from Exercise 11.

13. A **safety property** is an invariant property that specifies that a particular bad behavior never happens; for example, a safety property of the turnstile problem is that the number of entries into the zoo is never more than the number of entry fees paid. A **liveness property** is a property that specifies that a particular behavior eventually happens; for

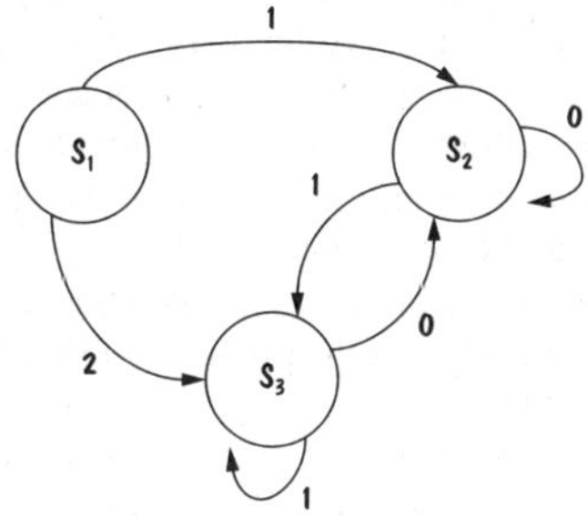

FIGURE 4.33 Original system for Exercise 11.

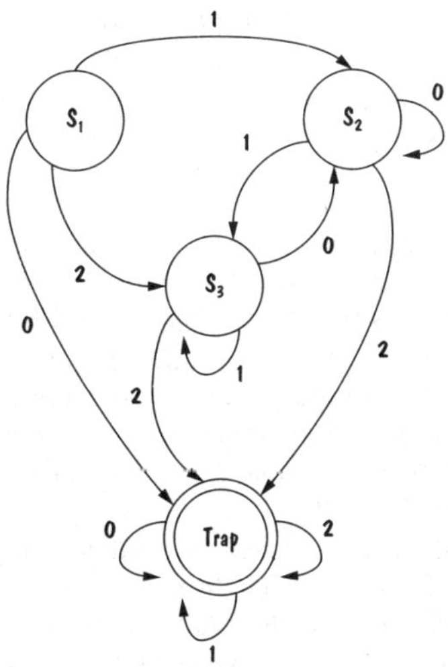

FIGURE 4.34 Complete system with trap state for Exercise 11.

example, a liveness property for the turnstile problem is that when an entry fee is paid, the turnstile becomes unlocked. Similarly, a liveness property for the library system is that every borrow request from a `Patron` who has no outstanding library fines succeeds. These three properties, when expressed in logic, look like the following:

```
□ (num_coins ≥ num_entries)
□ (insert_coin ○ barrier=unlocked)
□ ( (borrow(Patron,Pub) ∧ Patron.fines = 0)⇒
        ◇∃ Loan. [Loan.borrower=Patron ∧ Loan.Publication = Pub] )
```

List safety and liveness properties for your automated banking machine specification from Exercise 11. Express these properties in temporal logic.

14. Prove that your safety and liveness properties from Exercise 13 hold for your state-machine model of your automated banking machine specification from Exercise 11. What assumptions do you have to make about the ABM's environment (e.g., that the machine has sufficient cash) for your proofs to succeed?
15. The class diagram for the library problem is shown in Figure 4.5. Suggest three to four more classes that will make the system more complete. Explain briefly each class and suggest three possible attributes and operations.
16. Write a decision table that specifies the rules for the game of checkers.
17. If a decision table has two identical columns, then the requirements specification is redundant. How can we tell if the specification is contradictory? What other characteristics of a decision table warn us of problems with the requirements?
18. Write a Parnas table that describes the output of the algorithm for finding the roots of a quadratic equation using the quadratic formula.
19. Write a set of UML models (use-case diagram, MSC diagrams, class diagram) for an on-line telephone directory to replace the phonebook that is provided to you by your phone company. The directory should be able to provide phone numbers when presented with a name; it should also list area codes for different parts of the country and generate emergency telephone numbers for your area.
20. Draw data-flow diagrams to illustrate the functions and data flow for the on-line telephone directory system specified in the previous problem.
21. Write a Z specification for a presentation scheduling system. The system keeps a record of which presenters are to give presentations on which dates. No presenter should be scheduled to give more than one presentation. No more than four presentations should be scheduled for any particular date. There should be operations to Add and Remove presentations from the schedule, to Swap the dates of two presentations, to List the presentations scheduled for a particular date, to List the date on which a particular presenter is scheduled to speak, and to send a Reminder message to each presenter on the date of his or her presentation. You may define any additional operations that help simplify the specification.
22. Complete the partial SDL data specification for the library problem in Figure 4.20. In particular, write axioms for nongenerator operations `unreserve`, `isOnLoan`, and `isOnReserve`. Modify your axioms for operation `unreserve` so that this operation assumes that multiple requests to put an `item` on `reserve` might occur between two requests to `unreserve` that item.
23. Pfleeger and Hatton (1997) examined the quality of a system that had been specified using formal methods. They found that the system was unusually well-structured and easy to test. They speculated that the high quality was due to the thoroughness of the specification, not necessarily its formality. How could you design a study to determine whether it is formality or thoroughness that leads to high quality?

5 Designing the Architecture

In this chapter, we look at
- views of software architecture
- common architectural patterns
- criteria for evaluating and comparing design alternatives
- software architecture documentation

In the last chapter, we learned how to work with our customers to determine what they want the proposed system to do. The result of the requirements process was two documents: a requirements document that captures the customers' needs and a requirements specification that describes how the proposed system should behave. The next step in development is to start designing how the system will be constructed. If we are building a relatively small system, we may be able to progress directly from the specification to the design of data structures and algorithms. However, if we are building a larger system, then we will want to decompose the system into units of manageable size, such as subsystems or modules, before we contemplate details about the data or code.

The software architecture is this decomposition. In this chapter, we examine different types of decomposition. Just as buildings are sometimes constructed of prefabricated sections based on commonly needed architectural constructs, some prefabricated software architectural styles can be used as guidelines for decomposing a new system. Often, there will be multiple ways to design the architecture, so we explore how to compare competing designs and choose the one that best suits our needs. We learn how to document our decisions in a software architecture document (SAD) as the architecture starts to stabilize, and how to verify that this architecture will meet the customer's requirements. The steps we lay out result in a software architecture that guides the rest of the system's development.

5.1 THE DESIGN PROCESS

At this point in the development process, we have a good understanding of our customer's problem, and we have a requirements specification that describes what an acceptable software solution would look like. If the specification was done well, it has focused on function, not form; that is, it gives few hints about how to build the proposed system. **Design** is the creative process of figuring out how to implement all of the customer's requirements; the resulting plan is also called the **design**.

Early design decisions address the system's **architecture**, explaining how to decompose the system into units, how the units relate to one another, and describing any externally visible properties of the units (Bass, Clements, and Kazman 2003). Later design decisions address how to implement the individual units. To see how architecture relates to both design and requirements, consider again the example in which Chuck and Betsy Howell want to build a new house. Their requirements include

- rooms for them and their three children to sleep
- a place for the children to play
- a kitchen and a large dining room that will hold an extendable table
- storage for bicycles, lawn mower, ladder, barbecue, patio furniture, and more
- a place for a piano
- heating and air conditioning

and so on. From the requirements, an architect produces preliminary designs for the Howells to consider. The architect may start by showing the Howells some generic plans based on different styles of houses, such as two-story colonials and bungalows, to get a better feel for what style the Howells would prefer. Within a particular architectural style, the architect may sketch out various design alternatives. For instance, in one design, the kitchen, dining room, and children's play space may share one large open area, whereas another design may locate the play space in a less public part of the house. One design may emphasize large bedrooms, and another may reduce bedroom size to make room for an additional bathroom. How the Howells choose from among the design alternatives will depend on their preferences for a design's distinguishing characteristics, such as the utility and character of the rooms' layouts, or the estimated cost of construction.

The resulting design is the house's architecture, as suggested by Figure 5.1. Most obviously, the architecture describes the skeletal structure of the house, the locations of walls and support beams, and the configuration of each room. It also includes plans for

FIGURE 5.1 Architectural plans.

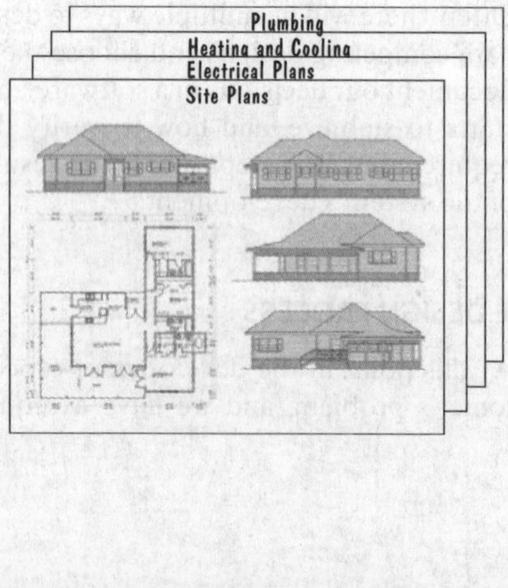

sufficient heating and cooling, and the layout of air ducts; maps of water pipes and their connections to the city's water mains and sewer lines; and maps of electrical circuits, locations of outlets, and the amperage of circuit breakers. Architectural decisions tend to be structural, systematic, and systemic, making sure that all essential elements of the requirements are addressed in ways that harmonize customer needs with the realities of materials, cost, and availability. They are the earliest design decisions to be made and, once implemented, are the hardest to change. In contrast, later design decisions, such as those regarding flooring, cabinetry, wall paint, or paneling, are relatively localized and easy to modify.

Difficult to change does not mean impossible. It is not unusual or unreasonable for the architecture or specifications to change as the house is being built. Modifications may not be proposed on a whim, but instead on a change in perception or need, or in reaction to new information. In the Howells' house, engineers may suggest changes to reduce costs, such as moving bathrooms or the location of the kitchen sink, so that they can share water pipes and drains. As the Howells think about how rooms will be used, they may ask that a heating duct be rerouted, so that it does not run along the wall where they plan to put their piano. If there are construction-cost overruns, they may scale back their plans to stay within their budget. It makes sense for the Howells to raise these issues and to change their specifications now, rather than be stuck with a house that displeases them, does not suit their needs, or costs more than they can afford. Indeed, a customer, in concert with the developers, will often modify requirements well after the initial requirements analysis is complete.

In many ways, designing software resembles the process of designing a new house. We are obligated to devise a solution that meets the customer's needs, as documented in the requirements specification. However, as with the Howells' house, there may not be a single "best" or "correct" architecture, and the number of possible solutions may be limitless. By gleaning ideas from past solutions and by seeking regular feedback from the customer, designers create a good architecture, one that is able to accommodate and adapt to change, that results in a product that will make the customer happy, and that is a useful reference and source of guidance throughout the product's lifetime.

Design Is a Creative Process

Designing software is an intellectually challenging task. It can be taxing to keep track of all the possible cases that the software system might encounter, including the exceptional cases (such as missing or incorrect information) that the system must accommodate. And this effort takes into account only the system's expected functionality. In addition, the system has nonfunctional design goals to fulfill, such as being easy to maintain and extend, being easy to use, or being easy to port to other platforms. These nonfunctional requirements not only constrain the set of acceptable solutions, but also may actually conflict with each other. For example, techniques for making a software system reliable or reusable are costly, and thus hinder goals to keep development costs within a specified budget. Furthermore, external factors can complicate the design task. For example, the software may have to adhere to preexisting hardware interface specifications, work with legacy software, or conform with standard data formats or government regulations.

There are no instructions or formulae that we can follow to guarantee a successful design. Creativity, intelligence, experience, and expert judgment are needed to devise a design that adequately satisfies all of the system's requirements. Design methods and techniques can guide us in making design decisions, but they are no substitute for creativity and judgment.

We can improve our design skills by studying examples of good design. Most design work is **routine design** (Shaw 1990), in which we solve a problem by reusing and adapting solutions from similar problems. Consider a chef who is asked to prepare dinner for a finicky patron who has particular tastes and dietary constraints. There may be few recipes that exactly fit the patron's tastes, and the chef is not likely to concoct brand new dishes for the occasion. Instead, the chef may seek inspiration from favorite recipes, will substitute ingredients, and will adapt cooking methods and times as appropriate. The recipes alone are not enough; there is considerable creativity in the making of this meal: in choosing the starting recipes, in adapting the ingredient list, and in modifying the cooking instructions to accentuate flavors, textures, and colors. What the chef gains by starting from proven recipes is *efficiency* in quickly settling on a plan for the meal and *predictability* in knowing that the resulting dishes should be similar in quality to dishes derived previously from the same recipes.

Similarly, experienced software developers rarely design new software from first principles. Instead, they borrow ideas from existing solutions and manipulate them into new, but not entirely original, designs. By doing so, developers can usually arrive at a suitable design more quickly, using the properties of the borrowed solutions to assess the properties of the proposed design. Figure 5.2 shows several sources from which developers can draw when looking for guidance in designing a new system.

There are many ways to leverage existing solutions. One extreme is **cloning**, whereby we borrow a whole design, and perhaps even the code, making minor adjustments to fit our particular problem. For example, a developer might clone an existing system to customize it for a new customer—though, as we will see, there are better ways of producing variations of the same product. Slightly less extreme is to base our design on a **reference model**: a standard generic architecture for a particular application domain. A reference model suggests only how we decompose our system into its major

FIGURE 5.2 Sources of design advice.

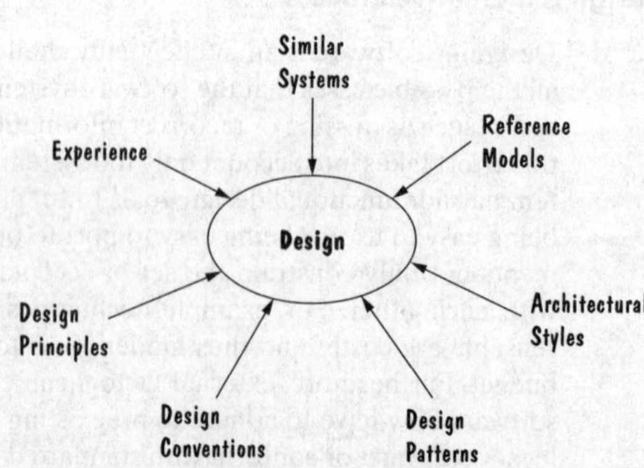

components and how those components interact with each other. The design of the individual components and the details of their interactions will depend on the specific application being developed. As an example, Figure 5.3 shows the reference model for a compiler; the specifics of the parser, semantic analyzer, optimizations, and data repositories will vary greatly with the compiler's programming language. There are existing or proposed reference models for a variety of application domains, including operating systems, interpreters, database management systems, process-control systems, integrated tool environments, communication networks, and Web services.

More typically, our problem does not have a reference model, and we create a design by combining and adapting generic design solutions. In your other courses, you have learned about generic, low-level design solutions such as data structures (e.g., lists, trees) and algorithm paradigms (e.g., divide-and-conquer, dynamic programming) that are useful in addressing entire classes of problems. Software architectures have generic solutions too, called **architectural styles**. Like reference models, architectural styles give advice about how to decompose a problem into software units and how those units should interact with each other. Unlike reference models, architectural styles are not optimized for specific application domains. Rather, they give generic advice about how to approach generic design problems (e.g., how to encapsulate data shared by all aspects of the system).

Sometimes, improving one aspect of a software system has an adverse effect on another aspect. For this reason, creating a software system design can raise several orthogonal issues. Good software architectural design is about selecting, adapting, and integrating several architectural styles in ways that best produce the desired result. There are many tools at our disposal for understanding our options and evaluating the

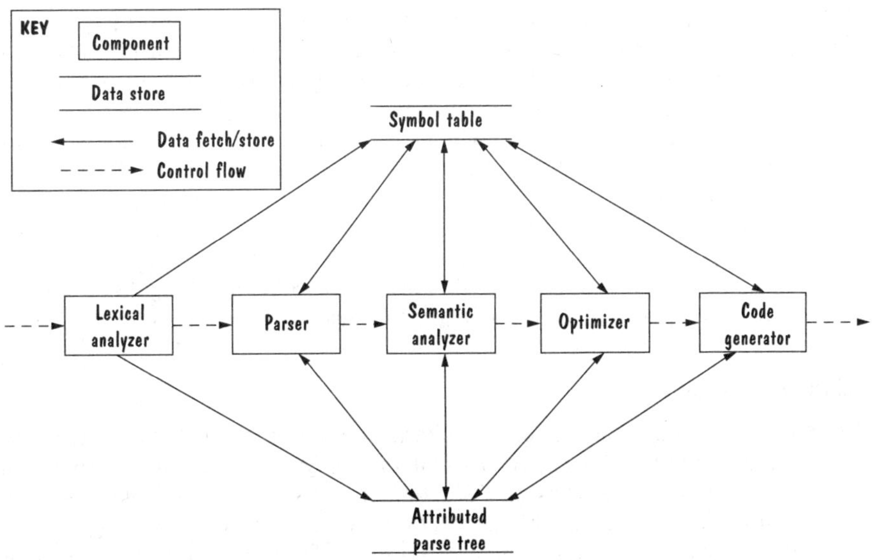

FIGURE 5.3 Reference model for a compiler (adapted from Shaw and Garlan 1996).

chosen architecture. **Design patterns** are generic solutions for making lower-level design decisions about individual software modules or small collections of modules; they will be discussed in Chapter 6. A **design convention** or **idiom** is a collection of design decisions and advice that, taken together, promotes certain design qualities. For example, abstract data types (ADTs) are a design convention that encapsulates data representation and supports reusability. As a design convention matures and becomes more widely used, it is packaged into a design pattern or architectural style, for easier reference and use; ultimately, it may be encoded as a program–language construct. Objects, modules, exceptions, and templates are examples of design and programming conventions that are now supported by programming languages.

Sometimes, existing solutions cannot solve a problem satisfactorily; we need a novel solution that requires **innovative design** (Shaw 1990). In contrast to routine design, the innovative design process is characterized by irregular bursts of progress that occur as we have flashes of insight. The only guidance we can use in innovative design is a set of basic **design principles** that are descriptive characteristics of good design, rather than prescriptive advice about how to design. As such, they are more useful when we are evaluating and comparing design alternatives than when we are designing. Nevertheless, we can use the principles during design to assess how well a particular design decision adheres to them. In the end, innovative design usually takes longer than routine design, because often there are stagnant periods between insights. Innovative designs must be more vigorously evaluated than routine designs, because they have no track record. Moreover, because such design evaluation is based more on expert judgment than on objective criteria, an innovative design should be examined by several senior designers before it is formally approved. In general, an innovative design should be superior to competing routine designs to justify the extra cost of its development and evaluation.

So should we always stick with tried and true approaches, rather than explore new ways of designing systems? As with other skilled disciplines, such as music or sports, it is only through continuous learning and practice that we improve our design skills. What distinguishes an experienced chef from a novice is her larger repertoire of recipes, her proficiency with a wide range of cooking techniques, her deep understanding of ingredients and how they change when cooked, and her ability to refashion a recipe or a meal to emphasize or enhance the desired experience. Similarly, as we gain more experience with software design, we understand better how to select from among generic design solutions, how to apply design principles when deviating from generic solutions, and how to combine partial solutions into a coherent design whose characteristics improve on past solutions to similar problems.

Design Process Model

Designing a software system is an iterative process, in which designers move back and forth among activities involving understanding the requirements, proposing possible solutions, testing aspects of a solution for feasibility, presenting possibilities to the customers, and documenting the design for the programmers. Figure 5.4 illustrates the process of converging on a software architecture for a proposed system. We start the process by analyzing the system's requirements specification and identifying any

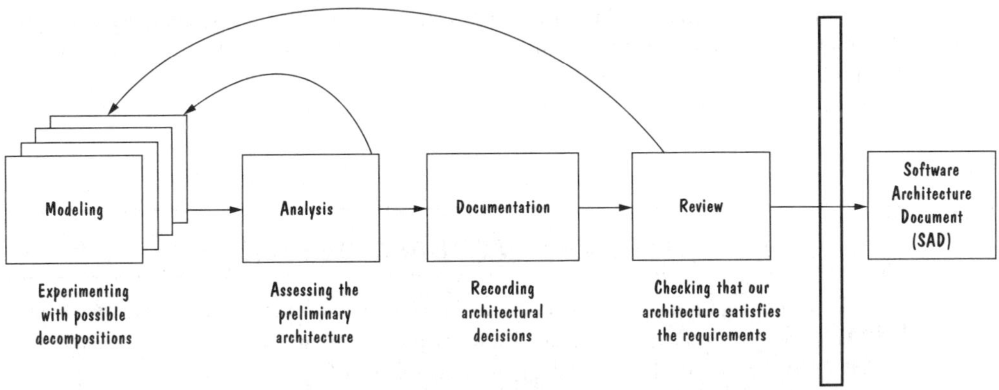

FIGURE 5.4 Process for developing a software architecture.

critical properties or constraints that the eventual design must exhibit or reflect. These properties can help us identify which architectural styles might be useful in our design. Different properties will suggest different architectural styles, so we will likely develop several architectural plans in parallel, each depicting a single facet or **view** of the architecture. The multiple views in software design are analogous to the blueprints that the Howells' architect produced for their house.

During the first part of the design phase, we iterate among three activities: drawing architectural plans, analyzing how well the proposed architecture promotes desired properties, and using the analysis results to improve and optimize the architectural plans. The types of analysis we perform at this stage focus on the system's quality attributes, such as performance, security, and reliability. Thus, our architectural models must include sufficient detail to support whatever analyses we are most interested in performing. However, we do not want our models to be too detailed. At the architectural stage, we focus on system-level decisions, such as communication, coordination, synchronization, and sharing; we defer more detailed design decisions, such as those that affect individual modules, to the detailed design phase. As the architecture starts to stabilize, we document our models. Each of our models is an architectural view, and the views are interconnected, so that a change to one view may have an impact on other views. Thus, we keep track of how the views are related and how they work together to form a coherent integrated design. Finally, once the architecture is documented, we conduct a formal design review, in which the project team checks that the architecture meets all of the system's requirements and is of high quality. If problems are identified during the design review, we may have to revise our design yet again to address these concerns.

The final outcome of the software architecture process is the SAD, used to communicate system-level design decisions to the rest of the development team. Because the SAD provides a high-level overview of the system's design, the document is also useful for quickly bringing new development team members up to speed, and for educating the maintenance team about how the system works. Project managers may use the SAD as the basis for organizing development teams and tracking the teams' progress.

Software architecture and architecture documents play a less clear role in agile development methods. There is an inherent conflict between software architecture, which documents the system's load-bearing, hard-to-change design decisions, and the agile goal of avoiding irreversible decisions. This conflict is discussed further in Sidebar 5.1.

SIDEBAR 5.1 AGILE ARCHITECTURES

As we noted in Chapter 4, it can sometimes be helpful to use an agile process when there is a great deal of uncertainty about requirements. In the same way, agility can be helpful when it is not yet clear what the best type of design might be.

Agile architectures are based on the four premises of agile methods as stated in the "agile manifesto" (see http://agilemanifesto.org):

- valuing individuals and interactions over processes and tools
- valuing working software over comprehensive documentation
- valuing customer collaboration over contract negotiation
- valuing response to change over following plans

Agile methods can be used to generate an initial design that describes essential requirements. As new requirements and design considerations emerge, agile methods can be applied to "refactor" the design so that it matures with the understanding of the problem and the customer's needs.

But architectural generation is particularly difficult using agile methods, because both complexity and change must be managed carefully. A developer adhering to agile methods is at the same time trying to minimize documentation and to lay out the variety of choices available to customers and coders. So agile architectures are based on models, but only small features are modeled, often one at a time, as different options and approaches are explored. Models are often discarded or rebuilt as the most appropriate solution becomes clear. As Ambler (2003) puts it, an agile model is "just barely good enough": it "meets its goals and no more."

Because agile methods employ iteration and exploration, they encourage programmers to write the code as the models are being produced. Such linkage may be a significant problem for agile architectures. As Ambler points out, although some agile methods advocates have high confidence in architectural tools (see Uhl 2003, for instance), others think the tools are not ready for prime time and may never be (see Ambler 2003).

A bigger problem with agile methods is the need for continuous refactoring. The inherent conflict between an architecture's representing a significant design decision and the need for continuous refactoring means that systems are not refactored as often as they should be. Thomas (2005) calls the refactoring of large, complex systems high-risk "wizard's work," particularly when there is a great deal of legacy code containing intricate dependencies.

5.2 MODELING ARCHITECTURES

In modeling an architecture, we try to represent some property of the architecture while hiding others. In this way, we can learn a great deal about the property without being distracted by other aspects of the system. Most importantly, the collection of models helps us to reason about whether the proposed architecture will meet the specified requirements. Garlan (2000) points out that there are six ways we can use the architectural models:

- to understand the system: what it will do and how it will do it
- to determine how much of the system will reuse elements of previously built systems and how much of the system will be reusable in the future
- to provide a blueprint for constructing the system, including where the "load-bearing" parts of the system may be (i.e., those design decisions that will be difficult to change later)
- to reason about how the system might evolve, including performance, cost, and prototyping concerns
- to analyze dependencies and select the most appropriate design, implementation, and testing techniques
- to support management decisions and understand risks inherent in implementation and maintenance

In Chapter 4, we described many techniques for modeling requirements. However, software architecture modeling is not so mature. Of the many ways to model architectures, your choice depends partly on the model's goal and partly on personal preference. Each has pros and cons, and there is no universal technique that works best in every situation. Some developers use the Unified Modeling Language (UML) class diagrams to depict an architecture, emphasizing subsystems rather than classes. More typically, software architectures are modeled using simple box-and-arrow diagrams, perhaps accompanied by a legend that explains the meaning of different types of boxes and arrows. We use this approach in our examples. As you build and evaluate real systems, you may use another modeling technique. But the principles expressed in boxes and arrows can easily be translated to other models.

5.3 DECOMPOSITION AND VIEWS

In the past, software designers used decomposition as their primary tool, making a large problem more tractable by decomposing it into smaller pieces whose goals were easier to address. We call this approach "top down," because we start with the big picture and decompose it into smaller, lower-level pieces. By contrast, many of today's designers work on the architecture from the bottom up, packaging together small modules and components into a larger whole. Some experts think that a bottom-up approach produces a system that is easier to maintain. We will look more carefully at these maintenance issues in Chapter 11. As architectural and design approaches change over time, and as we gather more evidence to support claims of maintainability and other quality characteristics, we will have a better understanding of the impact of each design approach.

Some design problems have no existing solutions or components with which to start. Here, we use decomposition, a traditional approach that helps the designers understand and isolate the key problems that the system is to solve. Because understanding decomposition can also shed light on the best ways to test, enhance, and maintain an existing system, in this section, we explore and contrast several decomposition methods. Design by decomposition starts with a high-level description of the system's key elements. Then we iteratively refine the design by dividing each of the system's elements into its constituent pieces and describing their interfaces. We are done when further refinement results in pieces that have no interfaces. This process is depicted in Figure 5.5.

Here are brief descriptions of some popular design methods:

- **Functional decomposition:** This method partitions functions or requirements into modules. The designer begins with the functions that are listed in the requirements specification; these are system-level functions that exchange inputs and outputs with the system's environment. Lower-level designs divide these functions into subfunctions, which are then assigned to smaller modules. The design also describes which modules (subfunctions) call each other.
- **Feature-oriented design:** This method is a type of functional decomposition that assigns features to modules. The high-level design describes the system in terms of a service and a collection of features. Lower-level designs describe how each feature augments the service and identifies interactions among features.
- **Data-oriented decomposition:** This method focuses on how data will be partitioned into modules. The high-level design describes conceptual data structures, and lower-level designs provide detail as to how data are distributed among modules and how the distributed data realize the conceptual models.
- **Process-oriented decomposition:** This method partitions the system into concurrent processes. The high-level design (1) identifies the system's main tasks, which

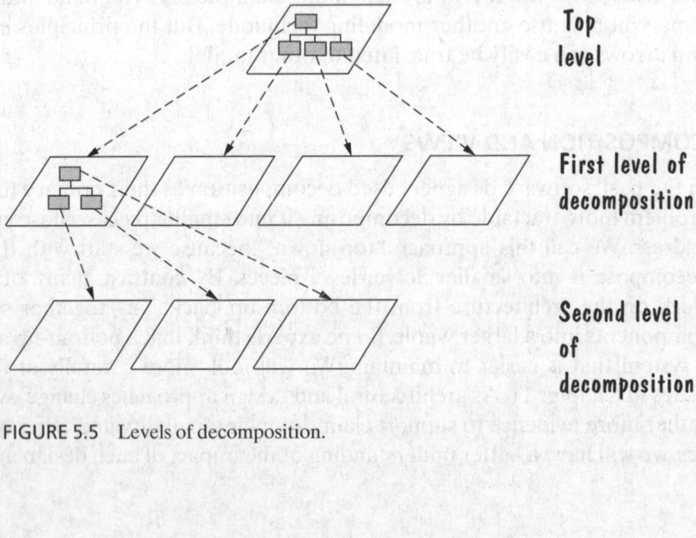

FIGURE 5.5 Levels of decomposition.

operate mostly independently of each other, (2) assigns tasks to runtime processes, and (3) explains how the tasks coordinate with each other. Lower-level designs describe the processes in more detail.

- **Event-oriented decomposition:** This method focuses on the events that the system must handle and assigns responsibility for events to different modules. The high-level design catalogues the system's expected input events, and lower-level designs decompose the system into states and describe how events trigger state transformations.
- **Object-oriented design:** This method assigns objects to modules. The high-level design identifies the system's object types and explains how objects are related to one another. Lower-level designs detail the objects' attributes and operations.

How we choose which design method to use depends on the system we are developing: Which aspects of the system's specification are most prominent (e.g., functions, objects, features)? How is the system's interface described (e.g., input events, data streams)? For many systems, it may be appropriate to view several decompositions, or to use different design methods at different levels of abstraction. Sometimes, the choice of design method is not so important and may be based on the designer's preferences.

To see how decomposition works, suppose we want to follow a data-oriented design method. We start with the conceptual data stores that were identified during requirements analysis. This analysis included externally visible operations on these data, such as creation, queries, modifications, and deletion. We design the system by clustering the conceptual data into data objects and operations on those objects. We further decompose complex data objects into aggregations of simpler objects, with the simplest objects storing one type of data. Each object type provides access operations for querying and manipulating its data. This way, other parts of the system can use the object's stored information without accessing the data directly. The resulting design is a hierarchical decomposition of objects. The design differs from the requirements specification because it includes information about *how* system data are to be distributed into objects and *how* objects manipulate data values, and not just information about *what* data will be manipulated by the system.

No matter which design approach we use, the resulting design is likely to refer to several types of software units, such as **component, subsystem, runtime process, module, class, package, library**, or **procedure**. The different terms describe different aspects of a design. For example, we use the term **module** to refer to a structural unit of the software's code; a module could be an atomic unit, like a Java class, or it could be an aggregation of other modules. We use the term **component** to refer to an identifiable runtime element (e.g., the parser is a component in a compiler)—although this term sometimes has a specific meaning, as explained in Sidebar 5.2. Some of the above terms designate software units at different levels of abstraction. For example, a system may be made up of subsystems, which may be made up of packages, which are in turn made up of classes. In other cases, the terms may overlap and present different views of the same entity (e.g., a parser might be both a component and a high-level module). We use the term **software unit** when we want to talk about a system's composite parts without being precise about what type of part.

SIDEBAR 5.2 COMPONENT-BASED SOFTWARE ENGINEERING

Component-based software engineering (CBSE) is a method of software development whereby systems are created by assembling together preexisting components. In this setting, a **component** is "a self-contained piece of software with a well-defined set of interfaces" (Herzum and Sims 2000) that can be developed, bought, and sold as a distinct entity. The goal of CBSE is to support the rapid development of new systems, by reducing development to *component integration*, and to ease the maintenance of such systems by reducing maintenance to *component replacement*.

At this point, CBSE is still more of a goal than a reality. There are software components for sale, and part of software design is deciding which aspects of a system we should buy **off the shelf** and which we should build ourselves. But there is still considerable research being done on figuring out how to

- specify components, so that buyers can determine whether a particular component fits their needs
- certify that a component performs as claimed
- reason about the properties of a system (e.g., reliability) from the properties of its components

We say that a design is **modular** when each activity of the system is performed by exactly one software unit, and when the inputs and outputs of each software unit are well-defined. A software unit is **well-defined** if its interface accurately and precisely specifies the unit's externally visible behavior: each specified input is essential to the unit's function, and each specified output is a possible result of the unit's actions. In addition, "well-defined" means that the interface says nothing about any property or design detail that cannot be discerned outside the software unit. Chapter 6 includes a section on design principles that describes in more detail how to make design decisions that result in modular designs.

Architectural Views

We want to decompose the system's design into its constituent programmable units, such as modules, objects, or procedures. However, this set of elements may not be the only decomposition we consider. If the proposed system is to be distributed over several computers, we may want a view of the design that shows the distribution of the system's components as well as how those components communicate with each other. Alternatively, we may want a view of the design that shows the various services that the system is to offer and how the services operate together, regardless of how the services are mapped to code modules.

Common types of architectural views include the following:

- **Decomposition view:** This traditional view of a system's decomposition portrays the system as programmable units. As depicted in Figure 5.5, this view is likely to be hierarchical and may be represented by multiple models. For example, a software unit in one model may be expanded in another model to show its constituent units.

- **Dependencies view:** This view shows dependencies among software units, such as when one unit calls another unit's procedures or when one unit relies on data produced by one or more other units. This view is useful in project planning, to identify which software units are dependency free and thus can be implemented and tested in isolation. It is also useful for assessing the impact of making a design change to some software unit.
- **Generalization view:** This view shows software units that are generalizations or specializations of one another. An obvious example is an inheritance hierarchy among object-oriented classes. In general, this view is useful when designing abstract or extendible software units: the general unit encapsulates common data and functionality, and we derive various specialized units by instantiating and extending the general unit.
- **Execution view:** This view is the traditional box-and-arrow diagram that software architects draw, showing the runtime structure of a system in terms of its components and connectors. Each **component** is a distinct executing entity, possibly with its own program stack. A **connector** is some intercomponent communication mechanism, such as a communication channel, shared data repository, or remote procedure call.
- **Implementation view:** This view maps code units, such as modules, objects, and procedures, to the source file that contains their implementation. This view helps programmers find the implementation of a software unit within a maze of source-code files.
- **Deployment view:** This view maps runtime entities, such as components and connectors, onto computer resources, such as processors, data stores, and communication networks. It helps the architect analyze the quality attributes of a design, such as performance, reliability, and security.
- **Work-assignment view:** This view decomposes the system's design into work tasks that can be assigned to project teams. It helps project managers plan and allocate project resources, as well as track each team's progress.

Each view is a model of some aspect of the system's structure, such as code structure, runtime structure, file structure, or project team structure. A system's architecture represents the system's overall design structure; thus, it is the full collection of these views. Normally, we do not attempt to combine views into a single integrated design, because such a description—comprising multiple overlays of different decompositions—would be too difficult to read and keep up-to-date. Later in this chapter, we discuss how to document a system's architecture as a collection of views. The documentation includes mappings among views so that we can understand the big picture.

5.4 ARCHITECTURAL STYLES AND STRATEGIES

Creating a software architectural design is not a straightforward task. The design progresses in bursts of activity, with the design team often alternating between top-down and bottom-up analysis. In top-down design, the team tries to partition the system's key functions into distinct modules that can be assigned to separate components. However, if the team recognizes that a known, previously implemented design solution might be useful, the team may switch to a bottom-up design approach, adapting a prepackaged solution.

Often, our approaches to solving some problems have common features, and we can take advantage of the commonality by applying generalized patterns. Software **architectural styles** are established, large-scale patterns of system structure. Analogous to architectural styles for buildings, software architectural styles have defining rules, elements, and techniques that result in designs with recognizable structures and well-understood properties. However, styles are not complete detailed solutions. Rather, they are loose templates that offer distinct solutions for coordinating a system's components. To be specific, architectural styles focus on the different ways that components might communicate, synchronize, or share data with one another. As such, their structures codify constrained interactions among components and offer mechanisms, such as protocols, for realizing those interactions. In the early stages of software development, architectural styles can be useful for exploring and exploiting known approaches to organizing and coordinating access to data and functionality. In general, by constraining intercomponent interactions, architectural styles can be used to help the resulting system achieve specific system properties, such as data security (by restricting data flow) and maintainability (by simplifying communication interfaces).

Researchers are continuously analyzing good software designs, looking for useful architectural styles that can be applied more generally. These styles are then collected in **style catalogues** that an architect can reference when considering the best architecture for a given set of requirements. A few of these catalogues are listed at the end of this chapter.

In the rest of this section, we examine six architectural styles commonly used in software development: *pipe-and-filter, client-server, peer-to-peer, publish-subscribe, repositories*, and *layering*. For each style, we describe the software elements comprising the style, the constraints on interactions among elements, and some properties (good and bad) of the resulting system.

Pipe-and-Filter

In a pipe-and-filter style, illustrated in Figure 5.6, system functionality is achieved by passing input data through a sequence of data-transforming components, called **filters**, to produce output data. **Pipes** are connectors that simply transmit data from one filter to the next without modifying the data. Each filter is an independent function that makes no assumptions about other filters that may be applied to the data. Thus, we can build our system by connecting together different filters to form a variety of configurations. If the format of the data is fixed—that is, if all of the filters and pipes assume a common representation of the data being transmitted—then we can join filters together in any configuration. Such systems have several important properties (Shaw and Garlan 1996):

- We can understand the system's transformation of input data to output data as the functional composition of the filters' data transformations.

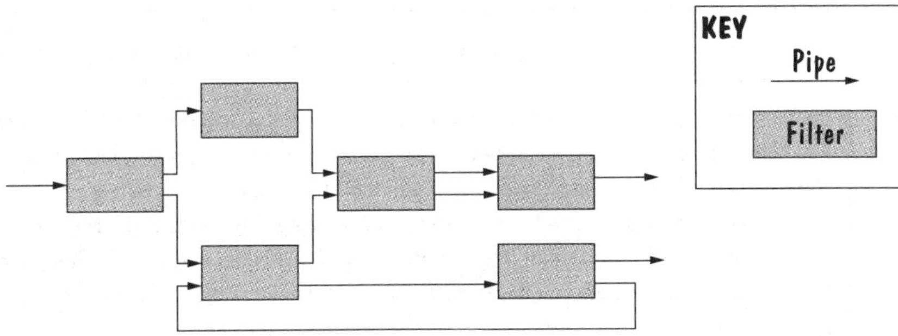

FIGURE 5.6 Pipes and filters.

- Filters can be reused in any other pipe-and-filter style program that assumes the same format for input and output data. Examples of such filters and systems include image-processing systems and Unix shell programs.
- System evolution is relatively easy; we can simply introduce new filters into our system's configuration, or replace or remove existing filters, without having to modify other parts of the system.
- Because of filter independence, we can perform certain types of analyses, such as throughput analysis.
- There are performance penalties when using a pipe-and-filter architecture. To support a fixed data format during data transmission, each filter must parse input data before performing its computation and then convert its results back to the fixed data format for output. This repeated parsing and unparsing of data can hamper system performance. It can also make the construction of the individual filters more complex.

In some pipe-and-filter style systems, the filters are independent data-transforming functions, but the representation of data passed between filters is not fixed. For example, old-style compilers had pipe-and-filter architectures in which the output of each filter (e.g., the lexical analyzer or the parser) was fed directly into the next filter. Because the filters in such systems are independent and have precise input and output formats, it is easy to replace and improve filters but hard to introduce or remove filters. For example, to remove a filter, we may need to substitute a stub that converts the output from the previous filter into the input format expected by the next filter.

Client-Server

In a client-server architecture, the design is divided into two types of components: clients and servers. **Server** components offer services, and **clients** access them using a **request/reply protocol**. The components execute concurrently and are usually distributed across several computers. There may be one centralized server, several replicated servers distributed over several machines, or several distinct servers each offering a different set of services. The relationship between clients and servers is asymmetric: Clients know the identities of the servers from which they request information, but servers

SIDEBAR 5.3 THE WORLD CUP CLIENT-SERVER SYSTEM

In 1994, the World Cup soccer matches were held in the United States. Over a single month, 24 teams played 52 games, drawing huge television and in-person audiences. The games were played in nine different cities that spanned four time zones. As a team won a match, it often moved to another city for the next game. During this process, the results of each game were recorded and disseminated to the press and to the fans. At the same time, to prevent the likelihood of violence among the fans, the organizers issued and tracked over 20,000 identification passes.

This system required both central control and distributed functions. For example, the system accessed central information about all the players. After a key play, the system could present historical information (images, video, and text) about those players involved. Thus, a client-server architecture seemed appropriate.

The system that was built included a central database, located in Texas, for ticket management, security, news services, and Internet links. This server also calculated games statistics and provided historical information, security photographs, and clips of video action. The clients ran on 160 Sun workstations that were located in the same cities as the games and provided support to the administrative staff and the press (Dixon 1996).

know nothing about which, or even how many, clients they serve. Clients initiate communications by issuing a *request*, such as a message or a remote-procedure call, and servers respond by fulfilling the request and *replying* with a result. Normally, servers are passive components that simply react to clients' requests, but in some cases, a server may initiate actions on behalf of its clients. For example, a client may send the server an executable function, called a **callback**, which the server subsequently calls under specific circumstances. Sidebar 5.3 describes a system implemented using the client-server style.

Because this architectural style separates client code and server code into different components, it is possible to improve system performance by shuffling the components among computer processes. For example, client code might execute locally on a user's personal computer or might execute remotely on a more powerful server computer. In a multitier system, like the example shown in Figure 5.7, servers are structured hierarchically into application-specific servers (the middle tiers) that in turn use servers offering more generic services (the bottom tier) (Clements et al. 2003). This architecture improves the system's modularity and gives designers more flexibility in assigning activities to processes. Moreover, the client-server style supports reuse, in that servers providing common services may be useful in multiple applications.

Peer-to-Peer

Technically, a **peer-to-peer** (P2P) architecture is one in which each component executes as its own process and acts as both a client of and a server to other peer components. Each component has an interface that specifies not only the services it provides, but

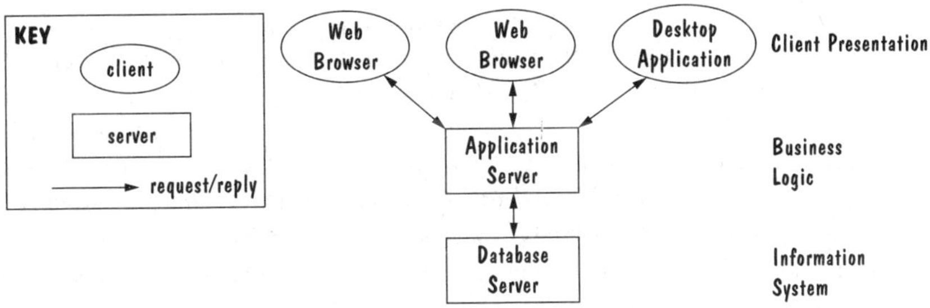

FIGURE 5.7 Three-tiered client-server architecture.

also the services that it requests from other peer components. Peers communicate by requesting services from each other. In this way, P2P communication is like the request/reply communication found in client-server architecture, but any component can initiate a request to any other peer component.

The best known P2P architectures are file-sharing networks, such as Napster and Freenet, in which the components provide similar services to each other. What differs among components are the data each component stores locally. Thus, the system's data are distributed among the components; whenever a component needs information not stored locally, it retrieves it from a peer component.

P2P networks are attractive because they scale up well. Although each added component increases demands on the system in the form of additional requests, it also increases the system's capabilities, in the form of new or replicated data and as additional server capacity. P2P networks are also highly tolerant of component and network failures, because data are replicated and distributed over multiple peers. Sidebar 5.4 describes the pros and cons of Napster's P2P architecture.

SIDEBAR 5.4 NAPSTER'S P2P ARCHITECTURE

Napster, the popular music-sharing system, uses a P2P architecture. Typically, the peers are users' desktop computer systems running general-purpose computing applications, such as electronic mail clients, word processors, Web browsers, and more. Many of these user systems do not have stable Internet protocol (IP) addresses, and they are not always available to the rest of the network. And most users are not sophisticated; they are more interested in content than in the network's configuration and protocols. Moreover, there is great variation in methods for accessing the network, from slow dial-up lines to fast broadband connections.

Napster's sophistication comes instead from its servers, which organize requests and manage content. The actual content is provided by users, in the form of files that are shared from peer to peer, and the sharing goes to other (anonymous) users, not to a centralized file server.

This type of architecture works well when the files are static (i.e., their content does not change often or at all), when file content or quality do not matter, and when the speed and reliability of sharing are not important. But if the file content changes frequently (e.g., stock prices or evaluations), sharing speed is key (e.g., large files are needed quickly), file quality is critical (e.g., photographs or video), or one peer needs to be able to trust another (e.g., the content is protected or contains valuable corporate information), then a P2P architecture may not be the best choice; a centralized server architecture may be more appropriate.

Publish-Subscribe

In a publish-subscribe architecture, components interact by broadcasting and reacting to events. A component expresses interest in an event by **subscribing** to it. Then, when another component announces (**publishes**) that the event has taken place, the subscribing components are notified. The underlying publish-subscribe infrastructure is responsible both for registering event subscriptions and for delivering published events to the appropriate components. **Implicit invocation** is a common form of publish-subscribe architecture, in which a subscribing component associates one of its procedures with each event of interest (called **registering** the procedure). In this case, when the event occurs, the publish-subscribe infrastructure invokes all of the event's registered procedures. In contrast to client-server and P2P components, publish-subscribe components know nothing about each other. Instead, the publishing component simply announces events and then waits for interested components to react; each subscribing component simply reacts to event announcements, regardless of how they are published. In models of this kind of architecture, the underlying infrastructure is often represented as an event bus to which all publish-subscribe components are connected.

This is a common architectural style for integrating tools in a shared environment. For example, Reiss (1990) reports on an environment called Field, where tools such as editors register for events that might occur during a debugger's functioning. To see how, consider that the debugger processes code, one line at a time. When it recognizes that it has reached a set breakpoint, it announces the event "reached breakpoint"; then, the system forwards the event to all registered tools, including the editor, and the editor reacts to the event by automatically scrolling to the source-code line that corresponds to the breakpoint. Other events that the debugger might announce include entry and exit points of functions, runtime errors, and comments to clear or reset the program's execution. However, the debugger is not aware of which tools, if any, have registered for the different events, and it has no control over what the other tools will do in response to one of its events. For this reason, a publish-subscribe system will often include some explicit invocations (e.g., calls to access methods) when a component wants to enforce or confirm a specific reaction to a critical event.

Publish-subscribe systems have several strengths and weaknesses (Shaw and Garlan 1996):

- Such systems provide strong support for system evolution and customization. Because all interactions are orchestrated using events, any publish-subscribe component can be added to the system and can register itself without affecting other components.

- For the same reason, we can easily reuse publish-subscribe components in other event-driven systems.
- Components can pass data at the time they announce events. But if components need to share persistent data, the system must include a shared repository to support that interaction. This sharing can diminish the system's extensibility and reusability.
- Publish-subscribe systems are difficult to test, because the behavior of a publishing component will depend on which subscribing components are monitoring its events. Thus, we cannot test the component in isolation and infer its correctness in an integrated system.

Repositories

A **repository** style of architecture consists of two types of components: a central data store and associated data-accessing components. Shared data are stockpiled in the data store, and the data accessors are computational units that store, retrieve, and update the information. It is challenging to design such a system, because we must decide how the two types of components will interact. In a **traditional database**, the data store acts like a server component, and the data-accessing clients request information from the data store, perform calculations, and request that results be written back to the data store. In such a system, the data-accessing components are *active*, in that they initiate the system's computations.

However, in the **blackboard** type of repository (illustrated in Figure 5.8), the data-accessing components are *reactive*: they execute in reaction to the current contents of the data store. Typically, the blackboard contains information about the current state of the system's execution that triggers the execution of individual data accessors, called **knowledge sources**. For example, the blackboard may store computation tasks, and an idle knowledge source checks a task out of the blackboard, performs the computation locally, and checks the result back into the blackboard. More commonly, the blackboard stores the current state of the system's computation, and knowledge sources detect pieces of the unsolved problem to tackle. For example, in a rule-based system, the current state

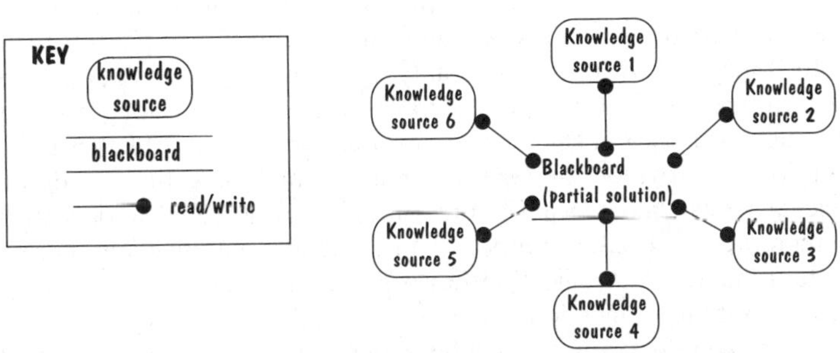

FIGURE 5.8 Typical blackboard.

of the solution is stored in the blackboard, and knowledge sources iteratively revise and improve the solution by applying rewriting rules. The style is analogous to a computation or proof that is written on a real-world blackboard, where people (knowledge sources) iteratively improve the write-up by walking up to the blackboard, erasing some part of the writing, and replacing it with new writing (Shaw and Garlan 1996).

An important property of this style of architecture is the centralized management of the system's key data. In the data store, we can localize responsibility for storing persistent data, managing concurrent access to the data, enforcing security and privacy policies, and protecting the data against faults (e.g., via backups). A key architectural decision is whether to map data to more than one data store. Distributing or replicating data may improve system performance, but often there are costs: adding complexity, keeping data stores consistent, and reducing security.

Layering

Layered systems organize the system's software units into layers, each of which provides services to the layer above it and acts as a client to the layer below. In a "pure" layered system, a software unit in a given layer can access only the other units in the same layer and services offered by the interface to the layer immediately below it. To improve performance, this constraint may be relaxed in some cases, allowing a layer to access the services of layers below its lower neighbor; this is called **layer bridging**. However, if a design includes a lot of layer bridging, then it loses some of the portability and maintainability that the layering style offers. Under no circumstances does a layer access the services offered by a higher-level layer; the resulting architecture would no longer be called layered.

To see how this type of system works, consider Figure 5.9, which depicts the Open Systems Interconnection (OSI) reference model for network communications (International Telecommunication Union 1994). The bottom layer provides facilities for transferring data bits over a physical link, like a cable—possibly unsuccessfully. The next layer, the Data Link Layer, provides more complex facilities: it transmits fixed-sized data frames, routes data frames to local addressable machines, and recovers from simple transmission errors. The Data Link Layer uses the bottom Physical Layer's facilities to perform the actual transmission of bits between physically connected machines. The Network Layer adds the ability to transmit variable-sized data packets, by breaking packets into fixed-sized data frames which are then sent using the Data Link facilities; the Network Layer also expands the routing of data packets to nonlocal machines. The Transport Layer adds reliability, by recovering from routing errors, such as when data frames are lost or reordered as they are routed (along possibly different paths) through the network. The Session Layer uses the Transport Layer's reliable data-transfer services to provide long-term communication connections, over which lengthy data exchanges can take place. The Presentation Layer provides translation among different data representations, to support data exchanges among components that use different data formats. The Application Layer provides application-specific services, such as file transfers if the application is a file-transfer program.

In the OSI example, each layer raises the level of abstraction of the communication services that are available to the next layer, and hides all of the details about how

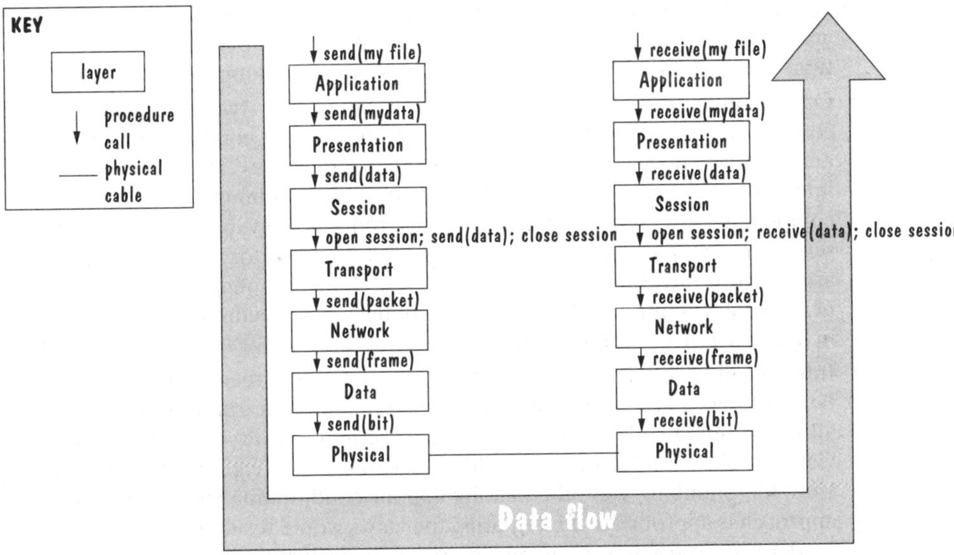

FIGURE 5.9 Layered architecture of OSI model for network communications.

those services are implemented. In general, the layering style is useful whenever we can decompose our system's functionality into steps, each of which builds on previous steps. The resulting design is easier to port to other platforms, if the lowest level encapsulates the software's interactions with the platform. Moreover, because a layer can interact only with its neighboring layers, layer modification is relatively easy; such changes should affect at most only the two adjacent layers.

On the other hand, it is not always easy to structure a system into distinct layers of increasingly powerful services, especially when software units are seemingly interdependent. Also, it may appear that layers introduce a performance cost from the set of calls and data transfers between system layers. Fortunately, sophisticated compilers, linkers, and loaders can reduce this overhead (Clements et al. 2003).

Combining Architectural Styles

It is easiest to think about an architectural style and its associated properties when we consider the style in its purest form. However, actual software architectures are rarely based purely on a single style. Instead, we build our software architecture by combining different architectural styles, selecting and adapting aspects of styles to solve particular problems in our design.

Architectural styles can be combined in several ways:

- We might use different styles at different levels of our system's decomposition. For example, we might view our system's overall structure as a client-server architecture, but subsequently decompose the server component into a series of layers. Or a simple intercomponent connection at one level of abstraction may be refined to be a collection of components and connectors at a lower level of decomposition.

For instance, we might decompose one architecture's publish-subscribe interactions to elaborate the components and protocols used to manage event subscriptions and to notify subscribing components of event announcements.

- Our architecture may use a mixture of architectural styles to model different components or different types of interactions among components, such as the architecture shown in Figure 5.10. In this example, several client components interact with each other using publish-subscribe communications. These same components use server components via request/reply protocols; in turn, the server components interact with a shared data repository. In this example, the architecture integrates different styles into a single model by allowing components to play multiple roles (e.g., client, publisher, and subscriber) and to engage in multiple types of interactions.
- Integration of different architectural styles is easier if the styles are compatible. For example, all the styles being combined might relate runtime components, or all might relate code units. Alternatively, we may create and maintain different views of the architecture, as building architects do (e.g., the electrical wiring view, the plumbing view, the heating and air conditioning view, and so on). This approach is appropriate if integrating the views would result in an overly complex model, such as when components interact with each other in multiple ways (e.g., if pairs of components interact using both implicit invocation and explicit method calls), or if the mapping between the views' components is messy (i.e., is a many-to-many relationship).

If the resulting architecture is expressed as a collection of models, we must document how the models relate to one another. If one model simply shows the decomposition of an element from a more abstract model, then this relationship is straightforward. If, instead, two models show different views of the system, and if there is no obvious mapping between the two views' software units, then documenting the views' correspondence is all the more important. Section 5.8 describes how to record the correspondences among views.

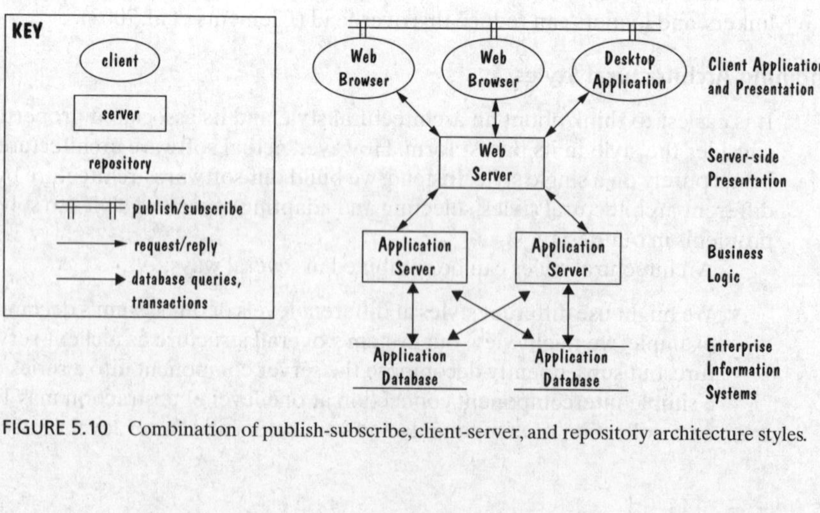

FIGURE 5.10 Combination of publish-subscribe, client-server, and repository architecture styles.

5.5 ACHIEVING QUALITY ATTRIBUTES

In Chapter 4, we saw that software requirements are about more than the proposed system's functionality. Other attributes, such as performance, reliability, and usability, are carefully specified, reflecting the characteristics that users want to see in the products we build. As we design our system, we want to select architectural styles that promote the required quality attributes. However, architectural style offers only a coarse-grained solution with generally beneficial properties; there is no assurance that a specific quality attribute is optimized. To assure the support of particular attributes, we use **tactics** (Bass, Clements, and Kazman 2003): more fine-grained design decisions that can improve how well our design achieves specific quality goals.

Modifiability

Modifiability is the basis of most of the architectural styles presented in this chapter. Because more than half of the full life-cycle cost of a system—including development, problem fixing, enhancement, and evolution—is spent after the first version of the software is developed and released, modifiability is essential. That is, above all, we want our design to be easy to change. Different architectural styles address different aspects of modifiability, so we must know how to select the styles that address our specific modifiability goals.

Given a particular change to a system, Bass, Clements, and Kazman (2003) distinguish between the software units that are directly affected by the change and those that are indirectly affected. The directly affected units are those whose responsibilities change to accommodate a system modification. We can structure our code to minimize the number of units requiring change. The indirectly affected units are those whose responsibilities do not change, but whose implementations must be revised to accommodate changes in the directly affected units. The difference is subtle. Both types aim to reduce the number of altered software units, but the tactics associated with each are different.

Tactics for minimizing the number of software units directly affected by a software change focus on clustering anticipated changes in the design:

- *Anticipate expected changes:* Identify design decisions that are most likely to change, and encapsulate each in its own software unit. Anticipated changes are not limited to future features that the customer would like to see implemented. Any service, functionality, or internal check that the system performs is susceptible to future improvement or obsolescence, and as such is a candidate for future changes.
- *Cohesion:* We will see in Chapter 6 that a software unit is cohesive if its pieces, data, and functionality all contribute to the unit's purpose and responsibilities. By keeping our software units highly cohesive, we increase the chances that a change to the system's responsibilities is confined to the few units that are assigned those responsibilities.
- *Generality:* The more general our software units, the more likely we can accommodate change by modifying a unit's inputs rather than modifying the unit itself. This characteristic is particularly true of servers, which ought to be general enough to accommodate all variants of requests for their services. For example,

an object that encapsulates a data structure should provide sufficient access methods to enable other objects to easily retrieve and update data values.

By contrast, tactics for minimizing the impact on indirectly affected software units focus on reducing dependencies among software units. The goal is to reduce the degree to which a change to a directly affected unit also affects the system's other units:

- *Coupling:* As we discuss in detail in Chapter 6, the level of coupling among software units is the degree to which the units depend on each other. By lowering coupling, we reduce the likelihood that a change to one unit will ripple to other units.
- *Interfaces:* A software unit's interface reveals the unit's public requisites and responsibilities, and hides the unit's private design decisions. If a unit interacts with other units only through their interfaces (e.g., calling public access methods), then changes to one unit will not spread beyond the unit's boundary unless its interface changes (e.g., if method signatures, preconditions, or postconditions change).
- *Multiple interfaces:* A unit modified to provide new data or services can offer them using a new interface to the unit without changing any of the unit's existing interfaces. This way, dependencies on the existing interfaces are unaffected by the change.

The above tactics apply when modifiability goals include reducing the cost of changing the design or implementation of our software. Another type of modifiability refers to our being able to modify a system after it is released, perhaps during set-up or on the fly during execution. For example, the process of installing Unix or Linux on a computer involves a complex configuration step in which many questions must be answered about the computer's hardware and peripheral devices to be supported, and which libraries, tools, application software, and versions of software are to be installed. Sidebar 5.5 describes a tactic, called **self-managing**, where the software changes on the fly in response to changes in its environment.

SIDEBAR 5.5 SELF-MANAGING SOFTWARE

In response to increasing demands that systems be able to operate optimally in different and sometimes changing environments, the software community is starting to experiment with self-managing software. It goes by several names (such as autonomic, adaptive, dynamic, self-configuring, self-optimizing, self-healing, context-aware), but the essential idea is the same: that the software system monitors its environment or its own performance, and changes its behavior in response to changes that it detects. That is, as its environment changes, the system may change its sensors. Here are some examples:

- Change the input sensors used, such as avoiding vision-based sensors when sensing in the dark.
- Change its communication protocols and interprotocol gateways, such as when users, each with a communication device, join and leave an electronic meeting.

- Change the Web servers that are queried, based on the results and performance of past queries.
- Move running components to different processors to balance processor load or to recover from a processor failure.

Self-managing software sounds ideal, but it is not easy to build. Obstacles include:

- *Few architectural styles:* Because self-managing software so strongly emphasizes context-dependent behavior, its design tends to be application specific, which calls for significant innovative design. If there were more general architectural styles that supported self-managing software, it would be easier to develop such software more rapidly and reliably.
- *Monitoring nonfunctional requirements:* Autonomic goals tend to be highly related to nonfunctional requirements. Thus, assessing how well the system is achieving these goals means that we have to relate the goals to measurable characteristics of the system's execution, and then monitor and dynamically evaluate these characteristics.
- *Decision making:* The system may have to decide whether to adapt on the basis of incomplete information about itself or its environment. Also, the system should not enter a perpetual state of adaptation if its environment fluctuates around a threshold point.

Performance

Performance attributes describe constraints on system speed and capacity, including:

- *Response time:* How fast does our software respond to requests?
- *Throughput:* How many requests can it process per minute?
- *Load:* How many users can it support before response time and throughput start to suffer?

The obvious tactic for improving a system's performance is increasing computing resources. That is, we can buy faster computers, more memory, or additional communication bandwidth. However, as Bass, Clements, and Kazman (2003) explain, there are also software design tactics that can improve system performance.

One tactic is improving the utilization of resources. For example, we can make our software more concurrent, thereby increasing the number of requests that can be processed at the same time. This approach is effective if some resources are blocked or idle, waiting for other computations to finish. For instance, multiple ATMs can simultaneously gather information about customers' banking requests, authenticate the customers' identification information, and confirm the requested transactions with the customers, before forwarding the requests to one of the bank's servers. In this design, the server receives only authenticated and confirmed requests, which it can process without further interaction with the customer, thereby increasing the server's throughput. Another option is to replicate and distribute shared data, thereby reducing contention for the data. However, if we replicate data, then we must also introduce mechanisms to keep the distributed copies in synch. The overhead of keeping data copies consistent must be more than offset by the performance improvements we gain from reducing data contention.

A second tactic is to manage resource allocation more effectively. That is, we should decide carefully how competing requests for resources are granted access to them. Criteria for allocating resources include minimizing response time, maximizing throughput, maximizing resource utilization, favoring high-priority or urgent requests, and maximizing fairness (Bass, Clements, and Kazman 2003). Some common scheduling policies are given below.

- *First-come/first-served:* Requests are processed in the order in which they are received. This policy ensures that all requests are eventually processed. But it also means that a high-priority request could be stuck waiting for a lower-priority request to be serviced.
- *Explicit priority:* Requests are processed in order of their assigned priorities. This policy ensures that important requests are handled quickly. However, it is possible for a low-priority request to be delayed forever in favor of new high-priority requests. One remedy is to dynamically increase the priority of delayed requests, to ensure that they are eventually scheduled.
- *Earliest deadline first:* Requests are processed in order of their impending deadlines. This policy ensures that urgent requests are handled quickly, thereby helping the system meet its real-time deadlines.

The above policies assume that once a request is scheduled for service, it is processed to completion. Alternatively, the system can interrupt an executing request. For example, a lower-priority request can be preempted in favor of a higher-priority request, in which case the preempted request is rescheduled for completion. Or we can use *round robin scheduling* that allocates resources to requests for fixed time intervals; if a request is not completely serviced within this time period, it is preempted and the uncompleted portion is rescheduled. How we choose from among these scheduling policies depends entirely on what performance property the customer wants to optimize.

A third tactic is to reduce demand for resources. At first glance, this approach may seem unhelpful, because we may have no control over inputs to our software. However, we can sometimes reduce demand on resources by making our code more efficient. Better yet, in some systems, we may be able to service only a fraction of the inputs we receive. For example, if some of the system inputs are sensor data rather than requests for service, our software may be able to sample inputs at a lower frequency without the system's missing important changes in the sensed environment.

Security

Our choice of architectural style has a significant impact on our ability to implement security requirements. Most security requirements describe what is to be protected and from whom; the protection needs are often discussed in a threat model, which casts each need in terms of the possible threats to the system and its resources. It is the architecture that describes how the protection should be achieved.

There are two key architectural characteristics that are particularly relevant to security: immunity and resilience. A system has high **immunity** if it is able to thwart an attempted attack. It has high **resilience** if it can recover quickly and easily from a successful attack. The architecture encourages immunity in several ways:

- ensuring that all security features are included in the design
- minimizing the security weaknesses that might be exploited by an attacker

Likewise, the architecture encourages resilience by

- segmenting the functionality so that the effects of an attack can be contained to a small part of the system
- enabling the system to quickly restore functionality and performance in a short time

Thus, several, more general quality characteristics, such as redundancy, contribute to the architecture's security.

A full discussion of security architectures is beyond the scope of this book; for a detailed discussion, see Pfleeger and Pfleeger (2006), where the architectural discussions are based on type of application, such as operating system, database, or user interface. No matter the application, some architectural styles, such as layering, are well-suited for any kind of security; they inherently ensure that some objects and processes cannot interact with other objects and processes. Other styles, such as P2P, are much more difficult to secure.

Johnson, McGuire, and Willey (2008) investigated just how insecure a P2P network can be. They point out that this type of architecture is at least 40 years old: the U.S. Department of Defense developed the Arpanet as a P2P system:

> TCP/IP, introduced in 1973, cemented the notion of direct host-to-host communication, with the network handling the mechanics of guiding the packets to their destination. Most of the protocols created since then (HTTP, SMTP, DNS, etc.) build on the idea that a host that needs data connects directly to the host that has it, and that it is the network's task to enable this. The techniques used by P2P file-sharing networking systems are simply an evolution of these principles.

Although a P2P network has advantages such as replication and redundancy, the underlying design encourages data sharing even when the data are not intended for open view.

To see how, consider that a typical P2P network involves users who place shareable items in a designated folder. You may think that a careful user's files would be safe. But there are many ways that data are unintentionally shared:

- The user accidentally shares files or folders containing sensitive information.
- Files or data are misplaced.
- The user interface may be confusing, so the user does not realize that a file is being shared. Good and Krekelberg (2003) found the KaZaA system to have this problem.
- Files or data are poorly organized.
- The user relies on software to recognize file or data types and make them available, and the software mistakenly includes a file or data that should have been protected.
- Malicious software shares files or folders without the user's knowledge.

Indeed, Krebs (2008) describes how an investment firm employee used his company computer to participate in LimeWire, an online P2P file-sharing network for people trading in music and videos. In doing so, he inadvertently exposed his firm's private files. These files included the names, dates of birth, and Social Security numbers for 2000 of the firm's clients, among whom was a U.S. Supreme Court Justice! The head of Tiversa, the company hired to help contain the breach said, "such breaches are hardly rare. About 40 to 60 percent of all data leaks take place outside of a company's secured network, usually as a result of employees or contractors installing file-sharing software on company computers" (Krebs 2008). Leaked often are files containing confidential company plans or designs for new products. So architectural considerations should address both conventional and unconventional uses of the system being developed.

Reliability

Sidebar 5.6 warns us that software safety should not be taken for granted. That is, we need to be diligent in our design work, anticipating faults and handling them in ways that minimize disruption and maximize safety. The goal is to make our software as fault-free as possible, by building fault prevention and fault recovery into our designs. A software system or unit is **reliable** if it correctly performs its required functions under assumed conditions (IEEE 1990). In contrast, a system or unit is **robust** if it is able to function correctly "in the presence of invalid inputs or stressful environment conditions" (IEEE 1990). That is, reliability has to do with whether our software is internally free of errors, and robustness has to do with how well our software is able to withstand errors or surprises from its environment. We discuss tactics for robustness in the next section.

SIDEBAR 5.6 THE NEED FOR SAFE DESIGN

How safe are the systems we are designing? The reports from the field are difficult to interpret. Some systems clearly benefit from having some of their functions implemented in software instead of hardware (or instead of leaving decisions to the judgment of the people who are controlling them). For example, the automobile and aviation industries claim that large numbers of accidents have been prevented as more and more software is introduced into control systems. However, other evidence is disturbing. For instance, from 1986 to 1997, there were over 450 reports filed with the U.S. Food and Drug Administration (FDA) detailing software defects in medical devices, 24 of which led to death or injury (Anthes 1997). Rockoff (2008) reports that the FDA established a software forensics unit in 2004 after it noticed that medical device makers were reporting more and more software-based recalls.

The reported numbers may represent just the tip of the iceberg. Because reports to the FDA must be filed within 15 days of an incident, manufacturers may not yet have discovered the true cause of a failure when they write their reports. For instance, one reported battery failure was ultimately traced to a software flaw that drained it. And Leveson and Turner (1993) describe in great detail the user-interface design problems that led to at least four deaths and several injuries from a malfunctioning radiation therapy machine.

The importance of software design is becoming evident to many organizations that were formally unaware of software's role. Of course, design problems are not limited to medical devices; many developers take special precautions. The Canadian Nuclear Safety Commission recommends that all "level 1" safety-critical software running in nuclear power plants be specified and designed using formal (i.e., mathematical) notations, "so that the functional analysis can use mathematical methods and automated tools" (Atomic Energy Control Board 1999). And many groups at Hewlett-Packard use formal inspections and proofs to eliminate faults in the design before coding begins (Grady and van Slack 1994).

Anthes (1997) reports the suggestions of Alan Barbell, a project manager at Environmental Criminology Research, an institute that evaluates medical devices. Barbell notes that software designers must see directly how their products will be used, rather than rely on salespeople and marketers. Then the designers can build in preventative measures to make sure that their products are not misused.

How do faults occur? As we saw in Chapter 1, a **fault** in a software product is the result of some human error. For example, we might misunderstand a user-interface requirement and create a design that reflects our misunderstanding. The design fault can be propagated as incorrect code, incorrect instructions in the user manual, or incorrect test scripts. In this way, a single error can generate one or more faults, in one or more development products.

We distinguish faults from failures. A **failure** is an observable departure of the system from its required behavior. Failures can be discovered both before and after system delivery, because they can occur in testing as well as during operation. In some sense, faults and failures refer respectively to invisible and visible flaws. In other words, faults represent flaws that only developers see, whereas failures are problems that users or customers see.

It is important to realize that not every fault corresponds to a failure, since the conditions under which a fault manifests itself as an observable failure may never be met. For example, fault-containing code may never be executed or may not exceed the boundaries of correct behavior (as with Ariane-4).

We make our software more reliable by preventing or tolerating faults. That is, rather than waiting for the software to fail and then fixing the problem, we anticipate what might happen and construct the system to react in an acceptable way.

Active Fault Detection. When we design a system to wait until a failure occurs during execution, we are practicing **passive fault detection**. However, if we periodically check for symptoms of faults, or try to anticipate when failures will occur, we are performing **active fault detection**. A common method for detecting faults within a process is to identify known **exceptions**—that is, situations that cause the system to deviate from its desired behavior. Then, we include **exception handling** in our design, so that the system addresses each exception in a satisfactory way and returns the system to an acceptable state. Thus, for each service we want our system to provide, we identify ways it may fail and ways to detect that it has failed. Typical exceptions include

- failing to provide a service
- providing the wrong service

- corrupting data
- violating a system invariant (e.g., security property)
- deadlocking

For example, we can detect data problems by identifying relationships or invariants that should hold among data values and checking regularly at runtime that these invariants still hold at runtime. Such checks can be embedded in the same code that manipulates the data. We say more in Chapter 6 about how to use exceptions and exception handling effectively.

Another approach to active fault detection is to use some form of redundancy and then to check that the two techniques agree. For example, a data structure can include both forward and backward pointers, and the program can check that paths through the data structure are consistent. Or an accounting program can add up all the rows and then all of the columns to verify that the totals are identical. Some systems go so far as to provide, and continuously compare, multiple versions of the whole system. The theory behind this approach, called **n-version programming**, is that if two functionally equivalent systems are designed by two different design teams at two different times using different techniques, the chance of the same fault occurring in both implementations is very small. Unfortunately, n-version programming has been shown to be less reliable than originally thought, because many designers learn to design in similar ways, using similar design patterns and principles (Knight and Leveson 1986).

In other systems, a second computer, running in parallel, is used to monitor the progress and health of the primary system. The second system interrogates the first, examining the system's data and processes, looking for signs that might indicate a problem. For instance, the second system may find a process that has not been scheduled for a long period of time. This symptom may indicate that the first system is "stuck" somewhere, looping through a process or waiting for input. Or the system may find a block of storage that was allocated and is no longer in use, but is not yet on the list of available blocks. Or the second system may discover a communication line that has not been released at the end of a transmission. If the second system cannot directly examine the first system's data or processes, it can instead initiate **diagnostic transactions**. This technique involves having the second system generate false but benign transactions in the first computer, to determine if the first system is working properly. For example, the second system can open a communication channel to the first, to ensure that the first system still responds to such requests.

Fault Recovery. A detected fault must be handled as soon as it is discovered, rather than waiting until processing is complete. Such immediate fault handling helps to limit the fault's damage, rather than allowing the fault to become a failure and create a trail of destruction. Fault-recovery tactics usually involve some overhead in keeping the system ready for recovery:

- *Undoing transactions:* The system manages a series of actions as a single **transaction** that either executes in its entirety, or whose partial effects are easily undone if a fault occurs midway through the transaction.
- *Checkpoint/rollback:* Periodically, or after a specific operation, the software records a checkpoint of its current state. If the system subsequently gets into

trouble, it "rolls" its execution back to this recorded state, and reapplies logged transactions that occurred since the checkpoint.

- *Backup:* The system automatically substitutes the faulty unit with a backup unit. In a safety-critical system, this backup unit can run in parallel with the active unit, processing events and transactions. This way, the backup is ready to take over for the active unit at a moment's notice. Alternatively, the backup unit is brought on-line only when a failure occurs, which means that the backup needs to be brought up-to-speed on the current state of the system, possibly by using checkpoints and logged transactions.
- *Degraded service:* The system returns to its previous state, perhaps using checkpoints and rollback, and then offers some degraded version of the service.
- *Correct and continue:* If the monitoring software detects a problem with data consistency or a stalled process, it may be easier to treat the symptoms rather than fix the fault. For example, the software may be able to use redundant information to infer how to fix data errors. As another example, the system may terminate and restart hung processes. Telecommunications systems operate this way, dropping bad connections with the expectation that the customer can reinitiate the call. In this manner, the integrity of the overall system takes precedence over any individual call that is placed.
- *Report:* The system returns to its previous state and reports the problem to an exception-handling unit. Alternatively, the system may simply note the existence of the failure, and record the state of the system at the time the failure occurred. It is up to the developers or maintainers to return to fix the problem later.

The criticality of the system determines which tactic we choose. Sometimes it is desirable to stop system execution when a fault affects the system in some way (e.g., when a failure occurs). It is much easier to find the source of the problem if system processing ceases abruptly on detecting a fault than if the system continues executing; continuing may produce other effects that hide the underlying fault, or may overwrite critical data and program state information needed to locate the fault.

Other times, stopping system execution to correct a fault is too expensive, risky, or inconvenient. Such a tactic would be unthinkable for software in a medical device or aviation system. Instead, our software must minimize the damage done by the fault and then carry on with little disruption to the users. For example, suppose software controls several equivalent conveyor belts in an assembly line. If a fault is detected on one of the belts, the system may sound an alarm and reroute the materials to the other belts. When the defective belt is fixed, it can be put back into production. This approach is certainly preferable to stopping production completely until the defective belt is fixed. Similarly, a banking system may switch to a backup processor or make duplicate copies of data and transactions in case one process fails.

Some fault-recovery tactics rely on the ability to predict the location of faults and the timing of failures. To build workarounds in the system design, we must be able to guess what might go wrong. Some faults are easy to anticipate, but more complex systems are more difficult to analyze. At the same time, complex systems are more likely to have significant faults. To make matters worse, the code to implement fault detection and recovery may itself contain faults, whose presence may cause irreparable damage.

Thus, some fault-recovery strategies isolate areas of likely faults rather than predict actual faults.

Robustness

When we learn to drive a car, we are told to drive defensively. That is, we not only make sure that we follow the driving rules and laws, but we also take precautions to avoid accidents that might be caused by problems in our surroundings, such as road conditions and other vehicles. In the same way, we should design defensively, trying to anticipate external factors that might lead to problems in our software. Our system is said to be **robust** if it includes mechanisms for accommodating or recovering from problems in the environment or in other units.

Defensive designing is not easy. It requires diligence. For example, we may follow a policy of **mutual suspicion**, where each software unit assumes that the other units contain faults. In this mode, each unit checks its input for correctness and consistency, and tests that the input satisfies the unit's preconditions. Thus, a payroll program would ensure that *hours_worked* is nonnegative before calculating an employee's pay. Similarly, a checksum, guard bit, or parity bit included in a data stream can warn the system if input data are corrupted. In a distributed system, we can check the health of remote processes and the communication network by periodically issuing a "ping" and checking that the processes answer within an acceptable time frame. In some distributed systems, multiple computers perform the same calculations; the space shuttle operates this way, using five duplicate computers that vote to determine the next operation. This approach is different from n-version programming, in that all of the computers run the same software. Thus, this redundancy will not catch logic errors in the software, but it will overcome hardware failures and transient errors caused by radiation. As we will see later in this chapter, we can use fault-tree analysis and failure-mode analysis to help us identify potential hazards that our software must detect and recover from.

Robustness tactics for detecting faults differ from reliability tactics because the source of problems is different. That is, the problems are in our software's environment rather than in our own software. However, the recovery tactics are similar: our software can rollback the system to a checkpoint state, abort a transaction, initiate a backup unit, provide reduced service, correct the symptoms and continue processing, or trigger an exception.

Usability

Usability attributes reflect the ease with which a user is able to operate the system. Most aspects of user-interface design are about how information is presented to and collected from the user. These design decisions tend not to be architectural, so we postpone a detailed discussion of this topic until the next chapter. However, there are a few user-interface decisions that do significantly affect the software's architecture, and they are worth mentioning here.

First and foremost, the user interface should reside in its own software unit, or possibly its own architectural layer. This separation makes it easier to customize the user interface for different audiences, such as users of different nationalities or different abilities.

Second, there are some user-initiated commands that require architectural support. These include generic commands such as *cancel, undo, aggregate*, and *show multiple views* (Bass, Clements, and Kazman 2003). At a minimum, the system needs a process that listens for these commands, because they could be generated at any time, unlike user commands that are input in response to a system prompt. In addition, for some of these commands, the system needs to prepare itself to receive and execute the command. For example, for the *undo* command, the system must maintain a chain of previous states to which to return. For the *show multiple views* command, the system must be able to present multiple displays and keep them up-to-date and consistent as data change. In general, the design should include facilities for detecting and responding to any expected user input.

Third, there are some system-initiated activities for which the system should maintain a model of its environment. The most obvious examples are time-activated activities that occur at defined time intervals or on specified dates. For example, a pacemaker can be configured to trigger a heartbeat 50, 60, or 70 times a minute, and an accounting system can be set up to generate monthly paychecks or bills automatically. The system must track the passage of time or days to be able to initiate such time-sensitive tasks. Similarly, a process-control system, such as a system that monitors and controls a chemical reaction, will maintain a model of the process being controlled, so that it can make informed decisions about how to react to particular sensor input. If we encapsulate the model, we will be better able to replace this software unit when new modeling technologies are invented, or to tailor the model for different applications or customers.

Business Goals

The system may have quality attributes that it is expected to exhibit. In addition, we or our customers may have associated business goals that are important to achieve. The most common of these goals is minimizing the *cost of development* and the *time to market.* Such goals can have major effects on our design decisions:

- *Buy vs. build:* It is becoming increasingly possible to buy major components. In addition to saving development time, we may actually save money by buying a component rather than paying our employees to build it. A purchased component may also be more reliable, especially if it has a history and has been tested out by other users. On the other hand, using a third-party or existing component places constraints on the rest of our design, with respect to how the architecture is decomposed and what its interfaces to the component look like. It can also make our system vulnerable to the availability of the component's supplier, and can be disastrous if the supplier goes out of business or evolves the component so that it is no longer compatible with our hardware, software, or needs.
- *Initial development vs. maintenance costs:* Many of the architectural styles and tactics that promote modifiability also increase a design's complexity, and thus increase the system's cost. Because more than half of a system's total development costs are incurred after the first version is released, we can save money by making our system more modifiable. However, increased complexity may delay the system's initial release. During this delay, we collect no payment for our product, we risk losing market share to our competitors, and we risk our reputation as a reliable

software supplier. Thus, for each system that we build, we must evaluate the tradeoff between early delivery and easier maintenance.

- *New vs. known technologies:* New technologies, architectural styles, and components may require new expertise. Past examples of such technological breakthroughs include object-oriented programming, middleware technologies, and open-systems standards; a more recent example is the prevalence of cheap multiprocessors. Acquiring expertise costs money and delays product release, as we either learn how to use the new technology or hire new personnel who already have that knowledge. Eventually, we must develop the expertise ourselves. But for a given project, we must decide when and how to pay the costs and reap the benefits of applying new technology.

5.6 COLLABORATIVE DESIGN

Not all design questions are technical. Many are sociological, in that the design of software systems is usually performed by a team of developers, rather than by a single person. A design team works collaboratively, often by assigning different parts of the design to various people. Several issues must be addressed by the team, including who is best suited to design each aspect of the system, how to document the design so that each team member understands the designs of others, and how to coordinate the resulting software units so that they work well when integrated together. The design team must be aware of the causes of design breakdown (Sidebar 5.7) and use the team's strengths to address them.

SIDEBAR 5.7 THE CAUSES OF DESIGN BREAKDOWN

Guindon, Krasner, and Curtis (1987) studied the habits of designers on 19 projects to determine what causes the design process to break down. They found three classes of breakdown: lack of knowledge, cognitive limitations, and a combination of the two.

The main types of process breakdown were

- lack of specialized data schemas
- lack of a meta-schema about the design process, leading to poor allocation of resources to the various design activities
- poor prioritization of issues, leading to poor selection of alternative solutions
- difficulty in considering all the stated or inferred constraints in defining a solution
- difficulty in performing mental simulations with many steps or test cases
- difficulty in keeping track of and returning to subproblems whose solution has been postponed
- difficulty in expanding or merging solutions from individual subproblems to form a complete solution

One of the major problems in performing collaborative design is addressing differences in personal experience, understanding, and preference. Another is that people sometimes behave differently in groups from the way they behave individually. For example, Japanese software developers are less likely to express individual opinions when working in a group, because they value teamwork more than they value individual work. Harmony is very important, and junior personnel in Japan defer to the opinions of their more senior colleagues in meetings (Ishii 1990). Watson, Ho, and Raman (1994) found a similar situation when they compared groupware-supported meeting behavior in the United States to that in Singapore. Parallel communication and anonymous information exchange were important for the American groups, but were not as important for the Singaporean groups, who valued harmony. In cases such as these, it may be desirable to design using a groupware tool, where anonymity can be preserved. Indeed, Valacich et al. (1992) report that preserving anonymity in this way can enhance the group's overall performance. There is a trade-off, however. Anonymity in some groups can lead to diminished responsibilities for individuals, leading them to believe that they can get away with making fewer contributions. Thus, it is important to view the group interaction in its cultural and ethical contexts.

Outsourcing

As the software industry seeks to cut costs and improve productivity, more software development activities will be outsourced to other companies or divisions, some of which may be located in other countries. In such cases, a collaborative design team may be distributed around the world, and the importance of understanding group behavior will increase.

Yourdon (1994) identifies four stages in this kind of distributed development:

1. In the first stage, a project is performed at a single site with on-site developers from foreign countries.
2. In the second stage, on-site analysts determine the system's requirements. Then, the requirements are provided to off-site groups of developers and programmers to continue development.
3. In the third stage, off-site developers build generic products and components that are used worldwide.
4. In the fourth stage, the off-site developers build products that take advantage of their individual areas of expertise.

Notice that this model conflicts with advising designers to shuttle among requirements analysts, testers, and coders, in order to enhance everyone's understanding of the system to be developed. As a development team advances through the stages of Yourdon's model, it is likely to encounter problems at stage 2, where communication paths must remain open to support an iterative design process.

Time zone differences and unstable Internet connections are just some of the challenges that can make it difficult for a distributed design team to coordinate its efforts. Yourdon (2005) has studied the trends and effects of outsourcing knowledge-based work, and he reports that distributed teams often use different development processes. Outsourced subteams are more likely to be staffed with junior developers who employ current best practices, whereas more mature subteams tend to use older methods that have proven effective on past projects. This mismatch of processes can be a source of contention. Also, outsourced subteams, especially those that work **offshore** (i.e., in another country), are less likely to know local business rules, customs, and laws.

Communication among distributed team members can be enhanced using notes, prototypes, graphics, and other aids. However, these explicit representations of the requirements and design must be unambiguous and capture all of the assumptions about how the system should work. Polanyi (1966) notes that intentions cannot be specified fully in any language; some nuances are not obvious. Thus, communication in a group may break down when an information recipient interprets information in terms of his or her understanding and context. For example, in person, we convey a great deal of information using gestures and facial expressions; this type of information is lost when we are collaborating electronically (Krauss and Fussell 1991).

This difficulty is compounded when we communicate in more than one language. For example, there are hundreds of words to describe pasta in Italian, and Arabic has over 40 words for camel. It is extremely difficult to translate the nuances embedded in these differences. Indeed, Winograd and Flores (1986) assert that complete translation from one natural language to another is impossible, because the semantics of a natural language cannot be defined formally and completely. Thus, a major challenge in producing a good software design is reaching a shared understanding among groups of people who may view the system and its environment in very different ways. This challenge derives not just from "the complexity of technical problems, but [also] because of the social interaction when users and system developers learn to create, develop and express their ideas and visions" (Greenbaum and Kyng 1991).

5.7 ARCHITECTURE EVALUATION AND REFINEMENT

Design is an iterative process: we propose some design decisions, assess whether they are the right decisions, perhaps make adjustments, and propose more decisions. In this section, we look at several ways to evaluate the design, to assess its quality and to gain insight into how to improve the design before we implement it. These techniques evaluate the design according to how well it achieves specific quality attributes.

Measuring Design Quality

Some researchers are developing metrics to assess certain key aspects of design quality. For example, Chidamber and Kemerer (1994) have proposed a general set of metrics to apply to object-oriented systems. Briand, Morasca, and Basili (1994) have proposed metrics for evaluating high-level design, including cohesion and coupling, and Briand, Devanbu, and Melo (1997) build on those ideas to propose ways to measure coupling.

To see how these measurements reveal information about the design, consider the latter group's coupling metrics. Briand et al. note that coupling in C++-like design can be based on three different characteristics: relationships between classes (e.g., friendship, inheritance), types of interactions between classes (e.g., class–attribute interaction, class–method interaction, method–method interaction), and the loci of ripple effects due to design changes (i.e., whether a change flows toward or away from a class). For each class in a design, they defined metrics that count the interactions between the class and other classes or methods. Then, using empirical information about the design for a real system and the resulting system's faults and failures, they analyzed the relationship between the type of coupling and the kinds of faults that were found. For example, they report that when a class depended on a large number of attributes that belonged to other classes that were not ancestors, descendants, or friends of that class, then the resulting code was more fault prone than usual. Similarly, when many methods belonging to `friend` classes depended on the methods of a particular class, then that class was more fault prone. In this way, design information can be used to predict which parts of the software are most likely to be problematic. We can take steps during the design stage to build in fault prevention or fault tolerance, and we can focus more of our initial testing efforts on the most fault-prone parts of the design.

Safety Analysis

We learned earlier about the importance of fault identification, correction, and tolerance in creating reliable and robust designs. There are several techniques that can be used during design to identify possible faults or their likely locations. **Fault-tree analysis**, a method originally developed for the U.S. Minuteman missile program, helps us to examine a design and look for faults that might lead to failure. We build fault trees that trace backwards through a design, along the logical path from effect to cause. The trees are then used to help us decide which faults to correct or avoid, and which faults to tolerate.

We begin our analysis by identifying possible failures. Although our identification takes place during design, we consider failures that might be affected by design, operation, or even maintenance. We can use a set of guidewords to help us understand how the system might deviate from its intended behavior. Table 5.1 illustrates some of the guidewords that might be used; you can select your own guidewords or checklists, based on your system's application domain.

Next, we build an upside-down tree whose root node is some failure that we want to analyze, and whose other nodes are events or faults that realize or lead to the root node's failure. The edges of the graph indicate the relationships among nodes. Parent nodes are drawn as logic gate operators: an *and*-gate if both of the child nodes' events must occur for the parent node's event to occur; an *or*-gate if one child's event is sufficient to cause the parent's event. Sometimes, an edge is labeled *n_of_m* if the system

TABLE 5.1 Guidewords for Identifying Possible Failures

Guideword	Interpretation
no	No data or control signal was sent or received
more	The volume of data is too much or too fast
less	The volume of data is too low or too slow
part of	The data or control signal is incomplete
other than	The data or control signal has another component
early	The signal arrives too early for the clock
late	The signal arrives too late for the clock
before	The signal arrives too early in the expected sequence
after	The signal arrives too late in the expected sequence

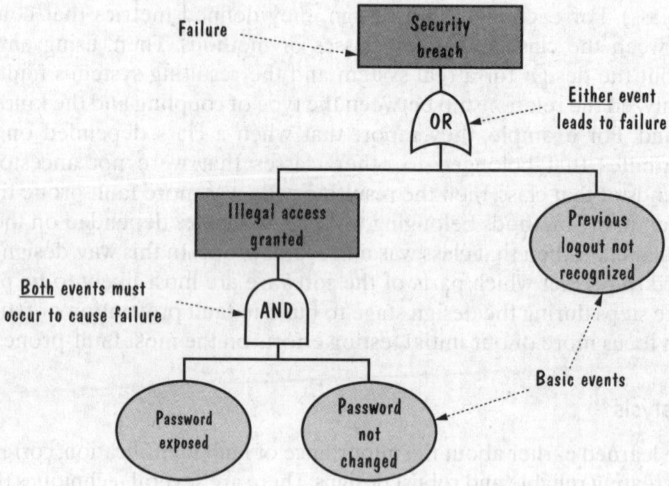

FIGURE 5.11 Fault tree for a security breach.

includes *m* redundant components, where *n* faulty components lead to the designated failure. Each node represents an independent event; otherwise, the analysis results may be invalid, especially with respect to compound faults.

For example, consider the fault tree presented in Figure 5.11. The tree shows that a security breach could occur either if a previous logout is not recognized (leaving the previous user logged in) or an unauthorized user gains access to the system. For the latter to happen, both of two basic events must happen: a valid user's password is exposed, and the password is not changed between the time of the exposure and the time an unauthorized user attempts to use it.

The concepts we have described can be applied to any system's hardware or software. The challenge is to identify key possible failures, and then trace backwards through the design, looking for data and computations that could contribute to the failure. Data-flow and control-flow graphs can help us trace through a design. As we saw in Chapter 4, a **data-flow graph** depicts the transfer of data from one process to another. The same ideas can be applied to an architectural design, to show what kinds of data flow among the design's software units. In this way, if one of the failures we are analyzing is data related, we can trace backwards through the data-flow graph to find the software units that could affect the data and thereby cause the fault. Similarly, a **control-flow graph** depicts possible transfers of control among software units. When applied to a design, a control-flow graph can show how a control thread progresses from one unit to the next during execution. If we are analyzing a failure that is related to computation or to a quality attribute, we can trace backwards through the control-flow graph to find the software units involved in that computation.

Once the fault tree is constructed, we can search for design weaknesses. For example, we can derive another tree, called a *cut-set tree*, that reveals which event combinations can cause the failure. A cut-set tree is especially useful when the fault tree is complex and difficult to analyze by eye. The rules for forming the cut-set tree are as follows:

1. Assign the top node of the cut-set tree to match the logic gate at the top of the fault tree.
2. Working from the top down, expand the cut-set tree as follows:
   - Expand an *or*-gate node to have two children, one for each *or*-gate child.
   - Expand an *and*-gate node to have a child composition node listing both of the *and*-gate children.
   - Expand a composition node by propagating the node to its children, but expanding one of the gates listed in the node.
3. Continue until all leaf nodes are basic events or composition nodes of basic events.

The **cut-set** is the set of leaf nodes in the cut-set tree. For example, consider the fault tree on the left side of Figure 5.12. G1 is the top logic gate in the fault tree, and its *or* condition leads us to expand its corresponding node in the cut-set tree to have two child nodes, G2 and G3. In turn, G2 in the fault tree is composed of both G4 *and* G5, so G2 in the cut-set tree is expanded to have a composition child node with label {G4, G5}. Continuing in this manner, we end up with the cut-set {A1, A3}, {A1, A4}, {A2, A3}, {A2, A4}, {A4, A5}. The cut-set represents the set of minimal event combinations that could lead to the failure listed at the top of the cut-set tree. Thus, if any member of the cut-set is a singleton event set, {A*i*}, then the top failure could be caused by a single event, A*i*. Similarly, the cut set element {A*i*, A*j*} means that the top failure can occur if both events A*i* and A*j* occur, and cut-set element {A*i*, A*j*, . . ., A*n*} means that failure can occur only if all of the composite events occur. Thus, we have reasoned from a failure to all possible causes of it.

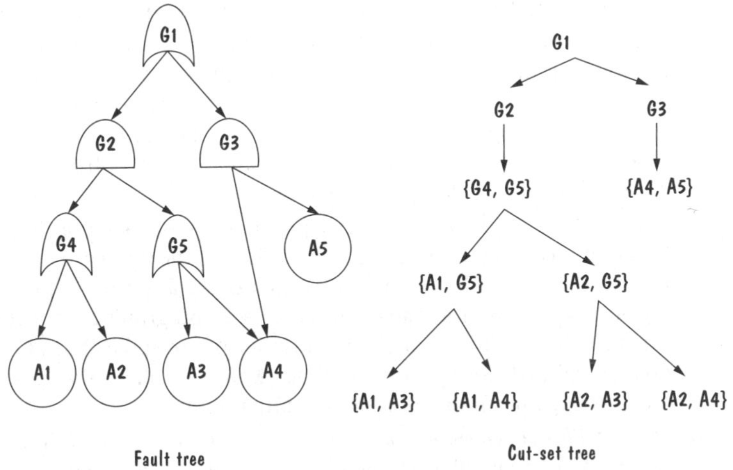

FIGURE 5.12 Cut-set tree generated from a fault tree.

Once we know the points of failure in our design, we can redesign to reduce the vulnerabilities. We have several choices when we find a fault in a design:

- Correct the fault.
- Add components or conditions to prevent the conditions that cause the fault.
- Add components that detect the fault or failure and recover from the damage.

Although the first option is preferable, it is not always possible.

We can also use fault trees to calculate the probability that a given failure will occur by estimating the probability of the basic events and propagating these computations up through the tree. But there are some drawbacks to fault-tree analysis. First, constructing the graphs can be time consuming. Second, many systems involve many dependencies, which means that analysis of the design's data-flow and control-flow graphs yields a large number of suspect software units to explore; it is difficult to focus only on the most critical parts of the design unless we have very low coupling. Moreover, the number and kinds of preconditions that are necessary for each failure are daunting and not always easy to spot, and there is no measurement to help us sort them out. However, researchers continue to seek ways to automate the tree building and analysis. In the United States and Canada, fault-tree analysis is used for critical aviation and nuclear applications, where the risk of failure is worth the intense and substantial effort to build and evaluate the fault trees.

Security Analysis

In Chapter 3, we saw how risk analysis is used to determine the likely threats to a project's cost and schedule. When designing the system's architecture, we must carry out a similar analysis, this time to address security risks. Allen et al. (2008) describe the six steps in performing a security analysis:

1. *Software characterization.* In the first step, we review the software requirements, business case, use cases, SAD, test plans, and other available documents to give us a complete understanding of what the system is supposed to do and why.
2. *Threat analysis.* Next, we look for threats to the system: Who might be interested in attacking the system, and when might those attacks occur? NIST (2002) lists many sources of threats, including hackers, computer criminals, terrorists, industrial espionage agents, and both naïve and malicious insiders. The threat activities might include industrial espionage, blackmail, interception or disruption of communications, system tampering, and more.
3. *Vulnerability assessment.* Security problems occur when a threat exploits a vulnerability. The vulnerability may be a flaw in the software design or in the code itself. Examples include failure to authenticate a person or process before allowing access to data or a system, or use of a cryptographic algorithm that is easy to break. Vulnerabilities can arise not only from mistakes but also from ambiguity, dependency, or poor error handling. Antón et al. (2004) describe a complete methodology for finding a system's vulnerabilities.
4. *Risk likelihood determination.* Once the threats and vulnerabilities are documented, we examine the likelihood that each vulnerability will be exploited. We must consider four things: the motivation (i.e., why the person or system is threatening), the

ability of the threat to exploit a vulnerability, the impact of the exploitation (i.e., how much damage will be done, how long the effects will be felt, and by whom), and the degree to which current controls can prevent the exploitation.

5. *Risk impact determination.* Next, we look at the business consequences if the attack is successful. What assets are threatened? How long will functionality be impaired? How much will recognition and remediation cost? Pfleeger and Ciszek (2008) describe RAND's InfoSecure methodology, which provides guidelines for recognizing and ranking various threats and vulnerabilities in terms of business impact. The highest rank is *business-ending*, where an organization or business would not be able to recover from the attack. For example, the business may lose the designs for all of its new products. The next category is *damaging*: a temporary loss of business from which it may be difficult but not impossible to recover. For instance, the business may lose sensitive financial data that can eventually be retrieved from backup media. The next lower category is *recoverable*; here, the business may lose its corporate benefit policies (such as life and health insurance), which can easily be replaced by the insurance providers. The lowest category is *nuisance*, where assets such as nonsensitive email are deleted from the server; restoration may not even be necessary.
6. *Risk mitigation planning.* The final step involves planning to reduce the likelihood and consequences of the most severe risks. InfoSecure performs this planning by first having us devise projects to address each risk. The projects specify both staff impact and policy impact. The projects are prioritized according to the business impact, considering both capital and overhead costs. A final list of projects to implement is based on likelihood of risks, business impact of mitigations, and cash flow.

Although the six security analysis steps can be applied to evaluate how well an architectural design meets security needs, these steps can also be applied later in the development process. Even when the system is operational, it is useful to perform a security analysis; threats and vulnerabilities change over time, and the system should be updated to meet new security needs.

Trade-off Analysis

Often, there are several alternative designs to consider. In fact, as professionals, it is our duty to explore design alternatives and not simply implement the first design that comes to mind. For example, it may not be immediately obvious which architectural styles to use as the basis for a design. This is especially true if the design is expected to achieve quality attributes that conflict with one another. Alternatively, different members of our design team may promote competing designs, and it is our responsibility to decide which one to pursue. We need a measurement-based method for comparing design alternatives, so that we can make informed decisions and can justify our decisions to others.

One Specification, Many Designs. To see how different architecture styles can be used to solve the same problem, consider the problem posed by Parnas (1972):

> The [key word in context] KWIC system accepts an ordered set of lines; each line is an ordered set of words, and each word is an ordered set of characters. Any line may be

"circularly shifted" by repeatedly removing the first word and appending it at the end of the line. The KWIC index system outputs a list of all circular shifts of all lines in alphabetical order.

Such systems are used to index text, supporting rapid searching for keywords. For example, KWIC is used in electronic library catalogues (e.g., find all titles that contain the name "Martin Luther King Jr.") and in online help systems (e.g., find all index entries that contain the word "customize").

Shaw and Garlan (1996) present four different architectural designs to implement KWIC: repository, data abstraction, implicit invocation (a type of publish-subscribe), and pipe-and-filter. The repository-based solution, shown in Figure 5.13, breaks the problem into its four primary functions: input, circular shift, alphabetize, and output. Thus, the system's functionality is decomposed and modularized. These four modules are coordinated by a master program that calls them in sequence. Because the data are localized in their own modules, and not replicated or passed among the computational modules, the design is efficient. However, as Parnas points out, this design is difficult to change. Because the computational modules access and manipulate the data directly, via read and write operations, any change to the data and data format will affect all modules. Also, none of the elements in the design are particularly reusable.

Figure 5.14 illustrates a second design that has a similar decomposition of functionality into sequentially called modules. However, in this design, the data computed by each computational module is stored in that module. For example, the circular-shift module maintains the index to keywords in the text, and the alphabetic-shift module maintains a sorted (alphabetized) version of this index. Each module's data are accessible via access methods, rather than directly. Thus, the modules form *data abstractions*. In a data abstraction, the methods' interfaces give no hint of the module's data or data representations, making it easier to modify data-related design decisions without affecting other modules. And because data-abstraction modules encompass both the

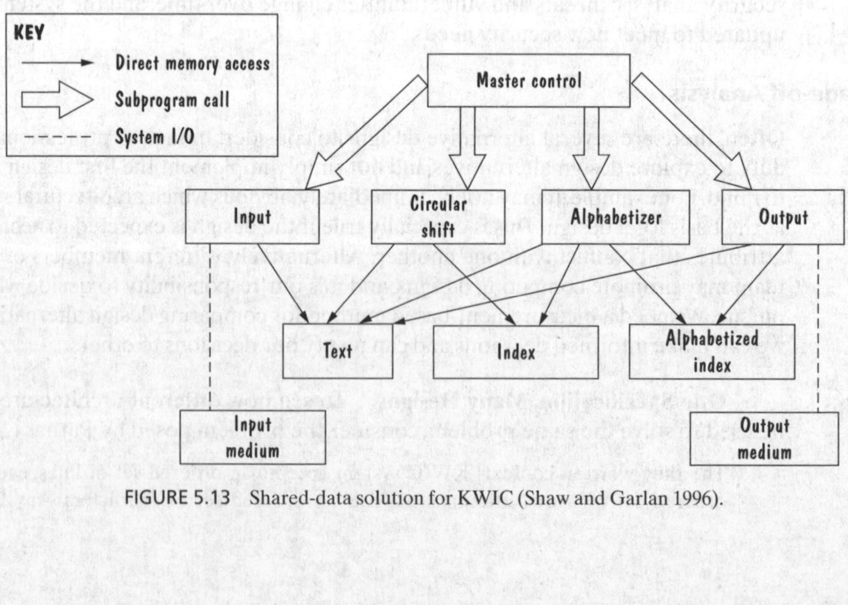

FIGURE 5.13 Shared-data solution for KWIC (Shaw and Garlan 1996).

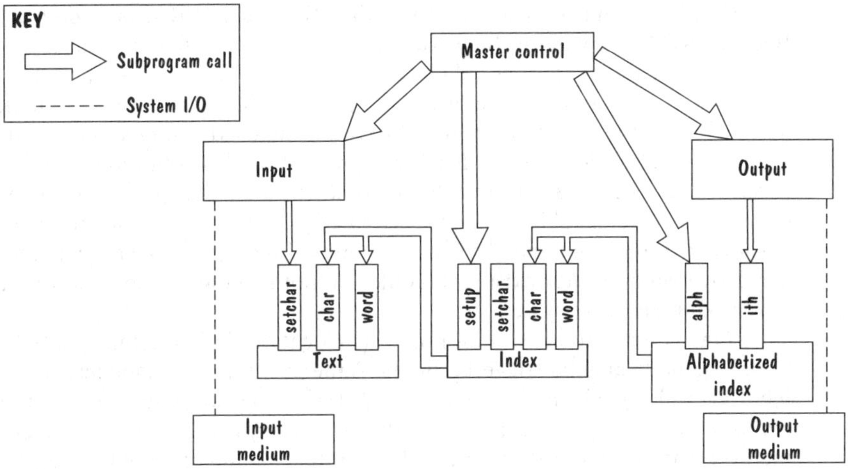

FIGURE 5.14 Data-module solution for KWIC (Shaw and Garlan 1996).

data to be maintained and the operations for maintaining the data, these modules are easier to reuse in other applications than modules from our first design. On the downside, changes to the system's functionality may not be so easy, because the functionality is so tightly coupled with the data. For example, omitting indices whose circular shifts start with noise words means either (1) enhancing an existing module, making it more complex, more context specific, and less reusable; or (2) inserting a new module to remove useless indices after they have been created, which is inefficient, and modifying existing modules to call the new module (Garlan, Kaiser, and Notkin 1992).

Instead, Garlan, Kaiser, and Notkin (1992) propose a third design, shown in Figure 5.15, in which the data are stored in ADTs that manage generic data types, such

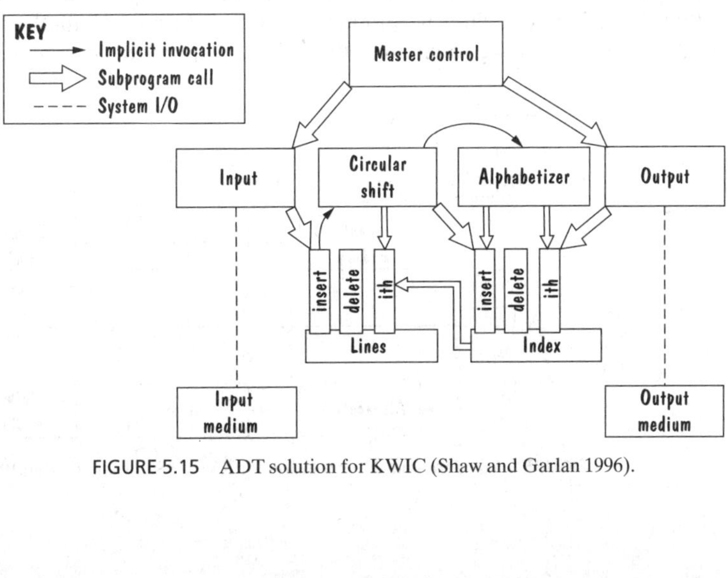

FIGURE 5.15 ADT solution for KWIC (Shaw and Garlan 1996).

as lines of text and sets of indices, rather than in KWIC-based data abstractions. Because ADTs are generic, they are even more reusable than data abstractions. Moreover, the data and operations on data are encapsulated in the ADT modules, so changes to data representation are confined to these modules. This design resembles the first design, in that the system's functionality is decomposed and modularized into computational modules. However, in this design, many of the computational modules are triggered by the occurrence of events rather than by explicit procedure invocation. For example, the circular-shift module is activated whenever a new line of text is input. The design can be easily extended, via new computational modules whose methods are triggered by system events; existing modules do not need to be modified to integrate the new modules into the system.

One complication with an implicit-invocation design is that multiple computational methods may be triggered by the same event. If that happens, all the triggered methods will execute, but in what order? If we do not impose an order, then the triggered methods may execute in any arbitrary order, which may not be desired (e.g., a method that expands macros in new lines of text should execute before a method that inserts a new line into the ADT). However, to control execution order, we must devise some generic strategy that applies to both current and future sets of methods triggered by the same event, and we cannot always predict what methods may be added to the system in the future.

This complication leads us to a fourth design, based on a pipe-and-filter architecture (Figure 5.16), where the sequence of processing is controlled by the sequence of the filter modules. This design is easily extended to include new features, in that we can simply insert additional filters into the sequence. Also, each filter is an independent entity that can be changed without affecting other filters. The design supports the reuse of filters in other pipe-and-filter applications, as long as a filter's input data is in the form that it expects (Shaw and Garlan 1996). The filters may execute in parallel, processing inputs as they are received (although the Alphabetizer cannot output its results until it has received and sorted all of the input lines); this concurrent processing can enhance performance. Unlike the other designs, a data item is no longer stored in any location, but rather flows from one filter to another, being transformed along the way. As such, the design is not conducive to changes that would require the storage of persistent data,

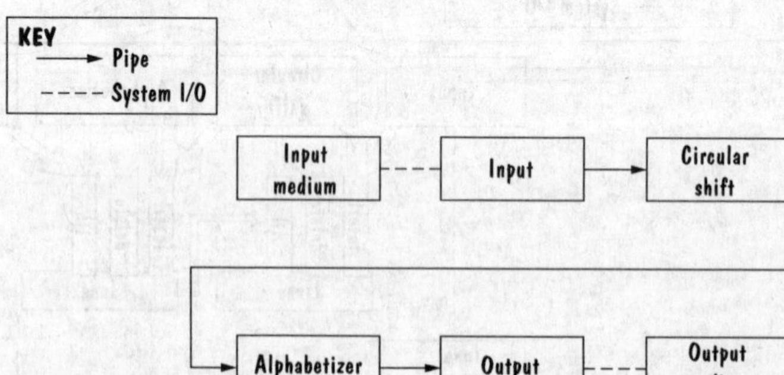

FIGURE 5.16 Pipe-and-filter solution for KWIC (Shaw and Garlan 1996).

TABLE 5.2 Comparison of Proposed KWIC Solutions

Attribute	Shared Data	Data Abstraction	Implicit Invocation	Pipe and Filter
Easy to change algorithm	–	–	+	+
Easy to change data representation	–	+	–	–
Easy to add functionality	+	–	+	+
Good performance	–	–	+	+
Efficient data representation	+	+	+	–
Easy to reuse	–	+	–	+

Source: Adapted from Shaw and Garlan (1996).

such as an *undo* operation. Also, there are some space inefficiencies: the circular shifts can no longer be represented as indices into the original text and instead are permuted copies of the original lines of text. Moreover, the data item is copied each time a filter outputs its results to the pipe leading to the next filter.

We can see that each design has its positive and negative aspects. Thus, we need a method for comparing different designs that allows us to choose the best one for our purpose.

Comparison Tables. Shaw and Garlan (1996) compare the four designs according to how well they achieve important quality attributes and then organize this information as a table, shown as Table 5.2. Each row represents a quality attribute, and there is one column for each of the proposed designs. A minus in a cell means that the attribute represented by the row is not a property of the design for that column; a plus means that the design has the attribute. We can see from the table that the choice is still not clear; we must assign priorities to the attributes and form weighted scores if we want to select the best design for our particular needs.

We start by prioritizing quality attributes with respect to how important the attributes are to achieving our customer's requirements and our development strategy. For example, on a scale of 1 to 5, where 5 indicates that an attribute is most desirable, we may assign a "5" to reusability if the design is to be reused in several other products.

Next, we form a matrix, shown in Table 5.3, labeling the rows of the matrix with the attributes we value. The second column lists the priorities we have determined for

TABLE 5.3 Weighted Comparison of Proposed KWIC Solutions

Attribute	Priority	Shared Data	Data Abstraction	Implicit Invocation	Pipe and Filter
Easy to change algorithm	1	1	2	4	5
Easy to change data representation	4	1	5	4	1
Easy to add functionality	3	4	1	3	5
Good performance	3	4	3	3	5
Efficient data representation	3	5	5	5	1
Easy to reuse	5	1	4	5	4
Total		49	69	78	62

each of the attributes. In the remaining columns, we record how well each design achieves each attribute, on a scale of 1 (low achievement) to 5 (high achievement). Thus, the entry in the cell in the ith row and jth column rates the design represented by column i in terms of how well it satisfies the quality attribute represented by row j.

Finally, we compute a score for each design by multiplying the priority of each row by the design's score for that attribute, and summing the results. For example, the pipe-and-filter design score would be calculated as $1 \times 5 + 4 \times 1 + 3 \times 5 + 3 \times 5 + 3 \times 1 + 5 \times 4 = 62$. The scores of the other designs are listed on the bottom row of Table 5.3.

In this case, we would choose the implicit-invocation design. However, the priorities and ratings, as well as the choice of attributes, are subjective and depend on the needs of our customers and users, as well as our preferences for building and maintaining systems. Other attributes we might have considered include

- modularity
- testability
- security
- ease of use
- ease of understanding
- ease of integration

Including these attributes (in particular, ease of integration) in our analysis might have affected our final decision. Other evaluators are likely to score the designs differently and may reach different conclusions. As we learn more about measuring design attributes, we can remove some of the subjectivity from this rating approach. But design evaluation will always require some degree of subjectivity and expert judgment, since each of us has different perspectives and experiences.

Cost–Benefit Analysis

Trade-off analysis gives us a means for evaluating design alternatives, but it focuses only on the technical merits of designs, in terms of how well the designs achieve desired quality attributes. At least as important are the business merits of a design: Will the benefits of a system based on a particular design outweigh the costs of its implementation? If there are competing designs, which one will give us the highest return on investment?

Suppose that we are responsible for maintaining the catalogue for a national online video rental company. Customers use the catalogue to search for and request video rentals, to identify actors in videos, and to access video reviews. KWIC is used to index catalogue entries for fast lookup by keywords in video titles, actors' names, and so on. The number of users, as well as the size of the catalogue, has been growing steadily, and the response time for querying the catalogue has gotten noticeably longer—to the point that users have started to complain. We have some ideas about how to improve the system's response time. Figure 5.17 shows the part of the system architecture that is affected by our proposed changes, including the impacts of our three ideas:

1. We could eliminate entries in the KWIC index that start with noise words, such as articles ("a, the") and prepositions. This change reduces the number of indices to

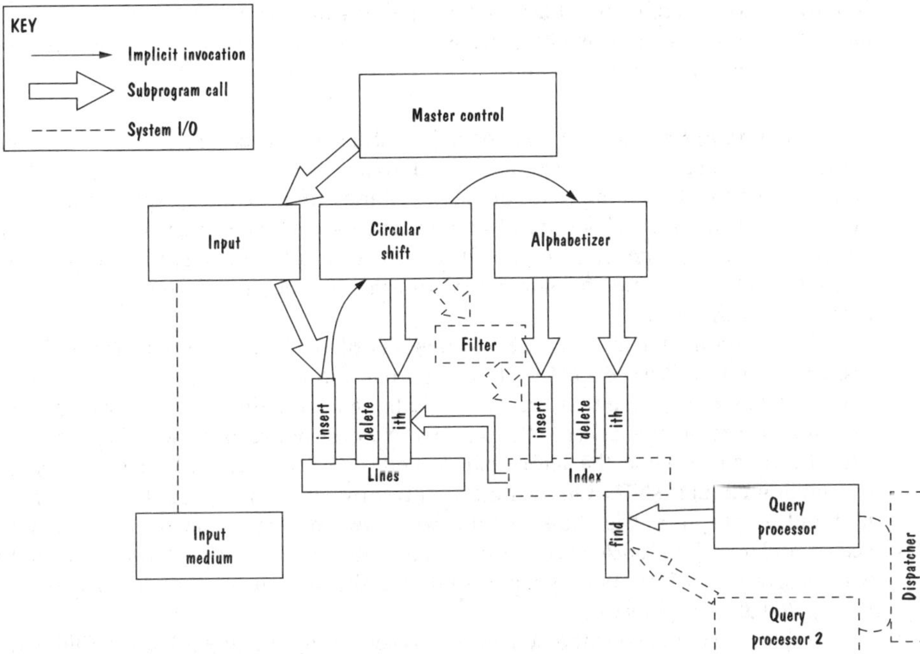

FIGURE 5.17 Proposed changes to KWIC.

be searched when servicing a lookup query. It would involve adding a filter module, between the circular-shift and sorted-indices modules, that aborts any request to store an index to a noise word. (The design changes involve a new Filter module, shown in dashed lines in Figure 5.17.)

2. We could change the representation of indices to be bins of indices, where each bin associates a keyword with the set of indices that point to lines that contain that word. This change reduces the time it takes to find subsequent instances of a keyword once the first instance (i.e., the bin) has been found. (The design changes the internal data representation within the Index module, shown in dashed lines in Figure 5.17.)
3. We could increase server capacity by adding another computer, Query Processor 2, that shares the task of processing queries. This change involves not only buying the server, but also changing the software architecture to include a Dispatcher module that assigns queries to servers. (The design changes shown involve a new Query Processor 2 and a Dispatcher, shown in dashed lines in Figure 5.17.)

All three proposals would improve the time it takes to lookup catalogue entries, but which one would be the most effective?

Most companies define "effectiveness" of a system in terms of value and cost: how much value will a proposed change add to the system (or how much value will a new system add to the company's business) compared with how much it will cost to implement the change. A **cost–benefit analysis** is a widely used business tool for estimating and comparing the costs and benefits of a proposed change.

Computing Benefits. A cost–benefit analysis usually contrasts financial benefits with financial costs. Thus, if the benefit of a design is in the extra features it provides, or in the degree to which it improves quality attributes, then we must express these benefits as a financial value. Costs are often one-time capital expenses, with perhaps some ongoing operating expenses, but benefits almost always accrue over time. Thus, we calculate benefits over a specific time period, or calculate the time it would take for benefits to pay for the costs.

For example, let us compute the benefits of the above design proposals, with respect to how well we expect them to improve the response time for querying the video catalogue. Suppose that the current catalogue contains 70,000 entries, and that the average size of an entry (i.e., the number of words per record, including the video's title, the director's name, the actors' names, and so on) is 70 words, for a total of almost five million circular shifts. On average, it currently takes the system 0.016 seconds to find and output all entries that contain two keywords, which means that the system accommodates about 60 such requests per second. However, at peak times, the system will receive up to 100 queries per second, and the system is eventually expected to handle 200 queries per second.

Table 5.4 summarizes the benefits of implementing the three designs. Eliminating noise words does not significantly improve performance, mainly because most of the words in an entry are names, and names do not have noise words. In contrast, adding a second server almost doubles the number of requests that the system can service per second. And restructuring the sorted-index data structure provides the greatest benefits, because it reduces the search space (to keywords rather than circular shifts), and because the result of the search returns all of the associated indices rather than just one.

Next, we compute the financial value of these improvements. The value of an improvement depends on how badly it is needed, so value might not increase proportionally with increases in quality. In some cases, a small improvement may be of little

TABLE 5.4 Cost–Benefit Analysis of Design Proposals

	Eliminate Noise Words	Store Indices in Bins	Add Second Server
Benefits			
Search time	0.015 sec	0.002 sec	0.008 sec
Throughput	72 requests/sec	500 requests/sec	115 requests/sec
Added value	$24,000/yr	$280,000/yr	$110,000/yr
Costs			
Hardware			$5,000
Software	$50,000	$300,000	$200,000
Business losses	$28,000+/yr		
Total costs first year	$78,000	$300,000	$205,000

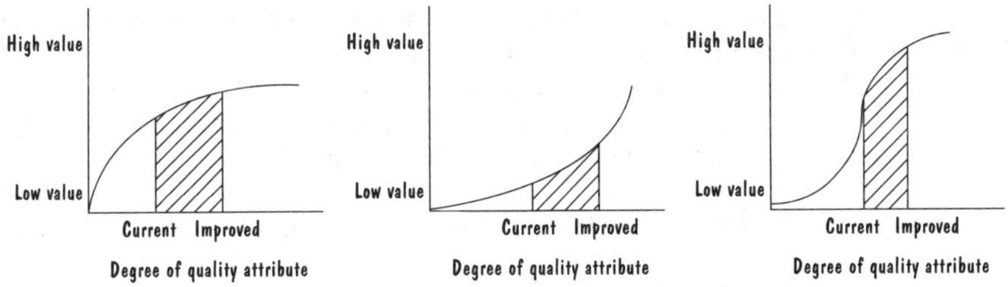

FIGURE 5.18 Value added by improving a quality attribute (Bass, Clements, and Kazman 2003).

value if it is not enough to address a problem; in other cases, small improvements are significant, and further improvements yield little additional value. Figure 5.18 shows several ways in which value may increase as a quality attribute improves. Given such a value function for a particular quality attribute for a particular system, the net value of an improvement is the area under the curve between the current and improved measures of the quality attribute.

For simplicity, suppose that every *additional* request per second that the system can process, up to 200 requests/second, would save the company \$2000 per year, based on retained customers and reduced calls to technical support. Given this value function, eliminating noise words would save the company \$24,000 per year, calculated as

$$(72 \text{ requests/second} - 60 \text{ requests/second}) \times \$2000/\text{year} = \$24{,}000/\text{year}$$

Adding a second server would save the company \$110,000 per year, calculated as

$$(115 \text{ requests/second} - 60 \text{ requests/second}) \times \$2000/\text{year} = \$110{,}000/\text{year}$$

The second design option would improve the system's throughput beyond what will be needed (the system will receive at most 200 requests per second). Therefore, the value added by changing to bin-based indexing is the maximum possible value:

$$(200 \text{ requests/second} - 60 \text{ requests/second}) \times \$2000/\text{year} = \$280{,}000/\text{year}$$

If there are multiple attributes to consider (e.g., the time it takes to update, reindex, and re-sort the catalogue), then a design's total financial added value is the sum of the added values ascribed to each of the attributes—some of whose added values may be negative if a design improves one attribute at the expense of a conflicting attribute.

Computing Return on Investment (ROI). The *return on investment* of making one of these design changes is the ratio of the benefits gained from making the change to the cost of its implementation:

$$\text{ROI} = \text{Benefits/Cost}$$

These costs are estimated using the techniques described in Chapter 3. The estimated costs of the proposed design changes in our example are shown in Table 5.4. In general, an ROI of 1 or greater means that the design's benefits outweigh its costs. The higher the ROI value, the more effective the design.

Another useful measure is the **payback period**: the length of time before accumulated benefits recover the costs of implementation. In our example, the payback period for restructuring the sorted-index module (design 2) is

$$\$300{,}000/\$280{,}000 = 1.07 \text{ of a year} = \text{approximately 13 months}$$

We return to calculations such as these in Chapter 12, where we investigate the best techniques for evaluating the return on investing in software reuse.

Prototyping

Some design questions are best answered by prototyping. A **prototype** is an executable model of the system we are developing, built to answer specific questions we have about the system. For example, we may want to test that our protocols for signaling, synchronizing, coordinating, and sharing data among concurrent processes work as expected. We can develop a prototype that implements processes as stubs and that exercises our communication protocols, so that we can work out the kinks and gain confidence in our plans for how the processes will interact. We may also learn something about the limits (e.g., minimum response times) of our design.

Prototyping offers different advantages in the design stage from those gained during requirements analysis. As we saw in Chapter 4, prototyping is an effective tool for testing the feasibility of questionable requirements and for exploring user-interface alternatives. The process of developing the prototype encourages us to communicate with our customers and to explore areas of uncertainty that emerge as we think about the system's requirements. As long as our customers understand that the prototype is an exploratory model, not a beta-version of the product, prototyping can be useful in helping both us and our customers understand what the system is to do.

In the design phase, prototyping is used to answer design questions, compare design alternatives, test complex interactions, or explore the effects of change requests. A prototype omits many of the details of functionality and performance that will be part of the real system, so that we can focus narrowly on particular aspects of the system. For example, a small team may generate a prototype for each design issue to be resolved: one prototype for modeling the user interface, one for certifying that a purchased component is compatible with our design, one for testing the network performance between remote processes, one for each security tactic being considered, and so on. The final design is then a synthesis of the answers obtained from the individual prototypes.

If a prototype is intended only to explore design issues, we may not give its development the same careful attention that we would give to a real system. For this reason, we frequently discard the prototype and build the actual system from scratch, rather than try to salvage parts from the prototype. In these cases, the **throw-away prototype** is meant to be discarded; its development is intended only to assess the feasibility or particular characteristics in a proposed design. In fact, Brooks (1995) recommends building a system, throwing it away, and building it again. The second version of the system benefits from the learning and the mistakes made in the process of building the first system.

Alternatively, we may attempt to reuse parts of the prototype in the actual system. By taking care in the design and development of the prototype's components, we can produce a prototype that answers questions about the design and at the same time provides building blocks for the final system. The challenge is to ensure that this style of prototyping is still fast. If the prototype cannot be built more quickly than the actual system, then it loses its value. Moreover, if too much effort is invested in developing a quality prototype, we may become too attached to the design decisions and other assets embedded in the prototype, and we may be less open to considering design alternatives.

An extreme version of this approach is called **rapid prototyping**, in which we progressively refine the prototype until it becomes the final system. We start with a prototype of the requirements, in the form of a preliminary user interface that simulates the system's responses to user input. In successive iterations of the prototype, we flesh out the system's design and implementation, providing the functionality promised by the initial user interface. In many ways, rapid prototyping resembles an agile development process, in that the system's development is iterative and there is continual feedback from the customer. The difference is that the initial prototype is a user-interface shell rather than the core of the operational system.

Boehm, Gray, and Seewaldt (1984) studied projects that were developed using rapid prototyping, and they report that such projects performed about as well as those developed using traditional design techniques. In addition, 45 percent less effort was expended and 40 percent fewer lines of code were generated by the developers who used prototypes. Also, the speed and efficiency of the systems developed with prototypes were almost the same as those of the traditionally developed systems. However, there are some risks in using rapid prototyping. The biggest risk is that by showing customers an operational prototype, we may mislead them into believing that the system is close to being finished. A related risk is that customers may expect the final system to exhibit the same performance characteristics as the prototype, which could be unrealistically fast due to omitted functionality, smaller scale, and communication delays. Also, because of the lack of documentation, prototyping as a development process is best suited for smaller projects involving smaller development teams.

5.8 DOCUMENTING SOFTWARE ARCHITECTURES

A system's architecture plays a vital role in its overall development: it is the basis on which most subsequent decisions about design, quality assurance, and project management are made. As such, it is crucial that the system's developers and stakeholders have a consistent understanding of the system's architecture. The SAD serves as a repository for information about the architectural design and helps to communicate this vision to the various members of the development team.

The SAD's contents depend heavily on how it will be used. That is, we try to anticipate what information will be sought by different types of SAD readers. Customers will be looking for a natural-language description of what the system will do. Designers will be looking for precise specifications of the software units to be developed. A performance analyst will want enough information about the software design, the computing platform, and the system's environment to carry out analyses of likely speed and load. Different team members read the SAD, each with a different purpose. For example, coders read the SAD to understand the overall design and make sure that each design feature or function is implemented somewhere in the code. Testers read the SAD to ensure that their tests exercise all aspects of the design. Maintainers use the SAD as a guide, so that architectural integrity is maintained as problems are fixed and new features implemented.

Given these uses, a SAD should include the following information:

- *System overview:* This section provides an introductory description of the system, in terms of its key functions and usages.
- *Views:* Each view conveys information about the system's overall design structure, as seen from a particular perspective. In addition to the views, we document also how the views relate to one another. Because the views are likely to be read by all SAD readers, each section is prefaced with a summary of the view and its main elements and interactions; technical details are addressed in separate subsections.
- *Software units:* We include a complete catalogue of the software units to be developed, including precise specifications of their interfaces. For each software unit, we indicate all of the views in which the unit appears as an element.
- *Analysis data and results:* This section contains enough details about the system's architecture, computing resources, and execution environment so that a design analyst can measure the design's quality attributes. The results of the analyses are also recorded.
- *Design rationale:* Design decisions must be explained and defended, and the rationale for the chosen design is recorded to ensure that project managers and future architects have no need to revisit design alternatives that were originally dismissed for good reason.
- *Definitions, glossary, acronyms:* These sections provide all readers with the same understanding of the technical and domain vocabulary used throughout the document.

In addition, the SAD is identified with a version number or date of issue, so that readers can easily confirm that they are working with the same version of the document and that the version is recent.

There are few guidelines, in the form of standards or recommended templates, for how to organize all of this information as a useful technical reference. For example, the IEEE recommendations for documenting software architectures, IEEE Standard 1471–2000, prescribe what information to include in an architectural document, but say little about how to structure or format the information. Thus, it makes sense to develop an in-house standard for organizing the SAD's contents, including guidance on the document's structure, contents, and the source of each type of information (e.g., whether the writer must collect or create the information). More importantly, a standard helps the reader know how to navigate through the document and find information quickly. Like other reference texts, such as dictionaries and encyclopedias, technical documentation such as the SAD is rarely read from cover to cover; most users use the SAD for quick queries about design decisions that are described at a high level in one part of the document but are described in detail elsewhere in the document. Thus, the SAD should be organized and indexed for easy reference.

As Bass, Clements, and Kazman (2003) note,

> One of the most fundamental rules for technical documentation in general, and software architecture documentation in particular, is to write from the point of view of the reader. Documentation that was easy to write but is not easy to read will not be used, and "easy to read" is in the eye of the beholder—or in this case, the stakeholder.

Given the many uses of the SAD, we have many readers to satisfy with a single document. As such, we may choose to split the SAD into different but related documents, where each piece addresses a different type of reader. Alternatively, we can try to merge all information into a single document, with directions to guide different readers to their information of interest. For example, we may suggest that customers read the system overview plus summaries of each view. By contrast, developers would be expected to read details of the software units they are to implement, the uses view to see how the units relate to the rest of the system, any other view that uses the corresponding architectural elements, and the mappings among views to see if the units correspond to other architectural elements.

Mappings among Views

How many and which views to include in the SAD depends on the structure of the system being designed and the quality attributes that we want to measure. At the very least, the SAD should contain a decomposition view showing the design's constituent code units, plus an execution view showing the system's runtime structure. In addition, a deployment view that assigns software units to computing resources is essential if we want to reason about the system's performance. Alternatively, we may include multiple execution views, each based on a different architectural style, if each of the styles reflects useful ways of thinking about the system's structure and interactions. For example, if our design is based on a publish-subscribe style, in which components are triggered by events, we may also include a pipe-and-filter view that depicts the order in which components are to be invoked.

Because our design is documented as a collection of views, we should show how the views relate to one another. If one view details an element that is a software unit in a more abstract view, then this relationship is straightforward. However, if two views show different aspects of the same part of the design, and if there is no obvious correspondence between the elements in the two views, then mapping this correspondence is essential. For example, it is useful to record how runtime components and connectors in an execution view map to code-level units in a decomposition view. Such a mapping documents how the components and connectors will be implemented. Similarly, it is useful to record how elements in one decomposition view (e.g., a module view) map to elements in another decomposition view (e.g., a layer view). Such a mapping reveals all of the units needed to implement each layer.

Clements et al. (2003) describe how to document a mapping between two views as a table, indexed by the elements in one of the views. For each element in the first view, the table lists the corresponding element(s) in the second view and describes the nature of the correspondence. For example, the indexed element *implements* the other element(s), or is a *generalization* of the other element(s). Because it is possible that parts of elements in one view map to parts of elements in the other view, we should also indicate whether the correspondence is partial or complete.

Documenting Rationale

In addition to design decisions, we also document **design rationale**, outlining the critical issues and trade-offs that were considered in generating the design. This guiding philosophy helps the customers, project managers, and other developers (particularly maintainers) understand how and why certain parts of the design fit together. It also helps the architect remember the basis for certain decisions, thereby avoiding the need to revisit these decisions.

Rationale is usually expressed in terms of the system's requirements, such as design constraints that limit the solution space, or quality attributes to be optimized. This section of the SAD lists decision alternatives that were considered and rejected, along with a justification for why the chosen option is best; if several alternatives are equally good, then those should be described too. The design rationale may also include an evaluation of the potential costs, benefits, and ramifications of changing the decision.

Good practice dictates that we provide rationale for lower-level design decisions, such as details about software-unit interfaces or the structure of a view, as well as overall architectural decisions, such as choice of architectural style(s). But we need not justify every decision we make. Clements et al. (2003) offer good advice on when to document the rationale behind a decision:

- Significant time was spent on considering the options and arriving at a decision.
- The decision is critical to achieving a requirement.
- The decision is counterintuitive or raises questions.
- It would be costly to change the decision.

5.9 ARCHITECTURE DESIGN REVIEW

Design review is an essential part of engineering practice, and we evaluate the quality of a SAD in two different ways. First, we make sure that the design satisfies all of the requirements specified by the customer. This procedure is known as **validating** the design. Then we address the quality of the design. **Verification** involves ensuring that the design adheres to good design principles, and that the design documentation fits the needs of its users. Thus, we validate the design to make sure that we are building what the customer wants (i.e., is this the right system?), and we verify our documentation to help ensure that the developers will be productive in their development tasks (i.e., are we building the system right?).

Validation

During validation, we make sure that all aspects of the requirements are addressed by our design. To do that, we invite several key people to the review:

- the analyst(s) who helped to define the system requirements
- the system architect(s)
- the program designer(s) for this project

- a system tester
- a system maintainer
- a moderator
- a recorder
- other interested system developers who are not otherwise involved in this project

The number of people actually at the review depends on the size and complexity of the system under development. Every member of the review team should have the authority to act as a representative of his or her organization and to make decisions and commitments. The total number should be kept small, so that discussion and decision making are not hampered.

The moderator leads the discussion but has no vested interest in the project itself. He or she encourages discussion, acts as an intermediary between opposing viewpoints, keeps the discussion moving, and maintains objectivity and balance in the process.

Because it is difficult to take part in the discussion and also record the main points and outcomes, another impartial participant is recruited to serve as recorder. The recorder does not get involved in the issues that arise; his or her sole job is to document what transpires. However, more than stenographic skills are required; the recorder must have enough technical knowledge to understand the proceedings and record relevant technical information.

Developers who are not involved with the project provide an outsider's perspective. They can be objective when commenting on the proposed design, because they have no personal stake in it. In fact, they may have fresh ideas and can offer a new slant on things. They also act as ad hoc verifiers, checking that the design is correct, is consistent, and conforms to good design practice. By participating in the review, they assume equal responsibility for the design with the designers themselves. This shared responsibility forces all in the review process to scrutinize every design detail.

During the review, we present the proposed architecture to our audience. In doing so, we demonstrate that the design has the required structure, function, and characteristics specified by the requirements documents. Together, we confirm that the proposed design includes the required hardware, interfaces with other systems, input, and output. We trace typical execution paths through the architecture, to convince ourselves that the communication and coordination mechanisms work properly. We also trace exceptional execution paths, to review the design measures we have taken to detect and recover from faults and bad inputs. To validate nonfunctional requirements, we review the results of analyses that have been performed to predict likely system behavior, and we examine any documented design rationale that pertains to quality attributes.

Any discrepancies found during the review are noted by the recorder and discussed by the group as a whole. We resolve minor issues as they appear. However, if major faults or misunderstandings arise, we may agree to revise the design. In this case, we schedule another design review to evaluate the new design. Just as the Howells would rather redo the blueprints of their house than tear out the foundation and walls later and start again, we too would rather redesign the system now, on paper, instead of later, as code.

Verification

Once we have convinced ourselves that the design will lead to a product with which the customer will be happy, we evaluate the quality of the design and the documentation. In particular, we examine the design to judge whether it adheres to good design principles:

- Is the architecture modular, well structured, and easy to understand?
- Can we improve the structure and understandability of the architecture?
- Is the architecture portable to other platforms?
- Are aspects of the architecture reusable?
- Does the architecture support ease of testing?
- Does the architecture maximize performance, where appropriate?
- Does the architecture incorporate appropriate techniques for handling faults and preventing failures?
- Can the architecture accommodate all of the expected design changes and extensions that have been documented?

The review team also assures that the documentation is complete by checking that there is an interface specification for every referenced software unit and that these specifications are complete. The team also makes sure that the documentation describes alternative design strategies, with explanations of how and why major design decisions were made.

An **active design review** (Parnas and Weiss 1985) is a particularly effective method for evaluating the quality of the SAD and determining whether it contains the right information. In an active review, reviewers exercise the design document by using it in ways that developers will use the final document in practice. That is, rather than reading the documentation and looking for problems, which is characterized as a **passive review process**, the reviewers are given or devise questions that they must answer by looking up information in the SAD. Each reviewer represents a different class of reader and is asked questions suitable to his or her use of a SAD. Thus, a maintainer may be asked to determine which software units would be affected by an expected change to the system, whereas a program designer may be asked to explain why an interface's preconditions are necessary.

In general, the point of the design review is to detect faults rather than correct them. It is important to remember that those who participate in the review are investigating the integrity of the design, not of the designers. Thus, the review is valuable in emphasizing to all concerned that we are working toward the same goal. The criticism and discussion during the design review are egoless, because comments are directed at the process and the product, not at the participants. The review process encourages and enhances communication among the diverse members of the team.

Moreover, the process benefits everyone by finding faults and problems when they are easy and inexpensive to correct. It is far easier to change something in its abstract, conceptual stage than when it is already implemented. Much of the difficulty and expense of fixing faults late in development derive from tracking a fault to its source. If a fault is spotted in the design review, there is a good chance that the problem is located somewhere in the design. However, if a fault is not detected until the system is operational, the root of the problem may be in several places: the hardware, the software, the design, the implementation, or the documentation. The sooner we identify a problem, the fewer places in which we have to look to find its cause.

5.10 SOFTWARE PRODUCT LINES

Throughout this chapter, we have focused on the design and development of a single software system. But many software companies build and sell multiple products, often working with different kinds of customers. Some successful companies build their reputations and their set of clients by specializing in particular application domains, such as business support software or computer games. That is, they become known not only for providing quality software but also for their understanding of the special needs of a particular market. Many of these companies succeed by reusing their expertise and software assets across families of related products, thereby spreading the cost of development across products and reducing the time to market for each one.

The corporate strategy for designing and developing the related products is based on the reuse of elements of a common **product line**. The company plans upfront to manufacture and market several related products. Part of the planning process involves deciding how those products will share assets and resources. The products may appear to be quite different from one another, varying in size, quality, features, or price. But they have enough in common to allow the company to take advantage of economies of scope by sharing technologies (e.g., architecture, common parts, test suites, or environments), assembly facilities (e.g., workers, assembly plants), business plans (e.g., budgets, release schedules), marketing strategies and distribution channels, and so on. As a result, the cost and effort to develop the *family* of products is far less than the sum of the costs to develop the products individually. The product-line notion is not particular to software; it has been used for years in all types of manufacturing. For example, an automobile company offers multiple models of cars, each with its own specifications of passenger and cargo space, power, and fuel economy. Individual brands have their own distinct appearance, dashboard interfaces, feature packages, and luxury options; the brand is targeted at a particular market and sold at prices within a particular range. But many of the models are built on the same chassis, use common parts from the same suppliers, use common software, are assembled at the same manufacturing plant, and are sold at the same dealerships as other models.

A distinguishing feature of building a product line is the treatment of the derived products as a **product family**. Their simultaneous development is planned from the beginning. The family's commonalities are described as a collection of reusable assets (including requirements, designs, code, and test cases), all stored in a **core asset base**. When developing products in the family, we retrieve assets from the base as needed. As a result, development resembles an assembly line: many of the components can be adapted from components in the core asset base and then plugged together, rather than developing each from scratch. The design of the core asset base is planned carefully, and it evolves as the product family grows to include new products.

Because the products in the product family are related, the opportunities for reuse abound and extend well beyond the reuse of code units. Clements and

Northrop (2002) describe why a number of candidate elements may belong in the core asset base:

- *Requirements:* Related products often have common functional requirements and quality attributes.
- *Software architecture:* Product lines are based on a common architecture that realizes the product family's shared requirements. Differences among family members can be isolated or parameterized as variations in the architecture; for example, features, user interfaces, computing platforms, and some quality attributes can be altered to address particular product needs.
- *Models and analysis results:* Models and analyses (e.g., performance analysis) of an individual product's architecture are likely to build on analyses of the product-line architecture. So it is important to get the product-line architecture right, because it affects the performance of so many associated products.
- *Software units:* The reuse of software units is more than just code reuse. It includes the reuse of significant design work, including interface specifications, relationships and interactions with other units, documentation, test cases, scaffolding code (i.e., code developed to support testing and analysis that is not delivered with the final product), and more.
- *Testing:* Reuse of testing includes test plans, test documentation, test data, and testing environments. It may also include the test results of reused software units.
- *Project planning:* Project budgets and delivery schedules of product-family members are likely to be more accurate than products developed from scratch, because we use our knowledge of the costs and schedules of past family members as guides in estimating the costs of subsequent members.
- *Team organization:* Because product-family members have similar design structures, we can reuse information from past decisions on how to decompose a product into work pieces, how to assign work pieces to teams, and what skill sets those teams need.

According to the Software Engineering Institute's Product Line Hall of Fame (at http://www.sei.cmu.edu/productlines/plp_hof.html), companies such as Nokia, Hewlett-Packard, Boeing, and Lucent report a three- to sevenfold improvement in development costs, time-to-market, and productivity from using a product-line approach to software development. Sidebar 5.8 describes one company's conversion to a software product line.

Strategic Scoping

Product lines are based not just on commonalities among products but also on the best way to exploit them. First, we employ strategic business planning to identify the family of products we want to build. We use knowledge and good judgment to forecast market trends and predict the demand for various products. Second, we **scope** our plans, so that we focus on products that have enough in common to warrant a product-line approach to development. That is, the cost of developing the (common) product line must be

SIDEBAR 5.8 PRODUCT-LINE PRODUCTIVITY

Brownsword and Clements (1996) report on the experiences of CelsiusTech AB, a Swedish naval defense contractor, in its transition from custom to product-line development. The transition was motivated by desperation. In 1985, the company, then Philips Elektronikindustier AB, was awarded two major contracts simultaneously, one for the Swedish Navy and one for the Danish Navy. Because of the company's past experiences with similar but smaller systems, which resulted in cost overruns and scheduling delays, senior managers questioned whether they would be able to meet the demands of both contracts, particularly the promised (and fixed) schedules and budgets, using the company's current practices and technologies.

> *This situation provided the genesis of a new business strategy: recognizing the potential business opportunity of selling and building a series, or family, of related systems rather than some number of specific systems. . . . The more flexible and extendable the product line, the greater the business opportunities. These business drivers . . . forged the technical strategy.*
> *(Brownsword and Clements 1996)*

Development of the product line and the first system were initiated at the same time; development of the second system started six months later. The two systems plus the product line were completed using roughly the same amount of time and staff that was needed previously for a single product. Subsequent products had shorter development timelines. On average, 70–80 percent of the seven systems' software units were product-line units (re)used as is.

more than offset by the savings we expect to accrue from deriving family members from the product line.

Product-line scoping is a challenging problem. If we strive for some notion of optimal commonality among the products (e.g., by insisting on reusing 80 percent of the code), we may exclude some interesting and profitable products that lie outside of the scope. On the other hand, if we try to include *any* product that looks related, we reduce the degree of commonality among the derived products, and consequently the amount of savings that can be achieved. A successful product line lies somewhere in the middle of these two extremes, with a core architecture that strongly supports the more promising products that we want to build.

In the end, a product line's success depends on both its inherent variability and the degree of overlap between its core asset base and the derived products. To obtain desired productivity-improvement numbers, each derived product's architecture must start with the product-line architecture, incorporating a significant fraction of its software units from the product line's core asset base. Then the product design adds easily accommodated changes, such as component replacements or extensions and retractions of the architecture. The less the final derived product has in common with the product line, the more the derived product's development will resemble a completely new (i.e., nonderived) product.

Advantages of Product-Line Architecture

A product-line architecture promotes planned modifiability, where known differences among product-family members are isolated in the architecture to allow for easy adaptation. Examples of product-line variability are given below:

- *Component replacements:* A software unit can be realized by any implementation that satisfies the unit's interface specification. Thus, we can instantiate a new product-family member by changing the implementations of one or more software units. For example, we can use a layered architecture to isolate a product family's interfaces to users, communication networks, other software components, the computing platforms, input sensors, and so on. This way, we can instantiate new family members by reimplementing the interface layers to accommodate new interfaces. Similarly, we can improve quality attributes, such as performance, by reimplementing key software units.
- *Component specializations:* Specialization is a special case of component replacement that is most strongly supported by object-oriented designs. We can replace any class with a subclass whose methods augment or override the parent's methods. Thus, we can instantiate new family members by creating and using new subclasses.
- *Product-line parameters:* We can think of software units as parameters in the product-line architecture, so that varying the parameters results in a set of possible system configurations. For example, parameters could be used to specify feature combinations, which are then instantiated as component additions or replacements. If parameters are the only source of product-line variation, then we can automatically configure and generate products by setting parameter values. See Sidebar 5.9 for a description of other work on generating product-family members automatically.

SIDEBAR 5.9 GENERATIVE SOFTWARE DEVELOPMENT

Generative software development (Czarnecki 2005) is a form of product-line development that enables products to be generated automatically from specifications. It proceeds in two phases: first, *domain engineers* build the product line, including mechanisms for generating product instances, and then *application engineers* generate individual products.

The domain engineer defines a **domain-specific language (DSL)** that application engineers then use to specify products to be generated. A DSL can be as simple as a collection of parameters, with a set menu of supported parameter values, or it can be as complex as a special-purpose programming language. In the former case, the engine for deriving product instances is a collection of *construction rules* (for selecting and assembling prefabricated components) and *optimization rules* (for optimizing the code with respect to the combination of parameter values specified). In the latter case, the product line includes a compiler that transforms a DSL program into a product, making heavy use of the product-line architecture and prefabricated components.

Lucent developed several product lines and generative tools for customizing different aspects of its 5ESS telephone switch (Ardis and Green 1998):

- ***forms*** that service-provider operators and administrators use to enter and change switch-related data about customers (e.g., phone numbers, features subscribed)
- ***billing records*** that are generated for each call
- ***configuration-control software*** that monitors and records the status of the switch's hardware components and assists with component transitions

Lucent created GUI-based DSLs that could be used to specify custom data-entry forms, billing-record contents, and hardware-interface specifications. It built compilers and other tools to generate code and user documentation. This technology allowed Lucent to customize its telephone switches as its customer base evolved from internal sales within AT&T to external and international service providers; as hardware technology evolved; and as feature sets grew.

- *Architecture extensions and retractions:* Some architectural styles, such as publish-subscribe and client-server, allow for easy feature additions and removals; these styles are useful in product lines that have varying feature sets. More generally, we can use *dependency graphs* to evaluate derived architectures. For example, a viable subarchitecture of the product-line architecture corresponds to a subset of the product line's modules plus all of the modules' dependencies. We want to limit architectural extensions to those whose effects on the architecture's dependency graph are strictly additive. In other words, we seek only those extensions that augment the product line's dependency graph with new nodes such that all new dependencies originate from the new nodes.

Documenting a product-line architecture is different from documenting the architecture for a specific system, because the product line is not in itself a product. Rather, it is a means for rapidly deriving products. Thus, its documentation focuses on the range of products that can be derived from the product line, the points of variability in the product-line architecture, and the mechanisms for deriving family members. The documentation of a given product is then reduced to a description of how it differs from or instantiates the product-line architecture, in terms of specific feature sets, component instances, subclass definitions, parameter values, and more.

Product-Line Evolution

After studying several industrial examples, Clements (Bass, Clements, and Kazman 2003) concludes that the most important contributor to product-line success is having a *product-line mindset.* That is, the company's primary focus is on the development and evolution of the product-line assets, rather than on individual products. Product-line changes are made for the purpose of improving the capability to derive products, while remaining backwards compatible with previous products (i.e., previous products are still derivable). Thus, no product is developed or evolves separately from the product line. In this sense, a company with a product line is like the farmer with a goose that lays golden eggs. Instead of focusing on the eggs, the company nurtures the goose, so that it will continue to lay golden eggs for years to come.

5.11 INFORMATION SYSTEMS EXAMPLE

So, what might be a suitable software architecture for the Piccadilly system? Certainly a key component would be the repository of information that needs to be maintained about television programs, program scheduling, commercial spots, agreements, and so on. In addition, the system should be able to process multiple heterogeneous queries on this information, in parallel, so that the information can be kept up-to-date and can be used to make important decisions about future commercial campaigns.

A typical reference architecture for an information or business-processing system is an n-tiered client-server architecture (Morgan 2002). Such an architecture for our Piccadilly system is depicted in Figure 5.19. The bottom layer is a data server that simply maintains all the information that Piccadilly must track for its own business as well as information about its competitors. The application programming interface (API) for this layer is likely to consist of basic queries and updates on these data. The middle layer consists of application services that provide richer, more application-specific queries and updates on the lower-level data. An example of an application-specific query might be to find all television programs that air at the same time as some Piccadilly program. The top layer of the architecture consists of the user interfaces through which Piccadilly's managers, accountants, television-programming specialists, and sales force use the information system.

In addition to the high-level architecture of the system, we also need to provide some details about each of the components. For example, we need to describe the data and relationships that the data server is to maintain, the application services that the application layer is to maintain, and the user interfaces that the presentation layer is to

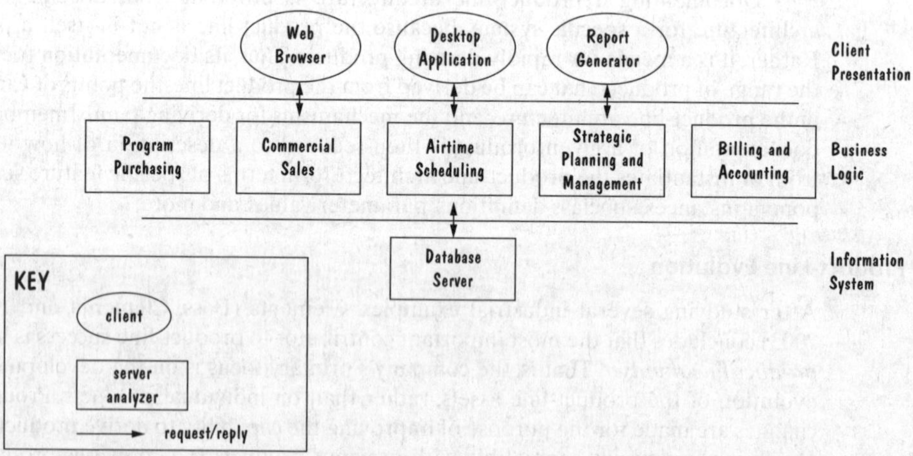

FIGURE 5.19 N-tier architecture of the Piccadilly system.

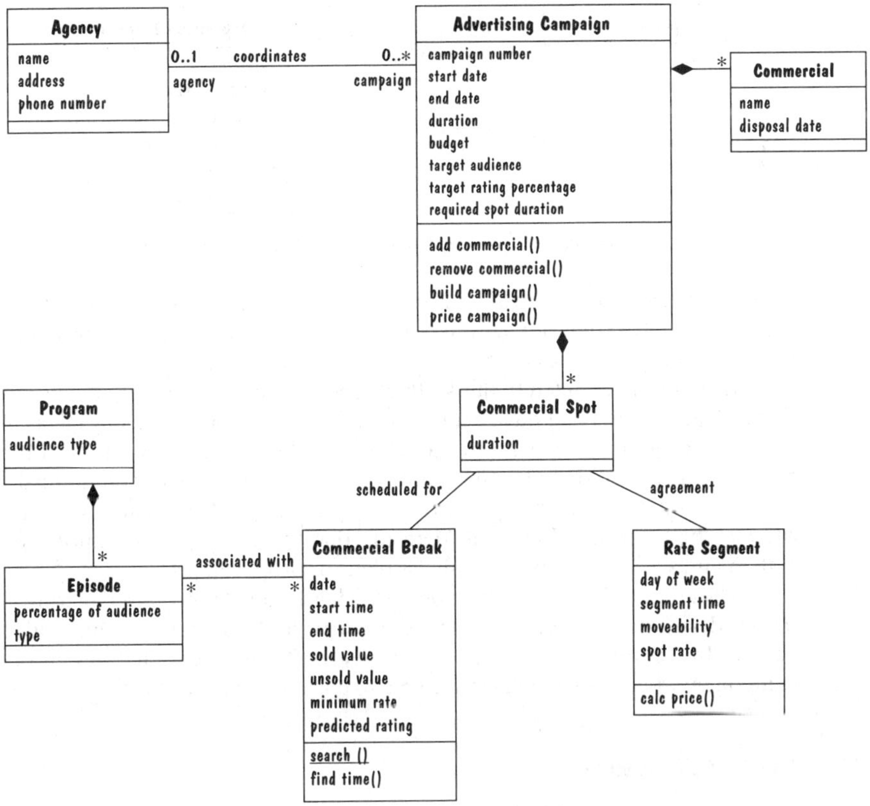

FIGURE 5.20 Partial domain model of the Piccadilly system.

provide. The domain model that we created in Chapter 4, as part of our elaboration of the system's requirements, can form the basis of the data model for the data server. The model is reproduced in Figure 5.20. We augment this model with additional concepts and relationships that arise as we work out the details of the application services. For example, a high-level description of the query to find the television programs that are aired at the same time as Piccadilly programs might look like the following:

```
Input: Episode
For each Opposition television company,
    For each Programming schedule,
          If Episode schedule date = Opposition transmission date
             AND Episode start time = Opposition transmission time
          Create instance of Opposition program
Output: List of Opposition programs
```

This function suggests new entities and relationships to be added to our data model, such as the concept of an opposition company. Each opposition company broadcasts its

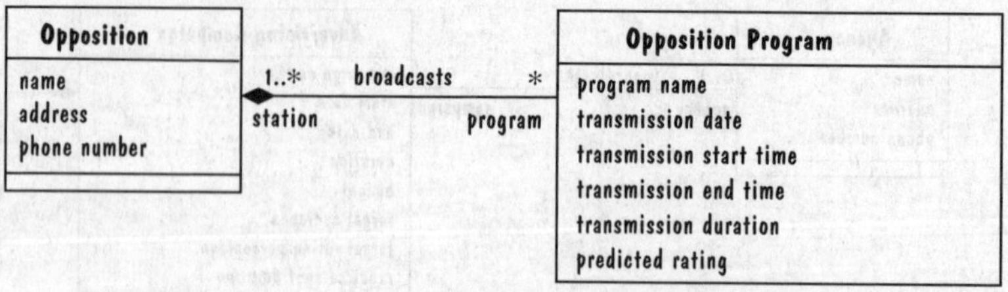

FIGURE 5.21 Newly identified concept of Opposition programs.

own programs, and each program has a time and date. We include this information in the data model, so that our system is able to issue queries on programs that air on competing stations. These new concepts are shown in Figure 5.21.

In addition, we need to think about how well our architecture meets any nonfunctional requirements that have been specified. For example, if the specialists in charge of television programming want to use the system to explore how different broadcasting schedules affect predicted ratings and corresponding prices of commercial spots, then our architecture needs to support the ability to undo edits. As another example, security may be a concern. We want to ensure that the competition cannot break into the system and access Piccadilly's business plans or proposed prices.

These models and descriptions are clearly high level. Architecture focuses on design decisions that require consideration of multiple components and their interactions. In Chapter 6, we narrow our focus to the more detailed design of individual components—each of which we are able to consider in isolation.

5.12 REAL-TIME EXAMPLE

One of the findings of the inquiry board that was set up to investigate the Ariane-5 accident was that the Ariane program in general had a "culture...of only addressing random hardware failures" (Lions et al. 1996) and of assuming that seemingly correct software was in fact correct. The board came to this conclusion partly because of the way the Ariane-5's fault-recovery system was designed. The Ariane-5 included a number of redundant components in which both the hardware equipment and the associated software were identical. In most cases, one of the components was supposed to be active; the other was to stay in "hot standby" mode, ready to become the active component if the current active component failed. But this architecture is not a good choice for this kind of system, because hardware failures are very different from software failures. Hardware failures are independent: if one unit fails, the standby unit is usually unaffected and can take over as the active unit. By contrast, software faults tend to be logical errors, so all copies of a software component have the same set of faults. Moreover, even if the software is not the underlying cause of a failure, replicated software components are likely to exhibit the same bad behavior in response to bad input. For these reasons, the hot standby redundancy in Ariane-5 is likely to recover only from hardware failures.

To see why, consider Table 5.5's list of sources of software failures (NASA 2004). Some of the software faults are internal to the software itself, and some are caused by

TABLE 5.5 Causes of Safety-Related Software Failures (NASA 2004)

Software Faults	Failures in the Environment
Data sampling rate	Broken sensors
Data collisions	Memory overwritten
Illegal commands	Missing parameters
Commands out of sequence	Parameters out of range
Time delays, deadlines	Bad input
Multiple events	Power fluctuations
Safe modes	Gamma radiation

input errors or erroneous events in the environment. Regardless of the source, most types of faults would adversely affect all instances of replicated software components that are processing the same input at the same time (with the exception of gamma radiation, which is a serious concern in software on spacecraft). As a result, software failures among replicated components in hot standby mode are rarely independent. This was the situation with the failed inertial reference systems (SRIs) on the Ariane-5: both units suffered the same overflow error, simultaneously.

The manner in which SRI problems were handled is another factor that contributed to the Ariane-5 accident. A key design decision in any software architecture is determining which component is responsible for handling problems that occur at runtime. Sometimes the component in which the problem occurs has information about its cause and is best suited to address it. However, if a problem occurs in a service component, it is often the client component (which invoked the service) that is responsible for deciding how to recover. With this strategy, the client can use contextual information about what goals it is trying to achieve when it determines a recovery plan. In the Ariane-5, the planned exception-handling strategy for any SRI exception was to log the error and to shut down the SRI processor (Lions et al. 1996). As we saw earlier in this chapter, shutting down or rebooting is an extreme error-handing strategy that is not advisable in critical systems. Another recovery strategy, such as working with the maximum value that the affected data variable would allow, might have kept the software operating well enough for the rocket to have achieved orbit.

5.13 WHAT THIS CHAPTER MEANS FOR YOU

In this chapter, we have investigated what it means to design a system based on carefully expressed requirements. We have seen that design begins with a high-level architecture, where architectural decisions are based not only on system functionality and required constraints but also on desirable attributes and the long-term intended use of the system (including product lines, reuse, and likely modification). You should keep in mind several characteristics of good architecture as you go, including appropriate user interfaces, performance, modularity, security, and fault tolerance. You may want to build a prototype to evaluate several options or to demonstrate possibilities to your customers.

The goal is not to design the ideal software architecture for a system, because such an architecture might not even exist. Rather, the goal is to design an architecture that meets all of the customer's requirements while staying within the cost and schedule constraints that we discussed in Chapter 3.

5.14 WHAT THIS CHAPTER MEANS FOR YOUR DEVELOPMENT TEAM

There are many team activities involved in architecture and design. Because designs are usually expressed as collections of components, the interrelationships among components and data must be well documented. Part of the design process is to have frequent discussions with other team members, not only to coordinate how different components will interact but also to gain a better understanding of the requirements and of the implications of each design decision you make.

You must also work with users to decide how to design the system's interfaces. You may develop several prototypes to show users the possibilities, to determine what meets performance requirements, or to evaluate for yourself the best "look and feel."

Your choice of architectural strategy and documentation must be made in the context of who will read your designs and who must understand them. Mappings among views help explain which parts of the design affect which components and data. It is essential that you document your design clearly and completely, with discussions of the options you had and the choices you made.

As a team member, you will participate in architectural reviews, evaluating the architecture and making suggestions for improvement. Remember that you are criticizing the architecture, not the architect, and that software development works best when egos are left out of the discussion.

5.15 WHAT THIS CHAPTER MEANS FOR RESEARCHERS

The architectures in this chapter are depicted as simple box-and-line diagrams, and we note that the modeling techniques discussed in Chapters 4 and 6 may also be useful in modeling the system. However, there are several drawbacks to representing the system only with diagrams. Garlan (2000) points out that informal diagrams cannot easily be evaluated for consistency, correctness, and completeness, particularly when the system is large or complex. Neither can desired architectural properties be checked and enforced as the system evolves over time. Thus, many researchers are investigating the creation and use of formal languages for expressing and analyzing a software architecture. These Architectural Description Languages (ADLs) include three things: a framework, a notation, and a syntax for expressing a software architecture. Many also have associated tools for parsing, displaying, analyzing, compiling, or simulating an architecture.

The ADL is often specific to an application domain. For instance, Adage (Coglianese and Szymanski 1993) is intended for use in describing avionics navigation and guidance, and Darwin (Magee et al. 1995) supports distributed message-passing systems. Researchers are also investigating ways to integrate various architectural tools into higher-level architectural environments, some of which may be domain specific. And other researchers are mapping ADL concepts to object-based approaches, such as the UML (Medvidovic and Rosenblum 1999).

Another area ripe for research is bridging the gap across architectural styles. Sometimes systems are developed from pieces that are specified in different ways.

DeLine (2001) and others are examining ways to translate a collection of different pieces into a more coherent whole.

Finally, researchers are continually challenged by systems that are "network centric," having little or no centralized control, conforming to few standards, and varying widely in hardware and applications from one user to another. "Pervasive computing" adds complications, as users are employing diverse devices that were not designed to interoperate, and even moving around geographically as they use them. As Garlan (2000) points out, this situation presents the following four problems:

- Architectures must scale to the size and variability of the Internet. Traditionally, one "assumes that event delivery is reliable, that centralized routing of messages will be sufficient, and that it makes sense to define a common vocabulary of events that are understood by all of the components. In an Internet-based setting, all of these assumptions are questionable."
- Software must operate over "dynamically formed, task-specific coalitions of distributed autonomous resources." Many of the Internet's resources are "independently developed and independently supported; they may even be transient," but the coalitions may have no control over these independent resources. Indeed, "selection and composition of resources [are] likely to be done afresh for each task, as resources appear, change, and disappear." We will need new techniques for managing architectural models at runtime, and for evaluating the properties of the systems they describe.
- We will need flexible architectures that accommodate services provided by private industry, such as billing, security, and communications. These applications are likely to be composed from both local and remote computing capabilities and offered at each user's desktop, which in turn can be built from a wide variety of hardware and software.
- End users may want to compose systems themselves, tailoring available applications to their particular needs. These users may have very little experience in building systems, but they still want assurances that the composed systems will perform in expected ways.

We are designing systems that are larger and more complex than ever before. Northrop et al.'s report (2006) on ultra-large scale systems explains our need to develop huge systems with thousands of sensors and decision nodes that are connected through heterogeneous and opportunistic networks and that adapt to unforeseen changes to their environment. These systems will need special architectural considerations, because current testing techniques will not work. Shaw (2002) discusses why it will be impossible for such systems to be absolutely correct, and that users and developers will need to soften their views and expectations about correctness. She suggests that we strive instead for sufficient correctness.

5.16 TERM PROJECT

Architecture is as much an artistic and creative endeavor as an engineering one. Different expert architects can take very different approaches to how they conceive and document their designs, with the results of each being solid and elegant. We can think of architects approaching their jobs along a continuum, from what is called task-centered to user-centered design. **Task-centered design** begins with thinking about what the system must accomplish. By contrast, **user-centered design** begins with the way in which a user interacts with the system to perform the required tasks. The two are not mutually exclusive and indeed can be complementary. However, one design philosophy often dominates the other.

As part of your term project, develop two different architectural approaches to the Loan Arranger: one that is task centered and one that is user centered. What architectural style(s) have you chosen for each? Compare and contrast the results. Which architecture is easier to change? To test? To configure as a product line?

5.17 KEY REFERENCES

There are many good books about software architecture. The first one you should read is Shaw and Garlan (1996), to provide a good foundation for how you learn about architecture and design. This and other books can act as architectural style catalogues, including Buschmann et al. (1996) and Schmidt et al. (2000). There are several books that address particular kinds of architectures: Gomaa (1995) for real-time systems, Hix and Hartson (1993) and Shneiderman (1997) for interface design, and Weiderhold (1988) for databases, for example.

More generally, Hofmeister, Nord, and Soni (1999) and Kazman, Asundi, and Klein (2001) discuss how to make architectural design decisions, and Clements et al. (2003) and Krutchen (1995) address the best way to document an architecture. In addition, the IEEE and other standards organizations publish various architectural standards.

You can read several product-line success stories at the Product Line Hall of Fame Web site (http://www.sei.cmu.edu/productlines/plp_hof.html), maintained by the Software Engineering Institute (SEI).

Scott Ambler has written extensively about the views of proponents of agile methods on architecture and agile modeling. See his Web site (http://www.agilemodeling.com) and his book on agile modeling (Ambler 2002).

5.18 EXERCISES

1. Review the four different architectural styles proposed by Shaw and Garlan (1996) to implement KWIC: repository, data abstraction, implicit invocation (a type of publish-subscribe), and pipe-and-filter. For each one, are the high-level components likely to have high or low cohesion and coupling?
2. What is the most common design model? Why?
3. For each of the architectural styles described in this chapter, give an example of a real-world application whose software design might incorporate that style.
4. What type of architectural style is represented by the NIST/ECMA model (shown in Figure 5.22) for environment integration? (Chen and Norman 1992).
5. Many of your class projects require you to develop your programs by yourself. Assemble a small group of students to perform an architectural review for one such project. Have

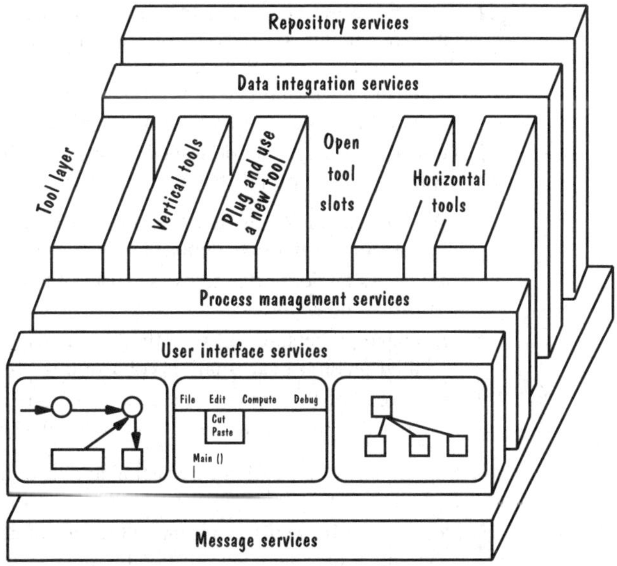

FIGURE 5.22 NIST/ECMA model.

several students play the roles of customers and users. Try to express all the requirements and system characteristics in nontechnical terms. List all the changes that are suggested by the review process. Compare the time required to make the changes at the architecture stage to that of changing your existing programs.

6. You have been hired by a consulting firm to develop an income tax calculation package for an accounting firm. You have designed a system according to the customer's requirements and presented your design at an architectural review. Which of the following questions might be asked at the review? Explain your answers.

   (a) What computer will it run on?
   (b) What will the input screens look like?
   (c) What reports will be produced?
   (d) How many concurrent users will there be?
   (e) Will you use a multiuser operating system?
   (f) What are the details of the depreciation algorithm?

7. List the characteristics of a system for which prototyping is most appropriate.

8. What are some of the most popular design methods? Which one is most likely to fit a complex real-time system? Why?

9. Explain why modularity and application generators are inseparable concepts. Give an example of an application generator with which you have worked.

10. List the characteristics you might include in an architecture evaluation table similar to Table 5.2. For each of the following systems, identify the weights you might use for each characteristic: an operating system, a word processing system, and a satellite tracking system.

11. Describe a telephone conversation using the OSI model.

12. Table 5.4 shows a cost–benefit analysis for three competing design proposals. The computation of benefits is based on projections that the rate of queries could increase to a peak of 200 queries per second. Suppose that, due to increased competition by other on-line companies, more recent projections estimate that there will never be more than 150 queries per second. How does this new information affect the original cost–benefit analysis?
13. For each of the systems described below, sketch an appropriate software architecture and explain how you would assign key functionalities to the design's components.
    (a) a system of automated banking machines, acting as distributed kiosks that bank customers can use to deposit and withdraw cash from their accounts
    (b) a news feeder that notifies each user of news bulletins on topics in which the user has expressed an interest
    (c) image-processing software that allows users to apply various operations to modify their pictures (e.g., rotation, color tinting, cropping)
    (d) a weather forecasting application that analyzes tens of thousands of data elements collected from various sensors; the sensors periodically transmit new data values
14. Suggest how the weather forecasting application in exercise 13(d) might detect faults in its data sensors.
15. Your university wants to automate the task of checking that students who are scheduled to graduate have actually satisfied the degree requirements in their respective majors. A key challenge in automating this task is that every degree major has its own unique requirements. Study the degree requirements of three disciplines at your university; identify which graduation requirements they have in common and where they diverge. Describe how the variability might be generalized so that checking the degree requirements of each major can be derived from the same product line.
16. Propose a redesign of your software architecture for the system of automated banking machines from the previous exercise so that it improves performance. Propose an alternate redesign that improves security. Does your strategy to improve performance adversely affect security, or vice versa?
17. Design a simple full-screen editor on a video display terminal. The editor allows text to be inserted, deleted, and modified. Sections of text can be "cut" from one part of the file and "pasted" to another part of the file. The user can specify a text string, and the editor can find the next occurrence of that string. Through the editor, the user can specify margin settings, page length, and tab settings. Then, evaluate the quality of your design.

6 Designing the Modules

In this chapter, we look at
- design principles
- object-oriented design heuristics
- design patterns
- exceptions and exception handling
- documenting designs

In the last chapter, we looked at strategies and patterns for creating a high-level architectural design of our software system. This type of design identifies what the system's major components will be, and how the components will interact with each other and share information. The next step is to add more detail, deciding how the individual components will be designed at a modular level so that developers can write code that implements the design. Unlike architectural design, where we have architectural styles to guide our design work, the process of creating a more detailed design offers us fewer ready-made solutions for how to decompose a component into modules. Thus, module-level design is likely to involve more improvisation than architectural design does; it relies on both innovation and continual evaluation of our design decisions, and we pay careful attention to design principles and conventions as we proceed.

In this chapter, we summarize the abundance of module-level design advice that exists in the literature. We begin with design principles: general properties of good designs that can guide you as you create your own designs. Then, we present several design heuristics and patterns that are particularly useful for object-oriented (OO) designs. OO notations and programming languages were developed specifically to encode and promote good design principles, so it makes sense to look at how to use these technologies to their best advantage. We also look at documenting a module-level design in a sufficiently precise way that allows the design to be implemented easily by other developers.

Your experience with module-level design from your previous programming courses may help you to understand this chapter. The design advice we include is based on the collective experience of a wide variety of developers building many types of systems. We have chosen advice based on quality attributes that the design is to achieve, such as improving modularity or ensuring robustness. This chapter can help you see *why* certain design principles and conventions are applicable, and then assist you in deciding *when* you should apply them.

To illustrate design choices, concepts, and principles, we introduce an example: automating a business, the Royal Service Station, that services automobiles. This example enables us to see that designing modules must reflect not only technological options but also business constraints and developer experience. Some aspects of our example were originally developed by Professor Guilherme Travassos, of COPPE/Sistemas at the Federal University of Rio de Janeiro, Brazil. More details plus other examples are available at Prof. Travassos's Web site: http://www.cos.ufrj.br/~ght.

6.1 DESIGN METHODOLOGY

At this point in the development process, we have an abstract description of a solution to our customer's problem, in the form of a *software architectural design.* As such, we have a plan for decomposing the design into software units and allocating the system's functional requirements to them. The architecture also specifies any protocols that constrain how the units interact with each other, and specifies a precise interface for each unit. Moreover, the architectural design process has already resolved and documented any known issues about data sharing and about coordination and synchronization of concurrent components. Of course, some of these decisions may change when we learn more about designing the individual software units. But at this point, the system's design is complete enough to allow us to treat the designing of the various units as independent tasks.

In practice, there is no sharp boundary between the end of the architecture-design phase and the start of the module-design phase. In fact, many software architects argue that a software architecture is not complete until it is so detailed that it specifies all of the system's atomic modules and interfaces. However, for the purposes of project management, it is convenient to separate design tasks that require consideration of the entire system from design tasks that pertain to individual software units, because the latter can be partitioned into distinct work assignments and assigned to separate design teams. Thus, the more we can restrict ourselves during the architecture-design phase to identifying the major software units and their interfaces, the more we can parallelize the rest of the design work. This chapter focuses on the detailed design of a well-defined architectural unit, looking at how to decompose the unit into constituent modules.

Once again, the software architecture-design decisions correspond to meal preparation decisions: degree of formality, number of guests, number of courses, culinary theme (e.g., Italian or Mexican), and perhaps main ingredients (e.g., meat or fish in the main course, and which seasonal vegetables). These decisions help to scope the set of possible dishes that we could make. And, like architectural decisions, they are fundamental to the planning and preparation of the entire meal; they are difficult to change in the middle of cooking. Plenty of open design questions will remain, such as which specific dishes to prepare, cooking methods for the meats and vegetables, and complementary ingredients and spices. These secondary decisions tend to apply to specific dishes rather than to the whole meal; they can be made in isolation or delegated to other cooks. However, secondary decisions still require significant knowledge and expertise, so that the resulting dishes are tasty and are ready at the appropriate time.

Although there are many recipes and instructional videos to show you how to move from ingredients to a complete meal, there are no comparable design recipes for progressing from a software unit's specification to its modular design. Many design methods advocate top-down design, in which we recursively decompose design elements into smaller constituent elements. However, in reality, designers alternate among top-down, bottom-up, and outside-in design methods, sometimes focusing on parts of the design that are less well understood and at other times fleshing out details with which they are familiar. Krasner, Curtis, and Iscoe (1987) studied the habits of developers on 19 projects; they report, and other evidence confirms, that designers regularly move up and down a design's levels of abstractions, as they understand more about the solution and its implications. For example, a design team may start off using a top-down method or an outside-in method that focuses first on the system's inputs and expected outputs. Alternatively, it may make sense to explore the hardest and most uncertain areas of the design first, because surprises that arise in clarifying an obscure problem may force changes to the overall design. If we are using agile methods, then the design progresses in vertical slices, as we iteratively design and implement subsets of features at a time. Whenever the design team recognizes that known design solutions might be useful, the team may switch to a bottom-up design approach in which it tries to tackle parts of the design by applying and adapting prepackaged solutions. Periodically, design decisions are revisited and revised, in an activity called **refactoring**, to simplify an overly complicated solution or to optimize the design for a particular quality attribute.

The process we use to work towards a final solution is not as important as the documentation we produce so that other designers can understand it. This understanding is crucial not only for the programmers who will implement the design but also for the maintainers who will change it, the testers and reviewers who will ensure that the design implements the requirements, and the specialists who will write user documentation describing how the system works. One way to achieve this understanding is by "faking the rational design process": writing the design documentation to reflect a top-down design process, even if this is not how we arrived at the design (Parnas and Clements 1986), as described in Sidebar 6.1. We discuss design documentation in more detail in Section 6.8.

6.2 DESIGN PRINCIPLES

With clear requirements and a high-level system architecture in hand, we are ready to add detail to our design. As we saw in Chapter 5, architectural design can be expressed in terms of *architectural styles*, each of which provides advice about decomposing the system into its major components. Architectural styles help us to solve generic problems of communication, synchronization, and data sharing. However, once we focus on decomposing individual components and software units into modules, we must address functionality and properties that are no longer generic; rather, they are specific to our design problem and therefore are less likely to have ready-made solutions.

Design principles are guidelines for decomposing our system's required functionality and behavior into modules. In particular, they identify the criteria that we should use in two ways: for decomposing a system and then for deciding what information to

SIDEBAR 6.1 "FAKING" A RATIONAL DESIGN PROCESS

In an ideal, methodical, and reasoned design process, the design of a software system would progress from high-level specification to solution, using a sequence of top-down, error-free design decisions resulting in a hierarchical collection of modules. For several reasons (e.g., poorly understood or changing requirements, refactoring, human error), design work rarely proceeds directly or smoothly from requirements to modules. Nonetheless, Parnas and Clements (1986) argue that we should behave as if we are following such a rational process:

- The process can provide guidance when we are unsure of how to proceed.
- We will come closer to a rational design if we attempt to follow a rational process.
- We can measure a project's progress against the process's expected deliverables.

Parnas and Clements suggest that we simulate this behavior by "writing the documentation that we would have produced if we had followed the ideal process." That is, we document design decisions according to a top-down process by (1) decomposing the software unit into modules, (2) defining the module interfaces, (3) describing the interdependencies among modules, and, finally, (4) documenting the internal designs of modules. As we take these steps, we insert placeholders for design decisions that we put off. Later, as details become known and deferred decisions are made, we replace the placeholders with the new information. At the same time, we update documents when problems are found or the design is revised. The result is a design document that reads as if the design process were purely top-down and linear.

The distinction between the actual design process and the ideal one is similar to the distinction between discovering the main steps of a new mathematical proof and later formulating it as a logical argument. "Mathematicians diligently polish their proofs, usually presenting a proof [in a published paper that is] very different from the first one that they discovered" (Parnas and Clements 1986).

provide (and what to conceal) in the resulting modules. Design principles are useful when creating innovative designs, but they have other uses too, especially in forming the basis for the design advice that is packaged as design conventions, design patterns, and architectural styles. Thus, to use styles and patterns effectively, we must understand and appreciate their underlying principles. Otherwise, when we define, modify, and extend patterns and styles to fit our needs, we are likely to violate the very principles that the conventions and patterns engender and promote.

The collection of software design principles grows as we "encode" our collective experience and observations in new design advice. For example, Davis (1995) proposes 201 principles of software development, many of which are design related. In this book, we restrict our discussion to six dominant principles: *modularity, interfaces, information hiding, incremental development, abstraction*, and *generality*. Each seems to have stood the test of time and is independent of style and methodology. Collectively, they can assist us in building effective, robust designs.

Modularity

Modularity, also called **separation of concerns**, is the principle of keeping separate the various unrelated aspects of a system, so that each aspect can be studied in isolation (Dijkstra 1982). **Concerns** can be functions, data, features, tasks, qualities, or any aspect of the requirements or design that we want to define or understand in more detail. To build a modular design, we decompose our system by identifying the system's unrelated concerns and encapsulating each in its own module. If the principle is applied well, each resulting module will have a single purpose and will be relatively independent of the others; in this way, each module will be easy to understand and develop. Module independence also makes it easier to locate faults (because there are fewer suspect modules per fault) and to change the system (because a change to one module affects relatively few other modules).

To determine how well a design separates concerns, we use two concepts that measure module independence: coupling and cohesion (Yourdon and Constantine 1978).

Coupling. We say that two modules are **tightly coupled** when they depend a great deal on each other. **Loosely coupled** modules have some dependence, but their interconnections are weak. **Uncoupled** modules have no interconnections at all; they are completely unrelated, as shown in Figure 6.1.

There are many ways that modules can be dependent on each other:

- *The references made from one module to another:* Module A may invoke operations in module B, so module A depends on module B for completion of its function or process.
- *The amount of data passed from one module to another:* Module A may pass a parameter, the contents of an array, or a block of data to module B.

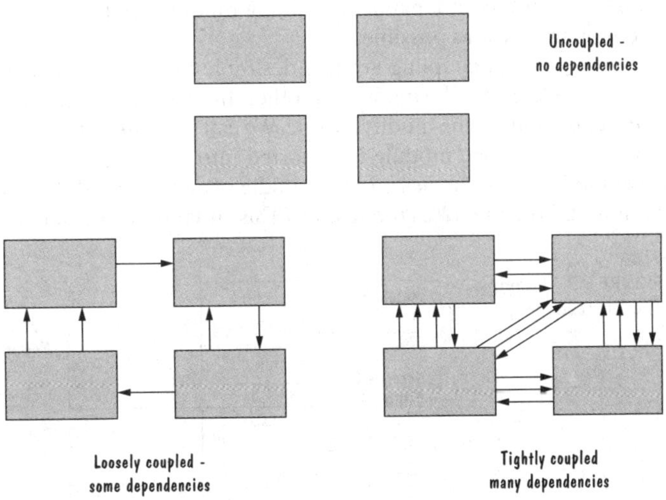

FIGURE 6.1 Module coupling.

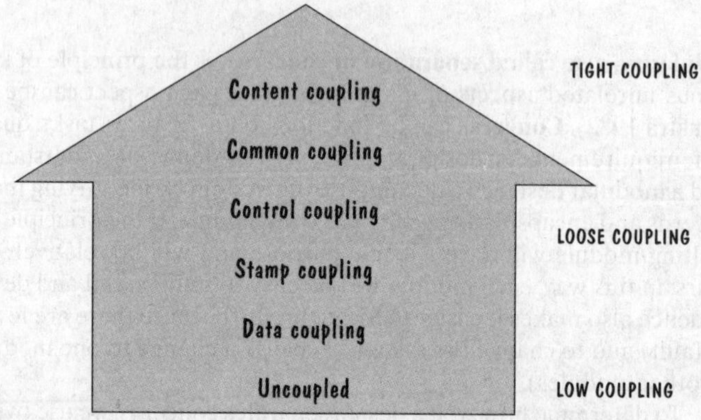

FIGURE 6.2 Types of coupling.

- *The amount of control that one module has over the other:* Module A may pass a control flag to module B. The value of the flag tells module B the state of some resource or subsystem, which procedure to invoke, or whether to invoke a procedure at all.

We can measure coupling along a spectrum of dependence, ranging from complete dependence to complete independence (uncoupled), as shown in Figure 6.2.

In actuality, it is unlikely that a system would be built of completely uncoupled modules. Just as a table and chairs, although independent, can combine to form a dining-room set, context can indirectly couple seemingly uncoupled modules. For example, two unrelated features may interact in such a way that one feature disables the possible execution of the other feature (e.g., an authorization feature that prohibits an unauthorized user from accessing protected services). Thus, our goal is not necessarily to have complete independence among modules, but rather to keep the degree of their coupling as low as possible.

Some types of coupling are less desirable than others. The least desirable occurs when one module actually modifies another. In such a case, the modified module is completely dependent on the modifying one. We call this **content coupling**. Content coupling might occur when one module is imported into another module, modifies the code of another module, or branches into the middle of another module. In Figure 6.3, module B generates and then invokes module D. (This situation is possible in some programming

FIGURE 6.3 Example of content coupling.

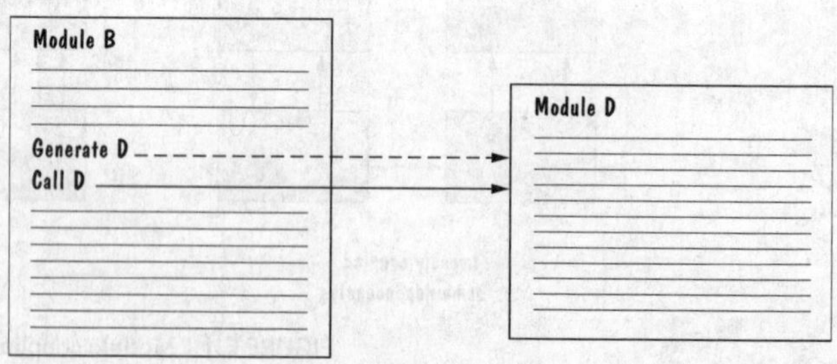

languages, such as LISP and Scheme.) Although self-modifying code is an extremely powerful tool for implementing programs that can improve themselves or learn dynamically, we use it knowing the consequences: the resulting modules are tightly coupled and cannot be designed or modified independently.

We can reduce the amount of coupling somewhat by organizing our design so that data are accessible from a common data store. However, dependence still exists: making a change to the common data means that, to evaluate the effect of the change, we have to look at all modules that access those data. This kind of dependence is called **common coupling**. With common coupling, it can be difficult to determine which module is responsible for having set a variable to a particular value. Figure 6.4 shows how common coupling works.

When one module passes parameters or a return code to control the behavior of another module, we say that there is **control coupling** between the two. It is impossible for the controlled module to function without some direction from the controlling module. If we employ a design with control coupling, it helps if we limit each module to be responsible for only one function or one activity. This restriction minimizes the amount of information that is passed to a controlled module, and it simplifies the module's interface to a fixed and recognizable set of parameters and return values.

When complex data structures are passed between modules, we say there is **stamp coupling** between the modules; if only data values, and not structured data, are passed, then the modules are connected by **data coupling**. Stamp coupling represents a more complex interface between modules, because the modules have to agree on the data's format and organization. Thus, data coupling is simpler and less likely to be affected by changes in data representation. If coupling must exist between modules, data coupling

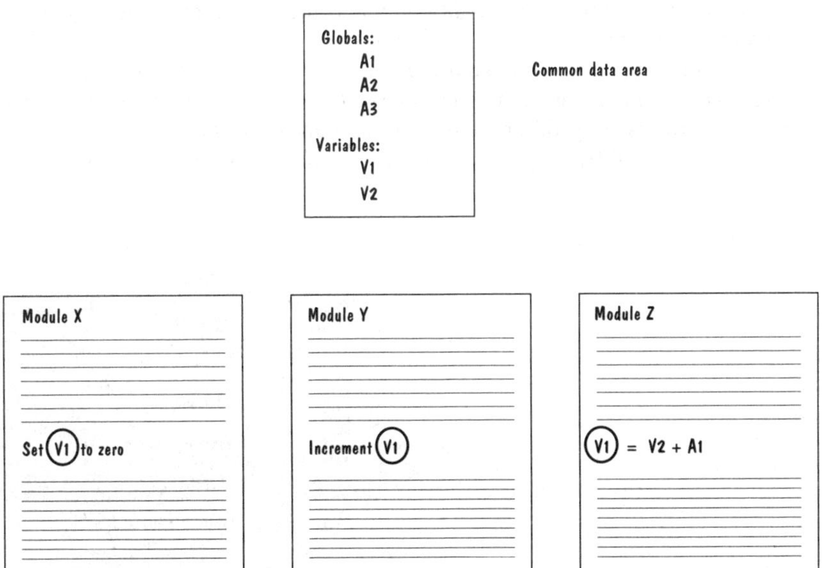

FIGURE 6.4 Example of common coupling.

is the most desirable; it is easiest to trace data through and to make changes to data-coupled modules.

Objects in an OO design often have low coupling, since each object contains its own data and operations on those data. In fact, one of the objectives of the OO design methodology is to promote loosely coupled designs. However, basing our design on objects does not guarantee that all of the modules in the resulting design will have low coupling. For example, if we create an object that serves as a common data store that can be manipulated, via its methods, by several other objects, then these objects suffer from a form of common coupling.

Cohesion. In contrast to measuring the interdependence among multiple modules, cohesion refers to the dependence within and among a module's internal elements (e.g., data, functions, internal modules). The more cohesive a module, the more closely related its pieces are, both to each other and to the module's singular purpose. A module that serves multiple purposes is at greater risk of its elements needing to evolve in different ways or at different rates. For example, a module that encompasses both data and routines for displaying those data may change frequently and may grow in different directions, as new uses of the data require both new functions to manipulate data and new ways of visualizing them. Instead, our design goal is to make each module as cohesive as possible, so that each module is easier to understand and is less likely to change. Figure 6.5 shows the several types of cohesion.

The worst degree of cohesion, **coincidental**, is found in a module whose parts are unrelated to one another. In this case, unrelated functions, processes, or data are combined in the same module for reasons of convenience or serendipity. For example, it is not uncommon for a mediocre design to consist of several cohesive modules, with the rest of the system's functionality clumped together into modules `MiscellaneousA` and `MiscellaneousB`.

A module has **logical cohesion** if its parts are related only by the logic structure of its code. As an example, shown in Figure 6.6, consider a template module or procedure that performs very different operations depending on the values of its parameters. Although the different operations have some cohesion, in that they may share some

FIGURE 6.5 Types of cohesion.

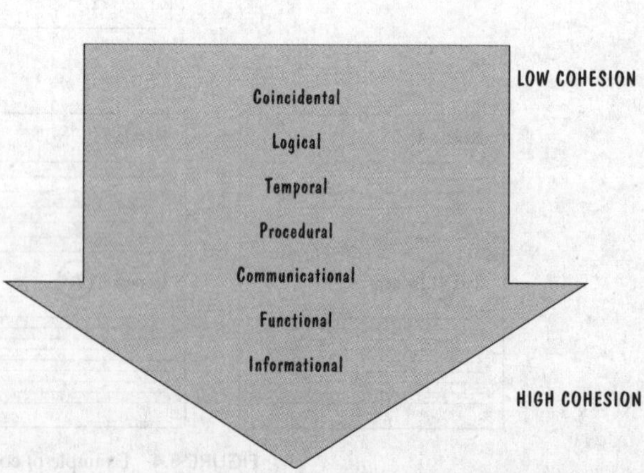

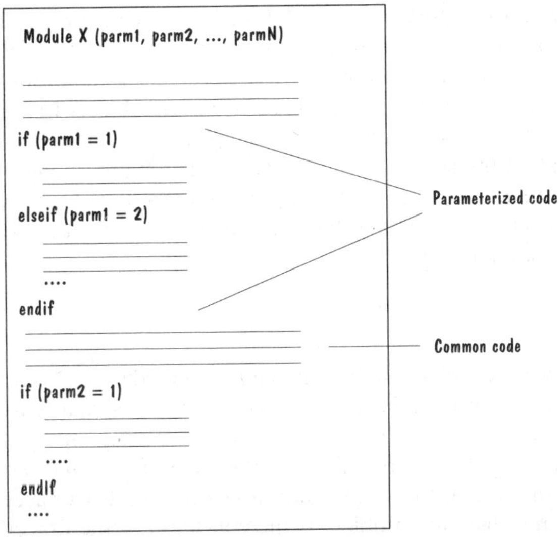

FIGURE 6.6 Example of logical cohesion.

program statements and code structure, this cohesion of code structure is weak compared to cohesion of data, function, or purpose. It is likely that the different operations will evolve in different ways over time, and that this evolution, plus the possible addition of new operations, will make the module increasingly difficult to understand and maintain.

Sometimes a design is divided into modules that represent the different phases of execution: *initialization, read input, compute, print output,* and *cleanup*. The cohesion in these modules is **temporal**, in that a module's data and functions are related only because they are used at the same time in an execution. Such a design may lead to duplicate code, in which multiple modules perform similar operations on key data structures; in this case, a change to the data structure would mandate a change to all of the modules that access the data structure. Object constructors and destructors in OO programs help to avoid temporal cohesion in initialization and clean-up modules.

Often, functions must be performed in a certain order. For example, data must be entered before they can be checked and then manipulated. When functions are grouped together in a module to encapsulate the order of their execution, we say that the module is **procedurally cohesive**. Procedural cohesion is similar to temporal cohesion, with the added advantage that the functions pertain to some related action or purpose. However, such a module appears cohesive only in the context of its use. Without knowing the module's context, it is hard for us to understand how and why the module works, or to know how to modify the module.

Alternatively, we can associate certain functions because they operate on the same data set. For instance, unrelated data may be fetched together because the data are collected from the same input sensor or with a single disk access. Modules that are designed around data sets in this way are **communicationally cohesive**. The cure for communicational cohesion is placing each data element in its own module.

Our ideal is **functional cohesion**, where two conditions hold: all elements essential to a single function are contained in one module, and all of that module's elements are essential to the performance of that function. A functionally cohesive module performs only the function for which it is designed, and nothing else. The adaptation of functional cohesion to data abstraction and object-based design is called **informational cohesion**. The design goal is the same: to put data, actions, or objects together only when they have one common, sensible purpose. For example, we say that an OO design component is cohesive if all of the attributes, methods, and action are strongly interdependent and essential to the object. Well-designed OO systems have highly cohesive designs because they encapsulate in each module a single, possibly complex, data type and all operations on that data type.

Interfaces

In Chapter 4, we saw that a software system has an external boundary and a corresponding interface through which it senses and controls its environment. Similarly, a software unit has a boundary that separates it from the rest of the system, and an interface through which the unit interacts with other software units. An **interface** defines what services the software unit provides to the rest of the system, and how other units can access those services. For example, the interface to an object is the collection of the object's public operations and the operations' **signatures**, which specify each operation's name, parameters, and possible return values. To be complete, an interface must also define what the unit requires, in terms of services or assumptions, for it to work correctly. For example, in the object interface described above, one of the operations may use program libraries, invoke external services, or make assumptions about the context in which it is invoked. If any of these requirements is absent or violated, the operation may fail in its attempt to offer its services. Thus, a software unit's interface describes what the unit requires of its environment, as well as what it provides to its environment. A software unit may have several interfaces that make different demands on its environment or that offer different levels of service, as shown in Figure 6.7. For example, the set of services provided may depend on the user privileges of the client code.

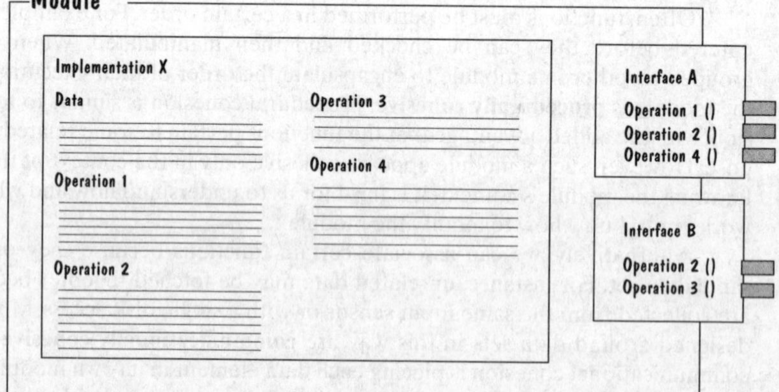

FIGURE 6.7 Example of interfaces.

Interfaces are the design construct that allows us to encapsulate and hide a software unit's design and implementation details from other developers. For example, rather than manipulate a stack variable directly, we define an object called *stack* and methods to perform stack operations *push* and *pop*. We use the object and its methods, not the stack itself, to modify the contents of the stack. We can also define **probes** to give us information about the stack—whether it is full or empty and what element is on top—without changing the stack's state.

The **specification** of a software unit's interface describes the externally visible properties of the software unit. Just as a requirements specification describes system behavior in terms of entities at the system's boundary, an interface specification's descriptions refer only to entities that exist at the unit's boundary: the unit's access functions, parameters, return values, and exceptions. An interface specification should communicate to other system developers everything that they need to know to use our software unit correctly. This information is not limited to the unit's access functions and their signatures:

- *Purpose:* We document the functionality of each access function, in enough detail that other developers can identify which access functions fit their needs.
- *Preconditions:* We list all assumptions, called **preconditions**, that our unit makes about its usage (e.g., values of input parameters, states of global resources, or presence of program libraries or other software units), so that other developers know under what conditions the unit is guaranteed to work correctly.
- *Protocols:* We include protocol information about the order in which access functions should be invoked, or the pattern in which two components should exchange messages. For example, a calling module may need to be authorized before accessing a shared resource.
- *Postconditions:* We document all visible effects, called **postconditions**, of each access function, including return values, raised exceptions, and changes to shared variables (e.g., output files), so that the calling code can react appropriately to the function's output.
- *Quality attributes:* We describe any quality attributes (e.g., performance, reliability) that are visible to developers or users. For example, a client of our software may want to know whether internal data structures have been optimized for data insertions or data retrievals. (Optimizing for one operation usually slows the performance of the other.)

Ideally, a unit's interface specification defines exactly the set of acceptable implementations. At least, the specification needs to be precise enough so that any implementation that satisfies the specification would be an acceptable implementation of the unit. For example, the specification of a *Find* operation that returns the index of an element in a list should say what happens if the element occurs multiple times in the list (e.g., returns the index of the first occurrence, or the index of an arbitrary occurrence), if the element is not found in the list, if the list is empty, and so on. In addition, the specification should not be so restrictive that it excludes several acceptable implementations. For example, the specification of the *Find* operation should not specify that the operation returns the first occurrence of an element when any occurrence would do.

Interface specifications keep other developers from knowing about and exploiting our design decisions. At first glance, it may seem desirable to allow other developers to optimize their code based on knowledge about how our software is designed. However, such optimization is a form of coupling among the software units, and it reduces the maintainability of the software. If a developer writes code that depends on how our software is implemented, then the interface between that developer's code and our code has changed: the developer's code now requires more from our software than what is advertised in our software's interface specification. When we want to change our software, either we must adhere to this new interface or the other developer must change her code so that it is optimized with respect to the new implementation.

A software unit's interface can also suggest the nature of coupling. If an interface restricts all access to the software unit to a collection of **access functions** that can be invoked, then there is no content coupling. If some of the access functions have complex data parameters, then there may be stamp coupling. To promote low coupling, we want to keep a unit's interface as small and simple as possible. We also want to minimize the assumptions and requirements that the software unit makes of its environment, to reduce the chance that changes to other parts of the system will violate those assumptions.

Information Hiding

Information hiding (Parnas 1972) aims to make the software system easier to maintain. It is distinguished by its guidance for decomposing a system: each software unit encapsulates a separate design decision that could be changed in the future. Then we use the interfaces and interface specifications to describe each software unit in terms of its externally visible properties. The principle's name thus reflects the result: the unit's design decision is hidden.

The notion of a "design decision" is quite general. It could refer to many things, including a decision about data format or operations on data; the hardware devices or other components with which our software must interoperate; protocols of messages between components; or the choice of algorithms. Because the design process involves many kinds of decisions about the software, the resulting software units encapsulate different kinds of information. Decomposition by information hiding is different from the decomposition methodologies listed in Chapter 5 (e.g., functional decomposition, data-oriented decomposition), because the software units that result from the latter encapsulate only information of the same type (i.e., they all encapsulate functions, data types, or processes). See Sidebar 6.2 for a discussion on how well OO design methodologies implement information hiding.

Because we want to encapsulate changeable design decisions, we must ensure that our interfaces do not, themselves, refer to aspects of the design that are likely to change. For example, suppose that we encapsulate in a module the choice of sorting algorithm. The sorting module could be designed to transform input strings into sorted output strings. However, this approach results in stamp coupling (i.e., the data passed between the units are constrained to be strings). If changeability of data format is a design decision, the data format should not be exposed in the module's interface. A better design would encapsulate the data in a single, separate software unit; the sorting

SIDEBAR 6.2 INFORMATION HIDING IN OO DESIGNS

In OO design, we decompose a system into objects and their abstract types. That is, each object (module) is an instance of an abstract data type. In this sense, each object hides its data representation from other objects. The only access that other objects have to a given object's data is via a set of access functions that the object advertises in its interface. This information hiding makes it easy to change an object's data representation without perturbing the rest of the system.

However, data representation is not the only type of design decision we may want to hide. Thus, to create an OO design that exhibits information hiding, we may need to expand our notion of what an object is, to include types of information besides data types. For example, we could encapsulate an independent procedure, such as a sorting algorithm or an event dispatcher, in its own object.

Objects cannot be completely uncoupled from one another, because an object needs to know the identity of the other objects so that they can interact. In particular, one object must know the name of a second object to invoke its access functions. This dependence means that changing the name of an object, or the number of object instances, forces us also to change all units that invoke the object. Such dependence cannot be helped when accessing an object that has a distinct identity (e.g., a customer record), but it may be avoided when accessing an arbitrary object (e.g., an instance of a shared resource). In Section 6.5, we discuss some design patterns that help to break these types of dependencies.

module could input and output a generic object type, and could retrieve and reorder the object's data values using access functions advertised in the data unit's interface.

By following the information-hiding principle, a design is likely to be composed of many small modules. Moreover, the modules may exhibit all kinds of cohesion. For example:

- A module that hides a data representation may be informationally cohesive.
- A module that hides an algorithm may be functionally cohesive.
- A module that hides the sequence in which tasks are performed may be procedurally cohesive.

Because each software unit hides exactly one design decision, all the units have high cohesion. Even with procedural cohesion, other software units hide the designs of the individual tasks. The resulting large number of modules may seem unwieldy, but we have ways to deal with this trade-off between number of modules and information hiding. Later in this chapter, we see how to use dependency graphs and abstraction to manage large collections of modules.

A big advantage of information hiding is that the resulting software units are loosely coupled. The interface to each unit lists the set of access functions that the unit offers, plus the set of other units' access functions that it uses. This feature makes the software units easier to understand and maintain, because each unit is relatively self-contained. And if we are correct in predicting which aspects of the design will change over time, then our software will be easier to maintain later on, because changes will be localized to particular software units.

Incremental Development

Given a design consisting of software units and their interfaces, we can use the information about the units' dependencies to devise an incremental schedule of development. We start by mapping out the units' **uses relation** (Parnas 1978b), which relates each software unit to the other software units on which it depends. Recall from our discussion about coupling that two software units, A and B, need not invoke each other in order to depend on each other; for example, unit A may depend on unit B to populate a data structure, stored in a separate unit C, that unit A subsequently queries. In general, we say that a software unit A "uses" a software unit B if A "requires the presence of a correct version of B" in order for A to complete its task, as specified in its interface (Parnas 1978b). Thus, a unit A *uses* a unit B if A does not work correctly unless B works. The above discussion assumes that we can determine a system's uses relation from its units' interface specifications. If the interface specifications do not completely describe the units' dependencies, then we will need to know enough about each unit's planned implementations to know which other units it will use.

Figure 6.8 depicts the uses relation of a system as a **uses graph**, in which nodes represent software units, and directed edges run from the using units, such as A, to the used units, such as B. Such a uses graph can help us to identify progressively larger subsets of our system that we can implement and test incrementally. A subset of our system is some useful subprogram together with all of the software units that it uses, and all of the software units that those units use, and so on. "Conceptually, we pluck a program P_1 out from the uses graph, and then see what programs come dangling beneath it. This is our subset" (Clements et al. 2003). Thus, the degree to which our system can be constructed incrementally depends on the degree to which we can find useful *small* subsets that we can implement and test early.

A uses graph can also help us to identify areas of the design that could be improved, with respect to enabling incremental development. For example, consider Designs 1 and 2 in Figure 6.8 as two possible designs of the same system. We use the term **fan-in** to refer to the number of units that use a particular software unit, and the term **fan-out** to refer to the number of units used by a software unit. Thus, unit A has a fan-out of three in Design 1 but a fan-out of five in Design 2. In general, we want to minimize the number of units with high fan-out. High fan-out usually indicates that the software unit is doing too much and probably ought to be decomposed into smaller, simpler units. Thus, Design 1 may be better than Design 2, because its components have lower fan-out. On the other hand, if several units perform similar functions, such as

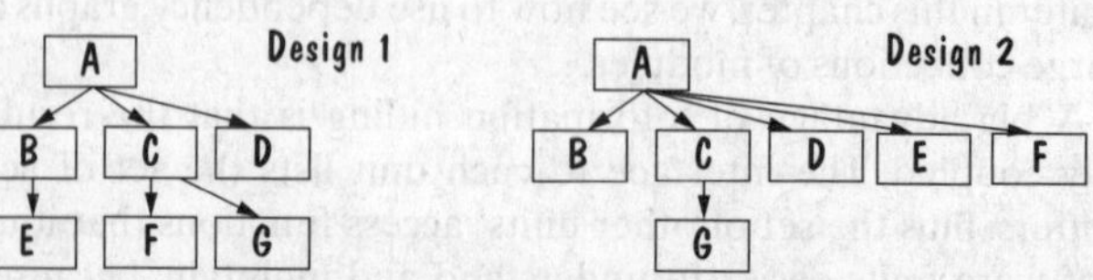

FIGURE 6.8 Uses graphs for two designs.

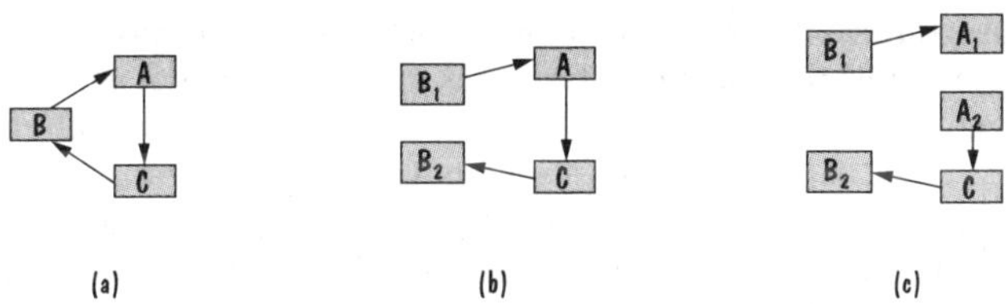

FIGURE 6.9 Sandwiching, to break a cycle in a uses graph.

string searching, then we may prefer to combine these units into a single, more general-purpose unit that can be used in place of any of the original units. Such a *utility* unit is likely to have high fan-in. One of our goals in designing a system is to create software units with high fan-in and low fan-out.

Consider another example, shown as a uses graph in Figure 6.9(a). The cycle in this uses graph identifies a collection of units that are mutually dependent on each other. Such cycles are not necessarily bad. If the problem that the units are solving is naturally recursive, then it makes sense for the design to include modules that are mutually recursive. But large cycles limit the design's ability to support incremental development: none of the units in the cycle can be developed (i.e., implemented, tested, debugged) until all of the cycle's units are developed. Moreover, we cannot choose to build a subset of our system that incorporates only some of the cycle's units. We can try to break a cycle in the uses graph using a technique called **sandwiching** (Parnas 1978b). In sandwiching, one of the cycle's units is decomposed into two units, such that one of the new units has no dependencies (e.g., unit B_2 in Figure 6.9(b)) and the other has no dependents (e.g., unit B_1 in Figure 6.9(b)). Sandwiching can be applied more than once, to break either mutual dependencies in tightly coupled units or long dependency chains. Figure 6.9(c) shows the results of applying sandwiching twice, once to unit A and once to unit B, to transform a dependency loop into two shorter dependency chains. Of course, sandwiching works only if a unit's data and functionality can be cleanly partitioned, which is not always the case. In the next section, we explore a more sophisticated technique, called **dependency inversion**, that uses OO technologies to reverse the direction of dependency between two units, thereby breaking the cycle.

The best uses graph has a tree structure or is a forest of tree structures. In such a structure, every subtree is a subset of our system, so we can incrementally develop our system one software unit at a time. Each completed unit is a correct implementation of part of our system. Each increment is easier to test and correct because faults are more likely to be found in the new code, not in the called units that have already been tested and deemed correct. In addition, we always have a working version of a system subset to demonstrate to our customer. Moreover, morale among developers is high, because they frequently make visible progress on the system (Brooks 1995). Contrast these advantages of incremental development to its alternative, in which nothing works until everything works.

Abstraction

An **abstraction** is a model or representation that omits some details so that it can focus on other details. The definition is vague about which details are left out of a model, because different abstractions, built for different purposes, omit different kinds of details. For this reason, it may be easier to understand the general notion of abstraction by reviewing the types of abstractions we have encountered already.

We discussed decomposition in Chapter 5. Figure 5.5 was an example of a *decomposition hierarchy*: a frequently used form of abstraction in which the system is divided into subsystems, which in turn are divided into sub-subsystems, and so on. The top level of the decomposition provides a system-level overview of the solution, hiding details that might otherwise distract us from the design functions and features we want to study and understand. As we move to lower levels of abstraction, we find more detail about each software unit, in terms of its major elements and the relations among those elements. In this way, each level of abstraction hides information about how its elements are further decomposed. Instead, each element is described by an *interface specification*, another type of abstraction that focuses on the element's external behaviors and avoids any reference to the element's internal design details; those details are revealed in models at the next level of decomposition.

As we saw in Chapter 5, there may not be a single decomposition of the system. Rather, we may create several decompositions that show different structures. For instance, one view may show the system's different runtime processes and their interconnections, and another view may show the system's decomposition into code units. Each of these *views* is an abstraction that highlights one aspect of the system's structural design (e.g., runtime processes) and ignores other structural information (e.g., code units) and nonstructural details.

A fourth type of abstraction is the *virtual machine*, such as that in a layered architecture. Each layer i in the architecture uses the services provided by the layer $i - 1$ below it, to create more powerful and reliable services, which it then offers to the layer $i + 1$ above it. Recall that in a true layered architecture, a layer can access only those services offered by the layer directly below it, and cannot access the services of lower-level layers (and certainly not the services of the higher-level layers). As such, layer i is a virtual machine that abstracts away the details of the lower-level layers and presents only its services to the next layer; the guiding design principle is that layer i's services are improvements over the lower-layers' services and thus supersede them.

The key to writing good abstractions is determining, for a particular model, which details are extraneous and can therefore be ignored. The nature of the abstraction depends on why we are building the model in the first place: what information we want to communicate, or what analysis we want to perform. Sidebar 6.3 illustrates how we can model different abstractions of an algorithm for different purposes.

Generality

Recall from Chapter 1 that one of Wasserman's principles of software engineering is **reusability**: creating software units that may be used again in future software products. The goal is to amortize the cost of developing the unit by using it multiple times. (**Amortization** means that we consider the cost of a software unit in terms of its cost per use rather than associate the full cost with the project that developed the unit.) **Generality** is the design principle that makes a software unit as universally applicable as possible, to increase the chance that it will be useful in some future system. We make

SIDEBAR 6.3 USING ABSTRACTION

We can use abstraction to view different aspects of our design. Suppose that one of the system functions is to sort the elements of a list L. The initial description of the design is

```
Sort L in nondecreasing order
```

The next level of abstraction may be a particular algorithm:

```
DO WHILE I is between 1 and (length of L)-1:
  Set LOW to index of smallest value in L(I),..., L(length of L)
  Interchange L(I) and L(LOW)
ENDDO
```

The algorithm provides a great deal of additional information. It tells us the procedure that will be used to perform the sort operation on L. However, it can be made even more detailed. The third and final algorithm describes exactly how the sorting operation will work:

```
DO WHILE I is between 1 and (length of L)-1
  Set LOW to current value of I
  DO WHILE J is between I+1 and (length of L)
    IF L(LOW) is greater than L(J)
       THEN set LOW to current value of J
    ENDIF
  ENDDO
  Set TEMP to L(LOW)
  Set L(LOW) to L(I)
  Set L(I) to TEMP
ENDDO
```

Each level of abstraction serves a purpose. If we care only about what L looks like before and after sorting, then the first abstraction provides all the information we need. If we are concerned about the speed of the algorithm, then the second level of abstraction provides sufficient detail to analyze the algorithm's complexity. However, if we are writing code for the sorting operation, the third level of abstraction tells us exactly what is to happen; little additional information is needed.

If we were presented only with the third level of abstraction, we might not discern immediately that the procedure describes a sorting algorithm; with the first level, the nature of the procedure is obvious, whereas the third level distracts us from the real nature of the procedure. In each case, abstraction keeps us focused on the purpose of the respective description.

a unit more general by increasing the number of contexts in which can it be used. There are several ways of doing this:

- *Parameterizing context-specific information:* We create a more general version of our software by making into parameters the data on which it operates.
- *Removing preconditions:* We remove preconditions by making our software work under conditions that we previously assumed would never happen.
- *Simplifying postconditions:* We reduce postconditions by splitting a complex software unit into multiple units that divide responsibility for providing the postconditions. The units can be used together to solve the original problem, or used separately when only a subset of the postconditions is needed.

For example, the following four procedure interfaces are listed in order of increasing generality:

```
PROCEDURE SUM: INTEGER;
POSTCONDITION: returns sum of 3 global variables

PROCEDURE SUM (a, b, c: INTEGER): INTEGER;
POSTCONDITION: returns sum of parameters

PROCEDURE SUM (a[]: INTEGER; len: INTEGER): INTEGER
PRECONDITION: 0 <= len <= size of array a
POSTCONDITION: returns sum of elements 1..len in array a

PROCEDURE SUM (a[]: INTEGER): INTEGER
POSTCONDITION: returns sum of elements in array a
```

The first procedure works only in contexts where global variables have names that match the names used within the procedure body. The second procedure no longer needs to know the names of the actual variables being summed, but its use is restricted to summing exactly three variables. The third procedure can sum any number of variables, but the calling code must specify the number of elements to sum. The last procedure sums all of the elements in its array parameter. Thus, the more general the procedure, the more likely it is that we can reuse the procedure in a new context by modifying its input parameters rather than its implementation.

Although we would always like to create reusable units, other design goals sometimes conflict with this goal. We saw in Chapter 1 that software engineering differs from computer science in part by focusing on context-specific software solutions. That is, we tailor our solution for the specific needs of our customer. The system's requirements specification lists specific design criteria (e.g., performance, efficiency) to optimize in the design and code. Often, this customization decreases the software's generality, reflecting the trade-off between generality (and therefore reusability) and customization. There is no general rule to help us balance these competing design goals. The choice depends on the situation, the importance of the design criteria, and the utility of a more general version.

6.3 OO DESIGN

Design characteristics have significant effects on subsequent development, maintenance, and evolution. For this reason, new software engineering technologies are frequently created to help developers adhere to the design principles we introduced in the last section. For example, **design methodologies** codify advice on how to use abstraction, separation of concerns, and interfaces to decompose a system into software units that are modular. OO methodologies are the most popular and sophisticated design methodologies. We call a design **object oriented** if it decomposes a system into a collection of runtime components called **objects** that encapsulate data and functionality. The following features distinguish objects from other types of components:

- Objects are uniquely **identifiable** runtime entities that can be designated as the target of a message or request.
- Objects can be **composed**, in that an object's data variables may themselves be objects, thereby encapsulating the implementations of the object's internal variables.
- The implementation of an object can be reused and extended via **inheritance**, to define the implementation of other objects.
- OO code can be **polymorphic**: written in generic code that works with objects of different but related types. Objects of related types respond to the same set of messages or requests, but each object's response to a request depends on the object's specific type.

In this section, we review these features and some of the design choices they pose, and we present heuristics for improving the quality of OO designs. By using OO features to their best advantage, we can create designs that respect design principles.

Terminology

The runtime structure of an OO system is a set of **objects**, each of which is a cohesive collection of data plus all operations for creating, reading, altering, and destroying those data. An object's data are called **attributes**, and its operations are called **methods**. Objects interact by sending messages to invoke each other's methods. On receiving a message, an object executes the associated method, which reads or modifies the object's data and perhaps issues messages to other objects; when the method terminates, the object sends the results back to the requesting object.

Objects are primarily runtime entities. As such, they are often not represented directly in software designs. Instead, an OO design comprises objects' classes and interfaces. An interface advertises the set of externally accessible attributes and methods. This information is typically limited to public methods, and includes the methods' signatures, preconditions, postconditions, protocol requirements, and visible quality attributes. Thus, like other interfaces, the interface of an object represents the object's public face, specifying all aspects of the object's externally observable behavior. Other system components that need to access the object's data must do so indirectly, by invoking the methods advertised in the object's interface. An object may have multiple interfaces, each offering a different level of access to the object's data and methods. Such interfaces are hierarchically related by type: if one interface offers a strict subset of the services that another interface offers, we say that the first interface is a **subtype** of the second interface (the **supertype**).

An object's implementation details are encapsulated in its class definition. To be precise, a **class** is a software module that partially or totally implements an abstract data type (Meyer 1997). It includes definitions of the attributes' data; declarations of the methods that operate on the data; and implementations of some or all of its methods. Thus, it is the class modules that contain the actual code that implements the objects' data representations and method procedures. If a class is missing implementations for some of its methods, we say that it is an **abstract class**. Some OO notations, including the Unified Modeling Language (UML), do not separate an object's interface from its class module; in such notations, the class definition distinguishes between public definitions (constituting the interface) and private definitions (constituting the class's implementation). In this chapter, we consider interfaces and classes to be distinct entities, because the set of objects satisfying an interface can be much larger than the set of objects instantiating a class definition. Graphically, we distinguish an interface or abstract class from other classes by italicizing its name and the names of its unimplemented methods.

Suppose we are designing a program that logs all sales transactions for a particular store. Figure 6.10 shows a partial design of a `Sale` class that defines attributes to store information associated with a sale (such as the list of items sold, their prices, and sales tax). The class implements a number of operations on transaction data (such as adding or removing an item from the transaction, computing the sales tax, or voiding the sale). Each `Sale` object in our program is an instance of this class: each object encapsulates a distinct copy of the class's data variables and pointers to the class's operations. Moreover, the class definition includes **constructor** methods that spawn new object instances. Thus, during execution, our program can instantiate new `Sale` objects to record the details of each sale as the sale occurs.

We also have **instance variables**, which are program variables whose values are references to objects. An object is a distinct value of its class type, just as '3' is a value of the `INTEGER` data type. Thus, an instance variable can refer to different object instances during program execution, in the same way that an integer variable can be assigned different integer values. However, there is a critical difference between instance variables and traditional program variables. An instance variable can be declared to have an interface type, rather than be a particular class type (assuming that interfaces and classes are distinct entities); in this case, an instance variable can refer to objects of any class that implements the variable's (interface) type. Moreover, because

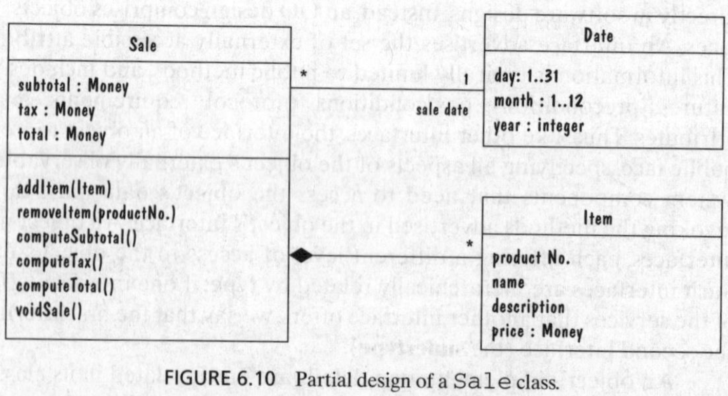

FIGURE 6.10 Partial design of a `Sale` class.

of the subtyping relation among interfaces, an instance variable can also refer to objects of any class that implements some ancestor supertype of the variable's (interface) type. The variable can even refer to objects of different classes over the course of a program's execution. This flexibility is called **dynamic binding**, because the objects to which the variables refer cannot be inferred by examining the code. We write code that operates on instance variables according to their interfaces, but the actual behavior of that code varies during program execution, depending on the types of objects on which the code is operating.

Figure 6.11 shows these four OO constructs—*classes, objects, interfaces*, and *instance variables*—and how they are related. Directed arrows depict the relationships between constructs, and the adornments at the ends of each arrow indicate the multiplicity (sometimes called the "arity") of the relationship; the **multiplicity** tells us how many of an item may exist. For example, the relationship between instance variables and objects is many (*) to one (1), meaning that many instance variables may refer to the same object at any point in a program's execution. Some of the other relationships merit mention:

- Each class encapsulates the implementation details of one or more interfaces. A class that is declared to implement one interface also implicitly (via inheritance) implements all of the interface's supertypes.
- Each interface is implemented by one or more classes. For example, different class implementations may emphasize different quality attributes.
- Each object is an instance of one class, whose attribute and method definitions determine what data the object can hold and what method implementations the object executes.
- Multiple instance variables of different types may refer to the same object, as long as the object's class implements (directly or implicitly via supertypes) each variable's (interface) type.
- Each instance variable's type (i.e., interface) determines what data and methods can be accessed using that variable.

Both the separation of object instances from instance variables and of interfaces from class definitions give us considerable flexibility in encapsulating design decisions and in modifying and reusing designs.

Support for reuse is a key characteristic of OO design. For example, we can build new classes by combining component classes, much as children build structures from building blocks. Such construction is done by **object composition**, whereby we define a

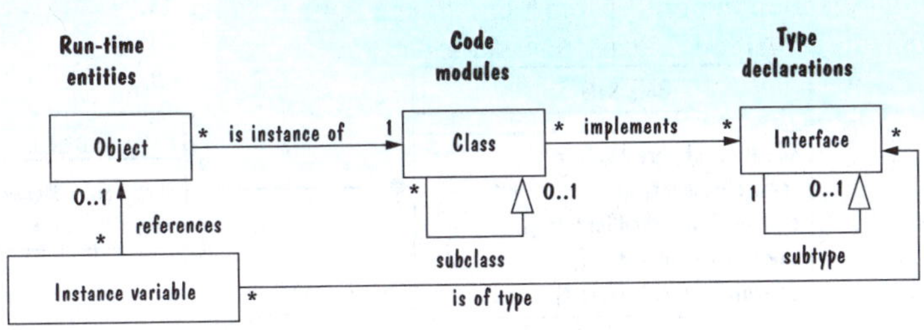

FIGURE 6.11 Meta-model of OO constructs.

class's attributes to be instance variables of some interface type. For example, the `Sale` class defined in Figure 6.10 uses composition to maintain an aggregated record of the `Items` sold, and uses a component `Date` object to record the date of the sale. An advantage of object composition is its support of modularity; the composite class knows nothing about the implementations of its object-based attributes and can manipulate these attributes only by using their interfaces. As such, we can easily replace one class component with another, as long as the replacement complies with the same interface. This technique is much the same as replacing a red building block with a blue one, as long as the two blocks are the same size and shape.

Alternatively, we can build new classes by extending or modifying definitions of existing classes. This kind of construction, called **inheritance**, defines a new class by directly reusing (and adding to) the definitions of an existing class. Inheritance is comparable to creating a new type of building block by drilling holes in an existing block. In an inheritance relation, the existing class is called the **parent class**. The new class, called a **subclass**, is said to "inherit" the parent class's data and function definitions. To see how inheritance works, suppose that we want to create a `Bulk Sale` class for recording large sales transactions in which a buyer qualifies for a discount. If we define `Bulk Sale` as an extension of our regular `Sale` class, as in Figure 6.12, then we need to provide only the definitions that distinguish `Bulk Sale` from its parent class, `Sale`. These definitions include new attributes to record the discount rates, and a revised method that applies the discount when totaling the cost of the sale. Any `Bulk Sale` object will

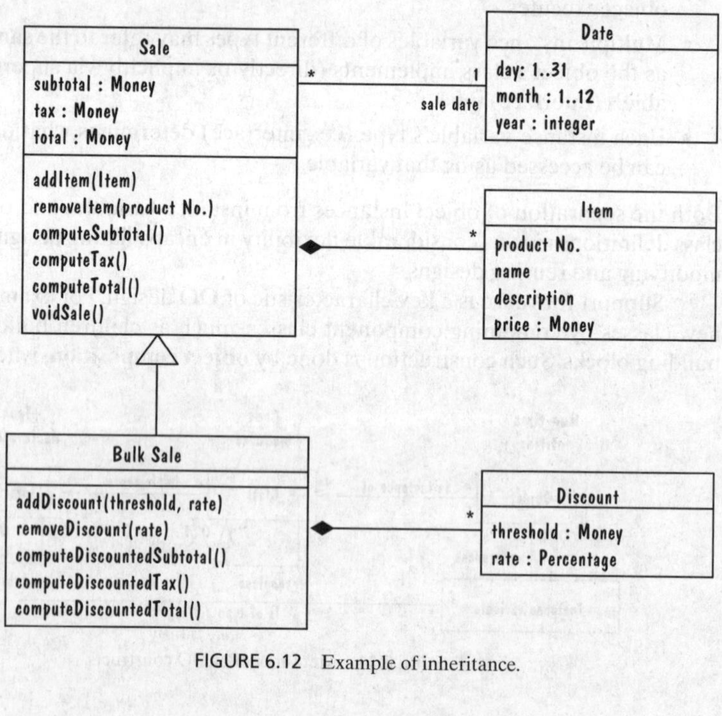

FIGURE 6.12 Example of inheritance.

comprise attributes and methods defined in the parent `Sale` class together with those defined in the `Bulk Sale` class.

Object orientation also supports **polymorphism**, whereby code is written in terms of interactions with an interface, but code behavior depends on the object associated with the interface at runtime and on the implementations of that object's methods. Objects of different types may react to the same message by producing type-specific responses. Designers and programmers need not know the exact types of the objects that the polymorphic code is manipulating. Rather, they need make sure only that the code adheres to the instance variables' interfaces; they rely on each object's class to specialize how objects of that class should respond to messages. In the `Sales` program, the code for finalizing a purchase can simply request the total cost from the appropriate `Sale` object. How the cost is calculated (i.e., which method is executed and whether a discount is applied) will depend on whether the object is an ordinary `Sale` or a `Bulk Sale`.

Inheritance, object composition, and polymorphism are important features of an OO design that make the resulting system more useful in many ways. The next section discusses strategies for using these concepts effectively.

Inheritance vs. Object Composition

A key design decision is determining how best to structure and relate complex objects. In an OO system, there are two main techniques for constructing large objects: inheritance and composition. That is, a new class can be created by extending and overriding the behavior of an existing class, or it can be created by combining simpler classes to form a composite class. The distinction between these two approaches is exhibited by examples similar to those of Bertrand Meyer (1997), shown in Figure 6.13. On the left, a `Software Engineer` is defined as a subclass of `Engineer` and inherits its parent class's engineering capabilities. On the right, a `Software Engineer` is defined as a composite class that possesses engineering capabilities from its component `Engineer` object. Note that both approaches enable design reuse and extension. That is, in both approaches, the reused code is maintained as a separate class (i.e., the parent class or the component object), and the new class (i.e., the subclass or the composite object) extends this behavior by introducing new attributes and methods and not by modifying the reused code. Moreover, because the reused code remains encapsulated as a separate class, we can safely change its implementation and thereby indirectly update the behavior of the new class. Thus, changes to the `Engineer` class are automatically realized in the `Software Engineer` class, regardless of whether the `Software Engineer` class is constructed using inheritance or composition.

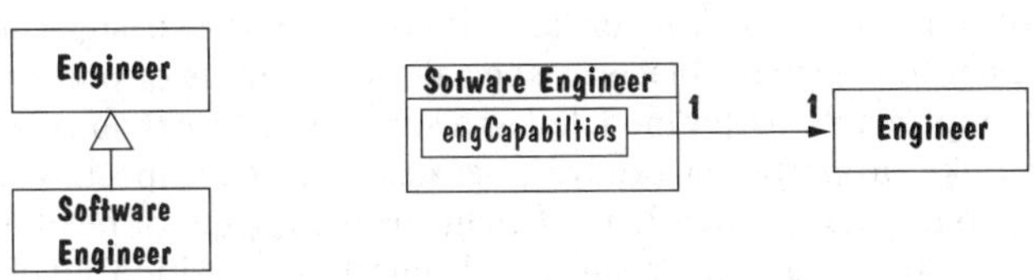

FIGURE 6.13 Class inheritance (left) vs. object construction (right).

Each construction paradigm has advantages and disadvantages. Composition is better than inheritance at preserving the encapsulation of the reused code, because a composite object accesses the component only through its advertised interface. In our example, a `Software Engineer` would access and update its engineering capabilities using calls to its component's methods. By contrast, a subclass may have direct access to its inherited attributes, depending on the design. The greatest advantage of composition is that it allows dynamic substitution of object components. The component object is an attribute variable of its composite object and, as with any variable, its value can be changed during program execution. Moreover, if the component is defined in terms of an interface, then it can be replaced with an object of a different but compatible type. In the case of the composite `Software Engineer`, we can change its engineering capabilities, including method implementations, by reassigning its `engCapabilities` attribute to another object. This degree of variability poses its own problems, though. Because composition-designed systems can be reconfigured at runtime, it can be harder to visualize and reason about a program's runtime structure simply by studying the code. It is not always clear which objects reference which other objects. A second disadvantage is that object composition introduces a level of indirection. Every access of a component's methods must first access the component object; this indirection may affect runtime performance.

By contrast, using the inheritance approach, the subclass's implementation is determined at design time and is static. The resulting objects are less flexible than objects instantiated from composite classes because the methods they inherit from their parent class cannot be changed at runtime. Moreover, because the inherited properties of the parent class are usually visible to the subclass, if not directly accessible, it can be easier to understand and predict the behavior of classes constructed using inheritance. Of course, the greatest advantage of inheritance is the ability to change and specialize the behaviors of inherited methods, by selectively overriding inherited definitions. This characteristic helps us to quickly create new types of objects that exhibit new behaviors.

In general, experienced designers prefer object composition over inheritance because of its ability to substitute component objects at runtime. When instance variables are defined in terms of interfaces rather than concrete classes, the variables can refer to objects of any type that implement the interface. As a result, the client code can be written without knowledge of the specific types of objects it uses or even the classes that implement those objects; the client code depends only on the definition of the interface. Such flexibility makes it easier to change or enhance capabilities in the future. For example, in the `Software Engineer` constructed by composition, we can satisfy the `Engineer` interface with any object that complies with the interface. We can define a new `Senior Engineer` class or subclass that has more capabilities and responsibility than a `Junior Engineer` has, and we can promote a `Software Engineer` to have senior engineering capabilities using a simple attribute assignment. This preference of composition over inheritance is not a definitive design rule, because sometimes it is easier to consider objects as specialized instances of one another. For example, a `Sedan` is probably better modeled as a subclass of `Car` than as a composite object that has car-like properties. Moreover, because object composition introduces a level of indirection, it may be overly inefficient for the degree of flexibility it offers. Thus, the choice between class inheritance and object composition involves trade-offs among design coherence, predictability of behavior, encapsulation of design decisions, runtime performance, and runtime configurability.

Substitutability

The use of inheritance does not necessarily result in subclasses that can be used in place of their parent class. Most OO programming languages allow subclasses to override the behaviors of their inherited methods, without regard to whether the result complies with the parent class's interface. As a result, client code that relies on the parent class might not work correctly when passed an instance of a subclass.

Consider a `BoundedStack` that is a specialized type of `Stack` that can store only a limited number of elements. The `BoundedStack` subclass not only introduces an attribute to record the bound on its size, but also overrides the behavior of the `push()` method to handle the case where an element is pushed onto a full stack (e.g., the `BoundedStack` might ignore the request, or it might push the bottom element off the stack to make room for the new element). A `BoundedStack` object is not substitutable for a normal `Stack` object, because the two objects behave differently when their respective stacks are full.

Ideally, a subclass must preserve the behavior of its parent class, so that client code can treat instances of it as instances of the parent class. This notion is best described by the **Liskov Substitutability Principle**, named after its inventor, Barbara Liskov, a pioneer in OO programming and data abstraction. According to the principle, a subclass is **substitutable** for its parent class if all of the following properties are satisfied (Liskov and Guttag 2001):

1. The subclass supports all of the methods of the parent class, and their signatures are *compatible*. That is, the parameters and return types of the subclass's methods must be substitutable for the corresponding parameters and return types of the parent class's methods, so that any call to a method of the parent class would be accepted by the subclass.
2. The subclass's methods must satisfy the specifications of the parent class's methods. The behaviors of the two classes' methods do not have to be the same, but the subclass must not violate the pre- and postconditions of the parent class's methods:
   - *Precondition rule:* The precondition of a subclass method must be the same as or weaker than the precondition of the parent class's method, so that the subclass method succeeds in all cases that the parent class method succeeds. We can represent this relationship as:

     $$pre_{parent} \Rightarrow pre_{sub}$$

   - *Postcondition rule:* In those cases where the precondition of the parent class method holds, the subclass method does everything that the parent method does, and may do more (i.e., the postcondition of the subclass method *subsumes* the postcondition of the parent class's method).

     $$pre_{parent} \Rightarrow (post_{sub} \Rightarrow post_{parent})$$

3. The subclass must preserve all declared properties of the parent class. For example, in UML, a subclass inherits all of the constraints on its parent class and all of its parent's associations with other classes.

If any of the above rules does not hold, then sending a message to an instance of the subclass might not give the same result as sending the message to an instance of the parent class. In the case of `BoundedStack`, the `push()` method does not simply extend the postcondition of its parent class's `push()` method; it has a different postcondition. Thus, the definition of `BoundedStack` violates the postcondition rule, and a `BoundedStack` object is not substitutable for a normal `Stack` object.

In contrast, consider `PeekStack`, another specialized type of `Stack` that allows users to peek at the contents of the stack rather than being able to view only the top element. A `PeekStack` subclass introduces a single new method, `peek(pos)`, that returns the value of the element at depth `pos` in the stack. Because `PeekStack` overrides none of the methods it inherits from `Stack`, and because the new method `peek()` never changes the object's attributes, it satisfies all of the substitutability rules.

The primary use of the Liskov Substitutability Principle is in determining when one object can safely be substituted for another object. If we conform to the principle when extending our designs and programs with new subclasses, we can be confident that the existing code will work with the new subclasses without modification. Despite this obvious advantage, in our study of design patterns we will encounter a number of useful patterns that violate the Liskov Substitutability Principle. As with most other design principles, substitutability is not a rigid design rule. Rather, the principle serves as a guideline for determining when it is safe *not* to reexamine the client modules of an extended class. Whenever we conform to the principle, we simplify the overall task of extending our design.

Law of Demeter

Although the design advice suggests that we prefer composition over inheritance, the resulting design may have multiple dependencies among classes. This problem occurs whenever a class that depends on a composite class also depends on all of the class's component classes. In our sales transaction example, consider a new class `Bill` that generates an invoice each month, listing all of the items sold that month to a particular customer. Suppose that each class in our design offers only services that manipulate that class's local attributes. Then to print the list of items sold, our `generateBill()` method must track down all of the appropriate `Item` objects:

```
For CustomerAccount c:
For each Sale c.s made to CustomerAccount c:
    For each Item c.s.i in Sale c.s:
        c.s.i.printName();
        c.s.i.printPrice();
```

In such a design, our `Bill` class accesses and thus depends directly on `CustomerAccount`, `Sale`, and `Item` classes. We must know the interfaces of all of them to invoke the appropriate methods correctly. Worse, we have to recheck our implementation of `generateBill()` whenever any of these classes is changed.

We can reduce these dependencies by including in each composite class methods for operating on the class's components. For example, we can add a `printItemList()` method to our `Sale` class, and add a `printSaleItems()` method to our `CustomerAccount` class. In this new design,

- our `generateBill()` method calls `printSaleItems()` in `CustomerAccount`
- `printSaleItems()` calls `printItemList()` in the appropriate `Sale` object
- `printItemList()` calls the print methods in the appropriate `Item` objects

This design convention is called the **Law of Demeter** (Lieberherr and Holland 1989), named after a research project called Demeter. It is also known more informally as the "Don't talk to strangers" design principle. The benefit of this convention is that client code that uses a composite class needs to know only about the composite itself and not about the composites' components. The difference between these two design alternatives and their resulting class dependencies can be visualized by the designs' induced dependency graphs, shown in Figure 6.14. In general, designs that obey the Law of Demeter have fewer class dependencies, and classes with fewer dependencies tend to have fewer software faults (Basili, Briand, and Melo 1995) and are easier to change (Li and Henry 1993).

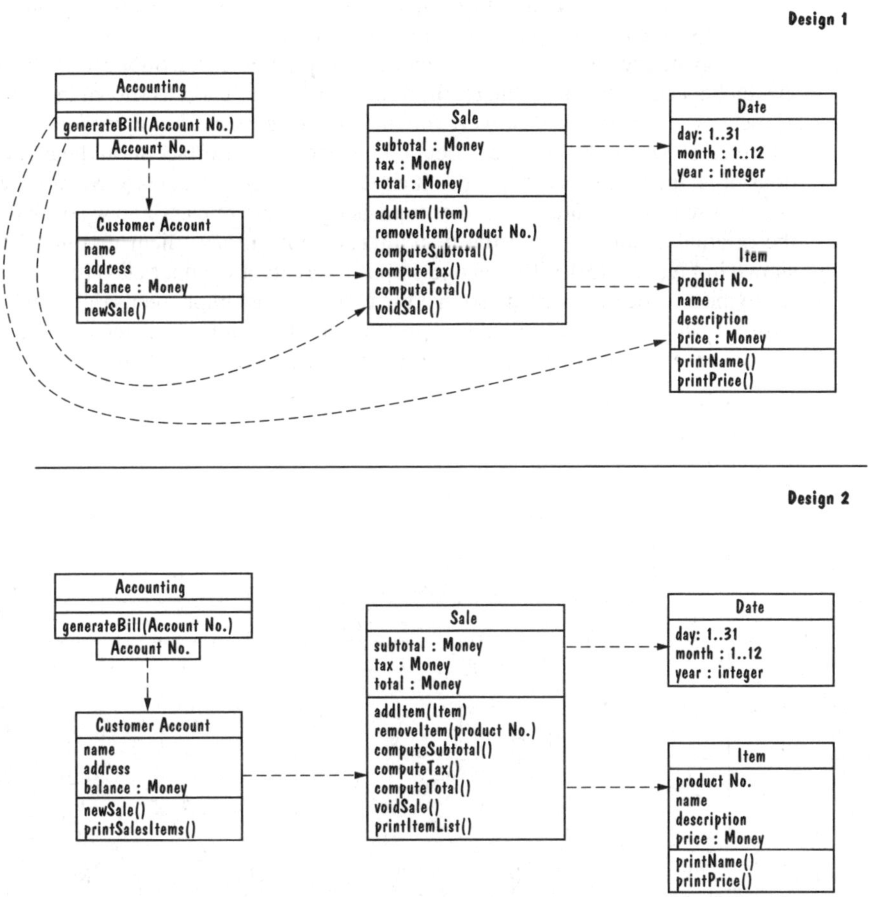

FIGURE 6.14 Contrasting designs and dependencies.

On the downside, such designs often use a **wrapper class** to add functionality without changing the implementations of existing classes. For example, we could have added `printItemList()` via a wrapper class associated with class `Sale`. Although wrapper classes ease the task of adding operations to composite classes, they can complicate the design and degrade runtime performance. Thus, deciding whether to adhere to the Law of Demeter involves evaluating trade-offs among design complexity, development time, runtime performance, fault avoidance, and ease of maintenance.

Dependency Inversion

Dependency inversion is our final OO design heuristic. It can be used to reverse the direction of a dependency link between two classes. For example, if a client class depends on some server class, we can use dependency inversion to revise the dependency, so that the server class depends on the client class instead. We might invert dependency to break a dependency cycle among classes, as we saw earlier in this chapter. Or we might rearrange our design so that each class depends only on classes that are more stable and less likely to change than it is.

Dependency inversion works by introducing interfaces. Suppose we have a design in which a client class uses the methods of some server class, as shown in Figure 6.15(a). The client depends on the server. The first step of dependency inversion is to create an interface on which the client can depend instead. This interface should include specifications of all the methods that the client expects from the server class. We modify the client class to use this new interface rather than using the server class, and we package together the original client class and the new interface into a new client module. The result is shown in Figure 6.15(b). The second step is to create a wrapper class for the server class (or to modify the server class), so that the wrapper class implements the interface created in step 1. This second step should be easy because the interface matches the specifications of the server class's methods. The resulting design, shown in Figure 6.15(c), induces a

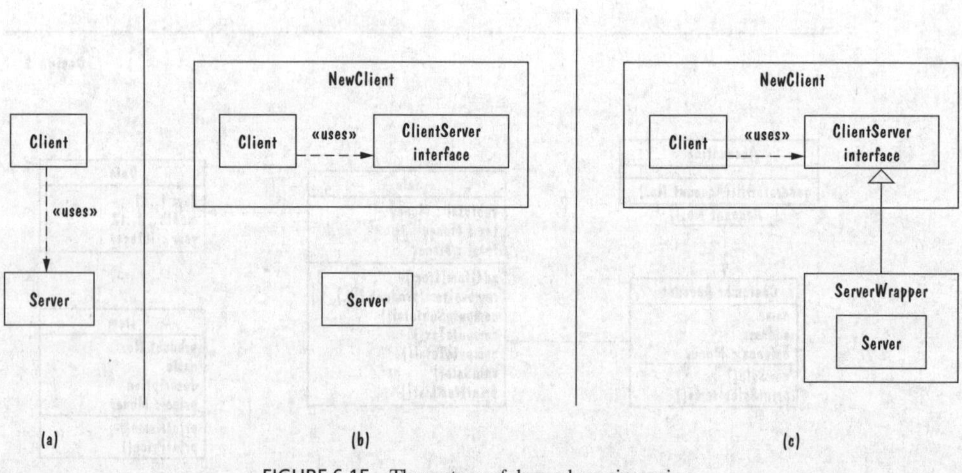

FIGURE 6.15 Three steps of dependency inversion.

dependency graph in which the newly wrapped server class depends on the new client package. In the original design, any change to the server code would cause us to reexamine and recompile the client code. In the new design, both the client code and the server code depend only on the new `ClientServerInterface`. A change to either class's implementation does not cause us to revisit or recompile the other class, so the new design is easier to maintain. As we will see, the dependency inversion principle is used in the definitions of several design patterns.

6.4 REPRESENTING OO DESIGNS IN THE UML

The UML is a suite of design notations that is popular for describing OO solutions. It can be tailored to fit different development situations and software life cycles. In fact, organizations such as the Object Management Group have adopted the UML as the OO notational standard. In this section, we review the UML constructs introduced in Chapter 4 and apply them to an example problem. For a more complete introduction to the UML, see Larman (1998).

The UML can be used to visualize, specify, or document a software design. It is especially useful for describing different design alternatives, and eventually for documenting design artifacts. UML diagrams include the dynamic view of the system, the static view, restrictions, and formalization. The dynamic view is depicted with use cases, lists of activities, interaction diagrams showing sequences and communication, and state machines to illustrate states and their changes. The static view is depicted with class diagrams, showing relationships (association, generalization, dependency, and realization) and extensibility (constraints, tagged values, and stereotypes). In addition, the static view shows packages and deployment. Restrictions and formalization are expressed with the Object Constraint Language (OCL).

UML in the Process

Because OO concepts apply to all parts of development, the UML can be used throughout the software development process. Figure 6.16 shows how the UML can be used in requirements specification, design, and coding. Notice that the UML makes use of many of the notations introduced in Chapter 4. Each notation makes explicit some aspect of the system, so that, in concert, the representations provide a detailed picture of the problem or its proposed solution. In the requirements process, **use case diagrams** describe the system to be built by describing the general processes that the system must perform. In addition, the use cases can embody the different scenarios that describe how the system will work and how the users will interact with the system. These diagrams can be supplemented by **UML activity diagrams**, which are a type of workflow process model for describing the activities that the business will perform, or with a **domain model** that defines the system's domain in terms of its entities. If the system is large, its software architecture can be modeled using UML **component diagrams**, to show the runtime components and their interactions, and UML **deployment diagrams**, to show how components are allocated computing resources.

Modular design begins with the UML **class diagram**. Classes and their relationships are first defined informally, as each scenario is worked out with the user, and

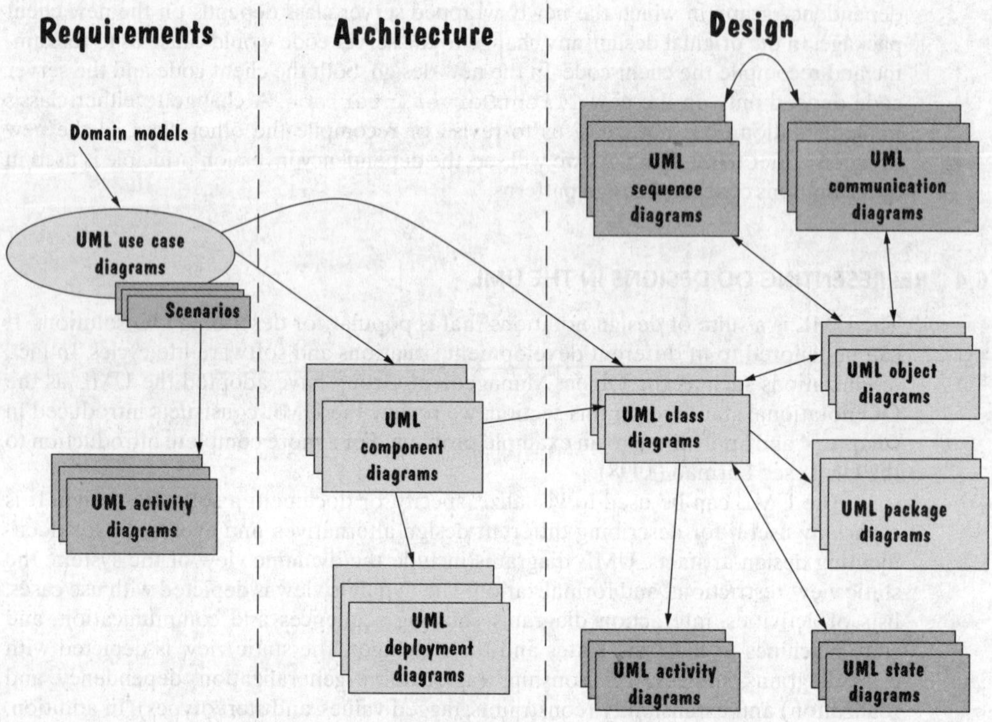

FIGURE 6.16 How the UML is used in the development process.

they become more detailed as design progresses. A set of structure and object diagrams describes how each class is associated with others, including inheritance relationships.

Next, design continues by addressing the dynamic aspects of the system. Initially, the interactions among classes are illustrated using simple **interaction diagrams**: sequence and communication diagrams. **Sequence diagrams**, introduced in Chapter 4, show how messages flow from one object to another, formalizing the informal descriptions of events in the requirements.

Communication diagrams show the same information, but from the context of an object diagram. As understanding improves, we assign responsibilities to individual objects. At this stage, we can use **activity diagrams** as a type of flowchart notation to describe complex operations. In concert with the activity diagrams, we develop **state diagrams** to show all possible states that an object can take, and the conditions under which objects execute their operations. The change from one state to another is triggered by a message (representing an event) that is sent from one object to another. Finally, we group the classes into packages, to make the design more hierarchical and easier to understand, and model the result in a **package diagram**.

In the rest of this section, we use the UML to generate an OO design for the Royal Service Station system, whose requirements are listed in Sidebar 6.4. The corresponding use case diagram, showing the system's essential functionality and the principal **actors** that interact with the system, is shown in Figure 6.17.

SIDEBAR 6.4 ROYAL SERVICE STATION REQUIREMENTS

1. The Royal Service Station provides three types of services to its customers: refueling, vehicle maintenance, and parking. That is, a customer can add fuel to the tank of his or her vehicle (car, motorcycle, or truck), can have the vehicle repaired, or can park the vehicle in the station parking lot. A customer has the option to be billed automatically at the time of purchase (of fuel, maintenance, or parking) or to be sent a monthly paper bill. In either case, customers can pay using cash, credit card, or personal check. Royal Service Station fuel is sold according to price per gallon, depending on whether the fuel is diesel, regular, or premium. Service is priced according to the cost of parts and labor. Parking is sold according to daily, weekly, and monthly rates. The prices for fuel, maintenance services, parts, and parking may vary; only Manny, the station manager, can enter or change prices. At his discretion, Manny may designate a discount on purchases for a particular customer; this discount may vary from one customer to another. A 5% local sales tax applies to all purchases.
2. The system must track bills on a month-to-month basis and the products and services provided by the gas station on a day-to-day basis. The results of this tracking can be reported to the station manager upon request.
3. The station manager uses the system to control inventory. The system will warn of low inventory and automatically order new parts and fuel.
4. The system will track credit history and send warning letters to customers whose payments are overdue. Bills are sent to customers on the first day of the month after the purchases are made. Payment is due on the first day of the succeeding month. Any bill not paid within 90 days of the billing date will result in cancellation of the customer's credit.
5. The system applies only to regular repeat customers. A regular repeat customer means a customer identified by name, address, and birthdate who uses the station's services at least once per month for at least six months.
6. The system must handle the data requirements for interfacing with other systems. A credit card system is used to process credit card transactions for products and services. The credit card system uses the card number, name, expiration date, and amount of the purchase. After receiving this information, the credit card system confirms that the transaction is approved or denied. The parts ordering system receives the part code and number of parts needed. It returns the date of parts delivery. The fuel ordering system requires a fuel order description consisting of fuel type, number of gallons, station name, and station identification code. It returns the date when the fuel will be delivered.

7. The system must record tax and related information, including tax paid by each customer, as well as tax per item.
8. The station manager must be able to review tax records upon demand.
9. The system will send periodic messages to customers, reminding them when their vehicles are due for maintenance. Normally, maintenance is needed every six months.
10. Customers can rent parking spaces in the station parking lot on a day-to-day basis. Each customer must request from the system an available parking space. The station manager can view a monthly report summarizing how many parking spaces were available or occupied.
11. The system maintains a repository of account information, accessible by account numbers and by customer name.
12. The station manager must be able to review accounting information upon demand.
13. The system can report an analysis of prices and discounts to the station manager upon request.
14. The system will automatically notify the owners of dormant accounts. That is, customers who did not make service station purchases over a two-month period will be contacted.
15. The system cannot be unavailable for more than 24 hours.
16. The system must protect customer information from unauthorized access.

UML Class Diagram

To see how the UML can be used, consider the system design of the Royal Service Station system. For simplicity, assume that the Royal Service Station consists of a single component, and thus is small enough not to warrant an architectural design. Then, we can generate a modular system design directly from the requirements in Sidebar 6.4. We begin with UML class diagrams. These diagrams describe the object types and their static relationships. In particular, we want to depict associations among objects (e.g., a customer is associated with a bill) and relationships between types and subtypes (e.g., diesel fuel is a subtype of type fuel). We want the diagrams to illustrate the attributes of each object, their individual behaviors, and the restrictions on each class or object.

The design process starts with a statement of the requirements. We try to extract nouns, looking for particular items that can suggest our first cut at object classes. We seek

- actors
- physical objects
- places
- organizations
- records
- transactions
- collections of things

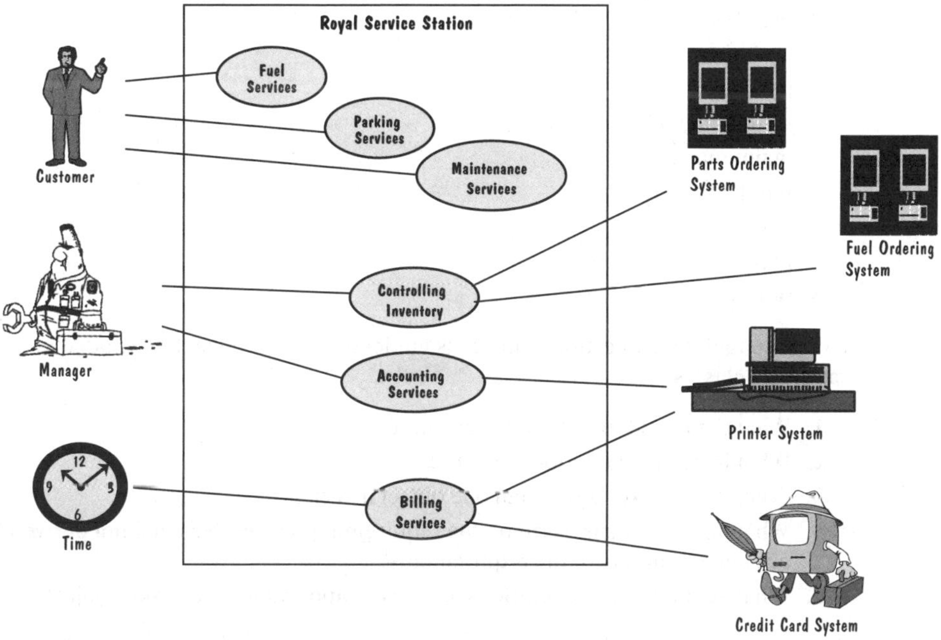

FIGURE 6.17 Use case diagram of the Royal Service Station system.

- operating procedures
- things that are manipulated by the system to be built

For example, consider this part of the first Royal Service Station requirement:

> A customer has the option to be billed automatically at the time of purchase (of fuel, maintenance, or parking) or to be sent a monthly paper bill. In either case, customers can pay using cash, credit card, or personal check. Royal Service Station fuel is sold according to price per gallon, depending on whether the fuel is diesel, regular, or premium. Service is priced according to the cost of parts and labor. Parking is sold according to daily, weekly, and monthly rates. The prices for fuel, maintenance services, parts, and parking may vary; only Manny, the station manager, can enter or change prices. At his discretion, Manny may designate a discount on purchases for a particular customer; this discount may vary from one customer to another. A 5% local sales tax applies to all purchases.

From this requirements statement, we can extract several tentative classes:

- personal check
- services
- paper bill
- discounts
- credit card

- tax
- customer
- parking
- station manager
- maintenance
- purchase
- cash
- fuel
- prices

The following questions can act as guidelines for what can be included in a list of candidate classes:

1. What data need to be "processed" in some way?
2. What items have multiple attributes?
3. When do we have more than one object in a class?
4. What information is based on the requirements themselves, and not derived from our understanding of the requirements?
5. What attributes and operations are always applicable to a class or object?

Answering these questions can help us to group the candidate classes and objects, as shown in Table 6.1.

Next, we examine other requirements to see what they add to our existing table of attributes and classes. For example, the fifth requirement states that,

> The system applies only to regular repeat customers. A regular repeat customer means a customer identified by name, address, and birthdate who uses the station's services at least once per month for at least six months.

Similarly, the ninth requirement says,

> The system will send periodic messages to customers, reminding them when their vehicles are due for maintenance. Normally, maintenance is needed every six months.

Thus, we have new candidate classes, such as regular repeat customer, name, address, and periodic messages. We can revise Table 6.1 as Table 6.2 to reflect this. However,

TABLE 6.1 Initial Grouping of Attributes and Classes: Step 1

Attributes	Classes
Personal check	Customer
Tax	Maintenance
Price	Services
Cash	Fuel
Credit card	Bill
Discounts	Purchase
	Station manager

TABLE 6.2 Initial Grouping of Attributes and Classes: Step 2

Attributes	Classes
Personal check	Customer
Tax	Maintenance
Price	Services
Cash	Parking
Credit card	Fuel
Discounts	Bill
Name	Purchase
Address	Maintenance reminder
Birthdate	Station manager

"regular repeat customer" is redundant, so we can leave it out. For the full set of requirements, we might expand our table to include all of the classes in Table 6.3.

Next, we identify behaviors that must be described in our design. From the requirements statements, we extract verbs. Again, we can look for particular items that suggest behaviors:

- imperative verbs
- passive verbs
- actions
- membership in
- management or ownership
- responsible for
- services provided by an organization

TABLE 6.3 Initial Grouping of Attributes and Classes: Step 3

Attributes	Classes
Personal check	Customer
Tax	Maintenance
Price	Services
Cash	Parking
Credit card	Fuel
Discounts	Bill
Name	Purchase
Address	Maintenance reminder
Birthdate	Station manager
	Overdue bill letter
	Dormant account warning
	Parts
	Accounts
	Inventory
	Credit card system
	Part ordering system
	Fuel ordering system

The behaviors will become actions or responsibilities taken by a class or object, or actions done to a class or object. For example, billing a customer is a behavior. The behavior is performed by part of the Royal Service Station system (i.e., the Royal Service Station system is responsible for billing), and the billing affects the customer.

To make it easier to manage the objects, classes, and behaviors, we use a UML diagram to describe their relationships. We can draw class boxes for our initial design for the Royal Service Station. Figure 6.18 shows the 17 classes we think we will need for our OO representation of a solution. Recall from Chapter 4 that the top segment of each box contains the class name, the middle segment lists the class's attributes, and the bottom segment lists the class's methods. Figure 6.19 summarizes the UML notation for denoting specific types of relationships between classes.

Let us examine our first attempt at a solution to the Royal Service Station problem. By comparing our design with the requirements in Sidebar 6.4, we see that the class diagram can be improved substantially. First, we can add an abstract `Message` class that combines the commonalities of the various types of letters and warnings. Similarly, we can create an abstract `Services` class that generalizes the different types of services (`Fuel`, `Maintenance`, and `Parking`) that the station offers. By creating the abstract classes, we take advantage of the polymorphism afforded by object orientation. For example, the `price()` method is common among all service classes, but the actual computation can be different, depending on which service is being purchased.

We can simplify the design by deleting the classes that depict adjacent systems—`Credit Card System`, `Part-Ordering System`, and `Fuel-Ordering System`—since they are outside of the boundary of our system. We can also remove the `Station Manager` class, because it is not related to any other classes.

The location of `discount` as an attribute of the `Purchase` class is inappropriate. The discount rate depends on the service being discounted as well as on the customer (who can be derived from the associated `Purchase` class). Thus, it is more appropriate to model `discount` as an association class.

There are other problems with our initial design: the service classes `Maintenance`, `Fuel`, and `Parking` are components of both the `Purchase` class and the `Inventory` class, and no object instance would ever simultaneously be a component of both the `Purchase` class and the `Inventory` class. Moreover, the information we need to maintain about the inventory is different from the information we are tracking about purchases. Thus, it is appropriate to represent these concepts as separate classes, keeping in mind that each purchase has an effect on the inventory. The resulting design is illustrated in Figure 6.20.

We need not stop here. By scrutinizing the second design further, we find that we can add a `Vehicle` class so that maintenance records and notifications are associated with vehicles being maintained. We also need operations to generate the reports and the reviewing capabilities described in the requirements. For example, the `Account` class requires an operation to allow the station manager to review account information on demand. Because such analyses apply to all objects of a class, rather than to individual objects, we mark them as being **class-scoped** by underlining the method names. Similarly, the tax rate in the `Purchase` class is a class-scope attribute: all purchases use the same tax rate. Finally, we add cardinality to the diagram, so that we have a better

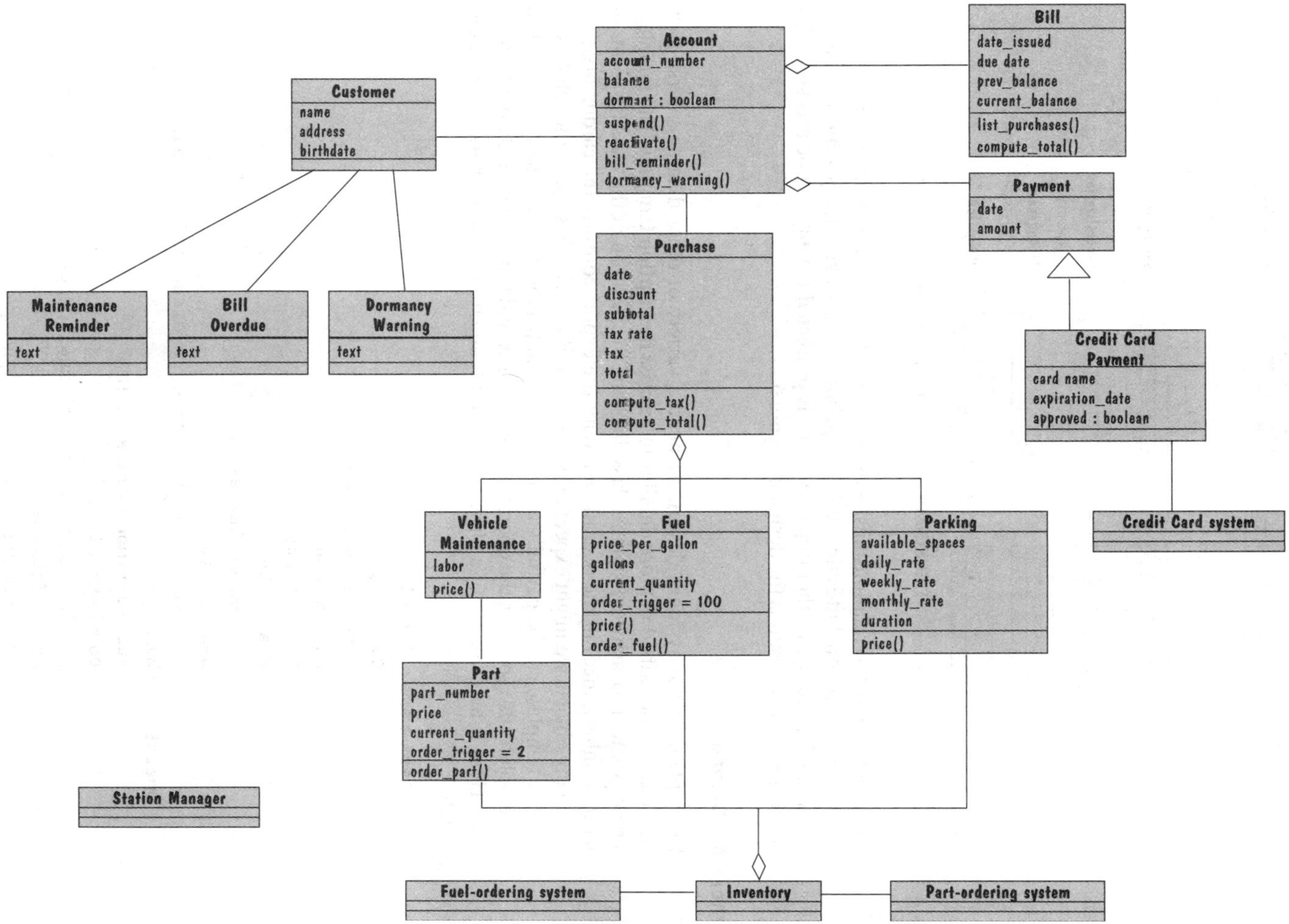

FIGURE 6.18 First cut at Royal Service Station design.

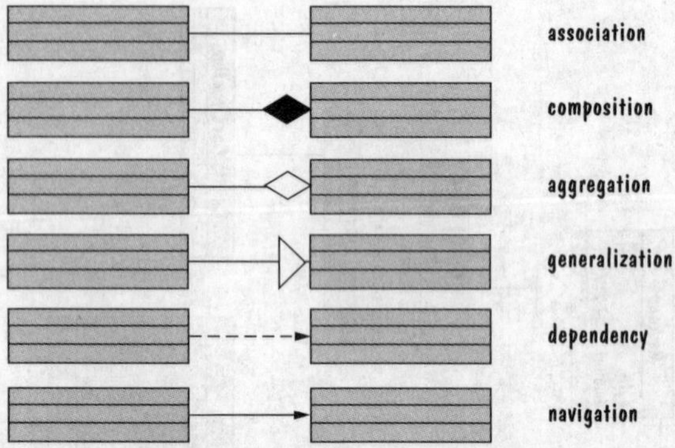

FIGURE 6.19 Types of class relationships.

understanding of the relationships between pairs of classes; at the same time, we indicate whether each attribute and method is **public**ly accessible (+), is **private** and cannot be accessed directly by other objects (−), or is **protected** (#) and can be accessed only by subclasses. The result is the design in Figure 6.21.

Other UML Diagrams

To supplement our system's design, we need a variety of other diagrams. First, each class must be described in more detail using a **class description template**. The template repeats some information from the class diagram: the position of the class (in terms of depth of inheritance) in the overall hierarchy, the export controls, the cardinality (i.e., how many objects we might expect in the class), and associations with other classes. In fact, the template can be partially generated automatically from the class diagram. But the template also specifies the operations in the class, and their public and private interfaces. Here is an example of a class description template for the `Refuel` class in our design:

```
Class name: Refuel
        Category: service
        External documents:
        Export control: Public
        Cardinality: n
        Hierarchy:
            Superclasses: Service
        Associations:
            <no rolename>: fuel in association updates
Operation name: price
        Public member of: Refuel
        Documentation:
            // Calculates fuel final price
        Preconditions:
            gallons > 0
```

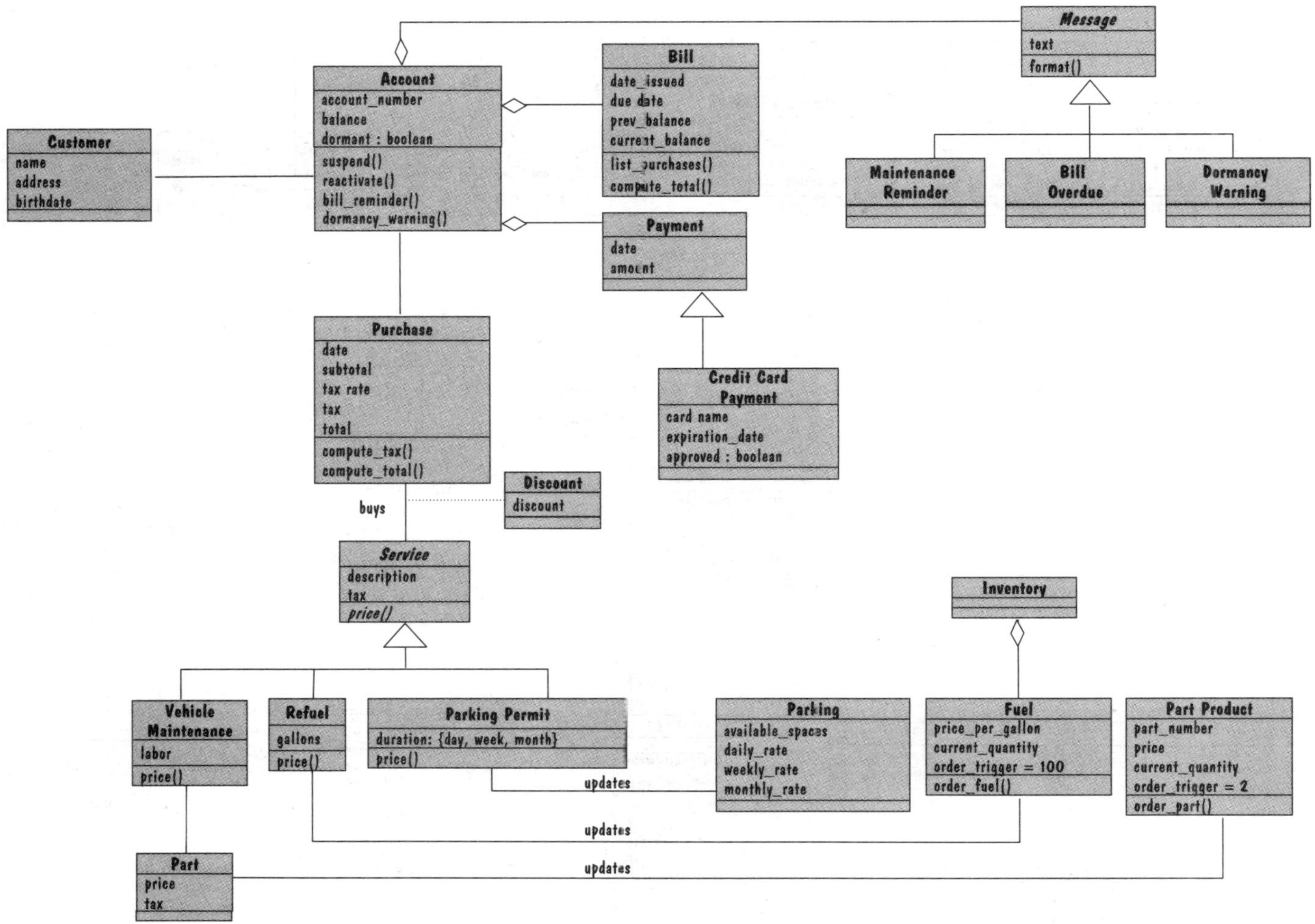

FIGURE 6.20 Second cut at Royal Service Station design.

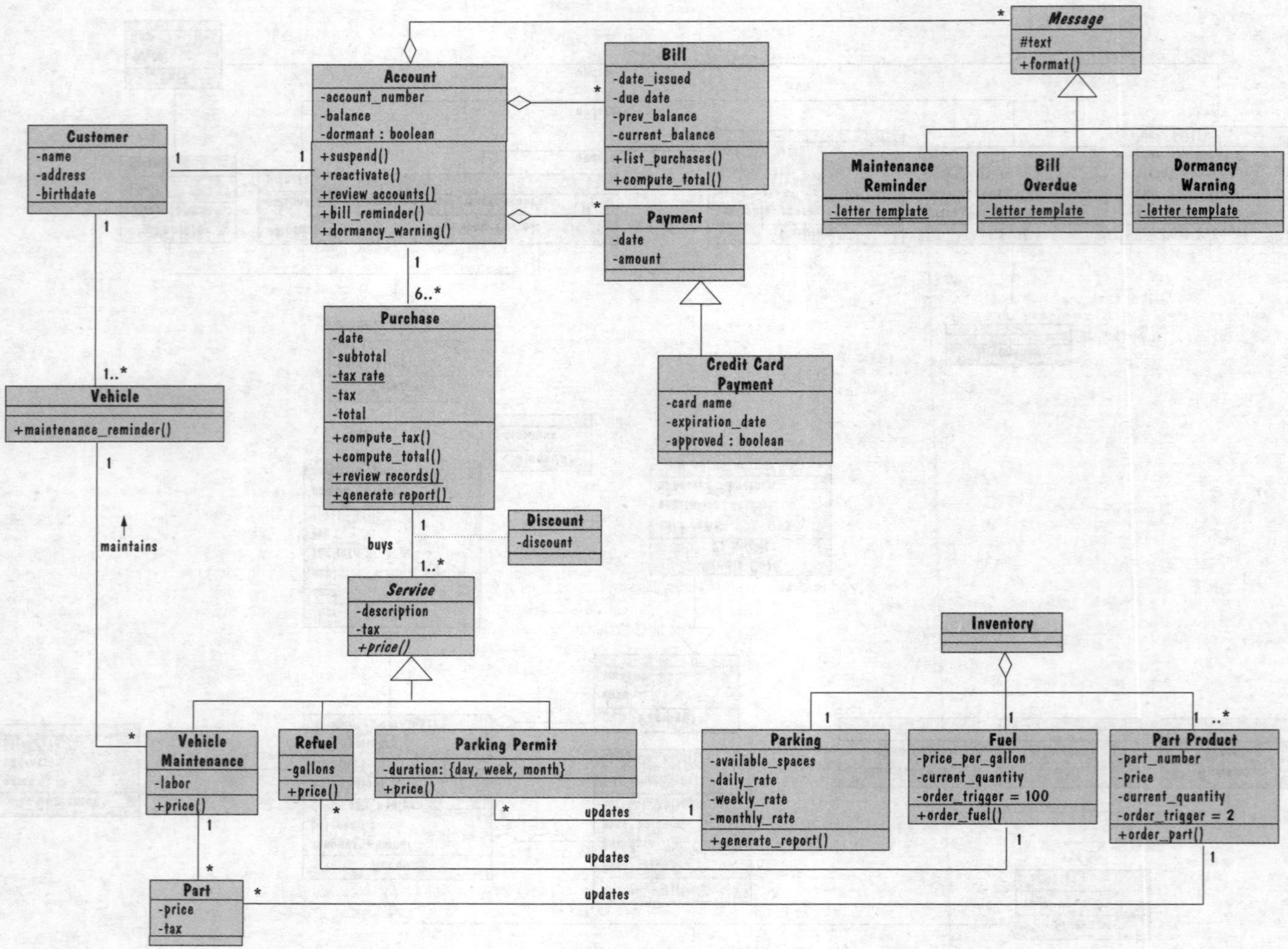

FIGURE 6.21 Third and final cut at Royal Service Station design.

```
            Object diagram: (unspecified)
        Semantics:
            price = gallons * fuel.price_per_gallon
            tax = price * purchase.tax_rate
            Object diagram: (unspecified)
        Concurrency: sequential
    Public interface:
        Operations:
            price
    Private interface:
        Attributes:
            gallons
    Implementation:
        Attributes:
            gallons
    State machine: no
    Concurrency: sequential
    Persistence: transient
```

Notice that the class description template lays the groundwork for the program design. In other words, the class description template includes information essential for programmers to implement the design as code. For example, the template contains formulas to be used in the class's operations and separates the public from the private interfaces. A **private interface** to a class is a mechanism that restricts access to class members; other objects cannot see the attributes or (some) methods for that class. A **public interface** allows access to some methods, but not to attributes, since a public attribute would violate the principle of encapsulation.

UML **package diagrams** allow us to view the system as a small collection of packages, each of which can be expanded to a larger set of classes. The package diagrams show the dependencies among classes that belong to different packages. We say that two items are **dependent** if changes to the definition of one may cause changes to the other. For example, two classes may be dependent if one class sends a message to the other, one class has data needed by another class, or one class uses another as a parameter in performing an operation. In particular, two packages are **dependent** if there is a dependency between a class in each of the packages. As with any good design, we want to minimize unnecessary coupling; thus, we want to keep dependencies to a minimum.

Packages and their dependencies are especially important during testing. As we will see in Chapters 8 and 9, we must design test cases to account for the different possible interactions among components. UML package diagrams help us to understand the dependencies and create our test cases. Figure 6.22 is an example of a UML package diagram for the Royal Service Station. In the figure, there are five major packages: accounting, transactions, services, inventory, and messages. Each of the packages is composed of classes from the design in Figure 6.21. For instance, the `Services` package consists of five key classes: `Service`, `Refuel`, `Vehicle Maintenance`, `Parking Permit`, and maintenance `Part`; the contents of the `Services` package are depicted in the figure to illustrate the connection between classes and packages but

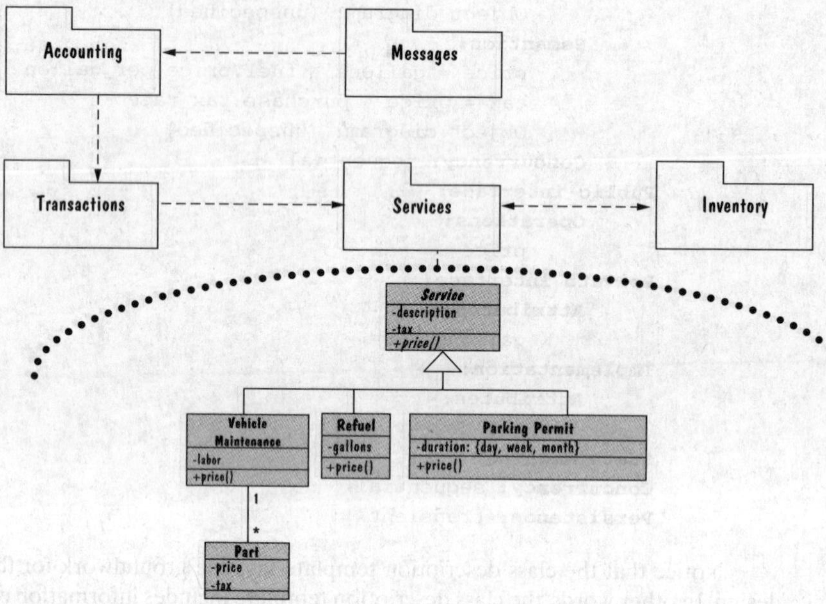

FIGURE 6.22 Package diagram for the Royal Service Station.

would not ordinarily be included in a package diagram. The dashed arrows show the package dependencies. For instance, the `Accounting` package depends on the `Transactions` package. As you can see, the package diagram gives a high-level overview of the system and highlights the high-level dependencies.

To model dynamic behavior, we create **interaction diagrams** that describe how operations and behaviors are realized by the objects in the design. We usually generate one interaction diagram for each use case to identify the exchange of messages between the system and the external actors that typically occur in that use case.

There are two kinds of interaction diagrams: sequence and communication. A **sequence diagram** shows the sequence in which activities or behaviors occur. An object is depicted as a box at the top of a vertical line, known as the object's **lifeline**. A narrow box on the lifeline indicates a period of time when the object is actively computing, usually in response to a received message. An arrow between two lifelines represents a message between the two objects, and it is labeled with the message's name and sometimes with the condition that must be met for the message to be sent. An asterisk on the arrow indicates that the message is sent many times, to several different receiving objects. When the message arrow loops back to its starting box on the same object, the object is sending a message to itself. Figure 6.23 is an example of a sequence diagram for the Royal Service Station, showing the use case for the `Refuel` class.

A **communication diagram** also depicts a sequence of messages between objects, but it is superimposed on an object model and uses the links between objects as implicit communication channels. As with sequence diagrams, the objects are icons, and arrows are used to depict the messages. However, unlike sequence diagrams, the sequence of

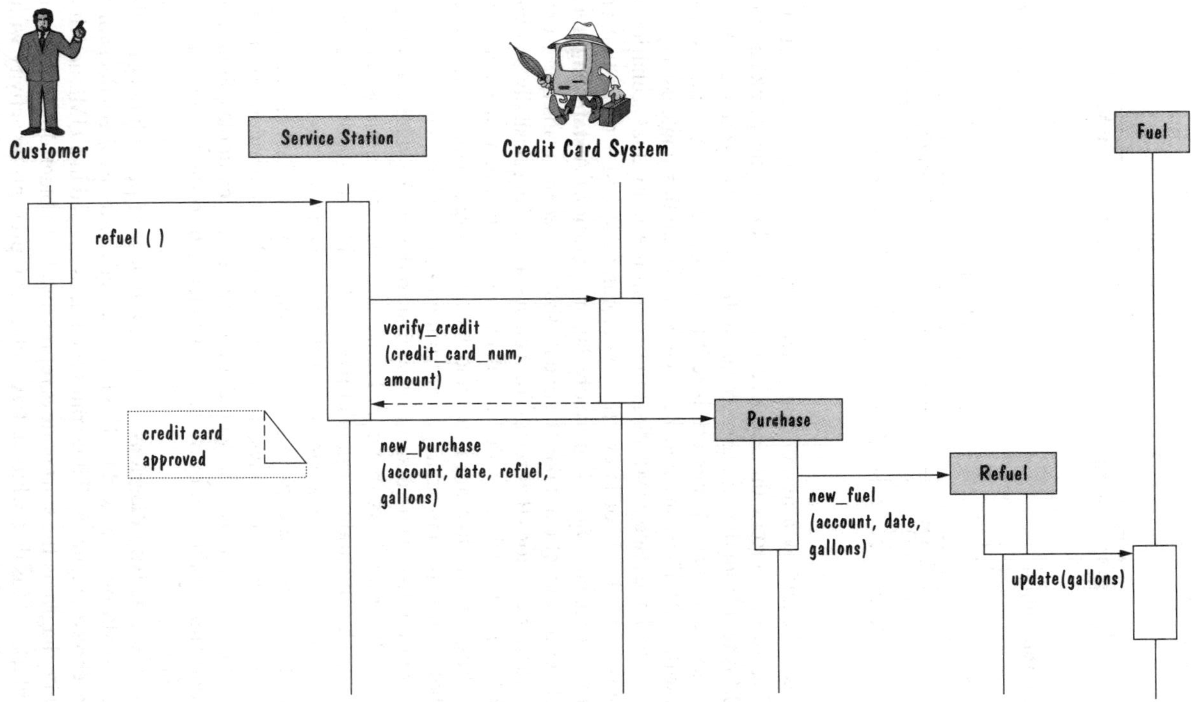

FIGURE 6.23 Sequence diagram for the `Refuel` use case.

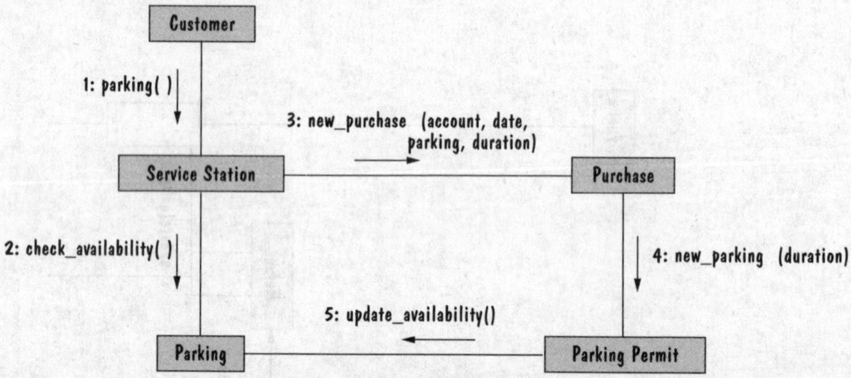

FIGURE 6.24 Communication diagram for the `Parking` use case.

messages is indicated by a numbering scheme. For example, the communication diagram in Figure 6.24 shows the `Parking` use case. First, the `parking()` message, labeled "1," is sent from the `Customer` class to the `Service station` class. Then, the `check_availability()` message is sent from `Service station` to `Parking`; it is labeled with a "2." There are five messages sent within this single use case.

So far, we have used UML diagrams to capture individual scenarios. The UML supports two more kinds of interaction diagrams, state and activity, that are used to model the dynamic behavior of entire objects or operations. A **state diagram** shows the possible states an object can take, the events that trigger the transition from one state to the next, and the actions that result from each state change. Usually, an object state is related to a set of attribute values, and events occur when messages are sent or received. Thus, a state diagram is needed only for classes where the objects exhibit dynamic behavior with many changing attribute values and messages.

The notation for a state diagram is similar to that of the state transition diagrams introduced in Chapter 4. As shown in Figure 6.25, the start node is represented by a black dot, and the end node is a smaller black dot inside a white dot. A rectangle represents a state, with an arrow showing a transition from one state to another. A condition is noted with a bracketed expression next to an arrow. For instance, if no payment is made to an account within 90 days, the account becomes delinquent. We can now build state diagrams for the Royal Service Station classes. As examples, Figure 6.25 shows the state diagram for the `Account` class and Figure 6.26 shows the state diagram for the `Fuel` class.

We can use **activity diagrams** to model the flow of procedures or activities in a class. When conditions are used to decide which activity to invoke, a decision node represents the choices. Figure 6.27 illustrates the notation used in a UML activity diagram. As with state diagrams, the start node is represented by a black dot, and the end node is a smaller black dot inside a white dot. A rectangle represents an activity, with an arrow showing transitions from one activity to another. In this example, after activity B is performed, a decision must be made. If one condition is satisfied, X is output to some other class. Otherwise, activity C or D (or both) is invoked. The long horizontal bar above

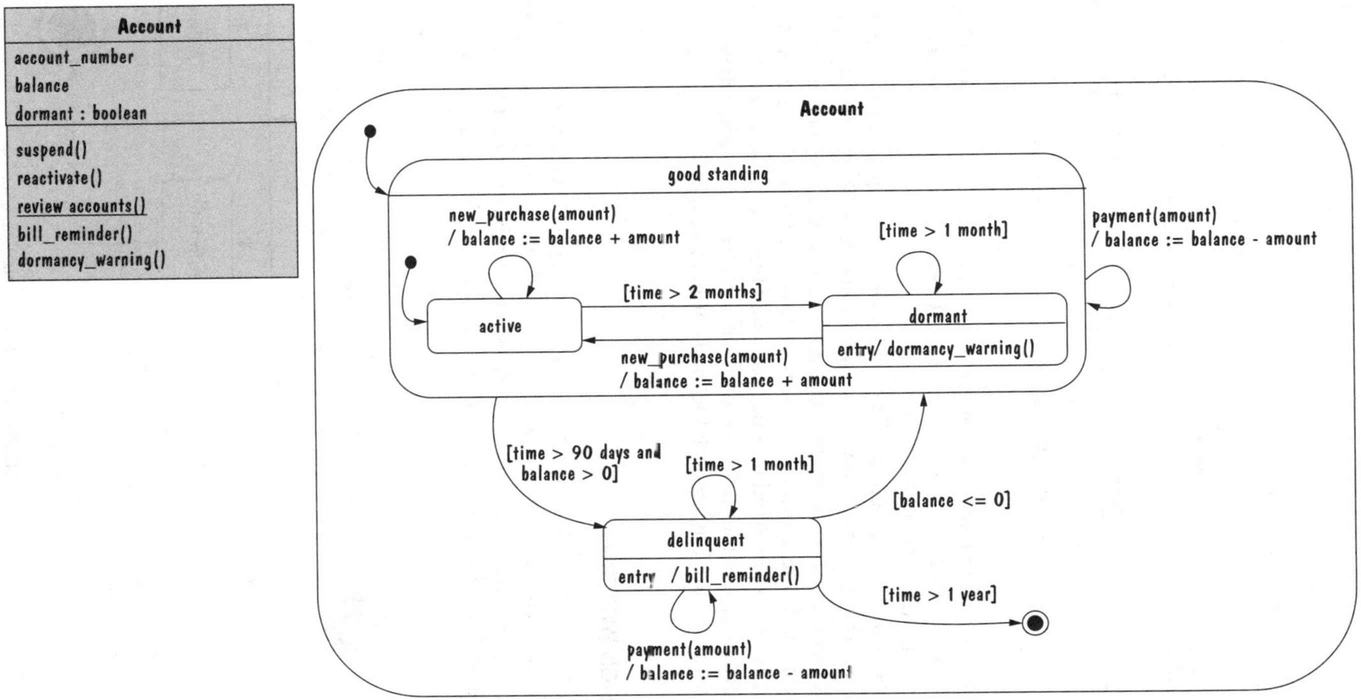

FIGURE 6.25 State diagram for the `Account` class.

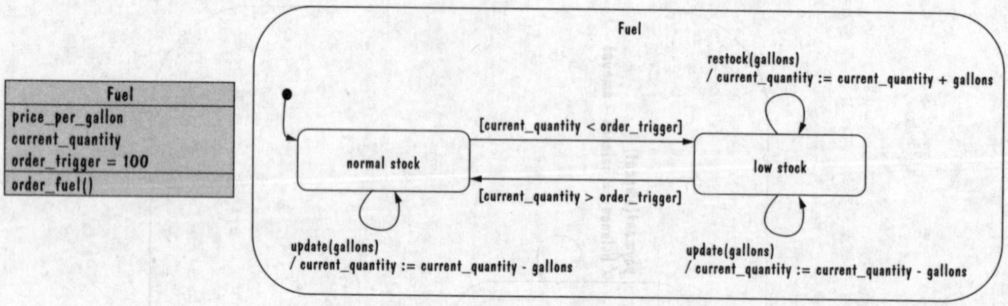

FIGURE 6.26 State diagram for the `Fuel` class.

activities C and D indicates that a message from one activity (in this case, B) can be broadcast to other activities (in this case, C and D). Then C and D are invoked separately, serially, or in parallel.

We can draw an activity diagram for the `Inventory` task of reordering supplies whenever the stock runs low. As shown in Figure 6.28, the activity diagram may have two decisions: one to verify that there is enough fuel, and another to verify that parts are in stock. If the inventory is short of either of these, the activity diagram indicates that activities are invoked to order parts and fuel. Notice that the horizontal bar allows both ordering activities to be initiated. This situation may arise when the station is busy and customers are buying both fuel and automotive parts.

6.5 OO DESIGN PATTERNS

As we can see from our experience with the Royal Service Station system, design is an inherently creative activity in which we iteratively devise potential solutions and then evaluate them. We have explored several design principles that act as criteria for assessing design decisions, thereby helping us evaluate design quality and choose among

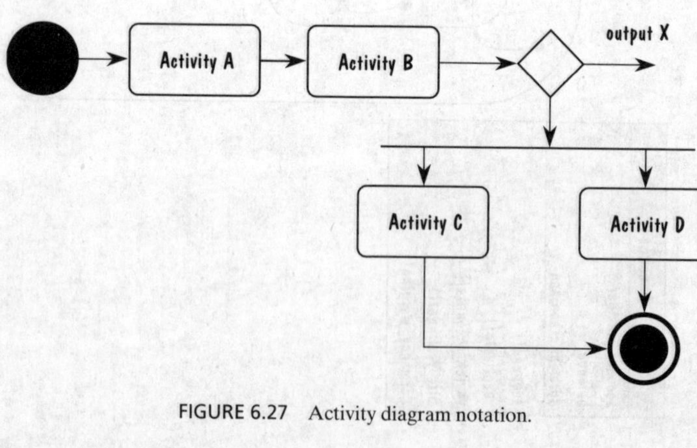

FIGURE 6.27 Activity diagram notation.

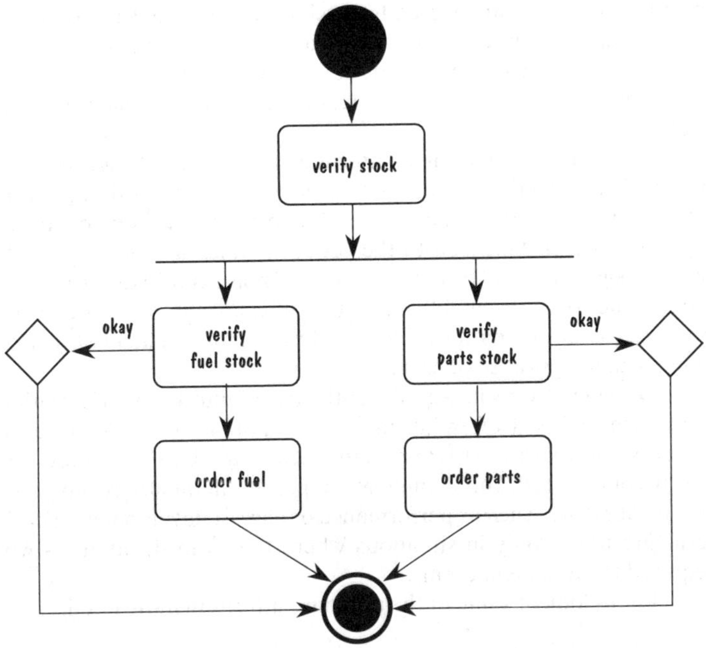

FIGURE 6.28 Activity diagram for `Inventory` operation.

competing design alternatives. While extremely useful, these principles provide no prescriptive advice about creating or refining our designs. In fact, no design aids can provide such advice. Instead, we can study examples of good designs and try to apply their lessons to creating and evaluating our own designs. Just as we can read high-quality literature to improve our vocabulary and writing skills, so too can we examine superior designs to improve our own design skills. The richer our design knowledge and experience become, the more we can draw ideas from them when we are presented with a new problem to solve.

When learning how to build physical structures, students of architecture learn to use collections of architectural patterns as the basic building blocks of new designs. In the same way, we can use a collection of *design patterns* to help us build a new software design. The collection presented by Gamma et al. (1995) is a good place to start. These patterns document design experience that can be studied in isolation. Each pattern can be adapted for reuse in new contexts. In fact, it was not until the software development community began to catalogue reusable designs as design patterns, architectural styles, and reference architectures that software engineering gained credibility as a true engineering discipline.

A **design pattern** codifies design decisions and best practices for solving a particular design problem according to design principles, some of which were identified earlier in this chapter. Design patterns are not the same as software libraries; they are not packaged solutions that can be used as is. Rather, they are templates for a solution that must be modified and adapted for each particular use. This adaptation is similar to the way that elementary data structures, such as queues and lists, must be instantiated and specialized for each use. The design patterns provide more specific guidance than design principles do, but they are less concrete and detailed than software libraries or toolkits.

The main goal of design patterns is to improve a design's modularity. In fact, each pattern is designed to encapsulate a particular type of design decision. The decision types vary widely, from the choice of algorithm that implements an operation to the type of object instantiated to the order in which a collection of objects is traversed. Some design patterns structure a design to make future design changes easier to implement. Other patterns enable a program to change its structure or behavior at runtime. The original design patterns identified by Gamma et al. (1995) are listed in Table 6.4, along with the purpose of each.

Design patterns make substantial use of interfaces, information hiding, and polymorphism, and they often introduce a level of indirection in a clever way. Because the patterns add extra classes, associations, and method calls, they sometimes can seem overly complicated. This complexity improves modularity, even at the expense of other quality attributes such as performance or ease of development. For this reason, the patterns are useful only in situations where the extra flexibility is worth the extra cost required to implement them.

Let us look at some of the popular patterns in more detail.

Template Method Pattern

The Template Method pattern aims to reduce the amount of duplicate code among subclasses of the same parent class. It is particularly useful when multiple subclasses have similar but not identical implementations of the same method. The pattern addresses this problem by localizing the duplicate code structure in an abstract class from which the subclasses inherit. To be precise, the abstract class defines a **template method** that implements the common steps of an operation, and declares abstract **primitive operations** that represent the variation points. The template method calls the primitive operations at points where its behavior depends on the object being involved. The subclasses override the primitive operations to realize subclass-specific variations of the template method.

To see how the Template Method pattern works, consider the task of printing a purchase record, including an itemized list of the services purchased, in the Royal Service Station system. Each line item should include a description of the service purchased, the price, and the tax on that item. The code to print an item's description or tax is the same for all types of services, but the computation of an item's price varies greatly among the services. Applying the Template Method pattern, we create a single method, called `list_line_item()`, in the `Services` class that prints the line item fields. This method calls a local abstract method `price()` to print the item's price. Each of the service subclasses overrides the `price()` method to reflect how the price for that service is computed (e.g., the price of a maintenance visit is the sum of the prices of the new automotive parts plus the cost of the labor). Then, when `list_line_item()` is called for a particular object, the price is computed appropriately. The resulting design is shown in Figure 6.29.

TABLE 6.4 Gamma et al. (1995) Design Patterns

Pattern name	Purpose
Creational Patterns	**Class Instantiation**
Abstract factory	Groups collections of dependent objects with a common theme
Builder	Separates construction from representation
Factory method	Creates objects without specifying exact class, deferring instantiation to subclasses
Prototype	Clones an existing object from a prototype
Singleton	Restricts object to one instance with a single point of access
Structural Patterns	**Class and Object Composition**
Adapter	Wraps interface of one object around the incompatible interface of another object, to allow both objects to work together
Bridge	Separates an abstraction from its implementation
Composite	Composes several objects into a tree structure so that they can act uniformly
Decorator	Adds or overrides responsibilities dynamically
Façade	Provides a unified interface to simplify use
Flyweight	Similar objects share data/state to avoid creating and manipulating many objects
Proxy	Provides placeholder for another object to control access
Behavioral Patterns	**Class and Object Communication**
Chain of responsibility	Delegates commands to chain of processing objects, allowing more than one to handle a given request
Command	Creates objects to encapsulate actions and parameters
Interpreter	Implements special language by representing grammar to interpret sentences in the language
Iterator	Accesses objects sequentially without exposing underlying representation
Mediator	Defines an object to encapsulate how a set of objects interact, providing only that object with detailed knowledge of other objects
Memento	Restores an object to its previous state
Observer	Publish/subscribe, allowing several objects to see an event and change state appropriately
State	Object alters its behavior when internal state changes
Strategy	Selects one of a family of algorithms at runtime
Template method	Defines an algorithm skeleton, then subclasses provide concrete behavior
Visitor	Separates algorithm from object structure by putting hierarchy of methods into a separate algorithm object

In this manner, the Template Method pattern provides the operation's skeleton, and the various subclasses fill in the details. This approach allows the subclasses to specialize the steps of an operation rather than overriding the entire operation. It also allows the parent class to limit the degree of variation in subclasses' versions of the method.

Factory Method Pattern

The Factory Method pattern is used to encapsulate the code that creates objects. Normally, we try to construct our designs so that when modules relate to other modules, they rely on interfaces rather than on explicit class types. However, we cannot rely on

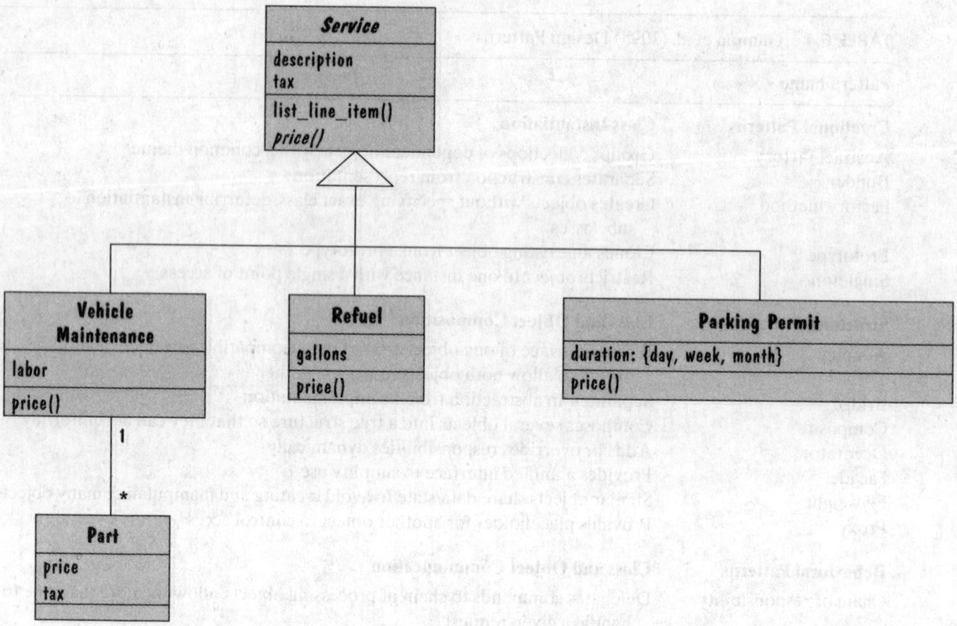

FIGURE 6.29 Application of the Template Method pattern to `price()`.

an interface during object creation; here, the constructor of the appropriate class must be called in order to create an object instance. By encapsulating the object creation code, the rest of our design can rely on abstract types and interfaces.

The Factory Method pattern is similar to the Template Method pattern. In this case, the similar but not identical methods are the constructor methods that instantiate objects. We create an abstract class that defines an abstract constructor method (the Factory Method). The subclasses override the Factory Method to construct specific concrete objects.

Strategy Pattern

The Strategy pattern allows algorithms to be selected at runtime. It is useful when various algorithms are available to an application, but the choice of best algorithm is not known until the application is running. To do this, the pattern defines a family of algorithms; each one is encapsulated as an object, so that they are interchangeable from the application's point of view. The application acts as a client, selecting an algorithm as needed.

For example, suppose that we want to decide at runtime which user-authentication algorithm to use, depending on the login request that we receive (e.g., rlogin vs. ssh request in UNIX). Figure 6.30 shows how we can use the Strategy pattern to support several authentication policies, and to choose from them dynamically. First, we implement each policy as a method of its own class. It is unlikely that the different policies

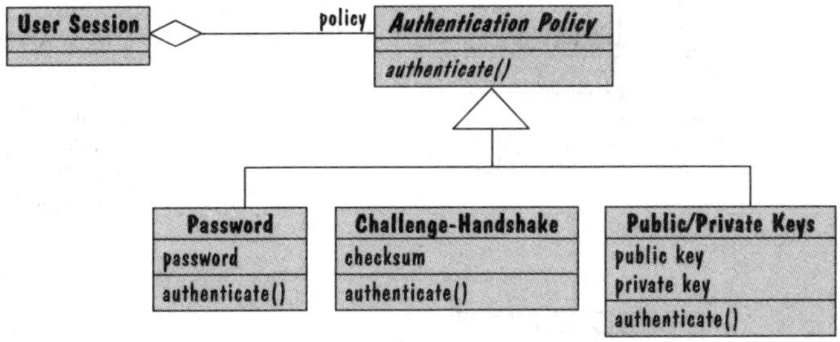

FIGURE 6.30 Application of the Strategy pattern to defer decision on authentication policy.

have the same signatures, but we can simplify the signatures and store the parameters as local member variables. Then, we create an abstract class, `Authentication Policy`, general enough to act as a superclass for all the concrete policy classes. Finally, the `User Session` class has a member variable, policy, of type `Authentication Policy`. This variable can be set to any of the concrete policy objects. Invoking the policy is achieved by executing the variable's method:

```
policy:= new Password(password);
policy.authenticate();
```

Decorator Pattern

The Decorator pattern is used to extend an object's functionality at runtime; it is a flexible alternative to using inheritance at design time to create subclasses that support new features. The key to the Decorator pattern is that each feature that decorates a base class is constructed in such a way that

1. the decorator is a subclass of the object it decorates
2. the decorator contains a reference to the object it decorates

The first property ensures that the decorated object will be accepted wherever the original object is accepted, including as the base for another decorator feature. The second property ensures that each decorator is like a wrapper: it provides new functionality while still including the original object as a component. Thus, successive decorators can be applied to the same object, each one adding a new outer wrapper to the decorated object.

To see how the Decorator pattern works, consider the design of a simple information system for a movie rental company, shown in Figure 6.31. In this example, the base object is an `Account`, and the decorators are various features to which the users can subscribe. The abstract `Decorator` class, as prescribed, is a subclass of the base object `Account`. It also has a member variable named `component` that corresponds to the account being decorated. Each possible feature of an account is a subclass of `Decorator`. A feature is applied by creating an instance of the feature and making its `component` member the account that subscribes to the feature. A second feature is applied by creating that feature object and making its `component` member the already

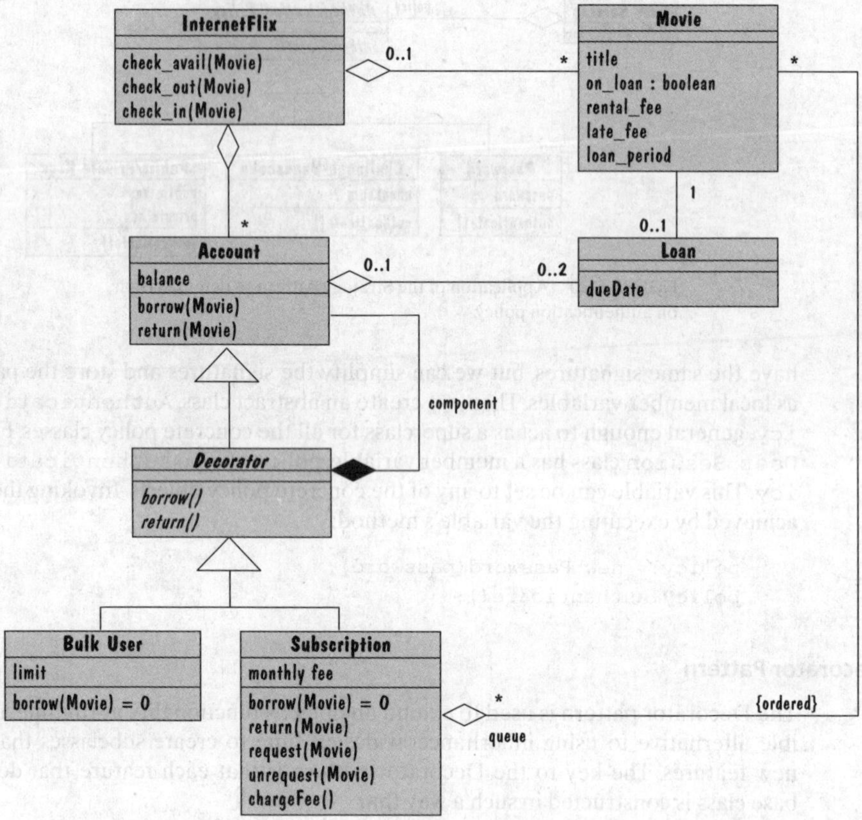

FIGURE 6.31 Application of the Decorator pattern to add features to `Account`.

decorated account. In this way, an account can have any number of decorators applied to it; it can even have the same decorator applied more than once (which makes sense for some features).

Observer Pattern

The Observer pattern is an application of the publish–subscribe architecture style. It is particularly useful when our software needs to notify multiple objects of key events, and we do not want to hard-code into our solution which objects are to be notified.

We can see how the Observer pattern works by examining a simple text editor that offers multiple views of a document being edited. The page being edited might be displayed in the primary window. Miniature thumbprints of several pages may be displayed alongside the edited one, and a toolbar may show metadata about the text (e.g., font family, font size, text color). The views represented by the different windows should be synchronized, so that changes to the text are immediately reflected in the associated thumbprint, and changes to the font size are realized immediately in the text.

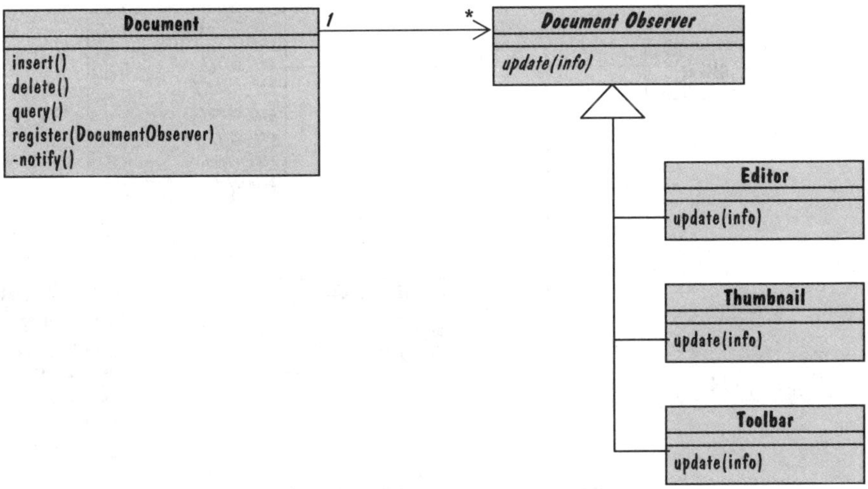

FIGURE 6.32 Application of the Observer pattern to synchronize views in editor.

We could design the system so that each view is explicitly updated whenever the document is changed. But we could employ a more efficient design by having the system publish notifications of updates, and having modules register to receive the notifications. This type of design uses an Observer pattern and is shown in Figure 6.32. There are several important constraints on this design. First, the design needs facilities for registering and notifying observer modules. Second, the observer modules must agree on an interface for the notifications, which is declared in the `Document Observer` abstract class.

Composite Pattern

A **composite object** is a heterogeneous, possibly recursive, collection of objects that represents some composite entity. For example, Figure 6.33 shows a class diagram for mathematical expressions that are modeled as tree-like structures of nodes representing various operators and variable operands. The Composite pattern promotes the use of a single uniform interface that applies to any of the composite object's elements. In Figure 6.33, the abstract class `Expr` provides this interface. This pattern's advantage is that client modules deal only with the new interface; they do not need to know how the composite object's data nodes are structured. Moreover, clients are not affected by changes to the composite object's class structure.

The Composite pattern conflicts with the Liskov Substitutability Principle, because the only way for the composite object's new interface to be uniform is for its set of methods to be the union of all the possible components' methods. As a result, subclasses may inherit meaningless operations. For example, the `Variable` subclass inherits operations to access left and right operand nodes. As such, the Composite pattern emphasizes *uniformity* of composite nodes over *safety* in knowing that each composite element reacts appropriately to any message that it can receive.

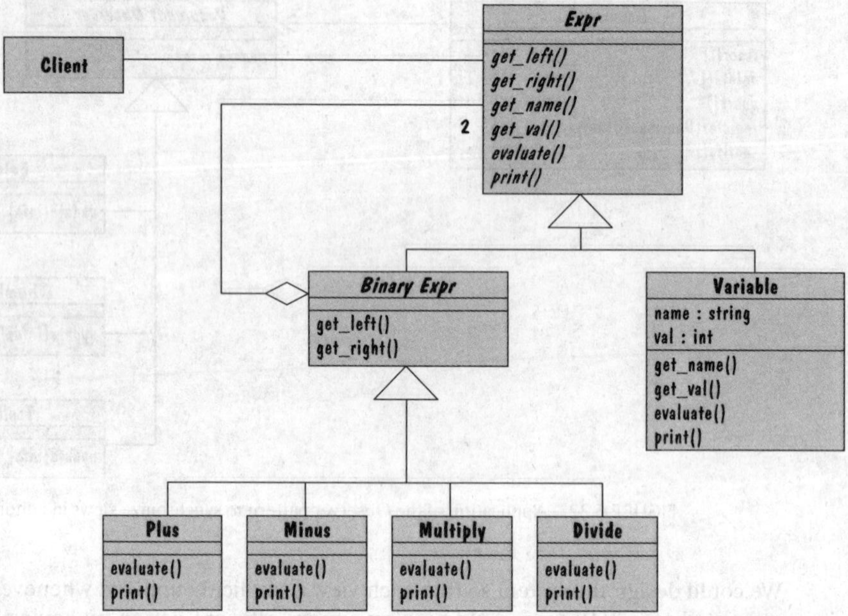

FIGURE 6.33 Application of the Composite pattern to represent mathematical expressions.

Visitor Pattern

Although the Composite pattern reduces coupling between client modules and a composite object, it does nothing to alleviate the task of adding new functions that operate over a composite object. For instance, the operations in Figure 6.33 are distributed over the various components, appearing as methods in each of the component types. Each of these methods contributes a fraction of the overall computation of an operation. Adding a new operation requires adding a new method to every class in the composite object.

The Visitor pattern reduces this problem by collecting and encapsulating these operation fragments into their own classes. Each operation is implemented as a separate subclass of an abstract `Visitor` class, and this subclass has methods that apply the operation to each component type. In addition, each class in the composite object has a single method for performing operations over the composite. In Figure 6.34, this method is named `accept()`. The method takes as a parameter a `Visitor` object that encapsulates the operation being applied.

Figure 6.35 shows how the composite object and visitor objects work together. To evaluate composite expression *e*, we invoke *e*'s `accept()` method, passing an `Evaluation` object as the parameter. The `accept()` method responds by invoking the appropriate `Visitor` method, according to *e*'s class type. For example, the `accept()` method in class `Plus` always calls `VisitPlus()`. The invoked `Visitor` method then operates on *e*. As the operation progresses, the `Visitor` operation is repeatedly passed to the `accept()` methods of various elements in the composite object; those elements call the type-appropriate methods in the `Visitor`; then the type-appropriate methods operate on the elements.

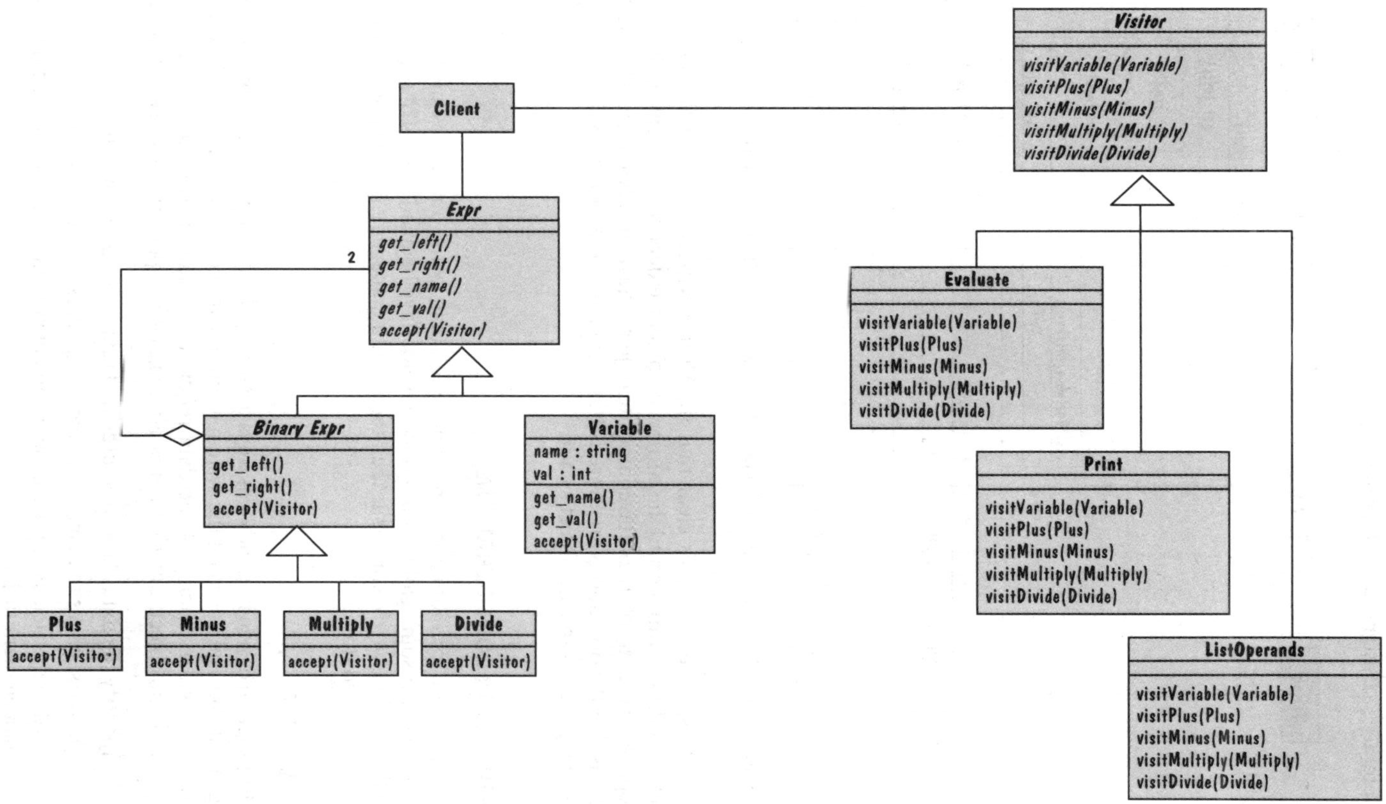

FIGURE 6.34 Application of the Visitor pattern to implement operations over composite.

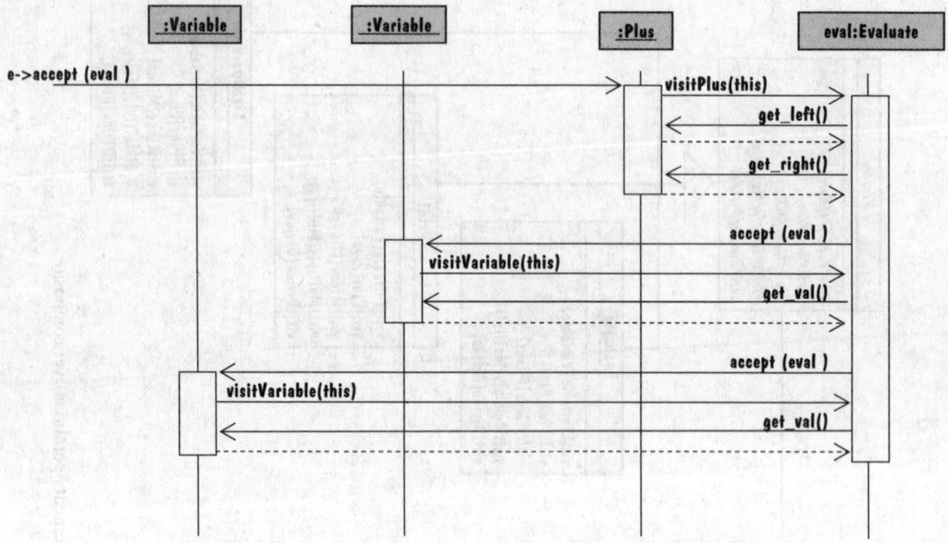

FIGURE 6.35 Execution of the visitor operation `Evaluate()` on expression $e = a + b$.

This example makes clear that the Visitor pattern does not eliminate coupling between the operations and the composite object; indeed, the designs of the operations depend on the structure of the composite object. The main advantage of the Visitor pattern is that the operations are more cohesive, and new operations can be added without touching the composite object's code.

6.6 OTHER DESIGN CONSIDERATIONS

There is more to creating the program design than laying out classes and interfaces. We must consider some global issues that may not have been addressed in the architecture. In this section, we explore issues related to data management, exception handling, user interfaces, and frameworks.

Data Management

The program design must address ways to store and recover persistent objects. Data management takes into account the system requirements concerning performance and space. From our understanding of the data requirements and constraints, we must lay out a design for the objects and for their operations. We can perform this task in four steps:

1. Identify the data, data structures, and relationships among them.
2. Design services to manage the data structures and relationships.
3. Find tools, such as database management systems, to implement some of the data management tasks.
4. Design classes and class hierarchies to oversee the data management functions.

An OO solution can use conventional files or relational databases, but it interfaces most easily with OO databases. To see how, consider the tracking of vehicle maintenance and parts at the Royal Service Station, as shown in Figure 6.36. If we were to use conventional files, we would have to set up a file for each class, and then program links among the files to enable us to perform the tasks required of the system. Using an object-relational database makes our job a bit easier because the structure of our class diagram suggests the database relations that we need to define. As shown in the figure, we must set up tables: one for each class and association in our model. For example, we will need not only a part table and a maintenance table, but also a part-by-vehicle table. In this way, object-oriented or object-relational databases establish a close correspondence between our OO design and the resulting database tables.

Exception Handling

We learned in Chapter 5 to program defensively by proactively identifying exceptions (situations that could cause our software to deviate from its normal behavior) and including exception handling that returns the system to an acceptable state. In practice, a great deal of implemented industrial code is devoted to input validation, error checking, and exception handling. Because embedding this error-checking code within the normal program-application logic distracts from the coherence of the overall functional design, many programming languages support explicit exception handling constructs that help to separate error checking and recovery from the program's main functionality.

Meyer (1992a) provides an example to show how exception handling can be embedded in a design. Suppose we are sending a message over a network. We know

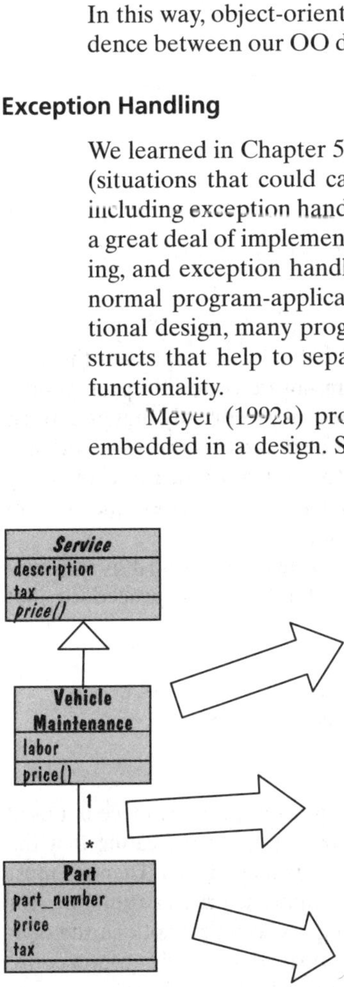

vehicle maintenance	ID	description	tax	labor
	1	oil change	0.25	5
	2	rotate tires	0.25	5
	3	replace timing belt	5	100

Maintenance X part	ID	part_number
	1	1X782
	2	-
	3	F895ERT

part	part_number	price	tax
	1X782	8	.40
	P3291	20 0	10
	E89WWY	34	1.70

FIGURE 6.36 Implementing the classes using an object-relational database.

that if the procedure fails, we want to transmit again, giving up after 100 unsuccessful attempts. We can include this information in our design in the following way:

```
attempt_transmission (message: STRING) raises TRANSMISSIONEXCEPTION
    // Attempt to transmit message over a communication line using the
    // low-level procedure unsafe_transmit, which may fail, triggering an
    // exception.
    // After 100 unsuccessful attempts, give up and raise an exception
local
    failures: INTEGER
try
    unsafe_transmit (message)
rescue
    failures := failures + 1;
    if failures < 100 then
        retry
    else
        raise TRANSMISSIONEXCEPTION
    end
end
```

In the above example, all of the procedure's normal behavior is located in the `try` clause. Alternatively, we could separate safe code from unsafe code, and protect only the unsafe code inside a `try-rescue` construct. This strategy not only makes explicit which aspects of our design are potentially unsafe, but also narrows the scope of anticipated failures; the resulting construction allows us to offer more targeted recovery schemes in the matching `rescue` clause. Notice that one possible recovery mechanism is to raise a new exception to be passed to the calling code.

An effective use of exceptions is to make our programs more robust by weakening modules' preconditions. Consider the following interface for a procedure that performs division:

```
division(dividend,divisor: FLOAT): FLOAT raises DIVIDEBYZEROEXCEPTION
  ensure: if divisor=0 then raise DIVIDEBYZEROEXCEPTION,
          else result = dividend / divisor
```

By using exceptions, we can design the interface with no preconditions. Had we not used exceptions, the above interface would have needed a precondition indicating that the procedure works correctly only if it is called with a nonzero-valued divisor. Then, we must rely on the calling code to not pass an invalid divisor; this approach risks a runtime error if the calling code is negligent or incorrect in its checking. By using exceptions, the division procedure does not need to trust the calling code. Instead, the division procedure checks the value of divisor itself, issuing a clear warning (in the form of a raised exception) back to the caller if there is a problem. However, not all preconditions are so easily checked. For example, it would not be cost effective to check that a list is sorted properly before performing a binary search because the check would take longer than the savings achieved by the binary search; instead, during the search, we could perform sanity checks to confirm that each element encountered is sorted properly with respect to the previous element encountered. In general, exceptions are most useful for eliminating preconditions that can be easily checked.

Designing User Interfaces

Let us look more closely at designing a user interface. We must consider several issues:

- identifying the humans who will interact with the system
- defining scenarios for each way that the system can perform a task
- designing a hierarchy of user commands
- refining the sequence of user interactions with the system
- designing relevant classes in the hierarchy to implement the user-interface design decisions
- integrating the user-interface classes into the overall system class hierarchy

The first step in user-interface design is laying out the interaction on paper. To do this, we determine how paper flows in the existing system; the paper documents may suggest comfortable user interfaces in the automated system. For example, the left-hand side of Figure 6.37 shows the paper bill that Manny uses at the Royal Service Station. Now, to automate his billing process, we may suggest a screen like the one on the right-hand side.

If Manny agrees to the screen design, the next step involves designing one or more classes to implement the screen. We may decide to use the design shown in Figure 6.38. Notice that this design includes classes for an okay button and a text box. These objects are not likely to have entered our initial conversations with Manny when we derived our use cases from his requirements. They reflect our solution, not his problem. It is common for the set of objects and classes to grow as we move through the life cycle from problem understanding to solution generation. This expansion of classes and hierarchy is another important reason to consider design flexibility as we devise our solution.

Frameworks

No one way of designing is best for all situations. The only guideline that applies to all systems is this: design for change. No matter what system we are building, it is likely to change at some time or other. There are many techniques and technologies to help us make the system more flexible and maintainable. For example, **toolkits** are sets of related, reusable classes that provide well-defined sets of functions. Toolkits are much like the subroutine libraries of procedural languages. As such, we may employ a toolkit to build the user interface from buttons and windows rather than write the code anew ourselves.

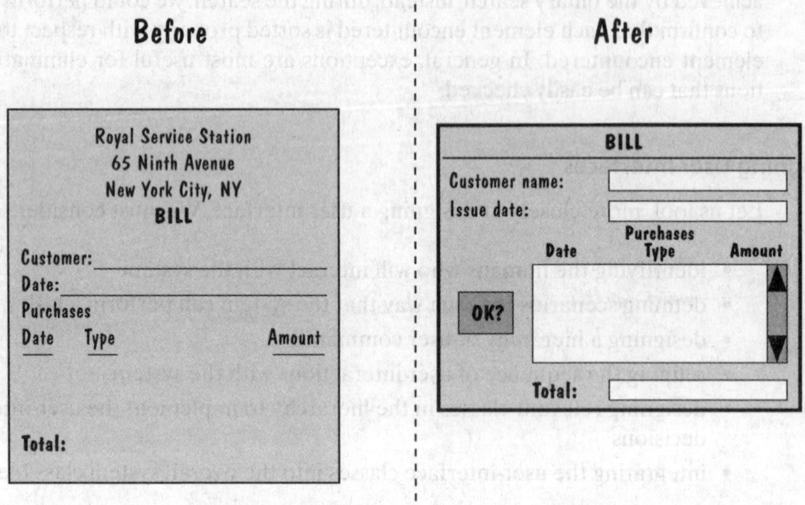

FIGURE 6.37 Transition from paper to screen.

Frameworks and *patterns* are also design aids. They differ from a toolkit in that they are more focused on design reuse than on code reuse. As we saw earlier in this chapter, a pattern is a template of abstract architectural elements that can be used to guide us in generating our design. Every pattern has a context and forces defined with it. The context explains the situations in which the pattern would be appropriate. The forces are elements of the context that vary to some degree. If our situation matches a pattern's forces and context, the pattern is well suited for our application. However, patterns are not as useful if they constrain a design that needs to be flexible.

A **framework** is a large reusable design for a specific application domain. For example, frameworks exist for building graphical editors, web applications,

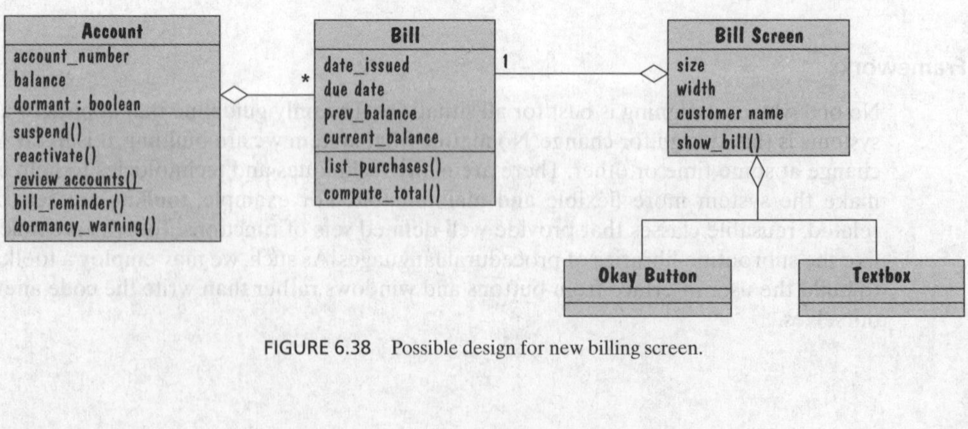

FIGURE 6.38 Possible design for new billing screen.

database-centric systems, accounting systems, and more. A framework often includes a substantial code base that is reused as well. We can think of a framework as a partially completed application missing some lower-level modules; we add modules to the framework to complete and specialize it for a particular application. Unlike software product lines, which are developed by a company for its own use, frameworks tend to be publicly available resources like software libraries and toolkits. Libraries are lower-level software units that we can incorporate into our programs, whereas software frameworks tend to be high-level architectures and modules whose low-level details need to be filled in. The use of frameworks and toolkits makes it easier for nonexperts to implement specialized code and improves the quality of the resulting code.

6.7 OO MEASUREMENT

Once we have an OO design of a system, we want to be able to measure its properties. For example, we have seen that there are desirable characteristics of designs such as low coupling and high cohesion, and that we can measure several aspects of design complexity. We want to measure these kinds of characteristics of OO systems, and we want the measurements to be useful for understanding, control, and prediction. In this section, we look at several kinds of OO measurement.

OO Size Measures

OO systems tend to grow in size as we move from requirements analysis to design to code and test. In this respect, they are no different from systems developed using a different paradigm. However, unlike other paradigms, with an OO approach, we use the same or similar language throughout each stage of the life cycle, making it convenient to measure size in the same terms from a system's inception to its delivery and maintenance.

Researchers have taken advantage of this common vocabulary when measuring size and making predictions based on size. For example, Pfleeger (1991) used objects and methods as a basic size measure in her effort-estimation approach; she found that her method was more accurate than COCOMO in predicting the resulting effort needed to build several OO systems. Olsen (1993) applied this technique to a commercial project, and the estimates were extraordinarily accurate. The advantage of assessing size in the same terms throughout development is clear: the estimation technique can be reapplied during development, and the estimate inputs are directly comparable. In other words, it is easy to see what the initial size is, and to track its growth over the product's life.

Lorenz and Kidd (1994) have described additional OO size measures that offer a finer level of detail. They defined nine aspects of size that reflect not only the general "bulk" of the system but also how the class characteristics affect the product. First, they look at the product in terms of its use cases. Each use case is associated with a scenario that describes a task performed by the system. Lorenz and Kidd count the number of scenario scripts (NSS) in the use cases. They report that this measure is correlated with application size and number of test cases. For this reason, NSS is useful in at least two ways. As a size measure, it can feed an estimation model for predicting project effort or duration. As a test case estimate, it helps the test team prepare test cases and allocate resources for future testing activities.

Next, Lorenz and Kidd count the number of key classes (i.e., domain classes) in the system. This measure is intended to evaluate high-level design, suggesting how much effort is needed to build the system. They also tally the number of support classes, this time targeting low-level design and the likely effort needed. The average number of support classes per key class and the number of subsystems are useful for tracking the structure of the system being developed.

Lorenz and Kidd also define size in terms of an individual class. Class size is the sum of the total number of operations and the number of attributes; here, we count inherited features as well as features defined in the class. In a metric that evaluates the effects of inheritance, they consider not only the class's depth in the inheritance hierarchy (with depth = 1 being the root), they also count the number of operations overridden by a subclass (NOO) as well as the number of operations added by a subclass. From these, they define a specialization index, SI:

$$SI = (NOO \times \text{ depth}) / (\text{total number of class methods})$$

Each of these metrics can be applied during the different stages of development, as shown in Table 6.5. The number of use case scripts and number of key classes can be measured very early, during requirements capture. This type of size measurement is typically more concrete and accurate than the requirements-counting schemes used in more traditional development, pleasing project managers who must allocate resources early.

Let us apply these measures to the Royal Service Station problem. Figure 6.39 shows the overview of our OO analysis of the problem. Reviewing Sidebar 6.4 and the ovals in this figure, we see that there are six ovals, representing the six key use cases we envision for this system. So, using Lorenz and Kidd's metrics, the NSS is equal to 6.

TABLE 6.5 Lorenz and Kidd Metrics Collection in Different Phases of Development

Metric	Phase				
	Requirements Description	System Design	Program Design	Coding	Testing
Number of scenario scripts	X				
Number of key classes	X	X			
Number of support classes			X		
Average number of support classes per key class			X		
Number of subsystems		X	X	X	
Class size		X	X	X	
Number of operations overridden by a subclass		X	X	X	X
Number of operations added by a subclass		X	X	X	
Specialization index		X	X	X	X

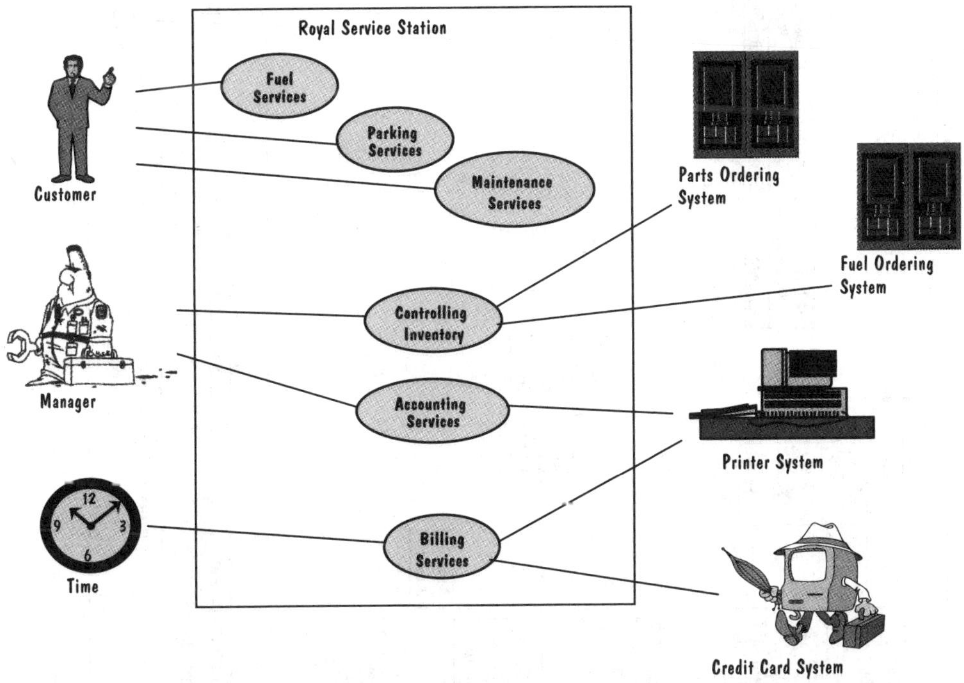

FIGURE 6.39 Use case diagram of the Royal Service Station.

We can calculate some of the remaining measures by referring to the class hierarchy of the system design represented in Figure 6.40. The table at the left of the figure lists the maximum and minimum values for each of the five Lorenz and Kidd metrics derived from this design. We can use these measures as a baseline from which to evaluate growth as the system evolves.

OO Design Quality Measures

Chidamber and Kemerer (1994) have also devised a suite of metrics for OO development. Their work is more focused on design quality than on size, so it complements the work of Lorenz and Kidd. In addition to size measures such as weighted methods per class, depth of inheritance, and number of children, Chidamber and Kemerer measure the coupling between objects, the response for a class, and the lack of cohesion in methods (LCOM). Table 6.6 shows where each of these metrics can be collected and used during development. Because they are widely used and have become a standard to which other OO metrics are compared, let us look more closely at some of the Chidamber–Kemerer metrics.

We noted in Chapter 5 that we can measure aspects of design quality, such as complexity. As we will see in Chapter 11, there are also several ways to measure the complexity of a piece of code. Chidamber and Kemerer leave the definition of complexity open, so

Metric	Min	Max
Number of Key Classes	21	21
Class Size	0	9
Number of Operations Overridden	0	1
Number of Operations Added	0	0
Specialization Index	0	1

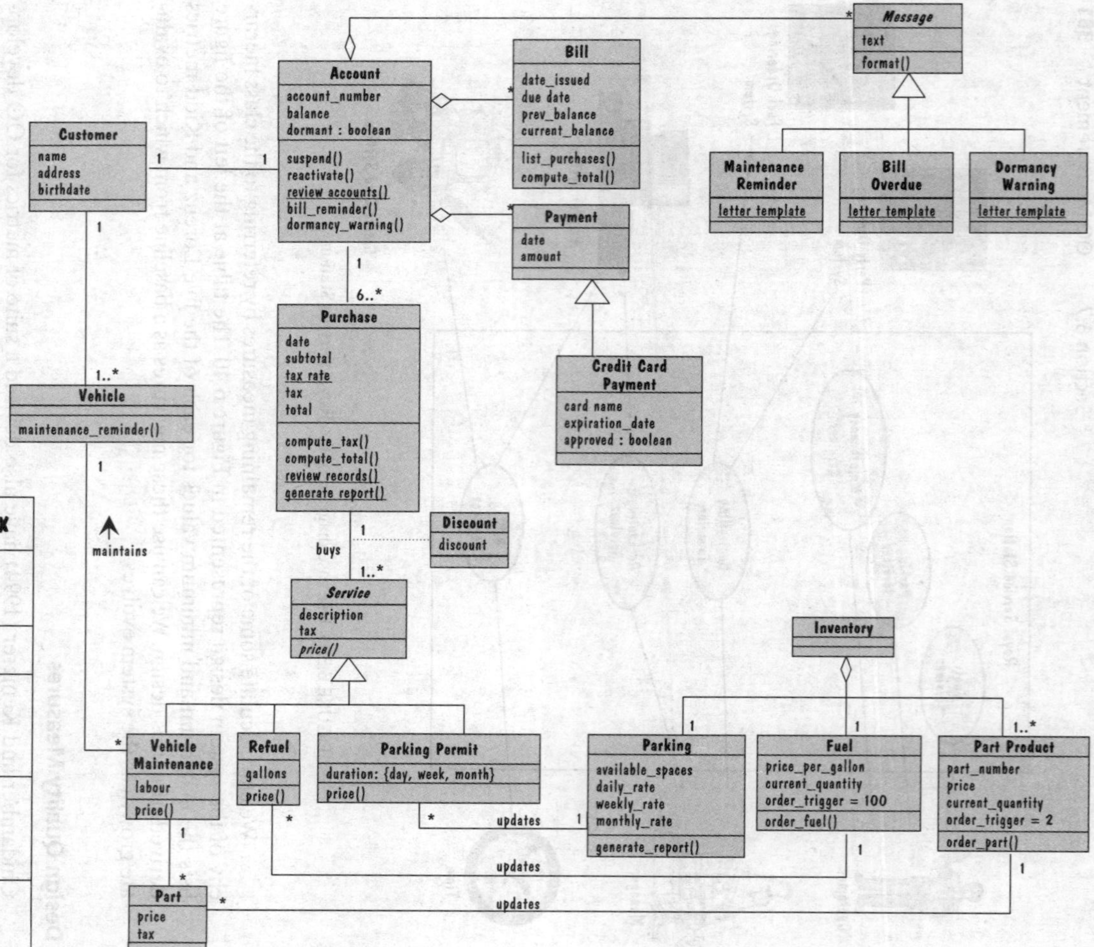

FIGURE 6.40 Class hierarchy for Royal Service Station, plus Lorenz and Kidd measures.

TABLE 6.6 Chidamber and Kemerer Metrics Collection in Different Phases of Development

Metric	System Design	Program Design	Coding	Testing
	Phase			
Weighted methods per class	X	X		X
Depth of inheritance	X	X		X
Number of children	X	X		X
Coupling between objects		X		X
Response for a class		X	X	
Lack of cohesion of methods		X	X	X

that the developers can choose a complexity measure appropriate for the project. Then, Chidamber and Kemerer use the number of methods, n, with the complexity of each method, c, as a weight in defining a weighted complexity measure for classes:

$$\text{weighted methods per class} = \sum_{i=1}^{n} c_i$$

That is, we sum the set of method complexities to find the total complexity for the class. If the complexity of each method is 1, then the complexity is simply the number of methods in the class. The number of methods and the complexity of methods suggest the amount of time and effort needed to build and maintain the class; the larger the number of methods, the more the effort and the greater the impact on the children of the class.

They also consider a class's depth in the inheritance hierarchy (with depth=1 being the root): the deeper a class is in the hierarchy, the more methods it is likely to inherit. This characteristic makes the class harder to understand and harder to maintain. Another metric is the number of immediate subclasses subordinated to the given class. This measure is an indication of the degree of variability of the parent class, and thus is another indicator of the ease of maintenance, testing, and reuse.

We can apply these concepts to the architecture for the Royal Service Station. In Figure 6.41, we see part of the design relating to accounts, bills, and payments. For the `Bill` class, the weighted methods metric is 2, and the depth of inheritance and the number of children are each 0.

The coupling between a `Bill` and other objects is 1, because the `Bill` class is associated only with the account being billed. However, coupling between an `Account` object and associated objects is 5, as we can see from the five arrows entering or leaving the box representing that class. As we noted earlier in this chapter, excessive coupling in any design is undesirable; we want to maximize the independence of each class, so that it is easier to develop, maintain, test, and reuse.

Calculating the degree of cohesion in methods is more complicated. Consider a given class C with n methods, M_1 through M_n. Suppose I_j is the set of instance variables used by the method M_j. Then there are n such sets, one for each of the n methods. We can define P to be a collection of pairs (I_r, I_s) where I_r and I_s share no common members,

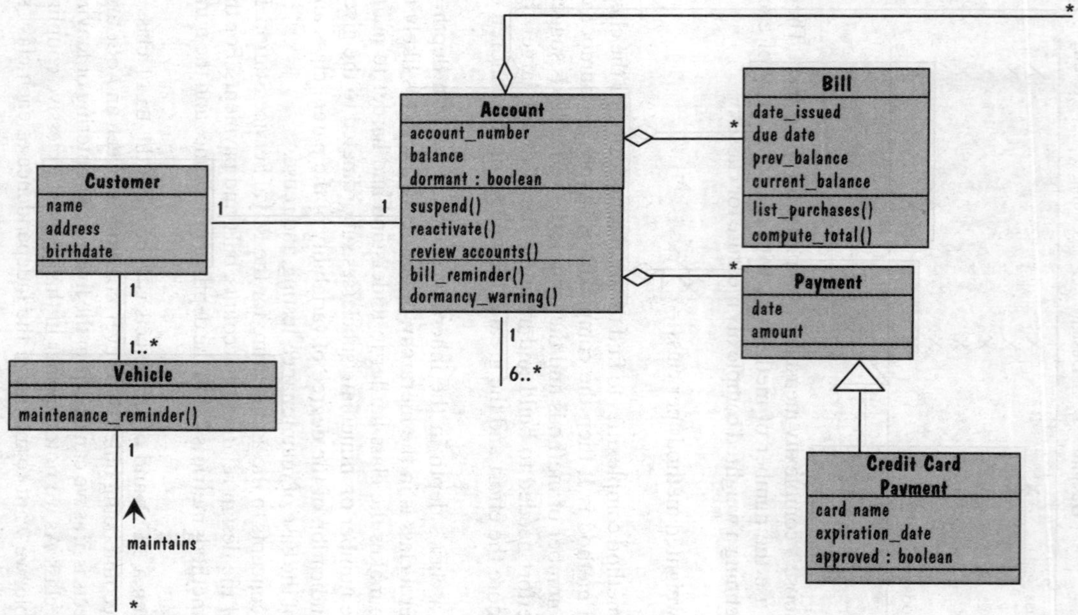

Metric	Bill	Payment	Credit Card Payment	Account	Customer	Vehicle
Weighted Methods / Class	2	0	0	5	0	1
Number of Children	0	1	0	0	0	0
Depth of Inheritance Tree	0	0	1	0	0	0
Coupling Between Objects	1	2	1	5	2	2

FIGURE 6.41 Chidamber–Kemerer metrics applied to the Royal Service Station class design.

and Q is the collection of pairs (I_r, I_s) where I_r and I_s share at least one common member. More formally, we define P and Q in the following way:

$$P = \{(I_r, I_s) \mid I_r \cap I_s = \emptyset\}$$
$$Q = \{(I_r, I_s) \mid I_r \cap I_s \neq \emptyset\}$$

We define the LCOM for C to be $|P| - |Q|$ if $|P|$ is greater than $|Q|$. Otherwise, LCOM is zero. In plainer language, the LCOM is the degree to which there are more pairs of methods that do *not* share variables than there are pairs of methods that do share variables. The metric is based on the notion that two methods are related if they share an instance variable. The larger the number of related methods, the more cohesive the class. Thus, the LCOM metric is a measure of the relatively disparate nature of the methods in the class.

Another metric, the response for a class, is the set of methods that might be executed in response to a message received by an object in that class. If many methods can be invoked when a message is received, then testing and repair become far more difficult. So designers should attempt to keep response for a class low and to view high values as an indication that additional scrutiny of the class and its implementation is warranted.

We can also use the Chidamber–Kemerer metrics to evaluate design changes. Consider the part of the module design for the Royal Service Station, shown in Figure 6.42, that is extended with user-interface modules. We can see from the table in the figure that the coupling between objects for the `Bill` class has increased from one to two, but the other metrics for bill, account, and payments have stayed the same.

The metrics help to identify problematic areas of the design. For each metric listed below, a higher value indicates greater likelihood of faults in the corresponding code:

- the larger the weighted complexity of a class (i.e., the system is more complex and therefore harder to understand)
- the more children a class has (i.e., there is greater variability in the class' hierarchy and therefore more code to implement and test)
- the larger the depth of the class's inheritance (i.e., attributes and methods are inherited from a larger collection of ancestor classes, thus the class is harder to understand)
- the larger the response for a class (thus, there are more methods to implement and test)

These guidelines were suggested in an empirical evaluation of C++ code done by Basili, Briand, and Melo (1995). Li and Henry (1993) studied these metrics too, adding two of their own to a preliminary set defined by Chidamber and Kemerer:

- **message-passing coupling:** the number of method invocations in a class's implementation
- **data abstraction coupling:** the number of abstract data types used in the measured class and defined in another class of the system

Li and Henry showed how these metrics can be used to predict the size of changes in classes during maintenance.

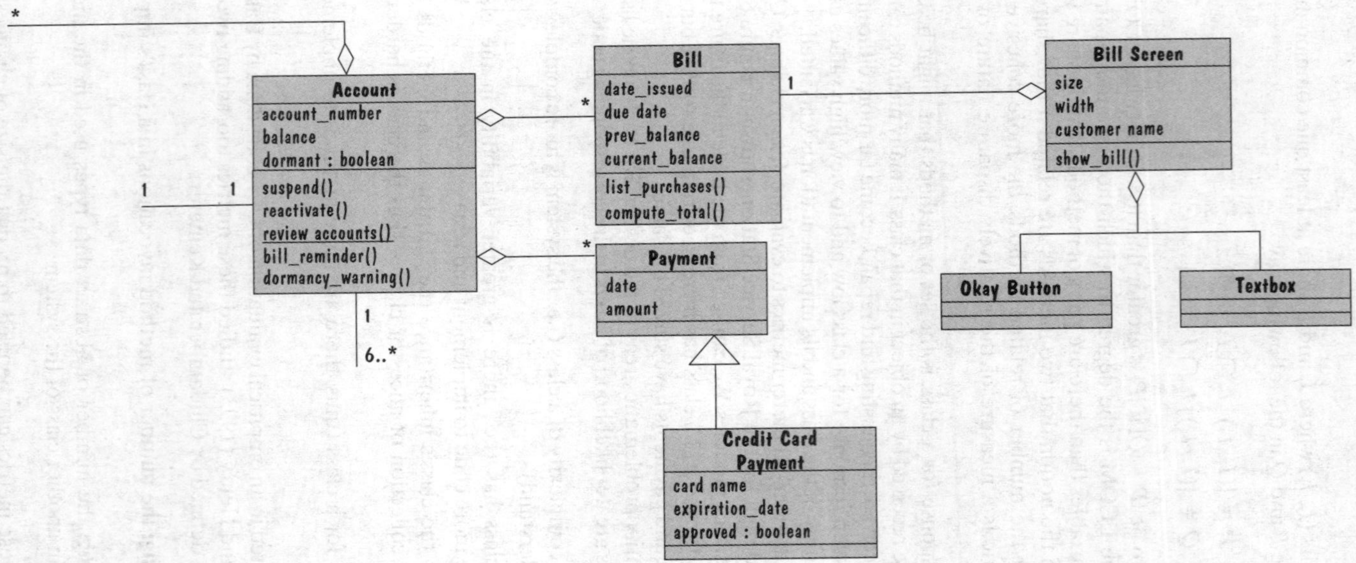

Metric	Bill	Payment	Credit Card Payment	Account	Bill Screen	Okay Button	Textbox
Weighted Methods / Class	2	0	0	5	1	0	0
Number of Children	0	1	0	0	0	0	0
Depth of Inheritance Tree	0	0	1	0	0	0	0
Coupling Between Objects	2	2	1	5	3	1	1

FIGURE 6.42 Chidamber–Kemerer metrics applied to a modified Royal Service Station design.

Metric	Min	Max
Average operation size	5	5
Average number of parameters per operation	0	4

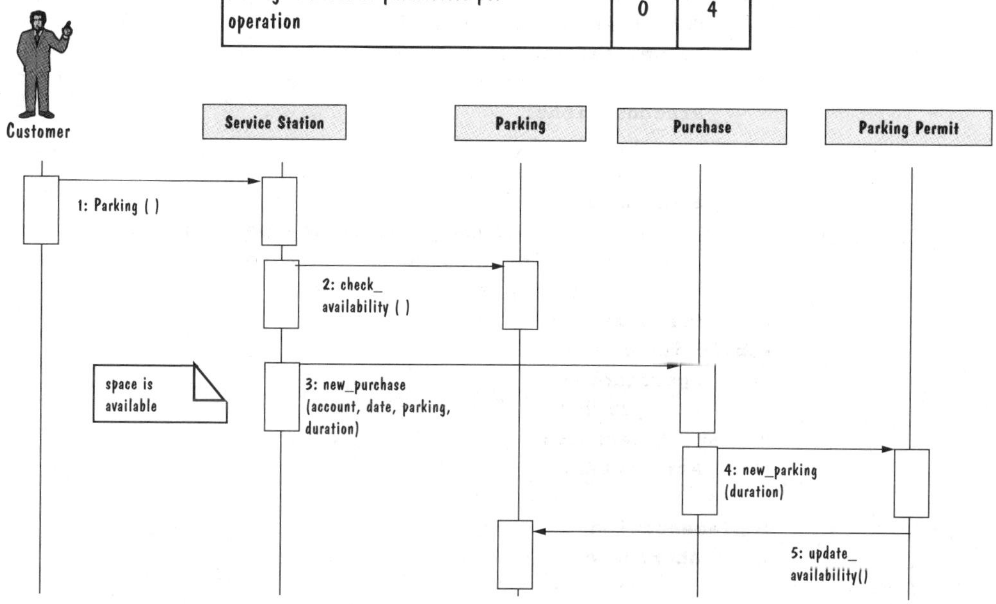

FIGURE 6.43 Measuring from a sequence diagram.

Travassos and Andrade (1999) suggest other possible metrics for OO systems. The number of messages sent by an operation can be used to calculate the average operation size. Similarly, it may be useful to know the average number of parameters per message. Each operation itself can be evaluated in terms of a host of complexity measures that apply equally well to non-OO development. The above measures are shown in Figure 6.43, applied to a sequence diagram for the Royal Service Station. Since the operation represented has five messages, the maximum and minimum operation sizes are the same: five. We can see that the fourth message requires four parameters, and the first message requires none, so the average number of parameters per message can range from zero to four.

We can also derive measurements from a class description. For example, consider this template for the refuel class:

```
Class name: Refuel
            Category: service
            External documents:
            Export control: Public
            Cardinality: n
```

```
        Hierarchy:
            Superclasses: Service
        Associations:
            <no rolename>: fuel in association updates
Operation name: price
        Public member of: Refuel
        Documentation:
            // Calculates fuel final price
        Preconditions:
            gallons > 0
            Object diagram: (unspecified)
        Semantics:
            price = gallons * fuel.price_per_gallon
            tax = price * purchase.tax_rate
            Object diagram: (unspecified)
        Concurrency: sequential
Public interface:
        Operations:
            price
Private interface:
        Attributes:
            gallons
Implementation:
        Attributes:
            gallons
State machine: no
Concurrency: sequential
Persistence: transient
```

From this template, we can find Lorenz and Kidd's class size, calculated as the total number of operations plus the number of attributes (including inherited features). Here, the class size is four. We can also evaluate a class in terms of more traditional measures, such as fan-in (the number of classes calling this class) and fan-out (the number of classes called by this class). Such measures can assist us with baselining and tracking, so we can observe growth in complexity and evaluate proposed changes.

Where to Do OO Measurement

There are many ways to measure OO systems, and the "best" set of metrics is yet to be identified. It is important to remember that measurement is valuable only when we can apply it to increase our understanding, prediction, or control. Any or all of the metrics presented here, or others in the literature or that you devise for your own projects, can be helpful, depending on ease of collection and relevance to the problem you are trying to solve. We can examine the metrics presented in this chapter to determine which ones are best captured from the various OO-related documents we have described.

TABLE 6.7 Where to Capture OO Metrics

	Phase				
Metric	Use Cases	Class Diagrams	Interaction Diagrams	Class Descriptions	Package Diagrams
Number of scenario scripts	X				
Number of key classes		X			
Number of support classes		X			
Average number of support classes per key class		X			
Number of subsystems					X
Class size		X		X	
Number of operations overridden by a subclass		X			
Number of operations added by a subclass		X			
Specialization index		X			
Weighted methods in class		X			
Depth of inheritance		X			
Number of children		X			
Coupling between objects		X			
Response for a class				X	
Lack of cohesion in methods				X	
Average operation size			X		
Average number of parameters per operation			X		
Operation complexity					
Percent public and protected		X		X	
Public access to data members		X		X	
Number of root classes		X			
Fan-in/fan-out		X			

As you can see in Table 6.7, there are metrics related to many types of documents, including use cases, class diagrams, interaction diagrams, class descriptions, state diagrams, and package diagrams. In general, measurement supports development by highlighting potential problems. Just as each type of diagram or chart reveals an issue or perspective that enhances our understanding of the problem or solution, each metric provides a different perspective on the design's quality and complexity that can help us anticipate and address problem areas of the software during development and maintenance.

6.8 DESIGN DOCUMENTATION

In Chapter 5, we discussed how to capture the details of the system architecture in a Software Architecture Document (SAD). The SAD acts as a bridge between the requirements and the design. In the same way, the program design acts as a bridge from the architectural design to the code, describing the modules in enough detail that programmers can implement them in a way that is consistent with the SAD, with good design principles, and with what the users expect to see in the final product (i.e., according to the requirements).

There are many ways to document the design. Much of it depends on developer preference and experience, and on the needs of the programmers and maintainers whose work depends on careful, complete documentation. In this section, we explore a particular approach to documentation, called *design by contract*, that uses the documentation not only to capture the design but to encourage interaction among developers.

In everyday life, a contract is written between two parties when one commissions the other for a particular service or product. Each party expects some benefit for some obligation: the supplier produces a service or product in a given period of time (an obligation) in exchange for money (a benefit), and the client accepts the service or product (a benefit) for the money (an obligation). The contract makes all obligations and benefits explicit. In building software, a contract is an agreement between a module's provider and its user, as shown in Figure 6.44.

In **design by contract**, each module has an interface specification that precisely describes what the module is supposed to do. Meyer (1997) suggests that design by contract helps ensure that modules interoperate correctly. This specification, called a **contract**, governs how the module is to interact with other modules and systems. Such specification cannot guarantee a module's correctness, but it forms a clear and consistent basis for testing and verification. The contract covers mutual obligations (the preconditions), benefits (the postconditions), and consistency constraints (called **invariants**). Together, these contract properties are called **assertions**.

As the module provider, we uphold our end of the contract as long as

- our module provides (at the least) all of the postconditions, protocols, and quality attributes that are advertised in the interface specification
- our code requires from its environment no more than what is stated in the interface's preconditions and protocols

As a software-unit user, we uphold the contract as long as

- our code uses the unit only when the unit's specified preconditions and protocols are satisfied
- our code assumes no more about the unit's behavior than is stated in its interface's postconditions, protocols, and invariants

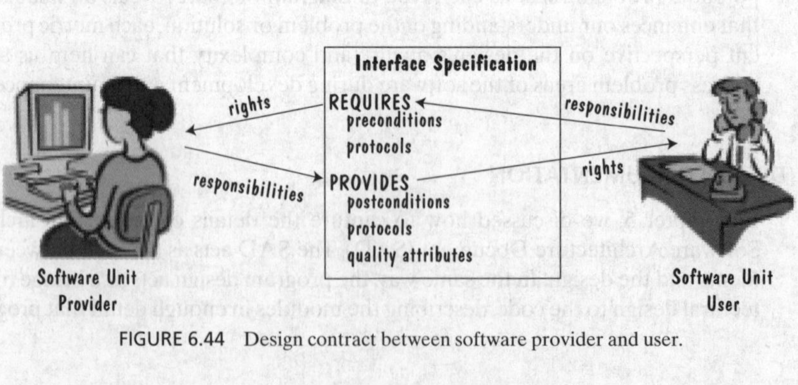

FIGURE 6.44 Design contract between software provider and user.

As we maintain the software system, the interfaces continue to apply: a software unit can be replaced by any new implementation that adheres to the unit's interface specification. Thus, contracts help us adhere to the substitutability design principle.

For example, consider a software unit that maintains a dictionary of elements indexed by a key. The provider of the software unit is responsible for providing operations to maintain the dictionary's contents. The software unit's users are responsible for invoking those operations correctly. For example, to insert a new entry into the dictionary:

1. The client ensures that the dictionary is not already full, that the element has a valid key, and that the dictionary does not already have an element indexed by that key.
2. The provider inserts elements into the dictionary.
3. If an element to be inserted has an invalid or duplicate key, no action is taken.

We can formalize this contract by being more precise about various responsibilities. Meyer (1992a) suggests a format in which a `require` clause specifies a method's precondition and an `ensure` clause specifies a method's postcondition:

```
// Implements data abstraction dictionary that maps String keys to Elements
    local
        count: INTEGER
        capacity: INTEGER
        dictionary: function that maps Key to Element
    insert(elem: Element; key: String)
        // Insert elem into dictionary
        require: count < capacity and key.valid() and not has(key)
        ensure: has(key) and retrieve(key) == elem
    retrieve(key: String): Element
        // Returns the element indexed by key
        require: has(key)
        ensure: result = dictionary(key)
```

Contracts also specify class invariants, which are properties over the instance variables that hold after every method invocation, including immediately after the constructor method creates each object of the class. For example, the above dictionary should never have duplicate entries:

```
invariant: forall (key1, Element1) and (key2, Element2) in dictionary,
           if key1<>key2 then Element1<>Element2
```

Class invariants are especially useful for testing the correctness of our design and testing design changes.

Contracts can be constructed for all types of designs. For example, suppose we are using data abstraction to design an OO system that controls the flow of water into reservoirs and out through dams. We may have classes of objects, such as `Dam`, `Reservoir`, and `River`. We can ask questions about the objects, such as `is_empty` and `is_full` for a reservoir, and we can issue commands, such as `empty` or `fill`. Our design can specify preconditions and postconditions; for instance, we may write

```
local
    gauge: INTEGER
    capacity: INTEGER
fill()
    //Fill reservoir with water
    require: in_valve.open and out_valve.closed
    ensure: in_valve.closed and out_valve.closed and is_full
is_full(): BOOLEAN
    // Tests whether reservoir is full
    ensure: result == (0.95*capacity <= gauge)
```

A contract can be compared with subsequent implementations to prove mathematically that the two are consistent. In addition, the contract's assertions provide a basis for testing. Class by class, the testers can determine the effects of each operation on each assertion. Moreover, when the design is changed in some way, each assertion can be checked to see if it is weakened or strengthened by the change.

6.9 INFORMATION SYSTEMS EXAMPLE

We saw in Chapter 5 how to structure the architecture of the Piccadilly system as a client–server system. But that design considered only the initial decomposition of the system into its major components. Now we need more detail about the individual components, so that programmers can implement the elements of the architecture as code. For example, the design needs more information about how to handle situations in which programs are on at similar but not identical times. For instance, a Piccadilly program that is televised from 9 PM to 10:30 PM may overlap with programs that air from 8 PM to 10 PM and from 10 PM to 11 PM. We must also decide how to handle faults; in this case, the *Opposition schedule* may contain an invalid date, such as February 31, or an invalid time, such as 2900 hours. Our lowest level of detail should include module interface specifications, so that programmers can be assigned to code and test individual modules. Nevertheless, this example shows that we must consider and combine a variety of complementary design techniques to formulate a solution that meets all of the customer's needs.

As we decompose our design into modules, we may need to reorganize which data and operations we combine into modules, to improve cohesion and coupling in the overall design. For example, at the end of Chapter 5, we identified a number of domain elements and relationships that the Piccadilly database will need to maintain, including the concept of `Opposition Program` shown in Figure 6.45. However, if we look at the models carefully, we see that there is considerable commonality in what we originally thought were disjoint concepts. In particular, the information and operations that we associate with Piccadilly television programs are the same as those that we associate

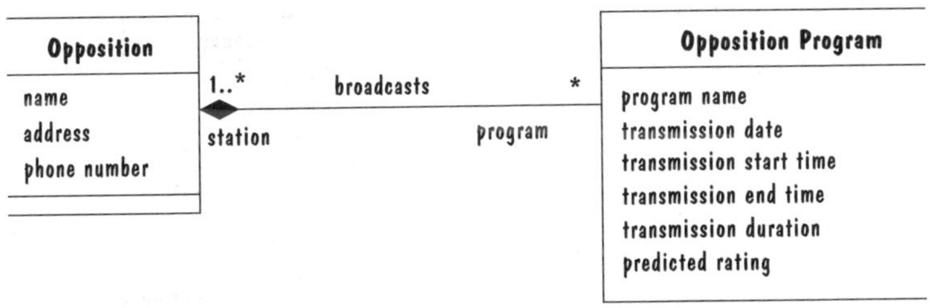

FIGURE 6.45 Data model of `Opposition Programs` broadcast by Piccadilly's competition.

with the programs broadcast by opposition stations. Figure 6.46 shows how we might integrate these concepts and their respective associations into a single `Program` class. With this refactoring, we avoid the extra work of implementing and testing separate versions of the same concept; we also avoid the headache of trying to maintain both versions of the class as it is modified or enhanced in the future.

In general, whether we are working on the design of a to-be-developed system or are enhancing an existing software system, we need to reevaluate and refactor the design's modular structure continually in order to minimize the coupling between modules.

6.10 REAL-TIME EXAMPLE

The proponents of OO development often tout the objects' reuse potential. As we have seen, the Ariane-5 system reused the inertial reference software (SRI) from Ariane-4. Had Ariane-5 been implemented using an OO approach, the reuse would have been in terms of either composition or inheritance. In a compositional approach, the SRI is viewed as a black box and is called from the main system, returning appropriate values for use in other parts of the Ariane-5 system. In an inheritance approach, the SRI structure and behavior are open to view, inheriting as much structure and behavior from parent classes as possible. A compositional approach is not likely to have prevented the disaster that occurred, since the black box would not have made the overflow problem visible. On the other hand, an inheritance-based reuse might have exposed the SRI design vulnerabilities to the Ariane-5 designers. They might at least have seen the unprotected exception and the comment stating that the exception would never be raised. Then, they might have reexamined this assumption and taken preventive action.

6.11 WHAT THIS CHAPTER MEANS FOR YOU

This chapter has described both program design and some OO development processes that support it. We have seen the need for modular designs that allow development teams to work in parallel on the design, implementation, and testing of separate software units. Each unit is described in terms of an interface that exposes what other programmers need to know to use the unit, while hiding design decisions that might change

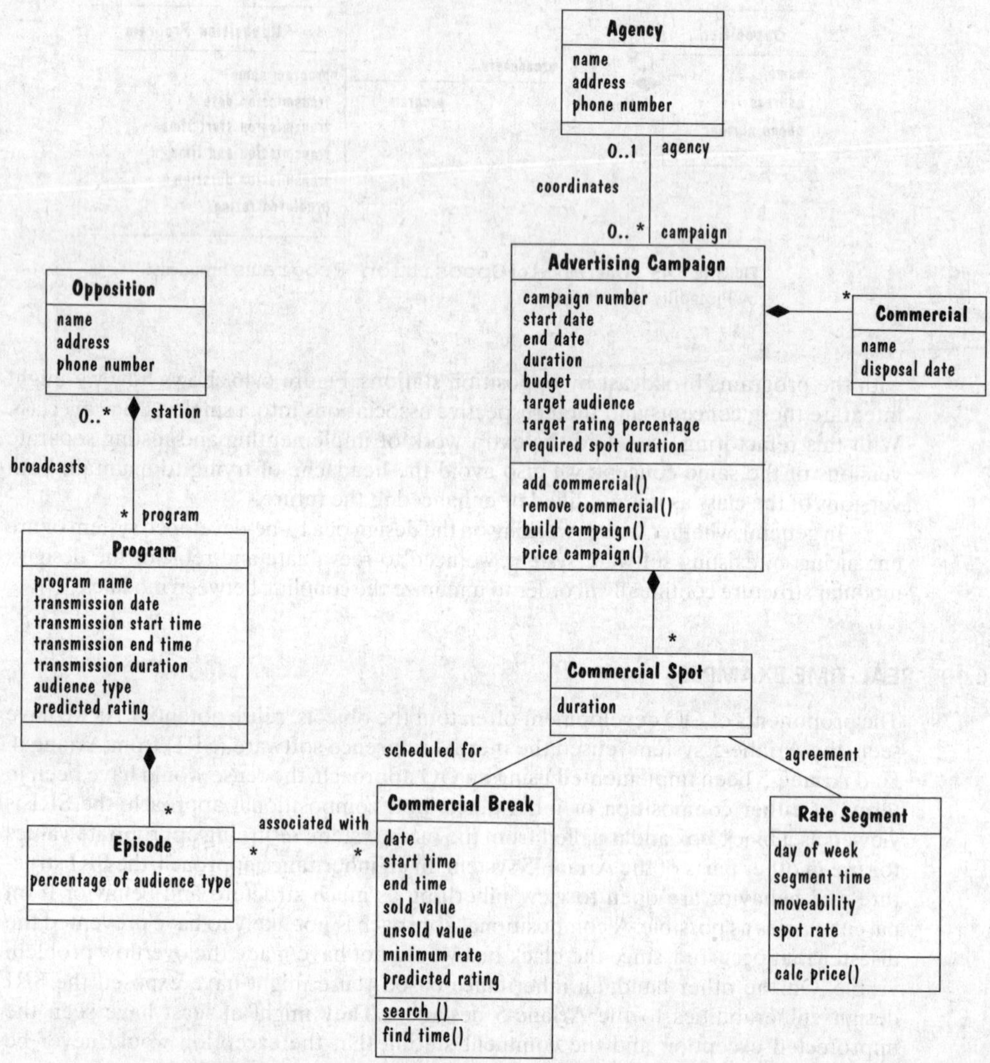

FIGURE 6.46 Integrated data model that merges `Programs` and `Opposition Programs`.

in the future. Such interfaces must include quality attributes as well as functionality, so that other programmers can determine whether the unit meets all of their requirements, including nonfunctional requirements.

We have presented several design principles useful in helping to keep your designs modular, reusable, and secure, and some design patterns that support the design principles. At the same time, we have introduced several metrics that are commonly used to measure size and design characteristics of OO artifacts. These measurements help us not only to predict resource allocation for development, testing, and maintenance; they also act as warnings when the system is becoming complex and difficult to understand.

6.12 WHAT THIS CHAPTER MEANS FOR YOUR DEVELOPMENT TEAM

The design process describes the system components using a common language with which to communicate. Object orientation is a particularly appealing basis for such design, because it allows us to describe and reason about the system from its birth to its delivery in the same terms: classes, objects, and methods. This consistency of terminology enables you to anticipate the size and structure of a system well before the design is complete. It simplifies the traceability across artifacts; you can see how a domain object in the requirements becomes an object in the design and then an object in the code, for instance.

A consistent notation makes it easier for your team to understand the implications of using a particular object or class—especially when you are constructing a system from someone else's OO components. Moreover, consistency assists the maintainers and testers, enabling them to build test cases and monitor changes more easily. And because the requirements, design, and code are expressed in the same way, it is easier for you to evaluate the effects of proposed changes to the requirements or designs.

6.13 WHAT THIS CHAPTER MEANS FOR RESEARCHERS

Both program design and the OO approach have been fertile fields for software engineering research. Design principles are heuristics for improving designs, but relatively little research has been done to evaluate whether following the principles actually results in consistently high-quality code over the life of a system. Similarly, object orientation has been embraced but not often rigorously compared with other development paradigms in terms of quality (especially security). Indeed, traditional ways of evaluating a system have been inappropriate or inadequate for object orientation. Projections based on lines of code are being replaced by prediction methods that take advantage of the characteristics of classes and hierarchies. In particular, research on fault prediction has produced new, more OO ways of estimating the number of problems remaining in designs or code.

Other researchers are evaluating the best ways to exploit the best characteristics of object orientation. How deep should the hierarchies be? When is composition better than inheritance for reuse? What are the best ways to take advantage of inheritance and polymorphism? Coupled with these research areas is a continuing effort to find good ways to measure the OO process and its products.

6.14 TERM PROJECT

Review your requirements for the Loan Arranger system. How would they change were they to be implemented as OO requirements? How would these changes make the system easier to fix or change? Next, review the characteristics of OO systems. Would any of these characteristics be beneficial for the Loan Arranger? Finally, develop an OO design for the Loan Arranger. Will it be easy to test the resulting implementation? To change? Why?

6.15 KEY REFERENCES

There are several good books that provide detailed instructions on how to think about systems in an OO way. Gamma et al. (1995) provide an overview of how to think of systems in terms of design patterns. Books such as Booch (1994), Jacobson et al. (1995), and Rumbaugh et al. (1991) offer detailed information about how to specify, design, and code OO systems. These three approaches form the basis for the UML. The classic texts on the UML are *The UML User Guide* (Booch, Rumbaugh, and Jacobson 2005) and *The UML Reference Manual* (Rumbaugh, Jacobson, and Booch 2004). In addition, Larman (2004) offers an excellent primer on how to use the UML. Binder (2000) describes everything you ever wanted to know about testing OO systems; it is full of good examples and counterexamples.

The classic references on OO measurement include Chidamber and Kemerer (1994), Li and Henry (1993), and Lorenz and Kidd (1994). Travassos and Andrade (1999) tie together the goals of OO measurement with some sensible guidelines for OO development.

6.16 EXERCISES

1. What is the significance of Lorenz and Kidd's specialization index? What are the implications of a high specialization index? A low one? A major change in the index as the product evolves?
2. There is stamp coupling between two software units if one of those units passes complex data structures to the other unit (e.g., as parameters in a method call). Suggest a way to refine such a design to avoid stamp coupling.
3. In the Ariane-5 design, the developers made a conscious decision to leave out the exception handling for three of seven exceptions that could be raised. What are the legal and ethical implications of this decision? Who is legally and morally responsible for the disaster that resulted? Are the testers at fault for not having caught this design flaw?
4. For each type of cohesion, write a description of a component exhibiting that kind of cohesion.
5. For a project that you have already developed for another class, draw a system diagram of your software using multiple levels of interconnected components. How modular was your system? What kind of coupling did it exhibit? Were the components cohesive? Can your system be restructured to increase the cohesion and decrease the coupling of components?
6. Are there some systems that cannot be made completely functionally cohesive? Why or why not?
7. For each type of coupling, give an example of two components coupled in that way.
8. Can a system ever be completely "decoupled"? That is, can the degree of coupling be reduced so much that there is no coupling between components? Why or why not?
9. For each of the quality attributes in the quality models of Chapter 1, explain how the characteristics of good design contribute to the product quality. For example, how do coupling, cohesion, and modularity affect reliability and traceability?
10. Provide an interface specification for a module that serves as an English–French dictionary. The module should provide facilities for adding new words to the dictionary, looking up the pronunciation of a French word, and returning the French word that corresponds to an input English word.

11. A recursive component is one that calls itself or in some way refers to itself. Given the design guidelines presented in this chapter, is a recursive component a good or a bad idea? Why?

12. For a complex module that you have already developed for another project, specify the module at varying degrees of abstraction (according to the descriptions in Sidebar 6.3). How might each abstraction be distinctly useful?

13. You are required to write a module that takes as an input an array of integers and returns three numbers: the largest number in the array, the average of the numbers, and the smallest number. How might this module fail? How would you protect the module from failing?

14. Inexperienced OO programmers often implement the following class hierarchy, where a `Stack` class is defined to be a subclass of `List`:

```
CLASS List {
      data: array [1..100] of INTEGER;
      count: INTEGER:= 0;
METHODS
      insert (pos: 1..100; value: INTEGER);
            require: insert value into List at position pos
      delete (pos: 1..100)
            ensure: remove value stored at position pos from List
      retrieve (pos: 1..100): INTEGER;
            ensure: return value stored at position pos in List
}
CLASS Stack EXTENDS List {
METHODS
    push(value: INTEGER)
          ensure: append value to end of Stack
    pop(): INTEGER;
          ensure: remove and return value from end of Stack
}
```

Explain why this is a bad use of inheritance.

15. Consider the following four specifications to insert an element `val` into a list `list`. For each pair of specifications, state whether one is substitutable for the other. Defend your answer.

(a) **require:** `val` is not in `list`
ensure: `list` contains all of its previous values plus `val`

(b) **ensure:** if `val` is already in `list`, then `list` is unchanged; otherwise `list` contains all of its previous values plus `val`

(c) **ensure:** `list` contains all of its previous values plus `val`

(d) **require:** `list` is sorted
ensure: `list` contains all of its previous values plus `val`, and `list` is sorted

16. An alternate version to specification 15(a) would be (a´) below, which declares an exception rather than requiring that the list not already contain the element to be inserted:

(a´) **exception:** throws `DuplicateElem` if `val` is already in `list`
ensure: `list` contains all of its previous values plus `val`

Which version of specification, a or a´, is better, and why?

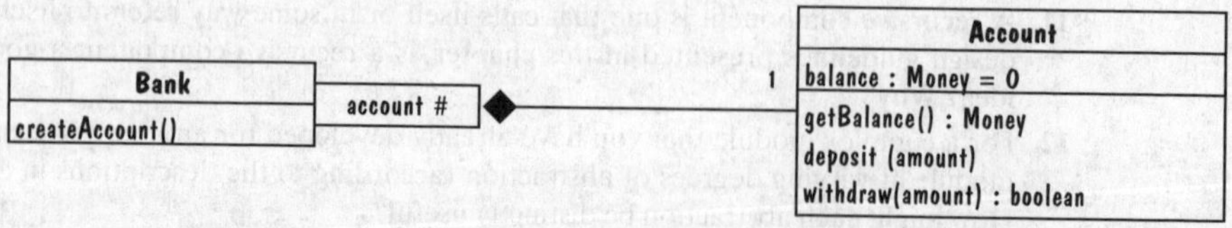

FIGURE 6.47 Design for banking system in Exercises 6.18 and 6.19.

17. Consider the following procedure interface for a module that sorts data:

```
PROCEDURE sort (a[] : INTEGER)
ensure: reorders elements so that they are in nondecreasing order
```

In what ways could this module be redesigned to improve its generality?

18. Consider a simplified OO design, shown in Figure 6.47, for a banking system. Accounts can be created at the bank, and money can be deposited and withdrawn from the account. An account is accessed by its account number. Use the Decorator design pattern to add two new banking features to the design:

(a) Overdraft protection: allows the customer to withdraw money when the account balance is zero; the total amount that can be withdrawn in this feature is a predefined credit limit.

(b) Transaction fee: charges the customer a fixed fee for each deposit and withdrawal transaction.

19. A bank must report to the government's tax institution all transactions (deposits and withdrawals) that exceed $10,000. Building on the initial design of the banking system from question 18, use the Observer design pattern to construct a class that monitors all Account transactions.

20. Rewrite the specifications in Section 6.8 (on design documentation) to use exceptions.

21. For one of your projects you are required to draw lines on a screen. You can choose between two modules: Module A is small, cheap, and easy to use. The other one, Module B is large, expensive, and more complex to use, but it provides additional functionality such as drawing polygons, drawing characters, and mouse support. What will be some of your considerations when choosing which module to use? Explain why.

22. Manny, the Royal Service Station manager, is going to expand his services to include an automated car washing system. The customer chooses the type of wash and specifies the type of car. The system computes the fee and displays the amount due on a control panel. The customer can then pay for the car wash. After payment, if the wash is currently busy, the system indicates that the customer must wait. Otherwise, the system indicates that the customer should drive the car into the car wash bay. How would you change the UML class diagram in Figure 6.21 to accommodate this new service?

23. Can an OO approach be used to develop any system? What are the strengths of object orientation? What are its weaknesses? Give an example of a system where object orientation would not be an appropriate development strategy.

7 Writing the Programs

> In this chapter, we look at
> - standards for programming
> - guidelines for reuse
> - using design to frame the code
> - internal and external documentation

So far, the skills we have learned have helped us to understand the customers' and users' problem and to devise a high-level solution for it. Now, we must focus on implementing the solution as software. That is, we must write the programs that implement the design. This task can be daunting, for several reasons. First, the designers may not have addressed all of the idiosyncrasies of the platform and programming environment; structures and relationships that are easy to describe with charts and tables are not always straightforward to write as code. Second, we must write our code in a way that is understandable not only to us when we revisit it for testing, but also to others as the system evolves over time. Third, we must take advantage of the characteristics of the design's organization, the data's structure, and the programming language's constructs while still creating code that is easily reusable.

Clearly, there are many ways to implement a design, and many languages and tools are available; we cannot hope to cover all of them in this book. In this chapter, we present examples from some of the popular languages, but the guidelines are generally applicable to any implementation. That is, this chapter does not teach you how to program; rather, it explains some of the software engineering practices that you should keep in mind as you write your code.

7.1 PROGRAMMING STANDARDS AND PROCEDURES

During your career, you are likely to work on many different software projects, writing code in many application domains using a variety of tools and techniques. Some of your work will also involve evaluating existing code, because you want to replace or modify it, or to reuse it in another application. You will also participate in formal and informal reviews to examine your code and others'. Much of this work will be different from the programming you have done for your classes. In class, your work is done independently, so that your instructor can judge its quality and suggest improvements. However, in the wider world, most software is developed by teams, and a variety of jobs are required to generate a quality product. Even when writing the code itself, many people are usually involved, and a great deal of cooperation and coordination is required. Thus, it is very important for others to be able to understand not only what you have written, but also why you have written it and how it fits in with their work.

For these reasons, you must know your organization's standards and procedures before you begin to write code. Many companies insist that their code conform to style, format, and content standards, so that the code and associated documentation are clear to everyone who reads them. For example, Sidebar 7.1 describes Microsoft's approach to programming standards.

Standards for You

Standards and procedures can help you to organize your thoughts and avoid mistakes. Some of the procedures involve methods of documenting your code so that it is clear and easy to follow. Such documentation allows you to leave and return to your work without losing track of what you had been doing. Standardized documentation also helps in locating faults and making changes, because it clarifies which sections of your program perform which functions.

SIDEBAR 7.1 PROGRAMMING STANDARDS AT MICROSOFT

Cusumano and Selby (1995, 1997) have studied software development at Microsoft. They point out that Microsoft tries to blend some aspects of software engineering practice into its software development cycle while preserving the creativity and individuality that hackers usually exhibit. Thus, Microsoft must find ways "that structure and coordinate what the individual members do while allowing them enough flexibility to be creative and evolve the product's details in stages." Because of market pressures and changing needs, Microsoft teams iterate among designing components, building them, and testing them. For example, team members revise both the types of features and their details as they learn more about what the product will do.

However, flexibility does not preclude standards. Nearly all of Microsoft's teams work at a single physical site, using common development languages (usually C and C++), common coding styles, and standard development tools. These standards help teams to communicate, to discuss the pros and cons of different design alternatives, and to resolve problems. Microsoft also requires its teams to collect a small set of measurements, including information about when failures occur and when the underlying faults are found and fixed. These measurements guide decisions about when to continue development and when to ship a product.

Standards and procedures also help in translating designs to code. By structuring code according to standards, you maintain the correspondence between design components and code components. Consequently, changes in design are easy to implement in the code. Similarly, modifications to code that result from changes in hardware or interface specifications are straightforward, and the possibility of error is minimized.

Standards for Others

Once your code is complete, others are likely to use it in a variety of ways. For example, as we shall see in later chapters, a separate team may test the code. Or another set of people may integrate your software with other programs to build and test subsystems and finally the whole system. Even after the system is up and running, changes may be needed, either because of a fault or because the customer wants to change the way the system performs its functions. You may not be part of those maintenance or test teams, so it is essential that you organize, format, and document your code to make it easy for others to understand what it does and how it works.

For example, suppose every program produced by your company begins with a section describing the program's functions and interfaces with other programs. The opening section might look like this:

```
*******************************************************
*
* COMPONENT TO FIND INTERSECTION OF TWO LINES
*
* COMPONENT NAME: FINDPT
* PROGRAMMER: E. ELLIS
* VERSION: 1.0 (2 FEBRUARY 2001)
*
* PROCEDURE INVOCATION:
*   CALL FINDPT (A1, B1, C1, A2, B2, C2, XS, YS, FLAG)
* INPUT PARAMETERS:
*   INPUT LINES ARE OF THE FORM
*        A1*X + B1*Y + C1 = 0 AND
*        A2*X + B2*Y + C2 = 0
*   SO INPUT IS COEFFICIENTS A1, B1, C1 AND A2, B2, C2
* OUTPUT PARAMETERS:
*   IF LINES ARE PARALLEL, FLAG SET TO 1.
*   ELSE FLAG = 0 AND POINT OF INTERSECTION IS (XS, YS)
*
*******************************************************
```

This block of comments tells the reader what the code does and gives an overview of the approach. To someone who is looking for a reusable component, this block is enough information to help decide if this code is what is being sought. To someone who is tracing the source of a failure, the block gives enough detail to help decide if this component is the likely culprit or even a co-conspirator.

A maintenance programmer reading blocks like this one will find the component that needs to be changed more easily. Once that component is located, if the data names are clear and the interfaces well-defined, the maintenance programmer can be sure that the change needed will not have any unexpected effects on other parts of the code.

Automated tools are available that can analyze the code to determine which procedures are called by this component and which procedures invoke it. That is, the documentation generated by the tools points up to the components that may invoke it and down to those called by the procedure. With information such as this, making a change to the system is relatively straightforward. At the end of this chapter, we examine an example of standards and procedures to see how they may direct our programming efforts.

Matching Design with Implementation

The most critical standard is the need for a direct correspondence between the program design components and the program code components. The entire design process is of little value if the design's modularity is not carried forward into the code. Design characteristics, such as low coupling, high cohesion, and well-defined interfaces, should also be program characteristics, so that the algorithms, functions, interfaces, and data structures can be traced easily from design to code and back again.

Remember that the system's general purpose is likely to remain the same throughout the software's lifetime, but its nature may change over time as customers identify enhancements and modifications. For example, suppose you are part of a team designing computer-aided displays for automobiles. The system you build will probably always be part of an automobile, but the menus and input devices may change, or new features may be added. These changes are made first to the high-level design and then are traced through lower design levels to the code that must be modified. Thus, the correspondence between design and code is essential. In later chapters, we will see that testing, maintenance, and configuration management are impossible without the links established by these standards.

7.2 PROGRAMMING GUIDELINES

Programming involves a great deal of creativity. Remember that the design is a guide to the function or purpose of each component, but the programmer has great flexibility in implementing the design as code. The design or requirements specification may suggest a programming language, either directly because it is specified by the designers or customers, or indirectly because of the constructs used. Language-specific guidelines are not addressed here, because there are many good books on the subject. Instead, we discuss several guidelines that apply to programming in general, regardless of the language.

No matter what language is used, each program component involves at least three major aspects: control structures, algorithms, and data structures. We examine each more closely.

Control Structures

Many of the control structures for a component are suggested by the architecture and design, and we want to preserve them as the design is translated to code. In the case of some architectures, such as implicit invocation and object-oriented design, control is based on system states and changes in variables. In other, more procedural designs, control depends on the structure of the code itself. For any type of design, it is important for your program structure to reflect the design's control structure. Readers should not have to jump wildly through the code, marking sections to which to return and wondering whether they have followed the right path. They should concentrate on what is being done by the program, not on the control flow. Thus, many guidelines and standards suggest that the code be written so that you can read a component easily from the top down.

Let us look at an example to see how restructuring can aid understanding. Consider the following program. Its control skips around among the program's statements, making it difficult to follow.

```
    benefit = minimum;
    if (age < 75) goto A;
    benefit = maximum;
    goto C;
    if (age < 65) goto B;
    if (age < 55) goto C;
A:     if (age < 65) goto B;
    benefit = benefit * 1.5 + bonus;
    goto C;
B:    if (age < 55) goto C;
    benefit = benefit * 1.5;
C:     next statement
```

We can accomplish the same thing in a format that is easier to follow by rearranging the code:

```
if (age < 55) benefit = minimum;
elseif (age < 65) benefit = minimum + bonus;
elseif (age < 75) benefit = minimum * 1.5 + bonus;
else benefit = maximum;
```

Of course, it is not always possible or practical to have exactly a top-down flow. For example, reaching the end of a loop may disrupt the flow. However, it is helpful whenever possible to have the required action follow soon after the decision that generates it.

We saw in previous chapters that modularity was a good design attribute. Its same advantages carry through to the code as well. By building a program from modular blocks, we can hide implementation details at different levels, making the entire system easier to understand, test, and maintain. In other words, we can consider a program component itself to be modular, and we can use macros, procedures, subroutines, methods, and inheritance to hide details while enhancing understandability. Moreover, the more modular the code component, the more easily it can be maintained and reused in other applications; modification can be isolated to a particular macro, subroutine, or other subcomponent.

Thus, in writing your code, keep in mind that generality is a virtue; do not make your code more specialized than it needs to be. For instance, a component that searches a string of 80 characters of text for a period can be written so that the input parameters include the length of the string and the character to be found. Then, the component can be used again to search a string of any length for any character. At the same time, do not make your components so general that performance and understanding are affected.

Other design characteristics translate to code components, such as coupling and cohesion. When you write your programs, remember to use parameter names and comments to exhibit the coupling among components. For instance, suppose you are writing a component to estimate income tax. It uses the values of gross income and deductions provided by other components. Instead of commenting your code with

```
Reestimate TAX
```

it is better to write

```
Reestimate TAX based on values of GROSS_INC and DEDUCTS
```

The second comment explains how the calculation is tied to data items in other components.

Your code must enable the reader to discern which parameters, if any, are being passed to the component and back again. Otherwise, testing and maintenance will be extremely difficult. In other words, dependence among components must be visible. By the same token, just as the system components were designed to hide information from one another, the subcomponents of your program should hide calculation details from each other. For example, in the earlier string-searching program, the text-searching component must contain information about how the specified character is sought. But the calling components need not know how the character is found, only that it is found and where it is. This information hiding allows you to change the searching algorithm without disturbing the rest of the code.

Algorithms

The program design often specifies a class of algorithms to be used in coding the component you are writing. For example, the design may tell you to use a Quicksort, or it may list the logical steps of the Quicksort algorithm. However, you have a great deal of flexibility in converting the algorithm to code, subject to the constraints of the implementation language and hardware.

One of the areas in which you have great discretion is the performance or efficiency of your implementation. Your instinct may tell you to make the code run as fast as possible. However, making the code faster may involve hidden costs:

- the cost to write the faster code, which may be more complex and thus take more time to write
- the cost of time to test the code, whose complexity requires more test cases or test data
- the cost of time for users to understand the code
- the costs of time to modify the code, if necessary

Thus, execution time is only a small part of the overall cost equation. You must balance execution time considerations with design quality, standards, and customer requirements. In particular, do not sacrifice clarity and correctness for speed.

If speed is important to your implementation, you must learn how your compiler optimizes your code. Otherwise, the optimization may take your seemingly faster code and actually slow it down. To see how this paradoxical situation can happen, suppose you are writing code to implement a three-dimensional array. You decide to increase efficiency by creating instead a one-dimensional array and performing all the indexing computations yourself. Thus, your code computes such variables as

```
index = 3*i + 2*j + k;
```

to calculate the position of an entry in a three-dimensional array. However, your compiler may perform its array indexing in the registers, so execution time is small. If the compiler uses an additive increment technique in the registers, rather than adding and multiplying for each position calculation, then your one-dimensional array technique may actually result in increased execution time!

Data Structures

In writing your programs, you should format and store data so that data management and manipulation are straightforward. There are several techniques that use the structure of the data to suggest how the program should be organized.

Keeping the Program Simple. The program's design may specify some of the data structures to be used in implementing functions. Often, these structures are chosen because they fit into an overall scheme that promotes information hiding and control of component interfaces. Data manipulation within a component can influence your choice of data structures in a similar way. For example, restructuring data can simplify a program's calculations. To see how, suppose you are writing a program to determine the amount of federal income tax due. As input, you are given the amount of taxable income and are told the following:

1. For the first $10,000 of income, the tax is 10%.
2. For the next $10,000 of income above $10,000, the tax is 12%.
3. For the next $10,000 of income above $20,000, the tax is 15%.
4. For the next $10,000 of income above $30,000, the tax is 18%.
5. For any income above $40,000, the tax is 20%.

Thus, someone who has a taxable income of $35,000 pays 10% of the first $10,000 (or $1000), 12% of the next $10,000 (or $1200), 15% of the next $10,000 (or $1500), and 18% of the remaining $5000 (or $900), for a total of $4600. To calculate the tax, you can include code in your component that reads in the taxable income and follows this algorithm:

```
tax = 0.
if (taxable_income == 0) goto EXIT;
if (taxable_income > 10000) tax = tax + 1000;
```

```
else{
    tax = tax + .10*taxable_income;
   goto EXIT;
}
if (taxable_income > 20000) tax = tax + 1200;
else{
    tax = tax + .12*(taxable_income-10000):
    goto EXIT;
}
if (taxable_income > 30000) tax = tax + 1500;
else{
    tax = tax + .15*(taxable_income-20000);
    goto EXIT;
}
if (taxable_income < 40000) {
    tax = tax + .18*(taxable_income-30000);
    goto EXIT;
}
else
    tax = tax + 1800. + .20*(taxable_income-40000);
EXIT: ;
```

However, we can define a tax table for each "bracket" of tax liability, as shown in Table 7.1, where we use a base figure and a percentage for each bracket.

Then, using the table, we can simplify our algorithm considerably:

```
for (int i-2; level=1; i <= 5; i++)
    if (taxable_income > bracket[i])
        level = level + 1;
tax = base[level]+percent[level]*(taxable_income-bracket[level]);
```

Notice how the calculations are simplified just by changing the way the data are defined. This simplification makes the program easier to understand, test, and modify.

Using a Data Structure to Determine a Program Structure. In the tax table example, the way we define the data dictates how we perform the necessary calculations. In general, data structures can influence the organization and flow of a program. In some cases, the data structures can influence the choice of language, too. For

TABLE 7.1 Sample Tax Table

Bracket	Base	Percent
0	0	10
10,000	1000	12
20,000	2200	15
30,000	3700	18
40,000	5500	20

example, LISP is designed to be a list processor, and it contains structures that make it much more attractive than some other languages for handling lists. Similarly, Ada and Eiffel contain constructs for handling unacceptable states called exceptions.

A data structure is said to be **recursive** if it is defined by identifying an initial element and then generating successive elements as a function of those previously defined. For example, a **rooted tree** is a graph composed of nodes and lines so that the following conditions hold:

1. Exactly one node of the tree is designated as the root.
2. If the lines emanating from the root are erased, the resulting graph is a set of non-intersecting graphs, each of which is a rooted tree.

Figure 7.1 illustrates a rooted tree, and Figure 7.2 shows how removing the root results in a set of smaller rooted trees. The root of each smaller tree is the node that had previously been connected to the original root of the larger tree. Thus, the rooted tree is defined in terms of its root and subtrees: a recursive definition.

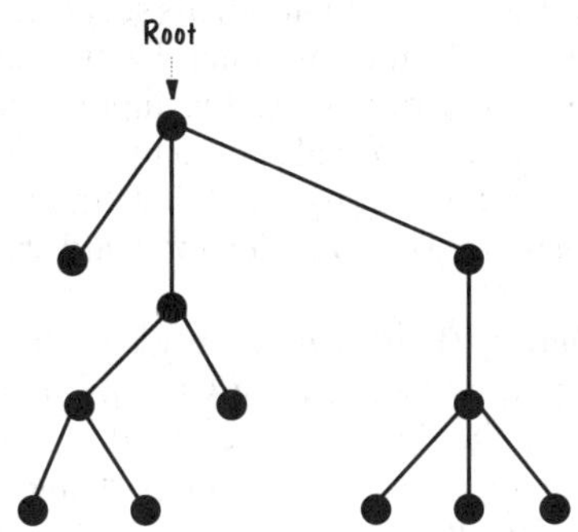

FIGURE 7.1 A rooted tree.

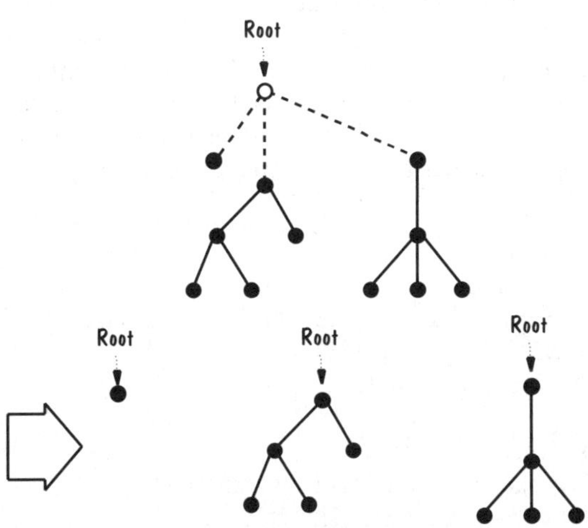

FIGURE 7.2 Subtrees of a rooted tree.

Programming languages such as Pascal allow recursive procedures to deal with recursive data structures. You may prefer to use recursive procedures for this type of data, since their use forces the burden of managing the data structure to be borne by the compiler rather than your program. The use of recursion may make the actual programming easier or may make your program more understandable. Thus, in general, you should consider the data structures carefully when deciding which language to use in implementing the design.

General Guidelines

Several overall strategies are useful in preserving the design quality in your code.

Localizing Input and Output. Those parts of a program that read input or generate output are highly specialized and must reflect characteristics of the underlying hardware and software. Because of this dependence, the program sections performing input and output functions are sometimes difficult to test. In fact, they may be the sections most likely to change if the hardware or software is modified. Therefore, it is desirable to localize these sections in components separate from the rest of the code.

An added benefit of localization is generalization of the overall system. Other systemwide functions to be performed on the input (such as reformatting or type checking) can be included in the specialized component, relieving the other components of the burden and thus eliminating repetition. Similarly, putting output functions in one place makes the system easier to understand and change.

Including Pseudocode. The design usually lays out a framework for each program component. Then, you add your creativity and expertise to build the lines of code that implement the design. For example, the design may be relatively language-independent, giving you many choices about the particular language constructs to use, how to use them, how the data will be represented, and so on. Since the design is an outline of what is to be done in a program component, it is useful to move in stages from the specified design to the code, rather than to translate the design immediately into code.

Pseudocode can be used to adapt the design to your chosen language. By adopting constructs and data representations without becoming involved immediately in the specifics of each command, you can experiment and decide which implementation is most desirable. In this way, code can be rearranged and restructured with a minimum of rewriting. For instance, suppose the design for a component of a text processing system states

```
COMPONENT PARSE_LINE:
 Read next eighty characters.
    IF this is a continuation of the previous line,
        Call CONTINUE
    ELSE determine command type.
    ENDIF
 CASE of COMMAND_TYPE
    COMMAND_TYPE is paragraph: Call PARAGRAPH.
    COMMAND_TYPE is indent: Call INDENT.
    COMMAND_TYPE is skip line: Call SKIP_LINE.
```

```
    COMMAND_TYPE is margin: Call MARGIN.
    COMMAND_TYPE is new page: Call PAGE.
    COMMAND_TYPE is double space: Call DOUBLE_SPACE.
    COMMAND_TYPE is single space: Call SINGLE_SPACE.
    COMMAND_TYPE is break: Call BREAK.
    COMMAND_TYPE is anything else: Call ERROR.
ENDCASE
```

Depending on the chosen language and your preference as a programmer, this design can be implemented in many ways. As the first stage in translating design to code, you might examine each type of command to determine what is involved in coding it. Using intermediate pseudocode, you might describe what you want your code to do in the following way:

```
PARAGRAPH:
   Break line, flush line buffer. Advance one line between
   paragraphs. If fewer than 2 lines left on page, eject. Set
   line pointer to paragraph indent
INDENT:
   Break line, flush line buffer. Get indent parameter. Set
   line pointer to indent parameter, set left margin to indent.
SKIP_LINE:
   Break line, flush line buffer. Get line parameter. Advance
   (parameter) lines or eject if not enough space left on
   current page.
MARGIN:
   Break line, flush line buffer. Get margin parameter. Set
   line pointer to left margin. Set right margin to margin.
PAGE:
   Break line, flush line buffer. Eject page. Set line
   pointer to left margin.
DOUBLE_SPACE:
   Set interline space to 2.
SINGLE_SPACE:
   Set interline space to 1.
BREAK:
   Break line, flush line buffer. Set line pointer to left
   margin.
```

However, by reviewing this pseudocode, you might see that the steps can be regrouped so that certain common functions follow one another:

```
FIRST:
    PARAGRAPH, INDENT, SKIP_LINE, MARGIN, BREAK, PAGE:
        Break line, flush line buffer.
    DOUBLE_SPACE, SINGLE_SPACE:
        No break line, no flush line buffer.
SECOND:
    INDENT, SKIP_LINE, MARGIN:
```

```
        Get parameter.
    PARAGRAPH, BREAK, PAGE, DOUBLE_SPACE, SINGLE_SPACE:
        No parameter needed.
THIRD:
    PARAGRAPH, INDENT, SKIP_LINE, MARGIN, BREAK, PAGE:
        Set new line pointer.
    DOUBLE_SPACE, SINGLE_SPACE:
        New line pointer unchanged.
FOURTH:
        Individual actions taken.
```

Having described the commands in this way, you may recognize that the FIRST and THIRD set of actions apply to the same group of commands. In addition, you notice that the line pointer depends on the left margin in all cases except when the command is PARAGRAPH. Using this information, you can write pseudocode in more detail:

```
INITIAL:
    Get parameter for indent, skip_line, margin.
    Set left margin to parameter for indent.
    Set temporary line pointer to left margin for all but
       paragraph; for paragraph, set it to paragraph
       indent.
LINE_BREAKS:
    If not (DOUBLE_SPACE or SINGLE_SPACE), break line, flush
       line buffer and set line pointer to temporary line
       pointer.
    If 0 lines left on page, eject page and print page header.
INDIVIDUAL CASES:
    INDENT, BREAK: do nothing.
    SKIP_LINE: skip parameter lines or eject.
    PARAGRAPH: advance 1 line; if < 2 lines on page, eject.
    MARGIN: right_margin = parameter.
    DOUBLE_SPACE: interline_space = 2.
    SINGLE_SPACE: interline_space = 1.
    PAGE: eject page, print page header.
```

Finally, you are ready to write code to implement the design:

```
//initial: get parameters
if ((command_type==INDENT) ||(command_type==LINE_SKIP)
        ||(command_type==MARGIN))
   parm_value=get_parm(input_line);
if (command_type = INDENT)
   left_margin:=parm_value;
if (command_type==PARAGRAPH) temp_line_pointer=paragraph_indent;
   else temp_line_pointer=LEFT_MARGIN;
```

```
//break current line, begin new line
if (not((command_type==DBL_SPC)||(command_type==SNGL_SPC))){
      break_and_flush_line( ) ;
      if (lines_left==0)
         begin_new_page();
      line_ pointer=temp_line_pointer ;
}
//actions for individual commands
switch(command_type){
   case LINE_SKIP:
      if (lines_left > parm_value)
      for (i=1; i<parm_value; i++)
          advance_line();
      else begin_new_page();
   case PARAGRAPH:
      advance_line();
      if (lines_left < 2)
         begin_new_page( ) ;
   case MARGIN: right_margin=parm_value;
   case DBL_SPC: interline_space=2;
   case SNGL_SPC: interline_space=1;
   case PAGE: begin_new_page
}//end switch
```

Thus, pseudocode has acted as a framework on which to construct the code. In briefing the code from the design in this way, notice that the design's organization has changed several times. Such changes must be reported to and approved by the designers, so that the links among requirements, design, and code can be documented and maintained.

Revising and Rewriting, Not Patching. When writing code, as when preparing a term paper or creating a work of art, you often write a rough draft. Then you carefully revise and rewrite until you are satisfied with the result. If you find the control flow convoluted, or the decision processes hard to understand, or the unconditional branches difficult to eliminate, then it may be time to return to the design. Reexamine the design to see whether the problems you are encountering are inherent in the design or in your translation to code. Look again at how the data are represented and structured, at the algorithms chosen, and at the decomposition.

Reuse. There are two kinds of reuse: **producer reuse**, where we are creating components designed to be reused in subsequent applications, and **consumer reuse**, where we are using components that were originally developed for other projects (Barnes and Bollinger 1991). Some companies have division-wide or company-wide reuse programs, with standards for evaluating and changing components; Sidebar 7.2 describes such a program at Lucent. The success of these programs suggests reuse

SIDEBAR 7.2 SELECTING COMPONENTS FOR REUSE AT LUCENT

Lucent Technologies initiated a companywide program to reuse software components (McClure 1997). As a consequence, the Workstation Software Development Department formed a Reuse Council to devise a strategy for selecting candidate components for its reuse repository. The Council consisted of seven people, representing all groups in the department. The Council created an inventory of components and formed a matrix with the features of all past and planned projects. Then, each feature was rated in terms of whether it had been implemented and was still needed, had been implemented but was no longer needed, or had not been implemented but was still needed. Those features that were needed and were common to more than one project were targeted for reuse. In fact, some were redesigned to make them more reusable.

The Council met every week for two hours to make component selections, inspect design documentation for those components already in the repository, and to monitor the levels of reuse in the department's projects.

guidelines for you. If you are a consumer for your current project, there are four key characteristics to check about the components you are about to reuse:

1. Does the component perform the function or provide the data you need?
2. If minor modification is required, is it less modification than building the component from scratch?
3. Is the component well-documented, so you can understand it without having to verify its implementation line by line?
4. Is there a complete record of the component's test and revision history, so you can be certain that it contains no faults?

You must also assess the amount of code you need to write so that your system can interface with the reused components.

On the other hand, if you are a producer of reusable components, you should keep in mind several things:

- Make your component general, using parameters and anticipating similar conditions to the ones in which your system will invoke your components.
- Separate dependencies so that sections likely to need change are isolated from those that are likely to remain the same.
- Keep the component interface general and well-defined.
- Include information about any faults found and fixed.
- Use clear naming conventions.
- Document the data structures and algorithms.
- Keep the communication and error-handling sections separate and easy to modify.

7.3 DOCUMENTATION

Many corporate or organizational standards and procedures focus on the descriptions accompanying a collection of programs. We consider **program documentation** to be the set of written descriptions that explain to a reader what the programs do and how they do it. **Internal documentation** is descriptive material written directly within the code; all other documentation is **external documentation**.

Internal Documentation

The internal documentation contains information directed at someone who will be reading the source code of your programs. Thus, summary information is provided to identify the program and describe its data structures, algorithms, and control flow. Usually, this information is placed at the beginning of each component in a set of comments called the **header comment block**.

Header Comment Block. Just as a good newspaper reporter includes the who, what, where, when, how, and why of a story, you must include the following information in your header comment block for each component:

1. what your component is called
2. who wrote the component
3. where the component fits in the general system design
4. when the component was written and revised
5. why the component exists
6. how the component uses its data structures, algorithms, and control

We can examine each of these pieces of information in more depth.

First, the name of the component must figure prominently in the documentation. Next, the block identifies the writer, with phone number or e-mail address, so that the maintenance and test teams can reach the writer with questions or comments.

During the system's lifetime, components are often updated and revised, either for fault correction or because requirements change and grow. As we will see in Chapter 11, it is important to track the revisions, so program documentation should keep a log of changes made and who made them.

Because the component is part of a larger system, the block should indicate how it fits in the component hierarchy. This information is sometimes conveyed with a diagram; at other times, a simple description will do. The header block should also explain how the component is invoked.

More detailed information is required to explain how the component accomplishes its goal. The block should list

- the name, type, and purpose of each major data structure and variable
- brief descriptions of the logic flow, algorithms, and error handling
- expected input and possible output
- aids to testing and how to use them
- expected extensions or revisions

Your organizational standards usually specify the order and content of the header comment block. Here is how a typical header comment block might look:

```
PROGRAM SCAN: Program to scan a line of text for a given
character
PROGRAMMER: Beatrice Clarman (718) 345-6789/bc@power.com
CALLING SEQUENCE: CALL SCAN(LENGTH,CHAR,NTEXT)
   where LENGTH is the length of the line to be scanned;
   CHAR is the character sought. Line of text is passed
   as array NTEXT.
VERSION 1: written 3 November 2000 by B. Clarman
REVISION 1.1: 5 December 2001 by B. Clarman to improve searching
   algorithm.
PURPOSE: General-purpose scanning module to be used for each
   new line of text, no matter the length. One of several text
   utilities designed to add a character to a line of text,
   read a character, change a character, or delete a character.
DATA STRUCTURES: Variable LENGTH - integer
   Variable CHAR - character
   Array NTEXT - character array of length LENGTH
ALGORITHM: Reads array NTEXT one character at a time; if
   CHAR is found, position in NTEXT returned in variable
   LENGTH; else variable LENGTH set to 0.
```

Other Program Comments. The header comment block acts as an introduction to your program, much as the introduction to a book explains its purpose. Additional comments enlighten readers as they move through your program, helping them understand how the intentions you describe in the header are implemented in the code. If the code's organization reflects a well-structured design, if the statements are formatted clearly, and if the labels, variable names, and data names are descriptive and easy to distinguish, then the necessary number of additional comments is small. That is, following simple guidelines for code format and structure allows the code to be a source of information about itself.

Comments have a place even in clearly structured and well-written code. Although code clarity and structure minimize the need for other comments, additional comments are useful wherever helpful information can be added to a component. Besides providing a line-by-line explanation of what the program is doing, the comments can also break the code into phases that represent major activities. Then, each activity can be divided into yet smaller steps, each only several lines in length. Pseudocode from your program design can serve this purpose and be embedded in the code itself. Also, when code is revised, programmers should update the comments to reflect the changes. In this way, the comments build a record of revisions over time.

It is essential that the comments reflect the actual code behavior. In addition, make sure that the comments add new information, rather than state what is already obvious from your use of good labels and variable names. For example, it is useless to write

```
// Increment i3
i3 = i3 + 1;
```

when you can add substantially more information by writing

```
// Set counter to read next case
i3 = i3 + 1;
```

Ideally, the variable names should explain the activity:

```
case_counter = case_counter + 1;
```

Usually, you begin coding by moving from the design to pseudocode, which in turn provides a framework for your final code and a basis for your comments. Be sure to write the comments as you write the code, not afterward, so you capture both the design and your intention. Beware of code that is difficult to comment; the difficulty often suggests that the design should be simplified before you finish coding.

Meaningful Variable Names and Statement Labels. Choose names for your variables and statements that reflect their use or meaning Writing

```
weekwage = (hrrate * hours) + (.5)* (hrrate) * (hours - 40.);
```

makes more sense to the reader than

```
z = (a * b) + (.5) * (a) * (b - 40.);
```

In fact, the *weekwage* example is not likely to need comments at all, and you are less likely to introduce faults.

Similarly, alphabetic statement labels should tell readers something about what the labeled sections of your program do. If the labels must be numeric, then be sure they are in ascending order and clustered by related purpose.

Formatting to Enhance Understanding. The format of your comments can help a reader understand the goal of the code and how the goal is reached. Indentation and spacing of statements can reflect the basic control structure. Notice how unindented code like this

```
if (xcoord < ycoord)
result = -1;
elseif (xcoord == ycoord)
if (slope1 > slope2)
result = 0;
else result = 1;
elseif (slope1 > slope2)
result = 2;
elseif (slope1 < slope2)
result = 3;
result = 4;
```

can be clarified by using indentation and rearranging the space:

```
if (xcoord < ycoord) result = -1;
elseif (xcoord == ycoord)
    if (slope1 > slope2) result = 0;
                 else result = 1;
elseif (slope1 > slope2) result = 2;
elseif (slope1 < slope2) result = 3;
else                  result = 4;
```

In addition to using format to display the control structure, Weinberg (1971) recommends formatting your statements so that the comments appear on one side of the page and the statements on the other. In this way, you can cover up the comments when testing your program and thus not be misled by what may be incorrect documentation. For example, the following code (from Lee and Tepfenhart 1997) can be read without comments by looking only at the left side of the page.

```
void free_store_empty()
{
    static int i = 0;
    if(i++ == 0)                          //guard against cerr
                                          //allocating memory
          cerr << "Out of memory\n";      //tell user
    abort();                              //give up
}
```

Documenting Data. One of the most difficult things for program readers to understand is the way in which data are structured and used. A data map is very useful in interpreting the code's actions, especially when a system handles many files of varying types and purposes, coupled with flags and passed parameters. This map should correspond with the data dictionary in the external documentation, so the reader can track data manipulation through the requirements and design to the code.

Object-oriented designs minimize or eliminate some of these problems, but sometimes this information hiding makes it even more difficult for the reader to understand exactly how a data value is changed. Thus, the internal documentation should include descriptions of the data structures and uses.

External Documentation

Whereas internal documentation is concise and written at a level appropriate for a programmer, external documentation is intended to be read also by those who may never look at the actual code. For example, designers may review the external documentation when considering modifications or enhancements. In addition, the external documentation gives you a chance to explain things more broadly than might be reasonable within your program's comments. If you consider the header comment block to be an overview or summary of your program, then the external documentation is the full-blown report. It answers the same questions—who, what, why, when, where, and how—using a system rather than a component perspective.

Because a software system is built from interrelated components, the external documentation often includes an overview of the system's components or of several groupings of components (the user-interface components, the database e.g., management components, the ground-speed-calculation components). Diagrams, accompanied by narrative describing each component, show how data are shared and used by one or more components; in general, the overview describes how information is passed from one component to another. Object classes and their inheritance hierarchy are explained here, as are reasons for defining special types or categories of data.

External component documentation is part of the overall system documentation. At the time the component is written, much of the rationale for the component's structure and flow have already been detailed in the design documents. In a sense, the design is the skeleton of the external documentation, and the flesh is supplied by narrative discussing the code component's particulars.

Describing the Problem. In the first section of the code's documentation, you should explain what problem is being addressed by the component. This section sets the stage for describing what options were considered for solutions and why a particular solution was chosen. The problem description is not a repeat of the requirements documentation; rather, it is a general discussion of the setting, explaining when the component is invoked and why it is needed.

Describing the Algorithms. Once you make clear why the component exists, you should address the choice of algorithms. You should explain each algorithm used by the component, including formulas, boundary or special conditions, and even its derivation or reference to the book or paper from which it is derived.

If an algorithm deals with special cases, be sure to discuss each one and explain how it is handled. If certain cases are not handled because they are not expected to be encountered, explain your rationale and describe any related error handling in the code. For example, an algorithm may include a formula where one variable is divided by another. The documentation should address cases where the denominator might be zero, pointing out when this situation might occur and how it is handled by the code.

Describing the Data. In the external documentation, the users or programmers should be able to view the data flow at the component level. Data flow diagrams should be accompanied by relevant data dictionary references. For object-oriented components, the overview of objects and classes should explain the general interaction of objects.

7.4 THE PROGRAMMING PROCESS

This chapter discusses guidelines, standards, and documentation. What kind of process do programmers follow to ensure that the code they produce is of high quality? Until recently, the programming process was not the focus of much research. As Whittaker and Atkin (2002) point out, software engineering researchers often assume that, given a good design, any programmer can translate the design into solid code. But good code is the result not only of a good design but also of skill, experience, and artfulness derived from imagination and good problem solving. To understand what processes support good programming practices, we begin by examining how to solve problems.

Programming as Problem Solving

Polyà (1957) wrote the classic book on how we solve problems. He points out that finding a good solution involves four distinct stages:

1. Understanding the problem
2. Devising a plan
3. Carrying out the plan
4. Looking back

To understand the problem, we analyze each of its elements. What is known? What is not known? What is possible to know? What is impossible to know? These questions address both data and relationships. Just as a good systems analyst frames a problem in terms of the system boundary, identifying what is inside the boundary and what is outside, a good problem solver must understand the conditions under which the problem must be solved. Then, once we can define the conditions, we ask if the conditions can be satisfied.

Sometimes it is helpful to draw a picture to enhance understanding. Programmers often do this by drawing a flow chart or diagram to show how a dynamically allocated data structure changes shape as various operations are performed on it. Such depiction helps us to identify various parts of the condition, and perhaps even to decompose the problem into smaller, more tractable problems. In a way, this reframing to gain understanding is a micro-design activity: the program design is viewed carefully and reorganized in pieces that are easier to address than the original framing of the design.

Next, a plan is devised to determine how a solution can be derived from what is known about the problem. What are the connections between the data and the unknowns? If no connection is immediately clear, then are there ways in which this problem is similar to other, better-known problems? It is here that we try to think of the current problem in terms of patterns: Is there a pattern or set of patterns that we can adapt to fit our problem?

We can try several techniques to find the right plan of attack:

- *Identifying a related problem:* Are there data, algorithms, libraries, or methods that we can use to attack our problem?
- *Restating the problem:* What are the key definitions? Can the problem be generalized or made more specific to make it more tractable? Can simplifying assumptions be made?
- *Decomposing the problem:* What are the essential elements of the problem? Can the data be partitioned into categories, so that each category can be processed separately?

Perkins (2001) suggests ways to brainstorm and arrive at what he calls the "Eureka" effect: recognizing the best solution. He wants us to rove through many different possibilities, stretching our minds to think even of implausible scenarios. We can also look for subtle clues that signal anomalies—reasons that a possible solution will not work. In addition to reframing the problem, Perkins suggests "decentering" from current fixations by examining every assumption and attitude. He tells us to think of creativity as a sophisticated form of questioning everything; we use our creativity to question proposed solutions and to find a better solution to our problem.

Once the plan of attack is chosen, Polyà tells us to carry it out. Step by step, we must verify that the solution—in our case our program—is correct. If necessary, we can use some of the techniques presented in Chapters 8 and 9 to evaluate each step, making sure that each logical statement follows from previous steps. When the solution is done, we look back and examine it, revisiting each part of the argument. At the same time, we evaluate the solution for its applicability to other situations. Is the solution reusable? Can it be used to solve a different problem? Should it become the basis for a pattern?

Any programming process that encourages these steps can enhance the speed at which we find a good solution. Libraries of programs, good documentation, and automated tools support a good process. As we will see in later chapters, reuse repositories, change management, and post-mortems also improve the process, particularly by analyzing our successes and failures and by encoding in our products and processes the recommendations from our analyses, so that programming is easier the next time around.

Extreme Programming

In Chapter 2, we learned about agile methods and the related philosophy of programming, called extreme programming. In extreme programming, there are two types of participants: customers and programmers. Customers represent the users of the eventual system. In this role, they perform the following activities:

- Define the features that the programmers will implement, using stories to describe the way the system will work
- Describe detailed tests that they will run when the software is ready, to verify that the stories were implemented properly
- Assign priorities to the stories and their tests

In turn, the programmers write code to implement the stories, doing so in the order specified by the customers' priorities. To assist the customers, the programmers must estimate how long it will take to code up each story, so that the customers can plan the acceptance tests. The planning occurs in two-week increments, so that trust builds up between customers and programmers. Martin (2000) points out that extreme programming involves more than just this dialog between programmers and customers; there are also dialogs between programmers as they pair program: sitting side by side at a workstation and collaborating on the construction of a single program.

Pair Programming

The concept of pair programming is one of the more radical of the agile method techniques, so we examine it in more depth in this chapter. In pair programming, a pair of programmers uses a single keyboard, display, and mouse. Each member of the pair assumes a very specific role. One person is the driver or pilot, controlling the computer and actually writing the code. The other person is the navigator, reviewing the driver's code and providing feedback. The two team members exchange roles periodically.

There are many claims made for pair programming, including improvements in productivity and quality. However, the evidence is thin and often ambiguous. For example, Parrish et al. (2004) report on the productivity impact of using pairs of developers. On average, the programmers in the study had 10 years of work experience. The study measured programmer collaboration as the degree to which pairs of programmers worked on the same module on the same day. Parrish and his colleagues found that "the high-concurrency pairs were significantly less productive despite the fact that they were experienced, methodology-trained programmers." Moreover, the study found, pairs were no more productive on later modules than on earlier modules. However, reports from the Software Engineering Institute (in evaluating the Personal Software Process) suggest that programmers using traditional methods get better as they do more programming, in terms of both productivity and quality. Concluding that pairs working together are not naturally productive, Parrish and his colleagues suggest that there are ways to use the role-based protocol of pair programming to help overcome the natural productivity loss that happens in pairs.

Other studies, such as Cockburn and Williams (2000), Nosek (1998), and Williams et al. (2000), suggest that pair programming produces code faster and with lower fault density than traditional individual programming. However, Padberg and Müller (2003) found that the cost-benefit ratio for pair programming depends on how large these advantages really are. In particular, they show that pair programming pays off only under strong market pressure, where managers encourage programmers to implement the next set of features quickly for the next release. Drobka, Noftz, and Raghu (2004) show mixed results: in one study, an extreme programming team was 51% more productive than the team using traditional approaches, but in another study, a non-extreme programming team was the more productive, by 64%. Many of these studies involve small, unrealistic projects; others may suffer from the so-called Hawthorne effect, in which behavior improves not because of better processes but because attention is being paid to the participants. We will see in Chapter 14 how to make decisions from these disparate and often conflicting pieces of evidence.

The other benefits of pair programming seem clear. Having an older, experienced programmer advise a novice while writing code can be a powerful learning experience. And having a second pair of eyes reviewing code as it is being developed can help to catch errors early. However, Skowronski (2004) points out that pair programming can inhibit essential steps in problem solving. He claims that the focus on the problem can be disturbed by the necessary interactions between pairs. "Agile methods could push people who excel at problem solving into the background, giving center stage to programming-team members who can talk well but might lack the analytical skills necessary to do the difficult design and coding tasks" (Skowronski 2004). Moreover, as Polyá (1957) and Perkins (2001) point out, good problem solvers need time alone, to think carefully, devise their plans, and analyze their options. This quiet time is not built into the pair-programming process.

Whither Programming?

As with almost anything, the answer may be "all things in moderation." Drobka, Noftz, and Raghu (2004) describe their use of extreme programming on four mission-critical projects. They found that extra steps were needed to adjust extreme programming to the realities of large-scale, mission-critical software. For example, with no architectural guidelines, each programmer had his or her own vision of what the overall architecture should be, and the visions differed considerably. Thus, the high-level architecture document was used as a roadmap to assist the developers in planning. Rather than use prioritized stories, the researchers found it essential to define baseline architectures, using documented scenarios to help describe key abstractions, and to define system boundaries. Finally, documentation was used to assist in communicating among team members. Strict agile-methods advocates eschew documentation, but Drobke, Noftz, and Raghu found it to be essential. So, too, were design reviews to ensure that the software being built would be maintainable over its likely 30-year life span.

Thus, in the future, programming is likely to be a blend of the good practices that have been advocated for decades and the flexible approaches being espoused by the agile-methods proponents. We will see in Chapter 14 that software engineers are defining a software engineering body of knowledge that describes the information and practices that a good software engineer should master in order to produce high-quality systems.

7.5 INFORMATION SYSTEMS EXAMPLE

Recall that in Chapter 6 we looked at designing the modules of the Piccadilly system. One aspect of the design involved finding television programs on competing channels, so that we could use information about them in our advertising campaign. This resulted in the design of a module that represents television `Programs`. According to our data model, the `Program` class will have attributes *program name, transmission date, transmission start time, transmission end time, audience type*, and *predicted rating*. We want to write a C++ function that finds all opposition programs that are broadcast at the same time as some given `Episode` of a Piccadilly program. One of the decisions we must make is how to pass information about an `Episode` to the function. There are several argument-passing mechanisms from which we can choose: passing a value, a pointer, or a reference.

If information about an `Episode` is passed by value, the actual value of `Episode` is not changed. Instead, a copy is made and placed on a local stack. Once the method terminates, the local values are no longer accessible to the method. One advantage of using this approach is that the calling component does not need to save and restore argument values. However, passing a value can use up a great deal of time and space if the argument is large. Moreover, this technique is not useful if the method must change the actual value of the argument. If we implement the method passing by value, it may look like this in C++:

```
void Match:: calv(Episode episode_start_time)
{
first_advert = episode_start_time + increment;
// The system makes a copy of Episode
// and your program can use the values directly.
}
```

Another alternative is to pass the argument as a pointer. No copy is made of the argument; instead, the method receives a pointer to an instance of `Episode`. If passed by pointer, the argument can be changed and the changed value persists after the routine terminates. The reference code might look like this:

```
void Match:: calp(Episode* episode)
{
episode->setStart (episode->getStart());
// This example passes a pointer to an instance of Episode.
// Then the routine can invoke the services (such as setStart
// and getStart) of Episode using the -> operator.
}
```

Finally, the argument can be passed as a reference. Pass by reference is like pass by pointer (e.g., the value of the argument can be changed), but the argument and its services are accessed as if it had been passed by value. The code might look like this:

```
void Match:: calr(Episode& episode)
{
episode.setStart (episode.getStart());

// This example passes the address of Episode.
// Then the routine can invoke the services (such as setStart
// and getStart) of Episode using the . operator.
}
```

Once you decide on your preferred way to handle the argument passing, you should document your choice both in the inline comments and in the external documentation. In that way, another programmer who might be reusing or updating your code will understand your low-level design decisions and keep the new code consistent with the old.

7.6 REAL-TIME EXAMPLE

We have seen that a major problem with the Ariane-5 software was its need to handle faults and failures appropriately. Such situations may influence the choice of implementation language. Coleman et al. (1994) discuss several object-oriented languages and their ability to deal with failures.

In Chapter 6, we learned that one popular way of handling a fault is to raise an exception. An **exception** is a condition that, when detected, causes control of the system to be passed to a special part of the code called an exception handler. In turn, the **exception handler** invokes code designed to fix the underlying fault or at least move the system to a state that is more acceptable than the exception state. Design by contract often includes specific exception-handling behavior in the contract.

The Eiffel language (Meyer 1992b) contains explicit exception-handling mechanisms. We learned in Section 6.6 that if an exception occurs when a method is executing, then special code, called **rescue code**, can be invoked to address the problem. We must make design decisions about how the rescue will work. Sometimes the rescue fixes the problem and tries to re-execute the method. In other cases, the rescue code finishes its work and then passes control to another exception handler; if the problem cannot be repaired, then the system reverts to a state in which it can terminate gracefully and safely. In a design by contract, the contract includes preconditions, an assertion, and postconditions. To handle exceptions, the Eiffel language also contains other postconditions that explain what the system state should be if the assertion is found to be false. Thus, had it been implemented in Eiffel, the Ariane-5 code could have contained postconditions that stopped the SRI subsystem before it caused the rocket to veer off course.

On the other hand, C++ compilers do not have standard exception handlers. Coleman et al. (1994) point out that Eiffel-style exception code can be implemented as

```
try
   {
   }
catch (...)
   {
   // attempt to patch up state
   // either satisfy postcondition or raise exception again
   }
```

Whatever language and exception-handling strategy are chosen, it is important to have a systemwide policy, rather than having different approaches in each component. Consistency of approach makes it easier to troubleshoot and trace a failure to its root cause. For the same reason, it is helpful to save as much state information as possible, so that the conditions leading to failure can be reconstructed.

7.7 WHAT THIS CHAPTER MEANS FOR YOU

In this chapter, we have looked at several guidelines for implementing programs. We have seen that you should consider the following when you write your code:

- organizational standards and guidelines
- reusing code from other projects
- writing your code to make it reusable on future projects
- using the low-level design as an initial framework, and moving in several iterations from design to code
- incorporating a systemwide error-handling strategy
- using documentation within your programs and in external documents to explain your code's organization, data, control, and function, as well as your design decisions
- preserving the quality design attributes in your code
- using design aspects to suggest an implementation language

There are many good books that provide specialized advice based on the particular implementation language you select.

7.8 WHAT THIS CHAPTER MEANS FOR YOUR DEVELOPMENT TEAM

Although much of coding is an individual endeavor, all of coding must be done with your team in mind. Your use of information hiding allows you to reveal only the essential information about your components so that your colleagues can invoke them or reuse them. Your use of standards enhances communication among team members. And your use of common design techniques and strategies makes your code easier to test, maintain, and reuse.

7.9 WHAT THIS CHAPTER MEANS FOR RESEARCHERS

There is a great deal of research needed on many aspects of programming.

- We need more information on the attributes of good programmers. Productivity can vary by a factor of 10, and quality is also highly variable. Understanding more about which characteristics lead to good code developed quickly will help us train developers to be more effective and efficient.
- It is difficult to identify components that have the best reuse potential. Measurement and evaluation are needed to help us understand which component attributes are the best predictors of reusability.
- We continue to need more research on language characteristics and their effect on product quality. For example, Hatton (1995) explains that some of the nonstandard aspects of C should be avoided in order to make software safer and more reliable.
- Automated tools are always helpful in generating code automatically, managing code repositories, enforcing design contracts, and providing templates for standard code structures. Researchers continue not only to build new tools, but also to evaluate existing tools for use in practical situations on large projects.

7.10 TERM PROJECT

In preceding chapters, you examined requirements for the Loan Arranger, and devised several designs to implement your solution to the described problem. Now it is time to implement the system. There are several areas that deserve particular attention, because they are more difficult than their requirements description makes them seem. One is the need to allow four loan analysts to use the system at once. This requirement should have suggested to you that it is necessary to design the Loan Arranger so that certain loans are locked while they are being considered for a bundle. What is the best way to implement this scheme? How can the implementation be done so that you can easily change the number of analysts allowed on the system at a given time?

A second implementation difficulty arises when you implement the bundling algorithm. How will your code find the best bundle to fit the criteria? Remember that you must respond to the user in a short period of time.

Finally, how does your choice of language affect the ability to meet the performance requirements?

7.11 KEY REFERENCES

There are several good books providing programming guidelines: Kernighan and Plauger (1976, 1978); Hughes, Pfleeger, and Rose (1978); Barron and Bishop (1984); Bentley (1986, 1989); and McConnell (1993).

Reuse repositories are available worldwide. Some of the more popular ones are

- ASSET (Asset Source for Software Engineering Technology)
- CARDS (Central Archive for Reusable Defense Software)
- COSMIC (Computer Software Management and Information Center)
- DSRS (Defense Software Repository System)
- Software Technology Support Center at Hill Air Force Base

Contact information for these and other reuse resources can be found on the book's Web page.

7.12 EXERCISES

1. If one person has written a component but others have revised it, who is responsible if the component fails? What are the legal and ethical implications of reusing someone else's component?
2. Give an example to show how a language designed for recursion makes list handling easier to understand than a language without such provision.
3. The most intuitive control statement is goto:
   if (condition) then goto (label).
   Yet, good structured programs do not use goto statements. Why?
4. You are asked to write a program to print out a yearly calendar. The user enters the year desired, and the output is a calendar for that year. Discuss how the representation of internal data will affect the way in which the program is written. Give several examples of data structures that might be used in such a problem. (*Hint*: Are your data structures cumulative or not? How is a leap year handled?)
5. In exercise 4 you were introduced to a program that prints out a yearly calendar. What are some of the special considerations regarding calendars that we have to keep in mind before we start programming? What are some of the possible faults that the program may have? How would you prevent them?
6. A list is a data structure that can be defined recursively. Give a recursive definition of a list. If you are familiar with a programming language that has recursive procedures (such as LISP or PL/I), explain how elements are added to and deleted from a list in that language.
7. How can control flow be documented for an object-oriented program?
8. The common algorithm for calculating the roots of a quadratic equation by the quadratic formula requires considering several special cases in your code. Write appropriate comments for this algorithm so that the comments make it easy to see the different cases and how they are handled. Write accompanying external documentation to explain this algorithm.
9. When code components are generated automatically by a tool or reused from a repository, how should coding, documentation, and design standards be enforced?

10. What are the advantages and disadvantages of using the same standardized language or tools across all applications in your organization?
11. Look at a program you have submitted as a project in another class. Can it be improved by using the suggestions in this chapter? If so, how? Does incorporating these suggestions make your program more or less efficient?

8 Testing the Programs

In this chapter, we look at
- types of faults and how to classify them
- the purpose of testing
- unit testing
- integration testing strategies
- test planning
- when to stop testing

Once you have coded your program components, it is time to test them. There are many types of testing, and this chapter and the next will introduce you to several testing approaches that lead to delivering a quality system to your customers. Testing is not the first place where fault finding occurs; we have seen how requirements and design reviews help us ferret out problems early in development. But testing is focused on finding faults, and there are many ways we can make our testing efforts more efficient and effective. In this chapter, we look at testing components individually and then integrating them to check the interfaces. Then, in Chapter 9, we concentrate on techniques for assessing the system as a whole.

8.1 SOFTWARE FAULTS AND FAILURES

In an ideal situation, we as programmers become so good at our craft that every program we produce works properly every time it is run. Unfortunately, this ideal is not reality. The difference between the two is the result of several things. First, many software systems deal with large numbers of states and with complex formulas, activities, and algorithms. In addition to that, we use the tools at our disposal to implement a customer's conception of a system when the customer is sometimes uncertain of exactly what is needed. Finally, the size of a project and the number of people involved can add complexity. Thus, the presence of faults is a function not just of the software, but also of user and customer expectations.

What do we mean when we say that our software has failed? Usually, we mean that the software does not do what the requirements describe. For example, the specification may state that the system must respond to a particular query only when the user is authorized to see the data. If the program responds to an unauthorized user, we say that the system has failed. The failure may be the result of any of several reasons:

- The specification may be wrong or have a missing requirement. The specification may not state exactly what the customer wants or needs. In our example, the customer may actually want to have several categories of authorization, with each category having a different kind of access, but has never stated that need explicitly.
- The specification may contain a requirement that is impossible to implement, given the prescribed hardware and software.
- The system design may contain a fault. Perhaps the database and query-language designs make it impossible to authorize users.
- The program design may contain a fault. The component descriptions may contain an access control algorithm that does not handle this case correctly.
- The program code may be wrong. It may implement the algorithm improperly or incompletely.

Thus, the failure is the result of one or more faults in some aspect of the system.

No matter how capably we write programs, it is clear from the variety of possible faults that we should check to ensure that our components are coded correctly. Many programmers view testing as a demonstration that their programs perform properly. However, the idea of demonstrating correctness is really the reverse of what testing is all about. We test a program to demonstrate the existence of a fault. Because our goal is to discover faults, we consider a test successful only when a fault is discovered or a failure occurs as a result of our testing procedures. **Fault identification** is the process of determining what fault or faults caused the failure, and **fault correction** or **removal** is the process of making changes to the system so that the faults are removed.

By the time we have coded and are testing program components, we hope that the specifications are correct. Moreover, having used the software engineering techniques described in previous chapters, we have tried to ensure that the design of both the system and its components reflects the requirements and forms a basis for a sound implementation. However, the stages of the software development cycle involve not only our computing skills, but also our communication and interpersonal skills. It is entirely possible that a fault in the software can result from a misunderstanding during an earlier development activity.

It is important to remember that software faults are different from hardware faults. Bridges, buildings, and other engineered constructions may fail because of shoddy materials, poor design, or because their components wear out. But loops do not wear out after several hundred iterations, and arguments are not dropped as they pass from one component to another. If a particular piece of code is not working properly, and if a spurious hardware failure is not the root of the problem, then we can be certain that there is a fault in the code. For this reason, many software engineers refuse to use the term "bug" to describe a software fault; calling a fault a bug implies that the fault wandered into the code from some external source over which the developers have no control. In building software, we use software engineering practices to control the quality of the code we write.

In previous chapters, we examined many of the practices that help minimize the introduction of faults during specification and design. In this chapter, we examine techniques that can minimize the occurrence of faults in the program code itself.

Types of Faults

After coding the program components, we usually examine the code to spot faults and eliminate them right away. When no obvious faults exist, we then test our program to see if we can isolate more faults by creating conditions where the code does not react as planned. Thus, it is important to know what kind of faults we are seeking.

An **algorithmic fault** occurs when a component's algorithm or logic does not produce the proper output for a given input because something is wrong with the processing steps. These faults are sometimes easy to spot just by reading through the program (called **desk checking**) or by submitting input data from each of the different classes of data that we expect the program to receive during its regular working. Typical algorithmic faults include

- branching too soon
- branching too late
- testing for the wrong condition
- forgetting to initialize variables or set loop invariants
- forgetting to test for a particular condition (e.g., when division by zero might occur)
- comparing variables of inappropriate data types

When checking for algorithmic faults, we may also look for **syntax faults**. Here, we want to be sure that we have properly used the constructs of the programming language. Sometimes, the presence of a seemingly trivial fault can lead to disastrous results. For example, Myers (1976) points out that the first U.S. space mission to Venus failed because of a missing comma in a Fortran do loop. Fortunately, compilers catch many of our syntax faults for us.

Computation and **precision faults** occur when a formula's implementation is wrong or does not compute the result to the required number of decimal places. For instance, combining integer and fixed- or floating-point variables in an expression may produce unexpected results. Sometimes, improper use of floating-point data, unexpected truncation, or ordering of operations may result in less-than-acceptable precision.

When the documentation does not match what the program actually does, we say that the program has **documentation faults**. Often, the documentation is derived from the program design and provides a very clear description of what the programmer would like the program to do, but the implementation of those functions is faulty. Such faults can lead to a proliferation of other faults later in the program's life, since many of us tend to believe the documentation when examining the code to make modifications.

The requirements specification usually details the number of users and devices and the need for communication in a system. By using this information, the designer often tailors the system characteristics to handle no more than a maximum load described by the requirements. These characteristics are carried through to the program design as limits on the length of queues, the size of buffers, the dimensions of tables, and so on. **Stress** or **overload faults** occur when these data structures are filled past their specified capacity.

Similarly, **capacity** or **boundary faults** occur when the system's performance becomes unacceptable as system activity reaches its specified limit. For instance, if the requirements specify that a system must handle 32 devices, the programs must be tested to monitor system performance when all 32 devices are active. Moreover, the system should also be tested to see what happens when more than 32 devices are active, if such a configuration is possible. By testing and documenting the system's reaction to overloading its stated capacity, the test team can help the maintenance team understand the implications of increasing system capacity in the future. Capacity conditions should also be examined in relation to the number of disk accesses, the number of interrupts, the number of tasks running concurrently, and similar system-related measures.

In developing real-time systems, a critical consideration is the coordination of several processes executing simultaneously or in a carefully defined sequence. **Timing** or **coordination faults** occur when the code coordinating these events is inadequate. There are two reasons why this kind of fault is hard to identify and correct. First, it is usually difficult for designers and programmers to anticipate all possible system states. Second, because so many factors are involved with timing and processing, it may be impossible to replicate a fault after it has occurred.

Throughput or **performance faults** occur when the system does not perform at the speed prescribed by the requirements. These are timing problems of a different sort: Time constraints are placed on the system's performance by the customer's requirements rather than by the need for coordination.

As we saw during design and programming, we take great care to ensure that the system can recover from a variety of failures. **Recovery faults** can occur when a failure is encountered and the system does not behave as the designers desire or as the customer requires. For example, if a power failure occurs during system processing, the system should recover in an acceptable manner, such as restoring all files to their state just prior to the failure. For some systems, such recovery may mean that the system will continue full processing by using a backup power source; for others, this recovery means that the system keeps a log of transactions, allowing it to continue processing whenever power is restored.

For many systems, some of the hardware and related system software are prescribed in the requirements, and the components are designed according to the specifications of the reused or purchased programs. For example, if a prescribed modem is used for communications, the modem driver generates the commands expected by the modem and reads commands received from the modem. However, **hardware and system software faults** can arise when the supplied hardware and system software do not actually work according to the documented operating conditions and procedures.

Finally, the code should be reviewed to confirm that organizational standards and procedures have been followed. **Standards and procedure faults** may not always affect the running of the programs, but they may foster an environment where faults are created as the system is tested and modified. By failing to follow the required standards, one programmer may make it difficult for another to understand the code's logic or to find the data descriptions needed for solving a problem.

Orthogonal Defect Classification

It is useful to categorize and track the types of faults we find, not just in code, but anywhere in a software system. Historical information can help us predict what types of faults our code is likely to have (which helps direct our testing efforts), and clusters of certain types of faults can warn us that it may be time to rethink our designs or even our requirements. Many organizations perform statistical fault modeling and causal analysis, both of which depend on understanding the number and distribution of types of faults. For example, IBM's Defect Prevention Process (Mays et al. 1990) seeks and documents the root cause of every problem that occurs; the information is used to help suggest what types of faults testers should look for, and it has reduced the number of faults injected in the software.

Chillarege et al. (1992) at IBM have developed an approach to fault tracking called **orthogonal defect classification**, where faults are placed in categories that collectively paint a picture of which parts of the development process need attention because they are responsible for spawning many faults. Thus, the classification scheme must be product- and organization-independent, and be applicable to all stages of development. Table 8.1 lists the types of faults that comprise IBM's classification. When using the classification, the developers identify not only the type of fault, but also whether it is a fault of omission or commission. A **fault of omission** is one that results when some key aspect of the code is missing; for example, a fault may occur when a variable is not initialized. A **fault of commission** is one that is incorrect; for example, the variable is initialized to the wrong value.

One of the key features of orthogonal defect classification is its orthogonality. That is, a classification scheme is **orthogonal** if any item being classified belongs to exactly one category. In other words, we want to track the faults in our system in an unambiguous way, so that the summary information about the number of faults in each class is meaningful. We lose the meaning of the measurements if a fault might belong to more than one class. In the same way, the fault classification must be clear, so that any two developers are likely to classify a particular fault in the same way.

TABLE 8.1 IBM Orthogonal Defect Classification

Fault Type	Meaning
Function	Fault that affects capability, end-user interfaces, product interfaces, interface with hardware architecture, or global data structure
Interface	Fault in interacting with other components or drivers via calls, macros, control blocks, or parameter lists
Checking	Fault in program logic that fails to validate data and values properly before they are used
Assignment	Fault in data structure or code block initialization
Timing/serialization	Fault that involves timing of shared and real-time resources
Build/package/merge	Fault that occurs because of problems in repositories, management changes, or version control
Documentation	Fault that affects publications and maintenance notes
Algorithm	Fault involving efficiency or correctness of algorithm or data structure but not design

SIDEBAR 8.1 HEWLETT-PACKARD'S FAULT CLASSIFICATION

Grady (1997) describes Hewlett-Packard's approach to fault classification. In 1986, Hewlett-Packard's Software Metrics Council identified several categories in which to track faults. The scheme grew to be the one depicted in Figure 8.1. The developers use this model by selecting three descriptors for each fault found: the origin of the fault (i.e., where the fault was injected in a product), the type of fault, and the mode (i.e., whether information was missing, unclear, wrong, changed, or could be done a better way).

Each Hewlett-Packard division tracks its faults separately, and summary statistics are reported on pie charts like the one in Figure 8.2. Different divisions often have very different fault profiles, and the nature of the profile helps the developers devise requirements, design, code, and test activities that address the particular kinds of faults the division usually sees. The overall effect has been to reduce the number of faults over time.

Fault classifications, such as IBM's and Hewlett-Packard's (see Sidebar 8.1), help improve the entire development process by telling us which types of faults are found in which development activities. For example, for each fault-identification or testing technique used while building the system, we can build a profile of the types of faults located. It is likely that different methods will yield different profiles. Then we can build our fault-prevention and -detection strategy based on the kinds of faults we expect in our system, and the activities that will root them out. Chillarege et al. (1992) illustrate

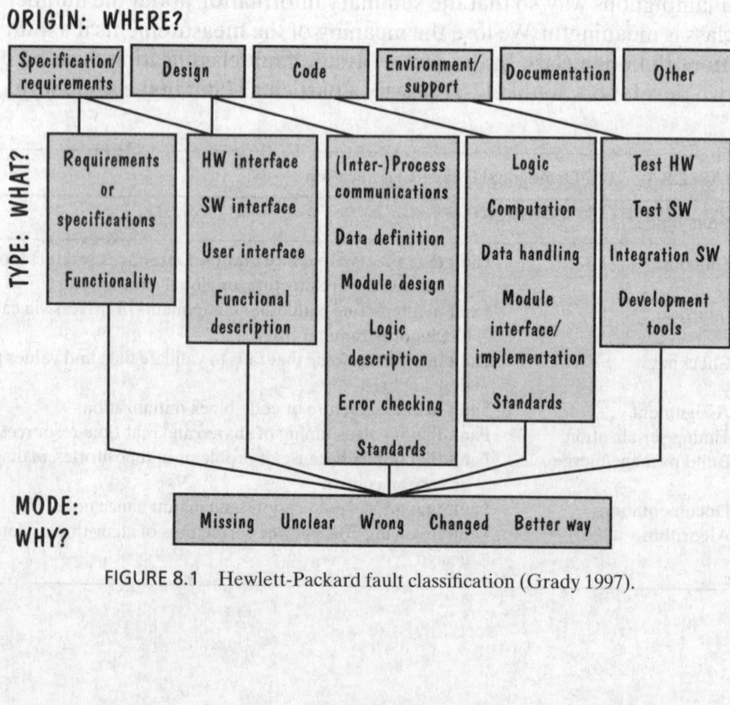

FIGURE 8.1 Hewlett-Packard fault classification (Grady 1997).

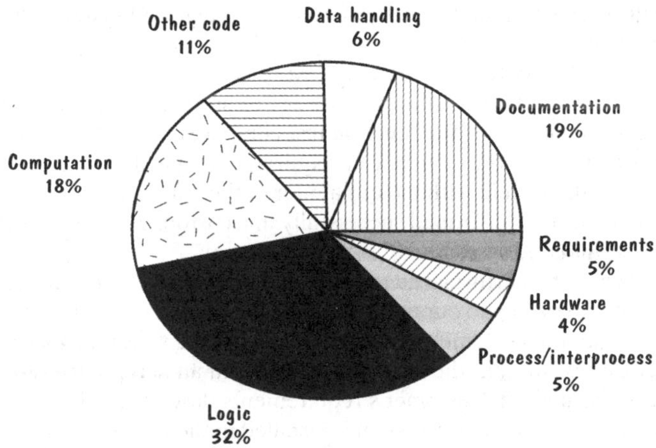

FIGURE 8.2 Faults for one Hewlett-Packard division (Grady 1997).

IBM's use of this concept by showing us that the fault profile for design review is very different from that for code inspection.

8.2 TESTING ISSUES

Many types of tests are done before we can release the system to the customer with confidence that it will work properly. Some tests depend on what is being tested: components, groups of components, subsystems, or the whole system. Other tests depend on what we want to know: Is the system working according to the design? The requirements? The customer's expectations? Let us consider some of these issues.

Test Organization

In developing a large system, testing usually involves several stages. First, each program component is tested on its own, isolated from the other components in the system. Such testing, known as **module testing**, **component testing**, or **unit testing**, verifies that the component functions properly with the types of input expected from studying the component's design. Unit testing is done in a controlled environment whenever possible, so that the test team can feed a predetermined set of data to the component being tested and observe what output actions and data are produced. In addition, the test team checks the internal data structures, logic, and boundary conditions for the input and output data.

When collections of components have been unit-tested, the next step is ensuring that the interfaces among the components are defined and handled properly. **Integration testing** is the process of verifying that the system components work together as described in the system and program design specifications.

Once we are sure that information is passed among components in accordance with the design, we test the system to ensure that it has the desired functionality. A **function test** evaluates the system to determine if the functions described by the requirements specification are actually performed by the integrated system. The result is a functioning system.

Recall that the requirements were documented in two ways: first in the customer's terminology, and again as a set of software and hardware requirements the developers could use. The function test compares the system being built with the functions described in the developer's requirements specification. Then, a **performance test** compares the system with the remainder of these software and hardware requirements. When the test is performed successfully in a customer's actual working environment, it yields a **validated system**.

When the performance test is complete, we developers are certain that the system functions according to our understanding of the system description. The next step is conferring with the customer to make certain that the system works according to customer expectations. We join the customer to perform an **acceptance test**, where the system is checked against the customer's requirements description. Upon completion of acceptance testing, the accepted system is installed in the environment in which it will be used; a final **installation test** is run to make sure that the system still functions as it should.

Figure 8.3 illustrates the relationship among these testing steps. No matter the size of the system being tested, the type of testing described in each step is necessary for ensuring proper functioning. In this chapter, we focus primarily on unit and integration testing, where components are tested by themselves and then merged into a larger, working system. In Chapter 9, we will look at the remaining steps in the testing process, collectively called **system testing**. In these later steps, the system is viewed and tested as a whole rather than as separate pieces.

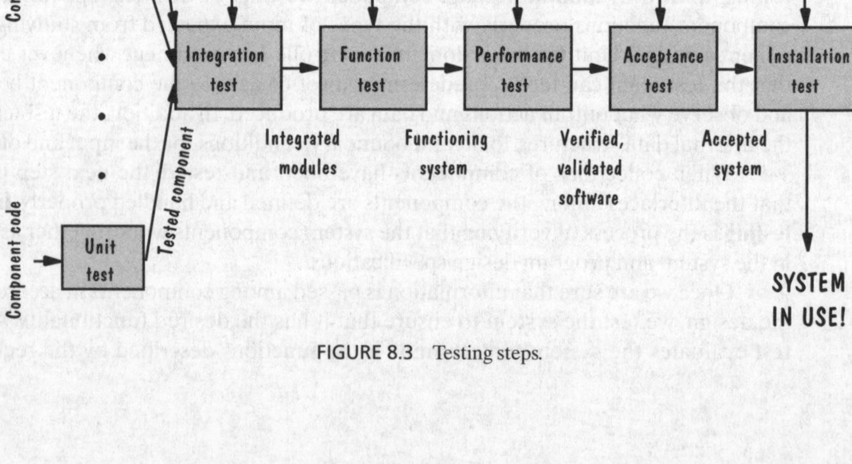

FIGURE 8.3 Testing steps.

Attitudes Toward Testing

New programmers are not accustomed to viewing testing as a discovery process. As students, we write programs according to the specifications given by our instructor. After having designed a program, we write the code and compile it to determine if any syntax faults are present. When submitting our program for a grade, we usually present our instructor with a program listing, data used as test input, and any output that shows how our program handled the input. The collection of code, input, and output acts as evidence that our code runs correctly, and we usually choose our input to persuade our instructor that the code functions as directed in our class assignment.

We may have considered our program only as a solution to a problem; we may not have considered the problem itself. If so, our test data may have been chosen to show positive results in certain cases rather than the absence of faults. Programs written and presented in this way are evidence of our programming skill. Thus, psychologically, we may consider a critique of our program to be a critique of our ability. Testing to show that our program works correctly is a way of demonstrating our skills to our instructor.

However, developing a system for customers is different. Customers are not interested in knowing that the system works properly under certain conditions. Rather, they are interested in being sure that the system works properly under all conditions. So our goal as a developer should be to eliminate as many faults as possible, no matter where in the system they occur and no matter who created them. Hurt feelings and bruised egos have no place in the development process as faults are discovered. Hence, many software engineers adopt an attitude known as **egoless programming**, where programs are viewed as components of a larger system, not as the property of those who wrote them. When a fault is discovered or a failure occurs, the egoless development team is concerned with correcting the fault, not with placing blame on a particular developer.

Who Performs the Tests?

Even when a system is developed with an egoless approach, we sometimes have difficulty removing our personal feelings from the testing process. Thus, we often use an independent test team to test a system. In this way, we avoid conflict between personal responsibility for faults and the need to discover as many faults as possible.

In addition, several other factors justify an independent team. First, we may inadvertently introduce faults when interpreting the design, determining the program logic, writing descriptive documentation, or implementing the algorithms. Clearly, we would not have submitted our code for testing if we did not think the code performed according to specification. But we may be too close to the code to be objective and to recognize some of the more subtle faults.

Furthermore, an independent test team can participate in reviewing the components throughout development. The team can be part of the requirements and design reviews, can test the code components individually, and can test the system as it is integrated and presented to the customers for acceptance. In this way, testing can proceed concurrently with coding; the test team can test components as they are completed and begin to piece them together while the programming staff continues to code other components.

Views of the Test Objects

Before we look carefully at unit testing, let us consider the philosophy behind our testing. As we test a component, group of components, subsystem, or system, our view of the test object (i.e., the component, group, subsystem, or system) can affect the way in which testing proceeds. If we view the test object from the outside as a **closed box** or **black box** whose contents are unknown, our testing feeds input to the closed box and notes what output is produced. In this case, the test's goal is to be sure that every kind of input is submitted, and that the output observed matches the output expected.

There are advantages and disadvantages to this kind of testing. The obvious advantage is that a closed box is free of the constraints imposed by the internal structure and logic of the test object. However, it is not always possible to run a complete test in this manner. For example, suppose a simple component accepts as input the three numbers *a*, *b*, and *c*, and produces as output the two roots of the equation

$$ax^2 + bx + c = 0$$

or the message "no real roots." It is impossible to test the component by submitting to it every possible triple of numbers (a, b, c). In this case, the test team may be able to choose representative test data to show that all possible combinations are handled properly. For instance, test data may be chosen so that we have all combinations of positive, negative, and zero for each of *a*, *b*, and *c*: 27 possibilities. If we know something about solving quadratic equations, we may prefer to select values that ensure that the discriminant, $b^2 - 4ac$, is in each of three classes: positive, zero, or negative. (In this situation, we are guessing at how the component is implemented.) However, even if a test in each of the classes reveals no faults, we have no guarantee that the component is fault-free. The component may still fail for a particular case because of subtleties such as round-off error or incompatible data types.

For some test objects, it is impossible for the test team to generate a set of representative test cases that demonstrate correct functionality for all cases. Recall from Chapter 7 the component that accepted adjusted gross income as input and produced the amount of federal income tax owed as output. We might have a tax table showing expected output for certain given inputs, but we may not know in general how the tax is calculated. The algorithm for computing tax depends on tax brackets, and both the bracket limits and associated percentages are part of the component's internal processing. By viewing this component as a closed box, we could not choose representative test cases because we do not know enough about the processing to choose wisely.

To overcome this problem, we can instead view the test object as an **open box** (sometimes called **clear box** or **white box**); then we can use the structure of the test object to test in different ways. For example, we can devise test cases that execute all the statements or all the control paths within the component(s) to be sure the test object is working properly. However, as we will see later in this chapter, it may be impractical to take this kind of approach.

For example, a component with many branches and loops has many paths to check. Even with a fairly simple logical structure, a component with substantial iteration or recursion is difficult to test thoroughly. Suppose a component's logic is structured so it

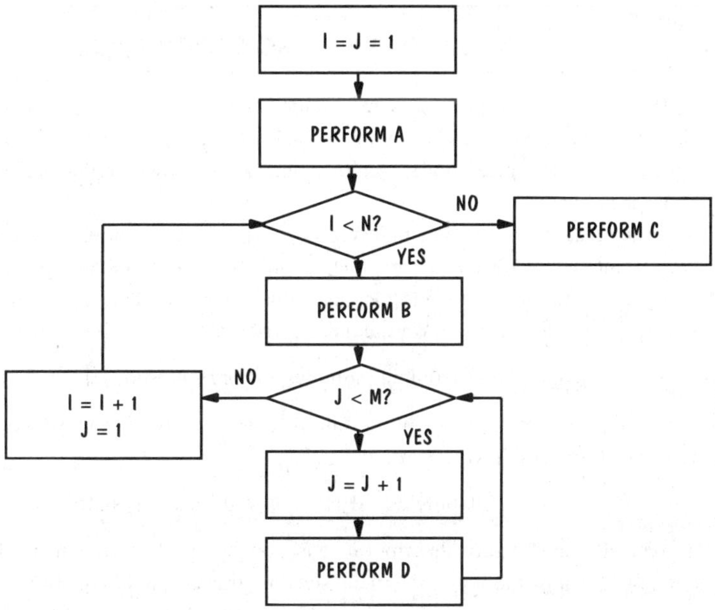

FIGURE 8.4 Example logic structure.

loops nm times, as shown in Figure 8.4. If n and m are each equal to 100,000, a test case would have to loop 10 billion times to exercise all logic paths. We can use a test strategy to exercise the loop just a few times, checking only a small number of relevant cases that represent the entire set of possibilities. In this example, we can choose a value for I that is less than n, another that is equal to n, and still another greater than n; similarly, we can look at J less than m, equal to m, and greater than m, and at combinations of these with the three combinations of values of I. In general, the strategy can be based on data, structure, function, or several other criteria, as we shall see.

When deciding how to test, we need not choose either open- or closed-box testing exclusively. We can think of closed-box testing as one end of a testing continuum and open-box testing as the other end. Any test philosophy can lie somewhere in between. Sidebar 8.2 shows us how some approaches, such as the box-structured approach, combine several points on the continuum to address a component from several perspectives. In general, the choice of test philosophy depends on many factors, including

- the number of possible logical paths
- the nature of the input data
- the amount of computation involved
- the complexity of the algorithms

SIDEBAR 8.2 BOX STRUCTURES

The box-structured approach to information systems ties together and extends the notions of open-box and closed-box views (Mills, Linger, and Hevner 1987; Mills 1988). This technique begins with a black-box view and extends it by stepwise refinement to a state box and then a clear box.

The black-box view of an object is a description of its external behavior in all possible circumstances. The object (a component, subsystem, or complete system) is described in terms of the stimulus it accepts, plus its stimulus history—that is, the record of how it has reacted to stimuli in the past. We can thus describe each response as a transition

(stimulus, stimulus_history → response)

Next, the state-box description is derived from the black box by adding state information. Each transition is written as

(stimulus, old_state → response, new_state)

Finally, the clear-box description adds a procedure that implements the state box; that is, it describes how the stimulus and old state are transformed to the response and new state:

(stimulus, old_state → response, new_state) by procedure

The procedure is written in terms of sequence, alternation, iteration, and concurrency. The progression from black box to clear box is useful not only in testing, but also in designing components, helping to turn a high-level description into a lower-level, more carefully described design.

8.3 UNIT TESTING

If our goal is to find faults in components, how do we begin? The process is similar to the one you use when testing a program assigned in class. First, you examine your code by reading through it, trying to spot algorithm, data, and syntax faults. You may even compare the code with the specifications and with your design to make sure you have considered all relevant cases. Next, you compile the code and eliminate any remaining syntax faults. Finally, you develop test cases to show if the input is properly converted to the desired output. Unit testing follows exactly these steps, and we examine them one at a time.

Examining the Code

Because the design description helps you to code and document each program component, your program reflects your interpretation of the design. The documentation explains in words and pictures what the program is supposed to do in code. Thus, it is helpful to ask an objective group of experts to review both your code and its documentation for misunderstandings, inconsistencies, and other faults. The process, known as a **code review**, is similar to the requirements and design reviews discussed in earlier chapters. A team is formed, composed of you as the programmer and three or four other technical experts; the team studies the program in an organized way to look for faults. The technical experts can be other programmers, designers, technical writers, or project supervisors. Whereas the design review team included customer representatives, the code review team contains no one from the customer's organization. Customers express requirements and approve the proposed design; they are interested in implementation only when we can demonstrate that the system as a whole works according to their description.

Code Walkthroughs. There are two types of code review: a walkthrough and an inspection. In a **walkthrough**, you present your code and accompanying documentation to the review team, and the team comments on their correctness. During the walkthrough, you lead and control the discussion. The atmosphere is informal, and the focus of attention is on the code, not the coder. Although supervisory personnel may be present, the walkthrough has no influence on your performance appraisal, consistent with the general intent of testing: finding faults, but not necessarily fixing them.

Code Inspections. A code inspection, originally introduced by Fagan (1976) at IBM, is similar to a walkthrough but is more formal. In an **inspection**, the review team checks the code and documentation against a prepared list of concerns. For example, the team may examine the definition and use of data types and structures to see if their use is consistent with the design and with system standards and procedures. The team can review algorithms and computations for their correctness and efficiency. Comments can be compared with code to ensure that they are accurate and complete. Similarly, the interfaces among components can be checked for correctness. The team may even estimate the code's performance characteristics in terms of memory usage or processing speed, in preparation for assessing compliance with performance requirements.

Inspecting code usually involves several steps. First, the team may meet as a group for an overview of the code and a description of the inspection goals. Then, team members prepare individually for a second group meeting. Each inspector studies the code and its related documents, noting faults found. Finally, in a group meeting, team members report what they have found, recording additional faults discovered in the process of discussing individuals' findings. Sometimes faults discovered by an individual are considered to be "false positives": items that seemed to be faults but in fact were not considered by the group to be true problems.

Inspection team members are chosen based on the inspection's goals, and sometimes a team member will have more than one role. For example, if the inspection is intended to verify that the interfaces are correct, then the team should include interface designers. Because the goal is the focus of the inspection, a team moderator, not the programmer, is the meeting's leader, using a set of key questions to be answered. As with walkthroughs, inspections criticize the code, not the coder, and the results are not reflected in a performance evaluation.

Success of Code Reviews. You may feel uncomfortable with the idea of having a team examine your code. However, reviews have been shown to be extraordinarily successful at detecting faults and are often included in an organization's list of mandatory or best practices. Remember that the earlier in the development process a fault is spotted, the easier and less expensive it is to correct. It is better to find a problem at the component level than to wait until later in the testing cycle, when the source of the problem may be far less clear. In fact, for this reason, Gilb (1988) and Gilb and Graham (1993) suggest inspecting early development artifacts, such as specifications and designs, not just code.

Several researchers have investigated the extent to which reviews have identified faults. Fagan (1976) performed an experiment in which 67% of the system's faults eventually detected were found before unit testing using inspections. In Fagan's study, a second group of programmers wrote similar programs using informal walkthroughs rather than inspections. The inspection group's code had 38% fewer failures during the first seven months of operation than the walkthrough group's code. In another Fagan experiment, of the total number of faults discovered during system development, 82% were found during design and code inspections. The early detection of faults led to large savings in developers' time. Other researchers report results from their use of inspections. For instance, Ackerman, Buchwald, and Lewski (1986) noted that 93% of all faults in a 6000-line business application were found by inspections.

Jones (1977) has studied programmer productivity extensively, including the nature of faults and the methods for finding and fixing them. Examining the history of 10 million lines of code, he found that code inspections removed as many as 85% of the total faults found. No other technique studied by Jones was as successful; in fact, none could remove even half of the known faults. More recent investigations by Jones (1991) suggest typical preparation times and meeting times, as shown in Table 8.2.

Grady (1997) explains that at Hewlett-Packard, planning for an inspection typically takes about two hours, followed by a 30-minute meeting with the team. Then, individual preparation involves two hours of finding faults and 90 minutes of recording the individual findings. The team spends about 30 minutes brainstorming the findings and recommending actions to be taken. After the faults have been fixed, the moderator of the inspection meeting spends an additional half-hour to write and release a summary document. Sidebar 8.3 describes how software developers at Bull Information Systems investigated ways to reduce resources needed for inspections but maintain their effectiveness.

Jones (1991) summarizes the data in his large repository of project information to paint a different picture of how reviews and inspections find faults, relative to other

TABLE 8.2 Typical Inspection Preparation and Meeting Times (Jones 1991)

Development Artifact	Preparation Time	Meeting Time
Requirements document	25 pages per hour	12 pages per hour
Functional specification	45 pages per hour	15 pages per hour
Logic specification	50 pages per hour	20 pages per hour
Source code	150 lines of code per hour	75 lines of code per hour
User documents	35 pages per hour	20 pages per hour

SIDEBAR 8.3 THE BEST TEAM SIZE FOR INSPECTIONS

Weller (1993) examined data from three years of inspections at Bull Information Systems. Measurements from almost 7000 inspection meetings included information about 11,557 faults and 14,677 pages of design documentation. He found that a three-person inspection team with a lower preparation rate did as well as a four-person team with a higher rate; he suggested that the preparation rate, not the team size, determines inspection effectiveness. He also found that a team's effectiveness and efficiency depended on their familiarity with their product: the more familiarity, the better.

On the other hand, Weller found that good code inspection results can create false confidence. On a project involving 12,000 lines of C, the requirements and design were not reviewed; inspections began with the code. But the requirements continued to evolve during unit and integration testing, and the code size almost doubled during that time. Comparing the code inspection data with the test data, Weller found that code inspections identified mostly coding or low-level design faults, but testing discovered mostly requirements and architectural faults. Thus, the code inspection was not dealing with the true source of variability in the system, and its results did not represent the true system quality.

discovery activities. Because products vary so wildly by size, Table 8.3 presents the fault discovery rates relative to the number of thousands of lines of code in the delivered product. The table makes it clear that code inspection finds far more faults than most other techniques. However, researchers continue to investigate whether some types of activities find different categories of faults than others. For example, inspections tend to be good at finding code faults, but prototyping is better for identifying requirements problems.

After Fagan published his guidelines for inspecting code at IBM, many other organizations, including Hewlett-Packard (Grady and van Slack 1994), ITT, and AT&T (Jones 1991), adopted inspections as a recommended or standard practice. Descriptions of the successful application of inspections continue to appear in the literature, and some are referenced on this book's Web site.

TABLE 8.3 Faults Found During Discovery Activities (Jones 1991)

Discovery Activity	Faults Found per Thousand Lines of Code
Requirements review	2.5
Design review	5.0
Code inspection	10.0
Integration test	3.0
Acceptance test	2.0

Proving Code Correct

Suppose your component has been coded, examined by you, and reviewed by a team. The next step in testing is to subject the code to scrutiny in a more structured way to establish its correctness. For the purposes of unit testing, a program is **correct** if it implements the functions and data properly as indicated in the design, and if it interfaces properly with other components.

One way to investigate program correctness is to view the code as a statement of logical flow. If we can rewrite the program using a formal, logical system (such as a series of statements and implications about data), then we can test this new expression for correctness. We interpret correctness in terms of the design, and we want our expressions to follow the precepts of mathematical logic. For instance, if we can formulate the program as a set of assertions and theorems, we can show that the truth of the theorems implies the correctness of the code.

Formal Proof Techniques. Let us look at how a formal proof works. We convert the code to its logical counterpart in a series of steps:

1. First, we write assertions to describe the component's input and output conditions. These statements are combinations of logical variables (each of which is true or false), connected by the logical connective symbols displayed in Table 8.4.

For example, suppose a component accepts as input an array T of size N. As output, the component produces an equivalent array T', consisting of the elements of T arranged in ascending order. We can write the input conditions as the assertion:

$$A_1\text{: } (T \text{ is an array}) \ \&\ (T \text{ is of size } N)$$

Similarly, we can write the output as the assertion

$$\begin{aligned} A_{\text{end}}\text{: } & (T' \text{ is an array}) \ \&\ (\forall\, i \text{ if } i < N \text{ then } (T'(i) \le T'(i+1))) \\ & \&\ (\forall\, i \text{ if } i \le N \text{ then } \exists\, j(T'(i) = T(j)) \ \&\ (T' \text{ is of size } N)) \end{aligned}$$

2. Next, we draw a flow diagram depicting the logical flow of the component. On the diagram, we denote points at which a transformation takes place.

Figure 8.5 shows such a diagram for a component where a bubble sort is used to rearrange T into ascending order. In the figure, two points are highlighted to show

TABLE 8.4 Logical Connectives

Connective	Example	Meaning
Conjunction	$x \,\&\, y$	x and y
Disjunction	$x \vee y$	x or y
Negation	$-x$	not x
Implication	$x \rightarrow y$	if x then y
Equivalence	$x = y$	x equals y
Universal quantifier	$\forall\, x\, P(x)$	for all x, condition $P(x)$ is true
Existential quantifier	$\exists\, x\, P(x)$	for at least one x, $P(x)$ is true

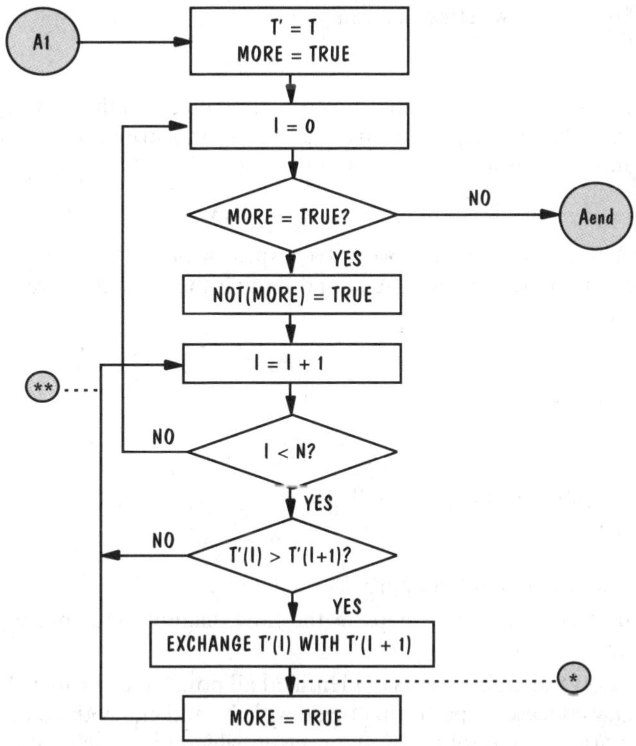

FIGURE 8.5 Flow diagram for array rearrangement.

where the transformations take place. The point marked with a single asterisk can be described as an assertion in the following way:

$$[(\text{not}(\text{more}) = \text{true}) \ \& \ (i < N) \ \& \ (T'(i) > T'(i+1))] \\ \rightarrow [(T'(i)) \text{ is exchanged with } T'(i+1)]$$

Similarly, the point marked with a double asterisk can be written as

$$[(\text{not}(\text{more}) = \text{true}) \ \& \ (i \geq N)] \rightarrow [T'(i)\text{sorted}]$$

3. From the assertions, we generate a series of theorems to be proven. Beginning with the first assertion and moving from one transformation to another, we work our way through to ensure that if one is true, then the next one is true. In other words, if the first assertion is A_1 and the first transformation point is A_2, then our first theorem is

$$A_1 \rightarrow A_2$$

If A_3 is the next transformation point, then the second theorem is

$$A_2 \rightarrow A_3$$

In this way, we state theorems

$$A_i \rightarrow A_j$$

where A_i and A_j are adjacent transformation points in the flow diagram. The last theorem states that a condition of "true" at the last transformation point implies the truth of the output assertion:

$$A_k \rightarrow A_{end}$$

Alternatively, we can work backward through the transformation points in the flow diagram, beginning at A_{end} and finding the preceding transformation point. We prove first that

$$A_k \rightarrow A_{end}$$

and then that

$$A_j \rightarrow A_{j+1}$$

and so on until we have shown that

$$A_1 \rightarrow A_2$$

The result of either approach is the same.

4. Next, we locate loops in the flow diagram and specify an if-then assertion for each.

5. At this point, we have identified all possible assertions. To prove the program correct, we locate all paths that begin with A_1 and end with A_{end}. By following each of these paths, we are following the ways in which the code shows that the truth of the input condition leads to the truth of the output condition.

6. After identifying all paths, we must verify the truth of each one by proving rigorously that the input assertion implies the output assertion according to the transformations of that path.

7. Finally, we prove that the program terminates.

Advantages and Disadvantages of Correctness Proofs. By constructing an automatic or manual proof in the manner described above, we can discover algorithmic faults in the code. In addition, the proof technique provides us with a formal understanding of the program, because we examine its underlying logical structure. Regular use of this approach forces us to be more rigorous and precise in specifying data, data structures, and algorithmic rules.

However, a price is paid for such rigor. Much work is involved in setting up and carrying out the proof. For example, the code for the bubble-sort component is much smaller than its logical description and proof. In many cases, it takes more time to prove the code correct than to write the code itself. Moreover, larger and more complex components can involve enormous logic diagrams, many transformations, and verification of a large number of paths. For instance, nonnumerical programs may be more difficult to represent logically than numerical ones. Parallel processing is hard to handle, and complex data structures may result in very complex transformation statements.

Notice that the proof technique is based only on how the input assertions are transformed into the output assertions according to logical precepts. Proving the program correct in this logical sense does not mean that there are no faults in the software. Indeed, this technique may not spot faults in the design, in interfaces with other components, in interpreting the specification, in the syntax and semantics of the programming language, or in the documentation.

Finally, we must acknowledge that not all proofs are correct. Several times in the history of mathematics, a proof that had been accepted as valid for many years was later shown to be fallacious. It is always possible for an especially intricate proof argument to be invalid.

Other Proof Techniques. The logical proof technique ignores the structure and syntax of the programming language in which the test program is implemented. In a sense, then, the technique proves that the component's design is correct but not necessarily its implementation. Other techniques take the language characteristics into account.

One such technique, **symbolic execution**, involves simulated execution of the code using symbols instead of data variables. The test program is viewed as having an input state determined by the input data and conditions. As each line of the code is executed, the technique checks to see whether its state has changed. Each state change is saved, and the program's execution is viewed as a series of state changes. Thus, each logical path through the program corresponds to an ordered series of state changes. The final state of each path should be an output state, and the program is correct if each possible input state generates the proper output state.

We can look at an example to see how symbolic execution works. Suppose we are testing these lines of a program:

```
a = b + c;
if (a > d) taskx();        // PERFORM TASKX
else tasky();              // PERFORM TASKY
```

A symbolic execution tool will note that the condition, $a > d$, can be either true or false. Whereas the conventional code execution would involve specific values of a and d, the symbolic execution tool records two possible states: $a > d$ is false and $a > d$ is true. Instead of testing a large number of possible values for a and d, symbolic execution considers only these two cases. In this way, large sets of data are divided into disjoint equivalence classes or categories, and the code can be considered only with respect to how it reacts to each category of data. Considering only equivalence classes of data, represented as symbols, greatly reduces the number of cases considered in a proof.

However, this technique has many of the same disadvantages as logical theorem proving. Developing a proof may take longer than writing the code itself, and proof of correctness does not ensure absence of faults. Moreover, the technique relies on a careful tracing of changing conditions throughout the program's paths. Although the technique can be automated to some extent, large or complex code may still require the checking of many states and paths, a time-consuming process. It is difficult for an automated symbolic execution tool to follow execution flow through loops. In addition, whenever subscripts and pointers are used in the code, partitioning into equivalence classes becomes more difficult.

Automated Theorem Proving. Some software engineers have tried to automate the process of proving programs correct by developing tools that read as input

- the input data and conditions
- the output data and conditions
- the lines of code for the component to be tested

The output from the automated tool is either a proof of the component's correctness or a counterexample showing a set of data that the component does not correctly transform to output. The automated theorem prover includes information about the language in which the component is written, so that the syntax and semantics rules are accessible. Following the program's steps, the theorem prover identifies the paths in several ways. If the usual rules of inference and deduction are too cumbersome to be used, a heuristic solution is sometimes employed instead.

Such theorem-proving software is nontrivial to develop. For example, the tool must be able to verify the correct use of unary and binary operations (e.g., addition, subtraction, negation), as well as of comparisons involving equality and inequality. More complex laws such as commutativity, distributivity, and associativity must be incorporated. Expressing the programming language as a set of postulates from which to derive theorems is very difficult.

Suppose these difficulties can be overcome. Using trial and error to construct theorems is too time-consuming for any but the most trivial of components. Thus, some human interaction is desirable to guide the theorem prover. Using methods frequently employed when developing an expert system, an interactive theorem prover can work with its user to choose transformation points and trace paths. Thus, the theorem prover does not really generate the proof; rather, it checks the proof outlined by its user. Symbolic-execution-based tools have been developed to evaluate code in small programs, but there is no general-purpose, language-independent, automated, symbolic-execution system available.

Can the ideal theorem prover ever be built, assuming the existence of a machine that is fast enough and an implementation language that can handle the complexities of the problem? The ideal theorem prover would read in any program and produce as its output either a statement confirming the code's correctness or the location of a fault. The theorem prover would have to determine if an arbitrary statement in the code is executed for arbitrary input data. Unfortunately, this kind of theorem prover can never be built. It can be shown (in Pfleeger and Straight [1985], for example) that the construction of such a program is the equivalent of the halting problem for Turing machines. The halting problem is unsolvable, which means not only that there is no solution to the problem, but also that it is impossible ever to find a solution. We can make our theorem prover solvable by applying it only to code having no branches, but this limitation makes the tool applicable only to a very narrow subset of all programs. Thus, although highly desirable, any automated theorem prover will only approximate the ideal.

Testing Program Components

Proving code correct is a goal to which software engineers aspire; consequently, much related research is done to develop methods and automated tools. However, in the near future, development teams are more likely to be concerned with testing their software rather than with proving their programs correct.

Testing vs. Proving. In proving a program correct, the test team or programmer considers only the code and its input and output conditions. The program is viewed in terms of the classes of data and conditions described in the design. Thus, the proof may not involve executing the code but rather understanding what is going on inside the program.

However, customers have a different point of view. To demonstrate to them that a program is working properly, we must show them how the code performs from outside the program. In this sense, testing becomes a series of experiments, the results of which become a basis for deciding how the program will behave in a given situation. Whereas a proof tells us how a program will work in a hypothetical environment described by the design and requirements, testing gives us information about how a program works in its actual operating environment.

Choosing Test Cases. To test a component, we choose input data and conditions, allow the component to manipulate the data, and observe the output. We select the input so that the output demonstrates something about the behavior of the code. A **test point** or **test case** is a particular choice of input data to be used in testing a program. A **test** is a finite collection of test cases. How do we choose test cases and define tests in order to convince ourselves and our customers that the program works correctly, not only for the test cases, but for all input?

We begin by determining our test objectives. Then, we select test cases and define a test designed to meet a specific objective. One objective may be to demonstrate that all statements execute properly. Another may be to show that every function performed by the code is done correctly. The objectives determine how we classify the input in order to choose our test cases.

We can view the code as either closed box or open box, depending on the test objectives. If closed box, we supply the box with all possible input, and compare the output with what is expected according to the requirements. However, if the code is viewed as an open box, we can examine the code's internal logic, using a careful testing strategy.

Recall the example component to calculate the roots of a quadratic equation. If our test objective is demonstrating that the code functions properly, we might choose test cases where the coefficients a, b, and c range through representative combinations of negative numbers, positive numbers, and zero. Or we can select combinations based on the relative sizes of the coefficients:

- a is greater than b, which is greater than c
- b is greater than c, which is greater than a
- c is greater than b, which is greater than a

and so on. However, if we acknowledge the code's inner workings, we can see that the logic depends on the value of the discriminant, $b^2 - 4ac$. Then, we choose test cases that represent when the discriminant is positive, negative, and zero. We may also include test cases for nonnumeric data. For example, we may input the letter 'F' as a coefficient, to determine how the system reacts to something nonnumeric. Including the three numeric cases, we have four mutually exclusive types of test input.

In this fashion, we use the test objective to help us separate the input into equivalence classes. That is, the classes of data should meet these criteria:

1. Every possible input belongs to one of the classes. That is, the classes cover the entire set of input data.
2. No input datum belongs to more than one class. That is, the classes are disjoint.
3. If the executing code demonstrates a fault when a particular class member is used as input, then the same fault can be detected using any other member of the class as input. That is, any element of the class represents all elements of that class.

It is not always easy or feasible to tell if the third restriction on the classes can be met. We can loosen the third requirement so that if a data element belongs to a class and reveals a fault, then the probability is high that every other element in that class will reveal the same fault.

Closed-box testing suffers from uncertainty about whether the test cases selected will uncover a particular fault. On the other hand, open-box testing always admits the danger of paying too much attention to the code's internal processing. We may end up testing what the program does instead of what it should do.

We can combine open- and closed-box testing to generate test data. First, by considering the program as a closed box, we can use the program's external specifications to generate initial test cases. These cases should incorporate not only the expected input data, but also boundary conditions for the input and output, as well as several cases of invalid data. For instance, if the component is coded to expect a positive input value, we may include a test case for each of the following:

- a very large positive integer
- a positive integer
- a positive, fixed-point decimal
- a number greater than 0 but less than 1
- zero
- a negative number
- a nonnumeric character

Some data are purposely chosen to be improper; we test with them to check that the code handles incorrect data gracefully.

Next, by viewing the program's internal structure, we add other cases. For example, we can add test cases to test all branches and to exercise as many paths as possible. If loops are involved, we may include test cases that loop once, many times, and not at all. We can also examine the implementation of algorithms. For instance, if the program does trigonometric calculations, we can include cases that test the extremities of the trigonometric functions, such as zero, 90, 180, 270, and 360 degrees. Or we may have input that causes a denominator to be set to zero.

Sometimes a system "remembers" conditions from the previous case, so sequences of test cases are needed. For example, when a system implements a finite-state machine, the code must recall the previous system state; the previous state plus current input determine the next state. Similarly, real-time systems are often interrupt-driven; tests exercise sets of cases rather than single ones.

Test Thoroughness. To perform a test, we decide how to demonstrate in a convincing way that the test data exhibit all possible behaviors. Let us see what choices we have.

To test code thoroughly, we can choose test cases using at least one of several approaches based on the data manipulated by the code:

- **Statement testing:** Every statement in the component is executed at least once in some test.
- **Branch testing:** For every decision point in the code, each branch is chosen at least once in some test.
- **Path testing:** Every distinct path through the code is executed at least once in some test.
- **Definition-use path testing:** Every path from every definition of every variable to every use of that definition is exercised in some test.
- **All-uses testing:** The test set includes at least one path from every definition to every use that can be reached by that definition.
- **All-predicate-uses/some-computational-uses testing:** For every variable and every definition of that variable, a test includes at least one path from the definition to every predicate use; if there are definitions not covered by that description, then include computational uses so that every definition is covered.
- **All-computational-uses/some-predicate-uses testing:** For every variable and every definition of that variable, a test includes at least one path from the definition to every computational use; if there are definitions not covered by that description, then include predicate uses so that every definition is covered.

There are other, similar kinds of testing, such as all-definitions, all-predicate-uses, and all-computational-uses. Beizer (1990) describes the relative strengths of these test strategies, as shown in Figure 8.6. For example, testing all paths is stronger than testing all paths from definition to use. In general, the stronger the strategy, the more test cases

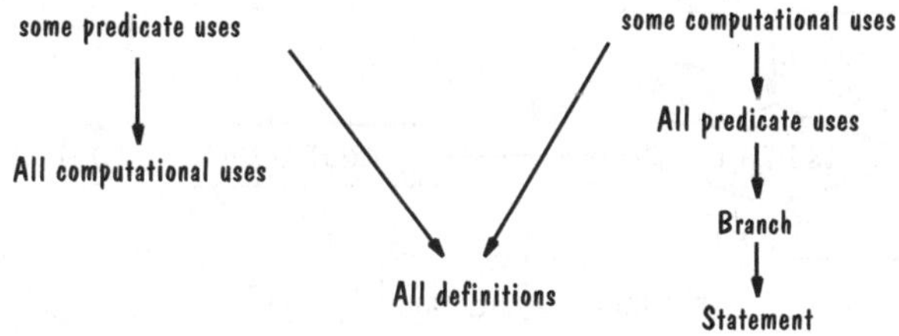

FIGURE 8.6 Relative strengths of test strategies (Beizer 1990).

are involved; we must always consider the trade-off between the resources available for testing and the thoroughness of the strategy we choose.

We are likely to do better with a strategy than with random testing. For example, Ntafos (1984) compared random testing with branch testing and all-uses testing on seven mathematical programs with known faults. He found that random testing found 79.5% of the faults, branch testing found 85.5%, and all-uses testing found 90%.

To see how the strategy affects the number of test cases, consider the example in Figure 8.7, which illustrates the logic flow in a component to be tested. Each statement, represented by a diamond or rectangle, has been numbered. Statement testing requires test cases that execute statements 1 through 7. By choosing *X* larger than *K* that produces a positive RESULT, we can execute statements

1-2-3-4-5-6-7

in order, so one test case suffices.

For branch testing, we must identify all the decision points, represented by diamonds in Figure 8.7. There are two decisions: one about the relationship of *X* to *K*, and another about whether or not RESULT is positive. Two test cases will exercise paths

1-2-3-4-5-6-7

and

1-2-4-5-6-1

and traverse each branch at least once. The first path uses the *yes* branch of the first decision point, and the second uses the *no* branch. Likewise, the first path uses the *yes* branch of the second decision point, and the second path uses the *no* branch.

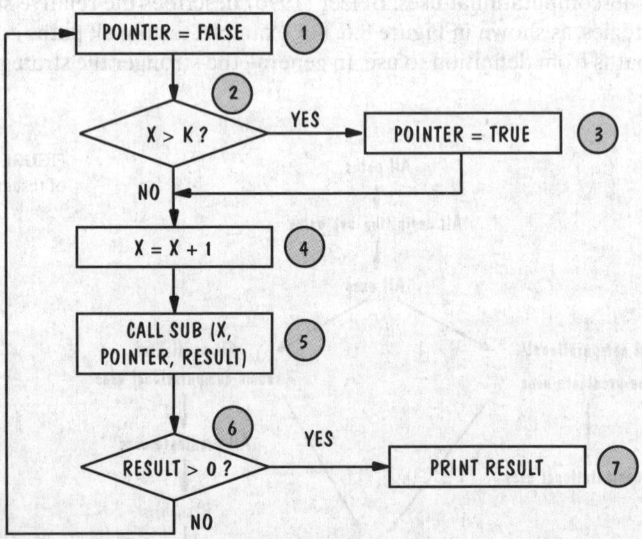

FIGURE 8.7 Logic flow.

If we want to exercise each possible path through the program, then we need more test cases. The paths

1-2-3-4-5-6-7
1-2-3-4-5-6-1
1-2-4-5-6-7
1-2-4-5-6-1

cover all the possibilities: two decision points with two choices at each branch.

In our example, statement testing requires fewer test cases than branch testing, which in turn requires fewer cases than path testing. This relationship is true in general. Moreover, the more complex a program, the more path test cases required. Exercise 10 investigates the relationship between the structure and order of decision points and the number of paths through the code.

There are many other test strategies that can be employed during unit testing. For example, secure applications are often tested by following each possible transaction to its end, employing a strategy called **transaction flow testing**. For a thorough discussion of testing strategy, see Beizer (1990).

Comparing Techniques

Jones (1991) has compared several types of fault-discovery methods to determine which ones are most likely to find certain categories of faults. Table 8.5 shows the results of his survey, organized by the development activity generating the fault. For example, if a fault is located in the code but is the result of a problem with the requirements specification, it is listed in the "requirements" column.

Jones (1991) also investigated which types of removal techniques were best in catching which kinds of faults. Table 8.6 shows that reviews and inspections were the

TABLE 8.5 Fault-Discovery Percentages by Fault Origin (Jones 1991)

Discovery Technique	Requirements	Design	Coding	Documentation
Prototyping	40	35	35	15
Requirements review	40	15	0	5
Design review	15	55	0	15
Code inspection	20	40	65	25
Unit testing	1	5	20	0

TABLE 8.6 Effectiveness of Fault-Discovery Techniques (Jones 1991)

	Requirements Faults	Design Faults	Code Faults	Documentation Faults
Reviews	Fair	Excellent	Excellent	Good
Prototypes	Good	Fair	Fair	Not applicable
Testing	Poor	Poor	Good	Fair
Correctness proofs	Poor	Poor	Fair	Fair

SIDEBAR 8.4 FAULT-DISCOVERY EFFICIENCY AT CONTEL IPC

Olsen (1993) describes the development of a 184,000-lines-of-code system using C, Objective C, assembler, and scripts at a company that provided automated assistance to the financial community. He tracked faults discovered during various activities and found differences: 17.3% of the faults were found during inspections of the system design, 19.1% during component design inspection, 15.1% during code inspection, 29.4% during integration testing, and 16.6% during system and regression testing. Only 0.1% of the faults were revealed after the system was placed in the field. Thus, Olsen's work shows the importance of using different techniques to ferret out different kinds of faults during development; it is not enough to rely on a single method for catching all problems.

most effective for discovering design and code problems, but that prototyping was best at identifying problems with requirements. Sidebar 8.4 illustrates why it is best to use a diverse set of techniques to discover faults.

8.4 INTEGRATION TESTING

When we are satisfied that individual components are working correctly and meet our objectives, we combine them into a working system. This integration is planned and coordinated so that when a failure occurs, we have some idea of what caused it. In addition, the order in which components are tested affects our choice of test cases and tools. For large systems, some components may be in the coding phase, others may be in the unit-testing phase, and still other collections of components may be tested together. Our test strategy explains why and how components are combined to test the working system. This strategy affects not only the integration timing and coding order, but also the cost and thoroughness of the testing.

The system is again viewed as a hierarchy of components, where each component belongs to a layer of the design. We can begin from the top and work our way down as we test, work from the bottom up, or use a combination of these two approaches.

Bottom-Up Integration

One popular approach for merging components to test the larger system is called **bottom-up testing**. When this method is used, each component at the lowest level of the system hierarchy is tested individually first. Then, the next components to be tested are those that call the previously tested ones. This approach is followed repeatedly until all components are included in the testing. The bottom-up method is useful when many of the low-level components are general-purpose utility routines that are invoked often by others, when the design is object-oriented, or when the system is integrating a large number of stand-alone reused components.

For example, consider the components and hierarchy in Figure 8.8. To test this system from the bottom up, we first test the lowest level: E, F, and G. Because we have

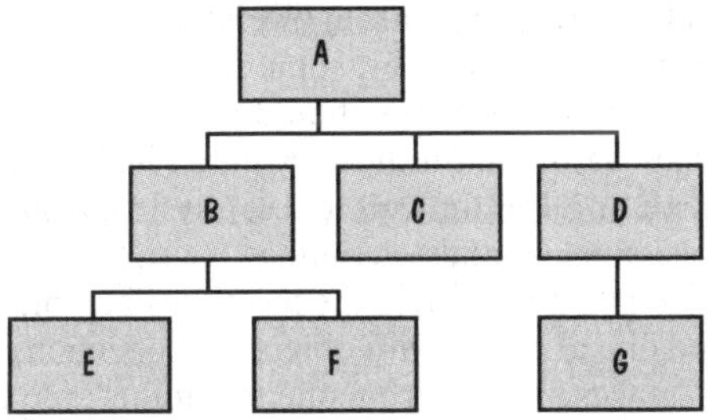

FIGURE 8.8 Example component hierarchy.

no components ready to call these lowest-level programs, we write special code to aid the integration. A **component driver** is a routine that calls a particular component and passes a test case to it. The driver is not difficult to code, since it rarely requires complex processing. However, care is taken to be sure that the driver's interface with the test component is defined properly. Sometimes, test data can be supplied automatically in a special purpose language that facilitates defining the data.

In our example, we need a component driver for each of E, F, and G. When we are satisfied that those three components work correctly, we move to the next higher level. Unlike the lowest-level components, the next-level components are not tested separately. Instead, they are combined with the components they call (which have already been tested). In this case, we test B, E, and F together. If a problem occurs, we know that its cause is either in B or in the interface between B and E or B and F, since E and F functioned properly on their own. Had we tested B, E, and F without having tested E and F separately, we might not have been able to isolate the problem's cause so easily.

Similarly, we test D with G. Because C calls no other component, we test it by itself. Finally, we test all components together. Figure 8.9 shows the sequence of tests and their dependencies.

A frequent complaint about bottom-up testing in a functionally decomposed system is that the top-level components are usually the most important but the last to be tested. The top level directs the major system activities, whereas the bottom level often performs the more mundane tasks, such as input and output functions or repetitive calculations. The top levels are more general, whereas the lower levels are more specific.

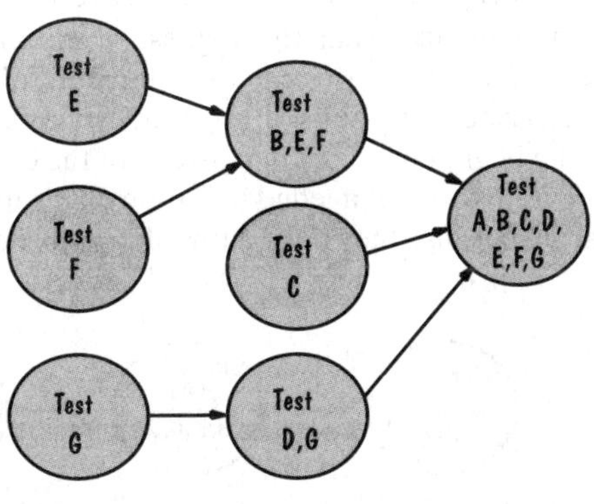

FIGURE 8.9 Bottom-up testing.

Thus, some developers feel that by testing the bottom levels first, the discovery of major faults is postponed until testing's end. Moreover, sometimes faults in the top levels reflect faults in design; obviously, these problems should be corrected as soon as possible in development, rather than waiting until the very end. Finally, top-level components often control or influence timing. It is difficult to test a system from the bottom up when much of the system's processing depends on timing.

On the other hand, bottom-up testing is often the most sensible for object-oriented programs. Objects are combined one at a time with objects or collections of objects that have been tested previously. Messages are sent from one to another, and testing ensures that the objects react correctly.

Top-Down Integration

Many developers prefer to use a **top-down approach**, which in many ways is the reverse of bottom-up. The top level, usually one controlling component, is tested by itself. Then, all components called by the tested component(s) are combined and tested as a larger unit. This approach is reapplied until all components are incorporated.

A component being tested may call another that is not yet tested, so we write a **stub**, a special-purpose program to simulate the activity of the missing component. The stub answers the calling sequence and passes back output data that lets the testing process continue. For example, if a component is called to calculate the next available address but that component is not yet tested, then a stub for it may pass back a fixed address only to allow testing to proceed. As with drivers, stubs need not be complex or logically complete.

Figure 8.10 shows how top-down testing works with our example system. Only the top component, A, is tested by itself, with stubs needed for B, C, and D. Once tested, it is combined with the next level, and A, B, C, and D are tested together. Stubs may be needed for components E, F, or G at this stage of testing. Finally, the entire system is tested.

If the lowest level of components performs the input and output operations, stubs for them may be almost identical to the actual components they replace. In this case, the integration sequence may be altered so that input and output components are incorporated earlier in the testing sequence.

Many of the advantages of top-down design and coding also apply to top-down testing. When functions in particular components have been localized by using top-down design, testing from the top down allows the test team to exercise one function at a time, following its command sequence from the highest levels of control down through appropriate components. Thus, test cases can be defined in terms of the functions being examined. Moreover, any design faults or major questions about functional feasibility can be addressed at the beginning of testing instead of the end.

Notice, too, that driver programs are not needed in top-down testing. On the other hand, writing stubs can be difficult, because they must allow all possible conditions to be

FIGURE 8.10 Top-down testing.

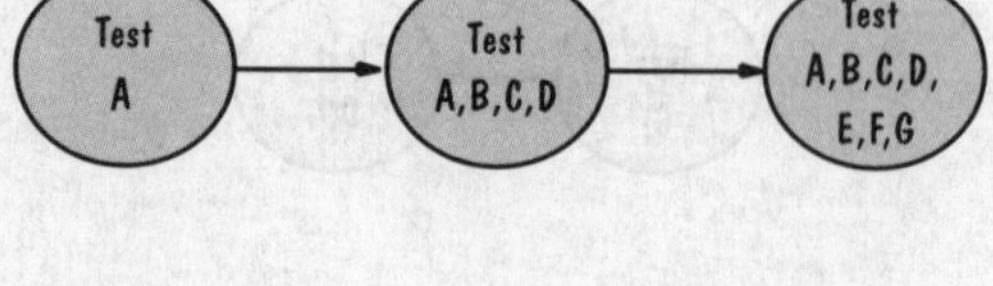

tested. For example, suppose component Z of a map-drawing system performs a calculation using latitude and longitude output by component Y. The design specification states that the output from Y is always in the northern hemisphere. Since Z calls Y, when Z is part of a top-down test, Y may not yet be coded. If a stub is written to generate a number between 0 and 180 to allow testing of Z to continue, the stub must be changed if the design is changed to allow southern hemispherical locations. That is, the stub is an important part of testing, and its correctness may affect the validity of a test.

A disadvantage to top-down testing is the possibility that a very large number of stubs may be required. This situation can arise when the lowest system level contains many general-purpose routines. One way to avoid this problem is to alter the strategy slightly. Rather than incorporate an entire level at a time, a modified top-down approach tests each level's components individually before the merger takes place. For instance, our sample system can be tested with the modified approach by first testing A, then testing B, C, and D, and then merging the four for a test of the first and second levels. Then E, F, and G are tested by themselves. Finally, the entire system is combined for a test, as shown in Figure 8.11.

Testing each level's components individually introduces another difficulty. Both stubs and drivers are needed for each component, leading to much more coding and many potential problems.

Big-Bang Integration

When all components are tested in isolation, it is tempting to mix them together as the final system and see if it works the first time. Myers (1979) calls this **big-bang testing**, and Figure 8.12 shows how it works on our example system. Many programmers use the big-bang approach for small systems, but it is not practical for large ones. In fact, since big-bang testing has several disadvantages, it is not recommended for any system. First, it requires both stubs and drivers to test the independent components. Second, because all components are merged at once, it is difficult to find the cause of any failure. Finally, interface faults cannot be distinguished easily from other types of faults.

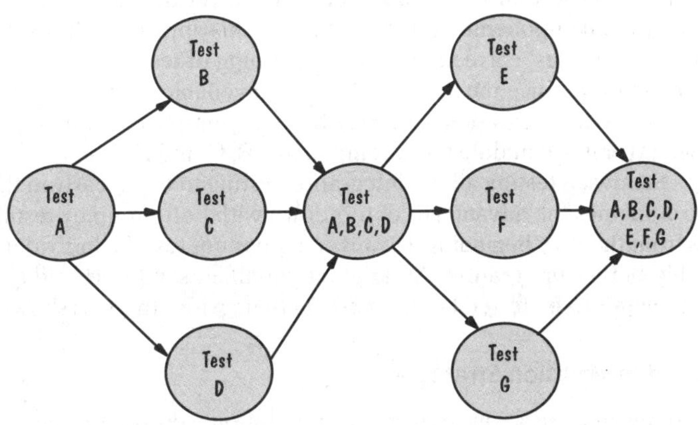

FIGURE 8.11 Modified top-down testing.

FIGURE 8.12 Big-bang testing.

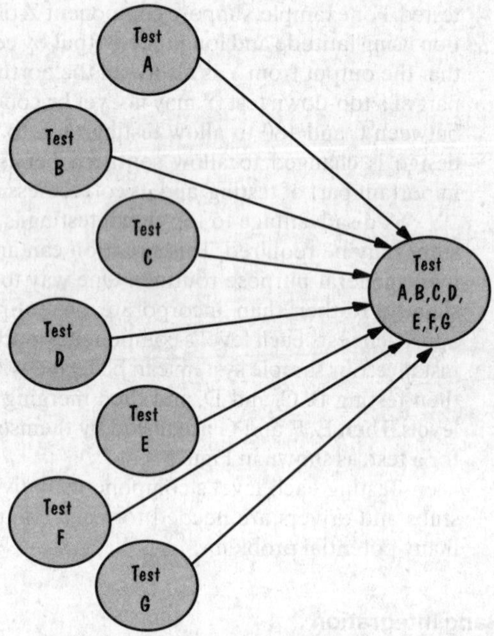

Sandwich Integration

Myers (1979) combines a top-down strategy with a bottom-up one to form a **sandwich testing** approach. The system is viewed as three layers, just like a sandwich: the target layer in the middle, the levels above the target, and the levels below the target. A top-down approach is used in the top layer and a bottom-up one in the lower layer. Testing converges on the target layer, chosen on the basis of system characteristics and the structure of the component hierarchy. For example, if the bottom layer contains many general-purpose utility programs, the target layer may be the one above, in which lie most of the components using the utilities. This approach allows bottom-up testing to verify the utilities' correctness at the beginning of testing. Then stubs for utilities need not be written, since the actual utilities are available for use. Figure 8.13 depicts a possible sandwich integration sequence for our example component hierarchy, where the target layer is the middle level, components B, C, and D.

Sandwich testing allows integration testing to begin early in the testing process. It also combines the advantages of top-down with bottom-up by testing control and utilities from the very beginning. However, it does not test the individual components thoroughly before integration. A variation, modified sandwich testing, allows upper-level components to be tested before merging them with others, as shown in Figure 8.14.

Comparison of Integration Strategies

Choosing an integration strategy depends not only on system characteristics, but also on customer expectations. For instance, the customer may want to see a working version as

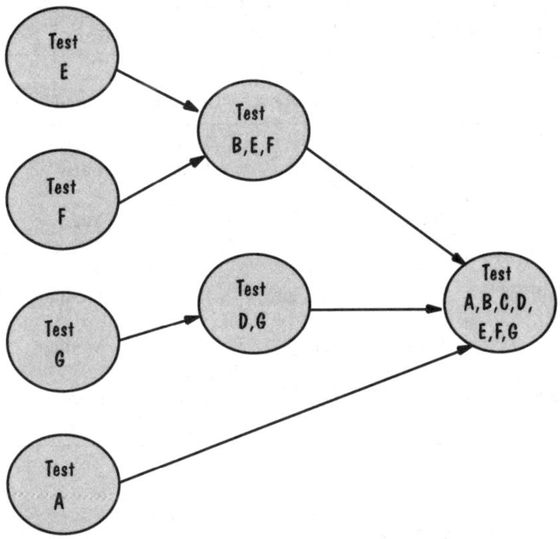

FIGURE 8.13 Sandwich testing.

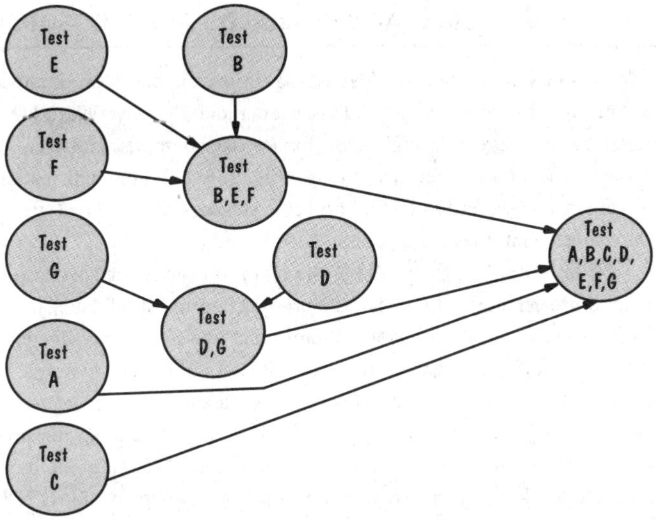

FIGURE 8.14 Modified sandwich testing.

soon as possible, so we may adopt an integration schedule that produces a basic working system early in the testing process. In this way, some programmers are coding while others are testing, so that the test and code stages can occur concurrently. Myers (1979) has composed a matrix, shown in Table 8.7, that compares the several testing strategies according to several system attributes and customer needs. Sidebar 8.5 explains Microsoft's strategy, driven by market pressures.

TABLE 8.7 Comparison of Integration Strategies (Myers 1979)

	Bottom-Up	Top-Down	Modified Top-Down	Big-Bang	Sandwich	Modified Sandwich
Integration	Early	Early	Early	Late	Early	Early
Time to basic working program	Late	Early	Early	Late	Early	Early
Component drivers needed	Yes	No	Yes	Yes	Yes	Yes
Stubs needed	No	Yes	Yes	Yes	Yes	Yes
Work parallelism at beginning	Medium	Low	Medium	High	Medium	High
Ability to test particular paths	Easy	Hard	Easy	Easy	Medium	Easy
Ability to plan and control sequence	Easy	Hard	Hard	Easy	Hard	Hard

SIDEBAR 8.5 BUILDS AT MICROSOFT

Microsoft's integration strategy is market-driven, based on the need to have a working product as quickly as possible (Cusumano and Selby 1995, 1997). It uses many small, parallel teams (three to eight developers each) implementing a "synch-and-stabilize" approach. The process iterates among designing, building, and testing components while involving customers in the testing process. All parts of a product are integrated frequently to determine what does and does not work.

The Microsoft approach allows the team to change the specification of features as the developers learn more about what the product can and should do. Sometimes the feature set changes as much as 30% or more. The product and project are divided into parts, based on features, and different teams are responsible for different features. Then, milestones are defined, determined by a partitioning of features into most critical, desirable, and least critical. The feature teams synchronize their work by building the product and by finding and fixing faults on a daily basis, as shown in Figure 8.15. Thus, the most important features are developed and integrated first, and each milestone includes "buffer time" to handle unexpected complications or delays. If the schedule must be shortened, the least important features are cut from the product.

No matter what strategy is chosen, each component is merged only once for testing. Furthermore, at no time should a component be modified to simplify testing. Stubs and drivers are separate, new programs, not temporary modifications of existing programs.

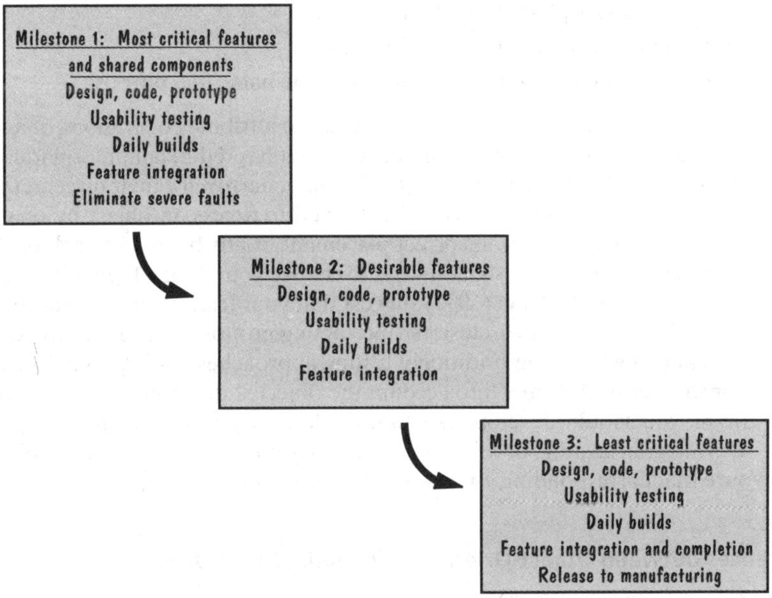

FIGURE 8.15 Microsoft synch-and-stabilize approach.

8.5 TESTING OBJECT-ORIENTED SYSTEMS

Many of the techniques we have described for testing systems apply to all types of systems, including object-oriented ones. However, you should take several additional steps to make sure that your object-oriented programs' characteristics have been addressed by your testing techniques.

Testing the Code

Rumbaugh et al. (1991) propose that you begin testing object-oriented systems by asking several questions:

- When your code expects a unique value, is there a path that generates a unique result?
- When there are many possible values, is there a way to select a unique result?
- Are there useful cases that are not handled?

Next, make sure that you check the objects and classes themselves for excesses and deficiencies: missing objects, unnecessary classes, missing or unnecessary associations, or incorrect placement of associations or attributes. Rumbaugh et al. (1991) provide some guidelines to help you identify these conditions during your testing. They note that objects might be missing if

- you find asymmetric associations or generalizations
- you find disparate attributes and operations on a class

- one class is playing two or more roles
- an operation has no good target class
- you find two associations with the same name and purpose

A class might be unnecessary if it has no attributes, operations, or associations. Similarly, an association might be unnecessary if it has redundant information or if no operations use a path. If role names are too broad or narrow for their placement, an association may be in the wrong place. Or if you need to access an object by one of its attribute values, you may have an incorrect placement of attributes. For each of these situations, Rumbaugh et al. (1991) suggest ways to change your design to remedy these situations.

Smith and Robson (1992) suggest that your testing should address many different levels: functions, classes, clusters (interacting groups of collaborating objects), and the system as a whole. The traditional testing approaches apply well to functions, but many approaches do not take into account the object states needed to test classes. At a minimum, you should develop tests that track an object's state and changes to that state. During your testing, beware of concurrency and synchronization problems, and make sure that corresponding events are complete and consistent.

Differences between Object-Oriented and Traditional Testing

Perry and Kaiser (1990) take a careful look at testing object-oriented components, especially those that are reused from other applications. The properties of object orientation are often thought to help minimize testing, but that is not always the case. For example, encapsulation isolates components that were developed separately. It is tempting to think that if a programmer reuses some components without change, and reuses others but with some changes, then only the modified code needs to be tested. However, "a program that has been adequately tested in isolation may not be adequately tested in combination" (Perry and Kaiser 1990). In fact, they show that when we add a new subclass or modify an existing subclass, we must retest the methods inherited from each of its ancestor superclasses.

They also examine the adequacy of test cases. For procedural languages, we can use a set of test data to test a system; then, when a change is made to the system, we can test that the change is correct and use the existing test data to verify that the additional, remaining functionality is still the same. But Perry and Kaiser (1990) show that the situation is different for object-oriented systems. When a subclass replaces an inherited method with a locally defined method with the same name, the overriding subclass must be retested, and probably with a different set of test data. Harrold and McGregor (1989) describe a technique for using the test case history of an object-oriented system to minimize the amount of additional testing. They first test base classes having no parents; the test strategy is to test each function individually and then test the interactions among functions. Next, they provide an algorithm to update incrementally the test history of the parent class; only attributes that are new or are affected by the inheritance scheme are tested.

Graham (1996a) summarizes the differences between object-oriented and traditional testing in two ways. First, she notes which aspects of object orientation make testing easier and which make it harder. For example, objects tend to be small, and the

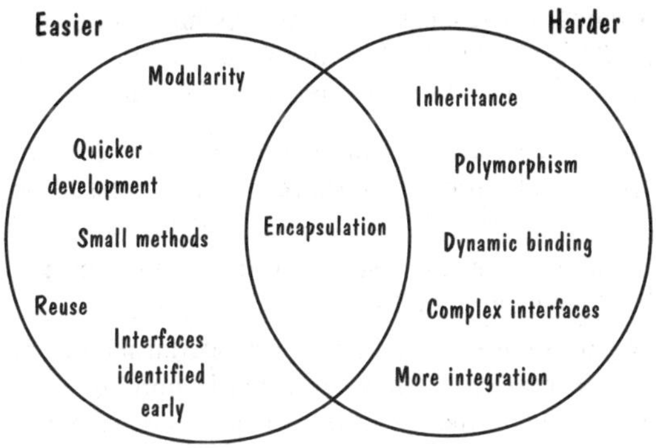

FIGURE 8.16 Easier and harder parts of testing object-oriented systems (Graham 1996a).

complexity that might ordinarily reside in the component is often pushed instead toward the interfaces among components. This difference means that unit testing is less difficult, but integration testing must be much more extensive. As we have seen, encapsulation is often considered a positive attribute of object-oriented design, but it also requires more extensive integration testing.

Similarly, inheritance introduces the need for more testing. An inherited function needs additional testing if

- it is redefined
- it has a specific behavior in a derived class
- other functions in that class are supposed to be consistent

Figure 8.16 depicts Graham's view of these differences.

Graham also looks at the steps in the testing process that are affected by object orientation. The diagram in Figure 8.17 is a Kiviat or radar graph that compares the differences between object-oriented and traditional testing. The gray polygon shows that

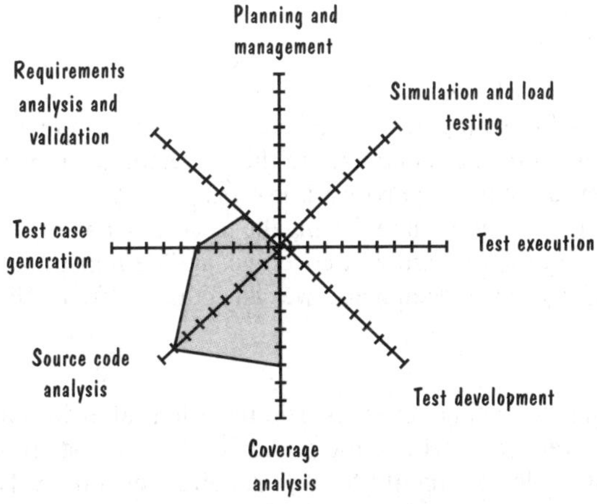

FIGURE 8.17 Significant aspects of the testing domain where object-oriented testing is different (Graham 1996a).

requirements analysis and validation, test case generation, source code analysis, and coverage analysis require special treatment. The farther the gray line is out from the center of the diagram, the more the difference between object-oriented and traditional testing.

- Requirements are likely to be expressed in the requirements document, but there are few tools to support validation of requirements expressed as objects and methods.
- Likewise, most tools that assist in test case generation are not prepared to handle a model expressed in objects and methods.
- Most source code measurements are defined for procedural code, not for objects and methods. Traditional metrics such as cyclomatic numbers are of little use when assessing the size and complexity of object-oriented systems. Over time, as researchers propose and test useful object-oriented measurements, this point of difference will diminish.
- Because it is the interaction of objects that is the source of complexity, code coverage measurements and tools are of less value in object-oriented testing than in traditional testing.

8.6 TEST PLANNING

As we have seen, much is involved in testing components and integrating them to build a system. Careful test planning helps us to design and organize the tests, so we are confident that we are testing appropriately and thoroughly.

Each step of the testing process must be planned. In fact, the test process has a life of its own within the development cycle, and it can proceed in parallel with many of the other development activities. In particular, we must plan each of these test steps:

1. establishing test objectives
2. designing test cases
3. writing test cases
4. testing test cases
5. executing tests
6. evaluating test results

The test objective tells us what kinds of test cases to generate. Moreover, the test case design is key to successful testing. If test cases are not representative and do not thoroughly exercise the functions that demonstrate the correctness and validity of the system, then the remainder of the testing process is useless.

Therefore, running a test begins with reviewing the test cases to verify that they are correct, feasible, provide the desired degree of coverage, and demonstrate the desired functionality. Once these checks have been made, we can actually execute the tests.

Purpose of the Plan

We use a test plan to organize testing activities. The test plan takes into account the test objectives and incorporates any scheduling mandated by the test strategy or the project deadlines. The system development life cycle requires several levels of testing, beginning with unit and integration testing, and proceeding to demonstrate the full system's functionality. The **test plan** describes the way in which we will show our customers that the software works correctly (i.e., that the software is free of faults and performs the functions as specified in the requirements). Thus, a test plan addresses not only unit and integration testing, but also system testing. The plan is a guide to the entire testing activity. It explains who does the testing, why the tests are performed, how the tests are conducted, and when the tests are scheduled.

To develop the test plan, we must know the requirements, functional specifications, and modular hierarchy of the system's design and code. As we develop each of these system elements, we can apply what we know to choosing a test objective, defining a test strategy, and generating a set of test cases. Consequently, the test plan is developed as the system itself is developed.

Contents of the Plan

A test plan begins with the test objectives, addressing each type of testing from unit through functional to acceptance and installation testing. Thus, the system test plan is really a series of test plans, one for each kind of test to be administered. Next, the plan looks at how the tests will be run and what criteria will be used to determine when the testing is complete. Knowing when a test is over is not always easy. We have seen examples of code where it is impossible or impractical to exercise every combination of input data and conditions. By choosing a subset of all possible data, we admittedly increase the likelihood that we will miss testing for a particular kind of fault. This trade-off between completeness and the realities of cost and time involves a compromise of our objectives. Later in this chapter, we look at how to estimate the number of faults left in the code, as well as identifying fault-prone code.

When the test team can recognize that a test objective has been met, we say that the test objectives are **well-defined**. It is then that we decide how to integrate the components into a working system. We consider statement, branch, and path coverage at the component level, as well as top-down, bottom-up, and other strategies at the integration level. The resulting plan for merging the components into a whole is sometimes called the **system integration plan**.

For each stage of testing, the test plan describes in detail the methods to be used to perform each test. For example, unit testing may be composed of informal walk-throughs or formal inspections, followed by analyzing the code structure and then analyzing the code's actual performance. The plan notes any automated support, including conditions necessary for tool use. This information helps the test team plan its activities and schedule the tests.

A detailed list of test cases accompanies each test method or technique. The plan also explains how test data will be generated and how any output data or state information will be captured. If a database is used to track tests, data, and output, the database and its use are also described.

Thus, as we read the test plan, we have a complete picture of how and why testing will be performed. By writing the test plan as we design the system, we are forced to understand the system's overall goals. In fact, sometimes the testing perspective encourages us to question the nature of the problem and the appropriateness of the design.

Many customers specify the test plan's contents in the requirements documentation. For example, the U.S. Department of Defense provides a developer with automated data systems documentation standards when a system is being built. The standards explain that the test plan

> is a tool for directing the . . . testing, and contains the orderly schedule of events and list of materials necessary to effect a comprehensive test of a complete [automated data system]. Those parts of the document directed toward the staff personnel shall be presented in nontechnical language and those parts of the document directed toward the operations personnel shall be presented in suitable terminology. (Department of Defense 1977)

We investigate the details of this test plan example in Chapter 9.

8.7 AUTOMATED TESTING TOOLS

There are many automated tools to help us test code components, and we have mentioned several in this chapter, such as automated theorem provers and symbolic execution tools. But in general, there are several places in the testing process where tools are useful, if not essential.

Code Analysis Tools

There are two categories of code analysis tools. **Static analysis** is performed when the program is not actually executing; **dynamic analysis** is done when the program is running. Each type of tool reports back information about the code itself or the test case that is being run.

Static Analysis. Several tools can analyze a source program before it is run. Tools that investigate the correctness of a program or set of components can be grouped into four types:

1. **Code analyzer:** The components are evaluated automatically for proper syntax. Statements can be highlighted if the syntax is wrong, if a construction is fault-prone, or if an item has not been defined.
2. **Structure checker:** This tool generates a graph from the components submitted as input. The graph depicts the logic flow, and the tool checks for structural flaws.
3. **Data analyzer:** The tool reviews the data structures, data declarations, and component interfaces, and then notes improper linkage among components, conflicting data definitions, and illegal data usage.
4. **Sequence checker:** The tool checks sequences of events; if coded in the wrong sequence, the events are highlighted.

For example, a code analyzer can generate a symbol table to record where a variable is first defined and when it is used, supporting test strategies such as definition-use testing. Similarly, a structure checker can read a program and determine the location of all loops, mark statements that are never executed, note the presence of branches from the middle of a loop, and so on. A data analyzer can notify us when a denominator may be set to zero; it can also check to see whether subroutine arguments are passed properly.

The input and output components of a system may be submitted to a sequence checker to determine if the events are coded in the proper sequence. For example, a sequence checker can ensure that all files are opened before they are modified.

Measurements and structural characteristics are included in the output from many static analysis tools, so that we have a better understanding of the program's attributes. For example, flow graphs are often supplemented with a listing of all possible paths through the program, allowing us to plan test cases for path testing. We are also supplied with information about fan-in and fan-out, the number of operators and operands in a program, the number of decision points, and several measures of the code's structural complexity. In Figure 8.18, we see an example of output from a static analysis program, comparing the findings for a particular piece of code with a large database of historical information. The comparison involves not only measurements such as depth of nesting, coupling, and number of decisions but also information about potential faults and uninitiated variables. Depictions like this one tell us how easy testing is likely to be and warn us about possible faults that we may want to fix before formal tests are run.

Dynamic Analysis. Many times, systems are difficult to test because several parallel operations are being performed concurrently. This situation is especially true for real-time systems. In these cases, it is difficult to anticipate conditions and generate representative test cases. Automated tools enable the test team to capture the state of events during the execution of a program by preserving a "snapshot" of conditions. These tools are sometimes called **program monitors** because they watch and report the program's behavior.

A monitor can list the number of times a component is called or a line of code is executed. These statistics tell testers about the statement or path coverage of their test cases. Similarly, a monitor can report on whether a decision point has branched in all directions, thus providing information about branch coverage. Summary statistics are also reported, providing a high-level view of the percentage of statements, paths, and branches that have been covered by the collective set of test cases run. This information is important when test objectives are stated in terms of coverage; for example, the London air traffic control system was required by contract to have 100% statement coverage in its testing (Pfleeger and Hatton 1997).

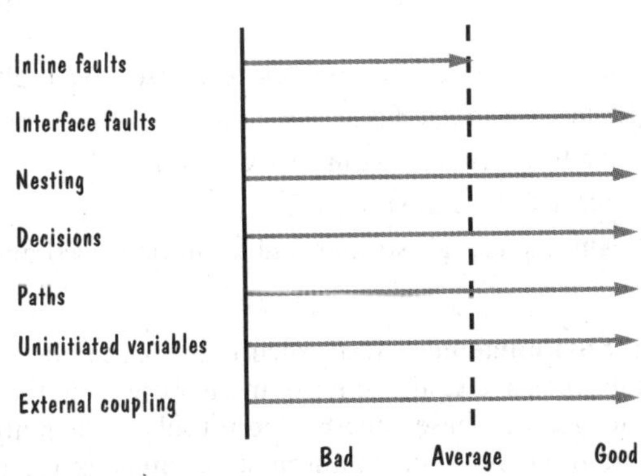

FIGURE 8.18 Output from static analysis.

Additional information may help the test team evaluate the system's performance. Statistics can be generated about particular variables: their first value, last value, minimum, and maximum, for example. Breakpoints can be defined within the system so that when a variable attains or exceeds a certain value, the test tool reports the occurrence. Some tools stop when breakpoints are reached, allowing the tester to examine the contents of memory or values of specific data items; sometimes it is possible to change values as the test progresses.

For real-time systems, capturing as much information as possible about a particular state or condition during execution can be used after execution to provide additional information about the test. Control flow can be traced backward or forward from a breakpoint, and the test team can examine accompanying data changes.

Test Execution Tools

The tools we have described so far have focused on the code. Other tools can be used to automate the planning and running of the tests themselves. Given the size and complexity of most systems today, automated test execution tools are essential for handling the very large number of test cases that must be run to test a system thoroughly.

Capture and Replay. When tests are planned, the test team must specify in a test case what input will be provided and what outcome is expected from the actions being tested. **Capture-and-replay** or **capture-and-playback** tools capture the keystrokes, input, and responses as tests are being run, and the tools compare expected with actual outcome. Discrepancies are reported to the team, and the captured data help the team trace the discrepancy back to its root cause. This type of tool is especially useful after a fault has been found and fixed; it can be used to verify that the fix has corrected the fault without introducing other faults into the code.

Stubs and Drivers. We noted earlier the importance of stubs and drivers in integration testing. Commercial tools are available to assist you in generating stubs and drivers automatically. But test drivers can be broader than simply a program to exercise a particular component. The driver can

1. set all appropriate state variables to prepare for a given test case, and then run the test case
2. simulate keyboard input and other data-related responses to conditions
3. compare actual outcome to expected outcome and report differences
4. track which paths have been traversed during execution
5. reset variables to prepare for the next test case
6. interact with a debugging package, so that faults can be traced and fixed during testing, if so desired

Automated Testing Environments. Test execution tools can be integrated with other tools to form a comprehensive testing environment. Often, the tools we describe here are connected to a testing database, measurement tools, code analysis tools, text editors, and simulation and modeling tools to automate as much of the test process as possible. For example, databases can track test cases, storing the input data for each test case, describing the expected output, and recording the actual output. However, finding evidence of a fault is not the same as locating the fault. Testing will always involve the manual effort required to trace a problem back to its root cause; the automation assists but does not replace this necessarily human function.

Test Case Generators

Testing depends on careful, thorough definition of test cases. For this reason, it is useful to automate part of the test case generation process, so that we can be sure that our cases cover all possible situations. There are several types of tools to help us with this job. **Structural test case generators** base their test cases on the structure of the source code. They list test cases for path, branch, or statement testing, and they often include heuristics to help us get the best coverage.

Other test case generators are based on data flow, functional testing (i.e., on exercising all possible states that affect the completion of a given function), or the state of each variable in the input domain. Other tools are available to generate random sets of test data, used mostly to support reliability modeling (as we will see in Chapter 9).

8.8 WHEN TO STOP TESTING

We noted in earlier chapters that software quality can be measured in many ways. One way to assess the "goodness" of a component is by the number of faults it contains. It seems natural to assume that software faults that are the most difficult to find are also the most difficult to correct. It also seems reasonable to believe that the most easily fixed faults are detected when the code is first examined, and the more difficult faults are located later in the testing process. However, Shooman and Bolsky (1975) found that this is not the case. Sometimes it takes a great deal of time to find trivial faults, and many such problems are overlooked or do not appear until well into the testing process. Moreover, Myers (1979) reports that as the number of detected faults increases, the probability of the existence of more undetected faults increases, as shown in Figure 8.19. If there are many faults in a component, we want to find them as early as possible in the testing process. However, the graph shows us that if we find a large number of faults at the beginning, then we are likely still to have a large number undetected.

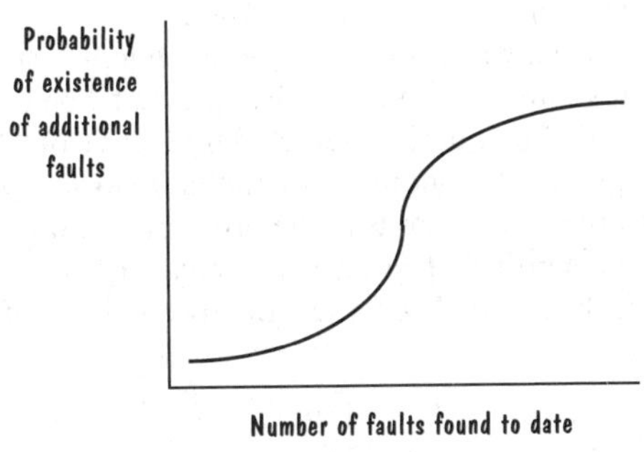

FIGURE 8.19 Probability of finding faults during development.

In addition to being contrary to our intuition, these results also make it difficult to know when to stop looking for faults during testing. We must estimate the number of remaining faults, not only to know when to stop our search for more faults, but also to give us some degree of confidence in the code we are producing. The number of faults also indicates the likely maintenance effort needed if faults are left to be detected after the system is delivered.

Fault Seeding

Mills (1972) developed a technique known as **fault seeding** or **error seeding** to estimate the number of faults in a program. The basic premise is that one member of the test team intentionally inserts (or "seeds") a known number of faults in a program. Then, the other team members locate as many faults as possible. The number of undiscovered seeded faults acts as an indicator of the number of total faults (including indigenous, nonseeded ones) remaining in the program. That is, the ratio of seeded faults detected to total seeded faults should be the same as the ratio of nonseeded faults detected to total nonseeded faults:

$$\frac{\text{detected seeded faults}}{\text{total seeded faults}} = \frac{\text{detected nonseeded faults}}{\text{total nonseeded faults}}$$

Thus, if a program is seeded with 100 faults and the test team finds only 70, it is likely that 30% of the indigenous faults remain in the code.

We can express this ratio more formally. Let S be the number of seeded faults placed in a program, and let N be the number of indigenous (nonseeded) faults. If n is the actual number of nonseeded faults detected during testing, and s is the number of seeded faults detected during testing, then an estimate of the total number of indigenous faults is

$$N = Sn/s$$

Although simple and useful, this approach assumes that the seeded faults are of the same kind and complexity as the actual faults in the program. But we do not know what the typical faults are before we have found them, so it is difficult to make the seeded faults representative of the actual ones. One way to increase the likelihood of representativeness is to base the seeded faults on historical records for code from similar past projects. However, this approach is useful only when we have built like systems before. And as we pointed out in Chapter 2, things that seem similar may in fact be quite different in ways of which we are not always aware.

To overcome this obstacle, we can use two independent test groups to test the same program. Call them Test Group 1 and Test Group 2. Let x be the number of faults detected by Test Group 1 and y the number detected by Test Group 2. Some faults will be detected by both groups; call this number of faults q, so that $q \leq x$ and $q \leq y$. Finally, let n be the total number of all faults in the program; we want to estimate n.

The effectiveness of each group's testing can be measured by calculating the fraction of faults found by each group. Thus, the effectiveness E_1 of Group 1 can be expressed as

$$E_1 = x/n$$

and the effectiveness E_2 of Group 2 as

$$E_2 = y/n$$

The group effectiveness measures the group's ability to detect faults from among a set of existing faults. Thus, if a group can find half of all the faults in a program, its effectiveness is 0.5. Consider the faults detected by both Group 1 and Group 2. If we assume that Group 1 is just as effective at finding faults in any part of the program as in any other part, we can look at the ratio of faults found by Group 1 from the set of faults found by Group 2. That is, Group 1 found q of the y faults that Group 2 found, so Group 1's effectiveness is q/y. In other words,

$$E_1 = x/n = q/y$$

However, we know that E_2 is y/n, so we can derive the following formula for n:

$$n = q/(E_1 * E_2)$$

We have a known value for q, and we can use estimates of q/y for E_1 and q/x for E_2, so we have enough information to estimate n.

To see how this method works, suppose two groups test a program. Group 1 finds 25 faults. Group 2 finds 30 faults, and 15 of those are duplicates of the faults found by Group 1. Thus, we have

$$x = 25$$
$$y = 30$$
$$q = 15$$

The estimate, E_1, of Group 1's effectiveness is q/y, or 0.5, since Group 1 found 15 of the 30 faults found by Group 2. Similarly, the estimate, E_2, of Group 2's effectiveness is q/x, or 0.6. Thus, our estimate of n, the total number of faults in the program, is $15/(0.5*0.6)$, or 50 faults.

The test strategy defined in the test plan directs the test team in deciding when to stop testing. The strategy can use this estimating technique to decide when testing is complete.

Confidence in the Software

We can use fault estimates to tell us how much confidence we can place in the software we are testing. **Confidence**, usually expressed as a percentage, tells us the likelihood that the software is fault-free. Thus, if we say that a program is fault-free with a 95% level of confidence, then we mean that the probability that the software has no faults is 0.95.

Suppose we have seeded a program with S faults, and we claim that the code has only N actual faults. We test the program until we have found all S of the seeded faults. If, as before, n is the number of actual faults discovered during testing, then the confidence level can be calculated as

$$C\begin{cases} = 1 & \text{if } n > N \\ = S/(S - N + 1) & \text{if } n \leq N \end{cases}$$

For example, suppose we claim that a component is fault-free, meaning that N is zero. If we seed the code with 10 faults and find all 10 without uncovering an indigenous fault, then we can calculate the confidence level with $S = 10$ and $N = 0$. Thus, C is 10/11, for a confidence level of 91%. If the requirements or contract mandates a confidence level of 98%, we would need to seed S faults, where $S/(S - 0 + 1) = 98/100$. Solving this equation, we see that we must use 49 seeded faults and continue testing until all 49 faults are found (but no indigenous faults discovered).

This approach presents a major problem: We cannot predict the level of confidence until all seeded faults are detected. Richards (1974) suggests a modification, where the confidence level can be estimated using the number of detected seeded faults, whether or not all have been located. In this case, C is

$$C\begin{cases} = 1 & \text{if } n > N \\ = \binom{S}{s-1} \Big/ \binom{S+N+1}{N+s} & \text{if } n \le N \end{cases}$$

These estimates assume that all faults have an equal probability of being detected, which is not likely to be true. However, many other estimates take these factors into account. Such estimation techniques not only give us some idea of the confidence we may have in our programs but also provide a side benefit. Many programmers are tempted to conclude that each fault discovered is the last one. If we estimate the number of faults remaining, or if we know how many faults we must find to satisfy a confidence requirement, we have incentive to keep testing for one more fault.

These techniques are also useful in assessing confidence in components that are about to be reused. We can look at the fault history of a component, especially if fault seeding has taken place, and use techniques such as these to decide how much confidence to place in reusing the component without testing it again. Or we can seed the component and use these techniques to establish a baseline level of confidence.

Other Stopping Criteria

The test strategy itself can be used to set stopping criteria for testing. For example, when we are doing statement, path, or branch testing, we can track how many statements, paths, or branches need to be executed and determine our test progress in terms of the number of statements, paths, or branches left to test.

Many automated tools calculate these coverage values for us. Consider this code from Lee and Tepfenhart (1997) to implement a computer game:

```
LISTING                                                 BRANCH   STATEMENT
                                                                  NUMBER
void                                                                 1
Collision::moveBall(Ball *ball)                                      2
{                                                                    3
    ball->change_position(final_loc),upperLeft());                   4
    int sf = 1;          //speed factor                              5
```

```
6     for(int i = 0; i<number_hit(); i++)            1 - 2
7     {
8       obstacle *hitptr=
9          (obstacle *) obj(i)->real_identity();
10      sf *= hitpte->respond_to_being_hit(this);
11    }
12    Point v = rebound(ball->get_velocity());
13    if(v.X() == 0 )                                3 - 4
14         v.X(1);
15    if(v.Y() == 0 )                                5 - 6
16        v.Y(-1);
17    ball->change_velocity(sf*v);
18  }
```

A tool may add to the listing a notation about where the branches are, as shown. Thus, branch 1 is the path taken when *i* is within the loop parameters in statement 6, branch 2 is the path taken when *i* is not in the loop parameters, branch 3 is the path taken when `v.X` is zero in statement 13, branch 4 is the path taken when `v.X` is not zero, and so on. An automated tool can calculate all of the paths to be covered by tests; in this case, there are 2^3, or 8, possibilities. Then, as testing progresses, the tool may produce a report like the ones in Tables 8.8 and 8.9, so we see how many paths are left to traverse in order to have path or branch coverage.

Identifying Fault-Prone Code

There are many techniques used to help identify fault-prone code, based on past history of faults in similar applications. For example, some researchers track the number of faults found in each component during development and maintenance. They also collect measurements about each component, such as size, number of decisions, number of operators and operands, or number of modifications. Then, they generate equations to

TABLE 8.8 Summary of Path Traversals

		This Test			Cumulative		
Test Case	Number of Paths	Invocation	Paths Traversed	% Coverage	Invocation	Paths Traversed	% Coverage
6	8	1	4	50	5	6	75

TABLE 8.9 Paths Not Executed

Test Case	Paths Missed	Total
6	1 2 3 4	4

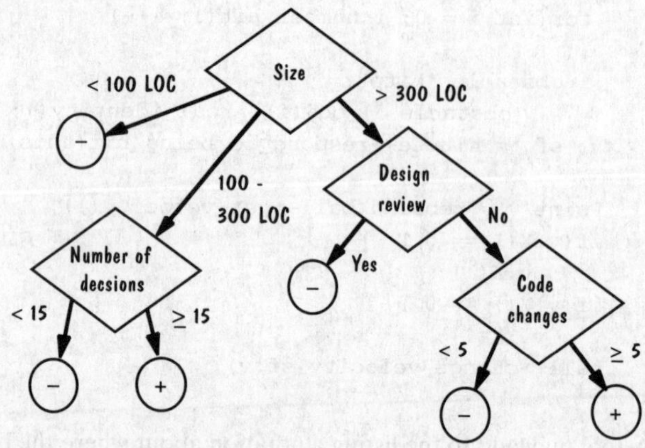

FIGURE 8.20 Classification tree to identify fault-prone components.

suggest the attributes of the most fault-prone components. These equations can be used to suggest which of your components should be tested first, or which should be given extra scrutiny during reviews or testing.

Porter and Selby (1990) suggest the use of classification trees to identify fault-prone components. Classification tree analysis is a statistical technique that sorts through large arrays of measurement information, creating a decision tree to show which measurements are the best predictors of a particular attribute. For instance, suppose we collect measurement data about each component built in our organization. We include size (in lines of code), number of distinct paths through the code, number of operators, depth of nesting, degree of coupling and cohesion (rated on a scale from 1 as lowest to 5 as highest), time to code the component, number of faults found in the component, and more. We use a classification tree analysis tool to analyze the attributes of the components that had five or more faults, compared with those that had fewer than five faults. The result may be a decision tree like the one in Figure 8.20.

The tree is used to help us decide which components in our current system are likely to have a large number of faults. According to the tree, if a component has between 100 and 300 lines of code and has at least 15 decisions, then it may be fault-prone. Or if the component has over 300 lines of code, has not had a design review, and has been changed at least five times, then it, too, may be fault-prone. We can use this type of analysis to help us target our testing when testing resources are limited. Or we can schedule inspections for such components, to help catch problems before testing begins.

8.9 INFORMATION SYSTEMS EXAMPLE

Suppose we are generating test cases to test the Piccadilly system's components, and we choose a test strategy that plans to exercise every path in a component. We may decide to write test scripts that describe an input and an expected outcome, and the test process will involve comparing the actual outcome with the expected outcome for each test case. If the actual outcome is indeed equal to the expected outcome, does that mean the component is fault-free? Not really. We may have what Beizer (1990) calls coincidental correctness in the component. To understand why, consider a component that has the following structure:

```
CASE 1: Y := X/3;
CASE 2: Y := 2X-25;
CASE 3: Y := X MOD 10;
ENDCASE;
```

If our test case uses 15 as the input for X, expects 5 as the output for Y, and actually yields Y equal to 5, we do not know which path was exercised; every case produces a Y of 5 for an X of 15! For this reason, test cases must be supplemented with markers that help the test team to identify which path is actually taken by the code. In this example, a path coverage tool would be very useful in tracking exactly which statements are exercised when each test case is run.

Because the Piccadilly system is an information system, we may in fact prefer to use a data-flow testing strategy rather than a structural one. We can identify each data element easily by using the data dictionary and then consider possible values for each. Strategies such as definition-use testing may be the most appropriate; we follow each data item through a component, looking for situations where the value of the data element can change, and verifying that the change is correct. Such testing can be supported by many automated tools: database repositories, test case generators, and test execution monitors that note each change in a datum's value. In fact, our test team may want to link the database that contains the data dictionary with other tools.

8.10 REAL-TIME EXAMPLE

The Ariane-5 system underwent a great deal of review and testing. According to Lions et al. (1996), the flight control system was tested in four ways:

1. equipment testing
2. on-board computer software testing
3. staged integration
4. system validation tests

The overall philosophy of the Ariane-5 testing was to check at each level what could not be achieved at the previous level. In this way, the developers hoped to provide complete test coverage of each subsystem and of the integrated system. Let us look at the postexplosion investigation to see why the testing during software qualification did not discover the SRI problems before the actual flight. (We will examine the integration and validation tests in Chapter 9.)

The investigators reported that "no test was performed to verify that the SRI would behave correctly when being subjected to the count-down and flight time sequence and the trajectory of Ariane-5" (Lions et al. 1996). In fact, the specification for the SRI software did not contain the Ariane-5 trajectory data among its functional requirements. In other words, there was no discussion in the requirements documents of the ways in which the Ariane-5 trajectory would be different from Ariane-4. The investigators noted that "Such a declaration of limitation, which should be mandatory for every mission-critical device, would have served to identify any non-compliance with the trajectory of Ariane-5."

Because the root cause is in the requirements, it could have been noticed quite early during the development process. Indeed, reviews were an integral part of the design and coding activities, and the investigators point out that they were "carried out at all levels and involved all major partners in the project (as well as external experts)." They concluded that

> . . . it is evident that the limitations of the SRI software were not fully analyzed in the reviews, and it was not realized that the test coverage was inadequate to expose such limitations. Nor were the possible implications of allowing the alignment software to operate during flight realized. In these respects, the review process was a contributory factor in the failure. (Lions et al. 1996)

Thus, the Ariane-5 developers relied on insufficient reviews and test coverage, giving them a false sense of confidence in the software.

There are several ways to improve the likelihood that reviews and test coverage are complete. One is to involve a nonexpert in the review process. Such a participant will question many of the assumptions that other reviewers take for granted—often wrongly. Another is to examine the completeness of test cases, either by asking an external participant to review them or by using a formal technique to assess the degree of coverage. As we will see in Chapter 9, the Ariane-5 developers had several other opportunities to find the SRI problem during testing, but it slipped through their safety net.

8.11 WHAT THIS CHAPTER MEANS FOR YOU

This chapter describes many techniques that you can use to test your code components individually and as they are integrated with those of your colleagues. It is important for you to understand the difference between a fault (a problem in the requirements, design, code, documentation, or test cases) and a failure (a problem in the functioning of the system). Testing looks for faults, sometimes by forcing code to fail and then seeking the root cause. Unit testing is the development activity that exercises each component separately; integration testing puts components together in an organized way to help you isolate faults as the combined components are tested together.

The goal of testing is to find faults, not to prove correctness. Indeed, the absence of faults does not guarantee correctness. There are many manual and automated techniques to help you find faults in your code, as well as testing tools to show you how much has been tested and when to stop testing.

8.12 WHAT THIS CHAPTER MEANS FOR YOUR DEVELOPMENT TEAM

Testing is both an individual and a group activity. Once a component is written, it can be inspected by some or all of the development team to look for faults that were not apparent to the person who wrote it. The research literature clearly shows that inspections are very effective at finding faults early in the development process. But it is equally clear that other techniques find faults that inspections often miss. So it is important for you to work with your team in an egoless way, using the many methods at your disposal, to find faults as early as possible during development.

Integration testing is a team activity, too, and you must coordinate with other team members in choosing an integration strategy, planning your tests, generating test cases, and running the tests. Automated tools are useful in these activities, and they help you and your teammates scrutinize the test results to identify problems and their causes.

8.13 WHAT THIS CHAPTER MEANS FOR RESEARCHERS

Researchers continue to investigate a large number of important issues associated with testing:

- Inspections are effective, but they can be made more effective in a variety of ways. Researchers are looking at the best ways to choose inspection team members, to review development artifacts, and to interact in group meetings to find as many faults as possible. Some researchers are comparing the use of the group meeting to lack of a group meeting, to see what a group meeting really accomplishes.
- Researchers continue to try to understand which techniques are best at finding what kinds of faults.
- The systems we are building are far more complicated and far larger than the systems built even just a few years ago. Thus, it is becoming more and more important to have automated tools to support our testing. Researchers are looking at ways to define test cases, track tests, and assess coverage completeness, and at the role of automation in these activities.
- Testing resources are usually limited, especially by schedules for market-driven products. Researchers continue to seek ways to identify fault-prone components, so that testing can be targeted at those first. Similarly, for safety-critical systems, researchers are building models and tools to ensure that the most critical components are tested thoroughly.

8.14 TERM PROJECT

The Loan Arranger requires a great deal of testing. Because the system is important to the economic health of the FCO, the customer wants the software delivered as soon as possible. Devise a test strategy that tests the Loan Arranger but uses a minimum of resources. Justify your strategy, and explain how you will know when to stop testing and turn over the system to the customer.

8.15 KEY REFERENCES

Testing has been the subject of several special issues of journals and magazines, including the March 1991 issue of *IEEE Software* and the June 1988 issue of *Communications of the ACM*. The September 1994 issue of *Communications of the ACM* discusses special considerations in testing object-oriented systems. And the January/February 2000 issue of *IEEE Software* addresses why testing is so hard. In addition, *IEEE Transactions on Software Engineering* often has articles that compare different testing techniques in terms of the kinds of faults they find.

There are several good books that describe testing in great detail. Myers (1979) is the classic text, describing the philosophy of testing as well as several specific techniques. Beizer (1990) offers a good overview of testing considerations and techniques, with many references to key papers in the field. His 1995 book focuses particularly on black-box testing. Hetzel (1984) is also a useful reference, as are Perry (1995), Kit (1995), and Kaner, Falk, and Nguyen (1993). Binder (2000) is a comprehensive guide to testing object-oriented systems.

There are many good papers describing the use of inspections, including Weller (1993 and 1994) and Grady and van Slack (1994). Gilb and Graham's book (1993) on inspections is a good, comprehensive, and practical guide. Researchers continue to refine inspection techniques, and to expand them to other process artifacts such as requirements. For examples of this work, see Porter et al. (1998) and Shull, Rus, and Basili (2000).

There are many automated testing tools available for you to use with your programs. Software Quality Engineering provides a variety of resources on its Web page, and publishes an electronic newsletter, StickyMinds, with information about the latest testing tools. It also organizes several annual conferences, including STAR (Software Testing, Analysis and Review) on the East Coast of the U.S. and STARWest on the West Coast. Information about particular tools can be found at vendor Web sites, such as Cigital and Rational Software. The Cigital site also contains a database of testing resources. Fewster and Graham's (1999) book discusses the issues involved in software test automation.

Other testing-related conferences sponsored by the IEEE Computer Society and the ACM are described at their Web sites. In addition, the American Society for Quality runs an annual World Congress for Software Quality, where testing and quality control are the key issues discussed.

8.16 EXERCISES

1. Let P be a program component that reads a list of N records and a range condition on the record key. The first seven characters of the record form the record key. P reads the key and produces an output file that contains only those records whose key falls in the prescribed range. For example, if the range is "JONES" to "SMITH," then the output file consists of all records whose keys are lexicographically between "JONES" and "SMITH." Write the input and output conditions as assertions to be used in proving P correct. Write a flow diagram of what P's logical flow might be and identify the transformation points.
2. You are required to perform black box testing on a module that calculates the average of an array of numbers. Suggest some test cases for the module.
3. What are the easiest detectable software faults? Why?

4. A program is seeded with 25 faults. During testing, 18 faults are detected, 13 of which are seeded faults and 5 of which are indigenous faults. What is Mills's estimate of the number of indigenous faults remaining undetected in the program?

5. You claim that your program is fault-free at a 95% confidence level. Your test plan calls for you to test until you find all seeded faults. With how many faults must you seed the program before testing in order to substantiate your claim? If for some reason you do not intend to find all seeded faults, how may seeded faults does the Richards formula require?

6. Discuss the differences in testing a business-critical system, a safety-critical system, and a system whose failure would not seriously affect lives, health, or business.

7. Suppose you are building a tax preparation system that has three components. The first component creates forms on the screen, allowing the user to type in name, address, tax identification number, and financial information. The second component uses tax tables and the input information to calculate the amount of tax owed for the current year. The third component uses the address information to print forms for federal, state (or provincial), and city taxes, including the amount owed. Describe the strategy you would use to test this system, and outline your test cases in a test plan.

8. Examine the fault categories in Hewlett-Packard's classification scheme, shown in Figure 8.1. Is this an orthogonal classification? If not, explain why, and suggest ways to make it orthogonal.

9. Complete the proof of the example in the text illustrated by Figure 8.5. In other words, write assertions to correspond to the flow diagram. Then, find the paths from input condition to output. Prove that the paths are theorems.

10. Suppose a program contains N decision points, each of which has two branches. How many test cases are needed to perform path testing on such a program? If there are M choices at each decision point, how many test cases are needed for path testing? Can the program's structure reduce this number? Give an example to support your answer.

11. Consider a program flow diagram as a directed graph in which the diamonds and boxes of the program are nodes, and the logic flow arrows between them are directed edges. For example, the program in Figure 8.7 can be graphed as shown in Figure 8.21. Prove that statement testing of a program is equivalent to finding a path in the graph that contains all nodes of the graph. Prove that branch testing is equivalent to finding the set of paths whose union covers the edges. Finally, prove that path testing is equivalent to finding all possible paths through the graph.

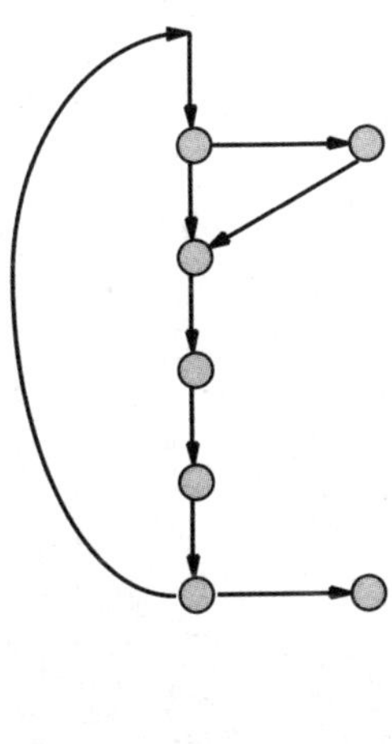

FIGURE 8.21 Graph for program in Figure 8.7.

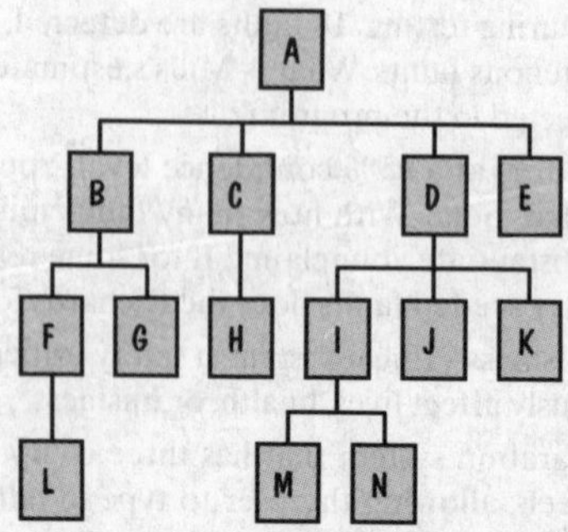

FIGURE 8.22 Example component hierarchy.

12. Programmable problem: Write a program that accepts as input the nodes and edges of a directed graph and prints as output all possible paths through the graph. What are the major design considerations for your program? How does the complexity of the graph (in terms of number of branches and cycles) affect the algorithm you use?
13. Figure 8.22 illustrates the component hierarchy in a software system. Describe the sequence of tests for integrating the components using a bottom-up approach, a top-down approach, a modified top-down approach, a big-bang approach, a sandwich approach, and a modified sandwich approach.
14. Explain why the graph of Figure 8.19 can be interpreted to mean that if you find many faults in your code at compile time, you should throw away your code and write it again.
15. If an independent test team does integration testing and a critical fault remains in the code after testing is complete, who is legally and ethically responsible for the damage caused by the fault?

9 Testing the System

In this chapter, we look at
- function testing
- performance testing
- acceptance testing
- software reliability, availability, and maintainability
- installation testing
- test documentation
- testing safety-critical systems

Testing the system is very different from unit and integration testing. When you unit test your components, you have complete control over the testing process. You create your own test data, design your own test cases, and run the tests yourself. When you integrate components, you sometimes work by yourself, but often you collaborate with some of the test or development team. However, when you test a system, you work with the entire development team, coordinating what you do and being directed by the test team leader. In this chapter, we look at the system testing process: its purpose, steps, participants, techniques, and tools.

9.1 PRINCIPLES OF SYSTEM TESTING

The objective of unit and integration testing was to ensure that the code implemented the design properly; that is, that the programmers wrote code to do what the designers intended. In system testing, we have a very different objective: to ensure that the system does what the customer wants it to do. To understand how to meet this objective, we first must understand where faults in the system come from.

Sources of Software Faults

Recall that a software fault causes a failure only when accompanied by the right conditions. That is, a fault may exist in the code, but if the code is never executed, or if the code is not executed long enough or in the appropriate configuration to cause a problem, we may never see the software fail. Because testing cannot exercise every possible condition, we keep as our goal the discovery of faults, hoping that in the process we eliminate all faults that might lead to failures during actual system usage.

Software faults can be inserted in a requirement, design, or code component, or in the documentation, at any point during development or maintenance. Figure 9.1 illustrates the likely causes of faults in each development activity. Although we would like to find and correct faults as early as possible, system testing acknowledges that faults may still be present after integration testing.

Faults can be introduced to the system early in development or late, such as when correcting a newly discovered fault. For example, defective software can result from faults in the requirements. Whether a requirement was ambiguous because the customer was unsure of a need or because we misinterpreted the customer's meaning, the result is the same: a system that does not work the way the customer wants it to work.

The same kind of communication mishaps can occur during system design. We may misinterpret a requirement and write an incorrect design specification. Or we understand the requirement but may word the specification so poorly that those who subsequently read it and use the design misunderstand it. Similarly, we may make assumptions about characteristics and relationships that are not shared by the other readers of the design.

Similar events can lead to program design faults. Misinterpretations are common when the system design is translated into lower-level descriptions for program design specifications. Programmers are several levels removed from the initial discussions with customers about system goals and functionality. Having responsibility for one "tree" but

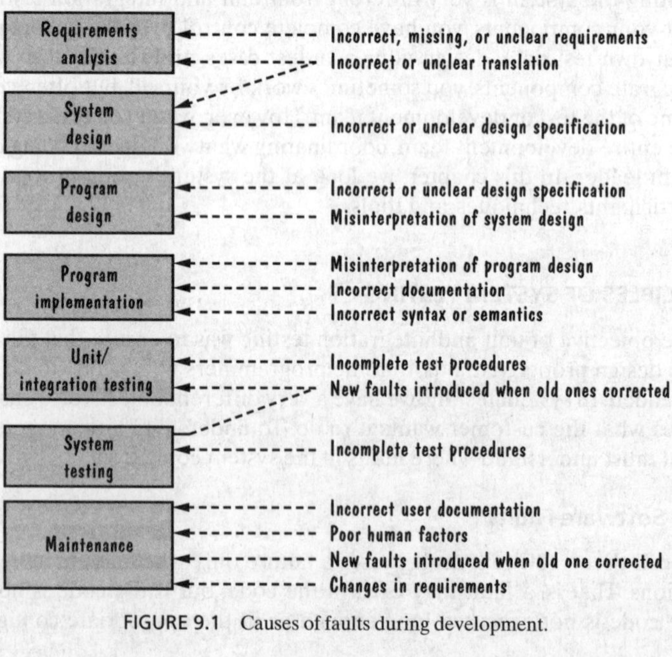

FIGURE 9.1 Causes of faults during development.

not the "forest," programmers cannot be expected to spot design faults that have been perpetuated through the first steps of the development cycle. For this reason, requirements and design reviews are essential to ensuring the quality of the resulting system.

The programmers and designers on our development team may also fail to use the proper syntax and semantics for recording their work. A compiler or assembler can catch some of these faults before a program is run, but they will not find faults when the form of a statement is correct but does not match the intention of the programmer or designer.

Once program component testing begins, faults may be added unintentionally in making changes to correct other problems. These faults are often very difficult to detect, because they may appear only when certain functions are exercised, or only under certain conditions. If those functions have already been tested when a new fault is inadvertently added, the new fault may not be noticed until much later, when its source may not be clear. This situation is likely to happen if we are reusing code from other applications, and we modify it to suit our current needs. The nuances of the code's design may not be apparent, and our changes may in fact do more damage than good.

For example, suppose you are testing components A, B, and C. You test each separately. When you test all three together, you find that A passes a parameter to C incorrectly. In repairing A, you make sure that the parameter pass is now correct, but you add code that sets a pointer incorrectly. Because you may not go back and test A independently again, you may not find evidence of the new fault until much later in testing, when it is not clear that A is the culprit.

In the same way, maintenance may introduce new faults. System enhancements require changes to the requirements, the system architecture, the program design, and the implementation itself, so many kinds of faults can be inserted as the enhancement is described, designed, and coded. In addition, the system may not function properly because users do not understand how the system was designed to work. If the documentation is unclear or incorrect, a fault may result. Human factors, including user perception, play a large role in understanding the system and interpreting its messages and required input. Users who are not comfortable with the system may not exercise system functions properly or to greatest advantage.

Test procedures should be thorough enough to exercise system functions to everyone's satisfaction: user, customer, and developer. If the tests are incomplete, faults may remain undetected. As we have seen, the sooner we detect a fault, the better; faults detected early are easier and cheaper to fix. Thus, complete and early testing can help not only to detect faults quickly, but also to isolate the causes more easily.

Figure 9.1 shows the reasons for faults, not evidence of them. Because testing aims to uncover as many faults as possible, it is concerned with where they may exist. Knowing how faults are created gives us clues about where to look when testing a system.

System Testing Process

There are several steps in testing a system:

1. function testing
2. performance testing
3. acceptance testing
4. installation testing

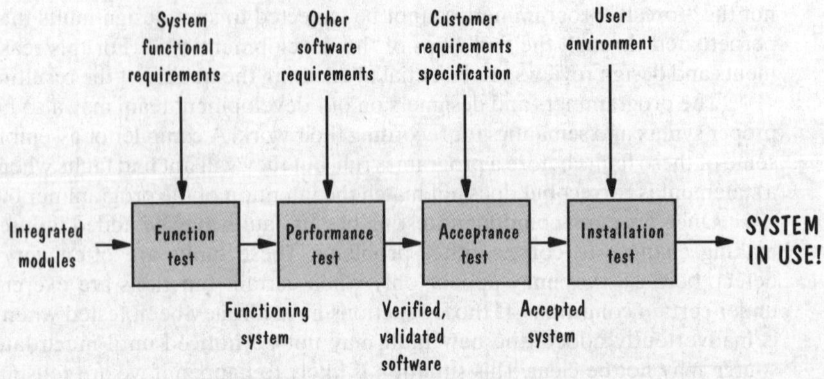

FIGURE 9.2 Steps in the testing process.

The steps are illustrated in Figure 9.2. Each step has a different focus, and a step's success depends on its goal or objective. Thus, it is helpful to review the purpose of each step of system testing.

Process Objectives. Initially, we test the functions performed by the system. We begin with a set of components that were tested individually and then together. A **function test** checks that the integrated system performs its functions as specified in the requirements. For example, a function test of a bank account package verifies that the package can correctly credit a deposit, enter a withdrawal, calculate interest, print the balance, and so on.

Once the test team is convinced that the functions work as specified, the **performance test** compares the integrated components with the nonfunctional system requirements. These requirements, including security, accuracy, speed, and reliability, constrain the way in which the system functions are performed. For instance, a performance test of the bank account package evaluates the speed with which calculations are made, the precision of the computation, the security precautions required, and the response time to user inquiry.

At this point, the system operates the way the designers intend. We call this a **verified system**; it is the designers' interpretation of the requirements specification. Next, we compare the system with the customer's expectations by reviewing the requirements definition document. If we are satisfied that the system we have built meets the requirements, then we have a **validated system**; that is, we have verified that the requirements have been met.

So far, all the tests have been run by the developers, based on their understanding of the system and its objectives. The customers also test the system, making sure that it meets their understanding of the requirements, which may be different from the developers'. This test, called an **acceptance test**, assures the customers that the system they requested is the system that was built for them. The acceptance test is sometimes run in its actual environment but often is run at a test facility different from the target location. For this reason, we may run a final **installation test** to allow users to exercise system functions and document additional problems that result from being at the actual site. For example, a naval system may be designed, built, and tested at the developer's site, configured as a ship might be, but not on an actual ship. Once the development site tests are complete, an additional set of installation tests may be run with the system on board each type of ship that will eventually use the system.

Build or Integration Plan. Ideally, after program testing, you can view the collection of components as a single entity. Then, during the first steps of system testing, the integrated collection is evaluated from a variety of perspectives, as previously described. However, large systems are sometimes unwieldy when tested as one enormous collection of components. In fact, such systems are often candidates for phased development, simply because they are much easier to build and test in smaller pieces. Thus, you may choose to perform phased system testing. We saw in Chapter 1 that a system can be viewed as a nested set of levels or subsystems. Each level is responsible for performing at least the functions of those subsystems it contains. Similarly, we can divide the test system into a nested sequence of subsystems and perform the system test on one subsystem at a time.

The subsystem definitions are based on predetermined criteria. Usually, the basis for division is functionality. For example, we saw in Chapter 8 that Microsoft divides a product into three subsystems based on most critical functions, desirable functions, and least needed functions. Similarly, a telecommunications system that routes calls may be divided into subsystems in the following way:

1. Routing calls within an exchange
2. Routing calls within an area code
3. Routing calls within a state, province, or district
4. Routing calls within a country
5. Routing international calls

Each larger subsystem contains all the subsystems preceding it. We begin our system testing by testing the functions of the first system. When all of the within-exchange functions are tested successfully, we proceed to test the second system. Similarly, we test the third, fourth, and fifth systems in turn. The result is a successful test of the entire system, but incremental testing has made fault detection and correction much easier than it would have been had we focused only on the largest system. For example, a problem revealed during function tests of calling within a state, province, or district is likely to be the result of code that handles state but not area code or exchange information. Thus, we can narrow our search for the cause to the code in subsystem 3 plus the code in 1 or 2 affected by 3. Had this problem been discovered only when all the subsystems were integrated, we could not easily pinpoint the likely source.

Incremental testing requires careful planning. The test team must create a **build plan** or **integration plan** to define the subsystems to be tested and to describe how, where, when, and by whom the tests will be conducted. Many of the issues we discussed in integration testing must be addressed by the build plan, including order of integration and the need for stubs or drivers.

Sometimes, a level or subsystem of a build plan is called a **spin**. The spins are numbered, with the lowest level called **spin zero**. For large systems, spin zero is often a minimal system; it is sometimes even just the operating system on a host computer.

TABLE 9.1 Build Plan for Telecommunications System

Spin	Functions	Test Start	Test End
0	Exchange	1 September	15 September
1	Area code	30 September	15 October
2	State/province/district	25 October	5 November
3	Country	10 November	20 November
4	International	1 December	15 December

For example, the build plan for the telecommunications system may contain a schedule similar to the one in Table 9.1. The build plan describes each spin by number, functional content, and testing schedule. If a test of spin n succeeds and a problem arises in spin $n + 1$, then the most likely source of the problem is related to the difference between spins n and $n + 1$, namely, the added functionality from one spin to the next. If the difference between two successive spins is small, then we have relatively few places to look for the problem's cause.

The number of spins and their definition depend primarily on our resources and those of our customer. These resources include not only hardware and software, but also time and personnel availability. A minimal system is placed in the earliest spin, and subsequent spins are defined by integrating the next most important or critical functions as early as is feasible. For example, consider the star network shown in Figure 9.3. The star's center is a computer that receives messages from several smaller computers, each of which captures data from sensors and transmits them for processing. Thus, the major functions of the central computer are translating and assimilating messages from the outlying computers. Since these functions are critical to the whole system, they should be included in an early spin. In fact, we may define the spins in the following way:

- Spin 0: test the central computer's general functions
- Spin 1: test the central computer's message-translation function

FIGURE 9.3 Star network example.

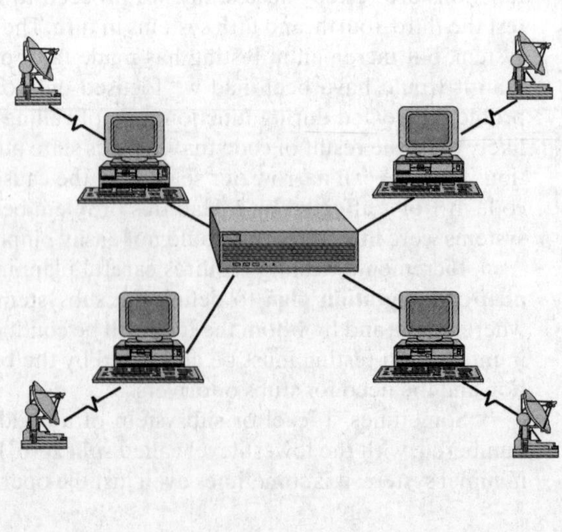

- Spin 2: test the central computer's message-assimilation function
- Spin 3: test each outlying computer in the stand-alone mode
- Spin 4: test the outlying computer's message-sending function
- Spin 5: test the central computer's message-receiving function

and so on.

The spin definitions also depend on the system components' ability to operate in the stand-alone mode. It may be harder to simulate a missing piece of a system than to incorporate it in a spin, since interdependencies among parts sometimes require as much simulation code as actual code. Remember that our goal is to test the system. The time and effort needed to build and use test tools might better be spent in testing the actual system. This trade-off is similar to that involved in selecting a test philosophy during unit and integration testing: Developing many stubs and drivers may require as much time during program testing as testing the original components they simulate.

Configuration Management

We often test a system in stages or pieces, based on spins (as before) or on subsystems, functions, or other decompositions that make testing easier to handle. (We look at these testing strategies later in this chapter.) However, system testing must also take into account the several different system configurations that are being developed. A **system configuration** is a collection of system components delivered to a particular customer. For example, a mathematical computation package may be sold in one configuration for UNIX-based machines, in another for Windows machines, and still another for Solaris systems. The configurations may be further distinguished by those running on certain kinds of chips or with particular devices available. Usually, we develop core software that runs on each, and we use the principles described in Chapters 5, 6, and 7 to isolate the differences among configurations to a small number of independent components. For instance, the core functionality may be contained in components A, B, and C; then, configuration 1 includes A, B, C, and D, and configuration 2 is A, B, C, and E.

Developing and testing these different configurations requires **configuration management**, the control of system differences to minimize risk and error. We have seen in earlier chapters how the configuration management team makes sure that changes to requirements, design, or code are reflected in the documentation and in other components affected by the changes. During testing, configuration management is especially important, coordinating efforts among the testers and developers.

Versions and Releases. A configuration for a particular system is sometimes called a **version**. Thus, the initial delivery of a software package may consist of several versions, one for each platform or situation in which the software will be used. For example, aircraft software may be built so that version 1 runs on Navy planes, version 2 runs on Air Force planes, and version 3 runs on commercial airliners.

As the software is tested and used, faults are discovered that need correction, or minor enhancements are made to the initial functionality. A new **release** of the software is an improved system intended to replace the old one. Often, software systems are described as version n, release m, or as version $n.m$, where the number reflects the system's position as it grows and matures. Version n is sometimes intended to replace version $n - 1$, and release m supersedes $m - 1$. (The word "version" can have two different meanings: a version for each type of platform or operating system, or one in a sequence of phased products. The terminology is usually understood from the context in which it is used. For example, a vendor might provide version 3 of its product on a UNIX platform and version 4 on a Windows platform, each offering the same functionality.)

The configuration management team is responsible for ensuring that each version or release is correct and stable before it is released for use, and that changes are made accurately and promptly. Accuracy is critical, because we want to avoid generating new faults while correcting existing ones. Similarly, promptness is important, because fault detection and correction are proceeding at the same time that the test team searches for additional faults. Thus, those who are trying to repair system faults should work with components and documentation that reflect the current state of the system.

Tracking and controlling versions are especially important when we are doing phased development. As we noted in earlier chapters, a **production system** is a version that has been tested and performs according to only a subset of the customer's requirements. The next version, with more features, is developed while users operate the production system. This **development system** is built and tested; when testing is complete, the development system replaces the production system to become the new production system.

For example, suppose a power plant is automating the functions performed in the control room. The power plant operators have been trained to do everything manually and are uneasy about working with the computer, so we decide to build a phased system. The first phase is almost identical to the manual system, but it allows the plant operators to do some automated record keeping. The second phase adds several automated functions to the first phase, but half of the control room functions are still manual. Successive phases continue to automate selected functions, building on the previous phases until all functions are automated. By expanding the automated system in this way, we allow plant operators slowly to become accustomed to and feel comfortable with the new system.

At any point during the phased development, the plant operators are using the fully tested production system. At the same time, we are working on the next phase, testing the development system. When the development system is completely tested and ready for use by the plant operators, it becomes the production system (i.e., it is used by the plant operators) and we move on to the next phase. When working on the development system, we add functions to the current production or operational system to form the new development system.

While a system is in production, problems may occur and be reported to us. Thus, a development system often serves two purposes: it adds the functionality of the next phase, and it corrects the problems found in previous versions. A development system can therefore involve adding new components as well as changing existing ones. However, this procedure allows faults to be introduced to components that have already been tested. When we write a build plan and test plans, we should address this situation and consider the need for controlling changes implemented from one version and release to the next. Additional testing can make sure that the development system performs at least as well as the current production system. However, records must be kept of the exact changes made to the code from one version to the next, so that we can trace problems to their source. For example, if a user on the production system reports a problem, we must know what version and release of the code are being used. The code may differ dramatically from one version to another. If we work with the wrong listing, we may never locate the problem's cause. Worse yet, we may think we have found the cause, making a change that introduces a new fault while not really fixing the old one!

Regression Testing. As we saw in Chapter 8, the purpose of testing is to identify faults, not to correct them. However, it is natural to want to find the cause of a problem and then correct it as soon as possible after discovery. Otherwise, the test team is unable to judge whether the system is functioning properly, and the continued presence of some faults may halt further testing. Thus, any test plan must contain a set of guidelines for fault correction as well as discovery. However, correcting faults during the testing process can introduce new faults while fixing old ones, as mentioned earlier.

Regression testing identifies new faults that may have been introduced as current ones are being corrected. A **regression test** is a test applied to a new version or release to verify that it still performs the same functions in the same manner as an older version or release.

For example, suppose that the functional test for version m was successful and testing is proceeding on version $m + 1$, where $m + 1$ has all the functionality of m plus some new functions. As a result, you request that several lines of code be changed in version $m + 1$ to repair a fault located in an earlier test; the code must be changed now so that the testing of $m + 1$ can continue. If the team is following a policy of strict regression testing, the testing involves these steps:

1. Inserting your new code
2. Testing functions known to be affected by the new code
3. Testing essential functions of m to verify that they still work properly (the actual regression testing)
4. Continuing function testing of $m + 1$

These steps ensure that adding new code has not negated the effects of previous tests. Sidebar 9.1 illustrates the dangers of not performing regression tests.

Often, the regression test involves reusing the most important test cases from the previous level's test; if regression testing is specified in the test plan, the plan should also explain which test cases are to be used again.

Deltas, Separate Files, and Conditional Compilation. There are three primary ways to control versions and releases, and each has implications for managing configurations during testing. Some development projects prefer to keep **separate files** for each different version or release. For example, a security system might be issued in two configurations: version 1 for machines that can store all of the data in main memory, and version 2 for machines with less memory, where the data must be put out to disk under certain conditions. The basic functionality for the system may be common, handled by components A_1 through A_k, but the memory management may be done by component B_1 for version 1 and B_2 for version 2.

SIDEBAR 9.1 THE CONSEQUENCEES OF NOT DOING REGRESSION TESTING

Not doing regression testing properly can have serious consequences. For example, Seligman (1997) and Trager (1997) reported that 167,000 Californians were billed $667,000 for unwarranted local telephone calls because of a problem with software purchased from Northern Telecom. A similar problem was experienced by customers in New York City.

The problem stemmed from a fault in a software upgrade to the DMS-100 telephone switch. The fault caused the billing interface to use the wrong area code in telephone company offices that used more than one area code. As a result, local calls were billed as long-distance toll calls. When customers complained, the local telephone companies told their customers that the problem rested with the long-distance carrier; then the long-distance carrier sent the customers back to the local phone company! It took the local phone companies about a month to find and fix the cause of the problem. Had Northern Telecom performed complete regression testing on the software upgrade, including a check to see that area codes were reported properly, the billing problem would not have occurred.

Suppose a fault is discovered in B_1 that also exists in B_2 and must be fixed to work in the same way. Or suppose functionality must be added to both B_1 and B_2. Keeping both versions current and correct can be difficult. The changes needed are not likely to be identical, but their results must be the same in the eyes of the user. To address this difficulty, we can designate a particular version to be the main version, and define all other versions to be variations from the main. Then, we need store only the differences, rather than all the components, for each of the other versions. The difference file, called a **delta**, contains editing commands that describe how the main version is to be transformed to a different version. We say that we "apply a delta" to transform the main version into its variation.

The advantage of using deltas is that changes to common functionality are made only to the main version. Furthermore, deltas require far less storage space than full-blown versions. However, there are substantial disadvantages. If the main version is lost or corrupted, then all versions are lost. More important, it is sometimes very difficult to represent each variation as a transformation from the main version. For example, consider a main version containing the following code:

```
...
26    int total = 0;
...
```

A delta file defines a variation that replaces line 26 with new code:

```
26    int total = 1;
```

However, suppose a change is made to the main version file, adding a line between lines 15 and 16. Then line 26 becomes line 27, and applying the delta changes the wrong command. Thus, sophisticated techniques are needed to maintain the correspondence between the main version and its variations, and to apply the deltas properly.

Deltas are especially useful for maintaining releases. The first release is considered to be the main system, and subsequent releases are recorded as a set of deltas to release 1.

A third approach to controlling file differences is to use **conditional compilation**. That is, a single code component addresses all versions. Conditional statements use the compiler to determine which statements apply to which versions. Because the shared code appears only once, we can make one correction that applies to all versions. However, if the variations among versions are very complex, the source code may be very difficult to read and understand. Moreover, for large numbers of versions, the conditional compilation may become unmanageable.

Conditional compilation addresses only the code. However, separate files and deltas are useful not only in controlling code, but also in controlling other development artifacts, such as requirements, design, test data, and documentation. Sidebar 9.2 illustrates how both deltas and separate files can be useful in organizing and changing large systems.

SIDEBAR 9.2 DELTAS AND SEPARATE FILES

The Source Code Control System, distributed with most versions of AT&T's UNIX, is intended to control a project's software baseline. It can also be used for other project-related documents, as long as they are in textual form. Using a delta approach, SCCS allows multiple versions and releases, and a programmer can request any version or release from the system at a given time. The baseline system is stored along with transformations. That is, for a given component, SCCS stores in one file the baseline code for version 1.0 of that component, the delta to transform it to version 2.0, and the delta to transform 2.0 to 3.0. Similarly, SCCS can store different releases, or a combination of version and release. Thus, any given release or version is always available for use or modification; SCCS just applies the appropriate deltas to derive it from the baseline. However, changing an intermediate version or release can lead to problems, since the delta for the next version or release is based on the previous version's text. On the other hand, SCCS's flexibility in handling multiple releases and versions means that a vendor can use SCCS to support many versions and releases simultaneously.

A programmer requests that a version or release be produced by SCCS by using the "get" command. If the programmer indicates with an "–e" switch that the component is to be edited, SCCS locks the component for all future users until the changed component is checked back in.

The Ada Language System (ALS) is a programming environment designed with configuration management as a key design factor (Babich 1986). It does not embrace a particular configuration management strategy. Instead, it incorporates UNIX-like commands that support configuration management tools. Unlike SCCS, ALS stores revisions as separate, distinct files. In addition, ALS freezes all versions and releases except for the current one. That is, old versions and releases may never be modified once a new version or release is made available to users.

ALS allows collections of related releases or versions to be grouped into a variation set. The variations can be based on a production version plus several development versions, or on a version with several subsequent releases. ALS also tags each file with attribute information, such as creation date, names of those who have charged it out, date of last testing, or even the purpose of the file. The system also keeps track of associations, so that all the files in a system, or all the files in a variation set, can be labeled.

The access control scheme for ALS involves locks to name people who are allowed to read, overwrite, append, or execute data in the file. The system also designates permission for certain tools to access or interact with a file.

Change Control. The configuration management team works closely with the test team to control all aspects of testing. Any change proposed to any part of the system is approved first by the configuration management team. The change is entered in all appropriate components and documentation, and the team notifies all who may be affected. For example, if a test results in modifying a requirement, changes are also likely to be needed in the requirements specification, the system design, the program design, the code, all relevant documentation, and even the test plan itself. Thus, altering one part of the system may affect everyone who is working on the system's development.

Change control is further complicated when more than one developer is making a change to the same component. For instance, suppose that two failures occur during testing. Jack is assigned to find and fix the cause of the first failure, and Jill is assigned to find and fix the cause of the second. Although the failures at first seem unrelated, Jack and Jill both discover that the root cause is in a code component called *initialize*. Jack may remove *initialize* from the system library, make his changes, and place his corrected version back in the library. Then Jill, working from the original version, makes her corrections and replaces Jack's corrections with hers, thereby undoing his! Regression testing may reveal that Jack's assigned fault is still uncorrected, but effort and time have been wasted.

To address this problem, the configuration management team performs change control. The team oversees the libraries of code and documents, and developers must "check out" copies when making fixes. In our example, Jill would not have been able to obtain a copy of *initialize* until Jack had replaced his version with a corrected, tested version. Or the configuration management team would have taken the extra step of consolidating Jack's and Jill's versions into one version; then, the consolidated version would have undergone regression testing as well as testing to ensure that both failures were eliminated.

An additional method for ensuring that all project members are working with the most up-to-date documents is to keep a single, definitive copy of each online. By updating only these copies, we avoid the time lag usually caused by distributing new or revised pages. In this way, the configuration management team still maintains some degree of control to make sure that changes to documents mirror changes to design and code. We may still have to "check out" versions in order to change them, and we

> **SIDEBAR 9.3 MICROSOFT'S BUILD CONTROL**
>
> Cusumano and Selby (1997) report that Microsoft developers must enter their code into a product database by a particular time in the afternoon. Then the project team recompiles the source code and creates a new build of the evolving product by the next morning. Any code that is faulty enough to prevent the build from compiling and running must be fixed immediately.
>
> The build process itself has several steps. First, the developer checks out a private copy of a source code file from a central place that holds master versions. Next, he or she modifies the private copy to implement or change features. Once the changes are made, a private build with the new or changed features is tested. When the tests are completed successfully, the code for the new or changed features is placed in the master version. Finally, regression tests ensure that the developer's changes have not inadvertently affected other functionality.
>
> Individual developers may combine their changes as necessary (sometimes daily, sometimes weekly, depending on need), but a "build master" generates a complete version of the product daily, using the master version of each source code file for the day. These daily builds are done for each product and each market.

may be told that some documents are locked or unavailable if someone else is working with them. Sidebar 9.3 describes how Microsoft uses private copies of source code to allow developers to test changes individually before changes are combined into the day's build.

Test Team

As we will see, the developers have primary responsibility for function and performance testing, but the customer plays a large role in acceptance and installation tests. However, the test teams for all tests are drawn from both staffs. Often, no programmers from the project are involved in system testing; they are too familiar with the implementation's structure and intention, and they may have difficulty recognizing the differences between implementation and required function or performance.

Thus, the test team is often independent of the implementation staff. Ideally, some test team members are already experienced as testers. Usually, these "professional testers" are former analysts, programmers, and designers who now devote all their time to testing systems. The testers are familiar not only with the system specification, but also with testing methods and tools.

Professional testers organize and run the tests. They are involved from the beginning, designing test plans and test cases as the project progresses. The professional testers work with the configuration management team to provide documentation and other mechanisms for tying tests to the requirements, design components, and code.

The professional testers focus on test development, methods, and procedures. Because the testers may not be as well-versed in the particulars of the requirements as those who wrote them, the test team includes additional people who are familiar with the requirements. **Analysts** who were involved in the original requirements definition and specification are useful in testing because they understand the problem as defined by the customer. Much of system testing compares the new system to its original requirements, and the analysts have a good feeling for the customer's needs and goals. Since they have worked with the designers to fashion a solution, analysts have some idea of how the system should work to solve the problem.

System designers add the perspective of intent to the test team. The designers understand what we proposed as a solution, as well as the solution's constraints. They also know how the system is divided into functional or data-related subsystems, and how the system is supposed to work. When designing test cases and ensuring test coverage, the test team calls on the designers for help in listing all possibilities.

Because tests and test cases are tied directly to requirements and design, a **configuration management representative** is on the test team. As failures occur and changes are requested, the configuration management specialist arranges for the changes to be reflected in the documentation, requirements, design, code, or other development artifact. In fact, changes to correct a fault may result in modifications to other test cases or to a large part of the test plan. The configuration management specialist implements these changes and coordinates the revision of tests.

Finally, the test team includes **users**. They are best qualified to evaluate issues dealing with appropriateness of audience, ease of use, and other human factors. Sometimes, users have little voice in the early stages of the project. Customer representatives who participate during requirements analysis may not plan to use the system but have jobs related to those who will. For instance, the representatives may be managers of those who will use the system or technical representatives who have discovered a problem that indirectly relates to their work. However, these representatives may be so removed from the actual problem that the requirements description is inaccurate or incomplete. The customer may not be aware of the need to redefine or add requirements.

Therefore, users of the proposed system are essential, especially if they were not present when the system requirements were first defined. A user is likely to be familiar with the problem because of daily exposure to it, and can be invaluable in evaluating the system to verify that it solves the problem.

9.2 FUNCTION TESTING

System testing begins with function testing. Whereas previous tests concentrated on components and their interactions, this first step ignores system structure and focuses on functionality. Our approach from now on is more closed box than open. We need not know which component is being executed; rather, we must know what the system is supposed to do. Thus, function testing is based on the system's functional requirements.

Purpose and Roles

Each function can be associated with those system components that accomplish it. For some functions, the parts may comprise the entire system. The set of actions associated with a function is called a **thread**, so function testing is sometimes called **thread testing**.

Logically, it should be easier to find the cause of a problem in a small set of components than in a large set. Thus, ease of testing calls for choosing carefully the order in which functions are tested. Functions may be defined in a nested manner, just as spins are defined in levels. For example, suppose a requirement specifies that a water-monitoring system is to identify large changes in four characteristics: dissolved oxygen, temperature, acidity, and radioactivity. The requirements specification may treat change acknowledgment as one of the many functions of the overall system. However, for testing, we may want to view the monitoring as four separate functions:

- acknowledging change in dissolved oxygen
- acknowledging change in temperature
- acknowledging change in acidity
- acknowledging change in radioactivity

Then, we test each one individually.

Effective function tests should have a high probability of detecting a fault. We use the same guidelines for function testing that we use for unit testing. That is, a test should

- have a high probability of detecting a fault
- use a test team independent of the designers and programmers
- know the expected actions and output
- test both valid and invalid input
- never modify the system just to make testing easier
- have stopping criteria

Function testing is performed in a carefully controlled situation. Moreover, since we are testing one function at a time, function testing can actually begin before the entire system is constructed, if need be.

Function testing compares the system's actual performance with its requirements, so the test cases for function testing are developed from the requirements document. For example, a word processing system can be tested by examining the way in which the system handles

- document creation
- document modification
- document deletion

Within each category, different functions are tested. For instance, document modification can be tested by looking at

- adding a character
- adding a word
- adding a paragraph
- deleting a character
- deleting a word
- deleting a paragraph
- changing the font

- changing the type size
- changing the paragraph formatting

and so on.

Cause-and-Effect Graphs

Testing would be easier if we could automatically generate test cases from the requirements. Work has been done at IBM (Elmendorf 1973, 1974) to convert the natural language of requirements definitions to a formal specification that can be used to enumerate test cases for functional testing. The test cases that result are not redundant; that is, one test case does not test functions that have already been tested by another case. In addition, the process finds incomplete and ambiguous aspects of requirements, if any exist.

The process examines the semantics of the requirements and restates them as logical relationships between inputs and outputs or between inputs and transformations. The inputs are called **causes**, and the outputs and transformations are **effects**. The result is a Boolean graph reflecting these relationships, called a **cause-and-effect graph**.

We add information to the initial graph to indicate rules of syntax and to reflect environmental constraints. Then, we convert the graph to a decision table. Each column of the decision table corresponds to a test case for functional testing.

There are several steps in creating a cause-and-effect graph. First, the requirements are separated so that each requirement describes a single function. Then, all causes and effects are described. The numbered causes and effects become nodes of the graph. Placing causes on the left-hand side of the drawing and effects on the right, we draw the logical relationships depicted in the graph by using the notation shown in Figure 9.4. Extra nodes can be used to simplify the graph.

FIGURE 9.4 Notation for cause-and-effect graphs.

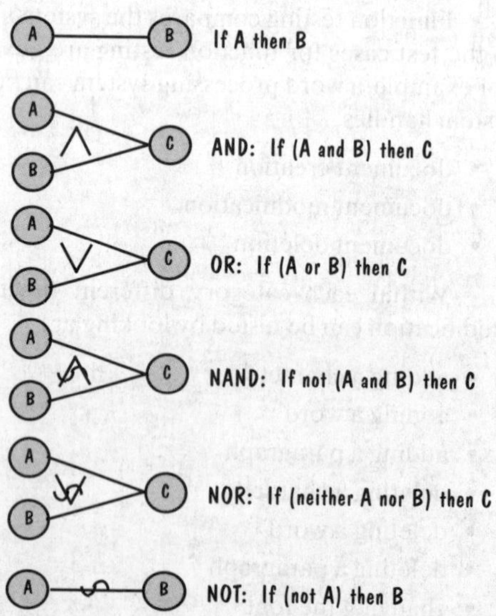

Let us work through an example to see how to build this type of graph. Suppose we are testing a water-level monitoring system that reports to an agency involved with flood control. The requirements definition for one of the system functions reads as follows:

> The system sends a message to the dam operator about the safety of the lake level.

Corresponding to this requirement is a design description:

> INPUT: The syntax of the function is LEVEL(A,B)
>
> where A is the height in meters of the water behind the dam, and B is the number of centimeters of rain in the last 24-hour period.
>
> PROCESSING: The function calculates whether the water level is within a safe range, is too high, or is too low.
>
> OUTPUT: The screen shows one of the following messages:
>
> **1.** "LEVEL = SAFE" when the result is safe or low.
> **2.** "LEVEL = HIGH" when the result is high.
> **3.** "INVALID SYNTAX"
>
> depending on the result of the calculation.

We can separate these requirements into five "causes":

1. The first five characters of the command "LEVEL."
2. The command contains exactly two parameters separated by a comma and enclosed in parentheses.
3. The parameters A and B are real numbers such that the water level is calculated to be LOW.
4. The parameters A and B are real numbers such that the water level is calculated to be SAFE.
5. The parameters A and B are real numbers such that the water level is calculated to be HIGH.

We can also describe three "effects":

1. The message "LEVEL = SAFE" is displayed on the screen.
2. The message "LEVEL = HIGH" is displayed on the screen.
3. The message "INVALID SYNTAX" is printed out.

These become the nodes of our graph. However, the function includes a check on the parameters to be sure that they are passed properly. To reflect this, we establish two intermediate nodes:

1. The command is syntactically valid.
2. The operands are syntactically valid.

We can draw the relationships between cause and effect, as shown in Figure 9.5. Notice that there are dashed lines to the left of the effects. These lines mean that exactly one effect can result. Other notations can be made on cause-and-effect graphs to provide additional information. Figure 9.6 illustrates some of the possibilities.

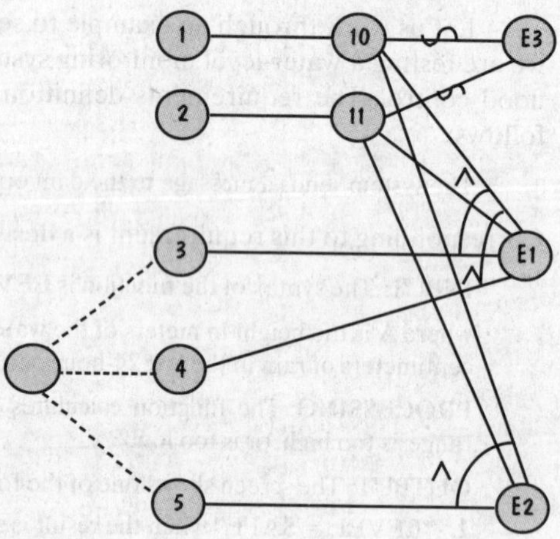

FIGURE 9.5 Cause-and-effect graph.

Thus, by looking at the graph, we can tell if

- exactly one of a set of conditions can be invoked
- at most one of a set of conditions can be invoked
- at least one of a set of conditions can be invoked
- one effect masks the observance of another effect
- invocation of one effect requires the invocation of another

At this point, we are ready to define a decision table using the information from the cause-and-effect graph. We put a row in the table for each cause or effect. In our

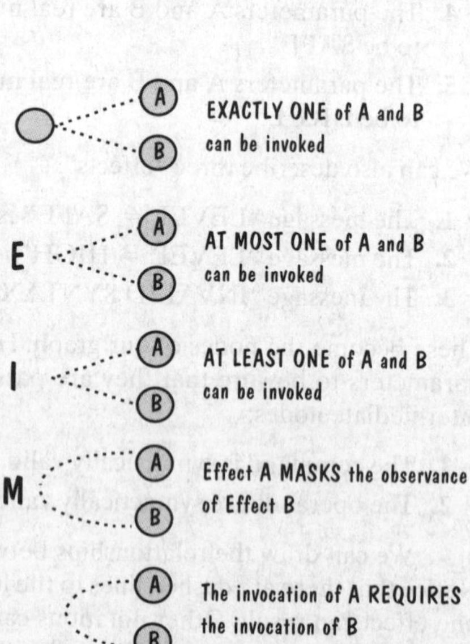

FIGURE 9.6 Additional graph notation.

example, our decision table needs five rows for the causes and three rows for the effects. The columns of the decision table correspond to the test cases. We define the columns by examining each effect and listing all combinations of causes that can lead to that effect.

In our LEVEL example, we can determine the number of columns in the decision table by examining the lines flowing into the effect nodes of the graph. We see in Figure 9.5 that there are two separate lines flowing into E3; each corresponds to a column. There are four lines flowing into E1, but only two combinations yield the effect. Each of the combinations is a column in the table. Finally, only one combination of lines results in effect E2, so we have our fifth column.

Each column of the decision table represents a set of states of causes and effects. We keep track of the states of other conditions when a particular combination is invoked. We indicate the condition of the cause by placing an I in the table when the cause is invoked or true, or an S if the cause is suppressed or false. If we do not care whether the cause is invoked or suppressed, we can use an X to mark the "don't-care" state. Finally, we indicate whether a particular effect is absent (A) or present (P).

For testing the LEVEL function, the five columns of Table 9.2 display the relationship between invocation of causes and the resultant effects. If causes 1 and 2 are true (i.e., the command and parameters are valid), then the effect depends on whether causes 3, 4, or 5 are true. If cause 1 is true but cause 2 is false, the effect is already determined, and we don't care about the state of causes 3, 4, or 5. Similarly, if cause 1 is false, we no longer care about the states of other causes.

Note that theoretically we could have generated 32 test cases: Five causes in each of two states yield 2^5 possibilities. Thus, using a cause-and-effect graph substantially decreases the number of test cases we must consider.

In general, we can reduce the number of test cases even more by using our knowledge of the causes to eliminate certain other combinations. For example, if the number of test cases is high, we may assign a priority to each combination of causes. Then, we can eliminate the combinations of low priority. Similarly, we can eliminate those combinations that are unlikely to occur or for which testing is not economically justifiable.

In addition to reducing the number of test cases to consider, cause-and-effect graphs help us predict the possible outcomes of exercising the system. At the same time, the graphs find unintended side effects for certain combinations of causes. However, cause-and-effect graphs are not practical for systems that include time delays, iterations,

TABLE 9.2 Decision Table for Cause-and-Effect Graph

	Test 1	Test 2	Test 3	Test 4	Test 5
Cause 1	I	I	I	S	I
Cause 2	I	I	I	X	S
Cause 3	I	S	S	X	X
Cause 4	S	I	S	X	X
Cause 5	S	S	I	X	X
Effect 1	P	P	A	A	A
Effect 2	A	A	P	A	A
Effect 3	A	A	A	P	P

or loops where the system reacts to feedback from some of its processes to perform other processes.

9.3 PERFORMANCE TESTING

Once we determine that the system performs the functions required by the requirements, we turn to the way in which those functions are performed. Thus, functional testing addresses the functional requirements, and performance testing addresses the nonfunctional requirements.

Purpose and Roles

System performance is measured against the performance objectives set by the customer as expressed in the nonfunctional requirements. For example, function testing may have demonstrated that a test system can calculate the trajectory of a rocket, based on rocket thrust, weather conditions, and related sensor and system information. Performance testing examines how well the calculation is done; the speed of response to user commands, accuracy of the result, and accessibility of the data are checked against the customer's performance prescriptions.

Performance testing is designed and administered by the test team, and the results are provided to the customer. Because performance testing usually involves hardware as well as software, hardware engineers may be part of the test team.

Types of Performance Tests

Performance testing is based on the requirements, so the types of tests are determined by the kinds of nonfunctional requirements specified.

- **Stress tests** evaluate the system when stressed to its limits over a short period of time. If the requirements state that a system is to handle up to a specified number of devices or users, a stress test evaluates system performance when all those devices or users are active simultaneously. This test is especially important for systems that usually operate below maximum capacity but are severely stressed at certain times of peak demand.
- **Volume tests** address the handling of large amounts of data in the system. For example, we look at whether data structures (e.g., queues or stacks) have been defined to be large enough to handle all possible situations. In addition, we check fields, records, and files to see if their sizes can accommodate all expected data. We also make sure that the system reacts appropriately when data sets reach their maximum size.
- **Configuration tests** analyze the various software and hardware configurations specified in the requirements. Sometimes a system is built to serve a variety of audiences, and the system is really a spectrum of configurations. For instance, we may define a minimal system to serve a single user, and other configurations build on the minimal configuration to serve additional users. A configuration test evaluates all possible configurations to make sure that each satisfies the requirements.

- **Compatibility tests** are needed when a system interfaces with other systems. We find out whether the interface functions perform according to the requirements. For instance, if the system is to communicate with a large database system to retrieve information, a compatibility test examines the speed and accuracy of data retrieval.
- **Regression tests** are required when the system being tested is replacing an existing system. The regression tests guarantee that the new system's performance is at least as good as that of the old. Regression tests are always used during a phased development.
- **Security tests** ensure that the security requirements are met. We test system characteristics related to availability, integrity, and confidentiality of data and services.
- **Timing tests** evaluate the requirements dealing with time to respond to a user and time to perform a function. If a transaction must take place within a specified time, the test performs that transaction and verifies that the requirements are met. Timing tests are usually done in concert with stress tests to see if the timing requirements are met even when the system is extremely active.
- **Environmental tests** look at the system's ability to perform at the installation site. If the requirements include tolerances for heat, humidity, motion, chemical presence, moisture, portability, electrical or magnetic fields, disruption of power, or any other environmental characteristic of the site, then our tests guarantee the system's proper performance under these conditions.
- **Quality tests** evaluate the system's reliability, maintainability, and availability. These tests include calculation of mean time to failure and mean time to repair, as well as average time to find and fix a fault. Quality tests are sometimes difficult to administer. For example, if a requirement specifies a long mean time between failures, it may be infeasible to let the system run long enough to verify the required mean.
- **Recovery tests** address response to the presence of faults or to the loss of data, power, devices, or services. We subject the system to a loss of system resources and see if it recovers properly.
- **Maintenance tests** address the need for diagnostic tools and procedures to help in finding the source of problems. We may be required to supply diagnostic programs, memory maps, traces of transactions, circuit diagrams, and other aids. We verify that the aids exist and that they function properly.
- **Documentation tests** ensure that we have written the required documents. Thus, if user guides, maintenance guides, and technical documents are needed, we verify that these materials exist and that the information they contain is consistent, accurate, and easy to read. Moreover, sometimes requirements specify the format and audience of the documentation; we evaluate the documents for compliance.
- **Human factors tests** investigate requirements dealing with the user interface to the system. We examine display screens, messages, report formats, and other aspects that may relate to ease of use. In addition, operator and user procedures are checked to see if they conform to ease of use requirements. These tests are sometimes called **usability tests**.

Many of these tests are much more difficult to administer than the function tests. Requirements must be explicit and detailed, and requirements quality is often reflected in the ease of performance testing. Unless a requirement is clear and testable, in the sense defined in Chapter 4, it is hard for the test team to know when the requirement is satisfied. Indeed, it may even be difficult to know how to administer a test because success is not well-defined.

9.4 RELIABILITY, AVAILABILITY, AND MAINTAINABILITY

One of the most critical issues in performance testing is ensuring the system's reliability, availability, and maintainability. Because each of these system characteristics cannot always be measured directly before delivery, this assurance is especially difficult; we must use indirect measures to estimate the system's likely characteristics. For this reason, we take a closer look in this section at testing for reliable, available, and maintainable systems.

Definitions

To understand what we mean by reliability, availability, and maintainability, consider an automobile. We think of a car as being reliable if it functions properly most of the time. We realize that some functions may stop working and that parts that wear out will need to be fixed or replaced. However, we expect a reliable car to operate for long periods of time before requiring any maintenance. That is, the car is reliable if it has long periods of consistent, desirable behavior between maintenance periods.

Reliability involves behavior over a period of time, but availability describes something at a given point in time. A car is available if you can use it when you need it. The car may be 20 years old and has required maintenance only twice, so we can call the car highly reliable. But if it happens to be in the repair shop when you need it, it is still not available. Thus, something can be highly reliable, but not available at a particular point in time.

Suppose your car is both reliable and available, but it was manufactured by a company that is no longer in business. This situation means that when your car fails (which, admittedly, is infrequently), the maintainer has great difficulty finding replacement parts. Thus, your car is in the repair shop for a very long time before it is fixed properly and returned to you. In this case, your car has low maintainability.

The same concepts apply to software systems. We want our software to function consistently and correctly over long periods of time, to be available when we need it, and to be repaired quickly and easily if it does fail. We say formally that **software reliability** is the probability that a system will operate without failure under given conditions for a given time interval. We express reliability on a scale from 0 to 1: a system that is highly reliable will have a reliability measure close to 1, and an unreliable system will have a measure close to 0. Reliability is measured over execution time, not real time (i.e., not clock time), in order to more accurately reflect system usage.

Similarly, **software availability** is the probability that a system is operating successfully according to specification at a given point in time. More formally, it is the probability that a system is functioning completely at a given instant in time, assuming that the required external resources are also available. A system that is completely up and running has availability 1; one that is unusable has availability 0. Availability is measured at points of clock time, not execution time.

Likewise, **software maintainability** is the probability that, for a given condition of use, a maintenance activity can be carried out within a stated time interval and using stated procedures and resources. It, too, ranges from 0 to 1. It is very different from hardware maintenance; hardware usually requires the system to be unavailable as maintenance is being carried out, but software maintenance can sometimes be done while the system is still up and running.

Because reliability, availability, and maintainability are defined in terms of failures, they must be measured once the system is complete and working. Software engineers usually distinguish known failures from new ones; that is, in determining reliability, we count only new failures, not the ones we know about but have not yet fixed.

In addition, we often assign a severity level to each failure, to capture its impact on the system. For example, the U.S. Military Standard MIL-STD-1629A distinguishes among four different levels of failure severity:

1. *Catastrophic:* a failure that may cause death or system loss.
2. *Critical:* a failure that may cause severe injury or major system damage that results in mission loss.
3. *Marginal:* a failure that may cause minor injury or minor system damage that results in delay, loss of availability, or mission degradation.
4. *Minor:* a failure not serious enough to cause injury or system damage, but that results in unscheduled maintenance or repair.

Failure Data

When we capture information about software failures, we make several assumptions about the software itself. In particular, we assume that, when the software fails, we will find the root cause of the problem and fix it. The corrections may themselves introduce new faults, however, or they may inadvertently create conditions, not previously experienced, that enable other faults to cause failures. In the long run, we hope to see improvements in software reliability. (That is, we hope to have longer and longer times between failures.) But in the short run, we may sometimes find shorter interfailure times.

We can monitor a system and record the interfailure times to show us whether reliability is growing. For example, in Table 9.3, we list the execution time (in seconds) between successive failures of a command-and-control system during in-house testing using a simulation of the real operational environment system (Musa 1979). Figure 9.7 graphs these data, and the long-term reliability growth is clear, because the interfailure times are generally increasing.

Notice that the times vary a great deal, with short times showing up often, even near the end of the data set. What do the data tell us about the system reliability? And how can we use these data to predict the length of time to the next failure? Before we can answer these questions, we must understand uncertainty.

Inherent in any set of failure data is a considerable amount of uncertainty. Even with complete knowledge of all the faults existing in the software, we cannot state with

TABLE 9.3 Interfailure Times (Read Left to Right, in Rows)

3	30	113	81	115	9	2	91	112	15
138	50	77	24	108	88	670	120	26	114
325	55	242	68	422	180	10	1146	600	15
36	4	0	8	227	65	176	58	457	300
97	263	452	255	197	193	6	79	816	1351
148	21	233	134	357	193	236	31	369	748
0	232	330	365	1222	543	10	16	529	379
44	129	810	290	300	529	281	160	828	1011
445	296	1755	1064	1783	860	983	707	33	868
724	2323	2930	1461	843	12	261	1800	865	1435
30	143	108	0	3110	1247	943	700	875	245
729	1897	447	386	446	122	990	948	1082	22
75	482	5509	100	10	1071	371	790	6150	3321
1045	648	5485	1160	1864	4116				

certainty when it will next fail. Our inability to predict the next failure derives from our lack of knowledge about how the software will be used; we do not know the exact inputs or the order in which they will be supplied to the software, so we cannot predict which fault will trigger the next failure. We call this **type-1 uncertainty**, reflecting uncertainty about how the system will be used. Thus, at any point in time, the time to the next failure is uncertain; we can think of it as a random variable.

A second fuzzy area, called **type-2 uncertainty**, reflects our lack of knowledge about the effect of fault removal. When we fix a fault, we do not know if our corrections are complete and successful. And even if we have fixed the fault properly, we do not know how much improvement there is in the interfailure times. That is, we are uncertain about the degree to which our correction increases the software's reliability.

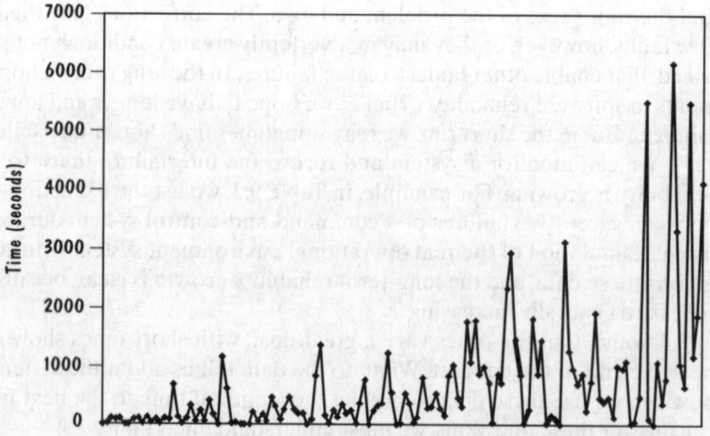

FIGURE 9.7 Graph of failure data from Table 9.3.

Measuring Reliability, Availability, and Maintainability

We want to express reliability, availability, and maintainability as attributes of the software, measured as numbers between 0 (unreliable, unavailable, or unmaintainable) and 1 (completely reliable, always available, and completely maintainable). To derive these measures, we examine attributes of the failure data. Assume that we are capturing failure data and that we have seen $i - 1$ failures. We can record the interfailure times, or times to failure, as $t_1, t_2, \ldots, t_{i-1}$. The average of these values is the **Mean Time to Failure (MTTF)**.

Suppose each underlying fault has been fixed and the system is again running. We can use T_i to denote the yet-to-be-observed next time to failure; T_i is a random variable. When we make statements about the reliability of the software, we are really making probability statements about T_i.

There are several other time-related data important to calculating availability and maintainability. Once a failure occurs, there is additional time lost as the faults causing the failure are located and repaired. The **Mean Time to Repair (MTTR)** tells us the average time it takes to fix a faulty software component. We can combine this measure with the mean time to failure to tell us how long the system is unavailable for use. That is, we measure availability by examining the **Mean Time between Failures (MTBF)**, calculated as

$$\text{MTBF} = \text{MTTF} + \text{MTTR}$$

Some practitioners and researchers propose measures for reliability, availability, and maintainability based on these means. For example, consider the relationship between system reliability and the mean time to failure. As the system becomes more reliable, its mean time to failure should increase. We want to use the MTTF in a measure whose value is near zero when MTTF is small, and nears 1 as MTTF gets larger and larger. Using this relationship, we can define a measure of a system's reliability as

$$R = \text{MTTF}/(1 + \text{MTTF})$$

so that it ranges between 0 and 1, as required. Similarly, we can measure availability so as to maximize MTBF:

$$A = \text{MTBF}/(1 + \text{MTBF})$$

When something is maintainable, we want to minimize the MTTR. Thus, we can measure maintainability as

$$M = 1/(1 + \text{MTTR})$$

Other researchers use surrogate measures to capture the notion of reliability, such as fault density (i.e., faults per thousand lines of code or faults per function point), when they cannot measure failures directly. Some researchers, such as Voas and Friedman (1995), argue that it is not the gross number of detected faults or failures that is important for software reliability, but the ability of a system as a whole to hide as-yet-undetected faults.

Reliability Stability and Growth

We want our reliability measure to tell us whether the software is improving (i.e., failing less frequently) as we find and fix faults. If the interfailure times stay the same, then we have **reliability stability**. If they increase, we have **reliability growth**. However, it is very difficult to predict when a system will fail. The prediction is a little easier for hardware than for software because, as noted in Sidebar 9.4, hardware reliability is distinctly different from software reliability. Hardware failures are probabilistic; we may not know the exact time of failure, but we can say that a piece of hardware will probably fail during a given time period. For example, if we know that a tire wears out in an average of 10 years, then we understand that the tire does not go from a failure probability of 0 on day 3652 (one day short of 10 years) to a failure probability of 1 on day 3653. Instead, the probability of failure increases slowly from 0, when we purchase the new tire, toward 1, as we approach 10 years of ownership. We can graph the probability's increase over time, and the shape of the curve will depend on the materials from which the tire was made, the tire design, the type of driving we do, the weight of the car, and more. We use these parameters to model the likely failure.

We take a similar approach when modeling software failure, defining a **probability density function** f of time t, written $f(t)$, that describes our understanding of when the software is likely to fail. For example, suppose we know that a software component will fail some time in the next 24 hours (because eventually a buffer will overflow), but that it is equally likely to fail in any 1-hour time interval. There are 86,400 seconds in 24 hours, so we can measure time t in seconds and define the probability

SIDEBAR 9.4 THE DIFFERENCE BETWEEN HARDWARE AND SOFTWARE RELIABILITY

Mellor (1992) explains why hardware failures are inherently different from software failures. Complex hardware fails when a component breaks and no longer functions as specified. For example, a logic gate can be stuck on 1 or 0, or a resistor short-circuits. The cause is physical (e.g., corrosion or oxidation), and the fault occurs at a particular point in time. To fix the problem, a part is either repaired or replaced, and the system can be restored to its previous state.

However, software faults can exist in a product for a long time, activated only when certain conditions exist that transform the fault into a failure. That is, the fault is latent, and the system will continue to fail (under the same conditions) unless the software design is changed to correct the underlying problem.

Because of this difference in the effects of faults, software reliability must be defined differently from hardware reliability. When hardware is repaired, it is returned to its previous level of reliability; the hardware's reliability is maintained. But when software is repaired, its reliability may actually increase or decrease. Thus, the goal of hardware reliability engineering is stability; the goal of software reliability engineering is reliability growth.

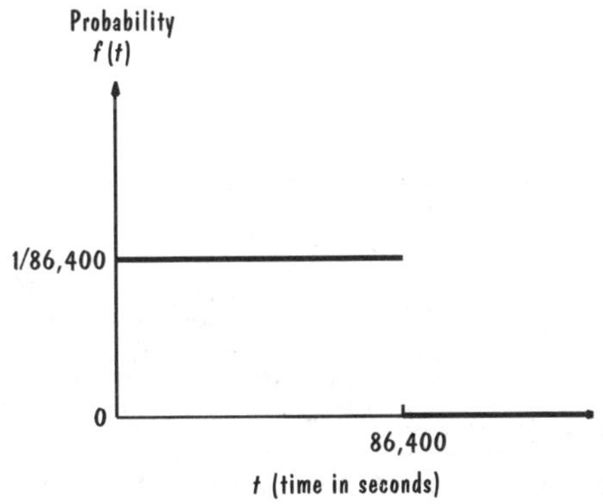

FIGURE 9.8 Uniform density function.

density function to be 1/86,400 for any t between 0 and 86,400, and 0 for any t greater than 86,400. We call this function **uniform** in the interval from $t = 0$ to 86,400 because the function takes the same value in that interval; it is depicted in Figure 9.8.

But not every density function is uniform, and one of the difficult problems in understanding and measuring reliability is capturing the failure behavior in an appropriate probability density function. That is, we can define a function $f(t)$ and use it to calculate the likelihood that a software component will fail in a given time interval $[t_1, t_2]$. Since this probability is the area under the curve between the endpoints of the interval, the probability of failure between t_1 and t_2 is

$$\int_{t_2}^{t_1} f(t)\ dt$$

In particular, the **distribution function**, $F(t)$, is the value of this integral over the interval from 0 to t. $F(t)$ is the probability that the software will fail before time t, and we define the **reliability function**, $R(t)$, to be $1 - F_i(t)$; it is the probability that the software will function properly up until time t.

Reliability Prediction

We can use the historical information about failures and failure times to build simple predictive models of reliability. For example, using Musa's data from Table 9.3, we can predict the time of next failure by averaging the previous two failure times to predict the third. That is, we observe from the table that $t_1 = 1$ and $t_2 = 30$, so we predict that the time to failure, T_3, will be the mean: $31/2 = 15.5$. We can continue this computation for each observation, t_i, so that we have:

- for $i = 4$, we have $t_2 = 30$ and $t_3 = 113$, so T_4 is 71.5
- for $i = 5$, we have $t_3 = 113$ and $t_4 = 81$, so T_5 is 97

and so on. What results is the gray line labeled "av 2" in Figure 9.9. We can extend this technique to include more of the historical data; the figure also shows what our

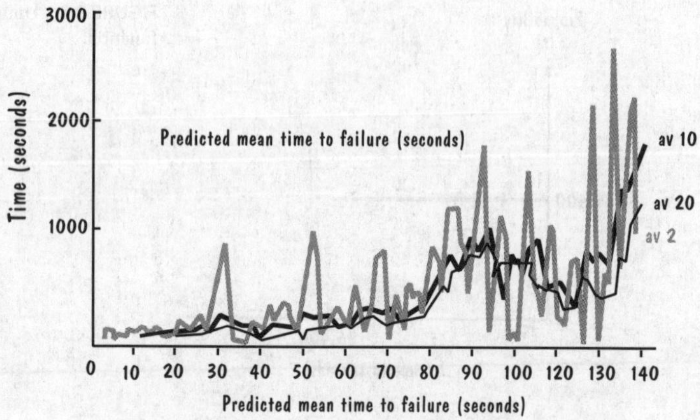

FIGURE 9.9 Predicting next failure times from past history.

predictions are like if we use the 10 previous failure times (av 10) and the 20 previous failure times (av 20).

However, researchers have suggested more sophisticated models of reliability that reflect our assumptions about software behavior as we find and fix faults. For instance, some models assume that the change in system behavior is the same regardless of which specific fault is fixed. But other models recognize that faults are different, and the effects of correction differ, too. For example, we may have different probability density functions for each correction, especially when we have reliability growth. As Fenton and Pfleeger (1997) point out, any system of prediction must include three elements:

- *a prediction model* that gives a complete probability specification of the stochastic process (e.g., the functions $F_i(T_i)$ and an assumption of independence of successive times)
- *an inference procedure* for the unknown parameters of the model based on the values of $t_1, t_2, \ldots, t_{i-1}$
- *a prediction procedure* that combines the model and inference procedure to make predictions about future failure behavior

In this section, we examine two popular reliability prediction models; for more models and more detailed information, see Fenton and Pfleeger (1997).

Good reliability models explicitly address both types of uncertainty about reliability. Type-1 uncertainty is handled by assuming that each fault is encountered randomly, so the time to the next failure is described using an exponential distribution. For example, Motorola uses an exponential distribution in its zero-failure testing approach (Sidebar 9.5). Thus, we can differentiate reliability models by the way they handle type-2 uncertainty.

SIDEBAR 9.5 MOTOROLA'S ZERO-FAILURE TESTING

Motorola uses a simple model called *zero-failure testing* that is derived from a failure rate function (Brettschneider 1989). The model assumes that the number of failures to time t is equal to

$$ae^{-b(t)}$$

for constants a and b. We can use the model to tell us how many hours the system must be tested in order to meet a reliability goal. Thus, the model requires three inputs: the target projected average number of failures (*failures*), the total number of test failures observed so far (*test-failures*), and the total number of test execution hours up to the last failure (*hours-to-last-failure*). The calculation for zero-failure test hours is

$$\frac{[\ln(failures/(0.5 + failures)] \times (hours\text{-}to\text{-}last\text{-}failure)}{\ln[(0.5 + failures)/(test\text{-}failures + failures)]}$$

For example, suppose you are testing a 33,000-line program. Up to now, 15 failures have occurred over the total test time of 500 hours. During the last 50 hours of testing, no failures have been reported. Your goal is to guarantee no more than an average of 0.03 failure per thousand lines of code. Based on the information you have, the projected average number of failures is 0.03 failure per 1000 times 33,000 lines of code, or 1. By using the preceding formula, the number of test hours needed to reach the goal is

$$\frac{[\ln(1/1.5)] \times 450}{\ln[(1.5/16)]} = 77$$

Thus, you should reach the desired level of reliability if you can test for 77 hours after the last detected failure without any more failures. Since you have already tested for 50 hours, you need only test for 27 hours more. However, if a failure occurs during the 27-hour period, you must continue your testing, recalculate, and restart the clock.

The Jelinski–Moranda Model. The **Jelinski–Moranda model** is the earliest and probably the best-known reliability model (Jelinski and Moranda 1972). It assumes that there is no type-2 uncertainty. That is, the model assumes that corrections are perfect (they fix the fault causing the failure, while introducing no new faults). Jelinski–Moranda also assumes that fixing any fault contributes equally to improving the reliability.

To see if the Jelinski–Moranda model portrays failure realistically, suppose we are examining software that has 15 faults, where 0.003 represents the degree to which fixing each fault contributes to the increase in reliability. Table 9.4 lists the mean time to the ith failure, plus a simulated set of failure times (produced using random numbers in the model). As i approaches 15 (the last remaining fault), the failure times become larger

TABLE 9.4 Successive Failure Times for Jelinski–Moranda

i	Mean Time to *i*th Failure	Simulated Time to *i*th Failure
1	22	11
2	24	41
3	26	13
4	28	4
5	30	30
6	33	77
7	37	11
8	42	64
9	48	54
10	56	34
11	67	183
12	83	83
13	111	17
14	167	190
15	333	436

and larger. In other words, the second column tells us the mean time to the *i*th failure based on past history, and the third column tells us the predicted time to the next (i.e., the *i*th) failure based on the Jelinski–Moranda model.

The widely used **Musa** model is based on Jelinski–Moranda, using execution time to capture interfailure times. It also incorporates calendar time for estimating the time when target reliability is achieved (Musa, Iannino, and Okumoto 1990). Musa tied reliability to project management, encouraging managers to use reliability modeling in many environments, particularly telecommunications.

The Littlewood Model. The **Littlewood model** is more realistic than Jelinski–Moranda, because it treats each corrected fault's contribution to reliability as an independent random variable. The contributions are assumed to have a gamma distribution. Littlewood uses two sources of uncertainty in his distribution, so we call his model **doubly stochastic**. The Littlewood model tends to encounter and remove faults with large contributions to reliability earlier than faults with a smaller contribution, representing the diminishing returns often experienced as testing continues. The Jelinski–Moranda model uses an exponential distribution for the times at which faults are discovered, but Littlewood's model uses a Pareto distribution.

Importance of the Operational Environment

We compare and contrast the accuracy of several reliability models in Chapter 13. Here, we look at the common assumption that a model accurate in the past will be accurate in the future, assuming the conditions of use are the same. Usually, our predictions are based on failures occurring during testing. But our testing environment may not reflect actual or typical system use.

Realism is even more difficult to capture when users have different modes of system use, different experience levels, and different operating environments. For example, a novice user of a spreadsheet or accounting package is not likely to use the same shortcuts and sophisticated techniques as an experienced user; the failure profiles for each are likely to be quite different.

Musa addressed this problem by anticipating typical user interaction with the system, captured in an **operational profile** that describes likely user input over time. Ideally, the operational profile is a probability distribution of inputs. When the testing strategy is based on the operational profile, the test data reflect the probability distribution.

An operational profile is often created by dividing the input space into a number of distinct classes and assigning to each class a probability that an input from that class will be selected. For example, suppose a program allows a user to run one of three different menu options: *create*, *delete*, and *modify*. We determine from tests with users that option *create* is selected twice as often as *delete* or *modify* (which are selected equally often). We can assign a probability of 0.5 to *create*, 0.25 to *delete*, and 0.25 to *modify*. Then, our testing strategy selects inputs randomly so that the probability of an input's being *create* is 0.5, *delete* is 0.25, and *modify* is 0.25.

This strategy of **statistical testing** has at least two benefits:

1. Testing concentrates on the parts of the system most likely to be used and hence should result in a system that the user finds more reliable.
2. Reliability predictions based on the test results should give us an accurate prediction of reliability as seen by the user.

However, it is not easy to do statistical testing properly. There is no simple or repeatable way of defining operational profiles. We see later in this chapter how cleanroom software development integrates statistical testing into its approach to building quality software.

9.5 ACCEPTANCE TESTING

When function and performance testing are complete, we are convinced that the system meets all the requirements specified during the initial stages of software development. The next step is to ask the customers and users if they concur.

Purpose and Roles

Until now, we as developers have designed the test cases and administered all tests. Now the customer leads testing and defines the cases to be tested. The purpose of acceptance testing is to enable the customers and users to determine if the system we built really meets their needs and expectations. Thus, acceptance tests are written, conducted, and evaluated by the customers, with assistance from the developers only when the customer requests an answer to a technical question. Usually, those customer employees who were involved in requirements definition play a large part in acceptance testing, because they understand what kind of system the customer intended to have built.

Types of Acceptance Tests

There are three ways the customer can evaluate the system. In a **benchmark test**, the customer prepares a set of test cases that represent typical conditions under which the system will operate when actually installed. The customer evaluates the system's performance for each test case. Benchmark tests are performed with actual users or a special team exercising system functions. In either case, the testers are familiar with the requirements and able to evaluate the actual performance.

Benchmark tests are commonly used when a customer has special requirements. Two or more development teams are asked to produce systems according to specification; one system will be chosen for purchase, based on the success of benchmark tests. For example, a customer may ask two communications companies to install a voice and data network. Each system is benchmarked. Both systems may meet a requirement, but one may be faster or easier to use than the other. The customer decides which one to purchase based on how the systems meet the benchmark criteria.

A **pilot test** installs the system on an experimental basis. Users exercise the system as if it had been installed permanently. Whereas benchmark tests include a set of special test cases that the users apply, pilot tests rely on the everyday working of the system to test all functions. The customer often prepares a suggested list of functions that each user tries to incorporate in typical daily procedures. However, a pilot test is much less formal and structured than a benchmark test.

Sometimes, we test a system with users from within our own organization or company before releasing the system to the customer; we "pilot" the system before the customer runs the real pilot test. Our in-house test is called an **alpha test**, and the customer's pilot is a **beta test**. This approach is common when systems are to be released to a wide variety of customers. For example, a new version of an operating system may be alpha tested at our own offices and then beta-tested using a specially selected group of customer sites. We try to choose as beta-test sites customers who represent all kinds of system usage. (Sidebar 9.6 warns of the dangers of using a beta version as the "real" system.)

Even if a system is being developed for just one customer, a pilot test usually involves only a small subset of the customer's potential users. We choose users whose activities represent those of most others who will use the system later. One location or organization may be chosen to test the system, rather than allowing all intended users to have access.

If a new system is replacing an existing one or is part of a phased development, a third kind of testing can be used for acceptance. In **parallel testing**, the new system operates in parallel with the previous version. The users gradually become accustomed to the new system but continue to use the old one to duplicate the new. This gradual transition allows users to compare and contrast the new system with the old. It also allows skeptical users to build their confidence in the new system by comparing the results obtained with both and verifying that the new system is just as effective and efficient as the old. In a sense, parallel testing incorporates a user-administered combination of compatibility and function testing.

Results of Acceptance Tests

The type of system being tested and the customer's preferences determine the choice of acceptance test. In fact, a combination of some or all of the approaches can be used.

SIDEBAR 9.6 INAPPROPRIATE USE OF A BETA VERSION

In July 1997, the U.S. National Aeronautics and Space Administration experienced problems with the Pathfinder lander that placed the Sojourner exploratory device on Mars. Pathfinder's software enabled it to land on Mars, release the Sojourner rover, and manage communications between Earth and the lander. However, because of failures related to stack management and pointers during task switching, the Pathfinder kept resetting itself, thereby interrupting its work for periods of time.

Sojouner contained a simple, serial-tasking 80C85 controller, and it worked quite well. But NASA had needed more complex software to manage the more complex functions of Pathfinder. During design, NASA chose a target processor first, and then found software to run on it. Consequently, NASA selected IBM's new radiation-hardened version of its R6000 processor, similar to the processor on the PowerPC. The 32-bit chip was attractive because using a commercial real-time operating system for it would have avoided the expense of building custom software. Thus, NASA's next step was to identify an operating system for Pathfinder.

Several operating systems were available, and NASA chose VxWorks from Wind River Systems (Alameda, California). When the selection was made, VxWorks was tested and available commercially for the PowerPC. However, a separate version for the R6000 was not yet ready. Consequently, Wind River Systems ported the PowerPC's version of the VxWorks operating system to the R6000, taking advantage of the portability of C code. The ported product was delivered to NASA in 1994.

When the R6000 version of VxWorks arrived, NASA froze the Pathfinder configuration at version 5.1.1, even though significant problems with the operating system had not yet been resolved. Thus, the Pathfinder software was really built around a beta-test version of its operating system, rather than around a fully tested, robust operating system (Coffee 1997).

Tests by users sometimes find places where the customer's expectations as stated in the requirements do not match what we have implemented. In other words, acceptance testing is the customer's chance to verify that what was wanted is what was built. If the customer is satisfied, the system is then accepted as stated in the contract.

In reality, acceptance testing uncovers more than requirements discrepancies. The acceptance test also allows customers to determine what they really want, whether specified in the requirements documents or not. Remember that the requirements analysis stage of development gives customers an opportunity to explain to us what problem needs a solution, and the system design is our proposed solution. Until customers and users actually work with a system as a proposed solution, they may not really know whether the problem is indeed solved. In fact, working with our system may help customers to discover aspects of the problem (or even new problems) of which they were not aware.

We have seen in previous chapters that rapid prototyping may be used to help the customer understand more about the solution before the entire system is implemented.

However, prototypes are often impractical or too expensive to build. Moreover, when building large systems, there is sometimes a long lag between the initial specification and the first viewing of even part of a system. During this time, the customer's needs may change in some way. For instance, federal regulations, key personnel, or even the nature of the customer's business may change, affecting the nature of the original problem. Thus, changes in requirements may be needed not only because they were specified improperly at the beginning of development, but also because the customers may decide that the problem has changed and a different solution is needed.

After acceptance testing, the customer tells us which requirements are not satisfied and which must be deleted, revised, or added because of changing needs. Configuration management staff identify these changes and record the consequent modifications to design, implementation, and testing.

9.6 INSTALLATION TESTING

The final round of testing involves installing the system at user sites. If acceptance testing has been performed on-site, installation testing may not be needed. However, if the acceptance testing conditions were not the same as the actual site conditions, additional testing is necessary. To begin installation testing, we configure the system to the user environment. We attach the proper number and kind of devices to the main processor and establish communications with other systems. We allocate files and assign access to appropriate functions and data.

Installation tests require us to work with the customer to determine what tests are needed on-site. Regression tests may be administered to verify that the system has been installed properly and works "in the field" as it did when tested previously. The test cases assure the customer that the system is complete and that all necessary files and devices are present. The tests focus on two things: completeness of the installed system and verification of any functional or nonfunctional characteristics that may be affected by site conditions. For example, a system designed to work aboard a ship must be tested to demonstrate that it is not affected by the severe weather or the ship's motion.

When the customer is satisfied with the results, testing is complete and the system is formally delivered.

9.7 AUTOMATED SYSTEM TESTING

Many of the test tools described in Chapter 8 are also helpful in system testing. Others are designed specifically to test large groups of components or to assist in testing hardware and software at the same time.

Simulation allows us to concentrate on evaluating one part of a system while portraying the characteristics of other parts. A **simulator** presents to a system all the characteristics of a device or system without actually having the device or system available. Just as a flight simulator allows you to learn to fly without an actual airplane, a device simulator allows you to control a device even when the device is not present. This situation occurs often, especially when the software is being developed off-site or when the device is being developed in parallel with the software.

For example, suppose a vendor is building a new communication system, consisting of both hardware and software, at the same time that software engineers are developing the driver for it. It is impossible to test the not-yet-completed vendor's device, so the device's specifications are used to build a simulator that allows us to test the expected interactions.

Similarly, a simulator is particularly useful if a special device is located on the customer's or user's site but testing is being done at another location. For instance, if you are building an automobile navigation system, you may not need the actual automobile to test the software; you can have your system interact with an automobile simulator instead. In fact, sometimes a device simulator is more helpful than the device itself, since the simulator can store data indicating the device's state during the various stages of a test. Then the simulator reports on its state when a failure occurs, possibly helping you to find the fault that caused it.

Simulators are also used to look like other systems with which the test system must interface. If messages are communicated or a database is accessed, a simulator provides the necessary information for testing without duplicating the entire other system. The simulator also helps with stress and volume testing, since it can be programmed to load the system with substantial amounts of data, requests, or users.

In general, simulators give you control over the test conditions. This control allows you to perform tests that might otherwise be dangerous or impossible. For example, the test of a missile guidance system can be made much simpler and safer using simulators.

Automation can also help in designing test cases. For example, Cohen et al. (1996) describe an Automatic Efficient Test Generator (AETG), developed at Bellcore, that uses combinatorial design techniques to generate test cases. In their combinatorial design approach, they generate tests that cover all pairwise, triple, or n-way combinations of test parameters. For instance, to cover all pairwise combinations, if x_1 is a valid value for a one parameter and x_2 valid for another, then there is a test case in which the first parameter is x_1 and the second is x_2. In one experiment, the test requirements for final release had 75 parameters, with 10^{29} possible test combinations. Using the AETG, the researchers generated only 28 tests to cover all pairwise parameter combinations. In another experiment, their technique generated tests that yielded better block and decision coverage than random testing. And a third study showed that the automated system revealed significant requirements and code faults that were not found using other testing means. Sidebar 9.7 describes another example of how test automation accelerated the test process.

9.8 TEST DOCUMENTATION

Testing can be complex and difficult. The system's software and hardware can contribute to the difficulty, as can the procedures involved in using the system. In addition, a distributed or real-time system requires great care in tracing and timing data and processes to draw conclusions about performance. Finally, when systems are large, the large number of people involved in development and testing can make coordination difficult. To control the complexity and difficulty of testing, we use complete and carefully designed test documentation.

SIDEBAR 9.7 AUTOMATED TESTING OF A MOTOR INSURANCE QUOTATION SYSTEM

Mills (1997) describes how his company uses automation to test a motor insurance quotation system. Each system contains risk profiles of approximately 90 insurers and products, enabling a broker to supply information about an automobile and its driver and to receive a quotation for insurance premiums. The input includes 50 fields, such as age, driving experience, area of the UK, type of use, engine size, and number of drivers. This information helps place the proposer in one of 20 areas, one of more than 20 vehicle groups, five classes of use, three types of insurance coverage, and 15 age groups. The quotation system tracks 14 products on 10 insurance systems, where each system is updated at least monthly.

Thus, the number of test cases needed to test the quotation system thoroughly is very large, and a big part of the testing process is deciding how many test cases are enough. Bates (1997) presents calculations to show that testing 5000 conditions for a system at National Westminster Bank requires 21,000 scripts; since each script takes three minutes to test manually, testing would take 7.5 months for one person on one platform! This situation is clearly unacceptable for the insurance system described by Mills, which involves more conditions and test scripts. The developers estimated that they could test at most 100 to 200 cases in batch mode, and the insurers directed the developers to run 100 random test quotes. But by using automated testing, a third party runs 30,000 planned test quotes per client on each quotation system every month. And the testing process takes less than one week to complete! Mills reports that the biggest difference between automated and manual testing, besides speed, is that many faults are found earlier in the testing process, leaving more time to fix them before the next version of the system is released.

Several types of documentation are needed. A **test plan** describes the system itself and the plan for exercising all functions and characteristics. A **test specification and evaluation** details each test and defines the criteria for evaluating each feature addressed by the test. Then, a **test description** presents the test data and procedures for individual tests. Finally, the **test analysis report** describes the results of each test. Figure 9.10 shows the relationship of the documents to the testing process.

Test Plans

In Chapter 8, we discussed the role of the test plan in laying out the patterns of testing for all testing activities. Now we look at how a test plan can be used to direct system testing.

Figure 9.11 illustrates a test plan's components. The plan begins by stating its objectives, which should

- guide the management of testing
- guide the technical effort required during testing

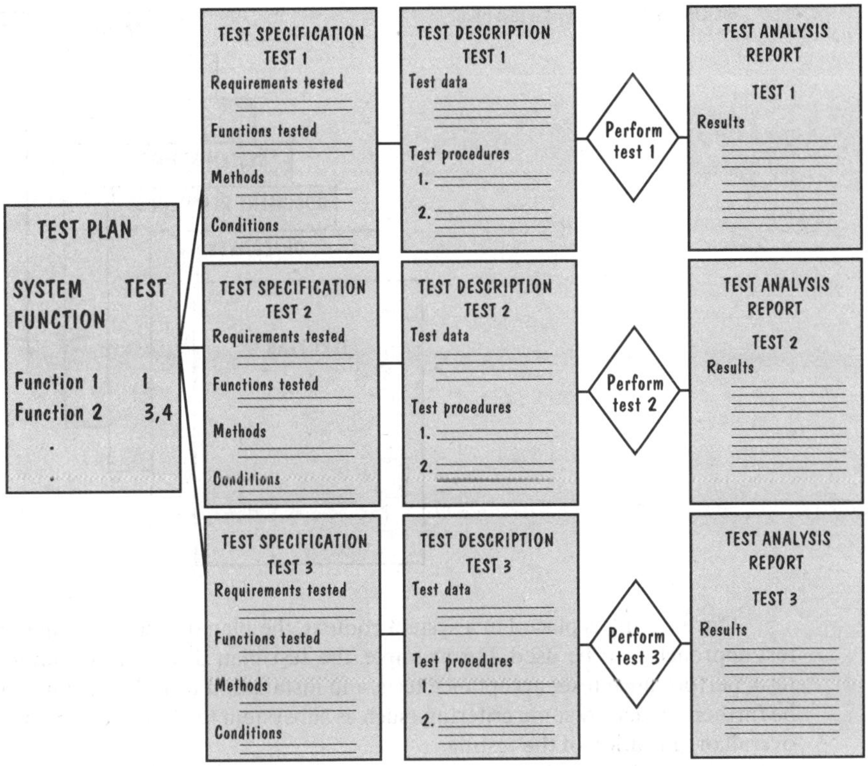

FIGURE 9.10 Documents produced during testing.

- establish test planning and scheduling, including specifying equipment needed, organizational requirements, test methods, anticipated outcomes, and user orientation
- explain the nature and extent of each test
- explain how the tests will completely evaluate system function and performance
- document test input, specific test procedures, and expected outcomes

Next, the test plan references other major documents produced during development. In particular, the plan explains the relationships among the requirements documents, design documents, code components and documents, and test procedures. For example, there may be a naming or numbering scheme that ties together all of the documents, so that requirement 4.9 is reflected in design components 5.3, 5.6, and 5.8, and tested by procedure 12.3.

Following these preliminary sections is a system summary. Since a reader of the test plan may not have been involved with the previous stages of development, the system summary puts the testing schedule and events in context. The summary need not be detailed; it can be a drawing depicting the major system inputs and outputs with a description of major transformations.

FIGURE 9.11 Parts of a test plan.

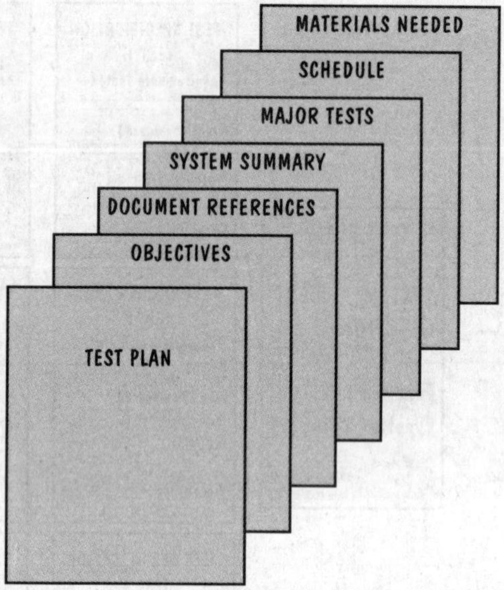

Once testing is placed in a system context, the plan describes the major tests and test approaches to be used. For example, the test plan distinguishes among function tests, performance tests, acceptance tests, and installation tests. If the function tests can be further divided by some criterion (such as subsystem tests), the test plan lays out the overall organization of the testing.

After explaining the component tests, the plan addresses the schedule of events. The schedule includes the test location as well as time frame. Often depicted as a milestone chart or activity graph, the test schedule includes

1. the overall testing period
2. the major subdivisions of testing, and their start and stop times
3. any pretest requirements (e.g., orientation or familiarization with the system, user training, generation of test data) and the time necessary for each
4. the time necessary for preparing and reviewing the test report

If testing is to take place at several locations, the test plan includes a schedule for each. A chart illustrates the hardware, software, and personnel necessary for administering the tests at each location, and the duration for which each resource will be needed. Noted, too, are special training or maintenance needs.

The plan identifies test materials in terms of deliverables (e.g., user or operator manuals, sample listings, tapes) and materials supplied by the site (e.g., special test apparatus, database tables, storage media). For example, if a test is to use a database management system to build a sample database, the test may require the users at the site to define data elements before the arrival of the test team. Similarly, if the test team requires any security or privacy precautions, the personnel at the test location may be required to establish passwords or special access for them before the test can begin.

Test Specification and Evaluation

The test plan describes an overall breakdown of testing into individual tests that address specific items. For example, if the system being tested has its processing distributed over several computers, the function and performance tests can be further divided into tests for each subsystem.

For each such individual test, we write a test specification and evaluation. The specification begins by listing the requirements whose satisfaction will be demonstrated by the test. Referring to the requirements documents, this section explains the test's purpose.

One way to view the correspondence between requirements and tests is to use a table or chart, such as Table 9.5. Note that the requirements listed across the top reference the number in a requirements document; the function on the left is mandated by the requirement in whose column the X is placed.

The system functions involved in the test are enumerated in the table. The performance tests can be described in a similar way. Instead of listing functional requirements, the chart lists requirements related to speed of access, database security, and so on.

Often, an individual test is really a collection of smaller tests, the sum of which illustrates requirements satisfaction. In this case, the test specification shows the relationship between the smaller tests and the requirements.

Each test is guided by a test philosophy and adopts a set of methods. However, the philosophy and methods may be constrained by other requirements and by the

TABLE 9.5 Test-Requirement Correspondence Chart

Test	Requirement 2.4.1: Generate and Maintain Database	Requirement 2.4.2: Selectively Retrieve Data	Requirement 2.4.3: Produce Specialized Reports
1. Add new record	X		
2. Add field	X		
3. Change field	X		
4. Delete record	X		
5. Delete field	X		
6. Create index		X	
Retrieve record with a requested			
7. Cell number		X	
8. Water height		X	
9. Canopy height		X	
10. Ground cover		X	
11. Percolation rate		X	
12. Print full database			X
13. Print directory			X
14. Print keywords			X
15. Print simulation summary			X

realities of the test situation. The specification makes these test conditions clear. Among the conditions may be some of the following:

- Is the system using actual input from users or devices, or are special cases generated by a program or surrogate device?
- What are the test coverage criteria?
- How will data be recorded?
- Are there timing, interface, equipment, personnel, database, or other limitations on testing?
- If the test is a series of smaller tests, in what order are the tests to be performed?

If test data are to be processed before being evaluated, the test specification discusses the processing. For instance, when a system produces large amounts of data, data-reduction techniques are sometimes used on the output so that the result is more suitable for evaluation.

Accompanying each test is a way to tell when the test is complete. Thus, the specification is followed by a discussion of how we know when the test is over and the relevant requirements have been satisfied. For example, the plan explains what range of output results will meet the requirement.

The evaluation method follows the completion criteria. For example, data produced during testing may be collected and collated manually and then inspected by the test team. Alternatively, the team could use an automated tool to evaluate some of the data and then inspect summary reports or do an item-by-item comparison with expected output. The efficiency and effectiveness measures described in Sidebar 9.8 can be used to assess the thoroughness of the tests.

Test Description

A test description is written for every test defined in the test specification. We use the test description document as a guide in performing the test. These documents must be detailed and clear, including

- the means of control
- the data
- the procedures

A general description of the test begins the document. Then, we indicate whether the test will be initiated and controlled by automatic or manual means. For instance, data may be input manually from the keyboard, but then an automated driver may exercise the functions being tested. Alternatively, the entire process could be automated.

The test data can be viewed in several parts: input data, input commands, input states, output data, output states, and messages produced by the system. Each is described in detail. For instance, input commands are provided so that the team knows how to initiate the test, halt or suspend it, repeat or resume an unsuccessful or incomplete one, or terminate the test. Similarly, the team must interpret messages to understand the system status and control testing. We explain how the team can distinguish among failures resulting from input data, from improper test procedures, or from hardware malfunction (wherever possible).

SIDEBAR 9.8 MEASURING TEST EFFECTIVENESS AND EFFICIENCY

One aspect of test planning and reporting is measuring test effectiveness. Graham (1996b) suggests that test effectiveness can be measured by dividing the number of faults found in a given test by the total number of faults found (including those found after the test). For example, suppose integration testing finds 56 faults, and the total testing process finds 70 faults. Then, Graham's measure of test effectiveness says that integration testing was 80% effective. However, suppose the system is delivered after the 70 faults were found, and 70 additional faults are discovered during the first 6 months of operation. Then, integration testing is responsible for finding 56 of 140 faults, for a test effectiveness of only 40%.

This approach to evaluating the impact of a particular testing phase or technique can be adjusted in several ways. For example, failures can be assigned a severity level, and test effectiveness can be calculated by level. In this way, integration testing might be 50% effective at finding faults that cause critical failures, but 80% effective at finding faults that cause minor failures. Alternatively, test effectiveness may be combined with root cause analysis, so that we can describe effectiveness in finding faults as early as possible in development. For example, integration testing may find 80% of faults, but half of those faults might have been discovered earlier, such as during design review, because they are design problems.

Test efficiency is computed by dividing the number of faults found in testing by the effort needed to perform testing, to yield a value in faults per staff-hour. Efficiency measures help us understand the cost of finding faults, as well as the relative costs of finding them in different phases of the testing process.

Both effectiveness and efficiency measures can be useful in test planning; we want to maximize our effectiveness and efficiency based on past testing history. Thus, the documentation of current tests should include measures that allow us to compute effectiveness and efficiency.

For example, the test data for a test of a SORT routine may be the following:

```
INPUT DATA:
Input data are to be provided by the LIST program. The program
generates randomly a list of N words of alphanumeric characters;
each word is of length M. The program is invoked by calling
      RUN LIST(N,M)
in your test driver. The output is placed in global data area
LISTBUF. The test datasets to be used for this test are as
follows:
Case 1: Use LIST with N=5, M=5
Case 2: Use LIST with N=10, M=5
Case 3: Use LIST with N=15, M=5
Case 4: Use LIST with N=50, M=10
Case 5: Use LIST with N=100, M=10
Case 6: Use LIST with N=150, M=10
```

```
INPUT COMMANDS:
The SORT routine is invoked by using the command
      RUN SORT (INBUF,OUTBUF) or
      RUN SORT (INBUF)

OUTPUT DATA:
If two parameters are used, the sorted list is placed in OUTBUF.
Otherwise, it is placed in INBUF.

SYSTEM MESSAGES:
During the sorting process, the following message is displayed:
      "Sorting...please wait..."
Upon completion, SORT displays the following message on the screen:
      "Sorting completed"
To halt or terminate the test before the completion message is
displayed, press CONTROL-C on the keyboard.
```

A test procedure is often called a **test script** because it gives us a step-by-step description of how to perform the test. A rigidly defined set of steps gives us control over the test, so that we can duplicate conditions and re-create the failure, if necessary, when trying to find the cause of the problem. If the test is interrupted for some reason, we must be able to continue the test without having to return to the beginning.

For example, part of the test script for testing the "change field" function (listed in Table 9.5) might look like this:

```
Step N:     Press function key 4: Access data file.
Step N+1:   Screen will ask for the name of the date file.
            Type 'sys:test.txt'
Step N+2:   Menu will appear, reading
                 * delete file
                 * modify file
                 * rename file
            Place cursor next to 'modify file' and press
            RETURN key.
Step N+3:   Screen will ask for record number. Type '4017'.
Step N+4:   Screen will fill with data fields for record 4017:
                 Record number: 4017     X: 0042 Y: 0036
                 Soil type: clay         Percolation: 4 mtrs/hr
                 Vegetation: kudzu       Canopy height: 25 mtrs
                 Water table: 12 mtrs    Construct: outhouse
                 Maintenance code: 3T/4F/9R
Step N+5:   Press function key 9: modify
Step N+6:   Entries on screen will be highlighted. Move cursor
            to VEGETATION field. Type 'grass' over 'kudzu' and
            press RETURN key.
Step N+7:   Entries on screen will no longer be highlighted.
            VEGETATION field should now read 'grass'.
```

```
Step N+8:   Press function key 16: Return to previous screen.
Step N+9:   Menu will appear, reading
                  * delete file
                  * modify file
                  * rename file
            To verify that the modification has been recorded,
            place cursor next to 'modify file' and press RETURN
            key.
Step N+10:  Screen will ask for record number. Type '4017'.
Step N+11:  Screen will fill with data fields for record 4017:
                  Record number: 4017      X: 0042 Y: 0036
                  Soil type: clay          Percolation: 4 mtrs/hr
                  Vegetation: grass        Canopy height: 25 mtrs
                  Water table: 12 mtrs     Construct: outhouse
                  Maintenance code: 3T/4F/9R
```

The test script steps are numbered, and data associated with each step are referenced. If we have not described them elsewhere, we explain how to prepare the data or the site for the test. For example, the equipment settings needed, the database definitions, and the communication connections may be detailed. Next, the script explains exactly what is to happen during the test. We report the keys pressed, the screens displayed, the output produced, the equipment reactions, and any other manifestation. We explain the expected outcome or output, and we give instructions to the operator or user about what to do if the expected outcome is different from the actual outcome.

Finally, the test description explains the sequence of activities required to end the test. These activities may involve reading or printing critical data, terminating automated procedures, or turning off pieces of equipment.

Test Analysis Report

When a test has been administered, we analyze the results to determine if the function or performance tested meets the requirements. Sometimes, the mere demonstration of a function is enough. Most of the time, though, there are performance constraints on the function. For instance, it is not enough to know that a column can be sorted or summed. We must measure the calculation's speed and note its correctness. Thus, a test analysis report is necessary for several reasons:

- It documents the results of a test.
- If a failure occurs, the report provides information needed to duplicate the failure (if necessary) and to locate and fix the source of the problem.
- It provides information necessary to determine if the development project is complete.
- It establishes confidence in the system's performance.

The test analysis report may be read by people who were not part of the test process but who are familiar with other aspects of the system and its development. Thus, the report includes a brief summary of the project, its objectives, and relevant references for this test. For example, the test report mentions those parts of the requirements, design, and implementation documents that describe the functions exercised in this test. The report also indicates those parts of the test plan and specification documents that deal with this test.

Once the stage is set in this way, the test analysis report lists the functions and performance characteristics that were to be demonstrated and describes the actual results. The results include function, performance, and data measures, noting whether the target requirements have been met. If a fault or deficiency has been discovered, the report discusses its impact. Sometimes, we evaluate the test results in terms of a measure of severity. This measure helps the test team decide whether to continue testing or wait until the fault has been corrected. For example, if the failure is a spurious character in the upper part of a display screen, then testing can continue while we locate the cause and correct it. However, if a fault causes the system to crash or a data file to be deleted, the test team may decide to interrupt testing until the fault is repaired.

Problem Report Forms

Recall from Chapter 1 that a fault is a problem in a system artifact that can cause a system failure; the fault is seen by the developer, and the failure is experienced by the user. During testing, we capture data about faults and failures in **problem report forms**. A **discrepancy report form** is a problem report that describes occurrences of problems where actual system behaviors or attributes do not match with what we expect. It explains what was expected, what actually happened, and the circumstances leading to the failure. A **fault report form** explains how a fault was found and fixed, often in response to the filing of a discrepancy report form.

Every problem report form should answer several questions about the problem it is describing:

- *Location:* Where did the problem occur?
- *Timing:* When did it occur?
- *Symptom:* What was observed?
- *End-result:* What were the consequences?
- *Mechanism:* How did it occur?
- *Cause:* Why did it occur?
- *Severity:* How much was the user or business affected?
- *Cost:* How much did it cost?

Figure 9.12 is an example of an actual fault report form from a British utility. Notice that a fault number is assigned to each fault, and the developers record the date when they were notified that a problem had occurred as well as the date when the

Fault Number	Week In	System Area	Fault Type	Week Out	Hours to Repair
...	...	...	...	...	...
F254	92/14	C2	P	92/17	5.5

FIGURE 9.12 Fault report form.

problem's cause was located and fixed. Because developers do not address each problem right away (e.g., because other problems have higher priority), the developers also record the actual number of hours needed to repair this particular fault.

However, the fault report form is missing a great deal of data. In general, a fault report form should address our list of questions with this kind of detailed information (Fenton and Pfleeger 1997):

- *Location:* within-system identifier, such as module or document name
- *Timing:* phases of development during which fault was created, detected, and corrected
- *Symptom:* type of error message reported or activity that revealed fault (e.g., testing, review, inspection)
- *End-result:* failure caused by the fault
- *Mechanism:* how the source was created, detected, and corrected
- *Cause:* type of human error that led to the fault
- *Severity:* refers to severity of resulting or potential failure
- *Cost:* time or effort to locate and correct; can include analysis of cost had fault been identified earlier in the development

Notice that each of these aspects of a fault reflects the developer's understanding of the fault's impact on the system. On the other hand, a discrepancy report should reflect a user's view of the failure caused by a fault. The questions are the same, but the answers are very different:

- *Location:* installation where the failure was observed
- *Timing:* CPU time, clock time, or other relevant measure of time
- *Symptom:* type of error message or indication of failure
- *End-result:* description of failure, such as "operating system crash," "service degraded," "loss of data," "wrong output," or "no output"
- *Mechanism:* chain of events, including keyboard commands and state data leading to failure
- *Cause:* reference to possible faults leading to failure
- *Severity:* impact on user or business
- *Cost:* cost to fix plus cost of lost potential business

Figure 9.13 is an actual discrepancy report form, mistakenly called a "fault" report. It addresses many of the questions in our list and does a good job of describing the failure. However, it contains a list only of the items changed, not a description of the underlying cause of the failure. Ideally, this form should reference one or more fault reports, so that we can tell which faults caused which failures.

We need more complete information in our problem report forms so we can evaluate the effectiveness and efficiency of our testing and development practices. Especially when we have limited resources, historical information captured in problem reports helps us to understand which activities are likely to cause faults, and which practices are good at finding and fixing them.

FAULT REPORT **S.P0204.6.10.3016**

ORIGINATOR: Joe Bloggs

BRIEF TITLE: Exception 1 in dps_c.c line 620 raised by NAS

FULL DESCRIPTION Started NAS endurance and allowed it to run for a few minutes. Disabled the active NAS link (emulator switched to standby link), then re-enabled the disabled link and CDIS exceptioned as above. (I think the re-enabling is a red herring.) (during database load)

ASSIGNED FOR EVALUATION TO: DATE:

CATEGORISATION: 0 ① 2 3 Design Spec Docn
SEND COPIES FOR INFORMATION TO:
EVALUATOR: [signature] DATE: 8/7/92

CONFIGURATION ID	ASSIGNED TO	PART
dpo_s.c		

COMMENTS: dpo_s.c appears to try to use an invalid CID, instead of rejecting the message. AWJ

ITEMS CHANGED

CONFIGURATION ID	IMPLEMENTOR/DATE	REVIEWER/DATE	BUILD/ISSUE NUM	INTEGRATOR/DATE
dpo_s.c v.10	AWJ 8/7/92	MAR 8/7/92	6.120	RA 8-7-92

COMMENTS:

CLOSED

FAULT CONTROLLER: [signature] DATE: 9/7/92

FIGURE 9.13 Discrepancy report from air traffic control system development (Pfleeger and Hatton 1997).

9.9 TESTING SAFETY-CRITICAL SYSTEMS

In Chapter 1, we looked at several examples of systems whose failure can harm or kill people. Such systems are called **safety-critical**, since the consequences of their failure are so severe. Anthes (1997) reported many other instances where software failures led to unacceptable levels of harm. For example, from 1986 to 1996, 450 reports were filed with the U.S. Food and Drug Administration, describing software faults in medical devices. And 24 of these reports involved software that led to death or injury. Among the problems reported were these:

- An intravenous medication pump ran dry and injected air into a patient.
- A monitor failed to sound an alarm when a patient's heart stopped beating.
- A respirator delivered "unscheduled breaths" to a patient.
- A digital display combined the name of one patient with medical data from another patient.

The problems are not necessarily indicative of declining software quality. Rather, they reflect the increasing amount of software being placed in safety-critical systems.

Unfortunately, we do not always understand how the software development process affects the characteristics of the products we build, so it is difficult for us to ensure

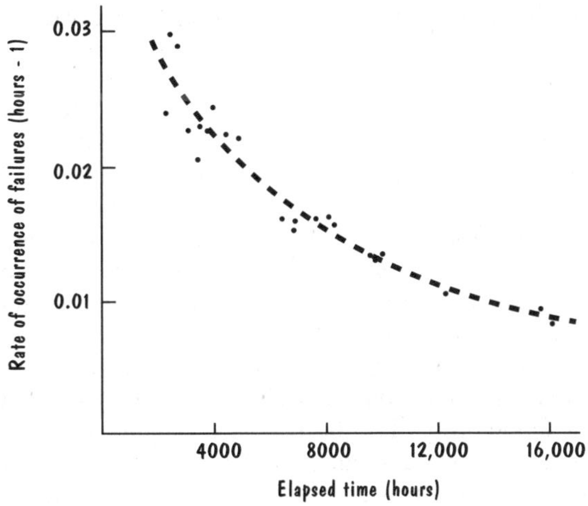

FIGURE 9.14 Estimates of rate of occurrence of failure derived from a Musa data set (Fenton and Pfleeger 1997).

that safety-critical systems are safe enough. In particular, we do not know how much each practice or technique contributes to a product's reliability. At the same time, our customers require us to reach ever-higher levels of ultra-high reliability.

For instance, the Airbus 320 is a fly-by-wire aircraft, meaning that software controls most of its vital functions. Because the airplane cannot tolerate failure of its fly-by-wire software, its system reliability requirement is a failure rate of 10^{-9} per hour (Rouquet and Traverse 1986). The software requirement must be even more restrictive.

The prescribed failure rate means that the system can tolerate at most one failure in 10^9 hours. In other words, the system can fail at most once in over 100,000 years of operation. We say that a system has **ultra-high reliability** when it has at most one failure in 10^9 hours. It is clear that we cannot apply our usual reliability assessment techniques in cases like this; to do so would mean running the system for 100,000 years (at least) and tracking the failure behavior. Thus, we must seek other practices to help assure the software's reliability.

Figure 9.14 shows us another way to look at the ultra-high-reliability problem. We have graphed failure data from a system in operational use; software and hardware design changes were implemented to fix the causes of the failures. In the graph, the Littlewood–Verrall model was used to compute the current Rate of Occurrence of Failures (ROCOF) at various times as testing proceeds. The dashed line, fitted manually, shows an apparently clear law of diminishing returns because the slope of the line flattens out, failures occur less and less frequently. That is, we must test for longer periods of time to make the system fail again, so reliability is increasing.

However, it is not at all clear what the ultimate reliability will be. We cannot tell if the curve is asymptotic to zero or whether we reach a nonzero reliability because we are introducing new faults as we fix old ones. Even if we felt confident that the system could reach ultra-high levels of reliability, we would still need to test for extraordinarily long periods of time to demonstrate our confidence.

In fact, even when we test a program for a long time without a failure, we still do not have the level of assurance we need. Littlewood has shown that if a program has worked failure-free for x hours, there is about a 50:50 chance that it will survive the next x hours before failing. To have the kind of confidence apparently needed for an aircraft such as the A320 would require a failure-free performance of the software for several billion hours (Littlewood 1991). Thus, even if the system had actually achieved its target reliability, we could not assure ourselves of it in an acceptable period of time.

Ensuring very high levels of reliability is a difficult but critical challenge that must be met if we hope to continue to use software in safety-critical systems. Many software engineers suggest that we should use formal verification techniques with our requirements, designs, and code. But formal evaluation of natural language is impossible, and important information may be lost if we translate natural language to mathematical symbols. Even formal proofs of specification and design are not foolproof, because mistakes are sometimes made in the proofs. For this reason, companies such as Baltimore Gas and Electric (Sidebar 9.9) rely on a combination of quality assurance techniques to try to catch or prevent as many faults as possible. Sidebar 9.10 lists additional industrial approaches to increasing safety. At the same time, researchers have been looking for other methods to help developers understand and ensure reliability. We will look at three of these techniques: design diversity, software safety cases, and cleanroom.

Design Diversity

Design diversity, introduced in Chapter 5, is based on a simple philosophy. The same system is built according to the same requirements specification but in several

SIDEBAR 9.9 SOFTWARE QUALITY PRACTICES AT BALTIMORE GAS AND ELECTRIC

In Maryland, the Baltimore Gas and Electric Company (BG&E) uses no special tools or techniques when it develops the safety-critical software that controls its two nuclear reactors. However, managers hope to ensure high reliability by checking the requirements definition thoroughly, performing quality reviews, testing carefully, documenting completely, and performing thorough configuration control.

To make sure all problems are caught early, the system is reviewed twice. Both the information systems group and the nuclear design engineering group conduct design reviews, code reviews, and system tests.

The United States government has issued federal Quality Assurance Criteria for Nuclear Power Plants, and software from BG&E's internal information systems group must comply with these regulations. Moreover, when a vendor supplies software to be used as part of the control system, BG&E sends an audit team to the vendor's development site, to ensure that the vendor has a software quality assurance program that meets the regulations (Anthes 1997).

SIDEBAR 9.10 SUGGESTIONS FOR BUILDING SAFETY-CRITICAL SOFTWARE

Anthes (1997) suggests several steps for building and testing safety-critical systems, as proposed by industry consultants:

- Recognize that testing cannot remove all faults or risks.
- Do not confuse safety, reliability, and security. A system that is 100% reliable still may be neither secure nor safe.
- Tightly link your organization's software and safety organizations.
- Build and use a safety information system.
- Instill a management culture of safety.
- Assume that every mistake users can make will be made.
- Do not assume that low-probability, high-impact events will not happen.
- Emphasize requirements definition, testing, code and specification reviews, and configuration control.
- Do not let short-term cost considerations overshadow long-term risks and costs.

independent ways, each according to a different design. Each system runs in parallel with the others, and a voting scheme coordinates actions when one system's results differ from the others'. The underlying assumption is that it is unlikely that at least three of the five groups of developers will write incorrect software for a given requirement, so high reliability is likely (Avizienis and Kelly 1984). Several systems have been built using this technique, including the software for the U.S. space shuttle and the Airbus A320 (Rouquet and Traverse 1986). However, there is empirical evidence suggesting that independently developed software versions will not fail independently; the diverse designs do not always offer reliability higher than that of a single version.

For example, Knight and Leveson (1986) performed an experiment in which 27 versions of a software system were developed independently. They examined the faults discovered in each system and found a high incidence of common ones. Knight and Leveson speculate that, because we train our software developers to use common techniques and common approaches to design, we can expect different designers and developers to make the same kinds of mistakes. Eckhardt and Lee (1985) discuss a theoretical scenario, based on the notion of varying the difficulty of different inputs, that supports these empirical findings.

Miller (1986) points out that, even if we build redundant systems that fail independently, we must still try to estimate the dependence between any two versions. He shows that this demonstration is as difficult as the problem of testing the resulting system as a black box, and claims this to be an essentially impossible task.

Software Safety Cases

Testing is necessarily connected to software's design and implementation. We can examine the design to help us define test cases, as well as to determine when we have considered all possible scenarios. Fenelon et al. (1994) suggest that we look at the quality of safety-critical systems by listing the system's goals, investigating how the design meets those goals, and ensuring that the implementation matches the design. Overall, we want the system to be **safe**, that is, free from accident or loss. We can decompose the safety goals and assign failure rates or constraints to each component of the design, so that satisfying each lower-level goal will "roll up" to allow us to meet safety goals for the entire system. In this way, we make a **safety case** for the system, making explicit the ways in which our software meets performance goals for safety-critical systems.

We can analyze a system from four different perspectives: knowing the cause or not, and knowing the effects or not. In each instance, we want to establish links between situations that lead to normal behavior and those that lead to potential failure. Table 9.6 illustrates steps we can take in each case. Used during design, these analyses help us plan ways to avoid failure; used during testing, they help us identify important test cases.

We saw in Chapter 5 how fault-tree analysis allows us to examine possible effects and trace them back to their likely root causes. **Failure Modes and Effects Analysis (FMEA)** complements fault-tree analysis by working from known failure modes to unknown system effects. We say that a **hazard** is a system state that, together with the right conditions, will lead to an accident. A **failure mode** is a situation that can give rise to a hazard. For example, the overflow in the Ariane-4 SRI is a hazard; it did not cause Ariane-4 to fail, because the associated conditions did not occur (but they certainly did on Ariane-5). The failure mode for Ariane-5 is the situation where the SRI ran longer than the period for which it was designed.

FMEA is highly labor-intensive and based on the experience of the analysts. It usually involves our performing an initial analysis of the software design, abstracting modes that might lead to failures. Then we look at how combinations of the basic failure modes might lead to actual failures. Sidebar 9.11 describes how FMEA, in concert with other techniques, might have improved the safety of Therac-25.

Hazard and operability studies (HAZOPS) involve a structured analysis to anticipate system hazards and to suggest means to avoid or deal with them. They are based on a technique developed by the Imperial Chemical Industries (UK) in the 1960s

TABLE 9.6 Perspectives for Safety Analysis

	Known Cause	Unknown Cause
Known effect	Description of system behavior	Deductive analysis, including fault-tree analysis
Unknown effect	Inductive analysis, including failure modes and effects analysis	Exploratory analysis, including hazard and operability studies

SIDEBAR 9.11 SAFETY AND THE THERAC-25

Between June 1985 and January 1987, a radiation therapy machine known as the Therac-25 was involved in six known accidents, causing death and serious injury resulting from massive overdoses. Leveson and Turner (1993) describe the machine, the accidents, and the software issues in great detail, and their article should be required reading for systems and software engineers who design and build safety-critical systems.

The software was written by a single person, using PDP-11 assembly language and reusing code from an earlier machine called the Therac-6. Some of the software was tested on a simulator, but most of it was tested as part of the larger system, using mostly integrated system tests (i.e., there was minimal unit and software testing).

Atomic Energy of Canada Limited (AECL) performed a safety analysis of the Therac-25 system. AECL began with a failure modes and effects analysis to identify single failures leading to significant hazards. Then, to identify multiple failures and quantify the results, it performed a fault-tree analysis. Finally, it hired an outside consultant to perform detailed code inspections of the software functions related to the most serious hazards: electron-beam scanning, energy selection, beam shutoff, and dose calibration. The AECL final report recommended 10 changes to the Therac-25 hardware, including interlocks to back up software control of energy selection and electron-beam scanning.

Leveson and Turner (1993) describe how the underlying cause of the problems was a timing error that was difficult to reproduce. They point out that most computer-related accidents result from requirements faults, not from coding faults, and they list several basic software engineering principles that were violated by the Therac-25:

- Documentation should be done as development progresses, not afterward.
- Software quality assurance practices should be an integral part of the development process. These practices should include standards that are set early and used to evaluate intermediate products.
- Simple designs are easier to understand, code, and test than complex ones.
- Software should be designed to anticipate failures and capture information about them.
- It is not enough to assume that system testing will catch software problems. Software should be tested extensively, as well as subjected to formal analysis, at the component and system levels before integration with the hardware.

to analyze the design of a new chemical plant. HAZOPS uses guide words as part of an extensive review process, in conjunction with an analysis of control and data flows between processing components, to help analysts identify hazards. Table 9.7 presents an example of guide words for a system where event timing, controlled by data and signals, is important for task coordination.

TABLE 9.7 HAZOP Guide Words

Guide Word	Meaning
no	No data or control signal sent or received
more	Data volume is too high or fast
less	Data volume is too low or slow
part of	Data or control signal is incomplete
other than	Data or control signal has additional component
early	Signal arrives too early for system clock
late	Signal arrives too late for system clock
before	Signal arrives earlier in sequence than expected
after	Signal arrives later in sequence than expected

Fenelon et al. (1994) have adapted HAZOPS to software situations with what is called the SHARD method. They base their guide words on three views of a hazard:

1. *Provision:* The software either provides a service when it should not or it does not provide a service when it should: omission/commission.
2. *Timing:* The service is either provided too soon or too late: early/late.
3. *Value:* The service is incorrect and it is either easy to see the fault or not: coarse incorrect/subtle incorrect.

This framework is expanded to a large set of guidewords, as shown in Table 9.8.

Once a failure mode is identified, we look for possible causes and consequences. When we find a meaningful cause and effect, we then look for strategies either to avoid the causes or to moderate the effects. During testing, we can select test cases to exercise each failure mode, so that we can observe whether the system reacts appropriately (i.e., does not lead to a catastrophic failure).

TABLE 9.8 SHARD Guide Words

Flow		Failure Categorization					
		Provision		Timing		Value	
Protocol	Type	Omission	Commission	Early	Late	Subtle	Coarse
Pool	Boolean	No update	Unwanted update	N/A	Old data	Stuck at . . .	N/A
	Value	No update	Unwanted update	N/A	Old data	Wrong tolerance	Out of tolerance
	Complex	No update	Unwanted update	N/A	Old data	Incorrect	Inconsistent
Channel	Boolean	No data	Extra data	Early	Late	Stuck at . . .	N/A
	Value	No data	Extra data	Early	Late	Wrong tolerance	Out of tolerance
	Complex	No data	Extra data	Early	Late	Incorrect	Inconsistent

Cleanroom

In the mid-1980s, researchers at IBM proposed a new software development process, designed to produce high-quality software with a high-productivity team. Their process, called **cleanroom**, reflects ideas used in chip production to keep faults at a minimum (Mills, Dyer, and Linger 1987).

Cleanroom Principles and Techniques. The cleanroom approach addresses two fundamental principles:

1. to certify the software with respect to the specifications, rather than wait for unit testing to find the faults
2. to produce zero-fault or near-zero-fault software

The principles are applied by blending several techniques discussed in this and earlier chapters. First, software is specified using box structures, introduced in Chapter 8. The system is defined as a black box, refined as a state box, and refined again as a clear box. The box structures encourage analysts to find omissions in requirements early in the life cycle, when they are easier and cheaper to fix.

Next, the clear-box specification is converted to an intended function, expressed in natural language or in mathematics, as appropriate. A correctness theorem defines a relationship, expressed as one of three correctness conditions, that describes the correctness of each intended function with respect to its control structures.

For example, the correctness conditions for common structures can be expressed in question form (Linger undated):

```
Control structures:            Correctness conditions:
Sequence                       For all arguments:
      [f]
      DO
         g:                    Does g followed by h do f?
         h
      OD
Ifthenelse
      [f]
      IF p                     Whenever p is true
      THEN                         does g do f, and
         g                     whenever p is false
      ELSE                         does h do f?
         h
      FI
Whiledo
      [f]                      Is termination guaranteed, and
      WHILE p                  whenever p is true
      DO                           does g followed by f do f, and
         g                     whenever p is false
      OD                           does doing nothing do f?
```

The project team reviews these relationships and verifies the correctness conditions with formal proofs of correctness. For example, a program and its subproofs may look like this (Linger undated):

```
Program:                     Subproofs:
[f1]                         f1 = [DO g1;g2;[f2] OD] ?
DO
    g1
    g2
    [f2]                     f2 = [WHILE p1 DO [f3] OD] ?
    WHILE
        p1
        DO [f3]              f3 = [DO g3;[f4];g8 OD]?
        g3
        [f4]                 f4 = [IF p2 THEN [f5] ELSE [f6] FI]?
        IF
            p2
        THEN [f5]            f5 = [DO g4;g5 OD] ?
            g4
            g5
        ELSE [f6]            f6 = [DO g6;g7 OD] ?
            g6
            g7
        FI
        g8
    OD
OD
```

This verification takes the place of unit testing, which is not permitted. At this stage, the software is certified with respect to its specification.

The final step involves statistical usage testing, where test cases are randomized based on probability of usage, as we saw earlier in this chapter. The results are used in a quality model to determine the expected mean time to failure and other quality measures. The researchers at IBM feel that traditional coverage testing finds faults in random order, whereas statistical testing is more effective at improving overall software reliability. Cobb and Mills (1990) report that statistical usage testing is more than 20 times as effective at extending MTTF than is coverage testing.

The Promise of Cleanroom. There have been many empirical evaluations of cleanroom. For example, Linger and Spangler (1992) note that first-time cleanroom teams at IBM and elsewhere produced over 300,000 lines of code with high productivity, involving a fault rate of 2.9 faults per thousand lines of code. They claim that this is an order of magnitude reduction from the 30 to 50 faults per thousand lines of their code developed traditionally. Moreover, "experience shows that errors left behind by correctness validation tend to be simple mistakes easily found and fixed in statistical testing, not the deep design and interface errors often encountered in traditional development" (Linger and Spangler 1992). The reported results are based on teams ranging

TABLE 9.9 NASA's SEL Study Results (Basili and Green 1994) © 1996 IEEE

Characteristic	Experiment	Case Study 1	Case Study 2	Case Study 3
Team size	Three-person development teams (10 experiment teams, 5 control teams); common independent tester	Three-person development team; two-person test team	Four-person development team; two-person test team	Fourteen-person development team; four-person test team
Project size and application	1500 lines of Fortran code; message system for graduate laboratory course	40,000 lines of Fortran code; flight-dynamics, ground-support system	22,000 lines of Fortran code; flight-dynamics, ground-support system	160,000 lines of Fortran code; flight-dynamics, ground-support system
Results	Cleanroom teams used fewer computer resources, satisfied requrements more successfully, and made higher percentage of scheduled deliveries	Project spent higher percent age of effort in design, used fewer computer resources, and achieved better productivity and reliability than environment baseline	Project continued trend in better reliability while maintaining baseline productivity	Project reliability only slightly better than baseline while productivity fell below baseline

from 3 to 50 members, with many kinds of applications developed in a large assortment of procedural and object-oriented languages.

The Software Engineering Laboratory at NASA's Goddard Space Flight Center put cleanroom to a rigorous test. It performed a series of controlled experiments and case studies to determine if some of the key elements of the cleanroom approach work as advertised. As you can see from the results in Table 9.9, cleanroom seems to work well on small projects but not on larger ones. Consequently, the SEL cleanroom process model evolved; in particular, the SEL process model was applied only to projects involving fewer than 50,000 lines of code and was changed for larger projects. In addition, SEL developers stopped using reliability modeling and prediction, because they had little data on which to base their projections. Basili and Green (1994) note that these studies, performed in a flight dynamics environment, have convinced them that key features of cleanroom led to lower fault rates, higher productivity, a more complete and consistent set of code comments, and a redistribution of developer effort. However, they caution that the SEL environment is different from IBM's, and that cleanroom must be tailored to the environment in which it is used.

Cautions about Cleanroom. Although much in the literature suggests that cleanroom improves software quality, Beizer (1997) suggests that we read the results with caution. He claims that cleanroom's lack of unit testing promotes dangerous malpractice, contradicting "known testing theory and common sense." According to Beizer, "you cannot find a bug unless you execute the code that has the bug," and orthodox cleanroom relies only on statistical testing to verify reliability, shunning unit testing of any kind. Morever, statistical usage testing itself can be misleading, as explained in Sidebar 9.12.

SIDEBAR 9.12 WHEN STATISTICAL USAGE TESTING CAN MISLEAD

Operational testing assumes that the highest manifestation of faults is in the most frequently occurring operations and the most frequently occurring input values. Kitchenham and Linkman (1997) point out that this assumption is true within a specific operation but not across the complete set of operations in a system. To see why, they describe an example where an operation sends print file requests to one of four printers. When the request is received, not all of the printers may be available. Three situations can occur:

1. A printer is available, and there are no internal print queues. This condition is called the *nonsaturated* condition.
2. No printer is available and there is no print queue; an internal queue must be initialized, and the request is put in the queue. This condition is called the *transition* condition.
3. No printer is available, a print queue already exists, and the print request is put in the queue. This condition is called the *saturated* condition.

From past history, we may know that a saturated condition occurs 79% of the time, a nonsaturated condition occurs 20% of the time, and a transition condition occurs 1% of the time. Assume that the probability of failure is the same for each of the three conditions: 0.001. Then the contribution of each mode to the overall probability of failure is (0.001)*(0.20) or 0.0002 for the nonsaturated condition, (0.001)*(0.79) or 0.00079 for the saturated condition, and (0.001)*(0.01) or 0.00001 for the transition condition. Suppose we have three faults, one associated with each condition. Kitchenham and Linkman (1997) show that, to have a 50% chance of detecting each fault, we must run 0.5/0.0002 = 2500 test cases to detect the nonsaturated conditional fault, 0.5/0.00001 = 500,000 test cases to detect the transition conditional fault, and 0.5/0.00079 = 633 test cases to detect the saturated conditional fault. Thus, testing according to the operational profile will detect the most faults.

However, they note that transition situations are often the most complex and failure-prone. For example, although take-off and landing occupy a small percentage of an airplane's operational profile, these operational modes account for a large percentage of the total failures. Thus, suppose that the probability of selecting a failure-causing input state is 0.001 each for saturated and nonsaturated conditions, but 0.1 for the transition condition. Then the contribution of each mode to the overall probability of failure is (0.001)*(0.20) or 0.0002 for the nonsaturated condition, (0.001)*(0.79) or 0.00079 for the saturated condition, and (0.1)*(0.01) or 0.001 for the transition condition. Converted to test cases, as before, we need 2500 test cases to detect a nonsaturated conditional fault, 633 to detect a saturated conditional fault, but only 500 to detect a transitional fault. In other words, using the operational profile would concentrate on testing the saturated mode, when in fact we should be concentrating on the transitional faults.

Beizer points out that cleanroom is never measured against

- proper unit testing done by addressing coverage goals
- testing done by software engineers trained in testing techniques
- testing performed by organizations that use test design and automated testing techniques
- proper integration testing

Moreover, cleanroom assumes that we are good at measuring software reliability. However, the reliability literature, summarized by the papers in Lyu's reliability handbook (1996), indicates that there are many problems with reliability engineering. In particular, as we have seen, we cannot guarantee that the operational profiles, essential to good modeling, are accurate or even meaningful.

Beizer describes the results of 24 empirical studies that have evaluated cleanroom, including Basili and Green's (1994), pointing out that they have several fatal flaws.

- The subjects knew they were participating in an experiment, so the Hawthorne effect may have influenced the results. That is, the fact that the participants knew their products were being evaluated may have caused the increase in quality, not the cleanroom technique itself.
- The "control" group of testers had no training or experience in proper testing methods.
- No coverage tools or automated techniques were used to support testing.
- Cheating was not controlled, so it is possible that cleanroom was actually applied to already debugged code.

By contrast, Beizer notes that no research has ever exposed current testing theory as being mathematically flawed. Since he finds the body of empirical evidence unconvincing, he suggests that retrospective empirical analysis can eliminate some of the bias (Vinter 1996). To compare two methods, we can develop software with the first method, recording all the faults discovered during the development process and the first year of use. Then, the second method could be applied to the code to see whether it reveals any of the faults already discovered. Similarly, a system developed using the second method could have the first method applied to it retrospectively.

The winner of this argument is yet to be determined. But Beizer raises some important issues and teaches us to be skeptical, not only of the software engineering techniques that are proposed to solve major problems of quality and productivity, but also of the evaluative techniques used to convince us that one technique is superior to another. We must take great care to test our theories and assumptions as well as our software.

9.10 INFORMATION SYSTEMS EXAMPLE

The concepts discussed in this chapter have practical significance for the developers of the Piccadilly system. The testers must select a method for deciding how to perform system testing, when to stop testing, and how many faults and failures to expect. These questions are not easy to answer. For example, the literature is not clear about what kind of fault density is expected or acceptable:

- Joyce (1989) reports that NASA's space shuttle avionics system had a defect density of 0.1 fault per thousand lines of code.
- Jones (1991) claims that leading-edge software companies have a fault density of 0.2 fault per thousand lines of code, or no more than 0.025 user-reported failure per function point.
- Musa, Iannino, and Okumoto (1990) describe a reliability survey that found an average density of 1.4 faults per thousand lines of code in critical systems.
- Cavano and LaMonica (1987) reference surveys of military systems, indicating fault density ranging from 5.0 to 55.0 faults per thousand lines of code.

So, setting goals for fault density, or computing stopping criteria, is difficult at best. As noted in Sidebar 9.13, hardware analogies are sometimes inappropriate for making decisions about quality. Instead, the Piccadilly developers would be wise to examine fault and failure records from past projects that are similar in some ways: language, functions, team members, or design techniques. They can build a model of fault and failure behavior, assess likely risks, and make projections based on the data that are captured as testing progresses.

There are many variables associated with Piccadilly system functions, because the price of advertising time is dependent on so many different characteristics: day of week, time of day, competing programs, number and kind of repeat advertisements, and more. Thus there are many different test cases to consider, and an automated testing tool may be useful for generating and tracking test cases and their results.

Bach (1997) suggests several factors to consider when selecting a test tool.

- *Capability:* Does the tool have all the critical features needed, especially for test result validation and for managing the test data and scripts?
- *Reliability:* Does the tool work for long periods of time without failure?
- *Capacity:* Can the tool work without failure in a large-scale industrial environment?
- *Learnability:* Can the tool be mastered in a short period of time?
- *Operability:* Is the tool easy to use or are its features cumbersome and difficult?
- *Performance:* Will the tool save you time and money during test planning, development, and administration?
- *Compatibility:* Does the tool work in your environment?
- *Nonintrusiveness:* Does the tool simulate an actual user, and in a realistic way?

Bach cautions us not to rely only on descriptions in users manuals or functions demonstrated at trade shows. To address each factor, it is important to use the tool on a real project, learning about how it works in our environment. The Piccadilly developers should evaluate several tools in their environment and select one that relieves them of the tedious process of generating all possible test cases. However, no tool will relieve them of the process of deciding which factors are important in distinguishing one test case from another.

SIDEBAR 9.13 WHY SIX-SIGMA EFFORTS DO NOT APPLY TO SOFTWARE

When we think of high-quality systems, we often use hardware analogies to justify applying successful hardware techniques to software. But Binder (1997) explains why some of the hardware techniques are inappropriate for software. In particular, consider the notion of building software to meet what is known as "six-sigma" quality constraints. Manufactured parts usually have a range or tolerance within which they are said to meet their design goals. For example, if a part is to weigh 45 mg, we may in fact accept parts that weigh between 44.9998 mg and 45.0002 mg; if a part's weight is outside this range, we say that it is faulty or defective. A six-sigma quality constraint says that in a billion parts, we can expect only 3.4 to be outside the acceptable range (i.e., no more than 3.4 parts per billion are faulty). As the number of parts in a product increases, the chances of getting a fault-free product drop, so that the chance of a fault-free 100-part product (where the parts are designed to six-sigma constraints) is 0.9997. We can address this drop in quality by reducing the number of parts, reducing the number of critical constraints per part, and simplifying the process by which we put together separate parts.

However, Binder points out that this hardware analogy is inappropriate for software for three reasons: process, characteristics, and uniqueness. First, because people are variable, the software process inherently contains a large degree of uncontrollable variation from one "part" to another. Second, software either conforms or it doesn't. There are no degrees of conformance, as in "doesn't conform, conforms somewhat, conforms a lot, conforms completely." Conformance is binary and cannot even be associated with a single fault; sometimes many faults contribute to a single failure, and we usually do not know exactly how many faults a system contains. Moreover, the cause of a failure may rest with a different, interfacing application (as when an external system sends the wrong message to the system under test). Third, software is not the result of a mass-production process. "It is inconceivable that you would attempt to build thousands of identical software components with an identical development process, sample just a few for conformance, and then, post hoc, try to fix the process if it produces too many systems that don't meet requirements. We can produce millions of copies by a mechanical process, but this is irrelevant with respect to software defects .... Used as a slogan, six-sigma simply means some (subjectively) very low defect level. The precise statistical sense is lost" (Binder 1997).

9.11 REAL-TIME EXAMPLE

We have seen in earlier chapters that problems with requirements and inadequate reviews contributed to the failure of Ariane-5's inertial reference software, SRI. The committee evaluating the failure also considered the preventative role that simulation might have played. They noted that it would have been impossible to isolate and test the SRI during flight, but software or hardware simulations could have generated signals related to predicted flight parameters while a turntable provided angular movements. Had this approach been taken during acceptance testing, the investigators think the failure conditions would have been revealed.

In addition, testing and simulation were being carried out at a Functional Simulation Facility, with the intention of qualifying

- the guidance, navigation, and control systems
- the redundancy of the sensors
- the functions of each rocket stage
- the on-board computer software's compliance with the flight control system

At this facility, engineers ran closed-loop simulations of the complete flight, including ground operations, telemetry flow, and launcher dynamics. They hoped to verify that the nominal trajectory was correct, as well as trajectories degraded using internal launcher parameters, atmospheric parameters, and equipment failures. During these tests, the actual SRIs were not used; instead, the SRIs were simulated using specially developed software. Only some open-loop tests were performed with the actual SRI, and just for electrical integration and communication compliance.

The investigators note that

> It is not mandatory, even if preferable, that all the parts of the subsystem are present in all the tests at a given level. Sometimes this is not physically possible or it is not possible to exercise them completely or in a representative way. In these cases, it is logical to replace them with simulators but only after a careful check that the previous test levels have covered the scope completely. (Lions et al. 1996)

In fact, the investigative report describes two ways in which the SRIs could have been used. The first approach might have provided an accurate simulation but would have been very expensive. The second was cheaper but its accuracy was dependent on the simulation's accuracy. But in both cases, much of the electronics and all of the software would have been tested in a real operating environment.

So why were the SRIs not used in the closed-loop simulation? First, it was felt that the SRIs were considered to have been qualified at the equipment level. Second, the precision of the navigation software in the on-board computer depended on the SRI's measurements. However, this precision could not have been achieved by using the test signals; simulating failures modes was thought to be better with a model. Finally, the SRI operated with a base period of one millisecond, but the Functional Simulation Facility used six milliseconds, further reducing simulation precision.

The investigators found these reasons to be valid technically. But they also pointed out that the purpose of a system simulation test is to verify not just interfaces, but also the system as a whole for the particular application. They concluded that

> there was a definite risk in assuming that critical equipment such as the SRI had been validated by qualification on its own, or by previous use on Ariane-4. While high accuracy of a simulation is desirable, in the FSF system tests it is clearly better to compromise on accuracy but achieve all other objectives, amongst them to prove the proper system integration of equipment such as the SRI. The precision of the guidance system can be effectively demonstrated by analysis and computer simulation. (Lions et al. 1996)

9.12 WHAT THIS CHAPTER MEANS FOR YOU

This chapter discussed many of the major issues in software testing, including those related to reliability and safety. As an individual developer, you should anticipate testing from the very beginning of the system's life cycle. During requirements analysis, you should think about system functions that will capture state information and data that will help you find the root cause if the software fails. During design, you should use fault-tree analysis, failure modes and effects analysis, and other techniques to help you avoid failures or moderate their effects. During design and code reviews, you can build a safety case to convince you and your colleagues that your software is highly reliable and will lead to a safe system. And during testing, you can take great care to consider all possible test cases, to automate where appropriate, and to ensure that your design addresses all possible hazards.

9.13 WHAT THIS CHAPTER MEANS FOR YOUR DEVELOPMENT TEAM

As an individual developer, you can take steps to ensure that the components you design, develop, and test work according to the specification. But often the problems that arise in testing derive from the interfaces among components. Integration testing is useful to test combinations of components, but system testing adds more realism—and more chance for failure to occur. Your team must keep communication channels open during this type of testing and make all assumptions explicit. Your team must examine carefully the system's boundary conditions and exception handling.

Techniques such as cleanroom require a great deal of team planning and coordination, in developing the box structures and in designing and running the statistical tests. And the activities involved in acceptance testing require close collaboration with customers and users; as they run tests and find problems, you must quickly determine the cause so that correction can allow testing to proceed. Thus, whereas some parts of development are solitary, individual tasks, testing the system is a collaborative, group task.

9.14 WHAT THIS CHAPTER MEANS FOR RESEARCHERS

There are many more approaches to testing than we have been able to describe here. Empirical research continues to help us understand which kinds of testing find which kinds of faults. This body of empirical work, combined with "testing theory," promises to make our testing more cost-effective.

Hamlet (1992) suggests several key issues for researchers to consider:

- In testing for reliability, clever ways of partitioning the system to guide testing may be no better than random testing.
- We need a better understanding of what it means for software to be dependable. It is possible that state explosion (i.e., the very large number of states that create a very large number of test cases) is not as critical as we think it is. We may be able to group related states and then pick sample test cases from the groups.

- We may be able to characterize those kinds of programs and systems for which the number of test cases is not forbiddingly high; we can say that these systems are more "testable" than those with an impossibly high number of cases to execute.
- Voas and Miller (1995) have defined a technique that examines a state's "sensitivity" to changes in the data state. Faults in insensitive states are likely to be difficult to detect by testing. Researchers must investigate how sensitivity relates to testing difficulty.

In addition, researchers should distinguish between testing to find faults and testing to increase reliability. Some researchers (such as Frankl et al. 1997) have demonstrated that using the first goal does not always meet the second one.

9.15 TERM PROJECT

We have discussed how designs may not be as diverse as we would like to think they are. Compare your design with those of other students or teams in your class. How are they different? How are they the same? For each kind of testing, would the similarities or differences in design help or hinder the discovery of faults in code?

9.16 KEY REFERENCES

There have been several special issues of *IEEE Software* focused on the topics covered in this chapter. The June 1992 and May 1995 issues looked at reliability, the March 1991 issue focused on testing, and the May 2007 issue addressed test-driven development.

The proceedings of the annual International Conference on Software Engineering usually has good papers on the latest in testing theory. For example, Frankl et al. (1997) examine the difference between testing to improve reliability and testing to find faults. Good reference books on testing include Beizer (1990); Kaner, Falk, and Nguyen (1993); and Kit (1995). Each provides a realistic perspective based on industrial experience.

There are several companies that evaluate software testing tools and publish summaries of their capabilities. For example, Grove Consultants in England, Software Quality Engineering in Florida, and both Cigital and Satisfice in Virginia do regular analyses of testing techniques and tools. You can find these and other resources on the Web to help with requirements analysis and validation, planning and management, simulation, test development, test execution, coverage analysis, source code analysis, and test case generation.

Software dependability and safety-critical systems are receiving more and more attention, and there are many good articles and books about the key issues, including Leveson (1996, 1997). In addition, the Dependable Computing Systems Centre in the Department of Computer Science, University of York, UK, is developing techniques and tools for assessing software dependability. You can get more information from its director, John McDermid, at jam@minster.york.ac.uk.

Usability testing is very important; a system that is correct and reliable but difficult to use may in fact be worse than an easy-to-use but unreliable system. Usability tests and more general usability issues are covered in depth in Hix and Hartson (1993).

9.17 EXERCISES

1. What is the importance of regression tests? As regression tests may be run several times, suggest a way to save time performing them.
2. Consider the development of a two-pass assembler. Outline its functions and describe how you might test it so that each function is tested thoroughly before the next function is examined. Suggest a build plan for the development, and explain how the build plan and testing must be designed together.
3. Suppose a mathematician's calculator has a function that computes the slope and intercept of a line. The requirement in the definition document reads: "The calculator shall accept as input an equation of the form $Ax + By + C = 0$ and print out the slope and intercept." The system implementation of this requirement is the function LINE whose syntax is LINE(A,B,C), where A and B are the coefficients of x and y, and C is the constant in the equation. The result is a printout of D and E, where D is the slope and E the intercept. Write this requirement as a set of causes and effects, and draw the corresponding cause-and-effect graph.
4. In Chapter 4, we discussed the need for requirements to be testable. Explain why testability is essential for performance testing. Use examples to support your explanation.
5. An air traffic control system can be designed to serve one user or many. Explain how such a system can have a variety of configurations, and outline how a set of configuration tests might be designed.
6. Give an example to show that testing is sometimes impossible without using a device simulator. Give another example to show the need for a system simulator.
7. A configuration management system is an important part of system testing. What are some of the key requirements of a good configuration management system?
8. Sidebar 9.6 describes two versions of VxWorks software, one for a 68000 chip and one for an R6000 chip. Explain the configuration management issues related to building one system for two different chips. Could the configuration management strategy have helped the vendor to port the 68000 version to the R6000?
9. A payroll system is designed so that there is an employee information record for each person who works for the company. Once a week, the employee record is updated with the number of hours worked by the employee that week. Once every two weeks, summary reports are printed to display the number of hours worked since the beginning of the fiscal year. Once a month, each employee's pay for the month is transferred electronically into his or her bank account. For each of the types of performance tests described in this chapter, describe whether it should be applied to this system.
10. Willie's Wellies PLC has commissioned Robusta Systems to develop a computer-based system for testing the strength of its complete line of rubber footwear. Willie's has nine factories in various locations throughout the world, and each system will be configured according to factory size. Explain why Robusta and Willie's should conduct installation testing when acceptance testing is complete.
11. Write a test script for testing the LEVEL function described in this chapter.
12. Outline a build plan for testing the Piccadilly system.
13. Certification is an outside source's endorsement of a system's correctness. It is often granted by comparing the system to a predefined standard of performance. For example, the U.S. Department of Defense certifies an Ada compiler after testing it against a long list of functional specifications. In the terminology of this chapter, is such a test a function test? A performance test? An acceptance test? An installation test? Explain why or why not.

14. When you develop a build plan, you must take into account the resources available to both developers and customers, including time, staff, and money. Give examples of resource constraints that can affect the number of builds defined for system development. Explain how these constraints affect the build plan.

15. What kinds of performance tests might be required for a word processing system? A payroll system? An automated bank teller system? A water-quality monitoring system? A power plant control system?

16. The following news release from CNN describes a software feature whose proper implementation might have prevented the crash of Korean Air Lines flight 801 in Guam in August 1997. What type of testing could have ensured that the feature was working properly in an appropriately sized area around Guam airport?

Software error plagued Guam airport radar system

August 10, 1997
Web posted at: 10:34 a.m. EDT (1434 GMT)
AGANA, Guam (CNN)—A radar system that could have warned the Korean Air jet that crashed in Guam last week that it was flying too low was hobbled by a software error, investigators said Sunday. The system, called an FAA Radar Minimum Safe Altitude Warning, issues an alert to officials on the ground who then tell the pilot that the plane is flying too low. But federal agents investigating the crash said the system—located at a U.S. military base on the island—was modified recently and an error was apparently inserted into the software. U.S. National Transportation Safety Board investigators said the error could not be pinpointed as the culprit in the crash, which killed 225 people, but it could have alerted the pilot to pull the jet to a higher altitude.

"Possibly . . . a Prevention"

"This is not a cause—it might have possibly been a prevention," said George Black, an NTSB member. Investigators were drawn to look into the system after an approach control operator told them he had not received an alert before the crash. The Federal Aviation Administration detected the error.

The altitude warning system is designed to cover a circular area with a radius of 55 nautical miles (102 kilometers). However, since the software was modified, the system only covered a mile-wide circular strip that ran the circumference of that area. Flight 801 was not covered when it crashed.

Black said the software was modified to stop the system from giving too many false alarms. "The modification modified too much," he said.

It was not immediately clear how long the error has existed or how many airplanes have landed at the airport since the modification. Investigators noted they were looking into whether other airports might be affected because the FAA supplies similar software equipment to airports throughout the U.S.

Airline Defends Pilot

News of the software malfunction came as Korean Air officials defended the pilot of the doomed Boeing 747 as a veteran who was more than capable of flying the plane. News reports have pointed to the possibility of pilot error. "Park Yong-chul was a veteran pilot with almost

9,000 hours of flight time," Korean Air said in a statement. The statement also showed Park's flight schedule and rest time in the week leading up to the accident. He had 32 hours and 40 minutes of rest before his last flight.

Korean Air Flight 801 crashed into a hillside overlooking Guam International Airport on Wednesday morning. There were 254 people on board, including 23 crew. Investigators say 29 people survived. Investigators have said the pilot had full control of the jet at the time of the crash, and are examining mountains of data and flight recordings to figure out why he was flying so low.

Even without the warning system, investigators said, the pilot had several other instruments on hand that could have told him that the plane was too close to the hillside. "This is just one piece," said lead investigator Gregory Feith. "Yes, it would have helped, but this is not as we know it the cause of the crash."

Other Problems Existed

The warning system was not the only malfunctioning piece of FAA equipment at the airport. The "glide slope," a portion of a landing instrument that guides planes to the runway, was out of service for regular maintenance. The airline has said it was aware of the absence of the instrument.

In issuing its statement, the airline said the combination of various equipment problems and bad weather could have caused the crash. "We are not yet ruling out the possibility of a sudden change in altitude caused by torrential rains, the breakdown of the glide slope or other elements, which combined, could have caused the accident," Korean Air said.

On Saturday, an airplane overshot the runway upon approaching the Guam airport, but managed to steady itself and land safely on a second attempt. It was not clear why the plane missed the runway on the first approach.

Recovery of bodies from the Korean Air crash has been hindered by the inaccessibility of the rocky, hilly crash site and the shattered condition of many of the corpses.

Correspondent Jackie Shymanski, The Associated Press and Reuters contributed to this report.

17. Working for ABC Software, you are responsible for conducting beta tests for a new release of a general purpose accounting system. Who would you invite to participate in these tests?

18. In this chapter, we have proposed a reliability measures in terms of mean time to failure, availability in terms of mean time between failures, and maintainability in terms of mean time to repair. Are these measures consistent with the definitions presented in this chapter? That is, if reliability, availability, and maintainability are defined as probabilities, will we get the same numbers as if we use the metrics? If not, can one be transformed into the other, or are there basic, irreconcilable differences?

19. A safety-critical system fails and several lives are lost. When the cause of the failure is investigated, the inquiry commission discovers that the test plan neglected to consider the case that caused the system failure. Who is responsible for the deaths: The testers for not noticing the missing case? The test planners for not writing a complete test plan? The managers for not having checked the test plan? The customer for not having done a thorough acceptance test?

20. Sometimes, customers hire an independent organization (separate from the development organization) to do independent verification and validation (V&V). The V&V staff examines all aspects of development, including process and product, to ensure the quality of the final product. If an independent V&V team is used and the system still experiences a catastrophic failure, who should be held responsible: the managers, the V&V team, the designers, the coders, or the testers?

21. In this chapter, we introduced two functions: the distribution function, $F(t)$, and the reliability function, $R(t)$. If the reliability of a system improves as we test and fix it, what happens to the graphs of these functions?

22. A test oracle is a hypothetical person or machine that can tell when actual test results are the same as expected results. Explain the need for including a test oracle in developing testing theory.

10 Delivering the System

In this chapter, we look at
- training
- documentation

We are nearing the end of system development. The previous chapters have shown us how to recognize a problem, design a solution, implement it, and test it. Now we are ready to present the customer with the solution and make sure that the system continues to work properly.

Many software engineers assume that system delivery is a formality—a ribbon-cutting ceremony or presentation of the key to the computer. However, even with turnkey systems (where the developers hand over the system to the customer and are not responsible for its maintenance), delivery involves more than putting the system in place. It is the time during development when we help users to understand and feel comfortable with our product. If delivery is not successful, users will not use the system properly and may be unhappy with its performance. In either case, users are not as productive or effective as they could be, and the care we have taken to build a high-quality system will have been wasted.

In this chapter, we investigate two issues key to successful transfer from developer to user: training and documentation. As the system is designed, we plan and develop aids that help users learn to use the system. Accompanying the system is documentation to which users refer for problem solving or further information. Examples of such documentation are available on this book's Web page.

10.1 TRAINING

Two types of people use a system: users and operators. We can think of them in the same way we think of chauffeurs and mechanics. The major function of an automobile is to provide transportation. A chauffeur uses a car to go from one location to another. However, a mechanic services or supports a car to enable the chauffeur to drive. The mechanic may never actually drive the car, but without the supplementary functions used by the mechanic, the car would not work at all.

In the same way, a **user** exercises the main system functions to help solve the problem described by the requirements definition document. Thus, a user is a problem solver for the customer. However, a system often has supplementary tasks that support major system functions. For example, a supplementary function may define who has access to the system. Another creates backup copies of essential data files on a periodic basis to enable recovery from system failure. These auxiliary functions are usually not performed directly by the users. Instead, an **operator** performs these functions to support the major work. Table 10.1 contains examples of user and operator functions.

Types of Training

Sometimes, the same person is both user and operator. However, user and operator tasks have very different goals, so the training for each job emphasizes different aspects of the system.

User Training. Training for users is based primarily on major system functions and the user's need to access them. For example, if a system manages a law firm's records, the user must be trained in record management functions: creating and retrieving records, changing and deleting entries, and so on. In addition, users must navigate through the records to access particular ones. If information is to be protected with a password or against accidental deletion, users learn special protection functions.

At the same time, users need not be aware of the system's internal operation. They can sort a set of records without knowledge of whether the sort is a shell sort, a bubble sort, or a quicksort. A user accessing the system may not need to know who else is accessing it at the same time or on which disk the requested information is being stored. Because these are support functions rather than primary ones, only the operator is concerned with them.

User training introduces the primary functions so that users understand what the functions are and how to perform them. Training relates how the functions are performed now (with the existing system) to how they will be performed later with the new one. Doing so is difficult, because users are often forced to block out familiar activities in order to learn new ones. (Psychological studies call this **task interference**.) The similar but subtle differences between old and new activities can impede learning, so we must design our training to take this difficulty into account.

TABLE 10.1 User and Operator Functions

User Functions	Operator Functions
Manipulating data files	Granting user access
Simulating activities	Granting file access
Analyzing data	Performing backups
Communicating data	Installing new devices
Drawing graphs and charts	Installing new software
	Recovering damaged files

Operator Training. The focus of operator training is familiarity with the system's support functions; this training addresses how the system works rather than what the system does. Here, task interference is less likely, unless the system closely resembles another system with which the operator has worked.

Operators are trained on two levels: how to bring up and run the new system, and how to support users. First, operators learn such things as how to configure the system, how to grant or deny access to the system, how to assign task sizes or disk space, and how to monitor and improve system performance. Then, operators concentrate on the particulars of the developed system: how to recover lost files or documents, how to communicate with other systems, and how to invoke a variety of support procedures.

Special Training Needs. Users and operators are usually trained in a concentrated and complete course in system use. Often, training begins with the basics: how the keyboard is configured, how menu selections are made, and so on; these and other functions are introduced slowly and investigated thoroughly. This complete training is offered during system delivery to those who will be using the system.

However, new users may later replace trained users, often because of changing job assignments. Training must be available at these times to show them how the system works.

Sometimes users want to brush up on things missed in the original training. Even when initial training is comprehensive, it may be difficult for users or operators to absorb everything taught. Users often like to review some of the functions originally presented in the initial training sessions.

You can appreciate the need for brushing up by remembering what it was like to learn your first programming language. You learned all the legal commands, but you remembered the syntax and meaning of some better than others. To master the language, you returned to your notes or textbook to review infrequently used commands.

A similar problem is encountered by infrequent system users. The knowledge gained in training can be easily forgotten for those system functions that are not exercised regularly. For example, consider a large corporation's word processing system. The system's primary users may be typists who type documents daily and route them from one location to another. Using the system often helps the typists remain familiar with most functions. However, the corporate president may use the system only once or twice a week to create a document or memorandum; the document is then put into final form by a typist. Training for an infrequent user is different from standard user training. The president has no need to know all the special features of the system; training for infrequent users can address only basic document creation and modification functions.

Operators encounter the same difficulty. If one system function is the semiannual storage of archival material on a separate disk, the operator may not remember the archive procedure after not having performed it for six months. Without review training, users and operators tend to perform only the functions with which they feel comfortable; they may not use other system functions that can make them more efficient and productive.

Similarly, specialized training courses can be designed for those who have special needs. If a system produces charts and reports, some users may need to know how to create the charts and reports, whereas others only want to access existing ones. Training can teach limited system functions or review just part of the total system activity.

Training Aids

Training can be done in many ways. No matter how training is provided, it must offer information to users and operators at all times, not just when the system is first delivered. If at some time users forget how to access a file or use a new function, training includes methods to find and learn this information.

Documents. Formal documentation accompanies every system and supports training. The documents contain all the information needed to use the system properly and efficiently. Existing in separate manuals or online, documents are accessible to users and operators as the system is functioning. The system manuals are often similar to an automobile owner's manual; they are references to be used when a problem or question arises. You may not read your car owner's manual from cover to cover before you put the key in the ignition and go for a drive; likewise, users and operators do not always read training documents before trying to use the system. In fact, one study showed that only 10% to 15% of the users in an intensive training program read the manual at all (Scharer 1983). Six months later, no one else had read the user manual, and replacement pages with revised information had not been filed in the manual. In this and many other cases, users may prefer well-defined icons, online help, demonstrations, and classes to learn how the system works.

Icons and Online Help. A system can be designed so that its interface with the user makes system functions clear and easy to understand. Most computer-based systems follow the example of Apple and Xerox in using icons to depict a user's choice of system functions. A click of the mouse selects an icon, and a second click invokes the function. Training for such systems is relatively simple, since the functions are more easily remembered by scanning the icons than by recalling commands and syntax.

Similarly, online help makes training easier. The user can scan additional information about a function's purpose or use without having to take the time to search through paper documents. Sophisticated online help that makes use of hypermedia technology allows the user to delve into collections of related online documents for as much detail as needed for understanding. However, as described in Sidebar 10.1, automated training requires the same kind of maintenance as any other software system.

SIDEBAR 10.1 TRAINING SYSTEMS ARE SOFTWARE, TOO

It is important to remember that computer-based training usually involves complex software, and that it has a downside. Oppenheimer (1997) points out that as users "concentrate on how to manipulate software instead of on the subject at hand, learning can diminish rather than grow." He explains that the use of techniques such as simulation can hide many of the assumptions we are making, rather than making them explicit and encouraging us to question them. The result is users who take things at face value, instead of realizing that they can change their working environment.

Demonstrations and Classes. Demonstrations and classes add individualization to training, and the users and operators respond positively. Users' needs are paramount, and the demonstration or class is focused on a particular aspect of the system. Demonstrations and classes are usually organized as a series of presentations, so that each class in the series teaches one function or aspect of the system.

Demonstrations and classes can be more flexible and dynamic than paper or online documents. Users may prefer a show-and-tell approach, whereby they try to exercise a demonstrated function. The demonstration can be a formal classroom presentation. However, computer-based or Web-based training has been very successful at demonstrating and teaching system concepts and functions.

Some training programs use multimedia in a variety of ways. For example, a videodisk, videotape, or Web site enaction can be used to demonstrate a function; then, the students try the function on their own computers. Other instructional software and hardware allow a teacher to monitor what each student is doing or to take control of a student's system to demonstrate a particular set of mouse clicks or keystrokes. The Requirements Laboratory at Imperial College (London) takes advantage of this type of technology.

Demonstrations and classes usually involve multiple forms of reinforcing what students are learning. Hearing, reading, and seeing how a function works help you to remember functions and techniques more easily. For many people, a verbal presentation holds attention longer than a written one.

A key factor in the success of demonstrations and classes is giving the user feedback. The trainer, whether on tape, on the Web, on television, or in person, offers as much encouragement as possible.

Expert Users. Sometimes it is not enough to see a demonstration or participate in a class. You need a role model to convince you that you can master the system. In this case, it is useful to designate one or more users and operators as "expert." The experts are trained in advance of other users and then used as demonstrators or helpers in the classroom. The other students feel more at ease because they recognize that the experts are users (just like them) who managed to master the techniques. Experts can point out places where they had difficulty but overcame it. Thus, experts convince the students that the impossible is really possible.

Expert users can also be floating instructors after the formal training period is over. They act as consultants, answering questions and making themselves available to others when problems arise. Many users who feel uncomfortable asking a question in class will not hesitate to call a more proficient user to ask the same question.

Expert users give feedback to the system analysts about user satisfaction with the system, the need for additional training, and the occurrence of failures. Users sometimes have trouble explaining to analysts why the system should be changed or enhanced. The experts learn the language both of the user and of the analysts, and thus help avoid communication problems that often occur between user and analyst.

Guidelines for Training

Training is successful only when it meets your needs and matches your capabilities. Personal preferences, work styles, and organizational pressures play a role in this success. A manager who cannot type or spell may not want the department secretary to know. A worker may be embarrassed or uncomfortable correcting a superior in class. Some students prefer to learn by reading, others by hearing, and still others by using a combination of techniques.

Individualized systems often accommodate this variation in backgrounds, experience, and preference. Whereas one student may be totally unfamiliar with a particular concept and may want to spend a great deal of time studying it, another may be familiar with the concept and skip over it. Even keyboarding skill can play a part: an exercise requiring substantial typing can be completed faster by an experienced typist. Since backgrounds vary, different training modules can address different types of students. Users who know how to use a keyboard can skip the modules on typing, and operators who are well-versed in computer concepts need not study the module on what each peripheral does. Review modules can be developed for those who are already familiar with some functions.

Material in a training class or demonstration should be divided into presentation units, and the scope of each should be limited. Too much material at once can be overwhelming, so many short sessions are preferable to a few long ones.

Finally, the location of the students may determine the type of training. Installation at hundreds of locations all over the world may require a Web-based system or a computer-based training system that runs on the actual installed system, rather than flying all prospective users to a central site for training.

10.2 DOCUMENTATION

Documentation is part of a comprehensive approach to training. The quality and type of documentation can be critical, not only to training, but also to the success of the system.

Types of Documentation

There are several considerations involved in producing training and reference documents. Each can be important in determining whether the documentation will be used successfully.

Considering the Audience. A computer-based system is used by a variety of people. In addition to users and operators, other members of the development team and the customer staff read documentation when questions arise or changes are proposed and made. For example, suppose an analyst is working with a customer to determine whether to build a new system or modify an old one. The analyst reads a system overview to understand what the current system does and how it does it. This overview for the analyst is different from one written for a user; the analyst must know about computing details that are of no interest to a user. Similarly, descriptions needed by operators are of no importance to a user.

For example, the S-PLUS package (version 3.0, from MathSoft, Seattle, Washington) came with several books, including *Read Me First*. Each book is designed for a different audience and has a different purpose. *Read Me First* begins with a Documentation

Roadmap, describing in four brief pages each of the other books included in the documentation:

- *A Gentle Introduction to S-PLUS* for the novice computer user
- *A Crash Course in S-PLUS* for the experienced computer user
- *S-PLUS User's Manual*, explaining how to get started, manipulate data, and use advanced graphics
- *S-PLUS Guide to Statistical and Mathematical Analysis*, describing statistical modeling
- *S-PLUS Programmer's Manual*, explaining the S and S-PLUS programming languages
- *S-PLUS Programmer's Manual Supplement* with information specific to a given version of the software
- *S-PLUS Trellis Graphics User's Manual*, describing a particular graphical feature to supplement the statistical analysis
- *S-PLUS Global Index*, providing a cross reference among the volumes of documentation

We must begin our design of the complete set of documentation by considering the intended audience. Manuals and guides can be written for users, operators, systems support people, or others.

User's Manuals. A **user's manual** is a reference guide or tutorial for system users. The manual should be complete and understandable, so sometimes it presents the system to users in layers, beginning with the general purpose and progressing to detailed functional descriptions. First, the manual describes its purpose and refers to other system documents or files that may have more detailed information. This preliminary information is especially helpful in reassuring users that the document contains the type of information they seek. Special terms, abbreviations, or acronyms used in the manual are included for easy reference.

Next, the manual describes the system in more detail. A system summary presents the following items:

1. the system's purpose or objectives
2. the system's capabilities and functions
3. the system's features, characteristics, and advantages, including a clear picture of what the system accomplishes

The summary need not be more than a few paragraphs.

For example, the *S-PLUS User's Manual* begins with a section called "How to Use This Book." The first paragraph explains the purpose of S-PLUS: "a powerful tool for data analysis, providing you with convenient features for exploratory data analysis, modern statistical techniques, and creating your own S-PLUS programs" (MathSoft 1995). It goes on to list the key techniques that a user will learn from this book:

- issuing S-PLUS commands
- creating simple data objects

- creating S-PLUS functions
- creating and modifying graphics
- manipulating data
- customizing an S-PLUS session

Every user's manual needs illustrations to support the text. For instance, a diagram depicting inputs and their sources, the outputs and their destinations, and the major systems functions help users understand what the system does. Similarly, a diagram accompanies a narrative about the equipment used.

The system functions should be described one by one, independent of the details of the software itself. That is, the user should learn what the system does, not how it does it.

No matter what functions are performed by the system, a user's manual functional description includes at least the following elements:

- a map of the major functions and how they relate to one another
- a description of each function in terms of the screens the user can expect to see, the purpose of each, and the result of each menu choice or function key selection
- a description of all input expected by each function
- a description of all output that can be created by each function
- a description of the special features that can be invoked by each function

For example, the major parts of the S-PLUS system are explained in the user's manual by noting that S-PLUS does both graphics and statistics. Then, each function is expanded so that users can understand them. The *S-PLUS User's Manual* describes the graphics functions first:

- scatter plots
- multiple plots per page
- histograms
- box plots
- separate symbols for groups
- legends
- normal probability plots
- pairwise scatter plots
- brushing
- three-dimensional graphics
- more detailed image plots
- other plots

and then the statistics functions:

- one- and two-sample problems for continuous data
- analysis of variance
- generalized linear models
- generalized additive models

- local regression
- tree-based models
- survival analysis

A complete and thorough user's manual is useless if you cannot find needed information quickly and easily. A poorly written user's manual results in frustrated users who are uncomfortable with the system and may not use it as effectively as possible. Thus, any techniques to enhance readability or access to information are helpful, such as glossaries, tabs, numbering, cross-referencing, color coding, diagrams, and multiple indices. For example, a table of function keys is much easier to understand than narrative describing their placement. Similarly, a simple chart such as Table 10.2 can help a user locate the proper keystroke combination.

Operator's Manuals. **Operator's manuals** present material to operators in the same fashion as user's manuals. The intended audience is the only difference between the operator's manual and the user's manual: users want to know the details of system function and use, and operators want to know the details of system performance and access. Thus, the operator's manual explains hardware and software configurations, methods for granting and denying access to a user, procedures for adding or removing peripherals from a system, and techniques for duplicating or backing up files and documents.

Just as the user is presented with the system in layers, so, too, is the operator. A system overview is described first, followed by a more detailed description of the

TABLE 10.2 Command Line Editing Keystrokes (from MathSoft 1995)

Action	Keystroke
Recall previous command	Up arrow
Next command	Down arrow
Recall tenth command back	Page up
Recall first command issued	Control + page down
Recall tenth command forward	Page down
Recall last issued command	Control + page up
End of line	End
Beginning of line	Home
Back one word	Control + left arrow
Forward one word	Control + right arrow
Clear command line	Escape
Erase left of caret	Backspace
Erase right of caret	Delete
Insert at caret	Type desired characters
Select left of caret	Shift + left arrow
Select right of caret	Shift + right arrow
Select to end of line	Shift + end
Select to start of line	Shift + home
Search for selected text	Function key 8
Copy selected text to clipboard	Control + delete
Cut selected text to clipboard	Shift + delete
Delete selected text	Delete

system's purpose and functions. The operator's manual may overlap the user's manual somewhat, since operators must be aware of system functions even though they never exercise them. For example, operators may never create a spreadsheet and generate graphs and charts from it. But knowing that the system has such capabilities gives the operator a better understanding of how to support the system. For example, the operator may learn the names of software routines that perform spreadsheet and graph functions, and the hardware used to draw and print the graphs. Then, if a user reports a problem with a graphing function, the operator may know whether the problem can be remedied with a support function or whether the maintenance staff should be notified.

General System Guide. Sometimes a user wants to learn about what the system does without learning the details of each function. For instance, the head of the audit department of a large company may read a system description to decide if the system is appropriate for her needs. This system description need not describe every display screen and the choices on it. However, the detail should allow her to decide if the system is complete or accurate for the company's needs.

A general system guide addresses this need. Its audience is the customer rather than the developer. The general system guide is similar to the system design document; it describes a solution to a problem in terms the customer can understand. In addition, the general system guide depicts the system hardware and software configuration and describes the philosophy behind the system's construction.

A general system guide is similar to the glossy, nontechnical brochure given to prospective customers by automobile dealers. The car is described in terms of type and size of engine, type and size of body, performance statistics, fuel economy, standard and optional features, and so on. The customer may not be interested in the exact design of the fuel injectors in deciding whether or not to buy. Similarly, the general system guide for an automated system need not describe the algorithms used to compute the address of the next record allocated or the command used to access that record. Instead, the guide describes only the information needed to create and access a new record.

A good general system guide provides cross-referencing. If readers of the guide want more information about the precise way in which a function is implemented, they find a reference to the appropriate pages of the user's manual. On the other hand, if readers want more information about system support, they can turn to the operator's manual.

Tutorials and Automated System Overviews. Some users prefer to be guided through actual system functions rather than read a written description of how the functions work. For these users, tutorials and automated overviews can be developed. The user invokes a software program or procedure that explains the major system functions step by step. Sometimes a document is combined with a special program; the user reads about the function first and then exercises the next step in the program to perform the function.

Other System Documentation. Many other system documents can be supplied during system delivery. Some are products of intermediate steps of system development. For example, the requirements documents are written after requirements analysis and updated as necessary. The system design is recorded in the system design document, and the program design document describes the program design.

The details of implementation are in the programming documentation that we described in Chapter 7. However, an additional document may help those who will maintain and enhance the system. A **programmer's guide** is the technical counterpart of the user's manual. Just as the user's manual presents a picture of the system in layers, from a system overview down to a functional description, the programmer's guide presents an overview of how the software and hardware are configured. The overview is followed by a detailed description of software components and how they relate to the functions performed. To help a programmer locate the code that performs a particular function, either because a failure has occurred or because a function must be changed or enhanced, the programmer's guide is cross-referenced with the user's manual.

The programmer's guide also emphasizes those aspects of the system that enable the maintenance staff to locate the source of problems. It describes system support functions such as the running of diagnostic programs, the display of executed lines of code or segments of memory, the placement of debugging code, and other tools. We will investigate maintenance techniques in more depth in Chapter 11.

Programmer's guides also help maintenance personnel implement system enhancements. For example, suppose a new site is to be added to the communications network. The programmer's guide points out those code modules dealing with communications; it may also explain the tools available for updating the code and corresponding documentation.

User Help and Troubleshooting

Users and operators refer to documentation to determine the cause of a problem and to call for assistance if necessary. Several types of user help can be provided, including reference documents and online help files.

Failure Message Reference Guide. If the system detects a failure, users and operators are notified in a uniform and consistent way. For example, if a user types two names or numbers, such as "3×," with no operator or other syntactic element between them, S-PLUS 3.0 produces the following failure message:

```
> 3 x
Syntax error: name ("x") used illegally at this point:
3 x
```

Or a user may be told that an expression is not a function:

```
> .5(2,4) Error: "0.5" is not a function
```

Recall that the system design proposes a philosophy for discovering, reporting, and handling failures. The variety of system failure messages is included in the design, and user documentation lists all possible messages and their meanings. Whenever possible, failure messages point to the fault that causes the failure. However, sometimes the cause is not known, or there is not enough room to display a complete message on the screen or in a report. Thus, a **failure message reference guide**, being the document of last resort, must describe the failure completely. A failure message on the screen may include the following information:

1. the name of the code component executing when the failure occurred
2. the source code line number in the component that was executing
3. the failure severity and its impact on the system
4. the contents of any relevant system memory or data pointers, such as registers or stack pointers
5. the nature of the failure, or a failure message number (for cross-reference with the failure message reference guide)

For example, a failure message may appear on the user screen as

```
FAILURE 345A1: STACK OVERFLOW
OCCURRED IN: COMPONENT DEFRECD
AT LINE: 12300 SEVERITY:
WARNING REGISTER CONTENTS: 0000 0000 1100 1010 1100 1010 1111 0000
PRESS FUNCTION KEY 12 TO CONTINUE
```

The user uses the failure number to refer to the reference guide, whose entry looks like this:

> Failure 345A1: Stack overflow.
>
> This problem occurs when more fields are defined for a record than the system can accommodate. The last field defined will not be included in the record. You can change the record size using the Record Maintenance function on the Maintenance menu to prevent this failure in the future.

Notice that the failure message reflects a particular philosophy for handling faults and failures. An alternative system design might have recovered from this failure automatically, either by prompting the user or fixing the record size behind the scenes. In the example presented, it is up to the user to resolve the problem.

Online Help. Many users prefer to have automated assistance at their fingertips, rather than having to locate a reference guide of some kind to help them. Some systems include an online help function. Often, the screen has a help function as a menu selection or a function key labeled "help" to be used when assistance or additional information is needed.

More detailed information can be displayed by selecting another icon or pressing another key. Some systems also refer you to a page in a supporting document. Thus, a user can get information directly from the automated system rather than having to search for it in a document.

Quick Reference Guides. A useful intermediate measure is a **quick reference guide**. This summary of primary system functions and their use is designed to be a one- or two-page reminder that users or operators can keep at the workstation. By referring to the guide, a user can find out how to perform commonly used or essential functions without having to read a lengthy explanation of how each works. Such a guide is especially useful when the user must remember special function key definitions or use codes

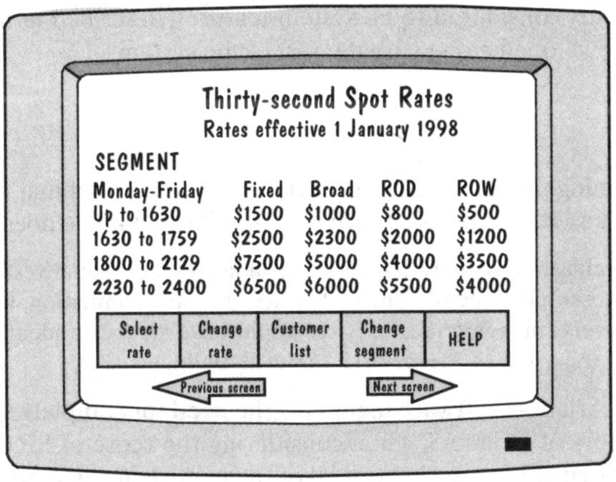

FIGURE 10.1 Piccadilly system screen.

and abbreviations (such as UNIX commands). In some systems, the quick reference guide is available on the screen and can be displayed by touching a function key.

10.3 INFORMATION SYSTEMS EXAMPLE

The Piccadilly system is likely to have many users who are familiar with television programming or advertising sales, but who are not necessarily well-versed in computer concepts. For this reason, the system should have extensive user documentation and help functions. Many people prefer to learn on the job rather than attend multiple-day training sessions, so the Piccadilly training can be done online, using actual system screens.

For example, users must learn how to change advertising rates, select rates to calculate advertising fees for a customer, and navigate around the system screens to provide additional information. A training system can present the user with the actual Piccadilly screens such as the one shown in Figure 10.1. Then, training software can be added to allow users to understand the nature and purpose of each system function. Suppose a user is reading the spot-rate screen, as shown. By clicking on the words "Spot Rates," the user can automatically bring up a training screen that describes the meaning of the term and points to additional help files that relate to spot-rate functions.

This training approach is useful not only for new users, but also for intermittent users who need reminders of how the rate changes work and, in general, how the system functions are executed. So the training, in fact, can be used by anyone at any time during the system's life.

Notice that this type of training software is very sophisticated. It must interact with the Piccadilly system to allow normal functions to work, and also to provide additional explanation and manipulation for training exercises. For this reason, training and documentation cannot be an afterthought; they must be designed as the rest of the system is designed, and maintained as the system grows and changes. The training software may require significant amounts of development time, all of which must be planned and tracked as a normal part of project management activities. In fact, training and documentation are usually considered to be system features, described in the requirements documents and developed along with the rest of the system.

10.4 REAL-TIME EXAMPLE

The investigators examining the reasons for the Ariane-5 failure noted that some of the assumptions about the reused Ariane-4 software were not present in the documentation:

> . . . the systems specification of the SRI does not indicate operational restrictions that emerge from the chosen implementation. Such a declaration of limitation, which should be mandatory for every mission-critical device, would have served to identify any non-compliance with the trajectory of Ariane-5. (Lions et al. 1996)

Thus, the reuse of Ariane-4 software highlights the need for complete system documentation. The designers of Ariane-5, when considering the reuse of SRI code from Ariane-4, should have been able to read about all of the underlying assumptions inherent in the code. In particular, the Ariane-4 documentation should have made explicit the fact that the SRI code was not intended to run for as long as it ran on Ariane-5. That is, the design decisions for Ariane-4 should have been captured in Ariane-4's SRI design documents and scrutinized carefully by the Ariane-5 designers. Having the design decisions in the documentation is much easier than forcing designers to read the code and understand its functions and limitations.

10.5 WHAT THIS CHAPTER MEANS FOR YOU

In this chapter, we have looked at the training and documentation necessary to support system delivery. As a developer, you should remember that

- training and documentation should be planned and tracked from the project's beginning
- training and documentation software should be integrated with the regular system software
- all training and documentation modules and documents should take into account the varying needs of different audiences: users, operators, customers, programmers, and others who work with or interact with the system

10.6 WHAT THIS CHAPTER MEANS FOR YOUR DEVELOPMENT TEAM

Your development team must not leave training and documentation for the last minute. Training and documentation can be planned as soon as the requirements analysis is complete. In fact, user's manuals should be written from the requirements at the same time that testers are writing scripts for system and acceptance testing. Thus, the trainers and documenters should maintain constant contact with all developers, so that changes to system requirements and design can be reflected in the documentation and training materials.

Moreover, updates to training and documentation can be planned early. The development team can put in place ways to access updates from a central location or to download them to users automatically from the Internet or Web sites. In particular, the documentation can be kept current, reporting on items such as known faults (and work-arounds), new functionality, new fault corrections, and other failure-related information. The updates can also remind users and operators of upcoming training courses, refresher courses, frequently asked questions, user group meetings, and other information useful to users, operators, and programmers.

10.7 WHAT THIS CHAPTER MEANS FOR RESEARCHERS

There is a large body of research about education and training, and software engineering researchers would be wise to study it when designing training and documentation for software-related systems. We need to know more about

- user and operator preferences for type of training and documentation
- the relationship between human–computer interfaces and retention of ideas
- the relationship between human–computer interfaces and personal preferences for learning
- effective ways to get information quickly and efficiently to those who need it

Researchers can also work on new ways to encourage interaction among users. For example, an online user group may help users to learn new tricks, to trade information about customizing an application and workarounds, and to understand the most effective ways to use the system.

10.8 TERM PROJECT

Write a user manual for the Loan Arranger system. The audience is the loan analyst. In your user manual, make reference to any other documentation you think should be available, such as online help.

10.9 KEY REFERENCES

The American Society for Training and Development (ASTD) supports conferences, training courses, and information about training and development. ASTD also publishes a magazine, *Training and Development*.

Price (1984) and Denton (1993) are useful books on how to write documentation for computer systems.

10.10 EXERCISES

1. Suppose a system's failure philosophy is to mediate the problem behind the scenes, without the user's knowledge. In a safety-critical system, what are the legal and ethical implications of not telling the user that a failure has occurred? Should the system report the failure and its corrective action?
2. In recent years we see a tendency to avoid printed manuals and integrate user manuals with the software. Explain how this trend changes the process of software development.

TABLE 10.3 BASIC Failure Messages

Number	Message
23	Line buffer overflow An attempt has been made to input a line that has too many characters.
24	Device time-out The device you have specified is not available at this time.
25	Device fault An incorrect device designation has been entered.
26	FOR without NEXT A FOR statement was encountered without a matching NEXT statement.
27	Out of paper The printer device is out of paper.
28	Unprintable error A failure message is not available for the condition that exists.
29	WHILE without WEND A WHILE statement was encountered without a matching WEND statement.
30	WEND without WHILE A WEND statement was encountered without a matching WHILE statement.
31–40	Unprintable error A failure message is not available for the condition that exists.

3. Prototyping allows the users to try out a working model of a system before the actual system is complete. Explain how prototyping can be counterproductive if it creates task interference during training.
4. The user of an automated system need not be familiar with computer concepts. However, knowledge of computers is beneficial for most operators. In what cases should the user of an automated system be unaware of the underlying computer system? Is this lack of awareness a sign of good system design? Give examples to support your answer.
5. Table 10.3 contains some of the failure messages in a reference guide for an actual BASIC interpreter. Comment on the clarity, amount of information, and appropriateness for user or operator.
6. Please look at error messages 26, 29, and 30 in Table 10.3. Why are these error messages different than the others? In what kinds of software products do we find this type of error message?

11 Maintaining the System

In this chapter, we look at
- system evolution
- legacy systems
- impact analysis
- software rejuvenation

In previous chapters, we investigated how to build a system. However, a system's life does not end with delivery. We saw in Chapter 9 that the final system is usually subject to continuing change, even after it is built. Thus, we turn now to the challenge of maintaining a continually evolving system. First, we review those system aspects that are likely to change. Then, we study the activities and personnel involved in maintaining a system. The maintenance process can be difficult; we examine the problems involved, including the nature of costs and how they escalate. Finally, we look at tools and techniques to help us improve a system's quality as it evolves.

11.1 THE CHANGING SYSTEM

System development is complete when the system is operational, that is, when the system is being used by users in an actual production environment. Any work done to change the system after it is in operation is considered to be **maintenance**. Many people think of software system maintenance as they do hardware maintenance: repair or prevention of broken or improperly working parts. However, software maintenance cannot be viewed in the same way. Let us see why.

One goal of software engineering is developing techniques that define a problem exactly, design a system as a solution, implement a correct and efficient set of programs, and test the system for faults. This goal is similar for hardware developers: producing a reliable, fault-free product that works according to specification. Hardware maintenance in such a system concentrates on replacing parts that wear out or using techniques that prolong the system's life. However, *whiledo* constructs do not wear out after 10,000 loops, and semicolons do not fall off the ends of statements. Unlike hardware, software does not degrade or require periodic maintenance. Thus, software systems are different from hardware, and we cannot use hardware analogies successfully the way we can for other aspects of software engineering.

Types of Systems

The biggest difference between hardware and software systems is that software systems are built to incorporate change. Except for the simplest cases, the systems we develop are evolutionary. That is, one or more of the system's defining characteristics usually change during the life of the system. Lehman (1980) has described a way to categorize programs in terms of how they may change. In this section, we look at how his categorization can be applied to systems, too.

Software systems may change not just because a customer makes a decision to do something a different way, but also because the nature of the system itself changes. For example, consider a system that computes payroll deductions and issues paychecks for a company. The system is dependent on the tax laws and regulations of the city, state or province, and country in which the company is located. If the tax laws change, or if the company moves to another location, the system may require modification. Thus, system changes may be required even if the system has been working acceptably in the past.

Why are some systems more prone to change than others? In general, we can describe a system in terms of the way it is related to the environment in which it operates. Unlike programs handled in the abstract, the real world contains uncertainties and concepts we do not understand completely. The more dependent a system is on the real world for its requirements, the more likely it is to change.

S-systems. Some systems are formally defined by and are derivable from a specification. In these systems, a specific problem is stated in terms of the entire set of circumstances to which it applies. For example, we may be asked to build a system to perform matrix addition, multiplication, and inversion on a given set of matrices within certain performance constraints. The problem is completely defined and there are one or more correct solutions to the problem as stated. The solution is well-known, so the developer is concerned not with the correctness of the solution, but with the correctness of the implementation of the solution. A system constructed in this way is called an **S-system**. Such a system is static and does not easily accommodate a change in the problem that generated it.

As shown in Figure 11.1, the problem solved by an S-system is related to the real world, and the real world is subject to change. However, if the world changes, the result is a completely new problem that must be specified.

P-systems. Computer scientists can often define abstract problems using S-systems and develop systems to solve them. However, it is not always easy or possible to describe a real-world problem completely. In many cases, the theoretical solution to a problem exists, but implementing the solution is impractical or impossible.

For example, consider a system to play chess. Since the rules of chess are completely defined, the problem can be specified completely. At each step of the game, a solution might involve the calculation of all possible moves and their consequences to determine the best next move. However, implementing such a solution completely is

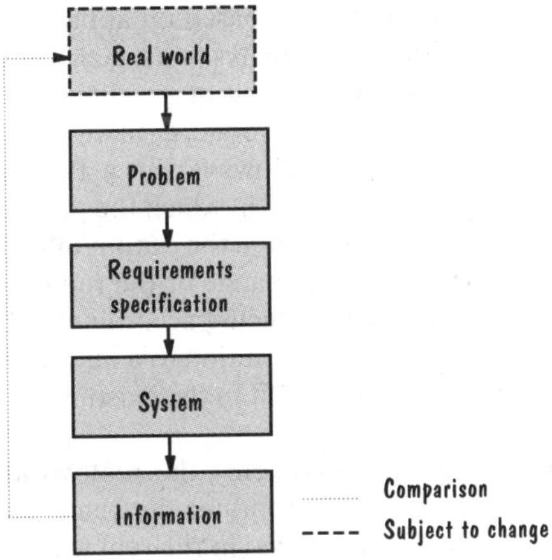

FIGURE 11.1 An S-system.

impossible using today's technology. The number of moves is too large to be evaluated in a practical amount of time. Thus, we must develop an approximate solution that is more practical to build and use.

To develop this solution, we describe the problem in an abstract way and then write the system's requirements specification from our abstract view. A system developed in this way is called a **P-system**, because it is based on a practical abstraction of the problem rather than on a completely defined specification. As shown in Figure 11.2, a P-system is more dynamic than an S-system. The solution produces information that is compared with the problem; if the information is unsuitable in any way, the problem abstraction may be changed and the requirements modified to try to make the resulting solution more realistic.

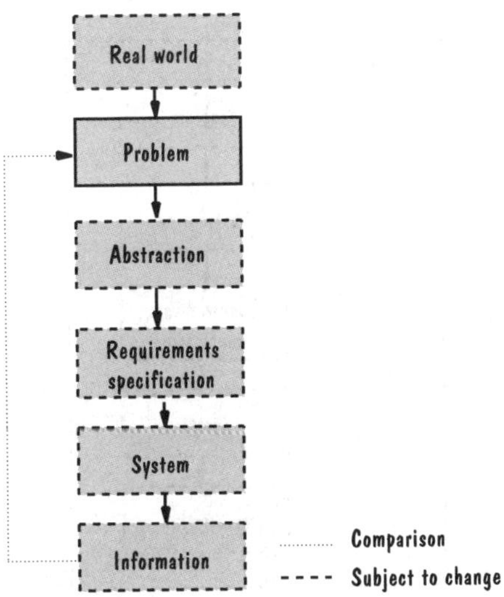

FIGURE 11.2 A P-system.

Thus, in a P-system, the requirements are based on approximation. The solution depends in part on the interpretation of the analyst who generates the requirements. Even though an exact solution may exist, the solution produced by a P-system is tempered by the environment in which it must be produced. In an S-system, the solution is acceptable if the specifications are correct. However, in a P-system, the solution is acceptable if the results make sense in the world in which the problem is embedded.

Many things can change in a P-system. When the output information is compared with the actual problem, the abstraction may change or the requirements may need to be altered, and the implementation may be affected accordingly. The system resulting from the changes cannot be considered a new solution to a new problem. Rather, it is a modification of the old solution to find a better fit to the existing problem.

E-systems. In considering S- and P-systems, the real-world situation remains stable. However, a third class of systems incorporates the changing nature of the real world itself. An **E-system** is one that is embedded in the real world and changes as the world does. The solution is based on a model of the abstract processes involved. Thus, the system is an integral part of the world it models.

For instance, a system that predicts a country's economic health is based on a model of how the economy functions. Changes occur in the world in which the problem is embedded. In turn, the economy is not completely understood, so the model changes as our understanding changes. Finally, our solution changes as the abstract model changes.

Figure 11.3 illustrates the changeability of an E-system and its dependence on its real-world context. Whereas S-systems are unlikely to change and P-systems are subject to incremental change, E-systems are likely to undergo almost constant change. Moreover, the success of an E-system depends entirely on the customer's evaluation of system performance. Since the problem addressed by an E-system cannot be specified completely, the system must be judged solely by its behavior under actual operating conditions.

FIGURE 11.3 An E-system.

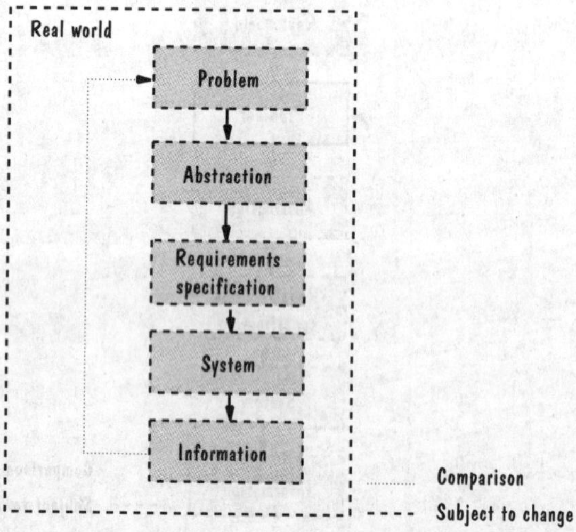

These categories show us the system elements subject to change. The greater the number of changeable elements, the more likely the need for system maintenance. In particular, since the problem generating an E-system may change, an E-system solution will probably undergo constant enhancement.

Changes During the System Life Cycle

By examining the system in light of its category (S, P, or E), we can see where during development change may occur, as well as how the change will affect the system. By its nature, an S-system problem is completely defined and unlikely to change. A similar problem may be solved by modifying the S-system, but the result is a completely new problem with a solution. If an S-system performs unacceptably, it is usually because it addresses the wrong problem. We react by redefining the problem and generating a new description of it; then we develop a new solution, rather than modifying the old system.

A P-system is an approximate solution to a problem and may require change as discrepancies and omissions are identified. In fact, as we compare and contrast the information produced by the system with the actual situation being modeled, we may change the P-system to ensure that it is economical and effective.

For a P-system, a model approximates a solution to the stated problem, so modification can occur during all stages of development. First, the abstraction may change. In other words, we alter the abstract description, and then change the requirements specification accordingly. Next, we modify the system design, redoing implementation and testing to incorporate the changes. Finally, we modify the approximate system and program documentation, and new training may be required.

E-systems use abstractions and models to approximate a situation, so E-systems are subject to at least the kinds of changes that a P-system may undergo. Indeed, their nature is more inconstant because the problem can also change. Being embedded in changing activities, E-systems may require that characteristics be built into the system itself to accommodate change.

Examples of changes to any type of system are listed in Table 11.1. For instance, a modification to the requirements during requirements analysis may result in a change to the specification. A modification to the technical design may require a change in the system design and perhaps in the original requirements. Thus, a change at any stage of development can also affect the results of previous as well as subsequent stages.

The software engineering principles suggested for system development also make change easier during maintenance. For example, having modularized the design and code components and cross-referenced the components with the requirements, you can easily trace a requirements change to the affected components and to the tests that must be redone. Similarly, if a failure occurs, you can identify the component containing the causes and then make corrections at all levels (design, code, and test) rather than just in the code. Thus, software engineering principles contribute not only to good design and correct code, but also to the ability to make changes quickly and easily.

The System Life Span

As software engineers trying to build a maintainable product, the first question we must ask ourselves is whether it is possible to build a system right the first time. In other

TABLE 11.1 Examples of Change During Software Development

Activity from Which Initial Change Results	Artifacts Requiring Consequent Change
Requirements analysis	Requirements specification
System design	Architectural design specification Technical design specification
Program design	Program design specification
Program implementation	Program code Program documentation
Unit testing	Test plans Test scripts
System testing	Test plans Test scripts
System delivery	User documentation Training aids Operator documentation System guide Programmer's guide Training classes

words, if we use highly cohesive components with low coupling, if the documentation is complete and up to date, and if the entire system is cross-referenced, will we need a maintenance phase? Unfortunately, the answer is yes. The reasons lie in the nature of the systems themselves. As we have seen, there is no way to guarantee that P-systems and E-systems will not require change. In fact, we must assume that they will change and then build them so that they can be changed easily.

Then, our next question must be: How much change can we expect? Again, the answer depends on the nature of the system. S-systems will have little or no change. P-systems will have much more, and E-systems are likely to change continually. For this reason, many software engineers prefer to call the maintenance stage of development the **evolutionary phase**. We speak of having **legacy systems**, built earlier when our needs and environment were different. As we will see, we must evaluate legacy systems and help them to evolve as our technology and business needs evolve. At some point, we may decide to replace a legacy system with a completely new one or to retire it simply because it is no longer needed.

Development Time vs. Maintenance Time. We can look at the development and maintenance times of other projects to get an idea of how long we can expect the evolutionary phase to be. According to Parikh and Zvegintzov (1983), the typical development project takes between one and two years but requires an additional five to six years of maintenance time. In terms of effort, more than half of a project's programming resources are spent on maintenance. A survey by Fjeldstad and Hamlen (1979) reports a similar split; 25 data processing organizations reported that they averaged 39% of effort in development and 61% in maintenance (correction, modification, and user support). Recent surveys report similar findings, and many developers count on the 80–20 rule: 20% of the effort is in development and 80% is in maintenance.

System Evolution vs. System Decline. When a system requires significant and continual change, we must decide if it is better to discard the old system and build a new one to replace it. To make that determination, we must ask several questions:

- Is the cost of maintenance too high?
- Is the system reliability unacceptable?
- Can the system no longer adapt to further change, and within a reasonable amount of time?
- Is system performance still beyond prescribed constraints?
- Are system functions of limited usefulness?
- Can other systems do the same job better, faster, or cheaper?
- Is the cost of maintaining the hardware great enough to justify replacing it with cheaper, newer hardware?

A positive answer to some or all of these questions may mean that it is time to consider a new system to replace the old one. The entire set of costs associated with system development and maintenance, from system creation to retirement, is called the **life-cycle cost**. Often, we make our decision to maintain, rebuild, or replace based on a comparison of life-cycle costs for the old, revised, and new systems.

Laws of Software Evolution. Our maintenance decisions are aided by understanding what happens to systems over time. We are interested in changes in size, complexity, resources, and ease of maintenance. We can learn a lot about evolutionary trends by examining large systems to see how they have changed. For example, Sidebar 11.1 describes the evolution of a large system at Bell Atlantic.

Throughout his career, Lehman has observed the behavior of systems as they evolve. He has summarized his findings in five laws of program evolution (Lehman 1980):

1. *Continuing change.* A program that is used undergoes continual change or becomes progressively less useful. The change or decay process continues until it is more cost-effective to replace the system with a re-created version.
2. *Increasing complexity.* As an evolving program is continually changed, its structure deteriorates. Reflecting this, its complexity increases unless work is done to maintain or reduce it.
3. *Fundamental law of program evolution.* Program evolution is subject to a dynamic that makes the programming process, and hence measures of global project and system attributes, self-regulating with statistically determinable trends and invariances.
4. *Conservation of organizational stability (invariant work rate).* During the active life of a program, the global activity rate in a programming project is statistically invariant.
5. *Conservation of familiarity (perceived complexity).* During the active life of a program, the release content (changes, additions, deletions) of the successive releases of an evolving program is statistically invariant.

SIDEBAR 11.1 BELL ATLANTIC REPLACES THREE SYSTEMS WITH ONE EVOLVING ONE

In 1993, Bell Atlantic (now known as Verizon) introduced the SaleService Negotiation System (SSNS) to replace three legacy systems that supported operators taking orders for new telephone-based services. The initial goals of the system were to minimize errors and to reduce the amount of time customer service representatives spend on the telephone with customers. But as the sales representatives used the system, management realized the system's great potential to provide on-screen cues reminding representatives of Bell Atlantic products that might meet the customers' needs. The goals of the system changed, from order-taking to needs-based sales.

The SSNS order process is much like an interview guided by the system. As the customer representative enters more information about the customer, SSNS prompts the representative about relevant products. Thus, as Bell Atlantic expands its product and service line, SSNS must be enhanced accordingly. SSNS has already been expanded to handle billing information, verify address and credit through remote databases, generate automatic service verification letters to customers, and give representatives information on service questions.

The system has also replaced archaic commands with plain English, and much of what was previously found in a 20-volume handbook is now online. The system has been customized in some states, since each state regulates telephone service differently. Some regulatory agencies required Bell Atlantic to disclose specific product information at the beginning of the interview, so the system has been tailored to do that, where necessary.

Originally written in C and C++ the system was modified with Java in the late 1990s to provide an intranet version accessible to mobile representatives. As regulations, products, technology, and business needs change, SSNS must evolve with them (Field 1997a).

The first law says that large systems are never complete; they continue to evolve. The systems grow as we add more features, apply more constraints, interact with other systems, support a larger number of users, and so on. They also change because their environment changes: they are ported to other platforms or rewritten in new languages.

The second law tells us that as they evolve, large systems grow more complex unless we take action to reduce the complexity. Many times, this increase in complexity occurs because we must make hasty patches to fix problems. We cannot take the time to maintain the elegance of a design or the consistency of approach throughout the code.

According to the third law, software systems exhibit regular behaviors and trends that we can measure and predict. Indeed, many software engineering researchers devote their study to finding these "universal truths" of software development and maintenance, much as physicists seek the Grand Unifying Theory.

The fourth law says that there are no wild or wide fluctuations in organizational attributes, such as productivity. Lehman points to Brooks's observations as support for this law (Brooks 1995). That is, at some point, resources and output reach an optimum level, and adding more resources does not change the output significantly. Similarly, the fifth law says that after a while, the effects of subsequent releases make very little difference in overall system functionality.

11.2 THE NATURE OF MAINTENANCE

When we develop systems, our main focus is on producing code that implements the requirements and works correctly. At each stage of development, our team continually refers to work produced at earlier stages. The design components are tied to the requirements specification, the code components are cross-referenced and reviewed for compliance with the design, and the tests are based on finding out whether functions and constraints are working according to the requirements and design. Thus, development involves looking back in a careful, controlled way.

Maintenance is different. As maintainers, we look back at development products, but also at the present by establishing a working relationship with users and operators to find out how satisfied they are with the way the system works. We look forward, too, to anticipate things that might go wrong, to consider functional changes required by a changing business need, and to consider system changes required by changing hardware, software, or interfaces. Thus, maintenance has a broader scope, with more to track and control. Let us examine the activities needed to keep a system running smoothly and identify who performs them.

Maintenance Activities and Roles

Maintenance activities are similar to those of development: analyzing requirements, evaluating system and program design, writing and reviewing code, testing changes, and updating documentation. So the people who perform maintenance—analysts, programmers, and designers—have similar roles. However, because changes often require an intimate knowledge of the code's structure and content, programmers play a much larger role in maintenance than they did in development.

Maintenance focuses on four major aspects of system evolution simultaneously:

1. maintaining control over the system's day-to-day functions
2. maintaining control over system modifications
3. perfecting existing acceptable functions
4. preventing system performance from degrading to unacceptable levels

Corrective Maintenance. To control the day-to-day system functions, we on the maintenance team respond to problems resulting from faults. Addressing these problems is known as **corrective maintenance**. As failures occur, they are brought to our team's attention; we then find the failure's cause and make corrections and changes to requirements, design, code, test suites, and documentation, as necessary. Often, the initial repair is temporary: something to keep the system running, but not the best fix. Long-range changes may be implemented later to correct more general problems with the design or code.

For example, a user may show us an example of a report with too many printed lines on a page. Our programmers determine that the problem results from a design fault in the printer driver. As an emergency repair, a team member shows the user how to reset the lines per page by setting a parameter on the report menu before printing. Eventually, our team redesigns, recodes, and retests the printer driver so that it works properly without user interaction.

Adaptive Maintenance. Sometimes a change introduced in one part of the system requires changes to other parts. **Adaptive maintenance** is the implementation of these secondary changes. For example, suppose the existing database management system, part of a larger hardware and software system, is upgraded to a new version. In the process, programmers find that disk access routines require an additional parameter. The adaptive changes made to add the extra parameter do not correct faults; they merely allow the system to adapt as it evolves.

Similarly, suppose a compiler is enhanced by the addition of a debugger. We must alter the menus, icons, or function key definitions to allow users to choose the debugger option.

Adaptive maintenance can be performed for changes in hardware or environment, too. If a system originally designed to work in a dry, stable environment is chosen for use on a tank or in a submarine, the system must be adapted to deal with movement, magnetism, and moisture.

Perfective Maintenance. As we maintain a system, we examine documents, design, code, and tests, looking for opportunities for improvement. For example, as functions are added to a system, the original, clean, table-driven design may become confused and difficult to follow. A redesign to a rule-based approach may enhance future maintenance and make it easier for us to add new functions in the future. **Perfective maintenance** involves making changes to improve some aspect of the system, even when the changes are not suggested by faults. Documentation changes to clarify items, test suite changes to improve test coverage, and code and design modifications to enhance readability are all examples of perfective maintenance.

Preventive Maintenance. Similar to perfective maintenance, **preventive maintenance** involves changing some aspect of the system to prevent failures. It may include the addition of type checking, the enhancement of fault handling, or the addition of a "catch-all" statement to a case statement, to make sure the system can handle all possibilities. Preventive maintenance usually results when a programmer or code analyzer finds an actual or potential fault that has not yet become a failure and takes action to correct the fault before damage is done.

Who Performs Maintenance. The team that develops a system is not always used to maintain the system once it is operational. Often, a separate maintenance team is employed to ensure that the system runs properly. There are positive and negative aspects to using a separate maintenance team. The development team is familiar with the code, the design and philosophy behind it, and the system's key functions. If the developers know they are building something that they will maintain, they will build the system in a way that makes maintenance easier.

However, developers sometimes feel so confident in their understanding of the system that they tend not to keep the documentation up to date. Their lack of care in writing and revising documentation may result in the need for more people or resources to tackle a problem. This situation leads to a long interval from the time a problem occurs to the time it is fixed. Many customers will not tolerate a delay.

Often, a separate group of analysts, programmers, and designers (sometimes including one or two members of the development team) is designated as the maintenance team. A fresh, new team may be more objective than the original developers. A separate team may find it easier to distinguish how a system should work from how it does work. If they know others will work from their documentation, developers tend to be more careful about documentation and programming standards.

Team Responsibilities. Maintaining a system involves all team members. Typically, users, operators, or customer representatives approach the maintenance team with a comment or problem. The analysts or programmers determine which parts of the code are affected, the impact on the design, and the likely resources (including time and effort) to make the necessary changes. The team is involved in many activities:

1. understanding the system
2. locating information in system documentation
3. keeping system documentation up to date
4. extending existing functions to accommodate new or changing requirements
5. adding new functions to the system
6. finding the source of system failures or problems
7. locating and correcting faults
8. answering questions about the way the system works
9. restructuring design and code components
10. rewriting design and code components
11. deleting design and code components that are no longer useful
12. managing changes to the system as they are made

In addition, maintenance team members work with users, operators, and customers. First, they try to understand the problem as expressed in the user's language. Then, the problem is transformed into a request for modification. The change request includes a description of how the system works now, how the user wants the system to work, and what modifications are needed to produce the changes. Once design or code is modified and tested, the maintenance team retrains the user, if necessary. Thus, maintenance involves interaction with people as well as with the software and hardware.

Use of Maintenance Time. There are varying reports of how maintainers spend their time among the several types of maintenance. Lientz and Swanson (1981) surveyed managers in 487 data processing organizations and found a distribution like the

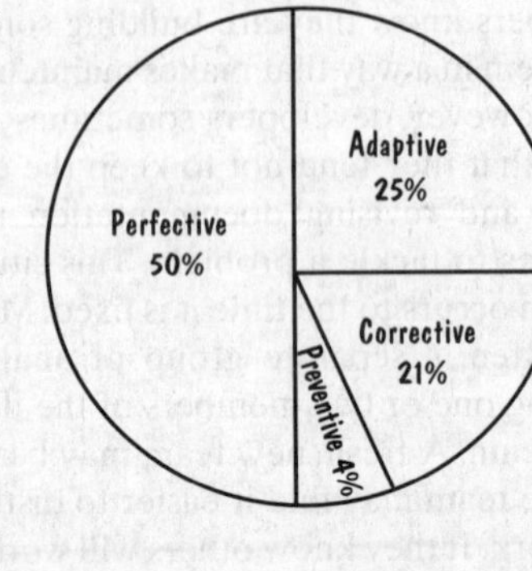

FIGURE 11.4 Distribution of maintenance effort.

one shown in Figure 11.4. Most of the effort was devoted to perfective and adaptive maintenance. Similar distributions are reported in other, later studies. But the distribution for a given organization depends on many things, including whether the system is an S-, P-, or E-system, and how quickly business needs change.

11.3 MAINTENANCE PROBLEMS

Maintaining a system is difficult. Because the system is already operational, the maintenance team balances the need for change with the need for keeping a system accessible to users. For example, upgrading a system may require it to be unavailable to users for several hours. However, if the system is critical to the users' business or operation, there may not be a window of several hours when users can give up the system. For instance, a life-support system cannot be disconnected from a patient so that maintenance can be performed on the software. The maintenance team must find a way to implement changes without inconveniencing users.

Staff Problems

There are many staff and organizational reasons that make maintenance difficult. The staff must act as an intermediary between the problem and its solution, tinkering and tailoring the software to ensure that the solution follows the course of the problem as it changes.

Limited Understanding. In addition to balancing user needs with software and hardware needs, the maintenance team deals with the limitations of human understanding. There is a limit to the rate at which a person can study documentation and extract material relevant to the problem being solved. Furthermore, we usually look for more clues than are really necessary for solving a problem. Adding the daily office distractions, we have a prescription for limited productivity.

Parikh and Zvegintzov (1983) report that 47% of software maintenance effort is devoted to understanding the software to be modified. This high figure is understandable when we consider the number of interfaces that need to be checked whenever a component is changed. For example, if a system has m components and we need to change k of them, there are

$$k^*(m - k) + k^*(k - 1)/2$$

interfaces to be evaluated for impact and correctness (Gerlich and Denskat 1994). So, even a one-line change to a system component may require hundreds of tests to be sure that the change has no direct or indirect effect on another part of the system.

User understanding also presents problems. Lientz and Swanson (1981) found that more than half of maintenance programmers' problems derived from users' lack of skill or understanding. For example, if users do not understand how the system functions, they may provide maintainers with incomplete or misleading data when reporting a problem's effects.

These results illustrate the importance of clear and complete documentation and training. The maintenance team also needs good "people skills." As we saw in Chapter 2, there are a variety of work styles. The maintenance team must understand how people with different styles think and work, and team members must be flexible when communicating.

Management Priorities. The maintenance team weighs the desires of the customer's management against the system's needs. Management priorities often override technical ones; managers sometimes view maintaining and enhancing as more important than building new applications. In other words, companies must sometimes focus on business as usual, instead of investigating new alternatives. But as management encourages maintainers to repair an old system, users are clamoring for new functions or a new system. Similarly, the rush to get a product to market may encourage us, as either developers or maintainers, to implement a quick, inelegant, poorly tested change, rather than take the time to follow good software engineering practice. The result is a patched product that is difficult to understand and repair later.

Morale. The Lientz and Swanson studies (1981) indicate that 11.9% of the problems during maintenance result from low morale and productivity. A major reason for low morale is the second-class status often accorded the maintenance team. Programmers sometimes think that it takes more skill to design and develop a system than to keep it running. However, as we have seen, maintenance programmers handle problems that developers never see. Maintainers are skilled not only in writing code but also in working with users, in anticipating change, and in sleuthing. Great skill and perseverance are required to track a problem to its source, to understand the inner workings of a large system, and to modify that system's structure, code, and documentation.

Some groups rotate programmers among several maintenance and development projects to give the programmers a chance to do a variety of things. This rotation helps avoid the perceived stigma of maintenance programming. However, programmers are often asked to work on several projects concurrently. Demands on a programmer's time result in conflicting priorities. During maintenance, 8% of the problems result from a programmer's being pulled in too many directions at once and thus being unable to concentrate on one problem long enough to solve it.

Technical Problems

Technical problems also affect maintenance productivity. Sometimes, they are a legacy of what developers and maintainers have done before. At other times, they result from particular paradigms or processes that have been adopted for the implementation.

Artifacts and Paradigms. If the design's logic is not obvious, the team may not easily determine whether the design can handle proposed changes. A flawed or inflexible design can require extra time for understanding, changing, and testing. For instance, developers may have included a component for input and output that handles only tape; major modifications must be made for disk access, because the disk is not constrained by the tape's sequential access. Similarly, the developers may not have anticipated changes; field and table sizes may be fixed, making them difficult to modify. The "year 2000 problem," where many developers represented the year as only two characters, is a good example of how simple but narrow design decisions can have a major effect on maintenance.

Maintaining object-oriented programs can be problematic, too, because the design often involves components that are highly interconnected by complex inheritance schemes. Incremental changes must be made with great care, since modifications can result in long chains of classes that hide others or that redefine objects in conflicting ways. Sidebar 11.2 describes more of the particular design trade-offs involved when maintaining object-oriented systems.

In general, inadequate design specifications and low-quality programs and documentation account for almost 10% of maintenance effort. A similar amount of effort is dedicated to hardware requirements: getting adequate storage and processing time. As a student, you understand the frustration of having a problem to solve but having no access to a workstation, or having to dial repeatedly to obtain remote access. Problems also arise when hardware, software, or data are unreliable.

Testing Difficulties. Testing can be a problem when finding time to test is difficult. For example, an airline reservations system must be available around the clock. It may be difficult to convince users to give up the system for two hours of testing. When a system performs a critical function such as air traffic control or patient monitoring, it may be impossible to bring it offline to test. In these cases, tests are often run on duplicate systems; then, tested changes are transferred to the production system.

In addition to time availability problems, there may not be good or appropriate test data available for testing the changes made. For instance, an earthquake prediction system may be modified to accommodate signals from a sensing device being developed. Test data must be simulated. Because scientists do not yet have a complete understanding of how earthquakes occur, accurate test data may be difficult to generate.

Most important, it is not always easy for testers to predict the effects of design or code changes and to prepare for them. This unpredictability exists especially when different members of the maintenance team are working on different problems at the same time. If Pat makes a change to a component to fix a data overflow problem while Dennis makes a change to the same component to fix an interface problem, the combination of changes may in fact cause a new fault.

SIDEBAR 11.2 THE BENEFITS AND DRAWBACKS OF MAINTAINING OBJECT-ORIENTED SYSTEMS

Wilde, Matthews, and Huitt (1993) have investigated the differences between maintaining object-oriented systems and procedural systems. They note several benefits of object orientation:

- Maintenance changes to a single object class may not affect the rest of the program.
- Maintainers can reuse objects easily, writing only a small amount of new code.

However, there are several drawbacks:

- Object-oriented techniques may make programs more difficult to understand because of the profusion of program parts. It is hard to discern the original designer's intent because of delocalization: program plans dispersed throughout many noncontiguous program segments.
- For the same reason, multiple parts can make it difficult to understand overall system behavior.
- Inheritance can make dependencies difficult to trace.
- Dynamic binding makes it impossible to determine which of several methods will be executed, so maintainers must consider all possibilities.
- By hiding the details of data structure, program function is often distributed across several classes. It is then difficult to detect and decipher interacting classes.

The Need to Compromise

The maintenance team is always involved in balancing one set of goals with another. As we have seen, conflict may arise between system availability for users and implementation of modifications, corrections, and enhancements. Because failures occur at unpredictable times, the maintenance staff is constantly aware of this conflict.

For computing professionals, another conflict arises whenever change is necessary. Principles of software engineering compete with expediency and cost. Often, a problem may be fixed in one of two ways: a quick but inelegant solution that works but does not fit the system's design or coding strategy, or a more involved but elegant way that is consistent with the guiding principles used to generate the rest of the system. As we noted earlier, programmers may be forced to compromise elegance and design principles because a change is needed immediately.

When such compromises are made, several related events may make future maintenance more difficult. First, the complaint is usually brought to the attention of the maintainers by a user or operator. This person is not likely to understand the problem in the context of design and code, only in the context of daily operations. Second, solving the problem involves only the immediate correction of a fault. No allowance is made for revising the system or program design to make the overall system more understandable or to make the change consistent with the rest of the system's components. These two factors combine to present the maintenance team with a quick repair as its limited goal. The team is forced to concentrate its resources on a problem about which it may have little understanding.

The team must resolve an additional conflict. When a system is developed to solve an initial problem, its developers sometimes try to solve similar problems without changing the design and code. Such systems often run slowly because their general-purpose code must evaluate a large number of cases or possibilities. To improve performance, the system can incorporate special-purpose components that sacrifice generality for speed. The special-purpose components are often smaller because they need not consider every eventuality. The resulting system can be changed easily, at a cost of the time it takes to modify or enhance the system or program design. The team must weigh generality against speed when deciding how and why to make a modification or correction.

Other factors that may affect the approach taken by the maintenance team include

- the type of failure
- the failure's criticality or severity
- the difficulty of the needed changes
- the scope of the needed changes
- the complexity of the components being changed
- the number of physical locations at which the changes must be made

All the factors described here tell us that the maintenance staff performs double duty. First, the team understands the system's design, code, and test philosophies and structures. Second, it develops a philosophy about the way in which maintenance will be performed and how the resulting system will be structured. Balancing long- and short-term goals, the team decides when to sacrifice quality for speed.

Maintenance Cost

All the problems of maintaining a system contribute to the high cost of software maintenance. In the 1970s, most of a software system's budget was spent on development. The ratio of development money to maintenance money was reversed in the 1980s, and various estimates place maintenance at 40% to 60% of the full life-cycle cost of a system (i.e., from development through maintenance to eventual retirement or replacement). Current estimates suggest that maintenance costs may have increased to up to 80% of a system's lifetime costs in the 2000s.

Factors Affecting Effort. In addition to the problems already discussed, there are many other factors that contribute to the effort needed to maintain a system. These factors can include the following:

- *Application type.* Real-time and highly synchronized systems are more difficult to change than those where timing is not essential to proper functioning. We must take great care to ensure that a change to one component does not affect the timing of the others. Similarly, changes to programs with rigidly defined data formats can require additional changes to a large number of data-access routines.

- *System novelty.* When a system implements a new application or a new way of performing common functions (such as the system described in Sidebar 11.3), the maintainers cannot easily rely on their experience and understanding to find and fix faults. It takes longer to understand the design, to locate the source of problems, and to test the corrected code. In many cases, additional test data must be generated when old test data do not exist.
- *Turnover and maintenance staff availability.* Substantial time is required to learn enough about a system to understand and change it. Maintenance effort suffers if team members are routinely rotated to other groups, if staff members leave the organization to work on another project, or if staff members are expected to maintain several different products at the same time.
- *System life span.* A system that is designed to last many years is likely to require more maintenance than one whose life is short. Quick corrections and lack of care in updating documentation are probably acceptable for a system with a short life; such habits can be deadly on a long-term project, where they make it more difficult for other team members to make subsequent changes.
- *Dependence on a changing environment.* An S-system usually requires less maintenance than a P-system, which in turn needs less adaptation and enhancement

SIDEBAR 11.3 BALANCING MANAGEMENT AND TECHNICAL NEEDS AT CHASE MANHATTAN

By the late 1990s, Chase Manhattan's Middle Market Banking Group had captured half of the market share of business banking services to small and midsize companies in the New York metropolitan area. To understand who its customers were, which bank products they used, and how they could be encouraged to buy more products in the future, the company developed the Relationship Management System (RMS), a system that gave salespeople a single interface to multiple types of middle-market customer data such as credit balance and transactions. RMS joined Chase Manhattan's legacy applications with PC/LAN/WAN technology to address the goal of freeing time for customer representatives to get to know their customers.

The system began in 1994 as an application developed by Chemical Bank. When Chemical merged with Chase in 1996, Chase decided to modify Chemical's system for use in the larger merged bank. The RMS system evolved in many steps. It was merged with another Chemical system, the Global Management System, and then combined with several other systems to eliminate duplication and link hardware platforms and business offices. RMS's Windows-based graphical user interface was developed, and the system was modified to allow it to run spreadsheets and print reports using Microsoft products. Then, the system incorporated Lotus Notes, so that data changes could be submitted only through a Notes application. Some parts of RMS were implemented in other Chase Manhattan banking units, and the system was deployed on an intranet to provide remote access to the bank's mobile sales force (Field 1997b).

than an E-system. In particular, a system dependent on its hardware's characteristics is likely to require many changes if the hardware is modified or replaced.

- *Hardware characteristics.* Unreliable hardware components or unreliable vendor support may make it more difficult to track a problem to its source.
- *Design quality.* If the system is not composed of independent, cohesive components, finding and fixing the source of a problem may be compounded by changes creating unanticipated effects in other components.
- *Code quality.* If the code is unstructured or does not implement the guiding principles of its architecture, it may be difficult to locate faults. In addition, the language itself may make it difficult to find and fix faults; higher-level languages often enhance maintainability.
- *Documentation quality.* Undocumented design or code makes the search for a problem's solution almost impossible. Similarly, if the documentation is difficult to read or even incorrect, the maintainers can be thrown off track.
- *Testing quality.* If tests are run with incomplete data or do not anticipate the repercussions of a change, the modifications and enhancements can generate other system problems.

Modeling Maintenance Effort. As with development, we want to estimate the effort required to maintain a software system. Belady and Lehman (1972) were among the first researchers to try to capture maintenance effort in a predictive model. They took into account the deterioration that occurs to a large system over time. A series of repairs and enhancements usually leads to fragmentation of system activities, and, in general, the system grows larger with each round of maintenance repair.

On very large systems, maintainers must become experts in certain aspects of the system. That is, each team member must specialize in a particular function or performance area: database, user interface, or network software, for example. This specialization sometimes leaves the team without any generalists; there is no single person with a systemwide perspective on how the system should function and how it relates to its requirements. The staff specialization usually leads to an exponential increase in resources devoted to maintenance. More people are needed to tackle the growing system, and machines and time must be made available to support them. And more communication is needed among team members to double-check their understanding of how the other system components or functions work.

At the same time, the system usually becomes more complex as a result of two things. First, as one fault is corrected, the fix may itself be introducing new system faults. Second, as corrections are made, the system structure changes. Because many repairs are made with the limited purpose of solving a particular problem, the coupling and cohesion of components, as well as the inheritance structure of an object-oriented system, are often degraded.

Belady and Lehman capture these effects in an equation:

$$M = p + K^{c-d}$$

M is the total maintenance effort expended for a system, and p represents wholly productive efforts: analysis, evaluation, design, coding, and testing. c is complexity caused by the lack of structured design and documentation; it is reduced by d, the degree to which the maintenance team is familiar with the software. Finally, K is a constant determined by comparing this model with the effort relationships on actual projects; it is called an **empirical constant** because its value depends on the environment.

The Belady–Lehman equation expresses a very important relationship among the factors determining maintenance effort. If a system is developed without software engineering principles, the value of c will be high. If, in addition, it is maintained without an understanding of the software itself, the value of d will be low. The result is that the costs for maintenance increase exponentially. Thus, to economize on maintenance, the best approach is to build the system using good software engineering practices and to give the maintainers time to become familiar with the software.

Current effort and schedule models predict maintenance costs using many of the same factors suggested by Belady and Lehman. For example, COCOMO II computes maintenance effort using a size variable computed as follows (Boehm et al. 1995):

$$\text{Size} = ASLOC(AA + SU + 0.4DM + 0.3CM + 0.3IM)/100$$

The variable $ASLOC$ measures the number of source lines of code to be adapted, DM is the percentage of design to be modified, CM the percentage of code to be modified, and IM the percentage of external code (such as reused code) to be integrated (if any). SU is a rating scale that represents the amount of software understanding required, as shown in Table 11.2. For example, if the software is highly structured, clear, and self-descriptive, then the understanding penalty is only 10%; if it is undocumented spaghetti code, it is penalized 50%.

TABLE 11.2 COCOMO II Rating for Software Understanding

	Very Low	Low	Nominal	High	Very High
Structure	Very low cohesion, high coupling, spaghetti code	Moderately low cohesion, high coupling	Reasonably well structured; some weak areas	High cohesion, low coupling	Strong modularity, information hiding in data and control structures
Application clarity	No match between program and application worldviews	Some correlation between program and application	Moderate correlation between program and application	Good correlation between program and application	Clear match between program and application worldviews
Self-descriptiveness	Obscure code; documentation missing, obscure, or obsolete	Some code commentary headers; some useful documentation	Moderate level of code commentary, headers, and documentation	Good code commentary and headers; useful documentation; some weak areas	Self-descriptive code; documentation up-to-date, well organized, with design rationale
SU increment	50	40	30	20	10

TABLE 11.3 COCOMO II Ratings for Assessment and Assimilation Effort

Assessment and Assimilation Increment	Level of Assessment and Assimilation Effort
0	None
2	Basic component search and documentation
4	Some component test and evaluation documentation
6	Considerable component test and evaluation documentation
8	Extensive component test and evaluation documentation

COCOMO II also includes a rating for the effort required to assess the code and make changes, as shown in Table 11.3. The more testing and documentation required, the higher the effort required.

Many of the issues regarding estimation during development apply equally to maintenance-related estimation. In particular, the best estimates are based on thorough histories of similar projects from the past. In addition, estimates must be recalculated as project and product attributes change; since legacy systems are continually evolving, the estimates should be made on a regular basis.

11.4 MEASURING MAINTENANCE CHARACTERISTICS

We have discussed several properties of software that make it easy (or not) to understand, enhance, and correct. Using these factors to measure software when it is delivered, we can predict the likelihood that our software is maintainable. During the maintenance process, measures can guide our activities, helping us evaluate the impact of a change or assess the relative merits of several proposed changes or approaches.

Maintainability is not restricted to code; it describes many software products, including specification, design, and test plan documents. Thus, we need maintainability measures for all of the products we hope to maintain.

We can think of maintainability in two ways, reflecting external and internal views of the software. Maintainability as we have defined it in this book is an external software attribute, because it depends not only on the product, but also on the person performing the maintenance, the supporting documentation and tools, and the proposed usage of the software. That is, we cannot measure maintainability without monitoring the software's behavior in a given environment.

On the other hand, we would like to measure maintainability before the software is actually delivered, so that we can get a sense of the resources required to support any problems that may occur. For this type of measurement, we use internal software attributes (e.g., those relating to the structure) and establish that they predict the external measures. Because this approach is not a direct measurement, we must weigh the practicality of the indirect approach with the exactness of the external approach.

External View of Maintainability

To measure maintainability as mean time to repair (as we saw in Chapter 9), we need careful records of the following information for each problem:

- the time at which the problem is reported
- any time lost due to administrative delay
- the time required to analyze the problem
- the time required to specify which changes are to be made
- the time needed to make the change
- the time needed to test the change
- the time needed to document the change

Figure 11.5 illustrates the mean time to repair the various subsystems for software at a large British firm. This information was useful in identifying subsystems causing the most problems and in planning preventive maintenance activities (Pfleeger, Fenton, and Page 1994). Tracking the mean time to repair with graphs like this one shows us whether the system is becoming more or less maintainable.

Other (environment-dependent) measures may also be useful, if available:

- the ratio of total change implementation time to total number of changes implemented
- the number of unresolved problems
- the time spent on unresolved problems

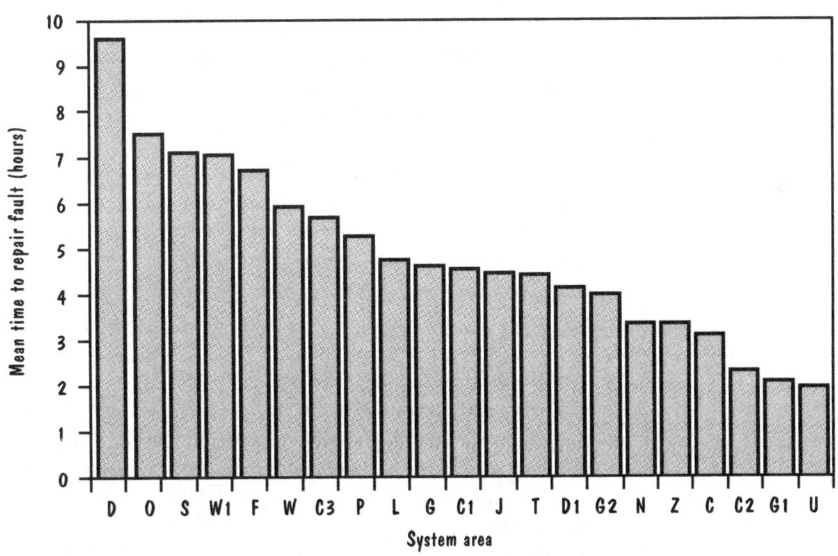

FIGURE 11.5 Mean time to repair faults by system area (Pfleeger, Fenton, and Page 1994) ©1996 IEEE.

- the percentage of changes that introduce new faults
- the number of components modified to implement a change

Together, these measures paint a picture of the degree of maintenance activity and the effectiveness of the maintenance process.

Internal Attributes Affecting Maintainability

Many researchers have proposed measures for internal attributes related to maintainability. For example, complexity measures described in earlier chapters are often correlated with maintenance effort; that is, the more complex the code, the more effort required to maintain it. It is important to remember that correlation is not the same as measurement. But there is a clear and intuitive connection between poorly structured and poorly documented products and their maintainability.

Cyclomatic Number. One of the most frequently used measures during maintenance is the cyclomatic number, first defined by McCabe (1976). The **cyclomatic number** is a metric that captures an aspect of the structural complexity of source code by measuring the number of linearly independent paths through the code. Based on graph-theoretic concepts, it is calculated by converting the code into its equivalent control flow graph and then using properties of the graph to determine the metric.

To see how the cyclomatic number is calculated, consider this C++ code from Lee and Tepfenhart (1997):

```
Scoreboard::drawscore(int n)
{     while(numdigits-> 0} {
            score[numdigits]->erase();
      }
      // build new score in loop, each time update position
      numdigits = 0;
      // if score is 0, just display "0"
      if (n == 0) {
            delete score[numdigits];
            score[numdigits] = new Displayable(digits[0]);
            score[numdigits]->move(Point((700-numdigits*18),40));
            score[numdigits]->draw();
            numdigits++;
}
while (n) {
            int rem = n % 10;
            delete score[numdigits];
            score[numdigits] = new Displayable(digits[rem]);
            score[numdigits]->move(Point(700-numdigits*18),40));
            score[numdigits]->draw();
            n /= 10;
            numdigits++;
      }
}
```

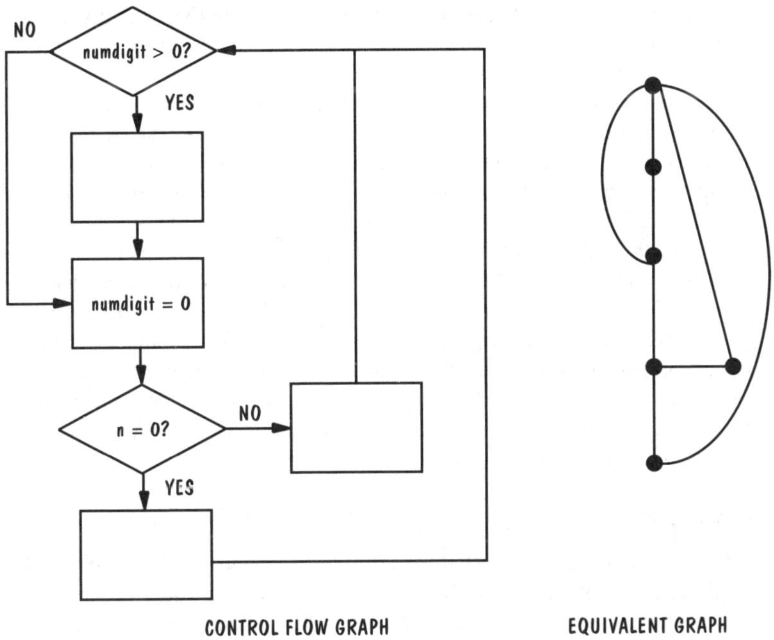

FIGURE 11.6 Example for cyclomatic number calculation.

The control flow graph is drawn on the left side of Figure 11.6. We can redraw this graph by assigning a node to each diamond or box and then connecting the nodes with edges, as is done in the original graph. The result is a graph with n nodes and e edges; in our example, n is 6 and e is 8. A result from graph theory tells us that the number of linearly independent paths through this graph is

$$e - n + 2$$

or 4 in our example. McCabe proved that the cyclomatic number is also equal to one more than the number of decision statements in the code. If we look at the preceding code fragment, we see two *while* statements and an *if* statement, so the cyclomatic number must be one more than 3, or 4. An easy way to calculate the cyclomatic number from the graph is to look at how the graph divides the plane into segments. In our example, the graph on the right divides the page into three pieces (the triangle, the semicircle, and the irregularly shaped piece to the right of the triangle) plus an extra piece for the rest of the page. Thus, the graph separates the plane into four pieces; that number of pieces is the cyclomatic number.

A similar calculation can be done from a component's design, so the cyclomatic number is often used to evaluate several design alternatives before coding even begins. The cyclomatic number is useful in many other contexts, too. It tells us how many independent paths need to be tested to give us path coverage, so it is often measured and used in determining testing strategy.

In maintenance, the number of independent paths, or equivalently, one more than the number of decisions, tells us how much we have to understand and track when we are examining or changing a component. Thus, many researchers and practitioners find it useful to look at the effect of a change or fix on a component's or system's cyclomatic number; if the change or fix results in a dramatic increase in the cyclomatic number, then the maintainers may want to rethink the design of the change or fix. Indeed, Lehman's second law of software evolution predicts that the cyclomatic number (and other complexity measures) will increase as the system evolves.

We should be cautious in using this or any other measure to represent all of software's complexity. It is true that an increase in the number of decisions or paths usually makes code harder to understand. But there are other attributes that contribute to complexity that are not captured by its structure. For example, the inheritance hierarchy of object-oriented programs can be quite complex, having ramifications not apparent when studying a single component out of context. Researchers continue to seek better methods for defining and measuring complexity, to help us in our quest to build simple, easy-to-maintain systems.

Other Product Measures

There are many product attributes that help us understand maintainability and predict likely sources of problems. Some organizations use rules based on component measures such as size. For example, Möller and Paulish (1993) show that, at Siemens, the smaller components (in terms of lines of code) had a higher fault density than the larger ones (see Sidebar 11.4). Other researchers have used information about depth of nesting, number of operators and operands, and fan-in and fan-out to predict maintenance

SIDEBAR 11.4 MODELS OF FAULT BEHAVIOR

Hatton and Hopkins (1989) studied the NAG Fortran scientific subroutine library, composed of 1600 routines totaling 250,000 executable lines of code. The library had been through 15 releases over more than 20 years, so there was an extensive maintenance history to examine. They were astonished to find that smaller components contained proportionately more faults than larger ones (where size was measured as static path count).

Hatton went on to look for similar evidence from other researchers. He notes that Möller and Paulish (1993) report the same phenomenon at Siemens, where size is measured as lines of code. Withrow (1990) describes similar behavior for Ada code at Unisys, as do Basili and Perricone (1984) for Fortran products at NASA Goddard.

However, Rosenberg (1998) points out that these reports are based on comparing size with fault density. Since density is measured as number of faults divided by size, size is part of both factors being compared. Thus, there may be a strong negative correlation between the two factors, masking the real relationship between faults and size. Rosenberg cautions us to take great care to understand the definition of measures before we apply statistical techniques to them.

SIDEBAR 11.5 MAINTENANCE MEASURES AT HEWLETT-PACKARD

Oman and Hagemeister (1992) have suggested that maintainability can be modeled using three dimensions: the control structure, the information structure, and the typography, naming, and commentary of the system being maintained. They define metrics for each dimension and then combine them into a maintainability index for the entire system.

This maintainability index was used by Coleman et al. (1994) at Hewlett-Packard (HP) to evaluate the maintainability of several software systems. First, the index was calibrated with a large number of metrics, and a tailored polynomial index was calculated using extended cyclomatic number, lines of code, number of comments, and an effort measure defined by Halstead (1977). Then, the polynomial was applied to 714 components containing 236,000 lines of C code developed by a third party. The maintainability analysis yielded a rank ordering of the components that helped HP to target the ones that were difficult to maintain. The results matched the HP maintainers' "gut feeling" about maintenance difficulty.

The polynomials were also used to compare two software systems that were similar in size, number of modules, platform, and language. The results again corroborated the feelings of HP engineers. In several subsequent analyses, the polynomial has continued to match the maintainers' intuition. But the measurements have provided additional information that supports make-or-buy decisions, targeting components for preventive and perfective maintenance, and assessing the effects of reengineering.

quality. Sidebar 11.5 describes an approach used at Hewlett-Packard to create a maintainability index.

Porter and Selby (1990) used a statistical technique called classification tree analysis to identify those product measures that are the best predictors of interface errors likely to be encountered during maintenance. The decision tree that results from the classification analysis of their data suggests measurable constraints based on past history:

- Between four and eight revisions during design and at least 15 data bindings suggest that interface faults are likely.
- Interface problems are probable in a component whose primary function is file management where there have been at least nine revisions during design.

These suggestions are particular to the dataset and are not intended to be general guidelines for any organization. However, the technique can be applied to any database of measurement information.

For textual products, readability affects maintainability. The most well-known readability measure is Gunning's **Fog Index**, F, defined by

$$F = 0.4 \times \frac{\text{number of words}}{\text{number of sentences}} + \begin{matrix}\text{percentage of words}\\ \text{of three or more syllables}\end{matrix}$$

The measure is purported to correspond roughly with the number of years of schooling a person would need in order to read a passage with ease and understanding. For large documents, the measure is usually calculated from a sample of the text (Gunning 1968).

Other readability measures are specific to software products. De Young and Kampen (1979) define the readability R of source code as

$$R = 0.295a - 0.499b + 0.13c$$

where a is the average normalized length of variables (the length of a variable is the number of characters in a variable name), b is the number of lines containing statements, and c is McCabe's cyclomatic number. The formula was derived using regression analysis of data about subjective evaluation of readability.

11.5 MAINTENANCE TECHNIQUES AND TOOLS

One way to lower maintenance effort is to build in quality from the start. Trying to force good design and structure into an already built system is not as successful as building the system correctly in the first place. However, in addition to good practice, there are several other techniques that enhance understanding and quality.

Configuration Management

Keeping track of changes and their effects on other system components is not an easy task. The more complex the system, the more components are affected by a change. For this reason, configuration management, important during development, is critical during maintenance.

Configuration Control Board. Because many maintenance changes are instigated by customers and users (as failures occur or as enhancements are requested), we establish a **configuration control board** to oversee the change process. The board is made up of representatives from all interested parties, including customers, developers, and users. Each problem is handled in the following way:

1. A problem is discovered by a user, customer, or developer, who records the symptoms on a formal change control form. Alternatively, a customer, user, or developer requests an enhancement: a new function, a variation of an old function, or the deletion of an existing function. The form, similar to the failure reports we examined in Chapter 9, must include information about how the system works, the nature of the problem or enhancement, and how the system is supposed to work.
2. The proposed change is reported to the configuration control board.
3. The configuration control board meets to discuss the problem. First, it determines if the proposal reflects a failure to meet requirements or is a request for enhancement. This decision usually affects who will pay for the resources necessary to implement the change.

4. For a reported failure, the configuration control board discusses the likely source of the problem. For a requested enhancement, the board discusses the parts of the system likely to be affected by a change. In both cases, programmers and analysts may describe the scope of any needed changes and the length of time expected to implement them. The control board assigns a priority or severity level to the request, and a programmer or analyst is made responsible for making the appropriate system changes.
5. The designated analyst or programmer locates the source of the problem or the components involved with the request and then identifies the changes needed. Working with a test copy rather than the operational version of the system, the programmer or analyst implements and tests the changes to ensure that they work.
6. The programmer or analyst works with the program librarian to control the installation of the changes in the operational system. All relevant documentation is updated.
7. The programmer or analyst files a change report that describes all the changes in detail.

Change Control. The most critical step in the process is number 6. At any moment, the configuration management team must know the state of any component or document in the system. Consequently, configuration management should emphasize communication among those whose actions affect the system. Cashman and Holt (1980) suggest that we must always know the answers to the following questions:

- *Synchronization:* When was the change made?
- *Identification:* Who made the change?
- *Naming:* What components of the system were changed?
- *Authentication:* Was the change made correctly?
- *Authorization:* Who authorized that the change be made?
- *Routing:* Who was notified of the change?
- *Cancellation:* Who can cancel the request for change?
- *Delegation:* Who is responsible for the change?
- *Valuation:* What is the priority of the change?

Notice that these questions are management questions, not technical ones. We must use procedures to manage change carefully.

We can aid change management by following several conventions. First, each working version of the system is assigned an identification code or number. As a version is modified, a revision code or number is assigned to each resulting changed component. We keep a record of each component's version and status, as well as a history of all changes. Then, at any point in the life of the system, the configuration management team can identify the current version of the operational system and the revision number of each component in use. The team can also find out how the various revisions differ, who made the changes, and why they made them.

From your perspective as a student, these configuration management conventions probably sound unnecessary. Your class projects are usually managed alone or by a small group of programmers, using verbal communication to track modifications and enhancements. However, imagine the chaos that would result from using the same techniques on the development and maintenance of a 200-component system. Often, large systems are developed by having independent groups work simultaneously on different aspects of the system; sometimes these groups are located in different parts of town or even in different cities. When miscommunication leads to a system failure, the configuration management team must be able to restore the system to its previous stable condition; this step can be taken only when the team knows who made exactly what changes to which components and when.

Impact Analysis

The traditional software life cycle depicts maintenance as starting after software is deployed. However, software maintenance depends on and begins with user requirements. Thus, principles of good software development apply to both the development and maintenance processes. Because good software development supports software change, change is a necessary consideration throughout the life of a software product. Moreover, a seemingly minor change is often more extensive (and therefore more expensive to implement) than expected. **Impact analysis** is the evaluation of the many risks associated with the change, including estimates of effects on resources, effort, and schedule.

The effects of manifold changes in a system can be seen in the resulting inadequate or outdated documentation, improperly or incompletely patched software, poorly structured design or code, artifacts that do not conform to standards, and more. The problem is compounded by increasing complexity, increasing time for developers to understand the code being changed, and increasing side effects that the change may have in other parts of the system. These problems increase the cost of maintenance, and management would like to keep this cost under control. We can use impact analysis to help control maintenance costs.

Pfleeger and Bohner (1990) have investigated ways of measuring the impact of a proposed change to determine the risks and weigh several options. They describe a model of software maintenance that includes measured feedback. The diagram in Figure 11.7 illustrates the activities performed when a change is requested, where the labeled arrows at the bottom represent measurements that provide information that managers can use in deciding when and how to make a change.

A **workproduct** is any development artifact whose change is significant. Thus, requirements, design and code components, test cases, and documentation are workproducts; the quality of one can affect the quality of the others, so changing them can have important consequences. We can assess the impact of the change for all workproducts. For each, **vertical traceability** expresses the relationships among the parts of the workproduct. For example, vertical traceability of the requirements describes the interdependencies among the system requirements. **Horizontal traceability** addresses the relationships of the components across collections of workproducts. For instance, each design component is traced to the code components that implement that part of the design. We need both types of traceability to understand the complete set of relationships assessed during impact analysis.

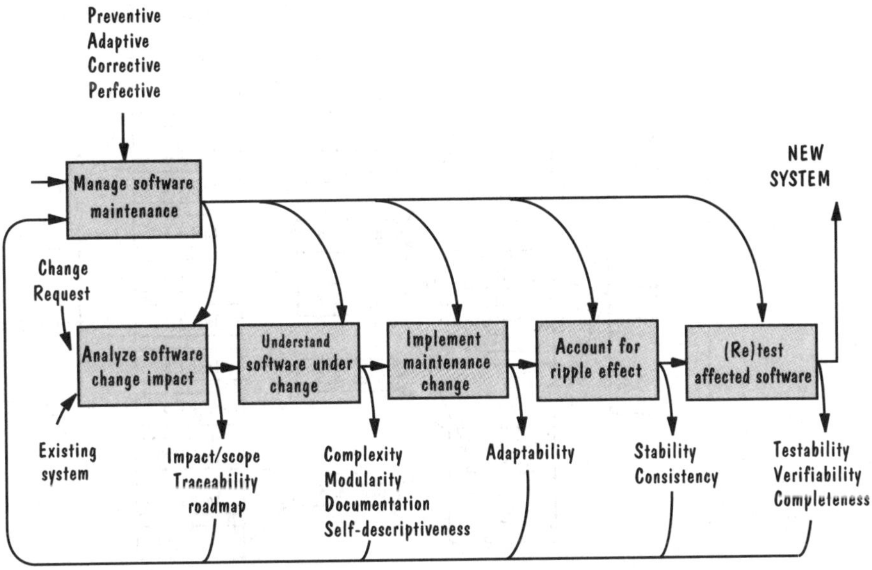

FIGURE 11.7 Software maintenance activities.

We can depict both horizontal and vertical traceability using directed graphs. A **directed graph** is simply a collection of objects, called **nodes**, and an associated collection of ordered pairs of nodes, called **edges**. The first node of the edge is called a **source node**, and the second is the **destination node**. The nodes represent information contained in documents, articles, and other artifacts. Each artifact contains a node for each component. For example, we can represent the design as a collection of nodes, with one node for each design component, and the requirements specification has one node for each requirement. The directed edges represent the relationships within a workproduct and between workproducts.

Figure 11.8 illustrates how the graphical relationships and traceability links among related workproducts are determined. We examine each requirement and draw a link between the requirement and the design components that implement it. In turn, we link each design component with the code components that implement it. Finally, we connect each code module with the set of test cases that test it. The resulting linkages form the underlying graph that exhibits the relationships among the workproducts.

Figure 11.9 illustrates how the overall traceability graph might look. Each major process artifact (requirements, design, code, and test) is shown as a box around its constituent nodes. The solid edges within each box are the vertical traceability relationships for the components in the box. The dashed edges between boxes display the horizontal traceability links for the system. Sidebar 11.6 describes how this approach was applied at Ericsson.

There is a great deal of evidence that some measures of complexity are good indicators of likely effort and fault rate (Card and Glass 1990). These notions can be

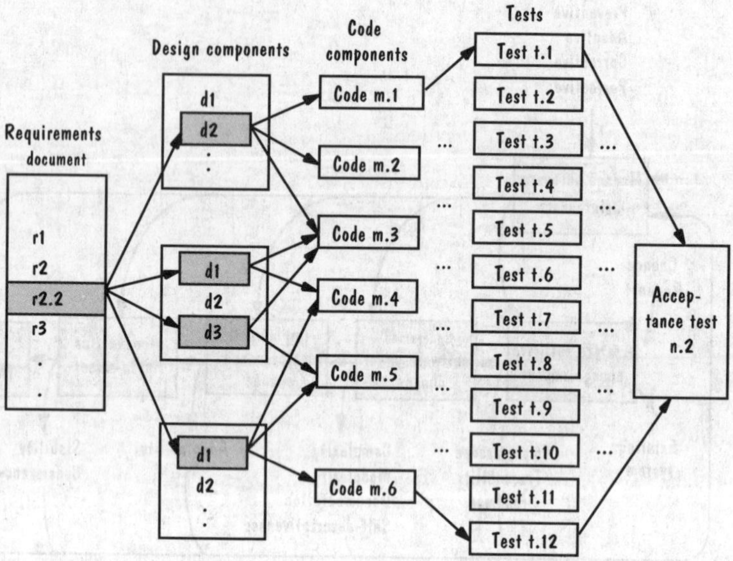

FIGURE 11.8 Horizontal traceability in software workproducts.

extended to the characteristics of the traceability graph to assess the impact of a proposed change. For example, consider the vertical traceability graph within each box of Figure 11.9. The total number of nodes, the number of edges for which a node is the destination (called the **in-degree** of the node) and for which the node is a source (called the **out-degree**), plus measures such as the cyclomatic number, can be evaluated before and

FIGURE 11.9 Underlying graph for maintenance.

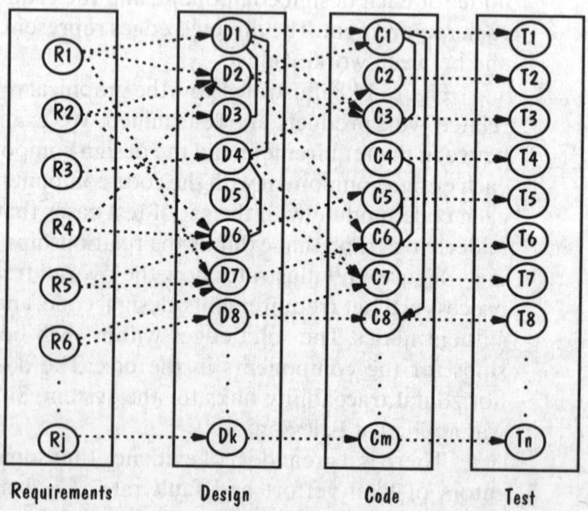

SIDEBAR 11.6 APPLYING TRACEABILITY TO REAL-WORLD SYSTEMS

Lindvall and Sandahl (1996) applied Pfleeger and Bohner's traceability approach to an object-oriented development project at Ericsson Radio Systems. As a result, they constructed a two-dimensional framework for traceability. The first dimension captures the items being traced. For example, they implemented five kinds of traceability:

- object-to-object
- association-to-association
- use case-to-use case
- use case-to-object
- two-dimensional object-to-object (incorporating inheritance)

The second dimension captures how the tracing is performed:

- using explicit links
- using textual references to different documents
- using names and concepts that are the same and similar
- using system knowledge and domain knowledge

The process of forming the links led to the discovery and correction of problems, as well as to the clarification of the meaning of many aspects of the system. They concluded from their research that "if traceability is an emphasized quality factor from the very beginning of the project, the documentation will be clearer and more consistent, a better understanding among design personnel is achieved, the inputs into the project will be more focused, and maintenance of the product will be less dependent on individual experts." However, some of their traceability work required a great deal of effort. Lindvall and Sandahl suggest that there are at least two situations that require significant effort:

- tracing items with no tools support for tracing links (as with association-to-association traceability)
- tracing in models that are partially inconsistent or underdocumented.

after the change. If the size and complexity of the graph seem to increase with the change, it is likely that the size and complexity of the corresponding workproducts will increase as well. Using this information, the configuration control board may decide to implement the change in a different way or not at all. Even if management decides to make the change as proposed, the risks involved will be understood more thoroughly with this measurement-based picture.

The vertical traceability measures are product measures that reflect the effect of change on each workproduct being maintained. Measures of characteristics of the horizontal traceability graph represent a process view of the change. For each pair of workproducts, we can form a subgraph of the relationships between the two: one relating requirements and design, another relating design and code, and a third relating code and test cases. We then measure the size and complexity relationships to determine adverse impact. Moreover, we can view the overall horizontal traceability graph to see if overall traceability will be more or less difficult after the change. Pfleeger and Bohner (1990) look at the minimal set of paths that span this graph; if the number of spanning paths increases after the change, then the system is likely to be more unwieldy and difficult to maintain. Similarly, if in- and out-degrees of nodes increase substantially, the system may be harder to maintain in the future.

Automated Maintenance Tools

Tracking the status of all components and tests is a formidable job. Fortunately, there are many automated tools to help us in maintaining software. We describe some types of tools here; the book's Web site has pointers to vendor sites and tool demonstrations.

Text Editors. Text editors are useful for maintenance in many ways. First, an editor can copy code or documentation from one place to another, preventing errors when we duplicate text. Second, as we saw in Chapter 9, some text editors track the changes relative to a baseline file, stored in a separate file. Many of these editors time- and date-stamp each text entry and provide a way to roll back from a current version of a file to a previous one, if necessary.

File Comparators. A useful tool during maintenance is a **file comparator**, which compares two files and reports on their differences. We often use it to ensure that two systems or programs that are supposedly identical actually are. The program reads both files and points out the discrepancies.

Compilers and Linkers. Compilers and linkers often contain features that simplify maintenance and configuration management. A compiler checks code for syntax faults, in many cases pointing out the location and type of fault. Compilers for some languages, such as Modula-2 and Ada, also check for consistency across separately compiled components.

When the code has compiled properly, the linker (also called a link editor) links the code with the other components needed for running the program. For example, a linker connects a *filename.h* file with its corresponding *filename.c* file in C. Or a linker can note subroutine, library, and macro calls, automatically bringing in the necessary files to make a compilable whole. Some linkers also track the version numbers of each of the required components, so that only appropriate versions are linked together. This technique helps eliminate problems caused by using the wrong copy of a system or subsystem when testing a change.

Debugging Tools. Debugging tools aid maintenance by allowing us to trace the logic of a program step by step, examining the contents of registers and memory areas, and setting flags and pointers.

Cross-Reference Generators. Earlier in this chapter, we noted the importance of traceability. Automated systems generate and store cross-references to give both the development and maintenance teams tighter control over system modifications. For example, some cross-reference tools act as a repository for the system requirements and also hold links to other system documents and code that relate to each requirement. When a change to a requirement is proposed, we can use the tool to tell us which other requirements, design, and code components will be affected.

Some cross-reference tools contain a set of logical formulas called verification conditions; if all formulas yield a value of "true," then the code satisfies the specifications that generated it. This feature is especially useful during maintenance, to assure us that changed code still complies with its specifications.

Static Code Analyzers. Static code analyzers calculate information about structural attributes of the code, such as depth of nesting, number of spanning paths, cyclomatic number, number of lines of code, and unreachable statements. We can calculate this information as we build new versions of the systems we are maintaining, to see if the systems are becoming bigger, more complex, and more difficult to maintain. The measurements also help us to decide among several design alternatives, especially when we are redesigning portions of existing code.

Configuration Management Repositories. Configuration management would be impossible without libraries of information that control the change process. These repositories can store trouble reports, including information about each problem, the organization reporting it, and the organization fixing it. Some repositories allow users to keep tabs on the status of reported problems in the systems they are using. Others, such as the tool described in Sidebar 11.7, perform version control and cross-referencing.

SIDEBAR 11.7 PANVALET

Panvalet is a popular tool used on IBM mainframes. It incorporates the source code, object code, control language, and data files needed to run a system. Files are assigned file types, and different files can be associated with one another. This property allows a developer to alter a string in one file, in all files of a given type, or in an entire library of files.

Panvalet controls more than one version of a system, so a file can have multiple versions. A single version is designated as the production version, and no one is allowed to alter it. To modify this file, the developer must create a new version of the file and then change the new file.

The files are organized in a hierarchy, and they are cross-referenced with each other. Each version of a file is associated with a directory of information about the version: its status with respect to the production version, the dates of last access and last update, the number of statements in the file, and the kind of action last taken with respect to the file. When the file is compiled, Panvalet automatically places the version number and date of last change on the compiler listing and the object module.

Panvalet also has reporting, backup, and recovery features, plus three levels of security access. When files have not been used for a long time, Panvalet can archive them.

11.6 SOFTWARE REJUVENATION

In many organizations with large amounts of software, maintaining those systems is a challenge. To see why, consider an insurance company that offers a new life insurance product. To support that product, the company develops software to deal with the insurance policies, policy-holder information, actuarial information, and accounting information. Such policies may be supported for dozens of years; sometimes the software cannot be retired until the last policy-holder dies and the claims are settled. As a result, the insurance company is likely to be supporting many different applications on a wide variety of platforms with a large number of implementation languages. Organizations in this situation must make difficult decisions about how to make their systems more maintainable. The choices may range from enhancement to complete replacement with new technology; each choice is intended to preserve or increase the software's quality while keeping costs as low as possible.

Software rejuvenation addresses this maintenance challenge by trying to increase the overall quality of an existing system. It looks back at a system's workproducts to try to derive additional information or to reformat them in a more understandable way. There are several aspects of software rejuvenation to consider, including

- redocumentation
- restructuring
- reverse engineering
- reengineering

When we **redocument** a system, we perform static analysis of the source code, producing additional information to assist maintainers in understanding and referencing the code. The analysis does nothing to transform the actual code; it merely derives information. However, when we **restructure**, we actually change the code by transforming ill-structured code into well-structured code. Both of these techniques focus solely on the source code. To **reverse engineer** a system, we look back from the source code to the products that preceded it, recreating design and specification information from the code. Broader still is **reengineering**, where we reverse engineer an existing system and then "forward engineer" it to make changes to the specification and design that complete the logical model; then, we generate a new system from the revised specification and design. Figure 11.10 illustrates the relationships among the four types of rejuvenation.

Of course, it is impossible to expect to re-create all intermediate workproducts from a given piece of source code. Such a task is comparable to re-creating a child's picture from an adult's. Nevertheless, some essential features of some of the workproducts can be enhanced or embellished. The degree to which information can be extracted from the final product depends on several factors (Bohner 1990):

- language(s) used
- database interface
- user interface
- interfaces to system services
- interfaces to other languages

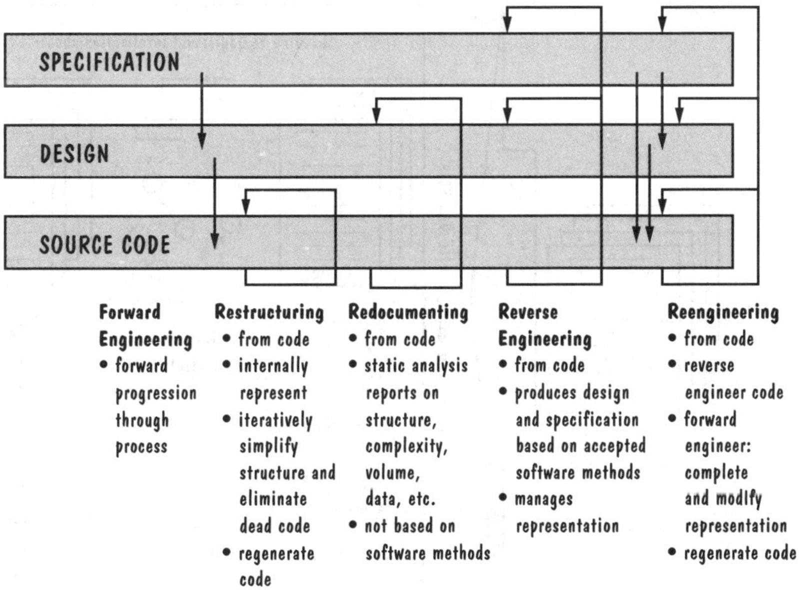

FIGURE 11.10 Taxonomy of software rejuvenation (Bohner 1990).

- domain maturity and stability
- available tools

The maintainers' ability, knowledge, and experience also play a large role in the degree to which the information can be interpreted and used successfully.

Redocumentation

Redocumentation involves static analysis of source code to produce system documentation. We can examine variable usage, component calls, control paths, component size, calling parameters, test paths, and other related measures to help us understand what the code does and how it does it. The information produced by a static code analysis can be graphical or textual.

Figure 11.11 illustrates the redocumentation process. Typically, a maintainer begins redocumentation by submitting the code to an analysis tool. The output may include

- component calling relationships
- class hierarchies
- data-interface tables
- data-dictionary information
- data flow tables or diagrams
- control flow tables or diagrams

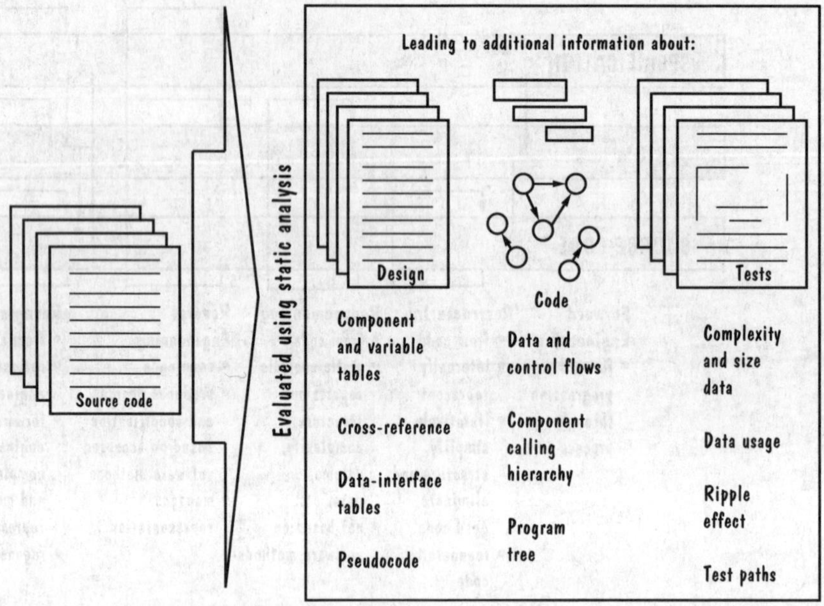

FIGURE 11.11 Redocumentation (adapted from Bohner 1990).

- pseudocode
- test paths
- component and variable cross-references

The graphical, textual, and tabular information can be used to assess whether or not a system requires restructuring. However, since there is no mapping between specification and restructured code, the resulting documentation reflects what is, rather than what should be.

Restructuring

We restructure software to make it easier to understand and change. Tools help us accomplish this task by interpreting the source code and representing it internally. Then, transformation rules are used to simplify the internal representation, and the results are recast as structured code. Although some tools produce only source code, others have supporting functions to generate structure, volume, complexity, and other information. These measurements are then used to determine the code's maintainability and to evaluate the effects of restructuring. For example, we hope that complexity measures will indicate a decrease in complexity after restructuring.

Figure 11.12 illustrates the three major activities involved in restructuring. First, static analysis provides information that we use to represent the code as a semantic network or directed graph. The representation is not necessarily read easily by humans; it is usually used only by an automated tool.

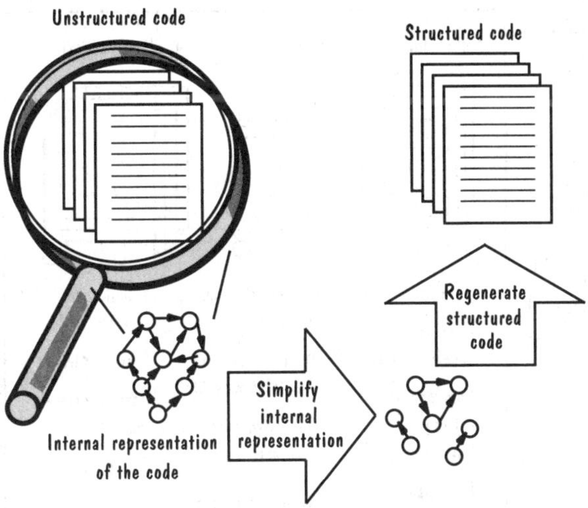

FIGURE 11.12 Restructuring (adapted from Bohner 1990).

Next, the representation is refined through successive simplifications based on transformational techniques. Finally, the refined representation is interpreted and used to generate a structured equivalent body of code for the system (usually for the same compiler).

Reverse Engineering

Reverse engineering, like redocumentation, provides specification and design information about the software system from its source code. However, reverse engineering goes further, attempting to recover engineering information based on software specification and design methods; this information is then stored in a form that allows us to manipulate it. The extracted information is not necessarily complete, because many source components are usually associated with one or more design components. For this reason, the reverse-engineered system may actually have less information than the original system.

Thanks to graphics workstations and storage management tools, much of reverse engineering can be automated. We can display and manipulate graphical designs and control a repository of data gathered by the tools we use.

Figure 11.13 depicts the reverse-engineering process. First, source code is submitted to a reverse-engineering tool, which interprets the structure and naming information and constructs outputs much in the same way as redocumentation. Standard structured analysis and design methods serve as good communication mechanisms to articulate the reverse-engineering information, such as data dictionaries, data flow, control flow, and entity-relationship-attribute diagrams.

The key to reverse engineering is its ability to abstract specifications from the detailed source code implementation. However, some significant obstacles remain before reverse engineering can be used universally. Real-time systems present a problem; the mapping between implementation and design is sparse because of frequent performance

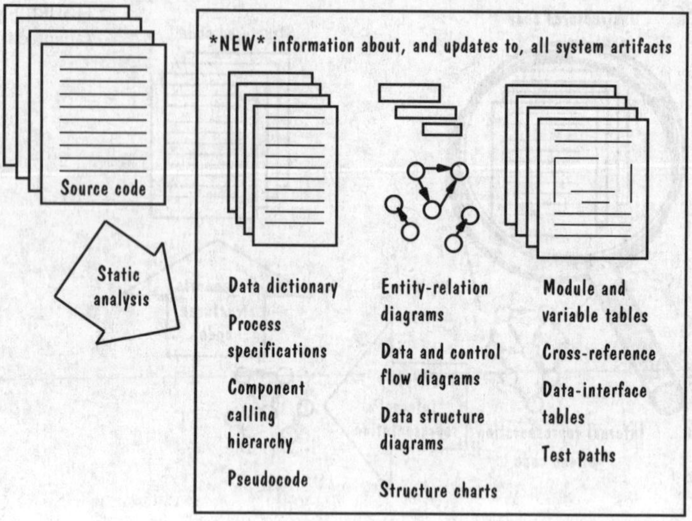

FIGURE 11.13 Reverse engineering (adapted from Bohner 1990).

optimizations. A second problem occurs when extremely complex systems are implemented with terse or incomprehensible naming conventions. When reverse-engineering tools are applied to these kinds of systems, the modeling information is of limited value.

Reverse engineering is successful when expectations are low. That is, tools do well in determining all related data elements and calls to a particular component. They can display complex system structure, and they recognize inconsistencies or violations of design standards.

Reengineering

Reengineering is an extension of reverse engineering. Whereas reverse engineering abstracts information, reengineering produces new software source code without changing the overall system function. Figure 11.14 illustrates the steps in this process. First, the system is reverse-engineered and represented internally for human and computer modifications based on current methods for specifying and designing software. Next, the model of the software system is corrected or completed. Finally, the new system is generated from this new specification or design.

Inputs to the reengineering process include source code files, database files, screen-generation files, and similar system-related files. When the process is complete, it generates all system documentation, including specification and design, and new source code.

Since fully automatic reengineering is unlikely in the near future, the process must involve a combination of transformation and human interaction. We can complete incomplete representations manually, and an experienced designer can enhance designs before the new system is generated. Sidebar 11.8 discusses the effort needed to reengineer a system, and how much must be done manually.

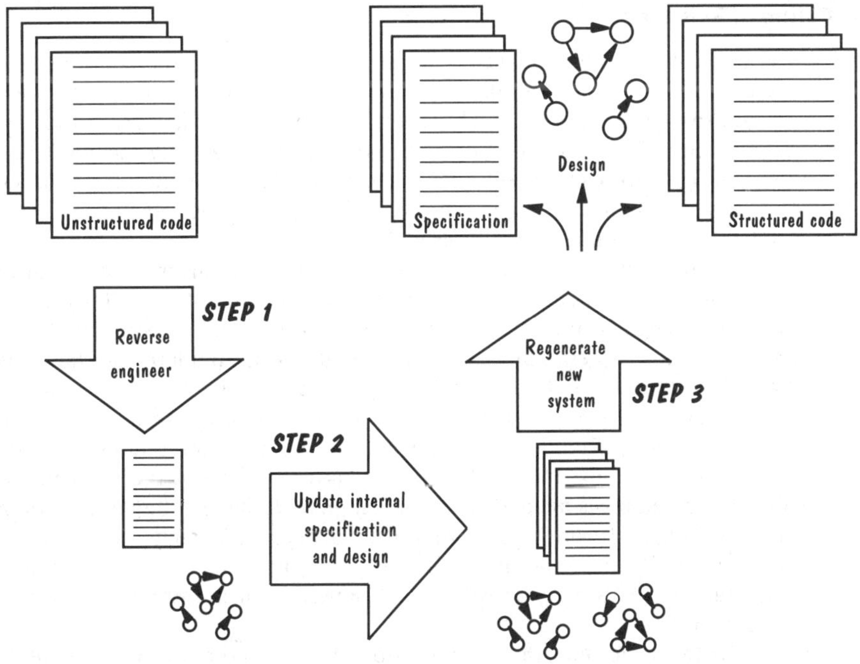

FIGURE 11.14 Reengineering (adapted from Bohner 1990).

SIDEBAR 11.8 REENGINEERING EFFORT

The U.S. National Institute of Standards and Technology (NIST) studied the results of reengineering 13,131 lines of COBOL source statements. The system, involving batch processing with no use of commercial off-the-shelf products, was reengineered using automatic translation. Ruhl and Gunn (1991) report that the entire reengineering effort took 35 person-months.

Boehm et al. (1995) point out that the original COCOMO model estimated 152 person-months for reengineering the same type of system, a clearly unacceptable level of accuracy. As a result, COCOMO II has been revised, based on other reengineering studies, to include a factor for automatic translation; the model calculates that automatic translation occurs at the rate of 2400 source statements per person-month.

The NIST study notes that the amount of code that can be translated automatically varies with the type of application. For instance, 96% of batch processing can be translated automatically, but only 88% of a batch processing application with a database management system can be translated automatically. By contrast, Ruhl and Gunn (1991) found that only half of an interactive application can be translated automatically.

The Future of Rejuvenation

Because software maintenance is not always as appealing to practitioners as new software development, issues like rejuvenation do not get as much attention as those related to new development. However, some advances have given more visibility to rejuvenation. Commercial reverse-engineering tools partially recover a software system's design; they can identify, present, and analyze information from the source code, but they do not reconstruct, capture, and express design abstractions that are not explicitly represented in the source code.

Source code information does not contain much information about the original design, so the remainder must be reconstructed from inferences. Thus, the most successful reverse-engineering attempts have been in well-understood stable domains such as information systems. Here, the typical system is standard, the language (usually COBOL) is relatively simple and well-structured, and there are many domain experts.

In other domains, design recovery is possible only with information from code, existing design documentation, personal experience, and general knowledge about the problem domain. Informal linguistic knowledge about the problem domain and application idioms is needed before a complete design can be understood and reconstructed. Thus, software rejuvenation will advance when technology and methods can capture rules, policies, design decisions, terminology, naming conventions, and other informal information. As we will see in Chapter 12, postmortems help us to record this information.

At the same time, the formalization of design notations and the introduction of domain models will broaden the information available to understand and maintain a software system. We can expect improvements in transformation technology to support more application domains, and more complete representations will allow more reengineering to be automated.

11.7 INFORMATION SYSTEMS EXAMPLE

Let us examine the relationship of the Piccadilly software to the real world to determine if Piccadilly is an S-, P-, or E-system. If Piccadilly were an S-system, its problem would have been completely specified; such a system is static and does not easily accommodate a change in the problem that generated it. However, it is clear that the problem itself may change dramatically. For example, the advertising regulations imposed by the British government might change as new laws are passed and old ones repealed. Or the television company's pricing strategy may change, or it may run special promotions to attract new advertisers. So the software cannot be an S-system; its inflexibility would require a completely new system each time the real-world constraints evolve.

If Piccadilly were a P-system, its solution would be based on an abstraction of the problem. Indeed, any method for determining the cost of advertising time is based on a model of various characteristics of television programming, including time of day, day of week, and number of additional advertising slots sold. However, a P-system requires a stable abstraction. That is, the model does not change; only information about the model changes. It is clear that our model may change, as new advertising strategies are suggested and as competition changes its models.

In S- and P-systems, the real-world situation remains stable, but an E-system changes as the world does; the system is an integral part of the world it models. This is clearly the case with the Piccadilly software, since the success of a particular advertising strategy may in fact affect the model itself. For example, suppose Piccadilly follows an initial advertising strategy that draws advertising revenue away from its competitors on Friday evenings from 9 to 11 P.M. The directors of the television company may decide to broaden the window in which advertisers are leaving the competition and signing up for Piccadilly. So the company changes its prices and runs a special promotion in a category not currently available with the present model. For instance, special rates may be given to advertisers who run a commercial message at 9 P.M. on Saturday as well as at 8 P.M. on Friday. Thus, there is continuous interaction between the real world and the abstraction; Piccadilly must be an E-system.

The implications for maintenance are particularly clear with respect to design. The initial Piccadilly design must be very flexible, and the design must not be allowed to degrade as the system evolves. Moreover, the television company directors may want to enhance the Piccadilly software with a simulation capability, so that they can view the likely effects of proposed changes in strategy.

11.8 REAL-TIME EXAMPLE

Maintainability is often measured in terms of mean time between failures, so preventing or mitigating failures should be a major goal of the maintenance team. One way to address this goal is to scrutinize the system's failure strategy. That is, we must ask ourselves what assumptions have been made about the best way to handle failures, and then see if we can change those assumptions to decrease the failure rate.

The investigative report after the Ariane-5 explosion points out that the developers focused on mitigating random failure. That is, the guidance given to developers of the inertial reference system (as all the software) was to stop the processor if any exception was detected. When the inertial reference system failed, it failed because of a design fault, not as a result of a random failure, so in fact the cessation of processing was correct according to the specification, but inappropriate according to the rocket's mission.

The investigative board emphasized this fact in its report. It said that

> The exception was detected, but inappropriately handled because the view had been taken that software should be considered correct until it is shown to be at fault. The Board has reason to believe that this view is also accepted in other areas of Ariane-5 software design. The Board is in favour of the opposite view, that software should be assumed to be faulty until applying the currently accepted best practice methods can demonstrate that it is correct. (Lions et al. 1996)

Thus, a critical next step for the Ariane software is to change the failure strategy and implement a series of preventive enhancements. Indeed, the board describes this task explicitly:

> This means that critical software—in the sense that failure of the software puts the mission at risk—must be identified at a very detailed level, that exceptional behaviour must be confined, and that a reasonable back-up policy must take software failures into account. (Lions et al. 1996)

Ariane-5 also provides us with a good example of the difficulty of testing and change control. It is clear that the European Space Agency cannot send up another rocket each time a software change is to be tested, so testing maintenance changes involves a complex series of simulations to evaluate the effects of the new or changed code. Similarly, because some software, such as the inertial reference system, exists in multiple versions (e.g., one for Ariane-4 and another for Ariane-5), then change control and configuration management must be invoked to ensure that successful changes to one version do not inadvertently degrade the functionality or performance of another version. The current inertial reference system for Ariane-4 performs as desired; changes needed for Ariane-5's SRI may not be appropriate for Ariane-4.

11.9 WHAT THIS CHAPTER MEANS FOR YOU

This chapter has introduced you to the key issues in software maintenance. We have seen how maintenance involves both technical and people-related problems. Maintainers must understand not only the software as it is, but also how it has been before and where it will evolve in the future. The major lessons we have observed are as follows:

- The more a system is linked to the real world, the more likely it will change and the more difficult it will be to maintain.
- Maintainers have many jobs in addition to software developers. They interact continually with customers and users, and they must understand business needs as well as software development. They also need to be good detectives, testing software thoroughly and hunting down the sources of failure.
- Measuring maintainability is difficult. To get a true measure of maintainability, we must evaluate the external behavior of a system and track the mean time between failures. But waiting until the system fails is too late, so we use internal attributes of the code, such as size and structure, to predict those parts of a software system that are likely to fail, based on past history. We use static code analyzers to help us in this identification process.
- Impact analysis builds and tracks links among the requirements, design, code, and test cases. It helps us to evaluate the effects of a change in one component on the other components.
- Software rejuvenation involves redocumenting, restructuring, reverse engineering, and reengineering. The overall goal is to make hidden information explicit, so that we can use it to improve the design and structure of the code. Although complete rejuvenation is unlikely in the near future, it is being used successfully in domains that are mature and well-understood, such as information technology.

11.10 WHAT THIS CHAPTER MEANS FOR YOUR DEVELOPMENT TEAM

Maintenance is definitely a team activity. A great deal of coordination must be used when checking out a component, changing and testing the component, and putting the revised component back into the working system. Moreover, many failures are the result of complex interactions among components, so you must communicate with your team members to get a big picture of how the software interoperates with its environment.

Your people skills are especially important during maintenance. As you seek the cause of a problem, you must talk with your colleagues, users, and customers, and each will have a different work style (as we saw in Chapter 2). So you must learn how to extract the information you need from documents and from people in the most effective ways possible, using your understanding of work styles.

11.11 WHAT THIS CHAPTER MEANS FOR RESEARCHERS

Maintenance is a ripe area of research. Many of our maintenance activities could be made easier or more effective if we were better at predicting the likely sources of faults. Researchers are looking for better ways to measure maintainability based on product information; they are developing new models to show us the interconnections among products, processes, and resources. Similarly, the models will help us know how much effort is needed to maintain a system and when it is appropriate to retire a legacy system or rejuvenate it.

Work continues on building tools to assist us in the maintenance process. Reengineering tools, change control and configuration management repositories, and project history databases are likely to become more sophisticated as researchers build prototypes based on empirical data.

Finally, researchers will continue to look at general laws of software maintenance, as suggested by Lehman (1980). They are eager to learn whether software engineering theory can confirm what empirical observation indicates in practice: namely, that the behavior of software systems evolution is consistent and predictable.

11.12 TERM PROJECT

Examine all your artifacts (requirements, design, code, test plans, documentation) for the Loan Arranger. How maintainable are they? If you had to design and implement the Loan Arranger again, what would you have done differently to make the product easier to maintain?

11.13 KEY REFERENCES

There are few up-to-date textbooks on software maintenance; most information is best sought in journals and conference proceedings. *IEEE Software*'s January 1990 issue had maintenance, reverse engineering, and design recovery as its theme; the January 1995 issue focused on legacy systems, and the January 1993 issue has a good article by Wilde, Matthews, and Huitt on the special maintenance problems of object-oriented systems. The May 1994 issue of *Communications of the ACM* is a special issue on reverse engineering. *Software Maintenance: Research and Practice* is a journal devoted entirely to maintenance issues.

The IEEE Computer Society Press offers some good tutorials on maintenance-related topics, including one on software reengineering by Arnold (1993), and another on impact analysis by Arnold and Bohner (1996).

Samuelson (1990) explores the legal implications of reverse engineering, asking whether such a practice is equivalent to stealing someone's ideas.

The International Conference on Software Maintenance is held every year, sponsored by the IEEE and ACM. You can order past proceedings from the IEEE Computer Society Press and look at information about the next maintenance conference by viewing the Computer Society Web site.

11.14 EXERCISES

1. Explain why a high degree of coupling among components can make maintenance very difficult.
2. Categorize the following systems as S-, P-, or E-systems. For each one, explain why it belongs in that category. Identify those aspects of the system that may change.
   (a) an air traffic control system
   (b) an operating system for a microcomputer
   (c) a floating-point acceleration system
   (d) a database management system
   (e) a system to find the prime factors of a number
   (f) a system to find the first prime number larger than a given number
3. There are three types of software systems: S-, P-, and E-systems. In the real world, what is the most likely type of software system? Why? Where can we find the other two types?
4. Examine a large program from one of your class projects. How must you add to the documentation so that someone else can maintain it? Discuss the pros and cons of writing this supplementary documentation as the program is developed.
5. Borrow a copy of a large program (more than 1000 lines of code) from a friend. Try to choose a program with which you are not at all familiar. How useful is the documentation? Compare the code with the documentation; how accurate is the documentation? If you were assigned to maintain this program, what additional documentation would you like to see? How does the size of the program affect your ability to maintain it?
6. As with the previous problem, examine a friend's program. Suppose you want to make a change to the code, and you must perform regression testing on the result to ensure that the program still runs properly. Are test data and a test script available for your use? Discuss the need to retain formal test datasets and scripts for maintenance purposes.
7. Explain why single-entry, single-exit components make testing easier during maintenance.
8. Is the Ariane-5 software an S-, P-, or E-system?
9. Does the McCabe cyclomatic number allow us to form an ordering of components according to quality? That is, can we always say that one component is more complex than another? Name some aspects of software complexity that are not captured by the cyclomatic number.
10. Suppose you are maintaining a large safety-critical software system. You use a model, such as Porter and Selby's, to predict which components are most likely to fail. Then, you examine those identified components carefully and perform perfective and preventive maintenance on each one. Soon after, the system undergoes a catastrophic failure, with

severe consequences to life and property. The source of the failure turns out to be a component that was not identified by your model. Are you at fault for neglecting to look at the other components?

11. Some computer science classes involve building a term project that begins as a small system and is continually enhanced until the result is complete. If you have worked on such a project, review your notes. How much time was spent defining and understanding the problem? How much time was spent implementing the code? Compare the categories of Table 11.2 with the time estimates for your project and comment on whether the differences are good or bad.

12. Review the characteristics of good software design. For each one, explain whether it will help or hinder software rejuvenation.

13. The following is a list of the version and configuration control functional criteria for configuration management tools for a British agency. Explain how each factor contributes to the ease of maintenance.

(a) Record versions or references to them.
(b) Retrieve any version on demand.
(c) Record relationships.
(d) Record relationships between versions to which the tool controls access and those to which it does not.
(e) Control security and record authorizations.
(f) Record changes to a file.
(g) Record a version's status.
(h) Assist in configuring a version.
(i) Relate to a project control tool.
(j) Produce reports.
(k) Control releases.
(l) Control itself.
(m) Archive and retrieve infrequently used files.

14. In Chapter 9 we saw the importance of configuration management in the testing phase of software development. State one reason why using such a system is important in the maintenance phase.

12 Evaluating Products, Processes, and Resources

In this chapter, we look at
- feature analysis, case studies, surveys, and experiments
- measurement and validation
- capability maturity, ISO 9000, and other process models
- people maturity
- evaluating development artifacts
- return on investment

In previous chapters, we have learned about the various activities involved in developing and maintaining software-based systems. Examples from industry and government have shown us that software developers use a large variety of methods and tools to elicit and specify requirements, design and implement systems, and test and maintain them as they evolve. How do we decide which technique or tool to use? How do we evaluate the effectiveness and efficiency of what we are already doing, so that we can tell if we are improving? When is one technique more appropriate than another for a given situation? And how do we demonstrate that our products, processes, and resources have the characteristics (such as quality) that we want them to have? In this chapter, we investigate techniques for evaluating products, processes, and resources; the next chapter presents documented examples of improvement based on following these techniques.

12.1 APPROACHES TO EVALUATION

As professionals, we are keen to evaluate our products and the ways in which we produce them. The evaluation techniques we use are similar to those in other disciplines: we measure key aspects of our products, processes, and resources and use this information to determine whether we have met goals for productivity, performance, quality, and other desirable attributes. But there are many kinds of studies, and it is important to understand which ones are most appropriate for telling us what we want to know.

We can think of an evaluation technique as being in one of four categories:

1. feature analysis
2. survey
3. case study
4. formal experiment

Feature Analysis

The simplest type of assessment is a **feature analysis**, used to rate and rank the attributes of various products so we can tell which tool to buy or method to use. For example, we may be interested in buying a design tool, and we list five key attributes that our tool should have:

1. good user interface
2. handles object-oriented design
3. checks for consistency
4. handles use cases
5. runs on a UNIX system

Next, we identify three possible tools and rate the criteria of each one from 1 (does not satisfy) to 5 (satisfies completely). Then, we examine the scores, perhaps creating a total score based on the importance of each criterion, as shown in Table 12.1. (We multiply the importance by the criterion score for each criterion and then sum.) Finally, based on the scores, we select t-OO-l as our design tool.

Feature analysis is necessarily very subjective, and the ratings reflect the raters' biases. It is useful for narrowing down which tools to buy, but it does not really evaluate behavior in terms of cause and effect. For example, feature analysis is not at all useful in determining which design technique is most effective at helping us build complete and consistent designs; in this case, we want to run controlled studies so that we can understand cause and effect.

TABLE 12.1 Design Tool Ratings

Feature	Tool 1: t-OO-1	Tool 2: ObjecTool	Tool 3: EasyDesign	Importance
Good user interface	4	5	4	3
Object-oriented design	5	5	5	5
Consistency checking	5	3	1	3
Use cases	4	4	4	2
Runs on UNIX	5	4	5	5
Score	85	77	73	

Surveys

A **survey** is a retrospective study to try to document relationships and outcomes in a given situation. Surveys are often done in the social sciences, where attitudes are polled to determine how a population feels about a particular set of issues, or a demographer surveys a population to determine trends and relationships. Software engineering surveys are similar in that we record data to determine how project participants reacted to a particular method, tool, or technique, or to determine trends or relationships. We can also capture information related to products or projects, to document the size of components, number of faults, effort expended, and so on. For example, we may compare the data from a survey of object-oriented projects with data from procedural projects to see if there are significant differences.

When performing a survey, we usually have no control over the situation at hand. Because a survey is a retrospective study, we record information about a situation and compare it with similar ones, but we cannot manipulate variables; for that, we need case studies and experiments.

Case Studies

Both case studies and formal experiments are usually not retrospective. We decide in advance what we want to investigate and then plan how to capture data to support the investigation. In a **case study**, we identify key factors that may affect an activity's outcome and then document them: inputs, constraints, resources, and outputs. By contrast, a **formal experiment** is a rigorous, controlled investigation, where an activity's key factors are identified and manipulated to document their effects on the outcome.

Both a case study and an experiment involve a sequence of steps: conception, hypothesis setting, design, preparation, execution, analysis, dissemination, and decision making. The hypothesis setting is particularly important, as it guides what we measure and how we analyze the results. The projects we select for inclusion in our study must be chosen carefully, to represent what is typical in an organization or company.

A case study usually compares one situation with another: the results of using one method or tool with the results of using another, for example. To avoid bias and make sure we are testing the relationship we hypothesize, we can organize our study in one of three ways: sister project, baseline, or random selection.

To understand the differences among the three types of case studies, consider an example. Suppose our organization is interested in modifying the way it performs code inspections. We decide to perform a case study to assess the effects of using a new inspection technique. To perform such a study, we select two projects, called **sister projects**, each of which is typical of the organization and has similar values for the independent variables that we have planned to measure. For instance, the projects may be similar in terms of application domain, implementation language, specification technique, and design method. Then, we perform inspections the current way on the first project and the new way on the second project. By selecting projects that are as similar as possible, we are controlling as much as we can. This situation allows us to attribute any differences in result to the difference in inspection technique.

However, if we are unable to find two projects similar enough to be sister projects, we can compare our new inspection technique with a general **baseline**. Here, our company or organization gathers data from its various projects, regardless of how different one project is from another. In addition to the variable information mentioned before, the data can include descriptive measures, such as product size, effort expended, number of faults discovered, and so on. Then, we can calculate measures of central tendency and dispersion on the data in the database, so we have some idea of the "average" situation that is typical in our company. Our case study involves completing a project using the new inspection technique and then comparing the results with the baseline. In some cases, we may be able to select from the organizational database a subset of projects that are similar to the one using the new inspection technique; again, the subset adds a degree of control to our study, giving us more confidence that any differences in result are caused by the difference in inspection technique.

We do not always have the luxury of finding two or more projects to study, especially when we are examining the first use of a new technique or tool. In this case, we may be able to use **random selection** to partition a single project into parts, where one part uses the new technique and the other does not. Here, the case study involves a great deal of control, because we are taking advantage of randomization and replication in performing our analysis. It is not a formal experiment, however, because the project was not selected at random from among the others in the company or organization. In this case, we randomly assign the code components to either the old inspection technique or the new. The randomization helps reduce the experimental error and balance out confounding factors (i.e., factors whose results affect one another).

Random selection is particularly useful for situations where the method being studied can take on a variety of values. For example, we may want to determine whether preparation time affects the effectiveness of the inspections. We record the preparation time as well as component size and faults discovered. We can then investigate whether increased preparation time results in a higher detection rate.

Formal Experiments

Formal experiments are the most controlled type of study and are discussed at length in Fenton and Pfleeger (1997). In a **formal experiment**, values of independent variables are manipulated, and we observe changes in dependent variables to determine how changes in the input affect changes in the output. For example, we may examine the effect of a tool or technique on product quality or programmer productivity; or we may try to discover the relationship between preparation time and inspection effectiveness.

In a formal experiment, several methods are used to reduce bias and eliminate confounding factors so that cause and effect can be evaluated with some confidence. For example, randomization is used to ensure that the selection of experimental subjects is not biased in any way by the selection technique. Often, we measure replicated instances of an activity, so that multiple data sets add to our confidence in the results we see. In other words, when we see something cause an effect several times, instead of just once, we are more certain that the effect resulted from the cause rather than by chance.

Formal experiments are designed carefully, so that the instances we observe are as representative as possible. For example, if we have novice, master, and expert programmers on a project, and we are comparing two techniques, we design our experiment so that all three types of programmers use each of the two techniques; then, we compare the results from all six combinations of programmer type and technique.

Preparing for an Evaluation

No matter what kind of evaluation we choose to do, there are several key steps to making sure we are focused and can identify the appropriate variables.

Setting the Hypothesis. We begin by deciding what we wish to investigate, expressed as a hypothesis we want to test. That is, we must specify exactly what it is that we want to know. The **hypothesis** is the tentative theory or supposition that we think explains the behavior we want to explore. For example, our hypothesis may be

> Using the cleanroom method produces better-quality software than using the SSADM method.

Whether we examine past records to assess what happened when a particular group used each method (a survey), evaluate a "snapshot" of our organization as it is using cleanroom (a case study), or do a carefully controlled comparison of those using cleanroom with those using SSADM (a formal experiment), we are testing to see if the data we collect will confirm or refute the hypothesis we have stated.

Wherever possible, we state the hypothesis in quantifiable terms, so that it is easy to tell whether the hypothesis is confirmed or refuted. For example, we can define "quality" in terms of the number of faults found and restate the hypothesis as

> Code produced using the cleanroom method has a lower number of faults per thousand lines of code than code produced using the SSADM method.

Quantifying the hypothesis often leads to the use of surrogate measures. That is, in order to identify a quantity with a factor or aspect we want to measure (e.g., quality), we must measure the factor indirectly using something associated with that factor (e.g., faults). Because the surrogate is an indirect measure, there is danger that a change in the surrogate is not the same as a change in the original factor. For example, faults (or lack thereof) may not accurately reflect the quality of the software: Finding a large number of faults during testing may mean that the testing was very thorough and the resulting product is nearly fault-free, or it may mean that development was sloppy and there are likely to be many more faults left in the product. Similarly, delivered lines of code may not accurately reflect the amount of effort required to complete the product, since that measure does not take into account issues like reuse or prototyping. Therefore, along with a quantifiable hypothesis, we document the relationship between the measures and the factors they intend to reflect. In particular, whenever possible, we use quantitative terms that are as direct and unambiguous at possible.

Maintaining Control Over Variables. Once we have an explicit hypothesis, we must decide what variables can affect its truth. Then, for each variable identified, we decide how much control we have over it. For example, if we are investigating the effect of a design method on the quality of the resulting software, but we have no control over who is using which design method, then we do a case study to document the results. Experiments are done only when we can manipulate behavior directly, precisely, and systematically. Thus, if we can control who uses the cleanroom method, who uses SSADM, and when and where they are used, then we can perform an experiment. This type of manipulation can be done in a "toy" situation, where events are organized to simulate their appearance in the real world, or in a "field" situation, where events are monitored as they actually happen.

In an experiment, we sample *over* the independent variables, so that we represent all possible cases. But in a case study, we sample *from* the variables, selecting values that are typical for the participating organization and its projects. For instance, an experiment involving the effects of language would choose a set of projects to cover as many languages as possible; by contrast, a case study might involve choosing a language that is used on most of the organization's projects.

Making the Investigation Meaningful. There are many areas of software engineering that can be analyzed using surveys, case studies, and experiments. One key motivator for using a formal experiment rather than a case study or survey is that the results of an experiment are usually more generalizable. That is, if we use a survey or case study to understand what is happening in a certain organization, the results apply only to that organization (and perhaps to organizations that are very similar). But because a formal experiment is carefully controlled and contrasts different values of the controlled variables, its results are generally applicable to a wider community and across several organizations. It is important to remember that we cannot control everything; software engineering experiments are not like biology or chemistry experiments. We must take into account the limitations and lack of control when deciding whether study results apply to a new situation.

12.2 SELECTING AN EVALUATION TECHNIQUE

Kitchenham, Pickard, and Pfleeger (1995) note that the differences among the research methods are also reflected in their scale. By their nature, since formal experiments require a great deal of control, they tend to be small, involving small numbers of people or events. We can think of experiments as "research in the small." Case studies usually look at a typical project, rather than trying to capture information about all possible cases; these can be thought of as "research in the typical." And surveys try to poll what is happening broadly over large groups of projects: "research in the large."

Key Selection Factors

Several general guidelines can help us decide whether to perform a survey, a case study, or a formal experiment. As we have seen, control is a key element in our decision. If we have a high level of control over the variables that can affect the outcome, then we consider an experiment. If we do not have that control, a case study is the preferred technique. But the level of control satisfies the technical concerns; we must also address practical concerns. It may be possible but very difficult to control the variables, either because of the high cost of doing so or the degree of risk involved. For example, safety-critical systems may entail a high degree of risk in experimentation, and a case study may be more feasible.

Kitchenham, Pickard, and Pfleeger (1995) point out that a formal experiment is especially useful for investigating alternative methods of performing a particular self-standing task. For instance, we can perform an experiment to determine if VDM is better than statecharts for specifying a set of requirements. Here, the self-standing task can be isolated from the rest of the development process, but the task is still embedded in the usual way the code is developed. Also, the self-standing task can be judged immediately, so that the experiment does not delay project completion. On the other hand, a case study may be preferable to a formal experiment if the process changes caused by the independent variables are wide-ranging, requiring the effects to be measured at a high level and across too many dependent variables to control and measure.

Another consideration is the degree to which we can replicate the basic situation we are investigating. For instance, suppose we want to investigate the effects of language on the resulting software. Can we develop the same project multiple times using a different language each time? If replication is not possible, then we cannot do a formal experiment. However, even when replication is possible, the cost of replication may be prohibitive. For example, if the study we want to do has a low replication cost, then an experiment is more appropriate than a case study. Similarly, if we have no control (i.e., the difficulty of control is high), then we should consider a case study.

What to Believe

Research reports contain conclusions of case studies, surveys, and formal experiments. But it is not always easy for us to tell which results apply to our circumstances. For example, consider the decision to move from COBOL to a fourth-generation language (4GL), one that is not as straightforward as it seems. In the 1980s, several interesting studies compared the use of COBOL with various 4GLs for implementing relatively simple business systems applications: Misra and Jalics (1988), Verner and Tate (1988), and Matos and Jalics (1989). The findings of these studies were fascinating but conflicting. Some showed productivity improving by a factor of 4 to 5 with 4GLs, whereas others found improvements of only 29% to 39%. Some showed that object-code performance degraded by factors ranging from 15 to 174 for 4GLs, but in some cases, the opposite happened: 4GLs produced code that was six times as fast as the equivalent COBOL!

When results conflict, how do we know which study to believe? We can use a series of questions, represented by the game board in Figure 12.1, to understand how to sort through these studies. The answers to the questions tell us when we have enough information to draw a valid conclusion about a relationship between factors. To begin, suppose our project team is interested in improving the quality of the code it produces. We want to determine which factors improve quality, so that our team can use appropriate techniques or tools to generate better code. First, we decide to measure quality by counting faults per thousand lines of code; then, we decide that a high-quality system is one having fewer than five faults per thousand lines of code. Next, we attempt to find out what affects code quality by examining population studies, where characteristics of a large population of developers are examined for associations among variables. For example, we read about a survey in another organization, reporting that code quality improves when the developers use a design tool. How do we know if this result is valid? It is possible that the study has fallen into pitfall 1, shown in Table 12.2.

Pitfall 1 is confounding factors, where it is impossible to tell which of two factors is causing the results that are observed. For example, if new programmers never use the design tool and experienced programmers always do, it is impossible to tell if the

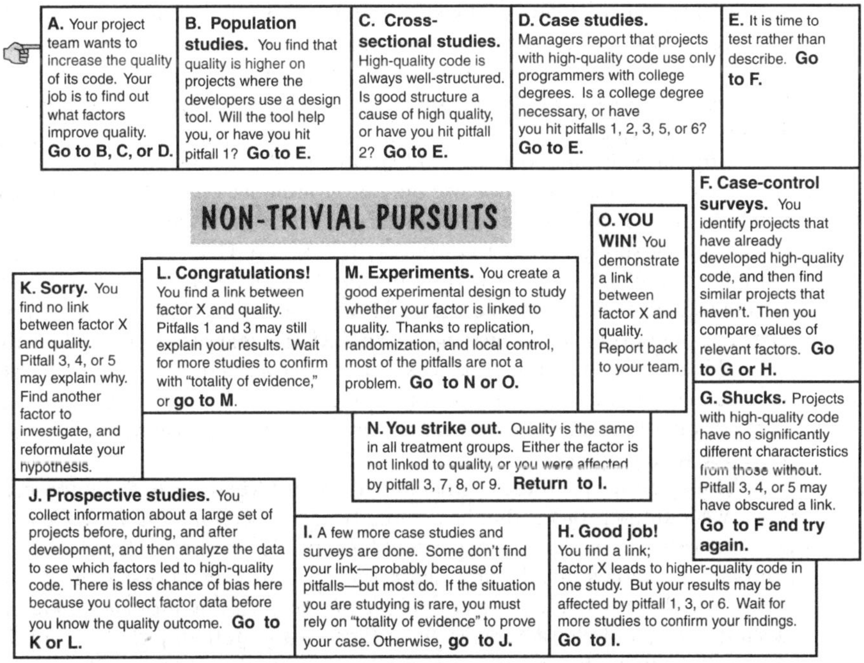

FIGURE 12.1 Investigation and evaluation (adapted with permission from Liebman 1994).

experienced programmers' code has fewer failures in the field because of the tool or because of their experience. Thus, when factors are confounded, it is possible that another factor is causing the quality to improve. If we cannot rule out confounding factors, we must do a more careful study, represented by box E in Figure 12.1.

However, suppose instead we look at a cross-sectional study (box C); that is, we select a representative sample of projects or products to examine. Suppose that by considering a cross-section of the code that our organization has produced, we find that

TABLE 12.2 Common Pitfalls in Evaluation (Adapted with Permission from Liebman 1994)

Pitfall	Description
1. Confounding	Another factor is causing the effect.
2. Cause or effect?	The factor could be a result, not a cause, of the treatment.
3. Chance	There is always a small possibility that the result happened by chance.
4. Homogeneity	No link is found because all subjects had the same level of the factor.
5. Misclassification	No link is found because the subjects' levels of the factor could not be accurately classified.
6. Bias	Selection procedures or administration of the study inadvertently bias the result.
7. Too short	The short-term effects are different from the long-term ones.
8. Wrong amount	The factor would have had an effect, but not in the amount used in the study.
9. Wrong situation	The factor has the desired effect, but not in the situation studied.

high-quality code is always well-structured. Is good structure a cause of good quality, or have we confused cause with effect (pitfall 2)? In fact, the good structure could be the result of some other action (such as use of a design tool or editor), and not a cause itself. Thus, we must do a more careful study, turning from descriptive investigations to ones that test hypotheses.

Alternatively, suppose we find a case study in the literature suggesting that projects with high-quality code use only programmers with college degrees. Before we conclude that a college degree is necessary in our organization, we must decide whether the result is subject to pitfalls 1, 2, 3, 5, or 6. That is, the high quality could be caused by a confounding factor, by confusing cause with effect, or simply by chance. Or the high-quality code could be the result of misclassification; perhaps all of the company's developers have college degrees, so having a degree will correlate with any other factor. Finally, the study might be biased; the programmers selected for the study might have been chosen exactly because they have degrees (i.e., the nondegreed developers were left out of the study), so we cannot draw a valid conclusion about the relationship of degree to high quality.

Thus, we turn to studies with a much higher level of control. Suppose, as noted in box F, we identify projects that have already developed high-quality code and then find projects with similar characteristics that have produced code of lower quality. Next, we compare the values of relevant factors to see if one or more factors distinguish the high- from the low-quality projects. If the projects with high-quality code have no significantly different characteristics from those without, then pitfall 3, 4, or 5 may have obscured the link. That is, there is a small possibility that chance led to no difference in the code, that all subjects had the same levels of each factor, or that we have misclassified some factors.

On the other hand, we may find that factor X led to high-quality code. If we are sure that confounding factors, chance, or bias has not influenced the study, then we may want to wait for more studies to confirm our findings.

Suppose that we do many more case studies and surveys, or we find several of them in the literature. Some do not exhibit the link between factor X and quality (probably because of pitfalls), but most of them do. If the situation in which we are studying these factors is rare (e.g., the application domain is new or the approach to solving the problem is rarely used), then we must rely on the "totality of evidence" to prove our case. That is, we must assume that most of the time we can rely on factor X to improve the code's quality.

If the situation is not rare, then we can do prospective studies. We collect information about a large set of projects before, during, and after development. Then, we analyze the data to see which factors lead to high-quality code. There is much less chance of bias in this type of study, since we collect factor data before we know the resulting quality. If we find no link between factor X and quality, chance, homogeneity, or misclassification (pitfalls 3, 4, and 5) might explain why. At this point, if we are certain that the pitfalls did not affect us, it is time to revise our hypothesis.

Alternatively, suppose we find a link between X and quality. The link may still be the result of confounding factors or chance, and we may want to wait for more studies to confirm the finding with "totality of evidence." But if we want stronger evidence that X leads to quality, we can run a formal experiment. By using good experimental design and controlling factors carefully, we can study whether factor X is linked to quality. By using techniques such as replication, randomization, and local control, we can avoid most of the pitfalls in Table 12.2.

When our experiment is complete, we may find that the quality is the same in all treatment groups; thus, either the factor is not related to quality, or we were affected by chance, or pitfall 7, 8, or 9. We probably need to conduct more studies. If our experiment indeed demonstrates a link between factor X and quality, we can report back to our project team about our discovery.

Thus, each of the various types of empirical investigations plays a part in learning how various process, product, and resource factors affect software quality. The type and number of studies depend on time, cost, practicality, and necessity. In particular, the more control, the stronger the study. To understand the difference between a collection of case studies and a collection of experiments, consider the difference between the juries of civil and criminal trials in the United States. For a civil trial, the jury must determine that a preponderance of evidence supports the plaintiff's case against the defendant. Thus, if only 51% of the evidence is in the plaintiff's favor, then the jury must find for the plaintiff. However, in a criminal trial, the jury must find evidence beyond a reasonable doubt—that is, the jury must be reasonably certain that the defendant is guilty. Similarly, if we are satisfied that the totality of evidence is convincing enough to switch to a new technique or tool, then a collection of case studies can support our decision. However, if cost or quality concerns (such as those involved in building safety- or business-critical systems) require that we have evidence beyond a shadow of a doubt, then we probably should look for experiments to support our decision, or even conduct experiments of our own.

This board game and its associated investigative pitfalls offer us guidelines in making decisions about software technology. But software engineering does not always present easily controlled situations, so we must be realistic and practical. Researchers control what they can, while understanding the possible effects of uncontrolled factors, to investigate the effectiveness of actions. We can evaluate their reported results and apply them appropriately to our own environment. Studies that we read about or perform ourselves can discover relationships in software development that can help us to make informed decisions and to build better products.

12.3 ASSESSMENT VS. PREDICTION

Evaluation always involves measurement. We capture information to distinguish different values of dependent and independent variables, and we manipulate the information to increase our understanding. In addition, measurement helps us to separate typical from unusual situations, or to define baselines and set goals.

Formally, a **measure** is a mapping from a set of entities and attributes in the real empirical world to a representation or model in the mathematical world. For instance, we consider the set of people and their attributes, such as height, weight, and hair color; then, we can define mappings that capture properties of people and preserve relationships. For example, we can say that Hughie is 2 meters tall, Dewey is 2.4 meters tall, and Louie is 2.5 meters tall. Then, we can manipulate the numbers or symbols in the mathematical world to obtain more information and understanding about the real world. In our example, we learn that the average height of the three is 2.3, so two of our set are above average in height.

Similarly, we can map hair color to the set {brown, blonde, red, black}; the symbols need not be numbers. We can use the hair-color mapping to generate distributions, telling us that 67% of our sample has brown hair and 33% black. A formal framework and description of measurement theory can be found in Fenton and Pfleeger (1997).

A large number of software measures capture information about product, process, or resource attributes. Fenton and Pfleeger describe the derivation and application of many of these measures. Finding the best one for the purpose at hand can be difficult, because candidates measure or predict the same attribute (e.g., cost, size, or complexity) in very different ways. For example, we saw in Chapter 5 that there are dozens of ways to measure design complexity. So the measurement can seem confusing: there are different measures for the same thing, and sometimes one can even imply the opposite of another! The source of the confusion is often the lack of software measurement validation. That is, the measures may not actually capture the attribute information we seek.

To understand software measurement validation, consider two kinds of systems (Fenton and Pfleeger 1997):

1. *Measurement systems* are used to assess an existing entity by numerically characterizing one or more of its attributes.
2. *Prediction systems* are used to predict some attribute of a future entity, involving a mathematical model with associated prediction procedures.

Informally, we say that a **measure is valid** if it accurately characterizes the attribute it claims to measure. On the other hand, a **prediction system is valid** if it makes accurate predictions. So not only are measures different from prediction systems, but also the notion of validation is different for each.

Validating Prediction Systems

We validate a prediction system in a given environment by establishing its accuracy by empirical means; that is, we compare the model's performance with known data in the given environment. We state a hypothesis about the prediction, and then we look at data to see whether the hypothesis is supported or refuted. For example, we may want to know whether COCOMO is valid for a given type of development project. We can use data that represent that type and then assess the accuracy of COCOMO in predicting effort and duration. This type of validation is well-accepted by the software engineering community. For example, Sidebar 12.1 describes the evaluation of reliability prediction models.

When validating models, acceptable accuracy depends on several things, including who is doing the assessment. Novice estimators may not be as accurate as experienced estimators. We also consider the difference between **deterministic** prediction systems (we always get the same output for a given input) and **stochastic** prediction systems (the output for a given input will vary probabilistically) with respect to a given model.

SIDEBAR 12.1 COMPARING SOFTWARE RELIABILITY PREDICTIONS

Chapter 9 described reliability prediction and presented several techniques and models for helping developers predict a system's likely reliability in the field. The software engineering literature contains many more techniques and models in articles showing how a model's application has been successful on a given project or in a particular domain.

However, the broader question of which model is best in a given circumstance has not been addressed very often. Lanubile (1996) describes work performed with Visaggio at the University of Bari (Italy) to replicate past studies and apply various techniques to 27 Pascal programs developed from the same information system specification; these programs contained 118 components to study. Lanubile and Visaggio defined a component to be high risk if its faults were discovered during testing, and low risk if no faults were discovered. Then, using independent variables such as fan-in, fan-out, information flow, cyclomatic number, lines of code, and comment density, they examined seven prediction techniques in terms of their false negatives (misclassifying a high-risk component as low risk), false positives (misclassifying a low-risk component as high risk), completeness (the percentage of high-risk components that were actually classified correctly), and wasted inspection (the percentage of identified components that were classified incorrectly).

Of the 118 components, two-thirds were used to define and tune the models, and the remaining one-third was used for validation. This approach is typical; the data used to build the model are called the **fit data**, and the remaining data that are used to test the model are called the **test data**. The results, shown in Table 12.3, show that none of the techniques was good at discriminating between the components with faults and those without. In fact, Lanubile and Visaggio compared the results to those obtained simply by flipping a coin for each component ("heads" is high risk, "tails" is low risk) and found no model to be significantly better at finding the high-risk components without wasting a lot of effort. They note that "publishing only empirical studies with positive findings can give practitioners unrealistic expectations that are quickly followed by equally unrealistic disillusionment." Further, they say that "a predictive model, from the simplest to the most complex, is worthwhile only if used with a local process to select metrics that are valid as predictors.

In a stochastic model, we allow for a window of error around the actual value, and the width of the window can vary. Prediction systems for software cost estimation, effort estimation, schedule estimation, and reliability have large margins of error; we say that they are very stochastic. For example, we may find that, under certain circumstances, our organization's reliability prediction is accurate to within 20%; that is, the predicted time to next failure will be within 20% of the actual time. We describe this window by using an **acceptance range**: a statement of the maximum difference between prediction and actual value. Thus, 20% is the model's acceptance range. Depending on the circumstances, we may find a large window too wide to be useful; for instance, the window may be too large for effective maintenance planning. Other managers may feel

TABLE 12.3 Results of Comparing Prediction Models (Lanubile 1996) © 1996 IEEE

Modeling Technique	Predictive Validity	Proportion of False Negatives (%)	Proportion of False Positives (%)	Proportion of False Classifications (%)	Completeness (%)	Overall Inspection (%)	Wasted Inspection (%)
Discriminant analysis	$p = 0.621$	28	26	54	42	46	56
Principal component analysis plus discriminant analysis	$p = 0.408$	15	41	56	68	74	55
Logistic regression	$p = 0.491$	28	28	56	42	49	58
Principal component analysis plus logistic regression	$p = 0.184$	13	46	59	74	82	56
Logical classification model	$p = 0.643$	26	21	46	47	44	47
Layered neural network	$p = 0.421$	28	28	56	42	49	58
Holographic network	$p = 0.634$	26	28	54	47	51	55
Heads or tails?	$p = 1.000$	25	25	50	50	50	50

comfortable with a large acceptance range, given the uncertainties of software development. We must always state in advance what range is acceptable before using a prediction system.

Models present a particularly difficult problem when we design an experiment or case study, because their predictions can affect the outcome. That is, the predictions become goals, and the developers strive to meet the goal, intentionally or not. This effect is common when cost and schedule models are used, and project managers turn the predictions into targets for completion. For this reason, experiments evaluating models are sometimes designed as "double-blind" experiments, where the participants do not know what the prediction is until after the experiment is done. On the other hand, some models, such as reliability models, do not influence the outcome, since reliability measured as mean time to failure cannot be evaluated until the software is ready for use in the field. Thus, the time between consecutive failures cannot be "managed" in the same way that project schedules and budgets are managed.

Prediction systems need not be complex to be useful. For example, Fuchs reports that weather predictions in Austria are accurate 67% of the time when they are based on the previous day's weather. Using sophisticated computer models increases this accuracy only by 3% (Fenton and Pfleeger 1997)!

Validating Measures

Validating a software measure is very different from validating a prediction system. We want to be sure that the measure captures the attribute properties it is supposed to capture. For example, does the cyclomatic number measure size or complexity? The **representation condition** says that the relationships among the numerical values of a measure correspond to the attribute's relationships we perceive in the real world. Thus, if we define a measure of height, then we must make sure that the height measure is larger for James than for Suzanne when James is taller than Suzanne. To validate a measure, we demonstrate that the representation condition holds for the measure and its corresponding attribute.

For example, suppose that a researcher defines a measure m that is claimed to measure the length of a program. To validate m, we must build a formal model that describes programs and a function that preserves our intuitive notions of length in relations that describe the programs. We can check to see that m behaves in expected ways. For instance, suppose we concatenate two programs P_1 and P_2 to yield a program whose length is the combined lengths of P_1 and P_2. Then m should satisfy

$$m(P_1, P_2) = m(P_1) + m(P_2)$$

Likewise, if program P_1 is longer than P_2, then

$$m(P_1) > m(P_2)$$

Many length measures can be validated in this way, including lines of code, a count of operators and operands, and a count of semicolons. The validation exercise assures us that measures are defined properly and are consistent with the entity's real-world behavior. When validating a measure, it is important to remember to view it in the context in which it will be used; a single measure may be valid for one purpose but not for another. For instance, the cyclomatic number may be valid for measuring number of independent paths but not for measuring ease of understanding (see Sidebar 12.2).

A Stringent Requirement for Validation

It is possible for a measure to serve both purposes: as an attribute measure and as input to a prediction system. For example, lines of code can measure program size and are sometimes useful as a predictor of faults. But a measure can be one or the other without being both. We should not reject a measure as invalid because it is not part of a prediction system. If a measure is valid for assessment, we call it **valid in the narrow sense** or **internally valid**. Many attributes are internally valid and are also useful in prediction. A measure is **valid in the wide sense** if it is both internally valid and a component of a prediction system.

Suppose we want to demonstrate that a particular measure is valid in the wide sense. We begin by stating a hypothesis to propose a specific relationship between the measure and an attribute. Then, we should conduct a carefully controlled experiment that shows that the relationship is confirmed by empirical data. The evidence must be more than a statistical correlation; we must demonstrate cause and effect. For example,

SIDEBAR 12.2 LINES OF CODE AND CYCLOMATIC NUMBER

It is easy to show that the number of lines of code is a valid measure of program size. However, it is not a valid measure of complexity, nor is it part of an accurate prediction system for complexity. Fenton and Pfleeger (1997) explain that the fault lies not with the lines of code measure, but with the imprecise definition of complexity. Although complexity is generally described as an attribute that can affect reliability, maintainability, cost, and more, the fuzziness surrounding its definition presents a problem in complexity research.

But problems with complexity do not prevent lines of code from being useful for measuring attributes other than size. For example, suppose there is a stochastic association between a large number of lines of code and a large number of unit testing faults. This relationship can help us select a testing strategy and reduce risk.

On the other hand, there are many studies that exhibit a significant correlation between lines of code and the cyclomatic number. Does this correlation prove that the cyclomatic number increases with size? If the cyclomatic number were a measure of size, then larger code would always be more complex code. It is easy to build a counterexample to this hypothesis. If we examine carefully the data that show the relationship between the cyclomatic number and lines of code, what we see is that the number of decisions in a component usually increases with code length.

we may claim that a measure of modularity is a good predictor of cost. To demonstrate that the measure is valid, we must model the relationship between modularity and development cost; the model must show all the factors that interconnect and affect modularity and cost. Then, we must show that a change in modularity always has a clear effect on cost. Only then can we judge whether measuring modularity is the same as measuring development cost.

Software engineers sometimes forget that statistical correlation is not the same as cause and effect. Just because marriage is strongly correlated with divorce does not mean that "is married" is a valid measure of divorce! Likewise, although there may be a statistical correlation between modularity and development costs, modularity may not be the only factor determining development cost. It is tempting to measure what is available and easy to measure, but as scientists, we must build models and capture complex relationships.

Courtney and Gustafson (1993) present a compelling statistical reason why we must be wary of the correlation approach. Unstructured correlation studies can identify spurious associations. For example, with a 0.05 significance level, we can expect a significant but spurious correlation 1 in 20 times by chance. So if we have 5 independent variables and look at the 10 possible pairwise correlations between them, there is a 0.5 probability of getting a spurious correlation! In situations like this, with no hypothesis about the reason for a relationship, we have no real confidence that the relationship is not spurious.

12.4 EVALUATING PRODUCTS

We have seen that software development produces a large number of artifacts: requirements, designs, code components, test cases, test scripts, user guides, cross-references, and more. In each case, we can examine a product to determine if it has desirable attributes. That is, we can ask whether a document, file, or system has certain properties, such as completeness, consistency, reliability, or maintainability. And we can use the notions of quality, such as the McCall model introduced in Chapter 1, to provide a framework for our questions.

Product Quality Models

There are several quality models that suggest ways to tie together different quality attributes. Each model helps us to understand how the several facets contribute to the whole. Often, we narrow our focus and think only about faults and failures; these models show us that quality is much broader. When we evaluate the quality of development products, we must see this bigger picture.

Boehm's Model. There are many software quality models, and Boehm and colleagues have constructed one of the best-known, shown in Figure 12.2. It is similar to McCall's in that it presents a hierarchy of characteristics, each of which contributes to overall quality (Boehm et al. 1978). Note that Boehm's notion of successful software includes the needs and expectations of users, as does McCall's; however, Boehm also includes characteristics of hardware performance that are missing in the McCall model. Let us examine Boehm's model in more detail.

Boehm's model begins with the general utility of the software. Thus, Boehm and his colleagues are asserting that first and foremost, a software system must be useful. If it is not, then its development has been a waste of time, money, and effort. We can consider utility in several ways, corresponding to the types of users who remain involved once the system is delivered.

The first type of user is the original customer, who is pleased with the utility of the system if it does what the customer wants it to do. However, there may be others who want to use the system on another computer or at another location. In this case, the system must be **portable** so that it can be moved from one computer to another and still function properly. The system should also be portable in a slightly different sense. Sometimes, an overall configuration remains the same, but the hardware or software is upgraded to a newer model or version. In this case, the system should be able to be moved to the new or different model or version without disturbing the functionality of the system. For example, if one programming language compiler is replaced by another compiler for the same language, the system's functions should not be degraded. Thus, the second type of user of a system is the one involved with this upgraded or changed system.

Finally, the third type of user is the programmer who maintains the system, making any changes that may be needed as customer requirements change or as errors are detected. Programmers must be able to locate the source of an error, find the modules that perform a particular function, understand the code, and modify it.

All three types of users hope that the system is reliable and efficient. As we noted in Chapter 9, **reliability** means that the system runs properly for very long periods of

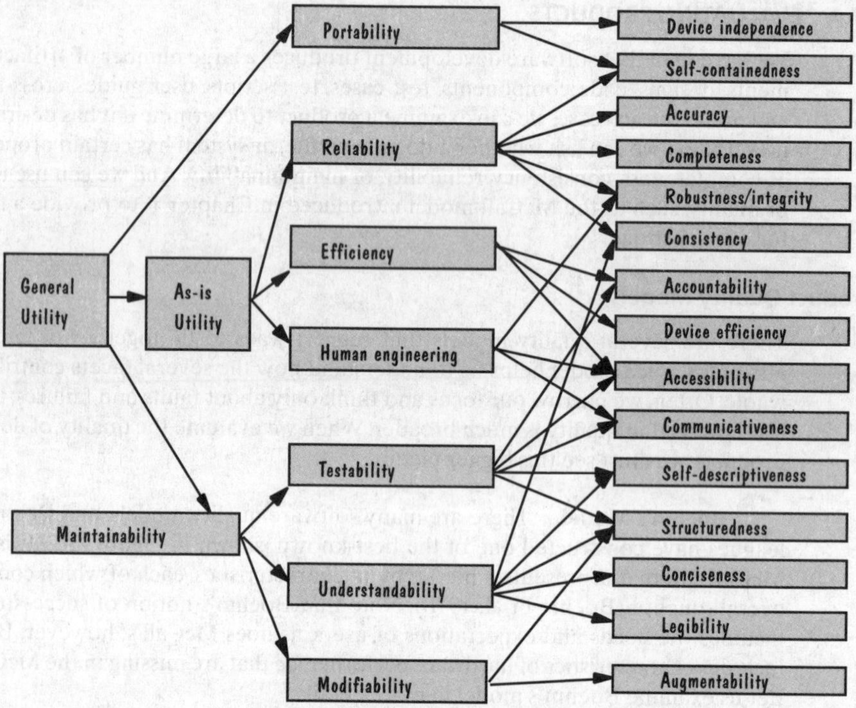

FIGURE 12.2 Boehm's quality model.

time without failure. According to Boehm's model, many software characteristics contribute to reliability, including accuracy, robustness, and completeness. In particular, if the system produces the correct result to the correct degree of accuracy, we say that the system has **integrity**, an attribute necessary for reliability. Moreover, if the same set of input data is submitted to the system many times under the same conditions, the results should match; this characteristic is called **consistency** of function.

At the same time, the system should produce its results or perform its functions in a timely manner, as determined by the needs of the customer. Thus, data should be accessible when needed, and the system should respond to the user in a reasonable amount of time.

Finally, the users and programmers must find the system easy to learn and to use. This human engineering aspect can sometimes be the most critical. A system may be very good at performing a function, but if users cannot understand how to use it, the system is a failure.

Thus, Boehm's model asserts that quality software is software that satisfies the needs of the users and programmers involved with it. It reflects an understanding of quality where the software

- does what the user wants it do
- uses computer resources correctly and efficiently

- is easy for the user to learn and use
- is well-designed, well-coded, and easily tested and maintained

ISO 9126. In the early 1990s, the software engineering community attempted to consolidate the many views of quality into one model that could act as a worldwide standard for measuring software quality. The result was ISO 9126, a hierarchical model with six major attributes contributing to quality (International Standardization Organization 1991). Figure 12.3 illustrates the hierarchy, and Table 12.4 defines the major attributes.

The standard recommends measuring the right-hand characteristics directly, but it does not give details about how the measurement is to be done.

One major difference between the ISO model and those of McCall and Boehm is that the ISO hierarchy is strict: each right-hand characteristic is related only to exactly one left-hand attribute. Moreover, the right-hand characteristics are related to the user view of the software, rather than to an internal, developer view.

These models, and many others, are helpful in articulating just what it is that we value in the software we build and use. But none of the models includes a rationale for why some characteristics are included and others left out, and for where in the hierarchy a particular attribute appears. For example, why do none of the models include safety? And why is portability a top-level characteristic in the ISO 9126 model, rather than a subcharacteristic? In addition, there is no guidance about how to compose lower-level characteristics into higher-level ones, to produce an overall assessment of quality. These problems make it difficult for us to determine if a given model is complete or consistent.

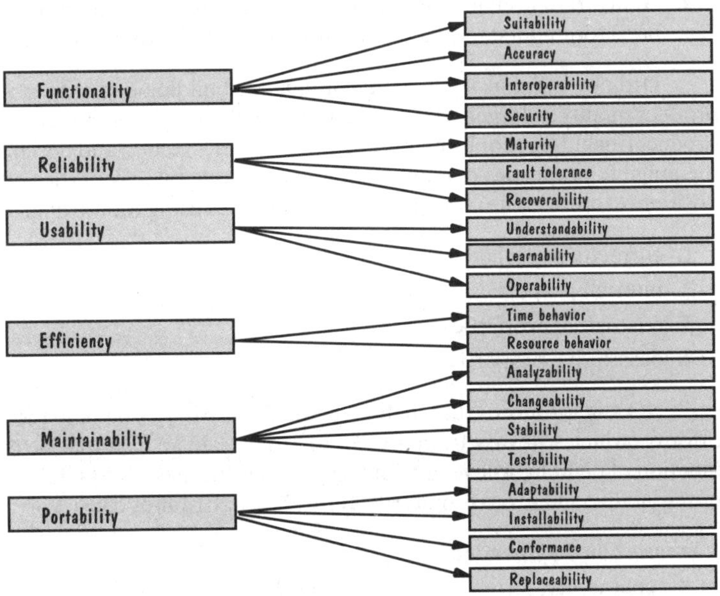

FIGURE 12.3 ISO 9126 quality model.

TABLE 12.4 ISO 9126 Quality Characteristics

Quality Characteristic	Definition
Functionality	A set of attributes that bear on the existence of a set of functions and their specified properties. The functions are those that satisfy stated or implied needs.
Reliability	A set of attributes that bear on the capability of software to maintain its performance level under stated conditions for a stated period of time.
Usability	A set of attributes that bear on the effort needed for use and on the individual assessment of such use by a stated or implied set of users.
Efficiency	A set of attributes that bear on the relationship between the software's performance and the amount of resources used under stated conditions.
Maintainability	A set of attributes that bear on the effort needed to make specified modifications (which may include corrections, improvements, or adaptations of software to environmental changes and changes in the requirements and functional specifications).
Portability	A set of attributes that bear on the ability of software to be transferred from one environment to another (including the organizational, hardware, or software environment).

Dromey's Model. Dromey has addressed these issues by proposing a way to construct a product-based quality model, all of whose lowest-level characteristics are measurable (Dromey 1996). His technique is based on two issues:

1. Many product properties appear to influence software quality.
2. Apart from a small amount of anecdotal, empirical evidence, there is little formal basis for understanding which lower-level attributes affect the higher-level ones.

Dromey suggests a generic technique for building a quality model. He notes that product quality is largely determined by the choice of components that comprise the product (including requirements documents, user's guides, and designs, as well as code), the tangible properties of components, and the tangible properties of component composition. Moreover, he classifies tangible qualities using four properties:

1. correctness properties
2. internal properties
3. contextual properties
4. descriptive properties

Next, he proposes that high-level quality attributes be only those that are of high priority (which will vary from project to project). In an example, he considers the combination of eight high-level attributes: the six attributes of ISO 9126, plus the attributes of reusability and process maturity. Reusability attributes consist of

- machine independence
- separability
- configurability

and process maturity attributes consist of

- client orientation
- well-definedness
- assurance
- effectiveness

To make these characteristics more tangible, Dromey combines the attributes with his framework to obtain the linkage shown in Figure 12.4. Then, he evaluates each type of software component in light of the framework; two examples are shown in Figure 12.5. The model is based on following five steps:

1. identifying a set of high-level quality attributes
2. identifying the product components
3. identifying and classifying the most significant, tangible, quality-carrying properties for each component
4. proposing a set of axioms for linking product properties to quality attributes
5. evaluating the model, identifying its weaknesses, and refining or re-creating it

Clearly, these steps can be used to produce models for requirements, designs, code, and other development products, and each model will reflect product and project goals.

Establishing Baselines and Targets

Another way to evaluate or assess a product is to compare it with a baseline. A **baseline** describes, in some measurable way, the usual or typical result in an organization or category. For example, we may say that the average or typical project in a company is 30,000 lines of code; we can also note that the typical project organization discovers one

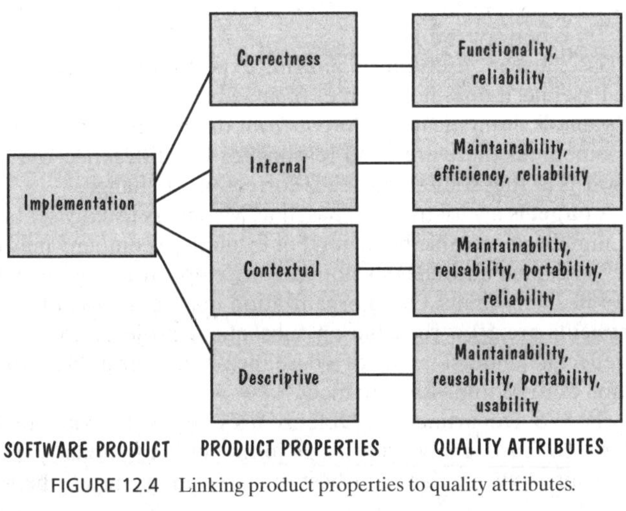

FIGURE 12.4 Linking product properties to quality attributes.

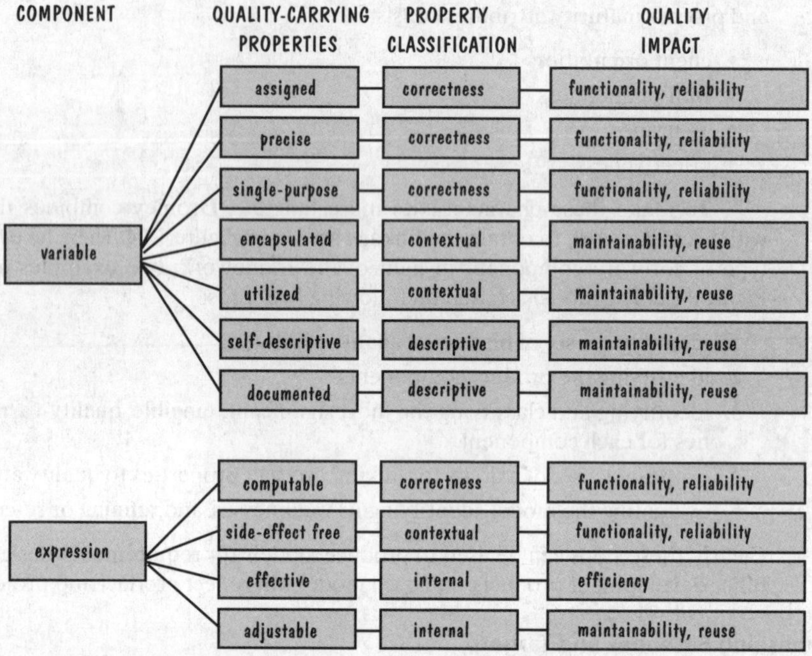

FIGURE 12.5 Product properties and their effect on quality.

fault per thousand lines of code in inspections and three faults per thousand lines of code in testing. Thus, 30,000 lines of code is the baseline size for that company, and three faults per thousand lines of code is the baseline fault discovery rate for testing. Other projects are compared against the baseline; code is smaller or larger, and fault discovery is better or worse.

Baselines are useful for managing expectations. When a particular value is close to the baseline, it does not warn us of any aberrant behavior. On the other hand, when some value is dramatically different from the baseline, we usually want to investigate why. Sometimes there are good reasons for the difference, but other times the difference warns us that something needs correction or change.

A **target** is a variation of a baseline. Managers usually set targets as ways of defining minimally acceptable behavior. For example, a company may declare that it will not deliver a product until the developers can demonstrate that they have removed at least 95% of its likely faults. Or an organization may set a target to develop systems whose components are 50% reusable on subsequent projects. Targets are reasonable when they reflect an understanding of a baseline, so that the goal is not so far from the actual situation as to be impossible to meet.

The U.S. Department of Defense uses targets to evaluate software. The Department of Defense analyzed U.S. government and industry performance, grouping projects into low, median, and best-in-class ratings. From their findings, the analysts

TABLE 12.5 Quantitative Targets for Managing U.S. Defense Projects (*NetFocus* 1995)

Item	Target	Malpractice Level
Fault removal efficiency	>95%	<70%
Original fault density	<4 per function point	>7 per function point
Slip or cost overrun in excess of risk reserve	0%	≥10%
Total requirements creep (function points or equivalent)	<1% per month average	≥50%
Total program documentation	<3 pages per function point	>6 pages per function point
Staff turnover	1% to 3% per year	>5% per year

recommended targets for Defense Department–contracted software projects, along with indicated levels of performance constituting what they called "management malpractice," shown in Table 12.5. That is, if a project demonstrates that an attribute is near or exceeds the malpractice level, then the department suspects that something is seriously wrong with the project.

Software Reusability

Reuse requires us to evaluate products from current and former development projects, to determine if they are the type and quality that we want for the next system we will be building. Thus, we look in depth at some of the reuse issues that may influence our evaluations.

Many of the software systems we build are similar to one another; every company probably has an accounting system, a personnel system, and perhaps a billing system, for example. There are commonalities among systems with a similar purpose. For instance, every personnel system includes data and functions relating to company employees. Rather than create every system anew, we can step back, evaluate components from other systems, and determine whether they can be adapted or even reused whole in the next system we build. Even when applications are very different, we must examine whether it is necessary to write yet another sort routine, search component, or screen input program. Software researchers believe that reuse has great potential for increasing productivity and reducing cost, and some efforts to apply reuse technology confirm their belief.

Types of Reuse. By **software reuse**, we mean the repeated use of any part of a software system: documentation, code, design, requirements, test cases, test data, and more. Basili (1990) encourages us to think of maintenance as reuse; we take an existing system and reuse parts of it to build the next version. Likewise, he suggests that processes and experience can be reused, as can any tangible or intangible product of development.

There are two kinds of reuse, as determined by the perspective of the reuser. **Producer reuse** creates reusable components, and **consumer reuse** uses them in subsequent systems (Bollinger and Pfleeger 1990). As consumers, we can either use a product whole, without modification (called **black-box reuse**), or modify it to fit our particular needs (called **clear-box reuse**). We perform black-box reuse often, when we use routines from mathematical libraries or build graphical interfaces from predefined sets of components. An important issue in black-box reuse is our ability to verify that a reused module performs its required function in an acceptable way. If the component is code, we want to be sure it is failure-free; if it is a test set, we want to be sure it thoroughly exercises the function for which it is intended.

Clear-box reuse (sometimes called **white-box reuse**) is more common but still controversial, because the effort to understand and modify the component must be less than the effort to write a new equivalent component. To address this problem, many reusable components are being built with many parameters, making them easier to tailor with an external view, rather than forcing developers to understand the internals.

Several advances in software engineering make reuse more feasible. One is the interest in and adoption of object-oriented development (OOD). Because OOD encourages software engineers to build a design around invariant components, many parts of the design and code can be applied to multiple systems. Another advance that encourages reuse is the increasing sophistication of tools that stretch their effects across the development life cycle. Tools that include a repository for the components developed for one system can encourage reuse of those components in a later system. Finally, language design can encourage component reuse. For example, Ada provides software restructuring mechanisms that support packaging, and its parameterization techniques can help to make software more general.

Approaches to reuse are either compositional or generative. **Compositional reuse** views reusable components as a set of building blocks, and development is done from the bottom up, building the remaining system around the available reusable components. For this kind of reuse, the components are stored in a library (often called the **reuse repository**). The components must be classified or catalogued, and a retrieval system must be used to scan and select components for use in a new system. For example, our repository might contain a routine to convert the time from 12- to 24-hour format (i.e., so that 9:54 P.M. becomes 2154 hours). Similarly, the Genesis database-management-system generator includes building blocks that allow us to construct a DBMS tailored to our needs (Prieto-Díaz 1993).

On the other hand, **generative reuse** is specific to a particular application domain. That is, the components are designed specifically to address the needs of a particular application and to be reused in similar applications later. For instance, NASA has developed a great deal of software to track satellites in orbit. Components to analyze ephemeris data may be designed to be reusable in several of NASA's systems. However, these modules are not good candidates for a general reuse repository, because they are not likely to be needed in other domains. Generative reuse promises a high potential payoff, and practice has focused on domain-specific application generators. Some of the best-known of these generators are Lex and Yacc, which are designed to help us generate lexical analyzers and parsers.

An underlying activity in both kinds of reuse is **domain analysis**, the process of analyzing an application domain to identify areas of commonality and ways to describe it (Prieto-Díaz 1987). Compositional reuse relies on domain analysis to identify common lower-level functions across a wide class of systems. A generative approach to reuse requires more active analysis activities; the domain analyst seeks to define a

TABLE 12.6 Aspects of Reuse (Adapted from Prieto-Díaz 1993)

Substance	Scope	Mode	Technique	Intention	Product
Ideas and concepts Artifacts and components Procedures, skills, and experience Patterns Architecture	Vertical Horizontal	Planned and systematic Ad hoc, opportunistic	Compositional Generative	Black-box, as is Clear-box, modified	Source code Design Requirements Objects Data Processes Documentation Tests

generic domain architecture and to specify interface standards among the architectural components.

These ideas lead to the notions of horizontal and vertical reuse. **Vertical reuse** involves the same application area or domain, but **horizontal reuse** cuts across domains. Reusing NASA's ephemeris routines is vertical, but reusing a sort program from a database system in a graphics package is horizontal.

Thus, there are many ways to view reuse, depending on our goals. Table 12.6 illustrates our many choices.

Reuse Technology and Component Retrieval. One of the biggest obstacles to reuse is the need to search through a large set of software products to find the best one for a particular need. The job is akin to sifting through a junkyard of books rather than visiting a library. The solution is **component classification**, where collections of reusable components are organized and catalogued according to a classification scheme.

It is possible to classify the components in a hierarchical scheme, much as books are organized in a library. A top-level category is divided into subcategories, which in turn are divided into subcategories, and so on, as shown in Figure 12.6. However, this approach is inflexible and new topics can be added easily only at the lowest level.

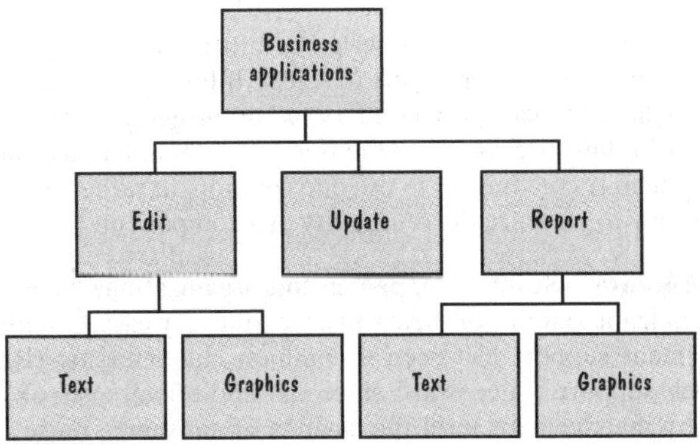

FIGURE 12.6 Example of a hierarchical classification scheme.

Moreover, extensive cross-referencing is necessary, since we must be able to find a text-handling routine under reporting as well as under editing, for example.

A solution to this problem is Prieto-Díaz's **faceted classification** scheme (Prieto-Díaz and Freeman 1987). Instead of using a hierarchy, each component is described by an ordered list of characteristics called facets. A **facet** is a kind of descriptor that helps to identify the component, and a collection of facets allows us to identify several characteristics at once. For example, the facets of reusable code may be

- an application area
- a function
- an object
- a programming language
- an operating system

Each code component is identified by an entry for each of the five facets. Thus, a particular routine might be labeled as

```
<switching system, sort, telephone number, Ada, UNIX>
```

The classification system is supported by a **retrieval system** or **repository**, an automated library that can search for and retrieve a component according to the user's description. The repository often has a thesaurus of synonyms to help us understand the terminology used in the classification. For example, the thesaurus may tell us to try using "search" as a synonym for "look up." In addition, a repository should address the problem of **conceptual closeness** to retrieve facet values that are similar to but not exactly the same as the desired component. For instance, if no "modify" component is found, we may be directed to "add" and "delete," which are similar.

The retrieval system can also record information about user requests. A volume of unmet requests of a certain type may trigger the librarian to suggest that a particular type of component be written. For example, if several users request a component to change a date from the U.S. format (11/05/98, or November 5, 1998) to the European format (05/11/98, or 5 November 1998) and no such component exists, the librarian can ensure that one is created. Similarly, if many developers search for components to draw geometric shapes but none is available, the librarian can identify good candidates and add them to the library.

Finally, the retrieval system can retain descriptive information about the component that aids us in deciding which components to select. Information about the component's source (e.g., where it was purchased or what project developed it), its reliability (the number of faults discovered or the number of hours it has run without failure), or previous usage may convince us to use one component rather than another. Sidebar 12.3 addresses how to measure the reusability of a component.

Experiences with Reuse. Several companies and organizations have been successful in reusing a significant amount of their software. In every case, committed and unconditional management support has been a common characteristic (Braun and Prieto-Díaz 1990). Such support is necessary, since the additional costs of producer reuse must be borne by management until the savings of consumer reuse outweigh

SIDEBAR 12.3 MEASURING REUSABILITY

How do we examine a candidate component and tell whether it should be placed in our reuse repository? Many managers would like a set of simple metrics that, when applied to the component, distinguish it as reusable or not. However, finding the right set of measurements is not as easy as it sounds. The measures must address a goal, usually related to quality, productivity, or time to market. And they must also reflect the perspective of the person asking the question; developers have different perspectives from top management. Pfleeger (1996) describes how the simple question of what to measure led to the generation of over 100 possible measurements—clearly, an unacceptable number of measurements to make.

But even if we had a good list of measurements, how do we know what limits to put on each? Is a small component more reusable than a large one? Is it better to reuse complex code than simple code? These research questions are being investigated in many different ways. Some organizations look at past history to determine the characteristics of the most reused components. Others select measurements based on "engineering judgment." The most promising approach was used at the Contel Technology Center, where an automated repository was organized using faceted classification. The repository tracked information about queries, such as which descriptors were used most often. It also recorded when a component was selected for use, when it was examined but not selected, and when it met a query but was not examined. Then, the repository administrator spoke with users to understand why certain components were not being used, and why other components were used a great deal. The measures, combined with the personal interaction, allowed the administrator to add new synonyms to the faceted classification, to modify components to make them more reusable, to delete components that were of no use to developers (thereby decreasing search time), and to find new components that were desirable but not yet incorporated in the repository.

them. Moreover, reuse often seems radical and threatening to developers who are accustomed to writing software from scratch. It is clear that many social, cultural, and legal issues are involved in reuse, as well as technical ones.

One of the first reported experiences with reuse is at Raytheon (Lanergan and Grasso 1984). The Missile Systems Division's Information Processing Systems Organization observed that 60% of its business applications designs and code were redundant and thus were good candidates for standardization and reuse. A reuse program was established, and over 5000 COBOL source programs were examined and classified into three major module classes: edit, update, and report. Raytheon also discovered that most of its business applications fell into one of three logical structures. These structures were standardized, and a library of reusable components was created. New applications are variations of the standard software structures, and they are built by assembling components from the library. Software engineers are trained and tested in using the library and in recognizing when a structure can be reused to build a new application. Reuse is then compulsory. After six years of reusing code in this way,

Raytheon reported that a new system contained an average of 60% reused code, increasing productivity by 50%.

One of the most successful reuse programs reported in the literature is GTE's. GTE Data Services established an Asset Management Program to develop a reuse culture in the corporation. The program was similar to those we have described so far. It began by analyzing existing systems and identifying reusable assets. Any software workproduct that could be partially or totally reused was a candidate asset. The collection of assets was then classified and catalogued in an automated library system. Several groups were created to maintain the library, promote reuse, and support reusers:

- a management support group to provide initiatives, funding, and policies for reuse
- an identification and qualification group to identify potential reuse areas and to identify, purchase, and certify new additions to the collection
- a maintenance group to maintain and update reusable components
- a development group to create new reusable components
- a reuser support group to assist and train reusers and to test and evaluate reusable components

Rather than making reuse compulsory, GTE established incentives and rewards. Programmers were paid up to $100 for each component accepted in the library, and royalties were paid to program authors whenever their components were reused on a new project. A "reuser of the month" award was created, and managers were given bonuses or budget enhancements for reaching reuse goals. In the first year of the program, GTE reported 14% reuse on its projects, valued at a savings of $1.5 million (Swanson and Curry 1987).

Nippon Novel, employing about 100 software engineers, began a reuse program that also used a cash incentive. It paid 5 cents (U.S.) per line of code to a developer who reused a component, and the creator of the component got 1 cent per line of code when it was reused. In 1993, the program cost the company $10,000, far less than the cost of writing the equivalent code (Frakes and Isoda 1994).

Other reuse programs have been started all over the world; most of them focus on code reuse. Sidebar 12.4 describes several reuse efforts in Japan. Government organizations such as the European Space Agency and the U.S. Department of Defense have large institutionalized reuse programs with component repositories. Commercial companies such as Hewlett-Packard, Motorola, and IBM have also invested heavily in reuse. And the European Community has sponsored several collaborative reuse efforts, including Reboot and Surprise. However, Griss and Wasser (1995) remind us that effective reuse requires neither widespread implementation nor sophisticated automation.

Benefits, Costs, and Reuse Success. Reuse offers the promise of increasing productivity and quality throughout the software development process. Productivity can be increased not only by reducing coding time, but also by reducing testing and documentation times. Some of the biggest cost reductions are offered by reusing requirements and design, since they have a ripple effect: reusing a design automatically encompasses code reuse, for instance. Moreover, reusing components may increase

SIDEBAR 12.4 SOFTWARE REUSE AT JAPAN'S MAINFRAME MAKERS

At the end of the twentieth century, most software development in Japan was done by mainframe manufacturers and their subsidiaries, so that is where we find the most software reuse. By the end of the 1980s, Nippon Electric Company (NEC), Hitachi, Fujitsu, and Toshiba had all established integrated software development environments supporting reuse.

NEC's Software Engineering Laboratory in Tokyo began its reuse program by analyzing its business applications. NEC standardized 32 logic templates and 130 common algorithms; then, a supporting reuse library was established to classify, catalog, document, and make them available. This library is part of NEC's Software Engineering Architecture, designed to enforce reuse in all development activities. Using three large-scale projects as controlled experiments, NEC reported an average productivity almost seven times that of a project that did not reuse software. The average quality of the products almost tripled (Nippon Electric Company 1987).

Hitachi also focused on business applications in COBOL and PL/1. The company used an integrated software environment called Eagle to allow software engineers to reuse standard program patterns and functional procedures (approximately 1600 data items and routines for input/output data conversion and validation). The patterns are used as templates, and the developers added their own code to modify them. Nevertheless, the ratio of generated to total lines of code was between 0.60 and 0.98 (Tsuda et al. 1992).

Fujitsu created an Information Support Center (ISC) for its electronic switching systems. The ISC is a regular library staffed with systems analysts, software engineers, reuse experts, and switching system domain experts. The library has a reference desk, a cross-reference between designers and coders, software archives, and commercial software. All software projects must use ISC in their development cycle by including ISC staff members in all design, and software reviews. Before the ISC program was created, only 20% of 300 projects were completed on schedule. Since the program's inception, 70% of the projects have been completed on time (Fujitsu 1987).

performance and reliability, because components can be optimized and proved before being placed in the repository.

A long-term benefit is improved system interoperability. The standardization involved in reuse may lead to uniform interfaces, making it easier to build systems that interact correctly. In particular, rapid prototyping based on a library of reusable components should be more effective.

There is only anecdotal evidence of reuse improvement. Some researchers have published descriptions of the positive effects reuse can have on development; very few have discussed the pitfalls and drawbacks. An example of good reuse analysis is Lim's (1994), describing reuse efforts at Hewlett-Packard. His careful assessment of two large reuse programs shows significant increases in quality and productivity and substantial decreases in time to market. Table 12.7 summarizes his findings.

TABLE 12.7 Quality, Productivity, and Time to Market at Hewlett-Packard (Adapted from Lim 1994) © 1996 IEEE

Project Characteristic	Hewlett-Packard Project 1	Hewlett-Packard Project 2
Size	1100 noncommented source statements	700 noncommented source statements
Quality	51% fault reduction	24% fault reduction
Productivity	57% increase	40% increase
Time to market	Data not available	42% reduction

TABLE 12.8 Costs to Produce and Reuse at Hewlett-Packard (Lim 1994) © 1996 IEEE

	Air Traffic Control System (%)	Menu- and Forms-Management System (%)	Graphics Firmware (%)
Relative cost to create reusable code	200	120 to 480	111
Relative cost to reuse	10 to 20	10 to 63	19

He also compared the costs to reuse and the costs to produce code on three projects. Table 12.8 shows his results, suggesting that there are in fact substantial additional costs in creating reusable code and in using it. Thus, we must balance the quality and productivity advantages with this extra investment in reusable components.

Joos (1994) offers a look into the management side of starting a reuse program. In explaining the pilot reuse studies at Motorola, she points out the need for good training, for managing expectations, and for obtaining up-front commitment to reuse. Sidebar 12.5 describes key success factors for reuse at NTT.

Pfleeger (1996) also presents a reuse tale, by formulating a composite of experiences with reuse programs that were not as successful as the ones described before. She suggests several key lessons learned from these attempts:

- Reuse goals should be measurable, so that we can tell if we have met them.
- Reuse goals can conflict, and management must resolve conflicts early and clearly. For example, as shown in Figure 12.7, a division manager's reuse goal may conflict with a project manager's goal, so no reuse ever gets done.
- Different perspectives may generate different questions. Whereas programmers ask specific technical questions, such as "Is this sort routine written in C++?" a vice-president is focused on the corporation as a whole and its position in the marketplace, asking, "Are we saving money yet?" Even when the questions are basically the same, we may get different answers. Different points of view reflect the different priorities of the participants in the reuse program.
- Every organization must decide at what level certain key questions are asked and answered. For example: Who pays for reuse? When expenses are incurred on one project in the hope that they will be recouped on future projects, they must reflect corporate choice and intent. And who owns the reusable components? Some

SIDEBAR 12.5 CRITICAL REUSE SUCCESS FACTORS AT NTT

Nippon Telephone and Telegraph began a software reuse project in its Software Laboratories that lasted four years and involved 600 engineers. As they implemented reuse, they learned a great deal about the importance of good management. They found that their critical success factors were (Isoda 1992)

- senior management commitment
- selecting appropriate target domains
- systematic development of reusable modules based on domain analysis
- investing several years of continuous effort in reuse.

level determines who owns them and who is responsible for their maintenance. Who builds the components? Another level must be responsible for the construction, population, and support of reuse libraries, as well as the measurement data generated by them. These questions are tied to the way the business is organized, so that profit-and-loss considerations are tied to investment and leveraging strategies. The questions and answers must be supported by measurement, so it is important to know who is asking and who needs the answer.

- Integrate the reuse process in the development process or participants will not know when they are supposed to be doing reuse.
- Tie measurements to the reuse process, so that the process can be measured and improved. Let business goals suggest what to measure.

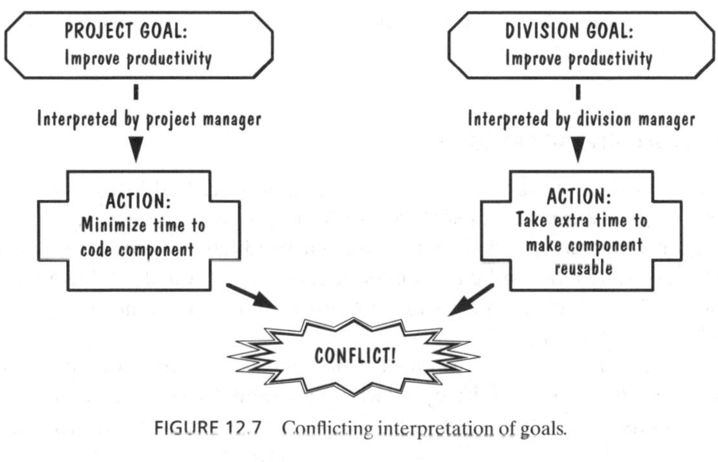

FIGURE 12.7 Conflicting interpretation of goals.

Pfleeger (1996) also poses questions that must be answered if reuse is to be successful:

- Is the model of reuse appropriate for the organization and goals?
- What are the criteria for success?
- How can current cost models be adjusted to look at collections of projects, not just single projects? Many of the decisions about potential cost savings require cost-estimation techniques involving several projects. But most commercial cost models focus on single projects, not on the collections of projects needed to justify reuse investment. Modified or new cost models are needed that can integrate aspects of multiple projects in order to support reuse decisions.
- How do regular notions of accounting (such as return on investment) fit with reuse? Those high in corporate management view reuse investment in the same terms as any other business investment. They want to discuss reuse options, indicators, and return on investment, not number of components, languages, or library search techniques. It is important for software engineers to be able to translate the language of reuse into the language of accounting, so that reuse investment can be compared with other possible corporate investment initiatives.
- Who is responsible for component quality? The scheme must be analyzed and organized to fit with the corporate culture. What happens when an author leaves the company? What happens when the component evolves or spawns multiple versions? What criteria are set for component quality, both for initial acceptance in the library and for maintaining the component as it changes over time?
- Who is responsible for process quality and maintenance? There is more to reuse than setting up libraries and filling them with components. Someone has to monitor the level of reuse, making sure that good components are identified, labeled properly, and used often. Someone has to cull the unused components and analyze them to determine why they are not used. Someone must evaluate the domain analysis process to determine if the components targeted are in fact highly reusable. And someone has to study the effect of reuse on the corporate bottom line to determine return on investment and future reuse policy. These ongoing activities may occur at different levels of the corporation, and they must be recognized as necessary parts of a reuse program.

12.5 EVALUATING PROCESSES

Many of the software engineering practices described in this book involve a process intended to improve our software in some way. Some processes, such as inspections or cleanroom, are supposed to improve our products in a direct and dramatic way. Other processes, such as configuration management or project management, affect the products indirectly by giving us more control and understanding about how our actions affect the resulting code.

The effort needed to enact a process varies. Some processes involve the entire software development life cycle, whereas others focus on a small group of activities. In either case, the effort must not be wasted; we want our processes to be effective and efficient. For example, we saw in Chapter 8 that we can evaluate our testing effectiveness by comparing the number of faults found in testing with the total number of faults found throughout our life-cycle activities. And the classification tree in Figure 8.20 shows that large components whose design has undergone review are not likely to have many faults; the classification tree analysis shows us that the design review process has been effective. In this chapter, we examine several other techniques for evaluating the effect that our processes have on the products they produce and on the people who produce them.

Postmortem Analysis

Every project is composed of a series of processes, each designed to meet a particular goal. For example, requirements engineering activities are intended to capture and compose requirements in a way that makes the requirements consistent and complete; review techniques aim to find faults well before testing activities. One way to evaluate our processes is to collect large amounts of data, not only during development, but also after the project is over; then, we can analyze the data to determine whether we are meeting our goals and to look for areas of improvement.

Petroski (1985) reminds us that we learn a lot from our successes, but we learn even more from our failures. Failure data are needed to present a balanced picture from which we can build models, so performing postmortem analysis is essential to good software engineering practice. Sidebar 12.6 lists many of benefits of deriving these "lessons learned."

A **postmortem analysis** is a postimplementation assessment of all aspects of the project, including products, processes, and resources, intended to identify areas of improvement for future projects. The analysis usually takes place shortly after a project is completed; however, a survey by Kumar (1990) notes that it can take place at any time from just before delivery to 12 months afterward (see Table 12.9).

As Collier, DeMarco, and Fearey (1996) note, "discovering which behaviors need changing is not a trivial task in complex systems, particularly on large, lengthy projects." They propose a postmortem process that is positive, blame-free, and encourages

TABLE 12.9 When Postimplementation Evaluation Is Done

Time Period	Percentage of Respondents (of 92 Organizations)
Just before delivery	27.8
At delivery	4.2
One month after delivery	22.2
Two months after delivery	6.9
Three months after delivery	18.1
Four months after delivery	1.4
Five months after delivery	1.4
Six months after delivery	13.9
Twelve months after delivery	4.2

SIDEBAR 12.6 HOW MANY ORGANIZATIONS PERFORM POSTMORTEM ANALYSIS

Kumar (1990) surveyed 462 medium-sized organizations (chosen from the top 500 of the Canadian Dunn and Bradstreet Index) that developed software for management information systems. Of the 92 organizations that responded, more than one-fifth did no postmortem analysis. And of those that did, postmortems were conducted on fewer than half of the projects in the organization. Kumar asked the managers why more postmortems were not done. Responses included unavailability of staff, shortage of qualified personnel, no evaluation criteria, and the pressures of work. However, those who responded noted several benefits of postmortems:

- verified that installed system met system requirements
- provided feedback to system development personnel
- justified adoption, continuation, or termination of installed system
- clarified and set priorities for needed system modifications
- transferred responsibility for system from developers to users
- reported on system effectiveness to management
- evaluated and refined system controls
- provided feedback to modify development methods
- verified economic payoff of system
- closed out the development project
- provided feedback for modification of project management method
- evaluated project personnel

communication among the participants. Their suggestions are based on more than 22 postmortems involving over 1300 project members. The process has five parts:

1. Design and promulgate a project survey to collect data without compromising confidentiality.
2. Collect objective project information, such as resource costs, boundary conditions, schedule predictability, and fault counts.
3. Conduct a debriefing meeting to collect information the survey missed.
4. Conduct a project history day with a subset of project participants, to review project events and data and to discover key insights.
5. Publish the results by focusing on lessons learned.

Survey. The survey is the starting point because its answers guide the rest of the postmortem analysis. It defines the scope of the analysis and allows us to obtain information that cuts across the interests of project team members. There are three guiding principles for administering the survey: do not ask for more than is needed, do not ask leading questions, and preserve anonymity. The first guideline is especially important. We want to minimize the time it takes a respondent to answer questions on the survey, so that more project members are likely to complete and return the questionnaire.

Sidebar 12.7 contains examples from the surveys administered by Collier, DeMarco, and Fearey (1996). The survey answers reflect the opinions and perspectives of the team members.

It is essential that we think about tabulating the results before we administer the questionnaire. Sometimes, the tabulation and analysis process suggests how a question should be reworded to clarify or expand it. Moreover, these questions are asked of every project, so we must be sure to express them in ways that are free of the particulars of any

SIDEBAR 12.7 SAMPLE SURVEY QUESTIONS FROM WILDFIRE SURVEY (COLLIER, DEMARCO, AND FEAREY 1996) © 1996 IEEE

Wildfire Communications developed a survey to assist in postmortem analysis; a Web pointer to similar materials is noted in the Key References section of this chapter. The survey contains eight categories of questions, with examples like these:

Category 1: Support and goals

Sample question: Were interdivisional lines of responsibility clearly defined throughout the project?

[ ] always [ ] sometimes [ ] rarely [ ] never

Category 2: Expectations and communications

Sample question: Did project-related meetings make effective use of your time?

[ ] always [ ] sometimes [ ] rarely [ ] never

Category 3: Issues resolution

Sample question: Were you empowered to participate in discussions regarding issues that affected your work?

[ ] always [ ] sometimes [ ] rarely [ ] never

Category 4: Information access

Sample question: Did schedule changes and related decisions involve the right people?

[ ] always [ ] sometimes [ ] rarely [ ] never

Category 5: Product specifications

Sample question: Was project definition done by the appropriate individuals?

[ ] always [ ] sometimes [ ] rarely [ ] never

Category 6: Engineering practices

Sample question: Was the build process effective for the component area you worked on?

[ ] always [ ] sometimes [ ] rarely [ ] never

Category 7: The big picture

Sample question: Considering time-to-market constraints, were the right trade-offs made between features, quality, resources, and schedule for this product?

[ ] always [ ] sometimes [ ] rarely [ ] never

Category 8: Demographics

Sample question: What was your primary function on this project?

[ ] quality assurance [ ] development [ ] marketing [ ] project management [ ] documentation.

given project. The collection of answers over a large set of projects enables us to look for trends, relationships, and areas ripe for improvement.

Objective Information. Next, we need objective information to complement the opinions expressed in the survey. Again, we want to collect data in a simple way that makes cross-project comparison easy to do. Collier, DeMarco, and Fearey (1996) suggest three kinds of measurements: cost, schedule, and quality. For example, cost measurements might include

- person-months of effort, reported by major roles or activities
- total lines of code, preferably by function
- number of lines of code changed or added, by function
- number of interfaces: total, added, changed, or deleted

Measuring schedule might include a report of the original schedule, a history of events that caused the schedule to slip, and an analysis of the accuracy of schedule predictions. Finally, quality can be measured as the number of faults found during each development activity and a depiction of the rate at which faults were found and fixed.

Ideally, much of this information is already available, having been collected during development and maintenance. But some organizations do a better job of measuring than others. The postmortem process can encourage teams to do more on the next project, once they realize that important questions can be answered with very little extra effort to collect and maintain data. Moreover, repeated measurements are more useful than one-time data capture. Measuring size or schedule change over time gives a team a better picture of progress than a single snapshot in the middle or at the end of development. So even when postmortem analysts cannot collect everything they would like to see, their current questions can still inspire improvement on later projects.

Debriefing Meeting. The debriefing meeting allows team members to report on what did and did not go well on the project. At the same time, project leaders can probe more deeply, trying to identify the root cause of both positive and negative effects. Often, the team members raise issues that are not covered in the survey questions, leading to discoveries about important relationships that were not visible during development. For example, team members may point out problems with using a particular requirements method for certain customers, because the customers' assumptions are not easily captured using that method. Or testers may discuss the problems encountered with having to assess performance on a development platform different from the operational platform.

The debriefing meeting should be loosely structured, with a chair to encourage attendance and keep discussion on track. For very large project teams, the debriefing meeting might be better conducted as a series of smaller meetings, so that the number of participants at each meeting does not exceed approximately 30. A key benefit of the debriefing meeting is a team member's ability to air grievances and have them be directed toward improvement activities.

Project History Day. Unlike the debriefing meeting, the project history day involves a limited number of participants. The day's purpose is to identify the root causes of the key problems experienced on the project. Thus, the participants include only those who know something about why the schedule, quality, and resource gaps occurred. For this reason, the history day team members may include staff outside of the development team; marketing representatives, customers, project managers, and hardware engineers are good candidates.

The participants prepare for the day by reviewing everything they know about the project: their correspondence, project management charts, survey information, measurement data, and anything else that may have bearing on project events. The first formal activity of project history day is a review of a set of schedule-predictability charts, as shown in Figure 12.8. For each key project milestone, the chart shows when the prediction was made about milestone completion, compared with the date of milestone completion itself. For instance, in the figure, someone predicted in July 1995 that the milestone would be met in January 1997. That prediction was the same in January 1996, but as the time grew closer to January 1997, the schedule prediction slipped to

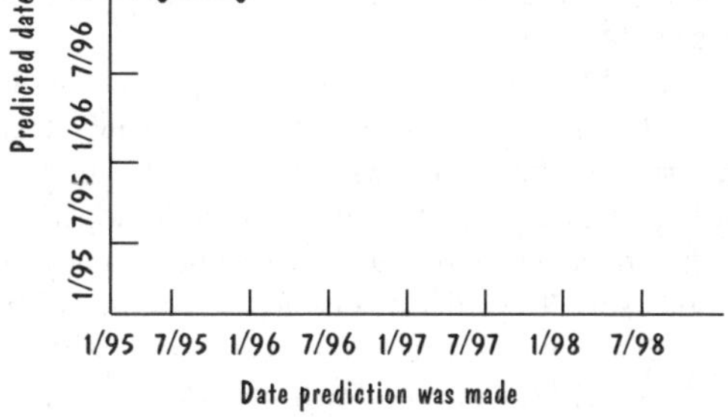

FIGURE 12.8 Schedule-predictability chart.

July 1997. Then, in July 1997 when the milestone was not met, the milestone was predicted to be met in January 1998. Finally, the milestone was indeed met in January 1998. The shape of the schedule-predictability chart tells us something about the optimism or pessimism in our estimates and helps us understand the need to estimate more accurately. The ideal situation is represented by a horizontal line.

The schedule-predictability charts can be used as illustrations, showing where problems occurred. They spark discussion about possible causes of each problem, and the focus of the team is on identifying an exhaustive list of causes. Then, using the objective data as support for each argument, the team narrows down each list of causes until it feels comfortable that it understands exactly why a problem occurred. Collier, DeMarco, and Fearey (1996) report that sometimes the initial list of causes can reach 100 items, and it can take several hours to analyze what really happened. By the end of project history day, the team has a prioritized list of the causal relationships surrounding approximately 20 root causes.

Publishing the Results. The final step is to share these insights with the rest of the project team. Rather than hold another meeting, the participants in project history day write an open letter to managers, peers, and other developers. The letter consists of four parts. The introduction is a project description that explains the general type of project and any information about whether or why the project was unique. For example, the letter may explain that the project involved building a telecommunications billing system, something for which the company is well-known. But this particular project used the Eiffel language for the first time, coupled with tools to assist in doing object-oriented design.

Next, the letter summarizes all of the postmortem's positive findings. The findings may describe not only what worked well, but also what can be used by other projects in the future. For instance, the project may have produced reusable code, new tools, or a set of tips on successful use of Eiffel that may be useful for subsequent similar developments.

Then, the letter summarizes the three worst factors that kept the team from meeting its goals. Usually, these factors are the top three items in the prioritized root cause list created during project history day.

Finally, the letter suggests improvement activities. Collier, DeMarco, and Fearey (1996) suggest that the team select one problem that is so important that it must be fixed before work starts on another project. The letter should describe the problem clearly, and suggest how to fix it. The problem description and solution should be supported by objective measurements, so that the developers can assess the magnitude of the problem and track changes as things improve.

Arango, Schoen, and Pettengill (1993) offer a broader approach to publishing the results of postmortem analyses. In their work at Schlumberger, they considered the reuse of everything from a project, including lessons learned. The Schlumberger researchers developed technology called project books and technology books, accessible by other developers on other projects, that share experiences, tools, designs, data, ideas, and anything that might be useful to someone else at the company. By using technology such as theirs, we can learn from each other and improve with each project, rather than continue to make the same mistakes and wonder why.

Process Maturity Models

In the 1980s, spurred by work at IBM, several organizations began to examine the software development process as a whole rather than focus on individual activities. Attempts were made by several researchers to characterize what it is that makes a process effective. From this work grew the notion of **process maturity**, where the development process incorporates feedback and control mechanisms so that its high-quality products are produced on time with few management surprises.

Capability Maturity Model. The **Capability Maturity Model** (CMM) was developed by the U.S. Software Engineering Institute (SEI) to assist the Department of Defense in assessing the quality of its contractors. The CMM, inspired by Deming's work (1989), had its beginning as the **process maturity model**, where an organization was rated on an ordinal scale from 1 (low) to 5 (high), based on the answers to 110 questions about its development process. Figure 12.9 summarizes the rise from low levels of maturity to higher ones.

Table 12.10 lists the 12 questions required for a level 2 (repeatable) assessment; if any of these questions was answered "no," then the organization was automatically assessed at a level 1, regardless of the answers to the 98 other questions.

There were many problems with this approach, and the CMM was developed to address them and replace the process maturity model. However, many of the basic principles of the original process maturity approach remain: the CMM uses a questionnaire to assess the maturity of a development project, supplements the questionnaire with requests for evidence to verify the answers, and generates a rating on a five-point scale. That is, the CMM describes principles and practices that are assumed to lead to better software products, and the model organizes them in five levels, providing a path to more process visibility and control, and to the improved products that should result. The model is used in two ways: by potential customers, to identify the strengths and weaknesses of their suppliers, and by software developers, to assess their own capabilities and set a path toward improvement.

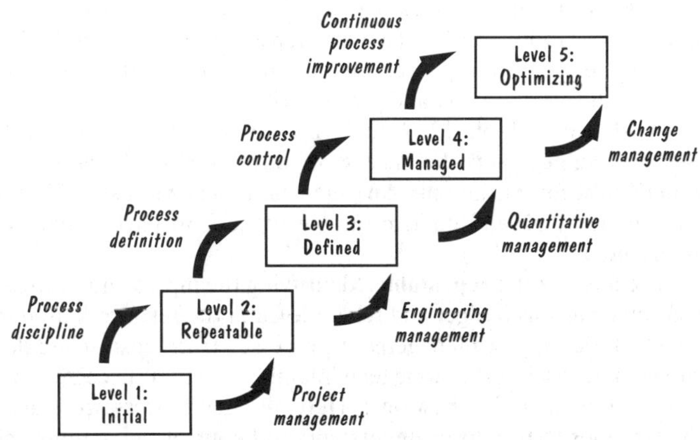

FIGURE 12.9 The Software Engineering Institute's levels of maturity.

TABLE 12.10 Required Questions for Level 1 of the Process Maturity Model

Question Number	Question
1.1.3	Does the Software Quality Assurance function have a management reporting channel separate from the software development project management?
1.1.6	Is there a software configuration control function for each project that involves software development?
2.1.3	Is a formal process used in the management review of each software development prior to making contractual commitments?
2.1.14	Is a formal procedure used to make estimates of software size?
2.1.15	Is a formal procedure used to produce software development schedules?
2.1.16	Are formal procedures applied to estimating software development cost?
2.2.2	Are profiles of software size maintained for each software configuration item over time?
2.2.4	Are statistics on software code and test errors gathered?
2.4.1	Does senior management have a mechanism for the regular review of the status of software development projects?
2.4.7	Do software development first-line managers sign off on their schedule and cost estimates?
2.4.9	Is a mechanism used for controlling changes to the software requirements?
2.4.17	Is a mechanism used for controlling changes to the code?

Each of the five capability levels is associated with a set of **key process areas** on which an organization should focus as part of its improvement activities. The first level of the maturity model, **initial**, describes a software development process that is ad hoc or even chaotic. That is, inputs to the process are ill-defined; where outputs are expected, the transition from inputs to outputs is undefined and uncontrolled. Similar projects may vary widely in their productivity and quality characteristics because of lack of adequate structure and control. For this level of process maturity, it is difficult even to write down or depict the overall process; the process is so reactive and ill-defined that visibility is nil and comprehensive measurement difficult. The project may have goals relating to improved quality and productivity, but managers do not know the current levels of quality and productivity.

As shown in Table 12.11, there are no key process areas at this level. Few processes are defined, and the success of development depends on individual efforts, not on team accomplishments. An organization at level 1 should concentrate on imposing more structure and control on the process, in part to enable more meaningful measurement.

The next level is **repeatable**, identifying the inputs and outputs of the process, the constraints (such as budget and schedule), and the resources used to produce the final product. Basic project management processes track cost, schedule, and functionality. There is some discipline among team members, so that successes on earlier projects can be repeated with similar new ones. Here, the key process areas are primarily management activities that help to understand and control the actions and outcomes of the process.

TABLE 12.11 Key Process Areas in the CMM (Paulk et al. 1993a,b)

CMM Level	Key Process Areas
Initial	None
Repeatable	Requirements management Software project planning Software project tracking and oversight Software subcontract management Software quality assurance Software configuration management
Defined	Organization process focus Organization process definition Training program Integrated software management Software product engineering Intergroup coordination Peer reviews
Managed	Quantitative process management Software quality management
Optimizing	Fault prevention Technology change management Process change management

The process is repeatable in the same sense that a subroutine is repeatable: proper inputs produce proper outputs, but there is no visibility into how the outputs are produced. Asked to define and describe the process, the development team can draw no more than a diagram similar to Figure 12.10. This figure shows a repeatable process as a simplified Structured Analysis and Design Technique (SADT) diagram, with input on the left, output on the right, constraints at the top, and resources on the bottom. For example, requirements may be input to the process, with the software system as output. The control arrow represents such items as schedule and budget, standards, and management directives, and the resources arrow can include tools and staff.

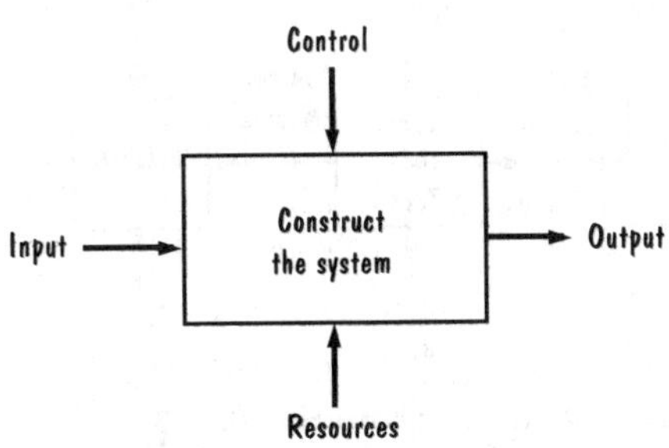

FIGURE 12.10 A repeatable process (level 2).

Since it is possible to measure only what is visible, Figure 12.10 suggests that project management measurements make the most sense for a repeatable process. That is, since all that is visible are the arrows, we can associate measurements with each arrow in the process diagram. Thus, for a repeatable process, measures of the input might include the size and volatility of the requirements. The output may be measured in terms of system size (functional or physical), the resources as overall staff effort, and the constraints as cost and schedule in dollars and days, respectively.

Improving the repeatable process leads to a **defined** process, where management and engineering activities are documented, standardized, and integrated; the result is a standard process for everyone in the organization. Although some projects may differ from others, the standard process is tailored to these special needs, and the adaptation must be approved by management. At this level of maturity, the key process areas have an organizational focus.

The defined level of maturity (level 3) differs from level 2 in that a defined process provides visibility into the "construct the system" box in Figure 12.10. At level 3, intermediate activities are defined, and their inputs and outputs are known and understood. This additional structure means that the input to and output from the intermediate activities can be examined, measured, and assessed, since these intermediate products are well-defined and visible. Figure 12.11 shows a simple example of a defined process with three typical activities. However, different processes may be partitioned into more distinct functions or activities.

Because the activities are delineated and distinguished from one another in a defined process, we can measure product attributes no later than level 3. Faults discovered in each type of product can be tracked, and we can compare the fault density of each product with planned or expected values. In particular, early product measures can be useful indicators of later product measures. For example, the quality of the requirements or design can be measured and used to predict the quality of the code. Such measurements use the visibility in the process to provide more control over development: if requirements quality is unsatisfactory, additional work can be expended on the requirements before the design activity begins. This early correction of problems helps not only to control quality, but also to improve productivity and reduce risk.

A **managed** process directs its efforts at product quality. By introducing detailed measures of process and product quality, the organization can focus on using quantitative

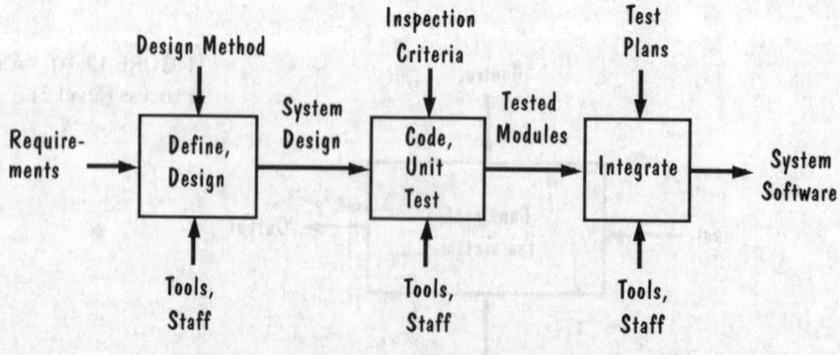

FIGURE 12.11 A defined process (level 3).

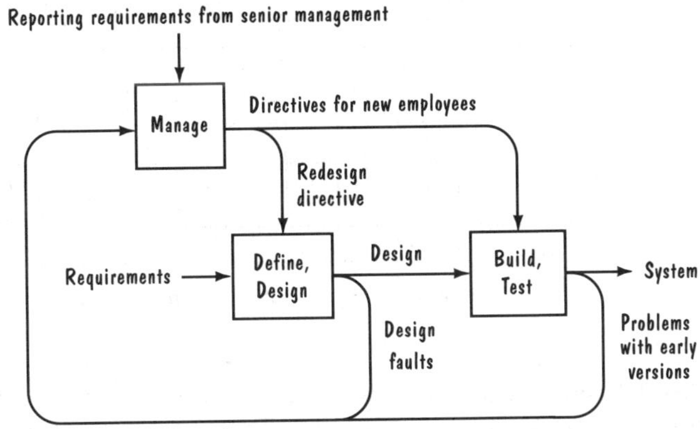

FIGURE 12.12 A managed process (level 4).

information to make problems visible and to assess the effect of possible solutions. Thus, the key process areas address quantitative software management as well as software quality management.

As shown in Figure 12.12, we can use feedback from early project activities (e.g., problem areas discovered in design) to set priorities for current activities (e.g., redesign) and later project activities (e.g., more extensive review and testing of certain code, and a changed sequence for integration). Because we can compare and contrast, the effects of changes in one activity can be tracked in the others. By level 4, the feedback determines how resources are deployed; the basic activities themselves do not change. At this level, we can evaluate the effectiveness of process activities: How effective are reviews? Configuration management? Quality assurance? Fault-driven testing? We can use the collected measures to stabilize the process, so that productivity and quality will match expectations.

A significant difference between levels 3 and 4 is that level 4 measurements reflect characteristics of the overall process and of the interaction among and across major activities. Management oversight relies on a metrics database that can provide information about such characteristics as distribution of faults, productivity and effectiveness of tasks, allocation of resources, and the likelihood that planned and actual values will match.

The most desirable level of capability maturity is **optimizing**, where quantitative feedback is incorporated in the process to produce continuous process improvement. In particular, new tools and techniques are tested and monitored to see how they affect the process and products. Key process areas include fault prevention, technology change management, and process change management.

To understand just how level 5 improves on level 4, consider Figure 12.13. The series of staggered boxes indicates a progression of processes, labeled $T_0, T_1, \ldots, T_n$ to indicate that the first box is the process used at time T_0, the second process is used at time T_1, and so on. At a given point in time, measures from activities are used to improve the current process, possibly by removing and adding process activities and changing the

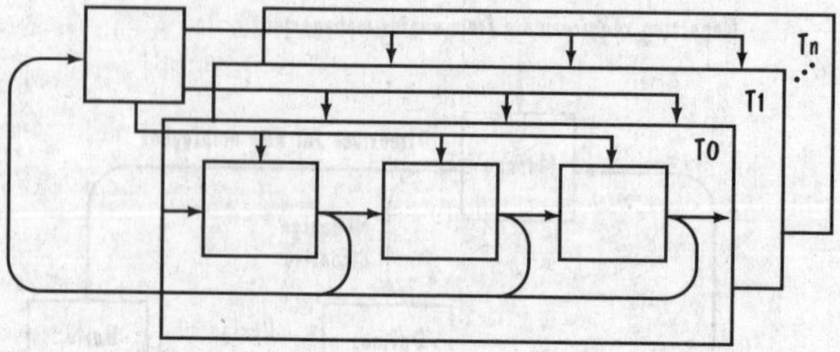

FIGURE 12.13 An optimizing process (level 5).

process structure dynamically in response to measurement feedback; the result is movement to the next process in the diagram. Thus, the process change can affect the organization and project as well as the process. Results from one or more ongoing or completed projects may also lead to a refined different development process for future projects. The spiral model is an example of such a dynamically changing process, responding to feedback from early activities in order to reduce risk in later ones.

For example, suppose we begin development with a standard waterfall approach. As requirements are defined and design is begun, measurements and verbal feedback may indicate a high degree of uncertainty in the requirements. Based on this information, we may decide to change the process to one that prototypes the requirements and the design, so that some of the uncertainty can be resolved before we make substantial investment in implementation of the current design. In this way, being able to optimize the process gives us maximum flexibility in development. Measurements act as sensors and monitors, and the process is not only under control but can also change significantly in response to warning signs.

It is important to remember that capability maturity does not involve a discrete set of five possible ratings. Instead, maturity represents relative locations on a continuum from 1 to 5. An individual process is assessed or evaluated along many dimensions, and some parts of the process can be more mature or visible than others. For example, a repeatable process may not have well-defined intermediate activities, but the design activity may indeed be clearly defined and managed. The process visibility diagrams presented here are meant only to give a general depiction of typical processes. It is essential to examine each project's process to determine what is visible. The figures and tables should not proscribe activities simply because the overall maturity level is a particular integer; if one part of a process is more mature than the rest, an activity or tool can enhance the visibility of that part and help to meet overall project goals, at the same time bringing the rest of the process up to a higher level of maturity. Thus, in a repeatable process with a well-defined design activity, design quality metrics may be appropriate and desirable, even though they are not generally recommended for level 2.

The CMM has another level of granularity not shown in the table: Each process area comprises a set of **key practices** whose presence indicates that the developer has implemented and institutionalized the process area. The key practices are supposed to provide evidence that the process area is effective, repeatable, and long-lasting (Paulk et al. 1993b).

The key practices are organized by these common features:

- *Commitment to perform:* What actions ensure that the process is established and will continue to be used? This category includes policy and leadership practices.
- *Ability to perform:* What preconditions ensure that the organization is capable of implementing the process? Practices here address resources, training, orientation, tools, and organizational structure.
- *Activities performed:* What roles and procedures are necessary to implement a key process area? This category includes practices on plans, procedures, work performed, corrective action, and tracking.
- *Measurement and analysis:* What procedures measure the process and analyze the measurements? The practices in this category include process measurement and analysis.
- *Verifying implementation:* What ensures that activities comply with the established process? The practices include management reviews and audits.

An organization is said to satisfy a key process area only when the process area is both implemented and institutionalized. Implementation is determined by the answers to the activities performed questions; the other practices address institutionalization.

SPICE. The CMM spawned a proliferation of process assessment methods, from Trillium (produced by Canadian telecommunications companies) to BOOTSTRAP (an extension of the CMM developed by a European Community ESPRIT project). This growth, and the application of process assessment techniques to products that were commercially sensitive, led the UK Ministry of Defence to propose an international standard for process assessment (Rout 1995). The new standard, ISO 15504 and called **SPICE** (Software Process Improvement and Capability dEtermination), harmonized and extended the existing approaches. Similar to the CMM, SPICE is recommended both for process improvement and capability determination. The framework is built on an assessment architecture that defines desirable practices and processes.

There are two different types of practices:

1. *Base practices* are essential activities of a specific process.
2. *Generic practices* institutionalize or implement a process in a general way.

Figure 12.14 illustrates how the SPICE architecture ties the two together and includes actual ratings for each. The left-hand side of the diagram represents functional practices involved in software development. This functional view considers five activities:

1. *Customer-supplied:* processes that affect the customer directly, support development and delivery of the products to the customer, and ensure correct operation and use
2. *Engineering:* processes that specify, implement, or maintain the system and its documentation
3. *Project:* processes that establish the project, coordinate or manage resources, or provide customer services

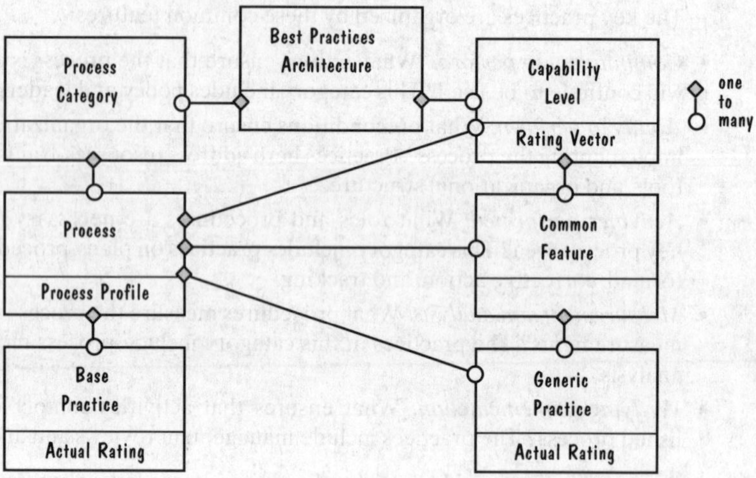

FIGURE 12.14 SPICE architecture for process assessment (Rout 1995).

4. *Support:* processes that enable or support performance of the other processes
5. *Organization:* processes that establish business goals and develop assets to achieve those goals

The right-hand side of Figure 12.14 shows a picture of management; the generic practices, applicable to all processes, are arranged in six levels of capability:

0. *Not performed:* failure to perform and no identifiable workproducts
1. *Performed informally:* not planned and tracked, depends on individual knowledge and identifiable workproducts
2. *Planned and tracked:* verified according to specified procedures, workproducts conform to specified standards and requirements
3. *Well-defined:* well-defined process using approved, tailored versions of standard, documented processes
4. *Quantitatively controlled:* detailed performance measures, prediction capability, objective management, and workproducts evaluated quantitatively
5. *Continuously improving:* quantitative targets for effectiveness and efficiency based on business goals, quantitative feedback from defined processes, plus trying new ideas

An assessment report is a profile; each process area is evaluated and reported to be at one of the six capability levels. Figure 12.15 is an example of how the profile is reported. The shading indicates the degree to which the activities were satisfied at each level.

Thus, whereas the CMM addresses organizations, SPICE addresses processes. As with the CMM, a SPICE assessment is administered in a carefully prescribed way, to minimize subjectivity in the ratings.

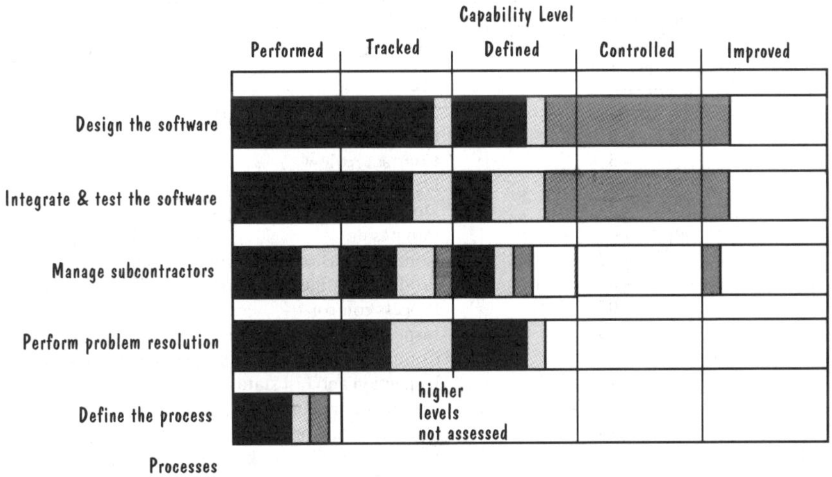

FIGURE 12.15 SPICE assessment profile (Rout 1995).

ISO 9000. The International Standards Organization (ISO) has produced a series of standards that collectively are known as **ISO 9000**. The standards specify actions to be taken when any system (i.e., not necessarily a software system) has quality goals and constraints. In particular, ISO 9000 applies when a buyer requires a supplier to demonstrate a given level of expertise in designing and building a product. The buyer and supplier need not belong to separate companies; the relationship can exist even within the same organization.

Among the ISO 9000 standards, standard 9001 is most applicable to the way we develop and maintain software (International Standards Organization 1987). It explains what a buyer must do to ensure that the supplier conforms to design, development, production, installation, and maintenance requirements. Table 12.12 lists the clauses of ISO 9001. Since ISO 9001 is quite general, there is a separate document, ISO 9000-3, that provides guidelines for interpreting ISO 9001 in a software context (International Standards Organization 1990).

Clause 4.2 of ISO 9001 requires an organization to have a documented quality system, including a quality manual, plans, procedures, and instructions. ISO 9000-3 interprets this clause for software, explaining how the quality system should be integrated throughout the software development process. For instance, clause 4.2.3 discusses quality planning across projects, and 5.5 addresses it within a given development project.

Similarly, clause 4.4 of ISO 9001 requires establishing procedures to control and verify design, including

- planning, design, and development activities
- defining organizational and technical interfaces
- identifying inputs and outputs
- reviewing, verifying, and validating the design
- controlling design changes

TABLE 12.12 ISO 9001 Clauses

Clause Number	Subject Matter
4.1	Management responsibility
4.2	Quality system
4.3	Contract review
4.4	Design control
4.5	Document and data control
4.6	Purchasing
4.7	Control of customer-supplied product
4.8	Product identification and traceability
4.9	Process control
4.10	Inspection and testing
4.11	Control of inspection, measuring, and test equipment
4.12	Inspection and test status
4.13	Control of nonconforming product
4.14	Corrective and preventive action
4.15	Handling, storage, packaging, preservation, and delivery
4.16	Control of quality records
4.17	Internal quality audits
4.18	Training
4.19	Servicing
4.20	Statistical techniques

Then, ISO 9000-3 maps these activities to a software context. Clause 5.3 addresses the purchaser's requirements specification, 5.4 looks at development planning, 5.5 at quality planning, 5.6 at design and implementation, 5.7 at testing and validation, and 6.1 at configuration management.

The ISO 9000 standards are used to regulate internal quality and to ensure the quality of suppliers. Typically, a contractor will subcontract for part of a system, based on the supplier's ISO 9000 certification. The certification process has a defined scope and is carried out by quality-system auditors. In the UK, ISO 9000 certification is performed under the auspices of the TickIT program, and there is a comprehensive TickIT guide to interpret and elaborate on the concepts and application of ISO 9000 (Department of Trade and Industry 1992).

Measurement is also part of ISO 9000, but it is not as explicit as in SPICE or the CMM. In particular, the strong emphasis on statistical process control found in SPICE and CMM is missing in ISO 9000. However, as with the other frameworks, the goals of the framework can easily be mapped to questions and metrics.

12.6 EVALUATING RESOURCES

Many researchers believe that the quality of our resources is a far more important factor in product quality than any technological breakthroughs we may make. For example, DeMarco and Lister (1987) discuss evidence that creativity, uninterrupted time, and good communication are necessary; they argue that cohesive teams build good products.

Similarly, Boehm's COCOMO models (1981, 1995) include parameters that adjust effort and schedule estimates based on staff attributes such as experience. His original research revealed that differences between high- and low-performance teams had the largest influence on project productivity. Thus, researchers argue that we should focus more on people and less on technology.

At the same time, software is usually built in a business environment. We are given resources such as time and money and asked to solve a business or societal problem. We must be able to evaluate whether we are using the appropriate levels of each. In this section, we examine two frameworks for evaluating these kinds of resources: a people maturity model for staff and a return-on-investment model for time and money.

People Maturity Model

It is notable that the CMM does not address issues relating to people and their productivity. Although named a "capability" model, the CMM is really designed to measure process capability rather than the capability of the people comprising the organizations. Curtis, Hefley, and Miller (1995) sought to remedy that omission by proposing a **people capability maturity model** for improving the knowledge and skills of the workforce.

Like the CMM, the people maturity model has five levels, where level 5 is the most desirable. Each level is tied to key practices that reflect how the organizational culture is changing and improving. Table 12.13 presents an overview of these levels and practices.

TABLE 12.13 People Capability Maturity Model (Curtis, Hefley, and Miller 1995)

Level	Focus	Key Practices
5: Optimizing	Continuous knowledge and skills improvement	Continuous workforce innovation Coaching Personal competency development
4: Managed	Effectiveness measured and managed, high-performance teams developed	Organizational performance alignment Organizational competency management Team-based practices Team building Mentoring
3: Defined	Competency-based workforce practices	Participatory culture Competency-based practices Career development Competency development Workforce planning Knowledge and skills analysis
2: Repeatable	Management takes responsibility for managing its people	Compensation Training Performance management Staffing Communication Work environment
1: Initial		

The lowest level represents a starting point, with much room for improvement. At the **initial** level, an organization takes no active role in developing the people who work for it. Management skill is based on past experience and personal communication skills, rather than on formal management training. Some people-related activities are performed, but without putting them in the larger context of motivation and long-term goals.

In an immature organization like a level 1, many managers do not acknowledge staff talents as a critical resource. Developers pursue their own goals, and there are few incentives to align the goals with those of the business. Knowledge and skills stagnate because employees move from job to job with no systematic plan for their growth.

Level 2 is the first step toward improving the workforce. Managers accept staff growth and development as a key responsibility, but only if they understand that organizational performance is limited by the skills of the individuals who comprise it. Thus, the focus of the **repeatable** level is to establish basic work practices among the various employees in a given unit or organization.

Among some of the simplest practices are those that support working in an environment without distraction. Steps are taken to improve communication and coordination, and managers take recruiting and selection very seriously. Managers make sure to discuss job performance with the staff and reward it when it is outstanding. Training is targeted to fill gaps in available skills, and compensation should take into account equity, motivation, and retention.

By level 3, the organization is beginning to tailor its work practices to its business. It begins this **defined** level of maturity by creating a strategic plan to locate and develop the talent it needs. The needs are determined by the knowledge and skills required by the business, considered to be organizational core competencies. In turn, staff are rewarded as they master core competencies and develop their skills. The thrust of these changes is to encourage staff to participate in meeting the company's business goals.

Mentoring plays a large role at level 4, the **managed** level of maturity. Not only are individuals encouraged to learn core skills, but teams are built around knowledge and skills that complement one another. Team-building activities lead to team spirit and cohesion, and many organizational practices focus on motivating and developing teams.

At this level, the organization sets quantitative goals for core competency growth, and performance is motivated across individuals, teams, and organizations. Trends are examined to determine how well the practices are increasing critical skills. Because of this quantitative understanding, staff abilities are predictable, making management much easier.

The **optimizing** level is the fifth and highest level of maturity. Here, individuals, managers, and the entire organization are focused on improving team and individual skills. The organization can identify opportunities to strengthen staff practices and does so, without waiting to react to a problem or setback. Data are analyzed to determine potential performance improvements, either by changing current practices or trying new, innovative techniques. Those new practices that offer the best results are implemented throughout the organization. In general, an optimizing culture has each staff member focused on every aspect of improvement: individual, team, project, organization, and company.

Curtis, Hefley, and Miller (1995) point out that the people maturity model

- develops capabilities
- builds teams and cultures
- motivates and manages performance
- shapes the workforce

The assessment framework is useful not only for evaluating a given organization, but also for planning improvement programs.

Return on Investment

In an ongoing attempt to improve software development, we select from among recommended methods and tools. Usually, limited resources constrain our choice; we cannot do everything, so we search for criteria for choosing the one(s) most likely to help us reach our goal. Thus, we must take a hard look at how software engineering developers and managers make decisions about technology investment.

Respected business publications often address the problem of technology investment. For example, an often-cited article suggests that any evaluation of an existing or proposed investment in technology be reported in several ways at once to form a "balanced scorecard": from a customer view (i.e., customer satisfaction), an operational view (i.e., core competencies), a financial view (i.e., return on investment, share price), and an improvement view (i.e., market leadership and added value) (Kaplan and Norton 1992). For example, Sidebar 12.8 describes some of the returns on investment at Chase Manhattan Bank. Favaro and Pfleeger (1998) suggest that economic value can be a unifying principle. That is, we can look at each investment alternative in terms of its potential economic value to the company as a whole. In fact, maximizing economic value can very well lead to increases in quality, customer satisfaction, and market leadership.

However, there are many different ways to capture economic value. We must decide which investment analysis approach is most appropriate for software-related investment decision making based on economic value. Investment analysis is concerned only with the best way to allocate capital and human resources. Thus, it is distinctly different from cost estimation or metrics; it weighs several alternatives, including the possibility of using capital markets to provide an expected annual rate of return. In other words, from a high-level corporate perspective, management must decide how a proposed technology investment compares with simply letting the money earn interest in the bank!

Not all investment analysis reflects this reality. Taking the perspective of a financial analyst, Favaro and Pfleeger (1998) look critically at the most commonly used approaches: net present value, payback, average return on book value, internal rate of return, and profitability index. They show that net present value (NPV) makes the most sense for evaluating software-related investments.

NPV expresses economic value in terms of total project life, regardless of scale or time frame. Since investment planning involves spending money in the future, we can think of the **present value** of an investment as the value today of a predicted future cash flow. The NPV calculation uses a **discount rate** or **opportunity cost**, corresponding to

SIDEBAR 12.8 RETURN ON INVESTMENT AT CHASE MANHATTAN

In Chapter 11, we learned about Chase Manhattan's RMS, a Relationship Management System that joined several legacy systems into one, to provide customer information to service representatives. The new system enables representatives to spend less time digging for data and more time getting to know customer needs.

The RMS development took a new approach. Developers were encouraged to talk with each other and with their customers, and the heightened communication led to a much better understanding of what was needed—in some cases, less was needed than the developers thought! Five different prototypes were built, and data were organized to maximize integrity.

One of the biggest paybacks on Chase Manhattan's technology investment was increased team cohesion. "The RMS development team stuck to a democratic approach to problem-solving. Priorities were voted on, and team members had to bow to the majority. That approach often resulted in compromise, but it also developed cross-functional collaboration and trust" (Field 1997b).

The project began in 1994, and by the end of 1996, RMS had been installed in 700 of Chase Manhattan's 1000 middle-market representative locations. But even without full deployment, RMS has increased customer calls by 33% and improved profitability by 27%. By protecting its old investments and encouraging communication among employees, Chase Manhattan accomplished four things:

1. It avoided huge investments in new hardware.
2. It provided more data more quickly to its service representatives.
3. It achieved an admirable return on investment.
4. It created cohesive teams that understand more about Chase Manhattan's business.

Denis O'Leary, executive vice-president and CIO, noted that "the challenge really is to get the business and IS groups to coalesce around a partnership that will endure and a technical infrastructure that is sturdy" (Field 1997b).

the rate of return expected from an equivalent investment in capital markets; this rate may change over time. In other words, the discount rate reflects how much money an organization can make if it invests its money in the bank or a financial vehicle instead of in software technology. Hewlett-Packard used NPV to evaluate investment in two multiyear corporate reuse projects.

The **net present value** is the present value of the benefits minus the value of the initial investment. For example, to invest in a new tool, a company may spend money for training and learning time, as well as for the tool itself. The NPV calculation subtracts these initial investment costs from the projected benefits.

TABLE 12.14 Net Present Value Calculation for Two Alternatives

Cash Flows	COTS	Reuse
Initial investment	−9000	−4000
Year 1	5000	−2000
Year 2	6000	2000
Year 3	7000	4500
Year 4	−4000	6000
Sum of all cash flows	5000	6500
NPV at 15%	2200	2162

The acceptance rule for NPV is simple: invest in a project if its NPV is greater than zero. To see how NPV works, consider the following situation. A company can create a new product line in two ways:

1. Base it on commercial off-the-shelf software (COTS). This choice involves a large initial procurement cost, with subsequent high returns (based on avoided work), but the COTS product will be outdated and must be replaced after three years.
2. Build the product with a reusable design. The reuse requires considerable up-front costs for design and documentation, but the long-term costs are less than normal.

The net present value calculation may resemble Table 12.14. The COTS alternative has a slightly higher NPV and is therefore preferred.

The NPV approach is sensitive to the timing of the cash flows; the later the returns, the more the overall value is penalized. Thus, time to market is essential to the analysis and affects the outcome. The size or scale of a project is also reflected in the NPV. Because NPV is additive, we can evaluate the effects of collections of projects simply by summing their individual NPVs. On the other hand, significant gains from one technology can mask losses from investment in another; for this reason, it is useful to evaluate each type of investment separately. In real-world practice, NPV is not used for naive single-project evaluation, but rather in the context of a more comprehensive financial and strategic framework (Favaro 1996).

12.7 INFORMATION SYSTEMS EXAMPLE

The Piccadilly system clearly adds value to the television broadcasters who commissioned it. The advertising time can be sold faster, the rates and schemes can be changed easily and quickly, and special offerings can be tailored to react to the competition. But how do we incorporate this added value? If revenues increase, then we can compare them with the money invested in the system's development. However, we may find ourselves in a situation where the revenues stay the same but would have gone down without such a system. That is, sometimes we must invest in technology to maintain our place in the market and stay viable, not to improve our position.

These issues should be addressed in a postmortem, in addition to the technical issues described in this chapter. In other words, a postmortem analysis must review the business as well as the technology, linking them together when appropriate to answer the question: "Is this system good for business?" The answer may not be easy, and it is certainly not easy to quantify. Sometimes new technologies are adopted not because they are the best for the job, but because good employees will leave if they are not trained in the latest techniques or tools. As managers, we must keep in mind that developers and maintainers are motivated by more than just their salaries. They also like constant challenge, recognition by their peers, and the opportunity to master new skills. So return on investment involves not only monetary reward and customer satisfaction, but also employee satisfaction. Investment in employees and teams can also be good for business.

12.8 REAL-TIME EXAMPLE

The Ariane-5 report is a fine example of a postmortem analysis. The investigation team followed a process similar to the one recommended by Collier, DeMarco, and Fearey (1996) and focused on the obvious need to determine what caused the fault that required exploding the rocket. The report avoided blame and complaint; instead, it listed the several steps that could have been taken during development that would have noticed the incipient problem: requirements reviews, design strategies, testing techniques, simulation, and more.

It is the next step that is not documented in the report: using the report's recommendations to change the way the next rocket is designed, built, and tested. As we will see in Chapter 13, we can compare the data from Ariane-5's postmortem with that of subsequent rockets to determine if any improvement has been made. Improvement is a continuous process, so we are likely to build a history from a series of postmortems; as we solve one problem, we address the next most critical problem until most of the major challenges have been met.

12.9 WHAT THIS CHAPTER MEANS FOR YOU

In this chapter, we have looked at ways to evaluate products, processes, and resources. We began by reviewing several approaches to evaluation, including feature analysis, surveys, case studies, and formal experiments. We saw that measurement is essential for any evaluation and that it is important to understand the difference between assessment and prediction. Then, we looked at how to validate measures; that is, we want to be sure that we are measuring what we think we are measuring and that our predictions are accurate.

Product evaluation is usually based on a model of the attribute of interest. We looked at three quality models to see how each one addressed particular concerns about how the different facets combine to form a whole. Then, we looked at software reuse, noting the issues that are raised when we must evaluate a component as a candidate for reuse.

Process evaluation can be done in many ways. Postmortem analysis looks back at completed processes to assess the root causes of things that went wrong. Process models, such as the capability maturity model, SPICE, and ISO 9000, are useful for asking questions about the control and feedback we have over the processes we use.

The CMM has inspired a host of other maturity models, including a people maturity model to assess the degree to which individuals and teams are given the resources and freedom they need to do their best. We invest other resources in our projects, too, including money and time. Return-on-investment strategies help us understand whether business is benefiting from investment in people, tools, and technology.

12.10 WHAT THIS CHAPTER MEANS FOR YOUR DEVELOPMENT TEAM

Many of the assessment models discussed in this chapter focus on team interaction. The process maturity models monitor team coordination and communication, encouraging measurable feedback from one process activity to another. These models help teams control what they do and make better predictions about what will happen in the future. Similarly, models such as the people maturity model evaluate whether individuals and teams are rewarded and motivated to do their best.

Feature analysis, case studies, surveys, and experiments encourage teams to share information, in hopes of understanding and verifying the relationships among products, processes, and resources. Teams must work together, during formal investigations as well as postmortem analysis, putting aside individual biases to determine the root causes of major problems that can be fixed in the future.

Finally, we have seen how return on investment includes investment in people as well as in technology. Skilled and motivated teams are likely to be more productive, carrying their experience and understanding from one project to the next.

12.11 WHAT THIS CHAPTER MEANS FOR RESEARCHERS

There is a great need for more empirical evaluation of software engineering practices and products. Researchers must adapt standard investigative techniques to the realities of software engineering. We cannot do the same project twice, once with a technique or tool and once without. So we must learn from our social science colleagues and adapt our research methods while learning as much as we can about how to be more effective.

Models and frameworks help us understand the relationships we are investigating. Researchers continue to propose new ways for us to view the various aspects of our products, processes, and resources; then, we evaluate the models and frameworks themselves to see how they match what we already know.

12.12 TERM PROJECT

Now that you have finished your Loan Arranger project, consider how you would evaluate the software and the development process used to build it. How good is the software? What measures can you use to demonstrate its quality? How would you compare the quality of the Loan Arranger software with that of another project you have completed?

Similarly, examine the process you used to produce the Loan Arranger. Would you consider it to be initial? Defined? Repeatable? Managed? Optimizing? What practices helped to make the project a success? A failure?

12.13 KEY REFERENCES

Evaluation techniques are quite complex, and there is more to discuss than was covered in this chapter. Fenton and Pfleeger (1997) contains three chapters on evaluation: one on techniques, one on data collection, and one on data analysis. Pfleeger and Kitchenham have a series of articles in *ACM Software Engineering Notes*, beginning in December 1995, discussing various investigative techniques in detail. Pfleeger (1999b) addresses the need to allow a technology to evolve as we study its effectiveness.

Information about maturity models abounds on the Web. To learn more about the CMMI (the Software Engineering Institute's current maturity model), see http://www.sei.cmu.edu/cmmi/general. Copies of the current SPICE standard are at http://www.iso.org/iso/home.htm.

Several issues of *IEEE Software* have been devoted to reuse, including May 1993 and September 1994. The latter contains a page-long list of the key papers and books on reuse through 1994.

ReNews, an electronic newsletter about reuse, is available at http://frakes.cs.vt.edu/renews.html.

There are several Web sites that contain documents and samples of postmortem products, including a concise, defined process, a sample survey, a sample tabulation of results, sample affinity diagrams, and a schedule-predictability tool. One example is at http://www.quality.amirex.com/pages/Software-Postmortem.html.

There are many conferences and workshops devoted to reuse. The major ones, sponsored by the IEEE Technical Council on Software Engineering, are the International Conference on Software Reuse and the Annual Workshop on Software Reuse. Information about back issues of their proceedings and announcements of upcoming conferences are available at the IEEE Computer Society Web site.

There are also several conferences and organizations related to evaluation. The International Symposium on Software Metrics, sponsored by the IEEE Computer Society, addresses issues of measurement and empirical investigation. Information about the latest conference is also on the Computer Society Web page. The International Software Engineering Research Network publishes studies of replicated investigations, and many of them are available from its Web site. Finally, the journal *Empirical Software Engineering* publishes not only studies, but also data and guidelines for empirical research.

12.14 EXERCISES

1. List some information that may be useful in recording the reuse history of a component. Be sure to include a rationale for each element in your list.
2. Which type of software reuse, black-box or clear-box, is more common? Evaluate the software that is required to run a large program from one of your class projects. Roughly, what percentage is reused? 20%? 60%? 98%? Why?

3. Suppose a postmortem analysis reveals that a particular developer is responsible for the major system problems. What kinds of improvement activities should be included in the recommendations to address this?
4. Examine the quality models described in this chapter: Boehm, ISO 9126, and Dromey. For each contributing characteristic of quality, discuss possible ways to measure the characteristic, and describe whether the measure is subjective or objective.
5. Examine the quality models in Figures 1.5, 12.2, and 12.3. How can models like these be used to prevent problems with product quality? Can measurement help to avoid such problems?
6. ISO 9126 is meant to be a general model of software quality that can be used by anyone involved with software. Is it sensible to have a general model? How does it help in comparing the quality of two different products? Are some products so unusual that ISO 9126 does not apply?
7. Computer security is usually considered necessary for a high-quality software product. How can computer security be defined in terms of the ISO 9126 model of quality?
8. Compare and contrast the McCall, Boehm, and ISO 9126 quality models. How do they differ from the developer's point of view? From the user's point of view?
9. Perform a postmortem on one of your own projects. What would you have done differently were you to do the project again? How do you know that these lessons will improve the next project you do?
10. Your organization is considering using a new COTS and you are required to calculate NVP. What are some of the considerations you need to take into account? How accurate can an NVP calculation be? Why?
11. The capability maturity model is used by many companies as an incentive to implement new practices. That is, organizations set goals and reward behavior to help them move up from level 1 toward level 5. What kinds of measurable goals can be set for each of the key process areas? How can these measures be used to track progress toward level 5?
12. Suppose you have implemented a new review technique during your requirements process. How could you evaluate its effectiveness? How would you control variables so that you are sure it is the new technique that is responsible for differences in quality or productivity?
13. The facets of a faceted classification scheme must be orthogonal. That is, the characteristic described by one facet cannot be described by using a combination of one or more other facets. Define a set of facets to classify the books in a software engineering library. How many facets do you need? How do you know when you have defined enough facets? Is each book description unique?

13 Improving Predictions, Products, Processes, and Resources

In this chapter, we look at

- improving predictions
- improving products by using reuse and inspections
- improving processes by using cleanroom and maturity models
- improving resources by investigating trade-offs

We have examined many software engineering techniques and tools, each of which is intended to help us build better products in better ways. In Chapter 12, we learned how to evaluate products, processes, and resources to determine which aspects of development and maintenance affect the quality of the products we build and maintain. We saw that several kinds of studies, supported by empirical evidence, enable us to set baselines from which to measure change and assist us in comparing and contrasting the effects of different techniques and tools. In this chapter, we look at how to combine careful evaluation with technology adoption to help us improve the way we use new technology. For example, it is not enough to adopt inspections and reviews because they seem like good ideas. It is better to examine our use of inspections and reviews to understand what makes them good and how to make them more effective.

We focus on four aspects of software engineering technology: prediction, products, processes, and resources. For each, we discuss several improvement strategies based on actual empirical study. The examples presented here are chosen to demonstrate the evaluation and improvement techniques used; they are not meant to be endorsements of particular techniques or strategies. As always, we suggest that you use and evaluate techniques and tools that seem the most appropriate for your own development and maintenance environments.

13.1 IMPROVING PREDICTIONS

We have seen throughout this book the need to predict many things: the effort and schedule of a proposed project, the number of faults in software, the reliability of a new system, the time required to test a product, and more. In each case, we want our predictions to be accurate. That is, we want the predicted value to be close to the actual value. In this chapter, we look at ways to improve the prediction process so that it yields more accurate estimates. We focus on reliability models, but the techniques are equally applicable to other kinds of prediction.

Predictive Accuracy

In Chapter 9, we examined several models that are used to predict the likely reliability of a software system. Then, in Chapter 12, we investigated the need to validate prediction systems, noting that we must compare the accuracy of the prediction with the actual reliability values. In this chapter, we take a close look at the accuracy of reliability models and investigate some techniques for improving that accuracy.

Abdel-Ghaly, Chan, and Littlewood (1986) compared several reliability models on the same dataset (the Musa dataset used in Chapter 9) and found dramatic differences among their predictions. Figure 13.1 illustrates their findings for several commonly used models. In the figure, "JM" designates the Jelinski–Moranda model introduced in Chapter 9; "GO" is the Goel–Okumoto model, "LM" is the Littlewood model, "LNHPP" is Littlewood's nonhomogeneous Poisson process model, "DU" is the Duane model, and "LV" is the Littlewood–Verrall model. Each model was used to generate 100 successive reliability estimates. Although each model exhibits increasing reliability on this dataset, there is substantial difference in the behavior of each prediction over time. Some models are more optimistic than others, and some are very "noisy," with large fluctuations in the predictions as testing proceeds.

It is not unusual for models to produce results like these, making it difficult for us to know how to use the models on our particular projects. We need to know which

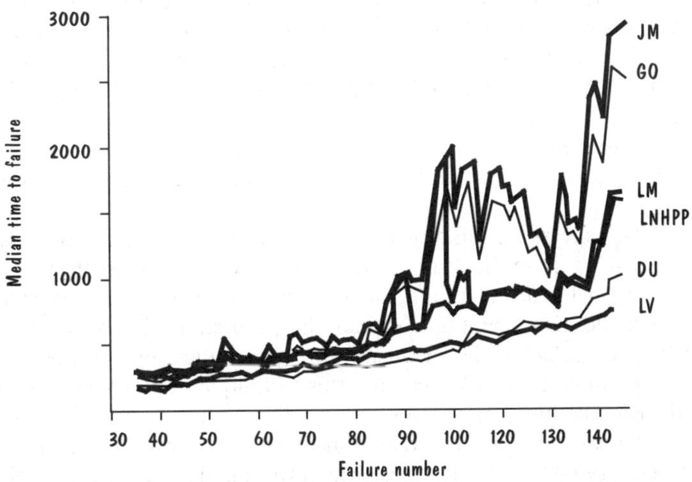

FIGURE 13.1 Results of applying reliability models to the Musa dataset.

model is most appropriate, and we must find ways of determining when the predictions are most accurate.

Predictions can be inaccurate in two different ways:

1. Predictions are **biased** when they are consistently different from the actual reliability of the product.
2. Predictions are **noisy** when successive predictions of a measure (such as median time to failure or mean time to failure) fluctuate more wildly than the actual reliability.

Of course, we do not know the actual reliability, so it is difficult for us to determine the amount of noise or bias in a prediction. However, Abdel-Ghaly, Chan, and Littlewood (1986) suggest several techniques for analyzing accuracy and helping us determine which model to use.

Dealing with Bias: The *u*-Plot

We deal with bias by comparing how often the observed times of failure are less than the predicted ones. That is, when a given model predicts that the next failure will occur at a particular time, we measure the actual time of next failure and compare the two. Suppose the clock starts at 0 and the first failure occurs at time t_1. The time to the next failure is t_2 and we continue to record interfailure times until we have observed n software failures, with interfailure times t_1 through t_n. We compare these times with the predictions (from the model) of T_1 through T_n. Then, we count the number of times that t_i is less than T_i; if this number is significantly less than $n/2$, then we are likely to have bias in our predictions. For example, in Figure 13.1, 66 of the 100 observations used with the Jelinski–Moranda model are smaller than the predicted median time to next failure. That is, the predicted medians are too large, so we say that the Jelinski–Moranda model is too optimistic on this dataset. Indeed, if we look only at the last 50 observations, we find that 39 of the actual times are smaller than the predicted times. So the increase in reliability predicted by the Jelinski–Moranda model is more than the actual increase. In the same way, we can analyze the Littlewood–Verrall model and see that it is consistently pessimistic in its predictions.

Intuitively, we expect to find the opposite. That is, we expect to have more accurate predictions as testing proceeds, as we find more faults, and as we know more about the data.

We express bias in a more formal way by forming a sequence of numbers $\{u_i\}$, where each u_i is an estimate of the probability that t_i is less than T_i. In other words, we estimate the likelihood that the actual observation was less than what we had predicted it would be. For example, consider the prediction system introduced in Chapter 9, where we predicted the mean time to next failure by averaging the two previously observed failure times. We can use this technique on the Musa data to generate values in the third column of Table 13.1.

We can calculate a distribution function for this data sequence (see Fenton and Pfleeger [1997] for details), from which we calculate the u values. Next, we construct a graph called a ***u*-plot**: we place the u_i values along the horizontal axis and then draw a

TABLE 13.1 Generating u_i Values for Predictions Based on the Musa Data

i	t_i	Predicted Mean Time to ith Failure	u_i
1	3		
2	30	16.5	0.84
3	113	71.5	0.79
4	81	97	0.57
5	115	98	0.69
6	9	62	0.14
7	2	5.5	0.30
8	91	46.5	0.86
9	112	101.5	0.67
10	15	63.5	0.21

step function, where each step has height $1/(n + 1)$ (assuming there are n u_is). Figure 13.2 shows the u-plot for the nine values shown in Table 13.1.

If we draw the line with slope 1 (i.e., a line at 45 degrees from the horizontal and vertical axes), we can compare it with the u-plot. If our predictions were perfectly accurate, we would expect the u-plot to be the same as this line. Thus, any differences between the line and the u-plot represent the deviation between prediction and actual observation. We measure the degree of deviation by using the **Kolmogorov distance** (the maximum vertical distance between the line and the u-plot), as shown in Figure 13.2.

To see how the u-plots work, consider the two most extreme models of Figure 13.1, the Jelinski–Moranda and the Littlewood–Verrall. We can measure the Kolmogorov distance (i.e., the greatest vertical distance) of each of their plots from the line of unit slope, as shown in Figure 13.3. The distance for Jelinski–Moranda is 0.190, which is significant at the 1% level; for Littlewood–Verrall, the distance is 0.144, significant at the 5% level. Thus, these two models are not very accurate on this dataset.

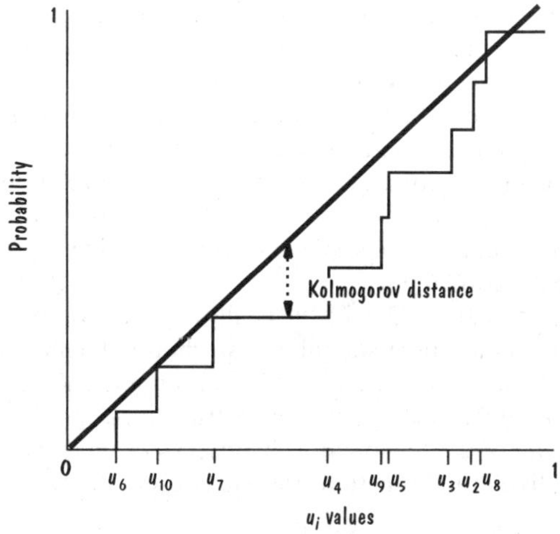

FIGURE 13.2 u-plot for values in Table 13.1.

FIGURE 13.3 Jelinski–Moranda (JM) and Littlewood–Verrall (LV) u-plots for 100 one-step-ahead predictions.

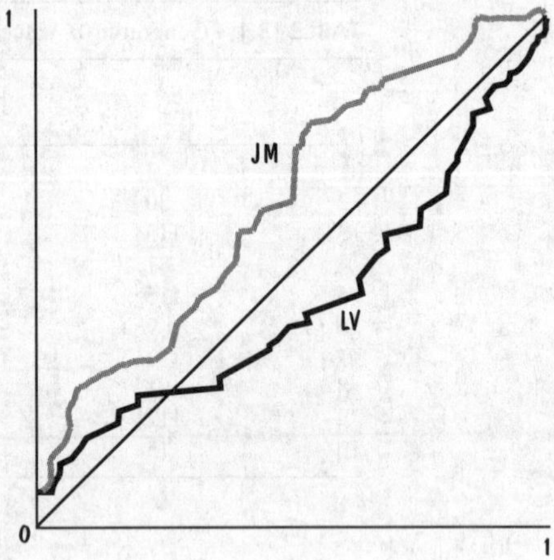

More important we can see that the plot for Jelinski–Moranda is always above the line, so there are too many small u values. In other words, when the u-plot is above the line, the model is too optimistic. Similarly, Littlewood–Verrall is too pessimistic because it is mostly below the line. We would like a model whose predictions are much closer to the line than either of these two models.

Dealing with Noise: Prequential Likelihood

It is not enough to eliminate bias in a model. If we have an unbiased but very noisy model, we may still have a model that is not very useful. To see how, consider a prediction generated by using the median of the three preceding interfailure times, t_{i-1}, t_{i-2}, and t_{i-3}. We predict the median time to failure T_i to be the median of t_{i-1}, t_{i-2}, and t_{i-3}; since the first three interfailure times are 3, 30, and 113, we set T_4 to be 30. Similarly, T_5 is 113 and T_6 is 81. These estimates are likely to be very far from the actual values, and they will fluctuate wildly even when the actual numbers have a much smoother behavior. Thus, we have a lot of noise in these predictions.

Sometimes, the fluctuations reflect the way in which the actual reliability fluctuates. For example, we may get significant fluctuation as we make changes to a system and introduce new faults. **Unwarranted noise** occurs when the actual reliability is not fluctuating but the estimates are. There is no technique sensitive to unwarranted noise, but we can use a more general technique, *prequential likelihood*, to handle noise and bias together, helping us to select a good model.

The prequential likelihood function (Dawid 1984) allows us to compare several different predictions on the same data source, so that we can choose the most accurate. (An overview of prequential likelihood can be found in Fenton and Pfleeger [1997], and a detailed description is in [Dawid 1984].) Using the Musa dataset and predictions generated by computing the mean of the two previously observed values, we can compute a sequence of prequential likelihood functions for each observation. The result is shown in Table 13.2.

TABLE 13.2 Prequential Likelihood Calculations

i	t_i	T_i	Prequential Likelihood
3	113	16.5	6.43E–05
4	81	71.5	2.9E–07
5	115	97	9.13E–10
6	9	98	8.5E–12
7	2	62	1.33E–13
8	91	5.5	1.57E–21
9	112	46.5	3.04E–24
10	15	101.5	2.59E–26
11	138	63.5	4.64E–29
12	50	76.5	3.15E–31
13	77	94	1.48E–33

We can use these values to compare the predictions from two models. Suppose we have two sets of predictions, one from model A and one from model B. We compute the prequential likelihood functions, PL_A and PL_B. Dawid (1984) proved that if PL_A/PL_B increases consistently as n (the number of observations) increases, then model A is producing more accurate predictions than model B.

To understand how to use prequential likelihood, we compute the functions for the Littlewood nonhomogeneous Poisson process model and the Jelinski–Moranda model, using the Musa dataset. The results are shown in Table 13.3, where n is the number of predictions on which the prequential likelihood ratio is based. For example, when $n = 10$, the ratio involves predictions $T_{35}, \ldots, T_{44}$; when $n = 15$, it involves $T_{35}, \ldots, T_{49}$. The ratio does not increase very fast until we exceed 60 observations; then the ratio becomes large very quickly. This analysis suggests that the Littlewood nonhomogeneous Poisson process model yields better predictions than the Jelinski–Moranda model.

Fenton and Pfleeger (1997) suggest caution when using this analysis technique. They tell us that "the fact that a particular model has been producing superior predictions in

TABLE 13.3 Prequential Likelihood Comparing Two Models

n	Prequential Likelihood LNHPP:JM
10	1.28
20	2.21
30	2.54
40	4.55
50	2.14
60	4.15
70	66.0
80	1516
90	8647
100	6727

the past is no guarantee that it will continue to do so in the future. However, experience suggests that such reversals on a given data source are quite rare. Certainly, if method A has been producing better predictions than method B in the recent past, then it seems sensible to prefer A for current predictions."

Recalibrating Predictions

We now have several ways to evaluate models, helping us decide which is best for our situation:

- examining the basic assumptions of each model
- looking for bias
- looking for noise
- computing prequential likelihood ratios

However, none of these techniques points to the best model. Moreover, models behave differently on different datasets; we can see very different results even on the same dataset. For example, consider the switching system data in Table 13.4. We can use it

TABLE 13.4 Musa SS3 Data, Showing Execution Time to Failure in Seconds, Read from Left to Right

107400	17220	180	32880	960	26100	44160	333720	17820
40860	18780	960	960	79860	240	120	1800	480
780	37260	2100	72060	258704	480	21900	478620	80760
1200	80700	688860	2220	758880	166620	8280	951354	1320
14700	3420	2520	162480	520320	96720	418200	434760	543780
8820	488280	480	540	2220	1080	137340	91860	22800
22920	473340	354901	369480	380220	848640	120	3416	74160
262500	879300	360	8160	180	237920	120	70800	12960
300	120	558540	188040	56280	420	414464	240780	206640
4740	10140	300	4140	472080	300	87600	48240	41940
576612	71820	83100	900	240300	73740	169800	1	302280
3360	2340	82260	559920	780	10740	180	430860	166740
600	376140	5100	549540	540	900	521252	420	518640
1020	4140	480	180	600	53760	82440	180	273000
59880	840	7140	76320	148680	237840	4560	1920	16860
77040	74760	738180	147000	76680	70800	66180	27540	55020
120	296796	90180	724560	167100	106200	480	117360	6480
60	97860	398580	391380	180	180	240	540	336900
264480	847080	26460	349320	4080	64680	840	540	589980
332280	94140	240060	2700	900	1080	11580	2160	192720
87840	84360	378120	58500	83880	158640	660	3180	1560
3180	5700	226560	9840	69060	68880	65460	402900	75480
380220	704968	505680	54420	319020	95220	5100	6240	49440
420	667320	120	7200	68940	26820	448620	339420	480
1042680	779580	8040	1158240	907140	58500	383940	2039460	522240
66000	43500	2040	600	226320	327600	201300	226980	553440
1020	960	512760	819240	801660	160380	71640	363990	9090
227970	17190	597900	689400	11520	23850	75870	123030	26010
75240	68130	811050	498360	623280	3330	7290	47160	1328400
109800	343890	1615860	14940	680760	26220	376110	181890	64320
468180	1568580	333720	180	810	322110	21960	363600	

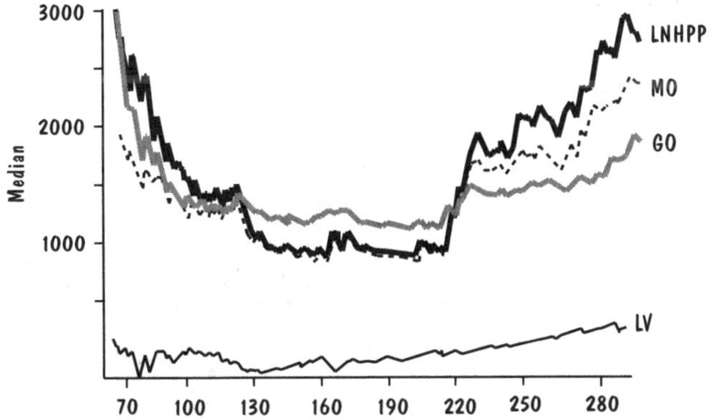

FIGURE 13.4 Reliability predictions of several models, using data from Table 13.4.

with several reliability models and plot some of the predictions (106 through 278), as shown in Figure 13.4. The figure shows that the Musa–Okumoto, Goel–Okumoto, and Littlewood nonhomogeneous Poisson process models have behaviors that are much the same, but Littlewood–Verrall is very different.

If we perform a prequential likelihood analysis, we find that the more pessimistic Littlewood–Verrall model is actually a better predictor than the others. We can also draw u-plots for these models, shown in Figure 13.5, showing that all of the models are very poor.

To deal with the overall inaccuracy of these models, we consider recalibrating them, learning from the inaccuracies as they occur. That is, we can use early understanding of a model's behavior to improve future predictions.

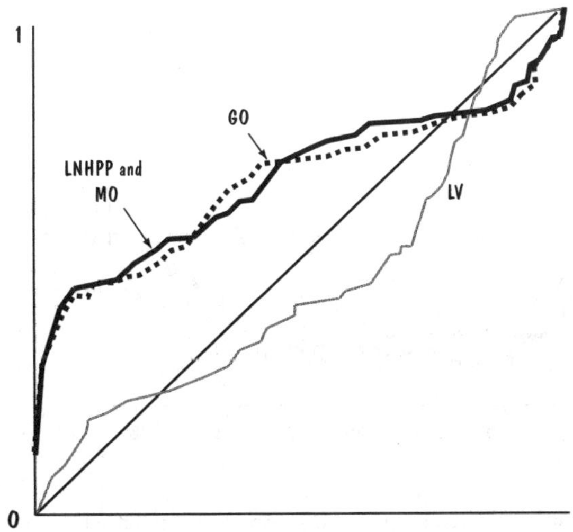

FIGURE 13.5 u-plots of models using data from Table 13.4.

FIGURE 13.6 *u*-plots for recalibrated models using data from Table 13.4.

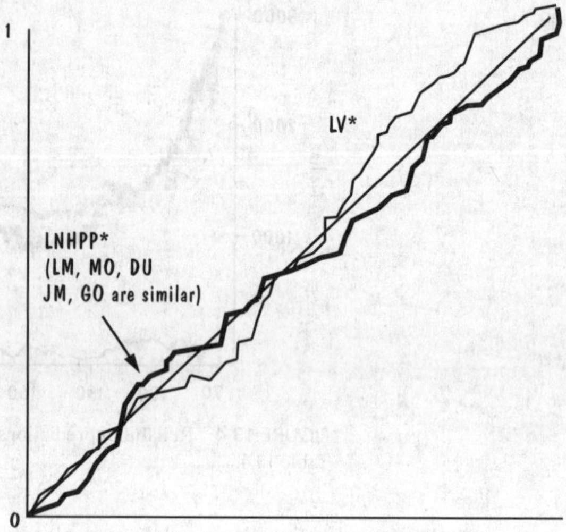

In particular, from a model M, we can learn from past errors and form a new prediction model, M^*, based on a *u*-plot. The recalibration procedure is beyond the scope of this book; see Fenton and Pfleeger (1997) for more information. However, we can look at the result of recalibration to see what difference it makes to the quality of the predictions. Figure 13.6 shows the *u*-plots for recalibrations of the models in Figure 13.5. After recalibration, the Kolmogorov distances are almost half of their original values.

We can also look at the predictions themselves, as shown in Figure 13.7. Here, there is much closer agreement among the recalibrated models than there was among the original models.

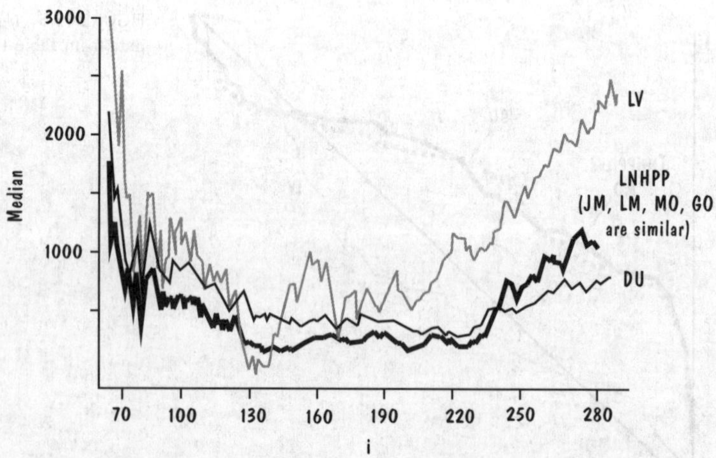

FIGURE 13.7 Predictions of recalibrated models using data from Table 13.4.

Thus, recalibration has yielded two key benefits:

1. models in closer agreement than before
2. new models with less bias than original ones

None of these techniques is particular to reliability modeling; we can use them to improve any prediction model. Thus, for any prediction system, we can use past behavior to build a model and then use the techniques introduced in this section to improve the predictions.

13.2 IMPROVING PRODUCTS

We have studied many examples of development and maintenance products: requirements specifications, design documents, code, test data, documentation, and user's guides, to name just a few. One of software engineering's goals is to use appropriate techniques to improve these products, making them easier to use, freer of defects, and more effective at doing the job they were intended to do.

In this section, we examine two product improvement strategies, inspections and reuse, to show how introducing them has yielded measurable improvements in industry products. We look at the effects of these techniques on fault density; Sidebar 13.1 describes how faults may be monitored during development.

Inspections

Barnard and Price (1994) report that AT&T was interested in using code inspections to improve its software quality. However, a search through the literature revealed wide variation in the percentage of faults removed by inspections: from 30% to 75%. In an effort to increase the percentage of faults removed, Barnard and Price used a set of nine measurements, generated by business needs and aimed at planning, monitoring, controlling, and improving inspections. The metrics tell AT&T not only whether the code quality is increasing as a result of inspections, but also how effective the staff is at preparing and inspecting code. Table 13.5 lists some of the measurements, with example values from two sample projects.

TABLE 13.5 Code Inspection Statistics from AT&T

Measurements	First Sample Project	Second Sample Project
Number of inspections in sample	27	55
Total thousands of lines of code inspected	9.3	22.5
Average lines of code inspected (module size)	343	409
Average preparation rate (lines of code per hour)	194	121.9
Average inspection rate (lines of code per hour)	172	154.8
Total faults detected (observable and nonobservable) per thousands of lines of code	106	89.7
Percentage of reinspections	11	0.5

SIDEBAR 13.1 MONITORING FAULT INJECTION AND DETECTION

Humphrey (1995) suggests several techniques for monitoring faults and measuring inspection effectiveness. He suggests that we create a fault database containing the program name, the fault number, and the type of fault. In addition, we should track the development activity during which the fault was injected into the product, the activity during which it was found and removed, and the time to find and fix the fault. This information helps us to understand where our faults are coming from and what kinds of activities should be improved. The improvement is done on two fronts: improving the activities where the injection is occurring, so that we can try to avoid injecting the fault in the first place, and improving the fault detection methods, so those faults that are injected are found as early as possible.

Humphrey also encourages us to calculate the "yield" of several review activities, much as Graham defined test effectiveness. For example, Table 13.6 shows how to track where faults were injected and where they were found. The table shows that four faults were found during design inspection, two of which were injected during planning and two during detailed design. During coding, two more faults were found, both of which originated in detailed design. Then three more faults are discovered during code inspection: one from detailed design and two more from the coding process. Similarly, five faults are discovered during compiling, four during testing and two after development is complete. If we analyze where these faults were injected, we can compute the yield of the two inspection processes as well as the total development yield. These numbers give us a better understanding of where faults are injected and how we can improve our product quality.

TABLE 13.6 Yield Calculation

		Faults Injected					
Activity	Faults Found	Design Inspection	Code	Code Inspection	Compile	Test	Post-Development
Planning	0	2	2	2	2	2	2
Detailed design	0	2	4	5	5	6	6
Design inspection	4						
Code	2			2	7	10	12
Code inspection	3						
Compile	5						
Test	4						
Postdevelopment	2						
TOTAL	20						
Design inspection yield		4/4 = 100%	4/6 = 67%	4/7 = 57.1%	4/7 = 57.1%	4/8 = 50%	4/8 = 50%
Code inspection yield				3/5 = 60%	3/10 = 30%	3/14 = 25.5%	3/16 = 18.8%
Total yield		4/4 = 100%	6/6 = 100%	9/9 = 100%	9/14 = 64.3%	9/16 = 56.3%	9/20 = 45%

For the first sample project, the researchers found that 41% of the inspections were conducted at a rate faster than Fagan's recommended rate of 150 lines of code per hour. In the second project, the inspections with rates below 125 found an average of 46% more faults per thousands of lines of code than those with faster rates. This finding means either that more faults can be found when inspection rates are slower or that finding more faults causes the inspection rate to slow. The information allows AT&T to tailor its inspection process so that more faults are found and products are thereby improved.

Weller (1994) reports a similar experience at Bull HN Information Systems. Bull software engineers track the actual faults found during development and compare them with the estimated faults they expected to find, as shown in Figure 13.8.

When fault density is lower than expected, the development team assumes it is for one of four reasons:

1. The inspections are not detecting all the faults they should.
2. The design lacks sufficient content.
3. The project is smaller than planned.
4. Quality is better than expected.

Similarly, if the fault density is higher than expected,

- The product is larger than planned.
- The inspections are doing a good job of detecting faults.
- The product quality is low.

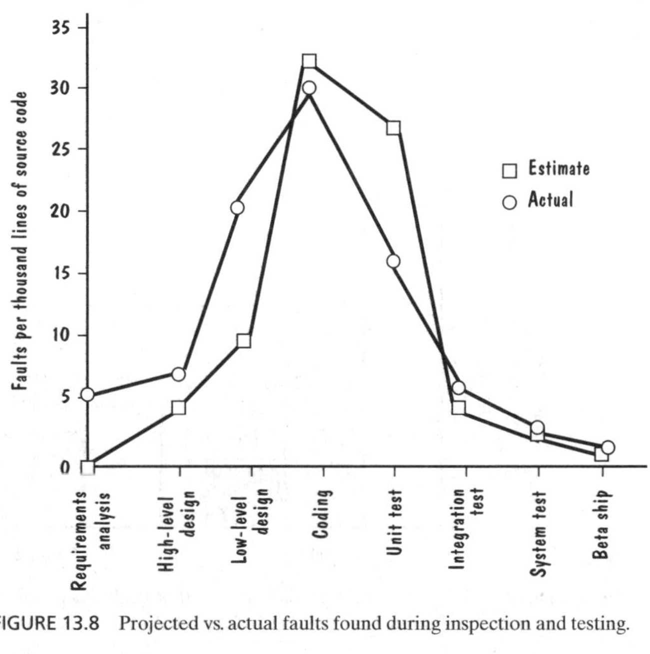

FIGURE 13.8 Projected vs. actual faults found during inspection and testing.

For example, if fault density is expected to be 0.5 to 1.0 fault per page as a result of inspection, and it falls below 0.1 to 0.2 fault per page, then the document may be incomplete. When the fault detection rate is below 0.5 fault per page, the team investigates to make sure that inspectors are taking enough time to prepare for an inspection.

Weller (1994) reports that there is a 7:1 difference in fault injection rates across projects. That is, some projects deliver products with seven times as many faults as others. But for the same team doing similar work, the fault injection rate stays about the same. By comparing expected faults with actual faults, Bull teams can determine how to find faults earlier during development, and how to make their inspection process more effective. The result is a gradual improvement in product quality.

Reuse

Reuse has long been touted as a method for improving product quality. By reusing products that have already been tested, delivered, and used elsewhere, we avoid making the same mistakes twice. We can take advantage of the efforts of other developers, and we use the fault and change histories of a design or code component to certify that it will work well in a new setting.

Surprisingly, there is little empirical information about the effects of reuse on quality. From his work at Hewlett-Packard, Lim (1994) shows us how reuse improves code quality. He performed two case studies to determine whether reuse actually reduces fault density. Figure 13.9 illustrates the dramatic difference between fault density in new code and in reused code. However, it is important to look at the fault density of the reused code combined with new code; many faults can be injected into the interfaces between the two.

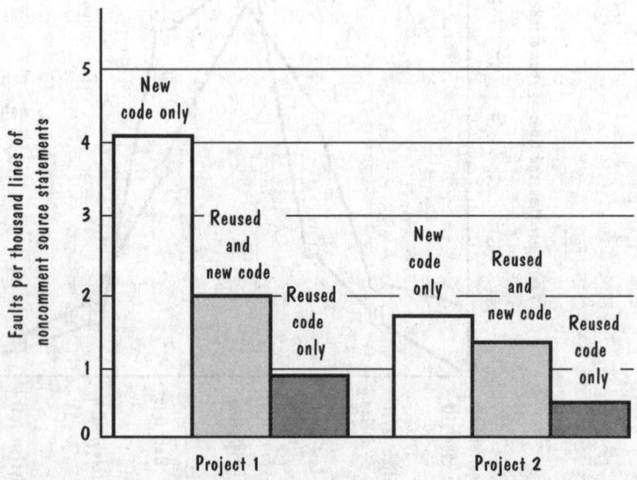

FIGURE 13.9 Effect of reuse on faults per thousand lines of noncomment source code.

Möller and Paulish (1993) investigated relationships involving fault density and reuse at Siemens. They found that reused components in which up to 25% of the lines of the original component had been modified had four to eight times more faults than components written from scratch. Thus, the quality increase promised by reusing components can be further improved if we are careful about how much code we modify. In some cases, we may not be able to avoid changing previously written code; if so, we can use supplementary techniques such as inspections or extra testing to ensure that the modifications do not introduce unnecessary faults.

13.3 IMPROVING PROCESSES

We have seen how software development processes can affect the quality of the products they produce. Models of process maturity are based on the notion that improving the process will automatically improve products, especially software. More narrowly focused processes, such as prototyping and cleanroom, are also aimed at reducing cost, improving quality, and shortening development or maintenance time. In this section, we look at investigations that improve the processes themselves, thereby indirectly improving products.

Process and Capability Maturity

We noted in Chapter 12 that there are several proposed models for improving the maturity of the overall development process, such as the CMM, ISO 9000, and SPICE. Many of these models have been embraced enthusiastically by some developers; others have resisted using them until they were made mandatory. In fact, the maturity models and their assessment methods are becoming de facto standards in many organizations. For example, minimum CMM scores are expected for some U.S. Air Force software contracts, and the scores have a significant effect on U.S. Navy contract decisions (Saiedian and Kuzara 1995). Rugg (1993) points out that "software capability—as measured in the submitted proposal and on site—counted as one-third of the weight for consideration to award the contract."

But ever since the introduction of process maturity models, there have been objections to their application and use. For example, Bollinger and McGowan (1991) noted many problems with the use of the original SEI process maturity questionnaire; in particular, they pointed out that limited questions captured only a small number of the characteristics of good software practice, and their yes/no answers made partial compliance impossible to measure. They also noted that the process maturity model assumes a manufacturing paradigm for software; as we discussed in Chapter 1, manufacturing and replication may be inappropriate analogies for software development.

Bollinger and McGowan (1991) also argue that the process maturity approach does not dig deep enough into how software development practices are implemented. For instance, certification at level 2 (repeatable) requires a "yes" answer to the question, "Do software development first-line managers sign off on their schedule and cost estimates?" This question means that a level 2 project must be managed by those who are willing to take responsibility for their estimates. However, there are no questions about whether managers assess the accuracy of their estimates or improve the estimation process as they learn more from process models and feedback. The danger in extracting only narrow information about key processes or practices is that it may paint a misleading picture of the project and its management. In this case, inappropriate models and inaccurate measurement are missed, and management may be "rewarded" with a level 2 assessment nevertheless.

Even with their drawbacks, do these maturity frameworks really work? Does moving up the maturity ladder automatically cause a developer to produce better software? For example, Pfleeger and McGowan (1990) suggest that improved maturity may lead to improved visibility into the inner workings of the process (see Sidebar 13.2). The U.S. Software Engineering Institute (SEI), as a promoter of the Capability Maturity Model, has undertaken an investigation of the effects of process improvement. Under the

SIDEBAR 13.2 PROCESS MATURITY AND INCREASED VISIBILITY

Pfleeger and McGowan (1990) have described how process maturity can affect an organization's or project's visibility into the process, and thereby its understanding of process issues. Although not strictly derived from the Software Engineering Institute's Capability Maturity Model, their notion of increasing visibility allows us to decide what makes sense based on what we can see in a picture of the process.

To see how this works, consider an example. Suppose our organization is concerned about requirements volatility. The goal of understanding the reasons for and effects of a requirements change suggests that our development group should measure both number of requirements and changes to those requirements. At the lowest level of visibility (akin to CMM level 1), the requirements are ill-defined. Here, we measure the number of and changes to each requirement as best we can. At the next higher level (similar to CMM level 2), the requirements are well-defined, but the process activities are not. At this stage, we can measure the number of requirements by type, as well as changes to requirements by type. Now, not only do we know how many requirements are changing, but we can also tell whether the changes occur primarily in the interface requirements, the performance requirements, the database requirements, or are distributed throughout the system specification. Actions taken based on these measurements have a more solid foundation and are more likely to be effective.

Similarly, at a higher level still (much like CMM level 3), the process activities are clearly differentiated; the project manager can tell when design is finished and coding starts, for example. Here, the requirements can be measured as before, including number of requirements and changes to requirements by type. But in addition, thanks to the defined activities, we can trace each requirement change to its corresponding design, code, or test component, enabling us to analyze the impact of the change on the rest of the system. The increased maturity of the process gives us more visibility, yielding a much richer body of information and a better understanding of the system than we had at lower levels.

TABLE 13.7 Aggregate Results from SEI Benefits Study (Herbsleb et al. 1994)

Category	Range	Median
Total yearly cost of software process improvement activities	$49,000 to $1,202,000	$245,000
Years engaged in software process improvement	1 to 9	3.5
Cost of software process improvement per engineer	$490 to $2004	$1375
Productivity gain per year	9–67%	35%
Early detection gain per year (faults discovered pretest)	6–25%	22%
Yearly reduction in time to market	15–23%	19%
Yearly reduction in postrelease fault reports	10–94%	39%
Business value of investment in software process improvement (value returned on each dollar invested)	4.0 to 8.8	5.0

auspices of the SEI, Herbsleb et al. (1994) collected data from 13 organizations representing various levels of capability maturity. By examining the changes in performance over time as software process improvement activities were implemented, the research team identified benefits in productivity, early fault detection, time to market, and quality. The results are shown in Table 13.7.

This study paints a very positive picture of software process improvement. However, we must be cautious about suggesting that the results indicate the general situation. The participating organizations volunteered to take part in the study; thus, this group did not form a random sample of the larger population. The projects were not characterized in a way that allows us to compare one with another, the process improvement efforts differed from one project to the next, and there was no measurement done to determine how representative the projects were. Although we can see that some software process improvement efforts were beneficial for this sample, we cannot conclude that software process improvement is beneficial in general.

It is not clear how the reported results should be viewed in the larger context of business value. The "value returned" in the Herbsleb study seems to be measured in terms of early detection of faults, reduction in time to market, and reduction of operational failures. But these characteristics do not address customer satisfaction or appropriate functionality. That is, they look at technical quality rather than business quality, so they paint only a partial picture of improvement. We cannot determine from these results whether adopting a maturity framework is good for business. As Sidebar 13.3 points out, there may be cases where high maturity can actually restrict business flexibility.

If the models and measurements are incorrect or misguided, the result can be misallocation of resources, loss of business, and more.

Card (1992) reports that inconsistent results were obtained from CMM assessments of the same organization by different teams; thus, we must wonder how reliable the CMM assessments are. Here, reliability refers to the extent to which the same measurement procedure yields the same results on repeated trials.

El Emam and Madhavji (1995) have further investigated reliability, asking

- How reliable are such assessments?
- What are the implications of reliability for interpreting assessment scores?

SIDEBAR 13.3 IS CAPABILITY MATURITY HOLDING NASA BACK?

Several researchers and practitioners have questioned whether the Capability Maturity Model helps us do better what we already do but does not allow us flexibility to try new things or to change and grow technically. To understand their concerns, consider the software in NASA's space shuttle. It was built and is maintained by an organization that has been rated level 5 on the CMM scale.

The software has been extraordinarily reliable, experiencing very few operational failures. However, the software is driven primarily by tables. Before each launch, NASA must develop new data tables to describe the launch and control the software. The process of updating these tables takes a great deal of time and effort, so it is a costly, time-consuming activity that can delay a launch date. The software development and maintenance process awarded the level 5 rating is the one that supports table revisions. It is possible that a major change in the development process, in part to overhaul the table-based approach and make the system more flexible, may result in a process that receives a lower CMM rating; if so, it may be possible that the prospect of another maturity evalution is discouraging the developers from trying a new, innovative approach. In other words, it is not at all clear whether reengineering or redesign of the space shuttle software will be hindered or helped by NASA's current optimized process.

They built a model of organizational maturity based on the CMM and several other popular models and performed a case study to address these questions. They found clear evidence of unreliability when measured along four dimensions: standardization, project management, tools, and organization. Moreover, when they investigated the relationship between organizational maturity and other attributes of process and product, they found a small, significant relationship between maturity and quality of service, but "no relationship was found with quality of products" and "a small negative correlation between the standardization and project management dimensions and the quality of projects."

The questions raised about process improvement frameworks are not particular to the CMM. Seddon (1996) delivers the same message in his report on the effects of ISO 9000 on several businesses in the UK. He says that "ISO 9000, because of its implicit theory of quality, will lead to common problems in implementation; problems which damage economic performance and which may inhibit managers from ever learning about quality's potential role in improving productivity and competitive position." Indeed, the UK's Advertising Standards Authority has ruled that the British Standards Institute must refrain from making claims that adherence to ISO 9000 will improve quality and productivity. In a newsletter that describes the case, Seddon notes that "In every case we have studied we have seen ISO 9000 damaging productivity and competitive position. The executives of each and every one of these organisations believed that ISO 9000 had been beneficial: they were all misguided" (ESPI Exchange 1996).

Thus, there are important measurement questions to be addressed in considering the use of these process and organizational frameworks. We must understand how

SIDEBAR 13.4 COMPARING SEVERAL MAINTENANCE ESTIMATION TECHNIQUES

De Almeida, Lounis, and Melo (1997) used machine learning algorithms to predict costly, fault-prone software components. Using fault data collected at NASA's Goddard Space Flight Center and product measures extracted from the Ada code, they classified components as being costly or not costly to correct. They found that inductive logic programming models were more accurate than top-down induction trees, top-down induction attribute value rules, and covering algorithms.

reliable and valid the measurements and models are, know what entities and attributes are being measured, and test the relationships between the maturity scores and the behaviors that "maturity" is supposed to produce or enhance.

Maintenance

In Chapter 11, we noted that maintenance costs are growing and often exceed development costs. Thus, it is important to investigate ways to improve the maintenance process, reducing cost while maintaining or improving quality. As Sidebar 13.4 points out, we have many models from which to choose; it is not clear which models are appropriate in a given situation. Henry et al. (1994) addressed that issue at the Government Electronic Systems Division of a major contractor, attempting to answer three questions:

1. How can we quantitatively assess the maintenance process?
2. How can we use that assessment to improve the maintenance process?
3. How do we quantitatively evaluate the effectiveness of any process improvements?

Using a method that employs common statistical tests (such as multiple regression, rank correlation, and chi-square tests of independence in two-way contingency tables) to quantify relationships among maintenance activities and process and product characteristics, they learned about the maintenance process; in particular, they looked at how requirements changes affect product attributes.

For example, the research team wanted a simple classification scheme for software components that would allow them to predict which ones were fault-prone. They created contingency tables based on the median values of faults corrected and the number of upgrades and upgrade-specification changes affecting a component. They found a significant correlation between faults corrected and upgrade impact, and used the relationship to rank the components. By selecting components for more careful scrutiny (such as more testing or extra reviewing) by their relationship to the median number of upgrade items affecting the component, they correctly identified 93% of the components with fault rates above the median.

Henry et al. (1994) also examined the relationship of several project attributes to engineering test failures. As a result of this analysis, the engineering test group changed its role and test strategy. Engineering testing now focuses on enhancement-to-enhancement regression testing, and the engineering test group now monitors the tests run by subcontractors, requiring detailed test reports.

The research group studying the maintenance process learned many lessons about maintenance, and their suggestions led to measurable process and product improvement. But they also learned a lot about the evaluation process itself. They note three things to keep in mind when evaluating improvement.

1. Use statistical techniques with care, because a single technique may not evaluate the true effect of process improvement. For example, when they considered only median and rank correlation of upgrade impact on product reliability, they saw no improvement. But when they used the mean and standard deviation, the improvement was clear.
2. In some cases, process improvement must be very dramatic if the quantitative effects are to show up in the statistical results. For example, the contingency tables used to classify components as fault-prone changed very little as the process was improved, until almost all the faults were removed.
3. Process improvement affects linear regression results in different ways. In particular, as the equations' accuracy increased, their effects on individual variables differed.

Cleanroom

NASA's Software Engineering Laboratory evaluated and improved processes for several decades. Basili and Green (1994) described how the SEL introduced new technology, assessed its effects, and took advantage of those tools and techniques that offered significant improvement. The SEL took into account the risks involved in using a new technology; where appropriate, the technique or tool was applied outside of the normal project environment, where its use would not threaten project goals.

These offline studies were usually performed as formal, controlled experiments or case studies. The SEL usually began with a small experiment, where the size permitted the variables to be controlled easily. Then, when experimental results looked promising, an industrial-strength case study verified that the small-scale results worked in real-world environments. Once the SEL was satisfied that a new technique would be good for NASA's developers and maintainers, it packaged the lessons learned so that others could understand and use the technology.

Basili and Green (1994) investigated the key processes involved in cleanroom, to see whether they would be beneficial at NASA. They organized their studies into five parts:

1. a controlled experiment comparing reading with testing
2. a controlled experiment comparing cleanroom with cleanroom-plus-testing
3. a case study examining cleanroom on a three-person development team and a two-person test team
4. a case study examining cleanroom on a four-person development team and a two-person test team
5. a case study examining cleanroom on a fourteen-person development team and a four-person test team

TABLE 13.8 Results of Reading vs. Testing Experiment 1

	Reading	Functional Testing	Structural Testing
Mean number of faults detected	5.1	4.5	3.3
Number of faults detected per hour of use of technique	3.3	1.8	1.8

The Experiments. In the first experiment, Basili and Green (1994) used fault seeding to compare reading by stepwise-abstraction, equivalence partitioning boundary-value testing, and statement-coverage structural testing. Their results are shown in Table 13.8.

They also considered the confidence in the result. After the experiment, the readers thought they had found about half of the faults, and they were approximately correct. But the testers thought they had found almost all the faults, which was never correct. Basili and Green (1994) speculate that exercising large numbers of test cases gives testers a false sense of confidence.

The readers also found more classes of faults, including interface faults, suggesting that the results would scale up to larger projects.

In the second experiment, Basili and Green (1994) acknowledged the traditional SEL reliance on testing. They felt it too risky to remove testing completely from the developers' control, so they designed their experiment to compare traditional cleanroom with cleanroom where testing was allowed. Among the findings were the following:

- Cleanroom developers were more effective at doing offline reading.
- Cleanroom-plus-testing teams focused more on functional testing than on reading.
- Cleanroom teams spent less time online and were more likely to meet their deadlines.
- Cleanroom products were less complex, had more global data, and had more comments.
- Cleanroom products met the system requirements more completely, and they had a higher percentage of successful independent test cases.
- Cleanroom developers did not apply the formal methods very rigorously.
- Almost all cleanroom participants were willing to use cleanroom again on another development project.

Because the major difference between the two teams was permission to do extra testing, Basili and Green (1994) suggest that members of the control group (cleanroom-plus-testing) did not take the time to learn and use the other techniques because they knew they could rely on testing.

The Case Studies. All three case studies involved the development of flight dynamics software. The first study's goal was to increase quality and reliability without increasing cost, as well as to compare cleanroom with the standard environment in the flight dynamics division. Because the SEL already had a baseline for flight dynamics development at NASA Goddard, researchers could compare the cleanroom results and study the differences. The cleanroom process was tailored, based on the results of the two experiments, so that it involved

- separation of the development and test teams
- reliance on peer review instead of unit testing
- use of informal state machines and functions to define the system design
- statistical testing based on operational scenarios

Basili and Green (1994) found that 6% of project effort shifted from coding to design when cleanroom was used. Also, whereas traditional developers spent 85% of their time writing code and 15% reading it, the cleanroom team spent about half its time on each activity. Productivity increased by 50% and the amount of rework decreased. However, the team had a difficult time using the formal methods, so they combined statistical testing with functional testing.

Learning from the first study, Basili and Green (1994) improved the formal methods training and provided more guidance in how to use statistical testing. In particular, they emphasized box structures instead of state machines. In this case study, they used a sister project design, comparing the cleanroom approach to a more traditional one. The results are summarized in Table 13.9.

The change and fault rates were clearly better for the cleanroom team, but there were some drawbacks. Cleanroom participants did not like using design abstractions and box structures, were uncomfortable with being unable to compile their code, and had difficulty coordinating developers and testers.

A third case study learned from the lessons of the first two. More cleanroom training was available, and a cleanroom process handbook was provided to the participants. The results have not yet been reported in the literature.

The Conclusions. The SEL's cleanroom experience teaches us several things. First, Basili and Green (1994) have shown us how to use a combination of experiments and case studies to compare a new technique with an existing one. They tailored both the technique and the investigative process to the organization involved and the results of previous studies. That is, they slowly modified the cleanroom approach as they learned how study participants reacted to the various cleanroom activities. And they used more than one type of case study, so that they could control as much variation as possible.

Their well-documented investigative work is typical of a mature organization. As new techniques and tools are adopted, the "typical" environment changes and improves.

TABLE 13.9 Results of SEL Case Studies

	Baseline Value	Cleanroom Development	Traditional Development
Lines of code per day	26	26	20
Changes per thousand lines of code	20.1	5.4	13.7
Faults per thousand lines of code	7.0	3.3	6.0

Basili and Green (1994) offer us valuable quantitative evidence of the effects of cleanroom at NASA Goddard. We can use similar studies to evaluate cleanroom in our own environments, but we are likely to get different results that reflect the abilities, needs, and preferences of our own organizations. The important lesson is not that cleanroom always works. Rather, it is that cleanroom can work, and that we must continue investigating to determine how to tailor it to make it work best for each particular situation.

13.4 IMPROVING RESOURCES

Many resources are required to produce good software. We must be supplied with appropriate equipment, tools, and techniques and given enough time to do the job. Some resources are fixed, leaving no room for improvement. For example, if a system must be developed on a particular platform or in a given language, our designs are sometimes limited. But other resources are highly variable, and understanding the variability helps us to improve them. For example, software engineers with equal training have very different abilities. We all know developers who are good at coding but terrible at testing or who are good designers but bad requirements analysts. Even within a category, there is variation; indeed, some programmers can write poor code quickly or good code slowly or just about anything in between!

Work Environment

Unfortunately, there is less in the literature about the human role in software engineering than about techniques and tools. Most of the quantitative analysis focuses on baselining programmer productivity or evaluating the trade-offs between cost and schedule. DeMarco and Lister are among the few researchers who have examined the way in which environment affects the quality of the work we do. They coined the term "peopleware" to designate the variability among developers and to emphasize that we can take steps to improve software quality by giving people the environment they need to do a good job (DeMarco and Lister 1987).

We noted in Chapter 3 the McCue (1978) study that recommended at least 100 square feet of dedicated work space per worker, 30 square feet of work surface per person, and noise protection. DeMarco and Lister's 1984 and 1985 surveys of programmers (DeMarco and Lister 1985) revealed that only 16% of the participants had the recommended minimum space and 58% said that their office space was not acceptably quiet. The work space results are shown in Figure 13.10.

To show how much the space and noise considerations matter, DeMarco and Lister analyzed the quality of a coding competition, comparing fault profiles for noisy and quiet offices. Workers who reported before the competition that their offices were quiet were 33% more likely to deliver fault-free code. And as the noise level gets worse, the trend appears to be stronger. DeMarco and Lister recommend simple, cost-effective measures for improving a developer's environment, such as voice mail and call-forwarding (to eliminate ringing telephones), and doors on offices (to reduce unnecessary interruptions).

It is commonly thought that small teams work better than large ones, because the number of communication paths increases dramatically as the team size goes up. Weller

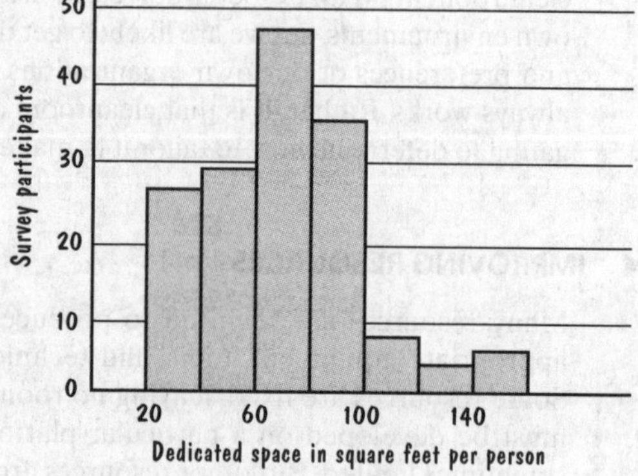

FIGURE 13.10 Floor space for developers, from DeMarco and Lister surveys.

(1993) confirmed this notion when he examined inspection data. As we saw in Chapter 8, a three-person inspection team can perform just as well as a four-person team. Sidebar 13.5 explains how users can be a valuable resource; we must not forget them when considering team size and communication paths.

DeMarco (1997) emphasizes the importance of team "jell," where team members work smoothly, coordinating their work and respecting each other's abilities. For this reason, he suggests that teams that have worked well together in the past be kept together for future projects. In addition, he urges us to use mediation to resolve conflicts, so that the team views itself as united on one side and the problem on the other side.

Cost and Schedule Trade-Offs

Time is a key resource. Given enough time, a development team can produce a high-quality product by designing carefully, testing thoroughly, and spending enough time with customers and users to ensure that all have a common understanding of the problem and its solution.

Unfortunately, time is not always available. Market pressures require us to sell products before our competitors do or offer services when our customers demand them. Coordination pressures force us to make our products available when other products are delivered, driven by integration and testing schedules. Thus, understanding the relationships among cost, schedule, and quality helps us plan our development and maintenance without sacrificing function or quality.

Many effort and schedule estimation models include this type of trade-off analysis. For example, COCOMO describes the interaction between effort and schedule and suggests nominal effort and schedule measures based on project parameters (Boehm 1981). Other models, such as Putnam's SLIM, illustrate the effects of compressing the schedule, usually resulting in an increasing need for staff. However, Brooks (1995) warns us that adding staff to a late project only makes it later. Similarly, Lister tells us that people under pressure do not think any faster, so there must be a minimum amount of time needed to perform a task well (DeMarco 1997).

SIDEBAR 13.5 VIEWING USERS AS A RESOURCE

In Chapter 11, we saw how Bell Atlantic built its SaleService Negotiation System (SSNS) to replace three legacy systems. By using on-screen prompts, SSNS guides sales representatives through an order cycle. The application created a more profitable relationship with Bell Atlantic's customers, making Bell Atlantic much more competitive in the marketplace (Field 1997a).

One of the reasons for SSNS's success was its developers' use of users as a resource. By forming a collaborative relationship between the information systems developers and Bell Atlantic's business managers, the SSNS team worked to define the problem carefully. Users pointed out problems and forced the information systems developers to address key issues. Information systems personnel encouraged users' input and listened carefully to their advice.

Performance issues were addressed by having the users work side by side with the software engineers. When the system was completed, some of the users were trained to be system advocates who explained the technology and trained others to use it. This mutual trust helped in the technology transfer, and users were eager to master the skills needed to use SSNS.

Abdel-Hamid (1990) uses systems dynamics models to investigate the effects of schedule compression. He notes that project scheduling is a continuous process; the project manager revises the schedule as more is known about a project. Thus, the final cost and completion time depend on an initial estimate and how realistic it is, and also on how resources are adjusted to address the initial estimate.

Abdel-Hamid (1990) applied his models to data from NASA Goddard Space Flight Center, looking at the effects of management's policies on project cost and on completion time. For example, Figure 13.11 shows the effect of two different hypothetical

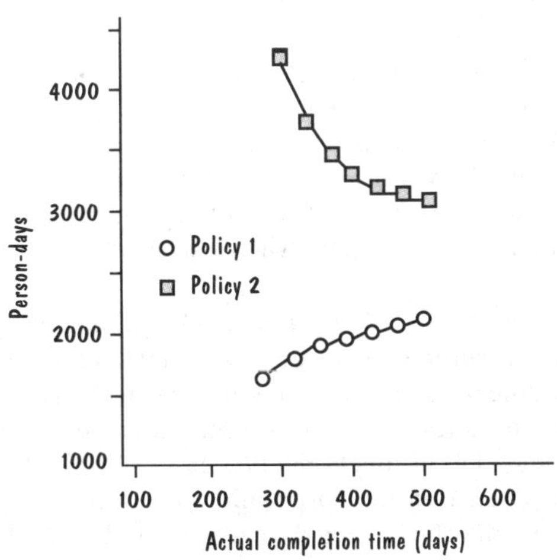

FIGURE 13.11 Trade-off between person-days and schedule for two management policies.

policies on the number of person-days to finish the project. The first policy, represented by circles, assumes that management will always adjust the workforce to the level necessary to keep the project on schedule. The second policy, represented by squares, eliminates the pressure of a maximum tolerable completion date. That is, schedule difficulties are addressed by extending the schedule, not by adjusting the workforce level. The trade-off behaviors are significantly different, and Abdel-Hamid's models help managers decide which policies to implement.

13.5 GENERAL IMPROVEMENT GUIDELINES

To stay successful, organizations should be flexible and grow. So, too, should their technology programs, whether they focus on reuse, measurement, inspections, or any other aspect of software engineering or management. Like anything else that is important to a company, a technology-based program requires strategic planning. The plan should address not only how technology will be used but also how it will improve an organization's products, processes, and resources.

Because things change over time, a strategic plan should be revisited periodically. Managers and developers should ask key questions:

- *Are the goals the same?* If the business goals have changed, then the technology program's goals may need to change with them. For example, initial goals may involve establishing a baseline for the organization or company. Once that is accomplished, goals relating to increased productivity may supersede them. Similarly, once productivity is increased, the company or division may want to focus on improving quality.
- *Are the priorities of the goals the same?* As one type of improvement is implemented successfully, other types may be selected for the next initiative. For example, initial high priorities may be assigned to goals involving test tool usage. But once test tool usage becomes part of the corporate development culture, requirements and design activities may become the focus of understanding and improvement.
- *Are the questions the same?* Questions that are relevant for the first stages of a program (e.g., how much should we invest in a technique?) may be replaced by questions of maturation (e.g., how much money and time are we saving by using the technique?). Similarly, technology transfer that is implemented by beginning with pilot projects may eventually generate new questions (e.g., what costs from the pilot project are likely to be incurred again when we introduce this technology companywide?).
- *Are the measurements the same?* As a development or maintenance process matures, the richness of the measurements needed to understand and control it increases. At the same time, some measures may no longer be necessary to collect, and they may be replaced by new ones. For instance, initial collection of size measures may be replaced by some kind of functionality measure. Similarly, as reuse becomes a widely accepted practice in the corporation, measures of reliability, availability, and maintainability may be collected to determine the effect of reuse

on corporate product quality. Measures related to customer satisfaction may also grow, from measures of the number of services requested and used to measures of interface and customer service quality.

- *Is the maturity the same?* The maturity of the development or maintenance process may improve, and with it the visibility needed to understand and measure new items. For example, initial attempts at data capture may not be automated, and the data may be stored in a simple spreadsheet. But as development grows and with it the size of a metrics database, an automated system may be developed to support it. With automation comes a finer level of granularity, as measurements can be made repeatedly over time and progress tracked. Thus, as maturity increases, the strategic plan can address issues at more detailed levels.
- *Is the process the same?* The development process may change dramatically over time. Feedback loops may be added for decision-making. Or prototyping may change the way in which products are developed and assessed. Each change has important implications for assessment and understanding, as well as for the issues addressed by the strategic plan.
- *Is the audience the same?* Many technology programs start small, often as a pilot in a department or division, and expand to the corporation slowly and carefully. As they do, the audience for understanding their effects changes from the programmers, managers, and department heads to the division heads and corporate executives. That is, the audience changes with the impact of the technology. It is important for the strategic plan to change, too, to reflect the questions and interests of the audience.

13.6 INFORMATION SYSTEMS EXAMPLE

Throughout this book, we have learned about Piccadilly's system for selling advertising time. Suppose the system is running well, and most maintenance changes reflect the needs of Piccadilly as its advertising campaigns change to meet business goals. What improvement strategies should the Piccadilly maintainers follow, so that they can make their changes quickly and without inserting faults in the software?

One key strategy is to perform perfective maintenance. The maintainers can examine the software's design, to see whether it can be made more flexible and more easily changed. Using a history of past changes, they can identify the components most likely to be affected by change and look at how much time past changes required.

Another strategy is to examine other similar software systems at Piccadilly. We have seen in this and previous chapters that companies such as Bell Atlantic and Chase Manhattan have replaced several legacy systems with one larger, more comprehensive one. Piccadilly analysts can take a broader, systems approach. How does the advertising system support the business? What other software systems interact with it? How can the systems be combined or enhanced to answer business needs faster or more effectively? In other words, the Piccadilly analysts should examine the system boundary and determine if it should be expanded to incorporate other problems.

13.7 REAL-TIME EXAMPLE

Improvement strategies are important at the European Space Agency, too. The Lions et al. (1996) report has suggested several improvements, including the following:

- The team should perform a thorough requirements review to identify areas where Ariane-5 requirements differ significantly from Ariane-4. In particular, the specification should contain the Ariane-5 trajectory data as a functional requirement.
- The team should do ground testing by injecting simulated acceleration signals in predicted flight parameters, using a turntable to simulate launcher angular movements.
- The guidance system's precision should be demonstrated by analysis and computer simulation.
- Reviews should become a part of the design and qualification process, carried out at all levels, and involving external experts and all major project partners.

These steps should be taken as part of a regression exercise whenever the code is changed. They should help to ensure that the failure modes that evaded detection in the past will not be missed in the future.

13.8 WHAT THIS CHAPTER MEANS FOR YOU

In this chapter, we have examined several techniques for improving predictions, products, processes, and resources. We have seen how predictions can be improved by using *u*-plots, prequential likelihood, and recalibration to reduce noise and bias. Products can be improved as part of a reuse program or by instituting an inspection process. Processes can be improved by evaluating their effects and determining relationships that lead to increased quality or productivity. For example, models can be developed, based on past history, to predict when components will be faulty; this technique reduces the time to maintain a system, and ultimately leads to higher-quality software. Similarly, process maturity frameworks may assist organizations in implementing activities that are likely to improve software quality, but careful controlled studies have not yet provided sufficient evidence. Finally, there is promise of improvement in resource allocation as we learn more about human variability and examine the trade-offs between effort and schedule.

As a developer or maintainer, these results affect you directly. To improve your surroundings and your products, you must be willing to participate in case studies and experiments and to give feedback to those who are trying to determine what leads to improvement. You must work closely with your customers and users to develop trust, so that they will feel confident about the system you are building for them. And you must work as part of a team, finding common ground when seeking solutions to problems.

13.9 WHAT THIS CHAPTER MEANS FOR YOUR DEVELOPMENT TEAM

The results described in this chapter suggest profound changes for your development team. Good predictions depend on a common understanding of the key issues affecting your team's effort and schedule. Good products and effective processes depend on the way in which your team works together in cohesive ways to get the job done. And good resources are essential for you to do your job right.

Several items reported here might affect your team in counterintuitive ways. If process maturity frameworks are indeed effective at improving software quality, then many of their recommended practices must become institutionalized across your team and your organization. It will be difficult to determine how much flexibility you are allowed before you forfeit your maturity rating. Similarly, if a "jelled" team should continue to work together across different projects, then you may produce better products but have fewer opportunities to work with new people on completely new problems.

On the other hand, the studies reported in this chapter emphasize the need for teams to check each other's work. Inspections, cleanroom, reuse, and other quality-related processes involve the careful scrutiny of one person or organization's work by another. These approaches encourage egoless development, where the focus is on product quality and process effectiveness rather than on individual accomplishment.

13.10 WHAT THIS CHAPTER MEANS FOR RESEARCHERS

Research on improvement issues is growing, as developers clamor for empirical proof that proposed technologies really work. This chapter illustrates the need for more surveys, case studies, and experiments; the Basili and Green example shows how a collection of studies can be organized to build on each other.

Research is also needed on frameworks for improvement, based on proven techniques and tailored for particular applications and domains. The general idea of maturity has spawned a series of related frameworks: a reuse maturity model, a CASE tool maturity model, and so on. These frameworks must be tied together so that practitioners have a better idea of which technologies to adopt and why.

Finally, software engineering researchers should jump into human factors research with both feet. We can understand more about resources issues such as team size, collaboration styles, and what makes a good working environment by learning from studies already performed in the social sciences. Then, we can assess which results apply to software engineers. Most researchers admit that human variability is a key factor in determining whether quality and schedule goals will be met; a better understanding of that variability will help us design techniques and tools to use that variability to our advantage.

13.11 TERM PROJECT

Consider how you and your team built the Loan Arranger project. What resource improvements would you have needed to do a better job? Training? Different skills? More time? More quiet in your workplace? Devise a list to present to your instructor, suggesting better ways to organize this project the next time it is assigned in class.

13.12 KEY REFERENCES

ISO 9000 certification is required in many countries. Seddon's book, The Case Against ISO 9000, plus other analyses of the standard, are available at http://www.systemsthinking.co.uk. By contrast, Micaela Martínez-Costa and Angel R.

Martínez-Lorente (2007) study data from 713 companies, finding that ISO 9000 can have very positive effects for some companies.

DeMarco and Lister continue to give updated seminars about the issues first raised in their *Peopleware* book, which they have recently updated and reissued. Information about the seminars and related materials can be found at the Web site of the Atlantic Systems Guild, http://www.systemsguild.com.

Evaluation and improvement are the subjects for many conferences and symposia. The Empirical Assessment of Software Engineering conference is organized by Keele University and attracts researchers interested in conducting case studies and experiments. More information is available at http://ease.cs.keele.ac.uk. The U.S. Software Engineering Institute and the various local Software Process Improvement Networks organize workshops related to maturity models. The journal *Software Process—Improvement and Practice* includes many articles about the effects of maturity models. Researchers continue to use empirical software engineering techniques to assess the effects of various maturity models, as well as the problems of interrater agreement and validity of the measurement instruments.

13.13 EXERCISES

1. Explain how systems dynamics might be used to examine the trade-offs between adequate computer security and acceptable system performance.
2. Suppose you are tracking the fault density in a series of similar products, so that you can monitor the effectiveness of the new inspection process you introduced. Over time, you find that the fault density decreases. Explain how you might determine whether the falling fault density is the result of inspections, increased understanding of the product, or sloppy inspection and development activities.
3. Can you think of two or three reasons why the different prediction models do not apply to all software projects? Explain.
4. Suppose your organization is considering rapid prototyping on its next project. Gordon and Bieman (1995) have catalogued the lessons learned about rapid prototyping from reports in the literature, and the results are not always clear. How would you design a process to introduce rapid prototyping, evaluate its effectiveness, and improve its use?
5. Telecommuting is becoming more and more popular. Your organization is considering allowing people to telecommute and you are required to make a preliminary evaluation on the effects of telecommuting on the work environment. What would be some of the issues you need to consider?
6. Abdel-Hamid's systems dynamics model takes into account the changes in project understanding as the project progresses. What are the pros and cons of capturing assumptions about these changes? How can we test our assumptions, so that we have more confidence in the results of the model?
7. The president of your company has learned about ISO 9000 and insists that the company become certified. She wants quantitative evidence that ISO 9000 has improved the company's processes and products. How would you measure the effect of ISO 9000 certification?

14 The Future of Software Engineering

In this chapter, we look at
- the Wasserman principles and how we have done
- technology transfer
- how researchers provide evidence for technology adoption
- decision-making in software engineering
- next steps in research and practice

In this book, we have examined in detail the many activities involved in engineering quality software. We have seen how to use well-defined processes to build software that meets customers' needs, improving the quality of their businesses and their lives. But to understand where we are headed, we can look back at how much we have accomplished in a relatively short period of time.

14.1 HOW HAVE WE DONE?

From the time in 1968 when the phrase "software engineering" was first used at a NATO conference until the present day when many companies realize that their products and services depend on building or using software, we have built a corpus of data, anecdotes, theories, and practices that have changed the lives of almost everyone. Because of the world's remarkable dependence on software, we are obligated as students, practitioners, and researchers to act responsibly and effectively. Part of our responsibility is to gain a greater understanding of what we do and why we do it and then use that knowledge to improve our practices and products.

We have taken great steps toward this overarching goal of improvement. Starting out as movers of bits and bytes, we now use complex languages to direct our digital systems. We have teased out patterns and abstractions to form reusable products and to fashion new approaches to design. We have applied formal methods to difficult, informally expressed problems to help make their complexities and conflicts more visible.

And we have built a vast array of tools to speed the more mundane tasks, to codify and categorize relationships, to track progress, and to simulate possibilities.

We have developed the wisdom to hide details when they obscure the essence of a problem (as with object-oriented development) or to make details explicit when they are needed for more complete understanding (as for clear-box testing). But we still have challenges ahead. We tend to provide great accuracy in the large: we can tell when a space vehicle will reach Mars, or when a chemical reaction will reach a critical stage. But we do not have accuracy in the small: we cannot tell precisely when a software product will fail again, or exactly how a user will exercise a system's functions.

Wasserman's Steps to Maturity

We began this book by presenting Wasserman's eight steps toward a more mature discipline of software engineering. Having examined current software engineering practices in more depth in the intervening chapters, we return to Wasserman's points as a roadmap for future work.

- *Abstraction.* We have seen how abstraction helps us to focus on the essence of a problem, and how it differs from transformation. We must continue to use abstraction to find patterns not only in designs and code but also in requirements, in work habits, in user preferences, in test cases and strategies, and in the general way we approach a problem and try to solve it. Abstraction can be the basis for new ways of learning, teaching, and problem solving.
- *Analysis and design methods and notations.* We still use a wide variety of methods and notations to represent our problems and solutions. Each of us has particular preferences, influenced by the ways we understand and learn. Some prefer pictorial representations, while others like text. Multimedia software also encourages us to represent things using color, sound, position, or other characteristics. But comfort and preference conflict with the goal of having a common notation understandable by all. The solution is not to abandon all but one method and notation. Rather, our goal should be to develop transformations from each representation and method to a common one, useful for discussion and archiving. Just as the European Union preserves its own languages but uses English for common communication and understanding, so can we find a common way to express our requirements and designs while preserving the value of alternative expressions.
- *User interface prototyping.* The role of the user becomes more and more important as we inject software into critical areas of our lives. We must learn how the user thinks about problems and exercises solutions, so that our software supports and encourages the appropriate user behaviors. We have seen examples of software that prevents users from doing their jobs, or prevents businesses from providing new products and services. By concentrating on user needs and business needs, we can build products that are more responsive and useful.
- *Software architecture.* Shaw and Garlan have shown us how different architectures reflect different solutions to the same problem. Each architectural solution has pros and cons, and we must allow the desirable characteristics of the solution to drive our choice of architecture. We have also seen how the identification of

architectural styles and patterns is in its infancy. We must expand our architectural study to gain a better understanding of patterns, components, and the meaning of style.

- *Software process.* There is no question that software process affects software quality as the process becomes more visible and controllable. But how that visibility and control affect quality is a subject for further study. We saw in Chapter 1 that software development is an art as well as a science, a form of creation and composition rather than manufacturing. We must learn how to use software process to enhance products without stifling creativity and flexibility. We must also learn which processes work best in which situations and understand what characteristics of the products and the people building them are the most important in process choice.
- *Reuse.* In the past, the reuse community has focused on reusing code from old applications, and on building new code to be reusable in several products rather than a single one. In the future, we must expand our horizons, looking for reuse opportunities throughout the development and maintenance processes. Several researchers view maintenance as an instance of reuse, and that perspective may help us to reuse our experience as well as our products. We must combine our expanding understanding of abstraction and architecture with the need to reuse whatever we can, so that we identify a much broader set of reuse opportunities. At the same time, we need to develop assessment techniques that help us understand the quality of a component or document; we want to be able to reuse an artifact with some degree of confidence that it will work as expected. These reuse issues apply not only to artifacts of in-house development and maintenance but also to commercial off-the-shelf products that we plan to integrate into our next software system.
- *Measurement.* Almost all of the activities described in this book involve measurement in some way. We need to know if our products meet quality criteria, and we hope that our practices are effective and efficient. In the future, we must measure key characteristics of our products, processes, and resources in ways that are unobtrusive, useful, and timely. We should measure productivity using characteristics other than code size, acknowledging that we are productive well before we start writing code. We should measure quality according to a broader framework, including customer satisfaction, business need, and factors in addition to faults and failures. And we should measure software engineer satisfaction, too, making sure that our jobs continue to be satisfying as we find new and better ways to build new and better products.
- *Tools and integrated environments.* For many years, developers looked for tools and environments that would make them more productive and effective. Now, after having invested millions of dollars in tools that have not lived up to their promise, developers are building and using tools with more realistic expectations. Our tools and environments can help us to automate mundane tasks, to make calculations unobtrusive, and to track relationships. In the future, we must look for tools that help us trace connections among products, so that we can perform impact analysis when a change is suggested. We must build measurement tools

that measure in the background and provide prompt feedback to the developers and managers who need information about products and progress. We need tools to help us simulate and understand parts of a problem, possible interfaces and architectures, and the implications of choosing one solution strategy over another. And we must use tools to support reuse, so that we can easily extract what we need from earlier developments and incorporate them into current products.

What Now?

This review of Wasserman's principles leads to at least two important issues we should be addressing as researchers and practitioners. First, we should consider how well we move our new software engineering ideas into practice. That is, when researchers have a good idea that offers promise of better software processes, resources, or products, do we do a good job at turning that idea into a technology that is useful and effective for practitioners? And knowing our track record at technology transfer, how can we improve it in the future?

Second, we must consider how well our research and practice support decision-making about processes, resources, and products. Each chapter in this book contains examples of necessary decisions during software development and maintenance. For instance,

- What software process should be used?
- How long will development take, and how many people will we need?
- How much should we reuse?
- What kind of testing should we do?
- How do we manage our risks?

How can we enhance our decision-making so that we have more confidence in our choices of technology and resources? The remainder of this chapter examines what we know and where we might head in the future.

14.2 TECHNOLOGY TRANSFER

Suppose we are about to start a new software development or maintenance project. Do we use a familiar, time-tested technology, or do we incorporate a new technology with great promise? Do we look for empirical evidence that a new technology works, or do we follow our gut feeling, our colleagues' advice, or vendor suggestions? Our choices probably depend on whether we see ourselves as technology producers or consumers, and also on whether we tend to focus on the problem to be solved or on its solution. For example, IBM developers ignored the "hot" technologies of the time and instead built the space shuttle with tried-and-true IBM 360 technology to minimize risk of failure. In doing so, IBM acted as a technology consumer, focusing on the stability of the solution rather than on intriguing new technologies. But companies such as Silicon Graphics and Tandem Computers, as technology producers, devised their own, special-purpose technologies rather than base their solutions on existing ones. When we talk about **technology transfer**, we mean both that technology producers create and use new technologies, and that technology consumers adopt and use them in new products and services.

No matter what we choose and why we choose it, we can find successful past examples of our own technology-selection strategy to support our thinking. Unfortunately, as we have seen in earlier chapters, we can also find past examples of failure. This success/failure puzzle wears at least two faces: technical and commercial. We may do a wonderful job in solving a problem, only to find that our project is not a commercial success. Or, to catch the window of opportunity, we may rush our product to release, so that it becomes a commercial success in the short term but fails in the long term due to lack of support and enhancement. Often we have a dual focus: we want to choose the right technology to solve the problem and do it in a way that appeals to customers who need to have that problem solved. In this section, we examine why and how we make technology-selection decisions. We also look at how the empirical software engineering described in Chapter 13 produces evidence to support those decisions. Does the evidence help or hinder the adoption of new technologies throughout organizations or market segments?

This book has described many kinds of technologies that we have at our disposal. As we noted in Chapter 1, the "technology" we choose to help us in our next project can be any method, technique, tool, procedure, or paradigm used in software development or maintenance. To know whether a technology is successful, we want to look at whether it solves a problem, whether it is commercially viable, and how long it takes for the technology to become accepted practice. We also want to know how to increase the odds that our technology choice is the right one.

How We Make Technology Transfer Decisions Now

In the mid-eighties, Redwine and Riddle (1985) described their findings when investigating the pace at which software technology matures and is accepted into practice. They gathered case studies related to many concepts and technologies that were initially developed in the 1960s and 1970s, including formal verification, cost models, and object-oriented languages such as Smalltalk. They found that "it takes on the order of 15 to 20 years to mature a technology to the point that it can be popularized and disseminated to the technical community at large" (Redwine and Riddle 1985). In the worst case, it took 23 years to go from concept formulation to a point where popularization could be considered; the best case took 11 years, and the mean time was 17 years. Once a technology was developed, it took an average of 7.5 years for it to become widely available.

Clearly, 17 years is too long to wait in a business where time-to-market pressures require new technologies to prove themselves quickly. For example, in 1997, half of Hewlett-Packard's revenues were generated by products introduced in the previous two years. Even if not all of these products involved new technology, the relationship between revenue and speed of change tells us that we must move new technologies to the marketplace far faster than in the past. Markets cannot wait a decade or two for technological innovation. For this reason, many development organizations grab promising new technologies well before there is clear evidence of proven benefit. For instance, the U.S. Software Engineering Institute's Capability Maturity Model was embraced by many companies well before the SEI and others began empirical investigations of the nature and magnitude of its process improvement effects. Similarly, many development teams are writing code in Java even as the Java standard is evolving.

In other cases, technology adoption is mandated when the technology seems to be so evidently beneficial that careful empirical evaluation is not considered to be necessary. The imposition of Ada as the standard Department of Defense programming language is one example of the use of standards to push technology adoption. Another is the British Ministry of Defence's insistence on the use of formal methods in the development of safety-critical systems, even when there was little evidence of the nature and extent of formal methods' benefits. Over time, Ada has lost its position as favorite language, as developers prefer to use other, sometimes newer, languages. By contrast, evidence is growing that formal methods lead to more solid software.

Using Evidence in Technology Decision-Making

To understand how technology decisions are actually made, we can turn to business schools and their marketing programs, focusing on what is known as "diffusion research." Rogers (1995), in studying technology transfer in many organizations (not just transfers related to software), notes that there are distinct patterns in the way and speed with which technology is adopted. The first people to adopt a technology are **innovators**; they probably comprise only 2.5% of the total likely audience, as shown in Figure 14.1. Rogers explains that innovators are "venturesome": they are driven by a desire to be rash and to do something daring. An innovator usually launches a new idea by importing it from outside of a system's normal boundaries. In this sense, an innovator is a gatekeeper for his or her organization. Innovators are also people movers, and they rely on personal contact to convince their colleagues to take a risk and try a new technology.

Early adopters are also quick to embrace a new technology. However, it is not just the technology itself that intrigues them. Rather, their interest is driven by their perception of the potential benefits that the new technology can bring to the business. Early adopters usually let someone else test the waters first. But when they read about the success of a technology in a respected publication, they build on someone else's success and introduce the technology to their own organizations. For instance, the Software Technology Support Center at Hill Air Force Base (Ogden, Utah) evaluates technology and reports its findings regularly; early adopters may wait for something promising to

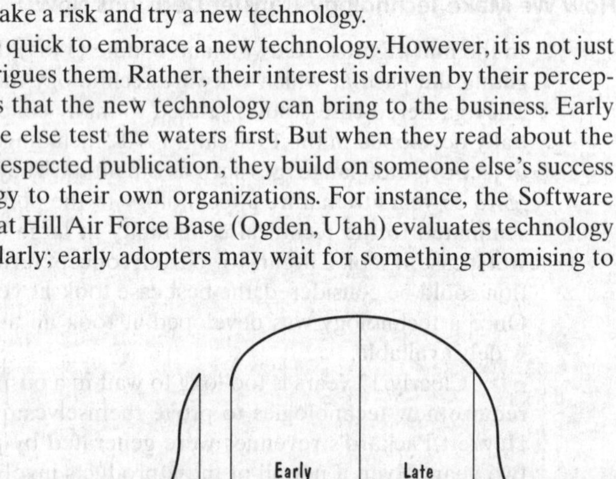

FIGURE 14.1 Adopter types and the chasm between the early and mainstream markets (Rogers 1995 and Moore 1991).

be reported by STSC and then embrace those tools or techniques that sound appealing. By making judicious technology decisions, early adopters decrease the uncertainty about the appropriateness or effectiveness of a new technology; they adopt it while personally informing colleagues of its past or present success.

The **early majority** is deliberate in decision-making, thinking for some time before welcoming a new technology. Driven by practicality, early-majority members make sure that the innovation is not a passing fad. In other words, they follow rather than lead, but they are willing to try new things demonstrated to be effective by others. Early-majority adopters can be convinced to try a technology not only when it has succeeded elsewhere but also when it is packaged with materials (such as training guides, help functions, and simple interfaces) that make adoption relatively smooth and painless.

Late-majority adopters are more skeptical. Adopting a new technology is usually the result of economic pressures or peer pressures. Most of the uncertainty about a new idea must be resolved before a late adopter will agree to try it. As a result, the late majority will wait until the new technology has become established and there is a sufficient amount of support available. Because late-majority adopters dislike uncertainty, they find it particularly appealing to rely on vendor advice. Thus, a vendor can use examples of other customers' experiences to help convince the late majority that the technology will work.

Finally, **laggards** are often averse to adopting something new, either with economic or personal justification. They jump on the technology bandwagon only when they are certain that a new idea will not fail, or when they are forced to change by mandate from managers or customers. Rules imposed by an organization, a standards committee, or a customer can encourage laggards to use a new technology when the other models fail.

Thus, successful technology transfer requires not only a new idea but also a receptive audience with a particular adoption style. Moore (1991) has looked at technology transfer from a marketing point of view. He highlights the chasm, shown in Figure 14.1, between the "early market" which requires little evidence, and the "mainstream market" which requires much more. The early market members are innovators and early adopters who are focused on the technology and its capabilities. They are willing to take risks in order to see how the technology works. Moore suggests that the early market is more interested in radical change, whereas the more conservative mainstream is more interested in incremental improvements to an existing way of doing things. That is, the early market takes great leaps and changes the way things are done, whereas the mainstream likes the current process but wants to tinker with it to make it more productive.

Evidence Supporting Technology Decisions

Researchers often perform investigative studies to support decisions about technology. A survey performed by Zelkowitz, Wallace, and Binkley (1998) highlights the often vast difference between the intended use of these studies and the way they are perceived by practitioners. Questioning 90 researchers and software practitioners about the value of various experimental methods necessary to validate a new technology, Zelkowitz et al. found that practitioners value most the methods that are relevant to their environment. That is, techniques such as case studies, field studies, and replicated controlled experiments were considered to be important to the decision-making process in choosing a new technology.

On the other hand, researchers prefer to perform studies involving reproducible validation methods that can be used in isolation in the laboratory, such as theoretical proof, static analysis, and simulation. They discounted methods that required interacting directly with practitioners. In other words, most researchers shunned the very methods that are most valued by practitioners: case studies, field studies, and experiments. Thus, researchers attempt to create a body of evidence for evaluating a technology, but practitioners seek a very different kind of substantiation of technical effectiveness. So the body of evidence provided by researchers is not likely to be taken seriously by the practitioners who are thinking about using the technology! The study shows us that successful technology transfer requires understanding the target audience and collecting a body of evidence that is relevant and credible to it.

What does this mean for both empirical software engineering research and software technology transfer in the future? It certainly means wasted research effort if things continue as they are now. And worse, it means that many of us will make technology decisions based on no evidence, little evidence, or even inappropriate evidence.

A Closer Look at the Evidence

Selling technological ideas requires an effective marketing strategy based on understanding the audience. As we have seen, the audience may have one of five distinct attitudes toward technology, and researchers should acknowledge the type of evidence sought by each one. But what do we know about putting evidential pieces together into a compelling argument? Fortunately, we can look to the legal community for guidelines about how to build compelling collections of evidence. Schum (1994) describes in great detail the analysis of evidence from at least two points of view: its source and its credibility. For example, we can place a piece of evidence in one of five categories:

- *Tangible evidence:* This type of evidence can be examined directly to determine what it reveals. Examples: objects, documents, demonstrations, models, maps, charts.
- *Testimonial evidence:* This type of evidence is supplied by another person, who can tell us how the evidence was obtained. Schum distinguishes three kinds of testimonial evidence: direct observation (the other person participated in the event and observed or perceived it directly), second-hand (she or he obtained the information from another source), and opinion (there is no primary source of information). Examples: requirements review reports, design walkthrough reports, journal articles.
- *Equivocal testimonial evidence:* The evidential provider does not remember the evidence exactly or supplies the information in probabilistic terms. Examples: operational profiles, reliability estimates.
- *Missing evidence:* The expected evidence cannot be found. Examples: reports from system maintainers who are no longer available to explain entries in problem reports; system developers who are no longer around to perform root cause analysis.
- *Accepted facts:* Information that is accepted without further need of proof. Examples: physical constants, mathematical formulae.

Evidence can be positive or negative. That is, it can provide proof of the advantages of a new technology, or it can show that there is no advantage or even a negative result.

Evidential credibility is assessed by looking at both its authenticity and accuracy. For example, testimonial evidence's credibility is directly related to the credibility of the provider. In turn, the provider's credibility depends on truthfulness (do we believe what the provider is telling us?), objectivity (is his or her perception influenced by expectations or other effects?), and observational sensitivity (how good is the measure or measuring device?).

Once we weigh each piece of evidence, we can combine the various pieces to see if, collectively, they support a conclusion about the technology. Sometimes this process is iterative; we come to a preliminary conclusion with some degree of confidence, and then we revise our conclusion and confidence level as new evidence is generated. If pieces of evidence are contradictory or conflicting, our conclusions must take this imperfect evidence into account. For example, some studies suggest that object orientation enhances reuse, whereas others do not. We can reach a conclusion about the value of reuse only by examining the nature of the evidential conflict. In the case of object orientation, the conflict may help us to distinguish the times when OO will help reuse from the times when it will hurt. That is, rather than dismiss a conclusion, a conflict may help to refine it. Similarly, larger bodies of evidence help to show us which variables are most important, and what aspects to consider when designing new studies.

Thus, we can have an evidential chasm that reflects Moore's marketing chasm: researchers must learn to produce evidence that is useful for practitioners. The evidence must be not only interesting but also credible to both researchers and practitioners. But what questions should the evidence try to answer? Rogers, Schum, and Moore provide clues about what kinds of evidence are suitable for whom. For example, Rogers (1995) notes that the relative speed at which a technology is adopted is based on several important things:

- *The nature of the communication channels used to increase awareness and knowledge of the technology.* Some types of adopters find some communication channels more credible than others. Innovators tend to rely on technical journals and reports from researchers and technical experts. Early adopters in turn ask the innovators to confirm a technology's credibility. Early- and late-majority members ask others in their social system, often by word of mouth or benchmarking visits.
- *The nature of the social system in which the potential user operates.* Innovators turn to technologists, but the mainstream market usually looks to the business community to see what its competitors are doing.
- *The extent of efforts to diffuse the technology throughout an organization.* The early market requires the least effort. However, the mainstream market requires not only information about the technology itself, but also packaging, user support, and testimonials from current adopters and users. Moore tells us that the technology itself is the "generic product," but the supporting materials help form the "whole product."
- *The technology's attributes.* Rogers suggests that the relevant attributes are
    - ◇ *Relative advantage:* To what degree is the new technology better than what is already available? Innovators answer this question in technical terms: is it faster, architecturally superior, or more maintainable? Early adopters look for

tangible evidence about the "whole product." Early-majority adopters seek information about the impact on the company, while late-majority adopters look at how the technology will increase market share. Thus, relative advantage reflects the advantage in four distinct areas—technology, product, company, and market—as each type of potential adopter widens the universe in which the decision-making is viewed.

- ◇ *Compatibility:* To what degree is the new technology consistent with existing values, past experiences, and needs of potential adopters? Because early market adopters are interested in radical change, they are not as interested in the answer to this question as those in the mainstream market. That is, the early market doesn't mind restarting from the ground up, but mainstreamers are reluctant to give up that with which they are already familiar.
- ◇ *Complexity:* To what degree is the new technology easy to understand and use? Early market adopters are more likely to be willing to learn completely new ways of doing things, even if more complex, in order to immerse themselves in newer, more exciting technology. But mainstreamers view ease of use as a necessary characteristic of a new technology.
- ◇ *Trialability:* Can the new technology be experimented with on a limited basis? Trying out the new technology is a must for early marketers. But many mainstreamers will try the technology only after others have built a solid case for the technology's advantages.
- ◇ *Observability:* Are the results of using the technology visible to others? The early market likes direct observation and tangible evidence. But mainstreamers prefer evidence only from organizations whose characteristics are like their own. For example, developers of banking software find evidence credible only when it comes from other banking organizations; case studies from telecommunications or defense firms leave them cold. Moreover, difficulties arise when the directly observed technology produces evidence of commercial advantage; in these cases, only second-hand evidence will be reported in the literature, if reported at all.

Figure 14.2 summarizes the types of evidence appealing to different audiences. The lower-left quadrant reflects innovators' interests, where the focus is primarily on the technology itself. Early adopters turn their attention to the broader notion of product, while mainstream market members are more interested in the company and the market. This figure makes it clear that different audiences look for very different kinds of evidence. Business school findings such as these help us ask the right questions about a technology (i.e., questions whose answers are interesting to the audience) and design the right kinds of studies to provide evidence that answers those questions.

New Models of Technology Transfer

The overriding goal of technology adoption is to improve at least one new product, process, or resource in some way. The evidence should help us to determine if the new technology causes improvement. We want to investigate the cause-and-effect relationship between the new technology and one or more variables of interest. Even if the benefit is the same as existing or competing technologies, we may choose the new technology

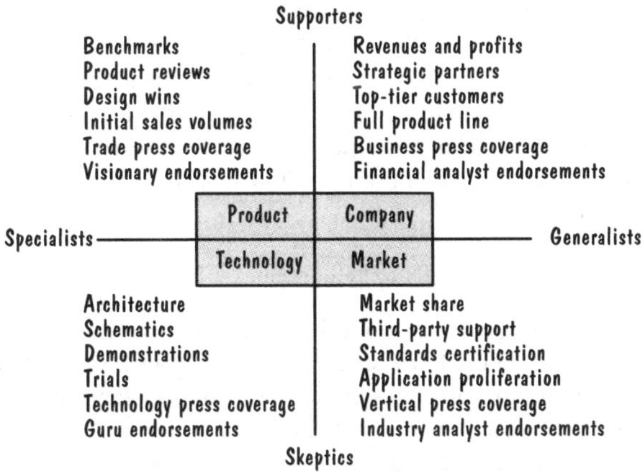

FIGURE 14.2 Evidence required for different audiences (adapted from Moore 1991).

simply because it reduces the uncertainty in cause and effect. In other words, we want the results of our development and maintenance processes to be more predictable.

To this end, we can put together these building blocks for technology transfer success to gain a better understanding of how technology transfer works in our individual organizations. Usually, such models include preliminary evaluation of a new technology, performed by those who use the technology for the first time, to see if it indeed solves the problem it was intended to address. This step should be sensitive to the organizational culture, so that a proposed technological solution can be viewed in the context of how it will be received by the organization or project that will use it. We should also identify promoters and inhibitors, so that we know who or what is likely to help or hinder technology adoption and effectiveness. For example, the adopter roles play a big part in determining the reception given to a particular technology, based on who is promoting it, whether similar technologies have been tried in the past, and how different the technology is from what is being performed currently.

This growing body of evidence should then be subjected to a more advanced evaluation, where we examine not only the technology but also the evidence itself. That is, to assess whether the body of evidence forms a compelling argument for using the technology, we look at the situations in which the technology has been used, compare the old ways to the new ways, and determine (using surveys, case studies, experiments, feature analysis, and other techniques) whether the evidence is conflicting, consistent, and objective. We want to know how "solid" a case we have for believing that the new technology will solve the business problem it addresses.

However, compelling evidence is not enough to ensure technology adoption. The marketing world tells us how to package and support the technology to make it "friendlier" and easier to understand and use. For example, tools and supporting written material go a long way in assisting a user to adopt a new technique or process. When the supporting infrastructure is in place to offer this assistance, the technology is "ready for prime time." That is, this packaged technology is finally ready for broader diffusion, so that we as a community can assess its adoption rate and evidence of effectiveness as more organizations report the results of their experiences.

In fact, we may need multiple models of diffusion, including iteration, based on the characteristics of the technology, the adopters, and the evidence. These models, plus the marketing and evidential concepts described in this chapter, offer us a vocabulary with which to discuss and understand key issues affecting the success of technology adoption and diffusion.

Next Steps in Improving Technology Transfer

We can no longer afford to make investments in technology whose adoption is either undesirable or not likely to be successful. Practitioners can help researchers take steps to understand the nature of successful technology transfer, and use that new understanding to build models and support for effective evaluation and adoption. In particular, some of the current empirical studies of software engineering technologies are loosely related and poorly planned: not a very good collective generator of a coherent body of evidence. If empirical software engineering researchers would organize studies so that each piece contributes a clear and significant result to the whole, the resulting body of evidence would be more compelling. That is, practitioners and researchers together must plan what to address in each study and how that study's result will contribute to the overall body of evidence.

At the same time, practitioners interested in using new technologies effectively can learn from the many studies already performed and apply their lessons to their own projects. Technology transfer inhibitors and promoters fall into three categories: technological, organizational, and evidential. For example, technology transfer is inhibited by lack of packaging, by lack of relationship to a pressing technical or business problem, and by difficulty of use and understanding. By contrast, a new technology can be promoted with tools, a well-understood context, and an understanding of clear potential benefit to those on the project now or who will use the resulting product later. In other words, the technology is easier to transfer if it is easy to use and easy to see how it will help.

Similarly, practitioners can evaluate current evidence and help researchers base new studies on existing findings. Whether practitioners are designing new studies or just participating in them, they should have credibility in the conveyors of information about the technology, be sure that the technology is clearly going to be the cause of anticipated effects, and apply the technology to a realistic problem in the field, not just a toy problem with no relevance to real work.

We do not know all we need to know about which software engineering technologies work best in which situations. And we cannot wait for years to know, given the blistering speed at which technology changes. But there are lessons to be learned, both from software engineering research and from other disciplines with similar interests in technology evaluation and transfer. We can take steps now both to speed up the rate of adoption and to build a credible body of evidence about the effectiveness of our practices.

14.3 DECISION-MAKING IN SOFTWARE ENGINEERING

Coupled with the need for evidence about new technologies is the need to make decisions about them. How do we decide what technologies to use on our next project?

How do we allocate the right resources to a team? And how do we weigh the risks of one choice over another? As with technology transfer, we can look to other disciplines to see how research on decision-making can help us improve our software engineering–related choices.

Lots of Decisions

Sometimes it seems as if software engineering is simply a string of pressured activities connected by decision-making and estimating. We plan our projects by estimating resources and risk. We assess projects by deciding if our processes were effective, our resources appropriate, and our products satisfactory. To test our products, we weigh alternatives when we cannot test everything. And change requests and maintenance require evaluating alternative actions, estimating needed resources, and analyzing risk.

We need not make our decisions in a vacuum. There are theories that support our decision-making from two points of view: descriptive and prescriptive. Descriptive theories provide evidence about how decisions are actually made, while prescriptive theories provide frameworks and methods to help decision-makers improve their performance in problem-finding and problem-solving, given real constraints. Figure 14.3 illustrates how many other disciplines contribute information to our decision-making.

Often, our decision-making involves at least two distinct steps. First, we make our choices individually. We predict or infer, we assign value to the different alternatives, and we assess different approaches as we make up our minds. Second, we contribute our findings to a group decision process. For example, to estimate the effort required for building a particular kind of software, each of us may make our own prediction before combining estimates to get an idea of what the group predicts. Moreover, this "group" may in fact be our projects, our organizations, or even our societies; each such decision has impact relative to the group it will reflect or affect.

	Descriptive theories	Prescriptive theories
Individual	Psychology Marketing Psychiatry Literature	Decision theory Economics Operations research Philosophy and logic
Group	Social psychology Organizational behavior Anthropology Sociology	Game theory Organizational behavior Clinical psychology and therapy Finance and economics
Organization	Organization theory Sociology Industrial organizations Political science	Planning and strategy Control theory and cybernetics Organizational design Team theory and economics
Society	Sociology Anthropology Macroeconomics	Legal philosophy Political science Social choice

FIGURE 14.3 Roots of decision sciences (adapted from Kleindorfer, Kunreuther, and Schoemaker 1993).

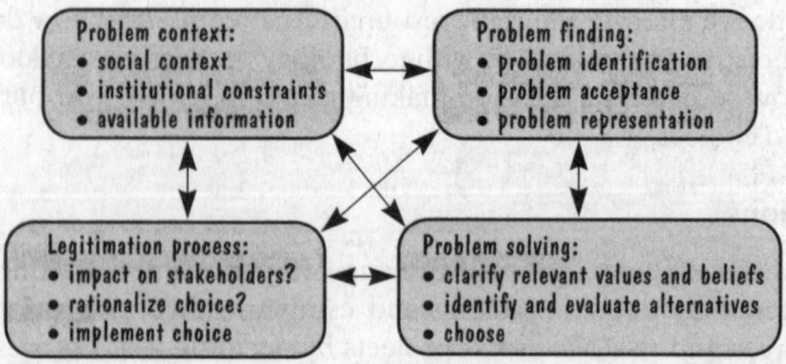

FIGURE 14.4 Aspects of decision-making (adapted from Kleindorfer, Kunreuther, and Schoemaker 1993).

Figure 14.4 shows us that many elements affect how we make up our minds. The context of the situation constrains both our understanding and our options. Within that context, we must understand and represent the problem before we try to solve it. Each option must be screened in several ways, to determine its likely effect on stakeholders, and its degree of rationality and realism. "Legitimation" is likely to be both highly significant and somewhat overlooked in the context of software engineering. It is conceivable that estimators and decision-makers may have a preference for estimates and decisions that can be more easily justified. This preference suggests a bias in favor of a particular approach, such as the use of algorithmic models over expert judgment. And the possible solutions must be viewed through a filter of our values and beliefs.

To see how we use these elements in our decision-making, consider the problem of choosing new office space. Table 14.1 represents five options. Each alternative is characterized by the rent in dollars per month, the distance in kilometers from home, the size in square meters, and a general, subjective rating of the quality of the space. (For instance, a high-quality space may have more light or higher ceilings than a lower-quality one.)

There are many rules we can use to select the best option. For example, we can choose the office with the lowest rent. Or we can choose the office closest to home. These rules reflect our values; someone who uses the first rule instead of the second may value money over time. Alternatively, we can use more complex rules. For instance, we can define "office value" to be a combination of rent and size, and we can balance it with the shortest travel time. Or, we can use a multistep approach, where first we set cutoff levels for rent and distance (such as, no more than $500 for rent, and no more than ten kilometers from home), and then balance the remaining attributes.

TABLE 14.1 Office Space Options

Office Option	Rent per Month	Distance from Home	Size (square meters)	Quality
1	$450	10 kilometers	4000	Medium
2	$475	15 kilometers	2500	High
3	$460	14 kilometers	1500	Average
4	$500	5 kilometers	1750	High
5	$510	7 kilometers	2500	High

Of course, our selection process can be still more sophisticated. For example, we can use domination procedures, where we eliminate alternatives that are "dominated" by better choices. However, this type of rule can lead to suboptimization; we may eliminate a pretty good choice if our cutoffs are arbitrary or not carefully considered. Or we can use conjunction (every dimension meets a defined standard) or disjunction (every dimension is sufficiently high). In these situations, there is no slack when the characteristic values are close to the threshold; we may discard a choice because the rent is over \$500, but in fact the other characteristics of the \$501 choice are far superior to those in other options.

Another strategy is to use elimination by aspects. Here, each attribute has a preassigned criterion value, and each attribute is assigned a priority. Attributes are then reviewed in terms of their relative importance. We can formalize this approach by using an additive value model, where we assign weights or priorities (w_j) to each attribute (x_j), and then sum the products of the weights and the attribute values $(v(x_j))$:

$$V = \sum_{j=1}^{n} w_j v(x_j)$$

Sometimes weights and comparisons are more easily made by adopting a pairwise approach, such as Saaty's Analytic Hierarchy Process, another example of a multicriteria decision aid.

Each of these approaches suggests the "right" choice, but it may not always be the optimum choice. Or it may involve many calculations or comparisons. In reality, we may use a heuristic approach that gives us a pretty good answer.

Group Decision-Making

So far, we have discussed characteristics related to the problem itself. Group decision-making is in some sense more difficult because aspects of group behavior influence how the decisions are made. Figure 14.5 illustrates some of the issues that must be considered when several people try to choose among alternatives. For example, trust, communication, and cooperation can affect the result; none of these is a factor in individual choice.

However, there are several group decision strategies to address these concerns. For example, dialectical strategies may allow one side to advance an argument, then the other side to speak. A third party may be employed to reconcile the differing viewpoints. Alternatively, brainstorming can be used to identify a full list of possibilities, including opportunities or threats. Nominal group techniques involve silent generation of ideas followed by a round robin, where ideas are shared one at a time and then evaluated spontaneously using silent voting. Or, social judgment approaches may be used to separate facts from judgments, or to distinguish science from values from social judgment.

When the group is an organization, the decision-makers must distinguish strategic from tactical and routine decisions. Strategic decisions affect the well-being and nature of the organization; typically, they involve new products, services, or markets, and senior management may play a significant role. Cost estimates can be part of strategic

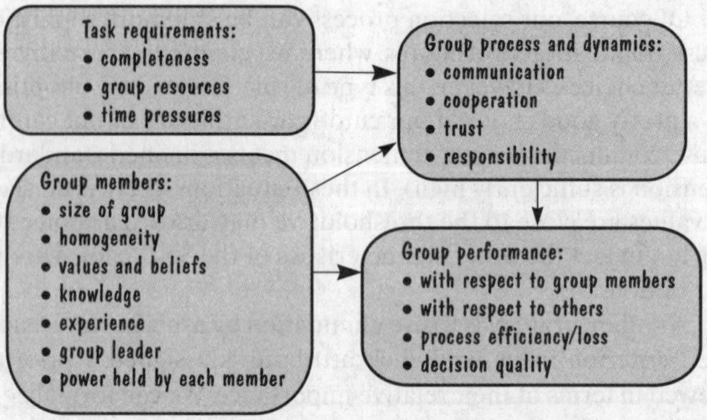

FIGURE 14.5 Issues in group decision-making.

decisions, especially when they are used to position a product in the marketplace. Tactical decisions affect pricing, employee assignments, customer interaction, or operations, but they do not affect the organization's financial bottom line or commercial direction to the same degree. A tactical cost estimate can be used to set the price for a new product where market share may not be an issue; for example, when one company division develops a product for another division, competition and pricing may not be of strategic importance.

Routine decision-making is usually more mundane: repetitive in nature, local in scope, and guided by organizational rules or policies. For instance, suppose a company supports its own reuse repository, where software engineers are rewarded for "depositing" a reusable component and "charged" for using a component that already exists in the repository. Determining the "price" of the component may be a routine task based on corporate guidelines.

How We Really Decide

The decision science and operations research literature is replete with examples of decision-making techniques. But which of those techniques do we really use when we make decisions? A survey reported by Forgionne (1986) indicates that we tend to use statistics and simulation, but very few of the more complex processes suggested in the textbooks.

There are many reasons why we often shun the more technically sophisticated approaches. The biggest impediments to their use are the difficulty of setting up the calculations and the combinatorial explosion of possibilities. Rather than hypothesize about the best way to make decisions, Klein (1998) has observed decision-makers at work, under pressure. In one study of 156 observations, he found that no one made use of preselected options (where the allowable options are identified ahead of time, and the decision maker simply chooses from among these). Eighteen decision-makers did a comparative evaluation, where an initial option was chosen, and then all other options were compared to it to see if it was the best one; here, the decision-makers were optimizing their action. Eleven decision-makers created a new option. But the rest used what

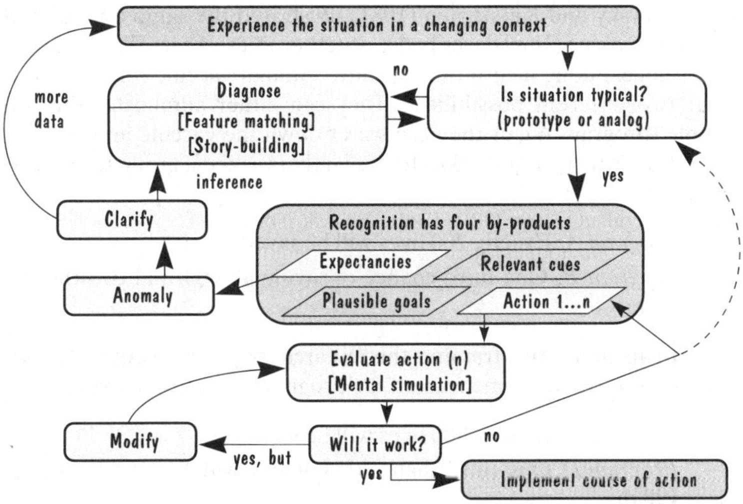

FIGURE 14.6 Recognition-primed decision model (adapted from Klein 1998).

Simon calls a satisficing strategy: they evaluated each option on its own merits until they found the first one that met their criteria for an acceptable solution.

After watching and interviewing firefighters, emergency medical technicians, soldiers, and others who make important decisions under pressure, Klein has suggested a "recognition-primed decision model," as shown in Figure 14.6, to describe how we really make decisions. He points out that we tend to keep a repository of examples in our heads, and we draw on these situations when we are confronted with a choice. We mentally refer to a past situation and compare the current one to see if it is similar. Rather than comparing all the options, we grab one that is "close," and we go through a process in our heads to justify to ourselves that it is "close enough" to be used as a basis for the current decision. At the same time, we use mental simulation to determine if the actions we propose to take will really work in this situation; when we don't think they will, then we back up, choose a different scenario, and perform the mental simulation again. Eventually, when we are satisfied that we have made the right choice, we act.

But decision-making and estimating are not as simple as the model suggests. Hershey, Kunreuther, and Schoemaker (1982) have demonstrated that the decision's context can bias the choice. To see how, consider these two questions:

Question 1: You have a 50% chance of losing \$200 and a 50% chance of losing nothing. Would you be willing to pay \$100 to avoid this situation?

Question 2: You can pay \$100 to avoid a situation where you may lose \$200 or nothing. Would you pay if there were a 50% chance of losing?

In their study, they asked each of two equivalent groups to answer the question with either "yes," "no" or "indifferent." Even though the two questions are equivalent, 6% of the group answering question 1 were willing to pay, but 32% of the group answering question 2 were willing to pay.

Tversky and Kahneman (1981) illustrated the same kind of bias in risk-analysis decision-making. They described a situation where a rare disease endangers 600 people in a village. Public health officials have enough vaccine for 200 people, and they consider two different possibilities. They can either administer the full vaccine to 200 people (program A), or they can water down the vaccine and hope that it will protect all 600 villagers (program B). The researchers asked a group to choose between the two programs, where

Program A: Exactly 200 lives will be saved.

Program B: One-third chance of saving all 600, and two-thirds chance of saving none.

In an alternative framing, the researchers asked an equivalent group to make the same choice, but this time framed the programs in terms of lives lost:

Program C: Exactly 400 lives will be lost.

Program D: One-third chance that no one will die, and two-thirds chance that 600 will die.

Even though the problems are mathematically identical, there was a dramatic difference in the responses. Seventy-two percent of the subjects shown the first framing chose A; only 22% of the subjects shown the second framing chose C.

In a similar study, people linked past actions to current decisions. To see how, consider the situation where you are going to the theater to see a play. When you get to the box office, you find that you have lost a $10 bill. Would you then pay $10 for the ticket to the play? Eighty-eight percent of the respondents said yes. But if, alternatively, when you get to the box office, you find that you have lost your $10 ticket, would you pay $10 for a new ticket? In this situation, only 46% would pay, even though the situations are mathematically identical.

Thus, it is important to consider contextual bias, especially when estimating effort or risk. The way in which the problem is framed can produce radically different results.

Steele's work (1999) has described a related phenomenon. He notes that expectation of performance or results can lead to a "stereotype threat." For example, if a particular group of people is told that it usually does not do well in a given situation, then the stereotype can actually result in poorer performance.

Other sources of bias can creep into decision-making. For example, people usually overvalue what they already own (called "status quo bias"). This phenomenon can influence an estimator to be overly optimistic about productivity in a familiar development situation. Similarly, probability and payoff interact: if probabilities are small, people look at payoff first; if probabilities are large, people look at probability and then payoff.

Individuals exhibit a marked preference for case-specific, or singular, information, as opposed to general statistical, or distributional, information. Busby and Barton (1996) focus on this preference when describing estimators who employed a top-down or work-breakdown approach to prediction. Unfortunately, this approach failed to accommodate unplanned activity, so that predictions were consistently underestimating by 20%. By definition, the case-specific evidence for each project will fail to account for unplanned activities, yet the statistical evidence across many projects suggests that unplanned activities are very likely to happen. Nevertheless, managers favored the singular evidence and would not include a factor for unplanned activities in their estimation process.

In addition, we must remember that recall is affected by both the recency and vividness of an experience. The further into the past a factor occurred, the greater the tendency of the recaller to discount its significance. In one sense, this diminishing significance may be sensible, given that the way in which we develop software has changed considerably over the years. On the other hand, many risks, such as requirements being modified or misunderstood, have changed little.

Anchoring-and-adjustment is another common technique employed by estimators. Here the estimator selects an analogous situation and then adjusts it to suit the new circumstances. However, there is considerable evidence to suggest that estimators are unduly cautious when making the adjustment. In other words, the anchoring dominates and then insufficient adaptation is made. This approach may be influenced by recall, in that the most suitable analogies may be overlooked because they are not recent.

A reluctance to appear negative can also affect expert judgment. DeMarco (1982) reminds us that "realism can be mistaken for disloyalty," leading to undue optimism in making predictions, both individually and in groups.

How Groups Really Make Decisions

Many organizations use group decision-making techniques to derive important projections or estimates. For example, the Delphi technique (see Sidebar 14.1) enables several estimators to combine their disparate estimates into one with which all can feel comfortable.

SIDEBAR 14.1 DELPHI TECHNIQUES

The Delphi technique was originally devised by the RAND Corporation in the late 1940s as a method for structuring group communication processes to solve complex problems. The U.S. government used Delphi to predict the future of the oil industry. Delphi is intended to capture informed judgment by keeping individual predictions anonymous and by iterating through several evaluations. Consensus is not essential. In fact, Delphi can also be used to educate its participants by drawing on multidisciplinary or diverse inputs.

The technique was subsequently refined and popularized by Barry Boehm (1981) for the more specific task of software project estimation. The major steps in the Delphi process include

1. A group of experts receives the specification plus an estimation form.
2. The experts discuss product and estimation issues.
3. The experts produce individual estimates.

4. The estimates are tabulated and returned to the experts.
5. An expert is made aware only of his or her own estimate; the sources of the remaining estimates remain anonymous.
6. The experts meet to discuss the results.
7. The estimates are revised.
8. The experts cycle through steps 1 to 7 until an acceptable degree of convergence is obtained.

While the technique is relatively well known and is featured in many software engineering textbooks, there are few published experiences of using Delphi for software prediction.

But the group dynamics can affect the quality of a decision or estimate. For instance, Foushee et al. (1986) found that it takes time for team members to learn to be productive together. The teams performed better at the end of their assignment than at the beginning, because they learned over time to work together effectively.

Group dynamics can also have negative effects. Asch (1956) tested the effect of colleagues on an individual's decision by presenting a subject with the lines shown in Figure 14.7. When individuals were asked which of the three lines on the right was the same length as the test line, almost all of the respondents answered correctly: line B. But when others in the room were present and gave the wrong answer, the number of errors rose dramatically, as shown in Table 14.2.

FIGURE 14.7 Example used in assessing group effects.

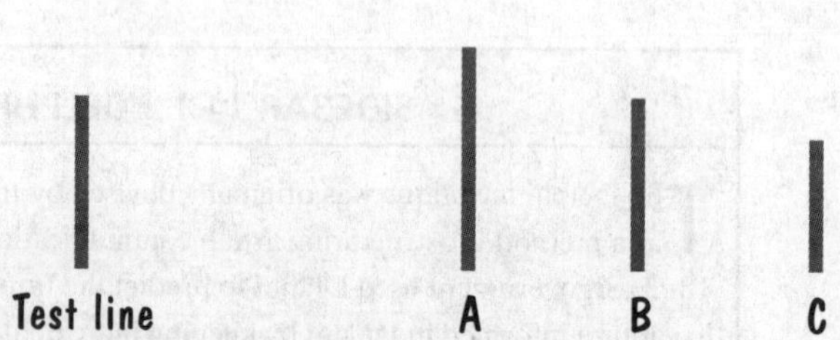

TABLE 14.2 Results of Asch (1956) Study

Condition	Error Rate
Subject is alone	1%
With one person who says A	3%
With two people who say A	13%
With three people who say A	33%
With six who say A and one who says B	6%

A Modest Observational Study

To examine group decision-making in software engineering, Pfleeger, Shepperd, and Tesoriero (2000) explored group approaches to effort estimation. They began with a pilot investigation at Bournemouth University. Twelve postgraduate students were organized into four teams having between two and four members. As part of the coursework, each team was required to capture requirements and develop a prototype for a simple information system. They then asked the team to predict the size of the prototype in lines of code. (To minimize counting problems, the researchers defined a line of code as a statement delimiter. Lines of code were chosen because they could easily be verified, not because of any other special significance.) The subjects were not constrained to any particular technique, although in practice they tended to use subjective judgment. Immediately afterwards, the subjects participated in Delphi meetings leading to two additional estimates.

Table 14.3 shows that both the median error and the spread or range of errors are greatest for the initial estimate. In other words, error was greatest prior to using the Delphi technique; the subsequent Delphi rounds led to a reduction in the differences between predicted and actual prototype sizes. As shown in Figures 14.8 and 14.9, three out of the four groups exhibited clear improvement, but the fourth group diverged from the true value as the process continued. This divergence was due in part to the dominance of one member of the group. Although the Delphi technique allows anonymity for individual estimates, it appears to be vulnerable to forceful individuals. Interestingly, this result is consistent with the behavioral theories described above. As we have seen, the group performance literature (e.g., Sauer et al. 2000) suggests that a major determinant of the outcome is the choice of decision scheme, as well as how the group makes use of its expertise.

Encouragingly, a similar observational study using postgraduate students at the University of Maryland yielded comparable results, in that successive rounds of the Delphi technique led to a substantial reduction in the range of estimates. In this case, the estimation task was a theoretical one, so the accuracy of the estimates could not be assessed. At Maryland, all the students were working practitioners with considerable experience; they were enrolled in a Master's of Software Engineering program. The class of ten was divided into three teams of three or four students each. As part of a more general project involving requirements elicitation, analysis, and estimation, the individuals on each team used two products, Data Salvage (an analogy tool developed at Bournemouth University) and Revic (a COCOMO-based tool developed for the U.S. Department of Defense), to generate initial estimates for their team project. Then, after a lesson in how to use the Delphi method, the students were observed and

TABLE 14.3 Estimation Errors from Three Rounds of Predicting Size

Estimate	Median Error	Minimum Error	Maximum Error
Initial	160.5	23	2249
Round 1	40	23	749
Round 2	40	3	949

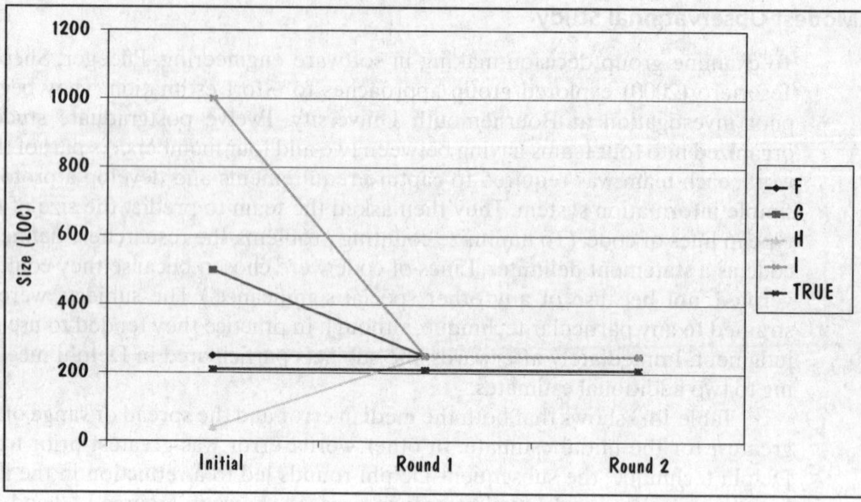

FIGURE 14.8 Convergent group estimates.

tape-recorded as they worked through two 20-minute Delphi rounds to converge on a team estimate. That is, each team was given the results of all the individual estimates not just for their team but from everyone in the class. Each team was asked to record its confidence in the new estimate and to document the assumptions it made in deriving the estimate. At the time of the study, the students were not aware that the researchers were interested in the dynamics of their discussion rather than the actual numbers they generated.

Pfleeger, Shepperd, and Tesoriero noticed several important trends across the teams. First, the spread from smallest to largest estimate decreased dramatically over

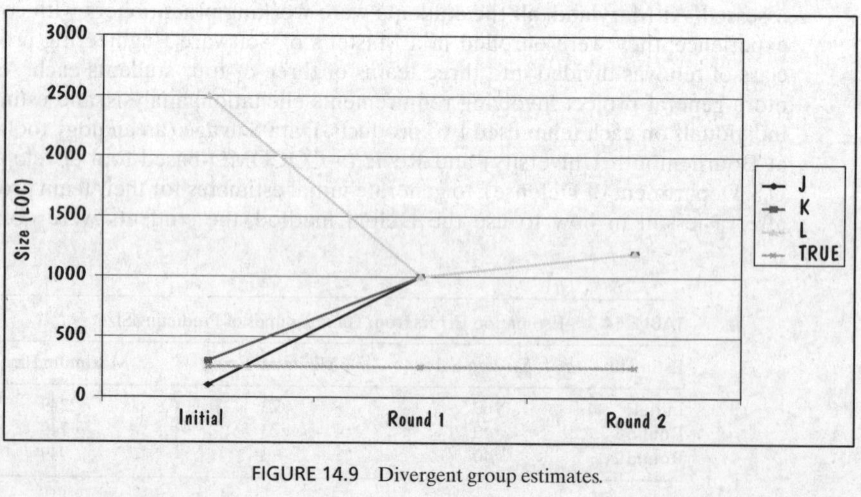

FIGURE 14.9 Divergent group estimates.

time. It went from 16,239 at the beginning of the first round to 10,181 at the beginning of the second, to 1520 at the end.

Second, there was a general growth in confidence as the students progressed through the Delphi discussions. That is, all students reported an increase in confidence with their estimate after the group discussions, regardless of their experience level. However, there was no evidence of any relationship between experience and confidence.

Because personality can play such a significant role in the Delphi discussions, each of the Maryland students completed a Myers–Briggs test. Myers–Briggs classifies each respondent on four scales: extroverted/introverted, sensing/intuition, thinking/feeling, and judging/perceiving. Thus, the results are reported as a four-letter combination, such as ISTJ, for introvert-sensing-thinking-judging, to describe the way in which the student typically responds to situations. The results for the second group were particularly interesting. Two members of this group were classified as ISTJ, a third was an ESTJ, and the fourth was an ISFJ. People with the ISTJ personality type tend to be precise and accurate, tending to follow rules and procedures and having excellent concentration. However, ISTJs do not like change and tend to be inflexible. ISFJs, like ISTJs, tend to be accurate, thorough, and careful with details, as well as resistant to change. Interestingly, ISFJ personalities tend to underestimate their own value. By contrast, ESTJs tend to be practical and results-oriented. They focus on a goal, becoming impatient with inefficiency and with those who do not follow procedures. Group 2's Delphi discussions focused on the details of the parameters of the Revic tool rather than on more global issues about the project in general. Perhaps the detail-oriented personality types of these group members led them to look more at the tool than at their own experiences. As can be seen from Table 14.4, Group 2 was the least confident in its final estimate, perhaps because of its team member personality types.

From a debriefing questionnaire that was administered after the study, it appears that the ten subjects had a favorable attitude toward Delphi, with all subjects reporting that the technique had increased their confidence in their estimate. When asked if each would consider using Delphi estimation techniques in a work situation, five said yes, four said maybe, and only one said no.

Table 14.5 lists the positive and negative issues identified by subjects in the debriefing questionnaire. They are sorted in decreasing order of frequency, so that the most commonly mentioned issues appear first. Notice that problems related to a dominant individual and lack of expertise were the most frequently cited disadvantages, while the benefits of different perspectives and the value of group discussion were the most frequently cited advantages.

TABLE 14.4 Maryland Group's Confidence in Final Estimate

Group	Number in Group	Median Confidence in Estimate	Range of Estimates
1	2	91	2
2	4	65	15
3	3	80	0
4	3	80	0

TABLE 14.5 Perceived Strengths and Weaknesses of the Delphi Technique

Weaknesses	Strengths
Can wrongly influence an individual and the impact of a dominant individual	Experts with different backgrounds/perspectives
Depends upon knowledge/expertise of individuals	Group discussion can correct mistakes
Risk of erroneous assumptions	Reconsideration
Group discussion made little difference to the result (consensus group)	Uses expert judgment
	Median better than mean
High variability in predictions	Provides comparison with other estimates
Inappropriate target, should use for more detailed problems	Anonymity/independence combined with group benefits

Lessons Learned

A number of lessons emerge from the two studies of Delphi estimation techniques. The first is that the subjects had a broadly positive attitude to the technique. Moreover, from the Bournemouth study, it is clear that the technique led to improved estimates. And in both studies, the technique clearly reduced the spread of estimates, even though six of the ten Maryland students reported negative effects of the group discussions. As researchers such as Klein point out, there are other, indirect benefits, including education and the development of a common vocabulary.

A second clear lesson is that personalities can dominate the discussion, even when the dominant participant is not correct, much as Asch found several decades ago. Moreover, the individual assumptions that formed the basis of initial estimates (i.e., the factors required as input by the tools used) were irrelevant in most of the subsequent group discussion. This result parallels findings reported in investigations of group meetings for reviews and inspections, where many individual findings are lost when not confirmed by others in the group. In particular, the focus of the Delphi discussions turns to the numbers themselves (rather than where those numbers come from), and to justifying gut feelings, as Klein suggests. In other words, anchoring-and-adjustment is alive and well in the Delphi technique.

We often assume that those with the most experience will provide the strongest influence on group discussions, leading to more realistic estimates. But in the Pfleeger, Shepperd, and Tesoriero studies, even the most experienced group (Maryland's Group 3) looked to the median for reassurance. And all students reported an increase in confidence that had no relationship to the experience of the team members. Thus, personality may dominate experience in Delphi discussions, a situation that does not often lead to realistic or accurate final projections.

Most of the existing research on estimation techniques has focused on the accuracy of individual estimates. However, most practitioners do their estimation in a group, either explicitly by relying on a technique such as Delphi, or implicitly by eliciting the opinions of their colleagues. For this reason, it is important to acknowledge the role of group dynamics in the estimation process, and indeed in group decision-making in general. We often assume that expertise and experience will dominate, that we have high-quality data in historical records of similar projects from which we can draw our analogies, and that we know how to tell when two projects are similar to one another. Unfortunately, many of these assumptions are wrong to some extent, and practitioners must rely on individual and group tools and techniques from which to generate a projection or a decision. Although we claim that objectivity is essential, in fact we are forced to rely on subjective and often fuzzy data and techniques to make our decisions. Observational studies, combined with a solid understanding of group dynamics, can help us to tailor our decision-making processes to the realities of personality and process and thus increase our confidence in the results.

Moreover, what we learn about decision-making in settings such as estimation can be applied in a wider context. We can learn how to be more effective at combining individual assumptions and opinions into a group consensus, and how to prepare and present evidence without bias.

14.4 THE PROFESSIONALIZATION OF SOFTWARE ENGINEERING: LICENSING, CERTIFICATION, AND ETHICS

Software engineering has come a long way. But it still has a very long way to go if it is to be considered as mature as other engineering disciplines. Several states in the United State are insisting that software "engineers" be trained and licensed, the same as other engineers. Several groups have convened to determine what constitutes the software engineering "core body of knowledge"—that is, the body of knowledge and skills that is reasonable to expect of any graduate of a university-level software engineering program or of any licensed professional. These efforts must answer difficult questions about the difference between software engineering and other computing disciplines. In this section, we examine the efforts to formalize, codify, and test for good software engineering practice. We also investigate the need for an ethical code to ensure that software engineers do the right thing when developing and maintaining software.

Focus on the People

Software engineering researchers first attempted to improve software quality by examining only the products of software development. As we have seen in earlier chapters, requirements, design, code, and related documents can be reviewed and verified, to determine if the products meet the quality standards set by customers and practitioners. But the difficulties and cost of assessing products (particularly of a final product that has been deployed) and the variation in products across domains make such quality assurance daunting. The next wave of improvement attempts involved the software process. Maturity models such as the CMM, international process standards such as ISO 9000, and other activities look not only at what is produced but also at how it is produced. Much as the finest chefs are trained to look at recipes and cooking techniques as well as the taste of the final dishes, software engineering researchers and practitioners saw process improvement as a means toward product improvement.

More recently, the software engineering community has turned its attention to the people building the software. In particular, efforts are under way to improve software engineering education and to investigate whether licensing or certification can lead to significant process and product improvements. For the most part, these efforts are a reaction to the large number of people who have entered the software profession without any formal education in software (e.g., self-taught student programmers just out of high school) and who promote themselves to clients and potential employers as software engineers. Efforts directed to this issue are not likely to improve the quality of safety-critical software, because the organizations that develop such products already hire well-qualified people, and they know how to evaluate the qualifications of their potential hires. Rather, efforts to "improve the practitioner" are intended to improve the average quality of software products and processes, to ensure that below-average practitioners meet or exceed minimum standards of software knowledge and competency, and to protect the public from unqualified practitioners.

Efforts in software engineering education are aimed at increasing the pool of well-qualified software developers; they are also aimed at building a pool of licensed professional engineers who understand the properties, capabilities, limits, and complexities of software and who have the expertise to build quality software components for engineered products (e.g., cars). The intent behind certifying or licensing software practitioners is to help to ensure that practitioners meet minimum standards of competency. We discuss each of these efforts in turn.

Software Engineering Education

Historically, software engineering has been considered a relatively small aspect of computer science. At best, a university computer science curriculum included a course on software engineering, usually offered in the junior or senior year. At the least, it included several lectures on the meaning and intent of software engineering. With the increasing emphasis on software quality and security, and with the recent push to professionalize software developers, universities have increasingly viewed software engineering as a distinct academic discipline. There are now many ways in which a student can navigate through a university curriculum and end up with a software engineering education:

- Specializing in software engineering as part of a computer science major
- Specializing in software engineering as part of a computer engineering major
- Specializing in software engineering as part of an engineering major
- Majoring in software engineering as a separate degree from computer science or computer engineering

As Table 14.6 shows, a software engineering program borrows from both computer science and engineering curricula. Computer science courses provide the technical knowledge and expertise needed to create and manipulate software artifacts: programming principles; data structures; algorithm paradigms; programming languages; grammars, parsing, and translation; concurrency and control structures; and the theoretical limits of computing. In addition, computer science and computer engineering courses cover key system components (e.g., computer architecture, operating system, middleware, networks) and key software components (e.g., databases, user interfaces), and how the design and implementation of these components can affect the performance, usability, and quality of our software.

TABLE 14.6 Software Engineering Involves Both Computer Science and Engineering

Computer Science	Engineering
Data management	Disciplined processes
Data patterns	Large, integrated systems
Data transformation	Coordinated teams
Algorithm paradigms	Nonfunctional properties (e.g., performance, reliability, maintainability, ease of use)
Programming languages	
Human–computer interaction	

From engineering, a software engineering curriculum borrows and adapts principles and practices that scale to large systems and that are aimed at producing successful products:

- Early planning and development activities that help to reveal errors early in the development process, when they are cheaper and easier to fix
- Systematic, predictable design and development processes that help to ensure that a software product is developed economically and that it is fit for use
- Consideration of nonfunctional properties, such as performance, maintainability, usability, economy, and time-to-market, that often determine whether a software product is acceptable

A traditional engineering education also includes a solid foundation in mathematics and science and an exposure to other engineering disciplines. Engineers use mathematics to model and analyze their designs. A science background is important because engineers must understand how to react to and control the physical world. Exposure to other engineering disciplines helps an engineer to understand and work more effectively with engineers from other disciplines, and to build components that interoperate better with other engineered components.

Software engineering courses build on these foundations in computing and engineering, and introduce the concepts that we cover in this book, including requirements elicitation, software design principles, technical documentation, project management, testing, and verification. In addition, a software engineering curriculum is likely to include nontechnical courses in communications, humanities, and social sciences. Software engineering projects tend to involve large numbers of people, so software engineers need to understand the dynamics of group interaction to know how to motivate individuals to pursue a common goal. They need to consider the impact of their technology on users and on society as a whole, and they may need to make decisions that take human and social values into account. They may also have to interact with specialists from other disciplines who have varied levels of software expertise. This work calls for strong communication, business, and reasoning skills.

As such, software engineering is more general, is more applied, and has a broader scope than computer science. At its core, computer science focuses on data, data transformation, and algorithms; advanced courses present designs and programming techniques for specific application domains. In contrast, software engineering focuses on building software products. It looks at all the activities involved in developing a software system from initial idea to final product. Moreover, software engineering design concepts tend to focus on general-purpose design principles, patterns, and criteria; advanced courses present design and analysis techniques that scale to large software systems.

Although it is tempting to try to classify software engineering as just another branch of engineering, this "natural" mapping has a fatal flaw: whereas most engineers produce physical artifacts that are deployed in the real world and obey physical laws, software engineers produce software artifacts that are deployed on computers (which are artificial worlds) and obey the laws and limits of computing. Most noticeably, a physical artifact has continuous behavior, which means that we can test the product in one situation and extrapolate how it will behave in related situations. Software artifacts cannot exhibit continuous behavior, which means that similar inputs may result in wildly different output values. Also, software is implemented using discrete-valued variables, and the imprecision introduced by such variables can accumulate in long computations. "Off by one" errors in other engineering disciplines are inconsequential, but such errors in software are disastrous. Thus, many of the traditional modeling and evaluation techniques in the engineer's standard toolkit are inappropriate for software. Software's flexibility and malleability belie its complexity; even small changes can have large effects, so design and testing are often far more difficult than in other engineering domains.

A software engineering undergraduate education cannot be completely comprehensive, because there are more courses needed than are possible in a four-year curriculum. Ideally, the perfect curriculum would include serious computing science depth, sufficient discrete mathematics for modeling and analyzing software, traditional engineering expertise in continuous mathematics and science, and software engineering knowledge and techniques, while still maintaining a shared experience with other branches of engineering. Thus, developers of software engineering programs have had to make difficult choices in deciding which combination of topics form an appropriate and feasible core curriculum for an undergraduate education in software engineering.

At the same time, people are entering the software industry via nonacademic routes, such as by learning how to program after studying another discipline like business, physics, or mathematics. Because practitioners with such varied academic backgrounds and varied work experiences are all calling themselves "software engineers," there has been a recent push to establish minimum requirements for such a designation. As a result, there have been a number of initiatives to define an underlying software engineering "body of knowledge": a detailed description of what someone should know in order to be called a software engineer.

Software Engineering Body of Knowledge

The intent behind defining a core body of knowledge is to establish within the software engineering community some agreement on the knowledge, skills, and expertise that every software engineer ought to possess. Some of the initiatives to define a body of knowledge for software engineering include:

- *Computing Curricula—Software Engineering (SE2004) (IEEE-CS and ACM 2004).* This joint effort between the Institute for Electrical and Electronics Engineers—Computer Society (IEEE-CS) and the Association for Computing Machinery

(ACM) is aimed at offering guidance on how to design curricula for undergraduate programs and specializations in software engineering. Its advice includes a core body of knowledge, called Software Engineering Education Knowledge (SEEK), that comprises the essential and desirable knowledge and skills that any software engineering program should try to include in its curriculum. Its body of knowledge includes knowledge from related disciplines (e.g., mathematics, computer science, engineering, economics) as well as from software engineering.

- *Software Engineering Body of Knowledge (SWEBOK) (IEEE-CS 2004).* This effort, sponsored by IEEE-CS and a number of industrial partners, is aimed at defining what a practicing software engineering professional ought to know. It focuses primarily on software engineering knowledge and on knowledge that a practitioner ought to have acquired from a combination of academics and four years of work experience.
- *Software Engineering Syllabus (CEQB 1998).* This effort by the Canadian Engineering Qualifications Board (CEQB) offers guidance to provincial engineering societies on how to assess the academic credentials of software engineering applicants seeking to become licensed professional engineers. Its body of knowledge is a de facto set of national guidelines for evaluating the undergraduate education of applicants who did not graduate from an accredited Canadian engineering program. Each provincial engineering society defines its own discipline-specific criteria for evaluating candidates who have nonengineering academic backgrounds, but it uses the CEQB syllabi as inputs in defining its criteria.

Because these efforts have different goals (e.g., the core of an undergraduate education vs. the knowledge expected of an established professional), they have different expectations of the breadth and depth of the knowledge and skills that constitute a software engineering body of knowledge. Table 14.7 shows a high-level view of the software engineering education knowledge (SEEK) (IEEE–CS and ACM 2004), and the *minimum* number of lecture hours that ought to be devoted to covering each knowledge area and unit. As can be seen, the SEEK includes not only principles considered to be proven guidelines for good practice but also technical knowledge of computer science, engineering, and software engineering that support and enhance the principles. Other parts of the SEEK (not shown) take the knowledge units listed in this table and decompose them into individual topics. Each topic is assessed as being essential, desirable, or optional to the core curriculum and is annotated with the degree to which students are expected to master the topic (e.g., to recall the knowledge, to understand the knowledge, to apply the knowledge in solving problems). For example, under Software Modeling and Analysis, the knowledge unit Modeling Foundations is decomposed into the topics

1. Modeling principles (e.g., abstraction, decomposition, views)
2. Pre- and post-conditions and invariants
3. Mathematical models and specification languages
4. Properties of modeling languages
5. Distinction between notations' syntax and semantics
6. Importance of models explicating all information

TABLE 14.7 SEEK Knowledge Areas and Knowledge Units (© IEEE-CS and ACM 2004)

Title	hrs	Title	hrs
Computing Essentials	**172**	**Software Verification and Validation**	**42**
Computer Science foundations	140	V&V terminology and foundations	5
Construction technologies	20	Reviews	6
Construction tools	4	Testing	21
Formal construction methods	8	Human–computer UI testing and evaluation	6
		Problem analysis and reporting	4
Mathematical and Engineering Fundamentals	**89**	**Software Evolution**	**10**
Mathematical foundations	56	Evolution processes	6
Engineering foundations for software	23	Evolution activities	4
Engineering economics for software	10		
Professional Practice	**35**	**Software Process**	**13**
Group dynamics/psychology	5	Process concepts	3
Communications skills (specific to SE)	10	Process implementation	10
Professionalism	20		
Software Modeling and Analysis	**53**	**Software Quality**	**16**
Modeling foundations	19	Software quality concepts and culture	2
Types of models	12	Software quality standards	2
Analysis fundamentals	6	Software quality processes	4
Requirements fundamentals	3	Process assurance	4
Eliciting requirements	4	Product assurance	4
Requirements specification and documentation	6		
Requirements validation	3		
Software Design	**45**	**Software Management**	**19**
Design concepts	3	Management concepts	2
Design strategies	6	Project planning	6
Architectural design	9	Project personnel and organization	2
Human–computer interface design	12	Project control	4
Detailed design	12	Software configuration management	5
Design-support tools and evaluation	3		

All of these topics are deemed essential, but only the first topic needs be mastered to the level of "application," where students should know how to apply these modeling principles in constructing their own models.

The core body of knowledge does not purport to be complete. Rather, it captures those practices and principles that are applicable to most software products, can be covered adequately in an undergraduate-level program, and provide some assurance of quality. However, application of these practices and principles does not guarantee that the result will be perfect software. In this sense, the body of knowledge reflects best-known practice, not perfection.

Licensing Software Engineers

As mentioned above, one of the intents behind defining a body of knowledge is to form a basis for evaluating the qualifications of practicing software engineers. This evaluation can take the form of licensing or certification. **Licensing** is a legal restriction on who is allowed to practice in a regulated profession, and the licensing process generally includes an evaluation of the candidate's knowledge and abilities. For example, in much of North America, provincial and state governments mandate the licensing of certain professionals, such as doctors, lawyers, and professional engineers, who are legally required to practice at a level consistent with public safety and welfare. In contrast, **certification** is a voluntary assessment that a practitioner may choose to undergo to demonstrate competency. We discuss certification of software engineers in the next section.

Most countries regulate the practice of certain professions, to protect the public from unqualified practitioners. Regulated professions tend to be those that can affect public safety (e.g., doctors, pharmacists, engineers, truck drivers) or that sell their services directly to the public (e.g., lawyers, accountants). Because software can affect health and well-being, and because software developers often sell their services and products to clients who cannot assess the developers' qualifications, many argue that the software profession ought to be regulated. This talk of regulation leads to the question of who exactly should be licensed and how. Engineering societies argue that software engineering is a branch of engineering and that its practitioners should be licensed as professional engineers (the American or Canadian title) or chartered engineers (the British title). In essence, they maintain that the means and authority for licensing software engineers already exists, in the form of the many state boards and professional engineering societies that currently license professional engineers. Computer societies argue that software engineering is too different from traditional branches of engineering for its practitioners to be evaluated according to engineering criteria, and that other organizations ought to be created or granted the authority to regulate the software profession. Below, we review the criteria for licensing professional engineers in the United States and Canada, and then we reconsider the arguments for and against the licensing of professional software engineers.

In North America, the engineering profession is regulated by states, provinces, and territories (hereinafter all called "states"); that is, each state has enacted laws that designate the authoritative body (e.g., government department, independent state agency, or self-regulating professional society) that regulates the engineering profession in that jurisdiction. Normally, a professional engineer cannot legally practice in a state without being licensed by its regulatory body, although most bodies have reciprocal agreements that allow an engineer who is licensed elsewhere to practice locally on a temporary basis. (This reciprocity is comparable to, although not exactly like, that for a driver's license, which is issued by the driver's home state but is recognized in other states.)

In the United States, the need for a license depends on the state in which an engineer practices. In general, licensing is mandatory for any professional who offers engineering services directly to the public and who participates in the design of structures and artifacts (e.g., roads, structures, nuclear plants) whose designs and plans must be submitted to state agencies for approval. Most U.S. engineers are not licensed. Often, they work for a company or for the federal government, so they are not offering services directly to the public. This distinction addresses the issue of responsibility; when an engineer designs a product or provides a service that fails, the engineer may not need a license if the employer is responsible for the effects of the failure. Moreover, most engineers do not use the title "engineer" outside of work, unlike physicians, who are always addressed as "doctor."

In Canada, any practicing engineer must be licensed as a professional engineer. Many jurisdictions define "engineering" by *practice* (what an engineer does) rather than by *title* (what an engineer calls herself or himself). In Ontario, the "practice of professional engineering" is defined in the **Professional Engineers Act** and comprises three tests:

- "any act of designing, composing, evaluating, advising, reporting, directing or supervising;
- wherein the safeguarding of life, health, property or the public welfare is concerned; and
- requires the application of engineering principles but does not include practicing as a natural scientist" (Queen's Printer for Ontario 2000).

Thus, anyone who is responsible for engineering work that could affect the safety, health, or well-being of the public is practicing engineering. Anyone who practices engineering without a permanent or temporary license is guilty of an offense and may be fined by the province.

With respect to practicing software engineers, the licensing laws in Canada and the United States are rarely enforced. This laxity is due partly to enforcement being complaint-driven, so that violations are often not detected until the practitioner's qualifications are questioned. It also reflects a lack of support for licensing by the government and by the software-development community, and this resistance is likely to continue as long as there are insufficient numbers of software engineers available to fill current job needs.

In both the United States and Canada, a professional engineer is evaluated within a specific engineering discipline, but he or she is licensed as a general "engineer," with no restriction in the title. Nevertheless, a professional engineer practicing beyond his or her area of competence may be subject to disciplinary action by the profession's regulatory board or society. This situation is analogous to that in the medical profession, where a doctor is licensed as a general "medical doctor" (M.D.), but is allowed to practice only within a specific area of expertise, such as surgery or internal medicine.

Figure 14.10 illustrates the three routes to becoming a professional engineer in Canada. The first step in the process is to satisfy the academic requirements. The choice of path depends on how much expertise is gained from academic study as opposed to on-the-job experience. The left-most path relies on graduation from an engineering program accredited by the Canadian Engineering Accreditation Board (CEAB), a board of the Canadian Council of Professional Engineers. Universities accredit their engineering programs to ensure that graduates begin their professional lives with the education needed to perform effectively. Graduating from an accredited engineering program is the easiest means of satisfying the academic requirement for licensure. The middle path includes graduation from an equivalent university honors program (e.g., an applied science program or an engineering program in another country), where "equivalence" must be demonstrated by confirmatory examinations. The right-most path requires successful completion of a special examination program, involving up to 20 examinations.

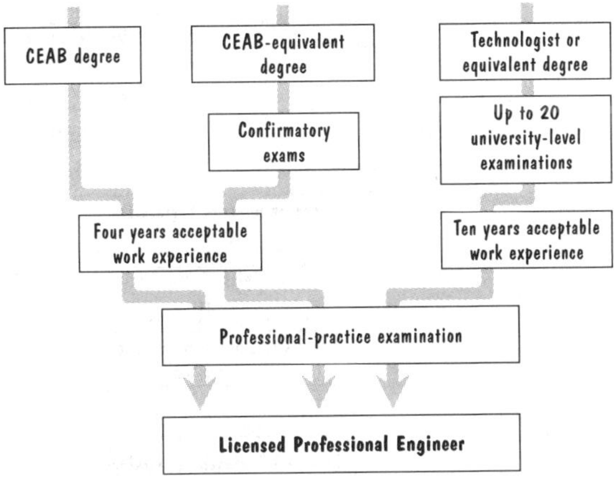

FIGURE 14.10 Routes to becoming a professional engineer (P.Eng.) in Canada.

The second step is to satisfy the engineering experience requirements. Nascent professionals need to practice their knowledge and skills before they are prepared to take primary responsibility for performing work in their field, so all three paths to a Canadian professional engineer's license require engineering experience. The paths that rely on strong academic backgrounds require four years of engineering experience. A candidate who did not graduate from an accredited engineering or equivalent program must accumulate ten years of experience before being considered for licensure. Up to one year of credit is given for post-graduate studies or military experience. (By contrast, U.S. physicians are required to have three years of supervised experience, called residency, before they can be licensed, and certified public accountants must work for a year for a board-approved organization before receiving their licenses.) Last, all candidates must write and pass a professional-practice examination that covers relevant provincial law, professional practice, ethics, and liability.

The licensing process in the United States is more difficult, in that all candidates must take confirmatory examinations. Moreover, there is no path based solely on experience (Figure 14.11). All professional engineers must have academic qualifications, preferably including graduation from an Accreditation Board for Engineering and Technology (ABET) accredited engineering program or its equivalent. (A CEAB-accredited program is considered an acceptable equivalent.)

Applicants who hold a degree from an ABET-accredited program require four years of engineering experience; other applicants require eight years of experience. The experience must demonstrate a clear use of engineering knowledge, engineering education, and engineering judgment, thereby indicating that the candidate is competent to take responsible charge of engineering work. The work must also be progressive, meaning that over time there is an increasing standard of quality and responsibility in one dominant discipline. Although working under the supervision of a licensed professional engineer is recommended, it is not a requirement for licensure.

No matter which path to licensure is followed, the candidate must pass an eight-hour examination in the fundamentals of engineering. This exam is usually taken

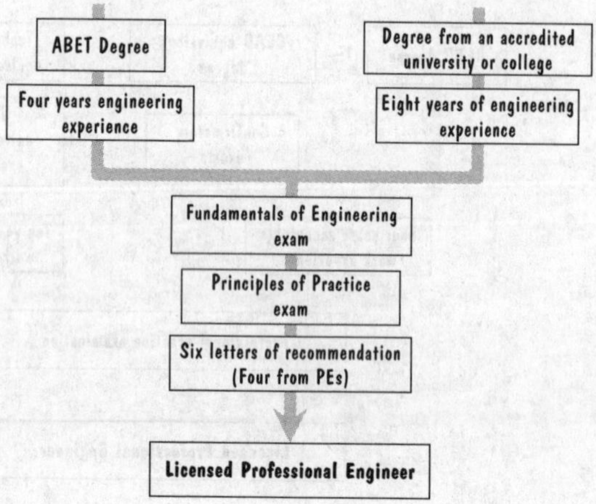

FIGURE 14.11 Professional engineer (PE) application process in the United States.

during a student's senior year of university, because the exam is very difficult to pass if taken well after the relevant courses were completed. The morning portion of the exam covers material common to all engineering disciplines, generally from the first two years of an ABET-accredited program, including chemistry, computers, dynamics, electrical circuits, engineering economics, ethics, fluid mechanics, material science, mathematics, mechanics of materials, statics, and thermodynamics. The intent behind this common exam is to ensure that every engineer knows something about other engineering disciplines, to facilitate communicating with engineers from other disciplines; this knowledge also helps to ensure that the engineer appreciates the level of expertise needed in different specializations, so as not to attempt to practice in a specialization in which she on he is not educated.

The afternoon portion of the exam tests competence in a specific discipline, reflecting the last two years of an ABET-accredited program. There are discipline-specific tests for civil, chemical, industrial, mechanical, and electrical engineering, or applicants can take a second general test that covers the same material as the morning exam, only in more detail. The intent behind the discipline-specific exam is to test competence in the applicant's area of specialization. At this writing, there is no discipline-specific exam for software engineering; there is not even one for computer engineering. A discipline-specific test is created only when there are at least 100 ABET-accredited programs in it that discipline, so no such software engineering exam is expected in the near future.

After no more than four years of experience, the candidate for licensure must pass a second examination, this time addressing the principles and practices of engineering in a discipline-specific topic. At this writing, there is also no principles of practice exam in software engineering.

The movement toward licensing software engineers is occurring in fits and starts. In Canada, some provinces, including Ontario, British Columbia, and Alberta, are licensing software engineers as professional engineers. In the United States, Texas and

Tennessee require the professional engineer designation before a practitioner can call himself or herself an "engineer," including software engineer. However, other jurisdictions are doing nothing. And in the United Kingdom, someone can be designated a chartered engineer simply by joining the British Computer Society.

There is not yet a great deal of momentum to encourage licensing. The reason goes beyond the shortage of software developers and includes differences of opinion on the state of the art in software engineering: Do we, as a profession, know how to develop certifiably correct and dependable software? Proponents advance several arguments for licensing software engineers:

- The practice of software engineering falls under statutes such as the Professional Engineers Act that require a governmental or institutional credential to practice (in Canada) or to sell services to the public (in the U.S.).
- Licensing software engineers would improve software quality by raising the average competence of practitioners.
- Licensing would encourage software developers to obtain a solid educational foundation for their practices.
- Licensing would encourage the use of best practices, even by those not licensed.
- Licensing would improve the engineering of software and the education of software engineers, thus advancing the professionalization of software engineering.

However, some practitioners argue that the profession is not (and may never be) ready for licensing. Their reasons include the following:

- There is no evidence that licensed software engineers produce and maintain the best software.
- Licensing may afford false assurance to the public that software developed by licensed professionals is of high quality.
- There is no widely accepted body of knowledge whose mastery would define competency in software engineering.
- Public safety would be best ensured by certifying the products rather than the processes or the producers. In other words, the proof of the pudding is in the eating.

Moreover, computer scientists and engineers continue to bicker over restrictions on who should be allowed to develop software. For example, licensing in Canada is required when engineering principles are applied, but where does computer science stop and software engineering begin? It is likely that licensing will eventually be enforced only for those software developers who build and maintain safety-critical or mission-critical systems, such as medical devices, nuclear power plant software, and software that involves modeling or controlling the physical world. However, should graduation from an accredited computer science program be considered sufficient academic background for licensure? Moreover, which software should be considered critical? Flaws in seemingly unimportant telephony software may bring down critical information infrastructure, and failures in mundane banking software may have adverse economic effects.

It is difficult to predict where software licensing will go in the near and long terms. The demand for well-qualified software specialists is likely to outstrip the supply of licensed software engineers for the foreseeable future. Governments and institutions may not become serious about licensing software professionals until the public demands better-quality software. However, licensing will not likely wait for software practices to mature to the point where we can guarantee the success and safety of our products. In this respect, the liability of software engineers may eventually be like that of doctors and lawyers, where we will be expected to follow "best practices" but not necessarily to produce perfect software.

In the meantime, governments may legislate the roles that distinguish computer scientists from software engineers, much as architects are distinguished from structural engineers. Practitioners may be exempt from legislation such as the Professional Engineers Act if the systems they build have little interaction with the physical world, such as financial, information, business, scientific, and entertainment applications. In addition, a limited license may be issued to individuals who have ten or more years of specialized experience; holders of such a license would be allowed to practice the narrow aspect of engineering (narrow with respect to both discipline and activity) in which they can demonstrate competence.

Certification

Certification is different from licensing. A **license** is a legal document that attests that the holder has met conditions set out by the government. **Certification** is the bestowing of a document that attests to a practitioner's competency based on passage of examinations, years of experience, or both; it is intended to inspire public confidence in the professional who holds it. A license is required for practice; a certificate is voluntary.

Certification is often administered and bestowed by a professional society. For example, the IEEE Computer Society offers certification as a certified software development professional (CSDP), and the Computer Information Processing Society (CIPS) has an information systems professional (ISP) certificate. Both certificates are intended to demonstrate that a practitioner satisfies minimum academic and practical-experience qualifications, and both require recertification every three years. To be recertified, practitioners must demonstrate that they have kept their skills up to date through courses, publishing, conferences, trade journals, and so on.

The Certified Software Development Society certification process, shown in Figure 14.12, requires that candidates hold a university degree and have ample experience (9000 hours) studying or applying software engineering concepts and techniques. This experience must fall within at least six of the following eleven areas:

- Professionalism and engineering economics
- Software requirements
- Software design
- Software construction
- Software testing
- Software maintenance
- Software engineering management

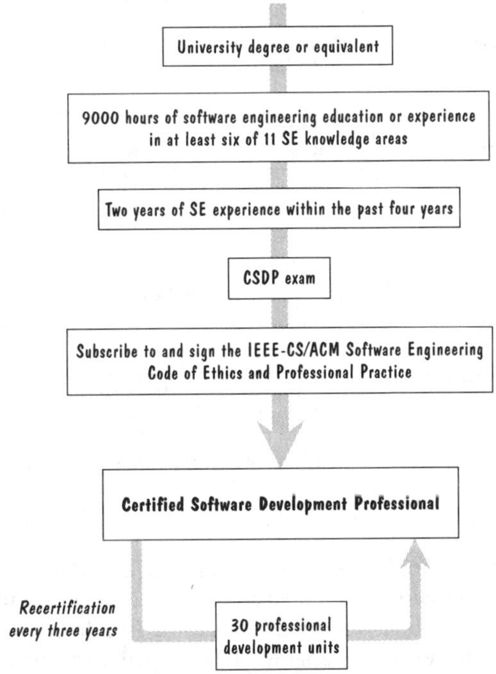

FIGURE 14.12 Certified Software Development Professional certification process.

- Software configuration management
- Software engineering process
- Software engineering tools and methods
- Software quality

In addition, the candidate must take an exam that covers the above 11 areas and must have recent work experience in a field related to software engineering. To remain certified, it is necessary to document professional-development units (PDUs) that have been completed in the past three years. PDUs can be claimed for educational activities (e.g., courses, conferences, seminars), articles or books written, presentations given, technical or professional service, self-study, or employment activities. A professional who applies for recertification after the three-year deadline for recertification may have to retake the CSDP exam.

The ISP certification process is considerably different. It requires experience that uses a significant level of knowledge about information technology (IT) and that exercises a high level of independent judgment and responsibility. Figure 14.13 shows the various combinations of degree and experience requirements that lead to ISP certification. A candidate who does not have a university- or college-level education in an IT-related area can satisfy the degree requirements by passing an exam offered by the Institute for Certification of Computer Professionals (ICCP). The ICCP exam includes

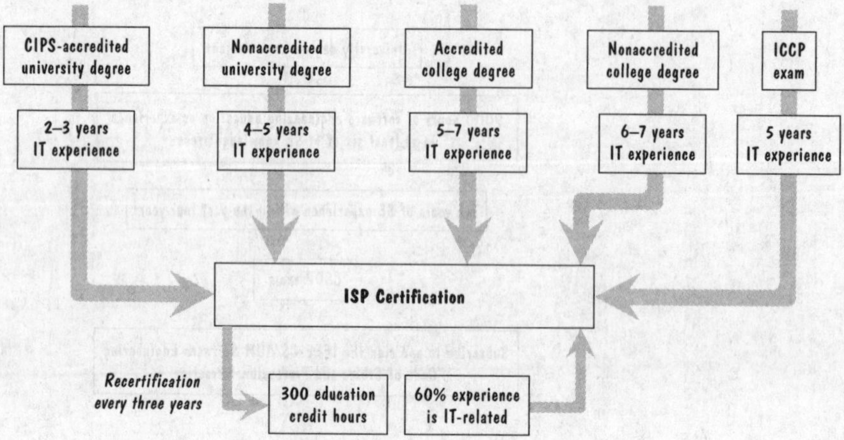

FIGURE 14.13 ISP certification process.

questions about core subjects, specialties, and programming languages. ISP certification requires its professionals to undergo recertification every three years. Candidates must demonstrate that their work continues to be IT-related. Candidates must also demonstrate continuing efforts to upgrade IT knowledge through classes, conferences, technical reading, publishing, mentoring, and so on; these efforts must sum to at least 300 hours of professional development over the three-year period.

Professional certification should not be confused with the certificates offered by software companies. For example, both Microsoft and Cisco have extensive certification programs to assess a user's competence in installing and using their operating systems and networking software. Such product- or vendor-specific certifications may demonstrate a user's proficiency in using particular company products, but they do not attest to the user's general proficiency as a software professional.

Code of Ethics

Engineers, and particularly software engineers, are sometimes chided for being so focused on a technical problem that they forget the human context in which it is embedded. For this reason, a code of ethics can be useful, if not essential, in ensuring that we understand and acknowledge the implications of our professional actions and activities. **A code of ethics** describes the ethical and professional obligations against which peers, the public, and legal bodies can measure a professional's behavior. The code has three key functions:

- It stimulates ethical conduct.
- It inspires public confidence in our profession.
- It offers a formal basis for evaluating actions and disciplining professionals who have agreed to adhere to the code.

Indeed, a code of ethics can inspire good behavior and can be used to challenge others' actions that deviate from the code. It can be supplemented with legal clout, so that code violations can be punished with license suspension or revocation.

There are several ways to determine and define ethical behavior; Baase (2002) discusses them in detail. A code of ethics can be prescriptive or descriptive. A prescriptive code is expressed in terms of rights and obligations. It spells out precisely what can and cannot be done. A descriptive code is expressed in terms of the virtues that the code intends to uphold. It is based on the assumption that the expressed values will act as a guide to appropriate behavior.

We can think of a code of ethics as the set of basic rules of integrity and fairness in our profession. For example, it can guide us in remaining loyal to our associates, employers, clients, and subordinates. The code is also a set of professional rules describing our responsibilities to those we serve. For instance, it may define rules of confidentiality or disclosure that help form our professional judgments about when and how to reveal information. An ethical code can also designate best practices, such as how much testing is adequate. Most professions embrace the notion of "due diligence," where a code describes when a practitioner can be said to have applied good judgment and commonly accepted good practice on behalf of a client or society.

The Association of Professional Engineers of Ontario (PEO) publishes a code of ethics, which imposes several duties on professional engineers:

- Duty to society
- Duty to employers
- Duty to clients
- Duty to colleagues and employees
- Duty to the engineering profession
- Duty to oneself

At the same time, the PEO has defined characteristics of professional misconduct:

- Negligence
- Harassment
- Failure to safeguard the safety, health, or property of a user
- Failure to comply with applicable statutes, regulations, standards, and rules
- Signing or sealing a document that a professional did not prepare or check
- Failure to disclose conflict of interest
- Performing a task outside one's area of expertise

The difference between a code of ethics and a definition of professional misconduct is a matter of degree; one is not the negation of the other. A code of ethics is a high standard of ethical behavior, above and beyond what is required by law. In contrast, professional misconduct is an offense punishable either by law or by a professional organization (e.g., suspending or revoking the offender's license or certification). Sidebar 14.2 lists the Software Engineering Code of Ethics published by the Association for Computing Machinery (ACM) and the Institute for Electrical and Electronics Engineers (IEEE).

Ethical choices are sometimes straightforward, but often they involve difficult choices. Ethical duties can conflict, and there may be no right answer—there may not even be a good choice. For example, if your colleague has a drinking problem that can affect engineering judgment, do you report this to your supervisor? If your colleague has a conflict of interest, do you report it? And if the product you are designing can have dire consequences (e.g., resulting in a better nuclear weapon), do you build it?

Professional Development

Regardless of whether we are licensed or certified, each of us has a responsibility to understand the latest discoveries about software engineering products, processes, and practices. Reading this book is one facet of this larger professional-development activity. Ongoing professional development maintains or improves our knowledge and skills after we begin professional practice; we become better practitioners, build better products, and provide better services.

There are many organizations offering help in our quest to learn about the state of the art and the state of the practice. Among them are international organizations, such as the Association for Computing Machinery (ACM) and the Institute for Electrical and Electronics Engineers (IEEE). Regional or national organizations are also essential; examples include the Canadian Society for Electrical and Computer Engineering (CSECE), the British Computer Society, and the Brazilian Computer Society. These and other organizations assist us in maintaining our competence by

- Developing standards
- Publishing research journals that extend our knowledge
- Publishing practitioner journals that facilitate technology transfer between researchers and practitioners
- Holding technical conferences that facilitate communication with colleagues
- Acting as a public representative for our interests
- Forming special-interest groups to explore focused topics

SIDEBAR 14.2 ACM/IEEE SOFTWARE ENGINEERING CODE OF ETHICS AND PROFESSIONAL PRACTICE (SHORT VERSION, © ACM/IEEE-CS 2004)

The short version of the code summarizes aspirations at a high level of abstraction. The clauses that are included in the full version give examples and details of how these aspirations change the way we act as software engineering professionals. Without the aspirations, the details can become legalistic and tedious; without the details, the aspirations can become high-sounding but empty; together, the aspirations and the details form a cohesive code.

Software engineers shall commit themselves to making the analysis, specification, design, development, testing, and maintenance of software a beneficial and respected profession. In accordance with their commitment to the health, safety, and welfare of the public, software engineers shall adhere to the following eight principles:

1. Software engineers shall act consistently with the public interest.
2. Software engineers shall act in a manner that is in the best interests of their client and employer, consistent with the public interest.
3. Software engineers shall ensure that their products and related modifications meet the highest professional standards possible.
4. Software engineers shall maintain integrity and independence in their professional judgment.
5. Software engineering managers and leaders shall subscribe to and promote an ethical approach to the management of software development and maintenance.
6. Software engineers shall advance the integrity and reputation of the profession, consistent with the public interest.
7. Software engineers shall be fair to and supportive of their colleagues.
8. Software engineers shall participate in lifelong learning regarding the practice of their profession and shall promote an ethical approach to the practice of the profession.

For example, the IEEE has nearly 360,000 members. Table 14.8 lists the 42 technical societies that comprise the IEEE. One subsidiary group, the IEEE Computer Society, focuses specifically on computer science and software engineering issues; it is the largest of the IEEE technical societies, with 98,000 members, and is the largest organization of computing professionals. The IEEE Computer Society sponsors dozens of technical conferences each year, alone and in concert with other organizations, enabling members to learn about the latest research. Its many technical publications, listed in Table 14.9, inform its membership about every aspect of computing. In addition, the IEEE Computer Society Press publishes books and conference proceedings. Other organizations, such as ACM, provide similar products and services.

Next Steps in Research and Practice

The future of software engineering is in our hands. We must study the ways we are similar to other engineers, so that we can learn from their experiences. And we must study the ways we are different, so that we can tailor our strategies, techniques, and tools to the unique problems that we encounter. More generally, we must make sure that we view software engineering in its broader setting, recognizing that quality software products and processes are generated by creative people working in teams, not by a manufacturing process stamping out widgets. To that end, we should embrace other disciplines, including the social sciences, so that our processes are tailored to take advantage of the best each engineer can offer, and our products are tailored to be as useful and helpful as possible to our customers. Finally, we must pay more attention to the consequences of our software

TABLE 14.8 IEEE Technical Societies

IEEE Aerospace and Electronic Systems Society	IEEE Instrumentation and Measurement Society
IEEE Antennas and Propagation Society	IEEE Lasers & Electro-Optics Society
IEEE Broadcast Technology Society	IEEE Magnetics Society
IEEE Circuits and Systems Society	IEEE Microwave Theory and Techniques Society
IEEE Communications Society	IEEE Nanotechnology Council
IEEE Components Packaging, and Manufacturing Technology Society	IEEE Nuclear and Plasma Sciences Society
IEEE Computational Intelligence Society	IEEE Oceanic Engineering Society
IEEE Computer Society	IEEE Power Electronics Society
IEEE Consumer Electronics Society	IEEE Power Engineering Society
IEEE Control Systems Society	IEEE Product Safety Engineering Society
IEEE Council on SuperConductivity	IEEE Professional Communication Society
IEEE Dielectrics and Electrical Insulation Society	IEEE Reliability Society
IEEE Education Society	IEEE Robotics & Automation Society
IEEE Electromagnetic Compatibility Society	IEEE Sensors Council
IEEE Electron Devices Society	IEEE Signal Processing Society
IEEE Engineering Management Society	IEEE Society on Social Implications of Technology
IEEE Engineering in Medicine and Biology Society	IEEE Solid-State Circuits Society
IEEE Geoscience & Remote Sensing Society	IEEE Systems, Man, and Cybernetics Society
IEEE Industrial Electronics Society	IEEE Ultrasonics, Ferroelectrics, and Frequency Control Society
IEEE Industry Applications Society	IEEE Vehicular Technology Society
IEEE Information Theory Society	
IEEE Intelligent Transportation Systems Council	

engineering decisions. Who is responsible when our software fails? What role should licensing and education play? Who bears the ethical and legal liability for our failures in requirements, design, implementation, and testing? As with any mature discipline, we must learn to take responsibility for our actions and our products.

14.5 TERM PROJECT

Your term project is completed. Consider the finished product from the point of view of technology transfer. How would you introduce the Loan Arranger to the loan analysts at FCO? Where do the loan analysts and their managers fit on the continuum of adoption described by Rogers? How does their classification suggest strategies for improving the user interface? training? support? product evolution?

14.6 KEY REFERENCES

General issues related to technology transfer are addressed at many conferences, including the International Conference on Software Engineering. The Redwine and

TABLE 14.9 IEEE Computer Society Publications

IEEE Transactions on Computers	IEEE Transactions on Visualization and Computer Graphics
IEEE/ACM Transactions on Computational Biology & Bioinformatics	Computing in Science & Engineering
IEEE Transactions on Dependable & Secure Computing	IEEE Annals of the History of Computing
IEEE Transactions on Information Technology in Biomedicine	**IEEE Computer**
IEEE Transactions on Knowledge and Data Engineering	IEEE Computer Graphics & Applications
IEEE Transactions on Mobile Computing	IEEE Design & Test of Computers
IEEE Transactions on Multimedia	IEEE Intelligent Systems
IEEE Transactions on Nanobioscience	IEEE Internet Computing
IEEE Transactions on Networking	IEEE Micro
IEEE Transactions on Parallel and Distributed Systems	IEEE MultiMedia
IEEE Transactions on Patterns Analysis and Machine Intelligence	IEEE Pervasive Computing
IEEE Transactions on Software Engineering	IEEE Security & Privacy
IEEE Transactions on Very Large Scale Integration (VI SI) Systems	**IEEE Software**
	IT Professional
	IEEE Transactions on Networking

Riddle (1985) paper remains the most comprehensive survey on software technology use to date. The U.S. Software Engineering Institute has published several technical reports on technology transfer. Recent papers discussing software technology transfer include Pfleeger (1999a), Pfleeger (1999b), and Pfleeger and Menezes (2000).

The social science literature is rich with information about group decision-making. Klein (1998) is a very readable introduction to the recognition-primed decision model. The January/February 2000 issue of *IEEE Software* addresses the more general question of what we can learn from other disciplines.

For information about the Delphi technique, see Linstone and Turoff (1975), and Turoff and Hiltz (1995).

Discussion of software engineering licensing is addressed in the November/December 1999 issue of *IEEE Software* and the May 2000 issue of *IEEE Computer*. Kaner and Pels (1998) consider who is responsible when software fails, and what you can do as a consumer when your software product does not work properly.

Other excellent references related to software certification and licensing include Allen and Hawthorn (1999), Canadian Engineering Quality Board (2001), Knight and Leveson (1986), Notkin (2000), Parnas (2000), and Shaw (1990). As you will see, many of the guidelines are in draft form, because licensing and accreditation issues are still being discussed in the software engineering community. The Professional Engineers Act, one of the statutes of the province of Ontario, can be found at http://www.e-laws.gov.on.ca/html/statutes/english/elaws_statutes_90p28_e.htm. A description of the University of Waterloo software engineering program is at http://www.softeng.uwaterloo.ca

An excellent discussion of ethics and the role of personal responsibility can be found in Baase (2002).

14.7 EXERCISES

1. You work for ABC Software, a company that develops and sells COTS, and your responsibility is the development infrastructure of the company. The main development tools the developers use are a C compiler, Configuration management system, Text editor, and Debugger.
   - **A.** Is ABC Software a technology producer or consumer? Explain.
   - **B.** Each of the four development tools has a new version and you need to decide if you want to use it or stick with the old and proven version. What will be some of your considerations common to all four tools? What will be your considerations specific to each tool?
2. Look at program you have submitted in another class. What technologies did you use? Try to recall the decision-making process: Why did you choose the technologies you did? Did you have alternatives? Could you submit the program using alternative technologies?
3. The January/February 2000 issue of *IEEE Software* contains an editorial by McConnell about software engineering's best influences:
   - reviews and inspections
   - information hiding
   - incremental development
   - user involvement
   - automated revision control
   - development using the Internet
   - programming languages: Fortran, COBOL, Turbo Pascal, Visual Basic
   - Capability Maturity Model for software
   - component-based development
   - metrics and measurement

   For each practice listed, analyze its likely technology adoption. Is it a best practice? What evidence supports its adoption? And what audience is addressed by the evidence?

Annotated Bibliography

Abdel-Ghaly, A.A., P.Y. Chan, and B. Littlewood (1986). "Evaluation of competing software reliability predictions." *IEEE Transactions on Software Engineering*, SE 12(9): 950–967.

Analyzes several reliability models. Introduces the notions of *u*-plots, prequential likelihood, noise.

Abdel-Hamid, Tarek (1989). "The dynamics of software project staffing: A system dynamics based simulated approach." *IEEE Transactions on Software Engineering*, 15(2) (February): 109–119.

Uses system dynamics models to simulate the effects of different staffing levels on a software development project.

——— (1990). "Investigating the cost/schedule trade-off in software development." *IEEE Software*, 7(1): 97–105, January.

——— (1996). "The slippery path to productivity improvement." *IEEE Software*, 13(4) (July): 43–52.

Suggests the use of systems dynamics to optimize resource use in software development projects.

Abdel-Hamid, Tarek, and Stuart Madnick (1991). *Software Project Dynamics: An Integrated Approach*. Englewood Cliffs, NJ: Prentice Hall.

Contains extensive system dynamics models of the software development process.

Ackerman, F., L.S. Buchwald, and F.H. Lewski (1986). "Software inspections: An effective verification process." *IEEE Software*, 6(3) (May): 31–36.

Adams, E. (1984). "Optimizing preventive service of software products." *IBM Journal of Research and Development*, 28(1): 2–14.

Analyzes a number of large software systems and shows that many software faults rarely lead to failures, whereas a small portion causes the most frequent failures.

Agile Alliance (2001). Principles of the Agile Alliance. http://www.agilealliance.org/.

Akao, Yoji (1990). *Quality Function Deployment: Integrating Customer Requirements Into Product Design*. Productivity Press, 1990.

Alexander, Christopher (1979a). *The Timeless Way of Building*. New York: Oxford University Press.

The first book to introduce the notion of design patterns in the context of architecture.

——— (1979b). *Notes on the Synthesis of Form*. Cambridge, MA: Harvard University Press.

Alford, M. (1977). "A requirements engineering methodology for real-time processing requirements." *IEEE Transactions on Software Engineering*, SE 3(1) (January): 60–69.

Article introducing SREM.

——— (1985). "SREM at the age of eight: The distributed computing design system." *IEEE Computer*, 18(4) (April): 36–46.

Allen, Frances, and Paula Hawthorn (1999). "ACM Task Force on Professional Licensing in Software Engineering." May. http://www.acm.org/serving/se_policy/report.html.

Allen, Julia H., Sean Barnum, Robert J. Ellison, Gary McGraw, and Nancy Mead (2008). *Software Security Engineering: A Guide for Project Managers*. Upper Saddle River, NJ: Addison-Wesley.

Ambler, Scott W. (2002). *Agile Modeling: Effective Methods for Extreme Programming and the Unified Process*. New York: John Wiley and Sons.

——— (2003). "Agile model driven development is good enough." *IEEE Software* (September/October): 71–73.

Ambler, Scott W. (2004a). "Agile Requirements Modeling." Official Agile Modeling Site, http://www.agilemodeling.com/essays/agileRequirements.htm.

——— (2004b). "Agile Software Development." Official Agile Modeling Site, http://www.agilemodeling.com/essays/agileSoftwareDevelopment.htm.

Andriole, Stephen J. (1993). *Rapid Application Prototyping: The Storyboard Approach to User Requirements Analysis*. New York: John Wiley.

Anonymous (1996). "In a hurry are we, sir?" *Pilot*.

Describes an unanticipated problem with radar software in a Harrier jet.

Anthes, Gary H. (1997). "How to avoid killer apps." *Computerworld*, July 7.

A good, accessible summary of some of the consequences of unsafe software design. Also available on the Web at http://www.computerworld.com/features/970707killer.html.

Antón, Philip S., Robert H. Anderson, Richard Mesic, and Michael Scheiern (2004). *Finding and Fixing Vulnerabilities in Information Systems: The Vulnerability Assessment and Mitigation Methodology*. MR 1601-DARPA. Santa Monica, CA: RAND Corporation.

Arango, Guillermo, Eric Schoen, and Robert Pettengill (1993). "Design as evolution and reuse." In *Proceedings of the Second International Workshop on Software Reusability* (Lucca, Italy, March 24–26). Los Alamitos, CA: IEEE Computer Society Press.

Discusses the use of technology books and project books to capture lessons learned on one project for reuse on others.

Ardis, Mark, and Janel Green (1998). "Successful introduction of domain engineering into software development." *Bell Labs Technical Journal*, 3(3) (July–September): 10–20.

Ardis, Mark A., John A. Chaves, Lalita Jategaonkar Jagadeesan, Peter Mataga, Carlos Puchol, Mark G. Staskauskas, and James Von Olnhausen (1996). "A framework for evaluating specification methods for reactive systems." *IEEE Transactions on Software Engineering*, 22(6) (June): 378–389.

An experience report, originally presented at the 17th International Conference on Software Engineering, that provides criteria for selecting from among several requirements specification techniques. It includes fundamental criteria and important criteria and shows how they apply across the development life cycle.

Arnold, Robert S. (1993). *Software Reengineering*. Los Alamitos, CA: IEEE Computer Society Press.

Arnold, Robert S. and Shawn Bohner (1996). *Software Change Impact Analysis*. Los Alamitos, CA: IEEE Computer Society Press.

Arthur, Lowell Jay (1997). "Quantum improvements in software system quality." *Communications of the ACM*, 40(6) (June): 47–52.

Discusses experiences in improving software at U.S. West Technologies. Points out some of the mistakes that were made, including focusing on the wrong goals.

Asch, Solomon (1956). "Studies of independence and submission to group pressure." *Psychological Monographs*, 70.

Associated Press (1996). "Pilot's computer error cited in plane crash." *Washington Post*, August 24, p. A4.

Atomic Energy Control Board (AECB) (1999). *Draft Regulatory Guide C-138 (E): Software in Protection and Control Systems*. http://www.nuclearsafety.gc.ca/pubs_catalogue/uploads/c138e.pdf.

News report of the role of computer error in a Colombian air disaster.

Avizienis, A., and J.P.J. Kelly (1984). "Fault tolerance through design diversity: Concepts and experiments." *IEEE Computer*, 17(8): 67–80.

Describes the notion of using several independently designed software systems that address the same requirements. The goal is to run all systems at once, using a voting procedure to take action based on the majority's results. This is the philosophy behind the U.S. space shuttle's redundant systems. See Knight and Leveson's (1986) paper for a conflicting view.

Baase, Sara (2002). *A Gift of Fire: The Social, Legal and Ethical Issues for Computers and the Internet*, 2nd ed. Upper Saddle River, NJ: Prentice Hall.

Babich, Wayne (1986). *Software Configuration Management*. Reading, MA: Addison-Wesley.

Good overview of the key issues involved in configuration management, with several case studies at the end of the book.

Bach, James (1997). "Test automation snake oil." In *Proceedings of the Fourteenth International Conference and Exposition on Testing Computer Software*, pp. 19–24 (Washington, DC, June 16–19).

Suggests guidelines for making sensible decisions about what test automation can and cannot do for you. Available from Frontier Technologies, Annapolis, MD.

Bailey, John W., and Victor R. Basili (1981). "A meta-model for software development resource expenditures." In *Proceedings of the Fifth International Conference on Software Engineering*, pp. 107–116. Los Alamitos, CA: IEEE Computer Society.

Baker, F.T. (1972). "Chief programmer team management of production programming." *IBM Systems Journal*, 11(1): 56–73.

First paper to suggest chief programmer team organization for software development projects.

Ballard, Mark (2006). "NHS IT cost doubled to £12.4 billion." *The Register* (16 June). http://www.theregister.co.uk/2006/06/16/nhsit_budget_overrun/.

Balzer, Robert (1981a). "Transformational implementation: An example." *IEEE Transactions on Software Engineering*, SE 7(1) (January): 3–14.

Describes transformational process model for software development.

——— (1981b). Gist Final Report (February). Los Angeles: University of Southern California, Information Sciences Institute.

Banker, R., R. Kauffman, and R. Kumar (1992). "An empirical test of object-based output measurement metrics in a computer aided software engineering (CASE) environment." *Journal of Management Information Systems*, 8(3) (Winter): 127–150.

Introduces the notion of object points for measuring the size of a system.

Barghouti, Naser S., and Gail E. Kaiser (1991). "Scaling up rule-based development environments." In *Proceedings of the Third European Software Engineering Conference* (Milan, Italy). *Lecture Notes in Computer Science*, no. 55, pp. 380–395. Amsterdam: Springer-Verlag.

Barghouti, Naser S., David S. Rosenblum, David G. Berlanger, and Christopher Alliegro (1995). "Two case studies in modeling real, corporate processes." *Software Process: Improvement and Practice*, 1(1): 17–32.

Barnard, J., and A. Price (1994). "Managing code inspection information." *IEEE Software*, 11(2) (March): 59–69.

Extensive quantitative study of introducing Fagan inspections at AT&T. Uses the goal-question-metric paradigm to determine what to measure.

Barnes, Bruce, and Terry A. Bollinger (1991). "Making reuse cost-effective." *IEEE Software*, 8(1) (January): 13–24.

A lovely survey paper that identifies some of the key issues in making reuse work.

Barron, D.W., and J.M. Bishop (1984). *Advanced Programming.* New York: John Wiley.

Basili, Victor R. (1990). "Viewing maintenance as reuse-oriented software development." *IEEE Software*, 7(1) (January): 19–25.

Basili, Victor R., Lionel Briand, and Walcelio Melo (1995). "A validation of object-oriented design metrics as quality indicators." *IEEE Transactions on Software Engineering*, 22(10) (October): 751–761.

Basili, Victor R., and Scott Green (1994). "Software process evolution at the SEL." *IEEE Software*, 11(4) (July): 58–66.

Describes the use of the quality improvement paradigm, case studies, and experiments to investigate the effects of reading techniques and of cleanroom. Especially useful for describing how to use different kinds of studies to assess a technology.

Basili, Victor R., and Barry T. Perricone (1984). "Software errors and complexity: An empirical investigation." *Communications of the ACM*, 27(1): 42–52.

Analyzes distributions and relationships derived from software changes data.

Bass, Len, Paul Clements, and Rick Kazman (2003). *Software Architecture in Practice*, 2nd ed. Boston, MA: Addison-Wesley.

A comprehensive text on how to create, document, and analyze a system's software architectures, with many good case studies.

——— (2003a). "Achieving qualities." In *Software Architecture in Practice*, pp. 99–128. Boston, MA: Addison-Wesley.

——— (2003b). "Software product lines." In *Software Architecture in Practice*, pp. 353–368. Boston, MA: Addison-Wesley.

Bates, Clive (1997). "Test it again—how long?" In *Proceedings of the Fourteenth International Conference and Exposition on Testing Computer Software* (Washington, DC, June 16–19).

Available from Frontier Technologies, Annapolis, MD.

Beck, Kent (1999). *Extreme Programming Explained: Embrace Change.* Reading, MA: Addison-Wesley.

Beck, Kent et al. (2004). "Manifesto for Agile Software Development." October. http://www.agilemanifesto.org.

Beizer, Boris (1990). *Software Testing Techniques*, 2nd ed. New York: Van Nostrand.

Second edition of one of the few comprehensive texts on software testing. Contains detailed descriptions of many specific strategies and takes the issues of measurement seriously.

——— (1995). *Black-Box Testing*. New York: John Wiley.

——— (1997). "Cleanroom process model: A critical examination." *IEEE Software*, 14(2) (March/April): 14–16.

Suggests that cleanroom ignores basic testing theory and is an irresponsible practice.

Belady, L., and M.M. Lehman (1972). "An introduction to growth dynamics." In W. Freiberger (ed.), *Statistical Computer Performance Evaluation*. New York: Academic Press.

Introduces one of the first mathematical models of software maintenance costs.

Bentley, Jon (1986). *Programming Pearls*. Reading, MA: Addison-Wesley.

——— (1989). *More Programming Pearls*. Reading, MA: Addison-Wesley.

Berard, Edward V. (2000). "Abstraction, encapsulation and information hiding," http://www. itmweb. com/essay550.htm.

Good essay on the differences among abstraction, encapsulation, and information hiding.

Berry, Daniel M. (2002a). "The inevitable pain of software development, including of extreme programming, caused by requirements volatility." *Proceedings of the Workshop on Time-Constrained Requirements Engineering (T-CRE)*. Essen, Germany (September): 9–19. Los Alamitos, CA: IEEE Computer Society Press.

Berry, Daniel M. (2002b). "The inevitable pain of software development: Why there is no silver bullet." In *Proceedings of Monterey Workshop 2002: Radical Innovations of Software and Systems Engineering in the Future*. Venice, Italy (October): 28–47. Los Alamitos, CA: IEEE Computer Society Press.

Bertolino, A., and L. Strigini (1996). "On the use of testability measures for dependability assessment." *IEEE Transactions on Software Engineering*, 22(2) (February): 97–108.

The authors examine the notion of testability as proposed by Voas and point out that there are potential dangers. By making a program highly testable, you may increase the probability that the program is fault-free but at the same time increase the probability that failures will occur if faults remain. They propose an improved model of testability.

Beyer, Hugh, and Karen Holtzblatt (1995). "Apprenticing with the customer: A collaborative approach to requirements definition." *Communications of the ACM*, 35(8) (May 1995): 45–52.

Bieman, James M., and Linda M. Ott (1993). Measuring Functional Cohesion, Technical Report TR CS-93-109. Fort Collins: Colorado State University, Computer Science Department.

Binder, Robert V. (1997). "Can a manufacturing quality model work for software?" *IEEE Software*, 14(5) (September/October): 101–105.

A Quality Time column that discusses why the six-sigma quality efforts are not applicable to software.

Binder Robert. (2000). *Testing Object-Oriented Systems*. Reading, MA: Addison-Wesley.

Bodker, K., and J. Pedersen (1991). "Workplace cultures: Looking at artifacts, symbols and practices." In J. Greenbaum and M. Kyng (eds.), *Design at Work: Cooperative Design of Computer Systems*, pp. 121–136. Hillsdale, NJ: Lawrence Erlbaum.

Boehm, Barry (2000). "Requirements that handle IKIWISI, COTS, and rapid change." *IEEE Computer*, 33(7) (July): 99–102.

Boehm, B.W. (1981). *Software Engineering Economics*. Englewood Cliffs, NJ: Prentice Hall.

This book is one of the first to approach software engineering from an "engineering" point of view. Boehm discusses the derivation and application of the COCOMO model for software effort and schedule estimation. It is of particular interest because Boehm based COCOMO on a large set of data from TRW, a defense contractor.

Boehm, B.W. (1988). "A spiral model for software development and enhancement." *IEEE Computer*, 21(5) (May): 61–72.

Describes a model for merging risk management procedures with software development life-cycle model.

——— (1989). *Software Risk Management*. Los Alamitos, CA: IEEE Computer Society Press.

Excellent tutorial on dealing with risk on software development projects.

——— (1990). "Verifying and validating software requirements and design specifications." In *System and Software Requirements Engineering*. Los Alamitos, CA: IEEE Computer Society Press.

——— (1991). "Software risk management: Principles and practices." *IEEE Software*, 8(1) (January): 32–41.

Good overview of risk management terminology, models, and examples.

——— (1996). "Anchoring the software process." *IEEE Software*, 13(4) (July): 73–82.

——— (2000). "Software cost management with COCOMO II." In *Proceedings of the International Conference on Applications of Software Measurement*. Orange Park, FL: Software Quality Engineering.

Boehm, B.W., J.R. Brown, J.R. Kaspar, M. Lipow, and G. MacCleod (1978). *Characteristics of Software Quality*. Amsterdam: North Holland.

Proposes definitions and measures for a range of quality attributes. This book describes a "model" of software quality that has since been referred to as Boehm's quality model.

Boehm, B.W., C. Clark, E. Horowitz, C. Westland, R. Madachy, and R. Selby (1995). "Cost models for future life cycle processes: COCOMO 2.0." *Annals of Software Engineering*, 1(1) (November): 57–94.

This paper describes the problems perceived in using the original COCOMO model and the techniques used to address them in a revised version of COCOMO.

Boehm, B.W., T.E. Gray, and T. Seewaldt (1984). "Prototyping versus specifying: A multi-project experiment." *IEEE Transactions on Software Engineering*, SE 10(3) (March): 290–302.

Boehm, B.W., and C. Papaccio (1988). "Understanding and controlling software costs." *IEEE Transactions on Software Engineering*, 14(10) (October): 14–66.

Böhm, C., and G. Jacopini (1966). "Flow diagrams, Turing machines and languages with only two formation rules." *Communications of the ACM*, 9(5) (May): 266.

Classic paper showing that any design can be written with only sequence, decision, and iteration—that is, without goto statements.

Bohner, Shawn A. (1990). Technology Assessment on Software Reengineering, Technical Report, CTC-TR-90-001P. Chantilly, VA: Contel Technology Center.

Lovely, clear description of how reengineering, reverse engineering, restructuring, and reengineering relate to one another. Unfortunately, it is available only from the author.

Bollinger, Terry B., and Clement L. McGowan (1991). "A critical look at software capability evaluations." *IEEE Software*, 8(4) (July): 25–41.

Clear, insightful paper questioning the underpinnings of process maturity. A must read for anyone considering adopting a process improvement strategy.

Bollinger, Terry B., and Shari Lawrence Pfleeger (1990). "The economics of software reuse: issues and alternatives." *Information and Software Technology*, 32(10) (December): 643–652.

Booch, Grady (1994). *Object-Oriented Analysis and Design with Applications*, 2nd ed. San Francisco, CA: Benjamin-Cummings.

Booch, Grady, James Rumbaugh, and Ivar Jacobson (2005). *The Unified Modeling Language User Guide*. Boston, MA: Addison-Wesley Professional.

Braun, Christine, and Rubén Prieto-Díaz (1990). Technology Assessment of Software Reuse, Technical Report CTC-TR-90-004P. Chantilly, VA: Contel Technology Center.

Brealey, R., and S. Myers (1991). *Principles of Corporate Finance*. New York: McGraw-Hill.

Brettschneider, Ralph (1989). "Is your software ready for release?" *IEEE Software*, 6(4) (July): 100–108.

Describes a simple model used at Motorola, called zero-failure testing.

Briand, Lionel C., Victor R. Basili, and William M. Thomas (1992). "A pattern recognition approach for software engineering data analysis." *IEEE Transactions on Software Engineering*, 18(11): 931–942.

Uses optimal set reduction for cost estimation.

Briand, Lionel C., Prem Devanbu, and Walcelio Melo (1997). "An investigation into coupling measures for C++." In *Proceedings of the Nineteenth International Conference on Software Engineering* pp. 412–421 (Boston, MA). May, 1997. Los Alamitos, CA: IEEE Computer Society Press.

Proposes a suite of measures for object-oriented designs. Demonstrates that some of these measures may be useful for fault detection.

Briand, Lionel C., Sandro Morasca, and Victor R. Basili (1994). Defining and Validating High-Level Design Metrics, Technical Report CS-TR-3301. College Park, MD: University of Maryland, Department of Computer Science.

Brodman, Judith G., and Donna L. Johnson (1995). "Return on investment (ROI) from software process improvement as measured by U.S. industry." *Software Process—Improvement and Practice*, 1(1): 35–47.

This paper examines the ways in which 33 organizations calculate return on investment from software. It shows great inconsistencies that make it impossible for us to amalgamate the results.

Brooks, Frederick P., Jr. (1987). "No silver bullet: Essence and accidents of software engineering." *IEEE Computer*, 20(4) (April): 10–19.

Brooks, Frederick P., Jr. (1995). *The Mythical Man-Month 20th Anniversary Edition*. Reading, MA: Addison-Wesley.

A classic book of essays, based on the author's experience building the OS-360 operating system. Many of his observations involve organizational dynamics, such as adding extra staff to a late project. Originally published in 1975.

Brownsword, Lisa, and Paul Clements (1996). "A case study in successful product line development." CMU/SEI-96-TR-016. Pittsburgh, PA: Software Engineering Institute, Carnegie Mellon University.

Busby, J.S., and S.C. Barton (1996) "Predicting the cost of engineering: Does intuition help or hinder?" *Engineering Management Journal*, 6(4): 177–182.

Buschmann, F., R. Meunier, H. Rohner, P. Sommerlad and M. Stal (1996). *Pattern-Oriented Software Architecture: A System of Patterns.* Chichester, UK: John Wiley & Sons.

Canadian Engineering Qualifications Board (CEQB) (2004). "Software Engineering Syllabus—2004." http://www.ccpe.ca/e/files/syllabus_4_20.pdf.

Canadian Engineering Quality Board (2001). "Core and Supplementary Bodies of Knowledge for Software Engineering: A report prepared for the CCPE as part of the CEQB Body of Knowledge Development Pilot Project." Draft version 0.4 (September 5).

Card, David N. (1992). "Capability evaluations rated highly variable." *IEEE Software*, 9(5) (September): 105–107.

Card, David N., V.E. Church, and William W. Agresti (1986). "An empirical study of software design practices." *IEEE Transactions on Software Engineering*, 12(2) (February): 264–271.

Card, David N., and Robert L. Glass (1990). *Measuring Software Design Quality*. Englewood Cliffs, NJ: Prentice Hall.

Interesting discussion of how a measure evolved based on the measure's goals and behavior.

Cashman, P.M., and A.W. Holt (1980). "A communication-oriented approach to structuring the software maintenance environment." *ACM SIGSOFT Software Engineering Notes*, 5(1) (January): 4–17.

Cavano, Joseph P., and Frank S. LaMonica (1987). "Quality assurance in future development environments." *IEEE Software*, 7(5) (September): 26–34.

Chen, Peter (1976). "The entity-relationship model: Toward a unified view of data." *ACM Transactions on Database Systems*, 1(1): 9–36.

Chen, Minder and Ronald J. Norman (1992). "A Framework for Integrated CASE," *IEEE Software*, 9(2): 18–22.

Chidamber, S.R., and C.F. Kemerer (1994). "A metrics suite for object-oriented design." *IEEE Transactions on Software Engineering*, 20(6): 476–493.

Chillarege, Ram, Inderpal S. Bhandari, Jarir K. Chaar, Michael J. Halliday, Diane S. Moebus, Bonnie K. Ray, and Man-Yuen Wong (1992). "Orthogonal defect classification: A concept for in-process measurements." *IEEE Transactions on Software Engineering*, 18(11) (November): 943–956.

Clements, Paul, F. Bachmann, Len Bass, David Garlan, J. Ivers, R. Little, Robert L. Nord, and J. Stafford (2003). *Documenting Software Architectures*. Reading, MA: Addison-Wesley.

Clements, Paul, and Linda Northrop (2002). *Software Product Lines: Practices and Patterns*. Boston, MA: Addison-Wesley.

Coad, Peter, and Edward Yourdon (1991). *Object-Oriented Analysis*. Englewood Cliffs, NJ: Prentice Hall.

Cobb, R.H., and H.D. Mills (1990). "Engineering software under statistical quality control." *IEEE Software*, 7(6) (November): 44–54.

Cockburn, Alistair (2002). *Agile Software Development*. Reading, MA: Addison-Wesley.

Cockburn, Alistair, and Laurie Williams (2000). "The costs and benefits of pair programming," *Proceedings of Extreme Programming and Flexible Processes in Software Engineering* (XP2000), Cagliari, Italy (June).

Coffee, Peter (1997). "Pathfinder made not so soft a landing." *PC Week*, July 19.

Coglianese, L., and R. Szymanski (1993). "DSSA-ADAGE: An environment for architecture-based avionics development." *Proceedings of AGARD'93* (May).

Cohen, David, Siddhartha Dalal, Jesse Parelius, and Gardner Patton (1996). "The combinatorial approach to automatic test generation." *IEEE Software*, 13(5) (September): 83–88.

Describes using combinatorial design to reduce test plan development from one month to less than one week.

Cole, M., and P. Griffin (1990). "Cultural amplifiers reconsidered." In D.R. Olson (ed.), *The Social Foundations of Language and Thought*, pp. 343–364. New York: W.W. Norton.

Coleman, Derek, Patrick Arnold, Stephanie Bodoff, Chris Dollin, Helena Gilchrist, Fiona Hayes, and Paul Jeremaes (1994). *Object-Oriented Development: The Fusion Method*. Englewood Cliffs, NJ: Prentice Hall.

Describes a method to integrate and extend the best features of OMT, Booch, CRC, and Objectory. Gives lots of well-explained examples.

Coleman, Don, Dan Ash, Bruce Lowther, and Paul Oman (1994). "Using metrics to evaluate software system maintainability." *IEEE Computer*, 27(8) (August): 44–49.

Describes use of metrics at Hewlett-Packard in guiding maintenance decisions.

Collier, Bonnie, Tom DeMarco, and Peter Fearey (1996). "A defined process for project postmortem reviews." *IEEE Software*, 13(4) (July): 65–72.

Compton, B.T., and C. Withrow (1990). "Prediction and control of Ada software defects." *Journal of Systems and Software*, 12: 199–207.

Report on software fault behavior at Unisys.

Computer Weekly Report (1994). "Sources of errors." August 12.

Conklin, Peter F. (1996). "Enrollment management: Managing the Alpha AXP program." *IEEE Software* 13(4) (July): 53–64.

Describes a project management approach that was very successful in developing Digital's Alpha chip.

Conte, S., H. Dunsmore, and V. Shen (1986). *Software Engineering Metrics and Models*. Menlo Park, CA: Benjamin-Cummings.

A nice survey and history of software metrics. Especially good section comparing cost estimation models.

Courtney, R.E., and D.A. Gustafson (1993). "Shotgun correlations in software measures." *Software Engineering Journal*, 8(1): 5–13.

Curtis, Bill, W.E. Hefley, and S. Miller (1995). People Capability Maturity Model, Technical Reports SEI-CMU-TR-95-MM-001 and -002. Pittsburgh, PA: Software Engineering Institute.

Curtis, Bill, Marc I. Kellner, and Jim Over (1992). "Process modeling." *Communications of the ACM*, 35(9) (September): 75–90.

A nice survey paper about different ways to model processes.

Curtis, Bill, Herb Krasner, and Neil Iscoe (1988). "A field study of the software design process for large systems." *Communications of the ACM*, 31(11) (November): 1268–1287.

Curtis, Bill, Herb Krasner, Vincent Shen, and Neil Iscoe (1987). "On building software process models under the lamppost." In *Proceedings of the 9th International Conference on Software Engineering*, pp. 96–103. Monterey, CA: IEEE Computer Society Press.

Important paper that suggests that we often model what is easy to model rather than what we need.

An evaluation of the significant activities on 17 software development projects.

Cusumano, Michael, and Richard W. Selby (1995). *Microsoft Secrets: How the World's Most Powerful Software Company Creates Technology, Shapes Markets and Manages People*. New York: Free Press/Simon and Schuster.

——— (1997). "How Microsoft builds software." *Communications of the ACM*, 40(6) (June): 53–61.

Interesting description of how Microsoft combines some good software engineering practices while preserving some aspects of the hacker mentality.

Czarnecki, Krzysztof (2005). "Overview of generative software development." In J.-P. Banâtre et al. (eds.), *Unconventional Programming Paradigms (UPP) 2004*, LNCS 3556, pp. 313–328.

Davis, Alan M. (1993). *Software Requirements: Objects, Functions and States*, rev. ed. Englewood Cliffs, NJ: Prentice Hall.

——— (1995). *201 Principles of Software Development*. New York: McGraw-Hill.

Dawid, A.P. (1984). "Statistical theory: The prequential approach." *Journal of the Royal Statistical Society*, A147: 278–292.

De Almeida, Mauricio, Hakim Lounis, and Walcelio Melo (1997). "An investigation on the use of machine learning models for estimating software correctability." Technical Report CRIM-97/08-81. Montreal: Centre de Recherche Informatique de Montréal.

DeLine, Robert (2001). "Avoiding packaging mismatch with flexible packaging." *IEEE Transactions on Software Engineering*, 27(2): 124–143.

DeMarco, T. (1978). *Structured Analysis and System Specification*. New York: Yourdon Press.

Clear and compelling argument for using structure during requirements analysis.

——— (1982). *Controlling Software Projects*. New York: Yourdon Press.

An entertaining, lucid argument for using measurement to understand and guide software projects. Includes a definition of "system bang" and a good discussion of the meaning of estimation.

——— (1997). *The Deadline: A Novel about Project Management*. New York: Dorset House.

DeMarco, T., and T. Lister (1985). "Programmer performance and the effects of the workplace." In *Proceedings of the Eighth International Conference on Software Engineering* (London). Los Alamitos, CA: IEEE Computer Society Press.

——— (1987). *Peopleware: Productive Projects and Teams*. New York: Dorset House.

Deming, W. Edwards (1989). *Out of Crisis*. Cambridge, MA: MIT Center for Advanced Engineering Study.

Denton, Lynn (1993). *Designing, Writing and Producing Computer Documentation*. New York: McGraw-Hill.

Department of Defense (1977). *Automated Data Systems Documentation Standards*. Washington, DC: DOD.

Department of Trade and Industry (1992). "TickIT guide to software quality management, system construction and certification using ISO 9001/EN 29001/BS 5750 issue 2.0." Available from TickIT project office, 68 Newman Street, London W1A 4SE, UK.

DeYoung, G.E., and G.R. Kampen (1979). "Program factors as predictors of program readability." In *Proceedings of the Computer Software and Applications Conference*, pp. 668–673. Los Alamitos, CA: IEEE Computer Society Press.

Dijkstra, Edsger W. (1982). "On the role of scientific thought." *Selected Writings on Computing: A Personal Perspective*. New York: Springer-Verlag.

Dion, Raymond (1993). "Process improvement and the corporate balance sheet." *IEEE Software*, 10(4) (July): 28–35.

Describes the effects of software process improvement and the SEI's Capability Maturity Model on corporate profit and loss.

Dixon, Rand (1996). *Client/Server and Open Systems*. New York: John Wiley.

An overview of client/server pros and cons, plus information about vendors supporting client/server and open systems architectural products.

Dressler, Catherine (1995). "We've got to stop meeting like this." *Washington Post*, December 31, p. H2.

Interesting article with suggestions about how to improve project meetings.

Drobka, Jerry, David Noftz, and Rekha Raghu (2004). "Piloting XP on four mission-critical projects." *IEEE Software*, 21(6) (November/December): 70–75.

Dromey, R. Geoff (1996). "Cornering the chimera." *IEEE Software*, 13(1) (January): 33–43.

A product quality model where all subcharacteristics are defined so that they can be measured and amalgamated into higher level characteristics.

Dutertre, Bruno, and Victoria Stavridou (1997). "Formal requirements analysis of an avionics control system." *IEEE Transactions on Software Engineering*, 23(5) (May): 267–277.

Describes a method for specifying and verifying a real-time system with PVS. Includes the formal specification of the functional and safety requirements. Demonstrates consistency and some safety properties.

Easterbrook, Steve, and Bashar Nuseibeh (1996). "Using viewpoints for inconsistency management." *IEEE Software Engineering Journal*, 11(1) (January), BCS/IEE Press: 31–43.

Eckhardt, D.E., and L.D. Lee (1985), "A theoretical basis for the analysis of multiversion software subject to coincident errors." *IEEE Transactions on Software Engineering*, SE–11(12): 1511–1517.

Ehn, P. (1988). *Work-Oriented Design of Computer Artifacts*. Stockholm: Almquist & Wiksell International.

El Emam, Khaled, and N.H. Madhavji (1995). "The reliability of measuring organizational maturity." *Software Process Improvement and Practice*, 1(1): 3–25.

Elmendorf, W.R. (1973). Cause-Effect Graphs in Functional Testing, Technical Report TR-00.2487. Poughkeepsie, NY: IBM Systems Development Division.

——— (1974). "Functional analysis using cause-effect graphs." In *Proceedings of SHARE XLIII*. New York: IBM.

Elssamadissy, A., and G. Schalliol (2002). "Recognizing and responding to 'bad smells' in extreme programming." In *Proceedings of the 24th International Conference on Software Engineering*, (May). Los Alamitos, CA: IEEE Computer Society Press.

Engle, Charles, Jr., and Ara Kouchakdjian (1995). "Engineering software solutions using cleanroom." In *Proceedings of the Pacific Northwest Quality Conference*. Portland, OR.

An example cited by Beizer as cleanroom orthodoxy that shuns unit testing.

ESPI Exchange (1996). "Productivity claims for ISO 9000 ruled untrue." London: European Software Process Improvement Foundation (October), p. 1.

Discussion of UK Advertising Standards Authority ruling that ISO 9000 certification does not ensure quality products.

Evans, M., and J. Marciniak (1987). *Software Quality Assurance and Management*. New York: John Wiley.

Fagan, M.E. (1976). "Design and code inspections to reduce errors in program development." *IBM Systems Journal*, 15(3): 182–210.

The original paper on Fagan inspections.

——— (1986). "Advances in software inspections." *IEEE Transactions on Software Engineering*, SE 12(7): 744–751.

An updated description of the classical Fagan inspection approach.

Favaro, John (1996). "Value based principles for management of reuse in the enterprise." In *Proceedings of the Fourth International Conference on Software Reuse* (Orlando, Florida). Los Alamitos, CA: IEEE Computer Society Press.

Favaro, John, and Shari Lawrence Pfleeger (1998). "Making Software Development Investment Decisions." *ACM Software Engineering Notes*, 23(5)(September): 69–74.

Fenelon, P., J.A. McDermid, M. Nicholson, and D.J. Pumfrey (1994). "Towards integrated safety analysis and design." *ACM Applied Computing Reviews*, 2(1) (July): 21–32.

A good survey of techniques for assessing software safety.

Fenton, Norman E., and Shari Lawrence Pfleeger (1997). *Software Metrics: A Rigorous and Practical Approach*, 2nd ed., London: PWS Publishing, 1997.

Fernandes, T. (1995). *Global Interface Design*. London: Academic Press.

Fewster, Mark, and Dorothy Graham (1999). *Automated Software Testing*. Reading MA: Addison-Wesley.

Field, Tom (1997a). "A good connection." *CIO Magazine*, February 1.

A description of how Bell Atlantic dealt with its legacy systems and upgraded customer service and products.

——— (1997b). "Banking on the relationship." *CIO Magazine*, February 1.

Describes how Chase Manhattan updated a legacy system and focused on interpersonal problems related to information technology.

Fischer, G., K. Nakakoji, and J. Ostwald (1995). "Supporting the evolution of design artifacts with representations of context and intent." In *Proceedings of DIS95, Symposium on Designing Interactive Systems* (Ann Arbor, MI), pp. 7–15 New York: ACM.

Fjeldstad, R.K., and W.T. Hamlen (1979). "Application program maintenance study: A report to our respondents." In *Proceedings of GUIDE 48* (Philadelphia).

Old but interesting survey of 25 data processing projects to look at the split between development and maintenance time.

Forgionne, G. A. (1986). *Quantitative Decision Making*. Belmont, CA: Wadsworth.

Forrester, J. (1991). "System dynamics and the lessons of 35 years." Working paper D-42241. Cambridge, MA: Massachusetts Institute of Technology, Sloan School of Management.

Description of the applications of systems dynamics since its creation.

Foushee, H.C., J. K. Lauber, M. M. Baetge, and D. B. Acomb (1986). "Crew performance as a function of exposure to high-density short-haul duty cycles," NASA Technical Memorandum 99322, Moffett Field, CA, NASA Ames Research Center.

Fowler, Martin (1999). *Refactoring: Improving the Design of Existing Code.* Reading, MA: Addison-Wesley.

Fowler, M., and K. Scott (1999). *UML Distilled: Applying the Standard Object Modeling Language*, 2nd ed. Reading, MA: Addison-Wesley.

Frakes, William B., and Sadahiro Isoda (1994). "Success factors of systematic reuse." *IEEE Software*, 11(5) (September): 15–19.

Introduction to a special issue on systematic reuse.

Frankl, Phyllis, Dick Hamlet, Bev Littlewood, and Lorenzo Strigini (1997). "Choosing a testing method to deliver reliability." In *Proceedings of the Nineteenth International Conference on Software Engineering* (Boston, MA), pp. 68–78. New York: ACM Press.

Interesting paper contrasting testing to find faults with testing to improve reliability.

Fujitsu Corporation (1987). Personal communication with Rubén Prieto-Díaz, as reported in Braun and Prieto-Díaz (1990).

Fukuda, K. (1994). *The Name of Colors* (*Iro no Namae*) (in Japanese). Tokyo: Shufuno-tomo.

Explains the cultural connotations associated with different colors. This information can be useful in considering user interface designs.

Gabb, Andrew P., and Derek E. Henderson (1995). "Navy Specification Study: Report 1—Industry Survey," DSTO-TR-0190, Draft 2.0a. Canberra: Australian Department of Defence, Defence Science and Technology Organisation.

A survey of companies involved in the development and supply of complex operational computer-based systems for the Australian Navy. Survey includes feedback on the quality of the Navy's requirements specifications.

Gamma, Erich, Richard Helm, Ralph Johnson, and John Vlissides (1995). *Design Patterns: Elements of Object-Oriented Software Architecture*. Reading, MA: Addison-Wesley.

An interesting and useful book that frames architecture in terms of the patterns we can discover.

Gane, C., and T. Sarson (1979). *Structured Systems Analysis: Tools and Techniques*. Englewood Cliffs, NJ: Prentice Hall.

A classic text in using structured analysis to capture requirements.

Garlan, David (2000). "Software architecture: A road map." In Anthony Finkelstein (ed.), *The Future of Software Engineering*, New York: ACM Press.

Garlan, David, Gail E. Kaiser, and David Notkin (1992). "Using tool abstraction to compose systems." *IEEE Computer*, 25(6) (June): 30–38.

Garvin, D. (1984). "What does 'product quality' really mean?" *Sloan Management Review*, (Fall): 25–45.

Discusses product quality from five perspectives: transcendental, user, manufacturing, product, and value-based.

Gerlich, R., and U. Denskat (1994). "A cost estimation model for maintenance and high reuse." In *Proceedings of ESCOM* 1994 (Ivrea, Italy).

German Ministry of Defense (1992). V-Model: Software lifecycle process model, General Reprint No. 250. Bundesminister des Innern, Koordinierungs- und Beratungstelle der Bundesregierung für Informationstechnik in der Bundesverwaltung.

Description of a process model used by the German defense department.

Ghezzi, Carlo, Dino Mandrioli, Sandro Morasca, and Mauro Pezze (1991). "A unified high-level Petri net formalism for time-critical systems." *IEEE Transactions on Software Engineering*, 17(2) (February): 160–172.

Gilb, Tom (1988). *Principles of Software Engineering Management*. Reading, MA: Addison-Wesley.

Gilb, Tom, and Dorothy Graham (1993). *Software Inspections*. Reading, MA: Addison-Wesley.

Good guide to what they are and how to get a program started in your organization.

Gomaa, Hassan (1995). *Software Design Methods for Concurrent and Real-Time Systems*. Reading, MA: Addison-Wesley.

Good, N.S., and A. Krekelberg (2003). "Usability and privacy: A study of KaZaA P2P file-sharing." In *Proceedings of the SIGCHI Conference on Human Factors in Computing Systems*. Ft. Lauderdale, FL (April 5–10).

Gordon, V. Scott, and James M. Bieman (1995). "Rapid prototyping: Lessons learned." *IEEE Software*, 12(1) (January): 85–95.

Grady, Robert B. (1997). *Successful Software Process Improvement*. Englewood Cliffs, NJ: Prentice Hall.

Lovely book that expands beyond software measurement to explain how Hewlett-Packard is working to improve its software company-wide.

Grady, Robert B., and Deborah Caswell (1987). *Software Metrics: Establishing a Company-Wide Program*. Englewood Cliffs, NJ: Prentice Hall.

An interesting and useful book that describes the corporate measurement program at Hewlett-Packard.

Grady, Robert B., and Thomas van Slack (1994). "Key lessons in achieving widespread inspection use." *IEEE Software*, 11(4): 46–57.

Explains how Hewlett-Packard is making inspections a standard practice.

Graham, Dorothy R. (1996a). "Testing object-oriented systems." In *Ovum Evaluates: Software Testing Tools* (February). London: Ovum Ltd.

Good overview of the differences between testing object-oriented and procedural systems.

——— (1996b). "Measuring the effectiveness and efficiency of testing." In *Proceedings of Software Testing '96* (Espace Champerret, Paris, France) (June).

Greenbaum, J., and M. Kyng (eds.) (1991). *Design at Work: Cooperative Design of Computer Systems*. Hillsdale, NJ: Lawrence Erlbaum.

Griss, Martin, and Martin Wasser (1995). "Making reuse work at Hewlett-Packard." *IEEE Software*, 12(1) (January): 105–107.

Grudin, J. (1991). "Interactive systems: Bridging the gaps between developers and users." *IEEE Computer*, 24(4) (April): 59–69.

Gugliotta, Guy (2004). "Switches failed in crash of Genesis." *Washington Post*, Saturday October 16, p. A3.

Guindon, Raymonde, H. Krasner, and B. Curtis (1987). "Breakdowns and processes during the early activities of software design by professionals." In *Empirical Studies of Programmers: Second Workshop*, pp. 65–82. New York: Ablex.

This study of designers on 19 projects identified causes of design breakdown, which are listed in Chapter 5 of this book.

Gunning, R. (1968). *The Technique of Clear Writing*. New York: McGraw-Hill.

Introduces a measure of understanding called the Fog index.

Hall, J. Anthony (1996). "Using formal methods to develop an ATC information system." *IEEE Software*, 13(2) (March): 66–76.

Describes decisions made about which formal method to use during which stages of a large air traffic control system development.

Halstead, Maurice (1977). *Elements of Software Science*. Amsterdam: Elsevier/North Holland.

Classic text applying (incorrectly) the concepts of psychology to program understanding. Some of his size measures have been useful, but others do not measure what he claims they measure.

Hamlet, Dick (1992). "Are we testing for true reliability?" *IEEE Software*, 9(4) (July): 21–27.

Provocative paper that argues that assumptions that hold for conventional reliability theory do not hold for software.

Harel, David (1987). "Statecharts: A visual formalism for complex systems." *Science of Computer Programming*, 8: 231–274.

Harrold, Mary Jean, and John D. McGregor (1989). Incremental Testing of Object-Oriented Class Structures, Technical Report. Clemson, SC: Clemson University.

Presents a technique for testing classes that exploits the hierarchical nature of the inheritance relation and reuses testing information for a parent class.

Hatley, D., and I. Pirbhai (1987). *Strategies for Real-Time System Specification*. New York: Dorset House.

This classic work describes Hatley and Pirbhai's real-time extensions to structured analysis.

Hatton, Les (1995). *Safer C: Developing Software for High-Integrity and Safety-Critical Systems*. New York: McGraw-Hill.

Excellent book describing the best ways to use C to develop high-integrity and safety-critical systems.

——— (1997). "Reexamining the fault density-component size connection." *IEEE Software*, 14(2) (March): 89–97.

Presents evidence that smaller components contain more faults than larger ones and suggests that this may be a universal principle in software engineering. In particular, he says that there may be a limit to the lowest fault densities we can achieve.

Hatton, Les, and T.R. Hopkins (1989). "Experiences with Flint, a software metrication tool for Fortran 77." In *Proceedings of the Symposium on Software Tools* (Durham, UK).

Heimdahl, Mats P.E., and Nancy G. Leveson (1996). "Completeness and consistency in hierarchical state-based requirements." *IEEE Transactions on Software Engineering*, 22(6) (June): 363–377.

Applies analysis algorithms and tools to TCAS II, the collision-avoidance system in U.S. airspace.

Heitmeyer, Constance L. (2002). "Software Cost Reduction." Technical Report, Naval Research Laboratory, Washington, DC. http://chacs.nrl.navy.mil/publications/CHACS/2002/2002 heitmeyer-encase.pdf.

Henry, Joel, Sallie Henry, Dennis Kafura, and Lance Matheson (1994). "Improving software maintenance at Martin Marietta." *IEEE Software*, 9(4) (July): 67–75.

Interesting study that shows how measurement was used to change maintenance behaviors at a large contractor site.

Herbsleb, James, Anita Carleton, James Rozum, J. Siegel, and David Zubrow (1994). Benefits of CMM-Based Software Process Improvement: Initial Results, Technical Report SEI-CMU-94-TR-13. Pittsburgh, PA Software Engineering Institute.

Herbsleb, James, David Zubrow, Dennis Goldenson, Will Hayes, and Mark Paulk (1997). "Software quality and the Capability Maturity Model." *Communications of the ACM*, 40(6) (June): 31–40.

Summarizes results of case studies and surveys to determine effects of implementing the CMM.

Hershey, John C., Howard C. Kunreuther, and Paul Schoemaker (1982). "Sources of bias in assessment procedures for utility functions." *Management Science*, 28: 936–954.

Herzum, Peter, and Oliver Sims (2000). *Business Component Factory: A Comprehensive Overview of Component-Based Development for the Enterprise*. New York: John Wiley.

Hetzel, William (1984). *The Complete Guide to Software Testing*. Wellesley, MA: QED Information Sciences.

Hillier, F.S., and G.J. Lieberman (2001). *Introduction to Operations Research*. San Francisco: Holden-Day.

A good, basic text about operations research techniques, including PERT and the critical path method.

Hix, Deborah, and H. Rex Hartson (1993). *Developing User Interfaces: Ensuring Usability through Product and Process*. New York: John Wiley.

Hofmeister, Christine, Robert Nord, and Dilip Soni (1999). *Applied Software Architecture*. Reading, MA: Addison-Wesley.

Hughes, C.E., C.P. Pfleeger, and L. Rose (1978). *Advanced Programming Techniques*. New York: John Wiley.

Good suggestions for writing crisp Fortran code, but much of the advice is language-independent.

Hughes, R.T. (1996). "Expert judgment as an estimating method." *Information and Software Technology*, 38(2): 67–75.

Humphrey, W.S. (1989). *Managing the Software Process*. Reading, MA: Addison-Wesley.

——— (1995). *A Discipline for Software Engineering*. Reading, MA: Addison-Wesley.

Humphrey, W.S., T.R. Snyder, and R.R. Willis (1991). "Software process improvement at Hughes Aircraft." *IEEE Software*, 8(4) (July): 11–23.

Hurley, Richard (1983). *Decision Tables in Software Engineering*. New York: John Wiley.

Describes how Hughes improved from capability maturity level 2 to level 3.

IEEE 610 12-1990 (1990). IEEE Standard Glossary of Software Engineering Terminology. New York IEEE Standards Press.

IEEE (1998). IEEE Standard 830–1998: IEEE Recommended Practice for Software Requirements Specification. Los Alamitos, CA: IEEE Computer Society Press.

IEEE-CS/ACM Joint Task Force on Software Engineering Ethics and Professional Practices (2004). "Software Engineering Code of Ethics and Professional Practice," Version 5.2. http://www.computer.org/tab/seprof/code.htm.

International Function Point User Group (1994a). *Function Point Counting Practices Manual*, Release 4.0. Westerville, Ohio: IFPUG.

——— (1994b). *Guidelines to Software Measurement*, Release 1.0. Westerville, Ohio: IFPUG.

International Organization for Standardization (1987). "ISO 9001: Quality systems model for quality assurance in design, development, production, installation and servicing." ISO 9001. Geneva: ISO.

Standard for measuring general process quality.

——— (1990). "Quality management and quality assurance standards. Part 3: Guidelines for the application of ISO 9001 to the development, supply and maintenance of software." ISO IS 9000-3. Geneva: ISO.

Standard for measuring software process quality.

——— (1991). "Information technology Software product evaluation: Quality characteristics and guidelines for their use," ISO/IEC IS 9126. Geneva: ISO.

Standard for measuring software product quality, using six high-level characteristics.

International Telecommunication Union (1994). Information Technology—Open Systems Interconnection—Basic Reference Model: The Basic Model, ITUT Recommendation X.200." http://www.itu.int/rec/T-REC-X.200-199407-I/en.

International Telecommunication Union (1996). "Message Sequence Chart (MSC)." ITU-T Recommendation Z.120 (November).

International Telecommunication Union (2002). "Specification and Description Language (SDL)." ITU-T Recommendation Z.100 (August).

Ishii, H. (1990). "Cross-cultural communication and computer-supported cooperative work." *Whole Earth Review* (Winter): 48–52.

Isoda, Sadahiro (1992). "Experience report of software reuse project: Its structure, activities and statistical results." In *Proceedings of the Fourteenth International Conference on Software Engineering*. Los Alamitos, CA: IEEE Computer Society Press.

Describes the CASE and reuse environments at Nippon Telephone and Telegraph.

Ito, M., and K. Nakakoji (1996). "Impact of culture in user interface design." In J. Nielsen and E. del Galdo (eds.), *International User Interfaces*. London: John Wiley.

Jackson, Michael (1995). *Software Requirements and Specifications: A Lexicon of Practice, Principles and Prejudices.* Reading, MA: Addison-Wesley.

A lovely little book that is meant to be thought-provoking and instructive. Each brief chapter addresses a facet of requirements analysis, forcing us to question our assumptions. Tom DeMarco calls this "Michael Jackson's best work ever."

Jackson, Michael, and Pamela Zave (1995). "Deriving specifications from requirements: An example," In *Proceedings of the Seventeenth International Conference on Software Engineering*, 15–24. Los Alamitos, CA: IEEE Computer Society Press.

Jacky, Jonathan (1985). "The 'Star Wars' defense won't compute." *Atlantic Monthly* (June): 18–30.

A description of the problems involved in building and testing the software for the U.S. Strategic Defense Initiative.

Jacobson, Ivar, M. Christerson, P. Jensson, and G. Overgaard (1995). *Object-Oriented Software Engineering: A Use Case Driven Approach*. Reading, MA: Addison-Wesley.

Jelinski, Z., and P.B. Moranda (1972). "Software reliability research." In *Statistical Computer Performance Evaluation* (ed. W. Freiburger), pp. 465–484. New York; Academic Press.

Jézéquel, Jean-Marc, and Bertrand Meyer (1997). "Design by contract: The lessons of Ariane." *IEEE Computer*, 30(1) (January): 129–130.

Johnson, M. Eric, Dan McGuire, and Nicholas D. Willey (2008). "The evolution of the peer-to-peer file sharing industry and the security risks for users." In *Proceedings of the 41st Hawaii International Conference on System Sciences*, p. 383. Honolulu. http://csdl2.computer.org/comp/proceedings/hicss/2008/3075/00/30750383.pdf.

Joint IEEE-CS/ACM Task Force on Computing Curricula (2004). "Computing Curricula—Software Engineering." http://sites.computer.org/ccse/SE2004Volume.pdf (October).

Jones, C. (1977). "Programmer quality and programmer productivity," Technical Report TR-02.764. Yorktown Heights, NY: IBM.

——— (1991). *Applied Software Measurement*. New York: McGraw-Hill.

Jones, S., C. Kennelly, C. Mueller, M. Sweezy, B. Thomas, and L. Velez (1991). *Developing International User Information*. Bedford, MA: Digital Press.

Joos, Rebecca (1994). "Software reuse at Motorola." *IEEE Software*, 11(5) (September): 42–47.

Describes what went right and wrong in their reuse program.

Joyce, Edward (1989). "Is error-free software possible?" *Datamation* (February 18): 53–56.

Jung, Carl (1959). *The Basic Writing of C.G. Jung*. New York: Modern Library.

Contains a description of personality preferences on two scales: introvert/extrovert and intuitive/rational. This framework is useful for understanding how project personnel interact.

Kaiser, Gail E., Peter H. Feiler, and S.S. Popovich (1988). "Intelligent assistance for software development and maintenance." *IEEE Software*, 5(3): 40–49.

A description of the MARVEL process modeling language.

Kaner, Cem, Jack Falk, and Hung Quoc Nguyen (1993). *Testing Computer Software*, 2nd ed. London: International Thomson Press.

Kaner, Cem, and David Pels (1998). *Bad Software*. New York: John Wiley.

Kaplan, R., and D. Norton (1992). "The balanced scorecard: Measures that drive performance." *Harvard Business Review* (January–February), pp. 71–80.

Karl J. Lieberherr, and I. Holland (1989) "Assuring good style for object-oriented programs." *IEEE Software*, 6(5) (September): pp. 38–48.

Kauffman, R., and R. Kumar (1993). "Modeling Estimation Expertise in Object-Based CASE Environments." New York: New York University, Stern School of Business Report.

Kazman, Rick, Jai Asundi, and Mark Klein (2001). "Quantifying the costs and benefits of architectural decisions." In *Proceedings of the Twenty-third International Conference on Software Engineering*, pp. 297–306. Los Alamitos, CA: IEEE Computer Society Press.

Introduction of object points as size measurement.

Kellner, Marc I., and H. Dieter Rombach (1990). "Comparisons of software process descriptions." In *Proceedings of the Sixth International Software Process Workshop: Support for the Software Process* (Hakodate, Japan) (October).

Summary of a modeling exercise that applied 18 process modeling techniques to a common problem.

Kemerer, C.F. (1989). "An empirical validation of software cost estimation models." *Communications of the ACM*, 30(5) (May): 416–429.

Good assessment of several cost models and their (lack of) accuracy.

Kensing, F., and A. Munk-Madsen (1993). "PD: Structure in the toolbox." *Communications of the ACM*, 36(4) (June): 78–85.

Kernighan, B.W., and P.J. Plauger (1976). *Software Tools*. Reading, MA: Addison-Wesley.

——— (1978). *The Elements of Programming Style.* New York: McGraw-Hill.

Kit, Ed (1995). *Software Testing in the Real World: Improving the Process*. Reading, MA: Addison-Wesley.

Kitchenham, Barbara A., and Käri Känsäla (1993). "Inter-item correlations among function points." In *Proceedings of the First International Symposium on Software Metrics* (Baltimore, MD). Los Alamitos, CA: IEEE Computer Society Press.

Kitchenham, Barbara A., and Steven Linkman (1997). "Why mixed VV&T strategies are important." *Software Reliability and Metrics Club Newsletter* (Summer): 9–10.

Kitchenham, Barbara A., Stephen G. MacDonell, Lesley M. Pickard and Martin J. Shepperd (2000). "What accuracy statistics really measure." Bournemouth University Technical Report, June.

Kitchenham, Barbara A., and Shari Lawrence Pfleeger (1996). "Software quality: The elusive target." *IEEE Software*, 13(1) (January): 12–21.

An introduction to a special issue on software quality, this article reviews some of the common software quality models and asks questions about what we really mean by "software quality."

Kitchenham, Barbara A., Lesley Pickard, and Shari Lawrence Pfleeger (1995). "Case studies for method and tool evaluation." *IEEE Software*, 12(4) (July): 52–62.

Kitchenham, Barabara A., and N.R. Taylor (1984). "Software cost models." *ICL Technical Journal*, 4(3):73–102.

Klein, Gary (1998). *Sources of Power*. Cambridge, MA: MIT Press.

Kleindorfer, Paul, Howard Kunreuther, and Paul Schoemaker (1993). *Decision Sciences: An Integrative Perspective*. Cambridge UK: Cambridge University Press.

Knight, John, and Nancy Leveson (1986). "An empirical study of failure probabilities in multiversion software." In *Digest of the Sixteenth International Symposium on Fault-tolerant Computing*, pp. 165–70. Los Alamitos, CA: IEEE Computer Society Press.

Assesses the claims of *n*-version programming, showing that *n* different designs share many of the same kinds of flaws.

Knight, John, Nancy Leveson, et al. (2000). "ACM Task Force on Licensing of Software Engineers Working on Safety-Critical Software." Draft (July). http://www.acm.org/serving/se_policy/safety_critical.pdf.

Knorr, Eric (2005). "Anatomy of an IT disaster: How the FBI blew it." *InfoWorld* (March 21). http://www.infoworld.com/article/05/03/21/12FEfbi_1.html.

Krasner, H., B. Curtis, and N. Iscoe (1987). "Communication breakdowns and boundary-spanning activities on large programming projects." In *Empirical Studies of Programmers*: Second Workshop, pp. 47–64. New York: Ablex Publishing.

Results from interviews conducted on 19 large software development projects to understand team- and project-level problems at MCC. Describes typical communications breakdowns in large programming projects, the cultural and environmental differences that create barriers to effective intergroup communications, and the boundary-spanning activities that coordinate five crucial topical networks of communication. Suggests more effective project coordination, including the use of tools for computer-supported collaborative software design.

Krasner, Herb, Jim Terrel, Adam Linehan, Paul Arnold, and William H. Ett (1992). "Lessons learned from a software process modeling system." *Communications of the ACM*, 35(9) (September): 91–100.

Describes experiences with SPMS, a software process modeling system.

Krauss, R.M., and S.R. Fussell (1991). "Constructing shared communicative environments." In L.B. Resnick, J.M. Levine, and S.D. Teasley (eds.), *Perspectives on Socially Shared Cognition*, pp. 172–200. Washington, DC: American Psychological Association.

Krebs, Brian (2008). "Justice breyer is among victims in data breach caused by file sharing." *Washington Post*, July 9, p. A1. http://www.washingtonpost.com/wp-dyn/content/article/2008/07/08/AR2008070802997_pf.html.

Krutchen, Phillippe (1995). "The 4+1 model view." *IEEE Software*, 12(6) (November): 42–50.

Kumar, Kuldeep (1990). "Post-implementation evaluation of computer-based information systems: Current practices." *Communications of the ACM*, 33(2) (February): 203–212.

Kunde, Diana (1997). "For those riding technology's wave, a new managerial style." *Washington Post*, February 9, p. H5.

Suggests that too much project management structure stifles designers' creativity.

Lai, Robert Chi Tau (1991). Process Definition and Modeling Methods, Technical Report SPC-91084-N. Herndon, VA: Software Productivity Consortium.

Technical report that defines a process and its component parts, describes a notation for process modeling, and then works through an extensive example.

Lanergan, R.G., and C.A. Grasso (1984). "Software engineering with reusable designs and code." *IEEE Transactions on Software Engineering*, SE 10(4) (September): 498–501.

Describes an early reuse project at Raytheon.

Lanubile, Filippo (1996). "Why software reliability predictions fail." *IEEE Software*, 13(4) (July): 131–137.

Interesting comparison of different prediction techniques that shows that none of them worked very well.

Larman, Craig (2004). *Applying UML and Patterns: An Introduction to Object-Oriented Analysis and Design,* 3rd ed. Upper Saddle River, NJ: Prentice Hall.

Lederer, Albert L., and Jayesh Prasad (1992). "Nine management guidelines for better cost estimating." *Communications of the ACM*, 35(2) (February): 50–59.

Describes the results of a large survey of cost estimation practices. Includes information about how often project managers use cost-estimation tools to assist in generating estimates.

Lee, Richard C., and William M. Tepfenhart (1997). *UML and C++ : A Practical Guide to Object-Oriented Development*. Upper Saddle River, NJ: Prentice Hall.

Lehman, M.M. (1980). "Programs, life cycles and the laws of software evolution." In *Proceedings of the IEEE*, 68(9)(September): 1060–1076.

Leveson, Nancy (1996). *Safeware*. Reading, MA: Addison-Wesley.

——— (1997). "Software safety in embedded computer systems." *Communications of the ACM*, 40(2) (February): 129–131.

Leveson, Nancy G., and Clark S. Turner (1993). "An investigation of the Therac-25 accidents." *IEEE Computer*, 26(7) (July): 18–41.

Definitive analysis of a famous software failure that resulted in loss of life.

Li, W., and S. Henry (1993). "Object-oriented metrics that predict maintainability." *Journal of Systems and Software*, 23(2) (February): 111–122.

Liebman, Bonnie (1994). "Non-trivial pursuits: Playing the research game." *Nutrition Action Healthletter*. Center for Science in the Public Interest, 1875 Connecticut Avenue NW, Suite 300, Washington, DC 20009-5728 (October).

Lieberherr, Karl J., and Ian M. Holland (1989). "Assuring good style for object-oriented programs." *IEEE Software*, 6(5): 38–48.

Lientz, B.P., and E.B. Swanson (1981). "Problems in application software maintenance." *Communications of the ACM*, 24(11): 763–769.

One of the first surveys to examine the characteristics of maintenance.

Lim, Wayne (1994). "Effects of reuse on quality, productivity and economics." *IEEE Software*, 11(5) (September): 23–30.

Describes reuse results at Hewlett-Packard. A careful, interesting study.

Lindvall, Mikael, and Kristian Sandahl (1996). "Practial implications of traceability." *Software: Practice and Experience*, 26(10) (October): 1161–1180.

Applies Pfleeger and Bohner (1990) traceability techniques to system at Ericsson Radio Systems. Shows that there are different kinds of objects and relationships that can be traced, and that the exercise of forming the links reveals important information (and often problems).

Linger, Richard C. (1993). "Cleanroom Software Engineering for Zero-Defect Software," *Proceedings of the 15th International Conference on Software Engineering*, IEEE Computer Society Press, pp. 2–13.

Linger, Richard C., and R. Alan Spangler (1992). "The IBM Cleanroom software engineering technology transfer program." In *Proceedings of the Sixth SEI Conference on Software Engineering Education* (San Diego, CA).

Linstone, H. and M. Turoff (1975). *The Delphi Method: Techniques and Applications*. Reading, MA: Addison-Wesley.

Lions, J.L., et al. (1996). Ariane 5 Flight 501 Failure: Report by the Inquiry Board. European Space Agency.

Report posted on the Web of the conclusions of the inquiry board into the crash of the Ariane-5 flight. Interesting discussion of the software design, testing techniques, and proposed remedies.

Lipke, W.H., and K.L. Butler (1992). "Software process improvement: A success story." *Crosstalk: Journal of Defense Software Engineering*, 38 (November): 29–31.

Liskov, Barbara, and John Guttag (2001). *Program Development in Java: Abstraction, Specification, and Object-Oriented Design*. Boston, MA: Addison-Wesley.

Littlewood, Bev (1991). "Limits to evaluation of software dependability." In N. Fenton and B. Littlewood (eds.), *Software Reliability and Metrics*. Amsterdam: Elsevier.

Lookout Direct (n.d.). User manual. www.automationdirect.com/static/manuals/lkdobjrefm/warning.pdf.

Lorenz, M., and J. Kidd (1994). *Object-Oriented Software Metrics*. Prentice Hall, Upper Saddle River, New Jersey.

Lutz, Robyn R. (1993a). "Targeting safety-related errors during requirements analysis." Proceedings of SIGSOFT Symposium on the Foundations of Software Engineering, *ACM Software Engineering Notes*, 18(5): 99–105.

Lutz, Robyn (1993b). "Analyzing software requirements errors in safety-critical, embedded systems." In *Proceedings of the IEEE International Symposium on Requirements Engineering*, pp. 126–133. Los Alamitos, CA: IEEE Computer Society Press.

Lyu, Michael (ed.) (1996). *Handbook of Software Reliability Engineering*. Los Alamitos, CA: IEEE Computer Society Press and New York: McGraw-Hill.

Wonderful compendium of the latest thinking on reliability measurement, modeling, and prediction.

Magee, J., N. Dulay, S. Eisenbach, and J. Kramer (1995). "Specifying distributed software architectures." *Proceedings of the Fifth European Software Engineering Conference*, ESEC'95 (September).

Manchester, William (1983). *The Last Lion*. Boston: Little, Brown.

First of three volumes that form a biography of Winston Churchill. This volume is notable, among other things, for its description of Churchill as an intuitive introvert.

Marca, David A., and Clement L. McGowan (1988). *SADT: Structured Analysis and Design Technique*. New York: McGraw-Hill.

Thorough introduction to SADT, including lots of examples of the process of using the notation.

Marcus, A. (1993). "Human communications issues in advanced user interfaces." *Communications of the ACM*, 36(4) (April): 101–109.

Martin, Robert C. (2000). "Extreme programming development through dialog." *IEEE Software*, 17(4) (July/August): 12–13.

Martin, Robert C. (2003). *Agile Software Development: Principles, Patterns and Principles*. Upper Saddle River, NJ: Prentice Hall.

Martinez-Costa, Micaela and Angel R. Martinez-Lorente (2007). "A Triple Analysis of ISO 9000 Effects on Company Performance," *International Journal of Productivity and Performance Management*, 56(5–6), pp. 484–499(16).

MathSoft (1995). *S-PLUS User's Manual*, Version 3.3 for Windows. Seattle, WA: MathSoft Corporation.

Matos, Victor, and Paul Jalics (1989). "An experimental analysis of the performance of fourth generation tools on PCs." *Communications of the ACM*, 32(11) (November): 1340–1351.

Mays, R., C. Jones, G. Holloway, and D. Studinski (1990). "Experiences with defect prevention." *IBM Systems Journal*, 29.

McCabe, T. (1976). "A software complexity measure." *IEEE Transactions on Software Engineering*, SE 2(4): 308–320.

This paper is the original reference for the cyclomatic number.

McCabe, T., and C.W. Butler (1989). "Design complexity measurement and testing." *Communications of the ACM*, 32(12): 1415–1425.

McCall, J.A., P.K. Richards, and G.F. Walters (1977). Factors in Software Quality, Vols. 1, 2, and 3, AD/A-049–014/015/055. Springfield, VA: National Technical Information Service.

One of the first papers to set forth a quality model, this paper presents the factor-criterion-metric approach to measuring software quality.

McClure, Carma (1997). *Software Reuse Techniques*. Englewood Cliffs, NJ: Prentice Hall.

McConnell, Steve (1993). *Code Complete*. Redmond, WA: Microsoft Press.

Good, sensible tips on design and implementation.

McCracken, D.D., and M.A. Jackson (1981). "A minority dissenting opinion." In W.W. Cotterman et al. (eds.). *Systems Analysis and Design: A Foundation for the 1980s*, pp. 551–553. New York: Elsevier.

McCue, G. (1978). "Architectural design for program development." *IBM Systems Journal*, 17(1): 4–25.

Describes the minimum amount of space a developer needs to work effectively.

McDermid, J.A., and D.J. Pumphrey (1995). A Development of Hazard Analysis to Aid Software Design, Technical Report. York, UK: University of York, Department of Computer Science, Dependable Computing Systems Centre.

Medvidovic, N., and D.S. Rosenblum (1999). "Assessing the suitability of a standard design method for modeling software architectures." In *Proceedings of the First Working IFIP Conference on Software Architecture (WICSA1)*, pp. 161–182. San Antonio, TX (February).

Mellor, Peter (1992). *Data Collection for Software Reliability Measurement, Software Reliability Measurement Series, Part 3*. London: City University, Centre for Software Reliability.

Notes to accompany series of three videotapes on software reliability, available from CSR at bi@csr.city.ac.uk.

Mendes, Emilia, and Nile Moseley (2006). *Web Engineering*. New York: Springer-Verlag.

Meyer, Bertrand (1992a). "Applying 'design by contract'." *IEEE Computer*, 25(10) (October): 40–51.

——— (1992b). *Eiffel: The Language*. Englewood Cliffs, NJ: Prentice Hall.

——— (1993). "Systematic concurrent object-oriented programming." *Communications of the ACM*, 36(9) (September): 56–80.

——— (1997). *Object-Oriented Software Construction*, 2nd ed. Englewood Cliffs, NJ: Prentice Hall.

Miller, Douglas R. (1986). "Exponential order statistical models of software reliability growth." *IEEE Transactions on Software Engineering*, SE 12(1): 12–24.

Mills, Harlan D. (1972). On the Statistical Validation of Computer Programs, Technical Report FSC-72-6015. Gaithersburg, MD: IBM Federal Systems Division.

Introduces the notion of fault seeding to estimate faults remaining in the code.

Mills, Harlan D. (1988). "Stepwise refinement and verification in box-structured systems." *IEEE Computer*, 21(6) (June): 23–36.

Mills, Harlan, Michael Dyer, and Richard Linger (1987). "Cleanroom software engineering." *IEEE Software*, 4(5) (September): 19–25.

Overview of IBM's cleanroom approach.

Mills, Harlan, Richard Linger, and Alan R. Hevner (1987). "Box-structured information systems." *IBM Systems Journal*, 26(4): 395–413.

Mills, Simon (1997). "Automated testing: Various experiences." In *Proceedings of the Fourteenth International Conference and Exposition on Testing Computer Software* (Washington, DC).

Interesting description of test issues involved in testing a motor insurance quotation system.

Misra, Santosh, and Paul Jalics (1988). "Third generation vs. fourth generation software development." *IEEE Software*, 5(4) (July): 8–14.

Miyazaki, Y., and K. Mori (1985). "COCOMO evaluation and tailoring." In *Proceedings of the Eighth International Software Engineering Conference* (London). Los Alamitos, CA: IEEE Computer Society Press.

Moad, Jeff (1995). "Time for a fresh approach to ROI." *Datamation*, 41(3) (February 15): 57–59.

Möller, Karl, and Daniel Paulish (1993). "An empirical investigation of software fault distribution." In *Proceedings of CSR 93*, Amsterdam: Chapman and Hall.

Presents results to show that smaller modules have a higher fault density than larger ones.

Moore, Geoffrey (1991). *Crossing the Chasm*. New York: HarperBusiness.

Morgan, Tony (2002). *Business Rules and Information Systems: Aligning IT with Business Goals*. Boston, MA: Addison-Wesley Professional.

Musa, John D. (1979). Software Reliability Data, Technical Report. Rome, NY: Rome Laboratories, Data Analysis Center for Software.

Musa, John D., Anthony Iannino, and Kazuhira Okumoto (1990). *Software Reliability: Measurement, Prediction, Application*. New York: McGraw-Hill.

Myers, Glenford J. (1976). *Software Reliability*. New York: John Wiley.

One of the first texts to look at software testing and reliability using empirical data.

——— (1979). *The Art of Software Testing*. New York: John Wiley.

Still one of the most valuable books to describe the philosophy of testing.

Nakakoji, K. (1994). "Crossing the cultural boundary." *Byte*, 19(6) (June): 107–109.

Discusses the importance of understanding culture in interface design.

NASA (2004). "NASA software safety guidebook." National Aeronautics and Space Administration technical report NASA-GB-8719.13 (March).

Discusses the relationship between management structure and project characteristics on successful projects.

National Science Foundation (1983). *The Process of Technological Innovation*. Washington, DC: NSF.

Netfocus: Software Program Manager's Network (1995). Washington, DC: Department of the Navy (January).

This newsletter describes the derivation of a metrics "dashboard" that depicts a small number of key measures. The dashboard is to be used by project managers to "drive" a software development project, telling the manager when the products are ready for release to the customer.

Newsbytes Home Page (1996). "Computer blamed for $500 million Ariane explosion." Paris (June 6).

Nippon Electric Company (1987). Personal communication with Rubén Prieto-Díaz, as reported in Braun and Prieto-Díaz (1990) (June).

NIST (2002). *Risk Management Guide for Information Technology Systems*. Gaithersburg, MD: National Institute of Standards and Technology Publication 800-30. csrc.nist.gov/publications/nistpubs/800-30/sp800-30.pdf.

Northrup, Linda, Peter H. Feiler, Richard P. Gabriel, John Goodenough, Richard Linger, Thomas Longstaff, Richard Kazman, Mark Klein, Douglas C. Schmidt, Kevin Sullivan, and Kurt Wallnau (2006). *Ultra-Large-Scale Systems: The Software Challenge of the Future*. Pittsburgh, PA: Software Engineering Institute, Carnegie Mellon. http://www.sei.cmu.edu/uls/summary.html.

Nosek, J. (1998). "The case for collaborative programming." *Communications of the ACM*, 41(3) (March): 105–108.

Notkin, David (2000). "Software Engineering Licensing and Certification," presentation at Computing Research Association Conference at Snowbird, Utah. http://www.cra.org/Activities/snowbird/00/notkin-crawk3-5.pdf.

Ntafos, S.C. (1984). "On required element testing." *IEEE Transactions on Software Engineering*, 10: 795–803.

Compares relative fault discovery effectiveness for several different testing strategies.

Nuseibeh, Bashar (1997). "Ariane 5: Who dunnit?" *IEEE Software*, 14(3) (May): 15–16.

Analyzes the cause of the Ariane-5 explosion from the point of view of different life-cycle activities. Concludes that risk management would have been the best approach to discovering the underlying problem early on.

Nuseibeh, Bashar, Joe Kramer, and Anthony Finkelstein (1994). "A framework for expressing the relationships between multiple views in requirements specification." *IEEE Transactions on Software Engineering*, 20(10) (October): 760–773.

Object Management Group (2003). "OMG Unified Modeling Language Specification," Version 1.5 (March).

Olsen, Neil (1993). "The software rush hour." *IEEE Software*, 10(5) (September): 29–37.

Interesting discussion of how metrics can be used to help manage the development process.

Oman, Paul, and J. Hagemeister (1992). "Metrics for assessing software system maintainability." In *Proceedings of the International Conference on Software Maintenance*, pp. 337–344. Los Alamitos, CA: IEEE Computer Society Press.

Describes a hierarchical model of maintainability, separated into three dimensions.

Oppenheimer, Todd (1997). "The computer delusion." *Atlantic Monthly* (July): 45–62.

Good discussion of the pros and cons of computer-based learning.

Osterweil, Leon (1987). "Software processes are software too." In *Proceedings of the Ninth IEEE International Conference on Software Engineering*, pp. 2–13. Los Alamitos, CA: IEEE Computer Society Press.

Controversial paper that suggests that given the right amount of understanding, a process language can describe a software development process, and then the process can be executed as a program.

Padberg, Frank, and Matthias M. Müller (2003). "Analyzing the cost and benefit of pair programming." *Proceedings of the Ninth International Software Metrics Symposium*, Sydney, Australia (September), pp. 166–177. Los Alamitos, CA: IEEE Computer Society Press.

Parikh, G., and N. Zvegintzov (1983). *Tutorial on Software Maintenance*. Los Alamitos, CA: IEEE Computer Society Press.

Although not a recent publication, contains information that still applies to maintenance projects.

Parnas, David L. (1972). "On criteria to be used in decomposing systems into modules." *Communications of the ACM*, 15(12) (December): 1053–1058.

Discusses the notions of abstraction and information hiding.

Parnas, David L. (1978a). "Some software engineering principles." *Infotech State of the Art Report on Structured Analysis and Design*, Infotech International.

Included in *Software Fundamentals: Collected Papers by David L. Parnas*. Boston: Addison-Wesley. 2001.

——— (1978b). "Designing software for ease of extension and contraction." In *Proceedings of the Third International Conference on Software Engineering*, pp. 264–277. Los Alamitos, CA: IEEE Computer Society Press.

——— (1985). "Software aspects of strategic defense systems." *American Scientist*, 73(5) (December): 432–440.

Describes the difficulties in ensuring that this type of system can work as required, with acceptable reliability and safety.

Parnas, David L. (1992). "Tabular Representation of Relations," Communications Research Laboratory Technical Report 260, CRL (October).

Parnas, David L. (2000). "Two positions on licensing." Panel position statement in *Proceedings of the 4th IEEE International Conference on Requirements Engineering* (June).

Parnas, David L., and Paul C. Clements (1986). "A rational design process: How and why to fake it." *IEEE Transactions on Software Engineering*, 12(2) (February): 251–257.

Parnas, David L., and David Weiss (1985). "Active design reviews: Principles and practices." In *Proceedings of the Eighth International Conference on Software Engineering*, pp. 215–222. Los Alamitos, CA: IEEE Computer Society Press.

Parris, Kathy V.C. (1996). "Implementing accountability." *IEEE Software*, 13(July)(4): 83–93.

Describes project management on the U.S. Department of Defense FX-16 airplane software project.

Parrish, Allen, Randy Smith, David Hale, and Joanne Hale (2004). "A field study of developer pairs: Productivity impacts and implications." *IEEE Software*, 21(5) (September/October): 76–79.

Paulk, Mark, B. Curtis, M.B. Chrissis, and C.V. Weber (1993a). "Capability maturity model for software, version 1.1," Technical Report SEI-CMU-93-TR-24. Pittsburgh, PA: Software Engineering Institute.

——— (1993b). "Key practices of the capability maturity model, version 1.1," Technical Report SEI-CMU-93-TR-25. Pittsburgh, PA: Software Engineering Institute.

Perkins, David (2001). *The Eureka Effect*. New York: W.W. Norton.

Perry, Dewayne E., and Gail E. Kaiser (1990). "Adequate testing and object-oriented programming." *Journal of Object-Oriented Programming*, 2(January/February): 13–19.

Examines Weyuker's testing axioms and shows that reusing objects is not as easy as it sounds. Some of the objects require extensive retesting.

Perry, Dewayne, and Carol Steig (1993). "Software faults in evolving a large, real-time system: a case study," 4th European Software Engineering Conference (ESEC 93), Garmisch, Germany, September 1993.

Perry, William (1995). *Effective Methods for Software Testing*. New York: John Wiley.

Peterson, James (1977). "Petri Nets." *ACM Computing Surveys*, 9(3) (September): 223–252.

Petroski, Henry (1985). *To Engineer Is Human: The Role of Failure in Good Design.* New York: Petrocelli Books.

Pfleeger, Charles P. (1997a). "The fundamentals of information security." *IEEE Software*, 14(1) (January): 15–16, 60.

Interesting article about how most requirements assume a benign universe, but security assumes it is hostile. Explains how to incorporate security in development.

——— and Shari Lawrence Pfleeger (2003). *Security in Computing*, 3rd ed. Upper Saddle River NJ: Prentice Hall.

——— (2006). *Security in Computing*, 4th ed. Upper Saddle River, NJ: Prentice Hall.

Classic text that addresses the key issues in computer security today, including networks, encryption, and how to describe and implement security requirements.

Pfleeger, Shari Lawrence (1991). "Model of software effort and productivity." *Information and Software Technology*, 33(3) (April): 224–232.

Description of effort estimation model based on counting objects and methods.

——— (1996). "Measuring reuse: A cautionary tale." *IEEE Software,* 13(4) (July): 118–127.

Describes reuse lessons learned at Amalgamated Inc., a composite of several organizations that have tried to implement reuse, with mixed success. Shows how important business decisions must be made before reuse questions can be addressed.

——— (1999a). "Albert Einstein and empirical software engineering." *IEEE Computer*, 32(10) (October): 32–37.

Addresses the need to allow technology to move forward as you study its effectiveness.

——— (1999b). "Understanding and improving technology transfer in software engineering." *Journal of Systems and Software*, 52(2) (July): 111–124.

——— (2000). "Risky business: What we have yet to learn about software risk management." *Journal of Systems and Software*, 53(3) (September): 265–273.

Looks at how other disciplines, including public policy and environmental policy, do risk management, and suggests ways to improve risk management for software projects.

Pfleeger, Shari Lawrence, and Shawn Bohner (1990). "A framework for maintenance metrics." In *Proceedings of the Conference on Software Maintenance* (Orlando, FL). Los Alamitos, CA: IEEE Computer Society Press.

Pfleeger, Shari Lawrence, and Thomas Ciszek (2008). "Choosing a Security Option: The InfoSecure Methodology." *IEEE IT Professional*, 10(5): 46–52.

Pfleeger, Shari Lawrence, Norman Fenton, and Stella Page (1994). "Evaluating software engineering standards." *IEEE Computer*, 27(9) (September): 71–79.

Shows how most software engineering standards are just guidelines and presents a case study of a British utility to evaluate the effectiveness of coding and maintenance standards.

Pfleeger, Shari Lawrence, and Les Hatton (1997). "Investigating the influence of formal methods." *IEEE Computer*, 30(2) (February): 33–43.

Case study of the use of formal methods in an air traffic control support system. Describes how formal methods affected product quality but also provides lessons learned about how to carry out such studies.

Pfleeger, Shari Lawrence, and Clement L. McGowan (1990). "Software metrics in the process maturity framework." *Journal of Systems and Software*, 12(1): 255–261.

Shows how different maturity levels imply process visibility and measurement.

Pfleeger, Shari Lawrence, and Winifred Menezes (2000). "Technology transfer: Marketing technology to software practitioners." *IEEE Software*, 17(1) (January/February): 27–33.

Pfleeger, Shari Lawrence, Martin Shepperd, and Roseanne Tesoriero (2000). "Decisions and Delphi: The dynamics of group estimation." In *Proceedings of the Brazilian Software Engineering Symposium*, João Pessoa, October.

Pfleeger, Shari Lawrence, and David W. Straight (1985). *Introduction to Discrete Structures*. New York: John Wiley.

Introductory text that describes the mathematics needed to understand computer science.

Polanyi, M. (1996). *The Tacit Dimension*. Garden City, NY: Doubleday.

Polyà, George (1957). *How to Solve It*, 2nd ed. Princeton, NJ: Princeton University Press.

Porter, Adam, and Richard Selby (1990). "Empirically-guided software development using metric-based classification trees." *IEEE Software*, 7(2) (March): 46–54.

Describes the use of a statistical technique to determine which metrics are the best predictors of an outcome. Very helpful for paring down a large set of collected metrics to those that provide the most useful information.

Porter, Adam, Harvey Siy, A. Mockus, and Lawrence Votta (1998). "Understanding the sources of variation in software inspections." 7(1): 41–79.

Price, Jonathan (1984). *How to Write a Computer Manual*. Menlo Park, CA: Benjamin-Cummings.

A wonderful description of how to write user documentation.

Prieto-Díaz, Rubén (1987). "Domain analysis for reusability." In *Proceedings of COMPSAC 87*. Los Alamitos, CA: IEEE Computer Society Press.

——— (1991). "Making software reuse work: An implementation model." *ACM SIGSOFT Software Engineering Notes*, 16(3): 61–68.

——— (1993). "Status report: Software reusability." *IEEE Software*, 10(3) (May): 61–66.

Prieto-Díaz, Rubén, and Peter Freeman (1987). "Classifying software for reusability." *IEEE Software*, 4(1) (January): 6–17.

Putnam, L.H., and Ware Myers (1992). *Measures for Excellence: Reliable Software on Time, within Budget*. Englewood Cliffs, NJ: Yourdon Press.

Queen's Printer for Ontario (2000). "Professional Engineers Act, R.R.O. 1990, Regulation 941, as amended." In *Revised Regulations of Ontario*, Toronto, Ont.

Redwine, S., and W. Riddle (1985). "Software technology maturation." In *Proceedings of the Eighth International Conference on Software Engineering*, pp. 189–200. Los Alamitos, CA: IEEE Computer Society Press.

Reiss, S.P. (1990). "Connecting tools using message passing in the Field Environment." *IEEE Software*, 7(4) (July): 57–66.

Describes a system that uses implicit invocation in its design.

Rensburger, B. (1985). "The software is too hard." *Washington Post National Weekly Edition*, November 11, pp. 10–11.

A newspaper report about why the Star Wars (Strategic Defense Initiative) software in the United States was too difficult to test properly.

Richards, F.R. (1974). Computer Software: Testing, Reliability Models and Quality Assurance, Technical Report NPS-55RH74071A. Monterey, CA: Naval Postgraduate School.

Discusses technique for estimating confidence in software based on fault history.

Rittel, H.W.J., and M.M. Webber (1984). "Planning problems are wicked problems." In N. Cross (ed.), *Developments in Design Methodology*, pp. 135–144. New York: John Wiley.

Robertson, James, and Suzanne Robertson (1994). *Complete Systems Analysis: The Workbook, the Textbook, the Answers*. New York: Dorset House.

Two volumes that give you a thorough grounding in the major requirements analysis techniques. Includes exercises and complete answers. (Republished in 1998 as a single volume.)

Robertson, Suzanne, and James Robertson (1999). *Mastering the Requirements Process*. Reading, MA: Addison-Wesley.

This book describes the requirements process completely, based on the Robertsons' Volere Requirements Process Model. Because the Robertsons continue to update their model, you can view the current version at the Atlantic Systems Guild Web site, http:// www. systemsguild.com.

Robinson, M., and L. Bannon (1991). "Questioning representations." In L. Bannon, M. Robinson, and K. Schmidt (eds.), *Proceedings of the Second ECSCW'91*, pp. 219–233. Amsterdam: Kluwar.

Rockoff, Jonathan D. (2008). "Flaws in medical coding can kill." *Baltimore Sun* (June 30).

Rogers, Everett M. (1995). *Diffusion of Innovations*, 4th ed. New York: Free Press.

Classic text on technology transfer. Describes fives types of people who adopt technology, and explains how to provide motivation to each type.

Rook, Paul (1993). *Risk Management for Software Development*, ESCOM Tutorial.

Good synthesis of risk management approaches.

Rosenberg, Jarrett (1998). "Five easy steps to systematic data handling." *IEEE Software*, 15(1) (January): 75–77.

Ross, D.T. (1977). "Structured analysis (SA): A language for communicating ideas." *IEEE Transactions on Software Engineering*, SE 3(1) (January): 16–34.

The first paper introducing Softech's SADT to the research community.

——— (1985). "Applications and extensions of SADT." *IEEE Computer*, 18(4) (April): 25–34.

Rouquet, J.C., and P.J. Traverse (1986). "Safe and reliable computing on board the Airbus and ATR aircraft." In *Proceedings of the Fifth IFAC Workshop on Safety of Computer Control Systems*, W.J. Quirk (ed.), pp. 93–97. Oxford: Pergamon Press.

Rout, T.P. (1995) "SPICE: A framework for software process assessment." *Software Process: Improvement and Practice*, 1(1) (August): 57–66.

Royce, W.E. (1990). "TRW's Ada process model for incremental development of large software systems." In *Proceedings of the Twelfth International Conference on Software Engineering*, pp. 2–11. Los Alamitos, CA: IEEE Computer Society Press.

Reports on use of Boehm's anchoring milestones and the Theory W model.

Royce, W.W. (1970). "Managing the development of large software systems: Concepts and techniques." In *Proceedings of WESCON* (August), Vol. 14, pp. A-1 to A-9.

The first publication to mention the waterfall model.

Rugg, D. (1993). "Using a capability evaluation to select a contractor." *IEEE Software*, 10(4) (July): 36–45.

Ruhl, M., and M. Gunn (1991). Software Reengineering: A Case Study and Lessons Learned, NIST Special Publication 500–193. Gaithersburg, MD: National Institute of Standards and Technology.

Reports on the results of reengineering over 13,000 lines of COBOL code.

Rumbaugh, James, M. Blaha, W. Premerlani, F. Eddy, and W. Lorenson (1991). *Object-Oriented Modeling and Design*. Englewood Cliffs, NJ: Prentice Hall.

Comprehensive guide to using OMT, the object management technique developed at Rational Corporation.

Rumbaugh, James, Ivar Jacobsonm, and Grady Booch (2004). *The Unified Modeling Language Reference Manual*. Boston, MA: Addison-Wesley Professional.

Russo, P., and S. Boor (1993). "How fluent is your interface? Designing for international users." In *Proceedings of the Conference on Human Factors in Computing Systems* (INTERCHI'93), pp. 342–347.

Sackman, H.H., W.J. Erikson, and E.E. Grant (1968). "Exploratory experimental studies comparing online and offline programming performance." *Communications of the ACM*, 11(1) (January): 3–11.

Interesting study showing that productivity can vary 10 to 1 among programmers.

Saiedian, H., and R. Kuzara (1995). "SEI capability maturity model's impact on contractors." *IEEE Computer*, 28(1) (January): 16–26.

Sammet, Jean (1969). *Programming Languages: History and Fundamentals*. Englewood Cliffs, NJ: Prentice Hall.

Classic text for understanding the issues involved in designing programming languages.

Samson, B., D. Ellison, and P. Dugard (1997). "Software cost estimation using an Albus Perceptron (CMAC)." *Information and Software Technology*, 39(1–2): 55–60.

Uses a neural net on the COCOMO dataset to perform cost estimation.

Samuelson, Pamela (1990). "Reverse-engineering someone else's software: Is it legal?" *IEEE Software*, 7(1) (January): 90–96.

Sauer, Chris, et al. (2000). "The effectiveness of software development technical reviews: A behaviorally motivated program of research." *IEEE Transactions on Software Engineering*, 26(1): 1–14.

Sawyer, K. (1985). "The mess at the IRS." *Washington Post National Weekly Edition*, November 11, pp. 6–7.

Newspaper's description of the difficulties in building a new software system for the U.S. Internal Revenue Service.

Scharer, L. (1983). "User training: Less is more." *Datamation* (July): 175–182.

Scharer, Laura (1990). "Pinpointing requirements." In *System and Software Requirements Engineering*. Los Alamitos, CA: IEEE Computer Society Press.

Schmidt, Douglas C., Michael Stal, Hans Rohert, and Frank Buschmann (2000). *Pattern-Oriented Software Architecture: Concurrent and Networked Objects*. New York: John Wiley and Sons.

Scholtes, Peter R. (1995). *The Team Handbook*. Joiner Associates.

Discusses the organization and impact of teams, including how to handle difficult team members.

Schum, David A. (1994). *Evidential Foundations of Probabilistic Reasoning*, Wiley Series in Systems Engineering. New York: John Wiley.

Applies legal thinking to the way we deal with evidence. Includes use of Bayesian probabilities to help decide when evidence is compelling.

Schwaber, Ken and Mike Beedle (2002). *Agile Software Development with Scrum*. Upper Saddle River, NJ: Prentice Hall.

Seddon, John (1996). ISO 9000 Implementation and Value-Added: Three Case Studies, Technical Report. London: Vanguard Consulting.

Seligman, Dan (1997). "Midsummer madness: New technology is marvelous except when it isn't." *Forbes*, September 8, p. 234.

Describes billing problems that resulted from a problem with Nortel software.

Shaw, Mary (1990). "Prospects for an engineering discipline of software." *IEEE Software*, 7(6) (November): 15–24.

——— (2002). "Self-healing: Softening precision to avoid brittleness." Position paper in *WOSS '02: Workshop on Self-Healing Systems* (November).

Shaw, Mary, and David Garlan (1996). *Software Architecture: Perspectives on an Emerging Discipline*. Upper Saddle River, NJ: Prentice Hall.

A wonderful book that describes some of the key issues in evaluating software design.

Shepperd, Martin (1997). "Effort and size estimation: An appraisal." *Software Reliability and Metrics Club Newsletter* (January): 6–8. London: Centre for Software Reliability.

Shepperd, Martin, Chris Schofield, and Barbara A. Kitchenham (1996). "Effort estimation using analogy." In *Proceedings of the Eighteenth International Conference on Software Engineering* (Berlin). Los Alamitos, CA: IEEE Computer Society Press.

Shneiderman, Ben (1997). *Designing the User Interface: Strategies for Effective Human-Computer Interface*, 3rd ed. Reading, MA: Addison-Wesley.

Shooman, M.L. (1983). *Software Engineering*. New York: McGraw-Hill.

Shooman, M.L., and M. Bolsky (1975). "Types, distribution and test and correction times for programming errors." In *Proceedings of the 1975 International Conference on Reliable Software*. New York: IEEE Computer Society Press.

Shull, F., I. Rus, and V. Basili (2000). "How perspective-based reading can improve requirements inspections." *IEEE Computer*, 33(7) (July): 73–79.

Shumate, K., and M. Keller (1992). *Software Specification and Design: A Disciplined Approach for Real-Time Systems*. New York: John Wiley.

Simmons, Pamela L. (1996). "Quality outcomes: Determining business value." *IEEE Software*, 13(1) (January): 25–32.

Simon, H.A. (1981). *The Sciences of the Artificial*. Cambridge, MA: The MIT Press.

Skowronski, Victor (2004). "Do agile methods marginalize problem solvers?" *IEEE Computer*, 37(10) (October): 120–118.

Smith, Bill (1993). "Six sigma design." *IEEE Spectrum* 30(9) (September): 43–46.

A good article describing how six-sigma design is used in manufacturing.

Smith, M.D., and D.J. Robson (1992). "A framework for testing object-oriented programs." *Journal of Object-Oriented Programming*, 5(3) (June): 45–54.

Software Engineering Coordinating Committee of the ACM and IEEE (2004). "Guide to the Software Engineering Body of Knowledge." http://www.swebok.org (October).

Spivey, J.M. (1992). *The Z Notation: A Reference Manual*, 2nd ed. Englewood Cliffs, NJ: Prentice Hall.

Describes a formal language for requirements specification.

Sreemani, Tirumale, and Joanne M. Atlee (1996). "Feasibility of model checking software requirements: A case study." *Proceedings of the 11th Annual Conference on Computer Assurance*, pp. 77–88.

Srinivasan, K., and D. Fisher (1995). "Machine learning approaches to estimating development effort." *IEEE Transactions on Software Engineering*, 21(2): 126–137.

Standish Group (1994). *The CHAOS Report*. Dennis, MA: The Standish Group.

——— (1995). *The Scope of Software Development Project Failures*. Dennis, MA: Standish Group.

Steele, Claude (1999) "Thin ice: Stereotype threat and black college students." *Atlantic Monthly* (August): 44–47, 50–54.

Steinberg, Daniel H. and Daniel W. Palmer (2004). *Extreme Software Engineering: A Hands-on Approach*. Upper Saddle River, NJ: Prentice Hall.

Stephens, Matt, and Douglas Rosenberg (2003). *Extreme Programming Refactored: The Case Against XP*. Berkeley, CA: Apress.

Swanson, Mary, and S. Curry (1987). "Results of an asset engineering program: Predicting the impact of software reuse." In *Proceedings of the National Conference on Software Reusability and Portability*. Los Alamitos, CA: IEEE Computer Society Press.

Describes the use of financial incentives for reuse at GTE Data Services in Tampa, Florida.

Swartout, W.R., and R. Balzer (1982). "On the inevitable intertwining of specification and implementation." *Communications of the ACM*, 25(7) (July): 438–439.

Teasley, B., L. Leventhal, B. Blumenthal, K. Instone, and D. Stone (1994). "Cultural diversity in user interface design: Are intuitions enough?" *SIGCHI Bulletin*, 26(1) (January): 36–40.

Teichroew, D., and E.A. Hershey III (1977). "PSL/PSA: A computer-aided technique for structured documentation and analysis of information processing systems." *IEEE Transactions on Software Engineering*, SE 3(1) (January): 41–48.

Introduces a language for recording requirements.

Theofanos, Mary F., and Shari Lawrence Pfleeger (1996). "Wavefront: A goal-driven requirements process model." *Information and Software Technology*, 38(1) (January): 507–519.

Presents a model of capturing the requirements based on measurement and goals.

Thomas, Dave (2005). "Refactoring as meta programming?" *Journal of Object Technology*, 4(1) (January–February): 7–11.

Trager, Louis (1997). "Net users overcharged in glitch." *Inter@ctive Week*, September 8.

Describes problems with inadequate testing of Nortel software.

Travassos, Guilherme H., and R. S. Andrade (1999). "Combining metrics, principles and guidelines for object-oriented design." In *Proceedings of the Workshop on Quantitative Approaches to Object-Oriented Software Engineering* (ECOOP99). Lisbon, Portugal.

Available at http://www.esw.inesc.pt/ftp/pub/esw/mood/ecoop99/.

Tsuda, M., et al. (1992). "Productivity analysis of software development with an integrated CASE tool." In *Proceedings of the International Conference on Software Engineering*. Los Alamitos, CA: IEEE Computer Society Press.

Describes reuse program at Hitachi.

Turoff, M., and S.R. Hiltz (1995). "Computer-based Delphi processes," in M. Adler and E. Ziglio, eds. *Gazing Into the Oracle: The Delphi Method and Its Application to Social Policy and Public Health*. London: Kingsley Publishers.

Tversky, Amos, and Daniel Kahneman (1981). "The framing of decisions and the psychology of choice." *Science*, 211: 453–458.

Uhl, Axel (2003). "Model driven architecture is ready for prime time." *IEEE Software* (September/October): 70–73.

University of Southern California (1996). *COCOMO II Model User's Manual*, Version 1.1. Los Angeles: USC.

U.S. Department of Defense (1994). *Military Standard: Software Development and Documentation*, MilStd-498. Washington, DC: DOD.

This is the current software development standard covering systems built by or for the U.S. Department of Defense.

Valacich, J.S., L.M. Jessup, A.R. Dennis, and J.F. Nunamaker, Jr. (1992). "A conceptual framework of anonymity in group support systems." In *Proceedings of the 25th Annual Hawaii Conference on System Sciences*, Vol. III: *Group Decision Support Systems Track*, pp. 113–125. Los Alamitos, CA: IEEE Computer Society Press.

Vartabedian, Ralph (1996). "IRS computer project has 'very serious problems,' Rubin Says." *Los Angeles Times*, March 29, p. D1.

Verner, June, and Graham Tate (1988). "Estimating size and effort in fourth generation development." *IEEE Software*, 5(4) (July): 15–22.

Vinter, Otto (1996). "The prevention of errors through experience-driven test efforts," Delta Report D-259 (January). Copenhagen.

Describes a retrospective technique for evaluating competing testing methods.

Voas, J.M., and Michael Friedman (1995). *Software Assessment: Reliability, Safety, and Testability*. New York: John Wiley.

Voas, J.M., and K.W. Miller (1995). "Software testability: The new verification." *IEEE Software*, 12(3) (May): 17–28.

Walden, Kim, and Jean-Marc Nerson (1995). *Seamless Object-Oriented Software Architecture: Analysis and Design of Reliable Systems*. Englewood Cliffs, NJ: Prentice Hall.

Walston, C., and C. Felix (1977). "A method of programming measurement and estimation." *IBM Systems Journal*, 16(1): 54–73.

Walz, Diane B., Joyce J. Elam, Herb Krasner, and Bill Curtis (1987). "A methodology for studying software design teams: An investigation of conflict behaviors in the requirements definition phase." In *Empirical Studies of Programmers*: Second Workshop, pp. 83–99. New York: Ablex Publishing.

Presents a method for analyzing processes involved in designing large-scale, computer-based systems, based on characterizing the design process to recognize the diversity of team members' underlying conceptualizations, to emphasize the transformation of abstract goals into concrete systems, and to distinguish between those breakdowns in the design process that are a part of the design function and those that are the results of the group process itself (within the design context).

Ward, P.T., and S.J. Mellor (1986). *Structured Development for Real-Time Systems*, 3 vols. New York: Yourdon Press.

Warmer, Jos, and Anneke Kleppe (1999). *The Object Constraint Language: Precise Modeling with UML*. Reading, MA: Addison-Wesley.

Wasserman, Anthony I. (1990). "Tool integration in software engineering environments." In F. Long (ed.), *Software Engineering Environments*, pp. 138–150. Berlin: Springer-Verlag.

——— (1995). "Towards a discipline of software engineering: methods, tools and the software development process," Inaugural Stevens Lecture on Software Development Methods. In *Proceedings of the Seventh International Workshop on Computer-Aided Software Engineering* (Toronto). Los Alamitos, CA: IEEE Computer Society Press.

Text of Wasserman's lecture about several key issues in software engineering today.

——— (1996). "Toward a discipline of software engineering." *IEEE Software*, 13(6) (November): 23–31.

A follow-on to Wasserman's Stevens Lecture, explaining why software development today is different from 10 or 20 years ago.

Watson, R.T., T.H. Ho, and K.S. Raman (1994). "Culture: A fourth dimension of group support systems." *Communications of the ACM*, 37(10) (October): 44–55.

Weiderhold, Gio (1988). *Database Design*, 3rd ed. New York: McGraw-Hill.

Weinberg, Gerald M. (1971). *The Psychology of Computer Programming*. New York: Van Nostrand Reinhold.

Seminal work about the way programmers think and how organizations help or hamper creativity and productivity.

——— (1993). *Quality Software Management: First Order Measurement*. New York: Dorset House.

Part of this book addresses work styles and team building.

Weiss, David, and Robert Lai (1999). *Software Product Line Engineering: A Family-based Software Development Process*. Reading, MA: Addison-Wesley.

Weller, E.F. (1992). "Lessons learned from two years of inspection data." In *Proceedings of the Third International Conference on Applications of Software Measurement*, pp. 2.57–2.69.

——— (1993). "Lessons from three years of inspection data." *IEEE Software*, 10(5) (September): 38–45.

Excellent empirical study showing data from more than 6000 inspection meetings. For example, compares defect-detection rates for different-size teams and different types of code.

——— (1994). "Using metrics to manage software projects." *IEEE Computer*, 27(9) (September): 27–34.

Wetherbe, J.C. (1984). *Systems Analysis and Design: Traditional, Structured, and Advanced Concepts and Techniques*. Eagan, MN: West Publishing.

Whittaker, James A., and Steven Atkin (2002). "Software engineering is not enough." *IEEE Software* 19(4) (July/August): 108–115.

Wilde, Norman, Paul Matthews, and Ross Huitt (1993). "Maintaining object-oriented software." *IEEE Software*, 10(1) (January): 75–80.

Williams, L., R. Kessler, W. Cunningham, and R. Jeffries (2000). "Strengthening the case for pair programming." *IEEE Software* 17(4) (July/August): 19–25.

Wilson, Peter B. (1995). "Testable requirements: An alternative software sizing measure." *Journal of the Quality Assurance Institute* (October): 3–11.

Wing, Jeannette M. (1990). "A specifier's introduction to formal methods." *IEEE Computer*, 23(9) (September): 8–24.

A good, clear introduction to formal methods, with pointers to many other resources.

Winograd, T., and F. Flores (1986). *Understanding Computers and Cognition*. Norwood, NJ: Ablex.

Withrow, Carol (1990). "Error density and size in Ada software." *IEEE Software*, 7(1) (January): 26–30.

Finds a U-shaped fault density curve comparing size and faults in Unisys Ada software.

Wittig, G.E., and G.R. Finnie (1994). "Using artificial neural networks and function points to estimate 4GL software development effort." *Australian Journal of Information Systems* 1(2): 87–94.

Wolverton, R.W. (1974). "The cost of developing large-scale software." *IEEE Transactions on Computers*, C23(6): 615–636.

Describes one of the early cost models, using a matrix of costs combined with project difficulty.

Wood, Jane, and Denise Silver (1995). *Joint Application Development*, 2nd ed. New York: John Wiley.

Yourdon, Edward (1982). *Managing the System Life Cycle*. New York: Yourdon Press.

——— (1990). *Modern Structured Analysis*. Englewood Cliffs, NJ: Prentice Hall.

——— (1994). "Developing software overseas." *Byte*, 19(6) (June): 113–120.

——— (2005). *Outsource*. Boston: Prentice-Hall.

Yourdon, Edward, and Larry Constantine (1978). *Structured Design*. Englewood Cliff, NJ: Prentice Hall.

Introduced the notions of coupling and cohesion for assessing design quality.

Zave, Pamela (1984). "The operational versus the conventional approach to software development." *Communications of the ACM*, 27(2) (February): 104–118.

Zave, Pamela, and Michael Jackson (1997). "Four dark corners of requirements engineering." *ACM Transactions on Software Engineering and Methodology*, 6(1) (January): 1–30.

Description of the operational specification approach to development.

Zelkowitz, Marvin V., Dolores R. Wallace and David Binkley (1998). "Understanding the culture clash in software engineering technology transfer," University of Maryland technical report (2 June).

Index